Purchased and Paid for by Do

Diana Sierazki

ASCH

8/19/90

To Doug & Susan Detrick,
my friends & esteemed colleagues, &
some of the most skilled hypnotherapists
I know.

D. Corydon Hammond

HANDBOOK

of

HYPNOTIC SUGGESTIONS
AND METAPHORS

An American Society of Clinical Hypnosis Book

A NORTON PROFESSIONAL BOOK

HANDBOOK

of
HYPNOTIC SUGGESTIONS
AND METAPHORS

EDITED BY

D. Corydon Hammond, Ph.D.

University of Utah
School of Medicine

W • W • NORTON & COMPANY • NEW YORK • LONDON

Printed in the United States of America

First Edition

Library of Congress Cataloging-in-Publication Data

Handbook of hypnotic suggestions and metaphors / edited by D. Corydon
  Hammond.
    p. cm.
   "An American Society of Clinical Hypnosis book."
   "A Norton professional book"—P.
   1. Hypnotism—Therapeutic use. I. Hammond, D. Corydon.
  RC495.H363 1990   615.8′512—dc20   90-31449

ISBN 0-393-70095-X

W. W. Norton & Company, Inc., 500 Fifth Avenue, New York, N.Y. 10110
W. W. Norton & Company, Ltd., 37 Great Russell Street, London WC1B 3NU

1 2 3 4 5 6 7 8 9 0

This book is dedicated with deep love and affection to my children,
Matthew, Erin, Christopher, and Mark

FOREWORD

Hypnotherapy is the application of hypnosis in a wide variety of medical and psychological disorders. Adequate training in psychotherapy is a prerequisite for practicing hypnosis, regardless of whether the clinician is a psychologist, physician, social worker, or dentist. In fact, training in psychotherapy and hypnotherapy is a never-ending process.

A text of this magnitude offers both the neophyte and the experienced clinician a tremendous, comprehensive reference. After receiving initial classroom or workshop training, additional training comes through reading, self-study and self-experience. This book represents a beacon for those desiring additional training in treating clinical problems. Having this reference available will give the new practitioner a very secure feeling.

This is a book for clinical practitioners. In fact, it will undoubtedly become *the* practical companion volume and supplement to comprehensive textbooks and courses on hypnosis. It provides the reader with the "how to" suggestions that therapists use with their patients. Rather than intellectually discussing the topic of hypnosis, this book gives therapists, physicians and dentists a sampling of what experienced clinicians actually say to their patients during hypnotic work. At last we have a book that helps answer the common query from our students: "But what do I say now that the patient is hypnotized?"

Every student and clinician who uses hypnosis will want to have this invaluable and comprehensive desktop reference. It represents the largest collection of therapeutic suggestions and metaphors ever assembled, with contributions from over 100 of the world's finest hypnotherapists. For those interested in the theoretical and research aspects of hypnosis, there are numerous other volumes that may be found in libraries. In my opinion, we are very fortunate in having this new text in which something so complicated has been made so much more understandable.

However, Dr. Hammond rightly emphasizes that this is not meant to be a cookbook of suggestions to be routinely used with certain problems. And simply the extensiveness of the suggestions he has compiled will tend to discourage anyone from mechanically applying the same paragraph of suggestions to everyone with a problem. His inclusion of empirical indications and contraindications for modules of suggestions is also intended to facilitate thoughtful treatment planning and the individualization of treatment.

What you will find here is a resource book from which you will be able to pick and choose suggestions that you clinically judge to be compatible with individual patients and with your own personal style of doing hypnosis. It is an eclectic book that models a wide range of styles of practice in clinical hypnosis. The tremendous breadth of suggestions will also serve as a stimulus to your creativity in preparing hypnotic suggestions and metaphors of your own. Chapter 2 will enhance your skills further through outlining the principles and guidelines for formulating successful hypnotic and posthypnotic suggestions.

Suggestions included in the book concern dozens of clinical problems. There are chapters and sections of suggestions on such medical topics as pain, hypnoanesthesia and hypnotic preparation for surgery, burns, emergencies, gastrointestinal disorders, cancer, chemotherapy, dermatologic complaints, obesity, smoking and addictions, childbirth training, obstetrical and gynecologic applications, insomnia, autoimmune diseases, and hemophilia.

Psychotherapists will find practical suggestions concerning habit disorders (e.g., nailbiting, trichotillomania), anxiety and phobic disorders, sexual dysfunctions and relationship problems, concentration, academic performance, sports, ego-strengthening to increase self-esteem and self-efficacy, posttraumatic stress disorders, multiple personality disorder, severely disturbed (e.g., borderline, schizophrenic) patients, and other emotional disorders. A chapter on hypnosis with children includes such clinical topics as pain and hypnoanesthesia, dyslexia, stuttering, enuresis, Tourette syndrome, school phobia, and asthma. Dentists will find useful suggestions concerning bruxism, TMJ, anxiety and phobic responses, pain control, thumbsucking, vascular control and gagging. There are also suggestions to be found on facilitating age regression, age progression, and time distortion. Each chapter represents the epitome of clinical expertise extant in our field.

This *Handbook* contains a wealth of original and previously unpublished suggestions that Dr. Hammond solicited from many of our most experienced hypnotherapists. In these pages you will also discover many of the finest suggestions that have appeared in books, chapters and journal articles over the last 30 years. For example, suggestions are included from throughout the back issues of the two most prestigious hypnosis journals in the world, the *American Journal of Clinical Hypnosis* and the *International Journal of Clinical & Experimental Hypnosis*. Dr. Hammond has done the work for us of reviewing tens of thousands of pages of books and journals, and then compiling in one place the practical clinical gems that he discovered.

This book was a massive undertaking. Tasks of this kind require literally hundreds of hours of personal sacrifice and effort. Very few people possess this dedication and scholastic capability. The present text is literally Herculean in scope, volume and content. The book is also unique in that neither Dr. Hammond nor any of his contributors will receive royalties from its publication. The book was literally a labor of love by all those who have contributed. It was donated to and accepted as an official publication of the American Society of Clinical Hypnosis. All royalties from its sale will go to the American Society of Clinical Hypnosis to promote further research and workshop training in clinical hypnosis throughout the United States and Canada.

Dr. Hammond is a master clinician of unusual breadth and talent who has become one of the giants in the field of clinical hypnosis. Part of his brilliance lies in the expertise that he has in integrating the practical contributions that are found in a great diversity of different orientations and approaches to hypnosis. Although he clearly makes scholarly and research contributions to the field, Dr. Hammond is primarily a clinician of the greatest magnitude, as exemplified by this text. Cory Hammond is one of the few people whom I know capable of authoring and compiling this type of text. People in the field will always be indebted for this yeoman challenge which he has completed in this magnificent presentation. His clinical breadth, extensive practical experience, and thorough knowledge of the field are truly reflected in this work. Dr. Hammond's book is destined to be a classic in the field that will be sought after for decades to come. It will rank as one of the greatest therapeutic contributions made in the fields of medicine, psychology, dentistry and allied fields.

Harold B. Crasilneck, Ph.D.
Past President, American Society of Clinical Hypnosis and the Society of
    Clinical and Experimental Hypnosis
Clinical Professor of Psychiatry and Anesthesiology, University of Texas
    Health Sciences Center, Dallas

CONTENTS

6. Anxiety, Phobias, and Dental Disorders   153

7. Hypnosis with Cancer Patients   199

8. Hypnosis with Medical Disorders   217

14. Concentration, Academic Performance, and Athletic Performance   433

16. Time Reorientation: Age Regression, Age Progression, and Time Distortion   509

INTRODUCTION

THIS IS A PRACTICAL resource book for clinicians. Although it is a large compilation of therapeutic suggestions and metaphors, I wish to emphasize from the outset that it is not intended as a "cookbook" of suggestions to be routinely used with various clinical problems. My own personal philosophy of hypnotherapy is to encourage therapists to individualize hypnotic suggestions to the unique personality, expectations, motivations and problems of the patient (Hammond, 1988a).

In the introductions to chapters I have often provided a scholarly overview of relevant research because I believe that it is important for clinicians to be aware of this literature. But this volume is not intended as a thorough text of the field of hypnosis. Rather, it is first and foremost a practical reference for clinical practitioners who are already trained in the use of hypnosis and a practical companion volume to comprehensive textbooks (e.g., Crasilneck & Hall, 1985; Hammond & Miller, in press; Watkins, 1987; Weitzenhoffer, 1989; Wester & Smith, 1984).

The intent of this book is to provide clinicians with models of hypnotic suggestions and metaphors from seasoned hypnotherapists who have diverse approaches and styles. Verbalizations for hypnotic induction and deepening techniques have not been included because they may be found abundantly in the texts identified above, as well as in the American Society of Clinical Hypnosis course text, *Hypnotic Induction and Suggestion* (Hammond, 1988c).

All too frequently we are only exposed to general descriptions of a therapeutic approach. As part of our training, we certainly need instruction in theory, history, assessment, guidelines and overall strategies. But if we are to function effectively as clinicians we also need exposure to the pragmatic nuts and bolts of what to say to patients. There is a deficit of such material in graduate education and students regularly complain that their training is not practical enough. This volume is designed to respond to that need and provide you with a look at what experienced clinicians actually tend to say to their patients during hypnotic work.

You will find suggestions that are highly indirect, permissive and metaphoric, and ones that are also very direct, forceful and authoritative. I must admit to having occasionally included a suggestion that I, personally, would probably not use with a patient, despite considering myself very eclectic and flexible. But there may be some readers who will appreciate and find certain of these same suggestions both helpful and compatible with their own style. As therapists we are as distinctive as our patients. It is hoped, therefore, that as you treat patients with specific problems you will find that you can pick and choose different paragraphs and modules of suggestions from various contributors and adapt them to your individual patient. The variety of suggestions will often provide you with alternative ways of communicating with a patient about a particular problem. We cannot always know for sure which ideas will produce the desired motivation. As Erickson (Rossi & Ryan, 1985) said, "You provide a multiplicity of suggestions: the more suggestions that you give, and the more simply you give them, the greater the possibility of getting some of them accepted. Your task isn't to force a patient to accept suggestions. Your task is to present a sufficient number of suggestions so that he will willingly take this one and that one" (p. 213).

In many ways hypnosis is the art of securing a patient's attention and then effectively communicating ideas that enhance motivation and change perceptions. There is nothing sacred about the phrasing of the suggestions in this volume. As Dr. Milton Erickson (Rossi & Ryan, 1985) taught, "I want all of you to be willing to disagree with my wording, because it's right for me but it may be wrong for you" (p. 216). You will undoubtedly find interesting ideas and concepts that appeal to you in the suggestions of many different contributors. But ofttimes you will probably find yourself wanting to convey the same idea a little differently, in your own way or in a manner that you believe will be more appealing to a particular patient. This is as it should be. In fact, this was another reason for compiling this volume—my belief that it will serve to stimulate your creativity in preparing your own suggestions and metaphors.

Alexander Hamilton once said, "Men give me some credit for genius, but all of the genius I have lies in this. When I have a subject in mind, I study it profoundly, day and night it is before me. I explore it in all its bearings. My mind becomes pervaded with it. The result is what some people call the fruits of genius, whereas it is in reality the fruits of study and labor." Part of the genius that was attributed to our Society's founding President, Dr. Milton H. Erickson, stemmed from this same kind of hard work and study. His sophistication and polish evolved from his discipline in carefully writing and rewriting suggestions and thoughtfully planning treatment (Hammond, 1984a, 1988b). He did this regularly for several decades of his life. Although this book will undoubtedly contain suggestions that you will find useful with patients or clients, it is also hoped that these materials will provide you with ideas and encouragement to thoughtfully prepare your own suggestions and metaphors.

The Underlying Therapeutic Philosophy: Integrative Hypnotherapy

Certainly this edited work reflects some of my own philosophy of psychotherapy, which is one of broad spectrum, eclectic treatment. Reliance on a limited range of methods and one approach appears to often be associated with inexperience as a therapist (Auerbach & Johnson, 1977; Fey, 1958; Parloff, Waskow, & Wolfe, 1978; Strupp, 1955; Wogan & Norcross, 1985). In fact, research has found that it is the most highly experienced therapists who ascribe to an eclectic approach (Norcross & Prochaska, 1982; Smith, 1982), refusing to be limited by adherence to only one orientation. Currently 30%-54% of psychotherapists from various disciplines identify themselves as eclectic (Norcross, 1986). It is my belief that not all patients need the same thing. Thus you will find a tremendous diversity in the suggestions represented in this book. In fact, when therapists tend to inflexibly use the same approach with all patients, there is evidence that destructive effects are much more likely to occur (Lieberman, Yalom, & Miles, 1973).

In the specialty area of hypnotherapy, we are beginning to witness an evolution similar to what has been seen in the broader field of psychotherapy where innumerable therapeutic schools and cults have sprung up. Various orientations to hypnosis have also begun to evolve. Unfortunately, we now see some clinicians who have begun to operate on the "one-true-light-assumption" that their specialized approach to hypnosis is *the* correct one. Similar to Erickson, I refuse to be limited by a unitary theory or orientation, either in psychotherapy or in my use of hypnosis. I value and encourage an openness to learning from all quarters. I am indebted to the work of many different master clinicians and hypnotherapists with highly divergent styles who have enriched my work in ways that would have never occurred if I limited myself to only one approach.

Thus I identify my approach to hypnotherapy as *Integrative Hypnotherapy* (Hammond & Miller, in press). This is an eclectic, multidimensional orientation that seeks to be comprehensive, incorporating methods from many hypnotic approaches. It is part of the emergent trend in psychotherapy, tracing its roots to pioneers like Thorne (1967), Wolberg (1954, 1967, 1987), Lazarus (1981), and more recently Beutler (1983), Prochaska and DiClemente (1984), Norcross (1986), and Hammond and Stanfield (1977). Depending upon the individual patient, direct, indirect, metaphoric, and insight-oriented techniques may be employed to alter behavior, affect, physiologic processes, imagery, perceptions, cognitions, and the internal dialogue of patients. Hypnosis is used to explore preconscious and unconscious functions, resolve historical factors, and utilize unconscious resources.

This method of working builds on the general philosophy of technical eclecticism (Lazarus, 1981; Hammond & Stanfield, 1977), encouraging the prescriptive use of techniques according to indications and contraindications derived empirically and by experimental validation, rather relying on theories. Unfortunately, research on effectiveness is far too often lacking and experimentally validated criteria commonly do not exist on indications, contraindications and the matching of techniques with patient variables. Thus strategy and technique selection currently remain implicit and primarily guided by empirical evidence and clinical experience. Hypnotherapy, like psychotherapy, is still more of an art and only embryonic in scientific development. Tentative and yet systematic and explicit guidelines need to be published concerning strategy and technique selection with different patients, and this process is currently under development (Hammond & Miller, in press).

Stemming from this therapeutic philosophy, you will find that I have often included some suggestive guidelines and indications for the use of the hypnotic suggestions and metaphors that have been included in the book. I have indicated when these guidelines were mine. The titles and subtitles throughout the text are in most cases mine also. They have been provided to allow you to more easily identify "modules" of suggestions that have a different theme or focus.

A necessary limitation of this book is that it focuses primarily on what we call suggestive hypnosis. Sometimes suggestive hypnosis is all that is needed to successfully treat a clinical problem. However, there are times when problems and symptoms are related to historical factors (e.g., trauma) and/or serve adaptive functions and purposes that are beyond conscious awareness. In these cases, delivering hypnotic suggestions and metaphors will be most effective following uncovering and age regression (abreactive) work. A comprehensive, integrative approach to hypnosis thus includes the use of exploratory and insight-oriented hypnotic techniques. These interventions, however, are much more difficult to model in a limited amount of space and consequently are only rarely included in this book. These methods may be studied by consulting Hammond and Miller (in press), Rossi and Cheek (1988), Brown and Fromm (1986), and Watkins (in press).

Finally, I wish to emphasize that hypnosis is often most effective when it is combined with other (nonhypnotic) interventions. Hypnosis is like any other medical or psychological technique or modality: it is not uniformly effective with all problems or all patients. Thus it is vitally important that we do not identify ourselves as "hypnotists," but rather as psychologists, physicians, dentists, social workers, marriage and family therapists, nurse anesthetists, etc., who use hypnosis as one mode of intervention along with our other clinical tools.

Furthermore, ethical practice requires that we only use hypnosis to treat problems that we are qualified to treat with nonhypnotic techniques. If one has not received advanced specialty training and supervision in practicing with children or in doing sex therapy, it seems ethically inappropriate to use hypnosis to work in these areas. Hypnosis training alone does not qualify us to work in subspecialty areas beyond our expertise. Similarly, merely learning a few hypnotic inductions and then seeking to apply suggestions gleaned from a volume like this is likewise deemed to be inappropriate. The reader is encouraged to seek specialty training and supervision in hypnosis from your local university or the American Society of Clinical Hypnosis workshops, and to study comprehensive textbooks.

The American Society of Clinical Hypnosis

PURPOSE AND DESCRIPTION

The American Society of Clinical Hypnosis (ASCH) was founded in 1957, with Milton H. Erickson, M.D., as the first president. Numbering almost 4,000 members, the ASCH is a nonprofit professional organization. Its purpose is to establish and maintain the foremost society in North America of professionals in medicine, psychology and dentistry dedicated to informing the public about the therapeutic effects of hypnosis and educating qualified professionals in the use of hypnosis for the benefit of humanity and themselves.

A central objective of the society is to provide and encourage educational programs to further, in every ethical way, the knowledge, understanding and acceptance of hypnosis as an important clinical tool. Thus, almost monthly, ASCH conducts beginning, intermediate and advanced training workshops at different locations throughout the United States and Canada, as well as an annual workshop. Approximately four dozen local Component Sections of the American Society of Clinical Hypnosis also provide ongoing professional interaction and educational programs.

Another key purpose of the society is to stimulate research and encourage scientific publication in the field of clinical hypnosis. Thus we also sponsor an annual scientific meeting, held in conjunction with the annual workshops. The American Journal of Clinical Hypnosis is published quarterly by the society. In addition to the professional papers and book reviews, the journal also includes abstracts of the worldwide hypnosis literature. A comprehensive computer search of references to worldwide publications is also included in each issue of the Newsletter, which is published five times a year. The ASCH Education and Research Foundation was established to encourage and promote both education and research.

Training Opportunities

REGIONAL WORKSHOPS

Eight or nine regional workshops are held yearly in different cities throughout the United States and Canada. This training is available to licensed psychologists, physicians, dentists, social workers, marriage and family therapists, and masters degree level registered nurses with advanced subspecialty training and certification. Medical residents and doctoral students in medicine, dentistry and psychology are also eligible to attend. Students, residents, interns, ASCH members, and full-time faculty members are eligible for discounted registration rates.

The regional workshops generally are conducted at three levels simultaneously: beginning, intermediate and advanced. A course text is available to participants and the workshops include the opportunity for several hours of supervised practice. The faculty is changed for each regional workshop, providing participants with models of a variety of styles of practice. Workshops generally begin Thursday evening and conclude at noon on Sunday. You may write for information at the address listed below.

ANNUAL WORKSHOPS AND SCIENTIFIC MEETING

Held in late March or early April each year, the annual meeting consists of two and one-half days of workshops and a two-day scientific meeting. A beginning and intermediate workshop is part of the program, and there is an extensive range of advanced workshop offerings. The 50-60 faculty members for the annual workshops include many of the finest teachers in the world. Professional papers in the scientific meeting cover a broad range of topics.

AMERICAN JOURNAL OF CLINICAL HYPNOSIS

Published quarterly, the *American Journal of Clinical Hypnosis* contains both experimental and clinical papers, book reviews, and abstracts of worldwide hypnosis literature that is in English or has English abstracts. Yearly subscriptions are available for $30. Subscription and advertising inquiries should be sent to the Business Manager, ASCH, 2200 E. Devon Ave., Suite 291, Des Plaines, IL. 60018, USA.

VIDEOTAPE LIBRARY AND AUDIOTAPES

Dozens of audiotapes of past workshops and scientific meeting presentations are available for purchase to professionals. In addition, the ASCH Videotape Library contains over 80 high quality videotapes of recognized authorities in the field demonstrating techniques. These videotapes are available for rental to members or Component Sections of the society.

BOOK SALES

For the convenience of members and attendees at workshops, ASCH maintains an inventory of many of the most respected volumes on different aspects of clinical hypnosis. In addition, the following three publications are available exclusively from ASCH:

1. *Hypnotic Induction and Suggestion*, edited by D. Corydon Hammond, Ph.D., is the ASCH course text for beginning and intermediate level workshops. This 134-page monograph is highly practical in nature and ideally suited for use in courses and seminars. A free instructor's copy is included with each class order of 20 or more books. It includes: verbalizations for 12 induction techniques; principles of induction and suggestion; a checklist assessment instrument for individualizing hypnosis; over 20 deepening techniques; guidelines and questions for rapid unconscious exploration through ideomotor signaling; 19 strategies for managing resistant patients; an annotated bibliography describing the contents of 135 books on hypnosis; preparing the patient; phenomena of hypnosis; stages and depth of hypnosis; self-hypnosis; adverse reactions; hypnosis and children; types of suggestions; and hypnotizability scales. It is available from ASCH for $15.00/copy plus $2.00 postage and handling.

2. *The ASCH Manual for Self-Hypnosis*, by D. Corydon Hammond, Ph.D. This 40-page manual is designed to provide your patients with the essential principles for using self-hypnosis. It will save you time in the

office, and patients who won't read a lengthy book will be willing to read this manual. Sections include: What is Hypnosis? Preparing for Self-Hypnosis; Preparing Hypnotic Suggestions; The Process of Self-Hypnosis; Deepening Your Hypnotic State; Spectatoring and Dealing with Distractions; Imagination: The Catalyst for Change; Having a Dialogue with Your Symptom; The Council of Advisers Technique; The Inner Adviser Technique; Mental Rehearsal and Age Progression; Erickson's Method of Self-Hypnosis; References for Further Reading. The cost is $5.00 (plus $2.00 shipping and handling on single orders), and quantity discounts are available to encourage its use with your patients.

3. *Learning Clinical Hypnosis: An Educational Resources Compendium.* "A unique, up-to-date volume on the methods and teaching of therapeutic hypnosis by D. Corydon Hammond and the acknowledged authorities of the American Society of Clinical Hypnosis. This is the *standard reference text* that belongs in the libraries of all medical, dental, and nursing schools, as well as graduate departments of Psychology and Social Work. Students and mature clinicians of all specialties will find an excellent orientation to the therapeutic art and leading edge of modern hypnosis right here!" Ernest L. Rossi, Ph.D.

This 393-page volume includes 265 pages of practical handouts and summaries of clinical techniques, 28 handouts on induction and deepening techniques, and 34 inductions for children. It includes sections on: foundations of knowledge, an overview of modules for teaching hypnosis and model course outlines, numerous alternatives for teaching demonstrations, many experiential learning exercises, formulating hypnotic suggestions, methods of unconscious exploration, age regression, methods of ego-strengthening, hypnotic strategies for pain management, specialized techniques and metaphors, resistance, and a comprehensive overview of commercially available audiovisual aids and resources. It is available for $37.50 (add $3.50 for shipping and handling).

COMPONENT SECTIONS

Approximately four dozen local component sections of ASCH provide support, professional interaction, and further training opportunities to members. Many component sections also allow masters degree practitioners membership status. Foreign affiliated societies offer still further opportunities for international exchange.

THE ASCH NEWSLETTER

Published five times a year, the Newsletter provides members with timely information about latest developments in the field and training opportunities. Clinically relevant information is frequently included, as well as a current literature computer search update.

Eligibility for ASCH Membership

To be eligible for membership, the applicant must have:

a. An M.D., D.D.S., D.M.D., D.O. or a Ph.D., or an equivalent degree (e.g., Ed.D. or D.S.W.) with psychology as the major study. (Doctoral level social workers and doctoral level marriage and family therapists frequently meet these requirements);
b. a doctorate from a university or college accredited by its appropriate regional accrediting body;
c. a license to practice in the state or province;
d. membership or eligibility for membership in a professional society consistent with his/her degree;
e. 40 hours of appropriate professional training and experience in clinical or experimental hypnosis.

To be eligible for associate membership, the applicant must have:

a. An M.D., D.D.S., D.M.D., D.O. or a Ph.D., or an equivalent degree (e.g., Ed.D. or D.S.W.) with psychology as the major study;
b. a doctorate from a university or college accredited by its appropriate regional accrediting body;
c. a license to practice in the state or province;
d. membership or eligibility for membership in a professional society consistent with his/her degree;
e. an associate member shall have two years' time allotted for acquiring the prerequisite clinical experience and training for full membership requirements.

To be eligible for student affiliate membership, the applicant must be:

a. A full-time student with a minimum of 45 completed graduate semester hours or 60 completed graduate quarter hours; and shall be (1) enrolled in a graduate program in active pursuit of a doctorate in medicine (M.D. or D.O.), dentistry or psychology, or (2) enrolled in a doctoral program where psychology is the major field of study;
b. pursuing his/her doctoral degree at a university or college fully accredited by the appropriate regional accrediting body to give such a degree.

For further information concerning membership, training, tapes or publications, please contact:
The American Society of Clinical Hypnosis
  2200 East Devon Ave., Suite 291
  Des Plaines, Illinois 60018
  (312) 297-3317

All royalties from the sale of this book have been donated to the American Society of Clinical Hypnosis to promote further training and research in hypnosis.

Acknowledgments

This book represents the compilation of many different people's styles and ways of working. Appreciation is extended to the dozens of master clinicians who freely contributed their work to ASCH for publication in this volume and in the 1973 *Handbook of Therapeutic Suggestions*. The finest suggestions from the 1973 volume have been retained in this book.

Thanks are also in order to Dr. Louis Dubin, past president of the American Society of Clinical Hypnosis, and to my colleagues on the Executive Committee of ASCH for encouraging this massive undertaking. I am also appreciative for the assistance of Drs. Michael Yapko, Valerie Wall, and Daniel Kohen for reviewing and providing feedback on some of the original material that was submitted. Most of all, I appreciate the sacrifices of my loving wife and companion, Melanie, who provided encouragement, endured this project along with me, and thoughfully helped proofread this volume.

FORMULATING HYPNOTIC AND POSTHYPNOTIC SUGGESTIONS

Iₙ ᴛʜɪs ᴄʜᴀᴘᴛᴇʀ ᴡᴇ ᴡɪʟʟ overview the major principles and guidelines involved in formulating effective hypnotic suggestions. Afterwards, we will discuss different types of suggestions that may be constructed and how to phrase suggestions. Finally we will examine the process of how you may present a series of suggestions in order to production different hypnotic phenomena. Keep in mind that hypnotic suggestions may be directed toward behaviors, emotions, sensations and physiologic processes, cognition, imagery, and relationships (Hammond & Miller, in press; Hammond & Stanfield, 1977). Suggestions may also focus on producing immediate responses within the hypnotic session or posthypnotic effects.

O Laws

Principles of Hypnotic Suggestion 32

1. ### ESTABLISH RAPPORT AND A COOPERATIVE RELATIONSHIP

Establishing a relationship with the patient must always be considered the first and most vitally important prerequisite for suggestions to be effective. Relating to the patient in a warm, understanding, caring and respectful manner reduces defensiveness and creates the trusting kind of climate that is necessary for hypnosis to be maximally effective. Because hypnosis is a cooperative venture, rather than something we do *to* the patient, it is crucially important to devote time to the human relationship dimension and not to simply concentrate on technical expertise in hypnosis alone.

2. ### CREATE POSITIVE EXPECTANCY

Experienced hypnotherapists are probably more effective than new students, at least in part, because they act utterly expectant and confident that their suggestions will occur. This inspires confidence in patients. Act and speak confidently.

There are times, as we will discuss shortly, when it is wise to phrase suggestions in a more permissive and indirect way. Exercise caution, however, that you do not speak in such a laissez faire manner that you are perceived as lacking confidence. This is a mistake common among hypnotherapists with limited experience and confidence, or who are trying to be overly permissive. Be careful about using words such as "perhaps," "maybe," "can," or "might" (Brown & Fromm, 1986). For instance, listen to the lack of conviction and confidence conveyed by these suggestions: "One of your hands *might* begin feeling lighter." "*Maybe* (*Perhaps*) your hand *can* float up." "*Perhaps* a numbness will develop in your hand." Compare the difference when you change the words to "will" and "is." "One of your hands *is* beginning to get lighter, and *will* begin to float up, lighter and lighter." As we will discuss under the principle of successive approximations, you can be permissive concerning the time required to develop a response, and still convey confidence. It is important to make the distinction between being confident and authoritative versus authoritarian and dominating.

THE LAW OF REVERSED EFFECT

The principle of reversed effect primarily applies to making suggestions to produce physiological effects. This "law" refers to the fact that the harder one consciously endeavors to do something, the more difficult it becomes to succeed. Have you ever tried to consciously will an erection or an orgasm? Or, how many times have you retired to bed too late and tried to help yourself to go to sleep, only to find yourself more wide awake? Just as we are unsuccessful at trying to *will* ourselves to perspire or salivate, we are generally unsuccessful in applying conscious willpower to produce therapeutic changes, especially physiologic changes.

As you formulate suggestions, emphasize imagination and imagery rather than appealing to the conscious will. For example, instead of simply verbally suggesting that a hand is becoming numb, you may have patients imagine putting their hand into the snow or into an icy cold stream, while simultaneously suggesting anesthesia. Alternatively, seek to evoke memories and images of life experiences where the phenomenon was experienced in the past. For example: "And one of the things that you don't know that you know, is how to lose the ability to feel. (This is a confusional statement that creates a sense of wonderment.) And yet you've experienced that many times—like when you've fallen asleep on a hand or an arm, and awakened to find it numb, or like when you've gone to a dentist and had novocaine or lidocaine injected—and I'm sure you know what those numb, leathery sensations feel like, do you not?" (These are truisms that evoke memories of the desired phenomenon.)

LAW OF CONCENTRATED ATTENTION: REPETITION OF SUGGESTIONS

This refers to the principle of repetition of suggestions. When we concentrate attention repeatedly on a goal or idea, it tends to be realized.

Thus, a classic principle in formulating important hypnotic suggestions is to repeat them several (e.g., three or four) times. Repetition of suggestion may be accomplished through using somewhat synonymous words and phrases. However, one of Milton Erickson's (1954/1980) contributions to hypnosis was his model of giving *both* direct verbal suggestions and also using metaphoric examples as an indirect method of repeating suggestions. Thus, Erickson often told a metaphor or two to "seed" an idea. He would then make a bridging association, identifying the relevance of the stories to the patient's problem, and finally, he would offer the patient direct suggestions.

THE PRINCIPLE OF SUCCESSIVE APPROXIMATIONS

In formulating hypnotic and posthypnotic suggestions, it is essential to not expect your patients to immediately produce various hypnotic phenomena. As therapists we often err in the same way as our patients: we hold magical expectations that hypnosis will produce instant results. We, like our patients, often want immediate gratification. But most clients do not "leap tall buildings in a single bound." Be patient as you seek to facilitate hypnotic phenomenon, and allow the client time to develop the desired response. It may be helpful, when responses are slow in coming, to mentally break the desired task down in your mind into intermediate steps to be facilitated. When you expect positive results, exude confidence, and are persistent in working to produce one the hypnotic phenomenon, the little bit of extra time will usually be rewarded.

Adjust your pace to your patient's rate of response. Thus you will want to avoid the authoritarian suggestions reminiscent of lay hypnotists and stage hypnotists: "You will immediately...," "In five minutes you will...," "By the time you awaken your pain will be *completely* gone." Respect the individuality of your patient and realize that different persons will require more time to respond to a suggestion. When giving suggestions for new patients, where you are not yet aware of their response potentials, it is, therefore, desirable to phrase the suggestions in more a fail-safe and permissive manner (Erickson & Rossi, 1979). We will discuss this further as we talk about different types of suggestions.

We should add, however, that you can be permissive concerning time, and yet still convey a confidence that patient's will, in their own time, respond to the suggestions. Some of the following types of words are permissive concerning time, but still contain the implication that the patient will respond: "soon," "before long," "yet," "beginning to notice," "shortly," "in its own way." For example: "And do you *begin* to notice the tingling and numbness beginning *yet*?" "*Soon* you'll sense a lightness *starting* to develop in that hand. And you can begin to wonder just *when* you'll *first* sense a twitch and sensation of movement in one of the fingers. And that hand's *becoming* lighter."

THE LAW OF DOMINANT EFFECT

This principle states that stronger emotions tend to take precedence over weaker ones. Thus, once again, rather than appealing to the conscious will, you will find it more effective to connect your suggestions to a dominant emotion. The famous defense attorney Clarence Darrow once described his prime courtroom strategy. He would seek to stir the emotions of the jury so that they wanted to decide the case his way, and then he would look for a technicality to give them to justify it. We as therapists may similarly be more influential by seeking to stir the emotions of patients and connect suggestions to them. It is my belief that this strategy is probably most effective with those patients who tend to emphasize their heart and emotions more than their intellect and rationality in decision-making. Related to this concept, you may at times seek to arouse an internal state of tension and anticipation in the patient that can be resolved only through producing the desired hypnotic response.

THE CARROT PRINCIPLE

As therapists we sometimes, in effect, try to push our patients from behind, toward a goal. But, like trying to push a mule toward our chosen destination, we find that some of our patients dig in their heels and resist our influence. Instead of pushing people from behind, we should be seeking to motivate them from in front, toward a goal. Therefore, as you formulate suggestions, interject comments about the patient's goals.

This principle encourages us to link the patient's motivations and goals with our suggestions, just as the Law of Dominant Effect encourages us to tie suggestions to strong emotions of the patient. By way of illustration, as part of a suggestion for deepening, you may state: "And you will sink deeper and deeper in the trance as that arm floats up toward your face, because you want to live to raise your children, and you want to become a nonsmoker." Along the same vein, when you work with a patient who gives more importance in his life to logic and reasoning (as contrasted with emotion), provide him with logical reasons (or even pseudo-rationales) for accepting your suggestions.

THE PRINCIPLE OF POSITIVE SUGGESTION

Rather than seeking to override existing motives or attitudes, create positive motivation and attitudes in your patients. This can sometimes be difficult to do, and in actuality, there is no research evidence to validate this principle. Thus you will notice that occasionally a contributor to this book resorts to a negative suggestion. Nonetheless, based on clinical wisdom, I recommend that whenever possible you should seek to change negative suggestions to positive ones. When this cannot be done, you may wish to precede the negative suggestion with an easily performed or accepted positive suggestion (Weitzenhoffer, 1989).

By way of illustration, instead of suggesting to a weight control patient, "You will not be hungry," (an unlikely, and even undesirable proposition), you may suggest: "And you'll be surprised to discover, how really comfortable you *will* be, because you'll simply become so absorbed in the things you're doing, that time will go by very rapidly, and suddenly, to your surprise, you realize that it's time for another meal." As another example, rather than suggesting, "You won't eat sweets or foods that are bad for you," you may suggest: "You will protect your body, treating it with kindness and respect, as if it were just like your precious, innocent little boy that you love, totally dependent upon your care and protection. You will protect your body, just as you protect and take care of your son." In talking to a child with a bedwetting problem, you talk about having a "dry bed" rather than about *not* wetting the bed.

9. THE PRINCIPLE OF POSITIVE REINFORCEMENT

Reinforce and compliment the patient both in and out of trance. "You're doing that very nicely." "Good. You're doing very well." "Umm hmm. That's right. And really enjoy the weightlessness of that hand, as it continues to float all the way up to your face." "You've worked very hard today, and I hope that your unconscious mind will take a real pride in how hypnotically talented you are, and in how much you've accomplished." As a further model of how you may compliment the hypnotized patient, note what Erickson (Erickson & Rossi, 1989) told a patient on two different occasions: "Also, after you awaken, I want you to have a very thorough appreciation of how very capably you have worked tonight." "I want you to know that I thank you for your generosity, your kindness, in permitting me to do things in my way. I appreciate it tremendously. It was very kind of you . . ." Social psychology research certainly suggests that compliments or praise will generally enhance patients' rapport and liking of us, and, therefore, their compliance to suggestions.

Certain suggestions may also be reinforced nonverbally. For example, in facilitating levitation, limb heaviness, or glove anesthesia, the hypnotherapist may reinforce verbal suggestions through very lightly stroking the patient's arm or hand two or three times: "And as I stroke that hand, you'll notice how the anesthesia begins to spread and flow through that hand." Similarly, you may "prompt" a patient who is slow in developing levitation, gently using an upward stroking motion under the forearm during inhalations, or lightly lifting the fingertips.

10. CREATING AN ACCEPTANCE OR YES-SET

For many years human relations experts and sales people have known the importance of obtaining an initial "yes" response from someone you are trying to influence. A powerful orator will seek to immediately obtain affirmative responses from the audience to create an acceptance set mentally. As early at 1936, Dale Carnegie emphasized this principle, referring to it as "the secret of Socrates." "His method? Did he tell people they were wrong? On, no, not Socrates. He was far too adroit for that. His whole technique, now called the 'Socratic method,' was based upon getting a 'yes, yes' response. He asked questions with which his opponent would have to agree. He kept on winning one admission after another until he had an armful of yeses. He kept on asking questions until finally, almost without realizing it, his opponent found himself embracing a conclusion that he would have bitterly denied a few minutes previously" (Carnegie, 1966, p. 144).

One particular type of hypnotic suggestion is particularly effective at eliciting a "yes-set": truisms. The truism, which will be discussed more fully later, is an undeniable statement of fact. For instance, "All of us have had the experience of walking along on a cold, winter day, and feeling the cold against our skin." Using suggestions in the form of truisms creates an acceptance set. This may be enhanced even further by interacting with the hypnotized patient. For example, continuing with the suggestion we just gave: "And I'm sure you've felt how cold the winter wind can be against your skin, have you not?" Most patient's will nod their head "yes." If an overt response was not immediately forthcoming, you could simply add, "You can simply gently nod your head up and down for yes, and back and forth for no. And you *can* remember how cold the winter's wind can feel against your face, can you not?" (Following a nod for "yes":) "And you remember how you can see your breath, like fog, in the cold air, don't you? (Patient nods.) And the longer you walk with your face or your bare hands exposed to that cold air, the more numb they feel, don't they? And so your mind remembers what that feeling of numbness is like." This type of sequence of undeniable experiences, where patients think or nonverbally indicate, "Yes, yes, yes, yes," makes it more difficult for them to not continue responding affirmatively to the suggestions that follow.

INTERACTIVE TRANCE AND CONFIRMING THE ACCEPTABILITY OF SUGGESTIONS

It is common for new hypnotherapists to expect that the patient should basically remain in a silent and passive role, while the therapist assumes full responsibility for single-handedly formulating suggestions and controlling the patient's experience. This is an error. We observe students frequently suggesting various types of internal (e.g., imagery, regression) experiences without any idea whether the patient is actually experiencing what was suggested.

You may involve the patient as an active participant in hypnotherapy in at least three ways. First, prior to hypnotic work, obtain patients' input and ideas about their interests, preferences, suggestions and the approach that they deem most likely to be effective. When your style of hypnotic work is congruent with the patient's expectations, you may anticipate a greater likelihood of success.

Second, you may obtain nonverbal feedback from the patient in the form of head nods, ideomotor finger signals, or even levitation as a signal to monitor progress. This type of suggestion has been called the implied directive. After giving posthypnotic suggestions, for example, you may suggest: "And if your unconscious mind is willing to accept this idea [or, "all of these ideas"], your 'yes' finger will float up to signal me." If a response is not forthcoming within the next 20 seconds or so, you may add,

"Or, if your unconscious mind isn't willing to accept all of these ideas, your 'no' finger can float up to signal me." In this manner you will be able to determine the acceptability of suggestions and whether resistance is present. Personally, I would rather know if there is resistance immediately so that we can work it through, rather than discovering it a week later.

Neophyte hypnotists too often practice what we might call, "When I wish upon a star therapy" — giving hypnotic suggestions and then hoping that they will magically have an impact on and be accepted by the patient. It seems far more desirable to regularly track patient progress, the acceptability of your suggestions, and the success of internal therapeutic work. Thus, after giving a hypnotic or posthypnotic suggestion, you may ask the patient: "Would that be all right?" "Is that acceptable to you?" "Do you understand?" "Do you understand this clearly?" "And is that all right?" "Would you be willing to do that?" This was a common practice of Dr. Milton Erickson. Once a suggestion is accepted, it commits the patient to a course of change and therapeutic movement.

The "unconscious" mind may also be consulted, as modeled two paragraphs above, to obtain a more involuntary commitment about the acceptability of suggestions. This is a regular practice in my therapeutic work. Once such confirmation is obtained, it is no longer necessary to be overly permissive or indirect in presenting suggestions to the patient. You have confirmed that resistance is not present, and you can, therefore, deliver the suggestions in a more positive, confident and forceful manner.

Obtaining commitments in hypnosis, whether conscious or unconscious, is a powerful therapeutic tool for increasing the effectiveness of suggestions. The reason seems to be that most people experience an internal pressure and need to feel and look consistent. Considerable social psychological research indicates that when someone makes an initial commitment, he is subsequently more willing to accept ideas related to the prior commitment (Cialdini, 1988). In fact, obtaining any kind of commitment at all seems to increase the likelihood of accepting subsequent ideas. This is the basis for the well-known sales strategy referred to as the "foot-in-the-door technique." Sales people usually start with a small, often seemingly innocuous request, realizing that a domino effect will often result once the change process is under way. Once inertia has been overcome, further movement is much easier to obtain. This is also the basis for the "yes-set" that we have already discussed.

Nonverbal responses may also be requested to determine when internal processes are being experienced or have been completed. Some examples will illustrate this process: "When you become aware of the numbness beginning to develop in your right hand, just gently nod your head up and down for yes." "And when your unconscious mind has identified a time in your past when you felt calm and confident, your 'yes' finger will float up to signal me." "And as you walk along in the mountains, the path will eventually lead you down by a creek or stream. And when you're walking along by that creek, just gently not your head up and down to signal me." Other illustrations will be given later as we discuss the implied directive as a type of suggestion.

Let's model the manner in which nonverbal signaling might be used in exploratory or abreactive work. Suppose that we have a female patient who was a victim of incest as a child, and that you have had the patient regress to the age of four, relive the experience and abreact the feelings. Some therapists might just assume that feelings have been resolved at this point, and simply give some posthypnotic suggestions. However, following abreaction and reframing, I consider it a more careful and thoughtful approach to interact with the patient and check concerning the resolution and acceptance of suggestions: "And now that you've released all those old, outdated feelings, is your unconscious mind now willing to let go of all those old, out-of-date feelings, so that they'll no longer influence you?" If an ideomotor signal for "yes" is obtained, you can more confidently suggest: "You can now let go of all those old feelings of anger, and hurt, and fear, and guilt. Just let go of all those outdated feelings, and when your unconscious mind can sense you letting go of them, your 'yes' finger will float up again." (Following a positive response:) "That's right. And your unconscious mind can finish letting go of all those old feelings, so that you will now be free of the effects of that experience. It will no longer influence how you think, or act, or feel. And I want to ask, can your unconscious mind now sense that all men are not like your father?" (After a positive response:) Good. You can now understand that all men are not like your father. And do you realize that your husband is not like your father?" (Again, following a positive response:) That's right, you can now appreciate that all men are not like your father. And you will begin to see men as individuals now, perceiving them as distinct individuals. All men are not like your father, and your husband is not like your father. And you are free now; free to relate to men as individuals, and free to relate to your husband as an individual. And those events that we've worked through will no longer influence how you think or act or feel. You are free now."

Finally, at times the patient may also be asked to verbally interact during hypnotic work. It is commonly believed that verbalizing "lightens" a hypnotic state, and, therefore, nonverbal signals often seem preferable. There are situations, however, when information is needed that cannot be conveniently conveyed through nonverbal ("yes" or "no") responses. When verbal interaction only occurs occasionally during hypnosis, it will not significantly alter the depth of trance. Furthermore, suggestions may be offered to minimize the "lightening" of the trance. For example, you may suggest: "You can speak in a hypnotic state, just as you can speak in the dreams of the night, without awakening. And remaining very deep in a hypnotic state, I want you to just verbally tell me, what are you experiencing right now?" Or, "And in a moment, I'm going to ask you to speak to me. And as you speak, simply the sound of your voice will take you into a deeper and deeper hypnotic state. So that as you speak, with every sound of your voice, and with every word that you speak, you'll go deeper and deeper into the trance."

Sometimes interactive trance is useful during induction and deepening. You may simply ask the patient to occasionally describe what he is hearing or seeing during an imagery experience. This allows you to tailor your input, rather than "operating blind." Similarly, in working to produce certain hypnotic phenomena, it may be useful to obtain interaction, and then accept and utilize whatever the patient offers you.

THE PRINCIPLE OF TRANCE RATIFICATION

In hypnosis it is vitally important to create a sense of positive expectancy in the patient. Trance ratification refers to the process of providing the patient with a convincer, that is, an experience or experiences that ratify for patients that they have been in an altered state of consciousness. It is interesting that sometimes even highly talented hypnotic subjects do not believe they have been hypnotized until they have a ratifying experience.

Trance ratification is a basic, yet often neglected, hypnotic principle. Through eliciting various hypnotic phenomena, patients may come to realize that they have undiscovered potentials beyond their conscious capacities. This realization increases patients' sense of self-efficacy and confidence that they have the inner resources needed to change (Bandura, 1977). It is recommended, therefore, that you provide from time to time a trance ratification experience for your patients.

For example, with a weight control patient, you might facilitate a glove anesthesia. Then, with the patient's permission, press on the hand with a sharp object, clamp a hemostat on the fleshy part of the hand below the little finger, or put a sterile needle through a fold of skin on the back of the hand. After inserting a needle or attaching a hemostat, ask your patient to open her eyes to briefly look at the hand. The suggestion may then be forcefully given: "I have had you do this to demonstrate to you the power of your own mind over your body. You have now witnessed the incredible power of your unconscious mind to control your feelings and your body. And you can know that, when your unconscious mind is so powerful that it can even control something as fundamental and basic as pain, that it can control anything having to do with your feelings and your body. You have far more potentials than you realize. And because of this power of your unconscious mind, your appetite and cravings will come under your control." Such an experience instills hope, belief and positive expectancy.

Some of the following hypnotic experiences are recommended as having value for providing trance ratification:

1. Glove anesthesia or analgesia.
2. Time distortion.
3. Limb catalepsy.
4. Arm levitation.
5. Limb heaviness.
6. Amnesia.
7. Ideomotor signaling.

8. Response to posthypnotic suggestion (e.g., for an itch; to not be able to stand up).
9. Recall of forgotten or even insignificant memories.
10. Ideosensory phenomenon: warmth, taste, smell.
11. Olfactory hallucination.

EXAMPLE OF SUGGESTIONS FOR TRANCE RATIFICATION.   As I have stated, the production of hypnotic phenomena serve to convince patients that they are in an altered state. In addition, successful response to such suggestions also appears to increase the patient's subsequent depth of trance. In the following suggestions for the treatment of warts, Crasilneck and Hall (1985) model for us, in a single treatment procedure, the use of a wide variety of trance ratification procedures: ideosensory phenomenon (heat, coolness); arm levitation; eyelid heaviness; response to posthypnotic suggestions for eyelid catalepsy and limb rigidity; glove anesthesia; and olfactory hallucination.

Please cup your right hand on your right knee. . . . That's it. . . . Now look at the knuckles of your hand and as you are doing so, your entire body will begin to relax thoroughly. . . . Pay no attention to other sounds . . . just concentrate on your right hand and my voice, realizing that nothing is beyond the power of your mind . . . and of the body. As I continue talking to you and as you continue staring at the back of your cupped hand, you will begin to notice things like the heat in the palm of your hand . . . and perhaps movement in one of the fingers. . . . As this occurs, slightly nod your head . . . yes . . . very good . . . and now you will notice that your hand is becoming very, very light . . . like a feather coming up toward your forehead . . . Good . . . Your hand starts to move upward . . . and as your hand continues to rise, keep looking at the back of your hand . . . but notice your eyelids are getting very heavy, very drowsy, and very relaxed. . . . Now when your hand touches your forehead . . . your eyes will be closed . . . you will be tremendously relaxed and capable of entering a deep level of trance. Your hand and arm comes up, up, up towards your forehead. . . . Now, your hand touches your forehead . . . your eyes are closed. . . . You can let your hand rest comfortably in your lap and normal sensation is returning to your right hand and arm. . . . Notice that your eyelids feel heavy . . . so heavy that even though you try to open your eyes for the moment . . . you can't. . . . Go ahead and try . . . but you cannot. . . . Try again . . . but the eyelids are shut tight. . . . Normal sensations return to the eyelids. . . . Now you will enter a much more sound and relaxed state. . . . Now I want you to raise your right hand. . . . That's it. . . . Extend it in front of you, and as I count to three, your arm will become rigid . . . hard . . . like a board soaked in water . . . like steel . . . so tight . . . so rigid . . . those muscles become steel. . . . One, tight . . . two . . . very rigid, and three, the whole arm, each finger . . . yes . . . become steel. . . . There . . . nothing can bend that arm or the fingers [as a further demonstration, at this point Crasilneck often has the patient use the other arm and feel the arm rigidity and their inability to bend it. Ed.] . . . showing you the power of your mind and body. . . . Now relax the arm and hand. . . . Normal sensation returns and still a much deeper and sounder state of relaxation.

I now give you the hypnotic suggestion that your right hand will develop the feeling that a heavy thick glove is on your right hand . . . as your hand has developed this sensation, move the forefinger of the right hand. . . . Good. . . . Now you will note some pressure in the forefinger . . . a dull sensation of pressure. . . . Open your eyes. . . . Now you see that in reality I'm sticking your finger severely with my nail file . . . but you are feeling nothing . . . correct? . . . Fine. . . . Normal sensation is returning to your hand. . . . I am now going to stimulate the middle finger. . . . As you feel this . . . nod your head, yes. . . . You see you pulled your hand back, which is an immediate and normal response. You are now aware of the tremendous control that your unconscious mind has over your body. . . . Now close your eyes again. . . . I now suggest that you can smell a pleasant odor of your choosing. . . . As you smell this, nod your head yes. . . .Good. . . . And now a very, very deep level of trance. . . . The pleasant odor leaves and still a more relaxed and deeper state of trance. . . . Nothing is beyond the power of the unconscious mind and these warts are going to leave completely and your skin will be void of them. . . . The area that I touch with this pencil . . . this area of warts now begins to feel very cool . . . cool . . . slightly cold. . . . As you feel this, nod your head. . . . Good. . . . Think the thought as I continue talking. . . . The area is cool. . . . The warts are going to leave. . . . The area is cool, and the warts will leave my body because of the power of my mind over my body. . . . Now just relax your thoughts . . . just pleasant, relaxed, serene thoughts. . . . Listen to me . . . my every word . . . *These warts are going to leave. . . . We have demonstrated the control of your mind over your body, and these warts will be gone very shortly.* . . . Your skin will feel slightly cool around the area of the warts for a day or so, and as the coolness fades, the warts will also begin to fade. And so, as I slowly count from ten to one, you will be fully awake . . . free from tension, tightness, stress and strain. These warts are going to fade out (pp. 374-375, reprinted with permission).

TIMING OF SUGGESTIONS AND DEPTH OF TRANCE

The timing of suggestions is something that is guided by clinical wisdom but which lacks research support at this time. Many leaders in the field have taught that you will have more impact by giving your most important suggestions last.

Although depth of trance has been discounted as unimportant by some, many senior clinicians have believed that when suggestions are given in a deeper hypnotic state, they will have more influence. Erickson (Erickson & Rossi, 1974/1980) certainly believed that it was important to devote sufficient time to adequately produce certain hypnotic phenomena and he instructed Rossi in this regard. "Erickson rarely gives therapeutic suggestions until the trance has developed for at least 20 minutes, and this only after hours of previous hypnotic training" (p. 89). Erickson often treated patients in time extended sessions where the patient might be in hypnosis for hours, and a large proportion of his famous case reports involved work in deep trance. In fact, his widow informed me that his favorite paper that he ever wrote was his chapter on deep trance (Erickson, 1954/1980). It is my own personal belief that subjects often tend to be more responsive in deeper trances.

THE PRINCIPLE OF INTERSPERSING AND EMBEDDING SUGGESTIONS

Suggestions may be subtly interspersed within stories, anecdotes, or "deepening" techniques. Words or phrases may be included, set apart by very brief pauses or changes in voice tone, that convey additional meanings and suggestions.

For instance, I was working with a woman for both obesity and marital problems. She had a noxious habit of interrupting rather than listening during interactions. Therefore, the following suggestions were given (and recorded on cassette tape for use in self-hypnosis). Notice where commas indicate very brief pauses. "It will be interesting for you to learn to listen, to your body. And as you listen, to your body, you can notice how you feel satisfied. And rather than interrupting, the natural balance of things, you can listen respectfully to feelings, and sensations of your body, noticing how soon you feel comfortably full and contented." Two problems were being addressed at once.

Personally, I find it useful to brainstorm ideas and phrases that convey the desired suggestions, and then to consult a comprehensive thesaurus to identify additional synonyms. What words and phrases convey attitudes, perceptions, feelings or qualities that are desirable for the patient? Then I contemplate how these words and phrases may be interspersed within an analogy, example, metaphor, or deepening technique. You are encouraged to read Erickson's (1966) example of the interspersal technique in the chapter on pain and to consult Erickson's collected papers (1980) for other masterful examples of this technique.

ERICKSON'S PRINCIPLES OF INDIVIDUALIZATION AND UTILIZATION

Milton Erickson emphasized the need to individualize hypnotic procedures. But many lay hypnotists and even some legitimate professionals assume that hypnotic response is only a trait and that individualization is, therefore, unnecessary. Thus, they mass produce popularized self-hypnosis tapes, presenting everyone with the same induction and suggestions. There is limited evidence, however, suggesting that hypnosis may be more effective when it is individualized (Holroyd, 1980; Nuland & Field, 1970) and takes into account the unique motivations, personality, interests and preferences of the patient. Furthermore, there is evidence in psychotherapy outcome research that failure to individualize therapy not only may result in poor outcome, but may be associated with psychological casualties (Lieberman, Yalom & Miles, 1973). Therefore, I have many of my patients take home a paper and pencil checklist of life experiences, interest and values (Hammond, 1985, 1988a). The checklist rapidly provides information to use in individualizing the induction, metaphors and suggestions.

As one example of individualization, we can determine by brief questioning (during or after hypnosis) which sensory modalities a patient is primarily able to imagine (visual, auditory, kinesthetic, olfactory). We may then tailor the imagery that we suggest accordingly. I also recommend questioning your patients after an initial hypnotic experience to obtain their feedback about how you can make the experience even more effective.

MYTH OF THE SUPERIORITY OF INDIRECT SUGGESTIONS.   As clinicians begin to study hypnosis, they commonly ponder over the question, "Should I be direct or indirect in my approach?" In recent years this has become one of the most controversial areas in hypnosis, particularly among workshop presenters and non-research-oriented writers; therefore, we will examine in some detail the existing evidence.

Some authors, particularly some of those identifying themselves as "Ericksonian," have assumed that indirect, permissive suggestions are always superior to direct suggestions. Some have even been so bold as to make statements like these: "Direct suggestion will bring only temporary relief, will intensify the transference relationship toward authority, and will increase repression of the conflict that led to the symptomatology" (Lankton & Lankton, 1983, p. 150), and "An Ericksonian hypnotist strives to be artfully indirect in all suggestions and interventions" (Lankton & Lankton, 1983, p. 251). "He [Erickson] noticed that direct suggestions were useful only to the extent that clients knew what they wanted, were congruent about wanting to accomplish it, and had the resources necessary to change available and organized. Clients seeking therapy rarely meet these criteria" (Lankton, 1985). Are indirect and permissive suggestions always superior?

Alman (1983) experimentally tested this assumption and to his surprise found that response to direct versus indirect suggestions was normally distributed—some patients responded better to very direct suggestions, and others were more responsive to permissive, indirect suggestions. Very similarly, McConkey (1984) found subjects were heterogeneous in their response to indirect suggestions—half were responsive to this type of suggestion and half were not. He speculated that "indirection may not be the clinically important notion as much as the creation of a motivational context where the overall suggestion is acceptable, e.g. by making the ideas congruent with other aims and hopes of the patient" (p. 312).

There have been some studies and uncontrolled case reports (Alman & Carney, 1980; Barber, 1977; Fricton & Roth, 1985; Stone & Lundy, 1985) that have reported superior effects for indirect suggestions, but several of these studies (e.g., Barber, 1977) had serious methodological flaws. The indirect condition that was used by Matthews, Bennett, Bean and Gallagher (1985), for example, was 34% longer than the direct condition, which appears to have accounted for the greater depth reported.

In contrast to the studies claiming greater potency for indirect suggestions, many other studies have failed to find a difference in effectiveness (e.g., Lynn, Neufeld, & Matyi, 1987; Matthews et al., 1985; Murphy, 1988; Reyher & Wilson, 1976; Spinhoven, Baak, Van Dyck, & Vermeulen, 1988). For instance, Barber's (1977) superior results with indirect suggestions have not been replicated with dental procedures (Gillett & Coe, 1984), with foot surgery (Crowley, 1980), obstetrical patients (Omer, Darnel, Silberman, Shuval, & Palti, 1988) or with pain in paraplegic patients (Snow, 1979). Furthermore, Van Gorp, Meyer and Dunbar (1985) used his procedure with experimental pain and found that traditional hypnotic suggestions were significantly more effective than indirect suggestions. Still other studies have likewise found that direct suggestions produce better posthypnotic response (e.g., Stone & Lundy, 1985).

Matthews and Mosher (1988) entered their study anticipating a superior response with indirect suggestions, and expecting that it would decrease resistance as hypothesized by Erickson and Rossi (1979). Subjects not only did not respond differently to either indirect inductions or indirect suggestions, but subjects receiving indirect suggestions were actually found to become more resistant! Lynn et al. (1988) likewise did not find that resistance was minimized by using indirect suggestion. Further testing the "Ericksonian" belief that indirect suggestions are superior with resistant and more independent patients, Spinhoven et al. (1988) examined the relationship of locus of control to preference for direct or indirect suggestions. Locus of control did not predict response to either direct or indirect approaches.

Sense of involuntariness of response to suggestions has also been discovered to be the same for direct and indirect suggestions (Matthews et al., 1985; Stone & Lundy, 1985). Furthermore, Lynn et al. (1988) actually found that sense of involuntariness and of subjective involvement was greater when direct suggestions were used. The later finding replicated the carefully controlled results of Lynn, Neufeld, and Matyi (1987).

Research (Matthews, Kirsch, & Mosher, 1985) has now carefully examined the Bandler and Grinder (1975) and Lankton and Lankton (1983) contention that using two-level communication and interspersing suggestions in a confusing dual induction produces superior results. If anything, they found the opposite. Not only was a double induction not more effective than a traditional induction procedure, but when it was used as the initial induction experienced by a subject, it was *less* effective and appeared to have a negative impact on later hypnotic experiences. Even Erickson (1964) would have probably predicted this, however, since he designed confusional procedures for primary use with consciously motivated but unconsciously resistant subjects.

So, let's return to our initial query, "Are indirect suggestions superior to direct hypnotic suggestions?" The weight of existing evidence clearly requires a response of "No." Indirect suggestions do *not* seem more effective than direct suggestions; in fact, direct suggestions may possess some advantages. Several studies (Alman, 1983; McConkey, 1984; Spinhoven et al., 1988) seem to indicate that some individuals will respond better to each type of suggestion, but most people fall in the middle of the distribution and may well respond equally well to either type of suggestion. The furor of the past decade over the belief that "indirect is always better" is rather reminiscent of the extensive research literature that has now failed to replicate the creative, but nonetheless unfounded tenets of NLP. As mental health professionals we may stand too ready to adopt unproven theories as truth.

It is thus my recommendation, in the light of current evidence, that we should keep our therapeutic options open and maintain the flexibility to use both direct and indirect suggestions. In light of the research, the debate over the preferability of one type of suggestion over the other may be "much ado about nothing." We are probably well advised to not spend so much time worrying about it. Erickson certainly felt free to use both highly directive and even authoritarian suggestions with some patients, and to use very permissive and indirect suggestions with others (Hammond, 1984).

We have no validated indications or contraindications for the type of suggestions to use. In fact, some of the widely accepted indications for when to use indirect suggestions (e.g., with resistant and more independent subjects) that evolved from clinical beliefs may be nothing more than folklore, since they have not received research support thus far. Hypnosis — like so much of psychotherapy — is still more art than science. We must therefore remain open and appropriately humble about what we actually know, rather than becoming prematurely entrenched in untested theories that may limit our options for intervention and learning.

What I am going to express now is only my tentatively held clinical belief, which may or may not prove to be accurate. In my own clinical work I tend to be more direct, straightforward, and forceful in giving hypnotic suggestions under the following circumstances: 1) When a good therapeutic relationship and rapport have been established with the patient; (2) When the patient seems motivated and nonresistant; (3) When the patient seems able to accept direction and authority, or is more dependent and used to accepting authority; (4) When the patient seems more highly hypnotically talented and is in a deeper hypnotic state; (5) When I am familiar with the hypnotic talents and capacities of the patient and am thus aware of the hypnotic phenomena she or he can manifest; and (6) When, upon questioning the patient, I learn that he or she seems to prefer and respond more positively to a direct approach. (In other words, a "work sample" of how the patient responds to different styles of suggestion is probably more valid than drawing inferences from unsubstantiated "personality" characteristics.)

UTILIZING PATIENT LANGUAGE PATTERNS.   Another method for tailoring hypnosis to patients is to incorporate their idiosyncratic syntax and styles of speech into the suggestions you give. Listen for phrases and words that the patient tends to use. For instance, during the initial evaluation a patient with relationship problems described himself as "very intelligent," and indicated, "I have a lot of common sense." He also used the phrase, "Take my own destiny in my own hands."

The phrases and concepts of this patient were incorporated into the following suggestions: "Now you are an intelligent person, an astute person, who can very level-headedly size up situations. And you can begin to realize that you have even further mental resources, beyond your conscious intellect. Your unconscious mind is very perceptive, and within you there is a great deal of intuitive common sense. Your unconscious mind perceives what needs to be done. And your unconscious mind will use these aptitudes, and will begin to give you spontaneous impressions about your relationships. As you interact with people, and as you observe other people interact, impressions, recognitions will spontaneously come into your mind, about what you do that's self-defeating in relationships. And you can trust that your unconscious mind has the common sense to recognize how you've been turning people off, without fully realizing it consciously. Your unconscious mind isn't about to let you just drift along, leaving your future to chance. It will bring images and impressions about your relationships into your mind, so that you can make intelligent decisions and changes. And rather than leaving your relationships to chance, you will find that you will begin to take your destiny into your own hands, realizing changes that need to be made."

When we are able to incorporate the patient's own language into suggestions, the ideas may feel more compatible and congruent to the patient. We are literally speaking the patient's language and thus the suggestions may conform more to the patient's pattern of thinking and make a more profound and lasting impression.

UTILIZATION.   Another facet of individualization is Erickson's principle of utilization. Erickson used this term to convey the importance of utterly accepting whatever occurs with the patient, and then seeking to use, displace, and transform it. In hypnosis, this is essentially the parallel of using empathy and respect to establish rapport in psychotherapy.

Thus if a patient yawns in a tired way, one may comment, "Have you ever noticed, how after a yawn, your whole body relaxes more deeply?" If a patient has some muscles jerk slightly in one leg during the process of induction, the therapist may say, "And you notice the little muscles jerk in your leg, which is a good sign that the tension is really flowing out of you, as your muscles relax." This intense observation and focus on the patient, in and of itself, creates rapport. But suggestions may then also reframe nonverbal behavior, making the attribution that it is evidence of hypnotic responsiveness. Patient behavior, even if it might be interpreted by some as problematic, is thus accepted and suggestions are connected to it.

A new patient complained that, in hypnotic attempts with a previous therapist, he could only enter a light hypnotic state because his mind kept wandering. Therefore, the following suggestions were offered during the induction: "And as we continue, undoubtedly your mind will begin to wander to thinking about other things [accepting his "resistant" behavior]. And different images may run through your mind. And that's perfectly all right, because for the next little while, your conscious mind doesn't have to do anything of importance. Just allow your unconscious mind to wander in whatever way it wants, because the only thing that matters, is the activity of your unconscious mind." The patient went into a profound, deep trance and experienced spontaneous amnesia for almost the entire session.

In individualizing hypnosis, you may also consider taking into account and utilizing the personality styles and needs of patients. In a highly competitive patient, for example, one might choose a dual levitation induction, while suggesting an attitude of curiosity about which hand will reach the face first. You are encouraged to thoroughly study the literature on utilization (Erickson, 1959; Erickson, 1980; Erickson & Rossi, 1979; Haley, 1973; Hammond, 1985).

THE LAW OF PARSIMONY

Finally, I wish to strongly encourage you to use the most parsimonious method and style of suggestion to accomplish the therapeutic task. Today, many hypnotists seem to be trying to make hypnosis much more complicated and difficult than it needs to be. This often stems from misinterpretations of Erickson's work (Hammond, 1984, 1988b). Esoteric, multiply embedded metaphors and confusional techniques are unnecessary with most patients, are often perceived as condescending, and usually meet the therapist's needs far more than the patients.

Types of Hypnotic Suggestions

Many of the types of suggestions we will discuss were conceptualized by Erickson and Rossi (1979). Some types were original with Erickson and some have been used for centuries. As I have indicated, there is no outcome research to suggest the superiority of any of these styles of suggestions. It is recommended, however, that you familiarize yourself with all of these types of suggestions to broaden your available repertoire for intervention.

In general, almost every one of the 14 types of suggestion may be used to facilitate any of the hypnotic phenomena (catalepsy, levitation, amnesia, dissociation, anesthesia, hyperesthesia, ideosensory activities, positive or negative hallucinations, hypermnesia, age regression, age progression, time distortion, depersonalization, induced dreams). One way to refine your skills in using the various suggestion types is to practice writing out several suggestions of each type for facilitating each one of the different hypnotic phenomena.

IMPLICATION

Implication is a difficult to define but important method of indirect suggestion. Rather than directly suggesting an effect, you may merely imply or assume that it will take place. For instance, in deepening a trance, you may ask, "What color are the flowers?" This implies and assumes that the patient is capable of visualizing. Similarly, a patient may be told, "*When you're aware of noticing some of the sounds of nature around you, like the wind in the trees and the birds singing, just nod your head.*" This implies that the patient will be capable of auditory imagination; the only question is "when" he will notice the sounds, not "if" he will hear them.

The hypnotherapist is well advised to be very cautious about the use of the words "if" and "try." "*If* your right hand is getting light, nod your head," implies that the patient may fail to obtain the desired response. Instead you may ask, "*Which* one of your hands feels lighter?" This implies that one hand does, in fact, feel lighter. "You can begin to wonder *which one* of your hands your unconscious mind will cause to develop a lightness, and begin to float up?" This implies that one hand will lift. The question has been shifted from "*will* one lift," to "*which* one will lift."

Contrast the prehypnotic suggestion, "Well, let's try to hypnotize you now," with the implications in the following suggestions by Erickson (Erickson & Rossi, 1975). "Would you like to go into trance *now or later*?" "Would you like to go into a trance standing up or sitting down?" "Would you like to experience a light, medium or deep trance?" "Which of you in this group would like to be *first* in experiencing a trance?" "Do you want to have your eyes open or closed when you experience trance?" (p. 152, emphasis added, reprinted with permission). These are therapeutic double binds, which will be elaborated in more detail later, but which change the question from "if" to "when" or "how." I have on occasion similarly asked a phobic patient, "Would you prefer that we get you over this problem with a rapid method that is more intense, or with a more gentle method that takes a little longer?" This offers the patient a double bind in that both alternatives are desirable and therapeutic, but it also assumes and implies that he *will* get better.

"And the numbness will begin to spread slowly at first," implies that later it will eventually begin to spread more rapidly. "Don't go into a trance quite so rapidly," implies that the subject is already entering trance. "We won't do anything to get you over your problem *today* [implication: we will in the future], but will simply give you the opportunity to experience hypnosis and see how soothing and calming it is" [implication: you will experience hypnosis]. Suggesting to a terminally ill or chronic schizophrenic patient that they send you a recipe when they return home implies that they *will* leave the hospital. "Have you ever been in a trance *before*," suggests through implication that they are about to enter a hypnotic state.

Consider the implications of the following double bind suggestions of Erickson (Erickson & Rossi, 1975), "Do you want to get over that habit this week or next? That may seem too soon. Perhaps you'd like a longer period of time like three or four weeks." "Before today's interview is over your unconscious mind will find a safe and constructive way of communicating something important to your conscious mind. And you really don't know how or when you will tell it. Now or later" (p. 153, reprinted with permission).

Another example of using implication by changing "if" to "when" may be found in my suggestions for induced erotic dreams in the chapter on sexual dysfunction and relationship problems.

Before moving on to discuss other types of suggestions, it may be instructive to listen to the words of Rossi (Erickson & Rossi, 1975) as he described the work of a master hypnotherapist:

Erickson does not always know beforehand which double bind or suggestion will be effective. He usually uses a buckshot approach of giving many suggestions but in such an innocuous manner (via implications, casualness, etc.) that the patient does not recognize them. While watching Erickson *offer* a series of double binds and suggestions, Rossi frequently had the impression of him as a sort of mental locksmith now gently trying this key and now that. He watches the patient intently and *expectantly*, always looking for the subtle changes of facial expression and body movement that provide an indication that the tumblers of the patient's mind have clicked; he has found a key that works much to his mutual delight with the patient. (p. 151)

19 TRUISM

A truism is a statement of fact that someone has experienced so often that they cannot deny it. These statements may be focused on motor, sensory, affective or cognitive processes, or on time. For example: "Most people enjoy the pleasant feeling of the warmth of the sun on their skin, as they walk along the beach."

TYPES OF PHRASING. The following types of phrases are often used with a truism. "Most people . . .; Everyone . . .; You already know . . .; You already know how to . . .; Some people . . .; Most of us . . .; It is a very common experience to . . .; Everybody . . .; You've known all along how to . . .; There was a time when you didn't . . .; Sooner or later . . .; Sooner or later, everyone. . . .; In every culture . . .; It gives everyone a sense of pleasure to. . . ."

20 NOT KNOWING AND NOT DOING

Suggestions of this type facilitate unconscious responsiveness rather than conscious effort. They assist patients to not try too hard (in accord with the Law of Reversed Effect), encouraging autonomous responding and dissociation. Here is an example of this type of suggestion: "You don't have to think, or reply, or try to do anything at all. In fact, it isn't even necessary to listen carefully to what I'm saying, because your unconscious mind will just inevitably hear everything I'm saying, without any effort on your part at all."

TYPES OF PHRASING. Some of the following phrases are commonly used with this type of suggestion: "You don't have to . . .; It isn't necessary to . . .; It isn't important . . .; You don't need to . . .; Without knowing it, you've . . .; You don't need to be concerned if . . .; Just allow it to happen . . .; Without really trying, it will just happen all by itself. . . ."

21 COVERING ALL POSSIBILITIES OF RESPONSE

Giving a suggestion that covers all the possible types of response that a patient may make is most valuable when you wish to focus patient responsiveness in a certain direction. This is a fail-safe approach because virtually any response is defined as successful and hypnotic. This is especially valuable when you don't know the patient well and are initially exploring his responsiveness and identifying his hypnotic talents. Here is an example of this type of suggestion: "Shortly your right hand, or perhaps it will be your left hand, will begin to get light and lift up, or perhaps it may develop a heaviness and press down, or maybe it won't even move at all, I can't really be sure. But you can simply notice very carefully what begins to happen [implication]. Perhaps you'll notice something in your little finger, or maybe it will be in your index finger that you first sense a movement or sensation, I really don't know. But the most important thing isn't even how it begins to move, but just to become fully aware of what begins to happen to that hand."

QUESTIONS

Suggestions in the form of questions may be used to focus attention and awareness, stimulate associations, facilitate responsiveness, and to induce trance. This type of suggestion is particularly valuable when the question is one that cannot be answered by the conscious mind. Questions, however, should not be used in a rigid manner, but should utilize ongoing patient behavior. Each question, for example, may suggest an observable response. Questions are, again, a fail-safe approach that you will want to use when you do not yet know the responsiveness and hypnotic talents of your patient, or perhaps when you anticipate resistance. Be careful, however, to avoid asking questions that communicate a lack of confidence and doubt. It is counterproductive, for example, to ask, "Is your hand getting numb?"

Several examples will illustrate this type of suggestion: "And the numbness, do you notice that beginning?" "And will that hand remain floating right there, or does it float up toward your face?" "Can you enjoy relaxing and not having to remember?" "Do you begin to experience the numbness in the fingers, or on the back of the hand first, or does it spread out from your palm?"

This type of suggestion, like the others we are discussing, may be used in producing any of the hypnotic phenomena, in induction or deepening, or as part of the treatment of almost any clinical problem. The following suggestions, reprinted with permission from Erickson and Rossi (1979), demonstrate the use of questions in doing an eye fixation induction and a levitation induction. Ordinarily we would use this type of suggestion occasionally and not exclusively as it is done here for illustrative purposes.

Would you like to find a spot you can look at comfortably? As you continue looking at that spot for a while, do your eyelids want to blink? Will those lids begin to blink together or separately? Slowly or quickly? Will they close all at once or flutter all by themselves first? Will those eyes close more and more as you get more and more comfortable? That's fine. Can those eyes remain closed as your comfort deepens like when you go to sleep? Can that comfort continue more and more so that you'd rather not even try to open your eyes? Or would you rather try and find you cannot? And how soon will you forget about them altogether because your unconscious wants to dream? (p. 29)

Can you feel comfortable resting your hands gently on your thighs? [As therapist demonstrates.] That's right, without letting them touch each other. Can you let those hands rest ever so lightly so that the fingertips just barely touch your thighs? That's right. As they rest ever so lightly, do you notice how they tend to lift up a bit all by themselves with each breath you take? Do they begin to lift even more lightly and easily by themselves as the rest of your body relaxes more and more? As that goes on, does one hand or the other or maybe both continue lifting even more? And does that hand stay up and continue lifting higher and higher, bit by bit, all by itself? Does the other hand want to catch up with it, or will the other hand relax in your lap? That's right. And does that hand continue lifting with these slight little jerking movements, or does the lifting get smoother and smoother as the hand continues upward toward your face? Does it move more quickly or slowly as it approaches your face with deepening comfort? Does it need to pause a bit before it finally touches your face so you'll know you are going into a trance? And it won't touch until your unconscious is really ready to let you go deeper, will it? And will your body automatically take a deeper breath when that hand touches your face as you really relax and experience yourself going deeper? That's right. And will you even bother to notice the deepening comfortable feeling when that hand slowly returns to your lap all by itself? And will your unconscious be in a dream by the time that hand comes to rest. (pp. 30-31)

As you begin to experiment with using this type of suggestion, you may find the following format beneficial in helping you initially generate suggestions.

> *Question Format For Suggestions*:
> CAN YOU (R) . . .
> DO YOU (R) . . .
>   (they)
> AND WOULD YOU LIKE TO . . .
>
> notice
> sense
> feel
> (your) unconscious
> hear
> taste
> smell
> listen
> remember
> imagine
> see
> experience
> pay attention to
> wonder
> choose
> let your
> let yourself

DOES _____
WILL ____*(it; you)*____
ARE YOU AWARE OF . . .

CONTINGENT SUGGESTIONS

Contingent suggestions connect the suggestion to an ongoing or inevitable behavior. This is a highly useful suggestion that has been used for well over a hundred years. Contingent suggestions may be used with both suggestions given during hypnosis and with posthypnotic suggestions where a trigger or cue for the suggestion is identified.

Here are some examples: "And as your hand lowers, you will find yourself going back to a time when _____ ." "And when you feel the touch of his body in bed, you will be surprised at the flood of erotic, intimate memories that come to mind."

Contingent suggestions are also closely related to the concept of "chaining" suggestions together, in a sense, making them contingent upon each other. It is commonly believed that suggestions may be made more effective by connecting them, as the following illustration demonstrates. [To a subject with an arm floating cataleptically:] "And as you become aware of the numbness beginning to develop in that hand, it will begin to float up even lighter toward your face, and your mind will begin drifting back through time to the beginning of that problem, and as the arm floats up higher, you drift further and further back through time." It is popularly believed that when two or more suggestions are linked together, it is more difficult to reject them.

TYPES OF PHRASING.   You will find some of the following types of phrases are often a part of contingent suggestions: "And when . . .; As . . .; As soon as . . ." You will also often use the words "until" and "then" as part of contingent suggestions: "If _____ then _____ ." In using this type of suggestion to trigger posthypnotic behaviors (or feelings, or thoughts), you will also need to identify inevitable cues or triggers. For examples: lying down in bed; tying a shoelace; brushing your teeth; seeing your house; hearing a song.

Contingent suggestions may also take the following forms:
"While you _____ you can _____ ."
"When you _____ please _____ ."
"Don't _____ until you _____ ."
"You won't _____ until _____ ."
"Why don't you _____ before you _____ ."
"The closer you get to _____ the more you can _____ ."
"After _____ you can _____ ."
"As you feel _____ you recognize _____ ."
"The feeling of _____ will allow you to _____ ."
"And as _____ occurs, _____ may occur more than you'd expect."
"And when you _____ ., you'll _____ ."

As soon as: your arm feels numb
            you can no longer feel your legs
            your unconscious knows _____
            you have gone back in time to . . .

            THEN, your arm will lower.

THE IMPLIED DIRECTIVE

The implied directive usually has three parts (Erickson & Rossi, 1979): (l) a time-binding introduction; (2) an implied suggestion for an internal response that will take place inside the patient; and (3) a behavioral response that will signal when the internal response or suggestion has been accomplished. This type of suggestion is particularly used for tracking progress during hypnosis.

FORMAT   The implied directive often conforms to the format: *"As soon as* [the time binding introduction] your inner mind has identified the circumstances when that problem developed [the internal process that is desired] your 'yes' finger will float up" [the behavioral signal].

PHRASING   Here are some illustrations, within the format that was just introduced, of how this type of suggestion may be phrased. *"As soon as . . .* (your entire hand feels very numb and anesthetized; you can no longer feel your legs; you can see _____ ; that memory has faded from your conscious mind; you know _____ ; your unconscious senses that your trance is deep enough to accomplish_____) . . . *then . . .* (your arm will float down; your finger will lift; you will awaken).

APPOSITION OF OPPOSITES

This type of suggestion, probably originated by Erickson in the 1930s, contains a balancing of opposites or polarities. For example: "As that right arm becomes more tense and rigid, the rest of your body becomes more and more relaxed." "As your right arm floats up, your left floats down." "As your forehead feels cooler, you'll feel your hands getting warmer." In this type of suggestion, you may also mention or suggest a physical metaphor, and then a psychological one.

PHRASING.   In formulating this kind of suggestion, you may find it helpful to consider some of the following polarities or opposites: warmth— coolness; tension—relaxation; anesthesia—hypersensitivity; wet—dry; floating—heaviness; light—heavy; full—empty; more—less; difficult (hard)—easy; older—younger.

NEGATIVES TO DISCHARGE RESISTANCE

Erickson (Erickson & Rossi, 1979) believed that the use of negatives could serve as a "lightning rod" to discharge minor inhibitions and resistance. He had begun using this type of suggestion by the 1930s and he believed in its clinical utility, but thus far we have no experimental validation for its effectiveness. Nonetheless, this type of suggestion is commonly used by many clinicians. Some examples will illustrate this type of suggestion.

"You will, *will you not?*"
"And you can, *can you not?*"
"You *can't* stop it, can you?"
"You can try, *can't* you?"
"You do, *don't you?*"
"And why *not* just allow that to occur?"
"And you really *don't* have to do _____ until _____ ."
"And you *won't* _____ until _____ ."
"You *don't* need to _____ ."
"_____ are you *not?*"
"_____ *doesn't* it?
"_____ *don't* you?"

THE BIND OF COMPARABLE ALTERNATIVES

This is a bind that *appears* to give a patient a free choice between two or more alternatives. However, both of the choices are essentially comparable and they will both lead the patient in the desired therapeutic direction. The choices offered in this type of suggestion may sound different, but are virtually the same, simply giving illusion of choice.

Here are several examples of a bind of comparable alternatives. The first three examples actually model prehypnotic suggestions. I have identified the hypnotic phenomena that some of the suggestions seek to elicit. "Would you rather go into trance sitting up or lying back in the recliner?" "Would you prefer to go into a trance gradually or more rapidly?" "Would you rather go into a light trance, a medium trance, or a deep trance?" *Levitation*: "And perhaps your left arm, or maybe it will be your right arm that will float up toward your face." *Age Regression*: "And you may remember a happy experience that happened when you were five years old, or perhaps you'd rather recall one from slightly later." *Analgesia or Anesthesia*: "You may choose to feel the pressure, or nothing at all." *Negative Hallucination*: "You can just be aware of the sound of my voice, or you can simply ignore everything else." *Time Distortion*: "Time may seem to pass quickly, or you may simply be unaware of its passing." *Anesthesia*: "Do you begin to experience the numbness more in the right hand, or in the left hand?"

CONSCIOUS-UNCONSCIOUS DOUBLE BIND

This type of suggestion seeks to utilize the patient's unconscious mind (or, depending upon one's theoretical frame of reference, uses the metaphor of the unconscious mind), bypassing conscious, learned limitations. Responses to this type of suggestion require patients to focus inwardly and initiate unconscious processes that are beyond their conscious control. In a double bind, behavioral possibilities outside the patient's usual range of conscious alternatives and voluntary responses are offered.

Here are several examples: "And if your unconscious mind is ready for you to enter trance, your right hand will begin to get light and float up. If your unconscious mind is reluctant for you to enter trance, your left hand will lift up." "And the unconscious mind can continue working on that problem and preparing you for our next session after you leave. And the really interesting, really curious thing, is that your conscious mind may or may not really be aware or even understand what's going on, depending on the preference of your unconscious mind. And as your unconscious mind is preparing you, and doing its work, your conscious will remain free to carry on all the many other things that you need to attend to each day."

CONFUSIONAL SUGGESTIONS

It is popularly believed that confusion will "depotentiate conscious mental sets" (Erickson & Rossi, 1979), allowing unconscious processes to occur more readily. Erickson (1964) believed that this type of suggestion was particularly indicated when a patient was consciously motivated but seemed unconsciously resistant to experiencing hypnosis. We will briefly introduce suggestions of this type.

SHOCK AND SURPRISE   Shock and surprise may be used to facilitate creative moments, stimulating the patient's unconscious mind to conduct an inner search and capturing the patient's attention. This may be done through interspersing certain shocking or surprising words and/or through the use of strategically placed pauses. For instance, after leaving a patient's hand floating cataleptic, the facilitator may suggest: "And what that hand is going to do next will surprise you," while then waiting expectantly. This method may be used for a surprise reinduction of hypnosis in a patient recently realerted: "Are you awake? Are you sure? And what do you begin to notice about your eyes . . . as they begin to flutter . . . and get heavier . . . and close, all by themselves." Another suggestion with a shock element would be to say, "It would be a *disaster*, if you didn't change directions, and arrived at where you are going."

DOUBLE DISSOCIATION DOUBLE BIND   This type of suggestion may include various other types of suggestions, and creates overload and confusion, depotentiating conscious sets. Careful observation and noting of patient responses to the alternatives may alert you to the hypnotic talents and tendencies of the patient.

This type of suggestion may take some of the following formats: "(In a moment) you can _____ but (you don't need to; even though; when; without knowing) _____ , or, you can _____*(do the opposite)*_____ , but *(or any of the other phrases above)* _____ ."

Here are a few illustrative examples. "In a moment you can awaken as a person, but it isn't necessary for your body to awaken. Or, you can awaken along with your body, but without being aware of your body." "In a moment you will open your eyes, but you don't need to wake up; or you can come fully awake when you open your eyes, but without an awareness of what transpired while they were closed." "You may choose not to remember, or you may choose just to forget, but choosing to forget is your choice in the same way as choosing not to remember that which you've chosen to forget." "As you remember to forget what it was that you were going to remember, you can just as easily forget what you were going to remember to forget."

PHRASING FOR A DOUBLE DISSOCIATIVE CONSCIOUS-UNCONSCIOUS DOUBLE BIND   This type of confusional suggestion may take the following format: "Your conscious mind _____ , while (or, and, since, as, because, at the same time) your unconscious mind _____ , or perhaps your unconscious mind _____ , while your conscious mind _____ ." Explained another way, the format may take either of two forms: (1) Conscious _____ , unconscious _____ , while (or, since) conscious _____ , unconscious _____ . (2) Unconscious _____ , conscious _____ , while unconscious _____ , conscious _____ .

Here are some examples: "Your conscious mind may think about solutions, while your unconscious mind considers their implications, or perhaps your unconscious mind will generate some solutions, while your conscious mind wonders what the results may be." "Your conscious mind may remember the details of those events, while your unconscious mind perceives the feelings, or your unconscious mind may recall what happened, while your conscious mind is only aware of strong feelings and not the reason for them." "Your conscious mind may be aware of the time available to complete the test, while your unconscious mind seems to have all the time it needs, or, your conscious mind may enjoy a relaxed pace without concern for time, while your unconscious monitors the time you have left and the speed of your work." "And when you open your eyes you can consciously see your mother sitting in front of you while your unconscious mind is aware of your feelings toward her, or perhaps your unconscious mind will hold the image of her while your conscious mind is encompassed in the feelings you have about her."

Do not be concerned if confusional suggestions initially seem overwhelming and too complex to master. They are by definition confusing, and are probably the least important type of suggestions to become skillful in using.

INTERSPERSAL OF SUGGESTIONS AND METAPHORS

This refers to bringing up topics and using words or phrases that "seed" ideas, focus attention, and indirectly influence the patient. Metaphors or anecdotes may serve to illustrate a point or tag a memory, to indirectly suggest or model solutions, to foster self-reflection and insight, to increase positive expectancy or motivation, to bypass resistance, to reframe or redefine a problem, and to intersperse suggestions while bypassing defenses (Zeig, 1980). Metaphors may be used, just like hypnotic suggestions in general, to facilitate behavioral, affective or cognitive-perceptual changes.

By way of illustration, you may describe to a patient the process, following an injury, of a scab forming for protection, while natural and internal healing processes take place. A scar may remain later, perhaps as a small reminder of a hurt, long ago, but which doesn't have to remain painful. This metaphor may be used to communicate ideas to a patient who has experienced trauma, incest, rape, or divorce.

Metaphors are another way of conveying suggestions, and they may be of particular value as a method of accomplishing repetition of suggestion without using identical words or phrases. When metaphors are delivered prior to giving more straightforward suggestions, this process has been popularly referred to as "seeding" an idea.

We may think about three basic styles of metaphors. Some hypno-therapists tell metaphoric stories out of their background of experience — for example, concerning previous patients or personal experiences. Another type of metaphor is the truism metaphor. These metaphors are commonly about nature or types of life experiences that are so universal that the patient cannot deny them. They thus establish a yes- or acceptance-set in the patient. Several of these types of metaphors that I use may be found in the sections of this book on sexual dysfunction and trauma.

Finally, some therapists (e.g., Lankton & Lankton, 1983; Gordon, 1978) make up metaphoric stories to fit a patient situation, often seeking to create characters and components that are parallel to aspects of the patient's circumstance.

My personal preference is clearly to utilize the first two types of metaphors, but no research exists to indicate that one is more effective than another. Making up stories seems to me, however, the opposite of therapist genuineness or authenticity — qualities which are consistently found to be important "nonspecific" factors in successful therapy and relationships (Hammond, Hepworth, & Smith, 1977; Truax & Carkhuff, 1967). Making up tales of the "once upon a time" variety may also seem condescending and, therefore, offensive to some patients. The use, and particularly the overuse, of such stories may thus run the risk of impairing the therapeutic alliance with the patient.

Erickson, who usually serves as the model for those who emphasize a metaphoric orientation to hypnosis, seems to have almost always used the first two types of metaphors. Furthermore, close colleagues who actually observed his therapy, as well as patients, have emphasized that metaphors were only occasionally used by him (Hammond, 1984). In fact, metaphors were estimated to represent no more than 20% of Erickson's hypnotic work (Hammond, 1988b). Metaphors have their place in our therapeutic armamentarium, but we must keep a balanced perspective and realize that therapy is more than storytelling.

A metaphoric story may be introduced by simply saying, "And let me give you an example," or "You may remember," or "Can you remember a time when . . .?" Also, and importantly, metaphors do not always have to be long and involved to make an important point. Consider, for example, this brief metaphor by Barker (1985): "Fleming's discovery of penicillin was serendipitous. He was working in his laboratory with some disease-causing bacteria. These were growing on a culture plate which became contaminated by a mold. Some investigators would probably have thrown the contaminated plate out, but Fleming took a look at it and noticed that the bacteria were dying where the mold was growing. This proved to be due to a substance produced by the mold, later named penicillin. So things should not always be taken at their face value" (p. 105, reprinted with permission). This metaphor makes a point, albeit briefly.

You will have an opportunity to review a variety of metaphoric styles in the chapters that follow and to determine the extent of your comfort with them. If you are particularly interested in refining this type of suggestion, you may wish to consult authors who have emphasized metaphors (Barker, 1985; Lankton & Lankton, 1989; Mills & Crowley, 1986; Witztum, Van der Hart, & Friedman, 1988; Zeig, 1980). You should also consult the section on Erickson's Interspersal Technique in the chapter on pain.

SYMBOLIC AND METAPHORIC IMAGERY

The term suggestions usually refers to verbal statements. The effects of imagery seem so powerfully in hypnosis, however, that it is my belief that we should acknowledge suggestions for imagery as a category of suggestion. The Law of Reversed Effect is a principle that encourages the use of imagery, particularly to bring about physiologic effects. For instance, having patients imagine what their pain looks like and then modify the imagery may produce analgesic relief. Imagining an agitated acid stomach and then modifying the imagery to images (and sounds, sensations and smells) of cool comfort often reduces gastric secretions. *Imagery modification* is a powerful hypnotic technique. Symbolic imagery may also be used to treat emotional problems, as you will see illustrated in the Silent Abreaction technique and others later in the book.

Finally, metaphoric imagery should also be noted. A patient's situation or idiosyncratic speech often suggests metaphoric imagery experiences. For instance, a patient may say, "I feel like I'm in a cave," or "I'm blocked and I don't know how to get past it," or "I'm trapped." Suggesting that the patient imagine himself in such a circumstance may be a valuable therapeutic method of evoking deeper emotions, clarifying situations, and facilitating the working through of conflicts.

The Phrasing of Suggestions

Hypnosis is essentially a refined way of communicating with a patient who is in a state of concentration. Becoming proficient with hypnosis requires that you master a new way of speaking and communicating, a hypnotic "patter." For this reason, as you study and watch hypnosis demonstrations, you are encouraged to write down phrases and suggestions that appeal to you. You will find it valuable to tape record workshops and demonstrations and subsequently study the language and phrasing of suggestions.

Some writers and teachers have emphasized the concept of going into a trance oneself, and simply "trusting the unconscious" to formulate suggestions and conduct hypnotherapy. This admonition stems from Erickson's discussing a particularly fascinating case where he did precisely this. However, before we can trust that something brilliant will flow out of our unconscious mind, we have to put something into it!

After 40 years of experience in compulsively writing, rewriting and carefully preparing suggestions (Hammond, 1984, 1988b), Erickson could certainly trust his unconscious mind to spontaneously contribute suggestions and ideas for intervention. This is the case with all experienced clinicians. Rollo May (1958) once said: "The therapist's situation is like that of the artist who has spent *many years* of disciplined study learning *technique*; but he knows that if specific thoughts of technique *preoccupy* him when he actually is in the process of painting, he has at that moment lost his vision . . . " (p. 85, emphasis added).

After thorough, careful study of the technique of hypnosis and of formulating suggestions, you will increasingly find that you can trust yourself to innovate spontaneously. In fact, as you progress you will undoubtedly be delighted with some of the creative and valuable suggestions that flow into your mind. However, the concept of "trusting the unconscious" should not be used to justify sloppy clinical work and a lack of thoughtful preparation or treatment planning.

I want to encourage you to invest considerable time in writing out suggestions and metaphors. Take concepts and ideas in this book that appeal to you and rewrite them and make them your own. Carefully consider where to put pauses and painstakingly examine the implications of your suggestions. Tape record your hypnotic work and listen afterwards to what you are actually saying and implying.

This kind of thorough study and preparation is crucial to becoming skilled at the art of hypnosis. It is my experience that many of the most highly polished hypnotherapists who seem to be "silver tongued" simply have the *appearance* of spontaneity. In most cases they have actually spent many long hours carefully formulating the suggestions and metaphors they use, and have then, in many cases, committed them to memory. This was certainly the case with Erickson, who for many years compulsively wrote and rewrote suggestions and metaphors to use with patients.

RHYTHM AND PAUSES   Most experienced practitioners speak with a rhythm and cadence when they do hypnosis, essentially speaking in phrases. This seems to encourage hypnotic response. A common error among new students is that they will tend to speak continuously, in a lecturing or conversational manner, without pauses.

It not only seems beneficial to speak in a rhythmic manner, but during the process of induction it is helpful to gradually slow down the rate at which you are speaking. Thus you will speak slower and in a more relaxed manner as the induction proceeds. There is an exception, however. Occasionally you may be working with an obsessional or resistant patient who is overanalytical of everything you say. With this type of patient it may be helpful, at least with important suggestions, to speak more rapidly so that they have less time to pick apart or resist suggestions.

EXAMPLES OF INTRODUCTORY HYPNOTIC PHRASING

In an effort to speed up your learning process, I will provide you with a list of many types of introductory phrases that are often used by hypnotherapists, particularly those with a more "Ericksonian" orientation. Repeated study of these phrases and the types of suggestions identified above will undoubtedly assist you to become smoother in your delivery of inductions and suggestions. It may be helpful to tape record these phrases and listen to them repeatedly. This will assist you in internalizing this new way of speaking.

And you can wonder . . .
Can you notice . . .?
And you can be pleased . . .
And you begin to wonder when . . .
With your permission . . .
Now I'd like you to have a new experience.
. . . In a way that meets your needs.
I want you to enjoy this experience.
And you will be surprised at . . .
Now of course I don't know for sure what you're experiencing. But perhaps
    you're . . .
It's going to be a pleasure to . . .
And I'd like to have you discover . . .
Perhaps even taking a special kind of enjoyment (in your ability to) . . .
And sooner or later, I don't know just when . . .
And I wonder if it will surprise you when . . .
I wonder if you'll be curious, as you notice . . .
You already know how to . . .
Perhaps you wouldn't mind noticing . . .
I would like you to discover something . . .
One of the things I'd like you to discover is . . .
And I want you to notice something that's happening to you.
At first . . ., but later . . .
Have you begun to notice that *yet*?
And I think you're going to enjoy being surprised that . . .
And I want you to notice something that's happening to you.
I wonder if you'll enjoy how naturally, how easily . . .
I wonder if you'd like to enjoy . . .
I wonder if you'll be surprised to discover that . . .
And I wonder if you'll be curious about the fact that you . . .
Perhaps noticing . . .
Perhaps beginning to notice . . .
And maybe you'll enjoy noticing . . .
I wonder if you've ever noticed . . .
Maybe it will surprise you to notice that . . .
I'd like you to let yourself become more and more aware of . . .

I'd like you to begin allowing . . .
And your unconscious mind can enable you to . . .
I wonder if you'll decide to . . . or . . .
In all probability . . .
Very likely . . .
And would you be willing to experience . . .?
You don't need to be concerned if . . .
It's so nice to know . . .
And do you notice the beginning of . . .?
It may be that you'll enjoy . . .
At times like this, some people enjoy . . .
One of the first things you can become aware of is . . .
And it appears that already . . .
Give yourself the opportunity (to see if). . . .
Perhaps sooner than you expect . . .
And if you wish . . .
And you can wonder what . . .
And, in an interesting way, you'll discover . . .
And its very rewarding to know that . . .
And, Chris, you know better than anyone that . . .
It's very positive and comforting to know . . .
You'll be fascinated and feel a strong compulsion to . . .
And that will probably remind you of other experiences, and other feelings
    you've had.
I would like you to appreciate the fact that . . .
I wonder if you'll be reminded . . .
I wonder if you'll be pleased to notice . . .
. . . by just noticing.
I wonder if you've ever noticed . . .
And while you wonder that, I want you to discover that . . .
I'd like you to begin allowing . . .
What's important, is the ability of your mind to . . .
I want to remind you of something that you probably already know, which
    is . . .
And as that occurs, you really can't help but notice . . .
So that it's almost as if . . .
Almost as if . . .
Almost as though . . .
Kind of like . . .
And that's just fine . . .
And that's all right . . .
That's okay.
All that really matters . . .
All that's really important . . .
I don't know if you're aware of these changes, and it doesn't really matter.
I wonder if you'll be interested, in learning how, to . . .
It may be that you're already aware of . . .
The really important thing is just to be fully aware of . . .

The Process of Suggestions in Facilitating Phenomena

I have adapted and modified (Brown & Fromm, 1986) eight steps that may be useful in conceptualizing how to structure a series of hypnotic suggestions that are designed to produce one of the hypnotic phenomenon.

1. *Focusing Attention.* It is recommended that a sequence of suggestions begin with something that captures or focuses the patient's attention. This may be done indirectly by simply speaking in a manner that compels or captures attention. For example, "Something is beginning to happen to one of your hands, but you don't know what it is yet." Such a suggestion creates a sense of wonderment, depotentiating conscious mental sets and focusing attention through evoking curiosity. After all, how often does anyone say something like that to most people?

   Attention may also be focused through a more direct suggestion. For example, in the case of formulating suggestions to facilitate arm levitation, one may say: "Concentrate on the sensations in your hands." Another illustration of a straightforward directive to focus attention prior to giving more important suggestions is to say, "I want the deepest part of your unconscious mind to listen very carefully. And when the deepest part of your mind is fully listening, your 'yes' finger can float up to signal me." Erickson often said, very simply, "Now I want you to listen very carefully."

2. *Enhancing Awareness of Immediate Experience.* Particularly when seeking to facilitate an immediate action or sensory hypnotic phenomenon (e.g., ideomotor or ideosensory activity, anesthesia), it can be valuable to increase the patient's awareness of his or her current experience. As a next step in arm levitation, for example, one may continue: "And you can simply tell me, which hand feels lighter?" or, "And notice the texture of your slacks, and the sensations that you notice in your fingers." This step, popularly referred to as "pacing," does not suggest an activity or experience, but simply points out or seeks to increase current awareness.

3. *Noting and Accepting Any New Aspect of the Experience or Leading the Subject.* Next, a suggestion is given to create an expectation and anticipation of a new experience. The therapist will now have an opportunity to note the patient's response to suggestion. Several suggestions will illustrate this step: "And one of your hands will begin to feel lighter than the other." "And a lightness will begin to develop in one of your hands. [pause] And you'll begin to notice a tendency to movement in one hand. And then a finger will begin to twitch or move, [pause] and then to float up." "You will begin to notice a numbness and anesthesia beginning to develop in your right hand. And *when* you notice the anesthesia beginning, just nod your head to let me know. [If no response is forthcoming, after 20 seconds, further suggestions may be given:] And I don't know if you'll begin to notice the numbness in your fingers,

or your palm or on the back of the hand *first*. But *when* you notice the numbness beginning, just nod your head. [If necessary, after another 30 second pause, you may ask:] Do you notice the numbness *yet*?"

4. *Introducing the Immediate (Process) Goal of the Suggestion*. The behavioral response or desired goal for the near future is next noted to the patient. "And as that lightness increases, *soon* that entire hand and arm will *begin* to float up, off your lap" [the immediate goal]. "And notice how that numbness begins to flow and spread through *that* entire hand ["that" is dissociative language, in contrast to saying "your hand."]. *Before long* that entire hand will become very numb, and leathery, and anesthetic. And when that entire hand feels very numb and anesthetized, just nod your head to let me know."

5. *Repetition of Suggestion and Reinforcing Partial Responses*. It is often important to be patient in seeking to obtain a hypnotic response. Use repetition of suggestion focusing on the intermediate responses that are needed to produce the full response you desire. "And that hand is getting lighter and lighter [said during inhalations], lifting, lifting, that's right [reinforcing a small twitching movement]. And that index finger twitches and lifts [further reinforcing the partial response to suggestion], and the other fingers will develop a lightness also, almost as if large helium balloons were being attached to each fingertip and the wrist with strings." Naturally, more significant responses to suggestion are also deserving of reinforcement. "That's right, and up it comes. And you can really enjoy the way it's effortlessly floating up."

6. *Encouraging Dissociation and Involuntary Response*. As the suggestive sequence continues, as modeled under step 4, it is important to shift to using dissociative language that will encourage a feeling of automatism and of responding involuntarily. For example: "And *the* hand is lifting; *it's* floating up, lighter and lighter. And *just allow that hand* to continue floating up *all by itself, at its own pace and speed*." The following suggestions illustrate this process in producing glove anesthesia: "Notice, with a sense of curiosity, how that numbness and anesthesia begin to flow and spread, all through *that* hand. Spreading and flowing in *its own way, without really trying, just allowing it to happen*."

7. *Building Anticipation and Expectation*. Occasionally in the process of giving suggestions to facilitate a phenomenon, it is helpful to create expectancy and build a sense of anticipation of a response that will soon occur. For instance: "And *soon* you'll *become aware of the tendency to movement*, and first one finger, and then another, will *begin* to develop a lightness. And *before long* you'll sense a finger twitch or move, and then it will begin to lift." "And something's *beginning to happen* to one of your hands, and *soon you'll become aware* of what it is."

8. *Accepting the Patient's Pace of Response*. Adjust to the patient's rate of response, whether it is rapid or slow. Begin by "pacing" the behavioral response, adjusting, accepting and commenting on it. Then, suggestions may be introduced to accelerate or slow down ("lead") the speed of response. When a levitation is beginning to occur very slowly, for example, be patient and continue to focus on and reinforce small,

minimal movements. Later, leading suggestions may be given. For instance, "And now it's as if some other force begins to push or pull that arm up. As if there's a large helium balloon under the palm, or attached with strings to each fingertip and to the wrist, and that hand and arm will begin to float up more rapidly, lighter and lighter [as the therapist very lightly strokes up the underside of the forearm, or very gently lifts the fingertips while the patient is inhaling.]."

HANDLING FAILURE TO RESPOND TO SUGGESTIONS

What do you do when there is no response to a suggestion? One option is to be accepting (e.g., saying "That's all right.") and then simply move on to something else, possibly with the suggestion that they will respond more fully next time. But perhaps the best strategy that I have discovered is to interact with the patient in trance. You may ask, "Remaining deep in trance, just tell me verbally, what are you experiencing?" You may discover that your suggestion was not clear to the patient or that he misinterpreted the suggestion. On the other hand, you may discover that some type of response has occurred that may then be accepted and utilized for therapeutic gain. For instance, after failing to obtain an ideomotor signal in response to suggestions, the inquiry may reveal that the patient feels a sensation in one finger, but that "it doesn't seem to want to float up." This may be accepted and utilized in the following manner: "That's just fine. Many people experience sensations instead of feeling a finger move. So whenever your unconscious mind creates a distinct sensation in that finger, it can represent a signal of 'yes,' you can then voluntarily lift it up to let me know." Be open to patient feedback when you make inquiries. You may learn something you need to modify, change or suggest to facilitate a successful response. Also, remember to be patient and reinforcing of partial responses.

It is also vitally important to accept that many patients seem to be natively talented at experiencing certain phenomenon, and may have difficulty experiencing others. It may be interpreted in this way to the patient, as a normal phenomenon, and this reduces perceptions of failure.

HYPNOSIS IN PAIN MANAGEMENT

INTRODUCTION

Evaluation and Assessment of Pain

ETHICAL PRACTICE requires that we have the technical knowledge to adequately evaluate patient needs. This means that the nonphysician treating pain patients must become familiar with medical evaluation and treatment alternatives. Pain patients should be required to obtain a physical examination and appropriate diagnostic studies prior to psychological intervention.

Similarly, it is vital for physicians and dentists to learn to evaluate more than the biophysical aspects of pain. Particularly with chronic pain patients, multidimensional assessment is required (Hammond & Stanfield, 1977), taking into account the physical-sensory, behavioral, affective, interpersonal-environmental, and cognitive (and adaptive function) components of the pain experience.

Interview evaluation may include: a description of the pain; history of the pain and whether it is acute or chronic; prior treatments, surgeries and medications and their effects; the impact of the pain problem on relationships, vocation, leisure activities, sexual activity, etc.; level of premorbid functioning; potential benefits of the pain ("If I could magically take away your pain today, how would your life be different? What would you be able to do that you can't do now?"); antecedents (environmental, temporal, emotional, cognitive) associated with exacerbation and improvement of pain; and level of depression.

We must remain aware that lifestyle variables such as bruxism, postural habits (e.g., from lengthy telephone use and video games), and environmental chemicals (Hall, 1980) may all contribute to pain problems. Last year a 53-year-old female patient consulted me with a 40-year history of severe, daily migraines. She had undergone almost every kind of medical and dental evaluation. But during the first interview it became apparent that her migraine headaches were usually present upon awakening in the mornings. Although she had no evidence of tooth abrasion from grinding, I asked her to consciously relax her jaw before retiring during the next week. The next week she had four migraines instead of seven. She was then taught self-hypnosis with suggestions for bruxism. The following week she only experienced one mild headache and she reported that it was the most comfortable week in 40 years! Her relief has continued. Despite the many intensive medical and dental evaluations, this behavioral factor that is responsive to hypnotic intervention had been overlooked.

Other cases may be cited, however, in which medical causes for pain were discovered that required medical treatment, not hypnosis. For instance, a large proportion of the women referred to me for the psychological treatment of dyspareunia (pain with intercourse) are said by their gynecologists to have no organic pathology. Experience has taught, however, that most gynecologists (who usually happen to be men) have not learned to do a detailed enough pelvic examination to identify organic causes of dyspareunia (Abarbanel, 1978; Kaplan, 1983). In my practice, when we have a specially trained gynecologist evaluate these patients, we find organic causes for dyspareunia in 70%-80% of the cases. The message is that we must not neglect thorough medical or psychological (behavioral, cognitive, environmental, affective) evaluation with pain patients. Pain is a complex disorder.

OBTAINING A SENSORY DESCRIPTION OF THE PAIN

Hypnotherapy with pain is facilitated by a detailed description of the following sensory aspects of the pain: (1) thermal sensations (e.g., degree of heat versus cold); (2) kinesthetic sensations and pressure aspects of the pain (e.g., dull, sharp, binding, itching, heavy, twisting, drilling, penetrating, stabbing, pounding); and (3) imagery of the pain (size, shape, color, texture, sound). One method for doing this is to obtain a detailed verbal description of the sensory components of the pain. This may be done in an interview in a manner that establishes rapport with the patient and leaves him or her feeling empathically understood. For example, I typically ask the patient to tell me which of the following adjectives describes an aspect of their pain:

Aching, beating, binding, biting, burning, caustic, cool, corroding, cramping, crushing, cutting, drilling, dull, flashing, flickering, gnawing, grinding, gripping, heavy, hot, itching, lacerating, nagging, nauseating, numb, penetrating, piercing, pinching, pounding, pulsing, rasping, searing, sharp, shooting, smarting, spasming, splitting, squeezing, stabbing, stinging, tearing, throbbing, tingling, twisting.

A detailed sensory description of the pain not only establishes rapport but also, more importantly, provides you with clues that may be valuable if techniques are used for replacement or substitution of sensations or for hypnotic reinterpretation of the pain experience. In addition, many of the pain descriptors listed above suggest imagery to both patient and therapist that may subsequently be used with the technique of imagery modification.

The qualitative aspects of pain may also be assessed through paper and pencil instruments such as the McGill Pain Questionnaire (Melzack, 1975) and the Low Back Pain Questionnaire (Leavitt, Garron, Whisler, & Sheinkop, 1978). It may likewise be enlightening to have patients draw their pain or at least to imagine in hypnosis what their pain looks like. Drawings may usefully assess the location of pain and will naturally also suggest images for later modification during hypnosis. Drawings to determine location of pain may particularly be facilitated by giving the patient a page with a line drawing of the front and back of the body, with instructions to identify or shade areas where pain is experienced.

OUTLINE OF HYPNOTIC STRATEGIES AND TECHNIQUES FOR MANAGING PAIN

In this chapter you will find a large number of hypnotic techniques discussed and modeled for you. You may find the following conceptualization of major hypnotic pain control strategies and the techniques that fall under these strategies to be useful in understanding these methods.

I. Unconscious Exploration to Enhance Insight or Resolve Conflict
    A. Ideomotor Signaling
    B. The Inner Adviser Technique
    C. Guided Imagery
    D. Hypnoprojective Techniques

II. Creating Anesthesia or Analgesia
    A. Direct or Indirect Suggestion
    B. Imagery and Imagery Modification
    C. Ideomotor Turn-off of Pain
    D. Gradual Diminution of Pain
    E. Interspersal Technique and Use of Metaphors
    F. The Clenched Fist Technique
    G. Increasing and Decreasing Pain

III. Cognitive-Perceptual Alteration of Pain
    A. Body Dissociation
    B. Symptom Substitution
    C. Displacement of Pain
    D. Replacement or Substitution of Sensations
    E. Reinterpretation of Sensations
    F. Unconscious Exploration of Function or Meaning of Pain
    G. Amnesia
    H. Time Distortion
    I. Massive Time Dissociation
    J. Increasing Pain Tolerance
        1. Posthypnotic Suggestions for Internal Dialogue
        2. Mental Rehearsal of Coping with Triggers and Pain
        3. Desensitization to Triggers that Exacerbate Pain
    K. The Inner Adviser Technique (to explore meaning and triggers of pain)

IV. Decreasing Awareness of Pain (Distraction Techniques)
   A. Time Dissociation
   B. Imagining Pleasant Scenes and Fantasies
   C. Absorption in Thoughts
   D. External Distraction Through Enhanced Awareness of the Environment
   E. Eliciting Mystical Experiences

STRATEGY AND TECHNIQUE SELECTION   How does one select which one of the strategies to use? My personal preference is to first determine with a technique from strategy I (e.g., ideomotor exploration) that an unconscious dynamic or past event is not a part of the problem. This can generally be assessed in one part of a single session, although if factors are uncovered they may require an interview or two to resolve. One problem with conventional pain assessment strategies (e.g., Karoly & Jensen, 1987) is that they neglect the possible role of unconscious variables as a potential cause of a pain problem. There are occasions when a pain problem, or part of a pain problem, may be associated with past trauma (e.g., incest) or serve unconscious purposes (e.g., for self-punishment). We may hypothesize that this may particularly be the case when the cause of the pain is unknown and cannot be causally related to any pathophysiologic process, where the pain seems more intense than would ordinarily be anticipated, and/or when pain lasts longer than is appropriate.

Hypnotherapy for pain should include a brief routine check (e.g., with ideomotor signaling) to determine if unconscious factors contribute to the problem (Hammond & Cheek, 1988; Rossi & Cheek, 1988).

When it has been determined that psychological and unconscious factors do not play a role in the problem, suggestive hypnosis may then be introduced. Thus it is next recommended that you determine whether strategy II techniques (e.g., suggestions for anesthesia, ideomotor turn-off of pain, imagery modification) are successful in alleviating or managing the distress. When these more straightforward techniques are not entirely effective, we may then experiment with the more complex techniques that fall under strategies III and IV. These techniques will be particularly beneficial when pain is chronic and where several pain sites are identified. Certain techniques (e.g., time dissociation, imagining pleasant scenes) are primarily useful with patients who can be inactive, at least for segments of the day. For instance, if a patient is imagining a future or past time when they were not in pain, this inward absorption precludes simultaneous interaction with people or the performance of vocational tasks. When working with more difficult, chronic pain patients who have several sites or types of pain, you may also find it helpful to begin by working with their least difficult or intense problem first. Begin with the problem where you anticipate the highest probability of success. Successful management of one pain area or problem will enhance patient self-efficacy and their belief that success may be anticipated with other problems (areas) as well. Success breeds success.

When time permits, it is also valuable to determine the hypnotic pain management techniques that the patient is most skilled in using and which techniques are most potent for them individually. You will probably find it most helpful initially to demonstrate pain control techniques to manage acute pain that is therapist-induced; for example, begin by creating glove anesthesia to block pain that is induced through the use of a hemostat or nail file.

There are a variety of suggestive hypnotic strategies for pain management that will be reviewed in the first part of this chapter. In successfully controlling organic pain, however, it is extremely important to have frequent reinforcement sessions early in treatment. In particular, it has been recommended (Crasilneck & Hall, 1985) that we should reinforce pain control as quickly as possible after the patient becomes aware of the return of pain. Thus, in the first 24-hour period it may be necessary to see the patient several times (e.g., every four hours) and self-hypnosis should be learned as rapidly as possible.

We should also not neglect the role of ego-strengthening as part of hypnotic work with chronic pain patients. Patients with chronic pain customarily also develop feelings of low self-esteem and self-worth that may be responsive to hypnotic suggestion. Furthermore, self-hypnosis provides such patients with an active self-management strategy that can return some sense of control and mastery to their lives.

Most of our patients are not capable of creating a complete anesthesia and removing all of their pain through hypnosis. However, even for those patients who are this hypnotically talented, we should only remove all pain in a small number of conditions: (1) dental anesthesia; (2) childbirth; (3) terminal illness (e.g., cancer pain); (4) when hypnosis is being used for surgical anesthesia; (5) phantom limb pain; and (6) possibly for treating shingles or arthritis attacks (Crasilneck & Hall, 1985). In other cases, we must remain cautious to leave some "signal" pain so that the patient will not injure himself and so that pain from the development of new symptoms or a worsening of the patient's condition will be perceived and reported.

Very importantly, as clinicians treating pain we must assume a realistic posture concerning the role of hypnosis. Hypnosis is like any other medical or psychological technique: it is not effective with every patient. Some patients obtain tremendous pain relief with hypnosis; others find it clearly helpful but are in need of still other methods of relief; some find that it reduces the affective components of pain (Price & Barber, 1987), making the sensory pain more tolerable; and some patients receive no benefit from hypnosis. Consequently we must also be familiar with nonhypnotic treatment options such as medications, nerve blocks and trigger point injections, physical therapy, transcutaneous electrical nerve stimulation (TENS), and biofeedback. When it comes to the treatment of pain, the hypnotherapist should not work in a vacuum. A multidisciplinary team is ideal, and interdisciplinary cooperation is vitally important.

CHAPTER OVERVIEW

The first part of this chapter will introduce you to a variety of hypnotic techniques for pain management and models of verbalizations for these techniques. Later, suggestions specific to several conditions such as migraine, arthritis, cancer and shingles will be presented.

Techniques of Hypnotic Pain Management

Joseph Barber, Ph.D.
Los Angeles, California

Though there are many ways of conceptualizing techniques of hypnotic pain management, and while different clinicians will certainly apply techniques differently, it is helpful to consider four basic methods of achieving hypnotic pain control:

1. *Analgesia or anesthesia* can be created in the hypnotized individual by simply suggesting that the perception of pain is changing, is diminishing, or that the area is becoming numb, so that the pain is gradually disappearing. It may be easier for a patient to notice growing *comfort* rather than diminishing pain; thus a specific feeling of comfort such as that associated with anesthesia can be suggested specifically, for example: *"You may remember the feeling of anesthesia from the past, and begin already imagining that such numbing comfort is beginning, just barely, to become more and more apparent."* Alternatively, the patient can be given a specific focus to notice diminishing pain. For instance, it may be helpful to ask the patient, before treatment, to rate his or her pain on a scale from 0 to 10, "0" representing no pain at all, and "10" representing the most pain imaginable. (Patients can rate their pain quite reliably, as Sternbach [1982] describes.) Following induction, the hypnotized patient may be told, *"Earlier, you were able to rate your pain, using numbers. I'd like you to look up, in the corner of your mind, right now, and notice what number you see, and notice that number beginning to change."* Further suggestions can be given for associating the number with the perception of pain, and for perceiving progressively diminishing magnitude of the numbers.

2. *Substitution of a painful sensation* by a different, less painful sensation can fre-

quently enable a patient to tolerate some persistent feeling in the area but not to suffer from it. A sensation of stabbing pain may be substituted with a sensation of vibration, for example: *"The stabbing needles might become, in a surprising way, somehow more dull, not quite so very hot, so that, at some point in the future, maybe in two minutes, maybe in two hours, you can notice the peculiar buzzing, or vibrating feeling of the blunt, warm needles."* For some patients, substitution is easier when the substituted feeling is not thoroughly pleasant; a burning neuralgic pain may become an irritating itch, for instance, or a tickle; a patient who needs for some reason to continue to be aware of the stimulus of the pain, for instance, may be better with this technique.

3. *Displacement of the locus of pain* to another area of the body, or, sometimes, to an area outside the body, can again provide an opportunity for the patient to continue experiencing the sensations, but in a less vulnerable, less painful area. The choice of the area is usually based on its lesser psychological vulnerability, and suggestions can leave the choice to the patient; for example: *"As you continue to pay careful attention to the discomfort in your abdomen, let me know when you first begin to notice the very slight movement of that feeling. . . . That's right, now just notice, as the movement continues, in perhaps a circular way, to increase . . . is it moving clockwise, or counterclockwise? . . . That's fine, now just continue to be curious as you notice how the feeling can continue to move, in an ever-increasing spiral, moving round and round your abdomen, and notice which leg it begins to move into . . ."* and so on, as the feeling is suggested to move into a limb, perhaps even to center in a single toe or finger, or to move outside the body altogether.

4. *Dissociation* of awareness can be created when the patient does not need to be very functional (e.g., during a medical or dental procedure) or when some condition renders

the patient virtually immobile (e.g., during the last stages of a terminal illness). The patient can be taught simply to begin to psychologically experience himself or herself as in another time, place, or state, as in a vivid daydream. For instance, one can suggest that the patient experience himself or herself as floating, and that *"your mind, your awareness, can just float easily outside your body, and move over by the window, so you can watch the world outside . . ."* or one can suggest that the patient float outside the room, and travel to any place he or she would enjoy.

EXAMPLE OF SUGGESTIONS FOR DECREASING NUMBERS TO CREATE COMFORT

A while ago, you were able to very accurately rate your pain, using a number from 0 to 10. Any time in the future that you would like to feel more comfortable, you can do so. All you have to do is to look up in the corner of your mind, and notice what number is associated with the level of pain you feel. Then, just watch . . . just watch as the number begins to change. I don't know exactly what that will be like. Maybe it will begin to quite slowly fade from your visual awareness, and as it does so a smaller number will begin to emerge from the background. For instance, if you feel and see an "8," you may begin to notice the lines of the "8" begin to fade, and "7" will become more apparent. Or maybe the curves of the "8" will begin to straighten and relax, and become more like the angles of the "7," until, after a while, the angularity of the "7" will take on the graceful curves of the "6." And maybe the "6" will, like the pages of a calendar in a movie, be blown by the wind, off into the darkness, leaving a "5." And maybe the "5" will begin to open, ever so gradually, and the line at the top will fade until you notice that there is no longer really a "5" there but rather a "4." Or, maybe some numbers will be skipped altogether, and

you might, more quickly than you expect, begin to have the impression of a lovely white swan, gliding along, the graceful long curve of its neck reminding you very, very distinctly of a "2." Or is it that, seeing a "2," you are reminded of a swan. And not only *reminded* of a swan, but, somehow, begin to feel almost as if you, too, are gliding gently along, the smoothness and grace more and more a part of your awareness. . . . And any time that you want to feel more comfortable than you do, all you have to do is look up in the corner of your mind and see the number you feel. And the number you feel is the number you see, and the number you see is the number you feel. And then just watch . . . just watch, as the numbers, and your feelings, begin to change. And a beautiful swan, or is it only the coolness of a "2," is so very much more easy to live with, is it not?

[The patient was thus given a posthypnotic suggestion for coping with future pain. However, in order not to lead the patient to expect too much from this new experience, no suggestion was given for complete pain relief (no "0" was suggested, for instance), and further caution was added:]

Now, I really don't know you very well, and you certainly don't know me well yet at all . . . so I really don't know how much relief you can expect, really expect, to feel when you leave my office. It may be that sometime later today, and I really don't know what time, maybe 10:30 this morning, or maybe just one second after noon, or maybe 6:18 this evening . . . I really cannot say what time it will be . . . I cannot predict the future . . . but maybe it would be interesting to you, or even enjoyable for you, to notice, at some time later today, but I don't know what time exactly, to just suddenly notice how much more comfortable you feel than you thought you might. But I don't know what to expect. I'd be really very surprised if you left here feeling much relief; I wouldn't be very surprised to later find out that you felt better later today. But listen . . . even if you feel better late today, either later this morning, or this afternoon, or even tonight, just before getting ready for bed, there is no reason to assume that this has anything at all to do with anything you and I may have done today. There is really no need to know how or why something happens in order to enjoy the fact of it. So there is no reason at all to assume any cause in particular. In fact, whatever relief you feel may be so very pleasing, so very enjoyable to you, you may not even care why it happens.

[The purpose of such suggestions was to obviate any expectations the patient may have had about my own expectations, as well as any doubts the patient may have had about the efficacy of hypnosis, and to diffuse issues of control or power which might have otherwise inhibited relief.]

ILLUSTRATIVE DISSOCIATIVE SUGGESTIONS WITH A RESISTANT CHRONIC PAIN PATIENT

I wonder, even as you continue to lie on the treatment table, if you would enjoy remembering some time, long ago, when you didn't hurt very much. Or maybe you can remember what it was like when the nerve block stopped the pain. That was really a great experience, and, though it might happen again, I really doubt that it could happen today. In fact, if you do feel better later today, on your way home, after you get home, while you're standing in the kitchen, or just as you're getting into your bed, it is unlikely that it is the result of anything we've done for you today. We're just getting to know you, and it seems unlikely that someone with a problem as complex as yours is going to experience much relief today, or, even if you do, it is probably just a lucky break, just a fluke. Who knows how much comfort you can have? I don't. Well, at least I don't know for sure. I'm sure you can have *some* relief. Who couldn't. But just how *much* is really as unclear to me as it is to you. I don't know you, I don't understand you, I don't feel your pain, I don't really understand your pain, so it would be really dumb for me to stand here and tell you that you're going to feel better today just because you're lying there listening to me with

your eyes closed, your body relaxing more and more with each breath you take. Whatever relief you might feel, either now, or later today, or tomorrow morning when it's time for you to awaken, that relief is just something that happens, and I don't know why, and I don't know how. You may have some idea about it, either while it's happening, or just after you discover feeling better, or maybe next month or next year. I don't know. After all, time is not only relative, but it is sometimes very confusing. Your mom is going to drive you home today, and when she does, while she is driving, and while you sort of daydream about what I've said to you, while this is happening, it is today, and you know what day this is. But tomorrow, today will be yesterday, and tomorrow will be today, and what was once today will be just that much farther in the past of your comfort, your relief, your hopes, your curiosity about what can be done for you, and better yet, what you might do for yourself. Now, as I leave the room, I want you to take whatever time you need to get up, after your mind has cleared and your eyes have opened, to get up, get your clothes on, go find your mom and do whatever else is necessary to get yourself gone to the comfort of your home. The receptionist will make an appointment for you to see me in a few days, and when I see you again, I will be really eager, really curious, to hear you tell me about the things you've been wondering about. Goodbye.

Altering the Quality of Discomfort: Example of Leg Pain

M. Erik Wright, M.D., Ph.D.

The following illustration shows how guided imagery can be used to assuage discomfort by reinterpreting its nature. It is taken from a case where it was important for the intensity of pain to become tolerable so that healing could be facilitated. Trance induction had already taken place. The therapist continued:

You have described this pain in your leg shin as being sharp and piercing, like a knife point sticking into the bone . . . A very distressing and uncomfortable experience . . . It would become more tolerable if this sudden, intense, sharp pain were replaced by a pain that did not come so unexpectedly, that gave you time to adjust yourself so that when it occurred, even if the new pain were not exactly comfortable. . . .

[The therapist begins to develop imagined conditions for modifying the pain:] Now visualize the left leg as being covered by thick layers of cotton . . . going around and around that part of the leg where the pain is most often experienced . . . See this cotton secured to your leg so that it won't slip off . . . The cotton is so thick and matted that nothing would be able to pierce through it, no matter how sharp it might be . . . [The therapist paces the process according to cues from the client:] Signal with your finger when you see this clearly . . . Good . . .

[The therapist continues building pain-reducing imagery:] Now see a sharp knife thrusting at the cotton layers, but it absolutely cannot penetrate through the cotton protection . . . You may sense the pressure transmitted through the cotton . . . It may feel like a dull pain, but it is mostly pressure and you are much better able to stand the amount of discomfort . . . When you have reached the tolerance level for this dull pain, see the knife being withdrawn from the cotton batting . . . The pressure is relieved, and the dull pain drops immediately. . . .

[The therapist gives control to the client for pain reduction and healing:] Now that your body does not have to prepare for the shock of the sharp pain, you will be able to use that spared energy to speed up the healing process . . . When the pain recurs, you can gradually build up the thickness of the cotton wadding so that the pressure becomes more tolerable and the dull pain continues to decrease. In time, you may feel only a sensitive area on the skin as the healing underneath continues.

Transformation of Pain

William L. Golden,
E. Thomas Dowd, and
Fred Friedberg

In physical transformation of pain, the pain is moved to a part of the body that is less central to the individual's activities or to a location that is so ridiculous that the person is enabled to treat it in a humorous fashion, thus making it easier to view the pain in a more detached manner. For example, lower-back pain could be transferred to the big toe, where it interferes less with daily activities. Or a headache could be moved to the little finger of the right hand or, more humorously, the left earlobe. This procedure is especially valuable in cases of chronic, intractable, benign pain, where there is often a need to retain the pain for psychological reasons. The client is thus not asked to give up the pain, but only to transform it. Often it is helpful to ask clients where they would like to move their pain, in order to involve them in the process.

Physical transformation of pain is accomplished as follows. After the subject is placed in a trance, he or she is instructed to touch the painful part of the body with (usually) the right hand and to transfer the pain to another part of the body by touching it with that hand. If desired, suggestions can also be made for a reduction of the pain in the new location. An instruction such as the following could be used:

You can slowly allow your right hand to move so that it touches your back at the most painful spot. . . . As it touches your back, you can be aware of the painful sensations flowing from your back into your hand. . . . Now slowly allow your hand to move toward your left shoulder, feeling the pain lessen as it does so. . . . As your hand touches your left shoulder, you can feel the pain move to your shoulder, but somewhat less than before. Now remove your hand and let it slowly drop to your lap, relaxing as it goes.

Pain can also be transformed into other sensations, and this procedure is likewise useful in cases of chronic, psychogenic pain. In addition, the signaling function of pain is retained, while the suffering and incapacitation associated with it are reduced. For example, suggestions can be given that the individual will experience an itching, tingling, or warm sensation in the place of and at the site of the pain rather than the pain itself. To some extent, this technique is based on the common observation that the label we attach to something might in part determine how we respond to it (a rose by another name might not smell as sweet), because the meaning of an event or object is partly a function of its name. For example, we might respond quite differently to a behavior labeled *aggressive* than to one labeled *forthright*, although the actual behavior could be the same in both cases. The client might be instructed as follows:

As you pay close attention to the sensations in your back [the location of the pain], you can become aware of a feeling of warmth, it will gradually replace all other feelings so that all you feel in that area is warmth. And you can allow that feeling of warmth to remain for as long as you have need of it.

Erickson's Suggestions for Pain Control

Milton H. Erickson, M.D.

INTRODUCTION

These practical suggestions were compiled from throughout the published papers and lectures of Dr. Erickson. They have been compiled according to technique. Although sometimes Erickson simply describes a technique, often his actual suggestions are provided. I believe that many of these suggestions will provide you with a valuable model for many of the more complex methods that we must occasionally resort to when more straightforward techniques are not successful. (*Ed.*)

TRUISMS FOR DEVELOPING ANESTHESIAS

Erickson discussed "the tremendous amount of learning you have acquired during your lifetime of experience in developing anesthesias throughout your entire body. For example, as you sit and listen to me now, you've forgotten the shoes on your feet . . . and now you can feel them; you've forgotten the glasses on your nose . . . and now you can feel them; you've forgotten the collar around your neck . . . and now you can feel it . . . You listen to an entertaining lecture, and you forget about the hardness of the chairs. But if it happens to be a very boring lecture, your chair feels so utterly uncomfortable. You sense those things. We've all had tremendous experience in developing anesthesias in all parts of our bodies" (Erickson, 1985, p. 228). "So how did you get that anesthesia for the shoes on your feet? Not because there is a drug put into the nerve; not because you were told to have the anesthesia; but because in your lifelong learning you have acquired the automatic ability to turn off sensations and to turn them on again" (Erickson, 1986, p. 120).

ANTICIPATION AND UTILIZING THE UNCONSCIOUS

A number of things may develop, some of which I have not mentioned. I hope you will notice and appreciate them, and then fit them into the goal that you wish to achieve. And I'd like to have you interested in the way these unexpected things can fit into the goal you wish to achieve (Erickson, 1985, p. 180).

REPLACEMENT, SUBSTITUTION OR REINTERPRETATION OF SENSATIONS

You tell your patients in the trance state to think over their pain. Maybe they can't cut out the *nagging* quality of the pain, but maybe they can cut the *burning* quality; maybe they can cut out the *heavy* quality. Or maybe they can keep the heavy, dull aspect of the pain, and lose the burning, the cutting, the lancinating, shooting qualities of the pain. And what have you done? You have asked your patients to take the total experience of pain and to fragment it into a variety of sensations; and as surely as your patients fragment their pain, . . . they have reduced it (Erickson, 1986, p. 81).

ALTERATION OF SENSATIONS.   You have aching pains in your legs that distress you very greatly; you are suffering from arthritis. But if you will examine those sensations, you will find, perhaps, a feeling of warmth; perhaps a feeling of coolness; perhaps a feeling of coldness; and now how about extending some of those sensations? (Erickson, 1986, p. 104).

I asked my patient to tell me whether I should take care of the cutting pain next — or should it be the burning pain, or the hard, cold pain, or the lancinating pain? What does the patient do in response to such a question? He immediately divides his pain experience, psychologically, into a great variety of separate kinds of pain . . . (Erickson, 1983, p. 223).

There are certain transformations that can be brought about here. You know how that first mouthful of dessert tastes so very good? And even the second mouthful still tastes good; but by the time you reach the sixty-sixth mouthful, it doesn't taste so good. You have lost the liking for it, and the taste of the dessert has changed in some peculiar way. It hasn't become bad; it has just "died out" in flavor. Now, as you pay attention to these various sensations in your body that you have described to me, I would like you to name the particular sensation that you want me to work on first (Erickson, 1983, pp. 225-226).

I want to know if that grinding pain is a rapid grinding pain or a slow grinding pain. Or, I can suggest an addition to the grinding: "If you will just pay attention to that grinding pain you will notice that it is a *slow* grinding pain." I have added my own adjective of *slow* to the patient's grinding pain, and if the patient does not accept *slow* I can slip over to *rapid* grinding pain. Why? Because anything that I do to alter the

patient's subjective experience of pain is going to lessen that pain . . ." (Erickson, 1983, p. 228).

And I explained to her with profound apologies that even though I had relieved the pain of her cancer by this numbness, I would have to confess that I was going to be an absolute failure in one regard. I would not be able to remove the pain from the site of the surgical scar. Instead of removing absolutely all of the pain, the best, the very best, that I could do would be to leave the scar area with an annoying, disagreeable, great-big-mosquito-like feeling. It would be something awfully annoying; something she would feel helpless about; something she would wish would stop. But *it would be endurable*, and I impressed that point on Cathy's mind. It took me four hours to accomplish everything (Erickson, 1983, p. 172).

DISPLACEMENT OF PAIN

Now, you've got cancer pain. Why not have another kind of pain also? Why not have pain out here in your hand? You have cancer pain in your body. It is very, very troublesome; it is very, very threatening; it is going to kill you. You know that. You wouldn't mind any amount of pain out here in your hand, because that wouldn't kill you. It is the pain in your torso that is going to kill you, and if you only had pain out here you could stand any amount." You can teach your pain to displace the pain from the torso out into the hand where it is gladly experienced, because it has lost its threatening quality. (Erickson, 1986, pp. 80-81).

AMNESIA FOR PAIN

One of the ways of dealing with unpleasant sensations is to forget them — like when you go to the movies and get all absorbed in the suspenseful drama on screen, and meanwhile you forget about your headache. You may not remember until three days later that you had a headache when you went into the cinema (Erickson, 1983, p. 226).

GRADUAL DIMINUTION OF PAIN

I can't take away all of your pain. That is asking too much of me; it is asking too much of your body. And if you lose 1 percent of that pain you would still have 99 percent of it left; you wouldn't notice the loss of 1 percent, but it would still be a loss of 1 percent. You could lose 5 percent of that pain. You wouldn't notice the loss of 5 percent, because you would still have 95 percent of the pain; but you would still have a loss of 5 percent. Now you could lose 10 percent of the pain, but that really wouldn't be noticeable because you would still have 90 percent of it; but you nevertheless would have a loss of 10 percent of your pain. [You continue to diminish the pain—down to 85 percent, 80 percent, 75, 70, 65, 60, and so on. Then you say:] You might even lose 80 percent of your pain, but I don't think that is quite reasonable, yet. I would be willing to settle for a loss of 75 percent. [And the patient is going to agree with you, regretfully. Then:] What is the difference between 75 and 80 percent, and sooner or later you can lose 80 percent, and maybe 85 percent; but first, let us settle for 80 (Erickson, 1983, p. 236).

DISORIENTATION AND CONFUSION TECHNIQUE WITH PAIN

"Let us see, is that pain in your right leg, or your left leg? . . . Let us see, which is your left leg and which is your right leg?" And you can get as confused as you get the child confused on this subject of where the pain is, and which leg is which. "And now is it on the outside side of your leg, or is it on the inside side of your leg?" . . . I discussed rightness and leftness, and centrality and dextrality, and so on, until the girl was so confused that she thought this hand was her right hand [her left hand], and this hand was her left hand [her right hand]—

because [the left hand] was the only hand that was left to write with! . . . What was my technique? I set up a body disorientation by teaching the patient to get very confused about the site of the pain, about the part of the body involved in the pain, and about the direction of the pain. You disorient the patient to the point where he simply does not know which side is which, and then you provide him with the orientation that you want for him. If you can move the pain to a place in the body where there is no organic cause for it, then you are in a position to produce hypnotic anesthesia for the pain at its actual site. You move the patient's subjective experience of the pain to the wrong area, bodily, because you can correct it more easily there; the patient has little resistance to accepting suggestions in the healthy area (Erickson, 1983, p. 235).

PAIN METAPHOR

. . . You can also cut down organic pain by minimizing your response to it. You see, in organic pain situations you have neurosynapses that are transmitting the pain. Through hypnosis you can spread those synapses apart—like sparks jumping a gap—until you have your synapses spread so wide apart that you get a jumping of the thing. At that point a certain maximal pain stimulation is necessary in order for the person to sense the pain (Erickson, 1985, p. 26).

General Principles for Alleviating Persistent Pain

Ernest L. Rossi, Ph.D. and
David B. Cheek, M.D.
Malibu, California, and Santa Barbara, California

Therapy for persistent pain states must be elastic and must conform to the understandings and needs of the patient and the patient's relatives. Often it must also fit into the needs and understandings of prior medical and surgical attendants in whom the patient has continued faith. It is best judgment to listen carefully to what the patient thinks can be done and what he or she expects the hypnotherapist to use as an approach to the problem. The patient is often in a hypnoidal state during the first moments of interview and may have insights of utmost value to impart. If the therapist can weather the initial critical interview and can have free rein, these are the general steps which have proven helpful:

1. Be sure the patient is unconsciously willing to be helped.
2. Discover when and what caused the illness or pain to be important in the very beginning [through ideomotor signaling]. This may relate to the distress of another person rather than to a personal experience with pain.
3. Determine the first moment at which the patient experienced the pain. Discover whether the patient was awake or asleep at the time. (*Sleep* means either natural sleep or a period of unconsciousness as from chemo-anesthesia.)
4. Discover what reinforced the importance of that initial pain. This may have been the statement of a doctor or the consternation of relatives at the time of initial illness or injury.
5. Ask if the patient now, at the time of interview, believes cure is possible. Orient tc the moment when this conclusion was drawn, regardless of the answer. Points of origin are significant whether optimistic or pessimistic.
6. Have the patient turn off all pain *at an unconscious level* and have a yes finger lift when this has been accomplished. Ask for a verbal report when it is *known consciously* that all pain is gone.
7. Ask the patient to turn the pain back on again but to make it twice as strong as it was at first. The patient may balk at this until it is made clear that the pain will again be turned off, and that it is helpful to know how to turn pain off by first learning how to turn it on. (Prior experience with uncontrolled fear of uncontrolled pain, a fear of the unknown.)
8. As soon as the patient has developed confidence in being able to turn the pain on and off, it is helpful to have him select a cue word or thought which will automatically turn off the pain. This is rehearsed several times in the office, but the patient is told to avoid trying it on his own until the instructor knows it is going to be successful. (There are several implications to this bit of instruction. Most important is the implied confidence that such a day will come. Next in importance is the warning that simple experiences in the office setting do not indicate that the task is now finished.)
9. A pseudo-orientation into the future is requested and the patient is asked to have the yes finger lift when he is forward to the time when there is good health and total freedom from pain. (Refusal to select a time may indicate discouragement or resistance which have not previously been apparent. Acceptance of a date commitment reinforces the other placebo elements of optimistic hope.)
10. Train the patient carefully with auto-hypnosis induction and simple use of brief periods for complete relaxation. This should be restricted to three minutes, at the most, from onset of a medium trance to the moment when the eyes feel like opening. The author insists that the patient stick to the time limits rather than drifting off into natural sleep or prolonged reverie. If too much time is lost during these exercises, the patient will tend to discredit results and will give up the rehearsals as a needless waste of time. The two- or three-minute exercises should be repeated after each meal and at bed time, four times a day. This is no more time than might be taken in smoking five cigarettes during the day.

It may suffice to make office appointments for one hour once a week if the patient is first seen during an interval of relative comfort. If the patient is in severe pain, the author usually arranges for admission to the hospital for a period of two or three days. This separates the patient from unrecognized triggering stimuli at home, permits more than one visit a day if necessary, and allows use of pain-relieving drugs to augment effects of suggestion.

Religious Imagery of Universal Healing for Ego-Strengthening and Pain

M. Erik Wright, M.D., Ph.D.

INTRODUCTION

It is commonly believed that anger, resentment and guilt take up a great deal of energy and may inhibit healing, as well as causing emotional turmoil. In fact, some research (Pennebaker, Kiecolt-Glaser, & Glaser, 1988) implies that releasing such feelings may produce both immediate and long-lasting effects on immune function.

In Wright's technique, you may also use ideomotor signals to have patients indicate when they feel they can forgive themselves. They may be asked to identify specific individuals they need to forgive, and to work inwardly on forgiving them and even praying for them, giving a signal when they feel they have let go of their negative feelings and resentments toward the person. It may then be suggested that they visualize the empty spaces where the guilt and resentment were, and imagine them being filled with love. It may be further suggested that they sense and feel the energy, which was wrapped up in keeping the resentment and guilt inside, being released and becoming available for healing. (*Ed.*)

SUGGESTIONS

There is a deep universal healing spirit within you and in the world that you can draw upon

for healing and for relief from pain . . . You must let yourself come closer to its essential meaning . . . Forgiveness and love are parts of this universal healing spirit . . . that release the inner tensions . . . free your body and your spirit from pain . . . Let your thoughts focus upon your feelings of forgiveness and love . . . Forgiving yourself . . . forgiving others . . . releasing the stresses within yourself that generate tension through anger, hatred, resentment . . . And as the spirit of forgiveness grows within you . . . these tensions are released . . . opening up the healing life forces . . . permitting you to connect with the love of others and love of self . . . and love of God . . . As you open up to this healing love . . . the awareness of the pain becomes distant . . . moving further and further away . . . diminishing in importance and in consequence . . . as the healing love flows through you. . . .

COMMENTARY.   Those who identify themselves with a particular religious group may invoke significant hypnotherapeutic images associated with their deep religious convictions. The client is encouraged to activate religious imagery that will evoke the most intense religious involvement, including religious ecstasy, with a consequent distancing from the ongoing pain experience. The procedures may not only emphasize relief from pain but also may provide considerable religious solace for the individual.

The "Sympathetic Ear" Technique with Chronic Pain

Barry S. Fogel, M.D.
Providence, Rhode Island

INTRODUCTION

Comprehensive approaches to the management of chronic pain attempt to reduce psychological rewards for pain behavior, of which secondary gains are a part. Commonly used methods include environmental manipulation in an inpatient setting, marital and family therapy to reduce interpersonal rewards for pain behavior in important relationships, formal instruction in alternate coping skills, and insight-oriented psychotherapy.

When a clinician is presented with an unrestricted invitation from a patient to treat pain by whatever means are necessary, the clinician often will opt for some combination of the above methods to deal with the operant aspects of pain; hypnosis might be used to directly reduce the intensity of the pain or to promote relaxation. However, the patient specifically requesting hypnotherapy of pain may be open to hypnosis, yet be relatively resistant to the introduction of other management approaches, particularly if they appear to be costly or to require the involvement of other individuals.

The seeker of self-hypnosis may be seeking *individual* mastery of the situation, through a mutative technique or experience, rather than seeking a program which requires ongoing submission to environmental manipulation suggested by another person. With patients who have settled upon hypnosis as their treatment of choice for psychological or ideological reasons, it may be useful for the therapist to use hypnosis itself to promote a cognitive restructuring that may mitigate the effect of secondary gain in sustaining pain behavior. Following such a restructuring, the patient may initiate a discussion of secondary gain with the therapist, eliminating the need for the therapist to confront the patient, possibly intensifying resistance or even leading to a defection from treatment.

Once the issue of secondary gain can be comfortably discussed directly, the therapist has the option of blending hypnosis with individual psychotherapy . . ., or making use of behavioral or family therapy techniques to directly reduce the operant reinforcers of the patient's pain behavior.

THE "SYMPATHETIC LISTENER" SELF-HYPNOTIC ASSIGNMENT

[Following hypnotic induction and deepening] Imagine a sympathetic listener, a sympathetic ear. The ear is eager to hear whatever you have to say—thoughts, feelings, complaints, ideas. . . . It wants to listen, and listens with perfect attention, without fatigue or judgment. Tell the ear all that concerns you now. . . . Each day take time to put yourself in a trance and talk to the sympathetic ear. As you talk to the sympathetic ear, you feel your concerns are fully and completely heard.

Reactivation of Pain-Free Memories: An Example of Intensifying and Relieving Pain

M. Erik Wright, M.D., Ph.D.

INTRODUCTION

Another approach to pain control is based on the following premises: People typically retain memories of a pain-free period in their lives, with its concomitant physical and emotional feelings of well being. A persistent pain experience, however, can submerge these memories. The psychotherapeutic premise is that clients who can recall these and intensify their chronic pain can also learn to diminish that pain perception, even to the point of eliminating it. The imagery invoked during hypnotic trance is based on this premise. The therapeutic process can proceed along the following lines.

ILLUSTRATIVE SUGGESTIONS

Therapist: You are familiar with your own signal for entering trance . . . So give yourself your signal to relax . . . to let yourself go all over . . . to feel yourself becoming light and free . . . Take the time you need to bring about a most comfortable feeling of calm and quietness within yourself . . . of the freeing up within yourself of muscle tension and inner tension . . . Raise your right index finger when you have reached that point . . . [The client does so shortly.] Fine. . . .

From what you have told me . . . you know that there was a time in your life when you felt well — physically, emotionally, and in every other way . . . when you knew what it meant to feel glad to be alive . . . when your body functioned easily and freely . . . [The therapist seeks permission to proceed:] Let's check with the inner part of your mind to see if it will be okay to go back to that time . . . to let the awareness of what it felt like to feel well return to you . . . Would the inner part of the mind use the finger signals in the way it has used them in the past? [The client lifts finger.] The "yes" finger went up slowly but definitely and remained up . . . Okay. . . .

[The therapist invites age retrogression in recalling wellness:] Drift yourself back through time to before the pain was part of your life . . . before the pain was in the picture . . . [Observer-participant dissociation is suggested:] Let part of you continue to remain with me in the here and now, while the other part of you goes back in time . . . Going back . . . going back . . . going back . . . When you are at that good time . . . let me know by your right index finger . . . [The therapist encourages elaboration of the feeling of well being:] Describe yourself . . . Tell how you feel in each part of your body . . . how it feels to feel good . . . Enjoy every moment of this feeling of well being . . . Let every cell of the body restore the awareness of this capacity to feel well, which is part of that cell but which has been submerged by stress feelings . . . This feeling is still a part of you . . . Nourish it . . . bring in colors . . . sounds . . . or any other sensations you wish to strengthen that feeling . . . Let yourself feel very comfortable . . . Now count from one to five slowly . . . and let all the psychological time take place that will revive these feelings of well being strongly in your mind . . . signal when you reach the count of five . . . [Soon the client signals.]

[The therapist seeks permission for the pain experience:] Is the inner part of your mind ready to move up in time to the beginning of a typical pain episode? . . . [The client responds with the finger signal.] The "yes" finger says it

is okay . . . [The therapist reassures the client:] No matter how intense the pain may become . . . you will be able to manage it . . . Observe what images are in your mind as the pain begins . . . Tell me what you are thinking of . . . what you are feeling . . . [Pain intensification is suggested:] Let this pain become stronger and more intense . . . Feel it in all its typical ways . . . Let the part that is with me in the here and now describe it, while the part that is going through the pain episode feels it in all its usual intensity . . . If you wish, now make that even more stressful than the usual experience . . . This is a bad episode . . . [Pain moderation begins:] When you have the full awareness of pain . . . start the turnoff . . . [Pain is supplanted with well being:] Let the inner well being flow into your body and clear out the pain sensations . . . quietness, calmness, the muscles letting go . . . turning off the pain . . . leaving it in the past . . . the images of relief filling you. . . .

[Posthypnotic suggestions are offered:] The conscious part of your mind and the inner part of your mind will remember the importance of what has just taken place . . . Not only were you able to permit the pain to flow into your body in its very typical way, but you were also able to clear the body of this pain, to have relief replace it and the well being feeling come back . . . [Homework is suggested:] This is an exercise that you will practice in between the pain episodes . . . Your skill at shutting off pain will increase . . . and then you will find yourself shutting off pain right in the early stages of your pain episodes . . . You will bring the pain into limits of feasibility that permit you to go on with your life . . . You can turn it off more and more as you gain confidence, and your life will expand once again. . . .

CONCLUDING COMMENTARY

In the reactivation model illustrated above, three phases are evident: the reactivation of pain-free memories, the reactivation and intensification of the chronic pain, and then the quieting of the pain experience.

Chronic Pain Syndrome

Richard B. Garver, Ed.D.

San Antonio, Texas

It is important, first, to help newly referred chronic pain patients to understand why they have been referred by a physician who determined that conventional medical treatment resources have been exhausted. In fact, the patient has often been told, "There is nothing more I can do for you; you have to learn to live with the pain." Although it is not meant to be so, this is often a negative suggestion.

I let patients know that I believe they are in pain, that they feel the pain, and that they are not seeing me because they are crazy or imagining things. But, I indicate that I am here to help them to change this pain pattern and that pain is a behavior like all other sorts of behaviors, and that we learn behaviors that are both productive and non-productive. Pain is sometimes a productive behavior when it protects us, but when it is reinforced and perpetuated by negative emotions such as anxiety and fear, it becomes self-perpetuating. Pain produces negative emotions. Negative emotions produce tension, and tension produces more pain. I also indicate that there is within the unconscious mind an established program of pain, which is reinforced by many things (primary and secondary gain), and this memory of pain adds to the perceived pain.

One of the first things that I do is to have patients produce a glove anesthesia and help them understand that they are really doing this, not I. They have produced this analgesic effect in their hand. This, of course, can be transferred to the affected areas. Other useful pain metaphors and suggestions follow.

SUGGESTIONS REINTERPRETING PAIN SENSATIONS

"You will experience other sensations that are more acceptable than pain, perhaps a gentle coolness or warmth, a lightness or heaviness, tingling, even numbness, or any combination of these that are more acceptable to you." [See the section on cancer patients below for further suggestions about reinterpreting sensations.]

GATE CONTROL THEORY METAPHOR

"The more sensations that your unconscious mind has options to produce, the more likely these other sensations are to occur. Your unconscious mind can relax all the nerve and muscle fibers in the area of your body where there is tension or pain. It can also interrupt the pathways which travel from the site of the injury, to the spinal cord, up the back of the spinal cord, through the brain stem and into the pain reception area. There are many, many gates which these pain impulses must pass through, and your unconscious mind can close many of these gates, reducing the number of nerve impulses that will finally reach the pain reception area, and so, you simply will be aware of less pain."

CONTROL SWITCH VISUALIZATION

"Your unconscious mind can also help you visualize this pain reception area, perhaps as a compartment or a lighted room. When there is a lot of pain being reported there, the light can be very, very bright; but you have a rheostat, a dimmer switch, which you can turn down. As you turn the light down, dimmer and dimmer, you will experience less and less pain. Perhaps you will even want to rate it on a scale of 1 to 10, with 10 being the most pain that you would ever be in. And the number that you feel will be the number you can see in your mind and in this pain reception area. If you feel an 8, you will see an 8. So the number you feel is the number you see, and the number you see is the number you feel. So see the number 7, and the number 6. As you lower the numbers, you will lower the pain. Remember the number you feel is the number you see, the number you see is the number you feel."

TIME DISTORTION

"Your unconscious mind can also distort time. You can tell your unconscious mind that the time that you feel pain will be perceived as the shortest amount of time. Perhaps an hour can even be like a minute, and the time of comfort can be much longer. So, whenever you do feel pain, you know that it will be over a very short period of time."

DISSOCIATION OF PAIN

"Also, if you like, you can leave the pain here and you can go somewhere else. You can leave your pain here, and go somewhere else where you are comfortable, and you can stay there for any amount of time that you would like. And, while you are gone, nothing will strengthen your pain; and so perhaps it will grow weaker and weaker, and by the time you return, there will be very little, if any, pain left at all."

COMPUTER PROGRAMMING METAPHOR

The computer metaphor of programming out all pain-related behaviors and programming in all comfort and control-related behaviors is a useful one. All the behavior that the patient associates with pain will be programmed out, and all behaviors that the patient associates with being comfortable and in control, both physically and emotionally, will be programmed in. A very good posthypnotic cue can also be used to reinforce this so that while the patient is in a normal waking state he may use a cue such as touching his right ear, which tells his unconscious mind to program in that positive comfortable behavior. If the situation he is in produces pain, tension or discomfort, he can touch his left shoulder, which is the unconscious cue for the unconscious mind to remember to program that behavior out. The exception to this, of course, is to always remind the patient that the unconscious mind will allow him to have pain that will keep him safe from injury, or that might prove beneficial for medical diagnosis. My emphasis with all of these pain patients is to emphasize and reinforce the fact that they are gaining more and more control of the pain, and that the pain is less and less in control of them.

HEADACHE PAIN

I use more relaxation of the nerve and muscle fibers in the area of the pain for tension headaches, and have found cooling the head and warming the hands useful for migraine headache pain. To help patients learn this feeling of cooling the head and warming the hands, I tell them to actually put themselves in that situation, to imagine putting ice packs around the head, and to place their hands in warm water and memorize the sensations. Self-hypnosis will thereby enable them to reproduce this at another time.

SUGGESTIONS WITH CANCER PATIENTS

Many of the same pain strategies apply with pain patients. However, for coping with the side effects of chemotherapy or radiotherapy, I suggest that the unconscious mind will potentiate the therapeutic effects of all treatment and minimize the adverse side effects. It is suggested that, in fact, "you can experience any number of different sensations instead of nausea or pain. A feeling of tingling, which often accompanies nausea, is one that you can focus on, and you will experience more tingling than nausea."

Some other very specific posthypnotic suggestions are also helpful. First, an environmental cue is established, for example, that when the patient enters the hospital or the treatment room or smells a particular odor, that will produce another effect (or several other effects) rather than any uncomfortable effects or sensations. A second very valuable suggestion is to establish a symptom awareness cue that is always present. It is suggested, "If you begin to feel even the slightest effect of an unwanted symptom, whether that be pain or nausea, that will be a feedback cue to the unconscious mind, to instead produce other behavior, other sensations that are acceptable." This is very important because the symptoms will often be there in one form or another unless all suggestions work perfectly, which they often won't. But, if the symptom occurs, the patient usually expects more of that symptom. It is very valuable when the symptom can be used instead to produce other sensations which are more comfortable.

The third suggestion is for a physical action cue. For example, by touching the forefinger and thumb together or touching the right ear, that will signal the unconscious mind to produce another sensation rather than the unwanted symptom. I tell the patient that this is very much like pushing the play button on a tape recorder so that the tape that you want played will begin to run. The physical action cue is the play button on that recorder.

Hypnotically Elicited Mystical States in Treating Physical and Emotional Pain

Paul Sacerdote, M.D., Ph.D.
Riverdale, New York

INDICATIONS AND CONTRAINDICATIONS

Sacerdote, expanding on the work of Fogel, Hoffer and Aaronson, provides us with two unique perceptual change techniques for eliciting mystical states. These methods are intended for patients suffering with protracted or recurrent physical pain and with accompanying emotional pain (anxiety, depression). They may hold particular value for patients with severe chronic pain problems, for example, from cancer and migraine. It is recommended that these techniques only be used by highly experienced hypnotherapists, after establishing a trusting rapport with the patient, with patients without severe psychopathology. These meth-

ods seem contraindicated, or should at least be used with utmost caution, with borderline or psychotic patients. Elicitation of mystical states will be useful primarily with deep trance subjects and with patients who are judged to have the capacity and security to temporarily suspend reality. Sacerdote primarily used these techniques after having a couple of hypnotic sessions with patients to determine their hypnotic talent and to provide them with experiences in primary process thinking through guided imagery and the use of induced dreams. (*Ed.*)

INTRODUCTION

For the purpose of this paper, mystical states are defined and operationally described as states of ecstasy, rapture, and trance. The experiencing subject finds himself perceptually, emotionally, and cognitively immersed in oceanic, universal feelings; i.e., in direct intuitive or supernatural communion with the universe or with a superior being. Visual (lights, colors, shapes), auditory (music), olfactory, and other sensations are often part of the experience, but the mystical states bypass ordinary sensory perceptions and logical understanding. Therefore, they cannot easily be described in terms of everyday reality. They are, by definition, ineffable — beyond verbal expression. In spite of these "inborn" difficulties of communication, patients usually attempt and partially succeed in giving some ideas of perceptual, emotional, and cognitive experiences which can only be described as mystical.

As this is a clinical paper, no useful purpose would be served by attempting to catalogue hypnotically elicited, mystical experiences along Fischer's (1971) continuum in his interesting "A cartography of the ecstatic and meditative states: The experimental and experiential feature of a perception-hallucination continuum are considered." (Incidentally, this cartography does not include hypnotic states!) Nor would the methods which I am about to describe or my patients' experiences be clarified if I were to spell them out in terms of Zen

Buddhist or other religious or philosophical terminology.

I find it of some use, however, to accept Aaronson's (1971) distinctions between an "introvertive mystical experience" and an "extrovertive mystical experience." The former culminates in the subjective experience of "nothingness"—the absolute void. The latter tends to expand the person's awareness to unlimited, universal experiences. To facilitate introvertive mystical experiences, Aaronson (1971) developed a progression of deepening verbalizations aimed at guiding trained Ss into abandoning identification of the senses, relinquishing ego-identification, and dispensing with usual logical categories of distinction. To achieve extrovertive mystical states, he used techniques aimed at expanding the ego across barriers of space and time.

The techniques which I have evolved and will describe were inspired by the original observations and experiments conducted by Fogel and Hoffer (1962), and by the more recent experiments of Aaronson (1968). In Fogel and Hoffer's experiment, a talented and well trained S was led into deep hypnosis and made to listen to an oscillator with the belief that its speed was constant. When, unknown to her, the speed was progressively increased, S became progressively more manic. When the speed was gradually decreased, depression set in, until, at speeds near zero, she retreated into a catatonic state. This experiment suggested that a person's behavior, mood, emotion, and cognition can be altered very radically through basic manipulations of the dimensions of time.

Aaronson (1968) gave to his trained, deep hypnotic Ss various posthypnotic suggestions. For instance, posthypnotic suggestions of a "restricted present" generally produced evidence of depression; suggestions of total absence of the present elicited a schizophrenic-like catatonic state. On the other hand, posthypnotic suggestions of "expanded" time—especially expanded present and expanded future—led his Ss to experiences of supreme serenity, during which the strictures and anxieties connected with passage of time disappeared. Similar suggestions involving "restriction" or "elim-ination" or "expansion" of space elicited comparable alterations of perception, emotion, mood, and cognition. These changes were dramatically illustrated by one S through drawings and paintings of the same scene, seen under different posthypnotically suggested time conditions or space conditions.

I have found it feasible to apply the above observations to the clinical area. The patient's conscious and subconscious needs, as well as our own understanding of such needs and our ability to follow and to guide him, determine the results: a schizophrenic-like experience, or a "conversion" occurrence, or a mystical state. For instance, an excellent S and superb student became belligerently paranoiac when she emerged from hypnosis; the opening of her eyes was the cue for the posthypnotic suggestion that, "upon coming out of hypnosis, distances would seem very short, people and objects would be close, clear, and distinct." Upon opening her eyes to this radically changed space, she had felt terribly closed-in and threatened. The same student was given the posthypnotic suggestion that, upon opening her eyes, she would find herself in a gently expanding space, with people and objects shining in marvelous luminosity. Upon emerging from hypnosis, she seemed to radiate ethereal serenity. She later described her experience as soothingly unreal, ineffable, without end or beginning, a wonderful universe without problems.

SUGGESTIVE VERBALIZATIONS

I will give some of the verbalizations which I currently utilize. It should be kept in mind that these are modifiable according to the patient's capabilities, needs, responses, and degree of hypnotic talent and training. Transference and countertransference obviously play an important role.

INTROVERTIVE MYSTICAL EXPERIENCES.   Usually the patient has been previously induced to a medium level of hypnosis by my method of "reversed hand levitation," which is based largely on concentrated attention with detachment.

The reversed hand levitation has generally the advantage, when compared with traditional levitation, of implicitly suggesting relaxation, deepening, and "letting go" (Sacerdote, 1970).

The patient who has responded well to previous inductions will already be able to experience dissociative phenomena and deep relaxation. When there is evidence for both, I repeatedly, patiently, and monotonously suggest:

Now, as every word travels from my lips to your ears to reach your brain, your body progressively enjoys more and more complete relaxation in every muscle and cell; and your mind delights in calm, clear, peaceful serenity. . . . You are now surrounded by a soothing atmosphere of absolute calmness . . ., protected from danger, disturbance, and fear. And while relaxation and peaceful serenity penetrate deeper and deeper to every cell of your body, we are safely surrounded in every direction by wider and wider transparent, concentric spheres of luminous serenity, of cheerful calmness . . . [The transparency which I explicitly mention communicates to the patient that he can see and be seen; that he is not emotionally isolated.] You are safely bathing and comfortably breathing in the center of these transparent spheres, while luminous calmness all around you penetrates even more deeply within your body and permeates your mind. . . . All voluntary and involuntary reactions and responses gradually fade and disappear. . . . Little by little, you become free of fears, of anxieties, of thinking, of feeling.

EXTROVERTIVE MYSTICAL EXPERIENCES. The patient who has similarly been led to a state of increasing dissociation and body relaxation is first guided by me through an imaginary climb to the top of a symbolic mountain:

Now finally you are at the top and you are able to look towards the sunny side of the mountain. . . . You notice the blue of the sky and the brightness of the sun. You enjoy the warmth of the sunshine on your shoulders and your back, on your arms and hands, on your legs and feet. You breathe in slowly and deeply the clean, pure, cool air. . . . In front of your eyes under the quiet blue sky you see the beautiful green valley; and beyond the valley a picturesque chain of mountains . . . and beyond that first chain, you distinguish another valley; and be-

yond it another chain of mountains . . . and then beyond, more and more valleys and more and more mountains and plains, and rivers, and lakes and oceans extending and expanding further and further out in every direction to receding horizons. . . . As the view continues to expand, your ears rejoice in the natural music of the wind, the rustling of grasses and leaves and tree branches, the singing of birds, the chirping of crickets, the tolling of bells; your nostrils smell all the fragrances of the trees, and the grasses, and the flowers . . . and your eyes watch in wonderment the continuously "expanding" view of the expanding future. . . .

WHY AND HOW SHOULD MYSTICAL STATES HELP TO RELIEVE PAIN?

The idea of eliciting extrovertive mystical states came to me while I was dealing with advanced cancer patients; they were raked with pain, beyond the reach of any further palliative treatment. I was familiar with the effects that the perception of expanded present, expanded future, and expanded space could have on the mood and reality perceptions of normal individuals. It seemed worthwhile to see if patients in pain, guided into symbolic, multisensory imagery, could be led to experience perceptions of expanding time and space. Such experiences might "free" them from the limits of time, from the restrictions of activity; death itself could become merely the completion of life, rather than an event to be feared. In the expanded present and future, people and objects could appear to the patients as bathed in luminous reflections. Synesthesias of colors, music, and fragrances would further distance them from the "reality" of pain, desperate illness, dependency, and depression. Mystical states could enable the patient to deal in entirely new ways with problems of guilt and punishment, of life and death. They might also encourage him to come to terms with these problems on a philosophical or theological basis.

The other approach, leading to "introvertive" mystical experiences, is based upon progressively deeper states of muscular relaxation and increasing psychological calm and serenity. The gradual restrictions of perceptions and responses suggested to the patient are also symbolized for him with the image of his body fully relaxed at the quiet center of concentric, luminous, serene spheres of wider and wider radius. Thus, a kind of sensory and emotional isolation is established which, in itself, can facilitate psychological and physiological dissociation of the loci of pathology from the thalamic and cortical centers of pain perception.

Active Control Strategy for Group Hypnotherapy with Chronic Pain

Timothy C. Toomey, Ph.D. and
Shirley Sanders, Ph.D.
Chapel Hill, North Carolina

INTRODUCTION

The following strategies and suggestions were used in a group hypnotherapy treatment format for working with chronic pain patients. Although only five subjects were used, the treatment was successful in reducing pain levels. (*Ed.*)

PRODUCTION OF PLEASANT, RELAXING IMAGES AND FANTASIES

Patients were encouraged to produce images of relaxation and comfort and to share these with the group. The responses frequently involved simple images of scenes which the patients reported when encouraged by the therapists and other group members. In contrast with traditional relaxation procedures which impose a technique on the patient, the therapists strove to employ the utilization methods described by Erickson (1959) which emphasize starting where the patient is and gaining gradual control over the symptom to demonstrate that change is possible.

Patients were given the following suggestions following the hypnotic induction:

Allow yourselves to imagine a scene of comfort and relaxation. A place where you can feel really secure and peaceful. You may see yourself alone or with another person or in a familiar or unfamiliar place. Let the scene present itself to you and allow yourself to see, smell, hear, touch, or taste anything of special interest to you. After a time, as you continue to experience your special place, with your eyes remaining closed, we will ask you to describe your scene to the rest of the group. You will retain a clear image of your special scene and will be able to recall it with ease anytime you like, especially when you begin to experience the onset of any pain. . . .

ENCOURAGEMENT OF IMAGES AND FANTASIES THAT EMPHASIZE CHOICE AND ALTERNATIVES

As a common feeling elicited from the chronic pain patients in the group was that of being "locked in" and overwhelmed by the pain, the use of a technique that emphasized choices and alternatives seemed important. Thus, patients were encouraged to have a dream while in trance of two roads, one leading to health, the other to sickness and disability. They were asked to image both roads, to describe them, to image choosing the road to health and what that entailed. Patients were given the following suggestion:

You are able to experience yourself at an intersection and can clearly see two paths leading from familiar to unfamiliar terrain. You know that both of these paths are meant for your steps alone. One of these paths is a *healthy* path and contains clues and directions for your recovery. While on this path some of you may experience a particular image or vision which is a clue to your healing and recovery. Allow yourself to be open to such an image. The other path is a *sickness* path and has sights and signs of the future should you choose this direction. Allow yourself to ask questions of any one you meet along both of these paths. After a time, we will ask each of you to share your journey with the rest of the group.

Frequently the "healthy path" generated images of people, activity, and interesting sights and sounds. The "sickness path" was usually dark, dreary, and isolated. While in trance, patients were encouraged to attend to the characteristic features of the healthy road as a way of obtaining cues for restoration—including people or activities they may have forgotten or neglected during their illness.

DETERMINATION OF SIGNALS OR CUES ASSOCIATED WITH ONSET OF SEVERE PAIN

Patients were encouraged to recall, while in trance, the feelings and thoughts associated with pain onset and disability behaviors. For one, it was a feeling of cramping and burning in the back; for another, it was a dull throbbing in the head. Patients were given the suggestion that such signals could be reinterpreted as reminders or cues for use of a coping strategy, e.g., pleasant imaging, deep breathing, muscle relaxation, instead of producing the usual cycle of self-depreciatory thought patterns and disability behaviors. Thus an effort was made to establish novel signal values for pain stimuli. Patients were given the following suggestion:

You are starting to experience an episode of pain. Be very attentive to any beginning clues that pain is coming. Some of you may feel a burning, others may feel cold, others a throbbing sensation. Imagine that your pain clues are changing to interesting, even pleasant, sensations. The burning becomes the warmth from a comforting fire; the cold becomes a refreshing breeze on a hot summer's day; the throbbing slows as your breathing becomes slow and regular and you imagine the ocean waves gently ebbing, and flowing on the shore. Now, as you become more comfortable and relaxed, no longer concerned with your pain, you have time to use any of the approaches you have learned in the group. You may wish to enjoy your special scene or allow your image of healing to do its work. Others may just want to enjoy deep regular breathing and deeper and deeper levels of relaxation and comfort. Take your time and enjoy the experience. You will be able to clearly recall this exercise and use it regularly whenever you notice any beginning clues of pain.

ENCOURAGEMENT OF PRACTICE AND ACTIVE EMPLOYMENT OF COPING STRATEGIES

In addition to incorporation in the patient's schedule of a time period each day for relaxing and enjoying pleasant images following self-induction of an hypnotic trance state, patients were encouraged to make active use of coping strategies during periods of pain or when they needed an extra boost to accomplish a difficult task. They were encouraged to view novel or difficult tasks, e.g., a new exercise-activity program or taking a plane trip, in a stepwise fashion and to use trance-induced coping strategies and images as means of simplifying complex tasks and reinforcing successful performance of each step. Although the approach described here is structurally very similar to techniques developed by self-control theorists and cognitive behavior modifiers (Meichenbaum, 1971; Turk, 1980), the emphasis on assisting the patient via the hypnotic environment to discover appropriate coping strategies is different. For example, "Imagine walking down the healthy path as you begin to walk the mile of prescribed exercise." "Focus on the pleasant and interesting sensation of air rushing past your limbs as you stand up, leave the house, and take your daily walk." Indeed, the patient actively participates in finding his own solutions.

Pain Strategies by Hypnotizability Level

David Spiegel, M.D., and Herbert Spiegel, M.D.
Stanford, California, and New York, New York

Instructions for pain control differ depending upon the hypnotizability of the subject. High hypnotizables are given instructions to use self-hypnosis to simply make the painful or affected area numb, or to imagine themselves floating above their body or even getting up and walking to another room while they are in pain.

Mid-range subjects are instructed to experiment with changing temperature of the affected body part, making it warm or cold by imagining that they are in a warm bath or rolling in snow, for example. Or, they may imagine that they are in the dentist's office receiving a shot of novocaine and that this numbness which they first experienced in the mouth can now be spread with their hand to the affected part of the body.

Low hypnotizable subjects are encouraged to use distraction techniques, focusing on competing sensations elsewhere in their body, for example, rubbing their fingertips together. All of these use the hypnotic state to focus on some competing sensation or image which involves teaching them to filter the hurt out of the pain rather than fighting the pain, at the same time producing a sense of floating relaxation.

Reinterpreting Pain as Protection

Charles B. Mutter, M.D.
Miami, Florida

[Various metaphors may be used with a patient in hypnosis to reinterpret pain as a protective mechanism rather than a debilitating one. The following metaphor is used while the patient is in hypnosis].

When you drive a car and it overheats, a red light signal goes on the dashboard . . . that signal tells you to pull the car over . . . to check the fan belt, the water pump, or radiator . . . because you know that if you continue to drive the car when it is hot, you can damage the motor. It is good to know that your car has a protective signal so that you know when to . . . cool it down . . . to avoid further damage. Think of your body as your car . . . that gets you through a lifetime . . . and it is good to

know . . . that you have all the protection you need . . . that if your red light goes on . . . you can cool it down.

Splinting Technique for Pain Control

Charles B. Mutter, M.D.
Miami, Florida

INDICATION

This technique is used to protect patients with chronic pain from overexerting or hurting themselves. It follows techniques given for pain control with patients who have chronic musculoskeletal disorders. These suggestions are used when the patient is in hypnosis.

SUGGESTIONS

Your unconscious mind has a sacred trust to protect your body. It knows the capacity of every cell, every organ, every system . . . and it will protect you by causing you to turn and twist or bend only within your physical capacity . . . and not beyond . . . so that when you attain comfort . . . you can move and keep that comfort for longer periods of time. As your body becomes stronger, your mind will then allow you to turn, twist, and bend to a greater degree . . . but only within those limits . . . so that when you gain comfort, you need not fear reinjuring yourself. Should you have any discomfort, it is merely your body protecting you . . . by giving you a signal that you have gone beyond those limits.

Erickson's Interspersal Technique for Pain

Particularly in cases of resistance and when he did not know a patient well, Milton Erickson would "seed" ideas through interspersing words or phrases within the context of a story or discussion. These embedded suggestions were typically set off by the use of a slightly different voice tone or a very brief pause.

Erickson (1966) masterfully used embedded suggestions in treating the cancer pain of a patient named "Joe." Joe was a retired farmer who had turned florist. Facial cancer had resulted in the loss of much of his face and neck due to surgery, ulceration, maceration and necrosis. He experienced intolerable pain for which medications were not very effective. A relative was urgently requesting that hypnosis be used, but Joe disliked even the mention of the word hypnosis. The patient was unable to speak and could only communicate through writing. We will now pick up on Erickson's account.

Despite the author's unfavorable view of possibilities there was one thing of which he could be confident. He could keep his doubts to himself and he could let Joe know by manner, tone of voice, by everything said that the author was genuinely interested in him, was genuinely desirous of helping him. . . . The author began:

Joe, I would like to talk to you. I know you are a florist, that you grow flowers, and I grew up on a farm in Wisconsin and I liked growing flowers. I still do. So I would like to have you take a seat in that easy chair as I talk to you. I'm going to say a lot of things to you, but it won't be about flowers because you know more than I do about flowers. *That isn't what you want.* [The reader will note that italics will be used to denote interspersed hypnotic suggestions which may be syllables, words, phrases, or sentences uttered with a slightly different intonation.] Now as I talk, and I can do so *comfortably*, I wish that you will *listen to me comfortably* as I talk about a tomato plant. That is an odd thing to talk about. It makes one *curious. Why talk about a tomato plant?* One puts a tomato seed in the ground. One can *feel hope* that it will grow into a tomato plant that *will bring satisfaction* by the fruit it has. The seed soaks up water, *not very much difficulty* in doing that because of the rains that *bring peace and comfort* and the joy of growing to flowers and tomatoes. That little seed, Joe, slowly swells, sends out a little rootlet with cilia on it. Now you may not know what cilia are, but cilia are *things that work* to help the tomato seek grow, to push up above the ground as a sprouting plant, and

you can listen to me, Joe, so I will keep on talking and *you can keep on listening, wondering, just wondering what you can really learn*, and here is your pencil and your pad, but speaking of the tomato plant, it grows so slowly. *You cannot see* it grow, *you cannot hear* it grow [suggestions for negative hallucinations], but grow it does — the first little leaflike things on the stalk, the fine little hairs on the stem, those hairs are on the leaves, too, like the cilia on the roots, they must make the tomato plant *feel very good, very comfortable* if you can think of a plant as feeling, and then *you can't see* it growing, *you can't feel* it growing, but another leaf appears on that little tomato stalk and then another. Maybe, and this is talking like a child, maybe the tomato plant does *feel comfortable and peaceful* as it grows. Each day it grows and grows and grows, *it's so comfortable, Joe*, to watch a plant grow and *not see* its growth, *not feel* it, but just know that *all is getting better* for that little tomato plant that is adding yet another leaf and still another and a branch, and it is *growing comfortably* in all directions. [Much of the above by this time had been *repeated many times*, sometimes just phrases, sometimes sentences. Care was taken to vary the wording and also to repeat the hypnotic suggestions. Quite some time after the author had begun, Joe's wife came tiptoeing into the room carrying a sheet of paper on which was written the question, "When are you going to start the hypnosis?" The author failed to cooperate with her by looking at the paper and it was necessary for her to thrust the sheet of paper in front of the author and therefore in front of Joe. The author was continuing his description of the tomato plant uninterruptedly, and Joe's wife, as she looked at Joe, saw that he was not seeing her, did not know that she was there, that he was in a somnambulistic trance. She withdrew at once]. And soon the tomato plant will have a bud form somewhere, on one branch or another, but it makes no difference because all the branches, the whole tomato plant will soon have those nice little buds — I wonder if the tomato plant can, *Joe, feel really feel a kind of comfort.* You know, Joe, a plant is a wonderful thing, and *it is so nice, so pleasing* just to be able to think about a plant as if it were a man. Would such a plant *have nice feelings, a sense of comfort* as the tiny little tomatoes begin to form, so tiny, yet so *full of promise to give you the desire to eat* a luscious tomato, sun-ripened, it's so *nice to have food in one's stomach*, that wonderful feeling a child, a thirsty child, has and can *want a drink, Joe*, is that the way the tomato plant feels when the rain falls and washes everything so that *all feels well*. [Pause.] *You know, Joe*, a tomato plant just flourishes each day *just a day at a time*. I like to think the tomato plant can*know the fullness of comfort each day*. *You know, Joe, just one day at a time* for the tomato plant. That's the way for all tomato plants. [Joe suddenly came out of the trance, appeared disoriented, hopped upon the bed, and waved his arms; his behavior was highly suggestive of the sudden surges of toxicity one sees in patients who have reacted unfavorably to barbiturates. Joe did not seem to hear or see the author until he hopped off the bed and walked toward the author. A firm grip was taken on Joe's arm and then immediately loosened. The nurse was summoned. She mopped perspiration from his forehead, changed his surgical dressings, and gave him, by tube, some ice water. Joe then let the author lead him back to his chair. After a pretense by the author of being curious about Joe's forearm, Joe seized his pencil and paper and wrote, "Talk, talk."] Oh, yes, Joe, I grew up on a farm, I think a tomato seed is a wonderful thing; *think, Joe, think* in that little seed there does *sleep so restfully, so comfortably* a beautiful plant yet to be grown that will bear such interesting leaves and branches. The leaves, the branches look so beautiful, that beautiful rich color, *you can really feel happy* looking at a tomato seed, thinking about the wonderful plant it contains *asleep, resting, comfortable, Joe*. I'm soon going to leave for lunch and I'll be back and I will talk some more. (pp. 205-206)

Erickson (1966) indicated that despite his "absurdly amateurish rhapsody" about a tomato plant that Joe had an intense desire for comfort and to be free from pain. This meant that Joe "would have a compelling need to try to find something of value to him in the author's babbling" (p. 207) which could be received without his realizing it. "Nor was the reinduction of the trance difficult, achieved by two brief phrases, 'think, Joe, think' and 'sleep so restfully, so comfortably' imbedded in a rather meaningless sequence of ideas" (p. 207). Joe was impatient and anxious to resume the talk after lunch. "When it was suggested that he cease walking around and sit in the chair used earlier, he did so readily and looked expectantly at the author.

You know, Joe, I could talk to you some more about the tomato plant and if I did you would probably go to sleep, in fact, *a good sound sleep*. [This opening statement has every earmark of being no more than a casual commonplace utterance. If the patient responds hypnotically, as Joe promptly did, all is well. If the patient does not respond, all you have said was just a commonplace remark, not at all noteworthy. Had Joe not gone into a trance immediately, there could have been a variation such as: "But instead, let's talk about the tomato flower. You have seen movies of flowers *slowly, slowly* opening, giving one *a sense of peace, a sense of comfort* as you watch the unfolding. So beautiful, *so restful* to watch. One can *feel such infinite comfort* watching such a movie."] (p. 207)

Joe's response was excellent and during the following month he gained weight and strength. Only rarely did he experience enough pain to need aspirin or demerol. A month later, Erickson visited again and after much casual conversation, "Finally the measure was employed of reminiscing about 'our visit last October.' Joe did not realize how easily this visit could be pleasantly vivified for him by such a simple statement as, 'I talked about a tomato plant then, and it almost seems as if I could be *talking about a tomato plant right now. It is so enjoyable to talk about a seed, a plant*'" (p. 208). As a result of these two extended sessions, Joe lived comfortably until his death over three months after the first contact.

One would be incorrect to assume that Erickson's primary therapeutic method was the use of interspersed suggestions within metaphors. Close long-term colleagues have estimated that not more than 20% of Erickson's work consisted of the use of metaphors (Hammond, 1984, 1988b). Erickson flexibly used both very direct and very indirect suggestions, depending on the clinical situation. However, the clinician should be aware that the patient's unconscious mind has the capacity to perceive meaningful suggestions offered in seemingly casual conversation or metaphoric stories. Metaphoric communication offers us one more avenue for therapeutic intervention.

The Setting Sun Pain Metaphor

Alexander A. Levitan, M.D.
New Brighton, Minnesota

[This metaphor is particularly indicated when the patient has described the pain as a flaming red sphere.]

See yourself sitting on a tropical beach at sunset. Notice the bright red sun as it descends on the far horizon. See the colors begin to change from orange to crimson, and then a deep, dark red-orange. Notice that as the sun approaches the water, there actually seems to be two suns, one in the sky and one in the water. See the sun gradually sink into the ocean. See the colors change from red to purple and then to blue. Notice the magical stillness that pervades everything just at sunset when the ocean is as smooth as glass and sounds seem to travel forever. Enjoy that delicious feeling of tranquility. Realize that that tranquility is available to you whenever you need it, on a moment's notice, merely by giving yourself your own personal signal to relax! Perhaps you might enjoy letting your finger and thumb come together to make a magic "O.K." sign and that can be your signal to experience immediate relaxation whenever you choose to employ it.

Mexican Food: Metaphor of the Body Adapting to Pain

D. Corydon Hammond, Ph.D.
Salt Lake City, Utah

INDICATIONS

This metaphor and the one that follows were designed for use with chronic pain patients. They were inspired by a metaphor by Milton Erickson (1983, p. 112) where he used a conceptualization that may be useful for patients, despite not being medically sound, of developing a callousness to the pain.

METAPHOR

I remember the first time that I ever ate Mexican food. I ate chili stew at Isleta Indian Pueblo in New Mexico. It contained so much red chili, that the broth of the stew was bright red. My nose started running, my eyes watered, and my mouth kept hurting and kept burning, no matter how much cold water I drank. I couldn't imagine how anyone could eat such hot chili. I was almost unaware of the taste, because the pain was so great.

But I spent the next year and a half living in New Mexico. And I'm not sure exactly when, or how, but my body changed and adapted. Or perhaps in part it was my mind that changed. Because, before long, that sensation of the hot chili in my mouth seemed different. Almost as if somehow, my mouth had developed a callous. Somehow my mouth adapted, so there was no longer pain, and I could just enjoy the taste. I had in a sense become callous to the pain, and yet remained pleasantly sensitive to the delicious flavor of the hot tamales or enchiladas or stew.

And you really should be willing to allow the nerves in the painful part of your body, to adapt, and develop callouses, just as I did in order to eat chili and Mexican food.

Metaphor of Callous Formation

D. Corydon Hammond, Ph.D.
Salt Lake City, Utah

It's interesting every spring when I begin to play golf again. After a long winter of not playing golf, in about early April I go up to the driving range and hit a bucket of balls. Before I'm done with a large bucket of balls, my hands are getting sore. And by the time I've hit a large bucket of balls, I have a few blisters on my hands. If the weather is rainy and cool the next week, it may be two weeks before I go back to the driving range to practice. And if I hit a large bucket of balls again, I'll develop blisters on my hands again.

But if I go to the driving range for a short time on Monday afternoon, and share a small bucket of balls with my son, and then go back on Wednesday and share another small bucket, and again for a short time on Friday and Saturday, blisters don't develop. When I gradually increase what I do, callouses gradually form. My body gradually adjusts. And before long I can play nine holes of golf, and my hands are only a little sore, and I don't have any blisters. And then before long, I can play eighteen holes of golf, comfortably, because my body has adjusted, and callouses have formed.

And in this same way, you can gradually allow callouses to form in your pain nerves, allowing your body to adapt gradually. And if I had a painful _____ , I'd be willing to spend just as much time allowing callouses to develop around those nerves, as I do allowing my hands and fingers to develop callouses.

Suggestions for Patients with Chronic Pain

Lillian E. Fredericks, M.D.
Palm Beach, Florida

[After appropriate induction of trance and deep relaxation, I use behavior modification with positive suggestions]:

You are so deeply relaxed and comfortable right now that you will be able to follow my suggestions with ease. You know with the use of hypnosis that you can alter perception, experience and memory, and you can regain control over your sensations. With this newly learned tool, you will be able to alter the course of events. Just like the person steering a sailboat can turn the rudder in such a way that the wind catches the sails, and the boat turns around and goes the opposite direction; so are you steering your boat of life and you can turn around and go the opposite direction. You can be relaxed, comfortable, and in control of your sensations.

WARMTH AND METAPHOR OF MELTING BUTTER OR CREME

You can change the sensation of discomfort to warmth [or cold if appropriate], and feel a warm comfortable tingling in your . . . [area of pain]. Let the sun shine on your [area of pain] and feel how the warmth penetrates the skin, the subcutaneous tissues, the muscles and all the way down to your bones. You can visualize a pad of butter or some soothing creme on your skin, and as it melts, so will your discomfort melt away. So good, so relaxing, so comforting. You can be very proud of your success and your ability to change your sensations at any time you wish, and to any degree you desire. And when you use self-hypnosis several times a day, you will notice that with practice you will be able to go deeper, and it will take less and less time to change and control your sensations. During the rest of the day you need not pay any attention to . . . [area of pain]. Your body knows how to make you breathe, and your heart to pump your blood around [etc.] completely, without your help. Pay all your attention to your work, your play, and your surroundings. You have learned a new skill and you can use it to see and hear and taste and touch in a new way. In a way which will be very pleasing to you.

When you walk through the woods, you will come to a fork in the road, and you can choose whether you want to go to the right or the left. Up to now you went unconsciously to the left. You did not know how to choose. Now you have the skill and the power to choose the right road, the road of comfort and to a productive and happy life.

Pain Reduction

Beata Jencks, Ph.D.
Murray, Utah

INTRODUCTION

The best approach for coping with pain is first to try to analyze its peculiar characteristics, differentiating it from other possible pains; then to decide what might change or alleviate it; and finally to experiment with appropriate imagery, relaxation, diversion, dissociation, or physical treatments like heat, cold, or massage.

ALLEVIATION OF DIVERSE PAINS

It must be remembered that all the following suggestions work with some, but not with others. Different exercises should be tried, and those which bring relief should be conscientiously practiced.

DULL ACHES.   These have been relieved by imagining during exhalations a hot water bottle which warms and relaxes, or by treating the aching area with warm water or alcohol, or even by imagining receiving a painkiller shot into it. Thinking of softening the area or feeling the pain "evaporate" during exhalations also proved helpful.

SHARP PAIN AND STABBING PAIN.   These have been partially relieved by imagining that the painful area was icy and very rigid, or by imagining that it was very soft, like foam rubber, so that the stabbing met with no resistance. This has not worked for stabbing pains so strong that they halted the breath.

BURNING PAIN AND PAINS FROM BURNS.   These can be relieved by thinking coolness and soothing lotions being applied during inhalations, and relaxation during exhalations. However, thinking coolness for burnt soles of feet may make it possible for the burn victim to walk, but the tissues will suffer additional damage. Common sense must always be a guiding factor for deciding whether pain reduction is beneficial or not.

CRAMPS.   These can be handled in at least three ways: relax as much as possible, tense as much as possible, or relax and tense alternately. Time the tensing with inhalations and the relaxing with exhalations. A cramp can also be waited out by concentrating exclusively on relaxing the body during exhalations in places which are not affected by the cramp. This has proven very helpful for getting rid of cramps without changing the position during yoga practice and for continuing swimming with a cramp. Lymph drainage massage is good for prevention.

LOCAL WARMTH.   Warm a hand, for instance on the abdomen or chest, and then put it on the painful area. Imagine during inhalations inhaling the warmth into the painful area and pain streaming out through it and away from it during exhalations.

COOLNESS.   Coolness or warmth can be attributes of one kind of pain and may be remedies for another kind. Usually the opposite is required for relief. Experiment while remembering that coolness, rigidity, and tensions are enhanced by inhalations, the opposites by exhalations.

ANESTHETIC.   Imagining strongly having a body part immersed in ice water or snow, or having been injected with a numbness-producing anesthetic, can evoke an effective anesthesia in dentistry and otherwise.

ARTHRITIC PAINS AND STIFFNESS.   Arthritic pains can be eased by imagining a warm shower over the shoulders and neck during exhalations, or a warm blanket over the knees. Cupping a painful area with a warm hand increases the effect. Imagine further that the afflicted area loosens up and becomes soft and warm during exhalations.

Before any movement, imagine moving the body parts involved in the movement, be it an arm for reaching or the legs for walking. Limber up the body in the imagination before getting up in the morning. Invigorate the limbs during inhalations while making imagined movements and relax during exhalations. Only then attempt to move in reality. Move then only during exhalations, since this avoids unnecessary body tensions and increases limberness. Inhale between movements. Hold the breath during movements only if the pain is excruciating. Lymph drainage massage is also helpful before getting out of bed. Also, get up from sitting and climb stairs during the exhalation phase. Halt during inhalations.

For bending, as for instance for tying shoelaces, bend as far as possible during one long exhalation. Wait and relax during several breathing cycles while the body adjusts to the position it reached. Then stretch a little further during another long exhalation. By thus bending stepwise, one may extend the reach a great deal.

Anticipation of relief is also helpful. If a hot bath or a hot whirlpool can ameliorate the pain, imagine going to the hot water. Imagine the anticipation very vividly during exhalations. Then imagine being in the hot water.

HEADACHES.   Distinguish the features of the headache. It can be in different places and have different qualities. It may be general, frontal, or one-sided, pressing, stabbing, nagging, dull, or pounding. Next, find body areas which are tense. Tension headaches can be due to tensions in the head itself or in the neck and shoulders, the spine, the small of the back, or even the legs. Do appropriate relaxation exercises and experiment to see if relaxation of certain body areas will reduce the headache.

For pressure headaches try the following. If the pain feels like a "board before the forehead," think of the area softening and becoming relaxed or warm during exhalations. During inhalations think that the bony walls of the skull expand or that coolness streams into the head. The thought of opening the head at the crown to "let fresh air in" also allayed or ameliorated pressure headaches. Experiment whether this works better for you during exhalation or inhalation. It differs. Also experiment whether coolness or warmth is better to ameliorate headaches.

RELIEVING DISCOMFORT IN THE CHEST AND ABDOMINAL AREA

The nonmedical clinician is reminded to always obtain careful medical evaluation, especially with conditions such as chest and abdominal pain, prior to providing hypnotherapy. (*Ed.*)

Start the relaxation at the throat. Exhale a few times slowly and deeply and imagine making the throat wide and open. Relax and think during exhalations "soft, gentle, wide, open," and so on, with respect to places inside the throat, chest, and abdomen. Do any or all of the following exercises according to need.

OPENING FLOWER.   Feel whether and where there is narrowness or tension in the throat. Imagine a flower bud opening in it, as in a time lapse film. Repeat this during two or three exhalations. Feel what happens to that throat region during the next two or three exhalations. Is there a widening? Softening? Moisture flowing?

INVERTED FUNNEL.   Imagine an inverted funnel, narrow above, wide and open below. Imagine this funnel starting at the mouth-throat junction. Feel during exhalations a widening, softening, and opening up toward the lower, wide open end of the funnel. Ascertain the place down to which the throat or chest opened up. Then start the narrow top of the funnel about an inch or two above that place, and repeat the widening, softening, and opening up during exhalations. Imagine that some liquid of pleasant temperature and consistency streams down the funnel. Relax in this manner the throat, chest, and abdominal cavity.

GUIDE ROPE.   Imagine the exhalation to be a guide rope along which you can glide, slide, or feel your way down into the chest cavity. Repeat this for about three consecutive exhalations. Relax while going down. Continue down into the abdominal cavity along the guide rope of the exhalation.

ELEVATOR.   Imagine riding down an elevator within yourself from the throat into the chest during exhalation. Make a stop at the place the elevator has reached at the end of the exhalation. Allow the inhalation to stream in passively. Then descend further during the next exhalation. Repeat, starting and stopping as necessary, and go down through the chest into the abdomen.

KNOT DISSOLVES. Remember the feeling of a "knot in the stomach," or actually create it by holding the breath and tensing inside. Then gently release the tenseness, or, for that matter, tenseness which was there without creating it, during successive exhalations by thinking "the knot dissolves." If no relief is felt, check if the jaw or base of the tongue are tense. Such tension is often related to stomach discomfort. Release these tensions.

SETTING SUN. Internal tensions can be reduced in the chest as well as in the upper and lower abdominal area by thinking of a setting sun during exhalations. Feel the gentle warmth, the red glow, the slow sinking, and allow the "inner space" to expand like a horizon, while the body walls seem to soften and expand elastically.

RELAXING THE LOWER ABDOMEN. Repeat first the widening of the chest and abdominal cavity. Then observe passively where discomfort makes itself known. Give such places a gentle, but deep finger pressure massage during deep exhalations. Wait passively, but attentively, until the body reacts. The abdomen usually "makes known" its reaction by air movements and pressure changes. Wait passively and then massage again where necessary.

RELIEF OF HEARTBURN. Think "cool" during inhalations and "calm and relaxed" during exhalations, or imagine drinking soothing cool milk with the thought of coolness during inhalations.

"Body Lights" Approach to Ameliorating Pain and Inflammation (Arthritis)

Ernest L. Rossi, Ph.D., and
David B. Cheek, M.D.
Malibu, California, and Santa Barbara, California

1. *Accessing and Transducing Symptoms into "Lights"*

a. **"See yourself standing in front of a full-length mirror. See tiny [colored] lights in different parts of your body. The colors represent the feelings of those parts. When you can see the total picture, your yes finger will lift to let me know."**

b. Scan the body, getting the color of each light and what that color represents to the patient. The process starts with unimportant parts of the body, ending with exploration of the organ or extremity suspected of having problems. For example, with rheumatoid arthritis, in which multiple joints are involved but some are more painful than others, one might proceed as follows, selecting the least painful for the first therapeutic approach. Confidence builds with each success from least to most painful.

   "Look at the entire image of yourself and let your unconscious mind select the joint you know to be the least inflamed, the least painful. When you know what it is, your yes finger will lift to tell me which joint and what color."

2. *Therapeutic Reframing*

a. **"Let your inner mind shift back to a time when there was a light that represents comfort and flexibility. When you are there, your yes finger will lift. [Wait for the signal.] Now come forward to the first moment that color (light) was put there in place of the comfortable light. When your yes finger lifts, please tell me how old you are and what is happening."**

b. **"Now, is there any good reason why you should continue with pain in that joint?"**

3. *Ratifying Therapeutic Gain*

a. **"Now that you know what has been happening, is your inner mind willing to let you turn off that unconscious pain and continue the process of healing?"** [If the answer is no, it will be necessary to orient to whatever factor is standing in the way, as in Step 2.]

b. **"Go forward now to the time when you will not only be free of the pain in that joint, but will have turned off the pain in** all the joints that have been troubling you—a time when you are no longer afraid of pain returning, when you are really well in every respect. When you are there, your yes finger will lift and you will see a month, day, and year, as though they were written on a blackboard." [This is done as a measure of the patient's confidence level.]

Suggestions with Postherpetic Neuralgia ("Shingles")

Diane Roberts Stoler, Ed.D.
Boxford, Massachusetts

INTRODUCTION

This script was developed for an 86-year-old man who had a severe case of shingles on his scalp which continued down to his left eye. He had been on pain medication for over six months with no relief and the physician was concerned about addiction and side effects of the drugs. He loved the ocean and was an ex-auto mechanic. The suggestions were given following induction and extensive deepening techniques.

SUGGESTIONS FOR SELF-HYPNOSIS

[The following suggestions for self-hypnosis were given during the induction-deepening process.] Each morning upon rising you can permit yourself to allow your body to become relaxed and in balance, then you will permit yourself to take one long deep breath in through your nose and out through your mouth while using the thumb and index technique. This will be a signal to go into the deepest level of hypnosis whereby you will feel your strength and confidence and knowledge that you can control the pain from the shingles and have the ability to heal the shingles all together.

SUGGESTIONS FOR PAIN CONTROL

You are peaceful, calm, relaxing deeper and deeper, deeper and deeper, deeper and deeper. As I talk to you, you continue to go into an even deeper state of relaxation. In the past you have had feelings of anxiety, doubts, fear, panic, and the sense of loss of control arises from flashbacks of reliving aspects of the shingles or from other past experiences which have evoked those kinds of feelings. All of these feelings and behaviors have interfered with your growth, sense of oneness, and natural healing processes and you acknowledging your uniqueness and goodness. If you experience any of those negative feelings as we're talking, either you can allow yourself to choose to look at what is causing those feelings at that time when you experience them, or you can imagine putting them into my locked file cabinet in my office. They will remain in the file cabinet in my office where they will be stored. These feelings will not surface and cannot be touched unless you choose to retrieve them to work on them yourself or in therapy, to help you learn to live and enjoy life. You will always know where they are because you have the control and you have chosen to place them there. By knowing this, if a flashback occurs, you have a way of having power to control those feelings and you no longer need to stuff them inside, but rather have a way of dealing with them to resolve them and help you to have greater control over your own life.

As you allow yourself to go deeper and deeper, you are realizing, perhaps for the first time, that you can allow yourself to take control over your body through your mind. You can become more relaxed and with this relaxation your body's healing mechanism can function appropriately and normally. And as your body responds in this deeply relaxed way, you are becoming aware that you can permit yourself, when needed, to take greater control over your body than you ever thought possible. You are acquiring confidence in yourself. You feel a realization growing within you of the fact that you have the ability to make changes, and these changes make your body healthier, and you can assist your body's normal healing functions with your relaxation and concentration.

You can allow yourself to activate the anti-viral mechanism via the Mystery Oil, to attack and kill all herpes virus, along with activating your white blood cells to attack and kill all bacteria on the turtle's back. The warmth of the sun will allow the scabs to heal, and with this awareness you can permit yourself to change the various dials on the alt meters to help you heal and to adjust the level of discomfort related to the pain in the various parts of your face and head. You can allow yourself to adjust these various meters so that you may achieve a comfortable level and by putting your thumb and index fingers together. This will be a signal to go into a deeply relaxed state, a deeply relaxed state.

As long as there are any signs or sensations of the pain near your eye, face or head you can allow yourself to adjust the various dials to produce a comfortable level for yourself, whereby you will feel pressure and no discomfort. And you will be aware of the causes and reason for the discomfort, but you need not feel a greater sensation than discomfort unless you do injury to that area, whereby you will feel pain.

As you turn the dial on the alt meter you will produce the feeling of pressure and by adjusting the volume control you can adjust the level of intensity from sharp, to dull, to total numbness. You will be able at all times to adjust and control the level of sensation to obtain the appropriate level for you to maintain comfort, whereby you feel sensation but no pain, pressure but no pain.

As the night settles in and the sun is setting in the west, your ability to take greater control of your life and the discomfort will increase, day by day, as you learn to concentrate your mind and relax more and more. If there is a psychological and/or physical reason for the pain you have been experiencing, this knowledge will come up through images, thoughts and dreams. With this information, you will be able to share it either with me or the necessary medical doctor.

With your relaxation and concentration, which activates your natural healing process, you will allow yourself a sense of strength and confidence which will fill your body. You have the ability to cleanse your body and help heal it, and with this knowledge comes a sense of calm, peacefulness and serenity. You permit yourself to enjoy the sounds of the birds and you become even more relaxed. As you listen to the sounds of the gulls and the sound of the ocean, you allow yourself a sense of joy and happiness which fills your body, and you can allow yourself to become even more relaxed.

Relaxation will give you that peace of mind and inner tranquility which will enable you to cope with the tensions and stresses of everyday living. You will be able to tolerate the persons, places or things that used to disturb you and annoy you. You will be there for you in all circumstances.

No one can bother you here. You have no cares or worries. You feel safe, secure, calm, peaceful and relaxed. There is a sense of peace with the environment around you. This spot is peaceful and serene. You feel calm, peaceful, confident. This spot is a safe, secure spot. No one can bother you here. You are peaceful, calm, relaxed; you go deeper and deeper, deeper and deeper and as I talk to you. You continue to go into an even deeper state of relaxation. Everything but my voice is becoming remote now, quite remote; nothing else but my voice seems important, nothing else is important, nothing else but my voice.

Suggestions to Reduce Pain Following Hemorrhoidectomies

Ernest W. Werbel, M.D.
San Luis Obispo, California

INTRODUCTION

The following suggestions were used before surgery and were reinforced the day following surgery. Eight of eleven patients receiving hypnosis reported no pain post-surgically, while three experienced moderate pain. In contrast, only two of eleven nonhypnotically treated patients reported no pain, four reported moderate pain, and five reported severe pain. Note Dr. Werbel's use of trance ratification procedures along with the suggestions. It is anticipated that when something like catalepsy, levitation, or glove anesthesia is used for ratification, that the success rate will be greater. (*Ed.*)

SUGGESTIONS

You are now in a relaxed state. An individual who is as relaxed as you are does not feel pain as acutely as a person who is tense. In fact, sometimes, he feels no pain at all. [Then one of the patient's hands is elevated. It usually remains in that position.] Please open your eyes and look at your elevated hand and note how perfectly motionless it remains, just as if you were a statue. Now close your eyes again. Your extremity remains motionless because you relax so well that your muscles are in equal tone and are not pulling against each other. [I then request the patient to look again at his motionless uplifted hand to convince him thoroughly that he is in a trance.] You relax wonderfully well. You are an excellent subject. Therefore, there is no need for you to feel pain following surgery. I want you to remember that there is *no need* for you to feel pain. You may feel pressure.

[Dr. Werbel then demonstrated glove anesthesia, after which he continued:] This shows that you need have no pain following surgery. Remember you need have no pain following surgery. If you have any pain at all it should be minimal. . . . When you have your first bowel movement be relaxed just as you are now and you need feel no pain. Remember, when you move your bowels following surgery, be relaxed as you are now and your bowels may move just as easily and comfortably as they did prior to surgery.

Suggestions for Pain Control

Don E. Gibbons, Ph.D.

DIRECT SUGGESTIONS FOR ALLEVIATION WITH SIGNAL PAIN

After the trance has been concluded, you will find that your pain is almost completely gone. There will still be a little discomfort remaining, just to serve as a reminder for you to take it easy; and you will still continue to let up as much as you need to for the healing to proceed properly. But the extra pain, which serves no useful purpose, is going to be completely taken away. And you are going to be greatly relieved at how much better you will feel.

SUGGESTIONS FOR HEADACHES

INTRODUCTION. I have had excellent results with the following suggestions, which use vestigial remnants of the diving reflex to alleviate the discomfort of migraine and other stress-induced headaches. By slowing the heartbeat and decreasing blood pressure by means of this technique, circulatory congestion in the head may be alleviated and the headache symptoms gradually cease. (Of course, suggestion also plays an important—and perhaps the *most* important—part in enhancing the effectiveness of this underlying physiological rationale.) [These suggestions will undoubtedly be most effective for patients who are familiar with and enjoy skin diving. (*Ed.*)]

The effect of the following suggestions may be enhanced by requesting the subject to assume a sitting position prior to the induction, and, as the "diving" suggestions are given, handing him a cloth moistened in cool water to hold against his face as he bends forward slightly and puts his head down.

SUGGESTIONS. Picture yourself now as a dolphin, swimming lazily along just below the surface of the sea. Feel the water above you gently warming your back; and feel the cooler water beneath you, as you swim lazily along. Just let yourself continue to swim slowly along, concentrating on the images and the sensations which you feel as you continue to listen to my voice, and soon you will be able to experience everything I describe to you just as if it were actually happening.

You think how refreshing it would be to dive down, all the way to the bottom. Let yourself begin to dive now, diving easily and gently, all the way down to the bottom. Feel the cooler currents against your face as you angle your body toward the bottom, and feel yourself beginning to adjust to the increasing depth and the pressure of the water around you as you continue to descend.

Any previous discomfort you may have felt is fading away now, as you feel the cool, soothing currents rushing by as you sink deeper and deeper, and your system continues to slow down in response to the increasing pressure and cold. The water continues to grow even colder now, as you continue to sink, but your body adapts to it easily and comfortably. You continue to drift down and down, sinking past seaweed forests and deep coral canyons, sinking all the way down to the bottom, almost there.

Now you find yourself drifting slowly along, exploring the bottom of the sea. Just savor the experience for a few moments and enjoy the cool freshness as you swim along.

In just a short while, I'm going to return you to your normal sense of time and place; but after you return, this feeling of peace and well-being will remain with you, and all traces of your previous headache will have vanished. Even after you have returned to your normal sense of time and place, you will continue to feel just as good as you do right now. So just continue to let yourself explore this undersea world for a moment or two, experiencing all the enjoyment and pleasure that goes with it; and soon it will be time to return you to the environment from which you left.

COMMENTARY.   After a moment or two has elapsed, suggestions may be given to the effect that the subject is slowly rising back to the surface, followed by suggestions that the scene is fading and that the subject is becoming fully aware of himself as a person once more, still in trance and still retaining the feelings of relaxation, peacefulness, and well-being which were part of his undersea experience. The trance may then be terminated in the usual manner, together with suggestions that the subject will continue to feel peaceful and relaxed, with no further trace of discomfort.

At the conclusion of the trance session, the subject may be instructed to repeat the foregoing imagery at the appropriate intervals by means of autosuggestion, either to ward off an oncoming headache or to alleviate one which has already begun. More responsive subjects should eventually be able to experience similar sensations merely by closing their eyes and silently repeating to themselves the word *dive*.

SUGGESTIONS FOR A PAINFUL CONVALESCENCE

INTRODUCTION AND INDICATIONS.   The following suggestions may be helpful in assisting a subject to get through a particularly stressful period, such as a painful convalescence, which is not unduly exacerbated by underlying personality conflicts or by various "secondary gain" factors. . . . These suggestions may also be employed, together with directly suggested sleep . . . to assist a seriously or terminally ill patient in coping with intervals of unusually severe discomfort. In the case of terminal illness, however, such suggestions should usually not be relied on to the extent that they may deny the patient sufficient time to accept and to come to terms with the fact of his own impending death; and other patients who may learn to use such techniques by means of autosuggestion should be cautioned not to employ them to avoid having to cope with problems which ought to be dealt with instead of merely being endured, such as the periodic drinking bouts of an alcoholic spouse.

TIME DISTORTION SUGGESTIONS.   As a result of what I am telling you now, your awareness of the passage of time is going to be changed, so that the days (or hours) will just seem to be flying past, and you are going to be pleasantly surprised at how swiftly they have gone. You will be able to carry out all of your routine activities in the usual manner, for this will have no effect on the speed with which you do things; but just as a few minutes can seem like an hour at times, and an hour seem like only a few minutes, your perception of the passage of time is being changed now, so that every minute that passes is going to seem much, much shorter than it actually is.

COMMENTARY.   As with other techniques, it may be necessary to repeat the foregoing suggestions at appropriate intervals (or to teach the subject to do so by means of autosuggestion) for them to remain effective for the desired length of time. But is should also be made clear to the subject that these suggestions are only intended to be effective for a limited period of time. This can most easily be accomplished by adding the following sentence each time the suggestions are administered, whether by the subject himself or by another:

"These suggestions will be effective only until _____ ,at which time your normal sense of the passage of time will be fully restored."

Suggestions for time condensation may also be used in conjunction with suggestions for emotional enrichment as a means of counteracting unpleasant or negative affect by directly suggestion the opposite sensations (Sacerdote, 1977).

Hypnosis for Migraine

Lillian E. Fredericks, M.D.
Palm Beach, Florida

I dissociate my patients to a cold place (in the winter to go skiing or walking in the mountains in the snow, etc.). I suggest that "the icy wind and snow is touching your forehead, and is making your temples colder and colder and colder. It feels as though you were holding an ice cube against your temples. It feels just like your hand feels when you hold a glass with your favorite drink in it. Do it right now, and feel how it gets colder, and colder, and colder, it gets tingly and numb, and sometimes even anesthetic so you cannot feel it anymore."

If the patient loves to take a bath: "You are now taking a bath, immersing yourself into this wonderfully warm and soothing water. You feel cozy and warm and comfortable all over. The only part of your body outside of the water is your head. As you turn the hot water faucet on to renew the water and make it even warmer, you notice that your temples are getting colder and colder and colder. As you feel your body getting hotter, notice your temples getting colder. A very good and comfortable feeling in your head. It becomes clearer, more lucid, and all the congestion disappears. The discomfort gradually drains out with the rest of the water in your tub, and you can just stay there and enjoy this comfortable feeling all over you.

[Never tell a patient, "You will just have to live with your pain." Subconsciously the patient will retain his/her pain because if there is no pain, he/she is not alive.]

Suggestions with Migraine

J.A.D. Anderson, M. A. Basker, and R. Dalton
London, England

INTRODUCTION

Using hypnotherapy, Anderson, Basker and Dalton (1975) obtained complete remission with 10 of 23 patients (in comparison with only three of 24 patients on prochlorperazine). Patients were taught self-hypnosis. They were provided with a simple explanation of migraine both in and out of hypnosis, including an emphasis that migraines result from abnormally swollen blood vessels in the scalp. They were also asked to visualize the arteries in the head and neck. The following suggestions were given.

SUGGESTIONS

Migraine is caused by . . . and always made worse by tension . . . thus making the arteries in the head congested and large. I want you to visualize the arteries in the head . . . picture them large and throbbing . . . now, as you relax and become less tense . . . each day . . . your arteries become smaller . . . smaller and smaller . . . more normal. The arteries stay normal . . . and your head feels comfortable. (p. 51)

Diminution Rather Than Elimination of Headache

Irving I. Secter, D.D.S., M.A.
Southfield, Michigan

[In accord with my findings on other comparable patients, I considered that permitting retention of a small amount of the illness, with instruction to have it at times when it is least disturbing, could be an effective measure of therapy. Accordingly, after this patient appeared to be in a satisfactory trance, I told him to take a few minutes time and if he so desired he could go into a deeper state of relaxation by breathing more slowly. I always give the patient sufficient time to become as deeply relaxed as desired. When I believe this has been accomplished, I give the following suggestions]:

Every time you are in bed ready to go to sleep, you will get the feeling you are getting a headache; as soon as you experience this feeling, you will breathe slowly, regularly, and deeply, as you are doing now; with each slow, regular, deep breath, the feeling that you are getting a headache will begin to subside, and then leave you completely. You will then go into a normal, natural, deep sleep; you will sleep the night through, and awaken refreshed at the correct, proper time, feeling very good, sound in body, sound in mind.

Suggestion for Symptom Substitution

Gary R. Elkins, Ph.D.
Temple, Texas

When you are ready to begin to resolve your problems, it may be possible to let go of the tension and pain. When you are ready, you can have some other symptom to replace the pain. The pain can fade and become less and less as you become more aware of another sensation that replaces it.

The Progressive Anesthesia Induction-Deepening Technique

D. Corydon Hammond, Ph.D.
Salt Lake City, Utah

INDICATIONS AND INTRODUCTION

This method, a modification of Watkins (1986) procedure, may be valuable with medical, cancer or burn patients who are experiencing considerable pain, as well as in hypnotic preparation for surgery. It may be more confidently used when the practitioner has facilitated glove anesthesia in the patient previously. In a talented subject, it may be used as the initial induction; in other cases, induction and deepening may precede the use of this method. There are several other options in using this technique. When a prior induction has been done and the anesthesia has spread through the entire body except the head, the patient may be given the following suggestions as part of his training: "Would you like to have a pleasant, surprising experience? In a moment, I'm going to have you awaken from trance, but you will only awaken from the neck up. Would that be all right? So that in a moment, as I instruct you to, you will only awaken from the neck up, and the rest of your body will remain asleep in a deep trance. You will only awaken from the neck up." After experiencing this for a minute or two, the patient is instructed to close his/her eyes and go into an even deeper state. The technique of having the patient's body remain in trance while the patient awakens may also be used with only one limb that is painful and which may also be made cataleptic. Watkins prefers to have each part of the body become rigid as it is anesthetized, removing only the rigidity after the entire body is numb.

SUGGESTIONS

Please concentrate on your right hand, and as you do so, a feeling of heaviness will begin to develop. As you notice that feeling of heaviness, please nod your head. [Pause] Good, and now as you keep focusing on that hand, and as I stroke it, you will begin to notice a numbness developing. [Lightly stroking the one hand, and pausing until a response is given.] Nod your head when you become aware of the numbness starting to develop. [Pause] Um hmm. And I'd like you to notice, with a kind of sense of curiosity, how that numbness and anesthesia begin to spread all through your hand, through the fingers, the palm, the back of the hand, all through the entire hand. [Pause] Notice how that numbness deepens more and more, and as it does so, it's such a pleasant feeling that it feels as if it's really too much bother to move even a finger. That hand just feeling a kind of heavy, relaxed, immobility, almost as if, it's going to sleep. Almost as if, it's beginning to sleep now, almost as though it's no longer a part of you. And as you're aware of that, your head will nod again. [Pause]

Now as I stroke your forearm, the numbness begins spreading into it too, as though something is flowing into it, bringing this feeling of numbness, and immobility to your forearm. [As this is being said, lightly stroke from the back of the hand through the upper forearm two or three times.] And you feel that numbness beginning to spread, do you not? And you can be rather fascinated by that. And when that anesthesia and kind of heavy, almost wooden-

like feeling has spread all the way up to your elbow, your head can begin to nod again. [Pause] [Repetition of suggestion may be used occasionally as needed.]

Would it be all right for that comfortable numbness to continue to spread? [After affirmative reply] All right. [Lightly stroking from the elbow to the shoulder] Gradually that numbness and immobility continues spreading upward, at its own pace and speed, through your elbow and into your upper arm. Flowing into your biceps, and your triceps, and then it will flow into your deltoid muscle. So that soon, it begins to feel as if that arm is asleep, [pause] almost as if the arm is detached somehow, [pause] as though it's no longer a part of you, but just resting motionless, there. When that feeling has spread through the entire arm up to your shoulder, your head can nod again. [Again, following pauses, use repetition as needed. The anesthesia may then be transferred across the shoulders and subsequently down the other arm, reinforced with light strokes. Then, without any further stroking (which could be construed as having sexual connotations), the anesthesia and sense of detachment are moved down through the rest of the body. Throughout this procedure, if it is being used as the initial induction, observe the patient's eyelids and utilize any heaviness or blinking that is noted. Thus eye closure may be facilitated at any time, or one may wait until the last part of the procedure when the anesthesia spreads to the head and face.]

Now feel that comfort, that still, quiet, rest and comfort spreading from your shoulders down, [pause] through your chest, [pause] through your back. [pause] A still, passive, comfort, spreading into your stomach, [pause] your lower back, [pause] your abdomen. Bringing a sense of rest, a sense of comfort and immobility, and stillness. Resting so quietly, that it's as if parts of your body are beginning to sleep now.

[Progress at the approximate pace the patient required through the earlier parts of their body, or ideomotor signals may be requested at different points in the progression. Use repetition as required. Facilitate the spread of anesthesia through the trunk, the right leg and foot, and then the left leg and foot. Continue using terms like: "quiet," "still," "motionless," "immobility," "wooden-like," "as if it's going to sleep," "feeling increasingly detached, almost separate from your body." Further suggestions may finally be given for the anesthesia to flow up the neck, across their head, and down through the patient's face.]

4

HYPNOANESTHESIA AND PREPARATION FOR SURGERY

INTRODUCTION

Role of Presurgical and Intraoperative Suggestions

THERE ARE A VARIETY of encouraging studies indicating that presurgical hypnotic suggestions and suggestions delivered while the patient is under anesthesia or in the recovery room may reduce postoperative pain and complications and speed recovery (Bonello et al., 1960; Bonilla, Quigley & Bowen, 1961; Doberneck, McFee, Bonello, Papermaster, & Wangensteen, 1961; Evans & Richardson, 1988; Goldmann, Shay, & Hebden, 1987; Kolough, 1962; Werbel, 1960).

AWARENESS UNDER CHEMICAL ANESTHESIA.   Milton H. Erickson (1963) made the pioneering observation in 1932 that anesthetized patients could perceive conversation at some level of awareness, and it was David Cheek (1959) who published the first paper on this topic. Since that time there have been numerous case reports of memories of both events and conversation that took place while the patient was under chemical anesthesia (e.g., Brunn, 1963; Goldmann, Shay, & Hebden, 1987; Hilgard, Hilgard, & Newman, 1961; Hilgenberg, 1981; Kumar, Pandit, & Jackson, 1978; Levinson, 1969; Rossi & Cheek, 1988; Saucier, Walts, & Moreland, 1983), some of which were confirmed as accurate by individuals who were present during the surgeries. Particularly impressive have been some of the reports about what we may call "fatty" comments where a surgeon made an insulting remark in reference to someone's weight during surgery (Bennett, 1988; Halfen, 1986). It is particularly impressive that such comments, unconsciously registered, seem capable of causing continuing psychosomatic problems (Rossi &

Cheek, 1988) and can be traumatic enough to cause postsurgical complications, depression and vegetative responses (Bennett, 1988; Goldmann, 1986). A lawsuit has now been settled out of court concerning a "beached whale" comment made by a surgeon around an anesthetized patient, which was recalled several days later by the patient and confirmed by a nurse who was present (Bennett, 1988).

Early case reports of awareness under anesthesia quickly led to recommendations to exercise caution about making derogatory remarks or inadvertently verbalizing negative suggestions in the presence of anesthetized patients. Furthermore, some anesthesiologists and surgeons began giving positive suggestions for speedy recovery, free of complications and pain, with positive results (Bonello et al., 1960; Bonilla et al., 1961; Doberneck et al., 1961; Evans & Richardson, 1988; Kolough, 1964; Werbel, 1960).

Wolfe and Millet (1960) reported on 1,500 patients where positive suggestions were delivered, and half of the patients required no postoperative pain medication! Hutchings (1961) described positive results from using positive intraoperative suggestions with 200 patients. He believed that children seemed even more responsive than adults, and indicated that 140 of the 200 patients required no pain medication after surgery and that 12 of 88 abdominal surgery patients needed no postoperative pain medication. Unfortunately, both studies lack control groups.

FAILURE TO REPLICATE STUDIES.   Such reports led to some investigations of memory retrieval that, in an effort to obtain experimental rigor, used recall of such things as unrelated nonsense syllables, poetry, music, or common words as their outcome measures. The memory for such information was often assessed a short time following surgery (Brice, Hetherington, & Utting, 1970; Browne & Catton, 1973; Dubovsky & Trustman, 1976; Eich, Reeves, & Katz, 1985; Lewis, Jenkinson, & Wilson, 1973; Loftus, Schooler, Loftus, & Glauber, 1985; Millar & Watkinson, 1983; Stolzy, Couture, & Edmonds, 1986). In general, these studies failed to find that surgical patients could recall what they heard during surgery. These results led reviewers (Dubovsky & Trustman, 1976) to conclude that surgical personnel need not curtail their operating room talk and that attempts to promote healing through suggestions delivered during surgery were not successful.

However, there were some serious methodological flaws in these studies (Bennett, 1988). For instance, these studies generally used information for recall that was not the least bit meaningful or relevant to the surgical patient. When more meaningful information has been used as a criterion measure, patients tend to recall far more (Bennett, 1988). Furthermore, as indicated above, some studies tested postsurgical patients relatively soon afterwards, but it has been found that, when there are longer periods (e.g., several days to several weeks) between surgery and postsurgical testing, there is greater recall of what occurred or was said during surgery (Adam, 1979; Bennett, 1988). Some failure to replicate studies have also used tape recordings, often of a voice unfamiliar to the patient (e.g., Abramson, Greenfield, & Heron, 1966; Bennett, Davis, & Giannini, 1984, 1985; Bonke & Verhage, 1984; Pearson, 1961). Prerecorded tapes have generally not produced positive results in enhancing recovery from surgery. Finally, some studies have asked for verbal recall of intraoperative suggestions, but this has been found to be more difficult to obtain. In contrast to verbal recall measures, when behavioral measures are utilized, significant results are generally found, as will be cited shortly.

CONSCIOUS RECALL OF SURGICAL EVENTS.   Hypnosis has proven effective in some cases in facilitating conscious patient recall of events or comments in surgery that were meaningful to the patient (Bennett et al., 1985; Cheek, 1959, 1966, 1981; Goldmann, Shay, & Hebden, 1987; Rossi & Cheek, 1988). For example, in an impressive study, Levinson (1965) staged a "surgical crisis" with ten dental patients under deep (stage 3) ether anesthesia. Four of the ten patients were able to recall the event under hypnosis. Thus, at least part of the time, hypnosis may promote recall of comments made during surgery. In particular, Cheek's (Rossi & Cheek, 1988) belief that a deeper level of consciousness is tapped through using the method of ideomotor signaling (Hammond & Cheek, 1988) to obtain recognition of disturbing events has received independent experimental validation (Bennett, 1988; Rath, 1982).

EFFECTS OF SUGGESTIONS UNDER ANESTHESIA.   Despite difficulty in recalling information consciously, even with the use of hypnosis, there is compelling evidence that suggestions delivered personally under surgical anesthesia do produce behavioral responses, even though there is conscious amnesia (e.g., Bennett et al., 1984, 1985; Goldmann, 1986). This validates that auditory messages are in fact perceived at some level of consciousness under anesthesia, despite the lack of conscious ability to remember. Furthermore, when an anesthetist addresses the patient by name and asks him or her to remember something, it may facilitate responsiveness even further (Bennett, 1988; Millar & Watkinson, 1983; Stolzy et al., 1986). Interestingly, in studies using tapes that also gave posthypnotic type suggestions for a behavioral response to a cue that would be presented later, significant levels of behavioral responses were still obtained (Bennett et al., 1984, 1985; Goldmann, Shay, & Hebden, 1987). The effectiveness of these personalized suggestions validates that messages are perceived, even though taped suggestions usually did not facilitate improved recovery.

Barber, Donaldson, Ramras, and Allen (1979) have also documented that subjects breathing 20%–40% concentrations of nitrous oxide had better response to posthypnotic suggestions than control subjects breathing oxygen. Mainord, Rath, and Barnett (1983) and Rath (1982) found fewer postsurgical complications in subjects receiving positive suggestions under deep surgical anesthesia. In fact, Rath (1982) found that patients receiving suggestions required less pain medication, had lower pain ratings, and were discharged from the hospital sooner, confirming other less rigorous studies (e.g., Kolough, 1964). Bensen (1971) reported on results of utilizing positive suggestions in the recovery room immediately following surgery. In 100 cases (primarily involving hemorrhoidectomies, dilettage and curettement, tonsillectomies, and some surgeries for removal of growths or tumors), 72% reported little or no postoperative pain, 98% experienced normal appetite and thirst, and bleeding was 90% controlled.

On a related note, it is also fascinating that studies have shown that suggestions delivered to sleeping subjects (Stage 1 REM sleep) may also produce behavioral responses to a cue (Evans, 1979; Evans, Gustafson, O'Connell, Orne, & Shor 1966, 1969; Perry, Evans, O'Connell, Orne, & Orne, 1978). As is usually the case in studies of suggestions given under surgical anesthesia, subjects were amnestic for the suggestions given during sleep, but the suggestions were nonetheless effective in producing the suggested behavioral responses.

HYPNOSIS WITH CHILDREN.   Collaborating the positive findings of Hutchings (1961), cited earlier, it should also be noted that hypnosis has often been successfully used as an adjunct to chemical anesthesia with children (Antich, 1967; Bensen, 1971; Betcher, 1960; Crasilneck, McCranie, & Jenkins, 1956; Cullen, 1958; Daniels, 1962; Jones, 1977; Kelsey & Barron, 1958; Marmer, 1959; Scott, 1969; Tucker & Virnelli, 1985; Wiggins & Brown, 1968). In fact, in a controlled study of the effects of hypnosis on anxiety and pain in children (ages 5–10), those receiving hypnotic preparation were found to be significantly less anxious and more cooperative, and they only required one-fifth as much postoperative pain medication as controls (Gaal, Goldsmith, & Needs, 1980).

In summary, the evidence seems unequivocal that presurgical hypnotic suggestions or verbal suggestions made while the patient is under chemical anesthesia (that are meaningful to the patient) will influence physiological, behavioral, and unconscious processes of the patient.

HYPNOANESTHESIA

It is well documented that hypnosis may actually be used as the sole anesthetic for both minor and major surgeries (August, 1960, 1961; Bowen, 1973; Elliotson, 1843; Esdaile, 1846/1976; Finer & Nylen, 1961; Lait, 1961; Marmer, 1959; Minalyka & Whanger, 1959; Monteiro & de Oliveira, 1958; Rausch, 1980; Steinberg, 1965; Tinterow, 1960). Some of these operations have included mitral commissurotomy, coarctation of the aorta, hysterectomy, thyroidectomy, hemorrhoidectomy, transurethral resection, dilation and curettage, mammaplasty, amputations, cesarean sections, tonsillectomies, and cholecystectomy. It should be noted, however, that the use of hypnoanesthesia as sole anesthetic is seldom necessary except under extenuating circumstances. Also, perhaps only 10%–20% of patients are sufficiently talented hypnotically to accomplish this.

Crasilneck and Hall (1985) cited the following indications for hypnosis in anesthesiology:

1. In situations where chemical anesthetic agents are contraindicated because of allergic reaction or hypersensitivity.
2. For certain surgical procedures during which it is desirable for the patient to be able to respond to questions or commands and when it is important to observe the patient's state of consciousness during surgery (e.g., stereotactic neurosurgical procedures, therapeutic embolizations of carotid and vertegral arteries, and for monitoring intraoperative spinal cord function).
3. With patients where fear and apprehension of general anesthesia are so significant that they may contribute to anesthetic risks.
4. When organic problems increase the risk of using chemical anesthetics and interfere with diagnostic or surgical treatment.

More commonly, hypnosis may be used in combination with chemical anesthesia. There is evidence that when hypnosis is used to augment chemoanesthesia, less general anesthesia is required (Bartlett, 1966; Crasilneck et al., 1956; Fredericks, 1980; Van Dyke, 1970). Hypnosis may also be very helpful in combination with local anesthesia (Crasilneck & Hall, 1985; Golan, 1975; Lewenstein, Iwamoto, & Schwartz, 1981).

SUMMARY

Hypnosis and positive suggestions may thus be used in the following capacities with surgical patients:

1. To reduce presurgical fear and apprehension, while simultaneously creating feelings of calm, optimism, motivation and increased cooperation.
2. To create hypnoanesthesia as the sole anesthetic for surgery in the rare instances when this is indicated.
3. Giving positive suggestions during surgery and in the recovery room to maintain calm, reduce complications, minimize pain (and the need for postoperative medication), facilitate appetite, reduce bleeding, enhance healing and speed recovery.
4. For analgesia or anesthesia to be used in combination with lower levels of chemical anesthetic agents.

In this section of the chapter you will have an opportunity to review the finest available suggestions and approaches that are used in the hypnotic presurgical preparation of patients, as well as suggestions to be used during and immediately following surgery. You will also find illustrations of suggestions to promote healing and for hypnoanesthesia. The reader interested in applications of hypnosis with burns and emergencies should also consult Chapter 8.

Preparation for Surgery

Lillian E. Fredericks, M.D.
Palm Beach, Florida

INTRODUCTION

Obviously you have to adapt the basic suggestions that follow according to each patient and the type of surgery the patient underwent. You obviously will not suggest that the patient is thirsty and hungry if he/she had a gastrectomy or bowel surgery, etc. Also, please never say to a postoperative patient, "You are finished," since the patient may take this literally, resulting in considerable anxiety or negative effects.

THE PREOPERATIVE VISIT

[After reading the chart and introducing myself to the patient]: What do your friends call you, Mr./Mrs . . .? May I call you . . .? [First name only] Where would you rather be right now? . . . [Patient's favorite place] . . . Would you like me to show you a way to go through tomorrow's surgery and anesthesia with comfort and safety? [Pause]

Just close your eyes and let all your muscles go limp and loose and relaxed, from the top of your head to the tip of your toes. That is very good. Now let's go to that lovely place of your choice, and thoroughly enjoy every minute. While you are there, feeling good and comfortable and happy, I will explain to you what will happen tomorrow, and how I will prepare you for a relaxed sleep so the surgeon can perform the operation to the best of his ability. Pay attention to my voice only. All other noises are unimportant to you; they are just like background music. [Tell the patient on his/her level of understanding, briefly, what you will do.]

I will be with you all the time, watch over you and make sure that you are comfortable and safe. When you are as nicely relaxed as you are now, you will need less anesthesia and you will awaken at the end of the operation as you awaken from a peaceful, natural sleep. You will be relaxed and pleased to feel so good, so happy, and so comfortable. All your physiological functions will return promptly and you will feel thirsty and hungry, and will look forward to your next meal.

After your surgery, you will do all the prescribed breathing exercises, and you will be a good and cooperative patient. You may feel some sensations in the operative area which will tell you that you are healing well. You will have a dry and comfortable wound and you will heal very promptly. Let these sensations be a signal to you to let that area go limp and loose, soft and relaxed. You will have time to rest and restore; so much time to enjoy all the care you are getting. You will enjoy your visitors and the planning for the return to your home. You will be able to eradicate from your mind any pain or problem you might have had prior to surgery. Just like sailboats going forward only, and enjoy all the things you can do again to make life more productive, more interesting, and more to your liking. You also will be surprised and pleased to see how short the hospital stay will seem to you.

POSTOPERATIVE SUGGESTIONS IN THE RECOVERY ROOM

Your operation has been completed and you are doing very well. You are healing and your immune system is working at full speed to prevent any infection. You are nicely relaxed and comfortable, thinking happy and pleasant thoughts. Your body and mind work together; your body reacts to the way you think and feel. You can breathe easily and deeply and with great comfort. You can cough and clear your throat any time you want to. You will be thirsty and hungry, and as you swallow, let that be a signal to your digestive tract to relax and function normally. Your wound will be dry and comfortable. Your body knows how to do all that, and you will be surprised how easy it will be to empty your bladder and move your bowels at the appropriate time. Feel good and happy knowing all is well.

Suggestions for Anesthesia and Surgery

Bertha P. Rodger, M.D.
Palm Harbor, Florida

PREOPERATIVE SUGGESTIONS

1. From the moment your medication is given, until you are back in your room again, you pay attention only to the voice that speaks directly to you. All other sounds seem pleasantly far away, a lulling, soothing sound . . . like background music . . . or the sound of waves gently lapping on the shore. That drowsy, dreamy, sleepy feeling increases with each sound . . . making you more comfortable.

2. Your medication can be the signal to start a pleasant daydream going of some pleasant activity in a special place where you feel safe, secure and contented.

3. The whole operative area remains soft, loose, limp and comfortable throughout the operation and afterward until completely healed.

4. You awaken in the recovery room as if from a restful, peaceful sleep, refreshed and pleasantly surprised to find your operation completed, your condition relieved, and healing already well under way.

5. The sensations you feel are those of healing, a little pulling that tells you the area is well put together again . . . slight cramping . . . a little heaviness or tingling reminds you that healing is already begun and acts as a signal to let the area become soft, loose and comfortable again . . . and to keep it that way.

6. You can recover quickly, completely, comfortably.

7. You can be pleased to find how easily you can pass water, move bowels, enjoy meals, breathe deeply. You can cough to clear your throat as needed and go on breathing gently, easily, deeply and comfortably.

8. You have time now to rest . . . to think of pleasant things like how nice it will be to feel like yourself again . . . Time to enjoy all the T.L.C. of the doctors, nurses and others working with you to help you get better fast.

9. You will be quite calm, comfortable and cooperative throughout, following all the easy instructions given to help you.

10. You can be pleasantly surprised to find it much easier than you anticipated . . . and be very thankful!

SUGGESTIONS DURING OPERATION

1. *As the patient is placed on the table*, blood pressure is taken, etc., repeat preoperative suggestions.

2. *Intubation*: "I'm going to slip in a soft airway while you take a deep breath."

3. Added *relaxation*: "Make the operative area soft, limp and comfortable."

4. *At closing of incision*:
   a. The operation is completed . . . your condition taken care of (relieved).
   b. You can look forward to getting better fast.
   c. The body is made to heal . . . and can do so quickly, comfortably, completely.
   d. All body functions return rapidly as the anesthesia wears off.
   e. You awaken smoothly, enjoy a rest period, respond to the voice speaking directly to you.
   f. You breathe easily, deeply, clear your throat and go on breathing easily, rhythmically, naturally.
   g. You can be glad that little soft tube is there doing work for you so function is rapidly restored.

5. *Intra-operative suggestions for cancer patient*
   a. The tumor has been removed. Now the immune system goes to work to complete healing. It can take care of any

remaining cells just as it knows how to take care of infection.

b. You can look forward to feeling much better, to getting better, to enjoying life fully.

c. Nothing need disturb you . . . nothing need bother you.

d. You can live all the rest of your life, making the most of it.

POSTOPERATIVE VERBALIZATIONS

1. You are now in the recovery room. Your operation is completed and healing is already well underway, your condition taken care of, you can get better now.

2. Pay attention only to the voice speaking directly to you. All other sounds seem very far away, soothing and lulling, like distant TV.

3. You can now recover quickly, completely, comfortably.

4. All body functions return rapidly as the anesthesia wears off. You can look forward to enjoying that good food and finding it so satisfying to drink fluids.

5. The sensations you feel will be those of the healing process . . . setting everything right . . . so you need not mind them. They remind you to keep the area soft, limp and comfortable.

6. You can breathe deeply and easily and swallow to clear your throat. This is the signal to your digestive system, "One-way— go straight on down." So it becomes more and more comfortable.

7. Your body knows how to bring enough blood to the area to bring the raw materials for healing . . . not enough to spill over nor to interfere with carrying away waste products.

8. Notice with pleasure how soon your body functions all return to normal . . . how easily and fully you regain control of your bladder and bowels . . . how much more comfortably you function than you anticipated.

SPECIAL NEEDS

1. You may feel some little discomforts . . . occasional cramping or pulling, a heaviness in the operative area from time to time. You can welcome these as part of the healing process and relax in response.

2. There may be a soft tube in your bladder (nose/mouth etc.) to keep it drained so it can function easily as soon as the tube is removed. You can be glad to know it is there working for you. It conforms to the contours of the area so you are aware only of a slight fullness.

3. You can keep your arm (with the I.V.) still so that the fluid you are getting can speed healing.

4. Whenever dressings need to be changed, you can keep the area soft, and limp like a Raggedy Andy doll so it will remain comfortable. You have time then for a pleasant daydream that makes it seem like a very short time and the time passes rapidly.

Hypnosis and the Anesthetist

John B. Corley, M.D.

The anesthetist visits the patient preoperatively. In a casual but personally conversational fashion he/she addresses the patient. He communicates those understandings and attitudes that he/she knows as an experienced anesthetist will be of most value in effecting within the patient that state of well-being most conducive to successful surgery and a favorable postoperative course. This communication is made slowly, thoughtfully, with pauses of varying length to meet the patient's needs in understanding. These pauses are indicated in the following material by the indicated spacing in the words employed.

I am Dr. Smith. . . .I am going to give you an anesthetic tomorrow . . . . I wanted to meet you. I wanted to check . . . a few simple things . . . myself . . . to make sure . . . everything goes smoothly . . . tomorrow morning.

The anesthetist then examines the patient exactly as he/she would under other circumstances, continuing the remarks:

Everything is fine. . . . I suppose everybody . . . is a little apprehensive . . . before an operation. . . . But you need not be. . . . You are in very good condition . . . for an operation . . . and you have an excellent surgeon. . . . You could not be in better hands . . . and, of course I'll be there too. . . . I promise I'll look after you . . . very carefully. . . . Everything, you will find . . . will go very smoothly. . . . Tonight the nurse will give you a sedative . . . to make sure you will relax . . . and have a good sleep . . . it always helps, doesn't it . . . to just relax . . . and not to worry unnecessarily? . . . Actually . . . it is much easier to relax . . . than most people ever realize. . . . Here . . . let me show you something . . . useful . . . and very pleasant. . . . Just close your eyes . . . for a moment . . . take a deep breath . . . and make yourself more comfortable . . . That's very good. . . . Now open your eyes . . . and let me place your hand . . . like this . . . [demonstrating] in front of your face. . . . Is that comfortable? . . . Good . . . now all you have to do . . . is to choose some spot . . . upon your hand . . . like that furrow there . . . and deliberately concentrate . . . on that spot . . . and just let your hand . . . do what it wants to do. . . . That's very good. . . . Notice how the fingers separate . . . how light appears between the fingers . . . how the fingers spread . . . spread far apart . . . just like a fan. . . . That's very good. . . . See how the hand itself . . . has now begun to move . . . towards your face. . . . Just let it. . . . As the hand comes closer . . . to your face . . . how comfortable . . . you begin to feel. . . . And actually, when the hand does touch your face . . . several pleasant things will happen. . . . Your hand will feel very comfortable . . . against your face . . . it will feel . . . as if it is stuck . . . with glue . . . very comfortable. . . . And your eyes will be so tired . . . you will find it very pleasant . . . as they close . . . and you take a deep, deep breath . . . and begin to relax all over. . . . That's very good . . . so pleasant . . . so comfortable . . . Just for a moment now . . . notice how pleasant it really is . . . when I touch you gently . . . on your shoulder . . . like this . . . [demonstrating]. Now the gentle pressure . . . of my hand . . . makes it so very easy . . . to take another deep, deep breath . . . and begin to let eoperating room . . . and you recognize my voice . . . and

especially when you feel my hand . . . upon your shoulder . . . just like this . . . [demonstrating] . . . you will be surprised . . . how very easy it will be . . . to recall how comfortable . . . you are now. . . . And you will be inclined . . . if you will allow yourself . . . to take a deep, deep breath . . . and become most comfortable . . . and very content . . . to leave everything to me. . . . It is pleasant, isn't it . . . to just lie there and relax . . . with your eyes closed . . . feeling warm and comfortable . . . and very safe . . . just letting yourself relax? . . . Just be indolent and lazy. . . . I will leave you . . . for a few minutes now. . . . I have to see another patient. . . . But I will be back . . . very soon. . . . While I'm gone . . . be comfortable . . . very comfortable . . . and just relax all over.

The anesthetist then leaves the room in accord with his statement to the patient. When he returns:

I'm back. . . . I'm glad to see . . . you were able . . . to relax so well. . . . It is very pleasant, isn't it?. . . . I just wanted to remind you . . . that everything is well in hand . . . for tomorrow morning. . . . You have an excellent doctor. . . . He is very good . . . as you already know . . . and you're very fit for the surgery. . . . And don't forget. . . .I will be there myself . . . to give your anesthetic . . . and to make sure . . . that everything . . . goes smoothly. . . . After the operation . . . you'll be pleasantly surprised . . . to find how well you'll really be. . . . You'll be able to breathe easily. . . . You will be able to pass your water. . . . You will be able to be remarkably relaxed . . . and very pleased to find it is all over. . . . Operations today . . . are very different . . . from what they used to be . . . I'm going to awaken you now. . . . Remember . . . when we meet in the operating room . . . and you recognize my voice . . . and especially . . . when I touch you on your shoulder . . . just like this . . . [demonstrating] . . . you will find it very easy . . . if you wish . . . to take a deep, deep breath . . . and be very comfortable. . . . I will count to 3. . . . When I do . . . you will awake. . . .completely awake and rested . . . very relaxed. . . . And when the nurse . . . tonight . . . brings you your sedative . . . you will take it . . . and find it very easy . . . to drift off to sleep . . . and sleep a very restful sleep. . . .1 . . . 2 . . . 3 . . . That's excellent. . . . Good night. . . . I'll see you in the morning.

Summary Steps for Preoperative Hypnosis to Facilitate Healing

Ernest L. Rossi, Ph.D., and
David B. Cheek, M.D.
Malibu, California, and Santa Barbara, California

1. *Initial training in anesthesia and well-being*
   a. Ideodynamic signaling for exercises in anesthesia and/or analgesia:
      "Your yes finger can lift when you can feel the numbness (coldness, stiffness, etc.)."
   b. Ideodynamic exploration and correction of misconceptions and fears about surgery.
2. *Accessing and utilizing inner resources*
   a. "After surgery of this kind, most patients are well and ready to go home in X days. Does your inner mind know it can facilitate healing so you may do even better than that?"
   b. "Let your inner mind now select a time when you've gone on a vacation. Your yes finger will lift when you are leaving; your no finger will lift when you are back in your home again. The injection you receive before surgery will be your ticket to leave on that trip. Your yes finger can lift when your unconscious knows this. All the sounds of the operating room will translate into background noises associated with your trip."
   c. "Your yes finger can lift when your unconscious knows it can ignore all conversation in the operating room unless I speak to you using your first name. I will keep informed about the operation but I want you to pay all your attention to the things you see, the people you are with, and the enjoyable food you eat during that trip. As you do this, you will be using all the normal biological processes for healing your body."
3. *Ratifying postoperative healing*
   a. "Does the inner part of your mind know that you can ignore sensations of dis-

comfort in the surgical area after you have regained consciousness?" (If the answer is no, it is time to check on possible resistance; but it may be only that more time and rehearsals are necessary.)
   b. "Elimination of postoperative pain with hypnosis allows the most rapid healing to occur because inflammation is minimized. Is your inner mind willing to work on this for the sake of yourself and the people who love you?" (A no answer indicates an unconscious need to suffer or to punish someone else. The source must be found and removed.)
   c. "Does your inner mind know you can go home as soon or even sooner than surgical patients who have had no preparation such as you have had?" (This projects your confidence in the patient's ability to do well. It strongly suggests that the patient will live through the surgery and will be going home.)

Ericksonian Approaches in Anesthesiology

Bertha P. Rodger, M.D.
Palm Harbor, Florida

EMERGENCY ROOM VERBALIZATIONS

You won't *mind* being *comfortable* while we work, will you? You *know* anything *hurts less* when you can relax even a little bit, or when you begin to distribute some of your attention elsewhere. [No one can argue with this. The truism initiates positive response, the important "yes-set" of mind.] You *know* the pleasant sensation of warmth on your skin when you stretch out in the sun in a favorite spot. You have *time* now to think about such things, to *let your mind wander . . .* and *wonder . . .* as you wander. You don't even have to pay attention to what I am saying. The deep part of your mind can listen to the voice speaking directly to you. All other sounds can deepen that sense of comfort that comes as you relax and rest so pleasantly.

PREPARATION FOR HYPNOANESTHESIA

The following verbalization is a mosaic which also illustrates a number of Erickson's teachings. Most ideas are drawn directly from Seminars on Hypnosis [led by Erickson and others in the 1950's, leading to the founding of the American Society of Clinical Hypnosis] or other workshop notes. Many have filtered through the lectures of others trained by him. It is no longer possible to sort out the sources of such contributions. Words, phrases, and approaches come spontaneously into use after long steeping in them.

A patient referred for learning hypnoanesthesia was somewhat diffident and apprehensive about hypnosis. Hence it seemed best to separate trance development from its use, as Erickson so characteristically did: "I really cannot hypnotize you. But at some time in the future when *you* are ready to learn to go into a trance, I can help you do so. Then you can learn to use it . . . and go on doing so all the rest of your life."

It made clear that the patient, not the facilitator, "does the hypnotizing," retaining control. Appearing to put it off to the nebulous future decreases its threatening aspect. Yet it leaves the matter open for change as readiness for it comes.

The anesthesiologist continues: "Meanwhile, there are some very interesting things you can learn that will help you. You can forget about hypnosis until you understand more about it and want to work with it. . . . There are certain things you already know about dealing with discomfort or pain that you can put to use right now — like the distraction that occurs when you give your full attention to a TV program,

tuning out everything else. You may even get so absorbed in what is going on that it seems as if you are really there, participating in the action. This is called 'dissociation.' It is just a matter of degree. So you have the choice of concentrating on the hurting — or turning to something more interesting. The more you do the latter, the less anything bothers you."

This falls within the realm of setting the stage for increasing collaboration. To go on with demonstrating a point is vastly more effective than remonstrating. It gives a firm basis upon which to build: "Tightening muscles seems to set nerves on edge so that discomfort increases. Tension always aggravates pain and can even cause it. Yet as much as 40% of pain is relieved by simple relaxation. You can test this out for yourself. Double up your fist and hold it very tightly. Pinch the back of your hand to discover how sharp it feels. Now make your hand go as limp and floppy as a Raggedy Ann doll and note how little a pinch bothers it now."

It's a little difficult to record on paper the grimace that accompanies the first pinch and the smile that goes with the second. Both are important. With the fact verified that helpful information is indeed being supplied, it is easier to proceed. This time a certain vagueness is introduced, producing slight confusion. Communication techniques use multiple levels of verbal content, voice variance, and nonverbal demonstration. All of these reinforce the changes in awareness and provide guidance.

To continue: "Turn your attention to the wealth of sensations you can sense in your hand . . . and to their changes. Just which part is the heaviest? Is it in the fingers? In the palm? Near the wrist? Where does it feel lighter? As if it might like to lift? To float upward? Does that tingly feeling start first in your fingers? Or the back of your hand? Is there a bubbly feeling along with this? Or does it feel stiff . . . as if it is made of wood . . . feeling only a slight vibration . . . if anything? *Notice* where it feels most comfortable of all . . . where nothing bothers it . . . nothing disturbs it. And that feeling of comfort is so pleasing . . . you wonder . . . how long it really needs to take . . . to spread even further . . . and deeper . . . through that whole area . . . and even beyond . . . for an extra margin . . . and how well it can remain . . . to keep you entirely comfortable. The comfort can stay as long as normal healing is going on. Your body knows how to heal. As you keep yourself comfortable . . . all the energy goes to the healing process. It's so good to be able to work so nicely with your body."

Numerous techniques are effected including: conviction of her ability to develop and retain control; raising her expectation of something desirable happening; showing her the creative choices; and focusing on the goodness of her body. All lead her to an experience of better functioning by her own skills.

STRUCTURING EXPECTATIONS

It is essential to pay attention to the patient's expectations. One who expects to feel *nothing* during treatment may be quite upset to feel *something*, interpreting any sensation as *pain*. Anticipating this is part of paying adequate attention to detail. It might be explained in this way. "*Analgesia* is like turning down the rheostat, the dimmer, to where sensation is tolerable, even comfortable. *Anesthesia* is like turning off the switch. It's possible you might feel a *little* something. *If* you were able to feel the incision, it would feel like a fingernail drawn lightly across the skin—a tickle or a trickle." Demonstrating this so lightly as to tickle makes it clear.

SUGGESTIONS FOR THE PATIENT IN LABOR

A frightened patient just admitted to labor room was on the verge of panic, becoming unmanageable. Grasping both her hands in the manner of a handshake, I spoke firmly to her, "If you *really* have to panic, you ought to do a good job of it! Come on . . . I'll help you. . . . Get your heart beating *faster* . . . pumping *harder* . . . *much* harder . . . and faster . . .

and *breathe* in little spasms . . . deeper . . . faster . . . get that *blood pressure* up higher. . . . It's so *very uncomfortable*, isn't it? So why don't you *stop halfway*? Wouldn't you really rather just let your eyes close? And snuggle down . . . just listen . . . to the voice that speaks directly to you . . . to tell you just what to expect . . . and how to respond . . . so as to keep yourself quite comfortable. . . ."

"You can let the time of the contraction seem to go by like a flash . . . so fast you hardly notice it except for timing it. The time between contractions can seem like a nice long time. So you have plenty of time to rest, relax and enjoy whatever you wish."

ALTERING PERCEPTIONS OF PAIN

"Erickson pointed out that when a child is hurt, it is in his entirety. Narrowing down the area to where the pain is actually felt and recognizing that all the rest of the body is free from pain enables easier management. Now a desensitization process can whittle away at it further. It is more readily accomplished a bit at a time, dimming sharpness, turning 'dull misery' into a 'wonderful weariness,' even a 'lovely lassitude' as that feeling is slowly attenuated. The 'red hot poker' effect can be cooled through 'real hot' to 'still too warm,' which is like moving away from the hot fireplace until it becomes 'comfortably warm' or 'pleasantly cool' or even 'numbingly cold'."

SOLILOQUY ON PAIN

"Give your full attention to your pain. *Try* not to let your mind wander from it—even for a moment. Find out *exactly* where it is located, exactly how it feels. Keep your mind fixed on it so you won't miss anything significant about it." [Starting with what the patient is already doing, giving full attention to his pain, the task is made more difficult by the effort it takes to keep such intense concentration. A point of no return is soon reached, after which the harder one tries, the less he succeeds. Erickson long ago observed that when he spotted an acquaintance walking ahead of him, he could catch up, get in step, then as he slowed his steps, speeded them, turned right or left, the other would go along with his assumption of leadership quite out of awareness. Such minute observation fostered his unique communication by indirect ways which avoid resistance.]

[Now mental imagery is introduced.] "There is a building in Boston containing a circular room with a bridge across its center. Standing on the bridge is like being on the inside of a globe, with colored maps of the world on the surrounding walls. Imagine walking into such a globe with a map of your pain on its walls, lighted from outside so you get a really good look at it. The color in the area of pain shows the intensity and concentration as well as the exact area covered." [A vivid picture, painted in "living color" is easily held, easily changed with the speed of thought to stir helpful associations. It allows a search for meaning or causation without bringing material to consciousness unless the patient is ready to do so. Mental energy is thus accumulated and directed usefully.]

"Watch what happens now, as a diluting color is put into the one representing pain. It begins to fade a little, turn paler. Some neutralization seems to be occurring, as if it's being suctioned out, washed out further, rendered more harmless. It looks better. You can see more clearly what was beside it, beneath it, behind it, around it, within it. You can also see relationships of timing . . . when it began . . . when it recurs . . . in relation to what . . . and to whom." [Putting the picture into a different frame allows broader vision, possibly the taking of a new road instead of continuing in the same old rut. Yet this is done without meddling. The patient can find his own meaning when he is ready, encouraged by this understanding support.] "You wonder how long its duration really needs to be . . . to fulfill its purpose as an alerting signal . . . that something is going on that might need attention . . . some care. It's like when a hot potato is tossed to you, you find that tossing it back is better

than burning your fingers. . . . It cools in the process enough to be handled comfortably."

"You tell me you have pain . . . and I know you really do have pain . . . and you know it hurts less when you relax. You *know* how to hurt. No one has taught you how *not* to hurt. I can do that. Simple relaxation can deal with as much as 40% of pain. That's almost half. As you learn to let the area go as soft, limp and floppy as a Raggedy Ann doll and keep it that way, you can *have* the pain or you can *halve* it!"

[Thus the patient is led away from being steeped in negative thinking and responses with alternatives couched in broad enough terms to allow for individual adaptation. He can learn to part with pain a little at a time or to trade it for a sensation less disturbing, less restrictive of function. While this re-education is going on, he has the option of *having* or *halving* the pain.]

PLAY ON WORDS

[To a cancer patient whose family was adamant that she not be informed of the diagnosis.] "You *know* you have pain . . . and many painful feelings too. And this pain . . . and the painful thoughts that go with it . . . can so fill your mind . . . as to drive out all other thoughts. You *know* you have pain . . . and you *know* that you know it . . . and *no* one can tell you any different. What you do *not know* . . . is that you also have areas of *no pain* . . . and you can *know* this *no-pain* . . . and the *time* of *no-pain* . . . can get *longer* and longer. . . . The *area* of no-pain can get *larger* and larger . . . so you have more and *more* no-pain . . . until you are entirely free!"

"You would like so much to say *no* to *all* pain. . . . You want your no to be a *good* no . . . the *right* no. There are many things *you* know . . . and you know others know them . . . and sometimes they *do not want* you to know *they* know them. So you do not let them know that you know them . . . to protect their feelings. There may be one person with whom you can share what needs to be shared . . . without distress to anyone. There are so many things you *do* know that will help you to say the *right no* . . . and let you become more and *more aware* of no-pain . . . until you consistently *feel no pain!*"

Examples of Preoperative Suggestions

Joseph Barber, Ph.D.
Los Angeles, California

1. You can enjoy an undisturbed, restful night's sleep.
2. You can awaken in the morning with feelings of calm and the anticipation of being well taken care of, and just let everyone else take complete care of you.
3. You can daydream as fully as you would like, with no need to pay attention to all the goings on in the hospital; you can ignore the noise and lights, and just be delighted (if not surprised) that there is really nothing to bother you, and nothing to disturb you.
4. During the comfort of anesthetic sleep, you can continue to let the doctors take care of you, but know that you can also do anything you need to do to increase your comfort.
5. Upon wakening, you can still let yourself daydream, without having to be clearly aware of anything except questions and requests directly made to you.
6. [If appropriate] You can enjoy comfortable, satisfying, deep breaths; free, effortless, urination; appropriate control of bleeding; uneventful healing.
7. You can be pleased to surprise the nurses when they don't get to give you medication for pain, and to enjoy noticing that there are no feelings to bother you or disturb you.

Preparation for Surgery

Sandra M. Sylvester, Ph.D.
Tucson, Arizona

INTRODUCTION

The following suggestions may be used in hypnosis with the patient, and may be tape recorded for the patient to use in tape-assisted self-hypnosis for reinforcement of the suggestions. (*Ed.*)

SUGGESTIONS

INTRODUCTION AND INDUCTION.   Hello, this is Dr. Sandra Sylvester and I am here to help you prepare for your surgery. What I am going to do at this time is to speak to you a little about surgery and the healing process and also give you some instructions that will help you become more comfortable and more relaxed as you prepare for your surgery.

Now, would you please lie in a position which is very comfortable for you. Take time to arrange your body, position your pillows, so that you feel poised and balanced and very comfortable and at ease. Take a few moments to do this. Adjust your head so that you are comfortable . . . your back . . . your arms . . . your feet . . . and legs. As we continue, if you would like to change your position to become even more comfortable, please feel free to do so.

The process of coming into the hospital for surgery is a very common and routine procedure for all of us here at the hospital. But for you it may be a once in a lifetime experience. And so, if I may, I would like to talk with you about what we have learned about the healing process so that you can prepare yourself in the best possible way for your surgery.

And so to begin: As you are lying in this comfortable position, look up at the ceiling and find a spot which is easy for you to see. Just any spot on the ceiling will do. Please continue to look at that spot while I continue to speak with you. Already as you are looking at that spot you may begin to perceive some very subtle changes in your vision. For example, you may notice that that spot becomes very easy to see. And you may also notice that the periphery of your vision surrounding that spot may begin to get hazy, so that as you keep that spot in focus, the rest of your vision moves out of focus. You may also notice that your eyes begin to tire and fatigue . . . and sometimes your eyes will indicate that by tearing. So you may notice your eyes watering a bit. You may notice that as your eyes blink, you sense a feeling of comfort come over your body in that brief moment when your eyes are closed. And as your eyes continue to tire, and they continue to blink, you will find more and more comfort and pleasure as your eyes are closing. And soon you will notice that it is more comfortable for you to just allow your eyes to close. When you notice that it is more comfortable for you to allow your eyes to close, let them close, so that you can notice the changes which occur when you have turned off your sense of vision.

FOCUSING ATTENTION AND UTILIZING HOSPITAL SOUNDS. One thing you may notice almost immediately is how easy it is to hear the words that I speak directly to you. It is also easy to hear and continue to hear all of the sounds around you. And yet, those sounds which are not important to you at this moment can fade into the background, and even though they are still there, they need not disturb you in any way. You can hear pages in the hallway and know that you do not need to listen to them. You may hear talking or sounds from your neighbor, the television set, snatches of conversations. While these go on, notice how pleasant it is to know that you need not bother to respond to anything unless it is directed specifically at you.

AUTOMATICITY, TRUSTING THE UNCONSCIOUS, AND DEEPENING. You may also notice how easy it is to begin to tune in to the rhythm of your breathing, noticing that when you are still, your body takes a rhythm of breathing which is most beneficial for you at this moment. As you

inhale and exhale, your chest goes up and down in a comfortable, easy rhythm. An interesting thing about your breathing is that you breathe day and night every moment of your life without having to think about it. Your autonomic nervous system directs and controls your breathing in a comfortable way; in a way that is so much better than you could ever do consciously; in a way that occurs without any effort on your part. Your body, in a sense, breathes by itself. As you continue to breathe, you may notice that each time you exhale, you can relax more and more. Each time you exhale you can feel as if you are sinking deeply into the support of the mattress. Each time you exhale you can feel as if you are letting go of more and more muscle tension. So that each time you breathe out, it is as if you are letting go of tightness and you feel your muscles becoming soft and loose. You may experience this as a comfortable feeling of heaviness, so that each time you exhale, you feel your body becoming soft and loose and heavy. If you notice that there is any part of your body which is still tense, which is holding on to tension, imagine as you exhale, that you breathe out through that body part which was holding tension and let your breath melt the tension so that, as you breathe out, those muscles too become soft and loose and comfortable. Take a few moments to make a tour of your body, taking time to notice if there is any tension anywhere within your body. If you notice any tension in your body, take a few moments of extra care, letting yourself breathe out through that part of your body and melt the tension away.

You may also notice that your heartbeat assumes a regular, even, rhythmical pattern, which is most beneficial for you at this time. You know again that your unconscious mind directs the beating of your heart day and night, every moment of your life whether you consciously think about it or not. It is the circulation of oxygenated enriched blood throughout your body which aids very much in the healing process. And so for these few moments, just feel the rhythm of your heartbeat. You may notice somewhere within your body a pulsing, regular, even rhythm. Sometimes your heartbeat may be so subtle that perhaps the only way to feel it is on a cellular level, for every single living cell in your body feels the regular influx of nutrients with every beat of your heart. This process also cleanses away all waste products in each and every cell in your body. And, as mentioned earlier, this process goes on automatically whether you think about it or not.

Your blood pressure lowers to a level which is best for you right now. Because you are lying down in a position of relaxation and comfort and you feel a certain sense of stillness, your blood pressure can lower. If you were to get up and move around, your blood pressure would rise so that you could carry on that activity. So the important thing about your blood pressure is that it be flexible, rising when you need it to rise and lowering when you are not doing anything which places a demand on your body.

UTILIZING INTERNAL DIALOGUE.   You may also notice that as I continue to speak with you, thoughts continue to drift through your mind, as if your thoughts are like drops of water in a river. And you know, sometimes those drops of water move very quickly in the form of white water rapids, bubbling over rocks, moving very quickly downstream. Yet, in the very same river, if you walk downstream far enough, you will come to a spot in the river where the water is so deep that it is almost impossible to detect any movement at all. In fact, perhaps you cannot see the water move until you wait and watch a leaf detach itself from a branch of a tree, begin to drift downward toward the surface of the water, touch the surface of the water, pause for just a moment and then begin its journey downstream. Feel the rhythm of your thoughts without bothering to pick out any one thought to think about. Just feel the gentle drifting rhythm of your thoughts as they drift through your mind like drops of water.

DEPOTENTIATING CONSCIOUSLY TRYING.   Know that at this moment there is nothing special for you to do, there are no demands being placed upon you, no expectations. There is no one to please, no one to satisfy. The only thing for you to do

right now is to feel and experience the rhythms going on within your body—feeling a sense of comfortable stillness, feeling a sense of quiet deep within you, allowing your unconscious mind to work freely and easily in this process of healing.

SUGGESTIONS FOR HEALING AND REFRAMING PAIN. One of the ways that your body heals itself is by circulating rich oxygenated blood to every single living cell in your body, filling that cell with nourishment and carrying away waste products and poisons, and filtering them outside of your body. This process is a process that you can participate in and facilitate. One of the ways that you can facilitate this process is to keep in mind that your body is constantly healing itself, sloughing off dead cells, nourishing that area, and growing new cells all of the time. As part of your healing process you will experience many different kinds of physical sensations. You may feel the sensation of stretching and shrinking as tissues join together and mend themselves. You may experience sensations of warmth as the healing process continues, or sensations of pressure as swelling begins to subside. It is important to know that, as your body heals itself, changes do occur and those changes may be perceived by you. You can cooperate with the work of your body by remaining calm, as you are now, continuing to breathe in a rhythmical easy rhythm, letting your breath enrich your blood supply, which in turn will carry nutrients to your cells, allowing your blood pressure to go to a level which is most beneficial to you now. If you are feeling any sense of discomfort, breathe in and out through that area so that your warm breath can soothe those muscles and allow them to feel soft and warm and relaxed. So let yourself rest and let your body take its time to heal.

Now, leaving you with these thoughts, allow yourself to continue to breathe, relaxing more and more with each breath, fully enjoying that feeling of deep comfort and peace. Allow the drifting of your thoughts to match the easy rhythm of your breathing as you inhale and exhale. Then, give to your unconscious the task of directing your healing process with the same efficiency that it directs your respiration, digestion, and circulation — knowing that your unconscious can direct your healing process, whether or not you consciously think about it.

REALERTING. In a few moments, you will begin to rouse yourself and reorient yourself to this room. You can begin to do so when, and only when, you are ready to do so, taking all the time you need; allowing yourself to retain that feeling of comfort and a sense of well-being. As you do begin to move around a bit, you may feel sensations returning to your hands and feet. Be curious as you open your eyes, and notice how bright the colors can appear. You can feel refreshed as if you have just awakened from a long and restful sleep.

I invite you to play this tape as often as you wish so that you can use it to help put yourself in the best possible mind-set for your surgery and for the healing process, which for the next few days and weeks will be your full-time job. Thank you.

Temperature Suggestion Following Chest/Abdominal Surgery

D. Corydon Hammond, Ph.D.
Salt Lake City, Utah

You will begin to get pleasantly warm now. We have placed a heat lamp over you, which will rapidly warm your body back to normal temperature, almost as if you were snuggled up warmly in bed, or resting comfortably in a warm bath.

Suggestions for Insertion of Needles or Short Procedures

Esther E. Bartlett, M.D.
Quincy, Massachusetts

[These suggestions may be used as waking suggestions with effectiveness, or with hypnosis for even greater effectiveness.]

I'm going to wash the skin [or mucous membrane] off with some cold, wet fluid that will wash away *most* of the feeling . . . right here [rubbing the area briskly and thoroughly with alcohol or any antiseptic], so that what I do is not a bit important to you . . . [giving the skin a few flicks of the fingernail to complete the anesthesia, washing again with the antiseptic and rapidly inserting the needle].

Switching Off the Senses

Bertha P. Rodger, M.D.
Palm Harbor, Florida

1. Assume a *COMFORTABLE* and *BALANCED* position. Allow your body *STAY STILL* and *NOTICE* how much quieter and more *COMFORTABLE* you become as the sense of *MOVEMENT*, is *SHUT OFF*.
2. *REST* your *EYES*, on a spot or *GAZE* into space, *NARROWING* the *FIELD* of *VISION*, decreasing *DISTRACTION*, with less stimulation from *OUTSIDE* your body, you *CENTER* it more and more on *INNER REALITIES*. You become *MORE QUIET*. Your body *KNOWS HOW* when you *SET THE STAGE* for it and *ALLOW* the quietness to come to you and *ALL THROUGH* you, very, very pleasantly. *NOTICE* these feelings. They are *UNIQUE* to you.
3. Let you eyes *CLOSE* and *STAY* closed. You begin to feel a familiar *DROWSY*, *DREAMY*, *SLEEPY* feeling. Yet you are neither asleep nor in the process of going to sleep. You are *ALERT* to whatever is *IMPORTANT*, *UNDISTURBED* by the unimportant. It is a *PURPOSEFUL FOCUSING* of attention. *DISCOVER* how infinitely more *COMFORTABLE* it is.
4. Pay attention to the *WEIGHT* of one *ARM* . . . perhaps your *DOMINANT* one. *SENSE* the heaviness of its bones, muscles, soft tissue, blood vessels. *NOTE* the pleasant feeling that it is really *TOO MUCH*

BOTHER to move even to lift a little finger! You feel a *LOVELY LASSITUDE*, perhaps even a *WONDERFUL WEARINESS*!

5. Note that *BOTH ARMS* are *ACTUALLY HEAVY*. Are they *EQUALLY* so? Which is heavier? Which is *LIGHTER*? Perhaps you *LIKE* the *LIGHTNESS* better? Pay attention to *ALL* the feelings of lightness. *REMEMBER* a time you felt a *DELIGHTFUL* lightness . . . of *FLOATING* . . . like a *FEATHER* on a gentle breeze . . . a *LEAF* on the water . . . a *BIRD* on the wind, soaring *EFFORTLESSLY*.

6. While you rest and relax so comfortably, *NO FEELING* need *DISTURB* you. You can *RECOGNIZE* any feeling but need not pay *ATTENTION* to it . . . nor *REACT* to it *UNLESS* it is *REALLY* important to do so. You can do whatever is *NEEDFUL* in response without being bothered by any feeling, physical or emotional.

7. *NO SOUND* need *DISTURB* you. There is no interference with hearing. You need not *REACT* to it *UNLESS* it is important. Many can sleep through a thunderstorm but awaken to the cry of a tiny baby. *ANY SOUND* can be the *SIGNAL* to go more deeply into the *STATE OF COMFORT*.

8. *NOTICE* that your *BREATHING* becomes more *CALM, DEEP AND EASY*. Your *HEART* beat becomes *CALM, STRONG*, and *REGULAR*. Measurements would show your *BLOOD PRESSURE* coming *TOWARD NORMAL* where it *STABILIZES*, responding appropriately to changing needs. A pleasant feeling of *WARMTH* pervades your entire being . . . as if your personal *THERMOSTAT* is turned to exactly the right temperature. *COMFORT FLOWS* through your whole being. You feel *CALM . . . CONTENTED . . . SAFE . . . SECURE*. These feelings *STAY* with you even when you return to another state of *ALERTNESS*.

9. As a way of *REORIENTING* yourself quickly and pleasantly . . . *WHEN* you are *READY* . . . you can say to yourself as you *BREATHE OUT* . . . "*WAKE*" . . . and as you *BREATHE IN* . . . "*UP*" . . . and return *FULL* of *VIGOR*.

Rapid Induction Analgesia

Joseph Barber, Ph.D.
Los Angeles, California

INTRODUCTION AND INDICATIONS

[Elicitation of cooperation] I'd like to talk with you for a moment to see if you'd like to feel more comfortable and relaxed than you might expect. Would you like to feel more comfortable than you do right now?

I'm quite sure that it will seem to you that I have really done nothing, that nothing has happened at all. You may feel a bit more relaxed, in a moment, but I doubt that you'll notice any other changes. I'd like you to notice, though, if you're surprised by anything else you might notice. OK, then . . . the really best way to *begin feeling more comfortable* is to just begin by sitting as comfortably as you can right now . . . go ahead and adjust yourself to the most comfortable position you like [Initiation of deep relaxation] . . . that's fine. Now I'd like you to notice how much more comfortable you can feel by just taking one very big, satisfying deep breath. Go ahead . . . big, deep, satisfying breath . . . that's fine. You may already notice *how good that feels* . . . how warm your neck and shoulders can feel. . . . Now, then . . . I'd like you to take four more very deep, *very comfortable* breaths . . . and, as you exhale, notice . . . just notice how comfortable your shoulders can become . . . and notice how comfortable your eyes can feel when they close . . . and when they close, just let them stay closed [Eye closure] . . . that's right, just notice that . . . and notice, too, how when you exhale, you can just *feel that relaxation beginning to sink in*. . . . Good, that's fine . . . now, as you continue breathing, comfortably and deeply and rhythmically, all I'd like you to do is to picture in your mind . . . just imagine a staircase, any kind you like . . . with 20 steps, and you at the top. . . . Now, you don't need to see all 20 steps at once, you can see any or all of the staircase, any way you like . . . that's fine. . . . Just notice yourself, at the top of the staircase, and the step you're on, and any others you like . . . however you see it is fine. . . . Now, in a moment, but not yet, I'm going to begin to count, out loud, from one to 20, and . . . as you may already have guessed . . . as I count each number I'd like you to take a step down that staircase . . . see yourself stepping down, feel yourself stepping down, one step for each number I count . . . and all you need to do is notice, just notice, how much more comfortable and relaxed you can feel at each step, as you go down the staircase . . . one step for each number that I count . . . the larger the number, the farther down the staircase . . . the farther down the staircase, the more comfortable you can feel . . . one step for each number . . . all right, you can begin to get ready . . . now, I'm going to begin. . . . [saying each number with the initiation of subject's exhalation, watching for any signs of relaxation and commenting on them] *ONE* . . . one step down the staircase . . . *TWO* . . . two steps down the staircase . . . that's fine . . . *THREE* . . . three steps down the staircase . . . and maybe you already notice how much more relaxed you can feel. . . . I wonder if there are places in your body that feel more relaxed than others . . . perhaps your shoulders *feel more relaxed* than your neck . . . perhaps your legs feel more relaxed than your arms. . . . I don't know, and it really doesn't matter . . . all that matters is that you feel comfortable . . . that's all. . . . *FOUR* . . . four steps down the staircase, perhaps feeling already places in your body beginning to relax. . . . I wonder if the deep relaxing, restful heaviness in your forehead is already beginning to spread and flow . . . down, across your eyes, down across your face, into your mouth and jaw . . . down through your neck, deep, restful, heavy . . . *FIVE* . . . five steps down the staircase . . . a quarter of the way down, and already begin-

ning, perhaps, to really, really enjoy your relaxation and comfort . . . *SIX* . . . six steps down the staircase . . . perhaps beginning to notice that the sounds which were distracting become less so . . . that all the sounds you can hear become a part of your experience of comfort and relaxation . . . anything you can notice becomes a part of your experience of comfort and relaxation . . . *SEVEN* . . . seven steps down the staircase . . . that's fine . . . perhaps noticing the heavy, restful, comfortably relaxing feeling spreading down into your shoulders, into your arms . . . [confusingly, permissively eliciting arm heaviness]. I wonder if you notice one arm feeling heavier than the other . . . perhaps your left arm feels a bit heavier than your right . . . perhaps your right arm feels heavier than your left . . . I don't know, perhaps they both feel equally, comfortably heavy. . . . It really doesn't matter . . . just letting yourself become more and more aware of that comfortable heaviness . . . or is it a feeling of lightness? . . . I really don't know, and it really doesn't matter . . . *EIGHT* . . . eight steps down the staircase . . . perhaps noticing that, even as you relax, your heart seems to beat much faster and harder than you might expect, perhaps noticing the tingling in your fingers . . . perhaps wondering about the fluttering of your heavy eyelids . . . [Each number, each suggestion of heaviness enunciated as though the hypnotist, too, is becoming intensely relaxed] *NINE* . . . nine steps down the staircase, breathing comfortably, slowly, and deeply . . . restful, noticing that heaviness really beginning to sink in, as you continue to notice the pleasant, restful, comfortable relaxation just spread through your body . . . *TEN* . . . ten steps down the staircase . . . halfway to the bottom of the staircase, wondering perhaps what might be happening, perhaps wondering if anything at all is happening [Integration of sighing with enunciation is helpful . . . watch for responsiveness] . . . and yet, knowing that it really doesn't matter, feeling so pleasantly restful, just continuing to notice the growing, spreading, comfortable relaxation . . . *ELEVEN* . . . eleven steps down the staircase . . . noticing maybe that as you feel increasingly heavy, more and more comfortable, there's nothing to bother you, nothing to disturb you, as you become deeper and deeper relaxed . . . *TWELVE* . . . twelve steps down the staircase. . . . I wonder if you notice how easily you can hear the sound of my voice . . . how easily you can understand the words I say [Suggestion to pay attention] . . . with nothing to bother, nothing to disturb . . . *THIRTEEN* . . . thirteen steps down the staircase, feeling more and more the real enjoyment of this relaxation and comfort . . . *FOURTEEN* . . . fourteen steps down the staircase . . . noticing perhaps the sinking, restful pleasantness as your body seems to just sink down, deeper and deeper into the chair, with nothing to bother, nothing to disturb . . . as though the chair holds you, comfortably and warmly . . . *FIFTEEN* . . . fifteen steps down the staircase . . . three-quarters of the way down the staircase . . . deeper and deeper relaxed, absolutely nothing at all to do . . . but just enjoy yourself [More and more directly suggesting enjoyment of the experience . . . more taking for granted the fact of the relaxation] . . . *SIXTEEN* . . . sixteen steps down the staircase . . . wondering perhaps what to experience at the bottom of the staircase . . . and yet knowing how much more ready you already feel to become deeper and deeper relaxed . . . more and more comfortable, with nothing to bother, nothing to disturb . . . *SEVENTEEN* . . . seventeen steps down the staircase . . . closer and closer to the bottom, perhaps feeling your heart beating harder and harder, perhaps feeling the heaviness in your arms and legs become even more clearly comfortable . . . knowing that nothing really matters except your enjoyment of your experience of comfortable relaxation, with nothing to bother, nothing to disturb [18-20 said more slowly, as though in increasing anticipation of being at the bottom] . . . *EIGHTEEN* . . . eighteen steps down the staircase . . . almost to the bottom, with nothing to bother, nothing to disturb, as you continue to go deeper and

deeper relaxed . . . heavy . . . comfortable . . . restful . . . relaxed . . . nothing really to do, no one to please, no one to satisfy . . . just to notice how *very comfortable* and heavy *you can feel*, and continue to feel as you continue to breathe, slowly and comfortably . . . restfully . . . *NINETEEN* . . . nineteen steps down the staircase . . . almost to the bottom of the staircase . . . nothing to bother, nothing to disturb you as you *continue to feel more and more comfortable*, more and more relaxed, more and more rested . . . more and more comfortable . . . just noticing . . . and now . . . *TWENTY* . . . bottom of the staircase . . . *deeply, deeply relaxed* . . . deeper with every breath you take . . . as I talk to you for a moment about something you already know a lot about . . . remembering and forgetting [Amnesia suggestions] . . . you know a lot about it, because we all do a lot of it . . . every moment, of every day you remember . . . and then you forget, so you can remember something else . . . you can't remember everything, all at once, so you just let some memories move quietly back in your mind . . . I wonder, for instance, if you remember what you had for lunch yesterday . . . I would guess that, with not too much effort, you can remember what you had for lunch yesterday . . . and yet . . . I wonder if you remember what you had for lunch a month ago today . . . I would guess the *effort is really too great* to dig up that memory, though of course *it is there* . . . somewhere, deep in the back of your mind . . . no need to remember, so *you don't* . . . and I wonder if *you'll be pleased* to notice that the things we talk about today, with your eyes closed, are things which you'll remember tomorrow, or the next day . . . or next week . . . I wonder if you'll decide to let the memory of these things rest quietly in the back of your mind . . . or if you'll remember gradually, a bit at a time . . . or perhaps all at once, to be again resting in the back of your mind . . . perhaps you'll be surprised to notice that the reception room is the place for memory to surface . . . perhaps not . . . perhaps you'll notice that it is more comfortable to remember on another day alto-gether . . . it really doesn't matter . . . doesn't matter at all . . . whatever you do, however you choose to remember . . . is just fine . . . absolutely natural . . . doesn't matter at all . . . whether you remember tomorrow or the next day, whether you remember all at once, or gradually . . . completely or only partially . . . whether you let the memory rest quietly and comfortably in the back of your mind . . . really doesn't matter at all . . . and, too, I wonder if you'll notice that you'll *feel surprised* that your visit here today is so much *more pleasant* and comfortable than you might have expected [Analgesia suggestions] . . . I wonder if you'll *notice that surprise* . . . that there are *no other feelings* . . . perhaps you'll feel cu-rious about that surprise . . . surprise, curiosi-ty . . . I wonder if you'll *be pleased* to notice that today . . . and any day . . . whenever you feel your head resting back against the headrest [Direct posthypnotic suggestion for analge-sia] . . . when you feel your head resting back like this . . . you'll feel reminded of how very comfortable you are feeling right now . . . even more comfortable than you feel even now . . . comfortable, relaxed . . . nothing to bother, nothing to disturb . . . I wonder if you'll be reminded of this comfort, too, and relaxation, by just noticing the brightness of the light up above . . . perhaps *this comfort and relaxation* will come flooding back, quickly and automat-ically, whenever you find yourself beginning to sit down in the dental chair . . . *I don't know* exactly how it will seem . . . I only know, as perhaps you also know . . . that your experi-ence will seem surprisingly *more pleasant*, sur-prisingly *more comfortable*, surprisingly *more restful* than you *might expect* . . . with nothing to bother, nothing to disturb . . . whatever you are able to notice . . . everything *can be a part* of being absolutely comfortable [Every sensa-tion creates the analgesic experience (nothing detracts from it)] . . . and I want to remind you that whenever [doctor's name] touches your right shoulder, like this . . . whenever it is appropriate, and only when it is appropri-

ate . . . whenever [doctor's name] touches your right shoulder, like this . . . or whenever I touch your right shoulder, like this . . . you'll experience a feeling . . . a feeling of being ready to do something [Posthypnotic sugges-tion for a variety of behaviors, but with pur-pose of developing a trance . . . and with im-plication for analgesia] . . . whenever I touch your right shoulder, like this . . . or whenever [doctor's name] touches your right shoulder, like this . . . you'll experience a feeling . . . a feeling of being ready to do something . . . perhaps a feeling of being ready to close your eyes . . . perhaps a feeling of being ready to be even more comfortable . . . perhaps ready to know even more clearly that there's nothing to bother, nothing to disturb . . . perhaps ready to become heavy and tired. . . . I don't know . . . but whenever I touch your right shoulder, like this . . . you'll experience a feel-ing . . . a feeling of being ready to do some-thing . . . it really doesn't matter . . . perhaps just a feeling of being ready to be even more surprised . . . it doesn't really matter . . . nothing really matters but your experience of comfort and relaxation . . . absolutely deep comfort and relaxation . . . with nothing to bother and nothing to disturb . . . that's fine. . . . And now, as you continue to enjoy your comfortable relaxation, I'd like you to notice how very nice it feels to be this way . . . to really enjoy your own experience, to really enjoy the feelings your body can give you . . . [Preparation for end to this comfortable expe-rience] and in a moment, but not yet . . . not until you're ready . . . but in a moment, I'm going to count from one to 20 . . . and as you know, I'd like you to feel yourself going back up the steps . . . one step for each number . . . you'll have all the time you need . . . after all, time is relative . . . feel yourself slowly and comfortably going back up the steps, one step for each number I count . . . more alert as you go back up the steps, one step for each number I count . . . when I reach three, your eyes will be almost ready to open . . . when I reach two, they will have opened . . . and, when I reach one, you'll be alert, awake, refreshed . . . perhaps as though you'd had a nice nap . . . alert, refreshed, comfortable . . . and even though you'll still be very comfortable and relaxed, you'll be alert and feeling very well . . . perhaps surprised, but feeling very well . . . perhaps ready to be surprised . . . no hurry, you'll have all the time you need, as you begin to go back up these restful steps. [Numbers on inhalation . . . lilting, arousing intonations . . . more quickly at first . . . watch for responsiveness] *TWENTY . . . NINETEEN . . . EIGHTEEN . . .* that's right, feel yourself going back up the steps . . . ready to be surprised, knowing what you had for lunch yesterday, and yet . . . *SEVENTEEN . . . SIXTEEN . . . FIFTEEN . . .* a quarter of the way back up, more and more alert . . . no rush, plenty of time . . . feel yourself becoming more and more alert [If no apparent arousal, slow down, inject more suggestion for arousal] . . . *FOURTEEN . . . THIRTEEN . . . TWELVE . . . ELEVEN . . . TEN . . .* halfway back up the stairs . . . more and more alert . . . comfortable but more and more alert . . . *NINE . . .* that's right, feel yourself becoming more and more alert . . . *EIGHT . . . SEVEN . . . SIX . . . FIVE* [After 5, increasingly slowly . . . repeat suggestions for arousal and positive experience] . . . *FOUR . . . THREE . . .* that's right . . . *TWO . . .* and *ONE . . .* That's right, wide awake, alert, relaxed, refreshed . . . that's fine. How do you feel? Relaxed? Comfortable?

Surgical and Obstetrical Analgesia

Ernest L. Rossi, Ph.D., and
David B. Cheek, M.D.
Malibu, California, and Santa Barbara, California

1. *Accessing unconscious control of analgesia*
   a. "Walk into an imaginary, cold lake until the water reaches your knees. When you feel the cold, your yes finger will life unconsciously. Tell me when you are feeling cold from your knees down."
   b. "When you are in cold water, you soon get used to it. It is no longer cold. You are about half as sensitive as you usually are. If you stubbed a toe or bumped your shin, you would feel a bump but there would be no pain. Your no finger will lift to let you know when you are half as sensitive as you were at first."
   c. "Now walk in until you feel the cold water up to your ribs. When you feel cold from your ribs to your knees, your yes finger will lift. When you are numb from your ribs down to your toes, your no finger will lift."
   d. "Now press your left thumb and index finger together. This associates instant coolness and numbness, and you will be able to do this with increasing speed every time you repeat this exercise."
   e. "Now loosen your pressure on the left hand, and press the index finger and thumb on your right hand to bring back, instantly, all the feelings that have been cool and numb."
   f. "Practice this at home until you know you can reproduce these sensation changes any time you wish."
2. *Therapeutic facilitation*
   a. Have patient repeat exercise until confidence is assured.
   b. Explain that making labor more like the work of sawing wood than like a long arduous experience will allow the baby to be born feeling welcome and free of guilt.
   c. "By turning off unconscious, painful stimuli, you will heal without inflammation and will be able to go home sooner."
3. *Ratifying and extending new ability*
   "Learning this skill will not only make your immediate task easier, but also will aid you in meeting unrelated tasks with confidence in the future."

Techniques for Surgery

William S. Kroger, M.D.
Palm Springs, California

REHEARSAL TECHNIC FOR SURGERY

[During a typical rehearsal session for abdominal surgery the patient is told:] Now your skin is being sterilized." [At this time the abdomen is swabbed with an alcohol sponge.] I am now stretching the skin and making the incision in the skin. [The line of incision is lightly stroked with a pencil.] Now the tissues are being cut. Just relax. You feel nothing, absolutely nothing. Your breathing is getting slower, deeper and more regular. Each side of the incision is being separated by an instrument. [The skin and the muscles are being pulled laterally from the midline.] Now a blood vessel is being clamped. [A hemostat is clicked shut.] You will feel absolutely no discomfort. You are calm, quiet and relaxed. Your breathing is getting slower, deeper, and more regular. Just relax! Now I am going deeper and entering the abdominal cavity." [For the peritoneum, suggestions of relaxation and assurances of complete pain relief are repeated several times.] Just relax. You are getting deeper and deeper relaxed: your heartbeat is getting slower and more regular. Just relax. You feel nothing, absolutely nothing. [The viscera are relatively insensitive to cutting. One does not have to worry about pain. However, the patient has to be prepared for the discomfort produced by pulling and torsion of the abdominal organs.]

[The steps for closure of the peritoneum, muscles, fascia and skin are also described in a similar manner. There are really only three times when pain can be expected: when the skin is incised, when the peritoneum is incised, and when one is tugging on the viscera.]

MAINTENANCE OF HYPNOANESTHESIA DURING SURGERY

[The following is a verbalization for maintaining hypnosis:] All the muscles in your body are relaxed, and, with every breath you take, you will find yourself going deeper and deeper relaxed. You are doing just fine. Just relax all the muscles of your abdomen and chest. You are breathing slower, deeper, and more regular. That's right. In and out . . . in and out. Going deeper and deeper relaxed. You feel nothing except a little pressure. The more relaxed you are, the less tension you have, the less discomfort you will have. [Frequently there is a slight trembling of the eyelids. This often is indicative of deep hypnosis. One can use this objective sign to deepen the hypnosis, as follows:] I notice that your lids are now trembling. That's a good sign. And, as they continue to tremble, you will go deeper and deeper relaxed. You will feel yourself falling, falling, deeper and deeper relaxed with every breath you take. Remember, if you want to open your eyes at any time, you may. Voices won't bother you.

[Production of catalepsy by light stroking of the skin frequently minimizes capillary bleeding, probably as the result of vasospasm. Here the law of dominant effect is put to use: a psychological suggestion is enhanced by a physiological effect. As the region that is going to be operated on is stroked light, I remark:] This area is getting very stiff, cold and numb. Think, feel and imagine that there is an ice cube on your skin. Now it is getting more numb and colder. Numb and cold. Very, very cold. [This verbalization and the stroking are most advantageous where bleeding from the skin is expected. If the hypnosis fails during surgery, one can easily switch to intravenous or inhalation anesthesia. It is always advisable to have these available for prompt use.]

POSTOPERATIVE VERBALIZATION FOR DEHYPNOTIZATION

[Patients are dehypnotized as follows:] You will feel just as if you have awakened from a deep sleep, but, of course, you were not asleep. You will be very, very relaxed. Any time in the future when I touch you on the right shoulder, if I have your permission, you will close your eyes and let your eyeballs roll up into the back of your head. Then you will count backward from 100 to zero slowly, and you will go deeper and deeper relaxed with every breath you take and every number you count. You will find that the period after your operation will be a very pleasant one. Should you have any discomfort in and around the wound, you may use the glove anesthesia which you learned to develop to "knock it out." You will be able to relax and sleep soundly. Should you require medication for sleep, it will make you very sleepy. You will not hesitate to eat the food given to you, and as a matter of fact, you will relish every bite. You will be very, very hungry. The more nutritious food you are able to consume, the faster your tissues will heal. I am going to count to five and you will open your eyes. [Dehypnotization should be done slowly:] You will feel completely alert, refreshed, and wonderful after you open your eyes. One, you are feeling fine. Two, more alert. Three, still more alert. Four, sound in mind, sound in body, no headache. Five, open your eyes. You feel wonderful.

EGO-STRENGTHENING: ENHANCING ESTEEM, SELF-EFFICACY, AND CONFIDENCE

INTRODUCTION

T HE CONCEPT OF "ego-strengthening" was popularized by John Hartland (1971). His ego-strengthening approach, reprinted later in this chapter, simply consisted of generalized supportive suggestions. Their purpose was to increase the patient's confidence and belief in him or herself, enhance general coping abilities, and minimize anxiety and worrying. It was his common practice to give ego-strengthening suggestions as part of almost every induction, seeking to reinforce self-reliance and a positive self-image.

Although not a practitioner of hypnosis, Bandura (1977) and others (e.g., Marlatt & Gordon, 1985) have emphasized the concept of self-efficacy: the expectation and confidence of being able to cope successfully with various situations. This has come to be a key concept in the emerging field of relapse prevention. Individuals with high self-efficacy perceive themselves as being in control.

In the helping professions we have a relatively limited number of interventions available to us for increasing self-esteem and self-efficacy. We may give patients positive feedback and compliment them, but they often discount such comments. Cognitive therapists of various persuasions have provided us with some methods for helping patients examine assumptions and irrational thinking patterns that undermine esteem. Traditional insight-oriented approaches to therapy examine the historic roots of one's self-image, and can be effective but sometimes rather time-consuming. Behaviorists (Bandura, 1981) emphasize that self-efficacy is increased by engineering success experiences for patients, but this is often quite difficult to accomplish. Roleplaying and mental rehearsal techniques which may also enhance coping abilities, have more recently been emphasized by behaviorists (Marlatt & Gordon, 1985) as methods for increasing self-efficacy expectations for specific situations.

Hypnotic techniques offer the clinician an abundance of other options for enhancing self-esteem and self-efficacy: rapid unconscious exploration and working through of the roots of self-image problems; obtaining unconscious commitments from the patient (as modeled by Barnett's approach); direct suggestions and indirect suggestions and metaphors; positively-focused age regression to successful and happy life experiences; age progression and mental rehearsal; hypnotic conditioning techniques (e.g., the clenched fist technique); symbolic imagery techniques; methods for altering imprinted ideas (as modeled in one of T.X. Barber's contributions); the use of trance ratification procedures to convince the patient of the power of his own mind and inner potentials; the use of personalized self-hypnosis tapes to provide regular reinforcement of suggestions; learning self-hypnotic self-management skills for coping with anxiety, anger or other emotions; hypnotic reinforcement of cognitive (e.g., rational-emotive) therapy concepts; and hypnotic reinforcement and facilitation through posthypnotic suggestions of positive internal dialogue and self-talk.

The enhancement of feelings of esteem and self-efficacy has been found to be a powerful tool in working with a great diversity of patients and problems: depression, low self-esteem, overemotionality, substance abuse, posttraumatic stress disorder and victimization; patients with developmental deficits, anxiety and phobic disorders, grief reactions, coping with chronic illness; athletes, business executives, students, children, and patients with eating and habit disorders. In this chapter you will find a tremendous diversity of options for increasing esteem and efficacy.

Ego-Strengthening

Moshe S. Torem, M.D.
Akron, Ohio

INTRODUCTION

John Hartland pointed out that only a few patients will let go of their symptoms before they feel confident and strong enough to do without them. Hartland's ego-strengthening techniques are comprised of positive suggestions of self-worth and personal effectiveness. I view ego-strengthening as analogous to the medical setting in which a patient is first strengthened by proper nutrition, general rest, and weight gain before a radical form of surgery is performed. At times his condition strengthens to the point that an infection is cured due to the strengthening of the patient's immune system. At times just the mere teaching of self-hypnosis for relaxation and calmness and the use of ego-strengthening techniques may be enough so that a patient's symptoms spontaneously disappear.

In my opinion, ego-strengthening is a technique that is indicated for all patients who come to us looking for an alleviation of their suffering regardless of what their symptoms are. It is like saying that healthy and good nutrition is helpful to all patients regardless of what their diagnosis or illness is. After I teach the patient self-hypnosis, I then introduce ego-strengthening suggestions. Later, I ask the patient to repeat after me specific statements of ego-strengthening. The following is a verbatim example of suggestions given, following induction, to a patient recovering from depression.

SUGGESTIONS

With each breath as you exhale, this calmness becomes stronger and stronger, spreading all the way from your head down to your toes, from top to bottom, inside out and outside in, immersing you in an ocean of calmness. An ocean of calmness . . . that's right. And as that continues, peace and serenity are taking you over, inside and outside, thus putting your mind and body in sync with each other. Creating a special state of internal harmony, and peace, and serenity. That's right. That's right. As you continue to sit here and listen to me, there is this center core within your unconscious mind that's logical and rational, cool and collected, calm and relaxed, clever and wise . . . the one that wants you to heal and recover and get well as a whole person. That's right, very intelligent and very knowledgeable. In fact, it knows so much that your conscious mind doesn't even know how much it doesn't know.

This center core within your unconscious mind has always been there with you, since the time you were a little child. It has helped you survive difficult predicaments in the past, and will continue to help you in the future. People refer to this center core in your unconscious as the inner guide or the internal adviser. Some refer to it as the higher self, and others as the guardian angel. But regardless of the name of what it is or how you call it, it has this very special function of guiding you from within, to continue to find your own way for self-actualization, your own way to learn the difference between the past and the present. This will allow you to remember what you need to remember about the past and what happened to you. And once you do remember, in fact, you have been an ingenious survivor, rather than a victim of unfortunate circumstances. That's right, and now you can let go of these memories. And know that you have

memories of the past, you know that you don't have to be the memories themselves. That's right. You can be free of the past and live better in the present, more adaptively, coping more effectively with the tasks of daily living . . . knowing that every day, in every way, you are continuing to get better and better, to see things more clearly, knowing that you are moving forward. Becoming stronger, wiser, improving your understanding of life and the purpose of living in your special role in your family and society.

You continue to strive for accomplishments, but at the same time, strike a very special balance between your career, life, and your family life. You strike a very special balance between time and energy you spend in accomplishing your goals, and the time and energy you spend in protecting and improving your relationships with other people. In doing that, you learn to accept yourself as you are, respect your thinking, your feelings, your emotions, and develop a sense of pride and self-worth. You become more authentic and develop greater courage to assertively express your needs in an adaptive way, as you relate to other people in the workplace and in the family. You develop a new sense of balance and moderation between leading a life of structure and commitment, and a life of playfulness and spontaneity. As you continue to move forward, you learn to accept yourself with grace and ease, viewing yourself in a positive light, developing greater confidence, your talents, your gifts, your skills, and your attitudes and abilities.

You have the capacity to visualize yourself in the future, living up to your dreams with a sense of joy and accomplishment. Now, all of the things I have said, you do not have to fully remember if you don't want to, or you don't need to remember them, but your unconscious mind and the center core will continue to guide you like an internal coach, even when you are asleep at night. This will continue every moment of the hour, every hour of the day and night . . . every day and night of the week . . . every week of the month . . . every month of the year, every year for the rest of your life.

And as you continue to move forward, you begin to realize that life is a journey, and that the goal of living is not traveling to a specific destination, but the journey itself becomes your destination, and the quality, grace, and form in which your travel on this journey we call life, is in itself the goal of living, and in doing so you are writing the book of your own journey.

Now take a deep, deep breath again. Let the air out slowly, that's right, and I want you to know that you have the capacity to use this specific technique for self-hypnosis on your own, anytime you want to. In doing so, you will reinforce again and again this specific technique, boosting your ego and your whole self, as a whole person. And now I will slowly count together with you from three to one, and when we get to one, your eyes open and they come back to focus. You will be fully alert, awake, and oriented, knowing exactly where you are and what you need. You will know what you want to do after the session to function adaptively in the tasks of your daily living, knowing that you have the capacity to do this again on your own as you come out of this exercise of hypnosis.

[The patient is then realerted. This technique is followed by a brief discussion of the patient's experience and what it was like. This will allow him to ask questions or clarify certain issues.]

An Example of Positive Suggestions for Well-Being

Sheryl C. Wilson, Ph.D., and
Theodore X. Barber, Ph.D.
*Framingham, Massachusetts, and
Ashland, Massachusetts*

[The illustrative suggestions, as presented below, are an example of the kinds of positive suggestions that we have used in conjunction with many other suggestions in the treatment of smoking and obesity.]

The key to your success is confidence . . . confidence in yourself . . . confidence in your ability to do . . . whatever you truly want to do . . . confidence that you can and will accomplish your goals through the power of your own mind . . . the power of your own thoughts. What you tell yourself has the greatest of power over your life. . . . What you tell yourself determines whether you feel cheerful, or gloomy and worried . . . and the way you feel, whether you feel joyous, or sad and worried, determines, to a great extent, the health and well-being of your physical body. When you are bothered and unhappy, your body simply cannot function properly. What you tell yourself has an enormous impact on your life. . . . What you tell yourself ultimately determines what you are and are not able to do.

Now, tell yourself that your life is just starting, and that from this day on you will begin to live fully, moment by moment, and really appreciate and enjoy being alive each moment. Tell yourself that you will no longer worry unnecessarily, either about things that happened in the past or about what might happen in the future, *unless* there is something constructive you can do to change them . . . because the past and the future exist only in our thoughts . . . life exists only in each moment. If you spend your moments worrying about the past or the future, these moments, which are your life, pass you by. So, let yourself become deeply involved in each moment . . . deeply involved in everything that is happening around you . . . less conscious of yourself—and more at peace with yourself and with the world. Tell yourself that with each passing day, you will feel happier, more content, more joyous, more cheerful, because you choose to feel this way by controlling your thinking. And because you feel this way, life will be more fun. . . . you will enjoy each day. . . . and you will become more and more healthy, as your body functions easily in a tension free environment.

Day by day, let yourself feel more alive, more energetic, and at the same time, less tense, less nervous, less worried or anxious. Tell yourself that your mind and body are relaxed, calm, and you are at peace with the universe. And because you are calm and at ease, you will have greater energy and your mind will be clearer, and sharper, and more focused. Consequently, you will be able to see problems in perspective and handle them easily, efficiently, effectively, and confidently, without becoming bothered or tired out.

Above all, stop telling yourself that you can't do something which you want very much to do [such as stopping smoking or losing weight]. As long as you tell yourself you can't do it, you can't. Instead, tell yourself that even if it is difficult, you will be able to do it. When you tell yourself that you can and will, you have taken the first step towards accomplishing what you want to accomplish. And you will find that you can and will accomplish your goal. These things that you will now be telling yourself will begin to affect your life more and more. They will affect the way you feel about yourself, and the way you feel about your life, and consequently will affect every aspect of your life.

Positive Suggestions for Effective Living

T. X. Barber, Ph.D.
Ashland, Massachusetts

INTRODUCTION

I'm going to present positive suggestions for effective living that we use with a wide variety of clients. These suggestions are especially made to emphasize that life can be a little different, that people can live more effectively; they can enjoy more, they can see things in a better way, they can feel better about themselves. We have found these kind of general suggestions to be useful with a wide variety of individuals. We use them when we're trying to help someone stop smoking, when we're trying to help someone lose weight, when we're trying to help somebody who's depressed. Almost always somewhere in the sessions, we give some of these kinds of suggestions. We make a tape for each client which includes these suggestions, tailoring the tape to fit that person's needs. It should be clear that these are by no means the only kind of suggestions that we use in our therapeutic endeavors. We use a wide variety of suggestions and a wide variety of procedures and techniques.

POSITIVE SUGGESTIONS FOR EFFECTIVE LIVING

[We begin by asking the client to sit quietly, close the eyes, and begin to relax. Then we go on somewhat as follows.]

Let yourself begin to relax and feel calm, with peace of mind. Just feel yourself at ease, tranquil, at peace, relaxed. Take a deep breath, just take a deep breath, and as you let out the breath, feel all the tensions leaving, you feel at peace, calm, and at ease. All bothers, worries, anxieties, just fading away, just gone far away. There's lots of time, feel your mind at peace, calm, at peace, relaxed and at ease—that your mind becomes calm, your mind and body are at ease, peaceful and relaxed. Become more and more ready to retain those ideas that I will give you, as you will let them go deep in the back of your mind, and you will use them as you wish throughout your life. Every day, beginning now, you'll feel this way, calm, and at peace, while you're interacting, while you're working, while you're doing, you'll still feel peaceful, calm and at ease. Be able to enjoy life now, with peace of mind, at peace with the universe, a feeling of peace and tranquility. And a feeling of it's so good to be alive, with peace of mind. At peace with everyone around you, relaxed and calm and at ease, and enjoying every moment of living. Starting now, a feeling of underlying happiness, and peace of mind can be with you, can be with everyone in the universe, because we make it ourself, as we let our mind be calm, and relaxed. As we become more calm, and relaxed, you feel a kind of underlying energy also. The relaxation and calmness fits in with energy, vitality, being fully alive, at all times and in all situations. More and more, starting today, you'll feel more and more calm, at ease, and at peace, feeling so good to be alive. So good to be vibrant, energetic, vital, healthy, and strong, alive and vibrant, able to flow with everything around you, every day, and to enjoy every day, more and more, to enjoy every aspect of every day, as you feel peaceful, and calm, and at ease, with energy, with vitality, feeling the strength and energy in your being, feeling the flowing and vibrations and energetic flow of your life.

SEEING AND APPRECIATING THE WORLD ANEW

With peace of mind, calm, and at ease, being able to look out at every part of the universe, at every person around you, at every flower and tree and plant, grass and children, and in a new way, as you begin, starting now, to see the world in a new way, with a freshness, and wonder, and awe of a little child. You begin now to see the world again as you once did when you were an unspoiled child, and you can regain that capacity again, to see and appreciate everything freshly, and naively, in a simple way as you can begin once again to see things anew, fresh, wonderful, clean. Now you can begin to look at every sunrise as if it's the first sunrise you've ever seen, and every sunset, and you will see the colors, and the wonder, and the beauty surrounding you again, as if it's the first time you've ever seen it.

Starting now, every bird that you see will be as if you've never seen a bird before, as if you're a new child, and you're beginning again to look with wonder and amazement at the world around you. You see every bird in a new way, and every tree, and the leaves on the tree, and the seeds on the tree, and the bark on the tree, and the green leaves and the sun shining, and the grass around you, you'll be able to see it in a new way, fresh, with wonder and awe. As you gain the capacity to appreciate everything as you once did. Everything that's become stale

over the years will no longer be stale for you, as you become aware again that we can be the way we were once, looking at each thing as miraculous, as beautiful, as wonderful as the first time we ever saw them, when we were children.

As if we're here now, again, for the first time. As if we're here from another planet. We've just landed and we see the wonders of the earth, and we see the people on the earth, and we see their hair, and their face, and their nose, and their skin, and the wonders of their being and their mind. And we see each person as if we've never seen this person before. We see them fresh and new, and we see all the wonderful aspects of their being. And we look again at every cloud and we feel every breeze. And we begin to feel the air around us, and we become more aware of the oxygen we breathe, and we become more aware of the colors and the details of the flowers and the trees, and the people, and the buildings, and the grass, and the books, and everything that surrounds us, every day, every person, every child, every adult, every person, every animal, every plant—we see it anew. Experiencing each moment in a new way, starting now, as if a fog has been lifted, as if everything is becoming sparkling clean, as if we've come from another planet and we look around, and we see, and we feel, and we experience in a new way, starting now, and every day. And this feeling will grow more and more as time goes on—you will be able to feel more and more at ease and calm and peaceful with vibrant energy, enjoying every aspect of your being, feeling strong, healthy, with peace of mind, calm mind, body at ease, and yet very vibrant and energetic, looking at everything in a new way, as if you've been here now, just a short time. You're beginning to experience the world again, fresh, clean, sparkling new, new perceptions, aware of everything around you freshly, once again. And this will grow every day.

With this new way of looking at life, you'll find every day that your energy will increase and you'll feel so healthy, and you feel healthy, and free, you'll feel all the tensions will leave. You'll feel at ease and calm, and free as you become more aware of the blood circulating in your body, and the strength in your muscles, and the wonders of your strong, healthy being. You begin to feel that you're living, you're beginning to live more and more, growing every day, becoming more aware, more filled with energy, more vibrant. Starting today, you'll begin to feel that life is just beginning, that your potential for living a very good life is there, and it will increase and you'll become more aware of the potential, and you'll become aware of how you can enjoy life more and more every day. And you'll look forward to every coming day as another exciting day that you can live fully, growing, changing, maturing, healthy, strong, vibrant, and energetic. You will realize that you have the potential to be happy, strong and much greater than you thought. That you have vibrant energy, that you're able to flow with everything around you, to be able to flow and move with every person, every individual you meet. You'll be able to feel with them, be able to feel with every animal, and every plant, and every part of the earth.

From this day on, you'll begin to live fully, moment by moment, every day. You'll get so much out of every day, more and more, starting now, every day, every hour, every second, will become more and more exciting, full, enthralling, amazing. You'll become more and more aware of the wonders of your being, yourself, the earth, and everything around you. You'll become more and more deeply involved in everything that is happening around you, the people you meet, the tasks you meet, and the children that you see, and everything that comes into your life. You'll be aware, and become more and more involved, like a child, living fully, enjoying every moment, being unself-conscious, feeling free. You'll be able to make more and more activities, and something like an enjoyable game, that you can play, and dance, and move, and enjoy. And your activities will be the way they were when you were a child, free and unspoiled, at ease, enjoying, able to get into things, more and more, as you were once able to be creative, ingenious, able to make everything into a fun game. You'll again

remember how to play and to have fun, by your own creativity and imagination, using your own ingenuity, able to regain your lost spontaneity, your naturalness, your freshness — it will come out and you will feel at ease with it.

CREATING HAPPINESS THROUGH CHANGING YOUR THINKING

Starting now, more and more, you will realize that happiness, and unhappiness, are due to your own thoughts, the way you think about situations. You will be able to shift your thoughts, the way you think about situations. You will be able to shift your thoughts to the positive aspects, and look at the positive aspects of living, enjoy every day. You will become more and more aware that if life's situations are not the way you always want them, you will work to change them, without frustration, without anger, without being bothered. You will work to change things that are not the way you want them, but you will do it with a calm, peaceful mind, being at ease and at peace with the universe.

You will become more and more aware that everyone has problems in living, but you will also be aware that as you become more mature, that you can face problems with a calm mind, with strength and determination, to work to improve them. When you cannot change things, you will accept them calmly, you will be aware that anger and frustration do not help. You'll realize that life is too precious and too wonderful to waste it in being bothered over little things, little annoyances. Starting today, you will work to change anything that is changeable that you can change with peace of mind, without being bothered, without frustration, without anger. You will be less and less worried about the future, problems of the future, dangers of the future which will never occur anyway. Most of the things you worry about won't happen anyway. You'll let the worries go, you'll enjoy the day, you'll let yourself go, you'll enjoy yourself, as worries drop out of your life.

LIVING WITH EMPATHY, RESPECT, AND HARMONY

And day by day, you'll find yourself more and more successful in living at peace with the universe, with yourself, with everything around you, with no unnecessary worries. As each day passes, you will feel more and more at peace, more and more lively, feeling alive, enjoying each moment, living now, today, enjoying every day more and more as you let these thoughts go to the back of your mind. They will be more and more this way, as you let them guide your life. You'll become increasingly able to meet the responsibilities of your life, and will be able to determine for yourself what the truly necessary activities are in life.

With ever increasing frequency, you'll become more and more deeply interested and aware of other people, seeing that other people have problems, and you will be aware of their problems, able to help them, as you become less and less concerned about yourself, and more concerned about others, more and more aware of the beauty of other individuals around you. As each day passes, you'll find yourself more aware of and concerned with the feelings of others. You'll be deeply interested in the people around you, more and more forgetting yourself, not concerned especially about yourself, not self-conscious, giving others your undivided attention, really interested in them, their life, what they think and say, feeling good, and relaxed, and happy, and natural.

You'll realize that everyone around you is more or less insecure, and doesn't feel perfectly secure with others. And you'll realize more and more that others want you to like them, they want to feel that they matter, that they're important. And once you realize this, it becomes more and more a part of your being, to be able to help others to feel good about themselves. You'll realize more and more that they're struggling to be happy, to love, to feel good about themselves, and you'll be able to empathize and feel with other individuals, to feel with their feelings and insecurity, with their desires to be kind, to be good, to do things for others also.

You'll feel with other individuals. You'll become more and more empathic as time goes on. You'll be able to help others, to help others to feel good, to help others enjoy life. And as you help others enjoy life, you'll be able to enjoy it yourself, more and more as time goes on.

GENERAL SUGGESTIONS FOR WELL-BEING

And each day, as you wake up in the morning, you'll have an inner feeling of excitement, a feeling of energy and underlying joy, eager to get up from bed and to get going. You feel so good, refreshed, awake, relaxed, with energy, an inner feeling of joy, and well-being, when you wake up in the morning. And throughout the day, a feeling of joy of living, of vibrant energy, and as you wake up in the morning it will be so good to begin to plan for the new day ahead. You'll feel refreshed, strong and healthy, as you'll have slept calmly and at peace, knowing that each day as life goes on, you will enjoy it more and more as you mature and become more and more aware of every beauty, and every mystery and amazing thing that surrounds you, as you become more and more aware of the amazing nature of the universe and life.

SUGGESTIONS FOR SLEEP

And each night when you go to bed, you'll be at ease and relaxed, you'll feel relaxed and calm knowing that every day is another adventure. Even though some days will have problems and things we don't like, every day will be an adventure. Starting now, as you go to bed every night, you'll be calm, and at ease, your mind and your body will be calm, tranquil and relaxed. You'll be able to sleep calmly, at peace, able to sleep the way you did when you were a baby—so calm, so relaxed, so completely at peace. You'll sleep so well. You'll be able to sleep soundly, knowing in the back of your mind, that day by day you're beginning to live more fully, more deeply. As time goes on, you will live with more and more wisdom, and you'll let yourself sleep the way a baby does, when a baby feels good and very secure. You'll sleep very well, and very calm, and when you wake up in the morning, you'll be fully rested, very refreshed and at peace.

SUGGESTIONS ABOUT WORK

You'll be at ease with your life and everything around you. You will be so glad and so happy to have another day to live and enjoy, every day. And when you're at work, you'll be able to focus on a task, and become absorbed and involved in the task at hand. You'll be able to also become absorbed and involved with the people around you. When you work, you'll be able to work well, and efficiently, able to concentrate, able to enjoy your work and able to enjoy the task.

ENHANCING PRESENT AWARENESS

And able to enjoy everything you do—the people around you, the food as you eat moderately and with peace of mind. Able to enjoy the water you drink, with peace of mind, calm and at ease, enjoying every aspect of the beautiful, wonderful earth. You'll be able to enjoy everything you see and touch, and you'll become more aware of touch and the beauties of touching. You'll become more and more aware of the fragrances and the aromas, and everything around you. And you become more aware of all the beauties of your senses, as you see, and hear, and touch, and smell, and feel. And you become more and more aware of people around you. You become more and more aware of their amazing nature, of the depths of their being, of their strivings and hardships and problems.

REINFORCEMENT OF EARLIER SUGGESTIONS

And as you become more and more aware that your life is only beginning, and of the potentials for living beautifully that are there all the time, you'll be able to have more and more calm, peace of mind, awareness, and a feeling of strength and health and energy, that will grow as the days pass. Your mind will be at peace and calm. You'll feel strong and healthy, and very vibrant and alive, and that feeling will pervade your being. You'll become more aware of it, but it will be there, at the back of your mind, starting now, every day.

Every day will be as if it's the first day in your life. You'll be able, more and more, to feel as if it's so wonderful, as you see things again in a fresh new way, experiencing everything in a fresh new way—the way you may have experienced it when you were a child, as you begin to look at the grass and the flowers, and the trees and the birds. You become aware of their delicate textures. You become aware of the details of their being. You become aware of the breeze every time it touches you. You become aware of everything you do with your hands, and the strength of your hands, and the wonderful manipulative ability of your hands, and the wonderful abilities of your body. You become more and more aware of so many things that you've taken for granted, and you begin to see them in a new way, no longer stale, no longer something that you're used to, no longer something that you just don't even notice— fresh as if you've just come to this earth. Starting anew.

And you begin to meet the challenges of life every day with a calm mind, a calm, peaceful mind. So good to be alive, and with this calmness, and feeling the strength of your being, the vitality and health flowing through your being, you'll be able to change those things that can be changed every day. But those things that can't be changed, you will accept with calmness and peace of mind, knowing that life can be so beautiful, no matter what problems you may face.

You'll become more and more absorbed in your work, in the people around you, consumed very much about the wonders of being able to think, and feel, and talk, and plan, and imagine, and in the wonders of your mind and your being, and being able to use them in your work and with people around you. Loving every individual and every creature that you see, and being more and more aware of nature. Living more and more fully, more and more deeply, every day, starting now. And as you let these thoughts enter the back of your mind, you'll feel, starting now, more and more at peace, calm, and at ease, with peace of mind. Vibrant, strong, and energetic body, and peace of mind. You begin to feel more and more at ease and calm and alive, and you see everything in a fresh, new way, new, beautiful. Your life will become more and more wonderful and exciting. You'll be able to fulfill the many, many potentials that you have starting now, so let these thoughts now go to the back of your mind. Let them guide your life as you wish. Let them guide your life, starting now, as you wish. Let them go to the back of your mind, and now, as you wish, you can become more and more alert to everything around you, more and more ready to begin to live with vibrant energy, and with peace of mind, as you become now more alert and ready to open your eyes, beginning now to open your eyes.

Suggestions for Raising Self-Esteem

T. X. Barber, Ph.D.
Ashland, Massachusetts

1. First, I look for and emphasize all of the manifest and latent positive characteristics that I can observe about the client. I am always able to find many such attributes, and I sincerely tell the client about them at intervals in our discussion, using statements such as the following:
   - You have done so much [or worked so hard or struggled so much] in your life.
   - You have been able to overcome so many

difficulties [misfortunes, illnesses, rejections, deaths of loved ones].
   - You have helped many people in your life.
   - You did well in a very difficult situation.
   - You really care about people.
   - You have much empathy and love for others that you have not been able to express.
   - You are a kind person.
   - You have so much that you haven't begun to use—so much more love, so much more competence, so much more ability to be at ease, to enjoy life, to live fully.

   In addition to interspersing these kinds of statements in our discussions, I also include them as suggestions in the hypnosuggestive procedures; for example, after the client has been given repeated suggestions of deep relaxation, he or she may be given a series of suggestions on various topics, interspersed with suggestions that "Starting now, you can begin to focus more on your strengths and positive aspects . . . you can become more aware of your ability to overcome obstacles . . . your caring and love for people . . . your growing ability to be at ease and to enjoy life," and so on.

2. A second hypnosuggestive approach that aims to enhance self-esteem derives from the fact that clients with low self-regard have typically been criticized by parents or other significant individuals in their early lives, and they have incorporated the criticisms into their self-images. In the therapy sessions, we trace back the destructive criticisms the clients have received from parents, siblings, or other important people "You're dumb, stupid, ugly, clumsy, rotten, no good," etc.). After we have uncovered some or many of the origins of the low self-esteem, I proceed as follows in a hypnosuggestive session. I first give to the client (and indirectly to myself) suggestions for deep relaxation and then, when the client and I are both relaxed with eyes

closed, I speak to the client from my "inner self"—for instance, somewhat as follows:

We understand now why you have felt you were unattractive, unintelligent, and not likable. It is clear now that your mother had a tremendous amount of resentment and anger and was unable to love you or anyone else because of her own father, who degraded her and made her feel totally unlikable and worthless. It's clear that *you were too young to understand* why your mother constantly put you down and screamed at you *and made you feel there was something wrong with you. You can now see how your negative feelings about yourself were due to negative suggestions you received constantly* from your mother, who was negative about everything and everyone because of her own misery. *Now you can begin breaking through the negative suggestions you have received, you can begin coming out of the negative hypnosis you have been in for so many years, and you can begin to be your true self that has been held down for so long. You can see more and more clearly that as long as you were negatively hypnotized and believed you were stupid, ugly, and no good, you reacted to events and people around you in a nonconfident, afraid way, which tended to confirm your own beliefs. You can now begin to let go of these negative suggestions and begin to be your own true self, realizing more and more each day that you are a good, kind, loving, and lovable person. Each day you can become less and less afraid, more and more at ease, more and more able to enjoy life and to be your true self.* [emphasis added]

3. As part of the hypnosuggestive approach to raising self-esteem, I make additional cassette tapes for the clients. These tapes, which are made when the client and I are in my office, begin with suggestions for deep relaxation, followed by specific suggestions that aim directly or indirectly to enhance self-esteem by guiding the clients to focus on their underlying strengths, virtues, and positive qualities. The clients are asked to listen to the cassette tape at home once a day during the forthcoming week, to let themselves relax deeply, and to let the ideas "go deep into your mind." Although these tapes are individualized for each client, they typically emphasize positive aspects of the client that have been neglected or suppressed and that can be released and expanded. Examples of the kinds of suggestions that are included in the hypnosuggestive tapes are as follows:

You have much caring and concern and love for others that you hold down and keep within you . . . You can begin now to let out these good feelings . . . allowing the kind, caring, good feelings to flow out to others . . . You can begin more and more to be your true self as you release your warmth and empathy toward others.

Starting now, you can be more and more aware of your true self that is being released, and you can stop criticizing yourself . . . You can stop blaming yourself for what you did that you should not have done or what you did not do that you should have done, and you can forgive yourself as you forgive others . . . You can be as kind to yourself as you are to others . . . as loving to yourself as you are to others . . . You can stop criticizing and blaming yourself, and you can be free—free, more and more, to be your true self.

Starting now, you can more and more allow yourself to be the person you can be . . . appreciating again and grateful again to be able to see, to hear, to smell, to touch, to be alive . . . Appreciating again as if it's your first day on earth, as if you've never felt the sun before, never heard a bird sing, never smelled a flower before . . . Grateful to be able to touch the rain and a stone, to hear the laughter of children and the sound of the sea, to smell the grass and appreciate tasty food, to see the colors of the earth and the stars . . . Appreciating again the strength and power in your body . . . Feeling the energy and health vibrating and flowing through your being . . . Feeling again the excitement and enthusiasm and the feeling of aliveness that has been suppressed for so long . . . more and more ready to enjoy, to have fun, to play and laugh and sing . . . More and more feeling good to be you and to be alive. [emphasis added]

Barnett's Yes-Set Method of Ego-Strengthening

Edgar A. Barnett, M.B., B.S.
Kingston, Ontario, Canada

INDICATIONS

This method of ego-strengthening is recommended following the use of other methods to enhance the patient's esteem; otherwise, patients with minimal self-esteem will usually fail to respond positively to step two and further work will be required. This method may be valuable in facilitating greater acceptance of one's own feelings and in promoting assertiveness and self-regard. Ideomotor finger signals should be established prior to using this method. (*Ed.*)

STEP ONE.   State a belief in humanity's worth and importance, seeking the patient's affirmation of this belief.

"Now, I want your unconscious mind to listen very carefully. And when the deepest part of your mind is listening carefully, your 'yes' finger can lift to signal me. [Pause] Good. And keep listening very carefully.

"I believe that every human being is unique and important. Do you agree?" [If the patient answers "no," exploration about this may be done with ideomotor signaling. Another approach is to say, "Even though you do not agree with me, do you believe me when I say that *I* believe that every human being is important and unique?"]

STEP TWO.   Persuade the patient to accept *himself* (herself) as an important and worthwhile human being.

"I believe that you, (patient's name), are unique and special—just as unique and important as any other human being. Do you agree?" [This question will typically be met with considerable thought and delay.]

When the patient answers "yes," ask: "Is there any part of your inner mind that does not entirely agree with me?" [This is a double check for a hidden ego state or part of the personality that is still negative. If such a part exists, undiscovered, it may sabotage the ego-strengthening suggestions.]

STEP THREE.   Help the patient to accept his/her feelings, and establish a yes-set. Then, let go of old, negative feelings.

"I know that all human beings have uncomfortable feelings as well as comfortable feelings, and I know that you have had feelings that are uncomfortable. I know that you have had feelings of sadness, like any other human being. If you agree with that, your 'yes' finger will float up to signal me. And you have had feelings of happiness, like any other human being. If you agree with that, again your 'yes' finger can lift. And you have had feelings of anger, just like any other person, have you not? And feelings of love, just like any other human being. [Wait for signal, and if necessary, ask, "Have you not?" or "Haven't you?"] Feelings of fear, just like any other human being. And feelings of safety and security, just like anybody else."

"Now, all of those feelings are normal, human feelings and you don't need to feel ashamed or guilty or embarrassed about any of them. I believe that you have the right to all of your feelings, whether or not they are unpleasant. Do you agree?" [If the answer is "no," seek to determine the reason. For example, perhaps anger is regarded as an unacceptable feeling. Reason with the patient, justifying the value of any type of feeling he or she regards as problematic.]

"I believe that you have as much right to your feelings of sadness as any other human being. If you agree, your 'yes' finger will float up again. [Pause] And you have as much right to your feelings of happiness as any other human being, do you not? [Pause] And you have as much right to your feelings of anger as anyone else; as much right to your feelings of love; as much right to your feelings of fear and to your safe feelings. Do you agree?"

"It is your privilege to have those feelings, and you don't need to feel guilty, ashamed or embarrassed about any of your normal human emotions. You have a right to keep them for as long as you need them. But you also have a right to let them go when you don't need them any more. And if you agree with all of this, your 'yes' finger will float up again." [Pause]

"And any of these old, out-of-date, uncomfortable feelings that you've been carrying around and which you no longer need can be let go. And if you feel that you are letting go of them right now, your 'yes' finger will float up. [Pause] And you can stay free of those old, out-of-date, uncomfortable feelings. You can finish letting go of them now. [Pause] You have a right to those feelings of hurt if you need them back; you have a right to have your feelings of anger back if you need them back at some time; you have a right to have your feelings of fear back any time you need them. But, when you don't need them any longer, you can feel happy, you can feel loving, and you can feel safe and secure."

"Now, I would like your unconscious mind to make a commitment that you will respect (patient's name) always. By that, I mean that you will respect his/her feelings. And if your unconscious mind is willing to do that, your 'yes' finger will float up. [Wait for 'yes' signal.] You'll like him/her because he/she has human feelings and a right to those feelings. And because you like him/her, you will listen to his/her feelings and not put him/her down for having them. He/she has a right to have them. And you will find ways of helping him/her to feel comfortable—good ways that are helpful. Never put him/her down for having uncomfortable feelings, for he/she has a right to them. Listen to them, respect them, like them. I want you to always protect him/her, as you have been doing in the best way that you could; but now, you have better ways of protecting him/her. Listen to his/her feelings. You've got better ways. You've found better ways. Always look for better ways to take care of (patient's name)."

"And don't allow people to put him/her down. He/she is just as good as anybody else.

No one has the right to put him/her down, so protect him/her from anybody who wishes to do that. Take care of him/her at all times. In fact, I want you to take care of him/her, but also to care for him/her. Care for (patient's name), love him/her. If your unconscious mind is willing to do all these things, your 'yes' finger will lift."

"And as you do all of these things, some wonderful things will happen: you feel very safe, very secure. It feels like you have the answer to so many things which used to puzzle you. You will feel so safe, so secure, that you will no longer let things get you down because you know how to handle them. You always did know, but you did not know you knew. And use the knowledge. You can use it to the best of your ability. And with that good knowledge, you can do the things that you really want to do. You will be able to do them because you feel friends with yourself. It's a nice thing to feel good friends with yourself. And if you are feeling friends with yourself right now, your 'yes' finger will lift." [pause]

"Continue to be friends with yourself. Continue to listen to yourself, hear yourself, and give yourself good advice. And take the good advice that you give yourself. And as you feel very good about yourself, I am going to ask you, please, to know that you don't need to put anybody else down. You don't have to put anybody else down, because you feel that you can respect other people, and respect them as having their problems and being human, just like you."

"And because you are feeling so good, today can be a very good day. I would like you to see yourself having a very good day. When you can see that, let your 'yes' finger lift. [Pause] Good. You feel so good. There's a nice, calm, relaxed, smiling feeling all through you. And keep that feeling. Keep it each day. Feel good about (patient's name), being the person you are, liking (patient's name), and taking care of him/her."

"I want you to know that you can remember what you need to remember at all times, and forget what you need to forget, because your unconscious mind will always remember everything that we have talked about. If that is understood, your 'yes' finger will lift. [Pause] It will keep all of the suggestions that we have agreed upon, so that your conscious mind does not have to bother with trying to remember all the many things that we have discussed. Your conscious mind can leave all of the remembering to your deep, inner, unconscious mind, so that when your open your eyes, your conscious mind can be free, to think about other things." [Awaken and distract the patient.]

Ego-Enhancement: A Five-Step Approach

Harry E. Stanton, Ph.D.
Hobart, Tasmania, Australia

INTRODUCTION

Opportunities to tailor the approach to handle specific problems occur within each of these five steps. Due to its flexibility, this approach to ego-enhancement may be used to help patients with a wide variety of presenting problems. Approximately 85% of my patients find that the ego-enhancement approach affords considerable relief. This is true whether they want to learn how to relax, overcome anxiety, sell more insurance, kick a football farther, or let go of habits such as smoking, overeating, and alcohol abuse. As it is basically gentle and nonintrusive in nature, ego-enhancement is a technique unlikely to cause harm and would seem capable of effective use with most patients finding difficulty coping with their life situations. However, as I have not employed the approach with patients suffering with severe character disorders, I am unable to comment on whether it would be similarly helpful and noninjurious in such a context.

THE GENERALIZED EGO-ENHANCEMENT TECHNIQUE

The technique embraces the following steps:

1. Physical relaxation induced by concentration upon the breath, following it as it flows in and out, letting go tension, tightness, and discomfort with each breath out. Patients are encouraged to develop a detached attitude, as if they are watching someone else breathing.

   The simple following-of-the-breath physical relaxation technique permits patients to "let go" specific problems, unwanted thoughts, and physical discomforts which have been discussed before induction is commenced. Thus, it serves as both the first step in trance induction and the commencement of therapy.

2. Mental calmness encouraged through imagining the mind as a pond, the surface of which is completely still, like a mirror. Thoughts are watched in a detached way, being allowed to drift through above the water, attention then being brought back to further contemplation of the water's stillness.

   In the "pond" mental relaxation step, patients may be encouraged to imagine the area above the water as their conscious minds and that below as their unconscious minds. Accordingly, they have the power to "drop into" the pond of their mind anything they desire. This may be formulated in terms of a trance-deepening suggestion, with the patient imagining a beautiful stone representing, say, mental calmness sinking down and down, deeper and deeper, until it comes to rest at the bottom of the pond. It is then suggested that the patient's mind locks around this calmness, a calmness which is to become a permanent part of his or her life. The same procedure may be followed with other stones, each one representing a specific suggestion relevant to the particular patient, and each one assisting the deepening of the trance as the stone sinks "down and down, deeper and deeper." As a normal practice, mental calmness, physical relaxation, confidence, and happiness comprise the "stones," but these may be replaced with others such as concentration, mental control, and healing where it seems appropriate. The "pond," then, provides a basic framework within which considerable flexibility is possible.

3. Disposing of "rubbish" as subjects imagine themselves "dumping" mental obstacles, such as fears, doubts, worries, and guilts, down a chute from which nothing can return. Physical obstacles, such as cigarettes and excess weight, may also be disposed of in this way.

4. Removal of a barrier representing everything that is negative in the lives of subjects. Embodied in this barrier are self-destructive thoughts, forces of failure and defeat, mental obstacles, and self-imposed limitations, everything which is preventing subjects from employing their lives as they would like. This barrier is destroyed through use of the imagination.

   The corridor, rubbish chute, and barrier metaphors may also be used to meet individual needs. Smokers may wish to discard their cigarettes, alcoholics their alcohol, and the obese may care to strip away their unwanted weight. Patients may also generate their own variations, this being one of the main benefits of the approach. . . . Similarly, they often put into the barrier negative aspects of their personalities which they have not mentioned in pre-trance discussion. However, because they feel these are holding them back, they decide for themselves that they should go into the barrier. Other specific negative influences which appear to be interfering with individuals' enjoyment of life are placed in the barrier by the therapist.

5. Enjoyment of a special place where subjects feel content, tranquil, and still. In this place they "turn off" the outside world. Once

patients find their special place, it is suggested that they think of themselves as they want to be, imagining themselves behaving the way they want to behave, and "seeing" themselves achieving the success they wish to achieve. Sometimes particular images to meet the expressed needs of patients will be suggested; on other occasions patients may generate their own material.

The "special place" visualization is a common aspect of many hypnotherapeutic treatments. One particularly useful pattern is to have patients imagining themselves going through a door which they can shut behind them to exclude the rest of the world. Suggestions may then be made that, in this place, they will be able to get into contact with the unconscious part of their minds which will then solve any problems they might have. One aspect of such solutions will be that things which have worried or upset them in the past will simply drop out of their lives as if they never existed. Because these things have now become so unimportant, patients will probably forget they were ever disturbed in this way. At this point, use may be made of an Ericksonian approach to the encouragement of amnesia by reminding patients of the frequency with which, in the past, they have forgotten people and possessions that, at one time, were very important to them. Once this importance has faded, so too does memory, a process that can take place with those things which used to worry and upset them.

As it is usually preferable for patients to be left free to choose their own special place, they can be told that when they pass through the door, a place will be waiting. This could be somewhere from their childhood where they enjoyed themselves while growing up, or perhaps a fantasy place, maybe even a comfortable emptiness. Wherever it is, beach, garden, lovely room, or a comfortable bed, in it the patient will feel happy, content, tranquil, and still.

Suggestions for Modifying Perfectionism

D. Corydon Hammond, Ph.D.
Salt Lake City, Utah

INDICATIONS

Perfectionism may be a part of many clinical syndromes, including depression (and low esteem), anxiety disorders, obsessive-compulsive disorder and personality, and type-A behavior. These are direct and cognitively oriented suggestions aimed at modifying perfectionistic tendencies. Cognitive, Adlerian and rational-emotive therapists may find these suggestions particularly compatible with their approaches. Many of these suggestions are for patients who are caught up in overcompetitiveness and striving for perfection. Those with a birth order as the oldest child and who feel that they must be first, best or superior, and second children who are caught up in the Avis Complex ("We're second, so we try harder.") may benefit from such suggestions. Some of the other suggestions may foster self-acceptance of one's humanness, despite making mistakes.

PERFECTIONISM, SUPERIORITY, AND OVERCOMPETITIVENESS

I wonder if you may be one of those people who feel that they can't settle for less than perfection, and perhaps even that you may as well not even try if you can't do something perfectly. Many people make themselves miserable by striving to be superior, the best, the first, or perfect. They become enslaved, striving for the mistaken goal of perfection and superiority. They mistakenly believe that the only thing worth being in life is a star—above other people, the best, the first, or perfect. That is a belief that will bring misery. Expecting perfection from yourself and others leads to disappointment and depression because we are all human and imperfect. When we have a goal of

perfection, we will just automatically feel inadequate, because we can't reach such a goal.

I think, however, that you can be pleasantly relieved, when you change your goal from perfection, to being competent and making a contribution. Life can be so much more enjoyable, so much more rewarding, when our goal is simply to do things well, and just keep gradually improving. I want you to appreciate the value, the benefit, of accepting yourself as imperfect, but in the process of growing, in the process of gradually learning and getting better and better.

PATIENCE WITH GRADUAL IMPROVEMENT AND CREDITING ONESELF

The natural process of change is generally a process of taking a series of steps. We roll over and learn to crawl before we learn to walk, or run, or ride a bicycle. We learn addition before we progress to multiplication or algebra. The natural order of things, is gradual growth and improvement. We don't have to be perfect, and certainly not overnight. We change by gradually walking up a series of steps; no one can leap up a whole staircase, far less leap a tall building in a single bound. We are human, and it is unrealistic to expect ourselves to be superhuman. And different people make progress in different ways. So I'd like to suggest that you be patient with yourself, because you're unique, and you have your own unique process of growth. And I'd like you to really enjoy, each small improvement, each small change. Experience changes fully, and take credit for the improvements and gains you make. I'd like you to just appreciate how *you* make changes, and not become impatient with how fast those changes take place.

CHANGING YOUR GOAL TO COOPERATION AND CONTRIBUTING

And as you accept the goal of being competent, and making a *contribution, instead of being perfect (superior), your relationships with people will become more gratifying, more harmonious.* People who strive to be the best or superior to others come to view the world as an unpleasant, competitive, dog-eat-dog jungle. People dislike them.

When your goal is to be *better than* others, you're forever competing, and continually insecure, because it's impossible to measure who's the best. But you can free yourself, from the tyranny of trying to be *better than* others. It can be so gratifying, so refreshing, to simply have the goal of making a contribution *to* other people. When you simply strive to improve, and make a contribution in life, people become friends, allies and confederates, instead of threatening competitors; we feel a fraternity and bond with people. The goal is now *cooperation*, not competition. And if your unconscious mind is willing to change your inner goal to growing, improving and making a contribution, instead of perfectionism and competitiveness, your "yes" finger will float up to signal me. [Await a response, and after 20 seconds if an affirmative response has not occurred, add, "Or your 'no' finger can float up if your unconscious mind is not willing to change your inner goal." If the latter is the case, ideomotor exploration may be employed concerning roadblocks to letting go of old, mistaken goals.]

What a relief! To be free of the burden of trying to be the best, or perfect (or superior). It's so much easier, *so* much more satisfying, *so natural*, to accept yourself as human, and in the process of improving and growing. No need to compete with anyone—there's no way to measure who's the best anyway.

And I wonder if you'll be surprised, at how attracted you *will now become*, how enthusiastic you'll become, about the goal of cooperating and working together and making a contribution, instead of trying to be perfect (or superior). And I wonder if you'll notice how spontaneously, how automatically you can find yourself cooperating with people, and thinking in terms of making a contribution. It will feel like such a relief—like becoming a member of the human family. And because your uncon-

scious mind has altered this inward, basic goal, you will find that all this will occur so easily, without your even thinking. And you can celebrate your humanness, and enjoy having the courage to be imperfect.

REFRAMING MISTAKE MAKING

We've all made mistakes. And I'm sure that you can recall a time when you made a mistake—a mistake that taught you something. Even though it may have been unpleasant, you can recall making a mistake that you learned something valuable from, can you not? [Negative to discharge resistance] [Assuming you get an affirmative head nod, you can proceed. Otherwise, you may enlist an unconscious search for such a time, with an ideomotor signal when such a memory is identified.]

And as you recall that memory, I want you to begin to appreciate the fact, that without having made mistakes like that, you would have never learned and progressed. As a kid, did you ever touch a light plug and get a shock that really kind of jolted you? Many of us had that experience, and we learned something very important from that, even though it was a very unpleasant jolt! And similarly, it's because you've had the pain of a burn, that you learned to be cautious with fire.

Your imperfect mistakes, have been *perfect* opportunities for a wealth of learnings, that have formed an *indispensable* foundation to build on. So don't be mistaken about mistakes; the more unpleasant it is, the more pleasant will be your learning.

And yet so many people are afraid to try, for fear they'll make mistakes. And when they do make a mistake, they try to cover it up for fear people will think less of them, or think they're weak or stupid. But I'd like you to appreciate the fact, that mistakes are not only tolerable, but are actually desirable, because we learn through making mistakes.

Have you ever been around someone who was afraid to admit they had made a mistake? [Brief pause for response] They're very tense and defensive, so they find it hard to grow and improve. What I'd like you to consider is the benefit, of having the courage to be imperfect.

I wonder if you've had the experience, I certainly have, of finding that when you see people make an error or mistake, that you can actually feel relieved, to see that *they're human too*. Most people feel more willing to have a relationship with someone who seems human, rather than perfect. And if someone does criticize you for making an honest mistake, it's probably because *they* are insecure.

I wonder if you might even find it an interesting growth experience, to tell friends about some mistakes you make, or about mistakes that you have made, instead of trying to hide and cover them up. In fact, wouldn't it be fascinating, as a way of giving you practice allowing yourself to be human and imperfect, if your unconscious mind were to arrange for you to make some minor mistakes? And while your unconscious mind may take a kind of pleasure in letting you be human, I don't know at first, if it will make you a little nervous, or if it will, in some strange sort of way, seem more fun and almost amusing, to find that you *can* make an occasional silly mistake. Or maybe it will just give you the feeling of, "Welcome to the human race." But deep inside, you can begin to get the feeling, that it *really is all right* to be human, and to make some mistakes, so that you can learn and grow more rapidly.

Suggestions Derived from Rational-Emotive Therapy

Harry E. Stanton, Ph.D.
Hobart, Tasmania, Australia

INDICATIONS

These suggestions may facilitate cognitive-perceptual changes and be particularly helpful with patients who operate on the kinds of irrational assumptions targeted for change in rational-emotive therapy. Individual paragraphs (themes) may be regarded as modules for use with patients who have particular difficulties. (*Ed.*)

SUGGESTIONS

Day by day you will increasingly do what you enjoy doing rather than what other people think you ought to do in life. It would be nice if other people approved of what you do, but it is not necessary to your happiness for you to be loved and approved of by almost everyone for almost everything you do. You know what it is that makes you happy, that makes life enjoyable and this is what you should do.

As each day passes, you will become increasingly competent as you try to better your own performance. Do things because they bring pleasure and rewards, but give up the notion of trying to be thoroughly competent, adequate and achieving. Try to *do* rather than do *perfectly*. Accept failures as undesirable but not dreadful. You are a worthwhile, valuable person because you exist as a human being, not because of how well you do something. You are worthwhile in yourself, quite apart from your performances.

Day by day you will find it easier and easier to accept that you are a fallible human being, and therefore, likely to make mistakes. You will be able to learn from your mistakes and be increasingly successful as a result. Because you can accept that as a human being you are fallible, you will find it completely unnecessary to blame yourself for anything, for self-blame is completely unhelpful and destructive.

When conditions are not as you would like them to be, you will be able, wherever possible, to change them for the better. When for the moment, things cannot be changed, you will be able to accept them calmly, realizing that anger and frustration would be making you miserable for nothing. It would be nice if things were going the way you want, but if they are not, it is not terrible, horrible or catastrophic. You will be able to accept the situation and determinedly work to improve it.

Day by day you will become more and more successful in feeding positive, happy thoughts into your mind. You will accept more and more strongly that you are responsible for your emotions, that you decide whether to be happy or miserable. It is not external events that make you happy or sad, but the attitude you take to these events. Your misery is caused by your irrational thinking and the negative sentences you speak to yourself.

Gradually you will find less and less need to worry about future problems and dangers, many of which are quite imaginary. You will be able to determine the real dangers about the things you fear and see what the probabilities are of their actually occurring. Most of the things we worry about never happen, so we make ourselves miserable for nothing. Day by day you will find yourself becoming more and more successful in overcoming such pointless worry.

As each day passes, you will become increasingly able to face up to the difficulties and responsibilities of life. You will be able to determine for yourself what the truly necessary activities of life are, and, no matter how unpleasant they may be, you will be able to perform them unrebelliously and promptly. As you do so, you will feel an ever growing sense of happiness and accomplishment.

With every passing day, the irrationalities of the past will influence your life less and less. You will reject more and more strongly the idea that the past is all important and you will realize very powerfully that just because something once strongly affected you, there is no reason why it should continue to do so indefinitely. You are a different person now from the one you were in the past and you can now successfully cope with things which may have previously upset you.

With ever increasing frequency, you will be able to accept people and things as they are, seeing that compromise and reasonable solutions are necessary. You will be able to give up the notion that it is catastrophic if perfect solutions to life's problems are not found.

As each day passes, you will find yourself making definite attempts to become vitally absorbed in some persons or things outside yourself. To make our lives happy and fulfilling we need a purpose, and you will be able to find such a purpose for yourself.

Suggestions for Raising Self-Esteem

Helen H. Watkins, M.A.
Missoula, Montana

INDICATIONS

The following suggestions were prepared for use with patients with low self-esteem. The suggestions should be given following hypnotic induction and deepening. These suggestions may be used in an office setting. It is also recommended that the session be tape recorded for later use by the patient at home. The suggestions labeled as "night tape" are for use by the patient immediately before going to sleep. It may be helpful in the "night tape" to use a lengthier induction-deepening process that may include such things as progressive relaxation and going down a long staircase for deepening. During the deepening process, the author also suggests, "For the present, you will not fall asleep, but will listen to the sound of my voice until the tape is finished." The "day tape" suggestions are for use in tape-assisted self-hypnosis during the day. (*Ed.*)

NIGHT TAPE SUGGESTIONS

THE SAFE ROOM.   You can see that in front of us is a hallway. And as you look down the hallway, you can see a door. That door is a door to a room of your own choosing, in which you will feel safe and comfortable. [Pause] As we come closer to the end of the hallway, you can see the door more clearly. This door will keep out all the negative messages, the words, the behaviors, that you perceived from your world as a child, which made you feel bad about yourself. There's no room here for such negative messages.

Look at the door very carefully, [pause] even the doorknob. And know that this is a room of your own choosing, in which you will feel safe, and comfortable. Early positive messages and experiences enter, but all negative messages must stay outside. And now I want you to open that door, and then close the door behind you. And look around that room, this safe room, that you can visit any time you wish, by just closing your eyes. Look around, and enjoy what you see there. [pause]

Now I'd like you to sit, or lie down someplace in that safe room, wherever you will be comfortable. And listen carefully to whatever I say to you. There is a life energy inside of you. It is unique to you. It is your life energy, not anyone else's. It is the energy from whence you came. Life energy has only one purpose: to help you reach your potential as an organism. It is protective; it is healing. And since it is healing and protective, it is therefore loving. I want you to experience that life energy of yours, by feeling a light above your head, a light from which issues warm streams of energy, warm streams of energy, that surround you like an imaginary cocoon, soft and pliable, that lets you move about, that protects you, like a cocoon.

Feel that life energy also penetrating every cell of your body, surrounding you, and penetrating you. This is your life energy. It represents your true self, your natural self, your essence — whatever you wish to call it. It belongs to no one but to you. It is protective; it is healing, and therefore loving. Within that life energy are no negative messages; they cannot exist there. Feel that positive life energy, coursing through every cell of your body, surrounding and protecting you. That life energy has sometimes been expressed within you, perhaps as a still inner voice, that many of us ignore; words of wisdom inside of us that we don't always listen to, but are really there to protect us. That still inner voice is a nurturing part of you. And that nurturing part is an

entity, that exists because it becomes a kind of spokesman, for that life energy, for that healing energy, for that essence, which is you.

That nurturing part of you is capable of healing, both mind, and body. It is capable of helping, healing those parts of you that are not happy, that don't feel good about themselves. And it is possible for that nurturing self, to seek out other parts of you, that are not happy, and help them, help them become happier, help them become more worthwhile in their own eyes, and most of all, help them to feel loved from the inside, not from the outside world.

To help this process, it is worthwhile for you to think about that nurturing part within you, and perhaps to visualize that process going on, as you go about your daily business. Visualize the process of that nurturing part helping out those, that are not so happy inside, in a way that comes naturally to you, in your mind's eye. And as you continue to do this, thinking about the nurturing part, you will stimulate that aspect of you, and it will become stronger within you.

As you go to sleep tonight, you will have a healing dream, [pause] a healing dream to heal mind, body and spirit. And that healing, nurturing part will know, what you need in a healing dream. And that healing dream will not only have an effect tonight in your dream, but will affect you during the day as time goes by. And as healing progresses, you will come to feel better about yourself, stronger, more self-confident, and therefore happier. And when you feel happier and better about yourself, the world will respond to you in more positive ways.

And now, in a moment I'm going to sign off, and you will find that you will drift into a natural sleep pattern, and when you awaken in the morning, you will be aroused just naturally from this sleep pattern. I'm signing off now. Sweet dreams. [Silence. Tape is left open-ended, allowing the patient to drift off to sleep.]

DAY TAPE SUGGESTIONS

Allow yourself to drift and float, drift and float. And listen to the sound of my voice, and what I'm going to be saying to you. Self-esteem is the way you think and feel about yourself. The more positive the feelings, the higher your self-esteem; the more negative the feelings, the more negative your self-esteem. Self-esteem affects the quality of your life. A high self-esteem can make you feel productive, capable, lovable, happy. Low self-esteem makes you feel unproductive, miserable, worthless, incompetent, unlovable. With low self-esteem, you may even be outwardly jovial, or you may act confident to the world, or you may be highly successful in your work. But inside, you cringe and say to yourself, "Boy, if that world out there only knew what I'm really like, they wouldn't want to get to know me. They'd probably just go away." And so you carefully polish up your cover, your facade, and stay on the alert, for fear you will be found out. What a miserable way to live. How do people get this way?

Well, let's take a trip, through your brain, where all of those notions are stored. Think of an area in your brain, containing all the experiences you have ever had in your lifetime. That area is not exactly a depository of *what* happened, but of what you learned from those experiences; that is, how you perceived them. For example, suppose at the age of two you spilled a glass of milk and you heard someone say, "Bad girl or bad boy!" From this experience, you might get the idea that *you* are bad, even though the person saying that did not mean that exactly. They were just upset at having to clean up the milk, and didn't want you to do it again.

But as a child, you can't help but think concretely; that is, literally. You conclude, "I am bad, or worthless, or I can't ever make it," or whatever that negative idea is. Therefore, the brain is always full of distortions from child thinking, which is just normally concrete and literal.

Check out that brain right now. Maybe you can see, or hear, or sense the messages that are there. They may not all be negative, but they are always a product of child thinking; that is, the perception of the child. I'll be silent for a

little bit, while you check out those messages from the past. [Pause for about one minute.]

Now let's take a trip into your past, and find out what faces go with those messages. Imagine that you are sitting in a pink compartment on a train, looking out the window. As you look around your compartment, for you are the only person sitting there, you notice that the compartment is pink all the way around, the ceiling, the walls, the furniture, so that you can almost feel the pinkness. The pinkness is strangely relaxing. That train will take you on a round trip into your past, all the way back to your birth, and then return to the present.

Now the train begins to move along, and pick up speed. But you have a control switch in front of you, and by moving that switch, you can control the speed of that train. You can even stop if you wish, to get a better view of some incident you want to study more carefully. Perhaps you want to look at the people in those scenes, and understand them better, and yourself. See them as human beings, with human faults, limitations and emotions. No one can be perfect, neither you nor I, nor any of the people in those scenes. In a while, I will sign off, so that you can go on this trip at your own speed. When the train reaches birth, take in a deep breath, and get in touch with the energy from whence you came. That energy from whence you came is your essence. It is protective, it is loving, it is your life energy, and it belongs only to you. Feel its power, its warmth, its protectiveness. Feel it as warm streams of energy, surrounding and penetrating you. It will give you strength on the trip back.

From birth, the train will head back on its return trip over the same scenery. However, on the return trip, you will be able to change your attitude toward these scenes, if you wish. You can even open a window and do something to change the event, [pause] because on that return trip, you are full of life energy, which helps you to be more confident and self-assured. Take the time you need for your trip; make it meaningful to you. Remember, you don't have to accept any more of those negative messages from the past. [pause] You can leave them back there. [Pause] When you return to the present, take a deep breath, and slowly open your eyes to become alert. Have a good, meaningful trip for yourself. Remember, you deserve it. This is [therapist's name] signing off. [Stop speaking and leave the tape open-ended.]

Suggestions to Facilitate Problem Solving

Don E. Gibbons, Ph.D.

INTRODUCTION

It is my own belief that the process of incubation may be facilitated by direct suggestion—if only because the subject is thereby made more confident that an effective solution will be forthcoming. At the conclusion of an induction, the following suggestions may be given.

SUGGESTIONS

In the coming days and weeks, your thoughts will often turn to the consideration of important decisions you have to make, and important problems for which you have as yet found no solution. Even when you are not consciously thinking about these topics, your mind will continue to deal with them so that, when your attention returns to them once more, you are going to be surprised and delighted at how many potentially useful ideas you are able to come up with; and some of these ideas are even likely to catch you by surprise at times, emerging into your awareness while you are thinking of something else. They might even enter your dreams at night, or you might wake up with some of these new ideas in mind; but regardless of how they make their appearance, they are going to be very helpful and beneficial to you.

Of course, You will always try to make sure that you have sufficient information on which to base any final decisions, and you will always want to check out these new ideas to make sure that they are practical, just as you would check out information from any other source. You will also continue to be aware that sometimes the best decision is a decision to wait or to secure additional information before acting. But nevertheless, you are going to be surprised and pleased at how much more clearly and creatively you are going to be able to think, and at how much more confidently and effectively you will be able to deal with the issues and problems which lie before you.

The Serenity Place

D. Corydon Hammond, Ph.D.
Salt Lake City, Utah

INDICATIONS

This is a permissive, indirect ego-strengthening method designed to increase patient coping abilities. It is useful with anxious patients, for patients with premenstrual syndrome, and with patients who are bright, insightful and self-directed. Along with induction and deepening, this procedure may be tape recorded for use in tape-assisted self-hypnosis. The open-ended conclusion allows the patient to remain in a deep trance for as long as needed, which can often produce profound feelings of calm and tranquility. Encourage the patient to allow the image to spontaneously appear, rather than searching consciously for the most ideal place. The process for arriving at the serenity place may be individualized, for example, through taking an elevator down and finding the special place when a door opens, floating there on clouds, or simply finding oneself there. Present the suggestions slowly and restfully. Commas are placed to suggest brief pauses.

SUGGESTIONS

Now, as you continue to relax, more and more deeply, just allow yourself to float across time and space. And in a moment, your unconscious mind is going to suddenly take you, to a very special place, that's associated with tremendous feelings of peacefulness, and tranquility, and safety, and happiness. It may be a place you've been before, or some special place that you find yourself in for the first time. And you can just allow such a place to spontaneously come into your awareness now. And as you find yourself there, give yourself the opportunity, to experience all the refreshing feelings of calm, and contentment, and security, and happiness, associated with this wonderful place. And I'm not really sure whether you'd rather just sit and rest back, and look at everything around you, or if you'd rather walk around some, and explore this special place, that's here right now, just for you. And I don't know for sure, the things that will stand out most for you—whether it will be the sounds in this special place, or the beauty of it. Perhaps you'll especially enjoy the sensations and feelings as you touch things, and maybe even the smells will be unusually pleasant.

And I wonder if you've already begun to notice the fact, that as you just experience, and enjoy this special place, you soak up and absorb these tranquil feelings. And you can just allow these feelings of deep contentment, and peace, and calm, to flow, all through you, to all parts of you, allowing all of you to experience these soothing feelings. And as each moment passes in this special place, these wonderful, invigorating feelings increase, and become more a part of you. And you can savor this place, and your enjoyment of it can be heightened, with every moment that you spend here. And as you rest here, and recharge your batteries, this experience may remind you of other places and experiences, where you've felt happy, and contented, and filled with peaceful feelings. [Pause]

And in this place of serenity and security, things can come into perspective. [Pause] You can be aware of actual feelings, with a correct sense of proportion, free from the distortions of a mood or set of circumstances. [Pause] As you rest in this place, things come into proper perspective. [Pause] And in this special place, independent of anything that I say, you can receive what you most need right now. Your unconscious mind knows what you most need. And I don't know exactly how you'll receive that. It may be that you gain a new perspective, or just find yourself feeling differently. [Pause] Or maybe, before awakening, you'll receive from your unconscious, a special gift, of an experience or a memory that gives you the understanding or the perspective or the feelings that you most need right now. [Pause] Or perhaps, you may hear, what you need. It may be that you hear a still voice, maybe a voice in your mind, or seeming to come from deep inside you, saying what you most need to hear, giving you the suggestions you most need to receive right now. [Pause]

And in a moment now, I'm going to stop talking. And you can remain in this special place of yours, for as long as you need. You can remain in this place of contentment, and happiness, and tranquility, for as long as you need, recharging your batteries, and soaking up these feelings, receiving what you need. And there's something that's going to be embedded and remain in your mind: you will know, that you can return to this special place of yours, whenever you need or want to. You will know, that whenever you need to rest, or replenish your strength and energy, that you can put yourself into a deep and peaceful hypnotic state, and return to this place.

And when you're ready to awaken, you can drift back across time and space, bringing these wonderful feelings, and this sense of perspective with you. And you'll awaken feeling well; refreshed, alert and clear-headed. And what you have experienced can remain with you, after you have awakened. Now, as I stop speaking, you can continue in this place, receiving what you need, for as long as you like.

Ego-Strengthening Suggestions

Richard B. Garver, Ed.D.
San Antonio, Texas

I know you have a conscious memory of what you have experienced and learned, but your unconscious mind has a much more complete record of everything that you have ever learned or experienced of any significance since you were born. I want to ask your unconscious mind to review all of that material, and it can do that much more quickly and completely than you could do it consciously. Review all of your learning and experiences; scan all of them and select only positive experiences and feelings. Review them, and strengthen them, and begin to make them available to you as your inner strength to cope with whatever you need to cope with now. And although you won't be aware of most of this consciously, it will be going on beneath the surface, just as your unconscious mind works on problems and continues to operate beneath your awareness most of the time. Perhaps you will be more aware of some of this, a small sample of it surfacing into your conscious awareness — perhaps an experience, a positive experience, that gives you a good feeling. It may be one that happened last week, last month, last year, or many years ago, but the thought of it makes you feel good about yourself. Then, perhaps occasionally a good feeling will surface, just a positive feeling, a feeling perhaps of being secure, confident, happy; or perhaps this feeling may be unattached to any particular experience, just a good feeling and you can enjoy it again, a feeling of inner strength. You'll begin to feel much better about yourself, and you will have the inner strength it requires to pursue some positive strategies that we have talked about, and where some of these may have been threatening before, now they will represent a challenge to you, and you will feel positive about taking a bit of a risk in meeting this challenge, and feeling good about it.

The Inevitability of Change

Robert C. Mashman, Ph.D.
Del Mar, California

INDICATIONS

These are nonspecific suggestions for change intended to activate the client's own abilities in selecting and implementing a necessary change. They are intended to potentiate the effect of subsequent suggestions. These suggestions define change as pervasive, positive, and unconsciously determined. In addition, they redefine feelings of anxiety and confusion as signs of positive unconscious activity. Discomfort is reframed as an epiphenomenon of natural, normal unconscious work.

SUGGESTIONS

Now *change* is something that exists throughout the universe and it is particularly characteristic of biological life. You may or may not know that every seven years almost all of the molecules that make up your body are cycled through. So that every seven years you are actually a completely new person. There are certain patterns that remain and that is why you are still recognizable to yourself and others.

Psychological change usually begins below awareness . . . from what might be described as a seed of change, a potentiality for change. A seed can be planted in our early or late childhood or perhaps even *today*, or it can be inherited as part of the genetic wisdom of our species. Up until recently developmental psychologists have paid attention mostly to childhood and adolescence, but it is now documented and recognized that adults go through developmental stages as well . . . throughout their entire lives. And there is remarkable consistency across people as to what the developmental stages are . . . and the order in which they appear, although each individual manifests the developmental issue differently.

This remarkable consistency in terms of adult development suggests that these particular changes come about as a result of a potentiality that is inherited, a seed that we inherit from our parents and even the species that preceded us. And when the conditions and the timing are correct, these seeds can develop and germinate below our awareness in our unconscious mind . . . and when that happens we may have a sense that something is going on below the surface.

In the days, weeks and months that follow, you may have a strange feeling, a sensation, an experience. If that should happen, you can take pleasure in knowing that your unconscious mind is working for you, that there is a necessary and useful change developing . . . and after that change is completed and has become part of your mental processes, that change will emerge into consciousness in the form of a new feeling or a changed behavior and you can understand — yes — that's what's been going on all along.

Change Is Necessary for Comfort

Robert C. Mashman, Ph.D.
Del Mar, California

INDICATIONS

These are further nonspecific suggestions for change intended to activate the client's own abilities in selecting and implementing a necessary change. Intended to potentiate the effect of subsequent suggestions, these suggestions utilize the client's own experience of a need for a physical readjustment in the hypnotic session as a metaphor for the process of readjustment in life. It is discomfort that informs us of the need for change. The suggestions redefine discomfort as a useful, unavoidable, and periodic part of life, and encourage flexibility and adaptability.

SUGGESTIONS

Understanding, more and more, that it is your ease and comfort that are important [said as the client readjusts his/her physical position], and in order to get more comfortable, you will shift your position when you would like. It is important to recognize that when you go through life, you will arrive in a certain situation, and you will find the most comfortable position for yourself, the most comfortable point of view, the comfortable understanding, and then you will feel good for a period of time.

But at some point the situation will change a little bit, or you will change yourself, and it will require an adjustment to remain comfortable. There is no one position, no point of view, there is no one understanding that will allow comfort forever . . . And so what is necessary to maintain your comfort as you proceed through your life is the ability to adjust your position from time to time . . . to see things a little bit differently, or to hear things in a way that is particularly useful, and to notice that your feelings can evolve and that, even though the same situation may present itself, the feelings that you have in response will be evolutionary.

An Abstract Technique for Ego-Strengthening

B. J. Gorman, M.B., Ch.B.

INTRODUCTION

One means of circumventing . . . critical faculty, which seems to be operative to some degree under all therapeutic situations, is to give suggestions in an indirect or abstract manner, in such a way that no direct suggestion is made, and therefore, the critical faculty is less likely to be activated. I have found that a modified form of Dr. John Hartland's excellent ego-strengthening (1971), delivered in this abstract manner, has been very effective. The general technique which I have used, altered, of course, to suit each patient, is as follows. . . .

This approach was first initiated when a patient commented upon the fact that certain words which I had used, such as "exactly" or "precisely" [e.g., from Hartland's ego-strengthening suggestions] had made him feel that I was setting too high a standard for him. I therefore dropped the authoritarian approach and now, almost exclusively, allow the patient to choose from the material which I present to him that which he needs. According to the circumstances, I may also soliloquize about such words as autonomy, wealth, happiness, etc. I have given in some detail the wording for "health," "success," and "motivation" to illustrate the mode of presentation which I have found most successful.

THE TECHNIQUE

You are now so deeply relaxed that your mind has become very receptive. In this state of deep relaxation the critical part of your conscious mind is also very deeply relaxed so that you *can* accept any ideas you *wish* to accept for your own good.

Because I wish you to remain in this uncritical state, I am not going to give you any direct suggestions with regard to any of your particular problems; I am only going to ask you to think about certain words and their meanings and associations for you. I want you to think lazily of these words, to turn them over in your mind, to examine them, to let them sink deeply into your subconscious mind until they become woven into the very fabric of your substance and of your self-image.

The first word I wish you to think about is the word *health*, and I want you now and always to couple it with the word *good*. What can the words *good health* mean? They can mean a sense of superb physical well-being, with strong heart and lungs, perfect functioning of all the organs, nerves, glands and systems of the entire body; firm, strong muscles, bones and joints; smooth, healthy, elastic skin and the absence of any ex-

cess fat or flesh; greatly increased resistance to all forms of infection or disease and an increasingly great measure of control of both the autonomic nervous system and the hormone glands which, between them, control all the functions and conditions of the body.

Good health means not only physical health but also a healthy attitude of mind in which the nerves are stronger and steadier, the mind calm and clear, more composed, more tranquil, more relaxed, more confident.

It can mean a greater feeling of self-esteem, a greater feeling of personal well-being, safety, security, and happiness than has ever been felt before.

It can mean complete control of the thoughts and emotions, with the ability to concentrate better and utilize all the vast resources of the memory and the full intellectual powers of the subconscious mind.

It can mean the ability to sleep deeply and refreshingly at night and to awake in the morning feeling calm, relaxed, confident and cheerful—and ready to meet all the challenges of the new day with boundless energy and enthusiasm.

The words *good health* can mean to you any or all of these things and more. These words have tremendous power. I want you to let them sink deeply into your subconscious mind, which always does reproduce in you your dominant thoughts.

The next word I would like you to think about is *success*. It may mean a sense of recognition, satisfaction and achievement in your chosen field in life; a happy, fulfilling sex life; a closely-knit, loving family circle; the ability to make firm friends and mix easily in a social setting, or the confidence and skill to speak well in public.

It may mean the ability to set and achieve goals in life which are realistic, worthwhile and progressive, and the motivation and determination to achieve those goals. It may mean the confidence to enable you to throw off your inhibitions, to be spontaneous, to express your feelings without fear or hesitation.

Success may mean wealth in terms of money and the things that money can buy, or security for yourself and your family. It can also show itself in the attitude of mind which gives inner happiness regardless of material possessions or circumstances.

It could mean the ability to overcome some particular problem; perhaps even some problem about which I do not know.

Whatever the word *success* means to you, I want you to use this word as an emotional stimulus to produce in you all the feelings which go with success.

Finally, I want you to think of the word *motivation*. What can it mean? It can mean the desire, determination and driving force to achieve a certain objective. It can mean a gradual but progressive strengthening of one's desire to be in charge of one's life; to destroy the old recordings of habit patterns; to play new music instead of old; to cease being a puppet of one's early conditioning and to become a creator of a new, healthy, happy, successful script in the play of life.

It can mean the gradual but progressive building of a stronger and stronger desire to stop [e.g., overeating or smoking, etc.] until the desire is so great that it is much stronger than the desire to [e.g., eat, smoke, etc.], and there is therefore no difficulty, hardship or discomfort in [e.g., losing weight, giving up smoking, etc.].

We have all been conditioned since birth to associate words with feelings. Words are therefore the tools which we are going to use to produce the feelings and results which we want. And these words are *health*, *success*, and *motivation*.

Learning to Feed Yourself: An Example of Age Regression to Experiences of Mastery

D. Corydon Hammond, Ph.D.
Salt Lake City, Utah

INTRODUCTION AND INDICATIONS

One method of ego-strengthening is through the use of direct suggestions. Another approach to ego-strengthening is to utilize experiences, particularly of mastery, in the personal life history of the patient. We may view the patient as having internal resources waiting to be tapped and utilized. This more indirect and experiential style was characteristic of Dr. Milton H. Erickson's method for enhancing esteem and self-efficacy. The example modeled here is one of moving from dependence to independence, as well as gaining mastery. Other early life experiences that may serve as a source of positive age regression include learning to walk, to talk, to read, to ride a bike, to roller skate, to swim, to drive a car, to skip rope, and to multiply and divide. The next contribution by Dr. Murray-Jobsis provides an excellent example of this approach in her suggestions about learning to crawl and walk. Hypnotic induction and trance-deepening should have been done prior to facilitating these experiences.

LEARNING TO FEED ONESELF

It might be interesting to allow your mind to drift back through time, as if you're growing younger and smaller, and smaller and younger. Allowing yourself to orient back to when you were a small infant. Just imagining as if you were a very small infant again, who still has to be fed by other people. And I'm not sure if you'll actually remember it exactly as it was, or if you'll only imagine it as if you were a baby again, and it doesn't really matter.

But I'd like you to find yourself in a high chair, or sitting and being fed. You are so small that someone else is feeding you. And it can be a very nice experience, to be fed. But when you're completely dependent on someone else, it can also be rather frustrating. Sometimes they may feed you too fast, and you really haven't had a chance to swallow the last bite before the next bite is already being put into your mouth. And your cheeks fill up with the food. And it's frustrating because you really can't tell them, except to push it out with your tongue. And at other times you feel full, and you really don't want any more, but they keep trying to feed you, even though you keep turning your head away. At other times, the person who is feeding you can get distracted with something. And you're really hungry, and you want that next bite that's sitting out there in the spoon, but it's not moving toward your mouth. And it's so frustrating to not be able to get it. [Pause].

And a little later, as you get a little bigger, you begin trying to feed yourself. And you take hold of that spoon or food, and maybe at first you thought it would be easy. But you quickly find that it won't go where you want it to go. It looked so easy. You want to get that food into your mouth, but somehow your hand won't do exactly what you want it to do. And you really can't quite figure out how to do it, how to get it there. You keep missing, and dropping the spoon, and you really can't get it up to your mouth. Sometimes it almost gets there, and then oh, it missed again! And finally someone helps you, and takes over and feeds you, and it must have seemed like such a relief. And I'm sure at first, that you must have felt very discouraged. You must have thought you'd never be able to feed yourself, like you saw other people do. But you really wanted to do things for yourself. And you didn't give up, and other people encouraged you. And before you knew it, you could do it yourself. And what a feeling that is, to master things that seemed impossible, and be able to do things for ourselves, without depending on others. There was a time when it seemed impossible to be able to do that for yourself, and now you don't even think about it. [A bridging association may now be made to the patient's problem.]

Ego Building

Joan Murray-Jobsis, Ph.D.
Chapel Hill, North Carolina

GENERAL MESSAGES

And it begins to become easier to imagine traveling through time and space in trance, beginning to explore and understand ourselves more fully. And in that understanding an acceptance of self, coming to know and understand and accept our strengths and our limitations. Coming to access our strengths and our sense of power without apology or fear, without worrying whether our strengths please or displease others. And acknowledging to ourselves our right to achieve our own personal best self. And at the same time acknowledging our need to accept limitations. Learning to discriminate between those limitations that can be changed through growth and learning, and those limitations that may be an inevitable part of human existence. And coming to an acceptance of our total selves with our strengths and our limitations. Knowing that we have a right and an obligation to be our best self. But also knowing that no one should ask us to be or do more than our best self.

EXPANDING MASTERY

And perhaps beginning to explore and expand the possibilities of competency and mastery that are available to us, continuing to explore and expand our boundaries for competency and mastery. And perhaps traveling back into past experiences, traveling back to some of the earliest times in childhood and infancy, to some of our earliest attempts at growth and mastery.

LEARNING TO CRAWL AND WALK.   Perhaps remembering and re-experiencing some of those early months of existence, of first beginning to crawl. Crawling across the floor. Feeling the excitement and the wonder of lifting the body off the floor and beginning to move. Feeling the strength and the power and the mastery of finally beginning to be able to move, not having to simply lie there waiting for someone to come. But being able to move, physically moving about, beginning to be able to explore things. And perhaps seeing the patterns beneath the fingers as the hands move across the floor crawling, the pattern of the carpet or the floor.

And feeling the excitement, the challenge, the mastery of being able to move about for the first time. And then perhaps reaching up to a chair or a table and pulling ourselves upright and standing for the very first time on two feet. And feeling once again that sense of mastery and excitement, struggle and accomplishment. And then still later taking that very first step, and wavering, and falling, but getting up again, and taking another first step, and falling. And so many steps and so many falls and failures. But always finding within ourselves the strength, the determination, to persevere, to endure all those falls and hurts and failures. And always getting back up and trying again. And from those first wavering steps we learned eventually to walk, and skip, and run, and jump, and after a while we hardly had to think about it at all.

And in those early months of existence, we were still free, not yet weighed down with those later fears of failure and of humiliation. And somehow as infants we knew instinctively that struggle and failure are a natural part of life and growth. And we knew that it is not avoidance of failure that leads to competence and growth; but rather it is learning from our failures, and perseverance, and willingness to take risks that allow us to grow and succeed. And even as the child learned to walk with steadier and steadier gait, so also can we as adults learn to walk through life—steadier and steadier, less fearful of our missteps and setbacks. So also can we as adults enhance our capacity for persevering our failures and expand our capacity for taking risks. And in so many ways, we can rediscover our capacity for growth, perseverance, risk-taking, allowing ourselves to move more freely and positively toward enhancing competency, mastery, growth, development.

EXPANDING JOY

And in similar fashion, beginning to explore and expand our capacity for joy in living. Beginning to explore all the ways in which we can experience joy in our everyday lives.

GLASS METAPHOR.   And most of us remember the story of the glass filled to the halfway mark, and how one person can look at that glass with great sadness and dismay, saying, "Oh, how awful, the glass is already half empty," and another person can look at that same glass with a great sense of joy and happiness and say, "How wonderful! The glass is still half full." And of course in both cases, the glass and the liquid are exactly the same, but the perceptions are dramatically different. And since how we feel about our existence is influenced by how we perceive our existence, then isn't it reasonable always to choose to perceive the fullness and satisfactions of life, and to distance from whatever losses, discomforts, or dissatisfactions may be an inevitable part of our existence? And in so many ways we can add to our sense of joy in life by choosing to perceive the fullness of life, perceiving all of the positives that are sent to us throughout our days, all of the positive responses, the compliments, the affirmations, all of the kind words and the smiles. Allowing ourselves to perceive them and perhaps distancing away from whatever inevitable negatives there may be. And most of us have in the past placed far too much emphasis on whatever negative or critical comments we've received in our daily lives. And most of us have been trained in a false sense of modesty to dismiss the positive comments that have come to us. And isn't it better wherever possible to help ourselves really focus on those positive messages and to dismiss or take less seriously some of the inevitable negative messages we get in our daily lives.

And perhaps also beginning to allow ourselves to perceive the joys in nature more fully, really noticing when there is a beautiful blue sky and high white clouds, or really noticing the scenery on the way in to work as we drive. Or when we take a walk, really noticing the trees, and the sky, and everything in nature. Seeing the beauty that is around us, beginning to allow ourselves to expand our capacity to see, and feel, and hear the beauty in nature. And in our personal interactions, seeing, and hearing, and feeling the beauty in our associations with loved ones, family, close friends, all of the good messages that come our way, perceiving them fully, expanding our capacity to perceive the joy in everyday living.

FREEDOM FROM DESTRUCTIVE COMPETITION AND ANXIETY

THE COMPETITIVE GAMES IN OUR FAMILY OF ORIGIN. And in addition to expanding our capacity for joy, for experiencing joy in living, we can also begin to explore the possibility of freeing ourselves from destructive forms of competition and destructive forms of anxiety. And very often we learn our patterns of competition in our early years, in our early years with our family. And sometimes we learn that we must always lose. Sometimes we compete for mother's approval and discover that mother's approval costs us father's love. Or sometimes we compete for father's approval and discover that in winning his approval we lose mother's love. And so we begin to discover that we lose by whatever action we take. And sometimes we compete with brothers and sisters for parents' love. And sometimes we discover that in winning our parents' love, we lose the love of our brother or sister. And again there's the feeling of somehow always losing. And in some families things are so destructive and mixed up that everyone competes, and no one wins.

And we begin to notice that the rules of competition are unfair, that the rules of the game are loaded. And the only way to deal with this destructive kind of competition is to step out of the game, refuse to play the game, and instead of seeking approval from others, we begin to set our own standards of approval. We learn to step out of the destructive game, and set our own standards of approval. We begin to get a sense of self, and to be able to define values, and to set our own standards. And then we begin to let go of the old habit of automatically competing, and we begin to judge whether the competition is fair. And we begin to discriminate, and select the competitions that are meaningful, and to determine whether win-

ning is worthwhile, and we set our own standards of approval.

And similar to freeing ourselves from destructive competitions, we also can expand the possibilities of freeing ourselves from destructive forms of anxiety. Again as we begin to examine the past, looking at the origins of our anxiety, we discover that anxiety hangs on us as if it were a weight around our neck, weighing us down and making it difficult for us to function.

MOUNTAIN METAPHOR.   And one of the ways we can begin to help free ourselves from these destructive anxieties is to begin to see our anxiety as if it were a mountain. And when we stand close to that mountain, it seems overwhelming. But we can imagine getting into a car and driving some distance from that mountain. And when we are far enough away, we can stop, get out of the car, and turn around and look back, and from this distance that mountain seems much less overwhelming. And from this distance we can begin to imagine different ways of getting beyond that mountain. Perhaps we discover a path around one or the other side of the mountain. Or perhaps we discover a tunnel through the base of the mountain. We might even discover that we can fly over the mountain. But in any event, from this distance that mountain of anxiety seems much less overwhelming. And we begin to discover that some of the anxieties become insignificant; some even disappear. And those that remain become much more manageable from this perspective. Everything does indeed become easier.

REFRAMING ANXIETY.   And then we may notice that anxiety consists of several component parts. And some of these component parts of anxiety are really quite positive, consisting of excitement and challenge and interest and energy, the kind of energy that gets us "up" for a performance. And when we think about it, we begin to realize that life would be very boring if we had no challenge, and if we had no anxiety at all. Even as children we sought challenge and excitement: riding roller coasters, learning to ride a bicycle. And without these challenges life would be dull and boring. So it's really only the excessive levels of anxiety that we experience as destructive, the excessive levels of anxiety that interfere with our performance. And these excessive levels of anxiety can be managed by distancing, while at the same time beginning to allow ourselves to experience and even enjoy the healthy, moderate levels of anxiety—to enjoy the challenges. Redefining the moderate levels of anxiety as energy, and interest, and excitement. And then with this new perspective, everything becomes easier.

The Ugly Duckling Metaphor

Roy L. Rummel, Ph.D.
Dayton, Ohio

Once upon a time a mother duck sat hatching her eggs. One egg was larger; it was the last to hatch. Her duck friends said, "Be careful about that egg; it's probably a turkey. Turkeys'll give you nothing but trouble. Why not spend your time and energies mothering your new babies that are hatched. Forget that big, old turkey egg." The mother duck was determined to follow her best instincts, however, and she kept sitting on it, and it finally hatched. There it was, not a baby turkey, but a big, gangly duckling.

Now she's got this big, awkward kid, along with all her beautiful brood! In the barnyard her friends continued to make many a snide remark about this peculiar and ugly creature, but like God, with nurturing devotion in her heart, she kept loving them all, giving her mother duck's best. Time went on. Her big fellow got bigger and bigger, but so often he felt like an outcast. His ugly appearance was shunned by all his peers, and the gangs and cliques in the barnyard shot him down with many slings and arrows of adversity. . . .

Finally, one spring day, after what seemed an eternity, he was moving around the pond near the castle, and over across the way he spotted this magnificent, regal-looking swan floating with such grace and beauty it made his sad heart flutter. He thought, if only I could be just a little beautiful with just a fraction of that loveliness. Then all of a sudden, he happened to look down into the water beside him and behold! There was a mirror-image, a reflection, of himself. No longer was he the ugly duckling; he too was a swan, a creature of stately elegance.

The ugly duckling, transformed into a beautiful swan, can symbolize the growth and changes in all of us. When there are emotional hangovers of ugliness from the past, when we might have been like an ugly duckling at least to ourselves in some ways, through loving care and affirmations we also change, and we become transformed. . . . Our destiny is to be fully and completely alive, full of loving ourselves and loving others, and we grow and develop toward that destiny. . . . Now relax, and let this picture of the ugly duckling transformed into a beautiful swan inspire and energize you toward a richer, more abundant life, as you take a few moments of silence to reflect about the growth and transformations taking place inside yourself. . . . That moment of silence begins . . . now.

The Prominent Tree Metaphor

Alcid M. Pelletier, Ed.D.
Grand Rapids, Michigan

INDICATIONS

A metaphor like this may be subtly disguised as a "deepening" technique ("to help you go still deeper"). During trance "deepening," before therapeutic work is usually done, patients are less likely to engage in the defensive monitoring and editing of suggestions. This type of metaphor may be particularly useful with patients who have been through trauma, deprivation, and difficult life circumstances. In such cases you could also discuss the early process of the tree's growth from a seed, encountering the hot sun, learning to bend before the strong winds, being weighed down by the rains and snow, the animals that may try to devour it, learning to grow around obstacles, the process and periods of growth and latency, and the development of a hard outer bark to protect the tenderness within. (*Ed.*)

INTRODUCTION

One should discuss which fantasized scenes most relax a patient. This method avoids using guided imagery which may exacerbate patient phobias or allergies. A prominent tree can be introduced in any nature scene. For the present example let us say a fairly intelligent patient has selected a walk through a field of moderately tall grass. . . . The therapist counts 20 steps, pausing occasionally to call attention to tall blades of waving grass, colors, gentle breezes, etc., to deepen the trance.

THE METAPHOR

. . .Ten . . . eleven . . . twelve, now *see* to *your* right or your left *stands a tall strong tree.* Thirteen . . . fourteen, the tree is *so fascinating* that you walk around *admiring* it. Fifteen . . . sixteen, *hear* the birds *singing* in the tree. The sound of the birds singing along with the sound of the wind through the leaves and the wind through *your* clothing is so *relaxing.* Seventeen . . . eighteen, *see* the tree, how *fascinating*, how tall and strong. *Examine it carefully.* Notice the outcropping of the *roots* reaching out across the soil and disappearing into the ground. *Imagine the roots spreading deep* into the ground to *firmly anchor* the tree. *See* how *tall* the trunk is with a few twists and turns, the scars and rough edges that are the result of the tree's *struggle to survive* against the wind, the hail and the *storms of life. The struggle to survive made it stronger.* Notice how *high and far* the branches *reach* into the sky. *Imagine* the branches *offering shelter* to the birds and shade to *man.* You know the leaves *obtain energy* from the sun through the process of photosyn-

thesis. *Imagine* the energy going through the cambium layers of the tree to the roots which obtain nitrates from the soil. *Imagine,* the *whole being, exchanging within itself,* to *give life, strength and health to the whole being.* Nineteen . . . twenty, as you *admire* that tree, *imagine yourself* like *that* tree, *tall and strong, firmly rooted and grounded. You,* like *that* tree have been made *stronger* by the vicissitudes of life. Like the tree's branches *you reach out* for help and *energy.* You too, can offer *shelter* and *help* to others. Within *you,* are the various *functional* systems to make the *whole you stronger and healthier.* But *now, think deeply, you are more* than that tree. *You can think, you have mobility, you can be discreet, you can make decisions, you can love and be loved, you can do so many, many things* that tree cannot do. Sense *your power, your strength, your abilities.* Be *grateful for you.* Think of *all you are!* Now please, *relax deeper and deeper* as *you* contemplate your strength. [At this point, if it is necessary, the therapist may utilize other ego-strengthening suggestions.]

The Seasons of the Year: A Metaphor of Growth

Lawrence R. Gindhart, Ph.D.

INTRODUCTION AND INDICATIONS

This metaphor was designed for a patient who wanted to "grow up," and may serve as an indirect method for facilitating personal "growth." Repetitions have been excluded from the written version, but should be included in presenting this to a patient. (*Ed.*)

THE METAPHOR

March is now, [patient's name], the time for beginning the growth that has ceased for so long—through the long cold winter. As you wonder, as you understand, as you listen to my voice, and as you hear every word I say, you can feel more and more relaxed as you listen to my voice. More and more relaxed—and comfortable—even warm—as you listen—and relaxed, as you listen, as you understand—as you become aware. And you can hear, you can listen, you can understand, and be aware as you relax and feel very comfortable—even as we talk about some things that won't seem to make much sense at first.

You know, [patient's name], in winter so much stays dormant for such a long time. The growth that once was, just had to stop, and wait—a long time waiting for the growth and the warmth of spring. You know, [patient's name], we could talk about trees—about how they must feel after waiting for such a long time—without growing. Just waiting for the right time—for springtime—to grow. And you know, [patient's name], about the cold and the barrenness and the aloneness and the misunderstanding those trees must endure before they greet the long awaited springtime and especially March. *Now, [patient's name], March* is a special time. You can feel the comfort of knowing about the strength from the fluid of *growth* that *begins to build* and *builds deep* in the roots of that which has been dormant for so long. Do you know, [patient's name], you can feel so good, so comfortable, so warm, as you sense the feelings of growth—beginning deep in those roots—and you can continue to feel it—beginning deep in those roots. And you can continue to feel it beginning deep, comfortable and strong—and strength, [patient's name], comes from knowing it begins soon. Soon, of course, can be any time—an hour from now—a day from now. Certainly, during that time—even in a moment—especially in March. Can you imagine—can you see clearly—and feel how peaceful you feel—*as you see the growth building deep* in those roots—as you become increasingly aware, as the energy of growth moves ever upward from deep in the roots. And can you—now—*[patient's name] —feel the special sense of pride that growing things feel* in springtime. You can *then—feel that special way as you notice the very budding of growth* that

comes early in spring—especially in March. Of course, it is very comforting to know that growth, especially *this special kind of rapid growth which always takes the right amount of time*—just the right amount of time—sometimes very fast—sometimes slower—*against odds*—often very rapidly—sometimes slower—it perseveres and it can and will take all the time it needs. That rapid growth occurs along with the budding—along with the unfolding of leaves—until *all is just right—when so much is in bloom*. And the blooming of flowers, and the unfolding of leaves, tells you all is growing—at just the right rate—in just the right amount of time. *When so much is in full bloom you will have the very satisfying feeling of confidence that growth is just as it should be.* The *things that grow always do, [patient's name]* , you know, *they always do*—and they don't forget what they learned when they had to stop growing—for a while. It took a lot to endure the misunderstanding of winter. Yes, it seems odd to talk about growth, trees, springtime and March—but, *growth occurs, [patient's name]* , *and you can feel it*, especially in March, even *now*.

Confidence Building

H. E. Stanton, Ph.D.
Hobart, Tasmania, Australia

THE CLOUD

Visualize a normal white, soft, fluffy cloud hovering over your head into which you will be able to place all the reasons, direct and indirect, which you think have contributed to your lack of confidence. These reasons are the unconscious "computer" programs which are maintaining your unwanted behavior. Thus, they need to be erased.

Let your mind drift in a pleasantly relaxed way and, whenever any reason for your lack of confidence, no matter how trivial, comes into your mind, put it into the cloud. As you do so, your unconscious mind will put in other reasons of which you are unaware, causing the cloud to become increasingly dark. When you have put in every reason you are able to think of, it will be inky black.

Look at the black cloud containing all these negative programs and, as you do so, somewhere behind it you will see a source of light. At first quite dim, it will become increasingly bright. That light is really a sun, the sun of your own desire to be free of everything that has been preventing you from living life to its fullest.

The light grows stronger and brighter until it begins to burn away the black cloud. As this is happening, you will become increasingly aware of the warmth of the sun so that, as the cloud burns away completely, leaving no trace of either cloud or anything it contained, you will be able to bask in this warmth, feeling the sun's rays penetrating every cell of your body, bringing a wonderful sense of self-assurance and self-confidence.

THE PYRAMID

Imagine yourself back in ancient Egypt, standing in the desert before the cave-like entrance to a large pyramid. As you enter, you find yourself in a downward sloping passageway, well lit with torches. Feeling a sense of security and confidence, you follow this passageway as it takes you deeper and deeper into the heart of the pyramid.

At the very end of the passage is a vast storeroom filled with treasures of all descriptions. This is the storehouse of all the vast untapped resources, all the potential for good and for achievement, which you have not yet turned to your advantage. All of this treasure is rightfully yours, for it has been stolen from you through force of circumstance. However, unless you carry it back into the world outside to enjoy and to share with others, it will eventually be sealed up within the room and lost forever.

Naturally, you attempt to gather this treasure, for it is rightfully yours. Yet, you cannot.

Some force is preventing you, a force emanating from a huge black statue in the center of the room. This statue, powered by a brilliant jewel embedded in its forehead, is the embodiment of all the negative forces of failure and defeat within you. It has been placed in the room as the guardian of the treasure, making all other guardians unnecessary.

To free this vast storehouse of your potential so that you can become the person you are capable of being, you must first overcome the negative tendencies, the forces of failure and defeat, within you which are acting to prevent this, these tendencies being personified and embodied in the guardian statue.

Go to the statue and knock the jewel from its forehead. As it lies on the ground, its lustre fades, so that it looks dark and ugly like a piece of coal. This can be stepped upon and crushed into black dust. Its power gone, the statue may then be pushed so that it falls and breaks into many pieces.

You are now free to gather up as many of the treasures as can be carried, taking it with you as you retrace your steps up the passage to the entrance. There is no need to attempt to take all the treasure, for you will be able to return to this treasure room whenever you want to. No matter how much you may take, or how many times you return, the room will never be empty.

Step outside into the warm sunshine, and return to the world of your everyday life with the treasures you have gathered. These treasures, which can be anything you want them to be, will reveal themselves in new habits, new ideas, and new directions.

On any occasion when you feel a lack of confidence in your ability to do something, think of the pyramid and the treasures it contains. As you do, you will feel a sense of confidence, strength, and power surging through you, filling you with the certainty that you are capable of accomplishing the task about which you were doubtful.

THE LAKE

INDICATIONS.   This image may feel more compatible to a patient who enjoys the mountains and certain leisure activities like swimming, canoeing or rowing. Imagery of walking in the mountains may be used for deepening before using this symbolic imagery experience. The patient may be asked to give a head nod or ideomotor signal when he/she is engaging in using some method to get across the lake, and when the other side is reached. Patients may also be asked to verbalize which activity they have selected for crossing the lake. (*Ed.*)

SUGGESTIONS. See yourself standing on the shore of a lake, looking out over the water. Where you stand, it is a dreary and depressing scene, the water rough and treacherous, whipped into waves by wind and rain. Yet, the other side of the lake is quite different, with people enjoying the bright sunshine and lively atmosphere. This is the shore of health and normality.

Visualize yourself crossing the lake in some way that requires considerable effort. Rowing a boat, paddling a canoe, or even swimming would be possibilities. Not only are the waves and wind to be combatted. Other obstacles will attempt to impede your progress from the shore of dreariness to the shore of brightness, but these you overcome. If the distance seems too great, or your efforts are exhausting, you can use the islands dotting the surface of the lake as temporary resting places.

When you finally reach the bright shore, as you will, you feel a tremendous surge of confidence, a belief in your ability to live your life as you want to, coping effectively and happily with whatever your environment provides.

Increasing Determination: The Snowball

H. E. Stanton, Ph.D.
Hobart, Tasmania, Australia

Picture yourself standing at the top of a tall snow-covered mountain, looking down into a valley below. In this valley is the place you have been attempting to reach. Though your journey has brought you as far as this mountaintop, further progress towards your objective is blocked, for all along the mountainside are numerous barriers and obstacles. These represent everything standing between you and the attainment of your goals.

Bend down and pick up a handful of snow. Examine this. You will find it to be soft and powdery, comparable, in a way, to your own determination which has, at times, lacked firmness and strength.

Add more snow, packing it more tightly in your hands, compressing it into a snowball which is firm, round, and hard. As you do so, feel your own assertiveness and determination becoming stronger and firmer too, as hard and as firm as the snowball being prepared for its trip down the mountainside. Walk over to a very steep incline at the side of the mountain and gently roll the snowball down it, straight at the obstacles below. Quite slowly the snowball rolls down the mountainside, growing in size as it does so, until it attains the proportions of a large boulder. It then becomes an avalanche, sweeping everything before it as it continues on its journey to the bottom.

The way is now clear. As all obstacles have been swept away, you can begin to descend the mountainside where your courage and determination have gone before to clear a path. As you imagine yourself striding purposefully down the mountain, you will know that, in your own mind, your determination is continuing to grow, as did the snowball, until it will become sufficiently strong to sweep away every obstacle in its path. You will then be able to attain whatever goals in life you have set, just as easily as you can now imagine yourself descending that mountainside.

Suggestions for Emotional Enrichment

Don E. Gibbons, Ph.D.

INTRODUCTION AND INDICATIONS

Many people consistently go at life with such an air of grim determination that they eventually lose, or at least severely blunt, their capacity to experience joy and a zest for living — not merely abandoning their sense of childlike wonder, but also the deeper, richer experiences of fulfillment which are characteristic of the fully functioning adult. . . .

The following postinduction suggestions are not designed to induce excessive or inappropriate affect, nor are they intended to elicit strong emotion merely for its own sake. Rather, they are designed for use as a set of "toning up" exercises for sufficiently suggestible subjects who are familiar with their aims and purposes: as a means of strengthening and heightening the capacity for positive emotional response, and as a method of counteracting occasional tendencies toward depression when such tendencies are primarily the result of habit or of failure to maintain a sufficiently optimistic outlook on life. When combined with appropriate suggestions of time expansion, these suggestions may also be useful as a means of providing a temporary substitute for persons who are presently addicted to mood- altering drugs. They may also be used as a method of pain control by allowing the subject to experience the opposite emotions. A similar approach has been employed for this purpose by Sacerdote (1977).

SUGGESTIONS

Now, as you continue to listen to my words, you find yourself being mentally transported to the center of a large, green meadow which lies at the foot of a tall mountain. But this is no ordinary mountain looming up before you; for this is a mountain of pure joy, and you are about to climb all the way to the top of it.

Now you are beginning to climb the mountain of joy. And as you climb, you can feel this joy coursing through every fiber of your being, as the level of joy within you continues to rise.

Now, you are about to be transported to greater heights of pleasure than you ever dreamed possible. As you continue soaring farther and farther into trance, you are already

beginning to breathe more rapidly in anticipation of the joys which will soon be yours; for soon your entire body will be quivering with pleasure and tingling with delight. As you continue soaring farther and farther into trance, your ability to respond to experience of every kind is becoming infinitely keener. Your entire body is becoming exquisitely more sensitive and more responsive with every breath you take.

You are beginning to breathe even faster now, as your capacity for experience multiplies itself over and over. And the higher you climb, the higher you want to climb and the stronger the effects of my words become.

And as your entire body continues to grow more sensitive and more responsive with every breath you take, you are also becoming more free, more open, and more accepting of every type of experience. You are becoming totally and completely *free,* as your responsiveness continues to grow and your breathing comes still faster in anticipation of the joys which will soon be yours. And the higher you go, the higher you want to go and the stronger the effects of my words become.

And now, as your responsiveness and sensitivity continue to increase within an atmosphere of total freedom, we are beginning to release all of the vast, untapped resources of feeling and emotion which lie within you. Probing the depths of your innermost self, and releasing every wonderful, positive emotion for your exquisitely tuned body to savor and experience to the fullest.

And the higher you go, the higher you want to go and the stronger the effects of my words become.

Great waves of pleasure, ecstasy, and delight are gushing forth from the innermost depths of your being like water from behind a bursting dam, overwhelming you completely as your breathing comes still faster and your heart begins to pound.

But there is never any sense of strain or fatigue; for the heights which you are able to achieve in trance are truly without limit. And the higher you go, the higher you want to go and the stronger the effects of my words become.

You are being guided all the way to the peak of the mountain by the sound of my words alone; and as I continue, you will feel wave after wave of ecstasy building up from the depths of your being and rolling endlessly forth like breakers upon an ocean shore. Each successive wave, as it comes crashing forth, will carry you still higher, leaving you ever more sensitive and more responsive to the one which is to follow.

And the higher you climb, the higher you want to climb and the stronger the effects of my words become.

The waves of joy will come faster and faster until they finally blend together into one vast tide. And when they finally fuse together and become one, they will carry you up to an ultimate peak of joy which is the fulfillment of all existence. And then you can sink back, happy and fulfilled, and able to experience joy more fully in your everyday life.

And each time this exercise is repeated, your capacity to experience joy will become greater, and your ability to *live* joyfully will be correspondingly enhanced.

Now, as you continue climbing on and on, you begin to sprint; for you are determined to reach the peak as soon as you can. And with every step, your speed increases. Running and running, breathing faster and faster, nearly bursting with delight as the level of joy within you continues to rise. And when you finally sink down upon the peak, a final burst of joy will explode within you like a rocket. Now you are very near the peak. Almost there. *Now!*

And as you sink down upon the peak and the joy begins to subside, it is followed by a boundless feeling of peace and tranquility, confidence and calm. You feel just as secure as a little baby nestled in its mother's arms. And as a result of having tapped into this vast potential for experiencing joy, you will be much more able to respond joyfully in everyday life situations; and each new day will contain new treasures of joy for you to discover and to experience.

Each time you climb this mountain of joy, you will be able to tap into more of this vast potential, and the joy which you are able to experience in your everyday life will be correspondingly enhanced.

Stein's Clenched Fist Technique

D. Corydon Hammond, Ph.D.
Salt Lake City, Utah

INDICATIONS

This is an ego-strengthening and hypnotic conditioning technique that can give patients a valuable coping method for altering problematic emotional states. Unconscious resources within the patient (e.g., feelings of confidence, happiness, calm, spontaneity) are accessed and then conditioned, so that they may be evoked by the patient whenever needed. This technique may be used for coping with anxiety, anger, cravings (smoking, food, alcohol, drugs), with compulsive disorders, in nailbiting, and with psychosomatic disturbances. In a sense, this method is like the behavioral methods of thought stopping and thought substitution, which can often be made more powerful and automatic through hypnotic conditioning. Failures may occur if this technique is used when unconscious adaptive functions are being served which need to be examined through exploration techniques (e.g., ideomotor signaling), or when strong hostility requires exploration and abreaction. The verbalizations modeled below are mine, but they are modeled after Dr. Calvert Stein.

THE TECHNIQUE

[First, identify the resource and feeling state needed by the patient. Following induction and deepening, the patient may be told:] Now I want your unconscious mind to search through your memories and identify a time when you felt (e.g., confident, happy, peaceful and calm, healthy, needed, accepted, competent, strong). Just allow your inner mind to identify a time when you felt _____ , no matter how brief the experience, or how long ago, and no matter how intimate or personal the experience, because it isn't necessary to tell me anything about it if you don't want to. And when your unconscious mind has identified that experience, just allow your "yes" finger to float up.

[After an ideomotor response:] Good. Now I'd like your unconscious mind to take you back through time to that experience. Just allow yourself to drift back to that experience, and when you are there, allow your "yes" finger to float up again. [Following an ideomotor response:] Good. And as you enjoy that experience again, you can begin to sense those feelings associated with it — feelings of _____ . And when you're aware of experiencing those feelings again, allow your "yes" finger to float up to signal me. [Pause for response] That's right. And notice how those feelings get *stronger*, as you enjoy that experience again, in complete privacy. [Pause]

And now as you feel these feelings, I'd like you to close your dominant hand into a *tight* fist, and as you do so, these positive feelings become *even stronger*. That's right, just close your dominant hand into a *tight* fist, as a sign and symbol of confidence and determination. This is the hand that you trust and depend on. And as you clench it tightly, feel the feelings of _____ becoming *even stronger*. And when you're aware of feeling those feelings even more strongly, just nod your head to let me know.

That's right, and just continue enjoying that experience, and these good feelings, allowing them to fill you, and to flow all through you. And as you continue experiencing these feelings, take several deep, refreshing breaths, while your unconscious mind *memorizes*, all of these wonderful feelings. Because in the future, whenever you close your dominant hand into a *tight* fist like this, you will feel once again, these feelings of _____ and _____ , flowing back over you and filling you. Whenever you want to experience these feelings again, all you

need to do is clench your dominant hand into a fist, and this same kind of memory and feelings, will come back into your experience.

[Identify two other experiences where the patient felt these same types of feelings, going through the same procedure and suggestions.]

And now you can feel pleased, and feel a sense of confidence in knowing, that you have learned a method for recapturing these feelings, *whenever you need them*. Your unconscious mind has *memorized* these feelings, these experiences, and they will remain just beneath the surface, as inner resources. And because of this conditioning, they will be readily available, *whenever* you need them. All that you'll need to do is to clench your _____ hand into a fist, as these memories, and positive feelings, wash back over you.

And I'd like you to demonstrate this for yourself now. In a moment, I want you to squeeze that (right, left) hand into a confident fist. And as you do so, notice, just notice how one of these same wonderful *memories*, and these *same feelings*, come back into your experience. Go ahead. [Pause] And enjoy this experience. [Pause] And the *stronger* you clench that fist, the more vivid the feelings become, do they not? [A double check] And I'd like you to appreciate, your own ability, to recapture these feelings, *whenever* you wish, knowing that they are *always there*, just beneath the surface for you.

Now allow that fist to relax, and allow yourself to drift into an even sounder, and deeper hypnotic state. [Deepen the trance.]

And now you're going to have an opportunity, to learn another method, which will allow you to even more effectively neutralize the feelings of _____ , and replace them with feelings of _____ and _____ . In a moment, I'd like you to permit yourself to remember an unpleasant experience, that made you feel _____ . It doesn't have to be so unpleasant that it makes you miserable. I don't want you to be *that* uncomfortable. But allow just enough of an unpleasant memory to come back, so that you begin to feel *some* of those feelings of _____ . [Pause] And when you're experiencing some of those unpleasant feelings, signal me with your "yes" finger.

All right. And now I want you to enjoy discovering something, *very* interesting. I want you to notice, how these negative feelings can be transferred and displaced, into your nondominant, (left, right) hand, as you close it into a fist. Close your (left) hand into a fist, and as you do so, be aware of how those unpleasant feelings and sensations funnel down, through your shoulder, your arm, your forearm, down into your (left) fist. Allow all those unpleasant feelings and sensations, those negative emotional and physical knots, to flow down into your _____ fist, condensing and concentrating there. Lock them up *tightly* in that fist, keeping them there until you're reasonably sure that all of them, or the majority of them, are in that fist, where *you* yourself have displaced and transferred them. You may not always be able to keep unpleasant feelings from appearing in your mind or body, but you'll be able to transfer them into your _____ fist, where *you can control them*. And when it feels as if all those unpleasant feelings, are collected into that fist, just nod your head to signal me.

Good. Now, since you're the one who put those feelings into that (left) fist, you're the person who can remove and neutralize them. And I want you to observe *how easy it is*, to get rid of those feelings, and *replace them* with positive feelings. I want you to squeeze your (dominant) hand into a strong, confident, happy fist. And as you do so, allow your (nondominant) hand to relax, *letting go* of all those unpleasant feelings. That's right. Just move those fingers around, allowing *all* those unpleasant feelings to flow out of your hand, as if they were just evaporating, or falling onto the floor. And you'll discover that the unhappy memory *disappears*, and is *replaced* by a *positive* one. And you can *enjoy* that happy memory again, in complete privacy, with that happy fist *tightly* closed, as a symbol of confidence, and strength, and determination. Enjoy taking several extra deep, relaxing breaths, as you just luxuriate in these positive feelings for a while. [Pause] And these good feelings *will*

remain with you, far *longer* than you might expect.

You now have a method for controlling your own feelings, and for creating this same sense of well-being, *whenever* you need to. So whenever you feel (negative feelings), just close your (nondominant) hand into a fist. As you do so, you'll feel all

those unpleasant feelings and sensations flowing, and funneling, and concentrating into your _____ hand. And after a short time, when it feels as though all those unpleasant feelings are locked up in that hand, then you can *neutralize* them. You can get rid of them, and then replace them with positive feelings, by simply squeezing your (dominant) hand into a tight fist, while you open your _____ hand, and *let go* of all the unpleasant feelings and sensations. And I want you to really *enjoy*, all the *positive* feelings, and *wonderful* memories that flow over you, and that will *increase*, the *tighter* you squeeze that _____ fist. And after a minute of two of clenching that fist, you'll discover that those pleasant, *good* feelings, *will remain with you*. Almost as if, by clenching that _____ fist, you've infused your *whole being* with *so many*, *good* feelings, with *so much* of those natural endorphin substances from your brain, that *for a long time*, there's just *nothing* to bother you, and *nothing* to disturb you.

Suggestions for Ego-Strengthening

John Hartland, M.B.

INDICATIONS

The suggestions that follow are *the* original ego-strengthening method, pioneered by the late John Hartland. Although they are extremely general, highly directive and authoritarian, they may nonetheless be useful with patients who are dependent and submissive to authority. Clinicians may also find certain concepts and ideas useful to adapt for individual patients, and to modify into a more permissive form. (*Ed.*)

SUGGESTIONS

You have now become *so* deeply relaxed . . . *so* deeply asleep . . . that your mind has become *so* sensitive . . . *so* receptive to what I say . . . that *everything* that I put into your mind . . . will sink *so* deeply into the unconscious part of your mind . . . and will cause so deep and lasting an impression there . . . that *nothing* will eradicate it. Consequently . . . these things that I put into your unconscious mind . . . will begin to exercise a greater and greater influence over the way you think . . . over the way you feel . . . over the way you behave.

And . . . because these things *will* remain . . . firmly imbedded in the unconscious part of your mind . . . after you have left here . . . when you are no longer with me . . . they will continue to exercise the same great influence . . . over your *thoughts* . . . your *feelings* . . . and your *actions* . . . *just* as strongly . . . *just* as surely . . . *just* as powerfully . . . when you are back home . . . or at work . . . as when you are with me in this room.

You are now so *very deeply asleep* . . . that *everything* that I tell you that is going to happen to you . . . *for your own good* . . . *will* happen . . . *exactly* as I tell you. And *every feeling* . . . that I tell you that you will experience . . . you *will* experience . . . *exactly* as I tell you. And these same things *will continue to happen* to you . . . *every day* . . . *just* as strongly . . . *just* as surely . . . *just* as powerfully . . . when you are back home . . . or at work . . . as when you are with me in this room.

During this deep sleep . . . *you* are going to feel physically *stronger* and *fitter* in every way. You will feel *more* alert . . . *more* wide awake . . . *more* energetic. You will become *much* less easily tired . . . *much* less easily

fatigued . . . *much* less easily discouraged . . . *much* less easily depressed. *Every day* . . . you will become *so deeply interested* in whatever you are doing . . . in whatever is going on around you . . . that your mind will become *completely distracted away from yourself*. You will no longer *think nearly so much about yourself* . . . you will no longer *dwell nearly so much upon yourself and your difficulties* . . . and you will become *much less conscious of yourself* . . . *much less preoccupied with yourself* . . . *and with your own feelings*.

Every day . . . your nerves will become *stronger and steadier* . . . your mind *calmer and clearer* . . . *more composed* . . . *more placid* . . . *more tranquil*. You will become *much less easily worried* . . . *much less easily agitated* . . . *much less easily fearful and apprehensive* . . . *much less easily upset*.

You will be able to *think more clearly* . . . you will be able to *concentrate more easily*. You will be able to *give up your whole undivided attention to whatever you are doing* . . . *to the complete exclusion of everything else*. Consequently, *your memory will rapidly improve* . . . and you will be able to *see things in their true perspective* . . . *without magnifying your difficulties* . . . *without ever allowing them to get out of proportion*.

Every day . . . you will become *emotionally much calmer* . . . *much more settled* . . . *much less easily disturbed*. *Every day* . . . *you* will become . . . and *you* will remain . . . *more and more completely relaxed* . . . and *less tense* each day . . . *both mentally and physically* . . . even when you are no longer with me.

And *as* you become . . . and *as* you remain . . . *more relaxed* . . . *and less tense* each day . . . *so* . . . you will develop *much more confidence in yourself* . . . more confidence in your ability to *do* . . . not only what you *have* . . . to do each day . . . but more confidence in your ability to do whatever you *ought* to be able to do . . . *without fear of failure* . . . *without fear of consequences* . . . *without unnecessary anxiety* . . . *without uneasiness*. Because of this . . . *every day* . . . you will feel *more and more independent* . . . *more able to 'stick up for yourself'* . . . *to stand upon your own feet* . . . *to hold your own* . . . no matter how difficult or trying things may be.

Every day . . . you will feel a *greater feeling of personal well-being* . . . *a greater feeling of personal safety* . . . *and security* . . . than you have felt for a long, long time. And because all these things *will* begin to happen . . . *exactly* as I tell you they will happen . . . *more and more rapidly* . . . *powerfully* . . . *and completely* . . . with every treatment I give you . . . you will feel *much happier* . . . *much more contented* . . . *much more optimistic in every way.* You will consequently become much more able to *rely upon* . . . *to depend upon* . . . *yourself* . . . *your own efforts* . . . *your own judgment* . . . *your own opinions.* You will feel *much less need* . . . to have to *rely upon* . . . or to *depend upon* . . . *other people.*

Suggestions for Self-Reinforcement

Don E. Gibbons, Ph.D.

INTRODUCTION AND INDICATIONS

The following suggestions are designed to assist an individual in developing a greater capacity for self-reinforcement so that he will be less dependent on external sources of reward—and hence, better able to determine the course of his own conduct. Of course, numerous concrete applications are possible.

SUGGESTIONS

Now I would like to help you to experience the feelings of satisfaction and achievement which come with the attainment of an important goal, so that you can learn to practice and strengthen these feelings and apply them to the attainment of other goals in your life. First of all, I would like you to think of a time in the past when you had just achieved something that was very important to you—something that gave you a strong sense of pride and accomplishment, and meant a great deal to you at the time. It may have been graduation from high school, or the day you got your first driver's license, or almost anything else you can think of, as long as it was something you really felt good about when it happened. Take your time, and as soon as you have thought of a situation which fits this description, you can signal me by raising the index finger of your right [or left] hand.

[After the subject has responded:] All right. Now let yourself get in touch with the feelings of achievement and satisfaction which you were feeling when you were actually in that situation. Let yourself go back and experience those feelings once more, and feel them growing even stronger as I speak. Growing and growing, and becoming clearer and stronger and more intense with every passing second. And all the time I am speaking to you, until the trance is over, these feelings are going to continue growing stronger by themselves.

And when the trance is ended, your normal, everyday mood will return. And of course, you will have no need to balance things out by feeling bad, just because you have been allowing yourself to feel so good. But because you have been able to recapture and to strengthen these feelings of pride and accomplishment, and the sense of deep personal satisfaction that goes with them, it will be much easier for you to feel good in the future over all the things you do that you ought to feel good about, and to give yourself a pat on the back whenever you have it coming.

Visualization of the Idealized Ego-Image

Maurice H. McDowell, Th.D.
Salem, Oregon

INTRODUCTION

Normally, I ask patients to read the first four chapters of Maltz's *Psycho-Cybernetics*. If they read the first four chapters, they normally will continue to read the rest of the book, and this makes an excellent background for therapy. After deep hypnosis has been obtained, the following suggestions are given to each patient.

SUGGESTIONS

Each person has several self-images. Your obvious, conscious self-image is largely a reflected image of how you feel significant people have reacted to or treated you. If you have felt that they treated you as a just, honorable, and decent person, you will tend to think of yourself in those terms. If, on the other hand, you have felt that they regarded you as a bad, lying, thieving, untrustworthy person of little value, you will tend to think of yourself in those terms.

You also have precise self-images: How you feel that your father feels toward you. What your mother would say about you if she were present now. Or, how would your favorite teacher evaluate you? How do you think the teacher you most dislike would evaluate you? What would your best friend say about you? [These various images were sometimes discussed with the patient for clarification. If any traumatic materials were elicited, a temporary amnesia was often instilled for follow-up at a later time.]

Now I want you to go way deep into your own mind and visualize the *real* you, the kind of a person you really are and can really become. I want you to look at it very carefully and to study it thoroughly and lock it into your conscious mind so that we can discuss it when I alert you.

I shall count to three, and the visualization will immediately appear in your mind. As soon as you have completed the visualization, please lift your right index finger to signal me that you have completed your part of this project and are willing to be alerted. . . .

[This technique has been used with over one hundred college students in their search for identity. It has been very helpful to a majority of the students.]

Cycle of Progress

Douglas M. Gregg, M.D.
San Diego, California

As you continue to relax, just letting yourself drift down deeper and deeper relaxed . . . you relax completely throughout every fiber of your being; relaxing physically, emotionally, mentally and spiritually. And as you relax so completely in this fashion, concentrating your mind, listening to each word that I say, you let each suggestion take complete and thorough effect to help you, deeply and automatically, on both the conscious and unconscious levels of mind activity. You extend the principles of relaxation and concentration which you now experience into your everyday life so that in every situation, and in every circumstance in which you find yourself, whether alone or with others, you relax and you concentrate your mind, automatically; no matter what you are doing, you find that more and more, day by day, you relax and you concentrate your mind. If you are doing something for fun or relaxation, you relax and you enjoy it more . . . you concentrate your mind casually and comfortably and get more out of what you are doing. If you are doing something that involves work or some serious project or activity, you relax and apply yourself more thoroughly, more effectively; you concentrate and do a better job. And so, every day in every situation and in every circumstance in which you find yourself, you relax and you concentrate, more and more and more. As you relax and concentrate, you evaluate everything thoroughly and completely; you reach decisions easily and readily; you act efficiently and effectively; and you build your self-confidence, your self-reliance, your self-acceptance, and your self-esteem. You become a stronger individual; you become self-sufficient. As this occurs, you feel more relaxed and you are capable of greater concentration.

Just drifting down now . . . way down . . . deeper relaxed. And you realize that as you are more relaxed and as you are capable of greater concentration, you evaluate things even more thoroughly and completely; you reach decisions even more easily and readily; you act even more efficiently and effectively and you continually build your self-confidence, self-reliance, self-acceptance, and self-esteem . . . growing stronger and more capable every day in all situations. As you do this, you feel even more relaxed and you are capable of even greater concentration. As you drift down deeper relaxed, you let all of these suggestions seat themselves deeply, permanently in your unconscious mind. And as you apply these principles in your life automatically every day, in every situation and in every circumstance in which you find yourself, whether alone or with others, you relax more and more deeply, you concentrate your mind more and more sharply and intensely, you evaluate thoroughly and completely, you reach decisions easily and readily, you act efficiently and effectively, and you continually build your self-confidence, self-reliance, self-acceptance, and self-esteem. And you continually find that you are capable of more relaxation and greater concentration and so on in a cycle of progress that grows, that deepens, strengthens and reinforces itself every day as you grow and become that person that you have always admired; the person you have always wanted to be: self-sufficient.

All of these suggestions are now implanted deeply, firmly and permanently in the deepest reaches of your unconscious, and they are part of your entire being to be used automatically by you to make your life more effective, more productive, more useful and happier as you learn to relax more and more, as you learn to concentrate your mind more and more. Helping you as you learn to relax, deeper and deeper relaxed . . . as you learn to concentrate your mind more and more intensely, more and more completely, just drifting deeper relaxed.

A Brief Ego-Strengthening Suggestion

William T. Reardon, M.D.
Wilmington, Delaware

You will be able to tolerate the persons, places, or things that used to disturb you and annoy you. You will be able to adjust yourself to your environment, even though you cannot change it.

A Future-Oriented Suggestion

P. Oystragh
Bondi, N.S.W., Australia

. . .and as this begins to happen, every day you will find yourself better able to . . . [include relevant suggestions] . . . and achieve for yourself that picture of yourself that you have in your mind's eye. As you want to be, as you can be, and as you will be.

You will be able to stand up for yourself, stand on your own feet and state your opinion or suggestion without embarrassment, without fear and without anxiety.

ANXIETY, PHOBIAS, AND DENTAL DISORDERS

INTRODUCTION

Anxiety and Phobic Disorders

THERE ARE MANY METHODS for working hypnotically with anxiety disorders. Occasionally, direct suggestions for relief of anxiety or phobias prove effective (e.g., Horowitz, 1970; Marks, Gelder, & Edwards, 1968; Naruse, 1965). When direct suggestions are ineffective, there are many other suggestive hypnotic techniques that may be productive. The patient may be taught to dissociate from anxiety-provoking circumstances. This may be accomplished through imagining floating away to a tranquil setting, feeling distant from tension-producing situations, or through age regression or age progression to more peaceful scenes and times (temporal dissociation). Contributions by the Spiegels, Stanton, Finkelstein, and Stickney model variations of such dissociative methods. Hammond's serenity place technique found in the ego-strengthening chapter is yet another example of scene visualization and dissociation for anxiety management.

Simply the process of induction and deepening generally relieves anxiety. Thus verbalizations for a progressive relaxation induction have been included as part of this chapter, although many other induction methods may produce anxiety reduction. Meares' contribution on the use of deep meditative trance, primarily facilitated through nonverbal methods, provides another option for anxiety management. This method is similar to the technique of prolonged hypnosis discussed in Chapter 8.

Hypnotically-facilitated systematic desensitization and mental rehearsal of successfully coping with tense situations are yet other methods for treating anxiety and phobic disorders (Clarke & Jackson, 1983). Advantages of hypnotic desensitization over traditional behavioral desensitization include enhanced scene visualization (Deiker & Pollock, 1975; Glick, 1970) and the ability to give posthypnotic suggestions to encourage behavioral responses to the situations that were imagined (Deyoub & Epstein, 1977; Gibbons, Kilbourne, Saunders & Castles, 1970).

Cognitive factors may be another important etiologic component of anxiety and phobic responses. When low self-esteem is determined to be an aspect of the problem, ego-strengthening methods may be employed. Any cognitive therapy interventions that are used at a conscious level may also be reinforced hypnotically. Thus in this chapter you will find Gurgevich modeling one of his methods for cognitive reframing. Rational-emotive therapy suggestions such as those found in this chapter and in the chapter on ego-strengthening may likewise be offered to anxious patients to modify their underlying assumptions and internal dialogue. Hypnosis may also be used to age regress patients to experiences immediately before they began to feel anxious (Crasilneck & Hall, 1985). This may aid in pinpointing the situations that elicit anxiety as well as the internal dialogue and imagery that evoke problematic responses. Age regression to times prior to the development of the phobia, when the patient was coping successfully, has also proven effective (Logsdon, 1960).

There are times, however, when a phobic response or generalized anxiety is caused by more than simply conditioning or irrational cognitions. In these cases unconscious exploration, through ideomotor signaling (Hammond & Cheek, 1988), ego-state therapy (Van der Hart, 1981), or hypnoprojective techniques (Gustavson & Weight, 1981; Schneck, 1966; Wolberg, 1948), has successfully identified conflicts, functions, purposes or past experiences that are beyond conscious awareness. When traumatic events are found to be associated with phobic reactions, it may be profitable to facilitate an age regression and abreact the feelings associated with the experience.

Finally, it should additionally be reinforced that hypnotic interventions may (and often should) be used in conjunction with more traditional psychotherapeutic and medical interventions. In the treatment of phobias or panic disorder, for example, hypnotic methods may be combined with medication, in-vivo desensitization, cognitive therapy, bibliotherapy, marital or systems therapy, imaginal desensitization, and assertiveness or social skill training to produce a broad spectrum treatment package (e.g., Barlow & Cerny, 1988; Lazarus, 1989). The suggestions by Ellis in this chapter are illustrative of how hypnosis may be used to reinforce nonhypnotic therapies.

There has been a tremendous amount published on hypnosis with phobic disorders, including a theme issue of the *American Journal of Clinical Hypnosis* in April 1981 and one book (Clarke & Jackson, 1983) focused on hypnotic treatment of anxiety and phobic disorders. We will not attempt in this introduction to provide a thorough review of an area as broad as anxiety, phobias and panic disorder. However, it seems important to note that, despite the fact that hypnosis is often useful in the treatment of anxiety and phobic disorders, careful evaluation and treatment are still essential (Crasilneck, 1980). At least 76 different phobias have been identified (Laughlin, 1967), and thus, the seemingly unitary category "phobic disorders" is far from a homogeneous grouping. Patients with phobias or anxiety disorders should not all automatically receive the same treatment. For instance, Fermouw and Gross (1983) emphasized the importance of considering the subtypes of social phobias, taking into account the difference between patients with high physiological arousal alone versus those with high cognitive and high physiological arousal.

The first section of this chapter will overview a variety of suggestions for facilitating anxiety relief. Suggestive procedures for the treatment of phobic disorders will be the next topic of this chapter.

DENTAL HYPNOSIS

There are many applications of hypnosis in dentistry. A large percentage of patients are anxious and fearful concerning dental work, some to the point of being phobic. Hypnotherapy prior to dental work, self-hypnosis training, and naturalistic (informal) hypnotic procedures may all prove calming for the patient. Suggestions that are found in other chapters of the book on pain, anesthesia, healing and working with children are certainly relevant to dentistry. Use of dental analgesia will reduce the need for chemical anesthetic agents, along with their risks and side effects. Hypnotic analgesia will prove particularly beneficial when medical conditions and allergies preclude the use of chemical anesthetic agents. Dentists will also want to consult Chapter 8 for suggestions to promote vascular control, for example, to control bleeding among hemophilia patients. Hypnotic suggestions may also be extremely effective in working with bruxism, temporomandibular joint syndrome, gagging, thumbsucking, nailbiting, tongue thrusting, and in adjusting to dentures. Hypnotic suggestions can additionally facilitate compliance to suggestions for brushing, flossing, adjusting to dentures, and wearing dental appliances. Finally, hypnosis can be of particular value in pediatric dentistry to facilitate cooperation, minimize misbehavior, and reduce pain and anxiety. Research (Barber, Donaldson, Ramras, & Allen, 1979) also suggests that the combined use of hypnosis with nitrous oxide may prove unusually effective, potentiating the effects of suggestions.

INDICATIONS AND CONTRAINDICATIONS FOR HYPNOSIS WITH TEMPOROMANDIBULAR JOINT SYNDROME AND BRUXISM.   Temporomandibular Joint Syndrome (TMJ) may cause symptoms of jaw pain, joint and muscle tenderness, abrasion of teeth (secondary to bruxism), and joint dislocation and/or sounds. TMJ, jaw clenching and bruxism may be an undiagnosed cause of headaches, particularly when the patient awakens with headaches. Clinicians who are not dentists should have potential TMJ problems evaluated by a dental or a maxillofacial specialist. Occlusal problems may result from abnormal malocclusion, and tooth grinding may stem from neoplasms, degenerative joint disease, congenital anomalies or trauma. The meniscus may also be displaced, worn down or torn.

Patients should be cautioned, however, that some dental specialists almost routinely suggest surgery without first trying more conservative treatments. Teflon joint implants that break down over time and require further surgery are also still being used. Nonhypnotic and nonsurgical treatments also include the use of removable splint and jaw appliances. However, placebo treatments often (40%–64%) provide lasting remissions and stress seems to be a prominent etiologic variable in both bruxism and TMJ. Thus hypnotic suggestions and self-hypnosis training may provide lasting relief for many patients. In this regard, many of the suggestive procedures included in the first part of this chapter for treatment of anxiety may be beneficial. Hypnotic approaches to TMJ and bruxism may include abreaction of emotions (e.g., anger), self-hypnosis training, and suggestive hypnosis. The final section of the chapter will present suggestions that have been used successfully by various clinicians for managing various dental problems, along with an overview of the areas in which hypnosis may be used in dentistry.

HYPNOSIS WITH ANXIETY

Progressive Relaxation Induction or Deepening Technique

D. Corydon Hammond, Ph.D.
Salt Lake City, Utah

FIXATION ON BODY AND BREATHING

I'd like you to begin by just resting back, very comfortably, and closing your eyes. Just rest back in the way that is most comfortable for you right now, just resting your hands on your thighs, or on the arms of the chair. And as you just settle back comfortably, this will be an opportunity for you to become even more comfortable, and to experience a hypnotic state, very easily, and very gently, and very comfortably.

And as you rest back, you can begin noticing the feelings, and sensations in your body right now. Just notice some of the sensations, that you can be aware of right now. For instance, you may become aware of the feel of the shoes on your feet; or you may notice the sensations in your hands as they rest there; or perhaps you may be aware of how the chair supports your body. And as you continue listening to me, and breathing easily and comfortably, and deeply, you may become aware of the sensations as you breath, noticing for example that the sensations are different when you breathe in [timed to inhalation], and when you breathe out [timed to exhalation]. Just notice those feelings as you breathe in [timed to inhalation], and fill your lungs; and then notice the sense of release, as you breathe out [said while exhaling simultaneously with the patient].

PROGRESSIVE RELAXATION

And now I'd like you to concentrate particularly on the feelings in your toes and feet. Just allow all the muscles and fibers in your toes and feet, to become very deeply relaxed. Perhaps even picturing in your mind's eye what that would look like, for all those little muscles and tissues to relax, loosely and deeply. Allowing yourself to get that kind of feeling you have when you take off a pair of tight shoes, that you've had on for a long time. And you can just let go of all the tension in your toes and feet, and feel the relaxation spread. [Brief pause]

And now imagine that this comfort and relaxation, is beginning to spread and flow, like a gentle river of relaxation, upward, through your ankles and all through your calves. Letting go of all the tension in your calves, allowing them to deeply, and restfully, and comfortably relax. And when it feels as if that comfort has spread all the way up to your knees, gently nod your head to let me know. [Pause] [After a response:] Good. [This signal is a double check that the patient is responding adequately and it also allows the facilitator to gauge the amount of time needed for purposes of timing the rest of the induction. A signal may also be given when the comfort has reached the top of the thighs.]

And allow that comfort to continue, flowing upward, into your knees, and behind your knees and through your knees, and into your thighs, letting go of all the tension in your thighs. Perhaps once again imagining what that might look like, for all those large muscles and tissues, to become soft and loose, and deeply relaxed. Perhaps already noticing that sense of gentle heaviness in your legs, as they just sink down, limply and comfortably. And when you notice that sense of heaviness in your legs, gently nod your head again. And continue to allow that comfort, to flow and spread upward, at its own pace and speed, into the middle part of your body. Flowing into your pelvis and abdomen and stomach, [pause] through your hips and into your lower back. Letting that soothing, deep comfort spread, inch by inch, up through your body, spreading from muscle group to muscle group. Gradually, progressively flowing into your chest, [brief pause] into your back, [brief pause], between your shoulder blades, and into your shoulders. Just allow all the tension to loosen, and flow away. As if somehow, just the act of breathing is increasing your comfort. As if somehow, every breathe you take, is just draining the tension out, of your body, taking you deeper, [timed to exhalations] and deeper, into comfort, with every breath you take. And allow that comfort to flow into your neck and throat. Perhaps imagining once again what that would look like, for all the little fibers and muscles in your neck and throat, to deeply, softly, comfortably relax. Let that relaxation sink deep into your neck. And it can gradually flow up your neck, up into your

scalp, and all out across your scalp, as if it's just bathing your head, with waves of comfort, and relaxation. And that relaxation can flow down, into your forehead, and like a gentle wave, down across your face, into your eyes, your cheeks, your mouth and jaw. Just let go of all the tension in your face, your mouth, your jaw, allowing those tissues and muscles to sag down, slack and relaxed.

And now allow that comfort to flow back down your neck, and across your shoulders, and down into your arms. Letting that comfort flow down your arms, through your elbows, [pause] through your wrists, through your hands and fingers, right down through your fingertips. Letting go of all the tension, and tightness, letting go of all the stress, and strain, all through your body. Just allowing your body to rest, and relax.

Hypnotic Treatment Techniques with Anxiety

David Spiegel, M.D., and
Herbert Spiegel, M.D.
Stanford, California, and New York, New York

Anxiety patients are taught to concentrate on developing a physical sense of floating relaxation, a sense of floating in some setting they associate with comfort, such as a pool, a bath, a lake, or a hot tub. They are then instructed to picture an imaginary screen in their mind's eye, with the picture on that screen initially a pleasant scene. They are thus taught that they can use their reservoir of memories and experiences to produce psychological relaxation and physical comfort rather than anxiety. They are then taught to picture what concerns them on this imaginary screen, using the center of the screen as a problem or receiving screen where they choose what particular anxiety-related problem they wish to work on. Then they are instructed to move some particular problem on which they wish to do further mental work onto the left, or sinister, side of the screen, where they picture their problem in greater detail. They then use the right side of the screen as a problem-solving screen, where they try out possible solutions. In this way, they are instructed to focus on particular aspects of the problem, making it possible to conceptualize solutions. Throughout this instruction, patients are interrupted if necessary to help them maintain a physical sense of floating comfort, thereby dissociating the psychological experience of stress from the physical experience of stress.

The Private Refuge

Selig Finkelstein, D.D.S.
Pleasantville, New York

INDICATIONS

This technique consists of a progressive relaxation procedure followed by downward movement and imagery of a safe place. These suggestions may be used for induction and deepening, and to assist patients where symptoms of anxiety and fearfulness are present. A variant of this technique is also valuable with multiple personality patients. (*Ed.*)

SUGGESTIONS

Relaxation is a mental process. You can begin by closing your eyes, but it helps to have something physical with which to work. Just wiggle your shoulders a little bit. That can give you a comfortable feeling of relaxation. Move that feeling of comfortable relaxation into your upper arms, through your elbows into your forearms, wrists, and hands, so that you have a comfortable, relaxed feeling from your right hand, up your right arm, through your shoulders to your left arm and left hand. Move the feeling of comfortable relaxation from your shoulders into your chest, stomach, hips and

upper legs, through your knees, into your lower legs, ankles and feet. Bring the feeling of comfortable relaxation from your shoulders into your neck and let it move into your head, until it fills your entire head with a comfortable, relaxed feeling. Take a deep breath and, as you breathe out, relax very deeply. [You can gently press the patient's shoulder as he/she exhales.]

Just imagine you are on the fifth floor of a very lovely building. This building has the interesting property that permits you to double your relaxation each time you descend to a lower floor. There are three ways of descending for you to choose from. There is a lovely elevator with very comfortable chairs to support you comfortably. There is an escalator, which has a comfortable chair for you to sit on as it goes down from floor to floor. There is a wide, carpeted stairway, that is brightly lit with lovely pictures on the walls. Through the windows you can see a lovely day outside.

As we descend, enjoy the increase in feelings of comfort and relaxation, which you can double with each successive floor. Now, we reach the fourth floor and continue down, reaching the third floor, and continue down as the relaxation intensifies, reaching the second floor, with relaxation deepening even more, and continue to the first floor.

You leave the building and enter an absolutely wonderful place, which is wherever you want it to be, and which you can change whenever you wish. In it are the things, and only the things you want, and you can change these also, as you wish. With you are the people, and only the people you want, and you can change them any time you choose, and you can even be by yourself, if you like.

Enjoy your special place, in a safe and lovely manner. This is your refuge, and now that you know where it is and how to get there, you can return to it any time you need to or want to.

When you wake up, you can feel refreshed and very good, and when I count to three, you can wake up, feeling terrific, because you are. One . . . two . . . three.

Imagery Scenes Facilitating Relaxation

H. E. Stanton, Ph.D.
Hobart, Tasmania, Australia

THE POOL

Imagine you are standing on a ledge overlooking a quiet pool, lifting a heavy rock high over your head. Watch the rock as you drop it into the water, observing, in slow motion, the splash and way it settles, sinking to the bottom of the pool. As it does so, imagine the water closing in above it, generating rippling circles spreading out all over the pool's surface. Continue to observe these ripples as they wax and wane until, finally, they fade away completely, returning the water to its initial state of mirror-like calm.

THE CLOUD

Feel that a warm cloud is bathing the entire center of your body. As it touches any part of you, it engenders a wonderful feeling of warmth and relaxation. Gradually the cloud spreads out from your center, touching every part of your body in turn, bringing a sense of energy, warmth, release of all tension, and peace. Once you are completely engulfed by the cloud, feel your body becoming increasingly light, so that it seems to float effortlessly, drifting upwards into the blue sky. Cushioned safely within this cloud, you can go to some special place where you feel at peace.

THE GARDEN

Imagine yourself standing on the patio of a lovely old house, enjoying the warm sun and the gentle breeze which fans your cheeks. From this patio, you notice that there is a flight of ten steps leading down into a beautiful sunken garden.

Go down these steps, one at a time, linking your downward movement to an exhalation of your breath, feeling that, with each step, you let go more and more. This sense of ever-growing calm has completely enfolded you by the time you reach the garden. [Pause]

And what a beautiful garden it is. You can see masses of multicolored flowers, an ornamental fountain, superb shrubs, and graceful trees. Perhaps you can smell the flowers, hear the songs of the birds and the sound of the water from the fountain splashing into the pool at its base, and feel the gentle warmth of the sun soaking into your body.

Island of Serenity

Edwin L. Stickney, M.D.
Miles City, Montana

INDICATIONS

This metaphor may be particularly indicated with anxious patients who feel threatened, overwhelmed, or intruded upon by others. It may be helpful in reducing patient defensiveness preparatory to exploration or in facilitating self-exploration and insight. (*Ed.*)

SUGGESTIONS

Now I want you to imagine that you are going to take a trip to an island. I am going to count to ten, and as I do, you will be able to make this journey. I don't know whether you will make it by plane, by boat, or by swimming as Donna Nyad did.

And now you begin the journey—One . . . going into a deeper and more relaxed state with each count.

Two. . . . etc.

Six . . . And now I need to tell you something about this island to which you are going. This island is *your island of serenity. It is very deep within you.*

Seven . . . going deeper and deeper. . . . This island is so *deep within you that it cannot be invaded.*

Eight . . . *deeper and deeper yet. . . . It cannot be invaded by anyone, it cannot be invaded by anything.*

Nine . . . deeper and more relaxed . . . so that when you are on this island you are safe. *Most of the time we need to guard ourselves, but you are so safe on this island that you may allow any feelings you wish to come out in the open and be recognized and deeply felt.*

Ten . . . *now you are on your island of serenity, and in the next few minutes you will be able to spend a whole day on that island.*

[Further visualizations and/or ego-strengthening suggestions may now be incorporated into this metaphor as needed.]

Deep, Meditative Trance: The Approach of Ainslie Meares, M.D.

INTRODUCTION AND INDICATIONS

The late Dr. Ainslie Meares was heavily influenced by Eastern meditative traditions. His distinctive approach was one of facilitating deep, meditative hypnotic states. He did this primarily through using nonverbal techniques and a minimum of verbal suggestions that would require conscious analysis. Concerning his use of touch, however, it must be remembered that Meares was a physician. Caution is urged with regard to the extent and nature of the touch utilized to minimize possible misinterpretation, transference or countertransference reactions. Meares believed that facilitating an extended state of profound quietness and stillness was very healing. He particularly utilized this approach with medical patients (e.g., cancer patients). The editor believes it is also a valuable technique that is indicated with anxiety states and premenstrual syndrome.

The following material was compiled and edited from Dr. Meares' contributions in the 1973 ASCH Syllabus and from his article in the

American Journal of Clinical Hypnosis. If you find this approach interesting, you will probably also want to consult the two contributions on prolonged hypnosis in Chapter 8 (Hypnosis with Medical Disorders). (*Ed.*)

I believe that the giving of specific hypnotic suggestions is poor quality hypnotherapy. This opinion is based on the experience of 1,130 patients treated by hypnosis. Of these, approximately 420 patients were treated primarily by hypnotic suggestion and approximately the same number by hypnoanalytic techniques, including both hypnography and hypnoplasty as well as verbal hypnoanalysis. The remaining 710 patients have been treated simply by deep relaxing hypnosis without any specific suggestions or hypnoanalysis at all. In this method, hypnosis is used to show the patient how to reduce his own anxiety. The rationale of the method is that symptoms are only maintained by anxiety. If the patient can reduce his anxiety, symptoms either disappear spontaneously or can be easily controlled by the patient. Thus the patient who wants to give up smoking or overeating becomes anxious when put to the test. This is shown by his restless, agitated apprehension. If he can be shown by relaxing hypnosis how to control this disquiet of his mind, he becomes master of his own destiny and is in a position to control his symptomatic behavior with little effort.

So, as I see it, the only therapeutic suggestions that we should use are those to help the natural mechanisms of the patient's mind to alleviate his anxiety. For this to be effective, the suggestions cannot be given by means of a logical verbal communication, as this would keep the patient alert and so prevent the essential atavistic regression. So the suggestions must be conveyed by the para-logical use of words, by unverbalized phonation and by touch.

At the beginning of the session, it is necessary to use a few words to allay the patient's immediate anxiety. But these words must be used in a way which does not evoke any critical thought in the patient, as such would keep the patient alert and so prevent the atavistic regression of true hypnosis.

So I say to the patient, "Good Easy Natural Letting yourself go Effortless All effortless and natural All through us Deeply All through our body All through out mind."

These verbal suggestions have very little logical content, but on the other hand they carry a significant para-logical meaning. They are said slowly. There are pauses between the phrases, and the pauses lengthen out into silences. From this there is an easy transition to suggestion by unverbalized phonation. "Ah Umm Umm." This continues into the sound that comes when I breathe out slowly in relaxed fashion. I do this, timing it with the natural rhythm of the patient's breathing.

The absence of any direct logical communication is very important. Any logical communication that I might make alerts the patient's critical faculties to evaluate what I have said, and so defeats the purpose of the procedure, which is to lead the patient to stillness of mind. Even such simple, but logical, ideas as, "Your arms are relaxed," have this effect, as the patient immediately thinks about the relaxation of his arms. Communication must be made in such a way that it does not provoke any intellectual activity in the patient. This is achieved by nonverbal phonation and by touch, and sometimes by single words or simple phrases which are merely reassuring and do not evoke critical mental activity in the patient. Thus the word, "Good," spoken slowly in a long exhalation, has this effect. Again, the phrase, "That's right," has a similar effect if spoken in a slow exhalation. Again, unverbalized phonation, a long natural, "Ummm," has meaning to the patient in the way of reassurance, and the knowledge that I am close by. The "Ummm" does not evoke any intellectual response. However, the main and most significant means of communication is by touch as something very natural, reassuring and helpful. The touch must never be tentative, or it will make the patient anxious.

The mind is simply allowed to be still. If we want our mind to be still, it is obvious that we cannot keep repeating a mantra. It is equally obvious that we cannot be aware of our breathing. If we are aware of our breathing, of course our mind is not still. It is important that this stillness of mind should develop in the absence of drowsiness and in the absence of physical comfort. At first, when the patient is learning this type of meditation, the stillness will not be complete. There will come moments of stillness followed by periods of mental activity, and then stillness again, which is experienced as a kind of ebb and flow in the naturalness of it all. Any attempt on the part of the patient to try to induce the stillness destroys the whole process. Many patients find that capturing the effortless quality is the most difficult part of the whole procedure. While all this is going on, other suggestions of relaxation are communicated by touch. I let my hands rest on the patient's shoulders, on his forehead, or on his abdomen where my hand moves easily but firmly with the patient's respiratory rhythm.

These nonspecific suggestions reduce the level of the patient's anxiety and no specific suggestions are given at all. By this means the patient learns to reduce his anxiety himself, and retains full personal responsibility for his better way of life.

If it is practicable, the cancer patient attends for a session of meditation each weekday morning for a month and then less frequently. Besides these sessions with me, the patient is required to practice daily at home. Meditation in a position of comfort produces a kind of drowsy numbness which is quite different from the crystal clear stillness of intensive meditation. So the patients are encouraged to practice their meditation in a posture of slight discomfort. Then, as the meditation comes, the slight discomfort is transcended and the patient is no longer aware that he is in a potentially uncomfortable or even painful posture. At the start I lead the patients into meditation while they are sitting in a comfortable chair. When they have learned the feel of it, they practice at home sitting on an upright chair or stool. This is enough to provide some very slight discomfort. They start to meditate. Then as the meditation comes they are no longer aware of the slight discomfort. Then they proceed to lying on the floor, kneeling, squatting on their buttocks or squatting cross-legged sitting on a cushion or book and then to squatting without any aid. The only purpose of the posture is to provide a degree of discomfort which is commensurate with the meditator's ability to transcend it.

The length of time spend in meditation depends on the patient's ability to do it. At the start, 10 minutes three times a day may be all the patient can manage. On the other hand, some patients who have been successful in bringing about a regression of their cancer have gotten into the way of meditating for two or three hours a day or more. . . . Those patients who come to like meditating do best.

Methods of Relaxed Breathing

Beata Jencks, Ph.D.
Murray, Utah

INTRODUCTION

Dr. Jencks has created a variety of innovative respiration techniques that may be beneficial in facilitating greater relaxation. She believes that utilizing imagination, along with suggestions in the form of single words or phrases, is particularly powerful when linked with the appropriate phases of the breathing cycle (see the Table below for details). The techniques may be used in the office setting, or recommended for use in self-hypnosis. These are also methods that may serve to focus attention and may be used for deepening techniques. (*Ed.*)

INSTRUCTIONS

While you are trying out or practicing many of the following exercises, keep in mind the effects listed in the Table. The instructions for the exercises should be modified by experimentation according to personal needs. For such experimentation the following instructions are helpful: (1) Do or imagine something only two or three times during consecutive breathing

rhythms; (2) use minimal real stimulation, but maximal involvement of the imagination; (3) observe a pause-for-feeling, or "creative pause," to allow time for the imagination to work and the body to react.

Experimentation should not be continued when the desired results are not obtained after a few trials. In this case other images should be substituted. However it should be kept in mind that different exercises and images may be effective at different times or under different circumstances.

TABLE
Physical, Physiological, and Psychological Feelings, Actions, and Images Related to the Breathing Rhythm

Exhalation	Inhalation	Holding the Breath
Physical and Physiological		
Relaxation	Increase of tension	Maintenance or increase of tension
Heaviness	Lightness	Unstable equilibrium
Calmness	Stimulation	Restlessness
Warmth	Coolness	Variability
Darkness	Brightness	Variability
Softness	Hardness	Rigidity
Moisture	Dryness	
Weakness, weariness	Strength, invigoration, refreshment	Momentary conservation of strength
Psychological		
Patience, endurance	Speed, being startled	Anxiety, oppression
Contemplation	Ready attention	Strained attention

(continued)

TABLE (continued)

Exhalation	Inhalation	Holding the Breath
Equanimity	Courage	Cowardice
Deep thought, concentration	Open-mindedness, creativity	Closed-mindedness
Introversion	Extroversion	
Boredom	Excitement	Keen interest
Satisfaction	Curiosity	Uncertainty
Depression	Cheerfulness	Nervous tension
Comfort	Exhilaration	Uneasiness
Generosity	Greed	Stinginess

Actions

Relax, release, let go, loosen	Tense, bind, tighten grasp	Hold on
Release pressure, stream, or flow out	Increase pressure, stream, or flow in	Maintain or increase pressure
Liquify	Solidify	Maintain consistency
Expand, widen, open	Contract, narrow, close	Dimension unchanged or congestion
Sink, descend, fall asleep	Ascend, levitate, rise, wake up	Maintain level
Lengthen	Shorten	Maintain length
Move or swing forward, strike, kick, punch, reach out	Move, draw, pull, or swing backward, haul in	Stop, stand, or hold still
Send, give, help, offer	Receive, take, demand	Keep, interrupt
Laugh, sigh, giggle	Sob, gasp	Smile, frown

LONG BREATH

Imagine inhaling through the fingertips, up the arms into the shoulders, and then exhaling down the trunk into the abdomen and legs, and leisurely out at the toes. Repeat, and feel how this slow, deep breathing affects the whole body, the abdomen, the flanks, and the chest. Do not move the shoulders while doing the long breath.

STONE INTO WELL

Imagine a deep well in your abdomen. Then imagine that you are dropping a stone into this well during a relaxed exhalation. Follow its fall. How long did the fall last? How deep did it fall? Where did it come to rest? Repeat.

BELLOWS

Breathe as if the flanks were bellows which are drawing in and pushing out. Inhale while the bellows are drawing in the air, exhale while the bellows contract and expel the air. Imagine that the air streams through the flanks freely.

HOLE IN THE SMALL OF BACK

Sit or lie comfortably and breathe normally and relaxedly. Disregard the chest and throat completely for a moment and imagine a hole in the small of the back, through which the breathed air flows in and out comfortably. Breathe deeply and relaxedly through the hole for three or four breathing cycles. Then just close the eyes for a moment, let the mind drift, and enjoy the feeling of deep relaxation.

SWING

Lie on your back and imagine a swing swinging with your respiration. Push the swing during one exhalation. Let it swing in its own rhythm. Do not push the swing all the time.

Permit it to swing by itself. Feel tensions swinging out during exhalation. Feel energy streaming in during inhalation.

PENDULUM

Inhale and halt the breath momentarily. Exhale and imagine that this sets a pendulum in motion. Permit the breathing to find its own rhythm. Allow it to swing or flow as it wants to do.

WAVES OR TIDES

Lie on your back and imagine ocean waves or tides flowing with your respiration. Allow them to flow out passively. Allow them to return passively. Do not push. They flow by themselves. Feel the passive flowing in and out of the waves or tides. Observe where you feel movement. Feel to where the waves are flowing. Feel from where the waves return. Do not prolong this exercise beyond two or three respiratory cycles. Then feel what happened in the body during the next two to three cycles. Get up from the lying position first to a sitting and then to a standing position during consecutive exhalations. This preserves the relaxation and prevents dizziness after deep relaxation.

Stand relaxedly, arms hanging easily at the sides, inhale and feel what is set in motion by the rising wave of inhaling. Then allow the wave of the breath to decline and fade, as if into a great distance. Repeat, and allow the arms to move easily with the breathing waves.

IMAGINED DRUG

Imagine that you are inhaling a broncho-dilator agent, which relaxes and widens the walls of the air passages in bronchi and lungs. Allow them to become soft like rags and relaxed, collapsing during the exhalations, and allow them to become widely expanded during the inhalations, while the air streams in easily.

BREATHING THROUGH THE SKIN

Concentrate on the forehead or any other body surface area and imagine inhaling and exhaling through the skin there. Exhale and feel something going out. Inhale and feel something coming in. Exhale through the skin and permit it to relax. Inhale through the skin and feel it refreshed and invigorated.

RELAXING THE DIAPHRAGM

The release of tensions will result spontaneously and unconsciously in slower, deeper exhalations. Such relaxed breathing is similar to that during sleep and during the waking state may be felt as "being breathed" rather than active breathing. The respiration is deepened when the tendons of the neck and shoulders are relaxed, the mouth-throat junction is felt as a wide open space, and exhalations are felt throughout the whole trunk, especially in the flanks and in the small of the back. Also imagining making movements with the joints, as in calisthenics, or using the vocal mechanism by humming, chanting, sighing, or growling will relax the diaphragm.

LOOSENING JOINTS

Work on the joints is especially effective for relaxing the diaphragm, since nerve cells which deepen the breathing rhythm reflexively are located around and in the joints. Allow any yawning, sighing, or changes in the breathing rhythm to occur naturally during joint exercises.

The following exercise is similar to F. M. Alexander's technique, and it is especially effective for the head-neck-shoulder region, which was the location with which he worked.

Sit in an armchair with a high back to rest the head, the arms well supported, the feet squarely on the floor with the knees bent at right angles, or lie on the floor on the back, with the legs drawn up, the feet on the floor. Then think each of the following phrases during an exhalation, disregarding the inhalations, or letting the air stream passively into the lungs as if a vacuum were filling gently. Use any or all and repeat as needed: Tell the shoulders to let go of the neck. . . . Tell the neck to let go of the head. . . . Tell the head to let go of the jaw. . . . Tell the throat to let go of the tongue. . . . Tell the eye sockets to let go of the eyes. . . . Tell the shoulders to let go of the upper arms. . . . Tell the elbows to let go of the lower arms. . . . Tell the wrists to let go of the hands. . . . Tell the hands to let go of the fingers. . . . Tell the spine and sternum to let go of the ribs. . . . Tell the lower back to let go of the pelvis. . . . Tell the hip joints to let go of the upper legs. . . . Tell the knees to let go of the lower legs. . . . Tell the ankles to let go of the feet. . . . Tell the feet to let go of the toes. . . .

Similar to this are some instructions in A. D. Read's (1944) relaxation method for natural childbirth. The practitioner is instructed to imagine, for instance, that the shoulders "open to the outside," the arms fall "out of the shoulder sockets," the back "sinks through the couch to the floor," the legs, knees, and feet "fall by their own weight to the outside," the head "makes an indentation in the pillow," the face "hangs from the cheekbones," and the jaw "hangs loosely." All of these involve the loosening of joints and are effective, especially if done during relaxing exhalations.

FILLING AND EMPTYING THE BOTTLE

This is a German version, taught to actors and singers, of a yogic exercise to relax and deepen breathing. Remember that, when liquid is poured into a bottle, the bottom fills before the middle and the top. When the liquid is poured out, the bottom will empty before the top. Imagine that the trunk is a bottle. Fill it with inhaled air, first the bottom and then higher and higher. During exhalation imagine the bottle tipped and the breath flowing out, emptying first the lower abdomen, then the upper, and finally the chest. Repeat, but no more than three times consecutively. Then resume normal breathing.

The Autogenic Rag Doll

Beata Jencks, Ph.D.
Murray, Utah

INDICATION

This may be used as an induction or deepening technique. It incorporates all the aspects of Schultz's autogenic training, but uses imagery instead of Schultz's intellectual formulas. It has proven valuable with anxiety, with children as well as adults, and in preparation for childbirth training. Individuals will respond best who can use visual and kinesthetic imagery. The procedure may be used on a self-hypnosis tape, and it may be presented in segments: introducing only the limb heaviness procedure first, and adding other components every few days. (*Ed.*)

HEAVINESS OF THE LIMBS.   Make yourself comfortable and allow your eyes to close. Then lift one arm a little, and just let it drop. Let it drop heavily, as if it were the arm of a Raggedy Ann [Andy] doll, one of those floppy dolls or animals. Choose one in your imagination. Choose a doll, an old beloved soft teddybear, a velveteen rabbit, a bean bag toy, or even a pillow or a blanket. Choose anything soft which you like. Lift the arm again a little and drop it, and then let is rest for a moment. . . .

Now think of your arm again, but don't lift it in reality, just in the imagination. Lift it in imagination and think that you are dropping it again, and do this while you breathe out. Let the arm go limp like a rag while you breathe out. . . .

And now work with the other arm. Use either your imagination or really lift it at first. It does not matter. But do not lift it too high, just enough to feel its heaviness, and let it drop, but gently and relaxedly. Learn to do it more and more in imagination only. And when you breathe out again, drop it, let it go soft, let it go limp and relaxed. . . .

Next lift both arms together, and allow them to drop, simply relax them, allow them to be limp and soft. . . .

Then lift one leg. Lift it only a little, just enough that you can feel its heaviness, and allow it to drop, limp and relaxed, limp and soft. . . . Do this always when you breathe out. Don't lift the leg too high, so that it does not hit too hard. Or better yet, lift it only in imagination. Do this a few times in your imagination only, and just let it become heavy and relaxed. . . .

Now do the same with the other leg. Lift it a little, and while you breathe out let it relax. Let it go soft like a rag. Let it drop like the leg of a giant rag doll. . . .

Feel free to move your legs or any part of your body to a more comfortable position any time you want to do so.

And now both legs together, lift them in your imagination, and let them relax, limp and soft, like a rag or a bean bag. . . .

And finally all limbs together, both arms and both legs, breathe out and allow them to be limp and relaxed, heavy and comfortable, like a giant rag doll, well supported by the chair, the sofa, or the floor.

WARMTH OF THE LIMBS.   Next imagine that you put your rag doll into the sun. Let it be warmed by the sun. The giant rag doll is lying very relaxedly. Feel how the sun is shining on it. Feel it on one arm first, and then on the other. See to it that the head of the rag doll is in the shade and kept cool, but all the limbs are sprawled out in the sun. Feel your arm, warm, soft, and relaxed. . . . And then feel the other arm, warm, soft, and relaxed. . . . And then let one leg be nicely warmed by the sun. . . . And then the other leg, nicely warmed, soft, and relaxed. . . . Remember, you are the giant rag doll, and you are lying in the sun; all your limbs are nice and warm, but your head is lying in the shade and is comfortably cool. . . .

HEARTBEAT.   And now that you are such a nicely relaxed rag doll, imagine you have within yourself something that is like a little motor, which makes you go all the time, and that is your heart. It just keeps you going all the time, day and night, whether you keep track of it or not.

And just as you walk or run, sometimes a little faster, sometimes slower, and sometimes skip along, just so that little motor in you sometimes goes a little faster, sometimes slower, and sometimes skips. That is quite normal. And now just feel, if you can, the rhythm of your heart. It does not really matter whether you can feel it or only imagine it, but think of your heart and say "thank you" to it. This organ works all the time for you, whether you think of it or not. So now just stay with it for a while, and say "thank you." . . . Thank your heart that it does such a good job for you. . . .

RESPIRATION.   Next, for a moment, pay attention to your breathing. The breathing rhythm, just like the heart, sometimes goes fast and sometimes goes slow. Allow it to go as slow or as fast, as shallow or as deep as it wants to. If you have to sigh, that is fine. If you want to inhale deeply, that is fine. Just follow the breathing. . . . And then, for a moment, just imagine that the air which you breathe streams in at the fingers while you breathe in, up your arms, and into your shoulders and chest; and then, while you breathe out, down into your abdomen, down into your legs, and out at your toes. And repeat this for two or three breaths. . . . Then imagine that you are floating, floating on an air mattress on the ocean, a big river, or a swimming pool. Let slow and gentle waves carry you up and down in the rhythm of your breathing.

INTERNAL WARMTH.   Now breathe into the palm of your hand and feel the warmth of your breath. Such warmth is within you all the time. Repeat it, and then put the hand down again and imagine. Imagine that you breathe this same kind of warmth into your own inside. . . . While you breathe out, imagine that you breathe that warmth down into your throat, down into your chest, down into your abdomen. . . . Just become nicely warm inside. . . . Or you may imagine that you are drinking something which really warms you nicely inside, or even that something like a warmly glowing ball is rolling around within you.

Allow it to warm your inside, so that it becomes all soft and relaxed.

COOLNESS OF THE FOREHEAD.   Bring one hand to the mouth and lick two fingers. Then stroke the moist fingers over your forehead. Just stroke your forehead and feel the coolness of the moisture. If you want to moisten the forehead again, feel free to do so. . . . And then, while you breathe in, feel the refreshing coolness of your forehead, and imagine again that giant rag doll or rag animal, lying with its head in the cool shade. . . .

Now just lie there and relax completely for a while, and think of the rag doll with its body warmed comfortably, relaxed in the sun. Feel again the gentle cradling of the waves of the breathing rhythm. And while breathing in feel the cool shade, the coolness on your forehead, and while breathing out feel your comfortably relaxed body.

ENDING THE ALTERED STATE OF CONSCIOUSNESS.   In time, become more and more aware of being refreshed during the inhalations. And when you decide it is time to end the state in which you are now, yawn and breathe in deeply and refreshingly while you stretch and flex arms and legs. And then open your eyes, look around and breathe in once more.

Hypnotic Suggestion/Metaphor to Begin Reframing

Steven Gurgevich, Ph.D.
Tucson, Arizona

INTRODUCTION

The following is spoken to the patient who is already in trance as a prelude to focusing on specific events that will be the focus of reframing or unbinding of affect. It is important to have already established ideomotor signaling and observation of physiological re-

sponses to trance-deepening so that the communicative rapport between therapist and subject remains clear and intact.

SUGGESTIONS

There were times in the past when you felt worried and frightened. Can you remember the feeling of being worried, the feeling of being frightened by your own thoughts? [Pause] Now, let yourself remember what followed that feeling. Can you remember the feeling of relief you experienced each time you began to think that everything is going to be fine—a feeling, a thought that everything is working out well, a feeling that everything is going to be fine. Such a wonderful feeling of relief and release from worry.

Each point in time is like a lens through which you see your world. The first day in school was different than the semester's end. The first time behind the wheel of an automobile felt different from the relaxing drive today. Some of your greatest pleasures today may have been first experienced with apprehension or tension. Now you may choose how you would like to feel about any past or present condition. As you relax more deeply, your unconscious mind selects the proper lens and the most comfortable frame. Sometimes you can tell your imagination what you are ready to begin enjoying. I don't know if your thoughts will change after your feelings, or if your feelings will follow more relaxing thoughts. But I know you are ready to enjoy a pleasant change, a wonderful feeling of release.

COMMENT

At this point, you would begin focusing upon specific events or conditions to reframe with the patient in trance. Also, at this point, suggestions can be offered for uncovering what events or circumstances need to be reframed in order to remove symptoms.

Rational-Emotive Suggestions About Anxiety

Albert Ellis, Ph.D.
New York, New York

INDICATIONS AND CONTRAINDICATIONS

These suggestions were excerpted from a published case with an anxious female patient. The case illustrates how any ideas that may be conveyed in a conscious state may also be reinforced in a hypnotic state. These suggestions may be of particular value with anxious and overemotional patients, who catastrophize and are very demanding of themselves and others. They will also be reinforcing when a cognitive therapy approach is being used for part of treatment. Some aspects of the suggestions may be offensive to religious patients, but could be modified for use with such individuals. The suggestions are also somewhat authoritarian at times. Some patients will like the forcefulness; but when working with someone who is very reactive to authority, you may want to phrase the suggestions more permissively. The suggestions were tape recorded for use in self-hypnosis, and were given following a progressive relaxation induction. (*Ed.*)

SUGGESTIONS

Your eyes are getting heavier and heavier and you want to let yourself sink, you're trying to let yourself sink, into a deeper, deeper, relaxed state. You want to let your whole body, especially your eyes, go *deeper* and *deeper* and *deeper into a totally free, warm, nice, flexible, relaxed state. And now you're letting yourself go deeper, deeper, deeper*. You want to fully relax and get your body out of your way and go *deep, deep, down deeper, down deeper*, into a fully, fully, fully free and easy relaxed state. You're only listening to the sound of my voice, that's all you're focusing on, and that's all you

want to hear — the sound of my voice. And you're going to do what I tell you to do, because you *want* to, you *want* to do it. You *want* to stay in this relaxed state and be fully aware of my voice and do what I tell you to do because you *want* to do it, you *want* to be relaxed. You *want* to rid yourself of your anxiety and you know that this will help you relax and listen, relax and listen, go into a fully free and relaxed state.

You're only focusing on my voice and you're going to listen carefully to what I'm telling you. You're going to listen carefully to what I'm telling you. You're going to remember everything I tell you. And after you awake from this relaxed, hypnotic state, you're going to feel very good. Because you're going to remember everything and use what you hear — use it for *you*. Use it to put away all your anxiety *about* your anxiety. You're going to remember what I tell you and use it everyday. Whenever you feel anxious about anything, you're going to remember what I'm telling you now, in this relaxed state, and you're going to fully focus on it, concentrate on it very well, and do exactly what we're talking about, relax and get rid of your anxiety, relax and get rid of your anxiety.

Whenever you get anxious about anything, you're going to realize that the reason you're anxious is because you are saying to yourself, telling yourself, "I *must* succeed! I *must* succeed! I *must* do this, or I *must* not do that!" You will clearly see and fully accept that your anxiety comes from your self-statement. It doesn't come from without. It doesn't come from other people. *You* make yourself anxious, by demanding that something *must* go well or *must* not exist. It's *your* demand that makes you anxious. It's always you and your self-talk; and therefore *you* control it and *you* can change it.

You're going to realize, "*I* make myself anxious. I don't *have* to keep making myself anxious, if I give up my demands, my musts, my shoulds, my oughts. If I can really accept what is, accept things the way they are, then I won't be anxious. I can always make myself unanxious and tense by giving up my musts, by relaxing — by wanting and wishing for things, but not *needing*, not *insisting*, not *demanding*, not *mus*turbating about them."

You're going to keep telling yourself, "I can *ask* for things, I can *wish*. But I do not *need* what I want, I never *need* what I want! There is nothing I *must* have; and there is nothing I *must* avoid, including my anxiety. I'd *like* to get rid of this anxiety. I *can* get rid of it. I'm *going* to get rid of it. But if I tell myself, "I *must* not be anxious! I *must* not be anxious! I *must* be unanxious!" then I'll be anxious.

Nothing will kill me. Anxiety won't kill me. Lack of sex won't kill me. There are lots of unpleasant things in the world that I don't like, but I can *stand* them, I don't *have* to get rid of them. If I'm anxious, I'm anxious — too damn bad! Because *I* control my emotional destiny — as long as I don't feel that I *have* to do anything, that I have to succeed at anything. That's what destroys me — the idea that I *have* to be sexy or I *have* to succeed at sex. Or that I *have* to get rid of my anxiety." In your regular life, after listening to this tape regularly, you're going to think and to keep thinking these things. Whenever you're anxious, you'll look at what you're doing to *make* yourself anxious, and you'll give up your demands and your musts. You'll dispute your ideas that "I *must* do well! I *must* get people to like me! They *must* not criticize me! It's terrible, when they criticize me !" You'll keep asking yourself, "Why *must* I do well? Why do I *have* to be a great sex partner? It would be *nice* if people liked me, but they don't *have* to. I do not *need* their approval. If they criticize me, if they blame me, or they think I'm too sexy, too damn bad! I do not *need* their approval. I'd *like* it, but I don't *need* it. I'd also *like* to be unanxious but there's no reason why I *must* be. Yes, there's no reason why I *must* be. It's just *preferable*. None of these things I fail at are going to kill me.

"And when I die, as I eventually will, so I die! Death is not horrible. It's a state of *no* feeling. It's exactly the same state as I was in before I was born, I won't feel *anything*. So I certainly need not be afraid of that!

"And even if I get very anxious and go crazy, that isn't too terrible. If I tell myself, 'I *must* not go crazy! I *must* not go crazy!' then I'll make myself crazy! But even if I'm crazy, so I'm crazy! I *can* live with it even if I'm in a mental hospital. I can *live* and not depress myself about it. *Nothing* is terrible even when people don't like me, even when I'm acting stupidly, even when I'm very anxious! *Nothing* is terrible! I *can* stand it! It's only a pain in the ass!"

Now this is what you're going to think in your everyday life. Whenever you get anxious about anything, you're going to see what you're anxious about, you're going to realize that you are demanding something, saying "It *must* be so! I *must* get well! I *must* not do the wrong thing! I *must* not be anxious!" And you're going to stop and say, "You know — I don't need that nonsense. If these things happen, they happen. It's not the end of the world! I'd *like* to be unanxious, I'd *like* to get along with people, I'd *like* to have good sex, but if I don't I *don't*! Tough! It is not the end of everything. I can always be a happy human *in spite of* failures and hassles. If I don't *demand*, if I don't insist, if I don't say, 'I must, I must!' Musts are crazy. My *desires* are all right. But, again, I don't *need* what I *want*." Now this is what you're going to keep working at in your everyday life.

You're going to keep using your head, your thinking ability, to focus, to concentrate on ridding yourself of your anxiety just as you're listening and concentrating right now. Your concentration will get better and better. You're going to be more and more in control of your thoughts and your feelings. You will keep realizing that *you* create your anxiety, *you* make yourself upset, and *you* don't have to, you never have to keep doing so. You can always give up your anxiety. You can always change. You can always relax, and relax, and relax, and not take *anyone*, not take *anything* too seriously.

This is what you're going to remember and work at when you get out of this relaxed state. This idea is what you're going to take with you all day, everyday: "*I* control me. I don't *have* to upset myself about anything. If I do upset myself, too bad. I may feel upset for a while but it won't ruin my life or kill me. And I can be anxious without putting myself down, without saying 'I must not be anxious!' At times I will make myself anxious, but I can give up my anxiety if I don't *demand* that I be unanxious."

And you're going to get better and better about thinking in this rational way. You'll become more in control of you. Never *totally* in control, because nobody ever is totally unanxious. But you'll make yourself much less anxious and able to live with it when you are anxious. And if you live with it, it will go away. If you live with it, it will go away. Nothing is terrible, not even anxiety. That's what you're going to realize and to keep thinking about until you really. really believe it.

Now you feel nice and free and warm and fully relaxed. In a few minutes I'm going to tell you to come out of this relaxed, hypnotic state. You will then have a good day. You will feel fine when you come out of this state. You will experience no ill effects of the hypnosis. You will remember everything I just said to you and will keep working at using it. And you will play this tape every day for the next 30 days. You will listen to it every day until you really believe it and follow it. Eventually you will be able to follow its directions and to think your way out of anxiety and out of anxiety *about* being anxious without your tape.

You will then be able to release yourself from anxiety by yourself. You can always relax and use the antianxiety technique you will learn by listening to the tape. You can always accept yourself *with* your anxiety and can stop telling yourself, "I must not be anxious! I must not be anxious!" Just tell yourself, "I don't *like* anxiety, I'll work to give it up. I'll conquer it. I'll control myself, control my own emotional destiny. I can always relax, make myself feel easy and free and nice, just as I feel now, get away from cares for a while and then feel unanxious. But I can more elegantly accept myself first with my anxiety, stop fighting it desperately, and stop telling myself it's awful to be anxious. Then I can go back to the original anxiety and get rid of it by refusing to awfulize about failing and vigorously disputing my irrational beliefs, 'I must do well! I must not be disapproved.'"

Stress Reduction Trance: A Naturalistic Ericksonian Approach

Eleanor S. Field, Ph.D.
Tarzana, California

INTRODUCTION

The following induction procedure utilizes the following process:

1. Focusing attention inward—inner approach.
2. Evoking pre-existing associations and mental processes.
3. Utilizing natural absorption and natural processes.
4. Utilizing natural resources.
5. Subconscious learning process (educational experience).
6. Use of dissociation, anticipation, confusion, exploration, double binds, universal experiences—the separation of the conscious and unconscious minds, metaphors.

SUGGESTIONS

I would like for you to take a few minutes to get yourself comfortable. Possibly you may want to take off your shoes, and you can do that too. And . . . I really DON'T KNOW . . . just what your eyes want to do at this moment. You MIGHT want to find a spot on the wall to look at, comfortably—not staring at anything—but just allowing it to occupy the center of your visual field . . . and WONDERING what is going to happen next. . . . You MIGHT feel more comfortable just . . . closing . . . your eyes in a peaceful sort of way—and either way you do it, I would just like for you . . . to let yourself . . . zero in on the idea of just . . .

being comfortable—and there have been many TIMES—many PLACES—many SITUATIONS where you have felt so COMFORTABLE that nothing else mattered except that comfort—and you might think of them now—and let your SUBCONSCIOUS mind . . . present to you . . . ONE SUCH SITUATION . . . where you really experienced the sense of physical and mental comfort.

And you CAN . . . recall . . . and RE-EXPERIENCE all the sensations—the sights—the sounds—the feelings . . . which go with being extremely comfortable—and you CAN RECALL where you FIRST EXPERIENCED . . . feeling profound relaxation . . . covering your body—the feeling of every muscle in that part of your body just loosening up—and just letting go—and lying flat like a limp rubber band—very deeply relaxed—and very LIKELY that part of your body that needed the relaxation most will re-experience it first—and the feeling of every nerve in that part of your body becoming . . . very quiet—peaceful—not doing any more than is absolutely necessary—and you can WONDER . . . what direction that relaxation is going to move through your body—whether you experience it all at once . . . like a flow of comfort peacefully moving through you. And soon you get the feeling that . . . you don't even have to be aware of it anymore. You can simply allow . . . yourself to become part of that relaxation . . . as it . . . becomes part of you.

And it will be very interesting for you to DISCOVER for yourself that you . . . don't even need to listen to me . . . because what your CONSCIOUS mind does now is not at all important. . . . Maybe . . . your CONSCIOUS mind just wants . . . to curl up in a corner and go to sleep for a while—or go as far away as it likes—the way you did as a kid in SCHOOL when you sat in the CLASSROOM and looked out the window . . . and allowed your mind to drift as far away from the CLASSROOM as it could get—some place you'd rather be—and you lost track of what was being said—and it didn't matter because your SUBCONSCIOUS mind was picking up everything which was

being said . . . as it is doing now—and your SUBCONSCIOUS mind is HERE WITH ME—AND IT CAN HEAR ME—and RESPOND in ITS OWN TIME—IN ITS OWN . . . COMFORTABLE WAY.

You CAN ENJOY whatever it is you are experiencing and—right now . . . you can enjoy whatever sensations—heaviness or lightness—warmth or coolness—and let them become part of your relaxation and comfort. You can . . . go as deeply as YOU need to—at this time—for WHATEVER it is your SUBCONSCIOUS mind wants to do to help you . . . ENJOY this experience. And you MIGHT ENJOY that experience of going so deeply into trance that it seems to you that you are just . . . ALL MIND without a body—a mind floating in space and time—completely free—able to move whenever and wherever it wants to go—THAT'S RIGHT.

And I WONDER what your subconscious mind wants to EXPLORE right now—what doors it wants to open—perhaps taking a look through the FILE CABINETS in the corner of that marvelous DATA PROCESSING SYSTEM that is your mind. Searching through the files and examining things that . . . stay the way they are—things that need to be updated—what needs to be erased—what items can be eliminated—and it is very comforting for YOU TO DISCOVER for yourself . . . that . . . you CAN really . . . let go . . . of what you don't need—and your SUBCONSCIOUS mind can do this in ITS OWN TIME . . . and . . . IN ITS OWN WAY—and you can continue to rest even more comfortably . . . just knowing . . . you CAN rely on your SUBCONSCIOUS mind to do the things that need to be done.

You CAN BEGIN TO EXPLORE . . . your CAPABILITIES . . . that you never had suspected you had—which have been there all the time—and find out for yourself a . . . very . . . deep . . . sense of just who and what you are—and what you are . . . capable of . . . doing all those things—perhaps you just weren't aware of them before—but your SUBCONSCIOUS MIND CAN MAKE THEM AVAILABLE TO

YOU . . . at the time that you need them. THAT'S RIGHT—and you can continue drifting along . . . very comfortably wherever you are in TIME AND SPACE—just enjoying the restfulness of not having to do anything in particular right now.

And I WONDER if you might begin to notice some change in the atmosphere around you—perhaps becoming more luminous—more transparent—spinning all around you in all directions . . . as far as you can see—and that atmosphere around you seems to be radiating a calmness you can experience with every one . . . of your senses—a calmness . . . moving all around you . . . and all over you . . . softly . . . moving itself into every fiber of your being . . . until you get the feeling that's all there is—nothing . . . else exists . . . for you . . . except that calmness—deep sense of peace—WEIGHTLESS SUSPENSION and you feel all the pressures dissipate—nothing to think about . . . and absolutely nothing to do except let yourself be—and on an even deeper level, experience a sense of your own being—who you are—what you are capable of—becoming more AWARE of your own INNER RESOURCES—and now you can ANTICIPATE the JOY of DISCOVERING those RESOURCES and WHAT YOU CAN DO—to make use of them to help yourself . . . and other people as well. . . .

And now, for the next few minutes—you CAN ALLOW yourself to relax—even more deeply—as your SUBCONSCIOUS MIND CONTINUES the important work it has started for you—working to reach an even deeper understanding—and whenever your subconscious . . . mind is finished . . . with what it needs to do at this time—it will find its own way of letting you know—and in your own time—at your own pace—and only when your subconscious mind is ready for you to do so—you can begin to drift back quietly—easily—from wherever it is you have been—reorienting yourself to . . . this time—this place—and become aware of feeling . . . very refreshed—alert—comfortable—and with a very deep sense . . . of having ACCOM-

PLISHED . . . something of tremendous importance—just for you—and you won't do it . . . until your subconscious mind is ready for you . . . to do so.

The Closed Drawer Metaphor

Brian M. Alman, Ph.D.
San Diego, California

Don is a salesman for a large printing company. His tensions and stress arise from a number of sources through the day. "I'd really like to go into a trance about eight or ten times on some days," Don reported. "Most of the problems hit me when I'm in the office. Now I have this drawer on the lower left of my desk for those problems."

What Don has done is given himself cues while in self-hypnosis that, whenever a problem comes up that stresses him, he will put his stress in that drawer. "I write down the name of the person or account or the supplier or sometimes just a word that describes the problem. Then I take two deep breaths, open the drawer, and put away both the slip of paper and the feelings of tension. Sometimes I also put away the throb I feel in my head that means a headache is on its way," Don said. "When I close the drawer I leave it all in there."

Once a week he throws out the old slips of paper and makes room for new calm and relaxed reactions. He also has a folder in his briefcase for situations that occur when he is in the field.

You may want to adapt this technique for yourself. Choose a drawer in your dresser at home or in your desk at work. Make it a place to deposit your tensions and stress, and when you close the drawer, you leave your unnecessary stress there. Use your imagery and visualization to reinforce the feeling of distance between you and the stress. [The patient may also imagine putting stresses in a drawer in self-hypnosis. (*Ed.*)]

He Who Hesitates is Lost: A Metaphor for Decision Making

Michael D. Yapko, Ph.D.
San Diego, California

INTRODUCTION AND INDICATIONS

An indirect strategy for facilitating decision-making and escape from ambivalence involves the use of metaphors that illustrate the truism, "He Who Hesitates Is Lost." The metaphor is used as a vehicle to encourage making an internal decision to act before external circumstances interfere. The following is an example of such a metaphor.

METAPHOR

A friend of mine recently went through an experience that really was most instructive . . . on a number of levels. . . . He had wanted to get a new job . . . one that paid more and afforded him great prestige . . . He applied for a job . . . one that involved moving to another city. . . . He wanted it very badly . . . but was uncertain about moving to make things happen . . . and he asked for a week to think the offer over . . . and they politely agreed he could take a week to decide . . . and a week of going back and forth in his feelings went by . . . and when they called him a week later . . . he asked if he could have three more days in order to decide . . . and when they called him three days later, he asked if he could have another day to decide . . . and they politely agreed he could have another day to decide . . . and when they called him the next morning and asked for his answer, he asked if he could tell them later that day . . . and they impolitely told him they gave the job to someone else apparently more enthusiastic about the opportunity . . . and he was quite upset because he wanted that job, but he made himself afraid . . . thinking of too many things to do at once . . . instead of knowing he could move and work and live one day at a time . . .

and there comes a time to take action . . . before the chance slips away . . .

COMMENTARY.   Any strategy that turns the depressing paralysis of ambivalence in a positive direction will also facilitate the recognition of one's abilities to make decisions in one's own behalf. In the above metaphor, the man loses an opportunity because of paralysis, not incompetence. The message is one that also addresses a global thought pattern, i.e., overwhelming oneself with all of what is involved. The client may thus learn that instead of focusing on the frightening aspects of what there is to lose by moving on, he or she can look at what will be lost by staying put.

De-Fusing Panic

Marlene E. Hunter, M.D.
Vancouver, British Columbia, Canada

INTRODUCTION

Many hypnotherapists are reluctant to interact with patients in trance. With techniques like this one, however, an interactive trance allows the therapist to obtain information about each part of the symptom complex. Thus the feedback obtained from interaction will permit greater individualization to the patient. (*Ed.*)

SUGGESTIONS

I am going to describe for you a way in which you can have some tools immediately available to you for relieving an anxiety attack. ['Immediately available' sounds good to any panic sufferer!]

You know how miserable it is to all of a sudden feel that coming on, so to have some sort of bandaid, as it were, that you could immediately use to relieve that feeling—that is very, very comforting. I'm going to describe such a situation.

In order to learn how to do that, I suggest that here, now, while you are very safe here in my office in hypnosis, you allow yourself to feel what one of those attacks feels like; *but* you can limit the feeling to just however much is okay for you to feel at this time. [Arranging the safe framework.]

Hypnosis is wonderful, you know, because you can make those restrictions. You're safe here in my office; just let yourself feel what one of those panic attacks feels like, knowing that you can limit those feelings to just whatever is okay, whatever feels manageable. That's right.

But whatever feels okay, let yourself feel that amount to the fullest, and take particular note of what happens first. Maybe the first thing you feel is a little fluttering in your chest, or your tummy; perhaps you notice your breathing is changing or your heartbeat is changing. Some people feel a little tension in the head, or your tummy is growling; maybe your hands become moist. [All people with panic attacks have some, if not most, of these symptoms; this reassures the subject that you do know how he or she feels.]

Just let yourself feel your own personal complex of feelings for those situations, remembering that you can limit it to just whatever feels okay for you to feel here, knowing that you are safe. But whatever is okay, let yourself feel that much to the *fullest*.

Then when you reach the fullest of that amount, whatever it is, hold that—just hold it——ahh, good for you. Now, bit by bit and one at a time, reverse EACH SYMPTOM. Start with your breathing. Breathing is something that we can deliberately change and regulate, so it is perhaps the best place to start. [Watch your subject carefully—*your* timing is important.] Let your breathing ease back, just concentrate on your breathing—that's the idea, you know how to do it, that's right.

As your breathing comes back into the comfortable zone again, you'll notice that your heartbeat is already beginning to do that too, because breathing and heartbeat go together.

When your breathing is comfortable again, wait a little longer; and when your heart rate feels comfortable again, then choose the next one—maybe that fidgety feeling in your hands, or maybe releasing the knot in your tummy—that's the idea; in the back of the neck there now—that's right, releasing each one by itself in turn until everything is back to normal again. See? You know exactly where to put your hands. That's it. When everything is easy again, take a deep breath and settle back down comfortably in the chair. [This patient moved her hands to her neck for comfort. Always utilize whatever the patient does, in a positive way.]

Just think of what you have learned in these last few minutes. You've learned at least two very important things: one is that you know exactly what to do with your hands, exactly where to put them, and exactly where that place is in your neck; you know exactly what to do, where to focus your attention. [Ego-strengthening.] The second thing you have learned is that *you can do it!* You have reversed each part of the symptom complex. Isn't that wonderful! I knew you could, and you've just proven it. [Positive reinforcement—the subject is doing it right.]

Now just to reinforce that, go through it again, again restricting the feeling to only what is okay to feel this morning right here in my office in hypnosis. You may feel comfortable about feeling a little more this time, because you know you can do it, but whatever is okay with you, limit it to that, that's right, and whatever is okay, let yourself feel that to the fullest, yes, that's right, that's right, that's it—hold it there. . . . [Once done, the subject will be more comfortable (and trusting) about doing it again.]

Then, when you are feeling it to the fullest once again, one by one, reverse each part in turn, usually starting with the breathing because it is something that we can have such definite control over; breathing comes first, then you yourself know how to proceed—the back of your neck, right in the pit of your stomach, that's right. One by one, it is important to do it one by one. [She again used her hands—on her neck, then her abdomen.]

That's it. Then, when everything is back to normal again, you can settle comfortably back in the chair, taking a deep breath. That's right. Just take care of that last feeling in the pit of your stomach. It's interesting, isn't it?—the way the feelings have a sort of a pattern. That's right, that's better—that shimmering feeling just letting you know that your muscles are relieving their tensions. That's good. [The patient gave a little movement.]

And then, when you are ready, breathe a very deep breath. What a relief! And just settle right back down. That's right. [Taking a deep breath and letting it out always relieves muscle tension.]

Congratulations! You see, you've done it twice and you've done it extremely well. And now you know that you have something you can do immediately, if ever you get stuck.

Next time, of course, we are going to be talking about *preventing* it happening at all,

but it is so comforting to know that you have something that you can do immediately—just like having that bandaid handy. [Positive reinforcement. Bandaid in place!] Something you can do right away, wherever you may be; one by one, reverse each part of that symptom complex, usually starting with the breathing because it is something that we can deliberately control. [Reassurance of further work.] And then, within a very short time (as you can tell), the symptoms ease away and you are back in perfect control again—in fact, YOU ARE IN CONTROL THE WHOLE TIME THAT YOU ARE REVERSING THAT SYMPTOM COMPLEX! Isn't that wonderful! Yes, you can regain control that quickly. That's marvelous. [Handing the control back to the subject.]

Next time we'll talk about preventing it from happening. In the meantime, you know now that there is always something that you can do, right away. That's good.

HYPNOSIS WITH PHOBIAS

Paradigm for Flying Phobia

David Spiegel, M.D., and
Herbert Spiegel, M.D.
Stanford, California, and New York, New York

Patients are taught to concentrate on three points: (1) to think of the plane as an extension of their body, very much like a bicycle or a car; (2) to float with the plane, so that they have a physical sensation of comfort associated with the experience of flying; (3) to concentrate on the difference between a probability and a possibility.

Thus anxieties about the flight can be processed from the point of view of putting them into the proper perspective rather than experiencing every adverse possibility as a probability. Patients are instructed to choose when to do this exercise but to use it in preparation for the flight, and during the flight either at speci-

fied times at some regular repeated interval or throughout the trip.

A Reframing Approach for Flight Phobia

Peter A. Bakal, M.D.
Schenectady, New York

INTRODUCTION

Dr. Bakal uses a three-session, individual hypnotherapy approach that is unique in that he addresses and reframes the negative suggestions about flying that are so prevalent in flight terminology. In his original article (Bakal, 1981), he reported excellent results with a series of 21 patients followed up for three years, and one qualified "success" with a patient who had only two sessions in two days before a flight to Hawaii. (*Ed.*)

REFRAMING SUGGESTIONS AND PROCEDURE

In the first session, prior to hypnosis, I point out all the wrong words used, unintentionally, by airlines to condition people to fear flying. Examples of such expressions include "terminal" for the airport building, "departure lounge" and the "last and final call" for the boarding call. I also remind patients that when they board a flight, one of the first messages they encounter is how to cope with a crash and how to use oxygen in case of an emergency. If all the wrong suggestions are combined, the patient gets the following picture: they arrive at the "terminal," see the "insurance desk," are asked if the place they are going is their "final destination," and they are told this is the "last and final call" for flight 146, "terminating at Kennedy Airport."

I remind patients to anticipate the noise of the gear going up and the flaps moving up and assure them that these are safe sounds to expect when the plane takes off. . . . The patients are taught to be critical of remarks from airline personnel—such as the pilot stating, "We are going to have some turbulence," and learn not to connect that with the image of air pockets, wings falling off, and planes crashing. They also learn what turbulence is and are encouraged to make the analogy to a bumpy road, a known condition which the patient could expect to handle in his own life experience. In another example, patients are warned that the pilot might say something like, "We have a thunderstorm on our radar and we will *try* to fly around it," thus evoking fears of thunderstorms, severe weather conditions, icing and such other situations.

The patients are told that, when the plane starts to descend, the change in the sound of the engines is similar to that of an automobile going downhill as the driver eases up on the gas

and the engine slows down. Also, veteran fliers will remember that the stewardess usually announces, "We are on our *final* approach and we will be on the ground in a few moments. Please stay in your seats until we arrive at the gate."

After the patient has consciously addressed the fact that he is constantly exposed to all these suggestions, hypnosis is induced. Although I use Ericksonian techniques, any technique would suffice. The patient is then led through a "flight." I like the "My-friend-John" approach. On the first session, I take "John" step-by-step through the flight, each time bringing to his subconscious attention these suggestive expressions so that he can address them and cannot deny that they exist. Then I take John on the plane after hearing, "last and final call." Finally, the plane moves, takes off. The following features are pointed out to the patient:

1. A lack of sensation of height.
2. The beauty of the city and countryside, night or day.
3. The slant of the airplane.
4. The statements made by the stewardess about crashing.
5. The sound of the gear retracting and the loud noise it makes when the holding bolts lock in.
6. The noise of the flaps and their purpose to aid in lift, and the sound when the plane reaches altitude and levels off and when the engines slow a bit, similar to the noise we expect with a car when it reaches the plateau at the top of a hill.
7. The pilot talking to them to warn of turbulence and thunderstorms.
8. The angle of the luggage racks in level flight (slightly upward).
9. The banking and tipping of the plane, similar to a car on a banked road.

John is now encouraged to settle down and enjoy the flight. When the plane starts its descent, the patient is taught to notice:

1. The luggage racks have now leveled off, the sound of the engines which have been slowed further. This is the same as an

automobile when it is ready to go downhill; the car slants down, you take your foot off the accelerator and decrease speed.

2. The stewardesses tell people to buckle their seat belts, put out cigarettes, and to put seats in the upright position, that they are on "the final approach" and will be "on the ground" shortly.

Each "wrong word" is pointed out. The landing is described. The flaps go down and the gear goes down with the usual loud sound. The plane lands and the pilot races the engine in reverse thrust to slow the plane down so that the brakes will become effective. Then the plane taxis up to the airport building known as the "terminal."

On the second visit, the patient again enters the state of hypnosis, is taken through the same situation. But this time, ideomotor responses are used as each situation is encountered. On the third trip, the patient verbalizes as he hears or sees each item on the flight.

Hypnosis with Phobic Reactions

Don E. Gibbons, Ph.D.

INTRODUCTION

Systematic desensitization may easily be adapted for use within a trance induction format (Gibbons, Kilbourne, Saunders, & Castles, 1970; Gibbons, 1971), as a means of alleviating phobic responses which are not due to unconscious symbolic substitutions or emotional displacements, and which are not primarily instrumental in the satisfaction of other needs. As an illustration of the manner in which this may be accomplished, the following suggestions are designed to alleviate a fear of flying which is simply the result of inappropriate past experience, or lack of appropriate experience, with flying itself. [Note: Clinicians may also obtain head nods or signals from the patient throughout such a rehearsal to monitor their comfort level. (*Ed.*]

REHEARSAL SUGGESTIONS WITH FEAR OF FLYING

First of all, I want you to make yourself quite comfortable and relaxed; and when you are feeling thoroughly peaceful, and completely comfortable in every way, you can signal me by raising the index finger of your right [or left] hand. So just let yourself relax completely now, and soon your finger will rise.

[After the subject has responded:]

That's fine. Just continue to relax even deeper now; and with every word that I utter, you will find yourself able to follow my suggestions more easily. Just let your imagination drift along with my words, and let yourself flow with the experience I describe, and soon you will be able to feel everything I suggest to you, just as if it were really happening.

Now, as you continue to relax more and more, I want you to picture yourself at home, getting ready to go to the airport. But the relaxation you are feeling now will remain with you, and if you should happen to feel any tension later on, you can just raise your index finger again, and I will take you back to an earlier part of the trip and we can proceed more slowly. So just picture yourself here at home, feeling very relaxed as you begin to pack and to make all the other preparations for your trip. And as you do, just notice how relaxed you are, and how calm you have become.

Now you are taking your luggage out to the car and putting it into the trunk. And now you are getting into the car, ready to go to the airport, and still feeling perfectly calm. All the details of the trip have been taken care of up to this point, and you can just relax and enjoy the drive.

You will be able to answer yes or no to my questions by shaking your head in the appropriate manner. You are still feeling very calm and relaxed now, aren't you?

[Pause. If answer is yes:]

That's fine. Now if you should happen to feel any anxiety at any time, you can just signal me by raising your index finger, and we can go back to an earlier stage in your journey and let you relax a little more deeply before going on.

But I doubt that you will need to do this, because you are still feeling so very deeply relaxed and calm.

Now you are pulling up to the airport and getting out of your car in order to give your luggage to an attendant who will see that it is checked onto your flight. You get back into your car and proceed to the parking area. You park your car and calmly stroll into the waiting room, feeling perfectly calm every step of the way. Now you are waiting in line at the ticket counter, picking up your ticket, looking at it, and now you are walking to the gate where you are to board your flight.

On the way to the gate, you pass a news-stand, where you notice a paperback book which looks extremely interesting. You stop a moment to purchase the book to take along with you on your flight. Now, still deeply relaxed, you are going through the security check on the way to the gate. You remain deeply relaxed as you think about the book you have just purchased, and about how interesting it appears to be.

Now you have completed the security check and you are approaching the gate. You give your ticket to the attendant, who stamps it and gives you your seat number. You take a seat in the waiting area and begin to thumb through the book, becoming more and more interested in it with each passing second. It looks like it is going to be one of the most interesting books you have ever read.

As your flight is called, you rise from your chair and prepare to board the plane along with the other passengers, still feeling very deeply relaxed and thinking about the fascinating book you have just started to read.

Now you enter the plane and make your way to your seat, still feeling perfectly calm and relaxed. You sit down and fasten your seat belt and open the book once more, quickly becoming so absorbed in your reading that you scarcely notice the takeoff.

You interrupt your reading long enough to enjoy the meal which is brought to you, and you are pleased to discover how good everything tastes. You are still deeply relaxed and you enjoy your meal thoroughly before returning to your book.

So absorbed in your book have you become once again that you are surprised to discover that the plane has landed and is taxiing up to the ramp.

You leave the plane, feeling relaxed and happy. You have had a very enjoyable flight, and you have remained perfectly calm during the entire trip. And now that you have seen how pleasant flying can actually be, you know that whenever you fly again in the future, you will have a similar relaxing and enjoyable experience in store for you.

Suggestions for Simple and Social Phobias

Michael A. Haberman, M.D.
Atlanta, Georgia

Phobic panic responses, as opposed to true panic disorder, occur following a psychological stressor. Usually, the anxiety response builds in anticipation of the event, which might vary from entering an elevator, airplane, or high place to giving a speech. The sine qua non of panic disorder is the onset of the panic attack without clear precipitant and then later the gradual onset of anticipatory anxiety and progressive limitation of activity. On the other hand, simple or social phobia has a clear and reproducible precipitant (e.g., entering an elevator or giving a talk) that leads to avoidance of a specific behavior. Panic disorder is treated with medication but phobias can respond to hypnosis and psychotherapy.

The essence of an anxiety response is that it is based on fear. A phobia concretizes that fear. Once established, the reinforcer to the avoidance is the reduction in anxiety when one moves away from the feared situation. Therefore, the person develops a conditioned response. Normal ego defenses erect walls to protect the personality from undue fear. Usually the origin of the phobia is unknown.

Hypnosis can approach these anxiety responses through a search of the unconscious using Watkins' affect bridge technique or by a more directly behavioral technique, such as relaxation coupled with systematic desensitization. The latter technique is extremely easy for a hypnotic operator. It involves only an induction and the suggestion for developing skill at self-hypnosis and relaxation of muscle tension coupled with suggestions that such relaxation (experienced as heaviness or a floaty feeling in the limbs, for example) indicates a lessening of fear and an increase of comfort.

You then use a fractionation technique during the first session. This technique involves helping the person alternately and repeatedly enter the hypnotic and waking state and is usually experienced as going deeper each time, which you also suggest to them.

Prior to inducing hypnosis the patient develops a hierarchy of situations gradually approaching the actual phobic situation, such that the first situation is the least anxiety-provoking (such as reading a travel magazine), to a bit more anxiety (thinking of taking an airplane), and then more anxiety-provoking (making a reservation). Gradually his visualizations then take him onto the plane itself, and then into the air. These form the basis of images. You can repeat the patient's own words during hypnosis.

As scenes are imagined, the therapist may obtain ideomotor finger signals when the patient is experiencing anxiety. At that point, the patient should be told to stop imagining the scene and to imagine a neutral stimulus. The anxiety response diminishes as you have the person take himself/herself deeper into trance before imagining the anxiety-provoking scene again. As you reintroduce the troubling scene, the anxiety response recurs but hopefully lessens.

In this manner, you gradually "desensitize" the individual to his fear in vitro. This must be followed by in vivo techniques (e.g., actual trips to the airport using self-hypnosis at appropriate times during the journey).

If the patient is less phobic and only gets anxious, for example, during the landing of an airplane, you can use a very different technique based more on the unique logic of hypnosis. A general theme in phobias is a fear of being trapped in a situation over which you have no control and which can be destructive to the self. This applies to airplanes or giving speeches. One needs to identify metaphors that the patient can use to concretize the concepts of freedom and control and power that they can use in hypnosis. Here is an example of how to apply the principles outlined above.

CASE 1.   Joseph is a 35-year-old salesman who must travel to both coasts in his job. After a few weeks of uneventful flying, a flight he is on experiences severe turbulence during which passengers are instructed to stay in their seats and fasten their seat belts. Joseph becomes frightened and notices his heart racing and his breathing becomes more labored. After the flight lands and he gets off the plane, he feels better but the next time he gets on a plane he is hypervigilant and consciously concerned over safety issues that he took for granted before. Over the next few weeks he flies four times and begins having anticipatory anxiety before leaving for the airport. He has anxiety attacks on the plane. Over the next few weeks, insomnia develops and he is anxious during the day, consciously afraid he will have to fly. He fears someone will find out and he will lose his job. He has no formal psychiatric history and he says, "I have always been able to handle things before. I don't know what to do."

You decide to use hypnosis. Joseph tells you he is fond of bicycling as a hobby. Joseph enters trance quickly and you might say: "I wonder if you can recall when you first learned to ride a bicycle. You may be thinking of a bike with training wheels or even a tricycle because that is how most people begin to learn how to control themselves. At first a grownup needed to walk next to you and steady the bike and you were very aware of your fear, but also of your excitement and your desire. A new world was opening up for you and you reached out for it. Remember how you practiced and practiced until somehow you forgot that you were afraid, forgot that there was ever a time you didn't know how to ride. You were in control. And all it took was practice and you learned to ride a bike as well as you could walk.

"And remember then when you first learned to drive a car, how scary it was to get behind the wheel and have to hit the gas and the brakes, and steer and watch the road. Remember there was a time you didn't want anybody to talk while you were driving, didn't want your concentration broken. Then suddenly you were driving and you couldn't remember how not to drive. You were in control. And you can learn to control your fear again just as you learned how to enter this relaxed state, just as you learned how to ride a bike and how to drive a car. You can permit yourself to be in control again. Just like you began to feel excitement instead of fear. And suddenly you weren't limited anymore in where you could go. You could travel far away from home knowing that you were in control, that you are in control now, of the depth of your relaxation, of the attention that you pay to the sound of my voice and the meaning of my words to your unconscious mind. If you choose you can achieve this state whenever you need to. Whenever you would like you can enter a deep state of relaxation, a state in which you are in control and you can permit yourself to go deeper and deeper as you breathe slowly and deeply. [Be sure the patient is doing this—otherwise, use what he is doing.] Whenever you need to you can enter this state of relaxation, deeply, easily, comfortably and always in complete control. Always in complete control."

Example of Treating Phobic Anxiety with Individually Prepared Tapes

M. Erik Wright, M.D., Ph.D.

INTRODUCTION

The following tape recording was prepared for a middle-aged woman who experienced de-

bilitating anxiety at the thought of going to a doctor or dentist, a store or restaurant, and so forth. When the anticipated anxiety became too great, she was able to calm herself sufficiently to carry out these activities by listening to the tape. She routinely kept the tape in her purse so that it would be available to her as needed. If she was in a situation that required privacy, she used earphones. She had practiced trance induction and relaxation procedures with the therapist in the past, and had described a number of reassuring scenes. These are imbedded in the relaxation process on the tape.

ILLUSTRATIVE TAPED SUGGESTIONS

[The therapist's voice is recorded on tape.] While sitting in a chair, as comfortably as you can, you can let your eyelids close, blinking a few times . . . and then very gently let them close. . . . As they close, let your whole body gradually begin to have a feeling of lightness . . . a feeling of lightness with the weight and heaviness going out of your shoulders and your chest, and then out of your abdomen . . . just letting go . . . letting your hands rest comfortably . . . feeling the air going in and out, from your abdomen, from your chest . . . Then feel the lightness in your hips, thighs, and legs . . . Just let go.

[The therapist introduces the idea of relaxing in a bath, a soothing experience for this client:] Let your thoughts take you to your bath where you are so very comfortable . . . just the right temperature . . . and relaxing very comfortably . . . with the same lightness of your body just floating and yet resting there . . . Very gently, quietly, letting go . . . Going deeper and more relaxed . . . [The therapist mentions a particular sensation that had been referred to by the client in the past:] Letting your stomach growl when it wants to . . . It has a right to make its own statement . . . Just feeling yourself getting lighter and freer . . . Very light and free. . . .

[The therapist introduces the idea of Wendy, the client's dog, a source of great pleasure and comfort:] And then, after a while, when you are out of the bath . . . feeling warm and relaxed . . . perhaps feeling Wendy near you, resting on your lap, or wherever she fits nicely . . . Just a sense of quiet peacefulness and letting go . . . Feeling secure . . . A sort of gentle peacefulness . . . Going deeper and deeper with each breath.

As you practice, two or three times a day, wherever you are, just feeling this free, and quiet, and secure feeling each time . . . then when you're very relaxed and quiet, you can go somewhere you want to . . . or take a trip . . . You can do some of the things that you need to do . . . or want to do . . . and enjoy the sheer pleasure of moving your body. . . .

Whenever you choose, you can spend ten minutes or twenty minutes or even longer, just letting go . . . feeling your shoulders easing up . . . listening to your quiet breathing . . . sensing the lightness and freedom of your body . . . There is no rush . . . There is no pressure . . . Just letting go . . . gently and quietly . . . So good to let go and not have any pressures or any tensions . . . Feeling good and whole. . . .

And as you relax, the inner mind is focusing your energy toward healing and mobilizing your health forces . . . not only for the health of your eyes and teeth, but for whatever else is needed . . . to heal, to recover your energy, to restore your sense of well-being and joy of living . . . Very quietly, very relaxed as you listen to my voice . . . going a step further each time that you practice going into this quiet space of your own . . . You can choose whatever images you want to . . . Wendy when you want her with you . . . or she may romp off when you want to be free . . . Very deeply relaxed, as long as you need to be. . . .

When you are ready to come back to the here and now, give yourself a signal . . . then very gently feel yourself coming back to the here and now . . . the calmness and good feeling persisting even when you are totally awake and going about your business.

Treatment of Lack of Confidence and Stage Fright

David Waxman, L.R.C.P., M.R.C.S.
London, England

The restoration of self-confidence is one of the easiest and most rapid results that can be achieved by hypnotherapy. The full ego-strengthening routine, suitably reinforced by specific suggestions appropriate to each individual case, has proved invaluable in the treatment of this condition.

[Begin with this, then proceed in the following manner:] "As you become . . . *more relaxed* and *less tense*, each day . . . *so* . . . you will remain *more relaxed* . . . and *less tense* . . . when you are in the presence of other people . . . no matter whether they be few or many . . . no matter whether they be friends or strangers.

"You will be able to meet them on equal terms . . . and you will feel much more at ease in their presence . . . *without* the slightest feeling of inferiority . . . *without* becoming self-conscious . . . *without* becoming embarrassed or confused . . . *without* feeling that you are making yourself conspicuous in any way.

"You will become . . . *so deeply interested* . . . *so deeply absorbed in what you are saying* . . . *that you will concentrate entirely upon this to the complete exclusion of everything else.*

"Because of this . . . *you will remain perfectly relaxed* . . . *perfectly calm and self-confident* . . . *and you will become much less conscious of yourself and your own feelings.*

"*You will consequently be able to talk quite freely and naturally* . . . *without being worried in the slightest by the presence of your audience.*

"*If you should begin to think about your-*

self . . . you will immediately shift your attention back to your conversation . . . and will no longer experience the slightest nervousness . . . discomfort . . . or uneasiness."

[When the patient is likely to be called upon to appear upon the stage, to make a speech or to deliver a lecture, the above may well be modified in the following manner:] *"The moment you get up to speak . . . all your nervousness will disappear completely . . . and you will feel . . . completely relaxed . . . completely at your ease . . . and completely confident. You will become so deeply interested in what you have to say . . . that the presence of an audience will no longer bother you in the slightest . . . and you will no longer feel uncertain . . . confused . . . or conspicuous in any way.*

"Your mind will become so fully occupied with what you have to say . . . that you will no longer worry at all as to how to say it.

"You will no longer feel nervous . . . self-conscious . . . or embarrassed . . . and you will remain throughout . . . perfectly calm . . . perfectly confident . . . and self-assured."

Whenever a speech or talk has to be given, or a stage appearance made, the patient must be impressed with the importance of making thorough preparation. The feeling that he has mastered his subject or become word perfect in his lines will help him enormously. It is always essential to rehearse it thoroughly before the actual performance. He should be instructed to speak slowly, clearly and deliberately, and to concentrate entirely upon what he is saying.

At every session, following the ego-strengthening phase, the subject is desensitized, as in other phobic problems, to the next situation along the hierarchy in which he is liable to feel the focus of attention.

The teaching of self-hypnosis, whenever possible, can prove invaluable in these cases. Not only can the patient be taught to visualize himself addressing an audience without difficulty, but he can also suggest to himself, during hypnosis, that he will gradually be able to do this without nervousness, self-consciousness or apprehension in real life.

Overcoming Anxiety over Public Speaking

Don E. Gibbons, Ph.D.

INDICATIONS

These suggestions were prepared for use when the patient has already begun to overcome anxiety and self-consciousness concerning public speaking. Once the patient begins to have successful speaking experiences, these suggestions may foster a more permanent diminution of anxiety. A very positive element of these suggestions is the acceptance, utilization and reframing of a modicum of anxiety, which research has demonstrated may enhance performance. (*Ed.*)

SUGGESTIONS

First of all, I would like you to allow yourself to express your fear of public speaking freely and openly for a moment, allowing it to escape like steam escaping from a safety valve, to relieve the pressure. So just picture yourself up there giving your talk, and let yourself feel all the anxiety for a moment, just as strongly as you can. Let your imagination go, and let yourself feel all the anxiety you have been holding back. Feel it surging to the surface. Let yourself feel it all and experience it all. *Now!*

And as I continue to speak, your fear is beginning to leave; for you have allowed most of it to escape by permitting yourself to express it openly. Your fear has been considerably weakened, and what little is left of it is going away completely. It's almost gone. Now your fear is completely gone, and you can feel a great sense of relief.

And whenever you are about to give any kind of public speech, you will be able to feel and experience all the anxiety that the speech may cause you; but this anxiety will always be felt *before* you are about to begin, so that by the time you actually start to speak, most of the anxiety will already have been released. And any remaining tension will be well within the range that is helpful — just enough to add live-liness and sparkle to your delivery, but not enough to detract from it or prevent you from doing your very best.

Because you are able to express all your unnecessary anxiety ahead of time, you will be able to concentrate completely on what you have to say as soon as your speech begins, without worrying about how you may look or sound to others. And as your talk progresses, you will soon become so engrossed in what you have to say that you will forget about yourself completely.

When your speech is concluded, you will be full of the warm feeling of accomplishment which comes from the certain knowledge that you have done well. And as time goes on, this realization of how well you are actually doing will cause your anxiety to become less and less, until it disappears completely.

SUGGESTIONS IN DENTAL HYPNOSIS

Suggestions with TMJ and Bruxism

Harold P. Golan, D.M.D.
Boston, Massachusetts

You will do this whole exercise with a sense of humor, sort of laugh at yourself and the rest of the world, knowing that you have this secret weapon to use whenever necessary. You may even smile at your teeth, jaws, tissues, realizing that they are going to be helped by what you are learning. You may use this knowledge for any medical or dental situation, injections, exami-nations, whatever.

[An explanation may be given to the patient that stressful situations occur every day which cause us to grit our teeth.] Whenever one of these anxiety-producing events happen or is go-ing to happen, such as an extremely hard exam-ination, a difference of opinion with a friend or parent, a difficult decision, you unconsciously grit your teeth. Now you have a way of handling the situation by keeping just enough nervous energy to do the task superbly well and spilling off the excess tension. When you go to sleep at night you will practice, saying something like this to yourself, "Nothing is important enough in life for me to eat myself up."

[Further instruction may explain that most gritting or bruxism happens during the night. The cause is that the subconscious mind re-members the stressful or anxiety-producing sit-uations which have occurred during the day or threaten to occur in the future and replays them many times during the night.] During the night the abnormal touch of your teeth will waken you, you'll smile, realize that your subconscious is protecting you, turn over and go right back to sleep, losing no sleep at all.

[Glove anesthesia and temperature change may then be produced for trance ratification. Following production of glove anesthesia and insertion of a 25-gauge needle through the skin on the back of the hand, the following sugges-tions may be given:] You are really wonderful at this. You have just demonstrated to me and to yourself that you have control over one part of your body. The only reason I chose the right hand is that it is visible and accessible. If you can control one part of your body, you can control any part of your body including your mouth. This is a big concept, control of your body rather than your body controlling you. You should be proud of yourself that you are so good at this modality. I'd like you to keep this feeling in your hand for five full minutes fol-lowing this state of relaxation as a further sign that something physical can happen from this marvelous mental process of yours.

Suggestions with TMJ

Ellis J. Neiburger, D.D.S.

The jaw clenching-muscle cramping-pain cy-cle of the temporomandibular joint syndrome can be reduced or eliminated by relaxation obtained by slightly opening the mouth. Inserting the tongue between the teeth tends in general to act as an accurate measure of interocclusal distance, and serves as a reminder of unconscious mandibular closure. Suggesting to the patient that whenever he clenches his jaw he will automatically insert his tongue between his teeth, averts the initialing state in the muscular tension-pain cycle.

"Whenever you grind your teeth or tighten your cheek muscles, you will want to keep your mouth slightly open, wide enough to place your tongue between your back teeth. This will help your muscles to become loose, loose. . . . This will stop your muscles from cramping. The longer your tongue stays between your teeth, the more your muscles will become loose, limp, like wet cotton."

Erickson's Suggestions with Bruxism

Milton H. Erickson, M.D.

Don't give the suggestion "when your head hits the pillow," because many people sleep without pillows. Instead, trigger it by "when you put your head down." Talk about "how nice it is to fall asleep instantly when you put your head down—the instant you are ready to go to sleep it is so delightful to go sound asleep into a deep physiological sleep. And whenever you go into a sound physiological sleep, there is the possibility that this night or the next night, that this week or the next week, you will grind your teeth. But from now on, whenever that does occur . . ." [Then make the bruxism inconvenient and unpleasant].

[The suggestion can also be to awaken whenever the teeth grinding occurs. Point out:] "It is a very nice thing to have a good grip of the hand, and people are so lazy about exercising—they always skip their calisthenics. Every time you grind your teeth, you exercise your grip until you get a really good grip." [This is particularly effective for children]. With a

small child you can reinforce these suggestions by tying a sponge rubber in the hand and endowing that sponge rubber with nice properties: "It will help your fingers to open and enable you to get a very strong arm."

[An alternative suggestion is for the bruxism patient to awaken whenever he grinds his teeth.] . . . he can go to sleep with gum tucked in between his cheek and his teeth. You explain that he must learn to sleep that way so that every time he grinds his teeth he will slip that gum in between his teeth, chew it for a while, then carefully tuck it back against his cheek and go back to sleep. [Transforms bruxism into a gum-chewing habit, and who wants to do this ordeal in the middle of the night.]

TMJ and Tension Headaches

Dov Glazer, D.D.S.
New Orleans, Louisiana

INTRODUCTION

For the next five minutes, experience a uniquely effective technique to enjoy a hypnotic trance. Simply listen to the suggestion, follow the instruction and be pleasantly surprised by the experience.

INDUCTION

TENSION.   Focus attention on your hands. Put the heels of the hands together and let the fingers touch each other. Raise the hands to the height of the jaw, elbows away from the body. Press the hands together. Press tight enough to feel the tension in the fingers, hands, arms, shoulders, neck, feel the tension around the jaw, face, head. Squint the eyes, wrinkle the forehead. Press tighter. Feel that tension!

RELAXATION.   Now relax: hands down, eyes closed. Take a deep breath through the nose and hold it, now gently release the air. Nice and comfortable, pleasantly relaxed. Lips together, jaw loose, limp and relaxed.

With eyes closed, arms and legs in a comfortable position, let the body sink gently into the chair. As the tension drains from the top of the head to the tips of the fingers, become aware of relaxed muscles around the head, temples, forehead, eyebrows, eyes, nose, cheeks, lips, chin, jaw, ears, neck, shoulders, arms, hands, fingers.

SUGGESTIONS

Sense the relaxation throughout. Feel warm. safe and secure. Float with the feeling, and once again, take a deep, deep breath through the nose and hold it, now gently release the tension. Nice and comfortable, pleasantly relaxed. More deeply relaxed.

Feel good and confident that relaxation is always just a breath away. Want it to happen, expect it to happen, it will happen. Enjoy the calmness, the tranquility and the serenity.

ALERT

Now as though waking up from a pleasant relaxed rest, feel naturally bright, alert and refreshed. Sound in mind, sound in body, sound in health. Eyes open, bright, alert and refreshed. Ready to proceed.

[Now that the muscles have been mentally relaxed, to further enhance relaxation, it is suggested that the patient follow the same path of relaxation by massaging the muscles from the top of the head to the tip of the fingers. The results are quite rewarding.]

Suggestions to Promote Dental Flossing

Maureen A. Kelly, D.D.S.,
Harlo R. McKinty, and
Richard Carr
Lincoln, Nebraska

These authors found that eight months following suggestions to promote dental flossing,

67% of patients, as compared with 15% of a control group, were found to have improved gingival health. The groups were given the following types of suggestions.

(1) "Suggestions involving oral health which explained the need for routine dental flossing to prevent periodontal disease and interproximal caries; (2) suggestions involving personal appearance which cited healthy looking gums, clean teeth, and the benefit of avoiding interproximal decay; and (3) suggestions dealing with social desirability which mentioned better smelling breath and a cleaner, more well-kept appearance."

Gagging

Harold P. Golan, D.M.D.
Boston, Massachusetts

INTRODUCTION

Gagging is an abnormal response of mouth and throat muscles to a normal stimulus either physical or psychological. It has been a problem in professional practice for persons who cannot swallow food or pills, brush their teeth, wear dental appliances, or react excessively to chemotherapy. Authorities have mentioned various methods of controlling this habit. They include authoritative waking suggestion, symptom removal by hypnotherapeutic suggestion, and brief hypnoanalysis (Erickson, Hershman, & Secter, 1961), as well as anesthesia (Hartland, 1966), ideomotor questioning and anesthesia (Cheek & LeCron, 1968), and direct suggestion (Hilgard & Hilgard, 1975). The following technique uses relaxation, temperature change and anesthesia for adults, and relaxation, temperature change and arm catalepsy relaxation for children.

THE TECHNIQUE

After an adequate physical and emotional history (Golan, 1987), hypnosis is explained as being a normal, natural physiological function, an altered state of awareness during which the patient will hear everything, be in control, and not be asked to do anything contrary to his or her wishes. Once patient permission is granted, induction consists of asking the patient to close his eyes, take a deep breath, hold it, and as he exhales slowly, let out all of the anxieties about this moment and problem. At the very beginning, you may briefly touch or raise the wrist to signal to the patient that some sort of change is happening. The following suggestions may then be offered:

Your body is your most prized possession. Only you can take care of it. You owe your body the respect of good health. Self-preservation is the first rule of life. With your new dentures, you'll look well. All those people surrounding you will see you smile. You'll eat well, being able to swallow everything, helping your digestion. Remember that adequate food is necessary for life itself.

Notice how good you feel right now, how your breathing rate has slowed. [The pulse is taken as this is being said.] Every muscle from the tip of your toes to the top of your head is relaxing, comfortably and easily. [Name the muscle systems.] You'll practice this in the privacy of your room or home, in the beginning, at least six times a day until it becomes second nature to you. It can be a moment, a minute, several minutes, or you can even put yourself to sleep this way. You'll be able to do this after a while with your eyes closed or open, because you'll have to eat or do what we have suggested here for treatment with your eyes open. You'll be in control even when you practice, because if there is any legitimate interruption such as the phone or someone calling you, you can open your eyes, capable of carrying out any of your daily activities perfectly well and cheerfully, just as you will at the end of this visit.

You'll be able to carry this out for any medical or dental reason whenever you need it. For the first time you'll be in control of your body, rather than your body controlling you. You'll smile, realizing an immense feeling of confidence and pride in yourself. You'll smile not only at the outside world, but at the tissues of your mouth and throat, using the new control you will learn. This relaxation is the most complete a body can experience.

Let's now mention the reasons gagging occurs. It can be a physical cause, such as being conditioned to gag by a physician's throat stick or choking on a piece of food like a fish bone. It can be psychological, such as an emotional situation which is frustrating, irritating, nauseating, connected with work, family, health, having teeth removed. You will be taught to control it whatever the cause may be.

At this time it is suggested to the patient that in order to test their creative imagination, they are being given a pseudo-injection in the back of the right hand with the blunt end of a pen:

You will know that feeling of numbness, pins and needles, cold which happens with an injection of novocaine. Allow this to spread across the back of your hand as though you have a glove of anesthesia, and stop it at the wrist.

The doctor, by observing, can see the veins begin to raise and stand out, and can also feel the temperature change. When he senses the area is anesthetized, he can insert a 25 or 27 gauge needle through the skin and leave it in place.

Remaining in this state of relaxation, in a few moments you may open your eyes, look down at the back of your right hand, smile at what you see there, close your eyes and go even deeper into this lovely state of relaxation, remembering what you saw.

For those who cannot legally insert a needle, you may suggest to the patient that he notice how cold his hand is, having him signal the change to you with an ideomotor signal, and then having him open his eyes in the same way described above, and notice how pale his hand is compared to the operator's hand and how his veins have raised because of the vaso-constriction from the cold. It is important for the patient to realize that he or she can cause a physical change by a mental process (Golan, 1986).

After removing the needle, suggest that the patient keep the anesthesia during the trance and for five minutes following hypnosis as a further sign that something physical can happen from the marvelous power of his or her mind. At this time, suggest that the patient transfer the anesthesia to his mouth, every portion of his mouth — hard palate, soft palate, throat, floor of the mouth, gingiva, and cheeks. Then, with a gloved finger, touch each portion. Have the patient emulate your touch. It will give him great confidence to be able to touch an area of the mouth, an action which previously caused him to gag.

In working with children, an arm catalepsy [rigidity] is suggested for trance ratification purposes. They may make an arm rigid, strong, tight, and then relax it. Explain to them that this is what they do when they gag, tightening their throat muscles and forgetting to relax them. Now that they know how to tighten and relax one part of their body, they can learn to do it to any part of their body, including their mouth. They, too, may open their eyes when you test their arm.

Control is mentioned again: if she can control her hand, she can control any part of the body, including the mouth. Whatever the original reason, physical or psychological, it can be controlled. If the reason was physical, the anesthesia or temperature change can do it; if psychological, the relaxation and anesthesia take care of the problem.

You may repeat some of the steps mentioned above which you consider important, since repetition of suggestions will enhance the total result. Motivation is increased by repeating suggestions about the wonderful, new appearance and function of dentures for this kind of patient, and the ability to eat properly for patients with problems swallowing. Suggestions may also be given for proper brushing and oral hygiene for patients who were not able to tolerate objects in the back of their mouths. Suggestions are tailored for each patient, taking into account the emotional history which was taken at the beginning. Finally, the trance may be ended by suggesting that the patient will have no feelings of tiredness or heaviness when he arouses himself:

You will be rested and refreshed, as though you had a very pleasant nap. You'll feel happy that you have found this medium, proud that you have the intelligence to do this, cheerful. Every nerve, blood vessel, and muscle will be vibrant and alive. The whole day will take on a rosy glow.

Repeat the suggestion of retention of the anesthesia for five full minutes after trance, assuring the patient the he can use the hand for any purpose during this time. Using a rising voice, make certain that the patient is completely aroused from trance during some of the repetition of dehypnotization. We then proceed at the patient's own pace after hypnosis, whether it be for x-rays, prophylaxis, operative procedures, surgery, or denture construction. As treatment proceeds, the need for formal induction and hypnosis decrease. Simple reinforcement may be necessary at crucial stages.

Imagery with Hypersensitive Gag Reflex

J. Henry Clarke, D.M.D., and Stephen J. Persichetti
Portland, Oregon

INTRODUCTION

Some dental patients have difficulty tolerating dental treatment because of a hypersensitive gag reflex. Direct suggestion has been used by some dentists. Desensitization may prove beneficial when anxiety and fear are the underlying etiology of the problem. Clarke and Persichetti, however, devised an imagery procedure for the treatment of a highly sensitive gag reflex in the absence of significant fear. (*Ed.*)

SUGGESTIONS

The patient may be asked to imagine "breathing through an opening in the neck (cricothyroid region). Our rationale is that it is difficult for these patients not to focus on the pharyngeal area. The image of an opening below that region allows them to focus on breathing, bypassing the 'gagging' area. It implies that the pharyngeal area is not so critical and need not be a problem. The image is related to the patient's primary concern with breathing, and therefore is easy for them to maintain. We also suggested cool, fresh air flowing in and out with no effort. . . .

"We have encountered some patients who disliked the image of breathing through 'a hole in the neck,' and we have then explored images such as a 'numb throat,' or breathing in some other creative way. The home use of audiotape, practice denture, and impression trays (or other practice techniques) is a form of desensitization—relaxing while simulating procedures that are usually anxiety-provoking. This also familiarizes the patient with the procedures for the next appointment. The patient goes through several rehearsals of the actual procedures. Acrylic practice dentures should be as thin and stable as possible; otherwise they may trigger the gag reflex. Combining the desensitization with the dental treatment reduces the number of appointments needed."

Denture Problems and Gagging

Donald R. Beebe, D.D.S.
Mentor, Ohio

INTRODUCTION

These suggestions were given to a patient who complained of problems with gagging the day after eight teeth were extracted and a denture made. (*Ed.*)

Mrs. L., your new denture is gagging you because it feels bulky and strange, and your recent extractions are causing you some discomfort and pain. You will no longer be troubled with these strange and bulky feelings, nor the discomfort and pain. For as I am talking to you these feelings and gagging difficulties will slowly fade away, you will find that when I wake you from this trance, that the denture will feel comfortable and that you will not gag anymore. Now I am going to count slowly from one to ten and when I reach ten all of your

gagging, discomfort and pain will have faded away.

One, your gagging and discomfort is starting to fade away. Two, it is fading more and more. Three, less gagging and discomfort. Four, gagging and discomfort fading more and more. Five, it is half gone. Six, gagging, discomfort and pain still fading. Seven, all of your dental difficulties are almost gone. Eight, your gagging problems are nearly gone. Nine. Ten, everything connected with your denture problems are normal. You no longer need to gag. I am going to count from one to three and at the count of three you will be wide awake, feeling refreshed and rested. Remember, your gagging problems will be gone as well as your other denture problems. One, coming awake. Two, eyes starting to open. Three, wide awake.

[The patient was instructed to return to my office in one week and told that she would be rehypnotized in the same manner and the same suggestions reinforced. The patient returned one week later and reported that she no longer had a problem with gagging. However, I rehypnotized her and reinforced the suggestions that had been given previously. Seven years later, this patient has never been troubled with gagging due to her denture.]

Suggestion with Gagging

Irving I. Secter, D.D.S., M.A.
Southfield, Michigan

The following is now frequently used. After the patient has learned to develop hypnoanesthesia on cue, he is told: "In the past the x-rays [or toothbrush, or whatever stimulus it may have been] has caused you to gag. From now on instead of causing you to gag it will cause an anesthesia to develop, which will prevent the gagging."

Gagging Suggestion

William T. Heron, Ph.D.

Mr. _____ , you are having trouble tolerating x-ray film in your mouth. You know, of course, that it is necessary to take the x-rays in order that the dentist may know how to proceed. That is the case, isn't it? [Pause for head response.]

When you are hungry, you enjoy food in your mouth, correct? [Pause for response. Of course everyone gives a positive response.]

All right. Now, when you have food in your mouth it touches your tongue, the inside of your cheeks, the roof of your mouth, but all of these touches are pleasant, aren't they? [Pause for positive response.] All right. Now, as the x-ray film touches your tongue and inside of your mouth, think of those touches as if it were food. Is that all right with you? [The dentist may now proceed with work, usually without too much difficulty.]

Control of Salivation

Irving I. Secter, D.D.S., M.A.
Southfield, Michigan

The flow of saliva increases when there is food in the mouth to be eaten. This is the beginning of the digestive process. There is now no food present to be digested. Therefore your excessive salivation is not useful and is undesirable. Visualize in your mind's eye a water faucet turned on full. Then see yourself turning the handle of the faucet until there is no more water coming through at all. Swallow the saliva which is in your mouth, and notice how dry your mouth becomes. Then turn the faucet on only enough for your mouth to become just moist enough.

Dental Phobias and Fears

Louis L. Dubin, D.D.S., Ph.D.
Philadelphia, Pennsylvania

EXPLORATION TECHNIQUE FOR DENTAL FEAR FROM A TRAUMATIC EXPERIENCE

[Following an appropriate evaluation of the patient and hypnotic induction:] I would like

you to visualize a large calendar that has the years on it, in addition to the months and days. And I want your mind to replicate a bear-cat scanner, and continue to scan the inner recesses until it lights up on the period of time and the incident that precipitated the problem. [Pause for identification of event.] I would now like to have you superimpose over this experience the type of experience that it can be, with modern techniques and skills, coupled with the kind of clinician you would enjoy, the way it can be— comfortable, secure and rapid. Whenever faced with any external or invasive technique, this new superimposed image will prevail, and a new security will embrace you.

PARESTHESIA FROM INDUCED ANESTHESIA OR NERVE DAMAGE BY MANIPULATION

I would like you to go back to that early time to recall the period when your lip had full sensation and functioned as intended. Now overlay this normal sensation over the unnatural feeling and feel how the change has returned you to comfort. [An ideomotor signal may be requested for when this internal response has occurred.] When either the chemo agent begins to dissipate or the nerve begins to regenerate, the hypnotic superimposition will begin to recede and the natural feeling will be reestablished. Thus during all the periods, there will never be anything but a natural feeling.

SUGGESTIONS FOR GAG REFLEX

1. While casually going about preparatory activity prior to a procedure, the clinician categorically and definitively states that it is impossible to gag while holding one's breath because of the physiologic and anatomic relationship of the human race. "Let me show you by introducing what has always troubled you: an x-ray film; a tongue depressor; or even an impression tray. [Each is used with the patient while he holds his breath, while the following suggestion is given.] And note how comfortable you feel, the loss of the troubled

sensation and the marvelous tolerance to the previous irritant.

2. [This procedure utilizes technical jargon and creates expectation of positive results from a "medical procedure." It is a naturalistic hypnotic procedure, assuming that the patient in the dental chair is already highly fixated and focused in attention. (*Ed.*)] [First note the severity of the gag by testing with no comment.] I am starting a process of tape that causes the shields on the receptor cells in the brain to drop, thereby not permitting awareness of the gag. I shall begin the tap through the occipital, parietal, temporal and frontal area on the left side of your head only, where the light pressure activates the dropping of the shield. [Following the application of pressure.] Now note the complete absence of any sensation of gagging. This may last permanently or have to be reinforced from time to time. So effective is it, that I can touch any portion of your throat and it is no more responsive than touching the skin on your hand.

BRUXISM AND CLENCHING DURING SLEEP

[Following appropriate evaluation and hypnotic induction:] Be aware of that comfortable feeling that you experience when there is an appropriate amount of space between your teeth — no contact. The intense pressure sets up a reaction in the temporomandibular joint which involves the nerves serving each entire side of the face and the head. The resultant symptoms mimic many other physical and anatomical abnormalities, resulting many times in excruciating pain and loss of function. Also, the premature wear of the facets of each tooth alters the occlusion, and if observed professionally, appears to have been caused by an aging process.

However, a mental protective mechanism will now be activated and constantly functioning. Whenever your teeth make contact while asleep, it will feel as if high powered stimuli suddenly appeared and you will be aroused from your sleep. Obviously, if you wish to enjoy an eve-

ning's sleep, the subconscious will discipline the conscious to keep the teeth slightly ajar. Just as the subconscious can alter the mental and physical response upon seeing or hearing a traumatic experience, so will it be effective here. All of this can be supplemented with a night guard constructed by your clinician.

ANESTHESIA AND ALTERATION OF PAIN AWARENESS

The following steps are used by the author in producing anesthesia/analgesia: (1) dissociation, (2) increased tolerance, (3) roleplaying, (4) recall.

INTRODUCTORY SUGGESTIONS. Take whatever number of deep breaths that you believe you require to return to that comfortable state that you enjoyed before. You will feel yourself descending or ascending several plateaus more than the previous time, and fully enjoying what you selected to experience; where and with whom, is your choice—either the experience you've had or would like to have, or in a location you've been to, or would like to be, either alone or with someone of your choice. It isn't necessary for you to be concerned about hearing my voice or listening for suggestions; enjoy your experience at the subconscious level.

DISSOCIATION. If you are frank and are truly enjoying an experience you've selected with all your senses involved, then all that transpires here will be of no consequence to you. If you are not here, all that happens here will not impact you. You will also have no recall back in the alert stage of what happened here, and only recall, if you wish, of the marvelous experience you selected.

INCREASED TOLERANCE. Note the degree of discomfort, on a scale of 0-10, that you are experiencing. Also note that if you would like to reduce it, you can participate in the resolu tion of the problem. You can, to whatever degree you wish or are capable, reduce it by "X" amount on the scale, therefore, noting the difference in comfort. Again, with your participation, you may do this on several occasions until you can go no further, noting, however, the obvious difference. Now, taking whatever number of breaths you require to arrive back at that comfortable secure state, picture yourself on a merry-go-round, passing that gold ring on each swing. Reach out, grasp and pull the ring, and depending on how effectively you pull it in, the tolerance that you've already achieved that is registered on the scale of 0–10 will alter considerably. You may be able to eliminate it completely or retain a tolerable level.

RECALL.   Do you recall the last time you experienced the comfort of the local anesthetic, the feeling of numbness of your lip to the midline, the loss of control and the inability to expectorate without dribbling down your chin? Do you also recall that whatever the doctor did, you had only awareness and no discomfort but only sensations of touch. All of this can also be experienced just as vividly.

Visualize taking off your glove on a sub-freezing day in the winter, and immersing your hand in the newly fallen snow. Feel the cold permeating from the tip of your fingers until it reaches your wrist, becoming colder and more intense, in fact, so intense that it is becoming intolerable, wanting to find relief.

One of your hands will float up toward your face now, and the index finger will touch the area that is to be anesthetized. When all of the anesthesia leaves the finger and hand, and drains into your face, the hand will return to your lap and the intensity of the cold will have completely anesthetized the gums, the teeth, tissues, both anterior and posterior, to he selected area. This area, like when it was previously anesthetized with a chemical and an injection, will have the same protective mechanism that frees you from all discomfort. It will last the same length of time that it always lasts when injected, and return to a natural feeling free of any post-discomfort, bleeding or swelling.

Illustrative Suggestions with Tooth Extraction

Selig Finkelstein, D.D.S.
Pleasantville, New York

RAPID RELAXATION INDUCTION

Mrs. M, before we start, I'm going to teach you how to relax. As you know, everything is easier when you are relaxed. While relaxation is a mental process, it does help to have something physical to work with, so shrug your shoulders a little. That's very good and that is all the actual physical movement you need to make. Mentally, move this feeling of relaxation from your shoulders into your upper arms, through your elbows into your forearms, wrists and hands, so that you have a comfortable relaxed feeling from your right hand up your right arm, across your shoulders, down your left arm to your left hand. It's all right to close your eyes now. Move the feeling of comfortable relaxation from your shoulders into your chest and stomach and hips . . . into your upper legs and through your knees into your lower legs, ankles and feet. Now move the feeling of comfortable relaxation from your shoulders into your neck and let it spread up into your head, until it fills your entire head with a comfortable relaxed feeling. Take a deep breath and as you breathe out, relax very deeply. You have noticed how relaxing it is when you breathe out, so you can become more deeply relaxed and comfortable each time you exhale.

ANESTHESIA SUGGESTIONS FOR TOOTH EXTRACTION

We do have a very effective surface anesthetic, which I am now applying to your tooth and gums. I'm squeezing it into the gum tissue and now, to make sure we have complete anesthesia, I'm going to push it under the gum around the tooth. Notice how the numbness increases as I push it firmly down further and further around the tooth. I'm now going to exert even more pressure to push the anesthetic material under the gum and down around the root of the tooth. The anesthesia has now become so profound you will not be able to feel the tooth being removed . . .

VASCULAR CONTROL, CLOTTING, AND NORMAL HEALING

The tooth is out, and you can let the socket fill with blood and clot normally. You can be pleasantly surprised at how little discomfort and swelling there will be as the tooth socket heals rapidly in a normal manner. When you open your eyes, you will feel refreshed and very good and very pleased with yourself, and when I count to three, you will open your eyes and feel terrific, because you are. One . . . two . . . three.

COMMENTARY

The suggestion for eye closure was made when she started to blink and seemed to be keeping her eyes open with an effort. The suggestion of powerful new topical anesthetic was made to give her trance logic a handle for interpreting any sensation as comfortable. The perceptual distortion was reinforced constantly as the elevator was applied to the tooth and finally as the tooth was removed. Until the tooth was removed, all the suggestions were to the effect that the anesthesia was being instituted and intensified. When the patient was told that it was so numb that she would not feel the extraction, the tooth had already been removed, so there was nothing that she could possibly feel.

The posthypnotic suggestion that the socket will fill with blood and clot and heal normally is readily accepted in the trance state, even though the exact physiological mechanism that makes this happen is unknown at the present time. Giving a subject the feeling of being refreshed and feeling good and being terrific when she opens her eyes gives her an incentive to come

out of trance. The trance state is a very comfortable and enjoyable state, and it is wise to give the subject an incentive to terminate it.

Dental Hypnosis

Victor Rausch, D.D.S.
Waterloo, Ontario, Canada

INTRODUCTION AND INDUCTION OF HYPNOSIS

To determine the appropriate formal induction technique suitable for a particular patient, let us ask ourselves one question: "At this time, is the patient experiencing acute physical pain or severe psychological distress?"

If the patient is not in immediate severe pain or distress, more permissive techniques such as progressive relaxation enhanced with ego-strengthening phrases are usually sufficient to produce the relaxation necessary to make the procedure comfortable for the patient.

Instructing the patient in a direct manner to take a deep breath, let the eyes close and let the whole body go limp as the breath is forcibly blown out produces a rapid relaxation response. The suggestion that "with each breath you take and with each word I say you relax deeper and deeper until nothing bothers, nothing disturbs" sets up an automatic deepening technique paced by the patient's breathing and the dental surgeon's voice. Specific suggestions can now be incorporated into the verbalization.

If the patient is in acute pain or experiencing severe psychological distress, the short, rapid, authoritarian instructive induction techniques are usually the most successful. For a patient in pain, the top priority is relief as quickly as possible. The patient's mind-set is such that he is less critical and readily accepts suggestions and commands which may under normal circumstances seem to be irrational.

The patient's need for the relief of pain or mental distress dictates the rapidity with which he or she will accept hypnotic suggestions and respond to them.

VERBALIZATION FOR TREATING A PATIENT IN SEVERE PAIN

"I realize you are in extreme discomfort and I can help you. For me to do that you must help me. Listen very carefully to what I say and follow my instructions. Do you understand? [Let the patient commit himself.] Good. Now, look at me and put your finger on the tooth that is hurting. Now, as I touch the area [place a finger on an area adjacent to the tooth where there is no inflammation and gently press], feel the pressure of my finger. The pressure feels good. As the pressure increases, your eyelids become heavy and close. Concentrate only on the pressure. In a few moments you will feel only the pressure. When that happens let this finger [touch and indicate a particular finger on one of the hands] twitch. It will move by itself to indicate to me when you feel only the pressure. [Wait for the ideomotor response.] That's good!

"The more pressure you feel, the more comfortable the tooth feels. Now, relax very deeply and become aware only of the good feeling of the pressure."

At this point the tooth can be surgically removed. The unacceptable feeling of pain has been integrated into the acceptable, pleasant feeling of pressure. Trust the ideomotor signal. Do the procedure. Often, as the forceps are engaged on the tooth in question, the pressure produced by the forceps acts as a deepening cue and causes the patient to go into very deep hypnosis.

OTHER DENTAL SUGGESTIONS FOLLOWING INDUCTION AND DEEPENING

ANESTHESIA AND BLEEDING CONTROL. "Nothing bothers, nothing disturbs—you are doing just fine—you are safe, comfortable, enjoying the feeling. Your body is safe, comfortable, totally relaxed, working automatically. You now let yourself flow with that feeling of relaxation so deeply that you need pay no attention to your body anymore.

"As I touch your teeth and the surrounding tissues, those areas become completely numb. Let this finger [indicate a specific finger by touching it] move by itself. It moves by itself when the areas I am touching are completely numb. [Stroke the area until the ideomotor signal is activated.] Good! [Teeth at this point may be surgically removed.] Let the sockets fill and the bleeding stop. Turn it off! [The denture may be fitted and inserted.]

EGO-STRENGTHENING AND TEACHING SELF-HYPNOSIS. "You have done extremely well. Enjoy a feeling of well-being and accomplishment. You now become aware of how good you are at hypnosis. After you leave here today, you can use self-hypnosis for your benefit anytime it is appropriate for you. Go through the same procedure we used today and you will respond as effectively and easily as you did today. Do you understand? Good."

POSTHYPNOTIC SUGGESTION. "In a few moments, I will ask you to allow yourself to come to complete alertness. After you do, your mouth remains completely comfortable. Your mouth heals rapidly. The denture feels good. You speak clearly. Nothing bothers, nothing disturbs. Do you understand? Good."

Suggestions for Operative Hypnodontics

William S. Kroger, M.D.
Palm Springs, California

PRODUCTION OF ANESTHESIA

[One should never assume that anesthesia is present, even though a patient may be in deep hypnosis. Always include this step to produce anesthesia first; then test before operating. The procedure is to take hold of the tooth to be treated between the index finger and the thumb, rocking it and at the same time depressing it in the socket, gently at first but gradually more firmly. While doing this say:] As I press down on this tooth, you will find that it is getting numb and losing all its feeling. It is beginning to feel as though you've had an injection. You will feel a tingling sensation . . . cold and numb . . .

TEST FOR ANESTHESIA.   [Take a sharp explorer and gently press into the gingival area around the tooth, saying:] I am pricking your gum with this point, but, you see, you feel absolutely no discomfort. [Stop, and say:] I shall do the same to the other side of your mouth, but you will feel a sharp pain there. [Then prick the gingival tissues on the normal side very lightly. Almost always, the patient will react with a sudden start. Now go back on the first side and indicate the difference to the patient. If there is any doubt in the operator's mind, either the hypnosis should be deepened and the above words repeated, or the patient should be given procaine and further tests should be made.]

The Let's Pretend Game

Lawrence M. Staples, D.M.D.

Some of my young patients like to play a game called "let's pretend" when they have to have their dental care. They shut their eyes when I tell them to, and they at first just pretend that they are at home, watching their favorite TV program, and they have fun while I am caring for and working on their teeth.

"Would you like to play a game like that," I asked Kathy, and she thought that would be fun. "All right, Kathy, I will draw a 'funny face' on your thumbnail. . . . Here are the eyes, and here is the mouth . . . and right between them will go the nose, and now a dimple in the chin. Hold your thumb in front of you and just look at that funny face so that is about all that you see . . . Just that funny face on your thumb. Pretty soon your eyes will be tired-like, and your eyelids will begin to feel so *VERY HEAVY* and tired-like, that they will feel like they do when you are tired. That is fine, just let them stay closed until I tell you to open them. You will not go to sleep, for you will want to

listen to what I am going to say, and it will be just so much fun.

"I want you to pretend — make believe — that is what the 'pretend game' is. You make believe that you are at home in your own living room and lying down looking at television. It can be just as real as can be. When you see the television screen you can nod your head so that I may know that you see the TV screen all lighted up, and your bestest TV program is coming on. . . . There it is now . . . and it is getting clearer and clearer. I want you to see every bit of the picture, and it can be just as good as it ever was when you saw it at home. I want you to tell me all about the picture . . . what people or animals, just what you saw, later, after I tell you to awaken. And all of the time that you are watching the television program, I'll be working on your teeth. You will hear some noise, and feel some pressure, but you will be having so much fun watching the picture that you will not mind anything that I do. Nod your head to let me know that you are having fun." [Kathy nods.]

I occasionally make some remark, such as: "I want you to tell me all about what you saw, and you know you can always close your eyes and see your favorite television program whenever you come to the dentist. . . . You will always want to have your dentistry done like this. Going to the dentist can always be fun because you have learned the game of 'let's pretend.'"

Then I said to Kathy: "In a moment I am going to say the letters . . . A..B..C..and the next time I say the letter C, you will open your eyes smiling and feeling very happy that you have had two cavities cared for and a little old root removed . . . and it has been a lot of fun . . . A . . . The picture is about over and it will just fade away . . . B . . . The picture has gone and the TV screen is dark, and now, smiling and happy . . . C . . . Your eyes will open and, oh boy, did you ever have fun!?"

My records show that later, as Kathy grew older, water skiing on one of the New Hampshire lakes took the place of the television, and Kathy told me how she learned to water ski one summer, and so I said: "Suppose you shut your eyes as you have done many times before when you were having dental care . . . let yourself become limp and loose and lazy-like, just as you have done before . . . sleepy-like and drowsy-like. . . . And suppose you see and feel yourself water skiing up on Merrymeeting Lake. . . . Imagine that you are in the water. . . . Daddy and his boat are in front of you and as you hold the rope, Daddy starts the motor and up you go on your skiis . . . just the way you did last summer. . . . And now Daddy makes the boat go a little faster, and away you go down the lake. . . . Be careful now, you are going to cross up over the waves that the boat is making. [As I said this, Kathy slightly lifted her toes as she would when going over a wave.] And now you are down near the end of the lake. Daddy is going make a turn." [And Kathy slightly moves her shoulders as she would do in balancing herself for making a change of direction.]

I chatted as I did her dental work, suggesting that she was going over the waves and making other turns, etc. At one point I suggested that one of her friends was out water skiing also, and I said: "Mary, over there has just taken a tumble . . . but you, Kathy, are such a good water skier that you don't fall. [This remark of praise brought a slight smile on Kathy's face.] Water skiing is so much fun up on Merrymeeting Lake, and it is also a lot of fun to close your eyes and daydream that you are waterskiing whenever you come for dentistry. You can always have your dentistry done this way. . . . And now, Kathy, your dentistry is finished for today, so I'll say A . . . B . . . C . . . and you will awake smiling and happy . . . A . . . Daddy's heading for the shore . . . B . . . you drop the rope; you are in shallow water now . . . and C . . . the daydream is all over—eyes open and you smile because that was a lot of fun."

Erickson's Approach with Bruxism in Children

Milton H. Erickson, M.D.

I think as soon as the child is old enough you really ought to take up with him the question of the feelings in his mouth, and the question of how the mouth works. Once you get the child interested in his own bruxism movement, sooner or later he will show it to you. You ask him to really memorize those feelings, and then you express the very pious hope that he *won't* awaken when he makes that bruxism movement during sleep. And you express this hope so nicely and so genuinely and so suggestively that you actually condition him to awaken by your subtle negative suggestion.

You can also suggest that he will be able to *hear* the bruxism; that he will awaken when he hears it; and that he will immediately comfort himself with the realization that he has a good pattern of going back to sleep whenever he awakens. But how many times does a person want to awaken in the middle of the night just to prove to himself that he can hear his bruxism, and that he can go right back to sleep!

Use of Fantasy or Hallucination for Tongue Thrusting

Irving I. Secter, D.D.S., M.A.
Southfield, Michigan

[First the hypnotized patient is asked to imagine (or hallucinate) an unpleasant, negative theater scene or a negative experience with the associated unpleasant feelings. Then he or she imagines a very happy scene or experience with the accompanying positive feelings. The patient is asked to signal with a head nod when he or she is experiencing the suggested scenes.]

Let the theater scene disappear for the time being. Be aware of the fact that you are sitting comfortably and relaxed in this chair.

Now we can talk about your tongue thrusting and how much nicer it will be for you when your teeth are straightened. Listen carefully. Every time you thrust your tongue into an improper position, you can re-experience the bad feelings that you had during that bad scene in the theater a short time ago. You can immediately put your tongue in a proper position, and the bad feelings can be immediately replaced by the wonderful feelings. Are you willing for this to happen? [Patient nods.] Would you be willing to try this a few times right now for practice?

Suggestions with Tongue Thrusting

Donald J. Rosinski, D.D.S.
New York Mills, New York

INTRODUCTION

[Following hypnosis and a thorough education of the nature of the problem.] At this point, the patient being in a very relaxed state and giving signs that he is willing to continue with the instructions, an explanation of the swallowing pattern is given. He is informed that the particular pattern which has brought him to our office is a holdover from infancy which has been allowed to become a habit for reasons in which we are not really interested. He is given the freedom to resolve for himself this aspect of the problem in the light of his intelligent adult evaluation of the explanation which is given. Assuming the strong motivation which has brought this patient to our office for assistance with his swallowing pattern, he is informed that we strongly believe that he wants and is willing to accept and act upon the re-education of his swallowing pattern.

SUGGESTIONS

Now, Paul, while your body is completely relaxed, and your mind completely free to concentrate upon the way in which you swallow, we can review for you the steps in swallowing. In doing this while the mind is completely attentive to the steps to be followed, we can be quite certain that these steps will be fed into the program of swallowing, and replace this troublesome way of swallowing which has been a holdover from infancy. We can allow the nerves in the tongue to become acquainted with the proper place for the tongue to be during swallowing.

You remember, Paul, that in proper swallowing, the tongue is supposed to make contact with a spot on the soft tissues of your palate directly behind the two front teeth. Now, Paul, allow your tongue to find this place, and to feel it, and to become comfortable with the way it feels. Notice particularly how well the tongue fits to this spot. Notice how much more relaxed your entire body becomes as your tongue becomes more familiar with this spot.

Now, Paul, allow the tongue to remain in contact with this special place, while your teeth and lips close together in preparation for swallowing. Notice how easily you can accomplish this when all of the muscles in and around your face and mouth are completely relaxed.

Pay close attention, now, Paul, to just how easy it is to complete the swallowing action while you are so completely relaxed. Notice that the tongue is able to maintain its contact with the palate during swallowing—without any extra stress on any of the muscles of your mouth—the lips are able to remain closed gently together without any need to fight the thrust of the tongue which you have had for all of these years.

Please continue to relax in this fashion, Paul, while you repeat this action a few times so that it becomes very completely imprinted in the memory banks of your subconscious mind—*so that each and every time you swallow from now on* [this is said slowly and repeated two or three times to ensure that the patient truly grasps its significance as a posthypnotic instruction] your subconscious mind will activate the nervous pathways which will enable you to swallow in this same relaxed fashion. You will find that this activity by the subconscious mind will replace very soon the past mode of swallowing.

You will also, Paul, become consciously aware of this progress, although only very dimly at first. As the newly learned pattern of swallowing becomes more comfortable, you will find this awareness growing in your consciousness, so that you will feel proud that you have been able to do such a good job on yourself when the orthodontist compliments your progress in treatment. But, most of all, Paul, you will have a feeling of accomplishment in knowing not only that you were able to learn this new pattern of swallowing, but also that you will have been able to do such a good job that there will not be any sliding back into this former pattern — you will have learned it well, and for good.

Paul, before we bring this trance to a close, I would like to know whether there is anything about the instructions which is not clear. Do you understand everything? [Upon ascertaining that the patient does understand the instructions, he can be roused from his state with instructions which also reinforce previously given posthypnotic instructions for swallowing and well-being in this regard.]

Now, Paul, since you fully understand what you must do to learn this new way of swallowing, we can end the appointment. I should like you to rouse yourself from this very relaxed state with a feeling of well-being that everything is normal. Also, you will feel refreshed from having relaxed in this fashion, and feel good in knowing that each and every time you swallow, the subconscious mind will take over to help you to swallow more easily, and without the problem tongue thrust.

HYPNOSIS WITH CANCER PATIENTS

INTRODUCTION

CANCER PATIENTS HAVE a variety of psychological and medical needs that may be addressed through hypnosis. Cancer and chronic illness may certainly have a negative impact on self-esteem and feelings of confidence. Thus hypnotic ego-strengthening methods that were discussed in Chapter 5 may be of value with these patients. In addition, simply the use of self-hypnosis to control symptoms provides the patient with a sense of mastery and counters feelings of helplessness and powerlessness. Pain is a prominent issue for some patients, and thus the suggestions in Chapter 3 may likewise be of benefit. The side effects of chemotherapy are popularly regarded as being almost as terrible as cancer itself. Certainly the side effects of anticipatory nausea, vomiting, diarrhea and loss of appetite may be successfully addressed through hypnotic suggestion (Walker, Dawson, Pollet, Ratcliffe, & Hamilton, 1988). You will find a variety of suggestions and metaphors in this section for treating these symptoms.

Anxiety and fear, discussed in the last chapter, are also important symptoms of many patients. Professionals in the fields of hypnosis and behavioral medicine widely believe that producing feelings of calm and tranquility allows the immune system to function at a maximal level, aiding the fight against cancer. For these reasons, self-hypnosis and approaches like Meares' deep meditative hypnosis or the method of prolonged hypnosis may be valuable therapeutic tools.

Although research evidence is anecdotal and limited, many health professionals similarly believe that hypnotic imagery may enhance the functioning of the immune system (Rossi, 1986; Simonton, Matthews-Simonton, & Creighton. 1978). We truly hope that this is the case and there is encouraging research about our ability to enhance cellular immunity (Hall, 1982-83). The field of psychoneuroimmunology (Ader, 1981) has experienced an explosion of exciting research that is beginning to identify factors like stress, depression (versus laughter), and loneliness (versus social support) that seem linked to diseases like cancer (Borysenko, 1987).

However, we must await further, more definitive evidence about the potentials, limits and active ingredients of hypnotic approaches with cancer. We very honestly don't know what works. Thus most of us use very different hypnotic approaches like those of both Meares and the Simontons, in the hope that they will be beneficial to at least some of our cancer patients. Assisting the patient in letting go of strong, unresolved feelings may also prove to be a key in enhancing the body's ability to fight and prevent cancer (Pennebaker, Kiecolt-Glaser, & Glaser, 1988).

I believe that we must strike a balance in our approach to cancer patients. We must remain optimistic, offering hope and treatment options that we believe may prove beneficial, and yet we must remain cautious not to make exaggerated claims to the public that imply that hypnosis is a cure for cancer. Historically, enthusiastic proponents of hypnosis have too often made grandiose claims, and then, when hypnosis has failed to live up to the false advertising, it has fallen into disrepute and disuse. We hope that we possess some keys, undoubtedly in need of refinement, that will open locks to free bodily responses that serve preventative functions and assist in the fight for life. At a minimum, hypnotic techniques will offer many of our patients' symptomatic relief from nausea, vomiting, pain, suffering, depression, and loss of self-worth—thus providing a higher quality of life during the time they sojourn with us. Later in this chapter you will also find that Levitan's Hypnotic Death Rehearsal Technique offers an alternative for assisting terminal patients to come to grips with their own impending death.

Clinical Issues in Controlling Chemotherapy Side Effects

William H. Redd,
Patricia H. Rosenberger, and
Cobie S. Hendler

We believe the control of chemotherapy nausea/emesis through hypnosis offers several advantages. Hypnosis during chemotherapy treatment makes the experience less stressful and the time pass more quickly. It requires no equipment unless a patient uses hypnosis tapes, and then only a tape recorder and audiotapes are required. Unlike antiemetic drugs, it does not produce aversive side effects. As a skill which patients can learn, it gives patients a personal sense of mastery and control over their problem, rather than an increased sense of helplessness resulting from further dependency on drugs. Hypnosis not only enables the patient to alleviate his or her experience of nausea, but also potentially benefits the patient in other areas. Finally, as a general relaxation technique, a patient may use hypnosis to reduce stress and anxiety. Its benefits extend beyond the control of nausea.

In spite of the many benefits hypnosis offers, we frequently encounter an initial reluctance on the patient's part to employ this technique. We find that many patients have the preconception that hypnosis is a mysterious technique allowing the therapist to influence or control the individual's thoughts or actions. Straightforward explanations of hypnosis alleviate many patient fears. In our introduction to hypnosis, we emphasize that patients control their hypnotic experience and that they become hypnotized only to the extent they allow themselves. Furthermore, we stress that it is a skill that individuals can master with practice, rather than a state which just "happens" every time they are hypnotized. To those patients searching for a technique which eradicates post-chemotherapy nausea with little effort on their part, this is a disappointment. To those patients who desire control over their acute nausea, this technique is eagerly embraced.

In addition to a general wariness toward hypnosis, some patients believe that a psychological intervention implies a psychological etiology of their problems. That is, if nausea can be controlled through hypnosis, the nausea must be psychological in origin, not the result of the toxic drugs. This suggests to some patients that they are emotionally and/or mentally "weak." In turn, they believe they should either "tough it out" or somehow gain psychological control over the nausea on their own. In response to this attitude, we discuss with patients the very real aversive side effects of chemotherapy and point out that psychological interventions can be useful in the treatment of physical problems.

Some patients are reluctant to devote the time necessary to practice hypnosis. It represents another interruption in a schedule already interrupted by physicians appointments and chemotherapy treatments. Some patients prefer to live with the nausea until it becomes unbearable rather than make a commitment to learning this technique. In addition to the inconvenience in their schedule, hypnosis serves as another reminder that they have cancer. For individuals actively seeking normalcy, any such reminder is not welcomed.

The importance of good rapport between therapist and patient cannot be underestimated. Hypnosis is an interpersonal event: both therapist and patient are active participants. This interpersonal element seems critical; we have found that patients must initially work with someone and be trained in hypnosis before hypnosis tapes are effective. Patients report they prefer to experience hypnosis with a therapist several times; it is only when they have identified and become comfortable with their hypnotic experience that they can "transfer" to audiotapes.

A final issue is the patient's dependence upon the therapist's presence during chemotherapy such that the patient resists progressing to self-hypnosis. Our research to date suggests that the presence of the therapist may be crucial to successful nausea/emesis control. However, it should be understood that in our initial work we included no formal training in self-hypnosis nor did we encourage the patients to use any methods of self-control. We are now investigating ways of maximizing patients' involvement in their nausea control by stressing patient independence from the outset, teaching patients to use audiotape recordings of hypnotic inductions during chemotherapy treatments, and training nurses to assist patients in nausea control.

Suggestions and Metaphors for Nausea

Alexander A. Levitan, M.D.
New Brighton, Minnesota

LAKE METAPHOR.   See yourself watching a lake high in the mountains. Notice that there is a storm raging. There are whitecaps and the skies are dark and cloudy. Then watch carefully as a solitary sunbeam penetrates the clouds. Soon others follow it and the dark storm clouds part to allow the sunshine to come streaming through. Soon there is bright sunshine everywhere. The surface of the lake is now tranquil and serene.

TURN OFF THE LIGHT.   See yourself as a house with many rooms. Find the room that contains the unpleasant feeling that you are experiencing now. [Pause] Turn off the light in that room. Tiptoe out of the room and quietly close the door and lock it so that those feelings don't bother you anymore.

SUGGESTION.   Whenever you practice relaxing, you will have the pleasant taste of mint in your mouth and it will replace any undesirable taste or feeling you may have.

MAGIC MIRROR.   See a magic mirror pass through your body at your upper abdomen such that all the nausea is below the mirror, and it doesn't bother you at all.

RESTAURANT METAPHOR.   See yourself planning to visit a new restaurant, one you've been looking forward to for a long time. See yourself dressing, then leaving the house with the person you'd most like to be with. See yourself arriving at the restaurant, being escorted to the table where everything is just as you hoped it would be. See yourself opening the menu, noticing all the wonderful things there are to eat. Be aware of that pleasant anticipatory hunger. Take an emotional snapshot of that feeling. That's the feeling you'll have whenever you practice relaxing, and it will substitute for any negative feelings you might have at the time.

Suggestions for Chemotherapy Patients

Alexander A. Levitan, M.D.
New Brighton, Minnesota

And I want you to take a moment to see the drugs helping you. You know that we are all here working together for your benefit. You're on the team, too. You are a member of our group. Feel the medicines going into your system. See them searching out any remaining cancer cells that might be anywhere in the body, anywhere in your abdomen. See them attacking those cells and destroying them. See the cancer cells dying. See the battle raging as one blow is delivered from one drug, then another blow from the other drug. Knocking out the cancer cells, destroying them totally. Then see your own defense mechanisms, your own white cells, your own antibodies going in there administering the final blows, cleaning up the breakdown products, the trash, the residue. See it

being taken up by the bloodstream and excreted from your body, expelled from your body in your urine and your stool. See the inside of your abdomen, healthy, clean, free of any hints of cancer cells. All of this is within your power. All of this you can do for yourself. It is a good feeling to be in control. It's nice to be in charge. It's nice to be the captain of the ship.

Now, while you are relaxing and enjoying the peaceful place you have chosen, I want you also to know that you can control the other feelings you have. Just as your learned to turn the pain switch off to your hand [when glove anesthesia was performed] so that you need not have any discomfort when the IV is set, you can turn off the switch that controls any unpleasant feelings in your stomach. Any hint of nausea can be turned off. Find the switch on the switchboard which controls that and turn that switch off. Let the light go out over the switch, let that feeling extinguish itself. Some people even like to think about a house, a house with all the rooms lighted. Find the room in the house that controls the stomach, and turn the light off. Let that feeling leave you totally and completely. Replace it instead with a comfortable, peaceful, pleasant feeling. Almost as if that part of the body didn't belong to you any longer. Almost as if you didn't even have to think about it. That's good. Enjoy that feeling and keep it there as long as you want. Know that it is available for you whenever you wish. You are in control, you can turn that switch off anytime you wish, and you can set the timer to leave it off as long as you like.

And if there ever should be any little hint of discomfort, any little hint that something isn't quite right, all you have to do is take a deep breath, let yourself relax and it will disappear. It will be replaced with the same feeling of peace and contentment you have now. And now, why don't you decide which hand you would like to numb up and, when you have fully numbed it up, that's fine, just let it become heavy, free of discomfort, free of painful sensations. Let the veins in the back of the hand dilate up. Let them become like swollen, full rivers. Let the needle go in properly into the vein when the IV is set. Let the vein and the skin wrap themselves tightly around the needle so that there will be no chance of any leakage, there will be no black and blue marks, no bleeding, and certainly no discomfort. That's fine. Just let that happen. OK. And when you're ready, let us know by raising the finger and we will set the IV. [There is no need to confine suggestions to anatomically or physiologically known functions. The mind has influence far beyond what we can accurately describe and explain. Glove anesthesia does not correlate with neuroanatomy and neither need these suggestions.]

Suggestions and Metaphors for Support and Ego-Strengthening in Cancer Patients

Billie S. Strauss, Ph.D.
Chicago, Illinois

Metaphors and suggestions must be such that they are meaningful to the patient at the particular time they are given. The patient must be able to relate to suggestions from the context of his or her previous experience, and suggestions must be ego-syntonic. Suggestions of mastery often are most effective when they reflect a previous time when the patient was competent and effectual.

A metaphor used with young adolescents with cancer to help them deal with depression around weakened functioning and the vast changes made in their lives is as follows:

Imagine a picture, broken into a thousand pieces. Now begin to pick up the pieces and put them back together again.

These children, metaphorically, felt that their lives were "broken into pieces" by the effects of the disease. They, often correctly, saw their lives as being devastated and felt helpless to continue with their daily routines. These children had worked picture puzzles when they were younger. Putting together a puzzle reflects mastery; the implication is that the child has mastered one situation, the puzzle and can in the same way, master another and cope with his or her present situation.

A suggestion used with adults who are struggling to cope with diagnosis or recurrence of cancer is as follows:

You'll find you have some strengths that you didn't know you had.

These adults were previously bright, well-functioning, and had considerable strength, so the suggestion "have some strengths" is ego-syntonic. The suggestions "You'll find" and "you didn't know you had" imply that the patient need not be aware of the strengths at present, but may experience them in the future.

General Suggestions for Self-Healing

Joan Murray-Jobsis, Ph.D.
Chapel Hill, North Carolina

INTRODUCTION

These suggestions for self-healing are applicable with other medical disorders besides cancer, but they have been included in this chapter because of their particular relevance to cancer. (*Ed.*)

SUGGESTIONS

And perhaps beginning to remember that inner, central core of existence, that place deep within the central part of mind and body, that place of inner harmony and inner calm, quiet stillness, a place of inner healing powers and life force. And remembering that from the very beginnings of existence, the mind and body have known how to heal themselves. The body knows how to heal over scrapes and wounds and injuries, how to generate new cells and new tissue whenever needed. And the body knows equally well how to regulate its own healthy functioning; regulating heart rate and breathing, and body temperature and blood pressure, all effortlessly, unconsciously, automatically maintained at moderate healthy levels. And the body knowing how to maintain its own healthy blood chemistry, maintaining the necessary hormonal and chemical components for a healthy functioning mind and body; maintaining and regulating the serotonin levels, the potassium, the endorphins, all the necessary hormonal and chemical components that allow for an active, alert mind and body, but without overexcitation, overstimulation. And in similar fashion, the body maintaining an immune system effortlessly, automatically, warding off invading organisms before they have a chance to gain a foothold. Building resistance, maintaining resistance, building antibodies, the white blood cells surrounding the invading viruses or bacteria, like white knights on white chargers. And the body knows how to regulate its metabolic system; the metabolism being designed to help us stabilize our bodies at a normal, moderate, healthy level. And in every way, mind and body working for health, healing, maintenance of healthy functioning. And somehow knowing of these inner resources, the strength, the growth, the healing, the life force, making everything easier.

Hypnotic Suggestions with Cancer

Jeffrey Auerbach, Ph.D.
Los Angeles, California

INTRODUCTION

The following suggestions, like the Simontons' approach, encourage the patient to actively fight the cancer through the use of imagery. Naturally, such suggestions may be individualized to the patient, and pauses may be included to allow time for the development of imagery. Patients may also be asked to interact and describe their experience and imagery, allowing suggestions to be more closely tailored to the patient's experience. (*Ed.*)

SUGGESTIONS

A cancer cell is a weak and confused cell. If it reproduces rapidly it may form a tumor. Normally cancer cells are quickly destroyed by the immune system. Recent research is demonstrating that imagery can assist immune system functioning. It is important for patients to communicate to the clinician their spontaneous imagery to the suggestions. This is important in terms of prognosis and also to help illuminate healing psychotherapeutic work that may be needed.

Allow yourself to become very warm and comfortable. Let any fear fade away . . . becoming very warm and relaxed . . . safe and secure. Begin your healing journey by first making yourself very small, as small as a drop of water, and then slip inside yourself through your mouth and down your throat. You can be inside a clear bubble that will protect you and supply you with everything you need. Allow yourself to become even smaller now and enter your bloodstream.

Circulate through your body and tell your immune system to release stronger and more effective white blood cells into your bloodstream. Let these white blood cells be represented by an animated or symbolic form. Watch them stream through your bloodstream, full of energy and sure of their purpose — to dissolve any unhealthy growth that they find. If you would like you can transmit messages of encouragement or direction to your immune system. . . . You might want to thank your immune system for the good job it is doing in the face of a challenger . . . or ask your immune system if there is anything you can do to help speed your healing.

From a safe vantage point, see any tumors being dissolved as your white blood cells surround and overcome any unhealthy growth. See the area being completely healed and then watch your immune system cells patrol through your body in a loving and protective way. See and feel yourself being restored to a state of ideal health and appreciate and love yourself for taking the time to love and heal in this way.

Hypnotic Suggestions with Cancer Patients

Harold B. Crasilneck, Ph.D., and James A. Hall, M.D.
Dallas, Texas

CONTROL OF CHEMOTHERAPY SIDE EFFECTS

Time will go by rapidly, your anxiety and fears will be much less . . . you can sleep for long periods of time during and following treatment . . . nausea and vomiting will be minimal; however, *if you have to vomit you can* . . . should you be asleep when you need to vomit you can awaken, vomit, and immediately go back to a deep, restful, peaceful sleep . . . time will pass by quickly . . . hours will seem like minutes . . . there will be little discomfort and vomiting will grow less with each treatment.

SUGGESTIONS WITH TERMINAL PATIENTS

You will be free of tension, tightness, stress and strain, you will be relaxed and at ease, and your body will be relatively free of discomfort. You will have a minimum of discomfort. . . . You will be relaxed . . . at ease. . . . You will have a feeling of well-being . . . sleeping when you desire . . . and reinforcing these suggestions yourself . . . as frequently as you desire. . . . You can eat well and enjoy the food

intake the doctor has ordered for you. . . . Discomfort, anxiety, and tension will be minimal and under control most of the time . . . you will be relaxed and at ease. . . . You can rest well, secure in the knowledge that your unconscious mind will allow you to be free of excessive tension and any physical or psychological discomfort.

[These suggestions may be reinforced as often as necessary with periodic and frequent self-hypnosis.]

TYPES OF SUGGESTIONS TAUGHT IN SELF-HYPNOSIS

I will be virtually free of pain. . . . I will eat as much as I can, enjoying my food. . . . I will sleep as often as I wish, going to sleep easily and awakening calm and refreshed. . . . I will be free of fear, calm and unafraid, with little anxiety or tension. . . . I can review as I wish the pleasant experiences of my past life, my family's affection, the warmth of my friendships . . . and past problems will fall into place, no longer of any great concern. . . . My body will respond maximally to any medical treatment that will prolong my life or increase my comfort. . . . I am calm and at ease . . . knowing that the immense power of my unconscious mind can help me both mentally and physically.

I have a built-in immune system . . . my immune system can block and destroy the cancer cells in my body. . . . I have a powerful built-in psychological immune system . . . and nothing is beyond the power of my unconscious mind. . . . My powerful built-in immune system can . . . and will destroy these cancer cells that have invaded my body. . . . My immune system can and will contain the tumor . . . arresting the growth . . . and finally destroy this invader of my body. . . . I can and will destroy these cancer cells because of the omnipotent power of my immune system and . . . my unconscious mind. . . . I will recover . . . I will get well. . . . I will get well. . . .

Imagery to Enhance the Control of the Physiological and Psychological "Side Effects" of Cancer Therapy

Simon W. Rosenberg, D.M.D.
New York, New York

INTRODUCTION

The selection of a variety of imagery from the patient's abundant garden of experience and fantasy can aid in controlling physiological processes. Analgesia or pain control may be obtained through a reduction of individual components of pain—i.e., experiential, anticipatory or actual pain stimuli. Local anesthesia obtained by hypnosis becomes useful for venipuncture, spinal taps, bone marrow aspiration or biopsy, injections, etc. An ability to maintain body rigidity is required for wound care and therapeutic or diagnostic radiology; body flaccidity may be required for examinations or diagnostic tests. The surgical patient often is aided by stimulation/suppression of appetite, gag reflex, salivation, bowel movement, urinary bladder function, etc. In addition, hemorrhage control may be crucial. Nausea and vomiting from cancer chemotherapy is often uncontrollable with medication. Hypnotic imagery for control of these physiological processes is used with consistent success. . . . The goals of ego-strengthening, faith enhancement, and reduction of secondary gain result in increased patient autonomy and cooperation. Experiencing a decreased sense of fear and anxiety, the patient reacts with less antagonism and resistance to the necessary, optimal therapy.

EXAMPLES OF SUGGESTIONS

[The following suggestions, excerpted from an individual case report, illustrate types of verbalizations that may be used. Induction and deepening had already occurred. It should be kept in mind that these suggestions were tailored to the individual patient, whose interests included snowmobiling, bowling, being outdoors in winter and at the beach in the summer. (*Ed.*)]

PAIN CONTROL FOR MOUTH, THROAT AND STOMACH.
Now picture the following: A winter scene at dawn in a safe, secure home or cabin in the woods. Have a relaxed, easy breakfast in front of a fireplace. A warm drink and nourishing food to remove the night's chill. So good to feel comfortable. Being warmly dressed, step outside feeling tip-top, into the invigorating air. Look around you. See each of the objects before you. Let them take on shape, dimension, texture. See each of their colors. Feel the warmth of the clothing—the refreshing coolness of the air. Hear the sounds of the woods—if only to allow the room noises of the nurses working or the intercom announcements to drift off—Perhaps all you can hear is the sound of quiet or even a dog's bark in the distance. Try to smell the fragrances of the woods in winter—a little more and a little bit more. Note how good it feels.

If you were to take off your glove, in your mind's eye, your hand might get numb. If you went on a warmed-up, well-tuned snowmobile through the woods, your cheek might feel a cool numbness with the wind and light snow flurries going refreshingly by. When they put in the central venous line this afternoon, and when they do the bone marrow tap, it will be interesting to think about that cool, comfortable numbness right in the area they're working. Wouldn't be surprised if you could make it numb even before they put the anesthesia in. George, you'll surprise yourself. I'm sure of it, George! Make it numb before they begin, if you want.

TIME DISTORTION.   [Time distortion was introduced as part of an undirected, open-ended use of the image used thus far.] I enjoy thinking about a snowmobile ride, down a new trail. One that can become a very familiar one. While you think about that snowmobile trail, I'd like to talk to you. You can control the speed and where you wish to go. Could even go in slow motion, like the old-time movies, or speed it up or go in reverse. As you take that ride, you can still listen to the things I'll say.

MOTIVATION AND EGO-STRENGTHENING.   Body and health are our most prized possessions. You're now working toward restoration of complete health. By mastering this technique, which you're so good with, George, you are regaining self-control. Just as you control how fast you snowmobile, you control your anxiety with relaxation.

There is no longer a need to worry about procedures. You can put it out of your mind if you like, until it's time. You'll be able to relax over it. Able to control the sting of needles, to take the hurt right out of it — pressure, but nothing more. No longer need to wait for pain pills or nausea meds. Once you've told the nurses or doctors, and only if it's appropriate, you can bring relaxation into that part of your body. You've become part of the treatment team. No need to be patient, or tolerate anything unpleasant. Not fighting the nurses or doctors anymore. Not delaying taking meds because now you're learning to handle each situation. Now unified to fight the disease and wipe out the bad cells.

INSTRUCTIONS FOR SELF-HYPNOSIS.   Now I've been talking a lot. You probably weren't paying complete attention but you heard everything. Now you're paying attention! You'll remember what we did so you can practice it four or five times a day. You're just an excellent patient and I know you will be able to master this thing so you can turn it on quickly, at a moment's notice. Remember to assume a comfortable position with arms and legs uncrossed. Take three slow, deep breaths. Hold. Feel the tension. Say "relax" and let the tension flow with each breath. Think about some safe, secure, comfortable place — might be the winter scene we talked about or any other scene. Perhaps the beach. See the objects — their shapes, texture, colors. Feel the warmth or coolness, moisture

or dryness. Hear the sounds. Smell the fragrances.

POSTHYPNOTIC SUGGESTIONS.   George, you will remember everything you need to. You will practice it four or five times a day and be able to achieve deeper relaxation each time more easily and quickly. You will feel better about yourself — a sense of accomplishment and mastery. Now you're able to control feeling instead of them controlling you. Feel just tip-top! Allow the day to take on a rosy glow. Feel the benefits of deep relaxation. As if having had a good night's rest. You will be able to go through the day more relaxed, more comfortable and secure in one's feelings. Look forward to the next session and think about reorienting to the room in a few moments.

POSTHYPNOTIC PHASE.   [After the patient was reoriented, he was encouraged to talk by saying:] Any questions? [After any needed clarification, reassurance and "waking" hypnotic suggestions were given.] George, you're such an excellent person for this. You did so well! I know you will practice what we've done and you'll benefit greatly from applying this when it is appropriate. I'll see you tomorrow. We can do another session, if you want. May not even need it.

IMAGERY AS A THERAPEUTIC MODALITY

Images do not intrinsically evoke specific effects; the practitioner's verbalization must include imbedded therapeutic suggestions. While there are no restrictions as to which images to use for a given desired result, the prehypnotic interview will often disclose which experiences of the patient might be revivified or what situations might be fantasized. Patients' likes and dislikes, as well as what things make them feel "good" or what they would really like to be doing, are important clues. Specific treatment goals should be elicited by asking the reason(s) hypnosis is desired. The winter woods scene used with this patient was carefully interwoven with both direct and indirect suggestions of "safe, secure; relaxed, easy breakfast; so good to feel comfortable; refreshing coolness; cool, comfortable numbness; regain self-control; control anxiety with relaxation; not fighting nurses or doctors; fight disease (pronounced ambiguously: disease); wipe out bad cells; rosy glow; etc."

SPECIFIC IMAGES.   Relaxation and anxiety control can be evoked with almost any trance induction or deepening imagery. The broad, green leaf detaching from the tree top, gently drifting on a breeze, as if in slow motion, and finally settling so easily it doesn't bend a single leaf of grass beneath the tree (per Albert Forgione, Ph.D.) can be modified to a colorful fall leaf, a winter snowflake, a speck of dust on a drop of water in a rainbow or the mist of a waterfall. Expansion to full vivification involving sight, sound, smell, taste and touch hallucination can easily introduce suggestions of time distortion (patient controls speed as in slow motion), dissociation (patient separates from the restraints of time, body, ideation, rumination or obsession), and selective amnesia (patient experiences the imagery instead of something perceived as painful or unpleasant). Other scenes of seashores, mountains, underwater or outer space are equally valid and widely used. Karen Olness' flying blanket . . . deserves special mention for use with children. This author often utilizes the imagery of a mare and its colt (or other animal/offspring pair). This image is readily accepted by children and serves the purpose of a strong metaphor (as the colt engages in its activity, the mother is near to make sure that all is well).

Analgesia and pain control involve reduction of the components of experiential (remembered or previously imagined), anticipatory or real (physically stimulated) pain. The first two of these are generally approached through relaxation, dissociation or behavioral desensitization. The actual pain may be reduced by removing the "hurt" from the "unbearable" through reinterpretation or suggestions of direct reduc-

tion, space and time contraction, transfer of analgesia/anesthesia to the area or transfer of the pain to another locus. Imagery of a cool, comfortable fog or light rain touching the cheeks, being breathed in and pleasantly numbing the tongue, mouth, throat, stomach, etc. has been particularly helpful and is expanded to a "fog of anesthesia" (as proposed by Andrew St. Amand, M.D.). This image can be adapted to induce local anesthesia, body rigidity or flaccidity, nausea and emesis control, stimulation or suppression of appetite, salivation, or bowel movement, urinary bladder release or retention, and even healing enhancement and tumor shrinkage/destruction.

The psychological goals of ego strengthening, motivation to recover, and reduction of secondary gain are obtained by including suggestions within the imagery. Visualizations of increased self-control, mastery of physiological control and autonomy are encouraged. Within the image the patient is in control of the sailboat, snowmobile, magic carpet, etc., or gains mastery of mountain climbing, swimming, running, etc., and this is linked with any control gained over the patient's physiological complaint.

Revivification of past accomplishments such as success with school, job, family, community or recreation shows previous ability to succeed. Abreaction may occur if the patient perceives this image as confirming the loss of some ability that was important to him. However, this can be a valuable therapeutic event to get the patient beyond the mourning stages of denial, anger and depression to acceptance and continuation of life. Imagery of value with this task involves regression back to early grade school when promotion to a new classroom meant chairs and tables seemed larger than life. The idea of looking through adult eyes at the same scene (with all of the accomplishments since grade school) is introduced. Thus the patient gains the perspective that, viewed from today, the obstacles of the past have been overcome, although they seemed insurmountable then. Childhood experiences of playgrounds, trips to relatives, vacations, etc., are variations on this theme (suggested by Harold Golan, D.M.D.).

Perhaps the most useful aspect of the imagery technique involves giving permission to experience all of the images that will allow the patients themselves to resolve any issues they need to, at the point in their "therapy" when they are ready. Within the image, patients interact with some "significant other" and are told what they need to hear to resolve their inner conflict. A related approach involves spiritual "awakening" or contact from which the patient gets the feeling of strength to survive and carry on.

Breast Cancer: Radiation Treatment and Recovery

Diane Roberts Stoler, Ed.D.
Boxford, Massachusetts

INTRODUCTION

This script was developed for inclusion on a self-hypnosis tape for a middle-aged woman with inflammatory breast cancer who had to have radiation implanted into her breast. The script was designed in two sections. The first part was designed to be used prior to the operation, in the waiting area, and during the operation. The second part was designed for use during the several days she needed to remain in the hospital with the radioactive implant inside and for her recovery at home. She worked with computers as part of her employment and loved the ocean.*

SUGGESTIONS

[These suggestions followed an imagery induction utilizing a beautiful, tranquil seashore, followed by deepening suggestions.]

*Special thanks and acknowledgment must be given to Dr. John C. Curnutte, M.D., Ph.D., The Scripps Institute, La Jolla, California, for his support, expertise and technical assistance in the area of oncology, especially for the current dynamics of how the immune system works for the destruction of cancer cells.

When you enter the hospital setting and during the holding period, you can allow your body to become relaxed and in balance. Then you will permit yourself to take one long deep breath in through your nose and out through your mouth while using the thumb and index technique. This will be a signal to go into the deepest level of hypnosis, whereby you will feel your strength and confidence and knowledge that you are a winner and can succeed. This one long deep breath will be a signal to give yourself the strength and confidence to reach the goal you have set for yourself. The time in the hospital and at home is for recovery and healing. The more you allow your mind and body to relax, the more rapidly this recovery will occur. You can permit yourself to allow your body to become relaxed and in balance. Your relaxation will allow your body to nurture itself and adjust, and thus come into balance to enhance your body's natural healing process. Your desire to recover, heal and return to an active life enables you to gain the inner strength and energy within you. With one long deep breath this will be a signal to give to yourself the strength and confidence to reach the goals you have set for yourself, to enhance the healing process. Your relaxation will enhance your healing process and receptivity to the words spoken by your physician, Dr. _____ . He will be speaking to you while you are under general anesthesia, and his words which will be technical language will be easily understood by you to enhance your healing process and your body's acceptance of the radiation. As the radiation is absorbed into your body, all healthy cells will be protected by a special coating, while all cancer cells anywhere in your body, whether you use the experimental medication or not, will be hypersensitive to the radiation and will be killed off. Not a single cancer cell will survive. Your love and acceptance of your own strength will allow you to mobilize your natural healing process to recover quickly.

Pay close attention to my voice. You have no cares, fears, worries or other negative thinking. Right now, all your cares, fears, worries and negative thinking will just drift away. They will go so far that you can barely feel or see them. Notice a boat off in the distance. You can put the thought and feelings of self-doubt, being scared, your excessive worry about the cancer, feelings of helplessness, being overwhelmed, not believing in yourself, and feelings of frustration onto that boat and allow it to drift off into the distance, off further and further away; so far and so distant that you barely notice it. Allowing it to be just a dot on the horizon. However, you do not let it totally disappear because you may choose to retain these feelings and retrieve them if you need them. But right now you have no need for them. As you let them go, you gain a sense of peace and calm flowing within your body.

You can allow yourself the pleasure of watching those feelings drift further and further away into the horizon. Notice that you do not allow them to entirely disappear, so that if you want those feelings, they will be there. But right now, you have no need for those feelings, so allow them to go off towards the horizon. These feelings will be there if you want them back or want to be in touch with them.

When you are entering the hospital setting and during the holding period, you can permit your body to become relaxed and in balance. Relaxation will give you that peace of mind and inner tranquility which will enable you to cope with the tensions and stresses of everyday living. It is possible there will be other noises in the waiting area, operating room or outside your room in the hospital. These noises will not disturb you; instead they will act as a signal to deepen your hypnosis. You will be able to adjust yourself to your environment, even though you cannot change it.

If there are people who are discussing something that is not beneficial to you, this will be a signal to go into an even deeper state and their voices will only be muted, white noise to your ears. You will remain calm, poised and relaxed. You will only attend to what Dr. _____ is saying to you to enhance your healing process and the body's acceptance of the radiation. As the radiation is absorbed into your body, all

healthy cells will be protected by a special coating, while all cancer cells anywhere in your body, whether you use the experimental medication or not, will be hypersensitive to the radiation and will be killed off. Not a single cancer cell will survive.

Time will pass quickly and pleasantly during your operation and your stay in the hospital. Each day that you are in your room will pass quickly and will be a signal to go into an even deeper hypnosis where your relaxation and concentration will enhance your healing process and your body's acceptance of the radiation.

Relaxation will give you that peace of mind and inner tranquility which will enable you to cope with your stay in the hospital and will enable you to enhance your healing process and your body's acceptance of the radiation. As the radiation is absorbed into your body, all healthy cells will be protected by a special coating, while all cancer cells anywhere in your body will be killed off.

Just imagine a mini computer screen which can monitor and have control over all sensations and control the poison to search and kill the cancer. If you want to monitor any sensation in your breast or any part of your body, you need only to turn on the screen. And if the sensation is due to radiation, the word or color violet will appear on the left hand side of the screen, with the level of intensity in words or numeral from 1-10. This left side is the input side. You can allow yourself to change the numerals to a comfortable level.

If the sensation is due to cancer in the body, the word or color black will appear on the left hand side of the screen, with the word or numeral of intensity from 1-10. On the right hand side of the screen you can type instructions to search and find the cancer, for the white cells and other immune systems to kill and release the needed poison to kill off the cancer cells, while adjusting the intensity level. Lastly, if the sensation is due to any reason other than stated, the word or color red will appear on the left hand side of the screen with its intensity level in numeral or word from 1-10. You can make the appropriate adjustment needed for complete comfort on the right hand side of the screen. In addition, by saying to yourself, "relax, calm, poise, courage" [conditioned cues for induction of self-hypnosis], you will allow yourself to relax, remain calm, and gain the inner strength and control to achieve your goal.

During your stay in the hospital, you will not need to feel any pain in your arms, legs, or breast, only pressure and some minor discomfort. Your ability to control your threshold of discomfort is under your control. You may feel pressure and some minor discomfort but no pain. If for any reason the medical staff does not do a procedure correctly, your body will be aware of it and it will register on your mini computer screen, so that you can inform them. Once you have told them, this will be a signal to allow yourself to go into a very deep state of hypnosis to enhance your healing process and body's acceptance of the radiation. As the radiation is absorbed into your body, all healthy cells will be protected by a special coating, while all cancer cells anywhere in you body will be hypersensitive to the radiation and will be killed off. Not a single cancer cell will survive.

You are peaceful, calm, relaxing deeper and deeper, deeper and deeper, deeper and deeper. As I talk to you, you continue to go into an even deeper state of relaxation. If feelings of fear or a sense of loss of control arises from a flashback or other past feelings that might interfere with your feeling alive, you can choose either to look at what's causing those feelings or to put them into your file in my office where they will be stored. These feelings will not surface and cannot be touched unless you choose to retrieve them to work on them in therapy, to help you learn to live and enjoy life. You will always know where they are because you have the control and you have chosen to place them there. By knowing this, if a flashback occurs, you have a way of having power to control those feelings and you no longer need to stuff them inside. Rather, you have a way of dealing with them to resolve them and help you to have greater control over your own life. When you return home, your sense of peace,

calm and strength will help in the healing process and your recovery time. Your concentration, relaxation, wisdom, and understanding, along with the support and love of your family and friends, helps you to activate your inner light, which is your energy, and your inner goodness, which is your strength. You can allow yourself to harness their energy to help your body's receptivity to enhance your healing process and your body's acceptance of the radiation.

As you allow yourself to feel the calmness within you and the awareness of the sun, you will allow yourself to feel a complete sense of peace and oneness within yourself. This calmness and relaxation will allow your body and mind to function more effectively. You feel a sense of joy and life within your soul. Allow yourself to settle back and listen to the sound and smells of the sea and shore. Listen to the waves rolling onto the shore line. You feel at peace. Let yourself sink deeper and deeper, deeper and deeper. Notice the warmth of the sun, experience the strength of the ocean surrounding you; within you a sense of control, comfortable peace and tranquility. You feel a sense of power, control, inner strength.

As you let yourself drift along deeper and deeper, you are becoming more and more relaxed, and as you are allowing yourself to become more relaxed, you permit your body to become limp and loose, and feel a sense of freedom and oneness with nature and the environment surrounding you.

You know that you can put yourself into hypnosis any time and any place where there is no danger to you or others; thus never while driving a car or cooking. Otherwise you can put yourself into hypnosis very quickly and with each trial and each time you will be able to go into hypnosis more rapidly that ever before. And the suggestions here or that you give yourself will last longer with each trial. You will always find hypnosis refreshing and relaxing. No one can put you into hypnosis without your agreeing to it. Otherwise you will always find hypnosis helpful in reaching your goal of taking greater control of your life.

Now allow yourself to go deeper and deeper than you have ever felt before. If for some reason you need to put yourself into hypnosis where it is not feasible to close your eyes, such as at work or in the middle of a stressful situation, by taking one long deep breath through your nose and breathing out through you mouth, you will permit yourself to go into a very deep state of hypnosis. At that point you will allow yourself to focus your mind on your body, picture the ocean, and repeat to yourself in your mind, "relax, calm, poise, courage." And you will be able to help yourself. You will remain calm, poised, and will respond more effectively to take care of and help yourself.

You will permit time for yourself and to take naps when your body feels fatigued. By taking two five- to ten-minute relaxation periods a day to picture yourself in the ocean or some other scene that brings inner peace, and a breather from the inner stress and turmoil, you will enhance the reaching of your goal of peace and calmness in your life and feelings of being in control.

Each time you listen to this tape, each time you reaccept the suggestions that are contained on this tape, they become more and more a part of you. Even though you may not consciously remember them, they will remain there in your unconscious, and they will work better and more effectively than ever before. You will permit yourself to accept the suggestions on this tape because you want to be cancer-free, and to be able to control various sensations in your body and to know what they mean. You will allow yourself to accept these suggestions because you want to feel stronger, more in control, relaxed, healthier and vigorous. Your desire to be cancer-free, to be strong, and to take control of your life is so great that it easily allows you to accept the suggestions contained on this tape.

Now you can allow yourself sink deeper and deeper, deeper and deeper. You can choose at this point either to fall asleep or to begin the procedure for bringing yourself back to your usual state of awareness. If you choose to fall asleep you will disregard the rest of this side of the tape; otherwise, when you are ready, you

can begin the procedure for bringing yourself back to your usual state of awareness. When you do, you will feel alert, refreshed and relaxed, calm, and refreshed, bright, sharp, physically better, emotionally better, mentally better and spiritually better than you have felt in a long, long time. The feelings of well-being will remain with you longer and longer with each trial and each time you listen to this tape. When you are ready, you can bring yourself back to your usual state of awareness.

Hypnosis as an Adjunct to Chemotherapy in Cancer

Sidney Rosen, M.D.
New York, New York

INDICATIONS AND CONTRAINDICATIONS

Dr. Rosen models for us his approach to assisting cancer patients who are undergoing chemotherapy. As I point out in Chapter 16, there have been suggestions of caution expressed about using age progression techniques with seriously depressed patients lest they project themselves into a very negative future that exacerbates feelings of hopelessness. This could be iatrogenic and increase suicide potential. Thus you are cautioned to use age progression thoughtfully in working with cancer patients, assessing their level of depression and suicide potential prior to intervention. (*Ed.*)

SUGGESTIONS FOR HEALING, COMFORT AND NAUSEA

[Following induction using Erickson's Early Learning Set.] You can become a bodiless mind. And as a bodiless mind you can travel anywhere at all in time or space. You can be three years old, or ten years old. You can enjoy comfort at any age. [Sometimes I will have the patients signal to me, with automatic movements, when they are comfortable. Then I may suggest:] Today's date is not 1983. Today is not July 18, 1983. And you are not in New York City, in Dr. Rosen's office. This is 1993 and I don't know where you are. You could be at home, you could be on a vacation trip. You could be with friends, your children, your grandchildren. I don't know where you are, or what you are doing. But you are comfortable, aren't you? You do feel good, don't you?

CASE EXAMPLE

After I get a positive response to age progression I may go even further into the future. For example, with one hospitalized woman, age 43, who had both breasts removed, I said during my first contact with her:

You are 80 years old—83 years old. And you can look back 40 years, seeing yourself at age 43. And you can realize that the period around age 43 was really a very important time in your life—a watershed, the time when you really began to understand the meaning of your life, the value of your life. A very important time for you. You can't say that you were actually lucky to have gotten cancer but, in a way, you feel that it was lucky for you.

I will then play with time:

You are age 83, looking back at yourself, at age 43. And you see what happened after you saw Dr. Rosen. How did you go through that period? How did you go through the chemotherapy? Was the chemotherapy upsetting to you? Did it take one week, did it take two weeks after you saw Dr. Rosen, before the chemotherapy was accepted as a matter-of-fact treatment? As a helper? Or did it take only one session before you felt better? Did it take a month? two weeks?

As I offer different times, I watch for responses and note them. Then I progress the patient, in the same way as I might bring her back from an early childhood regression:

And that young woman of 43 grows older, hour by hour, day by day, week by week, month by month, year by year—and really enjoys her life, doesn't she? Life has become very meaningful. She appreciated the value of every moment. Of course, as

Wordsworth said, "Into every life some rain must fall, some days will be dark and dreary." There were some times when things were not so hot. There were times when you thought that you were not going to be able to make it, to get through another hour, another day. But you got through those times, didn't you [again looking back from age 83]?

DISCUSSION.   After the general approach, outlined above, I might have the patient hypnotically review the entire chemotherapy treatment, using imagery, when possible.

The progression into the future has three possible effects:

1. It implies that the person will survive and thereby adds to a sense of hope. Hope has been associated with greater survival rates and greater longevity (Newton, 1982-3).
2. It is an indirect way of requesting the unconscious mind to devise ways of dealing with the side effects of therapy and with the psychological and physiological impact of the cancer.
3. Patients are left with some sense of mastery and a feeling of process as they preview responses over the immediate future and through the next few months of therapy. . . .

ILLUSTRATIVE SUGGESTIONS

[The following suggestions were given to a 63-year-old woman who had undergone a radical mastectomy and was soon to begin chemotherapy treatments. She had previously had fears that she might develop cancer, and associated her cancer with a kind of dirtiness or contamination. She believed the letter "c" was associated with negatives, e.g., cancer, calamity, contamination, chemotherapy. After a confusional induction, she was given time distortion and disorienting suggestions. Note the trance ratification procedures that Dr. Rosen utilizes. (*Ed.*)]

You know that St. Patrick's Day came last year and that it probably rained, as it always seems to do on St. Patrick's Day, this year, in 1981, just as it will in 1982 and as it did in 1979. You know that, a year or so ago, back in 1980, you were impelled to call Dr. Rosen, hoping that working with him would help you in dealing with some severe anxieties. When he didn't answer the telephone you decided that it wasn't the right time to do this. You don't know now, that two years from today you will actually be seeing Dr. Rosen, after some of your worst fears have materialized. You have a lot of conscious awareness of the importance of fantasy, the importance of listening to your own unconscious mind. When you do see Dr. Rosen, in March of 1982, you will want to be prepared to use whatever you have learned throughout your life so that you can redirect, not only your conscious thoughts, but your unconscious activity as well. You can do this by tapping that vast reservoir of unconscious learnings and extracting from it some of the most positive, the most helpful, the most creative experiences and moments. You can find yourself inspired, when the occasion arises, to lift yourself above yourself, or to take yourself outside of yourself, at times, or to go inside of yourself, in order to oversee or to direct those powerful healing forces which you know are present. You don't have to force those forces.

You don't have to force yourself to concentrate. All you need to do is make gentle requests of your unconscious mind. "I would like to ask my unconscious mind to help me to go through this experience comfortably and effectively." Once you have made that request you can let yourself go into a deeper trance, knowing that you have all the resources that you need. You can call on resources from inside and from outside—from your friends. You can allow them to nurture you, temporarily, putting aside your pride for a while, the feeling that you have to take care of everything, for yourself and for others. You can allow yourself to be sick, for a while, not needing to feel sick, but knowing that there is a cleaning up job to be done there, and that it will be done, as efficiently, as effectively and as comfortably as possible.

You know, deep down inside, do you not, that this will be done. It is not just a wish fulfillment, is it? You are going to be well very soon, are you not? I'm waiting for a signal. Yes! Like that! If you are wondering if that is just a wish fulfillment, that you are deliberately moving that thumb, try to stop it from going up, finding that the more you try to stop it the higher up it wants to go. That's right! Like that!

You can sense that force that is working inside you now. And that unconscious force that is working against you, too, can you not? That last force will become weaker and weaker as you become stronger.

You can have some understanding now of the question that was asked a long time ago. "What is the source of this unconscious part of you that is working against you now?" You can talk in words and tell me about it, if you like. [Patient: The source is fear. But it's not going to win—because fear is no good.]

Can you take that fear and wrap it up? Where is it located—in your left hand? Rather than try to fight against it, can you dispense with it, in some other way? Right now, when your hand becomes clenched so tightly, you can try to hold that fear in. The fingers and joints become locked tight. If you try to open that fist, the more you try to open it the tighter the fingers clench. That's right. Try to open it, finding that you can't. That's right. You can really feel the tightness, the tension. Locate all the tightness, all the tension from your body into that left hand; all of the despair. [A loud car horn is heard, persistently blowing outside the window.] And that damned irritating horn can make you feel more frustrated and angry, can't it—till you feel like smashing something—with that left fist . . . and when you've had as much of it as you can stand for now . . . yes, let it build up further . . . there are times when we are in severe pain, that we naturally and instinctively hold onto something, just as you are holding on now . . . in that left fist . . . until the fist itself becomes painful . . . the hand becomes achy. . . . When you don't want to stand it for another moment, just nod your head, once. . . . Now lean back and take a deep breath, and let the fist relax and open, letting out the fear, letting out the tension. Letting it out of your body. Letting it leave your mind . . . like that . . . yes. . . .

You focus on your breathing for a moment or two, letting yourself go into a more relaxed state, a deeper trance. Enter into your cocoon . . . and you are not alone here. You become more and more relaxed . . . and as you relax, more and more, you can listen to your unconscious messages . . . You've heard the negative ones. You have seen them . . . in your dream . . . but you can tune up the positive messages now, too . . . so that they become not only messages from your conscious mind, not only the grim determination of a very strong woman, to overcome this illness . . . it will become a voice from a very very deep source, which just quietly knows that you will become well . . . and safe . . . and able to proceed with the living of your life again . . . very, very soon.

I don't know what images are going to come to you . . . to represent this very positive feeling . . . but I do know that you will come up with some images that are meaningful to you . . . corrective images, clean, clear, perhaps celestial . . . certainly comforting. [Note the "good c's."] Can you see them, or hear them now? [She shakes her head "no."] Would you like me to supply some? All right . . . you have a vast repertoire of music . . . much more vast than mine. I do not want to limit you. You could think of "The Ode to Joy" . . . or a Schubert Mass . . . or even some Mozart . . . just scan through your repertoire . . . until you hit on some small piece of music that you can sense is a healing music for you. You can hear that, in your mind, more and more vividly, more and more clearly. You can see the orchestra. You can pick out various parts of the orchestra. . . . So, you will remember these and they will come back automatically. And they can be so vivid and so clear that you will be not quite sure—is there really an orchestra, or is it a record that I hear, or is it just in my own head? And it really doesn't matter. All that matters is that you know that you're creative, your healing forces are liberated, more and more. . . .

You can go into a deeper trance and can take a look into your future, if you like. You are with your family, your husband, and everything is back to normal, isn't it?

Or, are you involved in newer projects, that interest you? I [your husband] is well, is he not? You had fears, back in 1982, that he might not be. And he is 74 years old now, isn't he? No? How old is he? [Patient: 72.] Yes, but now it's 1984. He's 74. Can you see him being well, this year? And you are just a youngster—10 years younger.

And that chemotherapy is behind you. And that is a relief, isn't it? [Patient: Yes.] How did you go through it? Was it uncomfortable for you? Or were you able to utilize some of the things that you were working on with Dr. Rosen and others, to make it more comfortable? Did your hair fall out? That was not a serious problem, anyway, was it? You had the wig—a whole series of them, if you needed them . . . and what about the nausea that people talk about? Did you have much nausea? Or were you able to just take a deep breath, whenever you felt it beginning, and let that feeling go out of you . . . blow it out . . . instead of having to throw it up . . . remembering that there was a desire at one time to want to throw something up, in despair, wasn't there? Were you able to let go of that despair, in some other way? . . . to focus on feeling relaxed and comfortable . . . and safe . . . during the treatment and after the treatment? [Patient nods "yes."]

Hypnotic Death Rehearsal

Alexander A. Levitan, M.D.
New Brighton, Minnesota

INTRODUCTION

In response to the needs of certain patients and their families in our practice, a technique has been developed which has proven useful for those imminently facing death and in those manifesting marked anxiety about death. This technique has proven effective in defusing anxiety and correcting misconceptions regarding the death experience and the effect of death upon both the patient and the patient's family. This technique has been called death rehearsal. The approach varies according to the type of problem for which it is being employed and essentially represents a projection of the patient into the future with direct interaction and involvement of the therapist in the scene being visualized by the patient.

THE TECHNIQUE

A representative application of the death rehearsal technique might be for a cancer patient manifesting significant fear and anxiety over the actual mechanics of his or her own death. Characteristic anxieties expressed include the fear that the experience will be extraordinarily painful, extremely disruptive for the family, or that the patient will manifest cowardice during the terminal stages. A major associated fear is that of rejection and of dying alone and uncomforted because of the characteristic uneasiness manifested towards death by our society. Few patients have ever heard of the concept of "helping someone to die."

Under these circumstances we have found it useful to ask the patient whether he or she would like to learn a little about what it is like to die. Almost universally the patients respond affirmatively if the question is posed in a caring and solicitous fashion. A hypnotic trance is then induced by whatever method seems mutually acceptable to the therapist and the patient.

Once in a satisfactory state of relaxation, the patient is asked to project himself into the future and to visualize a point in time when his or her own death is immediately inevitable. He is then requested to give the therapist an ideomotor signal indicating that he or she has a visualization of that point in time. A suggestion is then given that the patient will be able to speak in a comfortable fashion and that each word spoken will serve to deepen the trance, thereby countering the normal tendency for a trance to lighten when the patient is asked to speak.

The patient is then asked to describe the circumstances of the scene visualized. He is encouraged to be as concrete as possible and to describe in minute detail not only the physical setting in which he finds himself but his thoughts and feelings as well. The hypnotherapist assists the patient by inquiring about specific details.

Representative questions might be: Where are you? Who is there with you? Are you afraid? Can you tell you are dying? Do you feel alone? Is there any pain? What is it like to die? What are those persons around you feeling? What are they saying? How do they react to your death? Is there an obituary in the newspaper? What does it say? Who is with your spouse after your death? Who visits you at the funeral home? What do they say? Who attends the funeral? What do they say or do? Who sends flowers? Who comforts or assists your family? What happens over the year after your death? Does anyone visit your grave on the anniversary of your death? What do they do or say? What has been the effect of your death upon your family, friends, business, etc.?

These questions are posed in a sympathetic, understanding, and accepting fashion. Where necessary, direction is given to the patient so

that the events described may be reframed in the most favorable fashion. If the patient's concept of death is integrated into his religious beliefs every effort is made to support his visualization of the death experience as long as it is not anxiety provoking. Reassurance is given to the patient that he will be kept comfortable at all times and will be attended by a group of loving and concerned family members or care providers according to his preference.

Should the patient visualize events that are totally inconsistent with reality, a gentle effort is made to direct his imagery to a more realistic circumstance. Where multiple interpretations of events are possible the patient is directed to the more favorable alternatives. If the spouse is visualized as being overwhelmed with grief or emotion it is suggested that it is helpful for a person to express these feelings rather than keep them locked within.

Alternatively, if a relative is visualized as showing little or no emotion, it can be pointed out that many people can experience deep feelings of love and affection without expressing them outwardly. In this fashion every effort is made to enable the patient to experience his own death in a setting of comfort and security while adhering to the realities of his particular circumstances. The death process is thus demystified and understood as a natural biologic event common to all mankind. . . .

Frequently, a death rehearsal will enable a patient to approach his own demise with equanimity, security, and control. The patient will often also express gratitude in having shared the death experience with the hypnotherapist and will take comfort in knowing that the hypnotherapist will be available for the actual experience as well should this be required.

In order to be of maximal assistance to the dying patient the hypnotherapist must become comfortable with his own mortality and the fact that he, too, will someday die. The act of "helping someone to die" must be clearly distinguished from the act of "causing someone to die." Death need not be perceived as a defeat for the therapeutic process but rather as a natural conclusion to a biologic chain of events.

8

HYPNOSIS WITH MEDICAL DISORDERS

INTRODUCTION

T HERE ARE A TREMENDOUS number of conditions and specialties in medicine where hypnosis may be beneficial. Thus Chapter 3 has focused on hypnosis with pain, Chapter 4 concentrated on hypnotic preparation for surgery and hypnoanesthesia, Chapter 7 centered on uses of hypnosis with cancer patients, Chapter 9 examines obstetrical and gynecologic applications of hypnosis, sexual dysfunctions are the focus of Chapter 11, and Chapters 12 and 13 elaborate hypnotic approaches with obesity, eating disorders, smoking and addictions. Medical conditions in children (e.g., pain, enuresis) are discussed in Chapter 15.

This chapter contains suggestions for use with other medical conditions such as dermatologic conditions, burns, emergencies (e.g., accident victims, critically ill patients, wound injection), vascular control (e.g., hemophilia, GI bleeding), sleep disorders, urinary problems (urinary retention, "bashful bladder"), ophthalmologic problems (e.g., lagophthalmos, blepharospasm), and neurologic complaints (stroke, involuntary muscle jerking, Bell's Palsy). The contribution by Jencks provides imagery and brief suggestions that may be used with a great diversity of conditions, including pulmonary complaints, nose and throat problems, ophthalmologic complaints, dermatologic conditions, and procedures to increase energy and facilitate feelings of invigoration and alertness. There are also a variety of suggestions concerning miscellaneous medical conditions that are included in this chapter: autoimmune disease, general suggestions for healing imagery, hypochondriasis, allergies, the use of prolonged hypnosis for psychosomatic disorders, asthma (suggestions for this may also be found in Chapter 15, Hypnotic Suggestions With Children), tinnitus, and difficulty swallowing pills. Before presenting suggestions that may be used in working with these various medical problems, a few introductory remarks will be made concerning some of these areas.

Hypertension, Gastrointestinal Disorders, Premenstrual Syndrome, and Psychosomatic Disorders

There are some conditions where hypnosis has proven particularly beneficial. While suggestions were not submitted in some of these areas, you should be aware of the potential benefits of hypnosis with these problems. One of these areas is hypertension. Hypertension has been benefited by deep muscle relaxation (e.g., Taylor, Farquhar, Nelson, & Agras, 1977), meditation (e.g., Benson, Rosner, Marzetta, & Klemchuk, 1974; Benson & Wallace, 1972) and hypnosis (Barabasz & McGeorge, 1978; Crasilneck & Hall, 1985; Deabler, Fidel, Dillenkoffer, & Elder, 1973; Friedman & Taub, 1977, 1978; Maslach, Marshall, & Zimbardo, 1972). Hypnotic procedures for control of hypertension include self-hypnotic training in relaxation and finger or hand warming. Consistent practice of self-hypnotic procedures several times each day is vitally important for success, and hypnosis may need to be combined with cognitive therapy, weight reduction, smoking cessation, and a regular exercise program for maintenance of change to occur.

Another particularly valuable area for the application of hypnosis is with gastrointestinal problems such as ulcers, irritable bowel syndrome, ulcerative colitis and Crohn's disease. Klein and Spiegel (1989) documented the ability of hypnosis to both stimulate and inhibit gastric acid secretion. When compared to no-hypnosis controls, for example, with hypnosis there was a 39% reduction in basal acid output and an 11% reduction in pentagastrin-stimulated peak acid output. Colgan, Faragher, and Whorwell (1988) studied the possible benefits of hypnotherapy in relapse prevention with duodenal ulcer patients. In a carefully controlled study, on one-year follow-up, 100% of control patients (who received medication until after ulcers were healed) had relapsed. But for patients who also received hypnotherapy, only 53% had relapsed.

A variety of studies have also impressively documented the value of hypnotherapy with irritable bowel syndrome (Byrne, 1973; Kroger & Fezler, 1976; Whorwell, Prior, & Faragher, 1984; Whorwell, Prior, & Colgan, 1987). Whorwell's group have now found long-term (mean 18 months) follow-up response rates on 50 patients with 95% success with classical cases, 43% with atypical cases, and 60% with cases exhibiting significant psychopathology. Patients over age 50 responded poorly (25% success), but patients below age 50 with classical irritable bowel syndrome were 100% successful. Gastrointestinal conditions appear to be stress-related illnesses (Fava & Pavan, 1976-77; Gerbert, 1980; Walker, 1983; Zisook & DePaul,

1977) and anecdotal evidence suggests the possible involvement of other emotional factors (e.g., repressed hostility and anger) (e.g., Walker, 1983) that may be responsive to hypnotherapy.

It should also be noted that premenstrual syndrome (PMS) patients may be benefited by self-hypnosis training (Hammond, 1988d). Hypnosis may assist these patients to reduce such primary symptoms as anxiety, overemotionality, and anger (Hammond, 1988e). PMS patients commonly feel "out of control," and experience diminished esteem and depression. Self-hypnotic techniques offer PMS patients a self-management skill that allows them to regain feelings of control, and it may be used to increase ego-strength and feelings of self-efficacy. Hypnosis may further assist such patients to cope with premenstrual cravings for sweets and salt, which seem to exacerbate the condition, and to cope with fatigue and insomnia.

A latter section of this chapter will introduce suggestions that may prove beneficial in promoting healing, and in treating other psychosomatic conditions and autoimmune diseases.

PHYSICAL MEDICINE, REHABILITATION AND NEUROLOGY. Crasilneck and Hall (1985) emphasized four prominent uses of hypnosis in neurology: (1) for differential diagnosis of functional versus organic problems; (2) to maximize functional ability even when full recovery is not possible; (3) for management of discomfort and pain; and (4) for enhancing motivation for rehabilitation (e.g., physical therapy) and recovery. They found that hypnosis may still be used with patients suffering from stroke and cerebrovascular accident, with the following modifications. The therapist should speak very slowly, use simple vocabulary, use increased repetition of suggestion, and persevere with the patient in spite of minimal response or negative countertransference. Hypnosis has been used with a variety of physical medicine, neurologic and musculoskeletal problems: phantom limb pain, spasticity (cerebral palsy, stroke, neurodegenerative conditions), movement disorders (e.g., tic, tremor, torticollis, blepharospasm, whiplash), seizures, hyperkinetic disorders, and problems with speech and swallowing.

Dermatologic Disorders

There are a variety of dermatologic disorders in which hypnosis may contribute to positive treatment outcome, including pruritus (excessive itching), acne, psoriasis, eczema, neurodermatitis, warts and herpes simplex.

Hypnotic interventions may include posthypnotic suggestions to reduce picking and scratching in acne, pruritus, eczema, and neurodermatitis. When suggestions are ineffective, exploration of unconscious dynamics may prove beneficial. This has particularly been found to be the case in patients with neurodermatitis. Hypnotic imagery of applying soothing and healing ointments or solutions (or in the case of Dr. Wright's contribution to this chapter, a soothing bath with cornstarch) is commonly beneficial with irritating conditions. Practicing self-hypnosis to reduce stress may likewise benefit conditions that are exacerbated by anxiety (e.g., herpes, acne, eczema, psoriasis). Warts and herpes may be positively affected through production of ideosensory changes (e.g., warmth, coolness, tingling) both in the office and through practice several times daily in self-hypnosis. Studies (e.g., Scott, 1960; Sinclair-Gieben & Chalmers, 1959; Surman, Gottlieb, & Hackett, 1972; Surman, Gottlieb, Hackett, & Silverberg, 1973; Tasini & Hackett, 1977) have shown particularly impressive effects in applying hypnosis to the treatment of warts. The successful impact of words and imagination on warts is of particular import considering the increasingly widespread routine use of powerful chemotherapy agents to treat warts.

Sleep Disorders

A small proportion of sleep disturbance is associated with sleep apnea or medical problems and will not be amenable to treatment by psychological techniques. The largest proportion of sleep disorders are associated with psychiatric disorders, or alcohol or drug dependence that will require broad-spectrum interventions with these disorders along with symptomatic disturbance. It is thus vitally important to carefully evaluate sleep disorders to assess the etiologic contributors. Depression, medical conditions (e.g., apnea, myoclonus), substance abuse, and overuse of caffeine or nicotine should all be ruled out prior to considering intervention with hypnotherapy.

There are, however, a proportion of insomnia patients whose sleep is disturbed by (1) cognitive overactivity and conditioned habit patterns incompatible with sleep (e.g., presleep patterns of worrying, rumination, compulsive analysis of the day's activities or planning for future events, reading, watching TV), (2) central nervous system excitation (anxiety, tension), and (3) underlying (unconscious) conflicts or fears that disrupt sleep. These patients may receive substantial benefit from hypnotherapeutic intervention.

Basic hypnotherapy strategies may involve: (1) self-hypnosis training to facilitate deep muscle relaxation; (2) use of additional self-hypnotic techniques to control cognitive overactivity (e.g., self-hypnosis tapes with monotonous activities such as hearing repetitive suggestions, listening to a metronome, walking down a long staircase, engaging in boring activities after becoming deeply relaxed); and, when the first two strategies are not successful within four or five interviews, (3) unconscious exploration of underlying functions or conflicts associated with the sleep disturbance.

Because use of the behavioral technique of stimulus control (Bootkin, 1977) has proven even more effective than relaxation procedures in treating insomnia, it is also recommended that this technique be routinely used in conjunction with hypnosis. Stimulus control instructions request that the patient: (a) Only sleep or make love in bed. Other activities, such as watching TV, reading, reviewing the day, planning activities of the next day, or eating must not occur in bed. If the patient begins to engage in these activities, he must decide if he wants to continue them, and if so, get up and go into the other room to engage in them. (b) If the patient is awake 20 minutes after retiring, she must get up and engage in a constructive activity. (c) The patient should only go to bed when he feels tired, never take naps during the daytime, and should set the alarm to awaken at the same time every morning.

Garver's contribution to this chapter emphasizes the recall of positive memories about sleeping, which may both relax and distract patients from other mental activities. Gruenewald's and Stanton's suggestions emphasize the use of imagery to promote relaxation and occupy mental attention. The Spiegels' approach encourages the patient to relax through experiencing floating feelings and then to distance themselves from thoughts by putting them on an imaginary screen. Zelling's contribution is unrelated to insomnia but offers an interesting approach for coping with snoring.

Burns and Emergencies

Crasilneck and Hall (1985) outlined five problem variables that may be addressed in hypnotherapy with burn patients: (1) the constant pain, (2) loss of appetite, (3) the necessity for repeated painful procedures, such as debridement, (4) contractures that result from lack of exercise due to pain, and (5) negativism and severe psychological regression that may slow rehabilitation. Their suggestions, along with those of several other experts in this area are presented later in the chapter.

There is widespread belief that trauma is trance-inducing, whether it stems from a serious automobile accident, burn, or myocardial infarction. Several suggestions have been reproduced in this chapter that may be offered to critically ill or emergency patients, acting on the assumption that they are already in a trance-like state and will not require a formal hypnotic induction.

Vascular Control Through Hypnosis

A variety of studies have documented that vascular flow and bleeding may be influenced and controlled through the use of hypnosis (e.g., LeBaron & Zeltzer, 1985; LaBaw, 1970, 1975; Bishay & Lee, 1984). This may be valuable in working with hemophilia patients, surgical and dermatologic procedures (e.g., dermabrasion), and in dental work. Several illustrative suggestions for this have also been included in this chapter.

HYPNOSIS WITH DERMATOLOGIC DISORDERS

Treatment of Pruritus

Michael J. Scott, M.D.
Seattle, Washington

In general, I use permissive suggestions and almost invariably gradually decrease the symptom over the course of several visits rather than at one session. I respect the patient's need for a symptom, such as functional pruritus. Only very rarely, when I am thoroughly convinced that a symptom is purely psychic in origin and the individual has no further need for it, do I employ dogmatic or authoritative suggestions such as, "Once this session is terminated you will no longer have any sensation of itching or any desire to scratch."

In dermatologic conditions, pruritus is the most frequently encountered complaint, so I will confine my reference to this particular symptom. The patient's scratching, in order to relieve the itchy symptom, is what invariably produces the undesirable side effects of excoriations, infections, etc. If we can eliminate or decrease the patient's desire to scratch, we can then shorten the course of many cutaneous disorders and frequently allow the natural healing processes to occur more readily. With this in mind, I often allow the patient to retain the symptom of itching, but decrease his desire or need to scratch through the use of several available methods. I may use hypnosis to gradually decrease the duration, intensity, or frequency of the pruritic attacks or his desire to scratch. I may offer symptom substitution, for example, suggest the sensation of pressure or dull, tolerable pain for the pruritus. I may hypnotically suggest other activities instead of scratching (such as physical exercises, verbal aggressiveness, painting, etc.).

With the above brief and incomplete background in mind, you can realize how my actual suggestions may vary considerably depending upon the patient, the situation, resistances, etc. However, some typical suggestions would be as follows:

Regardless of any itching sensations you feel, you will note that they no longer bother you in any way. You may still feel itchiness but you will no longer have any desire or need to scratch.

If a history reveals that a patient has his itchy spells when he arrives home from work at 5:30 p.m. and that they last until bedtime at 11:00 p.m., I may employ any of the following:

Until the next session you will note that the sensation of itchiness will last only from 5:30 p.m. to 8:00 p.m., and you will be completely free of symptoms for the last three hours of every evening.

At each subsequent session the times can be altered accordingly. You could use a different approach and alter the intensity of the pruritus, suggesting that it will become "progressively less severe every day" without changing the duration each night. You could similarly change the frequency by having it occur every other day instead of daily. With such techniques a previously intolerable pruritus may be decreased in intensity and frequency to a tolerable and comfortable level without depriving the patient of the symptoms entirely.

Instead of direct suggestion, one may recommend symptom substitution as follows:

Immediately upon coming home and changing clothes, you will go to the recreation room and devote three-quarters of an hour to the strenuous use of a punching bag. You will resume this activity for an additional half-hour later in the evening. You will then note that the sensation of itchiness will completely disappear and will no longer bother you.

In cases of generalized neurodermatitis, one may suggest:

Instead of scratching all over your body, you will now discover that by limiting your scratching to only your thighs, you will obtain the same relief and satisfaction you formerly derived from scratching all over your body.

In this way, with each visit we may gradually diminish the area involved and aid considerably in obtaining a cure. Merely changing the location of a visible, unsightly, functional dermatosis to a covered, invisible area of the body is often desirable and beneficial.

Erickson's Reframing Suggestion with Pruritus

Milton H. Erickson

"You're troubled by this itch. Naturally I don't know exactly what it is. I'm certain that you want *your itch for accomplishment to be kept. Your itch to do things can be kept. In fact, there are a number of itches that you want to keep. Any itch that you want to keep — be sure to keep it! Also let's be sure that you get rid of any itch you are willing to lose but no more than you are willing to lose.*"

Suggestions for Itching

Beata Jencks, Ph.D.
Murray, Utah

Itching may be controlled by imagining breathing through the afflicted skin area with the thoughts of "cool" or "still" during inhalations and "calm" or "relaxed" during exhalations. This has worked for heat rashes and certain allergic conditions. It may take considerable concentration to control bad allergic reactions in this manner. An additional aid is to involve the imagination generally for counteracting a skin condition, as for instance by thinking, "I am [exhalation] resting in a [inhalation] cool and refreshing, yet [exhalation] relaxing and comforting, [inhalation] relieving bath." Also thoughts of floating in the ocean, or even diving into cool water in a diving bell, were useful images evoked by trainees for reducing itching of skin areas.

Hypnotic Technique for Treating Warts

Harold B. Crasilneck, Ph.D., and James A. Hall, M.D.
Dallas, Texas

INTRODUCTION

Following hypnotic induction and deepening, Crasilneck and Hall (1985) lightly touch the area around a wart with a pencil while instructing the patient that he/she will feel a coolness or coldness in the area. It is suggested that this sensation will persist for approximately a day as the warts begin to diminish. These suggestions are reinforced in each subsequent session. The following suggestions model the authors' technique. Note the extensive use of hypnotic phenomena for purposes of trance ratification. (*Ed.*)

LEVITATION INDUCTION

Please cup your right hand on your right knee. . . . That's it. . . . Now look at the knuckles of your hand and as you are doing so, your entire body will begin to relax thoroughly. . . . Pay no attention to other sounds . . . just concentrate on your right hand and my voice, realizing that nothing is beyond the power of the mind . . . and of the body. As I continue talking to you and as you continue staring at the back of your cupped hand, you will begin to notice things like the heat in the palm of your hand . . . and perhaps movement in one of the fingers. . . . As this occurs, slightly nod your head . . . yes . . . very good . . . and now you will notice that your hand is becoming very, very light . . . like a feather coming up toward your forehead. . . . Good. . . . Your hand starts to move upward . . . and as your hand continues to rise, keep looking at the back of your hand . . . but notice your eyelids are getting very heavy, very drowsy, and very relaxed. . . . Now when your hand touches your forehead . . . your eyes will be closed . . . you will be tremendously relaxed and capable of entering a deep level of trance. Your hand and arm comes up, up, up towards your forehead. . . . Now, your hand touches your forehead. . . . Your eyes are closed. . . . You can let your hand rest comfortably in your lap and normal sensation is returning to your right hand and arm. . . .

TRANCE RATIFICATION PROCEDURES

EYELID CATALEPSY.   Notice that your eyelids feel heavy . . . so heavy that even though you try to open your eyes for the moment . . . you can't. . . . Go ahead and try . . . but you cannot. . . . Try again . . . but the eyelids are shut tight. . . . Normal sensations return to the eyelids. . . . Now you will enter a much more sound and relaxed state. . . .

LIMB RIGIDITY.   Now I want you to raise your right arm. . . . That's it. . . . Extend it in front of you, and as I count to three, your arm will become rigid . . . hard . . . like a board soaked in water . . . like steel . . . so tight . . . so rigid . . . those muscles become steel. . . . One . . . tight . . . two . . . very rigid, and three, the whole arm, each finger . . . yes . . . become steel. . . . There . . . nothing can bend that arm or the fingers . . . showing you the power of your mind and body. . . . Now relax the arm and hand. . . . Normal sensation returns and still a much deeper and sounder state of relaxation.

GLOVE ANESTHESIA.   I now give you the hypnotic suggestion that your right hand will develop the feeling that a heavy thick glove is on your right hand . . . as your hand has developed this sensation, move the forefinger of the right hand. . . . Good. . . . Now you will note some pressure in the forefinger . . . a dull sensation of pressure. . . . Open your eyes. . . . Now you see that in reality I'm sticking your finger severely with my nail file . . . but you are feeling nothing . . . correct? . . . Fine. . . . Normal sensation is returning to your hand. . . . I am now going to stimulate the middle finger. . . . As you feel this . . . nod your head, yes. . . . You see you pulled your hand back, which is an immediate and normal response. You are now aware of the tremendous control that your unconscious mind has over your body. . . . Now close your eyes again. . . . I now suggest that you can smell a pleasant odor of your choosing. . . . As you smell this, nod your head yes. . . . Good. . . . And now a very, very deep level of trance. . . . The pleasant odor leaves and still a more relaxed and deeper state of trance. . . .

IDEOSENSORY SUGGESTIONS FOR WART REMOVAL

Nothing is beyond the power of the unconscious mind and these warts are going to leave completely and your skin will be void of them. . . . The area that I touch with this pencil . . . this area of warts now begins to feel very cool . . . cool . . . slightly cold. . . . As you feel this, nod your head. . . . Good. . . . Think the thought as I continue talking. . . . The area is cool. . . . The warts are going to leave. . . . The area is cool, and the warts will leave my body because of the power of my mind over my body. . . . Now just relax your thoughts . . . just pleasant, relaxed, serene thoughts. . . . Listen to me . . . my every word . . . *These warts are going to leave. . . . We have demonstrated the control of your mind over your body, and these warts will be gone very shortly.* . . . Your skin will feel slightly cool around the area of the warts for a day or so, and as the coolness fades, the warts will also begin to fade. And so, as I slowly count from ten to one, you will be fully awake . . . free from tension, tightness, stress and strain. These warts are going to fade out.

Suggestions for Warts (Modeled after Hartland)

Don E. Gibbons, Ph.D.

Now I am going to stroke your hand, and as I do, you will gradually begin to be aware of feelings of warmth flowing from my hand into yours and flowing all through your hand, as these feelings of warmth continue to grow stronger and stronger with each passing moment. As I stroke your hand now, you will soon begin to notice these feelings of warmth flowing into your hand from mine, and as soon as you do, you can signal me by nodding your head. [After the subject has nodded his assent:] That's fine. Now, as the warmth continues to grow stronger, you are going to feel it becoming concentrated in the warts themselves. And soon the warts will begin to feel warmer than the rest of your hand. As I stroke the warts now, you can feel the warmth flowing into them from the rest of your hand. And as soon as you can feel the warmth in the warts themselves, you can signal me by nodding your head once more.

[After the subject has nodded his head once more:] Very good. Now, as you continue to feel the warmth flowing out of my hand and concentrating itself in the warts while I continue to stroke them, the warts are going to start to heal. And this healing process is going to continue until the warts are gone completely. Over the coming days, your warts are going to become flatter and smaller, and soon they are going to disappear completely. Before very long, they will be completely gone. Within a very short time, your warts will be gone completely.

Suggestions for Vaginal Warts

Diane Roberts Stoler, Ed.D.
Boxford, Massachusetts

INTRODUCTION

This script was written for a 26-year-old woman with recurring vaginal warts. She loved the ocean and was into holistic health. Imagery was used for extensive induction and deepening prior to giving the following suggestions. The last imagery scene was of a lush garden with a mountain stream flowing down through it.

SUGGESTIONS

You know that part of becoming healthier and happier is to allow yourself to enjoy only foods that are good for you. In this garden, if you become hungry there are all types of fruit trees growing here and vines, especially raspberries, strawberries, mangoes, pineapples, and oranges. The water is pure and cool; there are ponds which are spring fed. The water in one of the ponds is only for drinking and it has very special properties that allows your anti-viral and immune system to work at it best, to maintain and support your healing process so that you can remain free from illness and the vaginal warts. It is important that you drink 8–10 glasses of water per day to help your body remain free from the warts.

If any warts ever appear, your body will automatically search and find them, and will activate your anti-viral mechanism in your brain, along with decreasing the blood supply to any wart, anywhere on your body. Lastly you will permit yourself to feel the warmth of the sun and its heat in any area where the warts may appear and the warmth of the sun will dry them out immediately.

There are also other types of special ponds in this garden. You can go to any of these special ponds daily as part of your ongoing pursuit of health. They are ponds of positive emotions and strength—such as ponds of patience, humor, perseverance, calmness, kindness, endurance, high energy, wisdom and others. These ponds are warm, soothing and moss-lined, about the size of a bath tub, and you may take a dip in any of them when you need to replenish your supply of energy or positive emotions.

Another very special pond is the golden glitter pond. This pond is there for whenever you need to deal with warts or other bodily ailments, whether the causes are physical or emotional. You may take out this special clay and put it on whatever part of your body needs healing. The pond is warm, but not hot, and its healing energy penetrates through your skin and flesh to heal and rejuvenate your entire body with a soothing pleasant tingle.

There are no other people in the garden unless you want them there. No one can bother you here. You have no cares or worries. You feel safe, secure, calm, peaceful and relaxed. There is a sense of peace with the environment around you. This spot is peaceful and serene. You feel calm, peaceful, confident. This spot is a safe, secure spot. No one can bother you here. You are peaceful, calm, relaxed. You go deeper and deeper, deeper and deeper, and as I talk to you, you continue to go into an even deeper state of relaxation. Everything but my voice is becoming remote now, quite remote; nothing else but my voice seems important, nothing else is important, nothing else but my voice. [Further deepening suggestions are now offered.]

You can come anytime to this special garden and you can enjoy the fruit, the water, the various ponds to replenish your strength and positive energy, along with the very special golden glitter pond. This pond is there for whenever you need to heal bodily ailments. If there are any underlying imbalances that any ailments are symptomatic of, you will allow yourself to become aware of the reason for that ailment.

Suggestions with Condyloma Acuminatum (Genital Warts)

Dabney M. Ewin, M.D.
New Orleans, Louisiana

Your body has the capacity to overcome the wart virus and heal this infection. Focus your attention on the involved area and soon you will notice a sensation of warmth in the surrounding skin as the blood vessels dilate to bring in more antibodies and white blood cells to fight the infection, and more protein and oxygen to help build the new and normal tissue when the wart has gone away. When you feel the increased warmth, your left index finger will rise . . . [finger rises] . . . good. . . . Now your inner mind will lock in on this and maintain this warmth until the warts are healed and

your skin becomes normal in every way. You can forget about the warts and turn your conscious thoughts to other things, because your natural healing processes will cure the warts without your having any further concern about them.

Suggestions for Immunodeficient Children with Warts

M. F. Tasini and
Thomas P. Hackett, M.D.

"Let yourself feel relaxed and tired all over. Imagine doing something you like to do. Think of doing it now and how much fun it is. Take a few deep breaths—in and out—and imagine that as you let your breath out you get more and more relaxed. Feel your hand, the hand you write with, begin to tingle. Now it will start to get real light—like a feather. Imagine your hand is so light it will begin to rise up. Let it go. As it rises you will begin to feel very relaxed and good. Let it stay up for a while and then let it come down. As it comes down you continue to feel very relaxed and good." While in the trance state, the patients were told the following, "the warts will feel dry, they will then turn brown and fall off. They will not trouble you anymore." [Patients were seen for an average of three sessions.]

Evoking Helpful Past Experiences and Medical Treatments: Example with Skin Rash

M. Erik Wright, M.D., Ph.D.

INTRODUCTION

[The following example is that of a client who was beset with a recurring, highly irritating skin rash:] When you had this skin rash three years ago, you used to get great relief from soaking in a lukewarm bath in which you had dispersed half a box of cornstarch. Of course, when you are able to get into the bath water, you can truly enjoy the good feeling on your skin. However, there are many times, such as at work, when you cannot get into a bath to reduce the distress of the rash. When you find that your tolerance for the distress is becoming shaky, close your office door and give yourself an intense irritation-relief treatment.

RAPID INDUCTION AND SUGGESTIONS. [The therapist draws upon the client's ability to enter trance:] Close your eyes and give yourself the cue to relax and become quite drowsy. . . . Feel your body becoming lighter with each breath that you take . . . until you get the feeling of your body floating in your bathtub . . . and the water is at just the right temperature and you can see and feel the cornstarch dispersed throughout the water. . . . When you have reached that point . . . signal with your right index finger. . . . Very good. . . .

Feel the smooth, cool particles touch and coat your skin at every point where there is any irritation . . . and as the skin is coated by these particles, feel the coolness and the relief as the particles draw out the tenderness and irritation from each of the rash bumps. As the discomfort leaves, the skin energy is left to continue the healing. . . . Feel the active healing as the new cells on the surface of the skin replace the injured, irritated cells. . . . See, below the surface of the skin, how the blood is actively nourishing the healthy tissue growing on the skin . . . and the skin irritation subsides and becomes readily tolerable. . . .

[The therapist then offers a posthypnotic healing suggestion:] Let this cooling and healing continue even after you open your eyes, for as long as possible. . . . Each time that you repeat the exercise, the postexercise effect of cooling and healing regrowth will continue a bit longer. Soon you will not need the exercise at all, because the healing will have been completed. Give yourself the signal for arousal, feeling refreshed and comfortable.

Suggestions with Pruritus

William S. Kroger, M.D., and
William D. Fezler, Ph.D.
Palm Springs, California, and
Beverly Hills, California

IMAGERY OF SOFT COTTON.   You are enveloped in a layer of cotton which acts as a protective coating. This wonderful feeling will remain for several hours (or all day): your skin will feel fine until your next visit.

NEGATIVE SENSORY HALLUCINATION.   [The hypnotized patient is asked to imagine how the skin looks and feels in an area without lesions.] Look at your right wrist; you can begin to speculate on whether or not that area will look like your left wrist, which does not have any involvement. Now, keep looking at the left wrist; notice the texture of the skin—it also feels perfectly normal, does it not? [The patient nods his head in agreement.] Every time you look at this wrist you will observe that this area on your right wrist is becoming as normal-looking as your left wrist. You may also close your eyes, and in your "mind's eye" see or imagine that the lesions have disappeared—the skin is normal in appearance. However, you may keep just as much of the itching on the involved area of the wrist as you wish to retain. You do not have to get rid of this itching all at once, but rather, allow it to disappear slowly. [The patient is given another posthypnotic suggestion such as:] You might raise the question whether you wish this lesion [on the wrist] or that lesion [one near the elbow] to disappear first. Also, you might begin to consider the possibility of just when this will occur. Will it be tomorrow, a week from tomorrow, or several weeks from now? At any rate, the more you keep thinking about this under autohypnosis, the more likely the rash will go away.

Reducing Dermatologic Irritation

D. Corydon Hammond, Ph.D.
Salt Lake City, Utah

INDICATIONS

These suggestions are intended for use following induction and deepening with conditions like pruritus, eczema, neurodermatitis, and herpes simplex lesions. In the case of herpes lesions, the suggestions should be for the solution to produce a drying effect, to comfortably dry up the lesions.

SUGGESTIONS

And as you remain deeply relaxed, I want you to imagine that a cooling, healing salve or ointment is being gently spread over the affected areas of your skin. It is an ointment that pro-duces comfort . . . that promotes healing . . . that turns off the sensations in the affected skin areas, allowing more rapid healing to take place. And as this comforting, healing solution gently spreads over all the affected areas, you'll notice the underlying texture of the skin changing, softening, becoming more and more normal. Your skin changes to a comfortable, relaxed, normal color and consistency. Continue letting that soothing, healing ointment sink in, and allowing more to be spread on until there is a sense of complete comfort, and relief. And when your unconscious mind knows that this has influenced your skin sufficiently so that you will be able to maintain several hours of comfort, it will cause the index finger on your right hand to develop a lightness, and float up all by itself, as a signal to you. [Pause until the signal is given.] And within another minute or two you will become consciously aware of the comfort, and then you may awaken, realizing that you can apply this salve again in self-hypnosis, whenever you need to.

HYPNOSIS WITH BURNS AND EMERGENCIES

Suggestions with Burn Patients

Harold B. Crasilneck, Ph.D., and
James A. Hall, M.D.
Dallas, Texas

SUGGESTIONS

I am going to ask you to stare at this coin that I'm holding and as you do so, pay no attention to any other sounds or noises. You are aware that you are breathing more rapidly and also that as you stare intensively at this coin, your eyelids are beginning to blink and to feel heavy. As you feel them getting heavy and drowsy, just let them close . . . that's it . . . they are fluttering . . . closing and closed . . . closing and closed . . . and as I continue talking, you will enter a very deep level of hypnosis . . . for in so doing you are going to get well . . . a very deep and sound level. . . . As you are aware of this . . . nod your head. . . . Good . . . a deeper and a sounder state. . . . Now the finger that I touch will lose all feeling. . . . Now as that finger feels and is numb . . . nod your head, yes. . . . Good . . . Now open your eyes. . . . You will note that I am stimulating that finger very hard with the point of my nail file, but you have absolutely no sensation of pain. Pressure, but no pain. Now normal sensations return to your finger. As you feel the file just barely stimulating your finger, pull it away. . . . Good . . . relax . . . now you can realize the power of the mind over the body and if you can block pain . . . real pain . . . then, you can allow your body to respond to other suggestions equally well. You are now in a very deep state of relaxation. . . . You are going to hear some soft music that is pleasurable to you . . . and as this occurs, nod your head, yes. . . . Good . . . and now a very deep and relaxed state of mind and body. Because of the power of your mind over your body . . . you are going to be able to definitely increase your food intake. This food intake is going to help you to get well . . . it is an integral part of your rehabilitation, and you will eat all the food prescribed by your doctor. The food will taste good. . . . You will enjoy your food . . . realizing that with every mouthful you digest you are improving your physical and mental state. . . . Food intake is going to help you get well. . . . You will be hungry much of the time and you will eat not only the regular meals, but also the supplemental food ordered for you. *You will be hungry and your appetite will definitely increase . . . you will have a craving for each meal* because in your case food intake is an absolute necessity to health and you will eat every meal with enjoyment . . . knowing this food is making you get well very rapidly. As I slowly count from ten to one backwards, you will fully awaken . . . relaxed, at ease, and hungry.

Emergency Hypnosis for the Burned Patient

Dabney M. Ewin, M.D.
New Orleans, Louisiana

INTRODUCTION

The acutely burned patient arrives in the emergency room in a state of frightened anxiety, seeking prompt relief of the burning pain, and in a hypnoidal state that makes him highly susceptible to both good and bad suggestions. The body's response to the thermal injury is inflammation, causing progressive pathologic worsening (Hinshaw, 1963) of the injury. In sun burn, the first degree burn (redness) present on leaving the sun progresses to second degree (blister) in the ensuing 8-12 hours. The "standard" third degree (full-thickness) burn was shown by Brauer and Spira (1966) to be only

second degree for the first four hours. . . . The deeper dermal layers are not immediately killed by the heat, but rather later by the body's inflammatory response.

Chapman, Goodell, and Wolff (1959a,b) showed that inflammation is mediated through the central nervous system by release of a bradykinin-like substance which is released during the first two hours after the burn stimulus, but that the release of this enzyme is held in abeyance by icing the wound. They also showed that hypnotic suggestion can produce a blister (response without a true stimulus), and can prevent blistering when an experimental burn is placed on a hypnotically anesthetized arm (true stimulus without a response). Thus, the damaging inflammatory reaction can be blocked by *early* hypnosis, attenuating the ultimate depth and severity of the burn (Ewin, 1978, 1979).

During the first two days after a severe burn, inflammation causes large amounts of fluid to exude into the burned tissues from the bloodstream, requiring intravenous replacement to prevent shock and kidney shut-down. Since much of this fluid is later reabsorbed and can overload the cardiovascular system, standard fluid formulas aim at giving the least amount of fluid that will maintain both blood pressure and minimal urine output of 25 cc to 50 cc per hour (600–1,200 cc per 24 hrs.). Margolis, Domangue, Ehleben, and Schrier (1983) have shown that, in every case hypnotized before ten hours, the urine output on the second day was significantly elevated, averaging 3501 cc as opposed to 1,666 cc in matched controls. With the inflammatory edema limited, the calculated fluid was too much, and the extra had to be cleared through the urine.

When a newly burned patient arrives in the emergency room, his mind is concentrated and hypnosis is usually easy to induce. Since he may be a stranger to the physician, the first communication is an introduction and suggestion.

VERBALIZATION

Doctor: I'm Dr. _____ and I'll be taking care of you (pause). Do you know how to treat this kind of burn? [This question is to bring to his immediate attention that he doesn't, and that he must put his faith in the medical team. Precise wording is important because if you ask, "Do you know anything about treating burns?" he may know *something* and tell you about butter, Solarcaine, or kiss-it-and-make-it-well, which is a complete avoidance of recognizing the dependence.]

Patient: No. [The standard reply. In the rare instance of a physician or nurse who actually does know about burns, you simply use that knowledge to say, "Then you already know that you need to turn your care over to us, and that we will do our best."]

Doctor: That's all right, because we know how to take care of this and you've already done the most important thing, which was to get to the hospital quickly. You are safe now, and if you will do what I say, you can have a comfortable rest in the hospital while your body is healing. Will you do what I say? [This exchange lets the patient know that he is on the team and has already done his biggest job, so he can safely lay aside his fight or flight response (he's already fled to the hospital) which mobilizes hormones that interfere with normal immunity and metabolism. It includes a prehypnotic suggestion that he is safe and can be comfortable if he makes a commitment. His affirmative answer has made a hypnotic contract that is as good as any trance.]

Patient: Yes, or, I'll try. [Frightened patients tend to constantly analyze each sensation and new symptom to report to the doctor. By turning his care over to *us* (the whole team), he is freed of this responsibility and worry. Next, his attention is diverted to something he hadn't thought of before.]

Doctor: The first thing I want you to do is to turn the care of this burn over to *us*, so you don't have to worry about it at all. The second thing is for you to realize that *what you think* will make a great deal of difference in your healing. Have you ever seen a person blush, or blanch white with fear?" [Even dark-skinned

patients are aware of this phenomenon in light-skinned people.]

Patient: Yes.

Doctor: Well, you know that nothing has happened except a thought, an idea, and all of the little blood vessels in the face have opened up and turned red, or clamped down and blanched. *What you think* is going to affect the blood supply to your skin, and this affects healing, and you can start right now. You should have happy, relaxing, enjoyable thoughts to free up all of your healing energy. Brer Rabbit said "everybody's got a laughing place," and when I tell you to go to your laughing place, I mean for you to imagine that you are in a safe, peaceful place, enjoying yourself, totally free of responsibility, just goofing off. What would you do for a laughing place?" [The patient needs something he perceives as useful to occupy his time. The laughing place may be the beach, TV, fishing, golfing, needlepoint, playing dolls, etc. It becomes the key word for subsequent rapid inductions for dressing changes, etc., to simply "go to your laughing place."

Patient: Go to the beach . . . or . . .

Doctor: Let's get you relaxed and go to your laughing place right now, while we take care of the burn. Get comfortable and roll your eyeballs up as though you are looking at the top of your forehead and take a deep, deep, deep breath and as you take it in, gradually close your eyelids and as you let the breath out, let your eyes relax and let every nerve and fiber in your body go [slow and cadenced] loose and limp and lazy-like, your limbs like lumps of lead. Then just let your mind go off to your laughing place and . . . [visual imagery of laughing place]. [This short bit of conversation does not ordinarily delay the usual emergent hospital care. Most often, when the patient arrives in the emergency room an analgesic is given, blood is drawn, I.V. drips are started, and cold water applications are applied by the time the doctor arrives. If not, these can proceed even while the conversation takes place. A towel dipped in ice water produces immediate relief of the burning pain that occurs right after a fresh burn. Since frost bite is as bad an injury as a burn, the patient should not be packed in ice, but ice water towels are very helpful. In fact, Chapman et al. (1959a,b) showed that applying ice water to a burn holds the inflammatory response in check for several hours, so there is ample time to call for the assistance of a qualified hypnotist if the primary physician is not skilled in the technique of hypnosis.]

Doctor: Now while you are off at your laughing place, I want you to also notice that all of the injured areas are cool and comfortable. Notice how cool and comfortable they actually are, and when you can really feel this, you'll let me know because this finger (touch an index finger) will slowly rise to signal that *all* of the injured areas are cool and comfortable."

Doctor: [After obtaining ideomotor signal:] Now let your inner mind lock in on that sensation of being cool and comfortable and you can keep it that way during your entire stay in the hospital. You can enjoy going to your laughing place as often as you like, and you'll be able to ignore all of the bothersome things we may have to do and anything negative that is said. . . . Go to your laughing place.

In burns under 20%, the single initial trance generally suffices, while in larger burns, repeated suggestion helps control pain, anorexia, and uncooperativeness.

Since a thought can produce a burn (vide supra), continued feelings of guilt or anger can prevent healing and should be dealt with during emotional countershock a day or two after admission. If the patient is guilty, I stress the fact that it was unintentional and that he has been severely punished and has learned a lesson he will never forget or repeat. If he is angry, I point out that the goal is healing, and it does not interfere with his legal rights to get the best healing possible or to forgive the other person of evil intent. There is no place for anger at his laughing place, and he is instructed to postpone that feeling until healing has occurred.

It helps for the doctor to know what the laughing place is and to record it, because he may enhance it later with some visual imagery. This simple, rapid induction usually produces a profound trance almost immediately. By this time, the patient has iced towels on and the analgesic is taking effect so that he actually *is* cool and comfortable. It is much easier hypnotically to continue a sensation that is already present than it is to imagine its opposite. The suggestion "cool and comfortable" is anti-inflammatory, and if he accepts it he cannot be hot and painful. From now on, the word *injured* is substituted whenever possible for the word *burn*, because patients use the word "burning" to describe their pain. (Do not specify a particular area, hands, neck, etc., because, while these areas will do well, some spot you forgot may do poorly.)

I just leave the patient in trance and go ahead with his initial care, get him moved to the Burn Unit, and often he will drop off to sleep. On subsequent days, "Go to your laughing place," is all the signal the patient usually needs to drop off into a hypnoidal state and tolerate bedside procedures, physical therapy, etc.

Hypnosis in Painful Burns

R. John Wakeman, Ph.D., and
Jerold Z. Kaplan, M.D.

INTRODUCTION

BURNS WITH CHILDREN.   A burn injury is a devastatingly traumatic experience for anyone, regardless of age. The younger child often has greater difficulty in adjusting to routine (painful) procedures. He/she may have problems understanding why he/she must be submitted to torturous procedures and cannot easily project into the future with knowledge that it will all end soon. For these reasons, hypnosis utilization became a highly demanded and reinforcing alternative for the children, their parents, and the staff of our unit. Hypnotic training with younger children included such procedures as the "television screen" induction, dissociation to a "favorite place," and posthypnotic suggestions for "letting the body take a nap" when feeling discomfort.

SUGGESTIONS

[Ego-strengthening suggestions for improved self-esteem, body-image acceptance, hope, and coping skills for transition back into their families, homes, and communities were found to be quite effective in making the patient recovery period more positive. After the patient had achieved his or her deepest level of hypnosis, suggestions were included such as:] . . . and as the days go by . . . you will find that your attention . . . is less and less focused on your liabilities . . . your disabilities . . . or your changes of appearance . . . and more and more focused . . . on your assets . . . your strengths . . . and your inner resources . . . such as appreciation and pride in . . . your self-control . . . cooperation . . . intelligence . . . and inner fortitude . . . never allowing you to quit . . . or give up . . . and becoming more . . . and more . . . fully aware in attitudes . . . beliefs . . . and feelings . . . that despite your body's differentness from the way it was . . . you know that differentness is never a measure of worth . . . and although you may now be somewhat different . . . you are still . . . and will always be as worthwhile . . . as a human being . . . and driven to find new strengths . . . new abilities . . . and interests . . . in your life to come . . . accepting yourself more and more . . . as really the same person . . . that you were before . . . just stronger . . . with some differences . . . which do not detract from your worth . . . as a person . . . more and more able to understand other's failures in accepting "differentness" . . . more and more supportive of your family . . . in every way . . . finding it quite interesting that you seem to be less and less concerned . . . about how you have changed . . . about how you will live . . . and more and more focused

on what new . . . and exciting experiences lie ahead . . . more and more hope and positive anticipation . . . about your return home . . . your seeing friends . . . and your renewed energy to get as much out of life as possible in the years to come . . . and so on. . . . .

SUGGESTIONS PRIOR TO DEBRIDEMENT

[An example of a typical dissociation discourse after deepening has been achieved just prior to debridement is as follows:] . . . and as you continue to go deeper . . . and deeper . . . into that comfortable . . . relaxed state . . . as each moment goes by . . . you may be surprised at how easy it is for you to experience . . . the calmness, . . . comfort, . . . and pleasant relaxation . . . felt at your . . . special place [individual's scene – e.g., "boat races in San Diego"] . . . enjoying the surroundings . . . and going even deeper . . . letting your body relax . . . more and more completely . . . feeling the warm breeze . . . the gentle rocking of your boat . . . back and forth . . . back and forth . . . with each breath . . . you see all of the beautiful colors of each racing boat . . . counting the boats as they speed by . . . and going deeper . . . now feeling perfectly at ease . . . nothing to distract you . . . nothing to interrupt your pleasant experience . . . and knowing at all times . . . that all you have to do to return to this place . . . is raise your hand and arm . . . and as they grow heavy . . . you become deeply relaxed . . . deeply relaxed . . . completely comfortable . . . and can remain comfortable for a long time . . . even after leaving the beautiful scene . . . deeply comfortable . . . when exercising . . . when eating . . . when moving . . . you will find that sleeping is no longer a problem . . . you will be surprised at how much stronger you grow . . . each day . . . little by little . . . stronger and more relaxed . . . completely comfortable . . . even when you are no longer with me . . . even when you are not at this beautiful place . . . feeling better and better . . . without flaws . . . without apprehensions . . . only relaxation . . .

calmness . . . comfort . . . and self-confidence . . . and so on. . . .

Ideomotor Healing of Burn Injuries

Ernest L. Rossi, Ph.D., and
David B. Cheek, M.D.
Malibu, California, and Santa Barbara, California

If a patient is seen hours or days after experiencing a burn, proceed as follows, explaining the process as a means of eliminating inflammation and allowing healing to occur rapidly.

1. *Accessing inner healing resources*
   "Remember a time when you walked into cold water. It felt cold for a while until a time when you got used to it. That represents a degree of numbness. When you are feeling cold at an unconscious . . . level, your brain will shut down the messages that cause inflammation and interfere with healing.

   "Imagine standing in cold water up to your knees. When you are feeling that unconsciously, your yes finger will lift. When you are half as sensitive as normal, your no finger will lift.

   "Now, walk in further until the cold water is up to your hips. Your yes finger will lift when you are cold from your hips to your knees, and your no finger will lift when you are numb from your hips to your toes. Your right hand wrist will be below the water level and will also feel numb." [This will happen without explanation, even though the patient is lying in bed.]

2. *Self-testing of hypnotic analgesia*
   "Now you know how to make parts of your body alter sensations. Please place your cold, numb right hand over the burned area and experience the coldness and numbness flow into the burned area. When you know the burn is cold and numb, your yes and no

   fingers will lift to let you know how well you are doing."

3. *Ratifying and maintaining healing*
   a. **"That coldness and numbness will remain there for at least two hours. Then it may be necessary to repeat the exercise. You will get better each time you do it, and the result will last longer and work more effectively as you go along."**
   b. Any difficulty with this procedure may indicate a need to work through emotional problems.

Direct Suggestions in Emergencies with the Critically Ill

Ernest L. Rossi, Ph.D., and
David B. Cheek, M.D.
Malibu, California, and Santa Barbara, California

1. The critically ill are already in a state of hypnosis. Learn to recognize and utilize the spontaneous expressions of hypnotic behavior.
2. Avoid conversation and actions that might suggest pessimism. Suggest hope and optimism, but do so sincerely since the threatened human is canny in recognizing reassurance that is phony.
3. Collect your thoughts and marshal a plan of action before touching or speaking directly to the patient. You may be breathless in your hurry to get to the patient; you may not know exactly what to do. Take a few moments to give directions to bystanders. Your voice will be confident with them because you know more than they do. The quality of your voice will then give confidence to the patient in accepting reassurance from you. You also have gained time to control the expressions of your haste.
4. Tell the patient what has happened and that he will be all right. Outline what you are doing now and what your reason is for so

doing. This implies that you respect his knowledge and his ability to understand your actions. Allow time to outline what steps to take as you plan for the patient tomorrow and in the future. There is no better reassurance than the tacit suggestion that you expect a future for which to plan.

Instruction and promise of a future should be given to unconscious people, even when they show no pupillary reflex to light. Congratulate the unconscious person for being so relaxed, and tell him specifically how long you expect him to remain in this relaxed state before awakening with feelings of hunger and thoughts of food.

5. Give medication for pain if possible. This is a form of communication showing that you are interested in taking constructive action. Tell him what you are giving and for what purpose. The patient will know that it takes a little time before medication works; he will be able to focus attention better on your actions during the interval. The time taken in giving an injection allows you time to collect your thoughts and control any outward signs of alarm.

6. If he is able to talk, get the patient talking about work, hobbies or his family. The human mind can be taught to ignore pain and sources of shock if it is directed to concern itself with times and places where pain and fear did not exist.

SUMMARY OF DIRECT HEALING SUGGESTIONS IN EMERGENCIES

All injured, frightened, hemorrhaging, shocked, and unconscious people may be considered critically ill. They enter a hypnotic state spontaneously and need no formal induction.

1. *Accessing healing sources*
   a. Outline simply and briefly what you are going to do for them *now*.
   b. Designate a finger (by touching it lightly) to lift all by itself when the inner

healing source (mind, brain, etc.) carries out the following:
   c. **"Your inner healing source can let this finger lift when the bleeding (and/or pain, etc.) has been turned down by half."**
   d. **"That finger can lift again when your comfort can continue getting better and better in every way."**
2. *Therapeutic facilitation*
   a. **"Your inner mind knows exactly what it needs to do to continue recovery by returning your blood pressure (or whatever) to normal. It can lift a finger to indicate that healing is continuing now all by itself."**
   b. Congratulate the patient for being so relaxed and doing so well in allowing the healing to take place.
   c. Outline a series of steps (signs) by which the healing process will continue in the immediate future.
3. *Ratification with posthypnotic suggestion*
   "You will feel yourself going into a deep, comfortable sleep for four hours and then awaken feeling refreshed and alert with a good appetite." (Appropriate suggestions for each patient's particular situation are added at this point.)

Suggestions for Use of Spontaneous Trances in Emergency Situations

M. Erik Wright, Ph.D., M.D.

INTRODUCTION

In crisis or life-threatening situations (e.g., cardiac trauma, automobile accidents), patients typically enter spontaneous trances, fixated in their attention on their body and immediate environment. Unfortunately, negative suggestions are often made in emergency situations by bystanders, ambulance attendants, police and medical personnel. For instance, patients may hear: "You'd better hurry, this guy may not make it!" "Is this guy going to make it?" "Wow, look at that blood all over the place. This woman's a mess." At an annual scientific meeting of the American Society of Clinical Hypnosis, Wright presented results of an experiment where patients were randomly assigned to experimentally trained ambulance attendants versus untrained attendants. Crews trained to give positive suggestions had significantly fewer patients who were dead on arrival and their patients had a quicker recovery rate. This is a vitally important topic for further confirming research.

We believe that emergency personnel should be trained in giving positive suggestions, even to uncommunicative, stuporous patients.

These suggestions, the first paragraph of which are reprinted from Dr. Wright's book, illustrate suggestions used in his study. (*Ed.*)

SUGGESTIONS FOR AMBULANCE ATTENDANTS

[Ambulance attendants may be taught to give the following types of suggestions, speaking in a rather low-key manner, close to the ear of the patient.] You are in good hands now. You will be at the hospital shortly. Everything there is being made ready to help you. Let your muscles relax, let your mind begin to feel more secure and quiet. . . . Wherever this may be needed, let your blood vessels adjust to keep the blood circulating inside your blood vessels and to seal off leaks if they occur. . . . Wherever your skin is tight and tense, let it relax and permit the body's healing processes to begin to work. . . . As you listen to my voice, you will find yourself gradually becoming calmer. . . . Your breath will move in and out of your chest more freely and more regularly. . . . Your body has already begun to mobilize its healing powers and started to repair your hurt. . . . Everything that can be done to help you right here is now being done. Soon you will be at the hospital. The medical team has been told that you are on your way in. The team will take over with the hospital's resources to help you. . . .

[Other, similar suggestions were modeled by Dr. Wright in his scientific meeting talk:] Let your body concentrate on repairing itself and feeling secure. Let your heart, blood vessels, everything, bring themselves into a state of preserving your life. Bleed enough so that it will cleanse the wounds and let the blood vessels close down so that your life is preserved; your body weight, your body heat, everything is going to be maintained, and things are being made ready at the hospital. We are getting there as quickly and as safely as possible. You are now in a safe position. The worst is over. We are now taking you to the hospital.

SUGGESTIONS FOR CARDIAC EMERGENCY PATIENTS

This has been a terrible thing that has happened, but it is over and now it is time for the body to make use of itself and begin recovering. There are many things that will be able to be attended to later. Now the main thing is to let your body heal itself, relax, and begin to think in terms of what tomorrow may bring, of how good it is to be alive, and to be able to breathe and to be able to know that even with the tubes in your nose, there is life, and there is hope.

SUGGESTIONS AFTER STABILIZATION AT THE HOSPITAL

[Focusing on the body movements that are still there:] How good it is that you can focus and listen to me. There are a lot of things that we'll be able to talk about in the next week of learning when you can begin exercising, when you can begin to . . . [you lay out a program of future action, rather than a focus on the debit, the losses that have taken place. Now what you are offering is very limited and realistic in terms of what will be done.]

[By setting a framework of anticipation, the individual first detaches himself from the anxiety about the self and the number of secondary assaults so that the aftershock is lessened because you suggest that the heart, through learning how to make use of itself, is like it is shedding a load:] The attack has been a heavy load and it may shiver a little bit, but that is all right. [Thus, whatever may happen, you anticipate it so that you do not give rise to a new set of fears.]

COMMENTARY

Dr. Wright encouraged emergency personnel to translate to the patient the body experiences happening to him or her, such as the sense of pressure that comes and goes. He recommended talking with postcardiac recovery patients and with emergency physicians to learn about the subjective body experience of cardiac patients. The trained professional may then comment on the symptomatology and feelings of the patient (pacing), and then make comforting suggestions about it (leading). (*Ed.*)

Painless Wound Injection Through Use of a Two-finger Confusion Technique

Steven F. Bierman, M.D.

INTRODUCTION

Injection of local anesthetic into an open wound, in preparation for suturing, is in some ways like adding insult to injury. The procedure is painful and generally dreaded by patients. In recent years, physicians have turned to topic preinjection solutions in hopes of eliminating such discomfort (Pryor, Kilpatrick, Opp, et al., 1980). Although these solutions are often effective, especially in shallow wounds, their efficacy is limited in deeper wounds that require extensive debridement and layered closure. There is also the suggestion, albeit from animal studies, that tetracaine-adrenaline-cocaine (TAC) solution may predispose to wound infection (Barker, Rodeheaver, Edgerton, et al., 1982). This author has achieved reasonable success in this regard by using topical proparacaine, 0.5% solution. Here, the absence

of a vasoconstricting effect would argue against the likelihood of promoting infection. Nevertheless, results with both proparacaine and TAC have been imperfect.

Work with hypnosis led to the development of the present technique. No additional drugs are required, nor does the procedure require additional time. Instead, the patient's attention is focused away from the wound and distributed elsewhere. A discrimination task is assigned, and confusion is engendered by giving instructions ambiguously. The patient's consciousness is thus sufficiently preempted to permit injection without the perception of pain.

[It is recommended by the author that you draw a picture of a wound on a piece of paper and practice this technique with the paper to promote mastery. (*Ed.*)]

METHOD

A sterile field is prepared around the wound, and the patient is instructed that it would be best to direct his or her vision elsewhere. The physician, who usually engages in small talk while setting up, then says: "Now here's a *distinction* you can *learn*," emphasizing the italicized words. One finger of the physician's left hand is then placed to one side of the wound, a second finger to the other side. (Where the wound is long, a finger is placed on either side of the wound and gradually moved along its length as the injection proceeds.) With the physician using the right hand, the wound is then injected. All the while, the physician is delivering the following instructions and questions so as to maintain the state of distraction (notice that the play is on two words: "one," referring to finger #1 and to one finger—as opposed to two fingers—and "two," referring to finger #2 and to both fingers:)

Now, I'm going to place finger #1 here [on one side] and finger #2 here [on the other side]. And you can *feel finger #1* [wiggle finger] and finger #2 [wiggle finger], can't you? Now when I say *feel*, I mean the light *touch*, not the wiggle, so that whether I am moving finger #1 [wiggle #1] or finger #2 [wiggle #2] or two [wiggle both] or just moving one [wiggle

#2], you can still sense the touch of #1 [wiggle 1] or two [wiggle both]. Now at some time either one [wiggle #2] or both [wiggle both] will go *numb*, and what I want you to *pay attention* to is when one [wiggle #1] or two [wiggle #2] begins to *feel less*. And it's kind of like the old one [wiggle #1] — two [wiggle both].

At this point, the injection usually begins. The physician tries to keep the patient in a mild state of confusion while simultaneously directing the patient's attention to the side of the wound not being injected. It is best, therefore, to alternate the side one is injecting, being careful to do so unpredictably. For example, while injecting side #1, the physician may say:

Now I know you can *feel* the movement of *finger #2*, and I also know that if I stop moving one [stop #2] so that both one [wiggle — stop #1] and two [wiggle — stop #2] are still, you can still feel the touch of two [wiggle #2]; is that correct? Now what I don't know, and what I need you to tell me, is which finger, #1 or #2, is beginning to become more numb?

A similar tack may be taken when injecting side #2, with emphasis on the sensation under the contralateral finger.

At this juncture, the patient will generally comment. Whatever is said, the physician should respond sincerely and honestly. Common remarks by the patient are:

"I'm sorry, which is number one and which is number two?" The physician should respond by reiterating the initial instructions, more or less.

"Neither is becoming numb, I think." The physician should respond: "Neither is becoming numb, and yet you can *feel* finger #2 [wiggle #2] and two [wiggle both] and finger #1 [wiggle #1 . . .]" and so on.

"I'm feeling something else. . . ." The physician might respond: "You're feeling something else, yes, and yet what I want you to do is *pay attention* too to exactly when one of these fingers, #1 [wiggle #1] or #2 [wiggle #2] or two [wiggle both], is beginning to go *numb*. Now which finger [wiggling one after the other alternately] is beginning to *feel less?*

Any two-point discrimination of this sort will eventually accommodate to the perception of a single point. Moreover, instillation of local anesthetic in proximity to the two fingers will often effect some measure of numbness under either or both. So the target phenomenon will actually occur. Therefore, the physician can, and should, be earnest in his or her directions; the patient, sensing this, will be attentive and gratified upon discovering the effect.

To ensure success, the physician should attend scrupulously to three additional considerations. (1) The word *needle* is never volunteered: unless the patient asks specifically, the word is not used. Instead, one might ask for "a 30 gauge," a truncated phrase which always communicates the need sufficiently. (2) The needle is never shown. Lidocaine is drawn up into the syringe with the physician's back to the patient, thus concealing the dreaded point. These simple measures eliminate the verbal and visual cues that would otherwise recall previous unpleasant experiences and thus incite anticipation of the same. (3) The physician must be careful to avoid such negative suggestions as "now this is going to hurt," or "just a little prick now." As Erickson and Rossi (1976) have pointed out, "Every suggestion . . . requires that [the patient] act it out for himself to some degree." The suggestion, however well-intentioned, that pain is about to occur is self-fulfilling.

DISCUSSION

Thorough evaluation of the two-finger confusion technique would, of course, require a prospective, randomized, controlled experiment. Proparacaine 0.5% (or TAC) alone, for example, could be compared as preinjection anesthesia to proparacaine 0.5% (or TAC) plus the confusion technique. Initial results, however, warrant this preliminary report, for I have found that when administered in earnest, the two-finger method rarely allows for even the barest perception of the injection. In well over 50 cases where the technique has been used, no patient has ever described the injection of local anesthetic into a wound as painful; the vast majority have felt nothing and have been surprised to learn that an injection has been given. Thus, whereas an exact comparative study of available techniques would be nice, there is no question that use of the two-finger confusion technique can result in painless wound injection.

HYPNOSIS FOR HEALING, PSYCHOSOMATIC CONDITIONS AND AUTOIMMUNE DISEASES

General Approach to Physical Symptoms Caused by Stress

Carol P. Herbert, M.D., CCFP, FCFP
Vancouver, British Columbia

A permissive approach to self-hypnosis which emphasizes positive experiences of physical changes acts to reframe a negative self-image or previously confusing symptoms. I begin by briefly outlining the "fight or flight" response, then contrast the physical and emotional changes of the relaxation response. I ask the patient to choose a pleasurable visual or auditory image to focus his/her awareness.

"Take a couple of deep breaths in . . . and out . . . and on the out breath, notice a sense of comfortable heaviness beginning in one hand and arm. Repeat to yourself, 'My hand and arm are comfortably heavy,' several times. [Pause] Then allow your attention to pass to the other hand and arm and repeat, 'My hand and arm are comfortably heavy. Both my hands and both my arms are comfortably heavy.'"

The same suggestions are given for the lower limbs, ending with, "Arms and legs, hands and feet, comfortably heavy. Feeling quiet inside."

I do not use terms like "try" or "relax." In fact, I tell the patient that this is training in "how not to try hard to relax." I end the exercise by suggesting that the patient practice 5–10 minutes, three times daily, with complete alerting unless it is bedtime, by flexing and stretching the arms, inhaling sharply, and then opening the eyes. I encourage the patient to give positive self- suggestions during the last minute of the exercise.

I teach "warmth," "heartbeat," and "respiration" over the next three weeks, emphasizing self-awareness and encouraging reports of positive experiences of the physical self. [see Jencks, 1979).

This approach takes four one-half hour visits and is practical in a family practice office setting. I use this approach for conditions from insomnia to migraine. I may superimpose specific suggestions for particular symptoms, but have found that this general approach results in spontaneous remission of many symptoms, which is very powerful feedback to the patient to keep practicing. The patient is seen in follow-up at one month and two months, and then reinforced on routine visits for medical care.

Symphony Metaphor

Marlene E. Hunter, M.D.
Vancouver, British Columbia, Canada

INTRODUCTION

This metaphor is obviously particularly apropos for the musically inclined subject, but may be appreciated by many others also. There are many metaphoric concepts that may be included in such a metaphor, depending upon the concerns and problems of the patient: harmony and discord, orchestrating, rehearsal, leading and following, cooperation with each other and the importance of the different parts to each other, balance, tune and not in tune, fine tuning, the automaticity that comes after lengthy practice, picking up the tempo, etc. (*Ed.*)

SUGGESTIONS

Sometimes I like to think of the body as a symphony orchestra. A symphony orchestra makes beautiful music; but it is made up of many sections and each section is made up of many instruments. As you know, sometimes an instrument gets out of tune: a violin may break a string, or one of the reeds may need to be cleaned. [There are many possible problems.] Something needs to be done so that that instrument can produce beautiful music again. Or sometimes, when working on some composition, a whole section might be having trouble with the rhythm or with a difficult chord or harmonic, or the timing might be off.

But despite the fact that an instrument may need to be tuned or repaired, or a whole section might need to work on timing or rhythm, there is nothing wrong with the *orchestra*. [By implication, nothing is wrong with the *person*.] The orchestra is still as strong and vital as ever. It is simply that that instrument needs to be fixed, or that section has to practice more, and when they have done that, then the orchestra is once again harmonious, rhythmic, attuned to itself.

Well, the body is rather like that. If we think of the body as being composed of many "sections"—the digestive system, the respiratory system, the reproductive system, the cardiovascular system, the muscular system—all of these systems make up the symphony that is the body. And within each system, there are the various "instruments": in the digestive system there are the teeth and the mouth, and the esophagus where you swallow, and the stomach and the sphincter at the end of the stomach, and the various parts of the bowel; and then there are also the auxiliary organs like the liver. [One may change which system is described to suit a patient's symptomatology.] And all of these "instruments" make up that "section," just like the instruments in the sections of the orchestra.

So, although attention may need to be paid to one section or one instrument, yet the symphony—the body—is still wonderful, and still has all the potential for making beautiful music.

Think to yourself, "My body is like a symphony"—and feel the wonderful rhythms of your body pulsing softly to their own special beat within you, and harmony being restored.

Healing Imagery

Marlene E. Hunter, M.D.
Vancouver, British Columbia, Canada

INTRODUCTION AND INDICATIONS

Dr. Hunter's suggestions may facilitate healing in psychosomatic disorders (e.g., ulcers, colitis) or following accidents or surgery. The last sections describe images that may be suggested for use with patients whose clearest imagery capacity is visual, auditory, or kinesthetic. (*Ed.*)

SUGGESTIONS

All living things in the plant and animal world have one thing in common: all have within them, the most incredible capacity to HEAL. If you simply think of a wounded animal, or a damaged plant, you can affirm that statement for yourself. The animal—man included—recovers from wounds and illness; the plant grows new leaves or branches, and sometimes even has scars to remind the observer that once, it was wounded. [Universality of the capacity to heal.]

You also have this wonderful capacity. You also have this miraculous healing energy within you.

[Invitation to go deeper into trance.] Go now, deep within yourself: to the very center of yourself, to the source of that healing energy within you. Go to the very source of that healing energy; be aware of that energy that comes from the very center of yourself. Gather up that energy, and *direct it to that part of your body where you instinctively know it must be directed*! [You can trust your intuition.]

Each one of us has his or her own personal concept of that energy. [Everyone's concept is right for them.] For me, it is a source of light—a source of healing light, like the sun, a light that can be directed to the part of the body which needs healing, and suffuse that part of the body with its healing glow. It is a golden light, that surrounds and bathes the ill or wounded part of the body with that healing golden energy.

Discover YOUR own concept of what your healing energy is. Locate it deep within you, and direct it to wherever your body needs it.

Now FEEL, *sense* the healing that is already beginning within you. You can actually FEEL that healing. That's right. Direct that energy through your body, to wherever you intuitively know it is needed—knowing that you may even be surprised at the part of your body which you have intuitively chosen! [Positive suggestion for healing.] But knowing, also, that the subconscious mind has so much more information than the conscious mind has, the subconscious mind may know that some *other* part of the body, different from where your conscious mind would have thought, may need that healing first. Trust your subconscious mind to direct that energy; trust your intuitive response. [But generally it is better to let the subconscious do that itself.]

Now let your wonderful, creative imagination formulate an image, in your awareness, of what that ill or wounded part of your body is like—what it looks like, or feels like (kinesthetically or tactilely), or indeed even sounds like—discordant, harsh, hoarse, a grating sound perhaps, or thin and reedy with little substance. [Emphasizing the importance of self-trust.]

[Formation of images using all the senses; images must have personal meaning to be effective.] This image could be pictorial, as if you were looking at an anatomy book; or in three dimensions, like a piece of sculpture. It could be entirely symbolic, or graphic. Use your own talents to devise an image that has meaning for YOU.

Use all of your sensory awarenesses to formulate that image. Fill that image with all the detail you possibly can—what you see, hear, feel, touch, taste, smell. Remember color, and strength.

Then place that image, in your inner awareness, on one side. Now, begin to create another image: this image is of healing, of convalescence, of recovery. It is the image of what your body will be like—will look like, feel like, sound like when you are well again; restore harmony to your body, and power. Fill in all of THAT wonderful detail, in whatever kind of image is right for you, remembering that the image can be realistic or symbolic, two- or three-dimensional, whatever you instinctively know is congruent with your deep sense of self. [Ego-strengthening.]

Place this image beside the earlier one. Your task now becomes very simple: you simply need to evolve the first image into the second. [Simple expectation of success.]

Some people like to do this in a way similar to rifling through those little pictures in the upper corners of comic books—flipping the pages quickly so that the cartoons seem to move; some choose to make a video or movie of the process; some draw immediate images—short-term goals, as it were; some just sense the evolution of one into the other. [Triggers for the imagination.]

In your own hypnosis every day, reinforce this healing imagery. The more frequently you do that, the stronger the message that you are giving to your subconscious mind and thence to your body: I CAN BE WELL: I AM ALREADY ON THE ROAD TO RECOVERY! [Affirmations in imagery.]

HEALING IMAGERY—OTHER TECHNIQUES

1. COLOR.   Another type of imagery uses color extensively and gives it priority. Some people paint a picture in their imaginations—a picture in the colors of illness and disease. The healing imagery, then, involves painting a new picture, using the colors of health, or in changing the existing (in the mind's eye) picture as convalescence and healing ensue.

A variation is to simply perceive colors—in the shades and tones of woundedness or ill health—swirling about in various patterns; gradually the colors change, merging into the vibrant colors of full recovery. One thinks of this type of imagery with the artistically inclined (not necessarily artists).

2. MUSIC.   For those who use auditory imagery more extensively, music can be used to great advantage. The music of disease may be perceived as jarring and discordant—each subject will have his or her own ideas about that; many will hear (with their inward ear) a specific piece of music that fits their interpretation. The music may change suddenly or gradually, "letting it happen" or deliberately ending one and beginning another.

Pain which is perceived in auditory terms—e.g., throbbing—may be altered in this way, changing the image of the pain as the music changes. Personally, I have changed Heavy Metal (a throbbing ankle with torn ligaments) to a Mozart opera with great success! Similarly, musical representations of illness may change to those of health and happiness. These musical metaphors may be combined with the frequent use of words such as harmony, rhythm, attuned, tempo, etc. [Also see the Symphony Metaphor above.]

3. WIND, BREEZES.   The image of a soft breeze wafting away illness, bringing strength and a sense of well-being, is very pleasant. A brisk wind, blowing disease away, is more active and invigorating for some.

Alternatively, the concept of a storm, even a raging gale, as the terrifying or devastating illness, subsiding to a warm, healing breeze bringing peace and comfort, may describe some patients' situation more vividly.

4. HEALING WATER.   This could be, figuratively, swimming in a magic pool or immersing oneself in some sort of healing water. We sometimes talk of "taking the waters," referring to a spa or health resort. In that case the healing water is taken "within," rather than "without."

Healing water also has some reference to the safety of the womb, floating in the warm amniotic fluid. The link to baptism or being "born again" is another possibility to explore with some patients. Obviously one chooses the metaphor very carefully. A good history is the first essential, rapport a close second.

Healing imagery has an infinity of variation. Use your own creative imagination to present wonderful options to your patients.

Suggestions with Autoimmune Disease

Jeffrey Auerbach, Ph.D.
Los Angeles, California

INDICATIONS

In autoimmune diseases, like rheumatoid arthritis and lupus, the immune system attacks the body—the joints, internal organs or skin. In effect, the immune system is misguided or "confused." Hypnotherapeutic work may help stimulate healthy immune system functioning, where only foreign invaders or mutant cells are attacked. A general understanding of how autoimmune diseases operate will be helpful to the patient, and sometimes pictures of what the disease process and the immune system look like will help to facilitate the internal changes that are required for healing or remission.

SUGGESTIONS

Allow an image of yourself to become very, very small. Begin your healing journey by seeing yourself shrinking smaller and smaller until you're as small as a drop of water, and slip inside yourself through your mouth and down your throat. Then allow yourself to shrink even smaller until you are not much larger than a single cell, but fully protected by a sturdy and transparent bubble around you. Then slip into your bloodstream and travel to an area that is in need of healing. [Pause] What do you see? [Pause] From a very safe vantage point, you can observe your immune system in action. What are your white blood cells doing? [Pause] If any white blood cells are disturbing part of your body as opposed to only subduing foreign invaders or mutant cells, they will need educating.

You may want to have a dialogue with your immune system. "Why are you attacking me? . . . Let's live in peace. . . . What do we have to do to live in harmony? . . ."

Send a message from your safe vantage point to a wise, experienced and healthy white blood cell that understands the importance of not harming the joints, organs or skin. Watch this wise old cell explain effectively to the misguided cells how to recognize what not to attack. [pause] See the immune system leaving any damaged areas in peace, and watch, as in time lapse photography, those areas healing completely, and then watch yourself using that part of your body effectively and with pleasure.

Prolonged Hypnosis in Psychosomatic Medicine

Kazuya Kuriyama, M.D.
Japan

INTRODUCTION

Time-extended or prolonged hypnosis is not even mentioned in comprehensive textbooks on hypnosis. Therefore, although there is only limited experimentation with this approach (Kratochvil, 1970; Kuriyama, 1968; and two non-English publications from Germany and Czechoslovakia), it is being included in this volume to introduce a unique treatment option deserving of further investigation. Of possible relevance to this method are the studies of Barabasz and Barabasz (e.g., 1989), who in several reports have documented the ability to increase hypnotic susceptibility after only a few hours of REST: restricted environmental stimulation therapy. These results suggest that Kuriyama's approach may, at a minimum, enhance responsiveness to suggestion. There are also similarities between Kuriyama's approach and the independent method of the late Dr. Ainslie Meares reviewed in Chapter 6. (*Ed.*)

THEORY, TECHNIQUE, INDICATIONS, AND CONTRAINDICATIONS

The method is based on the following assumptions:

1. The human organism is endowed with spontaneous healing power with which to restore healthy mind and body.
2. The so-called hypnotic trance serves the functions of enhancing the healing force in the organism.
3. Especially in prolonged hypnosis, the self-recovering force is reinforced and the organism is set free from the strains of mind and body caused by the stress of the inner and outer world, and is helped to restore health.
4. Prolonged hypnosis stimulates the patient to develop an attitude to accept therapeutic approaches, such as suggestions and hypnotic working relationships, and respond to them in an active and self-regulatory manner.
5. The first assumption presupposes our basic belief in the human organism. This belief underlies any therapeutic endeavor, be it for physical or psychological disorders. The second assumption brings forward the nature of trance. Clinically speaking, we encounter many cases in which the so-called trance seems to exert strong therapeutic effect upon the human body. For example, in many cases mere induction into hypnosis can bring out marked improvement or more or less disappearance of symptoms without any therapeutic suggestions or interpretations being given. Often simply being in a trance seems to be very therapeutic.

As stated in the third and fourth assumptions, in prolonged hypnosis, which keeps the patient away from the stimuli and disturbances of the outer world and eliminates the tension state created by wrong learning, the inherent self-recovering force and the effect of the trance will be enhanced to an optimal level. Also, the feelings of security and satisfaction that come from the fact that the patient is treated well and long enough add to more favorable results.

THE METHOD.   After having induced the patient into deep hypnosis by ordinary inductive techniques, the following methods are in order.

1. Short-term prolonged hypnosis: Maintain the trance for two or three hours.
2. All-night prolonged hypnosis: Hypnotize the patient at night and maintain the trance, with which he goes into natural sleep, until the following morning when he wakes up from the hypnosis after washing his face.
3. All-day prolonged hypnosis: Maintain the trance as long as possible on the second day following the above all-night hypnosis.
4. Long-term prolonged hypnosis: Maintain the trance all day long, and, moreover, preserve it as long as the subject wishes; that is until he feels confident that he will recover. If necessary, the trance is to be continued for a few days or even for several weeks.

Method 1 is applied to some inpatients and outpatients by letting the patient lie down on the bed or sit relaxed in an easy chair. Some patients relax better themselves with the therapist close enough to be heard. Others do not do well unless the therapist visits them to help reinforce the trance occasionally. The other methods (Methods 2-4) are applied only to inpatients. Method 2 has turned out to be most practical and effective, apparently because the patients are not disturbed by day-time noises or visitors. In regard to method 3, it is important to take into consideration such factors as the patient's habits and personality traits and to maintain the trance according to the rhythm of his life. Method 4 is for specific conditions and needs very careful preparations.

When the individual is induced into prolonged hypnosis, the therapist needs to give a thorough explanation as to what it is like to be in the trance; that is, that there is no danger whatsoever, he can drink water or tea, go to the bathroom, and do any other necessary things under hypnosis. Also, the environmental manipulation needs to be arranged so that there should be no visitors during the treatment. The following is an example of suggestive words:

From now on you will be on the bed hypnotized for a long time. You are lying on the bed with your mind and body so relaxed, and comfortable. If you want to go to the bathroom or drink water, you will have no trouble doing so under hypnosis. And after coming back to bed, you will automatically go into a hypnotic state which is much deeper than when you left the bed. You are so comfortable that you will never feel that you woke from hypnosis, but rather that you wish to go into deeper hypnosis.

If the inpatients are to be hypnotized at night, the following suggestions need to be added.

You will be under hypnosis for a while, and then, you will gradually go into deeper and deeper sleep. You will never wake up until tomorrow morning when you will wake up from hypnosis only after you have washed your face. At that time, your head is clear and you will feel very good. You will enjoy breakfast very much.

In addition, depending on any special condition, proper suggestions or support need to be given.

TYPES OF DISEASES AND TREATMENT RESULTS.   Prolonged hypnosis can be used mainly for the following two situations: (a) cases from which a favorable outcome is expected by using prolonged hypnosis, and/or (b) when treatment has reached a deadlock with no further improvement, after the patient has improved to a certain stage by ordinary hypnotherapy.

Treatment results: The eight cases of bronchial asthma had suffered from severe attacks every day for several years with no noticeable improvement with various types of medical treatment, and thus had to be hospitalized. Five of them, persistent users of steroid hormone, were able to set themselves free from it in a relatively short time.

In some cases, only by keeping the patients in a so-called trance for many hours was marked improvement was observed. In others, the therapeutic effect was reinforced by proper suggestions during the course of treatment. At any rate, the author was able to observe marked improvement in many of the patients who had not responded to pharmacotherapy or standard hypnotherapy.

INDICATION AND CONTRAINDICATION.   This method is applicable to all cases where hypnotherapy is indicated. However, it seems to be of particular use in the following cases.

1. Bronchial asthma, organ neurosis and anxiety neurosis, which attacks during every day particularly during the night.
2. Angina pectoris, chronic stomach ulcer in which no immediate psychogenic factors are detectable, and where a good balance of mind and body seems to play an important role at present in bringing about favorable therapeutic outcomes.
3. Cases of chronic anxiety or tension, and those whose psychosomatic symptoms are perpetuated.
4. Cases where no effect can be expected by drug therapy or ordinary hypnotherapy.

Further Suggestions for Facilitating Prolonged Hypnosis

Stanislav Kratochvil, Ph.D.

[The following suggestions were given to subjects following hypnotic induction, deepening, and the production of a variety of hypnotic phenomena. (*Ed.*)]

1. You will remain in hypnosis until I repeat three times the word "zero." You cannot return to your normal state without this signal. Another person would be able to bring you back to your normal state only by repeating this word ten times.
2. You will behave and live in the hypnotic state in the same way as if you were not in hypnosis. You will be engaged in your ev-

eryday activity, talk with other people, eat and sleep normally at night, so that nobody will be able to find anything strange in your behavior; you won't be aware of any change, either.
3. With me you will be able to speak quite normally, too. My words will act upon you as a direct command only if I change the intensity of my voice, i.e., if I whisper or speak more loudly than usual.
4. As long as you remain in hypnosis, you won't be oriented in time. You will answer each question concerning the date, by the answer "January 1," being convinced that this is true. This is the only date you know from this moment in your hypnotic state.

Vascular Control Through Hypnosis

Emil G. Bishay, M.D., and Chingmuh Lee, M.D.
Torrance, California

INTRODUCTION

The following suggestions were used successfully in a study (Bishay & Lee, 1984) that documented the reduction in regional blood flow to the hands through production of hypnoanesthesia. Similar suggestions may facilitate vascular control in other parts of the body. (*Ed.*)

SUGGESTIONS

[Following induction utilizing relaxation, imagery, and a 20-step staircase for deepening:] Now you are so deeply relaxed, your whole body feels very relaxed, and very heavy. You have relaxed so well that you did not pay attention to the fact that you can feel your left hand getting heavier and heavier. You can feel it pressing on your left thigh . . . and you can't even move it. Your right hand, at the same time, is feeling as if it is being pulled up . . . as if there was a helium balloon attached to it with a strap and pulling it, very slowly, and slightly up.

As your right hand leaves your thigh, it is not going to go higher. It will feel cold and numb. You are going to actually start immersing your right hand in a bucket full of ice-cold water. It is getting colder and colder, more and more numb. You can hardly feel it. The tips of your fingers are very, very numb. . . . They are almost painful. The dorsum [back] of your right hand is very numb and cold. Move a finger on your right hand when you feel it really cold and very numb . . . That's nice . . . It is already pale and its veins are very collapsed. You can open your eyes, if you wish, and see how pale your right hand is . . . and remain in your deep trance.

Suggestion for Control of Bleeding

Milton H. Erickson, M.D.

In your present type of thinking, you do not believe . . . that you could control the flow of blood; that you could cut down on bleeding. Yet you know that the utterance of one single word right now could bring a flush to the face . . . And that is right, because your body has had a lot of experience in controlling the flow of blood, and it is so easy and so simple. And if you can control the flow of blood in your face, well, why shouldn't you be able to control it in your neck; and your neck does turn red and your forehead does turn red, and why not a little bit below. And consider the way in which your body has had experience in turning pale at the thought of something terrifying, and consider the way your body has had many experiences in turning red under heat and turning white under cold. Your body has had a lot of experience; there is a tremendous wealth of actual physiological experience that warrants the expectation that one could build up a hypnotic situation to control capillary flow of blood; and with that capillary flow of blood

you could also control salivary glands, or you could stimulate those glands. You can say a single word to someone that will produce tears. Those tears require an alteration of the flow of blood in the tear glands, and you don't even know how those tear glands are supplied with blood. There is a *wealth of knowledge that exists in your body*, of which you are totally unaware, and that will manifest itself when given the right psychological or physiological stimulation.

Suggestions for Control of Upper Gastrointestinal Hemorrhage

Emil G. Bishay, M.D.,
Grant Stevens, M.D., and
Chingmuh Lee, M.D.
Torrance, California

INTRODUCTION

Bishay, Stevens, and Lee (1984) used the following suggestions in an emergency room setting. The patient had a history of upper GI bleeding for three years and was admitted to the surgical ICU with a diagnosis of "recurrent peptic ulcer disease vs. stomach ulceration, incomplete vagotomy." After the patient was reassured that nothing would hurt her and no one would do anything to her against her will, she was told that if she could relax, her unconscious mind would help control the bleeding. The following suggestions were then given, which successfully controlled bleeding without surgical intervention. (*Ed.*)

SUGGESTIONS

As you lie comfortably in bed, all that you need to do is to close your eyes and take a series of real deep breaths . . . and as you exhale let your body relax as deeply as you can. . . . At the same time . . . imagine how it would feel if you were now lying on your back in some place in which you had pleasant memories . . . a beach perhaps. . . . Feeling the pleasant, cool sand under your back . . . and the lovely cool breeze on your face . . . enjoying an ice-cold drink which you are sipping slowly with great pleasure. . . . Listen to the calming waves . . . and the joyous laughter of kids playing far away. . . . The feeling that you can attain in your body is of complete and total relaxation. . . . Good! You are listening to my voice . . . and drifting into a very pleasant state of mind and body.

You know now that your "unconscious" is controlling your breathing . . . watch how deep and slow it is now. . . . Your unconscious mind is also controlling your pulse . . . your blood pressure and . . . your skin vessels . . . as I can see, these vital signs . . . have already been controlled by your unconscious mind . . . which is already taking very good care of your body. You can allow it to control your bleeding completely. It will cool down and close all the bleeding points in your stomach and esophagus effectively and safely . . . as if it is healing you while you are slowly sipping this refreshing ice-cold drink in your hand. . . . Notice how relaxed . . . comfortable and . . . secure you feel right now when you allowed your unconscious to help you. Your entire body is free from tension . . . and you feel so good! You are doing great! . . . and you have learned how to relax . . . whenever you need the help . . . of your unconscious . . . to make you feel safe . . . secure and happy. [Instructions for self-hypnosis were then given.]

Blood Perfusion Protocol

Lawrence Earle Moore, Ph.D.
San Francisco, California

STEP 1. PRE-INDUCTION TALK.   This is designed to facilitate the hypnotic induction by establishing rapport with the patient, correcting his misconceptions about hypnosis, and allaying his anxieties.

STEP 2. HYPNOTIC INDUCTION.   Typically this proceeds with a formal and direct induction procedure. Eye fixation is preferred because it establishes a precedent for the patient's narrowing focus of attention (later to be on a particular part of the body). This may be followed by progressive relaxation. Trance deepening is not necessary because a very light trance is sufficient for blood perfusion.

STEP 3. IMAGERY FOR PERFUSION.   After the patient has achieved an adequate trance, he/she is instructed as follows: "Picture your strong normal blood . . . flowing from your strong, normal heart . . . through a system of canals* to the desired area** . . . calm and comfortable . . . canals are expanding to facilitate the increased flow . . . pleasurable sensations . . . blood rushing to the desired area . . . you may already feel that area becoming warmer . . . comfortable . . . nothing to distract you now . . . enjoying the warmth and sensation of your healing blood flowing . . . your blood carrying all the building blocks of healing; protein, amino acids, vitamins, etc. . . ." [These suggestions are repeated over and over, with the possible introduction of time distortion.]

STEP 4. POSTHYPNOTIC SUGGESTIONS.   These are given for comfort, motivation, and increased ease and depth in subsequent hypnotic sessions. The desire for continued perfusion can be accommodated by suggesting that something commonly encountered in the patient's environment will trigger said perfusion. For example, the patient can be instructed to watch TV for some hours per day with the perfusion occurring and being maintained each time a commercial appears on the TV screen (clearly she must be prohibited from watching public or non-commercial channels). Hospital personnel (e.g., nurses or technicians) can also be a trigger.

---

*Here is an excellent place for utilization, e.g., a burned truck driver was told to view his arteries as freeways, a plumber as pipes, etc.

**The "desired area" is usually specified, e.g., left hand, right foot. Caution: the patient takes your suggestions *literally*.

HYPNOSIS WITH NEUROLOGICAL AND OPHTHALMOLOGICAL CONDITIONS

Teaching the Other Side of the Brain

Marlene E. Hunter, M.D.
Vancouver, British Columbia, Canada

INTRODUCTION AND INDICATIONS

These suggestions are designed for use in stroke patient rehabilitation, particularly where the damage has been to the left hemisphere, to facilitate recovery of function and feelings of hope. We do not presently have research validation that hypnosis can facilitate enhanced recovery of function, despite the clinical belief that this may be possible. Until we have evidence to the contrary, however, it seems that at worst the clinician has only wasted a few words while simultaneously instilling hope, motivation, and a sense on the part of the patient of being able to do something for himself. (*Ed.*)

SUGGESTIONS

You know that you have been able to perform many functions throughout your life — things like walking and talking and writing and feeding yourself. These became second nature to you many, many years ago. [You already have the information.] Then, three months ago when you had your stroke, you found that very suddenly you were unable to do those very things that you have done automatically for decades. [Calmly stating the fact.]

So the past three months have been very confusing and difficult, because of this strange and frustrating situation. [Acknowledging the feelings, reassuring that they are normal.] In particular, you have had a hard time speaking, because you seem to lose the words that you are looking for. This has been all the more exasperating and depressing because you have always been so articulate.

Your doctor has explained that the stroke affected the left side of your brain, the side where the speech center is located. That is why you are having trouble with your words. However, the *right* side of your brain is fine. [Opening up another possibility.]

Here is an interesting challenge for you, then — *teach the right side of your brain to do what the left side used to do!* [Often they are longing for a dramatic approach — here is one.]

This will be all the more interesting because the right side of the brain seems to be more active in the realm of imagery, music, and creativity, even though we know that both sides of the brain can perform all the various functions, and there is a tremendous cross-over in activity.

[Spoken very gently, but very intensely.] But this is just what you need! Think of the possibilities — the right side of the brain has all the potential that it needs to learn the various speech functions, and it has great powers of creativity, too! [Affirming the validity of the approach. Right side *specifically* designed for such a challenge.]

Because brain activity is physiological as well as mental, you will also need to focus very determinedly on mind/body communication. All the information about biochemistry and neurophysiology must be fully accessible to your subconscious mind, and the information that the subconscious holds must be accessible to the body.

So ask your subconscious mind and your body to get into strong communication, in order to cooperate and collaborate fully in this venture. The project, then, is this: the left side of your brain must teach the right side of your brain what to do, in order for you to find the words you want and speak clearly and freely again. [Restating the original suggestion in a new way: inner learning through inner teaching.]

Did you know that you have a bridge from one side of your brain to the other? You have.

[The concept of a bridge is reassuring—bridges ARE transportation routes.] It is called the corpus callosum. It is a very strong bridge connecting the two hemispheres of the brain. How wonderful that you have a bridge already there! It can be one of the routes that information can take as it is transferred from the left side to the right.

[Combining fact and imagery.] In your own way, create the image of this bridge in your mind, and envision or feel or hear or have the very strongest sense of information traveling across this bridge, from the left side of the brain, to the right.

When it gets to the right side, let it find the exact place to settle—somewhere accessible, where other information coming in, can find it easily and add to it. [The "right side" is symbolic.]

Then, when the information is safely lodged in the right side of the brain, again invoke that wonderful mind/body communication as you direct your right brain to *begin to use that information*! You can be very, very curious about how that will happen. Will you feel like speaking, and find that some promising sound comes forth? Will you say it all in your mind first, and then find the way to make your mouth and tongue work properly? How will it come about?

We know that this will probably take a very concerted effort over some period of time—after all, it took you some period of time to learn how to speak in the first place, so it is reasonable that it will take some length of time for your right brain to learn to do what your left brain has been doing. [Preparing for long effort.]

Stay patient, then—in the long run, this will be the shorter way. Stay patient and calm, and let the left side of your brain, teach the right side what to do. [Mildly confusing statement.]

Remember, too, that there are other ways of transferring information besides sending it across a bridge. [More creative imagery.] Send that information to catch a ride on a passing hormone, for instance. There is great hormone involvement in any learning process. This is

another opportunity for mind/body communication and collaboration.

And then there will be possibilities that only the deepest part of your subconscious mind knows about or has access to; so in your own hypnosis every day, remember to ask your subconscious to use ALL the information that it has, to help you in this challenging project. [Covering all bases.]

You know more than you know that you know. And learning what you already know is a wonderful experience. [Several words with multilevels of meaning are reiterated throughout, e.g., bridge, cross-over, creativity, "right side" etc.]

Once Learned, Can Be Relearned

Marlene E. Hunter, M.D.
Vancouver, British Columbia, Canada

INTRODUCTION

These suggestions were also prepared for use in stroke patient rehabilitation. A similar approach may also be used for the aphasic patient for relearning language and how to speak. These suggestions may also be combined with the previous ones. (*Ed.*)]

SUGGESTIONS

Today I'm going to talk about learning. But I'm going to talk about it in a rather different way. I'm going to talk about learning how to do *something you already know how to do!* [Catching attention with an unusual statement.]

[Setting the background for the statement.] When you were very small, just a baby boy, you had to learn how to walk; to get yourself up on your feet, standing straight, put one foot ahead of the other and take steps to get yourself to somewhere else from where you were.

Your conscious mind hasn't thought about that for decades. Walking came to be such an automatic thing, thinking about it was quite unnecessary. Your subconscious mind recognized, "I want to go over *there* . . .," your body took over, and you went.

[Invitation to realize all the ingredients.] However, a lot of learning, of trial and error, of finding out about the relationship of objects to other objects and most of all, of motor skills, were dedicated to learning to walk, for quite a long time before you were able to walk steadily and safely, to stop and start just when you wanted to and to go in the precise direction that you wanted to go.

Over the years, you have walked and walked and walked. Your body and your brain and your mind have collaborated so often on that activity called walking, that you know all there is to know about it. You even know how to walk backwards! [Curious ability!]

Six months ago a sudden, confusing and distressing thing happened to you: you had a stroke. [Acknowledging fact.] And that stroke affected the part of your brain that was involved in walking. Now your muscles apparently refuse to do what you tell them to do, and they are weak and flabby. You have been going to physiotherapy [physical therapy] diligently to regain your muscle strength in your legs and arms. [Reassuring that he has been doing his best.]

Yet, still your feet and ankles and knees and hips are obstinately staying put instead of going where you want them to go. [Recognizing frustration.] This has been very frustrating; and you know from some of our previous sessions, when we find something to be very frustrating, that indicates that we must look for a different approach. [A problem is an opportunity to do something different.]

Let us explore, then, a new avenue. We can do that by putting the whole situation into a new framework. [Reframing.]

When you were a baby, you learned how to do something you had not done before. Then how about—*again learning to do it*! [The invitation.] Now, THAT makes sense. After all, if

you can learn how to do it once (and when you were a baby, at that), you can learn how to do it again, when you have *all that previous experience about learning*. [Reflecting the opening statement.]

Yes. You have already learned how to learn how to walk. ["Learned how to learn how to . . ."—hypnotic emphasis and further emphasizes the "learn" throughout the script.] Therefore, you can relearn what you already have learned, calling on your subconscious to search out that previous learning and learn to put it to new use.

In order to do that searching, go further into hypnosis now. [Placing my thumb on his forehead again—deepening.] Use my thumb as a focusing point, and go "way down" into hypnosis, as far as you need to go to achieve what you need to achieve. That's right. Good.

Now, let your subconscious mind go back to the time when you were a small baby, just learning how to walk. [Regression.] Go back to the beginning of those lessons—and that beginning may even have been before you were born, when you were experiencing what it was like to move within the ocean of the amniotic fluid. Ask your subconscious mind to REVIEW ALL THAT LEARNING, and find out what you need to know again, as you relearn what you have already learned so many years ago. [Further emphasis, referring to earlier phrases.]

Feel again what it is like to learn how to walk. Let all your senses be clear as you re-experience that—the muscle tone, the awareness of something that you would later call strength, and sense of position, and of how you know your feet are on the ground; the exquisitely complicated movement of the foot as it lifts in a step and swings forward—all there for your subconscious mind and your body, together, to review and re-explore. [Kinesthetic imagery.]

Ask your subconscious mind to review all that old information many times a day, for as many days as it needs to, and then to *redirect that information to the present*. [The information is needed NOW.]

At the same time as your subconscious mind is reviewing that previous learning, you are regaining muscle strength through your therapy, so that soon the two approaches can merge, and you will begin to learn again what you have already known for many decades. [More mind/body communication.] Once learned, skills can be relearned. [Reinforcement.]

This new approach calls for the greatest possible collaboration between mind (conscious and subconscious) and body. Reinforce that collaboration every day in your own hypnosis, reminding yourself that you already know what you are now learning, and you are putting that knowledge to good use as you approach this worthwhile endeavor in this renewed and worthwhile way. ["You already know what you are learning"—referring again to the opening statement.]

Hypnosis with Blepharospasm

Joseph K. Murphy and
A. Kenneth Fuller

INTRODUCTION

Blepharospasm consists of an involuntary spasm and closure of the eyelids associated with involuntary contraction of the orbicularis oculi muscles due either psychological or organic causes. A variety of symptomatic treatment procedures have been followed, including medication, behavior modification, surgery, biofeedback and hypnosis.

HYPNOTHERAPY

The authors used both hypnosis and biofeedback in successfully treating a case. They age-regressed the patient to an enjoyable scene and "he was asked to see, feel, hear and experience himself 'functioning confidently, comfortably with natural blinking in a pleasant sit-

uation' from the past. . . . Go back to a pleasant time in your life before this eye problem began and experience what it is like to blink normally—naturally—remember what it feels like not to need to rub your eyes—enjoy knowing that at this time you have no need to open your eyes with your hands . . . [three-minute pause]. . . . It would be wonderful to bring back this feeling, this understanding, this ability to blink naturally and normally, would it not?"

They found that the patient was able to remain in hypnosis for an extended period without spasms, manual eye opening or eye rubbing. At that point, the patient was told, "Congratulations on your ability to control your eyelid movements. See, Mr. _____ you are in control—your eyes are opening and closing [timed to lid movements]—Now you are having no problem with spasms. . . . I'm curious to find out when you'll actually begin to notice that your eyes are opening and closing [again, suggestions paired with lid movements] naturally in your everyday life. . . . I hope that you will look forward to feeling confident in your ability to relax and to control your eye movements naturally. What I'd like to have you do is this: Why not avoid trying to force open your eyes. When you notice your attention being focused on eye spasms—why not—let that be a signal to RELAX [pause]—RELAX and wait for your eyes to open spontaneously—on their own . . . Just like you have done so well in today's session."

In another session the patient was taught self-hypnosis. He was also given repetitive posthypnotic suggestions for spontaneous eye opening, for relaxation, and for improving function. In still another session some of the following types of suggestions were given.

"You have shown exceptional ability to use hypnosis to RELAX. . . . You have shown good ability to use self-hypnosis. . . . You have demonstrated your ability to blink normally and naturally for extended periods of time using hypnosis. . . . I want you to really realize that you can continue to use these abilities in everyday life—even when you are no longer with me."

Hypnotherapy for Lagophthalmos

Jean Holroyd, Ph.D., and
Ezra Maguen
Los Angeles, California

INTRODUCTION

Holroyd and Maguen (1989) reported the only known successful treatment through hypnosis of a patient who was unable to close her eyelids at night. This condition caused corneal irritation and erosion. Lagophthalmos consists of incomplete eyelid closure, most commonly associated with thyroid ophthalmopathy, but also occurring with ectropion, conjunctival cicatricial diseases, facial nerve palsy, tumors involving the seventh nerve nucleus, and orbital space-occupying lesions. Nonhypnotic treatment for nocturnal lagophthalmos includes patching the eye to protect the cornea, use of lubricants and therapeutic soft contact lenses.

The patient was trained in self-hypnosis and it was suggested that "she could sleep very comfortably all night long with her eyelids completely closed" (p. 266). During the course of her treatment a self-hypnosis tape was also made for the patient to use nightly with "suggestions for relaxation, permissive suggestions for time and space dissociation, permissive amnesia suggestions, and the direct suggestion that her eyelids would be comfortably closed while she slept" (p. 266). The following types of suggestions were reinforced in about eleven appointments. A meaningful image for this particular patient was of her cats sleeping. (*Ed.*)

SUGGESTIONS

Your eyes can be *completely* closed while sleeping; they can close completely when you blink. Your eyelids can be comfortably closed all night, with your lids as if they were sealed. That part of your brain (or back of your mind) that takes care of your body (for eating, drinking, urinating) will keep your eyes closed while

you sleep. You will sleep very deeply, comfortably, with your eyes completely closed, like your cats.

When you are deeply relaxed your body functions optimally. Your eyes can produce more tears, just like actors and actresses. Tears will flow more liberally. They can be happy or neutral tears; they don't have to imply unhappiness. Your body takes in a *lot* of liquid, which goes into producing urine, sweat, blood, tears; it can secrete more tears. Your eyes will be very comfortable with the tear ducts producing more fluid. The ducts will become more active, alive, youthful; will produce more fluid like when you have a happy emotion—seeing a baby, a little kitten or a little puppy. The ducts will produce more and more liquid, day and night, and that will feel very comfortable to you. Your eyes will float very comfortably in that healthy liquid. When your eyes move during dreaming they will be bathed in fluid.

[Permissive amnesia suggestions were usually given:] You don't have to pay conscious attention to what I'm saying because what I say is taken in by your unconscious mind. As this material drifts into the back of your mind, you may forget it in your conscious mind. As you forget with your conscious mind, you'll *know* that it's in your unconscious mind. You may or may not remember what I have said; I have been talking to a deeper part of yourself.

Suggestions for Involuntary Muscle Jerking

Valerie T. Stein

INTRODUCTION

These suggestions were formulated and successfully used by Stein (1980) in treating a case of action (intention) myoclonus. The suggestions were used in four hypnotic sessions after induction, deepening, and suggestions for quietness, relaxation, calmness and internal peace. An audiotape to facilitate self-hypnosis was also made. Sessions were framed as "quiet time" and as a time for healing. Although only the subject of one case report, perhaps hypnosis may hold promise in working with this difficult disorder. I hope the inclusion of these suggestions will encourage such experimentation. (*Ed.*)

SUGGESTIONS

Imagine, now, that hovering over your body there is a globe of bright light; a sphere of warm energy that sends out rays of warmth and healing that penetrate every fiber of your being; body, mind, and spirit. Each ray enters into and merges with the very essence of your being. You can feel the warmth spreading throughout the totality of your body/spirit/mind. This sphere of light and warmth and healing has been sent to you from that which has created and maintains the universe. These rays are warming you, healing you, penetrating and joining with all that is you. Now imagine that these deeply warmly relaxing rays are tapping the powers of the universe and are healing and soothing your spirit, mind, and body. Imagine also, that the sphere itself slowly descends upon and into your being, merging with and becoming part of every aspect of your being, such that now the rays radiate outward from you, forming a glowing shield, encircling your essence. It is warming, relaxing, and healing at the deepest levels of your being. [Suggestions for relaxation, calmness, and quietness were continually repeated. Posthypnotic suggestions for calmness were given.]

Hypnosis with Bell's Palsy

Simon W. Chiasson, M.D.
Youngstown, Ohio

INTRODUCTION

Although we have only anecdotal, uncontrolled reports about the potential contribution of hypnosis with Bell's Palsy, Dr. Chiasson's experience is included for its potential benefit to clinicians. Furthermore, it is hoped that this report may encourage experimental evaluation of hypnotic intervention with Bell's Palsy. (*Ed.*)

THE TECHNIQUE

My results with hypnosis in the treatment of Bell's Palsy have been most rewarding and exciting. Bell's Palsy, along with other neuropathies, is fairly common in obstetrics. One of my friends, a neurosurgeon, claims that it is impossible to close the eye affected by Bell's Palsy or, otherwise, we must be dealing with something else. However, you can use an eye closure hypnotic technique and tell subjects to close their eyes and relax the eyelids so much that even if they try they cannot open them. Then by really trying they can open their eyes. It does not take any effort to close the eyes, but it takes a definite muscular effort to open the eyes. Therefore, I maintain that in Bell's Palsy the eye is kept open by muscle spasm and that when the patient relaxes, the muscle spasm disappears and the eye closes passively. When the hypnosis is discontinued the spasm returns and the eye remains open.

I merely give the explanation to the patient that the nerve is swollen and as the circulation improves the swelling will disappear and the nerve will come back to normal. I also mention taste in my suggestions because in some patients the capacity to taste is impaired on part of the tongue. A paresthesia is often experienced as the nerve is revitalizing. Therefore, I offer the explanation that the feeling of pins and needles is an alarm mechanism and that it is a good sign and means that the nerve is returning to normal. It would be inappropriate to have the patient create an analgesia again through hypnosis because that is what we are working to overcome. I simply tell the patient that since we know that normal function is returning, she might as well be comfortable while this is happening.

These explanations may not be physiologically accurate, but they seem to be reasonable explanations that are accepted by the patient, and they have produced effective results with five cases. I cannot infer from only five cases that hypnosis is the answer in treating Bell's

Palsy. However, I hope that others will pursue the use of hypnosis with this condition, although I also charge you not to neglect any traditional method of treatment.

HYPNOSIS WITH SLEEP DISORDERS

Suggestions with Sleep Disturbance

Richard B. Garver, Ed.D.
San Antonio, Texas

Your unconscious mind has a memory for virtually everything you do, and this includes your sleep behavior. It has a memory for good, high quality sleep, and it has a memory for sleep disturbance. Your unconscious will be selective in reviewing your sleep behavior, and will focus on the memory, the very positive memory, of good quality sleep, sleeping deeply and continually through the night and waking up refreshed in the morning.

[Always include the protective suggestion:] If you need to awaken through the night for an emergency or any physiological need, of course you will do so, but otherwise you will sleep through the night with good, comfortable sleep. Any memories of disturbed sleep will be ignored, and unless there is anything that's important that we need to know about that's keeping you from sleeping, you can sleep comfortably. If it is important that we need to know something that is interfering with your sleep, which is known by your unconscious mind, I suggest that it will surface into your conscious awareness before we meet again, so that you can tell me about it. Or, if we need to at another time, we can ask your unconscious mind exactly what it is that is interfering.

EXPLORATION OF UNCONSCIOUS DYNAMICS. I think it is important to explore unconscious dynamics only if necessary, and not just because the patient is very curious to know what might be interfering. I believe the unconscious mind usu-

ally wants to accept a more positive, comfortable, efficient, and effective program, so long as it does not cover up a problem or coerce a symptom away.

SUGGESTIONS TO POTENTIATE MEDICATION. [If it has been deemed beneficial for the patient to be taking a sleep medication for a brief time, another useful strategy is to give hypnotic suggestions to potentiate that drug:] Your unconscious mind will make the best use of these medications, directing them, using them to help you experience a very good quality of rested, continued sleep, until awakening refreshed in the morning. And your unconscious mind will memorize the therapeutic effect of this, and perhaps even the chemistry behind it, so that when you taper off the sleep medication, your unconscious mind will continue to produce the therapeutic effects of that medication.

Suggestions with Sleep Disorders

Doris Gruenewald, Ph.D.
Laguna Hills, California

INTRODUCTION

Following preliminary history gathering and assessment, the induction should be geared toward a relaxed, dream-like state, but always taking the patient's personality and defenses into account. Avoid motor tasks and emphasize fantasy, even if the patient has not shown much talent for it.

IMAGERY

Imagine yourself walking leisurely along a path that winds through . . . [choose the kind of scenery likely to appeal to the patient]. Feel the springy, soft ground under your feet . . . enjoy the green foliage . . . the light, gently weaving through openings . . . the increasing darkness as you enter deeper . . . deeper . . . [etc.]. Soon you see a fork in the path . . . one side leads to a place of deep relaxation, the other side leads more directly to sleep [adapt suggestions to the patient's needs]. You can choose which side you want to enter. [This choice is important for those who have trouble giving up control.] You want to enter the side of sleep. Soon you will feel even more drowsy than you already are . . . drowsier and drowsier . . . sleepier and sleepier. Soon you will drift off into a deep, natural, healthful sleep. [Repeat "sleep." The patient may actually fall asleep, in which case it is well to allow a brief period before awakening.]

STAIRCASE IMAGERY

Imagine yourself going down a softly carpeted stairway . . . slowly . . . step by step . . . you count each step until you are all the way down. [Therapist counts slowly to 10 or 20.] At the bottom of the steps you see a room, and you know that this room is there for you . . . for you alone. You enter this room. It's the most comfortable room imaginable and it looks exactly as you want it to be. [Describe if indicated.] There is a wonderfully inviting bed in this room. You realize immediately that it is there for you. [The patient's own bedroom may be used.] You lie down in the bed and enjoy the comfortable firmness [or softness] of the mattress, the silky feel of the sheets, the pillow adapting itself to the contours of your head. You sense, you know, that this is where you can sleep, as much as you want. Feel the pleasant drowsiness taking over more and more. Before long, you drift off into a natural, relaxing, restoring sleep . . . [etc.]. [If a tape is made of these suggestions, instruct the patient to arrange for automatic shut-off of the recorder.]

Visualization for Treating Insomnia

H. E. Stanton, Ph.D.
Hobart, Tasmania, Australia

1. Visualize a soft, black velvet curtain which has a warm, comfortable feeling about it. As thoughts enter your mind, allow these to drift across the curtain and disappear out of the other side of your mind, then return to a contemplation of the curtain. [Pause]
2. Then imagine yourself on the veranda or patio of a lovely house which has 10 steps leading down to a beautiful garden below. For each step you descend, allow yourself to let go more and more so that, when you reach the foot of the steps, you feel a sense of peace and relaxation. Enter the garden, noticing the colors of the flowers, the drifting clouds, the sound of birds singing, the rustle of leaves in the trees, and the pleasant warmth of the sun. [Pause]
3. Continue to visualize the garden, picturing yourself lying on the grass, enjoying the warmth of the sun on your face. As you lie there, watch the leaves as they fall slowly from the trees nearby, reminding you that it is possible to let go of old problems and worries, allowing them to drop away, just as old leaves drop away from trees, to make way for new growth.

THE TROPICAL ISLAND

In this tropical island fantasy, you visualize yourself standing beside a jungle pool into which a waterfall is splashing. You slide into the pool, finding the water warm and inviting. This warmth begins at your feet and calves, then your thighs, body, arms, and neck as you wade in further, immersing yourself completely.

As you swim towards the waterfall, you notice a flat rock, large enough to stand upon. This you do, allowing the warm water from the waterfall to cascade over your body, massaging it and soothing away all worries, tensions, and problems, leaving behind a wonderful sense of serenity. Every muscle, nerve, and fiber in your body is at peace.

Move out from under the waterfall and stretch out on the smooth, sun-warmed rock which is surprisingly comfortable. The warmth flows into your body from the rock and, together with the fresh air, the sunshine, and the soft jungle sounds in the distance, creates a comfortable, drowsy feeling within you, a feeling that becomes more and more all-encompassing as you drift off into the realms of sleep.

Hypnosis Techniques with Insomnia

David Spiegel, M.D., and
Herbert Spiegel, M.D.
Stanford, California, and New York, New York

[The Spiegels use a technique similar to their method with anxiety, experiencing floating while viewing an imaginary screen. (*Ed.*)] Patients are instructed that they cannot stop the flow of their thoughts if they are having trouble sleeping, but what they can learn to do is dissociate physical from psychological tension. They are instructed to use a screen to act as a traffic director for their own thoughts, projecting them out onto the screen rather than experiencing them within their body and thereby maintaining a high state of physical arousal that makes sleep more difficult.

Suggestions for Insomnia

Milton H. Erickson, M.D.

You use an awful lot of energy staying awake. You resort to every conceivable measure of preventing sleep. Now, if you sleep and rest yourself thoroughly, you will have an oversupply of energy. What would you really like to do with that energy? What constructive or instructive or developmental project would you like to undertake to use up that extra daily allotment of energy? You've got to direct it elsewhere [rather] than in keeping yourself awake. That nice rest each night is going to replenish your energy. How are you going to use it?

Snoring: A Disease of the Listener

Daniel A. Zelling, M.D.
Akron, Ohio

INDICATIONS AND CONTRAINDICATIONS

Where snoring is a serious problem, clinicians may want not only to treat the spouse as Zelling creatively suggests, but also to be alert to the possibilities of sleep apnea. Referral to a sleep lab will be necessary for accurate diagnosis of this condition. The suggestions that follow will undoubtedly prove most beneficial with patients who enjoy the ocean and sailing or ocean cruises. (*Ed.*)

INTRODUCTION

The myth is that snorers can or should be treated; the truth of the matter is: *snoring is a disease of the listener* and only the listener should be treated. A qualified medical hypnoanalyst can treat the listener not to be bothered by his or her spouse's snoring. After all, the engineer on an ocean liner, with all the noise of the engine room, can sleep when he is off duty. And with self-hypnosis and proper imagery, the listener can learn to ignore the noise or incorporate it into his or her own mental imagery. The imagery that I have found to be very effective is for the listener, in self-hypnosis, to imagine that he or she is on a large, wooden sailing vessel, falling asleep on the deck.

SUGGESTIONS

Have you ever been on a beautiful, ocean-going sailing vessel with the sting of a salty spray on your face? I want you to imagine, to picture in your mind's eye, or to just pretend that you're on a beautiful, large sailboat: The hull is knifing through a surging breaker. You hear the gulls and the creaking of the wooden mast under a full load of canvas: the clatter of the rigging; the squeak of the boom—all the sounds of the ocean and the sailboat. And you feel yourself lulled asleep on a beautiful sailing vessel. You listen to the creak of the wooden mast. It is so relaxing . . . so peaceful . . . the wind in your face; the salt spray from the ocean; and you are lulled to sleep . . .

You can use this image at night. At night when you go to sleep, the noises that surround you can fit into this image. Some of the noises of the house, some of the noises from other people can fit into this beautiful image, as you're on this large, old rigging sloop. So peaceful and tranquil. A quality ship on the high seas.

And you can let this ship take you wherever you want to go. Whether this is a pleasure trip on a Sunday afternoon to Cape Cod or the Bahamas, or yachting on the Riviera. Just close your eyes and allow yourself to be there in your mind's eye. The sounds of the ocean, the creaking of the mast, the sounds and sensations of a voyage. Hear the clatter of the rigging, hear the cries of the distant gulls. All the tension leaves your mind as the boat gently rocks you to sleep; floating . . . drifting . . . dreaming. So relaxed, so peaceful . . . Just sailing away . . . Sailing away . . . See the sun getting lower and lower on the horizon as the gentle rocking motion of the sailboat lulls you to sleep . . . Peaceful and tranquil . . . The creaking of the mast: so peaceful, so comforting. The buoys in the distance, the clanging of the bells on the buoys, as you continue your voyage, hear the bells, feel the rocking motion. Feel, hear and experience this pleasant voyage as you rest . . . really rest. And you can get back on board anytime you want. See what you're seeing now. Feel what you're feeling now, as the sounds fade and you drift. Peaceful and tranquil.

Always allowing yourself time to rest on your voyage of life, on the sea of life. The reassuring sounds of Mother Ocean that people have listened to since the beginning of time. Solid wood under your feet and a tall mast, swaying in the wind as you drift and float and dream, allowing the vessel to take you wherever you want to go as you continue to float and drift and dream.

MISCELLANEOUS MEDICAL APPLICATIONS

Hypnotic Techniques and Suggestions for Medical-Physical Complaints

Beata Jencks, Ph.D.
Murray, Utah

INTRODUCTION

The following suggestions and methods reflect Jencks' tremendous breadth of experience with not only hypnosis, but with autogenic training, yoga, mazdaznan, acupressure, massage, meditation, T'ai Chi, Zen, and other Eastern therapeutic measures. There is a simplicity about many of Jencks' procedures. For example, she emphasizes the use of breathing rhythms and often has patients repetitively think suggestions in the form of single words or phrases as they inhale and/or exhale. She has thoughtfully provided us with elegant therapeutic methods for working with a variety of medical conditions not commonly addressed in standard texts. Some of her suggestions are suitable to be given directly to patients, in the form of posthypnotic suggestions. Many specific suggestions for imagery are also provided. (*Ed.*)

NOSE AND THROAT DISORDERS

GATE.   Swallow hard and feel the place in the throat where the constriction during swallowing occurs. Imagine at that place a gate which can be opened and closed at will. Feel the gate closing when swallowing. Allow the gate to open wide during an exhalation. Imagine again the Lake in the Mouth [that the mouth is like a dark, warm cave with a lake at the bottom], and then imagine during exhalations opening a water gate at the place where you imagined the gate. Feel during exhalations the water from the imagined lake stream downward through the throat. Feel how far down into the chest it may flow during consecutive exhalations.

SHOWER OR WATERFALL IN THROAT.   Imagine a warm waterfall or shower running down inside the wide open throat during exhalations, or just think "warmth and moisture are flowing down." This is good for soothing sore or dry throats.

NOSE AND SINUSES.   Relax the jaw, throat and tongue. Think of the mucous membranes of the nose and sinuses during exhalations. Feel the air stream down. Disregard the inhalations for the present. Feel the spaces become wider during exhalations; feel them become moist; feel them warming.

Compare the effect of exhalations versus inhalations in the nose and sinuses. Feel the warmth and moisture during exhalations; feel the coolness and drying effect during inhalations. Feel widening, softening, and relaxation in the whole mouth-nose-eye area during exhalations. Feel constriction during inhalations.

For a running nose think "cool and dry" during inhalations and "calm" during exhalations, or disregard the exhalations. For a stuffy or dry nose think "warm, wide, and moist" during exhalations and "light" or "opening up"

during inhalations, or disregard the inhalations.

A cough or a tickle in the throat may be controlled by using both exhalations and inhalations. Thoughts like "calm," "warm," "moist," "comfortable," or "relaxed" should accompany exhalations, and "fresh," "cool," or "very still," inhalations.

OPHTHALMOLOGIC PROBLEMS

EYE COMFORT.   Close the eyes and note how they feel. Are they tense? Dry? Burning? Is there movement? Think of the hollows which surround the eyes. Are the eyes comfortable in their sockets? Consider what might do the eyes good in their present condition and choose from the following. For removing tensions, think "let go," or "loose" during exhalations. Also, the following should be thought or imagined during exhalations. To counteract dryness, imagine the eyeball swimming in a warm saline bath. For calming disturbing movements, think "calm and still," "a calming palm cups my eye," or "dark and comfortable." During inhalations, on the other hand, think "cool air streams through my eyelids," or "light and cool," or use both phases of the breathing rhythm by thinking for burning eyes "moist" during exhalations and "cool" during inhalations, or imagine the eyes "floating . . ." during exhalations, and add " . . . in cool water" during inhalations.

Sit back comfortably and work slowly. Exhale gently and close the eyes. Feel coolness gently streaming up the nose during inhalation. Exhale gently and relax the tissues around the cheekbones and above the eyes. Permit the eyes to move under the closed lids. Relax completely during a deep exhalation. Imagine during an inhalation that the inhaled air streams in through the closed eyelids, and think "my eyes are getting cool." Relax with an exhalation and repeat. Feel the forehead widen and expand above the eyes during inhalation. Relax during exhalation. Repeat. Sit back, relax for a moment, and allow the breathing to resume its natural rhythm.

Follow the above routine as close as possible, and incorporate whatever feels best from the following list of thoughts to be used during inhalations and exhalations respectively. The items in the two columns are interchangeable according to individual needs. Use any or all.

Thoughts During Inhalations
My eyes are getting cool.
My eyeballs shrink.
The space inside my forehead expands.
My eyes feel light.
The space between my eyelids and my eyeballs
    increases.
My eyesockets expand.
My eyelids become light and thin.
My eyelids float.
The visual center in the back
of my head seems refreshed.
The top of my head seems to
become wide and open.

Thoughts During Exhalations
My eyes are getting warm.
The pressure around my eyes feels relieved.
The space behind my eyes seems to enlarge.
My eyes become soft.
Moisture fills the space between my eyelids and
    my eyeballs.
My eyeballs are floating.
My eyelids become soft and warm.
My eyes sink back softly.
My eyes become very relaxed.
My chest and abdomen relax comfortably.

PULMONARY DISORDERS

MANAGING REAL AND APPARENT BREATHING RESTRICTIONS.   Work with the imagination is especially important for easing restricted breathing. Imagining anything that will remove a barrier or block, make something impenetrable permeable, soften a hard resistance, or change the direction of a movement may work. Greatest success is attained if the exercise is constructed according to the previous question, "What does the restriction feel like, and what, just in your imagination, could counteract this particular kind of restriction?" Success is highly individual.

SIEVE.   The diaphragm may be imagined as being permeable, so that whatever can be imagined to flow through it can do so. The movement during a relaxing "letting go" of the breath during exhalation may be felt as a streaming or flowing downward into the lower abdomen or down and out of the body. It can be felt while lying down, sitting, or walking and will always have a very relaxing effect. Just imagine the diaphragm to be a sieve. Feel during exhalations that something streams downward and outward or downward and inward. Relax deeply with the streaming and allow the abdomen to stay relaxed during the following passive inhalation.

TENNIS COURT.   If there is a feeling that not enough air can be inhaled, this exercise is helpful. Imagine that if the surface space of all air sacs of the lungs was spread out, it would cover an area approximately as large as a tennis court. Breathe, and imagine doing it "with the whole tennis court."

VERTICAL BREATHING.   This exercise works especially well for real physical restrictions, such as body casts or corsets, but also for being very still and calm for a long period of time as is necessary for an actor on stage when he plays being dead. Breathe very slowly and relaxedly while imagining that the breath moves up and down a vertical tube inside you. This tube can be between throat and pelvis, extend from the crown of the head to the toes, or even extend along the vertical axis of the body out into space.

RELIEVING SHORTNESS OF BREATH.   For relieving shortness of breath or the feeling of suffocating, press firmly under the nostrils with two fingertips. Breathe through the nose while moving the pressing fingers outwards toward the cheekbones.

TRAP DOOR.   To relieve a restricted feeling in the region of the diaphragm at the end of an exhalation, give the diaphragm a little push with the last breath, and imagine that the bottom were dropping out of the diaphragm, or that it were opening up like a lowering trap door to a room below.

INVIGORATION EXERCISES FOR ALERTNESS

[Jencks invigoration exercises are designed to produce alertness, a "lightness of the spirit," and feelings of being alive. Although many of the exercises involve imagery, some of the exercises may be done with the eyes open, performed in a short period of time, and do not involve hypnosis. (*Ed.*)]

SIMPLE INVIGORATION.   Imagine stretching the arms and legs and feel very much alive during inhalations. Also just inhale with an invigorating thought, such as "alive and anew," "aware and awake."

ENERGIZING.   Stretch and flex the limbs during inhalation while imagining energy rising up along the spine. Relax, and repeat.

ALERTNESS.   If the attention lapses during mental work, inhale and imagine that oxygen comes as energy into body and mind, and that it sweeps away all tiredness and "cobwebs of the mind."

AWAKE BREATHING.   If you are not alert enough to be adequate to an occasion or job at hand, your breathing may be too shallow. Allow the breathing to become as awake and aware as the task or situation demands, but at intervals revert to your natural rhythm, allowing sighing or yawning to occur naturally. Again and again enliven your breathing with refreshing inhalations.

SWEEPING OUT TIREDNESS.   Exhale forcefully and deeply and imagine that you are sweeping out, flooding out, or flowing out all slag, sludge, and foul air. Then inhale and imagine fresh, cool, vitalizing, invigorating air streaming in. Repeat as necessary.

BODY ALERTNESS.   Make a short, quick, alert survey of your body and ask: Do the shoulders allow alertness? Are the eyes alert? Are the ears fully awake and attentive? What about the chest, the arms? Drive out drowsiness where it lingers. Do groins, hips, and buttocks interfere with the alertness of the upper body? Are feet and legs aware and awake? Check once more the head-neck-shoulder region. Inhale and then resume your activity.

ENERGIZING WALK.   Do this in reality or in the imagination. Walk rhythmically, about four steps during inhalation, hold the breath for about four steps, and exhale during the next four steps. Adjust the speed of the steps to your physical and mental condition. However, take more steps during exhalations and/or holding the breath than during inhalations. Adjust the vigor of the inhalation to the need of the body. Very consciously end the real or imagined walk with a deep, refreshing, energizing inhalation.

CLEAN AIR.   Imagine walking through fog or smog during a long, slow exhalation. Then, during inhalation, imagine coming up and out of the fog or smog into clean, clear, snowy, sunny, cold mountain air.

JOGGING.   Imagine jogging leisurely on a good surface in a place which is pleasant and enjoyable. Let it have the right temperature, the right surface on which to run, the right landscaping. Breathe in rhythm with the imagined jogging.

MANHOLE.   Imagine jogging happily along or walking rather fast. Suddenly step into an open manhole. Let this surprise take away the breath. No harm was done, but you are really stirred up and awake.

COUNTERSTRETCHING.   Strengthen and energize the head and neck region by turning the head slowly right or left, the chin toward the shoulder, inhaling while turning the head and lowering it toward the shoulder and exhaling while bringing it back to the starting position. Do this so slowly that the motion is barely visible. Breathing in this exercise is opposite to that for relaxing the head and neck and is invigorating.

DOUBLE DOOR.   For invigoration of the shoulder and neck region, imagine a double door in the region of the shoulder blades. Allow its two parts to swing open widely during inhalations. Let them close during exhalations. Imagine that a cool, fresh breeze enters while it opens. Become calm and self-possessed while it closes.

FACE TREATMENT.   Imagine an invigorating massage of the skin of the face. Imagine drumming on it with the fingertips. Feel a water massage from a refreshing shower or raindrops, or feel little hailstones bouncing on different parts of the face. Feel the deeper tissues massaged during exhalations. Feel the fast, vibrating, exhilarating impact on the skin while inhaling in small, interrupted, almost gasping steps. End with a deep, refreshing inhalation.

ICE PLUNGE.   Imagine diving into a pool cold enough to stop the breath. Imagine coming out of the pool and relax. Inhale for new vigor and energy.

COLD SHOWER.   Inhale deeply in short steps and imagine the cold water of a shower beating on shoulders, head, chest, and neck. Feel the vibrations and the sting of the cold water jets. End with a deep, invigorating inhalation.

CLIMBING TO AWARENESS.   Imagine climbing stairs or a mountain during inhalations. With each step imagine climbing into greater and greater wakefulness and alertness. Keep the exercise short to prevent overventilation.

LIGHT BULB.   Imagine a little glowing, warm light bulb on top of your head. Make it float down the back of the head and along the spine during consecutive exhalations while allowing it

to warm every vertebra and melting any tensions. Then let it ascend during consecutive inhalations, filling the spine with energy and invigoration.

FINGER AND ARM INVIGORATION.   Invigorate the fingers with about five small, strong, flexing movements during a stepwise inhalation. Exhale while letting the hand relax, then repeat. Initiate movement of the arm, hand, and fingers from the shoulder blade region and imagine that the forearms or fingers, like those of a string puppet, are supported and moved by means of strings from an outside force. Remember that lifting and lightness are associated with inhalations. Permit the fingers to be soft, light, liquid, and sensitive, or heavy, precise, and hard like little hammers according to the work they must perform. Experiment with the breathing while doing this, so that it aids the actions.

INTEGRATION BREATH.   Imagine or do the following. Hold the arms straight down in front, hands folded, palms down. Raise the outstretched arms slowly above the head during inhalation. Feel the invigoration. Bring the folded hands behind the head and press the palms together about five times while holding the breath. During exhalation raise the arms with the folded hands to full height and slowly lower them to the starting position. Repeat three times.

MENTAL INVIGORATION.   Try any or all of the following. Imagine during an exhalation "shaking water off the fur," or "shaking dust off the mind." Then, during the following inhalation, allow clarity, order, and invigoration to enter body and mind.

Imagine during inhalations that coolness and vitality flow into the head. Relax the body during exhalations. End on a refreshing inhalation.

Relax completely during an exhalation. Allow the limbs to become heavy and the mind empty and floating. Then, during the ensuing inhalation, imagine or feel vibrations and think of physical and mental invigoration and re-newal. Repeat about three times.

Do the Long Breath [see this exercise in Chapter 6]. Then after an exhalation, inhale deeply and "send the invigoration up into the mind."

AWAKENING.   For awakening after sleep, or for coming out of a relaxed altered state of con-sciousness, inhale and make small stretching movements with fingers and toes. Either move several times during one long inhalation, or inhale stepwise while moving the fingers. Relax during exhalation. Lengthen the spine during inhalation. Feel it stretch and become longer. During exhalation relax again, but in a more refreshed manner. Then, during the next inha-lation, imagine plugging yourself into your new battery for recharging. Repeat this for several inhalations. Then stretch and flex the limbs, inhale, and start getting up. If young and healthy, get up with an inhalation to increase vigor and vitality. If weak and not so healthy, get up during an exhalation in order to preserve strength and avoid wasting energy.

CONSERVING AND INCREASING ENERGY

[In addition to the following exercises for enhancing energy level, Jencks advocates building as many rest periods as possible into one's daily routine and keeping the body as relaxed as possible. (*Ed.*)]

GOLDEN THREAD.   For being calm and relaxed, yet feeling alive, imagine a golden thread through the crown of the head and down the spine. Imagine that this thread is your center of calmness.

SOLAR PLEXUS OR STORAGE BATTERY.   The solar plexus is a network of nerve fibers, located at the level of the sternum, behind the stomach, in front of the spine. Its fibers radiate like a sun. The solar plexus region is a very good place for storing and conserving energy in the imagina-tion. Inhale and exhale while imagining charg-ing a battery there, or filling a reservoir with energy.

RESERVOIR OF ENERGY.   Create a reservoir for conserving and holding energy in the lowermost abdomen, in the region of the navel, or in the chest. Get energy during inhalations. Hold it, and possibly increase it while holding the breath. Think of endurance during long, slow exhalations. Imagine during inhalations that something starts glowing within you, or imag-ine a beam of light in the reservoir. Relax those parts of the body which are not involved in the building of the energy reservoir during exhala-tions. Use the reservoir as a place from which to draw energy in an emergency. Energy can thus be built up and "preserved" for several days before some event, in order to reach a peak of energy for a game day, a contest, or in a special event.

CALM BASE.   For being still and calm, inhale and exhale a few times deeply. Then find a comfort-able balance between relaxation, tension, and real or imagined support for the limb, the whole body, or the mind, whatever is to be the "calm base." From this base let well-aimed aggression proceed, be it in pistol shooting or in an argument.

PUMPING STRENGTH.   Breathe in and out sharply and imagine pumping energy and strength di-rectly into any body part or limb which needs it. End the pumping with an inhalation. If an exertion follows, hold the breath for this.

ATHLETIC WARM-UP.   The efficiency of a warm-up is increased and muscles remain more relaxed and invigorated if movements are consciously made as follows. For greater flexibility make forward movements and stretch, or overstretch, during exhalations. For invigoration make for-ward movements and stretch, or overstretch, during inhalations. Mix the two consciously during the warm-up. Inhalation also develops tension, and stretching during inhalation should alternate with relaxation during exhalation, so that the proper balance between the two is maintained.

PARTIAL RELAXATION AND INVIGORATION. Relaxation or invigoration alone may not be appropriate. Learn to combine invigoration of one part of the body, or tension of one part of the body, with relaxation of other parts. Remember that exhalation produces relaxation and inhalation produces invigoration or tension. Learn to bring a specific part of the body to the required state of invigoration or tension, and then relax the rest of the body. For example, relax shoulders and neck during exhalation, and during inhalation invigorate an arm for special movement, such as playing an instrument or a throw in athletics. Unnecessary tension in shoulders and neck hinders the freedom of the arm for easy, yet controlled, movement and must be released with exhalations.

ENDURANCE. Endurance may be increased by alternate relaxation and invigoration. If, for instance, an arm must be held for a prolonged time in a raised position, feel it light and invigorated during inhalations, feel it relaxed and easy during exhalations. Design your own exercises for increasing endurance using the entries in the table [found in Chapter 6].

EFFICIENT HANDS. To prevent tension while writing or working with the hands, imagine initiating the movements from the shoulder blade region or the elbows, not from the forearms or hands. Let the shoulders sink and relax the arms and hands repeatedly while working. Invigorate the fingers periodically by making small flexing and stretching movements.

DELEGATING ENERGY. Imagine the Rubber Joints [an exercise where ankle, knee and hip joints are imagined as flexible rubber] for relaxation and balance. Then, during an inhalation, gather the full breath and imagine during the next strong exhalation forcing all the inhaled oxygen into back, arm, fingers, or wherever energy is needed, for forethought, energetic action.

COUNTERACTING NAUSEA

Imagine inhaling "coolness" into the stomach area and exhaling through a place in the body as far removed from the stomach as possible. Then try to talk to the stomach and tell it to relax and calm down. Nausea is evoked by the parasympathetic nervous system. Do anything possible to divert the mind at the same time as stimulating the sympathetic nervous system.

GENITO-URINARY DISORDER

EXCRETION. The excretion of urine, feces, and menstrual flow can be influenced by the imagination and the breathing rhythm. The general rule is that increased excretion is evoked by thoughts of warmth, relaxation, or flow during exhalations. Decrease is effected by thoughts of tension, stoppage, or cold during inhalations. Depending on the purpose, inhale, tighten the muscles, and think "hold!" or "cold!" or relax during repeated exhalations and think "warm and comfortable" or "movement and flow are easy."

Paradoxical Self-Hypnotic Assignment for Chronic Urinary Retention or "Bashful Bladder"

Gerald J. Mozdzierz, Ph.D.
Hines, Illinois

[This approach was utilized in a case report, following self-hypnosis training through an eye-roll technique with the patient.] The patient was also given an "assignment" to go to the ladies' room at work every 45 minutes, preferably when others *would be present.* She was then instructed to "drop her drawers," position herself on the toilet seat, ready herself to void and then to roll her eyes upward and "let it happen." But, she was told that the purpose of the exercise was *not* to have her urinate but to have her more relaxed and accustomed to the restroom setting. She was to wait only a brief period for the relaxation to take effect (perhaps a minute or so), then leave. She was not to expect any urine output immediately.

Hypnosis in Postoperative Urinary Retention

Simon W. Chiasson, M.D.
Youngstown, Ohio

INTRODUCTION

There is not one gynecologist or surgeon who has not been plagued by the vexing problem of urinary retention, especially following extensive anterior colporrhaphy; however, it may occur following abdominal surgery or a hemorrhoidectomy. The problem may occur seldom or often, depending on the surgery performed or the individual involved in the procedure. I believe that the most frequent reason for the problem is the discomfort in the operative area, causing reflex bladder spasm. The only genuine anatomical obstructions are due to incorrect estimation in a sling procedure or overcorrection of the suburethral area with resulting spasm and edema.

This technique is not very time-consuming. It takes only about 10 to 15 minutes, time well spent in patient-physician relationship. I am reporting here the verbalizations used in successfully treated cases.

PROCEDURE AND SUGGESTIONS

CHIASSON'S INDUCTION. The patient is lying in bed, as comfortable physically as possible. She is properly oriented in understandings of hypnosis, and any special questions about hypnosis are answered. She is told to put her hand in front of her face, about 8 to 10 inches away, with the forearm parallel to the body. The fingers are held together and the hand is turned so that the patient is looking at the back of the hand. At this moment the verbalization is begun:

"Watch your hand and, as your fingers begin to separate, your hand will feel lighter and will gradually float down towards your face. When your hand touches your face, your eyes will close if they are not already closed, and you will become completely relaxed. [This is repeated until the desired effect is initiated.]

"As your hand comes closer and closer, your eyelids will get heavier and heavier. It doesn't matter which part of your hand touches your face: it may be your thumb, the back of your hand or your fingers, but when your hand touches your face, you will feel deeply relaxed.

"That's fine. Now that your hand has touched your face, let it move slowly down to your side and as you do so you can become even deeper and deeper relaxed. [The patient is then given suggestions to relax all muscles from the tip of the toes to the top of the head.]

"To help you get more deeply relaxed, imagine that you are standing at the top of a nice wide stairway with soft carpeting on the stairs, and as you come down the stairs you go deeper and deeper into relaxation.

"You step mentally on the first step and the carpeting is soft and thick, and the padding is thick underneath it. This gives you such a nice, pleasant, comfortable feeling that you want to transmit it to your whole body, and you feel more comfortable and more relaxed.

"You make every muscle in your body twice as relaxed as it was a moment before [each such suggestion for various muscle groups is timed with the patient's breathing and is given as she exhales]. Let your toes relax — feet — ankles — heels — legs — knees — thighs — hips — all the muscles in your pelvis — your abdomen (from your chest margin down to the middle of your thighs, inside and out, front and back) — all your chest muscles, and with each breath you go deeper and deeper — all your back muscles — your shoulders and arms — elbows and wrists — hands and fingers — all your neck muscles — every muscle in your face and even the muscles of your scalp and forehead. Nice and loose and relaxed, twice as relaxed as they were a moment ago.

"You get on the second step and the carpet is thicker and the padding is thicker and you feel more comfortable and more relaxed, and again you let every muscle become twice as relaxed as it was a moment ago.

"You get on the third step and the carpeting is so thick that it feels almost like sponge rubber. You go deeper, deeper and deeper, and again you let every muscle become twice as relaxed as it was a moment ago.

"When you get on the fourth step, the carpeting is so thick it feels as if you were walking on three to four inches of sponge rubber, and you feel more comfortable and more relaxed. You go deeper and deeper, and again you let every muscle be twice as relaxed as it was a moment ago.

"On the fifth step the carpeting is so thick it feels as if you were walking on air. You go deeper, deeper and deeper—and again, you let every muscle be twice as relaxed as it was a moment ago.

"On the sixth step it is as if there was no step at all, just as if you were walking on air. You feel more comfortable and more relaxed, no tension and no resistance. You go deeper, deeper and deeper.

"You get on the seventh step and it is just as if you were floating on a cloud—a nice soft, white, billowy cloud, and you feel more relaxed and go deeper, deeper and deeper.

"On the eighth step just imagine it pulling out wide like a big foam rubber mattress and your whole body melts right into it, right into it, and you get a pleasant, heavy feeling throughout your whole body. You go deeper and deeper.

"On the ninth step it is as if there were no step and no mattress, just as if you were floating along on 'Cloud Nine' with a pleasant, heavy, comfortable feeling and you go deeper, deeper and deeper.

"When you reach the tenth step you have reached the spot where, with every breath, you can go deeper and deeper until you reach the deepest point of relaxation for you at this particular time.

SPECIFIC THERAPEUTIC SUGGESTIONS. "As you continue to relax you will become aware of all of the relaxation in the pelvic muscles. The circulation will be better, your healing will progress more rapidly. When you feel the pressure building in your bladder and all the muscles around the neck of the bladder relaxing, raise your right index finger. [Alternately, an involuntary ideomotor signal may be called for. (*Ed.*)]

"That's fine. Now when I count to three and you become completely alert you can retain the relaxation in your pelvis, and you will be able to empty your bladder, and each time you will do it more and more easily."

Hypnotic Paradigm-Substitution with Hypochondriasis

Thomas Deiker, Ph.D., and
D. Kenneth Counts, Ph.D.

INTRODUCTION

These suggestions were used successfully in a single-subject design study (three sessions) in treating a 59-year-old woman with hypochondriacal neurosis. Her symptoms included weakness, low energy, nausea, diarrhea, and dizziness in the absence of medical ailments. Importantly, she also stated, "I haven't got any family or personal problems." She spent a great deal of time lying on the sofa. "The experimental paradigm-substitution sessions consisted of providing detailed cognitive beliefs relating to general mental health concepts, which were suggested to be incorporated amnestically between sessions." Although these illustrative suggestions were from only one session and are specific to the case, they illustrate a technique that may have potential benefit with hypochondriasis and that provides an alternative to uncovering and insight-oriented treatment methods. Since psychophysiologic complaints may both cover serious psychopathology or stem from organic conditions, however, clinicians are encouraged to do careful psychological and medical evaluation prior to using such techniques. (*Ed.*)

SUGGESTIONS

When you wake up you will feel as relaxed as you feel now, but there will be a change, an important change that will affect your daily life. The change will be in your mind, the way in which your mind works, the things that your mind thinks about. It's not that you will have no more problems, just the *kind* of problems you have, the kind of problems your mind thinks about, will be different. When you wake up you will think of yourself as a person with "problems in living." Everyone has problems in life. Problems in living. Sadness or nervousness bother most people at times. These feelings could have many sources, problems with family or friends. Feelings of loneliness or lack of purpose are other problems in living, or feelings that the future has little to offer. These are the problems that bother many people. Maybe some of these bother you. Maybe it's something else. You haven't had time to think about these important problems because of your other concerns. Now you will have time to do so, because your mind will be very curious to discover such problems in living in your own life, and you will be very eager to discuss them and solve them, because one of the changes in your mind will be much greater confidence in being able to solve these problems with hard work. Your other problems won't have gone away, but they will seem less important than these problems of living. You will feel good about yourself, proud of your courage and honesty in dealing with important problems in life. These problems will be just as important as your other problems, just as serious, interfere with your life just as much, will bring you the sympathy of those around you, but will be ones that you can solve, that hard work will overcome. Your other problems, your physical problems, worrying about physical problems has prevented you from being able to devote your energy to these more important problems in living. That is

another reason that physical problems, even though they are still there, will not seem as important, you won't spend as much time and effort thinking about those problems, not even important enough to spend time thinking or talking about.

Suggestions with Asthma

Don E. Gibbons, Ph.D.

If you ever feel any more attacks coming on, or even if one has already started, you will be able to place yourself in trance very rapidly, just by closing your eyes and silently repeating the necessary suggestions to yourself. Then you will be able to drive away the symptoms completely by slowly counting to fifty, with each count taking a deep breath and clenching your fists, and then unclenching your fists and letting your body relax as much as possible each time you let a breath out, silently repeating to yourself the word *calm* each time you exhale. And when the count is completed, you can terminate the trance in the usual way, feeling fine once more.

Suggestions for Prevention of Seasonal Allergies

Hans A. Abraham, M.D.
Palm Beach, Florida

The vast expanse of the United States has some blooming or pollinating plants at all times. There will be some pollens in the air at all times, not enough to cause symptoms. Nevertheless these minute amounts of pollens enter the system and will act similarly as the desensitizing injections from the allergist. There will be a gradual increase of the airborne pollens, desensitizing your body. When the pollen season in your area is upon you, you will be prepared, and although there may be some symptoms in the first year, they will not be enough to cause any disability. And season after season, the symptoms will be negligible until they have disappeared completely.

Erickson's Metaphor with Tinnitus

Milton H. Erickson, M.D.

Now I am going to give you a story so that you can understand better. We learn things in a very unusual way, a way that we don't know about. In my first year of college I happened to come across that summer a boiler factory. The crews were working on twelve boilers at the same time, and it was three shifts of workmen. And those pneumatic hammers were pounding away, driving rivets into the boilers. I heard that noise and I wanted to find out what it was. On learning that it was a boiler factory, I went in and I couldn't hear anybody talking. I could see the various employees were conversing. I could see the foreman's lips moving, but I couldn't hear what he said to me. He heard what I said. I had him come outside so I could talk to him. And I asked him for permission to roll up in my blanket and sleep on the floor for one night. He thought there was something wrong with me. I explained that I was a pre-medical student and that I was interested in learning processes. And he agreed that I could roll up in my blanket and sleep on the floor. He explained to all the men and left an explanation for the succeeding shift of men. The next morning I awakened. I could hear the workmen talking about that damn fool kid. What in hell was he sleeping on the floor there for? What did he think he could learn? *During my sleep that night I blotted out all that horrible noise of the twelve or more pneumatic hammers and I could hear voices. I knew that it was possible to learn to hear only certain sounds if you tune your ears properly. You have ringing in your ears, but you haven't thought of tuning them so that you don't hear the ringing* (p. 104). . . . And you think back; *there are a goodly number of times this afternoon when you stopped hearing the ringing. It is hard to remember things that don't occur. But the ringing did stop. But because there was nothing there, you don't remember it. . . . Now the important thing is to forget about the ringing and to remember the times when there was no ringing. And that is a process you learn.* I learned in one night's time not to hear the pneumatic hammers in the boiler factory—and to hear a conversation I couldn't hear the previous day. . . . I knew what the body can do automatically. [Pause] *Now rely upon your body. Trust it. Believe in it. And know that it will serve you well.*

Procedure with Difficulty Swallowing Pills

Irving I. Secter, D.D.S., M.A.
Southfield, Michigan

I want you to visualize someone other than yourself, who has the same problem you have. Signal that you can see this person sharply and clearly as if on a TV or motion picture screen, by letting your right index finger come up. [Patient signals.]

Notice this person is trying to swallow a pill. He chokes on it. His throat muscles tighten and he fails to swallow the pill. You know how he feels, don't you? Signal "yes" with your finger. [Patient signals.]

Is this person male or female? [Patient responds.] Observe now, our friend has been given the signal to "relax." He [or she] does so completely, mentally and physically. His throat muscles relax and he feels good all over. Note that you can share these feelings with him, too. Acknowledge this with the finger signal. [Patient signals.]

Now let our friend disappear from the picture and see yourself there in his place. OK? [Patient responds.] Now see yourself on the screen getting the signal to "relax." Do so completely, mentally and physically, both on the screen and in person. See yourself swallowing a pill without any difficulty and take pleasure in your success. From now on, whenever you need to swallow a pill or anything else that has given you difficulty, the touch of the pill to your tongue can be a signal for complete relaxation, and the pill can go down without any difficulty. Are you willing for this to happen? [Patient responds.]

Shall we practice this in the alert state?

Suggestion for Alleviating Hiccups

Gerald J. Mozdzierz, Ph.D.
Hines, Illinois

INTRODUCTION

This suggestion pertains to helping children and adults to rid themselves of a case of simple hiccups. This distressing symptom can interfere with a clinical interview or physical exam, and yet I have found that it can be quickly relieved. I have no knowledge of the derivation of this technique or if it has ever been described in publication form. I only know that I have used this approach to help any number of people to rid themselves of this oftentimes distressing spasming of the diaphragm which results in an abortive attempt to inhale.

THE TECHNIQUE

The technique begins with the common practice of eliciting the patient's permission. Thus the patient is asked if he/she would like to be rid of the hiccups. Most often the person will respond affirmatively. It is always better to elicit permission for such simple procedures since it demonstrates respect for the patient and greatly facilitates cooperation and therapeutic efficacy.

Next, the person is asked, "Please stare in my eyes and make every effort not to blink. That is all that is required. Breathe normally . . . that's right . . . just continue to stare in my eyes and breathe normally. That's right."

The suggestion above may be repeated over and over with simple variations. I have usually found the suggestion to be successful within one minute. I have no idea why the procedure is effective; I only know that it is very effective. One can speculate that the patient is completely distracted and, hence, relaxed by the eye fixation and attempting not to blink, so that normal breathing is returned.

The therapeutic effectiveness of the procedure can greatly enhance the credibility of the therapist for helping the patient to be relieved of this discomfort. Of course, the therapist should politely give credit to the patient for effecting the "cure."

HYPNOSIS IN OBSTETRICS
AND GYNECOLOGY

INTRODUCTION

HYPNOSIS HAS BEEN widely used in obstetrical care, particularly in hypnotic childbirth training. August (1960a), for example, performed more than 1,000 deliveries using hypnosis as the sole anesthetic. There are a variety of advantages that may result from the use of hypnosis in obstetrics. Hypnosis may be successfully used to reduce pain in delivery, reducing the need for medications and chemo-anesthesia, thereby eliminating its risks and post-delivery effects for both mother and child. It may additionally facilitate comfort in suturing the episiotomy. Hypnosis has proven successful as the sole anesthetic for childbirth in between 58% and 79% of cases (August, 1960, 1961; Fuchs, Marcovici, Peretz, & Paldi, 1983; Mody, 1960; Mosconi & Starcich, 1961), with an average among studies of 69%. Another potential advantage of hypnosis is seen in the widespread reports suggesting that it may reduce the average duration of labor by two to four hours (Abramson & Heron, 1950; Callan, 1961; Davidson, 1962; Fuchs et al., 1983; Mellegren, 1966).

Hypnosis has also proven extremely effective in the treatment of hyperemesis gravidarum, vomiting in the early stages of pregnancy. Success rates of 75% and greater are common with this problem (Fuchs, 1983; Fuchs, Brandes, & Peretz, 1967; Fuchs, Paldi, Abramovici, & Peretz, 1980; Henker, 1976).

Another important area of hypnosis application is in the care of patients with problems of premature labor. The incidence of premature labor has not decreased significantly in recent years (Caritis, Edelstone & Mueller-Heubach, 1979), despite advances in technology; hypnosis has the potential to enhance patient care and minimize risks and expenses for such patients. Hypnosis and self-hypnosis training may modify negative attitudes, anxieties and fears concerning childbirth. Zimmer, Peretz, Eyal and Fuchs (1988) recently found that mothers who used hypnosis for anxiety and stress management had fetuses who moved in a much more active manner than a control group.

More impressively, Omer (1987) and Omer, Friedlander and Palti (1986) have documented that brief hypnotic interventions produced significantly greater prolongation of pregnancy in women with premature labor than a medication treatment group, confirming earlier case reports (Lugan, 1963; Schwartz, 1963). Omer's approach to managing premature labor is presented later in this chapter.

Finally, it should be noted that hypnosis has also been used to promote and to suppress lactation (August, 1961; Cheek & LeCron, 1968; Kroger, 1977) in obstetrical patients.

Like any other therapeutic method, hypnosis has limitations. Obstetrical hypnosis requires that the patient have some hypnotic training prior to delivery, and, of course, not all patients will be adequately responsive to hypnosis. However, group hypnotic training is often conducted in a way that enhances rapport and satisfaction with patients and requires minimal time.

Hypnosis has also been used to treat a variety of gynecologic complaints. I have personally found hypnosis to be of considerable benefit in evaluating and treating dyspareunia (painful intercourse), and I have successfully treated (with long-term follow-ups) several chronic and resistant vaginitis (vaginal infection) cases. Hypnosis has been successfully used in the treatment of dysmenorrhea (painful menstruation) (Leckie, 1964), amenorrhea (Crasilneck & Hall, 1985; Erickson, 1960; Van der Hart, 1985), leukorrhea (vaginal discharge) (Leckie, 1964), pseudocyesis (false pregnancy), and post-menopausal symptoms (Crasilneck & Hall, 1985).

In approximately 50% of infertility cases the cause cannot be determined. It is widely believed that a proportion of these cases result from psychological factors—a belief that is reinforced by the common experience of couple's finally adopting a child out of frustration, only to conceive a child of their own a few months later. Unfortunately, we only have uncontrolled and anecdotal case reports (e.g., August, 1960b; Leckie, 1965; Muehleman, 1978; Wollman, 1960) of the potentially positive impact of hypnosis with resistant infertility. This is an area of potentially fruitful research.

We should also be aware that there is a variety of painful gynecologic procedures for which hypnotic analgesia may be helpful. Finally, there are several well-done investigative reports (Stalb & Logan, 1977; Willard, 1977; Williams, 1973) documenting that hypnosis may be used to induce breast growth. We do not yet know whether this phenomenon is mediated through vascular flow changes, endocrine effects, or a combination of the two, but it illustrates the power of mind-body interaction.

OBSTETRICAL HYPNOSIS: CHILDBIRTH TRAINING

Group Hypnosis Training in Obstetrics

Simon W. Chiasson, M.D.
Youngstown, Ohio

INTRODUCTION AND OVERVIEW

When I initially began using hypnosis, I treated patients on an individual basis. But after the original fascination wore off, I discovered that I was using up too much time. Therefore, I adopted a group training model with which I have been very pleased.

I consider the following aspects most important:

1. Group hypnosis training saves time for me.
2. I spend one and a half hours twice a month with the group and this allows a larger number of patients to achieve a greater depth in the hypnosis and to be exposed to a greater variety of techniques.
3. The patients are able to exchange experiences in the group.
4. The answers to questions by any member of the group help the entire group.
5. The spirit of competition helps some patients to attain a greater depth.
6. Group preparation is stressful for some patients. However, if patients who are rather anxious in groups are still able to achieve a hypnotic state under these conditions, they will have a better chance of achieving it in labor, which is another stressful condition.
7. The classes give a much better chance to educate the patient about the misconceptions that make labor and delivery such an ordeal.

I use a permissive technique that also enables me to help patients from outside my obstetrical practice. Many patients are referred to me with problems amenable to hypnosis. If I were to take time with each patient referred or asking for help with hypnosis, I would have to give up obstetrics and gynecology. However, I can accommodate a great number of these patients by teaching them hypnotic techniques in the group situation and then spending a short period of time with them on an individual basis.

I make no effort to induce my patients to use hypnosis. However, because of past patients who have used hypnosis and referrals for hypnosis, I still have a great many who choose this modality. Because of the understanding of hypnosis that the teachers of Lamaze have in our area, they no longer resist the use of hypnosis. At one time they felt that if a woman was using Lamaze she was controlling the situation, but if she was using hypnosis she was under someone else's control. I was able to demonstrate to them that their use of methods like eye fixation and breathing and counting were actually self-hypnosis. I helped them realize that no one actually hypnotizes a patient, but that we are teaching women how to go into a hypnotic state and use it for their own benefit.

I use a permissive approach with my patients. They are invited to come in and observe at least one class. At this time every effort is made to correct any misconceptions they may have concerning hypnosis and to give them a basic understanding of how hypnosis can be beneficial for them. It is explained that only 20%–35% of patients are able to go through labor and delivery using hypnosis alone. However, it is explained that, if they do need medication or anesthesia, less will be required than without hypnosis. They are informed that if they do not feel completely relaxed they may ask for medication to help them. They are told that they never have to feel that they are letting me down if they do not use hypnosis all through the delivery. After all, they are using hypnosis for their benefit, not mine.

I no longer use any one particular induction technique; rather, I seek to fit the technique to the individual. But, since I am using a group approach with about 20–25 patients, I have them close their eyes and I tend to use a counting technique, counting backwards from 100 to 0. I go from 100 to 80 in increments of 1, and then from 80 to O in increments of 5. I also offer suggestions after each count of 20. After counting down to 0, I ask them to picture themselves doing something they would find particularly enjoyable. It is suggested that, as this becomes more and more vivid, they can go deeper and deeper.

I no longer use dissociation to imaginal scenes during delivery. I used that technique in the very beginning. However, it seems silly to me to have a woman taking an imaginal trip 1,000 miles away on a beach, or even imagining sitting in a chair observing the birth process, while she is delivering. I believe that she should know that she is having a baby but that it does not have to be painful. Nevertheless, dissociational procedures are valuable when repairing an episiotomy, although even in this situation I give patients a choice of technique. I ask, "Do you want to simply picture yourself doing something enjoyable or do you want me to use a local anesthetic?"

TECHNIQUES AND SUGGESTIONS

The verbalizations I use for obstetrical patients vary with the problems. I usually give the following suggestions at every 20 number interval (e.g., at 80, 60, 40, 20, and 0) during the counting technique.

"The remainder of your pregnancy will be so much better. Your labor will be shorter, easier and safer. Your stay in the hospital will be so much better. When you are in labor and when you are in the hospital, you can use your contractions to get more and more relaxed, and to make every muscle in your bottom nice and numb, loose and relaxed. [These are the muscles that have to relax when the head is coming down and delivering.] If I put my hand (or if the nurse or your husband puts a hand) on your shoulder, you can use this as a signal to go deeper and deeper."

While the patients are deeply relaxed they are told about the "breakthrough periods," and how to use them to their advantage. First, when they are 6–7 cm. dilated, they may feel discouraged and that they are not getting anywhere or that no one is paying much attention to them. They may even feel nauseated. It is explained that if they are checked at this time and found to be 6–7 cm. dilated, then they should know that within a half an hour or less they will be completely dilated.

The second "breakthrough period" is just before they are completely dilated. They feel like pushing and if they push they feel uncomfortable because they are pulling down the whole uterus. It is not helpful to tell them not to push; instead they are told to take in a big breath and let it all out, or pant like a puppy, and then they cannot push. The last "breakthrough" is when the head comes through the cervix. Sometimes this occurs suddenly and with great force. They are told that this is what they were waiting for. If they have had a baby before, they will be ready to deliver in three or four contractions. If this is their first baby, they can use the contractions. "By pushing down, the more you push, the better it feels. And with each contraction, you can relax more and more, and make all the muscles in your bottom nice and numb, and loose and relaxed."

Patients are also told that when their contractions are 10 minutes or less apart, they should get ready to go to the hospital. "And when you get in the car, you can feel just as if you are sitting in this chair. And by merely putting your right hand on your left shoulder, and closing your eyes, picturing a color, and taking a deep breath, as you gradually let that breath out, and that hand sinks all the way to your side, you will be deeply relaxed." Patients are told to repeat the self-hypnotic induction again in the prep room to make the prepping and examination comfortable. "And each contraction and each background sound or noise will simply help you stay more relaxed." They are further told, "The remaining part of your pregnancy will be so much better. Your labor will be shorter, easier and safer, and your stay in the hospital will be so much better." They are also instructed to practice self-hypnosis.

I stress relaxation primarily, but glove anesthesia may be produced during a group session and transferred to the chin with suggestions to keep the numbness in the chin for five minutes after alerting from trance. This serves the purpose of providing trance ratification. It is pointed out that they can transfer the numbness anywhere.

I seek to see the patient in labor when she is 2½–3 cms. dilated. If I am delayed, however, our nurses and residents are familiar with supportive measures and are very helpful. If the patient is having difficulty relaxing, the resident usually asks what method she uses to relax, and during the process of explaining her self-hypnotic technique, the patient will usually induce a hypnotic state. If the patient needs medication it will usually not be until shortly before delivery, and then in most cases she will only require 25 mg. IV of Demerol.

SUGGESTIONS FOR HYPEREMESIS. "You can replace the dirty metallic taste in your mouth with a minty taste or the taste of your favorite toothpaste. And as you relax more and more, all your muscles will be twice as relaxed and your circulation improves on the inside and outside of your body, especially through your intestinal tract. As the circulation improves, all the peristaltic waves, the waves that move the food along the intestine, will be nice and smooth, beginning with the esophagus, the tube from the back of your throat to your stomach. And the food will go down nice and easy, and be broken up in the stomach and passed to the small bowel to be digested and absorbed. All the peristaltic waves will be nice and smooth. Each time you brush your teeth, you will reinforce the nice relaxed feeling and have this pleasant taste in your mouth."

EXCESS FLUIDS. "As the muscles relax more and more, the circulation improves on the inside and outside of the body, bringing the fluid back into circulation from the tissues, and helps the kidneys to work more effectively."

HEADACHES. "As the muscles relax, the circulation improves on the inside and outside of the body, especially through the brain. And since the circulation is normal, the vessels will not dilate or constrict; therefore, there should be no headaches."

Outline of Hypnotic Suggestions in Obstetrics

Bertha P. Rodger, M.D.
Palm Harbor, Florida

ADVANTAGES

- Versatility, flexibility, *adaptability* to individual and situation.
- Reduces or eliminates *drugs* for sedation, analgesia, anesthesia. *anxiety* and *pain* controlled without interference with physiology of mother/child.
- Answers *dependency* need, fostering mother's *maturity* as she learns to *pursue goal* despite suffering or difficulty. Satisfaction and *joy* in participating, whatever the circumstances.

PREPARATION

- Weekly *classes* of 10-20; question and discussion *save time*.
- Present as natural, *inborn ability* to control input for purpose of controlling output (behavior).
- Methods of *induction* and *deepening* taught as *auto*hypnosis.
- *Stages* of labor explained, special approaches suggested.
- Posthypnotic *suggestions* with a copy to *take home*. Rapport established with person of choice for *reinforcement* prn.

LABOR

- *Normal, psychological act* (as such, does not have to cause pain!).

- Does not have to be learned. *Body knows how!* Made to perform appropriately.
- Done *unconsciously* so the less attention to it, the better. *Muscles* of arms, legs, digestive tract, uterus, *contract* and do their work. *Recognize* the *pleasant sensations* of *hardening*: the feelings of accomplishment and *strength*.
- *Contractions = powerful* mechanism by which baby will be born into world. Hard work gives greatest satisfaction. *Look forward* to this result. Parents truly *co-creators* with God, bringing new life into the world.
- Term *"labor pain"* common. *Transpose* to *"contraction." True meaning* = a most useful device, a *tightening* and hardening which = *motor* part.
- *Welcomed* as each brings *goal* nearer. Stirs emotions of *placidity*.
- *Calmness* and pleasant *anticipation* of *fulfillment*. Use as a *signal* to go into *trance* as needed, relaxing excess tensions so *energy* goes where it's needed. Come *out* of trance as if from a pleasant *nap, refreshed* and *happy*. As *cervix* dilates from 1-10 cms., can go *deeper* and deeper and be *more* and more *comfortable*. (*Saves* both psychic and physical energy as both cervix and perineum relax in readiness for delivery.)
- *Full dilation: Familiar* sensation as head moves into birth canal. Signal to *notify attendant*. Important *step* forward. Now any discomfort in sacral area and thighs disappears spontaneously. Strong *desire to push* is *controllable* according to instructions. *Pressure* of descending head *numbs* unpleasant sensation (like elastic band on finger).

CONDUCT OF LABOR

Stage 1. Free to *enjoy* resting, relaxing, *reverie* of all the happy experiences leading up to your becoming a *co-creator* with God; *all love* in your life . . . whole *mosaic*. Can go into *trance* with each contraction, even

each procedure (enema, IV, etc.). Report unmistakable change to next stage.

Stage 2. Need to be doing something *active*. Counting Techniques, especially *pendulum* (e.g., counting a pendulum swinging from 1 to 100, or 2 to 99) or counting time in seconds, starting with 100, 99. Can *notice* how *pressure* actually does numb birth canal. Increasing *anticipation* of *seeing* baby . . . look forward to *holding* it. . . . Watch what is going on in the *mirror*.

Stage 3. Attention focused on *baby*, bath, footprinting, etc. Time to *review* with crystal clearness all the interesting and *delightful* sensations and experiences connected with having a baby so as to *share* when you wish.

Walking upright (as if with book on head) and *sitting squarely* numbs area of episiotomy nicely. (Minimizes irritation of rubbing buttocks).

Own doctor will tell you what *signs* to watch for, appraise you of what to expect, interpret what is happening and how you can help.

POSTHYPNOTIC SUGGESTIONS FOR LABOR AND DELIVERY

1. Each contraction can be considered as a pleasing occurrence, drawing you nearer to your goal . . . bringing a new love for your enjoyment.
2. You can feel it as a hardening, a tightening, a wonderful power working for you. You can welcome it, using it as a signal to go deeper into the state of comfort (trance).
3. The moment it starts to go, you can forget it completely. It has passed.
4. You need pay attention only to the voice speaking directly to you.
5. You can be quite calm, confident and cooperative throughout.
6. A pleasant sense of anticipation can replace any apprehension.
7. You can recuperate quickly, completely and comfortably.

ADDENDA

- You can feel your contractions to the point of satisfaction of your own curiosity, enabling you to share the experience with the rest of the female population who have had babies, assured thereby that you are really dealing well.
- You may feel it necessary to pay for this joyful experience with some pain, or need some TLC after it. Turn on your abdomen, relax into a lovely lassitude while gravity aids in draining all congested areas and realize you don't need those pills after all!
- Prolonged contraction of muscle in fear or in splinting causes it to ache just because of interference with its circulation.
- The odds are tremendously in favor of having a healthy, normal child, and doing it easily!
- Teach patient to deepen trance to count of 10 with the number 10 as the "deepest trance you can imagine." And then reports of the dilating cervix in cm. implies or can be given as a signal to deepen trance in a like manner.*

DEVICES TO AID COMFORT

1. Simple *relaxation*; trance prn: Can double the effect of medication, *halve* pain.
2. *Reverie*: Passes time quickly, pleasantly, sends messages to body to perform efficiently, heal rapidly.
3. *Time distortion*: Time of contraction passes "like a flash" leaving plenty of time between to rest and enjoy.
4. Deliberate *redirection* of attention from discomfort to *comfort*.
5. *Reinterpretation* of sensations in terms of familiar and pleasant.
6. Teach *glove anesthesia* and *transfer* (can do it mentally to difficult spot).
7. Revivify *saddle block* (epidural), tuning out any unpleasant part. trance.

---

*This suggestion comes from Belinda Novik, Ph.D.

8. *Dissociation* to another place, can "sit over there and watch."
9. *Posthypnotic Suggestions* provide helpful mind-set. *Reinforce* by reading at home in trance.
10. Feel sensation through *wall of numbness*.
11. As cervix *dilates 1–10 cms*, go *deeper* into comfort to count of 10.
12. *Counting* especially. Pendulum to occupy attention prn.

Suggestions for a Comfortable Delivery

Joseph Barber, Ph.D.
Los Angeles, California

When a woman wants to learn hypnosis for a comfortable delivery without chemical anesthesia, it is my practice to request that her husband participate in the process (as many husbands now participate in the delivery). At the outset I indicate to the couple that our goal is to enable them, as a team, to create as much comfort, excitement, and joy as possible during childbirth. I generally begin by hypnotizing the husband, asking that the wife pay close attention to the process. During hypnosis I suggest to the husband that while in the hypnotic state he is well able to know how to hypnotize his wife, since he can better empathize with her needs, for example:

"Now you know the comfort of this state, and, even though you remain in this state, feeling comfortable, you can enjoy watching your eyelids begin to open, and as you look over at your lovely wife, you can begin, even as you sometimes pay attention to me, you can begin to say things to her that you feel will help her to feel more of what you are feeling. You can begin now to share this experience with your wife."

As the husband begins, I serve as coach, providing additional cues and suggestions when needed, attempting to develop a state of mutual hypnosis for the couple. As this process continues, the husband is coached to provide suggestions to his wife for analgesia during labor and delivery, for example:

"You'll be doing hard work, but you've done hard work before. And there will sometimes be such a lot of pressure, maybe more than you can remember feeling before, but you don't need to be surprised by it. You can just notice how easily your mind seems to somehow ease the pressure, letting it spread and flow, without blocking, knowing that there are no other feelings to bother you or disturb you. And your physician can talk to you, and the nurse can talk to you, and you can easily pay attention to whatever you need, all the while letting the pressure come and go, sometimes feeling so excited that you're soon going to get to see your baby. And since you're preparing for this ahead of time, training your nervous system so that this natural experience can be quite comfortable enough, you can also know that you are preparing for any eventuality. So that, no matter what situation might occur, no matter if there are delays or surprises, or whatever, you still have the freedom and ability to do whatever is necessary for your comfort. And I'll be there with you, reminding you of what we're doing, if you forget. And you don't even have to pay attention to me if I'm distracting you. You can just do whatever you need. The noise, the lights, the unfamiliar feelings are all just a part of what is for you the most natural experience in the world. And you might sometimes find yourself thinking, as the work goes on, and as the pressure builds, you might sometimes enjoy thinking about later, either in a few minutes, or a few hours, about holding our baby outside your body, not inside, and getting to look at our baby. And whenever I squeeze your hand, like this, you can just let go and remember how really far away and quiet and comfortable you can feel, and how nice it is to be able to rest between work."

The husband is also taught how to provide noxious stimulation, such as squeezing the skin of his wife's inner thigh, for the purpose of their practice outside the office, so that the wife can experience analgesia in advance of labor and develop confidence in her ability to

create analgesia on her own. The couple is encouraged to practice daily and to return in a week, at which time their experience is discussed and any difficulties are explored and remedied. Generally, there are four such appointments.

A couple's relationship obviously plays a significant role in determining the pace and ultimate success of such a technique. In couples looking forward to the birth of their child and in women motivated to handle their delivery with hypnosis, this approach generally leads to quite happy results. Difficulties arise when the couple does not really want a child or if other aspects of the situation create fear or resentment. If, for instance, a woman wants her husband's support but he is unable or unwilling to give it, this issue must be faced before going further. A woman may learn to use her independence and autonomy in this situation; she may be able to locate an obstetrician willing to assist her in her use of her own psychological abilities, without the need to use her husband's help. Other difficulties arise if a woman has difficulty allowing her husband to help her, as was the case with one patient who initially giggled whenever her husband attempted to offer her suggestions; subsequent discussion revealed that the woman did not seriously believe her husband capable of any intellectual or emotional help to her in any situation. Our work became reoriented toward the wife's learning and practicing self-hypnosis and allowing the husband to "just share the experience," although by the time delivery occurred the couple had been able to move into the roles we originally attempted, and 15 hours of labor were experienced with little effort and no discomfort.

Advance training in pain control is easier than using hypnosis when pain is already being felt because learning to feel and maintain comfort is easier when pain, anxiety, and fatigue are not interfering. Certainly clinicians can help untrained patients during labor or other potentially painful experiences with hypnotic techniques, but in such cases attention needs to be paid initially to the fact of the discomfort and then to how it might change.

The Hypnoreflexogenous Technique in Obstetrics

A. Kenneth Fuller, M.D.
Gainesville, Florida

INTRODUCTION

Fuller's suggestions are adapted from the work of Werner, Schauble and Knudson (1982). They use a verbal conditioning technique to (1) overcome fear of delivery with positive feelings that reframe maternity as a special experience, (2) substitute the concept of contraction for pain, and (3) presumably reduce the excitability of the cortex through psychological sedation. You are referred to Werner's original article for further details concerning the rationale for these suggestions. (*Ed.*)

SUGGESTIONS

In the hypnoreflexogenous technique you may notice that we exalt maternity and enliven you with the emotion which the happy waiting and the precious moment of birth represent. You, through your own conscious and active participation, can maintain this emotion throughout labor. Each contraction can be considered as a pleasing occurrence which draws you constantly nearer to the goal of delivery, closer and closer — with you being able to actually see your baby and hold your baby, because a contraction is a motor part necessary in order for you to have your baby.

I want you to fully understand that this method works even for women who have had previous bad experiences and who may believe that drugs and anesthesia are the only ways to stop pain. You have the chance to understand that at any time during labor and delivery, you can readily have whatever medication you want, when you want it. This serves to help overcome your past fears. Probably medication will not be necessary, and if required will be only a small amount. In regard to the time of onset of labor, the uterus does not break the harmonious, hypnotic, relaxing calm of your body. When labor begins you will experience little or no discomfort. You may ask yourself, or your doctor, whether you may be in labor; the important thing is this: Your only symptoms are the natural contractions manifested only by periodic hardening of your womb. In some cases, where a complete blocking of discomfort is not obtained, women find discomfort so distributed that it is felt mainly at the level of the lower back as a discomfort similar to that during your period, or a heavy aching in both thighs. The back and upper thigh discomfort stops quickly and spontaneously when the dilation of the cervix is complete. You may look forward to this because it is a positive sign, indicating that the time of delivery is near.

After delivery you may vividly remember these words: "In the next few days you will pass your water without being catheterized; you will move your bowels without enemas; you will have a good appetite; the food will appeal to you; the nursing staff will appeal to you; you may have a few sutures, but they are not going to bother you — you will hardly know that they are there; the entire stay in the hospital will seem like a pleasant vacation." The effectiveness of your calm, fearlessness, motivation and training provided your child with the opportunity to be born without feeling any guilt for causing you any pain during labor and delivery.

You may benefit by entering hypnosis at some point — it is your right, your privilege to do so, if you wish, to stay in this state of pleasant expectation throughout labor and delivery. However, you will probably not need to enter hypnosis during labor, since you will not be uncomfortable. During the training sessions, you are being taught three techniques which produce the absence of pain and discomfort. First, you should understand and really understand that if at any time during labor or delivery you experience discomfort from an intense contraction of the uterus, automatically, without thinking, you will lapse into the deepest hypnotic state you can attain and remain in it as long as the contraction lasts, after which you will be completely comfortable again. Or, if the labor has gone on for quite a while and you would like a little nap, you may remain in the hypnotic state through several contractions or even through the rest of the labor and delivery.

Second, you can use the technique of allowing yourself to go to a pleasant place in your mind's eye. Really have a sense that you are there, that you are seeing the things that you see there, you are feeling the things that you feel there, you are hearing the things that you usually hear when you are at this place, enjoying yourself, being pleasant and comfortable. Continue to fully experience this and while you are there you may notice that you're noticing different sensations while you are in this place, this comfortable, pleasant, tranquil place where you can relax. While you are at this place nothing seems to bother you, you are just enjoying the moment there.

Third, why not learn to use a technique whereby you divide your body into two parts, an upper and a lower half. Now, I want you to include the uterus in the lower half. When you have done this, then you can awaken the upper half and learn to permit the lower half to remain asleep. . . . You may use these techniques in any stage of labor but usually, if needed at all, it will be at the end of the first stage for the lower backache type discomfort; during the second stage to push the baby out or to produce pain control for an episiotomy or any tear that might have occurred. The fact is you may not find it necessary to use any of these techniques at all. Now emphasis throughout hypnosis training in obstetrics is that you are not preparing to undergo a surgical procedure, but you are preparing to perform a normal, natural, physiological act.

Childbirth Suggestions

Larry Goldmann, M.D.
Fort Myers, Florida

1. Labor is a normal, physiologic process.
2. The contractions of the uterus are no different from the contractions of any other muscle of the body.
3. Surely you will feel the power of your contractions, but they are nothing more than muscular contractions.
4. Remember that each contraction carries you closer and closer to the delivery of your baby through a normal vaginal delivery.
5. Each contraction will be perceived as you desire, not as others would have you perceive them.
6. Your unconscious mind will cause you to become relaxed with each contraction—the stronger your contractions become, the deeper will be your relaxation.
7. Your husband's voice will be as relaxing to you as mine.
8. Your confidence in yourself and your partner will grow with each contraction.
9. You will look forward to each contraction, realizing that each one carries you closer and closer to the delivery of your baby.
10. Labor and delivery are exciting, enjoyable experiences that you can share with your partner in a relaxed, comfortable setting.
11. Remember that while you are in labor you are always in control.
12. You can have your baby your way—relaxed and completely in control.
13. You will find your husband's touch and voice to be relaxing and reassuring to you.
14. You will find that when your husband places his right hand on your left shoulder, you will become very deeply relaxed, when appropriate, without any effort on your part.
15. Just as you experience no discomfort when the muscles of your heart, intestine, or bladder contract, you will experience no discomfort when the muscles of your

uterus contract — for these are all normal physiologic functions.

Management of Antenatal Hypnotic Training

David Waxman, L.R.C.P., M.R.C.S.
London, England

SUGGESTIONS

In every confinement [labor], there are three separate and distinct stages. The first and longest of these is concerned with the necessary preparation for the birth of the child. This could not occur unless time were given for all the muscles to relax, and the passages to widen and dilate sufficiently to permit the passage of the baby. Once these are wide open, the second and more active state occurs. During this, the child descends through the passages, and eventually emerges and is born. When this has happened, there is still the final stage, which is not completed until the afterbirth [placenta] has come away.

Now, probably the first sign that you will have that labor has started is a slight show of blood, almost as if a monthly period were beginning. With this you will feel some weak contractions of the womb, with long intervals between them. Sometimes, the show does not occur, and the only sign of commencing labor is the presence of these weak, infrequent, but regular uterine contractions. When you first feel these, look at the clock and time them. No matter how long elapses between them, if they are occurring at regular intervals, you have probably started in labor, so either send for the midwife, or go straight into the hospital according to your previous arrangements. *You must not induce any hypnotic trance until this has been done.*

During this first stage, you will find that the contractions will be weak, and will not occur very often. They will gradually cause the passages to open up, but this is a slow process and takes time. They will cause so little discomfort to begin with, that the only thing you will need to do is to sleep as much as possible, and to relax. You will be able to do this by putting yourself to sleep and relaxing in hypnosis as you have been taught. Because of this, you will feel the contractions merely as pressure in your stomach, and they will not distress you at all. If anything, or anyone disturbs you, you will immediately put yourself straight off to sleep again, as a result of which your labor will progress more steadily and easily. You will remain perfectly calm and unworried, and not in the least bit afraid.

Later, as the passages open up, the contractions will become stronger, heavier and more frequent. You will not become frightened or try to resist this, because this is perfectly normal and helps the baby to be born. This is a sign that your labor is progressing well. You will be able to stay in your trance and remain relaxed by taking a series of deep, rapid, rhythmic breaths. With each of these, you will relax more and more completely. All tension will disappear and you will feel only the discomfort of heavier pressure from each contraction. You will not lose control, and will remain perfectly passive, allowing the contractions to do their own work, without trying to assist in any way.

A short pause may occur, after which the contractions will recommence with increased strength. About this time, the membranes will rupture and the waters escape. There is no need to become worried or alarmed about this, it merely means that you have entered into the second stage of your labor, and the actual birth . . . of your child is about to begin. Although the contractions become much heavier and more frequent, they will not frighten you, because soon it will be necessary for you to cooperate and help in getting your baby born. As the contractions continue, you will begin to feel an almost irresistible desire to assist by bearing down. No matter when this occurs, *you must not give way to it, until you are told to do so.*

If you do, you will delay the birth of your child, render it more difficult, and wear yourself out unnecessarily, without doing a scrap of good. As soon as you feel this urge, tell the midwife or nurse, but do not give way to it until she tells you to. When she does, take a deep breath, hold it as long as you can, and push down as hard as you can as long as each contraction lasts. If you have to breathe out before the contraction is over, take another deep breath as quickly as possible and continue to hold it and push down, since it is usually the last part of the contraction that produces most progress. You will find that this will greatly reduce the discomfort. Remember, as you bear down and push, how much you are helping to bring your baby into the world, because this could not be done without some hard work and physical exertion. It will be well worthwhile. In each interval, between the contractions, you will be able to relax completely, and sleep.

As the baby's head descends, and appears at the outlet, the final process of delivery is about to begin. At this point, you will be able to obey all instructions implicitly. Whenever you are told to stop pushing, you will stop pushing immediately, and indulge in rapid deep breathing instead. As a result of this you will relax more and more completely, and as the head presses down harder and harder on the outlet, the whole area will become quite numb and insensitive. You will experience a feeling of stretching, and the sensation of something passing through the outlet.

Although you will probably require no extra help, suitable drugs or anesthetics will be available if you feel the need of them. They will not be given to you unless you request them. You have only to ask. If, on the other hand, you wish to remain awake as your baby is born, you have only to say so. When you have seen the baby, and the afterbirth has come away, you will fall into a deep refreshing sleep. You will wake up from this feeling really fit and well, and remembering very little of what has occurred. Throughout the whole of your labor, you will be able to talk, or answer questions if necessary, without waking up from your deep, relaxed, hypnotic sleep. You will be able to cooperate in every way, but you will feel far too

sleepy and drowsy to become disturbed. You will carry out faithfully every instruction that you are given, just as effectively as if I had given them, myself.

EXPLANATION OF TRAINING

The main object of subsequent antenatal hypnotic training sessions is to condition the patient to become completely relaxed, both mentally and physically, whenever she enters the trance state, to remove fear and apprehension, and to instill suggestions of confidence and general and physical well-being. This conditioning is more effective if the patient is taught self-hypnosis and practices it regularly at home, thereby gaining much more confidence in her own power to control her reactions during the confinement.

When teaching self-hypnosis and in the course of each ordinary hypnotic induction, it is always advisable to couple suggestions of increased relaxation with deep, rhythmic breathing. Once this technique has been mastered by the patient, it will prove invaluable in the alleviation of pain and distress during her actual labor.

The suggestions to be impressed upon the patient's mind at each training session can easily be constructed from the detailed description of labor under hypnosis which has already been given to her. These should be selected and phrased to suit each individual case, in accordance with certain general principles:

1. Suggestions that the patient will continue to keep fit and well throughout her pregnancy.
2. That she will look forward to her confinement with pleasure and happiness, and not with dread and apprehension.
3. That everything is perfectly normal (provided, of course, that this fact has been clinically established).
4. That, during her labor, she will fall into a deep hypnotic sleep whenever she is told to do so, or upon a prearranged signal she gives herself to induce self-hypnosis, and all

subsequent suggestions will be both accepted and acted upon.

5. That each contraction of the womb will be felt as a not altogether unpleasant sensation. Even during the second stage, the feelings experienced will be simply those of increasing pressure, comparable in every way to ordinary physical exertion. Care must be taken not to abolish all her sensations, otherwise labor might well commence without the patient's becoming aware of the fact.

6. That every time she puts herself into a deep hypnotic sleep, she will be able to relax her muscles and relieve tension so completely that she will feel much less, and the delivery of the baby will become much easier.

7. That subsequently her breasts will more likely produce plenty of milk, so that she will be able to breast feed her child should she so wish, without difficulty. This last suggestion is likely to be successful since the commonest causes of deficient lactation are worry and fear. Hypnosis seems to abolish these by inducing an attitude of positive expectancy.

8. That once the confinement is over, and she has slept, she will wake up feeling perfectly fit and well, and may, if she so desires, remember little or nothing about it.

These specialized suggestions should be preceded by the usual ego-strengthening routine on every occasion. During the last six weeks of pregnancy, special emphasis is placed upon those suggestions relating to the patient's reactions and behavior, and the instructions she is to follow during her confinement.

If the practitioner, by any chance, will be unable to be present at the confinement, the patient must be placed posthypnotically *en rapport* with some other individual—doctor, nurse or midwife—with whose instructions she will comply as if they had been issued by the hypnotist. For this procedure to succeed, the deeper stages of hypnosis will have to be attained, and the individual to whom rapport is transferred fully informed as to the correct method of conducting a labor under hypnosis.

Erickson's Childbirth Suggestions

Milton H. Erickson, M.D.

Since you are a pregnant woman, you are expecting a baby, and you would like to have that baby in the way that is most comfortable to you. I want you to be sure to have it in the way that is most pleasing and most comfortable to you. If that means that you have to get a cramp in your arm from holding on to that grip, be sure to get that cramp because, you see, I don't know what kind of pain or distress you might want to have during the labor. All I know is that you want to have a very happy, very agreeable labor. You want to look upon the arrival of this child as a completely pleasing thing. Therefore, you might want a cramp in the right arm, a cramp in the left arm; you might want an itch on your leg; you might want to feel a labor contraction here and there. If you do want to feel a labor contraction I would like to suggest the following. You know that labor comes in three stages. The first stage gives you much more time to feel a labor contraction than the second or third stage. So if you really want to feel a labor contraction, do it in the first part of the first stage; because that gives you more time to study and to experience and to feel it. But, of course, you can also have a contraction that you feel in the second or the third stage, if you want to. In case you do wish to feel a labor contraction, I just want you to feel it in the most adequate way possible.

Being a medical man, I suggest the first stage, and the first part of the first stage; because that is the best time . . . to feel a labor contraction. But . . . [you can also] feel it in the second stage, or in the third stage. But in the third stage, you are going to be busy with a lot of other things. There is that impending question: What sex is the baby going to be?

An Ericksonian Approach to Childbirth

Noelle M. Poncelet, Ph.D.
Menlo Park, California

THE SETTING

The couple is seen in the third trimester of pregnancy when labor and delivery are immediate concerns. An audiotaped two-hour session usually suffices. I make clear I need not be present during labor and delivery. I am available for "booster" sessions or by phone if necessary. I request follow-up contact after the baby is born.

I send the woman's physician a letter that explains the nature of hypnosis and helps him or her recognize trance behavior. I make suggestions for ways the obstetrician can reinforce the trance, including a hand on the woman's shoulder, and/or simple sentences such as: "You are doing fine [first name]." I recommend lower trials of analgesic medication, if that is necessary, to avoid oversedation. I indicate that hypnotic training includes suggestions for appropriate responsiveness to interactions with the medical and nursing staff.

THE INFORMATION-GATHERING INTERVIEW

The information-gathering interview consists of two phases: (1) the identification of needs and "anchoring" of need fulfillment; and (2) fostering an understanding of hypnosis.

ANCHORING.   In order to tailor the hypnotic training to the unique characteristics of the couple, I proceed by first asking detailed information regarding: (1) their assumptions about the childbirth experience or their expectations if this is not their first pregnancy, and (2) their needs.

Questions about assumptions and expectations allow me to hear facts and myths transmitted by significant others and the health staff

and to determine if they are accepted to any extent by the couple (Poncelet, 1983). Particular attention is paid to metaphorical "organ" language. I question each spouse sequentially and treat them equally. Similarly, I question what their needs will be before, during, and after labor and delivery.

Most often the woman is quick to identify general needs, e.g., love and support from her mate and relief from pain. There is usually a pause when I ask her, "How will you recognize his love and support? What form do you wish his love and support to take?" I help her to identify whether she wants him to look at her, talk to her, touch her. What exactly does she want to hear? Where does she want to be touched? When? How much pressure? As I encourage her to create a totally satisfying sensory experience, I frequently am amazed at how specific many women can be, especially when invited to exclude some disagreeable behaviors.

It is delightful to observe the appreciative look of her husband as he sighs deeply and acknowledges the relief of knowing specifically how to be helpful. Many suggestions are elicited and the husband is then asked to state sincerely which behaviors he is willing to offer and which he would rather not. I will express disbelief at "blanket" acquiescence and will state that any need met out of obligation is poison to the relationship while those met out of desire are fertilizers. Helpful behaviors he agrees to are immediately rehearsed and anchored.

The process is then reversed and the husband is asked what his needs will be and how he would like his wife to best meet them. Stupefaction is a common response. Men have told me they do not need anything; this is not their time; all they want is to help their wife and make sure she is all right. I respectfully disagree and wonder aloud about their personal concerns and their isolation from the physical experience between their wife and child during the pregnancy. Tentatively first-time fathers begin to tune inward. Men who already have a child have less difficulty stating their inner experience. Needs can now be formulated, agreement elicited from the woman, and their needs can be anchored. Encouraging husbands to voice their concerns provides two crucial points of relief for the woman: It is a validation and explanation of a worried look on her husband's face or perceived concern in his voice. She is less likely to interpret these behaviors as rejection or criticism. Moreover, it prompts her to get away from her preoccupation with herself, and attend to his needs. . . .

Mutual anchoring of needs can occur at the visual, auditory, and kinesthetic levels in a way that is unique to each couple's needs. Anchoring is rehearsed in the office. It is a natural posthypnotic suggestion for a satisfying interaction and for personal comfort and relaxation during labor and delivery. Furthermore, clarifying and negotiating needs clear the way for privacy to be respected by each, since such withdrawal no longer is interpreted as rejection and abandonment.

KNOWLEDGE ABOUT HYPNOTIC EXPERIENCE.   The last part of the information-gathering interview focuses on the couple's knowledge of, and previous experience with, hypnosis. Successes, failures, myths and fears are carefully identified, again in behavioral terms. Experience with Lamaze and natural childbirth training, meditation, prayer and relaxation are acknowledged as useful and overlapping with the hypnotic state. Needs to be in control of the experience and complete responsiveness to the medical and nursing staff are stressed as being compatible (and in fact enhanced) in the hypnotic experience.

Such attention to the hypnotic experience is in itself the beginning of a naturalistic induction and, most often, signs of light trance behavior become evident at this point.

HYPNOSIS TRAINING

The partners are invited to enjoy the trance together, to make themselves even more comfortable than they already are. They are encouraged to readjust their body positions any time they wish to increase their comfort and relaxation. This is especially important because the pregnant woman may need to move if only in response to her baby shifting position. In fact, some pregnant women exhibit active trance behavior similar to that seen in hypnotized children; the main clue that a trance state has been experienced is the reorientation behavior seen as the trance is terminated (Poncelet, 1982).

EYE FIXATION.   Both are invited to focus on a "spot" on the ceiling in anticipation of the many ceiling fixtures they will see at home and in the hospital. Thus an orientation to the future is suggested. Experienced subjects are invited to recall their most satisfying trance, meditation, or relaxation training experience, while untrained subjects are specifically led toward eye closure. Other trance inductions may be used to meet the specific needs of either partner.

DISSOCIATION.   Dissociation is suggested to a *"favorite place filled with happy memories, where you have felt so relaxed, so comfortable, so safe. You can be by yourself or with each other, it does not matter."* They are encouraged to use the power of their imagination and to step into this place. Ideomotor finger signaling ratifies that this step has been accomplished and that trance is deepening.

RELAXATION.   Relaxation is suggested in a variety of ways. Always added is an invitation to *"focus on the most comfortable part of your body . . . and with each breath in, increase and spread the feeling of relaxation, with each breath out, let go of unnecessary tensions and concerns. They can be put on hold and dealt with later, just like dirty dishes in the sink sometimes need to wait for an appropriate time to be washed."* Thus, anxiety is not discounted but postponed.

TRANCE DEEPENING.   Deepening is achieved by the use of learning sets, suggestions about conscious and unconscious processes, truisms, and double binds. Many observations on the couple's trance behavior and appreciation of their accomplishments are also given.

PARTIAL AMNESIA FOR PREVIOUS CHILDBIRTH EXPERIENCE. At this point, suggestions are given to multi-para couples for retrieving the positive aspects of, and the lessons learned from, their previous childbirth experience and for forgetting what was "uniquely negative about those events."

PSEUDO-ORIENTATION IN TIME.   The couple is invited to *"think of the time soon in the future, the appropriate time only, when the baby will be ready to be born."* It is important in orientation to the future to stress that the rehearsal is for the future only and not an invitation to go into labor now. Perhaps she will recognize a contraction, the rupture of her membrane. There will be signals for her to feel very joyful, excited, curious, relieved that the time has come . . . and to go into a very soothing and comfortable trance. Therapeutic suggestions can be added: *"Your body knew how to learn to walk; how can childbirth not be the most satisfying, pleasurable experience when it is linked to your love for one another now and several months ago?"*

As her husband learns from his wife that labor has started, he is invited to use her message to go deeply into an active trance which will enable him to help himself, his wife, and the obstetrical team. He is invited to tap within himself the ancient genetic primary knowledge that he has about the childbirth experience. He is reminded that he is the product of one sperm and one egg, that he started as a female embryo before differentiating as a man. . . . Both are reminded of ways to meet the needs they have agreed upon and that are now available to them so that each can be maximally comfortable, confident, and present to the other.

ANALGESIA.   Contractions are described as *"the long abdominal muscles contracting while the cervix opens and the vaginal walls stretch. Your body knows what to do; your body leads, your*

mind observes and enjoys the experience." To maximize comfort, the metaphor of a switchbox in the mother's inner mind is offered. She is invited to identify the wires that connect every organ and the muscles involved in childbirth and to connect each one with a switch of a specific color. She is alerted to the light above the switch which goes on at the start of a contraction. This signal gives her the pleasure to recognize how well her body is working. She then can turn the switch off or lower it so that all she needs to feel is a *dull pressure, a numbing, cramping sensation, massaging her baby.*

AMNESIA.   She is encouraged to appreciate the work of each contraction and to recognize it as *completed* and therefore ready to be forgotten as she immediately becomes absorbed in other activities: preparing herself to go to the hospital, enjoying leisure, conversation, rest, dreaming, sleep.

POSTHYPNOTIC SUGGESTIONS.   The woman is encouraged to remain active during the first stage of labor, to follow her physician's advice on the proper time to go to the hospital, and to use the breathing and focusing techniques learned during childbirth training. She is invited to notice her trance and relaxation deepen with each contraction (or as she gets in the car, or at each traffic light, or as she approaches the hospital, talks to the insurance clerk, as she is greeted by the medical and nursing staff, as she sees uniforms, or when her physician and assigned nurse examine her, etc.) She is alerted to fluctuations of trance level as a normal phenomenon, especially in the lighter trance level necessary for verbal communication.

REFRAMING PAIN.   Both partners are invited to recognize that if contractions are one minute long, for example, *in one hour there will be twelve minutes of work for forty-eight minutes of comfort.* Therefore, boredom and fatigue are identified as unnecessary enemies and the couple is encouraged to play, move, listen to favorite music, dissociate to favorite places and rest.

REFRAMING ANXIETY. Anxious feelings are welcomed because "if you can say hello to them, you obviously will be able to bid them. . . ." I encourage the couple to observe their anxiety, to recognize its appropriateness, e.g., the contraction/release mechanisms of the body, fear of the unknown, concerns about the baby, doubt about parenting abilities. I suggest they seek information if it is needed. *"An 'A +' for your childbirth performance is not necessary; all that matters is to enjoy and fully experience a special shared moment. If you feel you need medication, trust yourself, and take some; you can be pleased to know you need less because you are using hypnosis."* Another metaphor is offered: *"Anxiety is like driving down the highway and coming to a railroad crossing. The light is flashing red and so, naturally, you stop, and listen. Before long you see the train coming from one side as you feel the ground tremble beneath you. You watch it crossing the highway and disappear out of your awareness as you proceed safely and cheerfully on your journey."*

REFRAMING HOSPITAL LANGUAGE. In the hypnotic state, any sentence is a potential positive or negative suggestion. At this point, with humor in my voice, I direct the couple's attention toward the peculiar way some people have of expressing themselves. *For example, if a nurse comes in and says: "Are you in much pain, honey?" or "You don't look uncomfortable yet!" or "How bad are your contractions?" or "You are only six centimeters dilated,"* I tell the couple to *immediately adjust such a potentially negative suggestion with tolerance and delight to: "How comfortable am I?" or "I am already six centimeters dilated with four more to go."* Similarly, in response to the well-meaning physician saying, "This is your last chance to receive medication before your baby is born, the woman is invited to think, "I have a choice: do I want medication?"

TIME DISTORTION. *"Welcome to the second stage of labor* [or "transition," if such terminology is used], *your baby is near! Your contractions are stronger and more powerful* [rather than more painful]; *they are closer to one another. Trust your body; it will know how to breath and flow with the pressure, if you let it use all it knows and has practiced."* Suggestions are given for time distortion so that in between contractions, time is experienced as relaxing and resting: *"Take a few moments . . ., all the time your unconscious needs to feel rested, regenerated with energy and refreshed."* Dissociation is particularly encouraged at this time.

REFRAMING THE STRAINING. The straining, the panting, the buildup of tension are linked gently to preorgasmic experience (when one can look and sound in pain and not experience it as such). Low vocalizing is a natural vehicle that can help push the baby down. She can use her energy as a powerful drive (Peterson calls it aggressive [1981]) *that will massage the baby down the stretched and flexible passage* without any harm to her or the baby (see Peterson, regarding the woman's fear that she will be ripped open and her baby's head be crushed). I prepare the woman for the possibility of experiencing the orgasmic-like pleasure, the "rush" and "joyful shaking" at the moment her baby rotates its head through her cervix and down her vagina. I reinforce that it will be a private and enormously satisfying experience.

Her husband is encouraged, if she so desires, to fondle her breasts during contractions (Gaskin, 1978), to massage her back and apply counterpressure, to squeeze her shoulders, her ankles with an intensity that parallels the contraction, using his own intuition and responding to her direction.

It follows naturally to talk about the joy of actively bringing her baby into the world as the couple focuses next on the pleasure of seeing the baby's head, hearing its sounds, feeling him/her in one's arms, on one's belly, close to one's breast.

REFRAMING THE NURSING EXPERIENCE. I describe the baby licking the nipple before suckling, the familiar sexual pleasure that facilitates vaginal contractions. I talk in general about the pleasure for their baby of enjoying both the feeding breast, full of milk, and the empty breast, the one that pacifies. I explain the delight for the baby of experiencing two different sensations. Here I offer the possibility for the man to consider comfortably giving in to his natural yearning for the nursing experience, if he so desires as some men do, and if social mores have not inhibited his capacity to recognize this need and to act upon it.

BLEEDING CONTROL. As the couple is absorbed in the trance state imagining the pleasure of discovering their newborn, it is easy to slip in some rather direct suggestions for prompt expulsion of the placenta, bleeding control, comfortable stitching of the episiotomy, if necessary, quick and effective contracting to pre-pregnancy shape, and speedy and smooth healing and recovery.

POSTHYPNOTIC SUGGESTIONS. Husband and wife are asked to share their unconscious experience of childbirth with their conscious mind upon awakening from the trance in the hospital.

Both are encouraged to appreciate what they have accomplished in this office and to take time to practice going into a trance with or without the audiotape of this hypnotic training session, with heightened confidence that they will pleasurably experience the birth of their baby.

TERMINATION OF TRANCE. Suggestions for re-orientation to the office are given. Comments, questions and clarifications are welcomed at the end of the session. Joyful anticipation is shared and my availability for "booster" sessions, if necessary, is made clear.

Childbirth Script

Diane Roberts Stoler, Ed.D.
Boxford, Massachusetts

Although this script is lengthy, it has been included to illustrate the manner in which repetition of suggestion is often included in actual work with patients. (*Ed.*)

INTRODUCTION

The childbirth script for labor, delivery and recovery was developed as part of the Stoler Program for Pain-Controlled Childbirth. It was based on previous childbirth scripts used in hypnosis, which have been revamped and restructured over a 10-year research period. The result of that research period is the present script, which provides women with a consistent, reliable and effective means of achieving the type of childbirth they have chosen to experience.**

CHILDBIRTH SCRIPT

[The script presented here was for a 36-year-old woman for her first pregnancy. She loved being at her grandmother's house near the ocean. The suggestions begin following an imagery induction to facilitate dissociation and deepening suggestions.]

DISTANCING FROM FEELINGS. Pay close attention to my voice. You have no cares or worries; right now, all your cares and worries will just drift away. Notice one of the fluffy clouds above you floating in the sky. You can allow yourself to put your nervous feelings, fear about the baby's health, fear of what people think, doubts about complications, loss of control, concern about your husband and all other negative scanning to be placed on that cloud, and allow it to drift away off into the distance, off, off, further and further away. So far and so distant that you barely notice it. Allowing it to be just a dot in the horizon, however, you do not let it totally disappear because you may choose to retain these feelings and retrieve them if you need them. But right now you have no need for them. You let them go and as you do you gain a sense of peace and calm flowing within your body.

You can allow yourself the pleasure of watching those feelings drift further and further away into the horizon. Notice that you do

_____

**For further information, write to Childbirth Inc., RFD#2, Boxford, MA 01921

not allow them to entirely disappear, so that if you want those feelings, they will be there. But right now, you have no need for those feelings, so allow them to go off towards the surface of the water. These feelings will be there if you want them back or want to be in touch with them; they are close at hand, but for the time being you can let them flow and be just within your grasp.

You are peaceful, calm, relaxed; you go deeper and deeper, deeper and deeper, and as I talk to you, you continue to go into an even deeper state of relaxation. Everything but my voice is becoming remote now, quite remote; nothing else but my voice seems important, nothing else is important, nothing else but my voice. What I say to you right now seems of interest, even though my voice may come to you from a dream, or it may change in quality, as you relax more and more, as you sink deeper and deeper into this lethargy. As you relax more and more, you allow yourself to sink deeper and deeper and deeper, deeper and deeper into this lethargy. As you relax more and more, more and more, more and more, you allow yourself to sink deeper and deeper, deeper and deeper, into a deeper state of relaxation. Just relax now. Relax. [Still further deepening suggestions are given.]

CHILDBIRTH SUGGESTIONS. You are bearing a child, the child is developing, growing, preparing for entry into this world. You will give birth to the baby with joy and relaxation. You have felt the movement of your child within you, growing, developing and preparing for entry into this world.

You will give birth to the baby with joy and relaxation. The process is a natural, effortless, and automatic one in which you will be relaxed and you know that you are courageous. Saying this will be a reminder to yourself to do your visualization and keep your mind active and to concentrate on the ocean and your visualization to enhance your ongoing health and healing process of your body. You will be able to adjust yourself to your environment, even though you cannot change it. You can do everything better when you are relaxed, whether it be physical,

mental or emotional. You can control your entire body with your mind. Your are relaxed and you have the ability to deliver your child in peace and relaxation. The act of bearing your child will be as natural and as easy as any other process of your body, like breathing in and out, breathing in and out, in and out, in and out, in and out. You will allow your body to flow rhythmically like the rhythmic flow of the breeze through the trees. Notice the leaves going back and forth, back and forth. You are relaxed and courageous. You know you are relaxed and courageous. You know the birth of your child is a joyful event in your life. You are courageous. You are relaxed. You are relaxed. You will be alert to hear your baby's first cry. You are relaxed and peaceful. You are courteous. You are relaxed and peaceful. You are composed. You are confident.

There is joy in you, and you feel strong, courageous, and there is an inner strength in your entire being. It is the birth of your child, and as you feel this strength and confidence, and vitality, you allow yourself to sink into an even deeper state of relaxation. When you are ready to go to the hospital after talking to your physician, you will notice that by saying to yourself, "Relax, calm, numb." You will be able to control and maintain harmony within your body.

IMAGERY FOR CONTROL OF COMFORT. You permit yourself to numb various areas just by picturing a switchboard with lights, heat sensors, dimmer switches, and on and off switches. Each light has a heat sensor under it, along with a dimmer switch and an on and off switch. This gives you complete control to adjust your body, your comfort level and sensation level. You have complete control to adjust the heat level and to adjust the dimmer switch. Thereby, by focusing on the various lights and adjusting the dimmer switch to any area on your body, you have complete control to adjust both the level and intensity of comfort you want. You have complete control for specific comfort and sensation levels. This ability, along with your thumb and index fingers together, will be a signal to go into a deeply relaxed state, a deeply relaxed state.

You will be able to control and regulate the degree of dullness, whereby you will feel pressure but not discomfort. This will allow you to be able to time your contractions.

At the onset of your labor you will dull all the nerves from just above your knees, front and back, to your pubic area, buttocks area, abdomen, lower back, upper back, chest cavity, just below your breast. If you can visualize an area like a barrel—from just below your breast to just above your knees, encircling your body—by adjusting the dimmer dial to the appropriate level of comfort, you will make it dull, where you will feel pressure and movement, but no sharp pain; pressure and movement, but no sharp pain. You have the ability to adjust the level of dullness in this area of your body throughout your labor. With the touch of your husband's hand (or the support person), on any part of your body, this will produce the required and desired amount of dullness. You will feel pressure and movement but no sharp pain, pressure and movement but no discomfort. You notice your contractions will be increasing and you will be able adjust the level of dullness by adjusting the dimmer switch to the level of intensity of sensation to the various parts of your body, to achieve the amount of sensation needed to feel the pressure and movement in a comfortable level, so that you can help the baby come out.

DEEPENING AS LABOR PROGRESSES.   You will know how far dilated you are by the rotation of the sun in the sky and the coolness of the air. At 1 cm., you notice the air becoming cooler, and by 10 cm. you will know that you are in transition when you may have a desire to go inside the house. But you will allow yourself to notice the setting sun in the west and choose to settle back in the grass and enjoy the beautiful sight. You allow yourself to go into an even deeper state of relaxation so that you may help yourself and your baby to arrive safely. At this point you feel of the gentle movement of the wind over your body and you allow yourself to settle comfortably in the grass cave which is safe and protected. This will fill your souls with joy and

happiness and this will encourage you to gain all your strength to go deeper and deeper into hypnosis to help yourself and your baby.

When you notice the sun setting in the west and the temperature drop, you know this will be a sign that you will be fully dilated, and you can gain more energy and the enthusiasm to push your baby into the world. At this point you can see your labor coming to completion. You will be aware to push your baby into the world. You can allow yourself to go into a very relaxed state, deeper than you have ever experienced before. By allowing yourself to go into this state, you permit your body to flow in its natural rhythms, and help and assist the natural movement of your muscles to gently, just like the natural gentle rhythm of movement of the distant ocean and the breeze through the trees surrounding, allow yourself to go deeper and deeper, and become more and more relaxed, and limp and loose like a Raggedy Ann Doll. At that point you will permit yourself to go deeper into this deep state of relaxation, whereby you can push your baby into the world with peace and tranquility.

TIME DISTORTION.   You allow yourself to drift back into a wonderful deep state of relaxation. You allow yourself to go deeper and deeper, deeper and deeper than ever before. Time will pass quickly and pleasantly (within 4–10 hours or maybe longer), and there will be no fatigue, nausea, or exhaustion because of your relaxation. As labor advances, each contraction will be represented in the gentle movement of the ocean in the distance, going back and forth, back and forth, allowing you to sink deeper and deeper. And each contraction means you are reaching your goal, allowing you to go deeper and deeper.

PERMISSION FOR AMNESIA.   You will remember only the things about labor and delivery that are pleasant; when the delivery is over, you will remember those things clearly and all other aspects of your labor and delivery will fade, with you coming closer and closer to the setting of the sun.

SUGGESTIONS FOR SOMNAMBULISTIC BEHAVIOR. You'll be able to move around the birth or labor room, use the bedpan or toilet, and still stay deeply hypnotized. In fact, you will go deeper and deeper, deeper and deeper, deeper and deeper during the process of delivery, than ever before. Opening your eyes will not bring you back to your usual state of awareness, but rather it will allow you to sink even deeper and deeper, deeper and deeper, deeper and deeper into this state of relaxation, concentration and peacefulness. It is possible there will be other noises, such as women moaning or other noises at the hospital or on the way to the hospital. These noises will not disturb you; instead they will act as a signal to deepen your hypnosis.

COMFORT WITH CONTRACTIONS. In the process of natural delivery, there will be no nausea, no sickness or pain, during or after labor. In childbirth the circular muscles of the lower part of the uterus relax and allow the longitudinal muscles of the upper part of the uterus to contract and push the baby down the birth canal.

SUGGESTIONS FOR CONTROL AND SELF-EFFICACY. As you relax you will permit yourself to go deeper and deeper. You will feel control to adjust the amount of dullness during labor and delivery, so that you can feel pressure and movement, but not pain. Your desire to take control and to make these adjustments is so strong because of two main reasons — you want to take control of your life and to help yourself and your baby. Therefore you desire to be able to control and adjust the dullness, so that you will permit yourself to feel only pressure and movement and no discomfort.

ENJOY THE MOVEMENT OF BABY. During labor and delivery you allow yourself to enjoy the movement of your baby. And with your eyes closed, you say to yourself, "Relax, calm, dull, courage." You let yourself sink deeper and deeper, deeper and deeper, deeper and deeper into hypnosis during labor than ever before. As the circular muscles relax and the long muscles push the baby into this world, this will be a signal to go deeper and deeper, deeper and deeper, and with each contraction, you will go deeper and deeper, deeper and deeper.

As you relax you will permit yourself to go deeper and deeper. You will feel control to adjust the amount of numbness during labor and delivery, so that you can feel pressure and movement, but not pain.

During labor and delivery you allow yourself to enjoy the movement of your baby. And with your eyes closed, you say to yourself, "Relax, calm, numb, courage." You let yourself sink deeper and deeper, deeper and deeper, deeper and deeper into hypnosis during labor than ever before. As the circular muscles relax and the long muscles push the baby into this world, this will be a signal to go deeper and deeper, deeper and deeper, and with each contraction, you will go deeper and deeper, deeper and deeper. You will be able to go deeper into hypnosis during labor than ever before, and each easy, gentle releasing breath and every uterine contraction will be a signal for you to go deeper and deeper, deeper and deeper. You will remain numb where you feel pressure and movement but no pain, pressure and movement but no pain.

When you will notice the sun starting to set and the sky colors becoming darker and deeper, you will allow yourself to realize that your positive energy will bring you strength and calmness to rejoice in the birth about to arrive. During labor and delivery you allow yourself to enjoy the smells and sounds of the flowers, the grass and the distant sea, and to feel of the warm sun over your body. As the sun is setting, you gain a sense of peace and harmony with the world around you and your body becomes more and more relaxed.

THE FINAL STAGE OF LABOR. And as you relax, the circular muscles relax and the long muscles push the baby into this world. This will be a signal to go deeper and deeper, deeper and deeper, and with each contraction you will go deeper and deeper, deeper and deeper. You will be able to go deeper into hypnosis during labor than ever before, and each breath and every uterine contraction will be a signal for you to go deeper and deeper, deeper and deeper. You will remain numb where you feel pressure and movement but no pain, pressure and movement but no pain. [Repetition of previous suggestions is now given.]

COMFORT EXCEPT FOR SIGNAL PAIN.   You will be able to respond appropriately, to help yourself and your child. Until the time when you need to push, you will allow your body to feel pressure and movement, but no pain, except if there may be damage to you or your baby. If you feel pain you will be able to report it to the nurse or some other person on the delivery team. They may need to know where the pain is located, so that they may help you. Then, once they have helped you, this will be a signal to allow yourself to become relaxed and to remain in a very deep state of hypnosis. After they have helped you, you will not need to feel the pain, but only pressure. You will remain calm and act appropriately to help yourself and your baby.

EDITING OUT NEGATIVE SUGGESTIONS.   If there are people who are discussing you or your child's progress, in a way that is not beneficial to you, this will be a signal to go even deeper, and their voices will only be a muted, white noise to your ears. You will remain calm, poised, and relaxed. You will, if needed, be able to instruct the labor and delivery team through your ability to separate body from mind, so that your body will feel totally heavy and limp, in a deep state of numbness, in order that you can respond in a very logical and appropriate manner to help you and your baby.

Once this has been accomplished you will be able to go and concentrate on the safe place in the grass near the house, ocean, the shore, the sky, or concentrate on the movement of your baby. You will permit yourself to take greater control by saying to yourself, in your mind, "Relax, calm, poise, numb." This will permit you to go back to a very deep state of relaxation, whereby you will feel pressure and movement but no pain, pressure and movement but no pain. If there is a need to be transported into

the delivery room or to have a cesarean birth because of some medical need for you or your baby, this will be a signal to reach an even deeper state, and by doing so, you will be helping yourself and your baby. You will only feel and continue to feel pain if it is needed to help you and your baby; however, as soon as the appropriate person acts to alleviate the problem, you will immediately go into a very deep state of relaxation, calm and total numbness. You will remain calm and act appropriately to help yourself and your baby.

COPING WITH ANXIETIES OR FEARS.   [Following deepening comments:] If during labor a scary anxiety arises regarding the hospital, from the memories of having your miscarriage, fears of not being able to bond with your baby, or fears that something will go wrong or any other flashback that might interfere, you can choose to put them into a box. Then tie a rope around it and place it at the bottom of the well, not too far away. This well has a very heavy lid that cannot be opened by anyone other than yourself. These feelings will not surface and cannot be touched unless you choose to retrieve them. You will always know where they are because you have placed them there and only you can retrieve them. These feelings cannot surface unless you choose to retrieve them, to work through the feelings in your therapy to help you make your life more productive and happier and healthier. You will always know where they are because you have the control and you have chosen to place them there. Allow yourself to settle back and listen to the sound, and movement, of the deep and the wonderful feeling of lying in the spring grass. Allow your body to feel heavy and limp, and to listen to the breeze through the trees and the distant ocean going back and forth, back and forth, back and forth in a melodious rhythm. You feel the warmth of the sun over your body. You feel at peace.

THE DELIVERY.   Opening your eyes will not bring you back to your usual state of awareness; rather, it will allow you to sink even deeper and deeper, deeper and deeper in this state of relaxation and peacefulness. When the delivery team announces that the baby is coming out, you will be able to open your eyes, and will be able to touch and assist your baby coming out into this world. Watching the birth of the baby, and seeing the blood and secretions will have no negative effect on you. Rather, you will watch in interest.

CONTROL OF BLEEDING AND PAIN.   By turning off your valves, you will be able to decrease the flow of blood, and by relaxing the perineum, you will be able to push through and stretch the perineum with little or no tearing. If you need to have an episiotomy, you can numb and decrease the flow of blood to the area. And the area will remain numb until the stitches are healed. After your delivery, the perineum will return to its size before the birth of your child so that you may enjoy an active and enjoyable sex life.

SUGGESTIONS FOR POST-DELIVERY COMFORT AND WELL-BEING.   If hemorrhoids appear, you will keep them numb in that area until they have gone. With your relaxation and concentration the flow of blood in the veins in your legs will virtually eliminate any and all varicose veins. After labor is over, you will feel only pleasantly tired, so you can relax and be able to void the urine in your body. You will sleep easily at any time in the hospital or at home. During and after delivery you will be happy, courageous, confident, proud, and you will have a wonderful feeling of accomplishment because you will be relaxed and happy. There will be no need for maternity blues. You will be able to calmly deal with your new baby at home, and the activities of your home life. You will feel only calmness, happiness, contentedness, a relaxed feeling, a feeling of accomplishment. If after delivery, after-contractions may occur, or if rectal discomfort develops, you will automatically be able to numb the areas of discomfort until those areas are healed.

SUGGESTIONS FOR LACTATION.   Your relaxation will allow the milk to develop quickly in your breasts. You can turn the valves to produce more milk quickly, and turn off the switches for any discomfort in the area. However, if an infection such as mastitis should occur, you will feel discomfort in order to inform your physician. But if there is no infection or major problem with the breast, other than general irritation, you will not feel pain or discomfort. When you have chosen to stop breast-feeding, you will be able to dry up the milk easily and comfortably by slowly turning off the valves to that area over the period of several days.

FURTHER SUGGESTIONS FOR SELF-EFFICACY.   [After further deepening comments:] Within you is a sense of control, comfortable peace and tranquility. You feel a sense of power, control, inner strength.

ONSET OF LABOR.   When labor begins the contractions may hurt; at that point, you will start timing the contractions. When they are continuous for a half-hour, coming every seven minutes, you will call the doctor. Based on what you are told you may choose to call the answering service if you want me or my support person to be with you at your delivery, so that she or I will be able to meet you at the hospital. When you start to dial the office number of the doctor, you will say to yourself, "Relax, calm, courage, numb." This will be a signal to adjust the dimmer switch to numb those parts of your body just below you breasts to just above your knees, in a barrel-like area that will surround that area. You will allow yourself to maintain the needed level of numbness whereby you will feel pressure and no discomfort.

Upon reaching the hospital, you will be able to maintain the needed level whereby the admitting nurse or a doctor agrees that you are in active labor. At that point, you will allow yourself to become even more numb, whereby you feel pressure and movement, but no discomfort.

If there is a traffic jam on the way to the hospital you can deepen your state by putting your thumb and index fingers together and taking one long, deep breath. This will act as a signal to allow you to go into a very deep state whereby you will achieve a very deep state of numbness, calm, and relaxation. You realize that by focusing your mind on your hand held monitor, and adjusting the dimmer switch, you can control the level of sensation and intensity you wish. You have complete control over how much dullness you want to have at any given time. Also, you may choose to have your husband or someone who is driving the car put his/her hand on your body, and by doing so you will achieve specific dullness to the area where he has touched.

If for some reason you are unable to leave your home and your husband is not with you and you are alone, by taking one long deep breath through your nose, and breathing out through you mouth, you will permit yourself to go into a very deep state of hypnosis. At that point you will allow yourself to focus your mind on your body and picture what areas you need to dull. With this focus and with picturing your scene, and repeating to yourself in your mind, "Relax, calm, courage, numb," you will be able to help yourself and your baby. You will remain calm and poised, and know that you have the ability to make decisions wisely to help you and your baby.

You will be able to visually go within yourself to monitor the progress of your baby, and your labor and delivery. You will be able to make, if possible, all the necessary phone calls to obtain assistance in your labor and delivery. You will feel relaxed, calm, and will maintain the needed level of dullness to deliver your baby, if necessary, in good health and tranquility. During this period you will allow yourself to focus on the movement of your baby, your body, and to picture yourself in your safe spot in the grass and how wonderful this feels. This calmness and relaxation will allow your baby to enter the world with an Apgar of possibly 9 or 10. You feel a sense of joy and life within your soul.

YOU MAY FEEL DESIRED SENSATIONS.   At any point during your labor you may wish to feel the actual labor and the strong contractions. You can choose to do so by saying to yourself that you want to experience the sensation. Once this has been accomplish, this will be a signal to allow yourself to dull the area and relax, and obtain a comfortable level to permit a comfortable level of pressure but no discomfort, and to allow yourself to go even deeper into hypnosis than you have ever been before.

COMFORT FOR MEDICAL PROCEDURES.   If at any time in the process there is the need for any kind of injection, for example, to place an intravenous tube, you can numb that area by focusing your mind and picturing the area. You may feel pressure, but no discomfort; pressure, but no discomfort. If for any reason the medical staff do not do a procedure correctly, your body will be aware of it, so that you can inform them; for example, if they do not put on the fetal monitor correctly or put in the IV correctly. Once you have told them, this will be a signal to allow yourself to go into a very deep state of hypnosis and to help yourself and your baby appropriately.

SUGGESTIONS FOR POST-DELIVERY CARETAKING.   After labor and delivery are over, and you have returned home, your sense of peace, calm, and strength will help in your recovery time and help you sleep, whether you have a vaginal or cesarean birth. Your inner strength, relaxation and desire will shorten the recovery period and help you to cope with the newborn's needs. You will remain relaxed and at ease.

You will eat only foods that are good for your body, such as complex carbohydrates, fruits, vegetables, and lean meat, while eliminating fats, sugar, and white flour. You will eat only when your body needs, not your emotions need, to be fed and nurtured. Therefore, you will eat only when your body is hungry, and only in small quantities. You will eat slowly and enjoy your food. You will gradually go back to a full exercise program that will bring health and contentment to you. This will help you reach your goal of ____ pounds that you have set for yourself. You will allow yourself to engage in activity—mentally, emotionally, and physically—that will bring to you health, longevity, and peace—mentally and physically and emotionally. You will permit time for yourself and time to take naps when your body feels fatigued. Your desire to achieve this goal in life will provide the strength and endurance for you to be able to reach your desired weight of ____ pounds.

By eating only when you are hungry, eating only the foods that are good for your body, eating small quantities, eating slowly and enjoying each and every morsel of food that you put into your mouth, and by exercising appropriately every day for a minimum of one 30-minute period, you will achieve your desired weight.

This calmness and relaxation will allow your body and mind to function more effectively. You feel a sense of joy and life within you soul. Let yourself sink deeper and deeper, deeper and deeper. Notice the warmth of the sun and the wonderful feeling of the world surrounding you. Within you is a sense of control, comfortable peace and tranquility. You feel a sense of power, control, inner strength.

SUGGESTIONS FOR SELF-HYPNOSIS.   You know that you can put yourself into hypnosis any time and any place except where there is danger to you or others, such as driving or cooking, where there could possibly be danger to you or others. Otherwise you can put yourself into hypnosis very quickly, and with each trial and each time you will be able to go into hypnosis more rapidly that ever before and the suggestions here, or that you give yourself, will last longer with each trial. You will always find hypnosis refreshing and relaxing. No one can put you into hypnosis without your agreeing to it. Otherwise you will always find hypnosis helpful in reaching your goal of taking greater control of your life.

If, for some reason, you need to put yourself into hypnosis where it is not feasible to close your eyes, such as at work, or when dealing with the baby, or in the middle of a stressful situation, you can put yourself into this wonderful feeling of calm and relaxation by taking one long deep breath through your nose. And as you breathe out through you mouth, you will permit yourself to go into a very deep state of hypnosis. At that point you will allow yourself to focus your mind on your body, picturing your scene, or any other peaceful and secure scene, and repeating to yourself in your mind, "Relax, calm, poise, courage," you will be able to help yourself. You will remain calm and poised and respond more effectively to take care and help yourself. [Suggestions are now repeated.]

Because you and I have worked on the various suggestions, along with the script I have developed to help you take greater control over your life, each time you listen to this tape, each time you reaccept the suggestions that are contained on this tape, the suggestions become more and more a part of you. Even though you may not consciously remember them, they will remain there in your unconscious, and they will work better and more effectively than ever before. You are letting yourself sink deeper and deeper, deeper and deeper.

Preparation for Obstetrical Labor

William S. Kroger, M.D.
Palm Springs, California

VERBALIZATION FOR GLOVE ANESTHESIA

[Glove anesthesia is produced as follows:] And now you will go into a deep, hypnotic state, way down, deeper and deeper! You are going to produce glove anesthesia. As I stroke this hand, it is going to get numb, heavy, and woodenlike. When you are sure that this hand has become numb, just as your gums would be after your dentist has injected procaine, you will then transfer this numbness to your face. *With every movement of your hand toward your face*, it will get more numb and woodenlike. [The hand moves to the side of the face.] When it touches your face, press the palm of your hand close to your face [The hand lifts and is pressed to the face], and when you are certain that that numbness has transferred from your hand to your face, drop your hand and your arm. You are going deeper and deeper relaxed with every breath you take. You can just feel that numbness being transferred from your hand to your face. That's fine. Just fine. Excellent. Now, after you are certain that the area on your face is numb, you can remove your hand and it will be normal but your face will be anesthetized.

[The glove anesthesia can be transferred to the abdomen by one or both hands. A posthypnotic suggestion can be given that the anesthesia can be transferred to the perineum at the appropriate time. As each site is anesthetized, the sensory proof of anesthesia can be demonstrated to the patient. However, one should remark:] Remember, you will know what I am doing, but you will feel no pain as I test for the degree of anesthesia. [This is consistent with what is known of the phylogenesis of the nervous system. Since pain is the most primitive of all sensations, it does not have as much cortical representation as the other senses. Discriminatory sensations such as touch, having been acquired later, have more representation in the cortex.]

MANAGEMENT OF LABOR

INTRODUCTION.   When labor actually begins, the patient induces autohypnosis. The physician also can induce hypnosis over the phone or through another physician to whom he has transferred the rapport. An assistant, such as a nurse, can do it by handing the patient a written order to go into a deep state of relaxation. How it is done depends on the kind of conditioning and the cues the patient received during her training program. If the patient has not mastered autohypnosis, the doctor's presence is necessary for maintaining the hypnosis. Suggestions are given for complete anesthesia of the abdomen, the perineum, and other hypersensitive areas.

The following is an actual verbalization taken from a tape recorder for the conduct of labor.

SUGGESTIONS DURING LABOR.   Now, Mary, you have been able to enter a deep state of relaxation through autohypnosis. Also, you have demonstrated that you can produce glove anesthesia and transfer this numb, heavy, wooden feeling to either side of the face. Now that you are in active labor, you will be able to develop the same anesthesia in both hands and transfer this numb, heavy, wooden feeling to the abdomen, in order to cut down the discomfort produced by your contractions [the word 'pain' is never used]. You will also develop anesthesia of any other area of the body that I pick out. such as the area between the vagina and the rectum. This area will be without any feeling for a considerable length of time. Each time you practice producing the glove anesthesia, you will be able to maintain it for long intervals. When labor starts, you will first feel an ache which will begin in the back and then it will move around to the side of your belly. At this time, you will be able to use the autohypnosis and place yourself in a deep state of relaxation. Remember, you need have no more discomfort than you are willing to bear. Your labor contractions will get stronger and longer, and that is a good sign that you are making progress. Even though you know that the labor contractions are there, you will not be able to feel them. If the glove anesthesia does not relieve your discomfort completely, please do not feel guilty about asking for drugs, which will be available.

HELPFUL SUGGESTIONS DURING LABOR

INTRODUCTION.   It takes years to become adept with forceps or to be a good vaginal operator. Likewise, the ability to be adept in producing, maintaining, and controlling the applications of hypnosis to obstetrics requires much practical experience. The most useful suggestions are given below. Misdirection of attention is used to mitigate the forcefulness of the labor contractions, as follows.

SUGGESTIONS. I want you to breathe deeply in the same manner in which you were trained during the prenatal classes. You will count the number of deep breaths or pants that you take with each contraction. In other words, as soon as you feel the contraction, start panting and keep a record of the number of breaths required for each contraction. Perhaps it might be 28 for the first one. In about 10 minutes, you should have another contraction which may last for 30 or 40 seconds; this one may require 30 deep breaths or pants. Keep an average between the first and the second by adding the total and dividing by two, which, in this case, would be 29. I want you to keep this average for all of your contractions. As they get closer and closer, you will notice that the average number of breaths will increase, indicating that labor is progressing nicely.

[The idea is to keep the patient's attention so concentrated on the addition and the division that she doesn't have time to think of the painful uterine contractions. Such a procedure can potentiate the use of hypnosis. This preoccupation undoubtedly explains to a degree the success of the natural childbirth method in which the woman spends a considerable amount of time thinking about whether or not she is carrying out this or that exercise correctly.]

Finally, when you are in the last stages of labor, you will push down when requested to do so. Naturally, the more you relax, the more effective each push will be. If you follow these suggestions you will get the most out of each contraction.

[Another way to deepen the hypnosis is to employ the husband's participation and post-hypnotic suggestions:] I am going to instruct your husband that each time you develop a contraction, he will squeeze your wrist with his forefinger and thumb. And, as he squeezes your wrist, this will be a cue, or a signal, that you will drop deeper and deeper relaxed with each deep breath you take.

[Backache in the sacral area causes considerable discomfort, especially if the fetus is in an occiput posterior position. Here, too, the husband's aid can be enlisted:] I want you to place the palm of your hand, with your fingers fanned out, over the small of your wife's back. You will press firmly over this area. You will start this at the beginning of each contraction and release the pressure only after the contraction has disappeared. [This maneuver often helps patients who complain bitterly of low back pain.]

If you do have more discomfort than you are able to tolerate, do not feel embarrassed if you have to moan. It will help relieve some of the tension. Also, if you wish to open your eyes, you may do so without interfering with the relaxed state you are in. As soon as you close your eyes, you will drop even deeper relaxed. You will not be bothered by any noises or sounds around you. As a matter of fact, you will become more and more concerned with your breathing and counting, and, as you become more involved in these, the sounds around you will fade into the distance. As the head of your baby descends down the birth canal, you will notice more of a desire to push. I have taught you how to breathe. You can grunt and bear down. Every contraction will be a signal for you to bear down harder. And, because you will be completely relaxed, you will obtain the maximal effect from each contraction. You can go through the rest of your delivery without any trouble. Remember, if you should require an anesthetic agent, it will be given to you. And, even if this is necessary, you will find that having a baby will be an exhilarating experience, especially if you are deeply relaxed.

[For the actual delivery, the patient can transfer the glove anesthesia to the perineum before it has been "prepped" or sterilized. She is instructed:] This area will remain completely numb and anesthetic. As you push down, with each deep breath you take this area will become more and more anesthetic. [One can also produce anesthesia by commenting:] As I stroke this area with my fingers, it will become numb and anesthetic, completely numb and anesthetic, just as if this area had been injected with procaine [lidocaine]. It will become just as numb and anesthetic as your jaws become after the dentist has blocked off a nerve. This area is getting very numb, heavy, and woodenlike.

[One can enhance the anesthetic effects of the above methods, after the vagina has been sterilized and the patient is ready for delivery, by the following suggestions:] I am now freezing all the skin between my thumb and forefinger. [Considerable pressure is exerted at this time.] Everywhere I touch my thumb and forefinger together, you will notice a numb, heavy, woodenlike sensation that will get more numb with each breath you take. [This, together with the delivery of the head, produces a considerable amount of pressure anesthesia which, in some patients who have a high pain threshold, is sufficient for the performance of an episiotomy.]

Suggestions with Untrained Patients in Labor

Nicholas L. Rock, M.D.,
T. E. Shipley, and C. Campbell
New Orleans, Louisiana

You seem uncomfortable and nervous about your labor, especially when you have a contraction. See how you tense up and fight these contractions? Now I am going to show you how you can relax your whole body by breathing correctly so you will be able to be more comfortable and endure the contractions and perhaps even sleep until your baby comes. It is very easy to do. All you have to do is cooperate and fix your eyes upon this target. . . . [At this point a fairly prominent object in the line of vision of the patient was used.] Keep your eyes on this target and no matter what happens do not move them away. If you do, bring your eyes back to the target and you will find it will make you much more comfortable. This whole procedure is very much like your everyday activities; for example, when you watch TV and are interested in the program, people come and go and you are not aware of them. Also, you may have experienced cutting your finger while cooking and not have noticed the pain or that it had been cut until afterwards. Or perhaps you might have seen a baby fall and hurt itself and cry but when the mother held it and kissed away the pain, the baby stopped crying. All this is a normal reaction of the human body; that is, by listening to my voice, watching the target, and trying to experience the things I tell you to, you will be able to relax your whole body, become more comfortable, and eventually fall asleep.

PREMATURE LABOR, MISCARRIAGE AND ABORTION

Hypnotic Relaxation Technique for Premature Labor

Haim Omer
Jerusalem, Israel

INTRODUCTION

Premature labor is the major cause of infant death and also results in costly hospitalization.

In a control group study, Omer documented that this hypnotic procedure combined with standard medication was clearly superior (p < 0.002) to a group receiving medications alone. Treatment was generally begun within three hours of hospitalization and lasted an average of three hours: one hour and a half on initial contact, and another hour and a half during the following days. Each patient also received an audiotape recorded especially for her with instructions to use it twice daily. (*Ed.*)

THE TECHNIQUE

[Following brief education about the nature of hypnosis:] An explanation of the physiological effects of hypnotic-relaxation was given as follows:

When you imagine a car accident your body reacts with signs of fright: Your heat beats faster; your muscles get tense; your blood pressure rises and so on. When you imagine a relaxed situation, for instance, a warm bath, your body also relaxes. The same is true with more specific images. When someone imagines that he is eating ice cream, the blood vessels in his stomach contract; when he imagines he is sipping hot tea from a cup, the blood vessels in his stomach dilate. It is thus possible to influence many bodily reactions in a desired manner. The goal of this hypnotic-relaxation exercise is to relax your whole body and your uterus in particular.

The therapist told the patient that the use of hypnotic-relaxation did not imply that contractions were due to psychological problems. The hypnotic-relaxation technique may influence physiological processes of physical as well as psychological origins.

If no other questions were asked, the therapist asked the patient if she was ready. If so, she was told to take a deep breath and close her eyes. . . . In what follows, the therapeutic procedure is described (schematically, whenever usual hypnotic techniques were used; in detail, whenever special interventions designed for this project were used).

A relaxation induction was utilized in which the therapist counted from 1 to 20 concentrating on various parts of the body. At the count of 10 the following suggestions were given:

I will now lay my hand lightly over your belly, and I will ask you to pay attention to the feeling of warmth which will develop under my hand. Now, pay attention to this warmth under my hand and imagine it slowly reaching your uterus. You can imagine this warmth spreading over your uterus, softening up every single corner and cell of your uterus, calming everything down slowly, as the sun relaxes and softens your muscles when you lie on a beach. This calmness may grow with every minute that goes by, with every breath you take.

These images were elaborated as the counting progressed to 15. At this point, suggestions were interspersed for trance deepening and further suggestions for uterine relaxation were given:

Maybe it is somewhat funny, but I may talk to your womb, and your womb . . . [here the women's name is inserted] can hear everything I say. Your womb . . . [the woman's name] hears me deeper and deeper, deeper than your conscious mind, your womb . . . [the woman's name] listens and understands everything that I say and may carry out those things that I am asking you to do. Your womb . . . [the woman's name] may rest so deeply, just as in a deep sleep and it . . . [the woman's name] can listen only to my voice and may know how to react so deeply to everything I say. The baby inside you may slowly become more comfortable, free; it has lots of space and nothing disturbs it; nothing presses upon it. Its small hands may float so freely, and you are so close to your baby that what happens to you passes over to your baby, and what happens to your baby passes over to you. You are so close to the baby that you can have a foggy feeling of the baby's foggy feelings and sensations. As the baby's hand becomes free and light it may start floating and moving [the therapist touches the woman's wrist and carefully raises it and moves it about, matching his motions to what he is saying. If catalepsy appears, the depth of hypnotic involvement can thus be checked]. It may get farther and farther away from the body, so lightly, so freely, so full of the open space surrounding it, and it may remain poised, floating, effortless, and it may slowly go down and rest, so deeply, so restful.

The counting progressed until 20 and a finger questioning procedure now took place:

Now I will ask you some questions about how your pregnancy will go on. You don't know the answer to these questions in any conscious way, but your body, deep inside you, knows the answers. The knowledge to answer these questions is there inside you, for your unconscious mind is very close to everything that happens to your body. You won't answer by speech, your body will show us the answers; your fingers will move and give us the answers. This finger [the index finger of the right hand was touched] will be the "Yes" finger, and this finger [the left hand index] will be the "No" finger. I will count to 30, and you can sink deeper and deeper, and with each count let your fingers become lighter and lighter as if they wished to rise all by themselves [the therapist counted to 30, giving suggestions for increased finger lightness and responsiveness]. The first question that I will ask you is whether deep inside your body and mind there is a readiness that the baby may go on growing inside you, inside your womb, until at least the beginning of the ninth month of pregnancy, until the 37th pregnancy week? [There is a short silent interval.] Slowly your fingers start to get that feeling, and they begin to move, that's right, lifting, more and more clearly, wonderful! [In 34 of 38 cases a positive answer was readily obtained, in two cases a negative one, and in three cases a no answer.] Now I will ask another question: Whether there is a readiness deep inside you to allow the baby to grow within you until the middle of the ninth month, say, the end of the 38th week? [There is a short silent interval. When a positive answer was obtained a third question was asked.] Now, maybe there is really a readiness deep inside you to let the baby remain and grow inside you to the very end of the ninth month? [There is another silent interval.]

Let us now ask another question: Is there a readiness deep inside you for your body to do everything to protect your pregnancy? For your body to learn how to move softly, to keep from making unnecessary efforts, to care for yourself slowly, softly, delicately? [There is a short interval.]

After this finger questioning procedure, a time progression was undertaken:

Please imagine that time is beginning to pass, a few hours have gone by, and you are now in the women's ward, away from the delivery room, and you may remember your hospitalization as something which took place a while ago, so that you are already used to it. Morning, noon and evening look very much alike as you rest in the hospital; a day has gone by, and you can feel calmer and better, and another day has gone by. Little by little a week has passed, and after while you go home, and with every hour that goes by and every day, your baby becomes

stronger and prettier. Another day and another day and some more and, look, another week has passed. Your baby's skin gets smoother, rosier, silk-like; another week goes by, and the line of his eyes and lips becomes more and more clear and beautiful. He gets stronger and bigger. One more week, and one more week, and the baby has all the space he needs and all the calm and time in the world. Somewhere in the middle of the ninth month you may look backwards and remember with your imagination how you have gone through all of those weeks, how you have succeeded in overcoming that crisis, how everything went on so smoothly, how your womb grew quiet and comfortable, how you found a funny kind of deep patience within you, the patience of a tree filling up its fruit with sweetness, a patience which filled up your body and mind. A feeling of timelessness, of having plenty of space around you, just like a tree allowing its fruit to ripen, to grow, to become full, to get its color, its sweetness, its juiciness, as if you had all the time in the world to allow your fruit to get totally ripe. And when you reach your day of delivery, somewhere by the end of the ninth month, everything is ready for an easy delivery. Surely you know how hard it is to pluck an unripe fruit from a tree, a green fruit, how stubbornly the fruit refuses to be plucked, how much you have to pull at it. Whereas a ripe fruit, when its time is come, when it is already beautiful, and full with its sweet scent, it is enough to give it a slight pull and it is out, for this happened at the right time. [If changes have appeared in the monitor as generally was the case, the therapist complimented the patient's womb for the achievement.] Now I am going to count backwards, from 30 to 1, and with each count all of the things I've said will slowly sink in your mind, like rain which slowly sinks into dry earth.

Dehypnotization proceeded by backward counting. During this process, suggestions were given to the effect that the patient would be influenced by the therapeutic messages even when not thinking about it. She was told that this influence would lead her to move around in a mild and self-protective way and that she would be able to remain calm even in the face of thoughts or events which would otherwise be disturbing. . . .

After the therapist had reviewed with the patient her reactions to the exercise, he tried to keep her mind involved associatively in the hypnotic process by telling her some thera-peutic anecdotes. These anecdotes are actually indirect suggestions for a continuation of preg-nancy, and are based on similar procedures by Erickson (Zeig, 1980). Here are two examples of such anecdotes:

(a) Natural scientists have long known that fe-males of many species are capable of influencing the timing of their delivery. The African wildebeests (a species of buffalo), for instance, live in large herds, sometimes consisting of hundreds of animals. This is a wandering animal, the wandering being a part of their defense against predators.

The female wildebeests are in heat for about one and a half months every year. This period is common for the whole herd. Pregnancy lasts for 11 months so that the calves should be delivered within a one and a half month period. Here a problem arises: Will the whole herd wait for each cow to deliver? This is a dangerous solution since the herd will then be liable to predation. Is it possible that the cow about to deliver will leave the herd and stay by itself? Of course this would leave her and her calf totally unprotected. The solution which nature devised for this problem is amazing. In a manner which is not well understood, all the cows deliver on the same day. In a few hours' time all of the calves are standing on their feet! The early ones . . . [the woman's name is inserted] postpone the delivery, whereas the late ones deliver earlier. This could be a story about wildebeests alone, but the fact is that their hormonal processes seem to be extremely sim-ilar to human ones. Everything a wildebeest can do with its uterus, it is quite possible that a woman can do as well. Only you don't know yet that you know how to do it. You just don't know consciously how it is that you are now calming your uterus, how your body is changing its timetable, postponing things, letting time go by.

(b) In some areas of South America there are some kinds of crickets which stay buried for 13 years as larvae deep inside the earth. Every 13 years they become crickets for one day and they go out of their holes for a giant honeymoon. The noise they make can be heard from enormous distances; the whole jungle is filled up with it. Sometimes a cricket comes out before its time. Something was wrong and it comes out something like a year or two too early. It gets out and starts chirping with great enthusiasm. The time, however, is still not ripe, and no answer comes. Slowly its chirping grows less and less fre-quent. Tzirrr, Tzirrr . . . Tzirrr . . . Tzirrr . . . [in Hebrew the word Tzir means also a uterine contrac-tion], slowly weakening, diminishing, fading out until it completely disappears.

After a few anecdotes, the therapist decided according to the uterine conditions whether to do another hypnotic-relaxation exercise. If con-tractions had disappeared, he would perform a similar exercise on the following day (without the finger questioning part) which he would record on cassette. If contractions were still present he would perform a second exercise on the spot. In this manner all women received at least two personal exercises. About half of them had the second exercise in the initial session, and another half had it the following day. These differences were not found to be related to outcome.

After the end of the woman's hospital stay (generally one week), the therapist contacted her by phone about once every two weeks to check how she was feeling and whether she was listening to the cassette.

Use of Immediate Interventions to Uncover Emotional Factors in Pre-Abortion Conditions

David B. Cheek, M.D.
Santa Barbara, California

In a retrograde study of abortion sequences some years ago, I found that more than half of the women started their bleeding and expulsive contractions during the night, usually between one and four in the morning. The majority of those who started during the day revealed, during age regression, their belief that the pro-cess really originated with troubled dreams repeated for several nights prior to the abor-tion.

Fortunately, thought sequences capable of causing abortion very rarely do so the first time around. They occur on repeated cycles of sleep and on successive nights of sleep. This gives the patient an opportunity to recognize that her sleep has been disturbed and to report this change in behavior to her doctor or midwife. Early intervention can prevent loss of a normal conceptus. The physician should know how to act at once during the first telephone call of alarm. In the case of a woman with a history of habitual abortion, it is far better to check out the emotional background *before* the patient begins the pregnancy.

Even if the process of bleeding and consciously perceived uterine contractions has already begun, there is usually time to expose the emotional cause and help the patient stop the progress toward abortion or delivery of a dangerously premature infant. But intervention must begin at once and should not be delayed by admission of the patient to a hospital. It can be handled over the telephone, any time, at home or even long distance when the patient is on a vacation trip.

All pregnant women, regardless of previous history, should know how to recognize that their sleep has been troubled and be shown how to check their own unconscious reactions to threatening dreams and deep sleep ideation. Their first line of correction is to ask for an ideomotor response to the question, "Is there an emotional cause for this?" If the answer is a yes with a finger signal or movement of a Chevruel pendulum, they can ask, "Now that I know this, can I stop my bleeding (or cramps) and go on with this pregnancy?"

If the answer suggests an organic beginning or inability to stop the process, there is still time to make a telephone call to the doctor or midwife who is capable of inducing hypnosis over the telephone, searching for the causal experience, and permitting the patient to make her corrections for the sake of her baby.

Consider this example: A woman who has not been to your office but has been referred to you for obstetrical care calls at 3 p.m. on Sunday to say that she has an appointment next week but started to bleed slightly this morning and is now having cramps. She would have called earlier but she did not want to bother you. She reports that her last period

started ten weeks ago, that this is a planned pregnancy but she has had five previous miscarriages of planned pregnancies, and she hopes that she might be able to carry this one. She is 30 years old and has been happily married for six years.

This is an emergency and you must act quickly if you are to be of help to her. You need not be concerned about her past history. She is frightened and is therefore already in a hypnoidal state. This enables her to respond strongly to positive, hopeful suggestions given honestly and authoritatively. We should use hypnosis permissively under peaceful circumstances, but authoritative commands are necessary during an emergency.

Explain that you will show her how to stop this process but that you need to know what has started this trouble. Say to her, "*Let the unconscious part of your mind go back to the moment you are starting the bleeding. When you are there, you will feel a twitching sensation in your right index finger. Don't try to recall what is going on. Just say 'now' when you feel that finger lifting up from where it is resting.*"

There is a double reason for this approach. Your words tell the patient that something can be done *right now* to prevent what has happened regularly before. The request for an unconscious gesture when reaching the moment that bleeding started centers her attention on what her finger might do and diminishes her acute attention to the contractions of her uterus and the fact that she is bleeding.

It may take less than 30 seconds before she says, "Now." You will probably notice that her voice is subdued, indicating that she has slipped into a deeper trance state. Say to her, "*Let a thought come to you about what your unconscious knows has started your bleeding. When you know it, your yes finger will lift again, and when it does please tell me what comes to your mind.*"

There may be another 30-second pause before she responds. Be quiet until she reports something such as: "I'm asleep after lunch. I'm dreaming that the doctor is saying he doesn't think I will be able to carry my baby because of all the other ones I have lost. He says we can try some hormones to see if that will help."

You answer, "*That index finger can represent a yes answer to a question. Your middle finger on the same hand can represent a no answer. This is like nodding your head unconsciously when you agree with someone or shaking your head if you disagree. I want to know, is the dream occurring* **after** *you have started bleeding?*"

She answers, "My no finger is lifting."

"*All right. This is a dream and your unconscious knows the dream is the cause of your bleeding. Sadness and fear can make a uterus bleed even when a woman is not pregnant. Is your inner mind willing now to stop the bleeding and let your baby go on developing normally?*"

The patient will usually find her yes finger lifting for this question, but if she gets a no, or some other finger, that might mean she does not want to answer; then you must ask her yes finger to lift when she knows why she feels this way. It is usually some feeling of guilt or defeatist belief system at work. Simple recognition permits her to remove that factor.

You conclude the telephone call with a deepening series of suggestions and directions to relax her abdomen, stop the irritability of her uterus, and fall asleep for about 10 minutes after hanging up. You ask her to call you back in one hour with a report. Do not say any more about bleeding. Just ask her to call you in one hour. The statement often used by doctors is, "Give me a call if your bleeding continues or gets worse." Such a statement is interpreted as meaning the doctor expects her to bleed, and she will do so. She has shown five previous times how well she can bleed and abort.

You explain that this does not mean she has to miscarry again. Bleeding occurs in 30% of pregnant women at some time during their pregnancy and has nothing to do with prognosis unless they become frightened.

This presentation is easily understood by a frightened patient. The statement of a way for communicating unconscious information is also telling the patient tacitly that discovery of the cause will permit correction of the problem. This diverts her total attention from the bleeding and uterine cramps to the more constructive area of what she can do to stop the trouble and get on with the pregnancy.

The questions and the unconscious review of significant events have led the patient further away from the thought that she might lose this pregnancy.

A marvelous protective action takes place by virtue of entering a hypnotic state at a time of crisis. Coagulation mechanisms return to a normal balance and all vegetative behavior is improved. There is no need to command bleeding to stop or the uterus to remain quiet, but it helps the patient to make better use of these protective functions when you show respect for this phenomenon by saying: "*Now this is something you dreamed. Would you agree that this dream does not need to threaten the life of your baby, and that you have a right to stop your bleeding and get on with your pregnancy?*"

Treating the Trauma of Prospective Abortion

Helen H. Watkins, M.A.
Missoula, Montana

INDICATIONS AND OUTLINE

This is a technique for use with newly pregnant women who are struggling with a decision concerning whether or not to have an abortion.

FIRST SESSION. Explore the pros, cons, facts, data, feelings, consequences, attitudes and beliefs.

SECOND SESSION. Explore the patient's feelings and attitudes with hypnosis.

THIRD SESSION. Following hypnotic induction, I have her visualize the fetus and speak to the fetus silently, expressing her conflict about the pregnancy. Then wait for a response, whether it is a feeling, something heard, or something seen. The patient repeats this process at home, usually by just closing her eyes, breathing to enter a relaxed state, focusing on her abdomen and stroking her abdomen gently.

CONSECUTIVE SESSIONS. If the patient decides to have an abortion and a medical appointment is made, then (first in my office and then at home) I have her speak to the fetus silently, explaining why she cannot give it birth and expressing her feelings to the fetus. If the woman senses a response of agreement from the fetus, then I have her begin the process of visualizing the fetus leaving her body in any way that comes to her. If the patient receives no response, then she makes the decision as to when the visualization of the abortion is appropriate. Sometimes the upcoming surgical procedure presses her for time; sometimes she simply senses the appropriate time.

It is surprising how often a response is forthcoming. I let the patient come to her own interpretation. No matter what happens physically, the patient finds emotional release in this procedure, and with emotional release comes a reduction of guilt.

Spontaneous miscarriages sometimes result. Women who experience this react with a sense of awe, respect for another energy system, and a sense of love by the fetus in agreeing to end its existence. It is a profound experience.

Perhaps these women experience the grief syndrome before the loss of the fetus, so that when the abortion is done the whole experience is finished. Many find a deeper sense of self, even deeper respect for life, looking forward to pregnancy in the future when the time is more appropriate. It is as if a force beyond their own comprehension understands their grief, their sorrow, and their desperation. Instead of potential tragedy, this process becomes a healing experience in their lives.

HYPEREMESIS GRAVIDARUM AND MISCELLANEOUS GYNECOLOGIC DISORDERS

Hypnotic Intervention with Hyperemesis Gravidarum

Ralph V. August, M.D.

INTRODUCTION

The late Dr. August used group training with obstetrical patients, and his groups included both experienced and new hypnotic subjects. He believed that by watching experienced subjects who entered hypnosis more quickly and easily, beginners learned self-hypnosis more quickly. He learned that hypnosis followed by suggestions for continuing comfort, "Just like you feel now," would control hyperemesis for two to ten days, and sometimes permanently. The following suggestions model those given in

front of the training group to a beginning subject who was also suffering with hyperemesis gravidarum. (*Ed.*)

SUGGESTIONS

You just concentrate your mind on my voice as I talk with you, as I make suggestions which will be beneficial to you. And as you count each breath, you will find with each deep breath, you relax deeper . . . and deeper . . . and so now you may be ready to concentrate your mind on your heart, and notice how, with each heart beat, you can feel yourself relaxing . . . deeper . . . and deeper . . . and deeper. So you can keep your mind on each heart beat, using each one to help you to go deeper . . . and deeper. And you may notice by now that your heart beats seem slower, more comfortable, more relaxed, more at ease. While you keep on relaxing, getting sleepier . . . and sleepier. And by now you may be ready for that which for you, Gail, is most important of all. Everyone else is aware of this . . . because, by now, you can concentrate your mind on your abdomen. Notice how your abdomen feels warm, relaxed, at ease. Feels so good that it feels like you could eat and drink anything you want . . . and I *know you can. It feels so good now* . . . it feels better than it's felt for quite some time. And some women may at this point be aware of the baby's movement or not, depending on what the baby happens to be doing. You will notice, Gail, that your abdomen and stomach just feel good . . . and that's all, because it is very, very early in your pregnancy. And you will notice now, it feels so good that you can ignore your abdomen and stomach altogether. You don't need to pay attention to them anymore because you know they feel good now, and you can continue to keep them feeling good, as I know you want to, and as now you can and will . . . while you keep on being as comfortable as you wish.

And by now you might feel as though your mind is floating on a cloud. Floating along . . . at ease . . . with your forehead cool, so that you can ignore everything down below. You don't need to pay attention to anything else in your body now . . . you just keep your mind in the clouds, and notice how good it feels. And you can do so, whenever you want to. All you need to do, Gail, is always just to sit back comfortably in a chair and say to yourself, "Gail, sleep." And every woman in this room knows all she ever needs do is to address herself by her own given name . . . when she does, just using the word *sleep*, she can relax completely . . . she knows that this sleep is a hypnotic sleep; in which you are just as aware as you want to be of the things around you, and you can ignore as much as you want to of everything else about you; in which you know that whenever you want to, all you need to do is to count to 3, and feel good, and you will be wide awake. And you can do so whenever you wish, and continue feeling good. Remember also,

Gail, that practice makes perfect, and you can practice doing this every day, as many times a day as you wish. And of course you, Gail, are also welcome to make your appointments for each week with our group; and when you have started gaining weight again, then you can go to your regular visits, which would be at the time of your regular obstetric visit, because it will be once a month for a while yet, until possibly about the eighth month . . . and of course today is December 18th. So each one of you is aware now of how comfortable you feel, and each one of you is aware of how easy it is to help yourself. Remember always that hypnosis is never what *I* do. It is never what anybody else or any other doctor does. It is what *you* do that counts. Where I fit into the picture is that I am a teacher showing you how.

This will help you to help yourself; and this, of course, will be my pleasure to help you to help yourself; and any time you want to, you count to 3, feel good, and are wide awake.

Control Of Hyperemesis

Larry Goldmann, M.D.
Fort Myers, Florida

PRE-INDUCTION DISCUSSION

1. Routine discussion of misconceptions about hypnosis.
2. Discussion of power of unconscious mind to control all body systems, i.e., respiration rate, heart rate, flight or fight responses, and alimentary function.
3. Discussion of physiology of alimentary tract, i.e., peristaltic motion, gastric empty, swallowing, etc.
4. Discussion of vomiting control center in brain.
5. Discussion of nutrition and its effect on pregnancy.
6. Find out from patient what her favorite food is, how she likes it prepared, and where she likes to eat it.

SUGGESTIONS ONCE IN TRANCE

1. The normal peristaltic motion of your bowel and esophagus move food down into the stomach then into and through the intestine for absorption of nutrients.
2. The unconscious mind controls the direction of peristalsis. The unconscious mind knows the path food is supposed to take.
3. The unconscious mind also knows how important nutrition is to the proper growth and development of your baby.
4. The unconscious mind also knows there are many times when the vomiting center of the brain needs to be stimulated, i.e., in case of food poisoning or intestinal flu, and it does this automatically. But during a normal physiologic state, like pregnancy, it knows that this center should be suppressed, because vomiting and nausea are counterproductive to good nutrition, which the unconscious mind knows is vital to a normal pregnancy outcome.
5. There may be times during the pregnancy when the unconscious mind feels there is a need for nausea, but these times will be short-lived, lasting 30 seconds or less, and will not interfere with your ability to eat, digest, and absorb your meals in a normal, profitable fashion, assuring you and your baby proper nutrition throughout the pregnancy.
6. Your unconscious mind knows that your pregnancy is a normal, physical state and does not and will not have any need for vomiting.
7. Your unconscious mind knows that good nutrition is essential to the normal progress of your pregnancy, and will work to assure you of this.
8. Now, I would like you to picture, very clearly, your favorite food, prepared as you like it. And see yourself with this food in a relaxed atmosphere, where you feel comfortable, safe, and secure. When you can vividly see and smell the food, please signal me.
9. Now, begin to eat your favorite food. I wonder how good it tastes, and how easily it goes down into your relaxed stomach, and does not cause any nausea or urge to vomit.
10. Feel how satisfying it feels to eat and digest your favorite meal, and know that you are giving vital nutrition to your normally developing infant — nutrition which cannot be obtained through IV feeding.
11. Now, at your own rate, finish your meal, and see how there is no sign of nausea or vomiting. Once you have finished your meal, please signal me.
12. Now, I would like you to begin to become more awake and aware, feeling very confident in your ability to eat and digest meals without any significant nausea and no vomiting, knowing that your unconscious mind will not allow you to vomit, because vomiting deprives both you and your baby of needed nutrition.
13. As you return to the awake, aware state, you will look forward to eating and enjoying your meals.

Suggestions for Hyperemesis

William T. Heron, Ph.D.

INTRODUCTION

The late Dr. Heron, working with Milton Abramson, M.D., developed the following suggestions for "morning sickness." They trained patients in a group, but these suggestions were given only to those suffering with hyperemesis. (*Ed.*)

SUGGESTIONS

Now, Mrs. C., you are resting comfortably and relaxed. Sometimes you have a little nausea and you would like to escape this difficulty. Let us point out that your physiology is under some strain because it is really taking care of two people — you and the baby. This increased strain does sometimes result in nausea. Now, after this if you should feel nauseated, all you need do is to sit or lie down for a few minutes. This resting your body will also rest your physiology, and the nausea will pass. All you need to do is to rest a few minutes, and the nausea will pass. Soon, as your physiology becomes accustomed to the increased load, the morning sickness will disappear completely.

Progressive Anesthesia Technique for Hyperemesis Gravidarum

D. Corydon Hammond, Ph.D.
Salt Lake City, Utah

INDICATIONS

The progressive anesthesia induction, the verbalizations for which are in Chapter 3 on pain management, may prove helpful with hyperemesis when other procedures have not met with complete success in treating hyperemesis. The disadvantage of this technique is that it will require the patient to remain immobile for a period of time. However, in cases of severe hyperemesis it is desirable to have periods of bed rest rather than continuing to vomit. In hypnotically talented and experienced subjects, it may be used as the induction, combining it with a progressive relaxation technique. In other cases, the procedure may follow induction and deepening by other methods. An alternative to this method is to ask the patient, after induction and deepening, "Would you like to have a pleasant, surprising experience? In a moment, I'm going to have you awaken from trance, but you will only awaken from the neck up. Would that be all right? So that in a moment, as I instruct you to, you will only awaken from the neck up, and the rest of your body will remain asleep in a deep trance. You will only awaken from the neck up." Refer to Chapter 3 (pp. 81–83) for the complete verbalizations of this technique.

Suggestions for Hyperemesis

Harold B. Crasilneck, Ph.D., and
James A. Hall, M.D.
Dallas, Texas

[After the patient is induced into a moderately deep hypnotic state, the authors demonstrate glove anesthesia for purposes of trance ratification. After removal of the anesthesia, the following suggestions are given. (*Ed.*)]

The nausea and the vomiting will simply discontinue. . . . You can and will digest foods easily without fear or excessive tensions or anxieties. . . . You simply will be relaxed and at ease; your mind and your body relaxed. . . . You can and will ingest and digest foods easily, with little or no nausea or discomfort.

Suggestions for Hyperemesis Gravidarum

David Waxman, L.R.C.P., M.R.C.S.
London, England

INTRODUCTION

Waxman uses hypnosis, sometimes combined with other medical measures, routinely in the treatment of hyperemesis. Exploration of psychological-emotional factors is recommended in resistant cases. (*Ed.*)

SUGGESTIONS

As you focus your attention on your stomach . . . *you will begin to experience a feeling of warmth, spreading into your stomach.* That feeling of warmth is increasing . . . with every word that I utter, warm and comfortable . . . warm and comfortable. . . . As soon as you feel that warmth . . . please raise your index finger. That's right. Now, put it down again.

And as your stomach feels warmer . . . it is beginning to feel more normal . . . more and more comfortable. All feelings of sickness are passing away completely . . . you no longer feel at all sick. Your stomach feels perfectly normal . . . and comfortable, in every way.

And in a few moments . . . when I count up to seven . . . you will open your eyes, and be wide awake, again. *You will wake up . . . with your stomach completely comfortable . . . without the slightest feeling of sickness or discomfort . . . and you will find that . . . when you wake up, each morning . . . you will not feel the slightest trace of sickness whatever . . . your stomach will remain perfectly normal . . . without the slightest discomfort of any kind.* And, with every one of these treatments . . . this trouble is going to disappear . . . more and more quickly . . . more and more completely.

Suggestions with Psychogenic Amenorrhea

William S. Kroger, M.D.
Palm Springs, California

REHEARSAL

Although this method does not always work, the author has on several occasions dramatically induced the menses by hypnosis. . . . Bleeding seldom can be initiated by direct suggestion. Rather, the technique is to ask the following questions: "Do your breasts get hot and heavy just before you are due to have your period? Do you feel like jumping out of your skin at this time? Is there any pain connected with the onset of the flow? If so, where is it? So you have a backache, or a feeling of pressure in the pelvic region? Are there any other symptoms associated with the onset of the flow?"

If the answers to the above questions are fed back to the hypnotized patient, one has an excellent chance of reestablishing the menses by this type of sensory-imagery conditioning. The verbalization used is as follows: "In about 2 weeks, you will find it most advantageous to feel all the sensations that you previously described and associated with your periods. Think

of the exact place where you have discomfort and pressure. Perhaps you might even imagine how 'jumpy' and irritable you felt just before your flow." [In this technique, a "dry run" or a rehearsal of the onset of menstruation under autohypnosis helps to reinforce the appropriate posthypnotic suggestions.

AGE REGRESSION.   Another technique is to utilize hypnotic age regression. The patient is regressed to her last period and asked to recall the specific sensations associated with it; if she wishes, she can choose the approximate date for the establishment of the menses. Suggestions must be made in a confident manner. However, the physician should never get himself "out on a limb" by guaranteeing that the menses will occur on a specific date. Rather, he can preface his remarks by saying, "If you are able to feel the sensations associated with your period, you have a good chance of having your period. Or, perhaps, you can begin to wonder whether it will be a day or two before the date you chose, or maybe the period will come on a week afterward."

Suggestions with Leukorrhea

F. H. Leckie, M.D.

INDICATIONS AND CONTRAINDICATIONS

Leukorrhea, a non-bloody vaginal discharge, may be responsive in some cases to hypnotic suggestion. However, at present we lack research evidence for this. Thus it is vitally important to obtain a gynecologic evaluation to rule out such causes as chronic cervicitis, eversion, erosion, genital infection, tumors, fistulas, and estrogen deficiency. (*Ed.*)

SUGGESTIONS

Deeply asleep—happy—calm—confident—relaxed. In the neck of the womb there are little glands which produce a slippery, clear secretion—this is normal and healthy. But various emotions, such as excitement, worry, fear, can make these little glands more active so that they produce more secretion; this excess secretion becomes noticeable as a discharge. You know that you have been examined and have been found to be normal; especially your womb, your ovaries, your front passage are normal. Because you are worried, anxious, tense, the little glands in the neck of your womb are producing more secretion. You can now learn to relax and control your feelings and emotions to free yourself from tension; in so doing, the little glands in the neck of the womb work

normally and your discharge clears. You feel better, more and more confident, and in control of your emotions. You are able to face all your problems and worries calmly and confidently. By counting up to four, slowly and confidently to yourself, when you feel excited and tense, you become calm and relaxed, and all your fears and worries fall away from you. You are now able to relax for sexual intercourse with your husband, and from now on you are able to have and enjoy full, normal sexual intercourse with him, free from all pain or discomfort, and you are able to achieve complete satisfaction and relief. Your discharge now clears.

HYPNOSIS WITH EMOTIONAL AND PSYCHIATRIC DISORDERS

INTRODUCTION

THIS CHAPTER IS DIVIDED into three sections. The first section consists of suggestive techniques that may be used with a variety of emotional disorders. Some of the contributions model "symbolic imagery techniques" that may be valuable in working through problems like guilt, anger, depression, fears, doubts, and anxieties. This section also includes two insight-oriented contributions for furthering self-insight. Stanton demonstrates how guided imagery techniques may facilitate self-understanding. Bresler's model of the inner adviser technique illustrates how this method may be used for self-exploration as well as symptomatic relief. Brown and Fromm's contribution demonstrates how suggestions may be used to enhance affective expression in emotionally underexpressive patients. Two metaphoric interventions are also included in this section.

The second section of the chapter models hypnotic suggestions that may be useful with severely disturbed patients, such as borderline, schizophrenic, bipolar, suicidal and emotionally labile patients. The final section of the chapter focuses on hypnotic interventions with post-traumatic stress disorder and multiple personality disorder patients.

Symbolic Imagery Techniques: Indications and Contraindications

There is a category of hypnotherapy techniques that I refer to as "symbolic imagery" techniques. It appears that a hypnotic state allows a suspension of our "generalized reality orientation" so that imagination may be used to powerfully influence thoughts and feelings. These techniques seem most effective with individuals who are responsive to both visual and, secondarily, kinesthetic imagery.

Thus, in hypnosis, imagery experiences that might otherwise seem superficial and silly may often produce potent therapeutic change. Watkin's (1980) silent abreaction procedure (see Chapter 16), in which a patient imagines demolishing a large boulder to safely vent resentment and anger, is an example of this category of techniques. Another clinically useful method is the red balloon technique (Walch, 1976). Some symbolic imagery techniques that were formulated by Dr. Harry Stanton may be found in this volume in the sections on ego-strengthening, anxiety, and sleep disorders. Hammond's master control room technique in the chapter on sexual dysfunctions is yet another example of a symbolic imagery procedure.

These methods are particularly suited for reducing problematic emotions, such as anger, resentment, guilt, pathological jealousy, compulsive cravings (e.g., for alcohol, drugs, cigarettes), and obsessional worries. Guided imagery techniques, as illustrated by Stanton's methods for facilitating self-understanding, may also be used for self-exploration and enhancement of insight. Working with emotional disorders, however, is all too frequently not as simple as suggesting them away or imagining them disappearing. Clinicians are advised to engage in careful assessment and history-taking prior to using hypnosis or any other therapeutic technique. Furthermore, training in hypnosis itself is insufficient preparation for treating psychological disorders. You should not use hypnosis to treat a condition you are not trained to treat with other, nonhypnotic methods.

Clinicians who work with emotional disorders will find, in many cases, that exploration (e.g., through ideomotor signaling or hypnoprojective techniques) of the underlying dynamics and abreactive work may be crucial preliminary steps that will increase the effectiveness and lasting benefits of these methods. Technique selection (Hammond & Miller, in press) will be dependent on: (1) the extent to which the emotional problems seem long-lasting versus recent and more delimited in scope; (2) the degree to which specific historical events and factors seem implicated; (3) the extent to which the preliminary history and assessment suggest secondary gains and adaptive functions may be involved in the emotional disorder; and (4) the initial expectations of the patient. When patients have expectations for the facilitation of insight or working-through (abreaction) of past events, and when problems seem more diffuse in origin, longer-term, and linked to internal dynamics and adaptive functions, more exploratory hypnotic techniques seem indicated initially. Insight-oriented hypnotherapy may sometimes require time, but in other cases may only take one, two or three sessions. Afterwards, symbolic imagery techniques may be very powerful and facilitative.

Hypnosis with Severely Disturbed Patients

Scagnelli (1976) noted three special problems and challenges for clinicians using hypnosis with schizophrenic patients:

1. The problem of control wherein these patients are intensely concerned with maintaining control and fear of loss of control. This fear may be

managed through allowing the patient to keep his eyes open, emphasizing self-hypnosis for self-control, and using a permissive hypnotic style.

2. Fear of closeness between patient and therapist, which necessitates the therapist's allowing the patient maximal freedom and independence, including freedom to reject the therapist and hypnosis.

3. Fear of giving up a negative self-concept for a more positive one, which may create resistance to ego-strengthening techniques.

Despite these unique challenges, patients with developmental deficits may be treated with the aid of hypnosis. There is such an increasingly large body of literature on the use of hypnosis with seriously disturbed patients that it is beyond the scope of this introduction to survey these articles. However, reviews of this area of treatment may be found in Murray-Jobsis (1984), Brown and Fromm (1986), Baker (1983a, 1983b, 1983c), and Copeland (1986). In addition, Hodge's contribution to this section provides a practical clinical overview on the topic of using hypnosis with psychotic patients.

Post-Traumatic Stress Disorder and Multiple Personality Disorder

Through the years there have been a variety of published works concerned with the psychotherapeutic treatment of the effects of traumatic stress. Following World War I, hypnosis and abreactive therapy became popular for rehabilitating troops suffering from "shell shock" (Shorvon & Sargant, 1947). Similarly, the impact of traumatic events in World War II encouraged a variety of publications on treatment of "war neurosis" (Grinker & Spiegel, 1943, 1945; Kardiner & Spiegel, 1947; Sargant & Slater, 1941; Watkins, 1949), as did the psychological casualties of the war in Vietnam (Figley, 1978; Van der Kolk; 1984). Our society has also grown more violent with the passage of time. Violent crimes and rape have increased, and we have now begun to recognize, believe in, and more accurately diagnose incest and childhood sexual abuse (Courtois, 1988; Russell, 1986). These events have lead us to more thoroughly appreciate the need for the treatment of post-traumatic stress disorders, whether they stem from war, child abuse, spouse abuse, cult abuse, terrorist actions or calamities of nature. It is the rare therapist who is not confronted with victims of some type of trauma.

Ever since the earliest work with PTSD, hypnosis has appeared prominently in the treatment literature as a modality that often produces beneficial results. Fascinatingly, as research has accumulated, we have discovered that childhood trauma and severity of punishment in childhood are related to both multiple personality disorder (a type of post-traumatic stress disorder) (Bliss, 1980; Coons, 1980) and high hypnotizability (Hilgard, 1970; Nowlis, 1969; Nash, Lynn, & Givens, 1984). Providing further support for these studies, Cooper and London (1976) learned that parents of high hypnotizable subjects rated themselves as more strict and impatient than parents of low hypnotizable subjects.

Thus it appears that trauma, especially early childhood trauma, encourages the use of dissociative processes, often leaving victims with higher hypnotic talent and capacity. This provides further suggestive evidence that hypnosis may often be an effective treatment modality with PTSD, and even more so in the treatment of multiple personality disorder—the most severe form of PTSD.

The selections in the latter part of this chapter will first provide you with illustrative suggestions that may be used with traumatic stress victims other than MPD patients. Herbert's contribution presents suggestions for use with assault victims in an emergency room setting and Ebert's material focuses on rape victims. Suggestions for the reframing of traumatic dreams, a common PTSD symptom, are provided by Mutter, and Havens' models an intervention with adult victims of abuse. A unique contribution by de Rios and Friedmann provides you with Spanish language suggestions for PTSD victims, along with the English translation of the suggestions.

The final part of this chapter concentrates on suggestions that may be useful with MPD patients. Kluft models for us fusion rituals and suggestions for containing the turmoil and dysphoria that are so often present in MPD patients undergoing therapy. Torem illustrates how ego-strengthening suggestions may be adapted for this population, and Price demonstrates his approach to exploration with MPD patients. Finally, I have provided some brief examples of metaphors that I use in selected circumstances with multiple personality patients. For a systematic, thorough study of the use of hypnosis with MPD, you are encouraged to refer to the following sources: Braun, 1984a, 1984b; Kluft, 1982, 1983, 1985, 1986; Putnam, 1989; Putnam, Guroff, Silberman, Barban, and Post, 1986.

SUGGESTIVE TECHNIQUES WITH EMOTIONAL DISORDERS

Hypnotherapeutic Technique for the Reduction of Guilt: The Door of Forgiveness

Helen H. Watkins, M.A.
Missoula, Montana

I hypnotize the patient, deepening by walking down stairs, and then suggest the following: "In front of us is a hallway at the end of which is the Door of Forgiveness. However, before you can reach the Door of Forgiveness, there may be other doors you may need to pass through. Look on either side of the hallway and tell me if you see any doors."

If the patient perceives doors on either side of the hallway, I ask, "To which door do you wish

to go first?" After the patient answers, we walk to the door and I ask the patient to describe the door. Then I ask, "Have you ever seen this door before?" The answer gives the patient a possible focus of where to go. I continue, "Would you open the door while we stand at the doorway looking in, and tell me what you see?" At this point, the patient becomes the observer and experiences as object whatever he or she sees in the room. If the patient walks into the room and participates in the scene, then the event is experienced as subject. The purpose of entering the room is to resolve some experience, some relationship out of the past which involves guilt. An emotional abreaction, therefore, may be involved. I am a supportive guide, but not an active participant. Whenever the patient feels finished, we close the door and come to the next one.

When there are no more doors to be seen, we walk to the Door of Forgiveness, and I say, "We are now at the Door of Forgiveness. As I open the door, walk to the middle of this place while I remain inside by the closed door. If you wish, let me know what happens." I am no longer a guide; I am simply a silent listener. In that way, the patient may share the forgiveness with me, but I am not the forgiver. The patient finds his or her own self-forgiveness. This technique may span several sessions.

Dumping the "Rubbish"

H. E. Stanton, Ph.D.
Hobart, Tasmania, Australia

THE LAUNDRY

Imagine yourself going into your laundry, filling the sink with water, opening a trap door in your head, pulling out the unwanted rubbish such as fears, doubts, anxieties, and guilts, and "dumping" it in the water, which becomes blacker and blacker as you do so. Finally, imagine yourself pulling out the plug and letting the inky water vanish down the sink.

ROOM AND FIRE

Imagine yourself on the tenth floor on an apartment building, waiting for the elevator. When it arrives, you enter and turn to face the door. To the right hand side of the door is a vertical indicator showing the floor numbers. At the moment, the number 10 is illuminated. The elevator begins its descent, smoothly, quietly, comfortably. As it reaches the ninth floor, the number 9 is illuminated, but the elevator continues on smoothly and effortlessly for this is yours alone; it will not be stopping to pick up anyone else. The numbers illuminate in turn as each floor is reached, your feelings of relaxation and comfort increasing as you approach

closer and closer to the ground level. When you reach the ground level you feel very much at ease, yet you can go still deeper, for on the indicator there remain three basement levels, B1, B2, and B3. As the elevator passes each of these floors you are able to let go still more, so that when you reach basement level 3, and the doors open, you are feeling a wonderful sense of ease and comfort.

In this state, you leave the elevator and, crossing a hallway, open the door to a room which you enter. This is a beautifully furnished room with a deep pile carpet and superb drapes. In this room is a large stone fireplace with a fire burning. Perhaps you can see the flames licking around the logs, hear the crackle and hiss, smell the smoke, and feel the glorious warmth soaking into every cell of your body.

Things you may not wish to keep in your life, such as fears, doubts, anxieties, hostilities, resentments, and guilts, can be imagined lying on a small table, in the form of accounts which have been paid. As there is no longer a need to keep these settled accounts around, you can pick them up and drop them onto the fire, one at a time, feeling a sense of release as they are transformed into ashes.

PROTECTION AGAINST NEGATIVE INFLUENCES

Imagine yourself putting on a beautiful golden helmet and closing the visor. Within this helmet you are safe from the negative influences of others. Their damaging suggestions, unable to penetrate this protection, simply bounce off harmlessly.

The Red Balloon Technique

D. Corydon Hammond, Ph.D.
Salt Lake City, Utah

INTRODUCTION AND INDICATIONS

This symbolic imagery technique, adapted from suggestions by Walch (1976), may particularly be helpful in reducing problematic emotions like anger, resentment, and guilt, as well as cravings. It will be primarily effective with patients who are responsive to both visual and kinesthetic imagery. The following verbalizations illustrate how I use this technique.

ILLUSTRATIVE SUGGESTIONS

I'd like you to imagine that you're walking along a path in a beautiful mountain setting. And as you walk, allow your comfort to increase, as you sink deeper and deeper into trance. And I really can't know for sure all the things you'll be noticing. Perhaps you'll particularly enjoy the contrasting shades of colors, or be aware of the tall trees, silhouetted against the blue sky, with peacefully drifting, fluffy clouds. I wonder if you'll notice a nearby mountainside, with interesting patterns of rocks and trees.

Many people enjoy the sounds of nature, like the sound of the wind in the trees, or of a nearby stream, or of birds singing. [Pause] Perhaps you'll notice the warmth of the sun against your skin, or the texture of things you touch along the way. As you walk, just take time to notice the things that interest *you*, as you drift deeper, and deeper into trance. [Pause]

And I'd like you to imagine that you're carrying a large pack on your back. Feel the weight and burden of it, and imagine that as you're walking, the pack is growing heavier with each step. That pack is filled with objects of some kind, objects that contain and have been infused with the heavy burden of all your excessive *(e.g., anger, guilt)* about *(e.g., your divorce)*.

And now the path begins leading up a rise, up a slight hill. And the pack is feeling even heavier. But you sense that a short distance ahead that you will come to the top of the hill. As you reach the top, the path leads into a large, open meadow, with beautiful green grass and wild flowers. And you can walk out into the meadow, noticing the beauty.

In the meadow you can also see a large, colorful, helium or hot air balloon, with a gondola underneath, and it is moored and tied down with large ropes. Walk over to it, and inside the gondola you'll notice a large basket or container of some kind, which you can unlatch, and which is empty inside.

Now, take off the heavy back pack, and drop it onto the ground. Are you tired of carrying around in your life that heavy burden of those feelings, which you've been carrying for so long? [Pause] Do you feel ready to get rid of those old, outdated feelings? [Pause] Good. Then, in a moment, I'm going to ask you to open that pack, and inside you'll find some kind of objects or containers, that have been infused with all of those excessive feelings of *(e.g., guilt, anger)*, that have been weighing you down. Open the pack, and see what kind of objects you find, that contain all that *(e.g., anger)*. What are they? [Pause].

Okay. Now, I'd like you to take those objects, slowly, one at a time, and toss them into that large basket in the gondola. And I think you're going to be pleased to notice, that with each object that you throw away, those feelings of _____ can decrease. And that will be such a relief! It's as if you're filling that basket up with all those feelings. As though you're cleansing yourself of all those excessive feelings, feeling increasing peace and comfort, increasing relief and freedom, with every object that you throw into that basket in the gondola. And by the time you've thrown away all of those objects, I think you're going to be surprised, or perhaps just enjoy, how free, how peaceful you can feel within yourself.

Now go ahead, and take the objects out of the pack and begin throwing them, one at a time, into that basket. And you can enjoy getting rid of those feelings. When you've thrown the last object into that basket, so that the basket is filled with all of those excessive feelings, allow the index finger on your right hand to float up to signal me.

[After the signal:] Good. Now close and latch the lid of the basket. And you can either untie those ropes or use a big knife or axe that you'll find nearby on the ground to cut those ropes. [Pause] And as you release that balloon, you can rest back on the comfortable grass, and watch it float up, into the sky, carrying away the basket, and all those excessive feelings of _____ that have burdened you. And with each movement and motion of the balloon up into the sky, you can feel an increasing sense of release, and relief. Free of those feelings, so that they will no longer have to influence your thoughts, or moods, or actions. Free of those feelings. Watch as the wind begins to carry the balloon farther, and farther away. Soon it will be out of sight, and when it's gone you can take a big deep breath, and then you can *really* enjoy the freedom, and relief, and peacefulness, of being rid of those feelings. And this relief, and peace, can flow and circulate all through you. And you'll be delighted to discover, that these feelings of freedom, and comfort, and well-being, can remain with you." [Another option some patients enjoy is to leave the feelings behind on the mountain, climb in the gondola, and float away themselves].

Edelstien's Fusion of Extremes Technique

D. Corydon Hammond, Ph.D.
Salt Lake City, Utah

INTRODUCTION

This method of Edelstien's (1981) is very similar to the gestalt therapy method of "integration of polarities." He advocates its use with reaction formations, "which cause us to behave in one way because we are afraid of behaving in the opposite way" (p. 121). In this technique, the patient visualizes two different individuals responding in opposite ways to a situation, and then visualizes these two persons merging into one, with the integrated person having the best characteristics of each. I have added some unconscious checks and commitments as elaborations to the technique.

THE TECHNIQUE

"In a few moments, I will describe a scene, and as I do so, you can experience it as though it were a dream, almost as if you were really observing it. And in a dream, you can see, and feel, and hear things, and they can seem very real, even though you're just lying there, very quietly, sleeping. And in a similar way, you can experience what I'm going to describe."

Now, present the patient with a visualization of the two extreme individuals. For example, one who is aggressive, and another who is passive and dependent. Describe each of the persons and their behavior *in some detail*, as the two individuals respond to the same setting or situation. Afterwards, have the patient see one of the individuals walking over, possibly taking the other person by the hand, and standing side by side. "And as they stand beside each other, a fascinating thing begins to occur. A bright light begins to shine on both of them, a warm, comforting kind of light. And as the light shines on them, their details begin to be obscured, and you sense them beginning to blend and merge together. Blending, and integrating, and fusing together into one person, a healthy, strong person."

Now describe this new person's characteristics, and how he/she is different from the two previous ones. "And she has the best qualities and characteristics of both of them. She is strong, and yet sensitive and considerate. She can be assertive and forceful when necessary, and yet compassionate and not overbearing," etc. The patient may now observe this model, prompted by the therapist, responding very positively to the previous situation.

"And as you think about the one person who is the integration and blending of the two, you can realize that this person is really very much like you. You can appreciate that you have these qualities, and the capacity to be this way, responding with the best qualities of each of those persons. It isn't necessary to act like either one of them alone. You have the best qualities of both.

"Now I want to ask your unconscious mind something, and please allow it to respond through your fingers, all by itself. Is your unconscious mind willing to allow you _____ to identify with that composite person, taking on the best characteristics, both the _____ and the *(specify the qualities)*?" [Pause for a response] "Good. Now I want the deepest part of your mind to listen to me carefully, and when the deepest part of your unconscious mind is listening very carefully, your 'yes' finger can float up." [Pause] "Good." [This step assumes that ideomotor signals have already been established.]

"Now your unconscious mind has made a commitment, to allow you to identify with the best characteristics of this composite person. And so in interesting ways, your conscious mind will notice how you're beginning to respond differently. Your *conscious* mind may doubt; it may question; but you will be unconsciously impelled to respond differently from the way you have in the past. And I wonder if you'll be curious, as you notice that you're beginning to feel more and more like the combination, like that integration of those two persons, and that you're finding it easier and easier to act as he/she would. And as that occurs, your conscious mind really can't help but notice—fascinated at how you're responding to these situations *(specify)* as if you were that combined person. At first, you may discover that these new responses happen suddenly and unexpectedly, before you have any opportunity to even think or resist. But after you've surprised yourself, by acting in these new ways, there will be a sense of deep inner satisfaction, of unconscious joy, and perhaps even amusement and delight. And soon, you'll begin to enjoy how naturally, how easily, you begin to act like the composite of the two women/men: _____, and _____, and *(specify the characteristics)*."

Scenes for Facilitating Self-Understanding

H. E. Stanton, Ph.D.
Hobart, Tasmania, Australia

INTRODUCTION

Stanton's techniques illustrate the manner in which guided imagery may be used to facilitate self-exploration and insight. Such exploration techniques may initially be introduced innocuously by presenting the imagery as a deepening technique that will seem nonthreatening. In using guided imagery (Hammond, 1988f), patients should be encouraged to "just let it happen," to allow it to happen "spontaneously." As an alternative to the structure that Stanton provides, the hypnotherapist may simply serve in an evocative role, offering implications and open-ended suggestions. For example: "When you enter this particular room, you'll find something very meaningful and significant there." "And soon you will discover something or someone relevant to what you're struggling with." When symbolic blocks are encountered, the therapist may suggest symbolic solutions. Guided imagery settings for exploration may also seek to incorporate interests of the patient (e.g., caves, mountain trails, scuba diving beneath the sea, cross-country skiing, using computers, music), or historic settings such as the patient's childhood home. If you are interested in other hypnotic techniques for facilitating insight you should refer to Brown and Fromm (1986), Freytag (1961), Hammond and Miller (in press), Rossi and Cheek (1988), Sacerdote (1978), Stein (1972), Watkins (in press), Wolberg (1964), and Wright (1987). (*Ed.*)

GANDOR'S GARDEN

Imagine walking down a forest path. The sun is shining, the birds are singing, and there is a feeling of warmth in the air. Without prior warning, you come upon a large mound of freshly dug earth on one side of which is a round, partly open, wooden door. Curious, you approach the door. Looking inside, you see a downward sloping tunnel which, though dark, does have a glimmer of light emanating from the far end.

You enter the tunnel, following it as it takes you down and down, deeper and deeper in the earth. As you do so, the light at the far end grows steadily brighter. Suddenly you emerge from the tunnel and, much to your surprise, you find yourself in a garden flooded with light coming from an ingenious system of skylights. High-pitched laughter comes from behind you and, turning, you see a smiling elf who, after introducing himself as Gandor, the owner of the garden, invites you to walk around and explore.

The first thing you notice is a tiny reflecting pool. As you gaze into it, you see an image of yourself as you would like to be, staring back at you. This idealized image then speaks, giving you some information about yourself of which you had been unaware. [Pause. A head nod may be requested after this information has been received, and remaining in trance, the patient may be asked to discuss the message received. If appropriate, further interaction may be promoted with Gandor. (*Ed.*)]

After absorbing this message, you continue walking along a pathway winding its way through the garden until you come upon a small child skipping rope. The child welcomes you with a smile, and, as you bend down to her, she whispers in your ear, telling you something about yourself that you had virtually forgotten. This is something relating to your own early years which needs to be remembered now to help you enjoy your present life more fully. [Pause. The patient may be asked if he/she would like to share what he/she has learned. (*Ed.*)]

You continue on your way, arriving at a small clearing where three butterflies are dancing joyfully in the air. They are humming a tune about happiness and what constitutes the true secret of being happy. You stop and listen to their song, then resume your walk. [Pause]

When you have almost reached the end of the path, you see an old man [or woman] sitting cross-legged on the verge. Though he appears to be sunk deeply in a meditative trance, he opens his eyes at your approach, as if he had been expecting you. Slowly and deliberately he begins to speak, conveying some especially wise advice on a matter about which you have been concerned. [Pause. A head nod may be obtained after the message has been received.]

Thinking about this advice, you return to your starting point. Gandor awaits you, em-phasizing that great insights will grow out of your experiences. He bids you farewell with an invitation to return as often as you desire to the magic garden. Taking your leave of Gandor, you retrace your steps along the tunnel, returning to the outside world with the wisdom you have received.

JIGSAW

Imagine that you are sitting at a table, a number of boxes before you. There are no pictures on their lids, but inside each one is a complete set of jigsaw pieces. Choose a box, empty out the contents onto the table and put the jigsaw together. As you put the pieces together, a picture will form, normally one which has some meaning for you, telling you something about yourself. Then go onto the other boxes, assembling the pieces found in each one, and create further pictures. These may be related to the first one, elaborating upon a single theme. Alternatively, they may indicate quite different concerns. [Feedback about each puzzle may be obtained as each picture is being put together, following each completed puzzle, or after the trance experience. (*Ed.*)]

THE THEATRE

Imagine yourself sitting in the stalls of a theatre waiting for the performance to begin. As you wait, you notice someone standing off to one side of the stage looking behind the closed curtain. Although you cannot see what is going on behind the curtain, this person is able to do so, and it is making him/her look very frightened, very unhappy. Slowly the curtains open, revealing to you the cause of this negative reaction.

Because of your tendency to project your own fears and problems onto this imaginary person, you are likely to gain increased insight into them. To focus on problems in particular, you could imagine the person looking very puzzled, then smiling happily as he/she found the solution to his/her problem by looking behind the curtain. Similarly, you could have the person looking very happy, or very confident, or very relaxed, as he/she looked behind the curtain. In this way you could gain further self-awareness.

Meeting an Inner Adviser

David E. Bresler, Ph.D.
Santa Monica, California

INTRODUCTION AND INDICATIONS

Working with inner advisers or guides is a popular therapeutic technique used by many therapists (Miller, 1977; Rossman, 1987; Samuels & Bennett, 1973; Zilbergeld & Hammond, 1988). This is primarily an insight-oriented hypnotherapy technique for uncovering information related to physical or psychological symptoms. Essentially, this method gives form and voice to the "unconscious" mind or inner wisdom of the patient. It is rather reminiscent of an "empty chair" technique that Perls (Fagan & Shepherd, 1970) used with dependent patients and patients about to terminate treatment. He had patients put their ideal therapist in an empty chair and interact with the "therapist," moving back and forth between chairs to play both roles. This method helped patients to understand that they know more than they know that they know, to use a phrase of Erickson's. The inner adviser technique similarly assists patients to elicit information that is already inside. It may also, however, be used to remove or control symptoms. For instance, sometimes an "adviser" may remove pain for the patient for varying periods of time.

Proper use of this technique requires an interactive trance in which you periodically question patients about who their adviser is and what their adviser says or does. This is not fully evident from the following script, but should be incorporated in clinical work. However, the following verbalizations by Bresler are a very fine model of how to begin doing "adviser

work" with patients and, in several instances, of how to work when there seems to be resistance and the adviser dialogue is not progressing smoothly. His dialogue does tend to favor an animal adviser. When you interact verbally with the patient and find that the adviser is a person, you will want to avoid suggesting that the patient sprinkle food or pet the adviser. For further information concerning other techniques with advisers, you may refer to Bresler (1979), Rossman (1987) or Hammond (1988f). If you are interested in the concept of using a council of advisers with a patient, you will find Napoleon Hill's (1963) description of his personal use of this technique fascinating. (*Ed.*)

INDUCTION

This tape contains a guided imagery exercise which will help you to make contact with an inner adviser who resides in your mind's eye. . . . Before beginning, take a moment to get comfortable and relax. . . . Sit upright in a comfortable chair, with your feet flat on the floor, and close your eyes. . . .

Take a few slow, deep, abdominal breaths . . . inhale . . . exhale . . . inhale . . . exhale. . . . Focus your attention on your breathing for a few minutes . . . and recognize how easily slow, deep breathing alone can induce a nice state of deep, gentle relaxation. . . .

Let your body breathe itself . . . according to its own natural rhythm . . . slowly . . . easily . . . and deeply. . . .

Now take a signal breath . . . a special message that tells the body you are ready to enter a state of deep relaxation . . . exhale. . . . Breathe in deeply through your nose . . . and blow out through your mouth. . . .

Remember your breathing . . . slowly and deeply. . . . As you concentrate your attention on your breathing, imagine a ball of pure energy or white light that starts at your lower abdomen and, as you inhale, it rises up the front of your body to your forehead . . . and, as you exhale, it moves down into your spine, down your legs, and into the ground. . . .

Again . . . imagine this ball of pure energy or white light rise up the front of your body to your forehead as you inhale . . . and as you exhale, it goes down your spine, down your legs, and into the ground. . . . Circulate this ball of energy around for a few moments . . . and allow its circulation to move you into even deeper states of relaxation and comfort. . . .

Each time you inhale and exhale, you may be surprised to find yourself twice as relaxed as you were a moment before . . . twice as comfortable . . . twice as peaceful. . . . For with each breath, every cell of your body becomes at ease . . . as all the tension, tightness, pain or discomfort drains down your spine, down your legs and into the ground. . . . Continue to circulate this ball of energy around for a few minutes. . . .

As you allow yourself to enjoy this nice state of deep, peaceful relaxation, return in your mind's eye to your personal place. . . . Let your imagination become reacquainted with every detail of this beautiful spot. . . . Sense the peaceful beauty all around you. . . . Stretch out . . . relax . . . and enjoy it. [Long pause]

MEETING THE ADVISER

As you relax in your favorite spot, put a smile on your face . . . and slowly look around. . . . Somewhere, nearby, some living creature is waiting for you . . . smiling and waiting for you to establish eye contact. . . . This creature may immediately approach you or it may wait a few moments to be sure that you mean it no harm. . . . Be sure to look up in the trees or behind bushes, since your adviser may be a bit timid . . . but even if you see nothing, sense his or her presence and introduce yourself. . . . Tell your adviser your name, and that you mean no harm, for you've come with only the friendliest intentions. Find out your adviser's name . . . the first name that comes to your mind . . . right now. . . .

Sprinkle some food out before you . . . and ask your adviser if he or she is willing to come over and talk with you for a few moments. . . .

Don't be alarmed if your advisor becomes quite excited and starts jumping up and down at this point. . . . Often, advisers have been waiting a long time to make this kind of contact. . . . Until now, your adviser has only been able to talk to you sporadically through your intuition. . . . Tell your adviser you're sorry you haven't listened more in the past, but that you'll try to do better in the future. . . . If you feel silly talking in this way, tell your adviser that you feel silly . . . that it's hard for you to take this seriously . . . but if you sincerely want your adviser's help, make that very, very clear. . . . Tell your adviser that you understand that, like in any friendship, it takes time for feelings of mutual trust and respect to develop. . . .

Although your adviser knows everything about you — since your adviser is just a reflection of your inner life — tell your adviser that you won't push for any simple answers to important questions that you may be dealing with. . . . Rather, you'd like to establish a continuing dialogue . . . so that anytime you need help with a problem, your adviser can tell you things of great importance . . . things that you may already know, but you may have underestimated their significance. . . .

If there's a problem that's been bothering you for a while, ask your adviser if he or she is willing to give you some help with it . . . yes or no? . . . Your adviser's response is the first answer that pops into your mind. . . . Pose your questions as you exhale . . . and the first response that comes into your mind as you inhale is your adviser's reply . . . an inspiration . . . ask your questions now. [Pause]

What did your adviser reply? . . . Ask any other questions that are on your mind. [Pause] Continue your dialogue for a few moments . . . asking your questions as you exhale . . . and listening to the response that pops into your mind as you inhale. [Pause].

Remember, your adviser knows everything about you, but sometimes — for a very good reason — he or she will be unwilling to tell you something. . . . This is usually to protect you from information you may not be ready to deal with. . . . When this occurs, ask your adviser what you need to do in order to make this information available to yourself. . . .Your adviser will usually show you the way. [Pause].

If there is something that you'd like your adviser to be thinking about between now and the next time you meet, tell this to your adviser now. [Pause] If there is anything your adviser would like you to think about between now and the next time you meet, find out what it is now. [Pause]

Set up a time to meet again . . . a time that's convenient for you and a time that's convenient for your adviser. . . . Be specific as to exact time and place. . . . Tell your adviser that, although these meetings are important to you, part of you is lazy or even reluctant to follow through. . . .

One way your adviser can help motivate you to continue to meet periodically is by giving you a clear demonstration of the benefits you can gain . . . a demonstration so powerful that you will be moved to work even harder in getting to know yourself. . . . If you are in pain, for example, ask your adviser if he or she is willing to take away that pain completely . . . right now, just for a few moments, as a demonstration of power. . . . If so, tell your adviser to do it . . . now. [Long pause]

Notice any difference? If you're willing to do your share of the work, by relaxing yourself and meeting periodically to set things straight, there's no limit to your adviser's power. . . . Ask for any reasonable demonstration that will be undeniably convincing to you of this power. . . .

You might be, for example, somewhat forgetful . . . and although you want to continue these meetings with your adviser, you might forget the exact time and place that you agreed to meet. . . . If so, ask your adviser to help you by coming into your consciousness just a few moments before it's time to meet, to remind you of the meeting.

Before leaving, tell your adviser you're open to having many different kinds of advisers . . . and that you will leave this totally up to your adviser's discretion. . . . Is there anything your adviser would like you to bring along with you

the next time you meet? . . . If so, find out what this is. [Pause]

See if your adviser will allow you to establish physical contact. . . . This is very important. . . . Just about every animal on the face of the earth loves to have its face stroked and its back scratched. . . . See if your adviser will allow you to make this contact now. [Pause] While making this contact, find out if there's anything else that your adviser would like to tell you . . . If so, what is it? [Pause]

Is there anything you would like to tell your adviser before you leave? . . . If so, do it now. [Pause]

In a moment, you will take the signal breath to return from this meeting . . . but before you do, tell yourself that each time you make contact with your adviser the communication will flow more and more smoothly . . . more and more easily . . . more and more comfortable. . . .

Tell yourself that when this experience is over, you will feel not only relaxed, rested, and comfortable, but also energized with such a powerful sense of well-being that you will be able to respond easily to any demands that may arise. . . .

To end this exercise for now, take the same signal breath that you used to begin it . . . exhale . . . breathe in deeply through your nose . . . blow out through your mouth . . . and be well.

Responsibility to a Fault: A Metaphor for Overresponsibility

Michael D. Yapko, Ph.D.
San Diego, California

INTRODUCTION AND INDICATIONS

This metaphor was used to enhance awareness in an adult woman of how she inappropriately took responsibility for her parents' actions. The theme of metaphors given to her was of someone being overly conscientious to such a degree that others were rendered powerless. (*Ed.*)

METAPHOR

The world of nature is enjoyed by almost everyone . . . people like the beauty and the diversity of animals, for example . . . but people do not realize that animals of all shapes, sizes, colors, and temperaments have to face certain realities . . . just as people do . . . animal families are not unlike human families in some ways . . . the establishment of a territory in which to live that is all one's own . . . the bonding of a family . . . the anticipation and finally the arrival of an offspring or two . . . the proud parents . . . the protective parents . . . and love takes a lot of different forms in the animal kingdom. . . . Consider the bears as an example of the wisdom of animals . . . a mother and her cubs are inseparable in their earliest weeks and months of life . . . if you really want to anger a bear . . . get near her cubs . . . she protects them fiercely . . . as she teaches them how to hunt for food . . . how to survive in the wilderness . . . how to live . . . and how to grow . . . and the cubs have time to play and be young . . . but they also know the seriousness of what they must learn . . . in order to be on their own eventually . . . and then one day, the mother will chase her cubs up a tree . . . and then abandon them . . . she leaves them on their own . . . to live for themselves . . . to grow and change and learn as their lives go on . . . and a huge part of her responsibility . . . is to reach a point of no longer having to be responsible for others . . . their lives are their own to live . . . and she knows she can't live it for them no matter how much she cares for them . . . and it may seem cold and callous on the surface . . . especially when one sees the desperate search of the cubs for their mother . . . but she has a greater wisdom . . . a broader perspective . . . and an intuitive sense that each life is valuable in what it allows its bearer to do . . . and what seems cruel on one level . . . is actually the greatest

gift of all on another, more important one . . . and I know of no recorded instances of an insecure mother bear preventing her cubs from becoming independent. . . .

COMMENTARY

If the client has issues surrounding abandonment, is feeling uncared for by others, or is assuming too much responsibility for others' feelings, the above metaphor can be useful, as can others with a similar theme.

Guilt and self-blame are closely related. Whereas the underresponsible individual tends to be a blamer (extropunitive), the overresponsible individual tends to be martyrish and intropunitive. The intensity of the self-blaming can be so great that it becomes the focal point of the person's mental energy, precluding awareness of other interpretations or perspectives. Guilt can be an incredibly profound agent of paralysis in an individual's life, and disrupting the overresponsible person's tendency to wallow in it is a key goal of treatment.

Different Parts: A Metaphor

Michael D. Yapko, Ph.D.
San Diego, California

INDICATIONS

This metaphor may be useful prior to the initiation of unconscious exploration, ego-state therapy, or unconscious negotiation with unconscious parts of a patient. It "seeds" the concept of unconscious parts or polarities of the self and that there can be motivations beyond our conscious awareness. It may be especially useful in working with children or teenagers. (*Ed.*)

METAPHOR

And I can tell you about a young boy I saw not long ago . . . who had been a model fourth grader . . . good grades, hard-working little fellow . . . and toward the end of the school year he underwent a transformation . . . he stopped doing his schoolwork . . . he stopped being nice to other children . . . he grew sullen and withdrawn . . . and nobody knew why . . . and then I saw him . . . and found out things of great importance to him . . . and he loved his teacher so much that he wanted her to be his teacher again . . . and he was trying to fail in school in order to stay with that teacher . . . and sometimes what seems odd on the surface, or even crazy, may make sense at a deeper level . . . but it became apparent that a part of him wanted to stay firmly put another year . . . but I also discovered a part of him that would be proud to be a big fifth grader . . . and I found a part of him that was quite curious about what fifth grade would be like . . . and I found another part of him that was excited about it being near the end of the school year . . . looking forward to a summer away from school . . . when there's lots of time to think and change one's mind . . . and another part that was sad at saying good-bye to friends for the summer . . . and there were lots of parts to this boy . . . and I wonder which part of him you would have talked to if you wanted to know that lots changes are part of growing . . . the curious part? . . . All I know is . . . when I talked about different parts of growing up . . . he listened very closely . . . and he's doing very well in fifth grade, you'll feel better knowing . . .

COMMENTARY

In the above metaphor, the idea is seeded that seemingly strange behavior can be purposeful, that change involves letting go, that there are different parts of self, and that the quality of one's experience is determined to a significant degree by which part(s) one focuses upon. The metaphor implies that one can focus on whichever part of oneself is best able to catalyze successful adjustment. The language of "parts" has now been introduced to the client, as has the concept of being able to selectively amplify or diminish parts of his or her experience in order to achieve a higher purpose.

Enhancing Affective Experience and Its Expression

Daniel P. Brown, Ph.D., and
Erika Fromm, Ph.D.
*Cambridge, Massachusetts, and
Chicago, Illinois*

Hypnosis has been used to induce specific emotions in normal subjects (Hodge & Wagner, 1964). In the clinical situation the hypnotherapist's task is not to suggest specific emotions to the patient but rather *to bring the patient's current emotional experience into full awareness.* Patients are often only dimly aware of the emotional undercurrent in interactions with others; the psychotherapy process is no exception. They become aware of emotions only at discrete moments in the ongoing exchange. Apart from these moments, they have little conscious awareness of the continuous affective experience. The therapist can help patients bring these underlying emotions to the point of consciousness (Rosen, 1953) and also help them to recognize the specific emotions accurately. To ease the entry of underlying emotions into awareness, the hypnotized patient is told, "Notice now what you feel as you experience this scene" or "When I count from one to five . . . by the time you hear me say, 'five' . . . you will begin to feel whatever emotion is associated with the [name symptom or problem]."

Bringing the undercurrent of feeling to the point of consciousness is only the first step. Many patients have difficulty in accurately recognizing certain affects and in verbalizing them. To enhance recognition and verbalization, the hypnotist says:

A specific feeling will become clear to you. . . . It will become clearer . . . and clearer. . . . You will be able to recognize exactly what this particular feeling is . . . and you will be able to describe it to me. . . . Now, what is it that you are now feeling?

It is especially important to give an open-ended suggestion — not to suggest a particular emotion to the patient but to amplify the patient's awareness of the emotion of the moment. Usually the patient will report experiencing a particular emotion. Should the patient continue to have difficulty finding words for the feeling, the hypnotist says:

I will count slowly from one to five . . . by the time I reach five, a word or two will come into your mind spontaneously . . . a word or two which exactly express what you are now aware of feeling . . . [Therapist counts]. . . . Now, tell me what it is you are feeling.

The hypnotherapist also helps the patient to experience the affect fully so that its visceral, cognitive, and motor (expressive) components are well integrated:

As the feeling becomes clearer and clearer to you, notice more carefully exactly how you experience this feeling in your body . . . notice what sensations you experience in your body as you feel [x] . . . notice where in your body you hold this feeling . . . notice the muscles in your face, and you will see just what muscles hold this feeling . . .now, notice what goes through your mind as you feel [x]. . . . You will discover certain thoughts, images, or memories spontaneously passing through your mind about this feeling.

Those instructions are standard procedure and can be employed whenever the patient describes a symptom or a behavioral problem, is involved in a fantasy production, or experiences some sort of shift in the psychotherapeutic process. By using this procedure strategically during the course of the therapy session, the therapist helps amplify a variety of affective experiences associated with the psychotherapeutic process.

Another technique used by the hypnotherapist is *affect intensification* (Rosen, 1953). The hypnotist says:

When I count slowly from one to five . . . with each number you will begin to feel "x" more and more intensely . . . with each number you hear, the feeling will grow stronger and stronger. . . . By the time I reach five, you will feel it in your body as strongly as it is possible to bear. . . . Now . . . one . . . two . . . three . . . four . . . five. Notice what you feel, and you will be able to describe it to me.

This technique is especially useful when a patient spontaneously reports a feeling emerging in the course of the therapy session. The therapist uses hypnotic suggestions to help the patient recognize the feeling within certain limits. To safeguard the patient from being overwhelmed, the therapist can use an ideomotor signal:

If at any point in the counting the intensity of the feeling seems too much to bear, the index finger of your hand will lift all by itself, and that will be your way of signaling to me not to count beyond that point.

Hypnosis can also *enhance affects* the patient has discovered. Affects are expressed through certain defined groups of facial muscles, supplemented by the limbs, through visceral responses largely mediated through the autonomic nervous system, and through complex behavioral patterns. The experience of an affect is not the same as its expression. It is not always necessary to encourage expression of the affect in behavior, though encouraging its communication in words is usually therapeutic. For example, the hypnotherapist should not say, ". . . and as the feeling gets stronger and stronger, you will find yourself compelled to do something." This kind of suggestion encourages discharge in the form of abreaction or acting-out. When the suggestion is worded this way, the expression of rage, sexual acting-out, or panic states is commonly observed (Rosen, 1953). The patient is likely to cry or laugh or have violent emotional outbursts, which are not themselves therapeutic. A better way to word the suggestions is to say, ". . . and as the feeling gets stronger and stronger, you will find an appropriate way to communicate it." This kind of suggestion encourages appropriate channels for expression, communication, and under-standing. Emphasis is on the therapeutic relationship, not on discharge itself. When suggestions are worded as we advise, the patient finds effective ways to communicate to the therapist the affective experience of the moment and to elicit an empathic response.

HYPNOSIS WITH SEVERELY DISTURBED PATIENTS

Can Hypnosis Help Psychosis?

James R. Hodge, M.D.

Akron, Ohio

INTRODUCTION

This is primarily a book of therapeutic suggestions. However, many misconceptions exist concerning whether hypnosis may be utilized with schizophrenic and psychotic patients. Therefore, I have decided to include Dr. Hodge's excellent, yet brief, introduction to this subject. (*Ed.*)

A French philosopher is reported to have stated that everything worth saying has already been said, but that because nobody was listening it has to be said again. Fortunately, new material may develop between the re-tellings.

To answer the title question, an additional series of questions must be asked and answers from the literature must be provided:

1. Can psychotic patients be hypnotized? For many years it was felt that they could not be, but recent evidence indicates that at least some can be (Baker, 1981, 1983c; Eliseo, 1974; Murray-Jobsis, 1985; Pettinati, 1982; Scagnelli-Jobsis, 1982; Spiegel, Detrick, & Frischholz, 1982).
2. Are special induction techniques necessary? Probably not (Baker, 1983c; Eliseo, 1974; Scagnelli-Jobsis, 1982). Both permissive and authoritarian approaches have been successful.

3. Are special treatment techniques necessary? Hypnosis by itself, like the passage of time, does nothing. What is done with and within hypnosis is what really matters. Treatment techniques should be designed for the individual patient. Many special techniques have been offered (Baker, 1981, 1983c; Brown, 1985; Scagnelli, 1976; Scagnelli-Jobsis, 1982). Hodge (1980) and Hodge and Babai (1982) have offered a general categorization of strategies and tactics of hypnotherapy, including some specialized techniques for psychotic patients. Scagnelli-Jobsis (1982) reports a number of cases in which hypnosis has helped when other methods were unsuccessful. "the use of hypnosis in psychotherapy requires three attributes in the therapist: experience in hypnosis and in psychotherapy, imagination, and courage to try both accepted and innovative techniques" (Hodge, 1980).
4. Can hypnosis be dangerous to the patient? There are always dangers in any procedure, but these are greatly lessened if the therapist will ". . . always practice within his area of competence—that is, he should use hypnosis only for conditions he would be willing and able to treat without the use of hypnosis" (Hodge, 1982). Conn (1972) and Scagnelli-Jobsis (1982), in her review of the theoretical and clinical literature, agree with the above. However, Kleinhauz and Beran (1984) report six cases of subjects who experienced trauma or psychopathological symptoms following the misuse of hypnosis, particularly for stage performances; and Smith and Kamitsuka (1984)

report a case in which the spontaneous use of self-hypnosis was misinterpreted as central nervous system deterioration. Interestingly, when each of these cases came to the attention of experienced hypnotherapists, the problems were quickly resolved. Scagnelli-Jobsis (1982) has reviewed the issues of concern about hypnosis with psychotic patients, and Watkins (1986) lists and describes the general dangers in the use of hypnosis. Complications are not always dangerous and can be handled by competent therapists. Actually, therapy with hypnosis generally tends to make the patient stronger and more effective (Scagnelli, 1976; Scagnelli-Jobsis, 1982), and this is the ultimate goal.

5. Is a special relationship necessary? Yes. Specifically there must be trust, a therapeutic alliance, and ego receptivity (Baker, 1983c; Scagnelli-Jobsis, 1982). Hodge (1980) emphasizes that "The effective use of hypnosis depends upon a positive therapeutic relationship; failure to develop this relationship is the primary contraindication to the use of hypnosis as well as the primary reason for its failure." Even if the patient has the ability to enter the trance, he must also have the willingness to enter it and the trust in the therapist to have the hypnotic and therapeutic experiences.

6. Is self-hypnosis effective? It is not only effective but desirable (Baker, 1983c; Scagnelli, 1976; Scagnelli-Jobsis, 1982). However, experience has shown that many patients either do not think to use it, do not use it, or find that it is less effective than when done with or by the therapist. I have found no really satisfactory explanation for this, but a hypothesis for further study comes from the words of Kleinhauz and Beran (1984) that, "During hypnosis the subject agrees to permit the hypnotist to become the sole channel of communication and source of interpretation of all internal and external stimuli impinging upon himself," and of Scagnelli-Jobsis (1982) that subjects are ". . . probably holding more of

their adult ego roles to themselves. At such times their self-monitoring ego would most likely be more prominent," and that ". . . ego receptivity (i.e., depth of altered states of consciousness) would be greatest when the subject trusts either the strength of his own overall ego, or the therapist's or both combined, to allow lowering of defenses, adaptive regression, and receptive access to previously defended material." Several of my own patients have reported unwillingness to use self-hypnosis, often (even when clearly necessary) for fear of becoming addicted to it ("I might like it too much"), for fear that it will wear out, or simply for fear that it won't work. Others have said, "I can just do it better in the presence of authority," and this is compatible with the above hypothesis, especially if we accept that all hypnosis is ultimately self-hypnosis. In any case there is a tendency for self-hypnosis to become more effective with reinforcement of successes, though not always.

7. Is the state of the illness important? Cases of treatment of acute psychosis, chronic psychosis, and organic brain syndromes have been reported (Baker, 1983c; Brown, 1985; Eliseo, 1974; Scagnelli, 1976; Scagnelli-Jobsis, 1982).

8. Is it necessary or desirable to limit the depth of trance? Probably not (Baker, 1983c; Eliseo, 1974; Scagnelli-Jobsis, 1982), but the depth of trance should be selected for the specific patient depending upon the goals to be achieved. Regression in the service of the ego, as well as other projective techniques (Hodge, 1980; Hodge & Babai, 1982) that can only be accomplished by deeper levels of trance, has been helpful.

9. Are there any special problems with hypnosis with schizophrenics? In terms of the patient, Scagnelli (1976) reports three issues: control, fear of closeness, and fear of releasing negative self-concepts. In terms of the therapist, he should always practice within his limits of competence with hypno-

sis and with the illness he is treating. In terms of hypnosis itself, Scagnelli-Jobsis (1982) lists four common concerns about the use of hypnosis with psychotics: hypnotizability, decompensation, preference for fantasy over reality with refusal to terminate trance, and excessive dependency. She states that all of these concerns have been able to be discounted when hypnosis is properly used for the appropriate patient.

Renurturing: Forming Positive Sense of Identity and Bonding

Joan Murray-Jobsis, Ph.D.
Chapel Hill, North Carolina

INDICATIONS

These suggestions, offered from an object relations framework, are designed for severely disturbed patients suffering with developmental deficits. The approach is basically one of facilitating age regression and providing the patient with nurturing early life experiences that may have been missed. (*Ed.*)

SUGGESTIONS

And then perhaps traveling back to some of those earliest memories of existence, those early weeks and months of existence, and beginning to create within our imagery and within ourselves a positive sense of living and loving, a positive sense of self that should have been, could have been, and would have been if we could have been there together. If I could have been there with you, the infant you, it would have been and should have been all of the good feelings. And we can create these feelings now, at least in part, in imagery.

THE EXPERIENCE OF BEING HELD

And we can begin to imagine the feelings of being held, feeling the arms, the warm strong arms. The feeling of being held snug and secure, tightly held against the warm soft breast. Feeling the rise and fall of the breast with the rhythm of the breathing, much like the rhythm of the ocean, constant, steady, always there. And the sound of the heartbeat, again like the rhythm of breathing, constant, steady. And the rhythm of the rocking, steady, soothing. And perhaps an awareness of the smell of the warmth of that nurturing body, and the taste of the warm sweet milk. And the feelings of fullness, and satisfaction, and well-being. And the feelings of loving and being loved, and warmth and security, and ease and well-being.

And from these early experiences and memories comes a sense of self that is secure, and loved, and loving. And in this beginning are the very beginnings of the sense of self: of well-being, comfort, ease, security, loving and being loved, and everything being well. And then everything does become easier.

DISCOVERING THE PHYSICAL BODY AND BOUNDARIES

And it becomes easier, from this sense of wholeness and wellness and well-being, to move on to those later weeks and months when we begin to discover this physical body that contains the sense of self. We begin to discover the sense of boundaries and limits of this physical being, this body that we exist within. We begin to discover an awareness of the skin that contains this body, and the physical movement that defines our body. The fingers, and the toes, and the face, that set the boundaries of this body. We discover the sensations of the skin, the sensations of touch, and holding, and stroking, and caressing. And we discover the sensations of movement, of reaching and stretching, and rocking, all the good sensations of the body. And we begin to discover the sensations of the internal body, sensations of food going into the mouth, and down into the stomach, and feelings of satisfaction. We begin to know and identify the physical being, the physical body that contains our sense of self, whole, satisfied, well-being, being loved, loving, wanted, secure.

RENURTURING: SEPARATION AND INDIVIDUATION

And then gradually we begin to understand and identify the boundaries and the limits containing this sense of self, and the separations between ourselves and that external environment. As we reach out and touch objects and let them go, we begin to discover the separateness between ourselves and those objects. And we begin to discover the separateness between ourselves and other physical beings. Discovering our physical being as separate from that other holding, protective, nurturing physical being, the holding, protective arms.

And even as we begin to discover a sense of separateness, of the boundaries and limits of our physical and emotional self, we also discover that our sense of separateness is experienced within an awareness of our earlier bonding and connectedness. And there is always an awareness and a memory of those early experiences of bonding and connnectedness, and of the well-being and the wholeness, loving and being loved and secure. Always an awareness of the bonding and connectedness, even as we begin to understand the separateness.

ACCEPTING THE IMPERFECT WORLD

But in the beginning, the awareness of that separateness can seem so painful. It can seem such a loss, and such an angry thing. Because it means the loss of that fantasy, the loss of the perfect, caring, nurturing parent, the symbiosis of being as if bound together, as if one. And it means the loss of the fantasy of the perfect world where all of our needs are met all of the time, whenever we need them, and where everything is exactly as we want it to be. And gradually we come to accept the loss of the fantasy, the loss of the perfect caretaker, nurturer. Gradually we come to accept the realities of the imperfect world, and the imperfect nurturing caretaker. We begin to accept the "good enough" nurturer, the "good enough" caretaker, and the "good enough" world that is the reality we are beginning to experience. A

reality where enough of our needs are met, where there is enough care, enough protection, enough loving concern. And where our feelings of anger and sadness and loss are allowed expression in a holding, loving, supportive, accepting environment. And so we experience our feelings, absorb them, grow beyond them, come to accept the realities of the imperfect world, giving up the fantasy of that perfect union of perfect care, everything, every need being cared for and met.

BEGINNING TO ENJOY SEPARATENESS

And gradually we begin to discover, perhaps to our surprise, that we may even begin to enjoy our sense of separateness. Perhaps we begin to discover that we may not really need that nurturing caretaker as much as we thought we did. We begin to develop capacities, competence, and mastery far beyond what we might have imagined. Because in the normal developmental process we seem to continuously grow and expand in our capabilities and mastery. And so we discover that we may not really need that nurturing parent quite as much as we once thought we did. And in similar fashion, we begin to discover, that perhaps we may not even *want* that nurturing parent as much as we once thought we did. We begin to discover that in our developmental growth and process of evolving, we begin to move toward curiosity and exploration, and challenge and growth, in ways that would have been so terribly limited by the old, fantasied, symbiotic union. A union so tight it would have prevented us from growing, and developing, and discovering all the potential of our individual identity. And in the normal course of development we begin to discover satisfactions in evolving and developing our own individual unique separateness. And we begin to discover strength from our experience of our original sense of connectedness and bonding. And the combination of strength and freedom that results from our bonding and the separateness begins to open a world of growth and satisfaction to us. And then it does begin to become satisfying to move into this "good enough" world with the "good enough" nurturing, caretaking parent. And we begin to grow in experience, and evolve into all of the satisfactions of developing into our own unique, very special human abilities, our own unique, special combination of abilities and capacities, and strengths and talents.

And gradually we begin to discover all sorts of adventures in that outside world. And we begin to discover other people, other children, other adults, who provide some of our needs and wants and care, alternative sources of solace and care and support. And alternative sources of interest and growth and excitement. And so we begin to move toward our natural evolution and development, discovering all of the other possibilities of bonding in the outside world that go beyond that original nurturing, caretaking, loving parent. And then things do seem to become easier, satisfying.

Suggestions for Creative Self-Mothering

Joan Murray-Jobsis, Ph.D.
Chapel Hill, North Carolina

In this hypnotic method, the patient is asked to imagine himself or herself as an infant or baby, and then to experience himself/herself mothering the little child. Dr. Murray-Jobsis believes that patients will usually perceive the infant as lovable and that this will help facilitate the process of beginning to love and reparent themselves. It provides some restitution for the lack of nurturing and mothering that some patients experienced, and it helps to foster self-love and self-acceptance. The suggestions that follow were taken from an actual case. (*Ed.*)

SUGGESTIONS

If you could have been the mother of that little girl, you would have loved her as she should have been loved, could have been loved.

When you look at that little girl Lisa, you know very well that she really was lovable and that she deserved all the love that every little girl has always deserved. If you had been there to be her mother, you would have done all of the things that a mother should do. You would have held her and cradled her and rocked her and sung songs to her and maybe talked to her of all of the love of poetry, of words, and music. You would have shared with her all of the happiness of running and playing, swinging and moving, all of the fun of living and learning and growing, and all of the fun of growing up strong and healthy and well loved. And little Lisa can still get some of those feelings of love from you, all of the feelings that you can give her, the mothering and the loving that she always deserved. The little girl Lisa was truly lovable, just as the grownup Lisa is now lovable.

Hypnotherapeutic Techniques with Affective Instability

Louis N. Gruber, M.D.

INTRODUCTION

There are many patients in psychiatry whose most characteristic feature is affective instability. . . . Diagnostically, these patients are often labeled as having "borderline personality disorder," or "cyclothymic disorder" or a major affective disorder, alone or in combination. . . . The basic principle of my psychotherapeutic approach using hypnosis can be found in Melitta Schmideberg's injunction concerning the "borderline" patient, "to be aware that the patient is dominated by . . . contrasts, because he can only be influenced therapeutically *if both sides are reached almost simultaneously*" (Italics mine) (1959). This is feasible with the hypnotic approach. Effective treatment of patients with affective instability must recognize:

— their suggestibility
— their sense of vulnerability to external influences

—their defensive clinging to negative mental states
—their creativity
—their desire for balance, stability, and self-control (even more than "feeling better").

Before the specific techniques are given, the patient must begin associating treatment with self-control and mastery. One must forcefully interrupt regressive behaviors (whining, weeping, slumping in the chair, diffuse hostility, sarcasm), and thus break up the negative mental set often associated to therapy. At the same time one gives recognition to the negative states and their validity. I may speak, for example, of the patient's "dark side" and "bright side," and the need to bring both of them into balance, "so that you can have more and more control over the working of your mind."

Patients are prepared for hypnosis by learning that it is a form of increased awareness which will give them greater control over their mental processes. I compare it to being so absorbed in a book or movie that one doesn't hear one's name called. Most patients are eager to get started.

A KINESTHETIC TECHNIQUE

I stumbled on this technique in desperation after more than ten years' work with a young woman. She had been phoning me almost daily complaining of depression, hopelessness, visual hallucinations, fantasies of committing mass murder, and warnings that "you're making me angry" in response to any therapeutic intervention. She responded immediately to the following technique and later asked why I had waited so long to teach it to her.

After gaining her total attention I brought her into trance by telling her a metaphorical story and announcing that she would now be receiving "special instructions." I then told her more or less as follows:

You undoubtedly have good reason to feel anger and bitterness. No one can really know how bad your childhood experiences were. Life has not worked out for you as you hoped. You have had much suffering and disappointment. In fact, your rage and anger can even be of value in certain situations. Sometimes even a little flash of that anger is all it will take for you to be left alone, or treated with greater respect. Now I want you to ponder those feelings, and then I want you to begin to focus and concentrate those feelings in one of your arms. That will be your anger arm, and as you now squeeze the fist on that side, you can feel those angry and bitter feelings growing stronger, under your complete control. . . . Now I want you to release that fist and consider for a few moments another kind of feeling. I want you to think of a situation in which you feel comfortable, confident and at peace . . . begin to feel the strength and comfort of that situation . . . and begin to focus and concentrate those feelings in your other arm. That will be your "strength and comfort arm," and as you now squeeze your fist tighter and tighter you can experience that feeling of strength and comfort growing stronger under your complete control. . . .

She left the session feeling greatly encouraged, and practiced the two evoked feeling states regularly as instructed. Improvement was noted in her daily life and she began to enjoy her therapy sessions. Although continuing to show instability, she was able to handle my departure from the area as well as her father's death over the next six months, stresses that would previously have been catastrophic for her.

AN IMAGERY TECHNIQUE

A visual imagery technique embodying the same basic principle (balanced evocation of two mental states) can be offered to patients who are outwardly in control but continue to swing between bouts of depression and giddy, unpleasant "highs."

A thirty-six year old man had been called manic-depressive and had a long history of erratically shifting symptom pictures. He was found to be quite suggestible and was interested in learning to regulate his own moods without drugs. He went easily into trance and was then instructed in the following two images:

First he was told to imagine, tied to one wrist, a bunch of large, brightly colored, powerful balloons, pulling him upward. Slight spontaneous arm levitation was ignored, and he was further told to imagine himself being lifted off the ground, slowly floating into the air, a few feet off the ground, then to window height, rooftop height, the height of the treetops, or high into the sky, "as HIGH as you comfortably wish to go," to look down from a comfortable height on the various scenes of his life with detachment and serenity.

When he signaled full experiencing of this image and its accompanying euphoria, he was instructed in the second image: "In your other hand, now, imagine a heavy rope, that is tied to a heavy iron anchor on the earth below you. Now as you pull that rope you can slowly come down, controlling your height, down to the height of the tree-tops, or the height of the ceiling, or a few feet from the ground, as low as you wish. And as you pull on that imaginary rope you can come down lower and lower and lower . . ."

The patient was instructed to place himself in trance and practice these visualizations on a regular basis, and he did so with enthusiasm. On one occasion, while practicing in bed, he went into a prolonged trance and "woke up" several hours later, "hanging on to my balloons" and feeling exhausted but euphoric. He let himself down with the imaginary rope and went to sleep. Therapy now proceeded rapidly with little "insight" but with an increasing sense of stability and self-confidence, and with active, realistic problem solving. As with the previous technique, evoked feeling states can be conditioned or "anchored" to various cues (Bandler & Grinder, 1978).

Hypnotic Suggestions to Deter Suicide

James R. Hodge, M.D.
Akron, Ohio

INTRODUCTION, INDICATIONS, AND CONTRAINDICATIONS

Some hypnotherapists have suggested that hypnosis is contraindicated or only to be used carefully by experienced therapists in working with depressed patients (e.g., Terman, 1980; Waxman, 1978) or in manic-depressive illness (Brown & Fromm, 1986) because the severity of depression may be exacerbated through uncovering of emotion-laden material. Nonetheless, in skilled hands and with patients who are depressed but not severely so, hypnosis may facilitate a rapid uncovering of vitally important etiologic factors.

Hodge (1972) has found that suggestions to deter suicide have seemed effective. He indicated: "Patients accept these suggestions quite easily, almost as if they do not believe them. They may or may not recall the suggestions before, during, or after a suicidal impulse; and they are frequently perplexed or even angry that something will happen to prevent their carrying out their suicidal attempts or that they will feel a need to contact me before carrying out such an attempt. Some remarks that patients have made have been of the nature of, 'I was getting all my pills ready to take them, but somehow I felt that I just had to call you,' or 'I was all ready to get in the car and go away to kill myself, but I felt I had to call you first.' Occasionally a patient will, while feeling suicidal, ask to be released from the obligation of the suggestion, but has invariably accepted the refusal" (p. 22).

Suggestive hypnosis certainly seems to possess a much lower risk of untoward effects than utilizing intense uncovering techniques or a method such as age progression. In the latter technique, the patient may imagine that the future continues to be negative and subsequently experience even greater feelings of hopelessness. Suggestions such as those recommended by Hodge (1972), however, seem to have little risk and may yield positive benefits. This is particularly the case when they are part of a broad-spectrum approach to the treatment of depression (e.g., medication, cognitive behavior therapy, etc.) and when Hodge's own excellent guidelines below are followed. The suggestions are very direct, and this clearly seems indicated in this type of situation. (*Ed.*)

RATIONALE

Most suicidal impulses are temporary and many are actually brief, especially if the problem can be identified and if there is someone available with whom the patient can discuss his problems and/or break up the suicidal ruminations. If the suicidal pattern of thought can be interrupted or if the patient can be given a "face saving way out," the suicidal danger may lapse. My main premises, then, in the wording of this suggestion are:

1. Hypnosis can and should only have a temporary deterring effect on a suicidal impulse. Ultimately the psychodynamics of the patient's suicidal tendencies should be worked out in psychotherapy so that such tendencies should not remain a way of life for him.
2. A direct and permanent confrontation-challenge to the patient that he *cannot ever* commit suicide would be bound to fail. The *"cannot ever"* implies a challenge and control that the patient must test regardless of the other dynamics of his suicidal tendencies; it is quite possible that he may overcome the effectiveness of such hypnotic suggestions.
3. A temporary deterrent is often all that is necessary to prevent a given suicide attempt permanently, especially if it gets the patient to the psychiatrist's office. At least it gives the psychiatrist a chance to work with the patient and to consider and arrange hospitalization if necessary. In case the suicidal pattern cannot be interrupted by discussion and analysis in the office, the patient has already agreed to enter the trance event though he may wish to commit suicide instead. Discussion and analysis in the trance may be effective even when it is not effective outside the trance. If this is not effective, however, it may be easier to protect the patient and to arrange for hospitalization while the patient is in a trance.
4. It gives the patient a realistic, logical, acceptable, and semi- compulsory alternative to suicide: Get an appointment with the psychiatrist.

SUGGESTIONS

In the future, though you may have some suicidal thoughts and feelings and impulses, you will not be able to carry out an actual suicide attempt until you have discussed it with me, in advance, and in my office. I do not know how you will prevent yourself from carrying out the suicidal impulse, but you will find a way. Do you understand? [The patient almost invariably agrees, but if he does not, I ask him what he does not understand and then explain it further.] Now, one other thing. I want you to agree with me that you will enter a trance at any time I *insist* on it even if you do not want to at that time. Will you agree to that? [Patients are sometimes reluctant to make such a promise, but I have had none of them refuse, and they have kept their promises quite well.]

[An alternative wording of suggestions to deter suicide attempts is modified from the suggestions I made to the patient described in my article on the treatment of dissociative reactions (Hodge, 1959):]

In the future while you may have some suicidal thoughts and feelings and impulses, you will be unable to carry out a suicide attempt unless you are in a hypnotic trance. The suicidal thoughts and/or feelings will serve as an *alert* to the possibility that you may be about to enter the trance, but you will not actually enter it unless (a) the feelings become *very* strong and you feel unable to handle them, (b) you actually begin to make preparations for a suicide attempt. In either of these situations you will enter the trance, will begin to feel better and more relaxed; and in any case you will be unable to commit suicide until you have actually contacted me and informed me that you are *in* a trance and have been planning suicide. If I am not available, you will continue to relax and to feel better in the trance and you may remain in it as long as is necessary to protect yourself until I am available. However, when you are aware that you are no longer suicidal, your trance will automatically terminate ten minutes later. Being in a trance will not prevent you from carrying out the necessities of your life. *To summarize*: The more suicidal you are, the more you will be compelled to enter a trance and to contact me. In the trance you will be unable to commit suicide unless I give you permission; the trance itself may be just the factor you need to break up your suicidal thoughts and to help you to relax and find better ways to handle your problems.

Hypnosis with Bipolar Affective Disorders

A. David Feinstein, Ph.D., and
R. Michael Morgan
Ashland, Oregon, and San Diego, California

INTRODUCTION

Feinstein and Morgan (1986) described a program for treating bipolar affective disorder patients with hypnosis. The five stages of their program include: (1) determining relevant medical and psychosocial parameters; (2) establishing rapport and a positive response set to the therapy; (3) introducing suggestions for electrochemical regulation; (4) teaching self-hypnosis; and (5) addressing self-concept. One innovative technique that they described is reprinted here. A number of studies, summarized by Feinstein and Morgan, have implicated electrochemical asymmetry in hemispheric lateralization in several major psychiatric disorders, including bipolar affective disorder. In addition, hypnosis has been found to spontaneously effect changes in hemispheric asymmetry (Frumkin, Ripley, & Cox, 1978). Feinstein and Morgan's technique encourages the development of balance through metaphoric suggestions for electrochemical balance.

We must bear in mind with this disorder, and many other conditions discussed in this volume, that we do not have research to document that hypnosis may make a positive contribution to treatment outcome. Neither do these authors

possess documentation that their suggestions lead to hemispheric changes (e.g., similar to lithium), although they propose that this is a hypothesis worthy of investigation. This, however, is not meant as a commentary on these authors; it is a commentary on the pre-scientific status of psychotherapy in general and hypnotherapy in particular. We must also keep in mind that it is possible that a metaphoric technique may produce beneficial behavioral change even if it does not produce hemispheric alterations. (*Ed.*)

INTRODUCING SUGGESTIONS FOR ELECTROCHEMICAL REGULATION

Before formulating suggestions for electrochemical hemispheric balance, suggestions for overall physical-emotional balance are introduced. Particular emphasis is placed on lifestyle imbalances that cause difficulties for the patient, such as relentless work activity or relationship patterns that swing from intensive involvements to no involvements at all. . . .

General suggestions for electrochemical balance precede the introduction of specifically tailored suggestions and imagery. A transcription taken from a typical session reads:

Your brain chemistry is balancing itself at the ideal level for you, for happiness, for attaining your goals in life. As each organ of your body continues to relax, you notice a new sense of balance between the two sides of your body, a balance which you can feel in your legs, your arms, your chest, your face, and now you sense it in your brain. As you notice this sense of balance, you may become aware of the circulation of your blood, seeing your blood pick up oxygen, feeling your blood circulate through your body and bringing even greater balance to your brain and to all the other organs of your body.

Specific suggestions and images for electrochemical balance are formulated based upon the patient's responses to these general suggestions. Tailoring these images to the patient's system of internal representation is critical to the effectiveness of the imagery. The images which were the most effective differed for each of the five subjects. The essential differences fell along a continuum from concrete, literal, kinesthetic imagery to abstract, symbolic, visual images. A kinesthetic image is apparent in the following instructions:

You will be imagining a chemical balance taking place in your brain. Direct your awareness to your brain; perhaps one part seems heavier than another part; perhaps one part seems warmer. As the chemical balance begins to take place, such feelings of warmth or heaviness may equalize throughout your brain. Allow this natural balance to occur now, knowing that the feelings of warmth or heaviness will fade away when the chemical balance is complete. As those feelings fade away, the balance remains.

CONTROL ROOM IMAGE.   An image that was on the abstract and symbolic end of the continuum was formulated for the male patient who had difficulty yielding control. He was taught to visualize himself on a swivel chair in a master control room which had dials, switches, and meters for every function of his being. [See Hammond's master control room technique in Chapter 11.] Two meters in particular revealed electrochemical status of the sides of his brain. He used imagery to adjust the dials, which brought the electrochemical status of both sides of the brain to their ideal, symmetrical levels. He later learned to use the control panel to influence other conditions such as physical pain.

BLENDING RIVERS IMAGE.   The imagery suggested by the therapist is, to the greatest possible extent, derived from the patient's internal world. For instance, the second patient, a naturalist, had described a favorite spot where two rivers merged into one. Under hypnosis she was told to imagine herself lying in the grass next to two mountain streams watching a brown leaf floating down one of the streams and a yellow leaf floating down the other: "The streams are flowing toward one another like streams of vital life chemicals in your brain. When the two streams merge, the leaves swirl together, becoming a single color, and the energies and chemicals in your brain blend in a natural harmony." In another instance, where several earlier images had not been effective, the therapist noted the patient's comment that her brain was "like a sponge that absorbs things" and had her formulate an image of one side of the brain being a sponge soaked in a liquid of one color, the other side being a sponge soaked in a liquid of another color, with suggestions of the two liquids flowing together to become a blended color.

The imagery finally arrived at for a given patient often combines both kinesthetic-literal and visual-symbolic modes, such as seeing a balance scale with beakers containing vital life chemicals on each end and sensing the scale coming into perfect balance as necessary chemicals are added to the beakers.

HYPNOSIS WITH POST-TRAUMATIC STRESS DISORDER AND MULTIPLE PERSONALITY DISORDER

Emergency Room Suggestions for Physically or Sexually Assaulted Patients

Carol P. Herbert, M.D., CCFP, FCFP
Vancouver, British Columbia

It is essential to recognize that many patients spontaneously enter trance following physical or sexual assault. In such situations, direct suggestion is helpful as follows:

1. "You did everything you could—now let me do what I can to help you."
2. "Your body is healthy and strong" (for children: "You will grow up to be a healthy, strong man/woman.")
3. "What happened is not your fault."
4. "It is a good thing that you told (someone)."

5. "You may find yourself remembering more and more details about what happened to you over the next few days. You may also dream about your experience. That is your inner mind's way of coping. Write down what you remember or tell someone."

It is important not to give inadvertent suggestions as to the identity of the assailant. Given the current legal climate, induction of hypnosis is not recommended in the emergency setting. However, it is permissible to encourage progressive muscle relaxation during physical examination or procedures (e.g., venupuncture).

Under no circumstances should patients be touched without explicit permission, as patients with a history of abuse may spontaneously dissociate or regress, especially if touch is perceived as sexual or as similar to the behavior of a past abuser.

Hypnotic Suggestions with Rape Victims

Bruce Walter Ebert
Beale Air Force Base, California

The following suggestions were adapted from Ebert (1988) for use with rape victims. After teaching a patient self-hypnosis, the following suggestions may be offered: "Take your time with this growing sense of power, control, and comfort because you will discover that, the more you relax with the techniques, the more the fears will simply fade away."

Another technique utilized by Ebert (1988) was to have the patient find the image that most represented strength to her. In one case a patient imagined her grandmother. She may then be instructed to take the strength she needs from this image/person, and told that this "is stored deeply inside and does contain your strength and power. You can utilize it whenever you choose by recalling this image when you need to *feel* strong, in control, and powerful."

Saying Goodbye to the Abused Child: An Approach for Use with Victims of Child Abuse and Trauma

Ronald A. Havens, Ph.D.
Springfield, Illinois

CONTRAINDICATIONS

This metaphoric procedure is not recommended for use with borderline personality disorder or with schizophrenic patients.

SUGGESTIONS

And now, as you sit there with your eyes closed, and begin to continue to allow your body to relax, your mind to relax, and experience the awareness of many different things, you may begin to wonder, as you drift down into a light trance or a deeper trance, exactly how deeply relaxed you might become later on.

But there really is no need to make an effort to try to be aware of exactly how deeply relaxed an arm or a leg might be, because you can continue to relax even more deeply later on while your unconscious mind does those things needed for you.

And so, as you continue to relax and to experience the peaceful calmness of a comfortable state of increasing relaxation, I can say many different things, including those things needed to help you discover the abilities and capacities you have to allow yourself to experience many different things.

And one of the things you may experience is an awareness that there are many different ways to heal a wound, a wound from long ago that never healed but remained behind tochange the way you think and feel. Kind of like a woman I know who always wondered why she was the way she was until one day when she discovered a child within—a sad child, an unhappy child, an angry, hurt child from long ago. A child she always heard in the background, a child she protected and did everything for today, a child who made her feel so sad and she would do anything to keep that child quiet, to keep that child happy, to give that child what it wanted and needed.

And I asked her what needed to be done and she said she needed to say *goodbye* to that child, she needed to *hug* that child, to *hold* that child, and to *tell* that child how very, very *sorry* she was that those things had happened to it. She felt so badly for the pain, so badly for the fear, so badly for the anger. But she knew she had to say goodbye. Finally, she had to leave it behind and go on with her life. She knew there was nothing she could do to save that child, to change the past, to undo what was. What was, was, and there was nothing she could do.

So she hugged that child and said goodbye, and walked away and cried and cried. The hardest thing she had ever done was to say goodbye, leave it behind, abandon it to the past. She felt awful, but she knew that was what she had to do. There was nothing she could do to change the past, nothing she could do to undo what that child went through.

But afterwards she was free, felt free, to do what *she* wanted. The child was gone and she was free, free of the past, free to be.

And so as you relax and drift upward toward the surface of wakeful awareness, your unconscious knows what you can do, your conscious knows it too, and you can feel the freedom of that relaxed letting go in your own way, even as you drift upwards now to the surface of wakeful awareness.

Reframing Dreams in PTSD

Charles B. Mutter, M.D.
Miami, Florida

In your sleep at night you dream. In those dreams you hear, you see, you move, you have many experiences, and a part of that experience is *forgetting* that dream after you awaken. Forgetting is an experience that is not unusual for anyone.

One of the nicest things about hypnosis is that in the trance state you can *dare* to look at, and think about, and see, and feel things, things that you wouldn't dare in the ordinary state.

It is hard for any person to think that he can be afraid of his own thoughts, but you can know that you have all the protection of your own unconscious which protects you in your dreams, permitting you to dream what you wish, when you wish, and keeping it as long as your unconscious thinks necessary or desirable.

Your unconscious mind is powerful and has a sacred trust to protect you. In your dreams, you can reframe any thought that you need to, to let you know that you survived all your past experiences, and all the powers that are behind you that have gotten you through this, continue to serve you as they do now in your waking state and even when you dream. Just as you are *now* able to allow your conscious mind to drift off into some pleasant place, your unconscious can listen to me and deal with other things at the same time and do what it needs to get this experience behind you, placing these old thoughts in the inactive file, and permitting you to go on with the rest of your life.

As you continue self-hypnotic skills, your unconscious mind will use this time to find out, explore things about you and your abilities, and solve any problems that you have. And this experience is yours; it belongs to you, and can be used in any way that you decide.

Suggestions and Metaphors for Post-Traumatic Stress Disorder and Pain Control (in Spanish)

Marlene D. de Rios, Ph.D., and
Joyce K. Friedman, Ph.D.
Fullerton, California, and Los Angeles, California

METAPHOR PRIOR TO HYPNOTIC INDUCTION (ENGLISH TRANSLATION)

I want to explain to you just what happens to you now that you have experienced an accident or burn trauma [substitute exact type of trauma or accident experienced by patient]. You see, the body responds in a very special way after you experience a trauma like the one you have just had. This trauma is felt in the body, especially in the muscle system.

You know, your blood flows through your veins and arteries very much like the irrigation canals you remember from your home country. That is, when we use very high-powered microscopes, we see that the arteries and veins have walls, very small so that the eye can't see them, but these walls are made up of muscles. The whole thing is like an irrigation canal you know so well in Mexico, you know, when the mud falls into the canal, the water cannot flow to irrigate the plants and crops. In this way, when you have an accident (trauma), the muscles of the walls of your arteries and veins get narrower and narrower until your blood doesn't flow as much and as quickly as it should. Just like the mud in the irrigation canal falling into the water, your arteries and veins get smaller and smaller and your hands get cold, and you get tense; it is like a little tiger ready to attack, that is the startle effect you feel very often.

Well, there are special exercises that I am going to teach you which will help you to communicate with your muscles. It appears to be a lie, but indeed it is true, that we can indeed control our own muscles and we can make these irrigation canals in our body open and we can allow our blood to flow normally the way it should. So, I will sit here in this chair, and you will sit over there and close your eyes and simply follow the words that I say. When I am finished, I will say to you, "Open your eyes." Do you understand? OK, let's begin.

INDUCTION AND SUGGESTIONS (ENGLISH TRANSLATION)

Pay attention to your breathing . . . breathe in, slowly, breathe out slowly, listen to the sound of my voice and try not to sleep, and with each breath that you take, feel yourself becoming more and more relaxed, more and more relaxed, calm and tranquil.

Feel the fresh energy, passing through your body, move that energy, little by little, through your body, from the top of your head, passing your forehead, your cheeks, feel your jaw relaxing, your mouth opening a little bit, as that energy passes to your shoulders. Take 10 seconds and feel that cool energy passing through your body, from the top of your head until your shoulders: begin now, 1, 2, 3, 4, more and more relaxed, calm and tranquil, 5, 6, 7, more and more relaxed, calm and tranquil, 8, 9, and 10.

Now, feel that cool energy passing through your body, move it little by little, inside your body, from the shoulders, passing through your chest, passing your back, until your waist, take 10 seconds to feel that fresh energy, passing through your body, move it little by little, into your body, from the shoulders until the waist. Begin now, 1, 2, 3, more and more relaxed, more and more relaxed, calm and tranquil, 4, 5, 6, very calm, 7, 8, 9 and 10, the most relaxed feeling that you have ever felt.

Now, feel the fresh energy passing through your body, move it little by little into your body, from the shoulders, passing your arm, passing your elbow, passing your wrist, until the tips of your fingers. Take 10 seconds to feel the fresh energy passing through your body, move it little by little, into your body, from the shoulders, until the tips of your fingers. Begin now. 1, 2, 3, more and more relaxed, calm and tranquil, 4, 5, and 6, more and more relaxed, calm and tranquil, 7, 8, 9 and 10, the most relaxed feeling that you have ever felt, as if you were floating on top of a pretty white cloud in a blue sky, so calm, so tranquil.

Now, feel the fresh energy pass into your body, move it little by little, into your body, from the waist, past your thighs, past your knees until your feet. Take 10 seconds to feel the fresh energy pass through your body, move it little by little, into your body, from the waist until the feet, begin now. 1, 2, 3, calm and tranquil, 4, 5, 6, more and more relaxed, calm and tranquil, 7, 8, 9, and 10, the most relaxed feeling you have ever felt.

Now, imagine that you are standing by the seashore, you feel very relaxed, calm, very happy, at ease, feel the breeze caress your face, smell the fresh air, feel the cool sand in your feet, more and more relaxed, more and more relaxed, calm and tranquil.

Now imagine that you are in a beautiful pine forest, it is a spring day, smell the fresh air, listen to the sound of the birds, see the flowers in all the colors, you feel very good, tranquil, calm, very calm, very tranquil.

SUGGESTIONS WHEN THERE ARE SLEEP PROBLEMS

Now, imagine that you are in your house, it is nighttime, you are sleeping in your bed. Imagine you are sleeping well, all night long, have happy dreams, pretty dreams, tranquil dreams, without waking up, breathing peacefully all night long, you feel very well, calm, tranquil, very relaxed.

SUGGESTIONS WHEN THERE ARE PROBLEMS OF PAIN

Now, imagine that you have a green pitcher of iced water, very cold, put your right hand inside the pitcher, and feel the cold passing to that right hand, until it is very numb, so that you don't feel it at all. Now, place that right hand on whatever part of your body is bothering you, and little by little, feel that coldness pass to your body, you feel very good, calm and tranquil, very relaxed.

SUGGESTIONS WITH PROBLEMS OF BODY IMAGE AFTER AN ACCIDENT OR INJURY

Imagine that you are in your house, in front of your mirror, how handsome (pretty) you are. You feel very tranquil; your hand is fine. Imagine that you are in your house, in front of your mirror, how handsome you are, how tranquil you feel.

METAPHORIC SUGGESTIONS FOR SELF-HYPNOSIS

You are like the eagle, king of the birds, king of all his dominion. Whenever you want, wherever you are, with the tape or without the tape, you know how to calm yourself. Simply close your eyes, pay attention to your breathing, won't you, and little by little, feel that fresh energy pass into your body, little by little. You are like the king eagle, king of all your dominion, because you know how to calm yourself, you know how to relax.

RE-ALERTING

Now, I am going to count from 1-10. Imagine that you are walking up a pretty staircase, and with each number that I say, feel that you are walking up the staircase, and you feel more and more alert with each step, very awake. 1, 2, 3, more and more alert, very happy, 4, 5, 6, very, very alert, more and more awake, 7, 8, 9, and 10, open your eyes.*

TRADUCCION EN ESPAÑOL: INDUCCION ANTES DEL HIPNOSIS

Quiero explicarle exactamente lo que le pasa ahora que Vd. ha experimentado un acidente o quemadura (substituya el tipo exacto de trauma o acidente experimentado por el paciente). Mire, el cuerpo responde al accidente de una manera especial como aquello que recientemente ha tenido Vd. Este trauma se siente en el cuerpo, especialmente en el sistema muscular.

Sabe, la sangre corre por sus venas y arterias tal como en los canales de irrígacion que Ud. recuerda de su tierra. Es decir, cuando utilizamos un microscopio de alto poder, vemos que las paredes de las arterias y las venas son muy pequenas que el ojo no puede verias, pero

---

*A tape of the suggestions given above for pain control and progressive relaxation is available from Dr. de Rios in Vietnamese, German, Spanish at the following address: Department of Anthropology, California State University, Fullerton, CA 92634, USA.

estas paredes estan hechas de musculos. Todo esto es como un canal de irrigacion que Vd. conoce tan bien en Mexico, Vd. sabe, cuando el barro cae dentro del canal, el agua no puede correr para irrigar a las plantas y las cosechas. De igual manera, cuando Vd. se acidenta, los musculos de las arterias y las venas se obstruyen de tal manera que su sangre no corre libremente. Justo, como el barro en el canal de irrigacion que cae al agua, igualmente sus arterias y sus venas se estrechan y sus manos se enfrian y Vd. se pone tenso. Es como un tigrillo listo para saltar en ataque. Esto es el susto que Vd. siente muy frecuentemente.

Ahora bien, hay ejercicios especiales que voy a enseñarie que le ayudarán a communicarse con sus músculos. Parece mentira, pero es la verdad, podemos controlar a nuestros propios musculos y podemos hacer que estos canales de irrigacion en neustro cuerpo se abran y podemos permitir que nuestra sangre corra normalmente. Pues, voy a sentarme aqui en la silla, y Vd. se sienta alli, y cierre los ojos y simplemente escuche a las palabras que yo digo. Cuando termino, voy a decirle, "abra los ojos." Comprende Vd.? Bien, empezamos. . . .

Preste atencíon a la respiracíon . . . aspire Vd. lentamente . . . expire Vd. lentamente, escucha el sonido de mi voz y procure no dormir . . . y con cada respiracíon, se va sentir mas y mas relajado, mas y mas relajado, calmo y tranquilo.

Siente la energia que es fresca, va a pasar por su cuerpo . . . tiene que moverla poco a poco, dentro su cuerpo . . . desde la corona de la cabeza, pasando la frente, pasando las mejillas, . . . la mandíbula relajada, la boco abre un poco . . . pasando el cuello hasta los hombros. Tome 10 segundos para sentir la energia va a pasar por su cuerpo, desde la corona de la cabeza hasta los hombros . . . empezamos ahora. 1, 2, 3, 4, mas y mas relajado, calmo y tranquilo, 5, 6, 7, mas y mas relajado, calmo y tranquilo, 8, 9 y 10.

Ahora, siente la energia que es fresca, va a pasar por su cuerpo, tiene que moverla poco a poco, dentro su cuerpo, desde los hombros, pasando el pecho, pasando la espaldo hasta la cintura tome 10 segundos para sentir la energia

que es fresca, va a pasar por su cuerpo, tiene que moverla poco a poco, de ntro su cuerpo . . . desde los hombros, hasta la cintura. Empezamos ahora, 1, 2, 3, mas y mas relajado, mas y mas relajado calmo y tranquilo, bien calmo, 7, 8, 9, 10 el mas relajado que nunca sentia.

Ahora, siente la energia que es fresca, va a pasar por su cuerpo, tiene que moverla poco a poco, dentro su cuerpo, desde los hombros, pasando el brazo, pasando el codo, pasando la muñeca, hasta las yemas de los dedos. Tome 10 segundos para sentir la energia que es fresca, va a pasar por el cuerpo, tiene que moverla poco a poco, dentro su cuerpo desde los hombros, hasta las yemas de los dedos. Empezamos ahora, 1, 2, 3, mas y mas relajado, calmo y tranquilo, 4, 5, 6, mas y mas relajado, calmo y tranquilo 7, 8, 9 y 10, el mas relajado que nunca sentia si fuera flotando encima de una nube bonita , blanco en un cielo azul, tan calmo, tan tranquilo.

Ahora, siente la energia que es fresca, va a pasar por su cuerpo, tiene que moverla poco a poco, dentro su cuerpo, desde la cintura, pasando los muslos, pasando la rodilla, hasta los pies, tome 10 segundos para sentir la energia que es fresca, va a pasar por su cuerpo, tiene que moverla poco a poco, dentro su cuerpo, desde la cintura hasta los pies, empezamos ahora, 1,2,3, calmo y tranquilo, 4,5,6, mas y mas relajado, calmo y tranquilo, 7,8,9 y 10, el mas relajado que nunca sentia.

Ahora, imagine Vd. que esta parado por la orilla del mar, Vd. siente relajado, calmo, bien a gusto, alegre, siente la brisa cariciar en su cara, huela el aire fresco, siente la arena fresca en sus pies descalzos, mas y mas relajado, mas y mas relajado, calmo y tranquilo.

Ahora, imagine Vd. que esta en un bosque bonito, de pinos, es un día de la primavera, huela el aire fresca, escucha el sonido de los pájaros, vea las flores de todos colores, Vd. siente muy bien, tranquilo, calmo, bien calmo, bien tranquilo.

(Si hay problemas con el dormir)

Ahora, imagine Vd. que esta en su casa, es noche, esta dormiendo en su cama, imaginese dormiendo bien, toda la noche, teniendo suenos alegres, bonitos, tranquilos, sin des pertarse, respirando con tranquilidad toda la noche, Vd. siente muy bien, calmo, tranquilo, bien relajado.

(Si hay problemas de dolor en el cuerpo)

Ahora, imagine Vd. que tiene un jarro verde de agua helada, bien helada, ponga Vd. la mano derecha dentro el jarro, y siente que el frio va pasando a la mano derecho, hasta que esta entumecida bien, que no lo siente. Ahora, tome la mano derecho a donde en su cuerpo esta molestando, y poco a poco siente la frialdad pasa al cuerpo, Vd. siente muy bien, calmo y tranquilo, bien relajado.

(Si hay problemas de desgusto del cuerpo después del acidente, injurio, etc.)

Imaginese que esta en su casa, frente su espejo, que lindo (guapo) esta, tranquilo, su mano esta bien, esta linda, imaginese que esta en su casa, frente su espe jo, que linda esta, que bonita, tranquila. . . .

Vd. es como el rey aguila, rey de todo su dominio, cuando quiere donde sea, con la cinta o sin la cinta, Vd. ya sabe calmarse, Vd. simplemente tiene que cerrar los ojos, hacer caso a la respiracíon, y poco a poco, siente la energia que es fresca va a pasar por su cuerpo, poco a poco, Vd. es como el rey aguilar, rey do todo su dominio, porque Vd. sabe calmarse, saba relajarse.

(Para despertarle al cliente)

Ahora, voy a contrar de 1 a 10, imaginese subiendo una escalera bonita, y con cada numero que digo, siente que esta subiendo la escalera, y se siente mas y mas alerto con cada peldaño, muy despierto, 1, 2, 3, mas y mas alerto, bien a gusto va, 4, 5, 6, mas y mas alerto, mas despierto, 7, 8, 9 y 10, abre los ojos.

A Fusion Ritual in Treating Multiple Personality

Richard P. Kluft, M.D.
Philadelphia, Pennsylvania

THE ROLE AND TIMING OF INTEGRATION

Integration is the process of undoing the dissociative dividedness of an individual suf-fering multiple personality disorder (MPD). It begins long before any personalities begin to lose the signs and/or sense of separateness and continues as an intrapsychic process of reorganization even after the personalities achieve unity. Fusion is the coming together of the several personalities into a unity and is said to occur after several indices of dividedness have not been observed for three months. Interventions which suggest and help bring about the occurrence of fusion at a particular point in time are often called fusion rituals; they often are facilitated by formal heterohypnosis.

Fusion rituals are ceremonies at a discrete point in time which are perceived by some MPD patients as crucial rites of passage from the subjective sense of dividedness to the subjective sense of unity. Some MPD patients, however, experience fusion as a spontaneous, abrupt or gradual process, and complete their treatments successfully without undergoing fusion rituals. Because such ceremonies are obvious and memorable landmarks in the treatment, they often are accorded an unfortunate overemphasis and unnecessarily invested with drama by both patient and clinician alike. In fact, a fusion ritual will not substitute for the hard work of other aspects of the therapy and is not a potent technique in and of itself. It is no more than an agreed-upon congenial formalization of work already accomplished. Some MPD patients' personalities fuse one at a time, some fuse in clusters, and some fuse all at once. Some personalities experience the process of fusion as a joining to or coalescence with specific other alters among the system of personalities; some simply cease to be separate.

The timing of a fusion should emerge from the intrinsic process and momentum of the therapeutic endeavor. It should never be undertaken because the therapist or patient is eager to see fusion achieved or hopes to find some form of short-cut. In essence, it is a permissive and positive intervention that is understood as tentative and framed in a manner that clearly states that, if the fusion does not hold, it is not a failure, but more an indication that there is more work to be done before a fusion would be appropriate. For this reason, it is not helpful to bypass resistances to fusion. They should be dealt with straightforwardly. A bypassed resistance or a procedure perceived as coercive virtually guarantees a rapid relapse into dividedness. In the long run, going slower and more gently speeds therapy and reduces both crises and failure experiences for both clinician and patient.

Useful considerations in the timing of an attempt at fusion are based on clinical experience. Fusion should occur when work on all reasons for the dividedness of the alters about to fuse has been completed, i.e., when the particular separateness in question no longer serves a meaningful function in the patient's ability to adapt to environmental and intrapsychic pressures. This is usually the case when the alters under consideration for fusion identify with one another, empathize with one another, and each accepts not only the other(s), but the other's (or others') memories and affects. At this point they often feel no need to remain separate. Although some alters experience fusion as a death, most which fuse successfully reach a sense of assurance that they will survive within the blended self of a united individual. Often when issues of survival have been negotiated with the first alters to fuse, the other alters perceive that the influences of fused personalities persist as contributions to an increasingly unified psyche, then such concerns cease to be pressing.

The wording of fusion rituals should be individualized rather than cookbookish. In general, one should be permissive and make it clear that the patient may interrupt the procedure at any time if discomfort is felt. It is useful to inquire about unsuspected remaining areas of conflict and concern before beginning. It is not uncommon for alters not involved in the proposed fusion, but opposed to it for some reason, to intercede. Usually they will withdraw after being allowed to verbalize their objections, but sometimes one must defer the procedure. Clinical experience indicates that images which suggest merger, union, and rebirth in which all aspects of all personalities are preserved as they come together are accepted much more readily than those which imply elimination, subtraction, death, or going away. I have described images of dance, embrace, shared activities, and the like, but most of my patients have preferred images of light or streams of water flowing together, or scenes in which the snow on mountain peaks melts and flows together into a lake on the surface of which all the mountains are reflected (Kluft, 1982). I have found science fiction scenarios quite useful in young boys (Kluft, 1985). Braun (1984) has described fantasies in which alters go to a library and read about and absorb one another, scenes of streams flowing together or of the mixing of red and white paint to form pink and the imagery of an antibiotic capsule dissolving and thereby circulating throughout the body and mind and becoming thoroughly absorbed.

As a concrete example of this process, I will share the wording of a recent and successful fusion ritual. This particular patient enjoyed the additional reassurance of a recheck and reinforcing ritual. What follows is a nearly verbatim ritual used with an MPD woman who had already fused many personalities during similar procedures. Joan and Anne are two alters in a patient named Claire (all pseudonyms). Joan and Anne have already been elicited by hypnosis. Each affirmed she had no more separate memories or issues which required further work, and each affirmed a readiness to join with and accept the other. The objections of an alter opposed to all fusion were dealt with by reminding it that its freedom of decision was being accepted and that alters who wanted to decide to join deserved similar consideration.

WHITE LIGHT SUGGESTIONS FOR FUSION

Please allow your eyes to roll up and your eyelids to flutter down and close. Let yourself go deep at the count of three—one, two, three. If at any time you want to stop or talk with me about something, raise your right index finger.

And now, deeper still at the count of four . . . (deepening by count until eight, and then) . . . as deep as you've ever been at the count of nine, and now deeper still at ten. That's right. Nod if you're ready. [Patient nods.]

OK. You all are in a beautiful clearing in the woods, a place of complete privacy and safety. All stand in a circle, take one another's hands, and now move toward the center of the circle. You'll find you have to let your arms slide gently around one another as the circle grows smaller. And as you get closer, already you can feel a pleasant warmth from the closeness, a sense of warmth and closeness that feels good to you all, even those who have no plans to join with one another today.

Above the center of the circle, a point of light is seen, which rapidly becomes brighter and more radiant, a warming, comforting, and healing form of light that rapidly becomes so beautiful, bright, and radiant that, although it does not hurt your eyes at all, is so luminous that each of you, no matter where you look, all you see is a beautiful field of light that engulfs you all. No matter where you look, there is no evidence of detail or separateness. And now the light seems to enter you as a warming current, and flows back and forth, forth and back, sharing with you all the experience of peace and well-being.

And now the current flows to Joan and Anne alone, back and forth between you. Back and forth, forth and back, and soon it takes with it all the memories, feelings, and qualities of Joan into Anne, and of Anne into Joan [this is elaborated]. Nothing is withheld, nothing is omitted [elaborate back and forth motif]. And now that all from each has flowed into the other, and all from the other has flowed into each, it seems so pointless to be separate. At three, the barriers between Joan and Anne gently crumble, and peacefully are washed away. All that was Anne flows into Joan, and all that was Joan into Anne. . . . And it's so easy and gentle because you already have become the same. Everything blending, joining, and mixing [elaborate]. And now everything settles gently and peacefully, joined now and forever at the count of two . . . that feels so natural, so right. . . .

And now the light recedes. All of you look around. Everyone feeling better, stronger, safer. Where there were Joan and Anne, there is a single individual, stronger, more peaceful, more resilient, and unified now and forever at the count of one. How do you feel? [The patient opens her eyes and says it went well.] OK. Close your eyes and rapidly go as deep as you were. You had said that the unified person would be called Joan. Joan, nod if you are there and OK. [Nods.] Anne, nod if you remain separate. [No nod.] Everyone else, raise the right index finger if anyone senses or knows Anne remains separate or notices anything amiss. [No signal.] OK, let this fusion be sealed and solid, now and forever, at the count of three . . . one, two, three. [The patient opened her eyes, and volunteered that she felt good.]

[This verbalization is only an example of what was congenial to one patient at one point in her treatment. It is offered as food for thought, but not as a tool for use with any other patient.]

Another Fusion Ritual

Richard P. Kluft, M.D.
Philadelphia, Pennsylvania

INTRODUCTION

Many patients with multiple personality disorder have had sufficient traumata that almost any set of images may be affectively loaded. The following is often sufficiently neutral, complex, and distracting that it is accepted and engrosses attention throughout the procedure across all alters, even those that are not participants in the fusion. Since it requires considerable concentration, it makes enough demands upon the patient to divert him or her from low to moderate levels of anxiety that may be attendant upon the fusion process. In this hypothetical example, three alters are joining into the total human being or the host personality, and the others are simply bystanders.

MODELED SUGGESTIONS

[After trance has been induced:] And now imagining yourselves on the side of a gentle sloping hillside that overlooks the sea, high up, near the top. Each of you will see it in the way that seems most peaceful, safe, and beautiful to him or to her. It is near the end of a very full and complete day. Much has been accomplished, and all of you can feel a great sense of satisfaction. You look down the hill, toward the sea, and there are three [the number of alters to fuse] rivers winding their way to the sea. You watch them flow, peacefully and calmly. The day is near its end. The sun is low over the horizon. As it becomes level on the horizon behind you, all of you are bathed with a beautiful light, that is so bright that unless you look ahead of you, down toward the sea, all you can see is a beautiful field of light. You can no longer see one another, only the rivers as they wind their way to the sea, and the rivers are golden, reflecting the sunlight behind you.

As the sun sinks lower, the gold on the surface of the rivers seems to move into the sea; in fact, by the time I count from one to ten, all of the gold in the rivers has flowed into the sea [count, and indicate the march of the gold into the sea]. The gold from all the rivers have joined the gold of the sun-covered sea—at three, all the gold of the rivers, all of their waters, is completely within the sea. At two, the flow of the water and the ebb and flow of the tide has blended them completely. At one, who could say this water came from one river or the other. All has become one, now and forever. And now, the sun is below the horizon, and what was gold has become purple, red, all of the colors of a beautiful sunset. All of you look around, and can be pleased to find that there are fewer of you who remain separate, and that those who do can feel the tremendous satisfaction of a job well done, and an even stronger sense of how all of you, at the right time and place, can find a way to be one.

Containing Dysphoria in MPD

Richard P. Kluft, M.D.
Philadelphia, Pennsylvania

INTRODUCTION AND INDICATIONS

Often the issue in treating MPD is not how to open things up but how to settle things down. Frequently an alter feels in too much pain to cope or fears that it cannot control its impulses. At such times, a variant of the following may be very useful and forestall a hospital admission, a suicide attempt, self-injury, or other counterproductive acting-out. It presupposes the patient's experience with some variant of the "safe room" technique and requires that at least one competent and trustworthy alter agrees to remain in charge in the interim. The patient is placed in a trance, and addressed as follows.

ILLUSTRATIVE SUGGESTIONS

And now, it is time for peace, time for safety. Each of you, in your own way, in your own safe place, a place that is completely secure from all danger of intrusion, from all hurt. And now, for those of you who are in pain, and for those of you who feel it is so very difficult to hold on, it is time for rest, for peace, and for relief. When I count to three, for those of you who would like to accept this time of restoration and healing, it is time to fall into a healing sleep, safe and secure. So, all of you in your own special places of safety, and now, for those of you who would like to, at one, go to the special place within that special place in which you can rest with peace. At two, lying down or reclining, closing your eyes and allowing pain to wash away, uncomfortable urges and pressures to dissolve, and permitting yourselves to drift toward sleep, a sleep that will last calmly and without disturbance until you actually enter my office for your next appointment. At that time, you will awaken, and be able to work on the problems that beset you. And now, it's time to sleep at the count of one. [As an added safety measure, it can be suggested that disruptive memories be put in a time-lock vault in between sessions.]

Modified Ego-Strengthening for MPD

Moshe S. Torem, M.D.
Akron, Ohio

The patient is guided into self-hypnosis and is then asked to repeat the following statements after the hypnotherapist:

1. I _____ deserve to live my life with respect and dignity.
2. I _____ deserve to live my life to the fullest.
3. I _____ am an adult, mature individual, intelligent, educated, clever, ingenious, tolerant, creative, and wish to get well.
4. Any emotional disagreements will be resolved on a psychological level through internal dialogue, writing in the journal, therapeutic sessions, writing poetry, and developing a new understanding of the difference between the past and the present.
5. Any internal conflicts will be resolved on a psychological level.
6. I _____ give my word of honor and vow that I will do no harm to myself externally, internally, passively or actively, intentionally or unintentionally, and I will resolve all my conflicts and emotional disagreements on a psychological level.
7. I _____ as a whole person, including all of my parts and ego-states as well, as alters and fragments, deserve to heal, recover, and to get well.
8. I _____ as a whole person give my word of honor and vow to do whatever is necessary in this therapy to heal, recover, and to get well.
9. Every day in every way, I continue on the road to full recovery. I gain new insight,

new understanding, and new energy in the determination to recover, heal, and get well.
10. Every day and every way, I am getting better and better.

Corporate Headquarters of the Mind

Donald A. Price, Ph.D.
Salt Lake City, Utah

INTRODUCTION AND INDICATIONS

The following is a visual imagery structure that I use very frequently with adults molested as children (AMACs) and multiple personality disorder (MPD) patients. Since most AMAC and MPD patients are quite visual and excellent hypnotic subjects, these internal structures and pictures are usually easy for them to visualize, and the effects are often quite remarkable. Some of the ideas are not original, and where I can remember their source, I have cited it.

At some point in a formal induction procedure, after teaching several hypnotic phenomena, such as ideomotor finger signals, and glove anesthesia, arm rigidity, etc., for deepening purposes, I give the following suggestion.

THE ELEVATOR OF YOUR MIND

Picture yourself getting on an elevator at the top of a tall building and pushing the down button. As the elevator descends floor by floor, you go deeper and deeper into trance and relaxation. I do not know with my conscious mind nor my unconscious mind, and you do not know with your conscious mind, but your unconscious mind knows just how deep you need to be in trance for us to work effectively today. Just continue to go down deeper with each floor, with each exhalation, with each passing second. When your unconscious mind knows you have reached the right depth of trance, the elevator will stop descending, and then move the "yes" finger.

Some elevators are old and you can feel them going down, deeper and deeper; more modern ones are so smooth you cannot feel them descend, but have to watch the numbers to know that you are going down; some of the very old ones and the very new ones you can see out and see that you are going down, deeper and deeper into trance. [Sometimes the elevator gets stuck, at which point one deals with resistance, usually some kind of fear, until the elevator starts descending again. With some patients, and after practice in using this image, you can suggest that they are on the "express elevator." These deepening suggestions may also be used as an introduction to any of the following metaphors.]

THE LOUNGE ROOM

[When the "yes" finger moves indicating that the person has reached the right depth, I suggest:] The elevator door opens, and we get off and go across the hall into a nice comfortable lounge room. Inside there is a large comfortable easy chair. Can you see that? Good; have a seat and make yourself very comfortable. In front of you is a large screen TV and a VCR. Can you see those? [If patient says they are unclear or fuzzy, I suggest: "Take some deep breaths to take you deeper into trance, and the picture will become clearer." It usually does.]

On one wall or the other, to your right or left, is a chalkboard. At the bottom of the board is a tray with a piece of chalk in it [source of chalkboard image is Bernauer Newton, Ph.D.]. This chalk is very special. It can help us by writing answers to questions we may have and provide us with directions. [At this time if we are in the uncovering process with an AMAC patient I will ask him/her:] Pick up a video cassette from the stack at the side of the chair. Our mind is very much like a giant video library. Take the tape that we need to review today. [If the patient does not know which tape to choose, I ask her to "ask the chalk to write on the board which tape to pick." Any time there is difficulty with retrieving the memories in this way, we ask the chalk to tell us why; it

usually does, and we may then proceed from there.]

Put the cassette into the VCR and when a picture starts to appear on the screen move the "yes" finger. [As the picture starts:] You can review the episode silently and then tell me what you have seen, or you can tell me as you are seeing it. [As the person gets into the memory I usually start talking in the present tense to help him/her *be there now*. Sometimes the picture will stop and it is obvious that there is more, but it will not proceed. This is a good time to ask questions through the chalk, such as, "Why did the picture stop?" or "Does another part of your mind have this information?"]

THE CORRIDORS OF YOUR MIND

[With patients who have or are suspected of having ego states or alter (multiple) personalities, after getting off of the elevator, I suggest:] As we walk down the corridor, look at the doors and see if there are any names on them. [If there are, I begin to ask if we can talk to the people behind the door. Sometimes a window or speakeasy hole needs to be placed into the door. The corridor image is often a way to begin to get a "map" of the alters. Find out how many doors there are, and how resistant the occupants are to talking. For non-MPD patients these corridors and doors may represent people and memories — locked in the rooms — of abusive events, or issues to be resolved.]

THE CONFERENCE ROOM

[Particularly with MPD patients, the conference room is a place to gather alters together for meetings and negotiations, to share feelings and information, as well as to decide who is ready to fuse, etc. The therapist need simply suggest:] I would like all (or certain alters) to gather in the conference room so we can discuss. . . .

THE COMMUNICATION ROOM

The communication room is particularly useful with MPD patients. When a new alter has been identified who does not know the other alters or host, but is willing to begin communication, the patient can be taken to the communication room and shown a row of "video phones" or even one "video phone" with the instruction: "All you need to do is punch the name of (host or alter) into the telephone and listen and watch on the screen to see what she looks like. Can you see her? Let her know you are there and are interested in talking with her now. Any time you need to tell her something, all you need to do is punch in her name and you will be in communication with her." Gradually, as the amnestic barriers are broken down, and alters communicate and see each other directly, internal communication is facilitated in a fairly nonthreatening way.

CENTRAL CONTROL OR CIRCUIT ROOM

After having identified and worked through important issues, imagery of the circuit room can help to formalize change. Attitudes and behaviors that have been linked by trauma or learning can be "unplugged" or "disconnected." Intensity (or feelings, pain, etc.) can be "turned down." Certain dysfunctional "plugs" may be removed and replaced with new functional "plugs." On-off switches (e.g., black/white, either/or attitudes and behaviors) can be replaced with light-dimmer type intensity switches. Suggestions like the following are often used:

Take the elevator down deep into your unconscious mind to that depth, that floor where we find the control room. [Pause] Let me know when we reach that depth by moving the "yes" finger. Now, look around and find a door that says Control Room, or Circuit Room, and let me know when you see it. . . . That's right. Now, let's go in, and look for that circuit board [plug, etc.] labeled [name of the issue being dealt with]. [If two issues are connected with each other that should not be connected, I suggest:] Notice that the plug labeled *(e.g., sex)* is connected by a wire to *(e.g., pain)*. Let's cut the wires. Take some wire cutters or an ax, whatever you need to disconnected the wires. [Sometimes the wires automatically go back together, or a plug is resistant

to being removed. All of this is material that the therapist with experience learns to respond to with creative suggestions, dealing with the resistance, whatever its nature. A cartoon showing a workman inside the brain amid a myriad of wall plugs, hanging plugs, and criss-crossed extension cords is often shared with the patient to introduce humor into the therapy.]

THE COMPUTER ROOM

I have found the visualization of a computer room to be particularly useful with cult victims who have actually been programmed with hypnosis, drugs, and torture. When attempting to change programs with such victims, the therapist must be prepared to deal with pain reactions that have been conditioned to any attempts at deprogramming. Other highly sophisticated brainwashing techniques, such as "backup" programs and programs that are protected by "screens" are also found. With experience, practice, luck and creativity, however, the therapist can learn to circumvent even the most devious brainwashing "programs." Recently a TV episode of Matlock depicted the creation of an "umbrella program" to surround a sophisticated security program, mimic it, and circumvent it by relaying information to a different person. A cult abuse patient had fortunately viewed this TV episode and I was able to create just such a program for her. Therapists who are caring and have a good therapeutic relationship with a cult victim have a power in their visualizations that the cult programmers and perpetrators of pain and abuse simply do not have. Eventually the caring, consistent, and genuine relationship, coupled with creative hypnotherapy, wins out. Many patients have experience with computers, which facilitates the use of imagery about computers.

Some patients, I have found, can use this imagery self-hypnosis to communicate with ego states (typing messages on the CRT of their mind). Very concrete suggestions are given such as: "Go down the elevator floor by floor, deeper and deeper into trance . . . etc. When you reach that depth of trance where the computer room of your mind is located, the elevator will stop. Get off of the elevator and look for a door that says 'Computer Room' . . . yes, that's it. We go in and sit down at the console. Now look around for the disk that has the program on it that is causing trouble (e.g., with overeating). Take out the disk, and let's look around for any other backup copies. Let's put them in a pile and burn them." New programs that the patient helps to create can then be typed into the console. Backup copies are always made.

For removing programs that have been installed through more complicated means, such as through electroshock during brainwashing or cult programming, a reversal of the programming with hypnotically compressed time can be effective. In this latter case I give the following suggestions while the person is in trance, even in the computer room:

Now we are going to completely remove this program, and the way we will do it is to go through the rite/programming episode backwards, using hypnotically compressed time. You will feel some pain, just as you did when the original program was installed, but it will go fast and will be minimal. [Since wires were sometimes attached to the victim's head, I will put my hands on each side of the patient's head, partly to restrain the seizure-like jerking as he abreacts, partly to simply use healing touch.] Now I will count *backwards* from 5 to 1, and by the time I finish counting, all of the program and pain will be removed. Now I will begin: 5 . . . 4 . . . 3 . . . 2 . . . 1. [If the patient is still in pain or trembling I will ask if there are backup copies of the program. If there is a nod for yes, I repeat the counting with the suggestion that this will remove all backup copies of the program. Usually the pain or abreaction stops and the patient becomes calm.]

GOING BACK UP THE ELEVATOR

Sometimes during the recall of a memory, during an abreaction, or other work with the above methods, a patient will appear to come out of the trance state and to seem as if they have finished and are alert in the present. Frequently this is not the case. Thus, routinely in concluding work with any of the above

procedures, the patient is told: "OK, now let's go back and get on the elevator and push the 'UP' button. As the elevator takes you back up, your breathing begins to return to normal, and as you reach the top floor, your breathing returns to normal. And as the door opens, your eyes open, and you find yourself oriented back in the present time, place and person." I have found that when this is not done, talented hypnotic subjects may still remain in a trance, or if they realert too fast, they may experience a headache, especially in MPD patients where there has been a lot of switching between alters. When this happens, simply suggest that they go back down, and come up the elevator more slowly.

Metaphors with Multiple Personality and Trauma Patients

D. Corydon Hammond, Ph.D.
Salt Lake City, Utah

SETTING A BROKEN BONE AND LANCING A WOUND

[This has proven to be a useful metaphor in preparing a victim of trauma for the painful abreactive work of reliving a past event.] The work that we have to do is very much like what must happen after a child breaks her leg, or an adult has a painful, infected wound that must be lanced. The physician doesn't want to cause the patient pain. But he/she knows that if he/she doesn't set the bone or lance the wound, the patient will continue to hurt for even longer, and will remain disabled and never recover properly and normally. It's hard and painful for the physician to do that procedure and create pain through setting that bone or lancing that wound. But it's an act of caring, that allows healing to take place.

And this process of facing painful memories and feelings from the past will be painful for a short time, just like setting a broken bone. But then you won't have to continue hurting from what happened, and healing will finally take place.

PRESSURE COOKER METAPHOR

[This metaphor is helpful with patients in crisis who have tremendous internal pressure, often from alter personalities who are overwhelmed with feelings. It may motivate patients to allow the controlled release of emotions, for example, through the technique of dissociating affect and content (Hammond, 1988f; Hammond & Miller, in press; Erickson & Rossi, 1979).]

Have you ever seen an old-fashioned pressure cooker? My grandmother used to have one. You would latch it shut, and turn up the heat, and the bubbling water and steam inside created tremendous pressure. After a while, some of that pressure had to be released or something would burst.

Right now you're experiencing tremendous pressure, from all the feelings inside. And it's important for us to use a safety valve to release that pressure, gradually, safely, in a protected and controlled way so that no one is harmed in an explosion of emotions.

A Projective Ideomotor Screening Procedure to Assist in Early Identification of Ritualistic Abuse Victims

D. Corydon Hammond, Ph.D.
Salt Lake City, Utah

It is certainly well-known that many MPD patients have a variety of fears and phobias, many of them stimulated by the nature of their traumatic experiences. It is the experience of many clinicians, however, that MPD patients who are victims of ritualistic abuse often have very idiosyncratic fears and phobias. As a tentative clinical tool for which there is currently no data on reliability or validity, I have begun asking hypnotized MPD patients about their fears. Ideomotor signals may be obtained so that any alter personality may indicate if he/she is afraid of an item, or individual personalities may be asked these questions. The italicized items below are believed to be more likely to elicit a fear reaction in ritualistic abuse victims. They have been embedded within a list of numerous other more common fears. Clinicians might also have patients rate the strength of the fear (e.g., on a 1-7 scale).

IDEOMOTOR FEAR INVENTORY FOR MPD PATIENTS

"Is anyone inside afraid of . . .?"
[Patients not diagnosed as MPD may be asked, "Is any part of you afraid of . . . ?"]

1. Heights
2. Doctors
3. Dentists
4. *Stars*
5. Speaking in Public
6. *Fire*
7. Being teased
8. *Knives*
9. Crowds
10. *Blood*
11. Sudden noises
12. Being criticized
13. *Being photographed*
14. *Dying*
15. Large open spaces
16. *Candles*
17. Sick people
18. *Feces*
19. Dogs
20. Cats
21. *Animals being hurt*
22. *Robes*
23. Being in an elevator
24. *A certain color* (specify)
25. Sight of deep water
26. Rope
27. *Colored rope*
28. *Certain animals*
29. Fences

30. *Masks*
31. *Eating certain things* (specify)
32. Birds
33. Enclosed places
34. *Coffins*
35. Airplanes
36. *Red meat*
37. Lightning
38. *Being shocked*
39. Being ignored
40. *Cemeteries*
41. *Crying*
42. Crossing streets
43. *People in a circle*
44. *Snakes*
45. *Spiders*
46. Journeys by car

47. People in authority
48. *Certain numbers* (specify)
49. *Goats*
50. Horses
51. Cows
52. *Digging in the dirt*
53. Snow
54. *People with a missing finger*
55. People with a deformity
56. *Nude men or women*
57. Taking a test
58. *Halloween*
59. Clouds
60. *Winter or summer solstice*
61. An eclipse of the sun
62. *The equinox*

HYPNOSIS WITH SEXUAL DYSFUNCTION AND RELATIONSHIP PROBLEMS

INTRODUCTION

T HE FIRST SECTION OF this chapter will present suggestions and metaphors for use in the treatment of sexual dysfunction. I have included many suggestions that I use in sex therapy since, unfortunately, very few suggestions were received from other clinicians. Although there are two volumes (Araoz, 1982; Beigel & Johnson, 1980) on this topic that describe useful procedures, there are very few actual suggestions modeled in the literature. The latter portion of the chapter provides suggestions that may be used in couples or family therapy and in general to enhance interpersonal relationships.

Hypnotherapy with Sexual Dysfunction

Far too many therapists with a superficial knowledge of sex therapy techniques (e.g., sensate focus exercises, the "squeeze" technique) have been willing to treat dysfunctional patients. An elementary knowledge of traditional sex therapy or hypnosis techniques that has been gleaned from a book or brief workshop is inadequate preparation for ethical practice. The hypnotherapist wishing to treat sexual dysfunctions must first master an extensive and complex body of literature on the evaluation of sexual disorders (Kaplan, 1983; Kolodny, Masters & Johnson, 1979; Krane, Siroky & Goldstein, 1983; Schover & Jensen, 1988; Wagner & Green, 1981). Afterwards, NIMH sponsored ethical standards mandate 50–100 hours of advanced supervision in sex therapy (Masters, Johnson, & Kolodny, 1977; Masters, Johnson, Kolodny, & Weems, 1980) to hold oneself out to the public as qualified to work with such referrals.

It should be noted that even well trained sex therapists are now finding the successful treatment of sexual disorders to be much more challenging than was originally believed. Initial reports (e.g., Masters & Johnson, 1970) in the field of sex therapy suggested an extremely high success rate. But recent effectiveness studies of behaviorally oriented sex therapy (DeAmicis, Goldberg, LoPiccolo, Friedman, & Davies, 1984) and surveys of certified sex therapists (Kilmann, Boland, Norton, Davidson, & Caid, 1986) have documented lower success rates than were originally suggested (Heiman & LoPiccolo, 1983). Methodological flaws have also been pointed out (Zilbergeld & Evans, 1980) in the work of Masters and Johnson (1970; Schwartz & Masters, 1988) that cast further doubt on the validity of the high success rates reported for their traditional approach. Sex therapists are struggling with difficult cases and finding that their traditional approaches are, in many cases, unsuccessful or only partially successful.

This seems due, at least in part, to the increased incidence of cases of inhibited sexual desire (ISD). This is a term originated by Lief (1977) to describe a syndrome that he and others (Frank, Anderson, & Rubinstein, 1978; Kilmann, et al., 1986; Lief, 1985; LoPiccolo, 1980; Schover & LoPiccolo, 1982) find is the most widespread sexual dysfunction. Recent estimates suggested that 50% or more of sex therapy clinic patients have the diagnosis of ISD (Shover & LoPiccolo, 1982). And yet this is perhaps the most complex and least successfully treated sexual complaint (Kaplan, 1979; Leiblum & Rosen, 1988; Zilbergeld & Ellison, 1980), typically requiring a greater number of treatment sessions than other dysfunctions (Kilmann et al., 1986; Leiblum & Rosen, 1988). It seems often to involve problems with communication and intimacy, traumatic sexual experiences, and negative parental models (Stuart, Hammond & Pett, 1986, 1987).

Since ISD is exceptionally widespread and traditional sex therapy highly limited in treating this problem, we perceived an increasing need for more effective treatment protocols. Hypnosis has been used in the treatment of sexual problems for a long time. Almost 50 years ago, Erickson and Kubie (1941) provided us with the earliest known case of the successful treatment of ISD with hypnosis. Hypnotic interventions with sexual dysfunctions (Araoz, 1980, 1982; Crasilneck, 1979, 1982; Hammond, 1984b, 1985c; Zilbergeld & Hammond, 1988) seem to hold considerable promise in sex therapy, although the literature consists exclusively of case studies and outcome reports on series of patients. However, a recent survey (Kilmann et al., 1986) indicates that the potential of hypnosis remains largely untapped by certified sex therapists, only 7% of whom use hypnosis in their clinical work.

ADVANTAGES OF HYPNOSIS IN SEX THERAPY.   The use of hypnosis in sex therapy has several unique strengths to recommend it. Hypnosis may be used in the treatment of the individual patient without a partner. Relatively few treatment options have typically been available for the single patient or those without cooperative partners, particularly if the therapist does not use sexual surrogates. Interestingly, the largest and most extensive follow-up reports on the use of hypnosis with sexual dysfunction have been on individual patients suffering with erectile dysfunction (Crasilneck, 1979, 1982). Crasilneck reported follow-ups on a larger number of impotent patients than any other sex therapy researchers, including Masters and Johnson, and with comparable outcome rates to those of Masters and Johnson (1970).

Hypnosis also offers techniques that allow rapid exploration and identification of underlying conflicts, unresolved feelings about past events, and factors beyond conscious awareness. For example, many patients have reported in an initial sex history that they had never experienced incest or sexual molestation. Later, however, early childhood sexual abuse was uncovered through the use of hypnosis. There are additionally times when adaptive functions are being served by sexual dysfunctions, of which the patient has only limited or no conscious awareness. A dysfunction, for instance, may serve as a way of protecting the patient against a fear (e.g., of infidelity), of punishing the self for past misbehavior, or of expressing anger toward a partner.

Learning self-hypnosis may provide patients with a sense of self-control and a technique for stress management. Physical and mental tension and fatigue often inhibit sexual interest and performance capacities. Some patients need a method for mentally "changing gears" and making a transition from a hectic day to being able to focus on sensual involvement. Self-hypnosis provides them with such a skill for anxiety reduction and decompression, as well as for the arousal of sexual passion through sexual imagery prior to sexual involvement.

Discouragement is a factor too often overlooked in sex therapy. Many patients simply no longer believe that they will ever be able to experience passion and interest or to perform adequately. However, perhaps due to the popularized images of hypnosis as mystical, some patients come to therapy with a belief that hypnosis can do for them what they cannot do for themselves: promote change. Hypnosis may be used to provide hope, increased feelings of self-efficacy (Bandura, 1977), and confidence that change can occur. "Trance ratification" procedures can convince patients of the power of their own mind and of hypnosis to help them. When patients feel an arm levitate and float up involuntarily, they are often convinced that this thing called hypnosis may, in fact, be capable of doing something for them. Similarly, when a glove anesthesia is created in a hand so that a needle may be painlessly put through a fold of skin on the back of the hand, patients are convinced that they have more potentials than they realized and that perhaps their mind is powerful enough to stir sexual desire, facilitate orgasm, or create erections.

We are well aware that some patients are endowed, either through heredity and/or early life experiences, with exceptional hypnotic capacity. For individuals with these native capacities, hypnosis can be an extremely powerful tool. When patients possess the capacity to focus and use their minds so powerfully, it seems a shame not to utilize their unique talents.

Hypnosis also offers us a variety of techniques for altering problematic emotions and increasing desired emotional states. Symbolic imagery techniques often allow patients to release pent-up feelings like anger and resentment, without further harming the relationship with the partner. For example, such a patient may experience himself gradually smashing a huge boulder in the mountains while simultaneously venting his angry feelings. Other patients may imagine breaking through a barrier, discarding old parental messages that evoke negative emotions, or placing feelings of guilt in the gondola of a hot air balloon and watching it float away. The chronically fatigued patient may imagine an energy transfusion or withdraw to a serene place in self-hypnosis. The master control room technique, found at the beginning in this chapter, has proven surprisingly effective in stimulating feelings of sexual desire, particularly after roadblocks to desire (e.g., relationship problems) have been removed.

In the treatment of secondary dysfunctions (e.g., inhibited sexual desire, erectile dysfunction), hypnotic age regression may revivify memories that help rekindle and recapture positive sexual and affectional feelings. Hypnosis and self-hypnosis can enhance the patient's ability to focus attention and increase sensory awareness, thereby facilitating increased arousal and pleasure. Hypnotic techniques can also aid in elucidating internal (cognitive, imagery) processes that are impossible to observe and difficult to explicate through discussion alone. Occasionally, for instance, spouses report a very unpleasant experience with assigned tasks like sensate focus, but they are unable to explain why or provide details about thoughts or images that may have interfered. Through hypnosis patients may be regressed to the sexual date several days earlier; as they mentally relive the experience, the suggestion may be offered, "Everything that you are thinking, mentally picturing, and experiencing, just say out loud." Patients are often able to provide details of what were elusive and unavailable internal processes.

LIMITATIONS OF HYPNOSIS.   Despite the many advantages of hypnosis, hypnosis is not a panacea and is frequently most effective when combined with other therapeutic methods. Although I use hypnosis with considerable frequency, I do not rely on or advocate the unitary use of hypnosis. As with any single treatment modality, there are also some limitations and cautions in the use of hypnotic techniques in this area.

First, hypnotherapists may experience the temptation to overemphasize an individual focus for treatment, neglecting important relationship factors that may be involved. Individual psychotherapy has been known for many years to have the potential to evoke pathological reactions in the untreated spouse (Kohl, 1962), and deterioration in the marital relationship appears to be a greater risk in individual marital therapy (Gurman & Kniskern, 1978a, 1978b). We find in sex therapy that, unless individually focused hypnosis is used in a context that involves the partner in assessment and in at least part of the treatment, there is a risk that some patients may feel singled out as the "identified patient," and relationship factors may be neglected. It is recommended, therefore, that the partner be included from the beginning in assessment. When I do individual hypnotic work, the mate is typically involved in behavioral assignments afterwards. If the individual work requires more than three or four sessions, it is further recommended that a conjoint session occur for one-half hour or an hour each month to maintain the spouse's feeling of involvement and input. The temporarily uninvolved partner is also encouraged to call between conjoint sessions if an individual or conjoint session is desired and/or to send feedback through the spouse.

It should also be noted that spouses may sometimes be present during hypnotic work. Some patients will feel self-conscious, as though they have an audience, and prefer not to have the spouse in attendance. However, occasionally a patient will feel more secure having his/her mate present. Inquire about this matter and respect the feelings of the patient. When a partner witnesses an age regression to a negative past experience(s), he/she will generally be more empathic and supportive of the mate. Some hypnotic techniques also focus on both partners simultaneously, such as mutual hypnosis. Both mates may also be age regressed to a wonderful experience, or the technique of pseudo-orientation in time into the future may be used to have them share a fantasy of having beautiful sexual experiences together. On the other hand, if the patient is being taught to enter a self-hypnotic state and create sexual fantasies to facilitate sexual desire, and the fantasies are about partners other than the spouse, an individual session will be desirable.

Variations in the native hypnotic talent level of patients provide an inevitable limitation to hypnotic work. Thus the 5%–10% of patients who either cannot or will not be hypnotized and realistically the other 10%–15% of patients who enter only very light trance states will be limited in their hypnotic capacity and unlikely to benefit from such treatment. Furthermore, even after being educated about the nature of hypnosis, a very small number of patients will not want to be hypnotized because of the widespread misconceptions about hypnosis. Thus hypnosis is like any other therapeutic technique: it will not be effective with everyone. Finally, we should note, once again, the need for controlled research in this area to accurately investigate the potentials of hypnotic treatment of sexual dysfunction.

Hypnosis with Interpersonal Problems

In the final section of the chapter you will find a variety of suggestions focused on relationships with spouses, families, and others. Although we cannot directly control the reactions of another person, hypnosis may be an aid in fostering healthier interactions with others and healthier perceptions of relationships. Hypnosis may also serve a number of functions in couples therapy. For example, it may be used to work through resistance and overcome stalemates in therapy. Hypnosis may assist in resolving problematic emotions, such as anger and resentment. Hypnotic exploration can uncover the hidden goals and unconscious expectations behind interaction patterns, as well as promote insight into parataxic distortions rooted in experiences with the family of origin. Certainly, hypnosis may also be used in the service of individual treatment needs with one partner from a marriage, for example, in resolving past trauma or learning self-hypnosis to cope with premenstrual syndrome.

HYPNOTHERAPY WITH SEXUAL DYSFUNCTIONS

The Master Control Room Technique

D. Corydon Hammond, Ph.D.
Salt Lake City, Utah

INDICATIONS AND CONTRAINDICATIONS

This technique was designed to be used in the treatment of inhibited sexual desire, ejaculatory inhibition, orgasmic dysfunction, erectile dysfunction, and sexual addictions. It seems most effective when hypnotic exploration has been done first to rule out or work through unconscious conflicts or resistance to change. This method may be easily adapted for application to eating disorders.

SUGGESTIONS

Now you are going to enter a very special room, a nerve center, a control room in the hypothalamus part of your brain. This is the control room for all your feelings and desires. As you find yourself in this room, notice all the panels of lights, lights of different colors. You may be aware of the sounds of the computers, the temperature of the room, and perhaps even a distinctive smell.

As you observe the banks of colored lights, you can notice the different panels. There may be one panel that regulates your appetite for food. And you can notice another panel that regulates your level of sexual desire and interest [or, arousal, erection]. And on those panels you'll see a dial, or I wonder if it's going to be a lever, or perhaps some other kind of control that can be set from 0-10. Zero is the level of no interest. Everyone has had the experience of not being hungry. Sometimes you're not interested in food, and not interested in sex. Ten is the level of strong desire or appetite. We all know

what it's like to really want and desire something. Nod your head when you see the panels and the dial.

Now look closely at the panel regulating sexual desire and interest [arousal, erection], and tell me, what number does it look as though it's set on? Um hmm. Now reach over and take hold of the dial or lever, and move it slightly, gradually. And as you do so, you're experiencing a different feeling. Be aware of that change in sexual desire [arousal]. [Brief pause] You may find it interesting to notice, how and where you begin to experience an increased desire [arousal]. [Pause] And now, as you get ready to turn the dial again, what number is the dial on? [Wait for response] And where would you like to turn it to? [Following response:] Okay, and as you turn the dial from (3) to (4), let me know when your body senses the difference.

[If resistance is encountered and the patient does not report an ideosensory experience, refer to the alternative phrasing for resistance section found later in the script, and then return to the text below.]

Um hmm. And move the knob from ____ to ____ , as you begin to experience the delight, or perhaps the exhilaration, of the desire [arousal] that's increasing. And those hormones are being set free, released, into your bloodstream, pulsing, and flowing all through your body, and especially concentrating in certain places. And you really don't need to know how to do this, because you know that you know how at an unconscious level. And you may be aware of how those hormones are stimulating sensations, very natural urges, and feelings, in such a fascinating way.

Let me know when it's all right to increase the dial one more level. [Pause for response] All right, turn the dial from ____ to ____ , as you effortlessly begin to appreciate, and savor the feelings of desire [arousal], circulating through you. And when would you like to increase the dial one more level?

NEGOTIATION, IDEOMOTOR COMMITMENT, AND POSTHYPNOTIC SUGGESTION

And would you like to increase the dial again, or leave it at this level? [Negotiate and allow the patient to determine the level where the dial is set. Ideomotor signaling may also be used to determine if it is acceptable with the unconscious mind to leave the dial at its current level for the following two weeks to determine how that feels. When an ideomotor commitment is obtained, reinforce the commitment with posthypnotic suggestions. When a commitment is not obtained, the following kinds of suggestions may be given.]

And you can feel relieved, and pleased, and perhaps even a pride in knowing that you'll now be able to regulate the level of your own sexual desire [arousal]. And you may choose to permit this change, so that you can leave it at either a moderate, or even a high level. Or, you may choose to allow your unconscious mind to modify it, depending on the appropriateness of the circumstances. From now on, you can be so satisfied, knowing that you can easily and automatically adjust that dial to regulate your level of desire and interest [arousal]. You may find it particularly surprising to discover, how *rapidly* you can increase your level of sexual desire [arousal], when you snuggle against your partner. So that when he/she cuddles you, in a pleasant way, you can become aware of interesting sensations that develop, and flow. And as you snuggle, pleasant sensations may spread more than you'd anticipate, as you recognize, perhaps with some surprise, how rapidly you can increase your level of sexual desire [arousal], when you're close to your partner.

ALTERNATE PHRASING WITH RESISTANCE

[When the patient does not notice feelings and sensations, you may suggest:] Isn't that interesting? That just proves how subtle those changes are. They're almost imperceptible when they first begin. And we really don't need to know what's going on. It's kind of like sometimes when we're watching a television program, or when a movie is really exciting, you become very absorbed and involved in it. And while you're sitting there, wrapped up in the show, you're not noticing your body's response. And yet as the tension builds in the movie, your body also gets very tense and tight, and adrenaline is being released. And then, after while, when the excitement of the show is over, and everything has turned out well, you suddenly become aware of the sense of relief and release, and all those feelings that you weren't even aware of. And these changes also begin subtly at first, as the hormones begin their work, and the nerves become more alert. And it's really not important for you to fully sense these changes, in *this* environment. [Now return to turning up the dial, saying:] And you may or may not notice the physical and subjective feelings associated with the hormones that are being set free. [Return to the primary text above.]

[Later, the resistant or less talented subject may be given the following types of suggestions:] And I'm not sure just when, or where, you'll begin to detect the difference. Your unconscious mind can bring about that awareness, of change, in a way that meets your needs. It may be that you suddenly and spontaneously become aware, that you feel urges, feelings, an impulse. Or, perhaps there will be a gradual growing sense of progressive changes, of a subtle, unhurried, natural evolution. And I don't know if you'll recognize those changes tomorrow, or Thursday, or next week. But in an interesting way, you'll realize that you *are* changing, in your own personal way.

[Still another optional suggestion that may be useful with a subject who resists turning up the dial significantly is to add:] And you can wonder, how soon it will be, until your unconscious mind has prepared, so that you'll be able to move that dial to a higher number, whenever you really want to.

Illustrative Suggestions in Sex Therapy

Bernie Zilbergeld, Ph.D.
Oakland, California

"The only important thing is the sensations you experience. So focus where you're being touched. Experience the texture, temperature, pressure and movement. Immersed in feeling and sensation. Nothing to do but to feel and experience the pleasure.

"It can be exactly as it was [name a time when things went well, e.g., before you moved to California; in Hawaii]. You can feel the same feelings, experience the same sensations and pleasure, and function just as you did then. Everything can be just as it was in Hawaii. Just as much pleasure, just as much fun. Everything exactly the same." [This suggestion may be used in conjunction with mental rehearsal or age progression.]

"I wonder if you know how really excited you can be, how truly, totally turned on, feeling arousal from your toes to your nose, in every nook and cranny of your being.

"I wonder if you can find a way of enjoying this. Some way of making it your own and enjoying it for your own interests, growth and pleasure. Some people get into it because they like giving pleasure to their partners. Some people because they feel it's an important skill for themselves. Some because they're curious about what they can learn. There are lots of ways of getting into this and enjoying it. I wonder what way you'll find.

"A man who can only give pleasure to his partner is halfway there. It's also necessary to be able to take pleasure for himself. To ask for it, direct it, focus on it, luxuriate in it, and be totally immersed in it. Learning to take and experience pleasure is so important to being a good lover.

"You can't give up control until you have it, so what you need to do is take more control. Ask for stimulation when you want it, and get it exactly, precisely as you want it. Be in charge and get just what you want, and enjoy the feeling of taking control, being the director of what happens to you.

"Just as you have been focusing on sensation in the last few moments, engrossed in the feelings in your chest, so you'll be able to become focused and immersed in sensation when your wife caresses your arms and legs.

"Just as you functioned well and had satisfying sex before your baby was born, so you'll be able to function well and have satisfying sex in the future. As it was before, so it shall be."

Hypnotherapy with Psychogenic Impotence

Harold B. Crasilneck, Ph.D.
Dallas, Texas

INTRODUCTION AND CONTRAINDICATIONS

Crasilneck's (1979, 1982) reports on the treatment of patients seen for erectile dysfunction represent the largest and most extensive follow-up reports on the use of hypnosis with sexual dysfunction. Crasilneck's (1982) outcome rate at 12-month follow-up for his last 100 consecutive patients treated was 87% with an average of 10 sessions. The return of good erectile function occurred on average following the fifth hypnotic session.

Hypnosis, particularly when combined with education of the patient and work with the spouse, may be extremely effective with this condition. Hypnosis also has the distinct advantage of dramatically expanding the range of intervention techniques available for treating the patient without a cooperative or available partner. Despite Masters and Johnson's (1970) original claims that 95% of erectile failure was psychogenic, recent research suggests that perhaps 40% of erection problems have an organic contributor (e.g., Krauss, 1983; Spark, White & Connoly, 1980). Therefore, before proceeding with hypnotherapy it is vital for clinicians to conduct careful diagnostic workups on erectile dysfunction patients. Most physicians, including urologists, do not conduct thorough and adequate evaluations for this condition. Nocturnal penile tumescence monitoring is perhaps the best single test for discriminating organic from psychogenic impotence. An adequate endocrine screen should include evaluating serum testosterone, LH, FSH, and prolactin levels. Doppler studies may be conducted to evaluate vascular involvement. Finally, a fasting glucose tolerance test should be conducted to determine if undiagnosed diabetes may be a contributor.

In addition, Crasilneck (1982) has advised: "It is expedient and judicious for the referring physician to realize that there are certain individuals who should not be hypnotized and that there are contraindications to the use of hypnosis with such people. The highly masochistic person, the extremely depressed male, the individual with a psychotic history and/or the person with a background of severe conversion reaction. In such cases, the decision must be made between the referring physician and the hypnotherapist. The assessment and evaluation of the patient prior to the use of hypnosis is foremost in every case" (p. 56). (*Ed.*)

HYPNOTIC TECHNIQUE WITH IMPOTENCY

As early as 1954, the author used hypnotic induction and the suggestion of catalepsy [arm rigidity] to one of the patient's arms, in order to demonstrate the control and strength his unconscious mind has over this part of his body. The patient is requested to open his eyes, feel the cataleptic arm with his normal hand (in order to prove that he had achieved this physiological cataleptic rigidity), and is told that this power which he displays over another part of his body could be easily transferred to his penis and premature ejaculations. Then, the patient is asked to close his eyes, told to enter a deeper level of trance, and that normal sensations would return to the rigid arm.

Repeated suggestions are made that if the patient could achieve such rigidity in his arm,

he could do so with his penis. When the patient is in a deep level of trance, the writer takes one hand of the patient and with the tip of a blunt nail file gently touches the fingers, and includes all areas front and back of the hand, up to the wrist, saying, "The fingers, the palm, the back of your hand up to the wrist will begin to lose feeling. Your hand will feel like a thick electrician's glove. When you have achieved this loss of feeling, this anesthetized feeling in your hand, nod your head." Then, during this trance state the writer requests that the subject open his eyes. The writer says, "See what I am doing. I am stimulating the middle finger of the anesthetized hand with this blunt nail file. The thick electrician's glove which envelops the hand prevents you from feeling any pain. Pressure, no pain. Pressure, no pain. Good. Now close your eyes. Normal sensation returns to the hand. All normal sensations return . . . good. Now as you feel me stimulate the middle finger, pull your hand away. . . ."

The writer then continues: "A deeper and a sounder, and a more relaxed state. The muscles in your body are relaxed and at ease. Free from tension and tightness and stress and strain. You have just observed that you are capable of obtaining catalepsy and rigidity in your arm. You have just observed that you are capable of controlling the perception of pain in your hand, and if one can control the cataleptic strength in a specific part of his body and control the perception of pain in a specific part of his body, so may he control the erection of his penis. You have complete control over every part of your body and you can and will control the erection in your penis."

The writer describes to the patient the psychology and physiology involved in an erection. "First there is the attraction and the foreplay." The writer holds up his index finger, squeezes it tightly and says, "Erection is a combination of psychology and physiology. It is a perception of the love object, a response, a stimulation, a gorging of blood and the trapping of blood. Then following ejaculation the trapped blood is released causing the penis to relax."

In such cases where premature ejaculation is a problem, the patient is told, "As you were able to control the perception of pain in your finger, so can you control the hypersensitivity in your penis which has caused you to ejaculate prematurely. Your fears and anxieties will be less and you will gain both intellectual and emotional insight into your problem."

Therapeutic sessions are weekly, thirty minutes per visit and on an individual basis. . . . The writer did not take as much of an authoritarian approach in the first study as he did in his second and third studies (1979 and 1981). It is now the writer's opinion that such an approach is necessary in the treatment of psychogenic impotency because the hypnotherapist transfers this dominant attitude to the patient who in turn exhibits authoritarian control over his own bodily functions. . . .

The impotent patient is encouraged by the writer to make every attempt to divulge his innermost, secret and cloistered sexual fantasies, not only to the therapist but also to his partner. That is, "What sexual fantasies turn you on more than anything you can think of?"

The patient is allowed the freedom to discuss all his libidinous feelings concerning his heretofore internalized, suppressed sexual caprices and encouraged to share these thoughts and feelings with his sexual partner. Many times he requests that his partner join him for a session or two, so that he may discuss these visionary fancies with his partner, while experiencing the supportive presence of the writer during the session. In most instances the patient has had complete trust and faith in his sexual partner to a point of mutual regard and respect for each other's feelings and welfare, because to this date only a few partners have been unwilling to participate in the subject's fantasies. In some cases the sexual partner, too, has revealed her own lascivious longings. . . .

The verbal expression of sexual fantasies by the patient is an important phase of treatment and the expressions of such fantasies are encouraged. Whenever feasible the therapist encourages the patient to bring these desires into reality with his sexual partner.

Suggestions for Spectatoring and Sensate Focus

D. Corydon Hammond, Ph.D.
Salt Lake City, Utah

INDICATIONS

These suggestions were prepared for use in conjunction with assigning sensate focus exercises, and to reduce pressure and "spectatoring" in patients with orgasmic dysfunction, erectile dysfunction, ejaculatory inhibition, and inhibited sexual desire.

SUGGESTIONS

As you're touched, you may notice there are times, that you begin watching yourself, almost as though you were a spectator across the room, curious to observe what's happening. Much like when we sort of observe ourselves when doing some new activity [*individualize*: like being consciously aware of a golf or tennis swing, or in driving a car with a different type of gear shift than we're used to]. Whenever we begin a process of change, many people feel a little nervous or embarrassed, and as a result it's really quite natural to briefly take the role of a spectator. But this will pass easily, and you can look forward to refocusing your attention back onto this body, and its pleasant sensations, and just effortlessly become absorbed in the feelings.

Whatever pleasant sensations you're aware of, you can just explore them and allow them to continue, giving yourself plenty of time. And when you feel pleasure or arousal for a few moments, and then lose those sensations, this is all right too. That is very normal and natural, especially when you're learning, to notice and appreciate such sexual feelings. And I wonder how you can focus on the feelings at the place where you are being touched. Allow your attention to remain on those feelings. If your thoughts momentarily wander, gently bring them back to your physical sensations, and follow your partner's touch with your mind.

And as you do so, just enjoy this opportunity, for you to discover and rediscover, the sensations, the fun, the pure pleasure of touching. And you really don't need to wonder about his/her reactions, because he/she will tell you if anything is unpleasant. So that leaves you free to just playfully touch him/her in ways that are fun, and interesting for you, and you can just use his/her body for your enjoyment.

There are so *very* many ways, that you've already learned how to trust your unconscious mind. If you allow it to do its job, it takes very good care of you. Each day, you speak and just say things spontaneously and automatically, without consciously having to think about how to pronounce each word or each syllable. In a similar way, without consciously having to think, your unconscious mind is continually regulating the flow of blood through thousands of miles of arteries and capillaries, to tissues and muscles that need the blood and its nutrients, causing chemical and nerve changes to close the right, appropriate capillaries, and open others. Simultaneously, it may be opening and closing the retina of your eye, adjusting to the light, while at the same time it is monitoring your blood levels of numerous hormones, and releasing more, when it's necessary.

Without any conscious thought, your unconscious mind coordinates 650 muscles, and more than 100 joints in intricate ways, so that you can walk, and maintain balance, without requiring any conscious thought about how far apart to place your feet, or which muscles to move. Your unconscious mind takes care of *all* that, independently. Consciously, you don't know how to *will* your body to perspire. But throughout each day, your unconscious regulates the temperature of your body, through creating perspiration just when it is needed.

I wonder whether you really need to put so much pressure on yourself? Maybe not? You've already learned that *trying* to help with your conscious mind, and worrying about how you're doing, will only interfere with your pleasure. Please recognize, that your unconscious mind can automatically take care of everything for you, freeing you to just relax and enjoy yourself. So you don't need to push the river, it will flow all by itself. So just let the goals be fun and pleasure. You can allow yourself to just get involved and participate in that pleasure, and your unconscious mind will take care of all the rest. And if occasionally your mind wanders, that's just natural, and you can just wait and see where it wanders to, and how it gently comes back to the pleasure. Just gently, and patiently, go back to enjoying and paying attention to your body's sensations, comfortably engrossed, satisfyingly absorbed in the pleasure from your body, savoring each touch.

SUGGESTIONS FOR SEXUAL AVERSION PATIENTS GIVEN SENSATE FOCUS OR MASTURBATION ASSIGNMENTS

Perhaps you will, be aware, of several different feelings. You don't have to experience arousal. It isn't even necessary, to be aware of pleasurable feelings right now. It's all right to just experience, whatever you experience. And I think you'll be pleased to discover, and you can learn, that there's nothing to bother you or disturb you. And some things may feel familiar, and some things may feel new and unfamiliar, and that's all right. That's the way we grow and develop. For now, you can just concentrate on places that feel different from other places, and notice the distinctive sense of different types of touch. And I really don't know what you'll notice, and it doesn't really matter *to me*. You may be aware of textures, and differing pressures. You may also be aware of warmth or comfortable coolness. You might even notice dryness or some moistness. And I wonder what you'll learn about the meaning of those things as you feel them, and I wonder how you're going to feel about what those things mean. Some things may feel soothing, and others more restful. Some relaxing, and some unusually interesting.

OTHER POSTHYPNOTIC SUGGESTIONS

And as more and more skin is exposed, your skin can feel more and more tantalizingly alive.

And as you sense his/her increasing arousal, *you* can feel more and more aware of the stimulus, which is stimulating in itself. As if somehow, the sounds and movements of his/her arousal are contagious, and are causing a warm flush to pulse and flow to your genitals. And it's like every rush of circulation, every movement of pleasure, increases your excitement.

And when he cuddles you, in a pleasant way you can become aware of the interesting sensations that develop and flow. And as you snuggle, pleasant sensations can spread — it's really fascinating — so much more than you'd anticipate.

Learn to trust your body. It doesn't need your help; it knows what to do, so stop trying to help, and just relax and enjoy. It isn't necessary to help, it can do it all by itself. So just remember that there is no way that you can fail, because the goal of sex is pleasure and sharing closeness.

Suggestions for Facilitating Sexual Fantasy

D. Corydon Hammond, Ph.D.
Salt Lake City, Utah

INDICATIONS

In traditional sex therapy, patients with performance dysfunctions are encouraged to absorb themselves in sexual fantasy when they are unable to attend to sensual sensations in the present moment and they begin to engage in spectatoring. These suggestions may facilitate this process and make it more automatic.

SUGGESTIONS

If at times you find that your mind is wandering elsewhere during sex, that may be a good time, to direct those thoughts so that your mind can drift off to a memory, or perhaps a fantasy, of something very arousing. So when you notice stray thoughts distracting you, you can use that as the time, for a very sensual, a very vivid, a very enticing daydream to just kind of flow into your mind.

And I don't know if that image will be from a movie you particularly liked, or from something you've read. Perhaps you'll find yourself picturing an especially erotic scene, noticing the sensual way a couple kiss, [pause] the way they lovingly caress each other, [pause] how they begin to gradually, seductively remove clothes. You feel as you remember what you're observing them doing. Perhaps playfully, seductively teasing each other, or tenderly beginning to explore the other's body, with lips, with fingers. Maybe noticing them beginning to move and responding to the pleasure, the sounds of pleasure you hear, the tender, loving things said to each other.

On the other hand, it's fine and fun to know that when stray thoughts distract you during sex, you don't need a movie of others. You may have some vivid memories of your own, that can come freely to mind; sensuous, erotic experiences you shared with someone in the past, or that you wish you had shared with someone. [Pause] And you can become deeply involved and absorbed in those memories, in enjoying the excitement of the interaction, feeling what you know how to feel and felt then, experiencing the excitement and pleasure. Memories can be so real. Many people can sense the texture and gentle softness of skin, silky and smooth; the feel of warm, pleasant curves, and the sensations of soft hair; hearing breathing, whispered words, sighs of pleasure. And it may be that you are even aware of the pleasant fragrance of cologne or someone's hair, along with the mounting pleasure and excitement.

At other times when your mind begins to wander, it could be fun to allow your unconscious mind to get involved in a fantasy, knowing something you might particularly enjoy. And I wonder if it might involve someone else, or perhaps be about the fun of making love in a different place. I don't know. I wonder whether your unconscious will decide that it will be a quicky, a brief image, or an involved, creative story; if it will be more sensual, or if it will be an elegant kind of romantic adventure. But it really doesn't matter. Doesn't matter at all. All that matters, is that you enjoy this gift, from your unconscious.

So during sex, whenever you notice your mind wandering elsewhere, and you think you might become distracted, that's the reason that it's time, for you to find very erotic, very sensual images coming into your mind. And you can be satisfied, with the good effects these fantasies will have on your sexual relationship.

OTHER SUGGESTIONS FACILITATING FANTASY

And his/her touch will probably remind you of other experiences. And that's all right, to just remember, *really* remember. Images of someone from long ago, images of something very exciting, can just come washing over you, when *(name)* begins to intimately touch you. As if, his/her touch is the signal, for your unconscious mind to spontaneously, automatically, remind you of your passionate, erotic experiences.

And when she touches your penis [or, when he kisses you], you can be surprised and pleased to find very sensual, erotic memories beginning to come, into your mind—exciting, sexual pictures that can absorb much of your attention. [Use repetition of these suggestions.]

SUGGESTIONS NORMALIZING FANTASY FOR THE INHIBITED PATIENT

Using fantasy is one way you can take responsibility for your own pleasure, instead of expecting your partner to do everything. And of course, people never actually do most of the things they fantasize about, but they can still vicariously enjoy some perhaps forbidden pleasures, in an exciting but safe way. And it's your partner who really reaps the benefits.

Changes in Preference Metaphor

D. Corydon Hammond, Ph.D.
Salt Lake City, Utah

INDICATIONS

This metaphor may be used with cases of sexual aversion or inhibited sexual desire. It may also be useful whenever you need to create a belief that change is possible, and that it can occur autonomously. Rather than simply being a concocted story, this illustrates a metaphor built around almost universal truisms that the vast majority of people have experienced and cannot deny. Commas have been used to encourage appropriate brief pauses, and italics are used to suggest words to be very slightly emphasized which generally contain implications and embedded suggestions.

THE METAPHOR

Most of us have some foods we like better than others. I can recall when I was a child, I loved certain foods. I remember how much I just loved pancakes, and the smell of hot, fresh pancakes cooking in the morning. And umm, after that warm, sticky feel of the syrup, a glass of cold milk tasted *so* good. And I recall the warm, comfortably full kind of feeling after eating them.

I don't know, when you were a child, what foods you liked. But *you* certainly remember, maybe not all of them, but some of them. I don't know, for instance, if when you were a child, you liked eating pancakes, or pizza, or even strawberries. Maybe there was a particular food that you liked *very* much. [Pause] I wonder how you are able to remember as a child, smelling the aroma, or seeing that food before you. Do you remember the taste of that food, the texture of it in your mouth as you relished it? Perhaps you remember the tingly juiciness of strawberries, and that feeling on your tongue. Or maybe you'd rather recall the crunchiness of fresh carrots out of the garden. For a moment, maybe you can just really enjoy the real memory of your favorite childhood foods again. [Pause]

Most of us as children, also had some foods that we disliked. I can recall as a child, how I hated several kinds of foods. I didn't like peas, and at that time I hated clam chowder and enchiladas. I was turned off by all salads, and mushrooms, and yuk, the thought of eating a lobster or clam was repulsive. I'm sure you can remember some of the different foods that you disliked. [Pause]

There were so many things *then*, that I didn't like, to eat. But you know, it's interesting, even surprising, how dramatically our tastes and preferences *can change*. Some of the foods that you avoided and disliked as a child, *can be enjoyed as an adult*. And what I notice *now*, is that the taste of an enchilada, and the slipperiness of a clam, *seems different*. I'm not sure how; I just know that, *it's different*. And we learn that what *was* unappealing, *can* become really *pleasant* and delicious.

And I guess that's because *it's a part of nature*, as we are continually growing and *changing*. Remember as children, we couldn't imagine how our parents could *enjoy* watching or listening to the news. It had no appeal to us *then*, but later, *that changed*. As a child, you can probably remember some television shows that you had no interest in. [Pause] Many of us just couldn't understand how anyone could enjoy a movie that was *romantic*. A love story had no appeal to us *then*. We had no desire, to see it. *At the time*, it seemed boring. But certain types of programs which once seemed uninteresting, as we changed, *can become enjoyable*.

And it was the same with certain kinds of movies, and with certain kinds of music. [Pause] We couldn't have imagined it at the time, but *we have changed*, in many ways that *we could have never predicted*. And most of the

time, we aren't even quite sure exactly how or when those changes came about. But one thing that we can be sure of, is that we will continue to change and to grow. Change is just a very natural part of life.

Metaphors for Going Out to Dinner and Back Scratching

D. Corydon Hammond, Ph.D.
Salt Lake City, Utah

INDICATIONS

This metaphor conveys the message that it is vitally important to take responsibility for your own sexual pleasure through communicating with your partner. It may be useful when patients have problems with orgasmic dysfunction, erectile dysfunction, or ejaculatory inhibition. It may be equally valuable for sexual enhancement with normal couples or individuals, and in modified form to encourage general assertiveness instead of mind reading in relationships.

SUGGESTIONS

You may enjoy just allowing your mind to drift back to an evening when you and your partner (spouse) went out for dinner, to an especially nice restaurant. Perhaps you recall arriving at the restaurant together, and how it looked, possibly aware of the smell of the food outside or as you entered. And can you kind of remember the details of the restaurant, perhaps aware of the sound of silverware and glasses, the sound of people talking in the background, of being taken to your table, and noticing the things around you, near where you're sitting. And perhaps you can recall looking over the menu, seeing the different selections, and their prices. Some of the entrees probably don't sound very inviting, but there are likely several things that appear *very* appealing. And at times like this we often talk, and look around, until finally the waiter or waitress comes to take the order.

Have you ever noticed how when the waiter or waitress comes, you just tell them what you'd like? You don't even have to think about it, you just say what it is you've decided you'd like. Now I'm sure that your husband/wife knows what you often like. But your tastes can be different from night to night. You don't really feel like liking the same thing every night. And you probably, don't think much, about giving your order for what you want to eat. I suspect you really wouldn't want your husband/wife to be the *only one* to see that menu, and to then place an order for you, making the assumption that he/she knows what you want, without consulting you. Because you both know that he/she can't read your mind.

And so you just naturally take the responsibility, for getting the kind of food that will satisfy your tastes and desires. It's just second nature. We've all learned to speak up, and you express your desires and indicate what will satisfy your preferences that particular evening. Because, after all, your husband/wife can't magically know what you want and desire from night to night. You're going to get tired of the same thing. *Anyone* would get tired of a diet of steak every night, and so sometimes lobster or Chinese food is just what you're ready for, and sounds much more appealing. So of course it's perfectly all right, completely natural, to help your husband/wife, so that he/she knows what it is you'd enjoy on different evenings.

There are lots of other situations when you really have to do the same kind of thing. You know that when you have an itch on your back, and you can't quite reach it, you don't expect your partner to know, unless you tell him/her. And of course, even when he/she knows you have an itch, he/she may not be able to find the right spot. So he/she needs you to guide him/her. And sometimes you want him/her to rub hard, and at other times you just want him/her to scratch lightly. There are times when it may feel better to be scratched back and forth, and sometimes you want him/her to rub

up and down. Sometimes in just one place; other times with very long strokes. And when you have an itch, and you guide them in just the right way, to just the right spot, it feels *so* good. But of course he/she can't know, unless you tell him/her. Even though he/she wants to please you, he/she needs you to tell him/her, *somehow*. If not by telling him/her verbally, then by the way you move. Sometimes you can guide someone with your hand, and sometimes you guide them just by being able to move your body.

And it would be really, really nice, for you to remember, that you are really the world's authority on only *one* thing. You are *the* world's authority on yourself, and on what's natural for you. You are the best teacher about what you want, and what gives you pleasure, and what will make you happy at any particular time.

And so sexually [or, in your marriage] . . . [And now make the bridging association to the patient's specific problem.]

Organ Transplant Metaphor

D. Corydon Hammond, Ph.D.
Salt Lake City, Utah

INDICATIONS

This is a metaphor that may be used in overcoming sexual myths and misinformation. It may also be used in correcting self-defeating introjects associated with nonsexual problems.

SUGGESTIONS

Some years ago, they began doing organ transplants, putting hearts and kidneys into people who needed them. What they began to discover was that when a foreign object, from someone else, was put into another person, that person's body would accept it, for a time. But then, after a while, his body would recognize it as not being his own, and the immune system would reject it.

In a very similar way, as children, with limited discrimination abilities and limited experience, we often took in ideas that were given to us by our parents and other people. They were someone else's concepts, but for a time, most of us accept them. But later on, as adults, our mature unconscious mind finally recognizes these ideas as not being our own, as foreign, and something that doesn't really fit for us. And our unconscious mind can reject those ideas, that were someone else's and may have fit for them, but that later are recognized as foreign, and that don't belong in us. And your unconscious mind can inwardly review, the ideas and concepts that you picked up from other people, and even without your full conscious awareness, can begin to determine which of those are compatible, and which are alien to you.

The Pee Shyness Metaphor for Sexual Dysfunction

D. Corydon Hammond, Ph.D.
Salt Lake City, Utah

INDICATIONS

This is a brief metaphor illustrating the concept that we cannot consciously will sexual response, but must allow it to happen and trust the unconscious. It may be used with performance problems such as erectile dysfunction, orgasmic dysfunction, and ejaculatory inhibition.

SUGGESTIONS

Many years ago, I used to work occasionally with drug abusers who were on parole. A condition of their parole was that they be in therapy, and that they be on urine surveillance. Twice a week they came to the clinic to leave a urine specimen. The urine specimen would be mailed to a lab, and if traces of drugs were

found in their urine, they might have their parole revoked.

These men had urinated tens of thousands of times before, without ever thinking about it, without every questioning their ability to urinate. But when one of us had to go into the restroom with them, to observe them urinate in a specimen bottle, they often couldn't get their urine flow started. When they felt pressure to perform, they couldn't. The harder they tried to will it to happen, the more they couldn't urinate.

We simply can't will our body to respond. It's kind of like when we've stayed up too late one night, and the harder we try to help ourselves go to sleep, the more wide awake we are. You can't will yourself to perspire. And in a similar way, we can't will an erection, or orgasm, or ejaculation. We simply have to allow it to occur . . . to simply trust our unconscious mind, to know what to do, and how to do it. The more we try to help out, the more we interfere.

Metaphoric Suggestions and Word Plays for Facilitating Lubrication

D. Corydon Hammond, Ph.D.
Salt Lake City, Utah

INDICATIONS

These suggestions may be helpful for those female patients who have problems with sexual arousal and, in particular, in becoming lubricated. Such patients experience dyspareunia secondary to the lack of lubrication. Commas have been placed to suggest brief pauses. [The author is indebted to Dr. Kay Thompson for her model and instruction many years ago in the use of word plays.]

SUGGESTIONS

I know and you know that you have been experiencing some difficulty lubricating. But I wonder if you have ever thought about the many different kinds of lubrication? What you may not know that you know, is that it's a very common experience to find ourselves around some really delicious food, and to notice that our mouth is involved in lubrication, because it's watering involuntarily. It isn't something we think about. When we're in the right circumstance, whether it's food or whatever, it just happens. And everyone knows that on a hot day, we will spontaneously perspire, whether we expect to or not. It isn't something that we can voluntarily control. It's just an intrinsic, innate part of us. Certain things like lubrication are just part of our natural make-up, the way they flow.

And there are many things that we know and do, without knowing that we know or do them. For instance, one of the things that most of us don't realize, is that during a baby girl's first day of life, without any conscious thought, even without any sexual arousal, her vagina lubricated and became wet, several times in fact. It's just sort of a natural body rhythm, that occurs in all women, each night of their lives. And you haven't realized that each night since you were born, that you've lubricated. It's just a fundamental quality. Although you aren't consciously aware of it, your unconscious knows that last night as you slept, your body responded on its own, and about every 100 minutes your lubricated, and became wet. Do you realize that that is about every hour and a half? You haven't realized that because you haven't had to pay any attention to it, because it just happens, *and you've known how to lubricate all your life.*

And your mouth knows how to water in an appropriate fashion in response to food, and your body knows how to perspire. And there are many reasons why you perspire. Sometimes you perspire when you are warm and overheated, and sometimes you will perspire with embarrassment. And you can lubricate in many situations, even when you don't have the opportunity to do anything about it. Your body has been doing it automatically ever since you were born. We really do know a lot of things we

don't know we know. And I know that your body has the know-how, without your needing to know. And you have no notion of how to will your body to do what it already knowingly knows how to do with no effort. And you don't need to consciously know. You've been saying no to a lot of things that you don't need to no, and maybe it's time for you to stop saying no, just so you can let yourself know that you know things that you didn't know you knew.

And I wonder if it will surprise you, as you simply enjoy playfully touching and being touched, to discover that warm wetness. Because you will find that as your husband/partner sensually touches you, and as you enjoy his body, and just concentrate on the pleasure, that your body will respond all by itself. Just like on a warm day when you spontaneously perspire, you will feel the warmth between your legs, and the wetness. And you will know what this lubrication means, what it stands for in terms of your caring, and the playfulness, and the readiness, knowing that you don't need to say no to that knowledge.

Suggestion for Ejaculatory Inhibition or Orgasmic Dysfunction

D. Corydon Hammond, Ph.D.
Salt Lake City, Utah

INDICATIONS

This suggestion is intended to reduce performance anxiety and pressure in patients suffering with orgasmic dysfunction or retarded ejaculation. The suggestion seeks to change the focus to *when* orgasm will occur, instead of *if* it will occur. This suggestion may be given in hypnosis while the patient is also being assigned traditional sex therapy tasks like sensate focus.

SUGGESTION

And you're not really sure when you'll ejaculate (come) with her/him. Do you think you'll ejaculate (come) with her/him by *(three days hence)*? I don't and I don't think you or *(partner's name)* do either. I don't expect that you'll come with her/him after you come to the next session, and you probably don't either. After all, you've had this habit for a while. I think we agree on that. I don't know if you'll ejaculate (reach orgasm) by accident soon after two more sessions, or if you'll come *soon* after three more sessions. I really don't know, and neither do you. Will it be earlier in an evening, or maybe in the morning when you're not so tired, or will it be later in an evening when you're so tired that you're not thinking about it and it just surprises you? I'm not sure; you're not sure; your unconscious mind isn't sure. But we *are* in agreement that it's surely unlikely to happen *for a while*, just as it's sure to happen after a while. So isn't it great that you can just have some fun with each other, and just enjoy some pleasure together.

Suggestion for Erection or Lubrication

D. Corydon Hammond, Ph.D.
Salt Lake City, Utah

INDICATIONS

This is an indirect suggestion that covers all possibilities, intended primarily for use with patients with erectile dysfunction. The suggestion also reframes any erectile difficulty as a message and cue to focus on fun and pleasure, rather than performance. It may also be useful in women with lubrication problems, and alternative phrasing for this (instead of erections) is included.

SUGGESTIONS

I wonder what kind of an erection (how much wetness) you are going to have at first? Maybe there will be hardly any erection (lubrication) at all. More likely, you may (notice some wetness) have an erection that comes and goes, or maybe you'll even be surprised to notice a full hard erection (how very wet you've become). But even if there's hardly an erection, that's all right, because that's a very important message from your body, that it's time to remember to enjoy the pleasure, and to have more fun, trusting all the rest to your unconscious mind.

Suggestions for Impotence and Anorgasmia

Leo Alexander, M.D.

ERECTILE DYSFUNCTION

[Some patients are so overly worried about their partner's pleasure that their worry impairs performance. Such individuals must receive permission to be *temporarily* selfish and to become absorbed in their own pleasure. The following suggestion seems particularly designed for such a patient. (*Ed.*)] "Sex will be enjoyment, not a performance—pure enjoyment! No thought of performance at all! Please her out of the bedroom, but in bed enjoy yourself!"

"Performance applies to study and work, but to nothing else. . . . In sex, enjoyment is primary. . . . This will become easier for you, every day, every week, every month, every year; you will achieve enjoyable, automatic mastery. . . . You will countermand all negative ideas about performance. . . . Just enjoy her— don't perform. Touch, kiss, and if anything happens, let it happen."

ORGASMIC DYSFUNCTION

[Once again, the following suggestion must be very selectively used with the woman who has focused primarily on giving pleasure, rather than learning to receive pleasure. She must learn to play at sex rather than working at it. (*Ed.*)] "First of all, you must please yourself. Please your man in any other way. Make him the most sumptuous breakfasts, the most fabulous dinners, shine his shoes, take his socks off, do whatever you want. But in bed, please only yourself . . . Sex should be pure enjoyment, without any thought!"

Suggestions for Induced Erotic Dreams

D. Corydon Hammond, Ph.D.
Salt Lake City, Utah

INDICATIONS

These suggestions were formulated for patients with inhibited sexual desire or sexual aversion. When such patients report that they experience nocturnal dreams, and especially when their value systems discourage or prohibit the reading or viewing of erotic material, these suggestions may be of value.

SUGGESTIONS

You already know how to experience stimulating dreams. And it's perfectly natural, following the kind of work we're doing, to have some pleasurable dreams. And the dreams of the night are a perfect occasion, to sort through understandings, and rehearse, preparing us for new experiences. And your unconscious mind has the ability to continue, independently, to work on increasing your sexual desire toward *(partner)*, through the dreams of the night.

I don't know what you'll dream about, and you don't either. Dreams are often so creatively surprising in their content. It may be that the dream will be like a romantic love scene, from a novel. For instance, you might have a dream where you are with your partner, and he's/she's saying very tender things to you, and very romantically seducing you. Perhaps the dream will involve people you know, or maybe some interesting people you've been close to in the past. [Pause] I'm not really sure whether you'll feel as if it's happening to you, and be completely involved, or if it will seem more as if you are intimately observing the very erotic scenes.

But what I do know is that it's not unusual, for people I work with to have very exciting, very erotic dreams. It's a very common experience, because every night we just inevitably dream, sometimes unknowingly, several dreams. And this is just a very natural process, that our unconscious mind uses, to work things through. It's been going on all our lives, will continue all our lives. It's just innate in you and in me.

And because your goal is to increase your sexual desire, in all probability, you will have an interesting experience tonight, while you're sleeping. I'm not absolutely sure about the particular night. I suspect it will be tonight, when you have the first erotic dream which you'll remember, but perhaps your unconscious mind will be inclined to wait until tomorrow night, or even the next night. I'd be somewhat surprised if your unconscious waited until *(e.g., Friday)* night to let you remember an erotic dream, but I'm not really sure. I expect that it will very likely be tonight or tomorrow night, that you have a very sexually stimulating dream, which is remembered. And perhaps you may have some doubts about it, until you awaken one morning. And at first, I don't know if you'll fully remember the relevant dream, or if you will just sense and know that something is different, even though you don't know quite what it is that you know.

And of course we're not responsible, for what occurs in dreams. The wonderful thing is, that your unconscious mind not only helps you, but it also protects you. Many times in the past, your unconscious has allowed you to forget parts of dreams after awakening. So even though you are not consciously responsible for the content of your dreams, *if part* of a dream would make you *too* uncomfortable or embarrassed, you may just find it difficult to remember everything after awakening. You've had that experience many times. And that will be all right, because those dreams will have already served their purpose, of stirring sexual feelings and desires and releasing hormones. And those desires will be carried with you into your day, where they will appropriately influence your thoughts and behavior. And even though you won't remember *all* your erotic and sexy dreams, in the mornings, you can still sense and know that something is different, even if you can't quite put your finger on precisely what it is.

And you don't even have to believe that you're going to have erotic dreams. One of the most interesting things about this is, that you don't even have to believe it's going to happen. In fact, it may even be fun for you to doubt that you're going to have such a dream, because if you didn't have a doubt, you wouldn't be able to be amused or surprised. And so you may even doubt it as you're driving home, and doubt it as you're going to sleep, right up until the moment you awaken one morning, with a realization. And most likely, you'll have your first erotic dream which you remember, tonight. I can't really be sure though. It may be _____ night or _____ night, although I think it's going to be tonight that you have a very erotic, exciting, stimulating dream which you remember.

But your unconscious mind can determine whether you recall the dream or not, or only part of it. But whether you consciously remember or not, is irrelevant, because your unconscious mind will enjoy it, and the next morning you will carry those warm desires and sexual interests into your day, and will realize, that something is different. And I don't think you'll want to have those romantic, stimulating dreams *every* night, but your unconscious mind will thoroughly enjoy scheduling some irresistibly tantalizing dreams, fairly often.

Suggestions with Sexual Dysfunctions

Don E. Gibbons, Ph.D.

INTRODUCTION

Gibbons (1979) uses the crystal gazing technique, one that was often used by Erickson, to enable a patient to visualize the successful resolution to a problem in the future. It will undoubtedly have the most impact on patients capable of amnesia. As an alternative to a crystal ball, the patient may be asked to visualize a stage in a theater, a movie screen, or a television screen. This technique is most likely to have applicability with dysfunctions where performance anxiety is involved, such as erectile dysfunction, ejaculatory inhibition, orgasmic dysfunction, or perhaps premature ejaculation. Ideomotor signals may be obtained from the patient to track their progress and experience of scenes. (*Ed.*)

THE CRYSTAL GAZING TECHNIQUE

Now I would like you to imagine yourself seated comfortably in front of a large crystal ball, gazing into its depths. Continue to visualize the crystal ball and to focus on it, and soon you will begin to see the images appear within. You will be able to describe everything you see, just as it occurs; and I will be able to guide and direct the images as they appear, or to suggest new images from time to time. Now you can picture the crystal ball very clearly in your mind, and as soon as you are ready, you can begin to describe the images as they appear. [Pause]

Now, as you continue to watch the crystal ball, you are gradually going to be able to see an image appear within it of yourself at some time in the near future, making love extremely well. I will not ask you to describe the scene; but as you continue to gaze into the crystal ball, you can see that both you and your partner are going to be fully and completely satisfied. And now, as this is occurring, the scene is beginning to fade, and the crystal ball is fading away too. And even though you will not be able to recall the memory of the crystal ball when the trance is over, you will still be aware that you are irresistibly headed for certain success; and that your future sexual experiences will be just as pleasurable, and just as enjoyable, as you have already seen that they will be in the crystal ball.

[Amnesia for the specific details of the experience is suggested so that factual discrepancies between the details of the visualized scene and the actual experience, when it does take place, will not negate the validity of the positive expectations engendered by this procedure.]

SUGGESTIONS WITH ERECTILE DYSFUNCTION AND PREMATURE EJACULATION

Please extend the index finger of your right [or left] hand straight out in the air in front of you. That's fine. Now, as I continue to speak, you will soon notice that your index finger is becoming very stiff and very rigid. And as it does, you will also find that you are completely losing all feeling in it. Soon your index finger will be just as stiff and just as numb as a bar of iron. It's becoming just as rigid and just as numb as an iron bar now. Your index finger is just as rigid as a bar of iron, and just as insensitive.

Now please clench your jaw firmly, three times in a row. And as you do, you notice that feeling is returning to your finger, even though it continues to be stiff and rigid. The feeling is returning completely now; and even though your finger remains as rigid as before, the feeling in it is entirely normal once again.

And now, in order to make the stiffness go away, all you have to do is to decide that you are ready for it to do so. And notice as you do that your finger has become completely flexible once again. Just bend it a couple of times to assure yourself of this fact, and then go ahead and put it down.

From now on, each time you are ready to have intercourse, you will find that at the proper time your penis has become just as stiff and just as rigid as your index finger was a moment ago. And it will also be just as numb, as stiff and as numb as a bar of iron.

You will be able to maintain your erection and prolong intercourse for as long as necessary to fully satisfy your partner. And when you are ready for normal feeling to return, you will only need to clench your jaw firmly three quick times in a row for this to happen. But even after your sensitivity does come back, you will still be able to maintain your erection as long as necessary so as to achieve your own orgasm.

[Additional sessions may be necessary until the subject has achieved the necessary control. When this has been accomplished, subsequent suggestions should emphasize retaining progressively more feeling in the penis until the subject has clenched his jaw three times, allowing more and more restraint to be developed, until finally such suggestions are no longer necessary.]

SUGGESTIONS WITH DISCREPANT OR INHIBITED SEXUAL DESIRE

Sometime during the next few nights, when you are asleep in bed with your partner, you are going to have a pleasant dream which you will find sexually very stimulating. The dream will be formed out of images and sensations which you find especially pleasant and arousing at the time, and you will be so excited by them that you will awaken even before the dream is completely over, fully aroused and ready to make love.

The arousing effects of the dream will persist for some time after you wake up. They will add new dimensions of richness and pleasure to your lovemaking, and they will enable you and your partner to discover new avenues of pleasure, and new channels of communication, which will deepen your relationship considerably.

You will be particularly pleased to find that your orgasm will be unusually profound and satisfying, and it will seem to last much longer than it usually does.

And you will continue to have dreams of this sort at appropriate intervals in the future, which will continue to enrich and deepen your relationship in just the same manner.

Suggestions for Premature Ejaculation

Milton H. Erickson, M.D.

INTRODUCTION, INDICATIONS AND CONTRAINDICATIONS

Premature ejaculation is the most easily treated male sexual dysfunction, with success rates generally in the range of 90%–95% (Stuart & Hammond, 1980) using traditional, behavioral sex therapy techniques. Due to the high effectiveness of the squeeze and stop-start techniques, hypnosis is certainly not the first treatment of choice for premature ejaculation problems. When more validated methods have failed, however, or when the patient does not have a cooperative partner to do behavioral assignments, then hypnosis is extremely helpful. In addition to suggestive hypnosis, uncovering methods such as ideomotor signaling may be used to explore underlying functions or resistances. Physical metaphors, such as creating a glove anesthesia and then suggesting a similar control of sensations in the penis, may likewise be effective. The rather elaborate and complex procedure below was successfully used in a suggestive hypnosis format by Erickson with a compulsive, single patient with premature ejaculation. This method seems primarily indicated when more parsimonious procedures have failed to produce satisfactory results in patients capable of deeper trances and experiencing amnesia. (*Ed.*)

THERAPEUTIC PROCEDURE

Therapy was begun by inducing a light trance in the patient and impressing upon him, most tediously, that the "light trance" was a most important measure. Its purpose, he was told

repetitiously, was to insure that he had both a conscious and an unconscious understanding of the fact that a deep hypnotic trance would settle once and for all time whether or not he could ever succeed in sex relations. Two hours of repetition of these general ideas resulted in a deep trance, but no effort was made to give him an awareness of this fact. An amnesia, spontaneous or one indirectly suggested, was desired for therapeutic purposes.

Then, as a posthypnotic suggestion, he was told that he must, absolutely must, get a wristwatch. If at all possible, this wristwatch should have an illuminated dial and illuminated hands. Absolutely imperative was the fact that the watch should have a second hand. The second hand, it was stressed over and over, would be absolutely necessary.

The second posthypnotic suggestion was given that he must and could, and would, thenceforth sleep with a night light at his bedside so that he could tell time to the very second at any time during the night, since he must, absolutely must, and would wear his wristwatch whenever he should happen to be in bed.

Solemn promises in relation to these demands were secured from the patient with no effort on his part to question the author's reasons for his various insistences.

It was then explained to him that he would continue his "useless inviting of girls to spend the night" with him. To this he also agreed, whereupon it was emphasized that only in this way could he find out what he "really, really, really would want to learn."

The next posthypnotic suggestion was presented most carefully, in a gentle yet emphatic tone of voice, commanding, without seeming to command, the patient's full attention and his full willingness to be obedient to it. This suggestion was a purportedly soundly based medical explanation of the expectable development, on an organic physiological basis, of his "total problem." This was the fact that his premature ejaculation, by virtue of body changes from aging processes, would be diametrically changed. The explanation was the following posthypnotic suggestion:

Do you know, can you possibly realize, can you genuinely understand, that medically all things, everything, even the worst of symptoms and conditions, must absolutely come to an end. *But not, but not, I must emphasize, not in the way a layman would understand?* Do you realize, do you understand, are you in any way aware, that your premature ejaculation *will end in a failure*, that no matter how long your erection lasts, no matter how long and actively you engage in coitus, you will fail to have an ejaculation for 10, for 10 long, for 15 long minutes, for 20, for 25 minutes? Even more? Do you realize how desperately you will strive and strive, how desperately you will watch the minute hand and the second hand of your wristwatch, wondering, just wondering if you will fail, fail, fail to have an ejaculation at 25 minutes, at 25½, at 26, at 26½ minutes? Or will it be at 27½, at 27½ minutes—at 27½, at 27½ minutes? [This last said in tones expressive of deep relief.]

And the next morning you still will not believe, just can't believe, that you won't fail to have an ejaculation, and so you will have to discover again, to discover again, if you really can have an ejaculation, but it won't be, it can't be, at 27½ minutes, nor even at 28, nor even at 29 minutes. Just the desperate hope will be in your mind that maybe, just maybe, maybe at 33 minutes, or 34, or 35 minutes the ejaculation will come. And at the time, all the time, you will watch desperately the wristwatch and strive so hard lest you fail, fail again, to ejaculate at 27 minutes, and then 33, 34, 35 minutes will seem never, just never, to be coming with an ejaculation.

And now, this is what I want you to do. Find one of the girls you are used to. Walk her to your apartment. When you come to the corner at 8th, even as you turn right [all of this was said with the utmost of intensity] try so very hard to keep your mind on the conversations, but notice that you can't help counting one by one the cracks in the sidewalk until you turn into the courtway and step upon the boardwalk. With complete intensity you are to try hard, very hard to keep your mind on the conversation, but keep counting desperately the cracks, the cracks between the boards, the cracks under you [to the unsophisticated, slang often gives opportunities for double meanings], all those cracks all along the way to your apartment until it seems that you will never, never, never get there, and what a profound relief it will be to enter, to feel comfortable, to be at ease, to give your attention to the girl, and then, and then, to bed, but not the usual—but the answer, the real, real, real answer, and from the moment you enter [pause] the apartment [pause] your mind will be on your wristwatch, the watch that, as time goes by, can, at long last, bring you the answer.

Quickly now, keep all that I have said in your unconscious mind—locked up, not a syllable, not a word, not a meaning forgotten—to be kept there, used, obeyed fully, completely. You can even forget me—just obey fully—then you can remember just me and come back and tell me that the wristwatch was right when it read 27½ minutes and when it read 33, 34, and 35.

Arouse now, completely rested and refreshed, understanding in your unconscious mind the completeness of the task to be done."

HYPNOTIC SUGGESTIONS FOR INTERPERSONAL RELATIONSHIPS

Hypnotic Ego-Assertive Retraining

David Waxman, L.R.C.P., M.R.C.S.
London, England

INTRODUCTION AND INDICATIONS

Ego-strengthening techniques are designed to enhance self-esteem and self-image. However, there are times when it is vitally important to correct a deficit in interpersonal skills through modeling and either rehearsal or covert, mental rehearsal (Bandura, 1969). Waxman's (1989) ego-assertiveness training provides modeling and mental rehearsal to promote feelings of self-efficacy and assertiveness in specific contexts. This method seems particularly indicated for patients who lack confidence and who are passive, unassertive, and threatened in specific interpersonal situations. (*Ed.*)

A TYPICAL EGO-ASSERTIVE ROUTINE

The patient is put in hypnosis and the trance state is deepened.

Proceed as follows:

You are completely calm and in a deeply relaxed state. I want you to see yourself at work and attending your weekly departmental meeting. You are sitting in the manager's office. The others are seated rather informally about the room. See that situation and confirm that you are there with the usual signal.

The patient raises his right index finger. Now ask the patient where he is sitting.

Patient: "On the chair by the door."

Therapist: "Are there any empty seats?"

Patient: "Yes, the armchair by the desk."

Therapist: "You are feeling totally calm and relaxed. Go and sit in the armchair . . . tell me when you are sitting in the armchair and feeling totally calm and relaxed."

After a few moments the patient will give the ideomotor signal.

Therapist: "You will remain totally calm and relaxed . . . and now the manager is opening the meeting . . ."

Therapist as manager (very assertively): "Good morning gentleman. We will have department reports first of all."

Therapist: "He's looking at you."

Therapist as manager: "What have you got to tell us?"

Therapist: "You feel completely calm and relaxed and full of confidence. Completely at ease and comfortable in yourself. Speak up now. Answer him . . ."

Patient: "Well sir, I think . . ."

Therapist: "Forget about sir—speak up—you don't think—you know—speak out!"

Patient: "We have two problems, I'm sorry to say."

Therapist: "Forget about being sorry, you have no reason to apologize! It's your department—you are in charge of it and you are in charge of yourself!"

Patient: "We have some problems regarding staff. Two of our typists are off sick and one is on holiday."

Therapist: "Stop apologizing—it's not your fault. Speak up."

Patient: "Personnel say that all replacements are on attachment elsewhere."

Therapist as manager (even more aggressively): "Then what are you going to do about it?"

Therapist: "Speak up and speak out (remain quite calm and relaxed)—It's your department. You are in charge of the department, of the situation and of yourself, now speak!"

Patient: "I'll get on to them and tell them that we must have immediate replacements."

Continue in this way simulating the manager speaking very aggressively and showing the patient that he can reply assertively but politely and remaining calm and in control throughout the interview.

A wide range of situations may be dealt with in this manner working through various aspects of the patient's life events.

It must be understood that assertive retraining involves dealing not only with the emotions of anxiety invoked by the pressure of some person or persons whom the patient may consider threatening in the authoritarian sense. It may also include the difficulties which many people experience with their peers or in achieving friendship, affection and love. The person may feel such a social misfit that even life itself may become unacceptable. He or she may act out and even indulge in antisocial behavior.

"Fruits & Vegetables": A Simple Metaphor for Understanding People Better

Gerald J. Mozdzierz, Ph.D.
Hines, Illinois

This is a simple metaphor for people who may be discouraged because they have been disappointed by a significant other person. The disappointment may have been experienced as a result of having exaggerated expectations or as a result of simply not knowing the obvious, namely, that people have their idiosyncrasies and limitations. The clinician can simply call this the "fruit and vegetable theory of people."

Once a client has expressed disappointment in someone and difficulty in understanding the behavior, feelings, or attitudes of the other person, the therapist may point out that the person in question is very much like a strawberry (or some other fruit, vegetable, or other living plant). As such, no matter what we may want that person to look like, taste like, be like, or act like, that person is a strawberry and will always be a strawberry. Yes, we may want that person to be more like a combination of peach, plum, raspberry and several other good things, but, in essence, some people are strawberries and we have to learn to accept them as such. When we do accept them as such, we become less disappointed that a strawberry looks like, tastes like, and acts like a strawberry. But then something else happens!

At this point in time, we become a little more able to enjoy the other person's essence of "strawberriness" and all the things that strawberries can be! Strawberry pie, strawberry shortcake, strawberry ice cream, strawberry soda, etc. In describing the fruit or vegetable, the clinician can be as simple or as elaborate and elegant as is called for by the client and the situation.

This simple metaphor is meant to suggest that other people can act like desirable and more undesirable fruits and vegetables as well. At times, the client will volunteer that the person with whom he has been having trouble is exactly like a horseradish root. Not much you can say about that, is there? Nevertheless, that troublesome person must be accepted for what he or she is, a horseradish root.

The metaphor is designed to help clients put other people into perspective. The focus of the metaphor may also be gently shifted so that the client begins to wonder what type of fruit or vegetable he or she is, whether he has been accepting himself for what he is, etc. Finally, the metaphor obviously includes a dimension of humor that helps others to see things with a twinkle.

Suggestions to Increase Interpersonal Effectiveness

Don E. Gibbons, Ph.D.

INDICATIONS

Dr. Gibbons designed these suggestions for improving social skills, enhancing assertiveness, and improving interpersonal relationships. They seem particularly indicated for egocentric patients who talk excessively about themselves. (*Ed.*)

SUGGESTIONS

This experience will provide you with a great deal more confidence in yourself, which will be reflected in the greater ease and skill with which you will be able to deal with others. You will be a great deal less aware of yourself, and a great deal more attentive to those around you. You will be much more interested in what other people have to say, and much more able to lose yourself in the topic of conversation.

As you come to derive more and more enjoyment out of talking to others, you will find yourself constantly alert for qualities, attributes, and achievements which are justly deserving of praise, and you will be able and willing to unstintingly provide it. At the same time, you will be able to exercise a great deal of restraint over any anger or impatience you may have over the shortcomings of other people. And if you should happen to feel that another person is unfairly taking advantage of you in some way, you will be able to phrase your objections kindly and tactfully, in a manner which will enable you to speak up for your own rights without becoming unduly emotional, and without the other party unnecessarily taking offense. As your confidence and skills improve, you will become vastly more sensitive to the emotional needs of those around you, and you will be able to find new sources of wisdom and understanding which will help you to meet those needs. There will be many people who will be able to look upon you as a friend to whom they can turn for comfort, for reassurance, and for advice, and there will be many whom you will be able to look upon as a friend in return. Your own life will consequently take on a great deal more meaning, and you will be able to enrich the lives of those around you considerably.

Suggestions for Difficulties in Interpersonal Situations

Kermit E. Parker, Jr., Ph.D.
Albuquerque, New Mexico

[Following hypnotic induction and deepening:] You know from past experience that as you achieve this level of comfort and relaxation, you can become physically more comfortable, and you're able to become mentally more comfortable as well. And in this process, your unconscious mind allows you the opportunity to grow, and to develop new attitudes and new feelings, and new ways of feeling about yourself and your circumstances.

In this state you can become more receptive, more creative, more aware of the abilities that you have within yourself. This hypnotic state allows you to gain confidence in yourself, to be in touch with that part of you that's confident and comfortable, and knows how you want to feel and behave. Within yourself, that quiet part of you that we sometimes call the unconscious, or that still, small voice, or that intuition within yourself, that knows you are an outgoing and warm and friendly person. These characteristics are abilities which you have, and your intuition can tell you that you can freely allow yourself to express those characteristics when it is appropriate, when it is called for.

CULTIVATING THE ABILITY TO LISTEN

And in being quietly confident, you find yourself being calm inside with the necessary amount of activation of your physiology and your mind, to be outgoing and warm, and friendly and talkative, without excessive activa

tion, without excessive energy, without nervous talking or laughter. And this is because you're aware that others need the opportunity to share with you about themselves, and your ability to listen, and your ability to give them that opportunity, creates a warm feeling for yourself . . .possibly a feeling of curiosity about them, that allows you to listen while they're talking, without interrupting, because what they're saying is interesting or important for them.

The Symbolic Imagery Letter Writing Technique

Mark S. Carich, Ph.D.
Centralia, Illinois

INDICATIONS AND CONTRAINDICATIONS

This is a cognitive behaviorally oriented hypnotic technique wherein the client writes an imaginary letter. The client is instructed, while in a hypnotic state, to imagine writing a letter pertaining to a specific topic. Expressing emotions through writing letters is a powerful technique that has been demonstrated not only to provide cathartic relief, but also to result in enhanced functioning of the immune system on both short- and long-term follow-ups of individuals writing about their feelings about traumas in their lives (Pennebaker & Beall, 1986; Pennebaker, Kiecolt-Glaser, & Glaser, 1988; Pennebaker & O'Heeron, 1984). Carich finds this technique valuable in working through resentments and anger, facilitating forgiveness of oneself or others, reducing guilt, letting go of and bringing a sense of closure over past relationships, fostering acceptance of a situation, and altering beliefs or perceptions about a problem. If it is to be done through self-hypnosis in an uncontrolled setting, this method seems contraindicated or should be used cautiously with suicidal, severely disturbed or unstable patients. (*Ed.*)

THE TECHNIQUE

Although this method may be used in nonhypnotic therapy [as Pennebaker has], it may also be used following hypnotic induction and deepening. The hypnotized client is instructed to imagine writing a letter to a specific person or about a specific topic. Naturally, the content and topic of the letter depend on the nature of the problem. For example, a grieving patient who has been angry and blaming God for years for the death of a loved one may be asked to write a letter about her feelings. The goal may be to vent and defuse the anger and come to an acceptance of the situation. The client may imagine writing the letter, verbalizing what is being mentally written as it's written. A deeper trance subject may actually write the letter in trance through the technique of automatic writing. Before the client is assigned the task of "writing" the letter, the therapist may "seed" ideas about emotionally letting go of the loved one, accepting the loss, obtaining a relief of her burden, letting go of anger and the past, and forgiving God and the deceased person.

While the client verbalizes the "letter," the therapist may offer suggestions to encourage cathartic relief and the letting go of outdated emotions and to reframe the situation. For example, some of the following types of suggestions may be given as the client "writes" the letter: "And as you express those feelings, allow yourself to accept his/her death." "As you write, notice the past is the past and does not have to bother you. You can let go of that pain." Rational-emotive suggestions may also be given to correct cognitive distortions.

ILLUSTRATIVE SCRIPT FOR SAYING GOODBYE

[Addressing the hypnotized subject:] What I would like you to do is to write a goodbye letter in your mind. Allow yourself to visualize and see a pad of paper. Do you see the paper? [Wait for confirmation.] Now visualize a pen. [Obtain confirmation. If there is resistance, use explor-atory methods to uncover the purpose of the block.] Good! Now imagine writing the goodbye letter, and as you begin to write, just say everything that you're writing out loud. And as you write, you'll begin to notice that heavy burden being lifted. [Suggestions for encouraging cathartic release of feelings and therapeutic, reframing suggestions may then be given.]

The Jazz Band Metaphor for Family Interaction

Philip Barker, M.B.
Calgary, Alberta, Canada

Let us now consider the functioning of a jazz band. . . . Jazz, an improvised music, depends for its quality and success on the constructive and creative interplay of different musicians, playing a variety of instruments. A jazz band has its different parts; there is usually at least a "rhythm section" and a "front line." These have distinct functions. The rhythm section lays down the beat of the music. The front line instruments are responsible for the melodic lines and their interplay. The front line may be further divided into different instruments or groups of instruments, for example brass instruments and reed instruments; the players of each must know what they are supposed to be doing, and how what they are doing is distinct from but at the same time fits in with what the other musicians are doing. The collective effort of the band as a whole also needs direction.

As you watch a jazz band playing you will see that the leader is continually giving instructions to the members of the band, setting the tempo for each tune; indicating when the musicians should take solos, and how long each should be; defining "riffs," which are repetitive musical patterns that the other musicians may play behind a soloist or at some other point during the performance of a piece; and of course letting the members of the band know when each tune should come to an end. Such instructions are often given quite unobtrusively, perhaps by a nod of the head, some other nonverbal cue or the use of a musical phrase or emphasis with which the musicians are familiar.

Sometimes the musicians have played together for so long that instructions are no longer needed. They know how their leader likes a certain tune played, who should take solos when, and so forth. Nevertheless, the leader's decisions and authority are still in operation, even though the band is functioning so well and is so experienced and well-rehearsed that few or no instructions need be given while they are playing. Some bands have dual leadership; this can work well, but it carries with it the risk of friction between the leaders.

COMMENTARY

Few, if any, therapeutic metaphors perfectly represent the clinical situations for which they are constructed, but there is a considerable resemblance between some aspects of the subsystems of a family and those of a jazz band. The metaphor of the functioning of a symphony orchestra could of course be used, as could many other forms of organization. A symphony orchestra has the same need for the smooth interaction of its different sections, and also the same need for leadership. But it probably provides a less exact metaphor for a family than a jazz band does; for one thing it plays predetermined, composed pieces, rather than creating its own musical structure as it goes along. Few families are as ordered and predictable as a symphony orchestra.

Playing in a jazz band is predictable only up to a point; things are changing all the time, as the individual musicians, operating within the overall framework of the group, define their own melody lines and create their own mini-compositions while they play. Also, when the members of a band stay together over a period of years, they develop new skills, learn new musical tricks and techniques, and extend their repertoire. In the same way the behaviors, as well as the emotional and physical states, of the members of a family are, typically, changing all the time. Thus constant adjustments must be made by each individual in the family, rather as jazz musicians adjust their playing according to what the other members of the group are doing. The families we see are all faced with the task of making progress through developmental stages. . . . In the same way, jazz bands develop over the years; an excellent example is that of the Duke Ellington Orchestra. This was a small group, playing relatively simple pieces when it was formed in the mid-1920s. It developed impressively between that time and 1974, when Ellington died. The changes in Ellington's orchestra and music were sometimes gradual, sometimes quite rapid. The organization had its ups and downs, sometimes losing key musicians, but gaining new recruits too, people who enriched the orchestra with their talents. It also had to cope with the loss to the armed forces of several of its members during the war. This process of development, and the vicissitudes encountered along the way, bear many similarities to a family's long-term development. A well-functioning family may be likened to a well-practiced band, whose musicians have played together for a long time, communicate well with each other, respect each others' roles and professional skills, understand the different functions of the members of the group, and have common objectives. Few, if any, instructions need be given to the musicians while such a band is playing. On the other hand, in a poorly functioning band there may be struggles for power, disagreements about the tempos at which tunes should be played, uncertainty about who has the final decision about what should be done when members disagree, competing desires to share the limelight, and a general lack of order and organization. When such problems exist the collective effort of the band suffers.

Golden Retriever Metaphor

D. Corydon Hammond, Ph.D.
Salt Lake City, Utah

INDICATIONS

This is a brief metaphor with a paradoxical message for selective use with a spouse (or premarital individual) who tends to pursue an uncommitted partner excessively, almost begging him/her for love.

THE METAPHOR

I don't know if you have ever trained or watched the training of a golden retriever. If you throw something out for the dog to retrieve, sometimes it will run out to fetch it, but then refuse to bring it back to you. You can coax and call it, but it refuses to come to you. If, out of frustration, you finally start to go after it, it will run away. But if you *accept* its behavior, and start to walk away, it will often decide to come to you. And sometimes relationships with people operate that way too.

The Pygmalion Metaphor

D. Corydon Hammond, Ph.D.
Salt Lake City, Utah

INDICATIONS

This metaphor may be useful in working with an individual who is perfectionistic, has exceptionally high expectations of his marital partner or fiance, and tends to be intolerant of differences rather than respecting them.

SUGGESTIONS

According to mythology, there was once a very accomplished sculptor who lived on the island of Cyprus. His name was Pygmalion. Pygmalion was a man with such specific and definite *expectations* that he *couldn't be satisfied*. He simply could not find a woman to equal his concept of beauty. So he found some very beautiful, pure white marble, and in his studio he sculpted *the image in his mind*. He created in stone his conception of a beautiful, perfect woman. He continued to search and look everywhere for this perfect woman to match his sculpture. But he was *so critical* that *he found something wrong with every woman* he saw. No one could match the statue's beauty. He was so in love with this *perfect image* from his mind that he finally prayed to the goddess Aphrodite, pleading with her to help him find a woman who would equal and be as lovely as his sculpture. But, being a wise goddess, Aphrodite knew that *Pygmalion's expectations were too high* and uncompromising. She knew that *no woman could ever live up to all his expectations*. So it is said that Aphrodite breathed life into the statue, and Pygmalion named her Galatea, and married his own creation.

And I wonder if many of our problems in relationships are not caused by being like Pygmalion—wanting our partners to be perfect clones of ourselves and our expectations, rather than *accepting and respecting differences*.

HYPNOSIS WITH OBESITY AND EATING DISORDERS

INTRODUCTION

Weight Control

Obesity appears to result from an addiction that is as difficult to treat successfully as drug dependency and smoking—and probably much more so. Stunkard and McLaren-Hume (1959), for instance, discovered that only 5% of obese patients lose weight without relapsing, and Brownell (1982) pointed out that the cure rate for many forms of cancer is greater than the success rate with obesity.

There are numerous case studies and reports of outcomes with a clinical series of patients (e.g., Crasilneck & Hall, 1985; Stanton, 1975; Aja, 1977) who were treated through hypnosis for problems with obesity. There are very few studies (Wadden & Flaxman, 1981) that have compared hypnotic with nonhypnotic treatments, but these have generally found no difference between hypnotic and nonhypnotic treatment (Wadden & Anderton, 1982). Unfortunately, the hypnotic approaches used in these studies were unsophisticated and relied simply on suggestive hypnosis. We must await further research to determine if hypnosis truly has something to offer beyond behavioral, low-calorie diet, and multidimensional treatment approaches and, if so, to what types of patients.

It is my clinical belief and experience that, although this is one of our greatest treatment challenges, hypnosis is of clear value with some obesity patients. Since this is an addictive disorder, you will undoubtedly find it helpful to consult some of the suggestions that are used with smoking in Chapter 13. The suggestions that are presented in this chapter offer the finest ideas available for suggestive hypnotic work with weight control. You should keep in mind, however, that success in many cases may require that you use hypnotic strategies for unconscious exploration and for internal conflict resolution in connection with (or prior to) suggestive hypnotherapy. A simplistic approach to a complex addictive problem, whether in hypnosis or psychotherapy, will seldom be effective.

Anorexia and Bulimia

Studies of hypnotizability (Pettinati, Horne, & Staats, 1985) have now documented that patients with bulimia possess higher hypnotic capacity than other patients. The greater dissociative capacity may enable these patients, in fact, to more easily induce vomiting. On the other hand, there is tentative evidence (Pettinati et al., 1985) that patients with anorexia nervosa may be less hypnotically responsive than other patients. Naturally these studies reflect averages; we should not conclude that all patients with bulimia will be responsive to hypnosis or that anorexics cannot be helped with hypnosis. There are, in fact, case reports of successful outcomes from treating anorexic patients through hypnosis (Thakur, 1984).

The last section of this chapter will provide some illustrative suggestions for altering body image and perception, as well as for treating eating disorders through suggestive hypnosis.

HYPNOSIS WITH OBESITY

Examples of Suggestions for Weight Reduction

Sheryl C. Wilson, Ph.D., and Theodore X. Barber, Ph.D.
Framingham, Massachusetts, and Ashland, Massachusetts

INTRODUCTION

The following suggestions are illustrative of suggestions that we have used as one part of a broad based program for the treatment of overweight. The suggestions are presented to the client in the office and are simultaneously tape recorded. The client is then given the cassette tape and is asked to listen to the tape daily. These illustrative suggestions, which are presented below in a generalized form, are tailored specifically for each client. These illustrative suggestions are derived from (a) an application of our theoretical framework (see Barber, Spanos, & Chaves, 1974) to the treatment of eating disorders, (b) the many writings

pertaining to obesity in the literature of behavior modification, and (c) the suggestions used in the treatment of overweight developed by many clinicians, especially by William S. Kroger (see Kroger & Fezler, 1976), Herbert Mann (1973), and Harold B. Crasilneck and James A. Hall (1985).

The suggestions below are typically given after relaxation suggestions and positive suggestions for well-being. The positive suggestions typically conclude as follows.

POSITIVE SUGGESTIONS FOR WELL-BEING

Day by day, you will have increased feelings of confidence, self-assurance as you realize that you can and will reach your desired weight. You can and will become a new, slender, more attractive, more energetic, more vivacious you . . . the real you.

CHANGING SELF-DEFINITION

In the past you have come to think of yourself as heavy, overweight, and unattractive. It is important that you now change the way that you think of yourself — this is as important as changing your eating habits. Picture yourself weighing _____ pounds [patient's ideal weight], standing in front of a full-length mirror, having just come out of the shower. Imagine that you are standing in front of a full-length mirror. See your reflection in the mirror, slender, streamlined, and attractive. When you see yourself slender and shapely standing in front of the mirror, raise your right index finger. [Pause and wait for the patient to raise the index finger.] Now, let yourself feel how very light you feel without all that unnecessary weight. Tell yourself that you can and will look and feel like this because this is the real you, which has been hidden and imprisoned by excess weight and which *you* are *now determined* to set free.

EATING AS AN ART

Eating can be an art. You can learn and use some special techniques for eating as a gourmet. When you use these techniques, you will enjoy food more and obtain pleasures in eating that are greater than you ever imagined possible.

This is how you can enjoy food infinitely more than you ever have enjoyed it in the past. Eat only at mealtimes, and when you eat, focus all your attention on your food. Do not watch TV or read, and unless absolutely necessary, do not engage in conversation. Before you begin eating, spend a few moments observing your food. Notice the colors and textures. Inhale deeply and enjoy the aromas. When you are ready to begin eating, take only small bits of food, place only small portions on your fork or spoon, or take very small bites of those foods that you hold in your hand, such as sandwiches. Focus your complete attention on the food you are eating. Don't let your thoughts wander. Become aware of all the taste buds on your tongue and how they are stimulated by each tiny bit of food. Chew your food many times, and move your food around in your mouth slowly with your tongue before finally swallowing it. By doing this you will satisfy all the

taste buds on your tongue and obtain greater pleasure from your food, enjoying each mouthful maximumly.

Each time that you swallow, focus your attention on all of the feelings and sensations in your stomach. As you continue eating, let yourself become aware of an ever increasing feeling of fullness in your stomach, so that when you have finished your meal, you will feel comfortably full, and completely satisfied until your next meal.

As you are focusing on all the subtle tastes in each bite that you take, and on the feeling of fullness in your stomach each time that you swallow, tell yourself that time is slowing down and there's lots of time. Each second is stretching out . . . far, far out. Notice how as you eat, there's so much time between each bite you take. And as you chew your food, slowly, notice how you feel as if every second is a minute and there's so much time . . . as if everything is in slow motion. When at last you've finished your meal . . . you will feel comfortably full and satisfied . . . as if you have been eating for hours.

So, instead of giving up food, or trying not to think about food, you can become a gourmet by learning to enjoy food to the utmost. You can do this first by becoming aware of the colors, textures, and aromas of your food, and then by taking only small bits of your food into your mouth and totally focusing on your food and all the subtle flavors as you chew your food slowly and move it slowly about your mouth with your tongue, as if in slow motion.

IMPORTANCE OF HUNGER

In addition to totally focusing on your food and eating as a gourmet, there is yet another aspect which is an integral part of the enjoyment of food, and this important aspect is *hunger*. You simply cannot totally enjoy food if you are not *really hungry* when you begin to eat. If you are not really hungry, when you begin to eat, your hunger will be satisfied with the first few bites of food. After that, you will not be able to truly enjoy eating your meal.

Hunger is nature's signal to tell us that we should begin searching for food. Years ago, this signal was very effective. People would feel hungry and by the time they found food and prepared it, they were *really hungry* and consequently they could really enjoy their food without gaining weight. But today, with our modern convenience foods, we can eat as soon as we feel hungry, and so we become overweight. We have learned from our culture that hunger is a bad thing, that one should not be hungry, and if we become hungry between meals, we often snack on something to satisfy our hunger. Consequently, we seldom know what real hunger is. Hunger is a bad thing only when someone is starving to death and is unable to obtain food. Otherwise, in normal everyday life, hunger helps us to enjoy our food when we eat. Whenever you feel hungry and it's not time for you to eat, tell yourself two things. Tell yourself, "My body is now using up some of the excess fat, the excess weight, that I want to lose." And tell yourself, "When it *is* time for me to eat my meal, this feeling of hunger will help me to enjoy it to the utmost." "Starting today, whenever you feel hungry, along with the feeling of hunger, you can have a feeling of real joy, an inner feeling of deep satisfaction, because whenever you feel hungry, you will know that you are accomplishing your goal . . . you are losing weight.

FEELINGS OF LIGHTNESS

Hold your right arm straight out in front of you, parallel to the floor. Concentrate on your arm and listen to me.

Imagine that the arm is becoming lighter and lighter, that it's moving up and up. It feels as if it doesn't have any weight at all, and it's moving up and up, more and more. It's as light as a feather, it's weightless and rising in the air. It's lighter and lighter, rising and lifting more and more. It's lighter and lighter, and moving up and up. It doesn't have any weight at all and it's moving up and up, more and more. It's lighter and lighter, moving up, more and more, higher and higher.

Now relax your arm and let it float back down. Now concentrate on your body and listen to me. Imagine that your whole body is becoming lighter and lighter, your head, your shoulders, your trunk are becoming lighter and lighter. It feels as if they don't have any weight at all. And as if you're floating suspended in the air. Let yourself feel light as a feather. Feeling lighter and lighter, rising and floating, feeling lighter and lighter. It feels as if you don't have any weight at all, and you're just floating pleasantly in space. You feel lighter, and lighter, floating and drifting lighter and lighter. And as you let yourself feel lighter and lighter, and as if you're floating and drifting along, think of how pleasant it will feel when you feel feathery light after you lose all the unnecessary weight you wish to lose.

AGE REGRESSION

[If the overweight patient was not overweight as a child, you can use age regression to reinstate in the patient the feeling of not being overweight; that is, of being the ideal weight. Tell the patient the following:]

By directing your thinking, you can bring back the feelings you experienced when you were in elementary school. Think of time going back, going back to elementary school, and feel yourself becoming smaller and smaller. Let yourself feel your hands, small and tiny, and your legs and body, small and tiny. As you go back in time, feel yourself sitting at a big desk. Notice the floor beneath you. Feel how good and healthy you feel, without any unnecessary weight to carry around. Notice how your clothes fit you comfortably, without binding or pinching. Feel how comfortable it is to sit at a desk without any protruding stomach to get in your way. Feel the top of the desk now, and you may feel some marks on the desk top, or maybe a smooth, cool surface. [Continue with age regression suggestions from the Creative Imagination Scale.] Now just feel how healthy and energetic you feel without any excess weight. [15–30 second pause] Now tell yourself its all in your own mind and bring yourself back to the present.

LOOK TOWARD THE FUTURE [AGE PROGRESSION]

Picture yourself slender and attractive, standing on a scale. Notice that the dial on the scale is pointing to _____ pounds [the patient's desired weight]. Feel how joyous, ecstatic, and overwhelmingly happy you feel as you realize that you can and will achieve your goal. Notice how healthy, vibrant, and alive you feel as you realize the full potential of your mind.

Whenever you think of eating something you're not supposed to eat, or eating at a time other then mealtime, picture yourself healthy and trim, and tell yourself that you do not want to eat this food, or that you do not want to eat at this time, because you want to get rid of the unnecessary weight you have so that the real you (slender, shapely, attractive and healthy) may be set free. Then let yourself feel the true deep inner satisfaction, security, and confidence you have, knowing that you can and will control the amount of food that you eat and that in this way you will take control of your life.

Don't worry or be anxious about losing weight. Worry and anxiety will not help you lose weight. Relax and tell yourself that you are now on a road that will lead to a new you . . . to a more attractive, healthier, more energetic, and more alive you. Feel an overwhelming sense of confidence and security rising up within you as you realize that you have taken control, taken charge of your life, and you will no longer allow yourself to be the victim of each tempting, fattening food that comes along.

Hypnotic Suggestions for Weight Control

T. X. Barber, Ph.D.
Ashland, Massachusetts

[These suggestions are offered following an induction, for example, emphasizing relaxation and imagery of a beautiful place.]

EGO-STRENGTHENING SUGGESTIONS

Your mind can be at peace. Just at peace, relaxed, calm and so comfortable. Lots of time. So much time, just more and more time. so good. You're breathing now easily and gently. You can feel yourself relaxing more and more. Your mind becomes calm, like a lake without a ripple. So calm and more and more at ease. It feels as if all the cares are just rolling away. And it can feel so good, as if nothing matters, nothing at all. Just a feeling of "I don't care." It's so nice to be alive, to have peace of mind, to be calm and relaxed, feeling so good. You can feel more and more peaceful. Floating so peacefully, so at ease, so calm. Lots of time, more and more time, so much time. Lots of time. So at ease. Mind becoming more and more clear and open, like a clear, beautiful lake that reflects the sky without a ripple. Just so at ease, feeling so good. A little drowsy, but so relaxed and at peace. You can become more and more at ease, calm and relaxed. Lots of time; so much time. You can feel this way whenever you wish by telling yourself and hearing these words: "I can be calm and I can be relaxed. I can feel so good to be alive." You can hear these words whenever you wish. You can feel calm, relaxed and so good to be alive. Starting now, in any situation, whenever you feel tenseness, any bother, and especially when you sit down to eat, you'll be able to hear these words. You'll be able to say them to yourself, and hear them in the back of your mind. You'll be able to say them to yourself and hear them in the back of your mind. You can be calm, relaxed, so calm and relaxed. It feels so good to be alive. You can feel calm and relaxed in every aspect of your life, in every day, all the time with your eyes open, walking, moving, working, all the time. You can feel in the back of your mind, the same feeling, this good feeling as you hear these words and say them to yourself. "I can be calm and I can be relaxed. It feels so good to be alive."

Starting now, you can start a new life. Ready to live in a new way, to enjoy every aspect of everything around you. To be aware of all the beauty of the earth. The beauty and goodness of being alive, to feel so aware, that you are conscious and aware, and able to think, and feel, and smell, and taste, and love, and experience. To be fully alive more and more, every day, as you feel this calm, relaxed mind, enjoying more and more, starting now.

Starting now you'll be able to flow with everything around you so much better, more and more all the time. Just flowing, experiencing, not hung up, not bothered, just enjoying the calm, relaxed mind, able to face life with its problems in a relaxed way. Flowing with the problems. Doing your best to be able to move with them and not be bothered. In the same way, starting now, if you feel any feelings of hunger, be able to flow with it, feel good about it. Say, "That's perfectly okay. I flow with the hunger so my body uses up the stored up food. I don't need it now. I already have it. I have plenty of fats and sugars, and ice creams and cakes, and chocolates stored up, and now I'll use them up. I flow with hunger as my body uses up the stored up food."

SUGGESTIONS FOR SELF-TALK

And you'll find another interesting thing starting now. Whenever you eat, be able to eat slowly, with reverence, in a relaxed way. You'll feel there is lots of time. You'll hear these words. You'll say them to yourself in the back of your mind. "I can be calm, relaxed, feeling so good to be alive. And there's lots of time. So much time." Now eat with reverence, knowing how wonderful it is to be alive, to be able to enjoy and to feel, experience, and be conscious and aware. "I eat with reverence, starting now."

If you ever have any feeling that you want these high calorie, rich, fat foods for the next few days and few weeks, this too will drop away. In the meantime, whenever you think of candies, cakes, chocolates, ice cream, and other high calorie, rich, unnecessary foods, you'll hear me say, "STOP." You'll hear it quite loud, you'll hear it over and over. You'll hear me say, "STOP! You're free. You're no longer an addict. You no longer need these. You don't have

to have these high calorie, rich, fattening foods. You're free now. You're no longer an addict. You no longer have to have them." You'll hear me say, "STOP," loud and strong in the back of your mind. You'll hear me say, "STOP" over and over. And after awhile, you'll internalize it, and it will be your own thoughts saying, "STOP," and saying, "You're free now. You're no longer an addict. You don't need them. You're free."

SUGGESTIONS FOR EXERCISE AND ACTIVITY

You can start a new life, enjoying everything around you. Enjoying being alive, feeling good to be alive, with a calm, peaceful mind. Relaxed, at ease, living with reverence of being alive, and enjoying every aspect of it. Determining today that you can make your life as good as you possibly can, in every way. Being aware of how good it is to move, and exercise and be active. How good it is to be strong and healthy, and have a wonderful, healthy body, and a healthy, wonderful, calm mind. Starting today, it can feel so good when you exercise, when you move, when you walk, when you work. You're going to feel good to be able to control your body, and to feel how good it is to be strong and healthy. And you'll increase the amount of exercise, of effort, of walking, of moving. You'll notice that it is going to feel real good as you become more and more alive. You'll begin to enjoy everything more, starting now, as if you've just come to the earth, and everything is new and fresh and sparkling clean. You'll be able to look around you and see the colors and the beauty of the earth. You'll be able to hear the music of the earth and everything that's around you, and everything that's alive.

REPETITION OF EARLIER SUGGESTIONS

You'll enjoy people more and every aspect of your life more as you flow with all the problems of living. You'll take them as they come with calmness, peace, relaxation, calm, feeling good to be alive. Starting today you can start a new life. More calm, relaxed, feeling good to be alive. Eating with reverence and living with reverence. Enjoying every aspect of the food as you eat slowly, moderately, with preplanning and foresight, as a conscious, aware, very much alive, human being. Whenever you feel any need, even any thought of high calorie, addictive foods, like candies and cakes, you'll hear me say, "STOP. You're free. You don't need them any more." And you'll be able to flow with the feeling of hunger as your body uses up the stored up food, knowing that you have plenty of sugars and fats and carbohydrates, all stored up. You'll be able to flow with it and feel good about it, as you flow with all the problems of living. You'll be able to feel good about being alive, moving, walking, working, and exercising. You'll feel so good, starting now.

Let these thoughts now go deep in your mind. They'll be there to help you as the days go by. As they go deep into your mind now, you begin to alert yourself. You become quite alert, very alert, more and more alert, as you open your eyes.

Hypnotic Strategies for Managing Cravings

D. Corydon Hammond, Ph.D.
Salt Lake City, Utah

INDICATIONS

These suggestions and strategies are designed to be used with urges and cravings commonly encountered in addictions and habit disorders. They have proved useful in working with smoking, obesity, alcoholism, drug dependency, and sexual addiction. These procedures may also prove valuable with other compulsive urges.

SUGGESTIONS ABOUT CRAVINGS

INTRODUCTION.   The following suggestions, for purposes of illustration, focus on a problem with overeating. The suggestions seek to reframe cravings and to facilitate positive self-talk. Cognitive behavior modification approaches offer us valuable strategies for impulse control. Unfortunately, cognitive therapy usually concentrates on only consciously teaching patients coping statements to say to themselves. Posthypnotic suggestions, however, may assist in making positive self-talk a more automatic process.

SUGGESTIONS.   You may be one of those people, who have mistakenly believed that cravings and eating urges occur because of physical withdrawal, and because you *need* to eat. But that isn't true. Most of our urges or hunger pangs are triggered by unrelated things, like the time of day, certain people whom we're around, a type of feeling, or the kids coming home. Some people also mistakenly think that if they experience a hunger pang, that hypnosis has worn off or failed. That's not true either. Cravings or urges are simply conditioned responses, that seldom last very long. And when you don't indulge them, they get weaker and weaker, and easier to ignore.

So when you feel a craving or hunger pang, you can talk to yourself in your mind, reminding yourself that, in a minute or two it'll go away. Hunger pangs are always fairly brief and time-limited. Many people don't realize that, and fear that they won't stop unless you eat. But urges to eat pass fairly quickly. So, whenever you feel a hunger pang or craving, you can hear a voice in your mind, reminding you, "It will go away in a minute or two." When you feel a craving, it can be as if a voice comes into your mind, or from deep inside you, reminding you, "I don't have to eat right now. This urge will stop shortly. Just wait a short time, and it'll go away." And your unconscious mind can and will so govern your conscious mind, that you'll remember that, urges or cravings will pass, and you don't have to indulge them. So you can become absorbed in doing something, and almost before you realize it, the cravings are gone. And that's going to be a delight, discovering that eating urges and hunger pangs quickly pass, and you can put off responding to them. And in a few minutes, much to your surprise, you suddenly realize you're comfortable again.

SYMBOLIC IMAGERY TECHNIQUES

The patient may be taught to use symbolic imagery in self-hypnosis for decreasing cravings. The red balloon technique [found in the Chapter 13] is an illustration of this method. In this technique, patients imagine gradually putting their cravings into the gondola of a hot air or helium balloon and then releasing it. Other symbolic methods may include slaying the urge like an enemy or picturing the sensations inside themselves, and then modifying the imagery until the urge decreases. The interests of patients may be utilized in individualizing the imagery that is selected.

SUGGESTIONS FOR IMMEDIATELY IMAGINING NEGATIVE CONSEQUENCES

Posthypnotic suggestions may be given to the effect that when the patient thinks about eating fattening foods, he/she will immediately have images come to mind of horrible and negative consequences that could occur in the future. This may likewise be used with smokers, sexual addicts, and substance abusers. For instance, they may imagine losing their spouse and family, losing their job in disgrace, etc. This method is essentially a hypnotically reinforced version of the cognitive therapy technique called covert sensitization.

COGNITIVE REFRAMING SUGGESTIONS FOR INCREASING IMPULSE CONTROL

Rational-emotive therapy (RET) concepts that are usually discussed at a conscious level

may also be reinforced hypnotically, and recorded on self-hypnosis tapes for patients. Spiegel and Spiegel (1978) have also provided some valuable suggestions about choosing to ignore urges or cravings, focusing instead on respecting the body. These suggestions encourage detachment and externalization of the urge. The following suggestions for increasing impulse control illustrate the adaptation of RET concepts along with some of Spiegels' ideas.

ILLUSTRATIVE SUGGESTIONS.   Most people don't like to be told, "You can't," or "You shouldn't." And we don't like it much better when we say those things to ourselves. Have you ever noticed that when we tell ourselves, "I can't eat that," that we often secretly want to rebel? But you'll be pleased to find, that you can talk to yourself in other ways, that are much more helpful. Instead of fighting or trying to deny an urge to eat or drink, you can admit it. But then realize that cravings are very brief, and will pass within a couple of minutes. Instead of thinking, "I'm dying for *(e.g., a doughnut)*," you can detach yourself from the urge to eat, and say something like, "I'm feeling an urge to eat. I wonder what the situation or feeling is that's triggering this desire?" You will realize, "It will pass in a moment. This craving is just a signal to let me know that I need to cope with this situation."

It's interesting to realize how sometimes we deceive ourselves. Maybe you can recall saying to yourself, when you're trying not to eat between meals, "This is *too* hard!" Of course it's hard, but what makes it *too* hard? Naturally it's difficult to learn new habits. But you've done many difficult things before. [Pause] Urges to eat will pass fairly quickly. So the only thing that makes it "*too* hard," is our irrationally telling ourselves that it is. But as you reaffirm your commitment, to respect and protect your body, so that *(cite their individual motivations)*, you will find your eating behavior changing.

You know, maybe you can remember once when something was difficult, and you said or thought to yourself, "I can't stand it!" And then you went and ate something tempting. We've all thought that before. But this is an irrational self-deception, and you don't want to stand under any misunderstandings. Of course we can "stand it." And you can keep in mind that if you don't eat a certain food, or at a certain moment, you're not going to explode. When we choose not to eat something, we're not going to evaporate. For a few moments from time to time, it may not be entirely pleasant or easy, but we *can* stand it. There is no logical reason why life *should always* be *perfectly comfortable*, pleasant and easy, for *every* moment. You can handle a little brief discomfort. We all can. And when we master things that are not easy, we feel very good about ourselves. Remember, you don't *"have to"* have a certain food, at some particular moment. You don't *need* it. Sometimes you *want* it, but you also *want* to be slender, and you *want* to respect your body so that you can live. So you can admit that sometimes you want a fattening food, and that it's not always entirely easy, but you can *choose* not to eat it, and not to eat right now, or you can eat something that's much better for you.

TRANCE RATIFICATION

Methods of trance ratification (e.g., glove anesthesia, limb rigidity, ideomotor phenomenon) may be used to increase patient confidence and feelings of self-efficacy. "And just as your inner mind is so powerful that it can even control something as fundamental and basic as pain, so you now know that it can control any of your feelings and desires, and anything about your body. And because of the incredible power of your unconscious mind, your urges and cravings will increasingly come under your control, and will grow less and less. Just as it controlled pain in your hand, so your cravings and desires for *(food, cigarettes, drugs, sex)* will come under your control." In the case of glove anesthesia, suggestions may be given for the anesthesia to remain after the patient

awakens and opens his/her eyes. After a minute or two, trance may be reinduced and the anesthesia removed. Then comments may also be made (in addition to the suggestions above) about the "power of the unconscious mind to control your body and feelings at any time, even when you are not in hypnosis."

Weight Control

David Spiegel, M.D., and
Herbert Spiegel, M.D.
*Stanford, California, and
New York, New York*

The instruction for weight control is similar to that used for smoking control. Subjects are given the following three points:

(1) For my body, too much food is damaging (or disfiguring); (2) I need my body to live; (3) I owe my body respect and protection.

Subjects are instructed to recognize that most of the food they eat nourishes their body, but an excess damages it, and that they can use self-hypnosis to learn to eat with respect for their body—eating with respect involves giving the body only the food it needs for nourishment and not forcing it to take in food which is damaging or disfiguring to it. They are further taught to concentrate on the concept of eating like a gourmet—savoring every aspect of the food they take in, the color, the texture, temperature, the aroma, the flavor, the seasoning—so that they learn that they can actually eat less but enjoy eating more when they concentrate fully on the food they eat. This includes eating slowly and eating without distraction such as the television or a newspaper. Other elements include, of course, a balanced diet and exercise. The plan is, again, to help patients restructure their approach to food, putting the emphasis on eating with respect rather than a temporary state of deprivation. This approach is applied primarily to patients who are within 20% of their ideal body weight.

Suggestions for Patients with Obesity Problems

Joan Murray-Jobsis, Ph.D.
Chapel Hill, North Carolina

INDUCTION

In working with problems of overeating and obesity, I typically will use an induction that employs progressive relaxation and an arm levitation. During the arm levitation, I suggest to the patients that they are experiencing an altered sense of perception—that at one point in time they have perceived their arm or their hand as if it were under their control, but that during the levitation they can perceive the arm or hand in an altered sense, as if it were dissociated and separate, floating and apart.

SUGGESTIONS

SHIFTING PERCEPTIONS AND REFRAMING.   [I later refer back to this experience of altered perception and suggest to the patient:] Since we can alter perception about something as real and concrete as a physical part of our body, our hand and our arm, then it must be an even simpler matter still to imagine altering perceptions about things such as ideas and thoughts and feelings. And then we can begin to imagine how we might alter our perception about ourselves and our perceptions about food, our thoughts and feelings and behaviors about food. Perhaps beginning to see ourselves as a slender thinking, feeling, eating person.

And you can see yourself off in a distant future time with some sense of perspective and distance, and begin to notice that you do indeed have choices. You can choose to give care and respect to this physical being within which you reside. And with that sense of care and respect, you can indeed choose healthy, caring eating patterns.

[Remind the clients about their ability to alter perception and then suggest:] When most people think about dieting, one of the first things they think about immediately afterward is deprivation. They think they have to be deprived of things that they want and like. But, in actual fact, all we really need to do to become the slender person we wish to become is to help ourselves *shift our perceptions* of our satisfactions about food. And instead of perceiving the old, destructive foods as satisfying, we shift our perceptions into new healthy, constructive patterns of eating that are satisfying. And so we begin by helping ourselves forget to remember the old destructive eating patterns, the old destructive satisfactions.

SYMBOLIC IMAGERY OF A CLOUD.   We might imagine putting all the old destructive foods—the fatty, greasy foods, the fast foods, the snack foods, the junk food, the excessively sweet foods, the excessive amounts of food—putting all that destructive food on a cloud. Finding it somewhat heavy and distasteful, all that excessive, heavy, greasy, sweet mixed-up food. And then we give the cloud a push and watch it float off into the distance, until eventually it floats so far away that it becomes a mere speck on the horizon, and we can scarcely remember the taste or the aroma or even the look of some of those old destructive foods, forgetting to remember those old destructive foods. And beginning to discover in their place all the healthy, positive foods that we can eat and enjoy, even as we become slender—finding satisfaction in lean meat and poultry, and fish and fruits and vegetables—the satisfaction of being free of the greasy, fatty foods and the difficulty with digestion that follows, and the satisfaction in being free of the excessively sweet, sticky food, and the highs and lows of high/low blood sugar rebounds. Feeling free from the addiction of eating sweets, the kind of addictive eating where one taste never seemed to satisfy, and there was always a need for another, and then another and another. And when we begin to unhook, when we refrain from taking that first taste of sugary food, we suddenly, within a very few days, begin to discover a sense of freedom from that addictive, compulsive, mindless, empty eating, where food was passed into the mouth and body almost untasted. We find ourselves free to choose, sometimes to eat, sometimes not to eat, sometimes to eat moderately, discovering the satisfaction and being comfortably full, but never again having to be overstuffed and bloated. You'll begin to discover that we have the capacity to find more lasting, more constructive satisfactions in life.

CHOOSING LONG-TERM, NOT SHORT-TERM REWARDS. The fleeting moment of the taste of a piece of food in the mouth was never meant to be much of a satisfaction. It's far too fleeting. We discover that we can indeed find healthier, more lasting, more constructive satisfactions: in hobbies and entertainment, or satisfactions in work and accomplishment, satisfactions in friends and loved ones, or even in comfortable, relaxing and easy solitude. We can create for ourselves far more lasting, constructive satisfaction, discovering healthy ways of soothing ourselves, distracting ourselves.

HANDLING EMOTIONS AND EMOTIONAL NEEDS DIRECTLY. And then we discover that we have the capacity of mind to begin to deal with our feelings directly, no longer needing to submerge feelings in food. We discover that the mouth never ever solved the problems of the mind, but that we have the capacity with our mind to deal with our feelings directly, to allow ourselves to experience feelings: feelings of anger, or frustration, or sadness, or boredom, or even joy. Discovering that we have the capacity to experience our feelings, to feel them, to resolve them, and that we no longer need to try to distance feelings or submerge them in food. And learning that we can deal far more effectively with our feelings with our mind rather than our mouths. We discover that we no longer need the excuse of food in order to take a break, that we can simply choose to allow ourselves break time, down time, rest time. We no longer need the crutch of food for concentration or for socializing.

We begin to discriminate between the body's real hunger for food for energy and the emotional hungers where food was eaten even when we were full. We learn that we can deal with our emotional hungers with our mind rather than our mouth.

INCREASING ACTIVITY LEVEL. And then we can begin to visualize ourselves in the coming days of the coming week following healthy, moderate eating patterns and activity patterns. Remembering the capacity to shift perception, we visualize ourselves following healthy moderate patterns of eating and activity throughout the day. Perhaps increasing activity, enjoying physical activity even more. Remembering that the body has the capacity to alter metabolism, automatically helping us find a more moderate, healthier weight level as the body was designed to do—balancing body weight by balancing food intake and calorie consumption, and setting that balance point at a more moderate, healthier weight level as it was intended. Reminding our body to activate the metabolic process, even as it depresses and suppresses appetite, finding that balancing point at a level that allows a healthy, moderate body weight.

VISUALIZING THE GOAL. And then beginning to visualize ourselves at a still more future time at some more slender weight, and beginning to experience all of the feelings of that more slender body, feeling a smaller, but stronger body, healthier, more self-confident, attractive, a sense of pride and accomplishment, feeling all of the good feelings. And knowing that we are indeed already becoming that future slender self, and that all it takes is time and perseverance, simply following the moderate, healthy, satisfying patterns that we are already developing. And we are already becoming that future slender self.

Computer Metaphor for Obesity

Richard B. Garver, Ed.D.
San Antonio, Texas

It is explained to patients that in order for them to really lose weight and keep it off, it is necessary for them to change their eating behavior, and not just go on a diet. Therefore, I use a computer metaphor and suggest to patients that before I see them again, they are to make a behavioral list for me. It is to consist of behaviors that they feel are negative or inappropriate eating behaviors. This "program out" list may include the kinds of foods they eat, emotional eating, binge eating, any sort of inappropriate or negative eating behavior.

Then, they are to make a list of "program in" behaviors—all those behaviors associated with positive, desired and appropriate eating behaviors. When the patient returns, these lists are discussed. The patient or I may add some behaviors, and together we decide what is to be programmed out and programmed in. Then, in the hypnotic session, the unconscious mind is asked to specifically program out and program in behaviors that were selected. It is suggested that, "These will continue to be reinforced, and since the programmed in behaviors will be used more, they will get stronger; the programmed out behaviors will be used less and less, and they will grow weaker, until the new eating behavior program is dominant."

This can be reinforced with audiotapes, self-hypnosis and, of course, individual therapy sessions. This computer metaphor works nicely with most behavior modification, but particularly with habit disorders. I also find it useful to use unconscious ideomotor signaling, both to uncover problem areas and also to validate patients' positive self-reports. Then, they can see that not only consciously but also unconsciously they are accepting the suggestions and processing them in a positive way.

Suggestions for Decreasing Food Intake

Harold B. Crasilneck, Ph.D., and James A. Hall, M.D.
Dallas, Texas

INTRODUCTION

Crasilneck and Hall (1985) have each of their obesity patients medically screened and then they assess their emotional stability. Patients are asked to keep a daily diary of food intake, and unless there are medical contraindications, they are asked to not consume over 900 calories daily. Patients are further asked to walk one mile daily (other daily exercise may be substituted). (*Ed.*)

SUGGESTIONS

You simply will not be hungry. . . . The limited food intake can and will satisfy your hunger needs. . . . You will eat slowly and enjoy the food you are eating . . . you will eat slowly, masticate your food slowly . . . you will enjoy every mouthful. . . . You will have a full feeling in your stomach much sooner than usual . . . and as you are aware of this full feeling in your stomach much sooner than usual . . . you will then discontinue eating. . . . You will be relaxed and at ease, free from tension, tightness, stress, and strain, free from excessive hunger. . . . Because of the power of your unconscious mind you will want to lose this weight. . . . You can and you will tolerate this diet with minimal desire for food. . . . You will be proud of every pound you lose and you will perceive yourself as becoming thinner, less obese, and more like you've wanted to be. . . . You will not continue a habit pattern of overeating in which you have been taking certain risks concerning your physical and psychological health . . . you will want to lose weight and you can lose weight. . . . Regardless of circumstances you will maintain your diet without fanfare or resentment . . . you simply will be relaxed and at ease, free from hunger and tension, and tightness. . . . The weight loss will be consistent and permanent.

ILLUSTRATIVE SUGGESTIONS FOR USE IN SELF-HYPNOSIS

I am lying here with my eyes closed, ruling out all other thoughts and feelings. I am now concentrating on my right hand, which is resting comfortably on my abdomen. . . . I am concentrating on the breathing of my abdomen, on the sensitivity of the fingers in my right hand . . . to the texture of the material in my clothing . . . my hand rises and falls with every breath I take . . . and I am beginning to enter a much deeper state . . . I am relaxed, free from tension, free from psychological stress and strain . . . every muscle, every fiber in my body is relaxing . . . from my head, shoulders, arms, torso, legs, feet, toes. . . . My breathing is comfortable and with every breath I take I am entering a much deeper, a much more relaxed state. . . . Now my right leg feels heavy . . . as I feel it, normal sensation returns to my right leg . . . a deeper and sounder state . . . my right arm becomes tense and rigid like steel . . . one, two, three . . . steel . . . this passes. . . . As I slowly count from 1 to 10, which I now start doing, I will progressively enter into the deepest state possible so that I can accept into my unconscious mind and put into effect with my unconscious mind these suggestions — food intake is no longer of great importance to me. . . . I will no longer overeat as I once did, in a hurried, forceful fashion. . . . I will eat extremely slowly, frequently pausing while I eat, respecting my body rather than gorging it with food . . . the loss of weight will have much more meaning to me than being grossly obese . . . and I am never going to be fat again! . . . I am going to respect my body, and I will not be excessively hungry. . . . I will enjoy eating, but I will not exceed the caloric count prescribed for me. . . . I am so very relaxed, and I am going to know a peace of mind in achieving this weight loss. . . . This weight loss will be permanent. . . . I will maintain my diet in my home and social situations under any conditions because I want to. . . . Now as I slowly count from ten to one I am slowly going to be awakened. . . . I am going to be refreshed, my thoughts will not be obsessed with food or food intake . . . but instead, I will be pleased with every pound that I lose. . . . I am now counting slowly, I am awakening, and I am fully awake at the count of one.

Historic Landmark Technique for Treating Obesity

William C. Wester, II, Ed.D.
Cincinnati, Ohio

INTRODUCTION

This is a circular hypnotic technique whereby the patient begins a journey at a certain point and then ends the journey at the same point. This technique can be used following a basic progressive relaxation technique, and a variety of direct and indirect suggestions can be given during the patient's imagined journey. The technique can be altered to fit the specific nature of the patient's problem. I will use the problem of obesity as an example of this treatment procedure. The brief example below can be embellished in any way. The procedure can be modified to be consistent with any hypnotic or therapeutic style. A recording of this procedure can be completed during the session and given to the patient to be played a minimum of once every other day until the next visit.

SUGGESTIONS

And now, I would like you to see yourself standing at the edge of a beautiful field. It's a gorgeous day, just the way you would like it to be. And even the field itself can be any kind of field you might wish it to be. A field of beautiful flowers, or perhaps a wheat field, with the wheat gently flowing with the breeze. Cutting across the field there is a path; it's very safe and secure and I'm going to ask you to walk along the path as I'm talking to you and simply enjoy this beautiful day. As you walk along the path, you can find yourself relaxing more deeply, thoroughly, and completely — feeling so good and so comfortable and so relaxed.

On the other side of the field you will notice that the path just continues across a meadow. Stay on the path, enjoying a gorgeous day, and just ahead you're going to come to a footbridge. Now there's just a couple of steps onto the footbridge; there's a bench built into the bridge where perhaps you would like to stop a moment and rest and relax even more completely. Beneath the bridge there's a brook. The water is crystal clear, it's quite shallow; you may even be able to hear the water trickling over the rocks. It's just so relaxing and so comfortable. Just enjoy that comfort and relaxation for a moment and then continue off the other side of the footbridge, staying on the path.

You'll notice up ahead that there is a marvelous old building, like an old castle. Along the side of the path there's a marker which indicates that this is a historical landmark, and visitors are welcome at all times. Stay on the path now, and as you approach the old building, there's a caretaker and the caretaker's spouse out working in the grounds, and you are really impressed. The grounds are just magnificent! Everything is hedged and weeded and pruned and mulched—just right. All of the various flowers and plantings are just beautiful. It's obvious to you that here are two people who take great pride in what they do, and have worked very hard to accomplish a goal important to them. You might even want to speak to them and acknowledge what a great job they have done. They indicate to you that the front door to this old building—this old castle—is left propped open, so that visitors can step inside and really enjoy the splendor of this magnificent, strong and sturdy structure. As you step inside the entrance way, you find yourself standing in a light source; it's not direct sunlight, but simply a light source and a very special feeling comes over your body.

There's a point in time when we really feel good, comfortable and totally relaxed. Some people describe it as a glow—that point in our life when things seem to be going quite well and we really feel good. Just allow that special feeling to come over your body, a feeling of deep comfort and deep relaxation. As you experience this feeling, recognize the degree to which your subconscious mind is going to allow you to maintain extremely high motivation, to

continue to control your eating habits and behaviors, and to develop new eating habits and behaviors appropriate to your goal. Each day, allowing you to feel and be more and more in control—in control, comfortable, confident, knowing what you're doing is a good and healthy and appropriate thing for you. Because you're going to be so much in control, you're going to feel relaxed, calm, less stressed, less tense, less anxious, less nervous, no need to overeat or to eat inappropriate foods. You're in charge and you're in control. And even when sitting down at a regular meal, you're going to find that your subconscious mind gives you a nice feeling of fullness much sooner than before, allowing you to eat appropriately and consistent with your goal. [Any other specific motivations provided by the patient during the prehypnotic interview can also be included at this time.]

Now take all of that strength, motivation, and control with you. Your subconscious mind is a very powerful part of you. Take all of that with you now and come back outside of the old castle, say goodbye to the caretaker and the caretaker's spouse; and begin walking back down along the path, back down to the footbridge, and as you come to the footbridge, I'd like you to pause for a moment, look down into the water, and see a reflection of yourself at your desired weight; see yourself right there, the way you would like to look and feel. Notice perhaps even what you're wearing and how good you feel about yourself. Just allow that image to be very clear and helpful to you, because each time that you even think about overeating, or eating inappropriate foods, that image is just going to pop into your mind, and continue to give you that added strength, control and motivation needed to keep those eating habits and behaviors consistent with your goal.

Take that image now and all of those feelings that you have with you from the old castle, and come off the other side of the footbridge and begin to walk back across the meadow, feeling so good and so comfortable, and so much in control and really looking forward to each pound that you lose, getting closer and closer to your goal. And now as you reach the edge of the field, I'm just going to count from one to five, and when I reach the number five, your eyes will open and you will be completely, completely alert; feeling good, feeling refreshed, completely, completely alert. One . . . two . . . a little more alert now, 3 . . . really feeling that control, and knowing that you're in charge of your eating habits and behaviors; four . . . a little more alert, almost completely alert now, and five . . . opening your eyes completely, completely alert.

Hypnosis in Weight Control

Herbert Mann, M.D.
San Jose, California

WEIGHT CONTROL SUGGESTIONS

As you relax comfortably, I am going to offer ideas and suggestions that will be most helpful in attaining deeper levels of relaxation and in controlling your desire for fattening food. It isn't really necessary for you to pay close attention to what I have to say. You may involve yourself in your own thoughts, your own body feelings, your own sensations. In its unique way, your subconscious mind listens and responds to new learnings and experiences. Your eyes are growing heavier, and a delightful feeling of deep relaxation is spreading through the muscles of your face, your neck, shoulders, and downward through your chest, back, abdomen, thighs, and legs.

Your attempts in the past to starve yourself into reducing body weight developed tension, anxiety, and frustration. That is all over. Now you have the wonderful opportunity to associate relaxation of body and mind with a relaxed attitude toward eating. You find yourself comfortably choosing only those foods that are good for you, and passing up the foods that are fattening. Each passing day you gain more and more confidence in your ability to control your food intake.

RATIFICATION THROUGH LEVITATION.   At this time I would like you to focus attention on feelings in your left hand. Imagine that colored balloons are tied to the fingers of your left hand and that several balloons are tied to your left wrist. Feel the lightness in your fingers and wrist as the balloons in their upward flight support the weight of your fingers and hand. As your hand feels lighter and lighter and you go more deeply relaxed, your subconscious mind will readily accept ideas for making your whole body lighter.

EATING IS AN ART.   Reduction of body weight can be accomplished by learning to thoroughly enjoy those foods that do not contribute to the formation of body fat while eliminating sweets and starches. Your enjoyment of those foods that are good for you can be markedly enhanced. To help you appreciate the pleasure in eating properly, I would like you to picture in your mind's eye a wine taster. You relax more deeply as your hand continues to rise toward your face and the image of a wine taster appears. He/she spends a little time holding a glass of wine toward the light and fully appreciates the beautiful color and clarity of the beverage. He/she permits himself the luxury of enjoying the delicate aroma and bouquet. Only then does he allow a few drops of the liquid to touch his lips and tongue, and to bring into play the sensitive taste buds. Taking full advantage of the organs of sight, smell, taste, he derives the most exquisite gustatory pleasure.

Eating is an art. You are learning to apply techniques that give you more satisfaction and enjoyment in eating than you have ever experienced in the past. You automatically find yourself eating slowly, appreciating the color and fragrance of those foods that are good for you. You take small bites of food and devote time to appreciate patterns of eating, and textures. As you establish new and delightful patterns of eating, you enjoy a feeling of release from anxiety and frustration, a feeling of increased confidence in your ability to achieve your goal.

As you continue to relax more deeply and comfortably, I will touch your left hand and lower it to your lap. The lightness disappears and you go deeper into trance and feel more confident in your ability to carry out instructions and recommendations. As time goes on you will find yourself eating only those foods that are good for you and that will permit your body to lose excess weight. [Specific foods that are acceptable and prohibited may be indicated.]

The change in your eating habits results in loss of excess weight, a more attractive figure, and increased pep and energy. You develop confidence in your ability to be a dynamic and effective person. Your subconscious mind has a tremendous capacity for learning, and as you continue to relax more deeply your new learnings automatically become an integral part of your total personality. You respond to ideas and suggestions that are most helpful in establishing a new point of view, a new orientation, a new way of life.

[As the patient's ability to operate within the hypnotic situation increases, self-hypnosis is used to reinforce therapeutic suggestions in daily home sessions. In a self-induced trance, the patient reviews ideas and suggestions that have been imprinted on the subconscious. By actively participating in the weight reduction program, patients learn to depend less on the therapist and more on their innate ego-strengthening capability.]

Your success in learning to relax and to experience various hypnotic phenomena may now be utilized in another learning process. Just as your subconscious mind learned to experience various sensations and activities, it can learn to control the pleasurable activity of eating. While you continue to relax more and more deeply and comfortably, I am going to offer you ideas that your subconscious mind can readily accept. In that way you will automatically change your eating habits so that you can comfortably lose excess weight, then continue through life eating pleasurably and sensibly while maintaining normal weight. You can accomplish this by eating food that is good for your body.

SAVORING FOOD LIKE A COFFEE TASTER.   You can learn to enjoy eating while making appropriate changes in eating habits that will result in weight loss. To help you do this, I would like you to picture in your mind a professional coffee taster raising a cup of coffee and spending a little time analyzing the reflections of light on the surface of the coffee, the color and clarity of the coffee. When you see this clearly, let me know by nodding the head. [Note: Raising a finger may be used in lieu of nodding the head.] Then the taster slowly raises the cup and spends a few moments enjoying the delicate aroma of the coffee. As you develop this image, you go into a deeper, delightful trance state, and as you go deeper and deeper relaxed you notice the coffee taster taking a sip of the beverage, bringing into play the sensitive organs of taste. By taking advantage of the organs of sight, smell, and taste, the coffee taster derives the utmost gratification from a small quantity of coffee. As you continue to go into a deeper, enjoyable trance state, it might be interesting for you to compare the coffee taster's unhurried appreciation of a small amount of coffee with another person who quickly gulps a whole cup of coffee without taking time to appreciate all the subtleties of good eating, his taste buds so overwhelmed by a large quantity of coffee rapidly consumed that he cannot appreciate the delicate flavor.

You can develop the habits of a professional taster taking time to concentrate on color, aroma, flavor, enjoying eating slowly, limiting yourself to small bites of food and developing a feeling of comfortable fullness after eating relatively small portions of food. You will pass up fattening foods because they become associated in your mind with being overweight. Eating properly is associated with pleasurable feelings, feelings of lightness, attractiveness and good health. As you continue to develop good eating habits, you will take pleasure in increasing physical activity and exercise. Eating properly helps develop a feeling of physical well-being and attractiveness. It diminishes mental and muscle fatigue so that you find yourself more alert and inclined to participate in that form of exercise and recreation that best fits your particular needs.

Weight Control Suggestions

Harry E. Stanton, Ph.D.
Hobart, Tasmania, Australia

[Following induction, deepening, and ego-strengthening suggestions:] And now I want you to have a clear mental image in your mind, of yourself standing on the scales and the scales registering the weight you wish to be. See this very, very clearly for this is the weight you will be. See yourself looking the way you would like to look with the weight off those parts of the body you want the weight to be off. See this very, very vividly and summon this image into your mind many times during the day; particularly just after waking in the morning and before going to sleep at night, also have it vividly in your mind before eating meals. And this is the way you will look, and this is the weight you will be. As you believe this, so it will be. When you have attained this weight, you will be able to maintain it, you will find yourself eating just enough to maintain your weight at the weight you would like to be. Until you *do* attain this weight you will find you have less, and less desire to eat between meals. In fact, very, very soon, you will have no desire at all, to eat between meals. You simply will not want to. Also you will find you will be content with smaller meals. There will be no sense of unhappiness or dissatisfaction, smaller meals will be quite satisfactory to you, and you will have no desire to eat large meals. Also you will have less, and less desire for high calorie, rich, unhealthy foods. Day by day, your desire for such foods will become less and less, until very, very soon, you will have no desire at all for rich, high calorie, unhealthy foods. Instead, day by day, you will desire low calorie, healthy foods, and these will replace the high calorie foods, the rich foods, you have eaten in the past. As you lose weight and approach closer and closer to the weight you wish to be, you will find yourself growing stronger and stronger, healthier and healthier. Your resistance to illness and disease will increase, day by day. With less weight you will feel better and better, and

your health will become better and better. Remember, too, that your own suggestions will now be just as effective as the suggestions I give you, either personally or by tape.

Miscellaneous Suggestions for Weight Control

William S. Kroger, M.D., and
William D. Fezler, Ph.D.
*Palm Springs, California, and
Beverly Hills, California*

EAT LIKE A GOURMET.   If you really wish to lose weight, you will roll the food from the front of the tongue to the back of the tongue and from side to side in order to obtain the last ounce of satisfaction and the "most mileage" out of each morsel and each drop that you eat. By doing this you will more readily satisfy the thousands of taste cells that are located all over your tongue (there is an appetite center located in the hypothalamus) and, as a result, less food will be required and your caloric intake will be immeasurably curtailed.

THINK THIN.   Second, you will "think thin"; that is, you will keep an image uppermost in your mind of how you once looked when you were thin. Perhaps you have a picture of yourself when you weighed less. If so, place this in a prominent position so that you will be continually reminded of the way you once looked. There is considerable basis for this suggestion. You undoubtedly are aware that, if a woman imagines or thinks that she is pregnant, her body will develop the contour of a pregnant woman; her breasts will enlarge and she may, in many instances, stop menstruating. Also, you may have at one time experienced a great deal of inner turmoil and lost weight in spite of the fact that you ate excessively. Cannot a frustrated lover also "pine away" for the beloved?

AVERSIVE CONDITIONING.   Third, you might like to think of the most horrible, nauseating, and repugnant smell that you have ever experienced. Perhaps it might be the vile odor of rotten eggs. In the future, whenever you desire to eat something that is not on your diet, you will immediately associate this disagreeable smell with it. Also, you might like to think of the most awful and disgusting taste that you may have had in the past. This, too, can be linked with fattening foods even when you merely think of them.

MOTIVATING YOURSELF.   Finally, for this session, remember that you cannot will yourself of lose weight. The harder you try, the less chance you will have to accomplish your aims. So relax— don't press. The next suggestion is to motivate you. Would you mind purchasing the most beautiful dress that you can afford? Hang it up in your bedroom where you can see it every morning and imagine yourself getting into it within a relatively short time. You can speculate how soon this will be. Now this is important! The dress you buy should be at least one or two sizes too small for you.

Further Suggestions for Management of Obesity

William S. Kroger, M.D.
Palm Springs, California

SUGGESTIONS FOR GLOVE ANESTHESIA

"Glove anesthesia" is another valuable dynamism for appetite control. It is extremely useful for minimizing hunger contractions. The patient places the hand "made numb" over the epigastrium. This technique has been employed in dentistry, for amelioration of pain in cancer, with surgical and obstetrical patients. . . . The technique for glove anesthesia is as follows:

Imagine that your right or left hand is in a pitcher, jug or bowl of ice water. You can practically feel the imaginary ice cubes bumping your hand. At first you will notice a numb, tingling sensation in the fingertips. As you imagine your hand in that cold, chilling ice water, the colder and more numb your fingers will become. So, if you wish to develop this numbness in your hand, just lift it toward the side of your face. If you wish to increase the numbness, suggest to yourself that with each motion of your hand toward your face it will get more numb and more wooden-like. [At this point the hand continues to move upward.] After each movement, pause to give your hand a chance to feel the suggestions of numbness. [The hand continues to move a short distance of an inch or two at a time, and to move steadily toward the side of the face.] If you wish more numbness of the hand, notice that the closer it approaches your cheek the more numb it will get. And when it finally reaches your cheek, just let the palm of your hand rest lightly against your cheek. Then allow the numbness to be transferred from your palm to the side of your cheek. After you are certain that your cheek has become very numb, only then will your hand drop to your side, and it will feel normal. However, the side of your face will feel just as if a dentist had injected novocaine into your gums. Remember how leathery and stiff one side of your face feels following an injection?

Such suggestions make full use of subtle techniques leaving the patient no alternative but to make the side of his face feel completely "anesthetized." After feeling the glove anesthesia he is convinced that the numbness of the cheek is genuine. This suggestion is given as follows:

Whenever you feel the onset of hunger, you can stop it by placing the anesthetized hand over the pit of your stomach to control the hunger pangs.

USING IMAGINATION

. . ."Think thin," that is, keep an image uppermost in your mind of how you once looked when your weight was normal. Pick your own good points (smile, eyes, hands, hair, complexion, etc.) and concentrate on how these will be enhanced by weight loss. Also, place a picture of yourself when you weighed less in a prominent position so it continually reminds you of the way you once looked.

Erickson's Suggestions with Obesity

Milton H. Erickson, M.D.

[With a severely obese young woman who already described herself as a "fat slob":] I really don't think you know how unpleasant your fatness is to you . . . so tonight when you go to bed, first get in the nude and stand in front of a full-length mirror and really see how much you dislike all that fat you have. And if you think hard enough and look through that layer of blubber that you've got wrapped around you, you will see a very pretty feminine figure, but it is buried rather deeply. And what do you think you ought to do to get that figure excavated?

THOROUGHLY ENJOY A SMALL PORTION

And I'd like you to enjoy it thoroughly and well. You know, it's just as easy to enjoy a small portion as it is a large portion. In fact, those . . . who eat a small portion will enjoy a small portion much more than you would a large portion. And you really will, because you won't even have to feel guilty about that small portion. You'll be perfectly delighted with it.

FAIL-SAFE QUESTIONS UTILIZING THE UNCONSCIOUS

And what will be the effective means of losing weight? Will it be because you simply forget to eat and have little patience with heavy meals because they prevent you from doing more interesting things? Will certain foods that put on weight no longer appeal to you for whatever reasons? Will you discover the enjoyment of new foods and new ways of preparing them and eating so that you'll be surprised that you did lose weight because you really didn't miss anything?

Negative Accentuation: Vivifying the Negative During Trance

M. Erik Wright, M.D., Ph.D.

INDICATIONS AND CONTRAINDICATIONS

Indications and guidelines concerning the use of aversive, negative hypnotic techniques are discussed to some degree by Dr. Wright below, but a few remarks seem appropriate. It is not currently fashionable to use aversive or negative hypnotic methods. But when more positive techniques do not produce success, and when the patient is very hypnotically talented and capable of experiencing ideosensory phenomena, aversion suggestions may potentially contribute to favorable outcomes. Aversive methods also seem to me to be indicated when they are congruent with the patient's expectations for therapy. Some patients want, expect and even request this type of suggestion. It seems reasonable in such instances to meet the patient's expectations and preferences by providing such suggestions, albeit preferably within the context of many other positively framed suggestions. Dr. Wright's approach to accentuating the negative provides a particularly balanced and thoughtful model for us. Dr. Stock's metaphor that follows also illustrates a subtle method for giving aversive suggestions. (*Ed.*)

INTRODUCTION

The client is asked to prepare a list of personally negative consequences of overeating and to rank them in order of increasing negative value. . . . Even though the client is the person who prepares the list of negative effects and chooses the one(s) to be initially elaborated, it remains prudent for the therapist to use either the Chevruel pendulum or the finger signaling technique to check whether accentuating the negative in fantasy would be acceptable to the client. An affirmative response confirms the client's readiness to accept the heightened stress that may be associated with negative accentuation during hypnotic trance. It also implies that the client recognizes the purpose of negative accentuation in facilitating better self-management of eating.

The particular client in the following demonstration was a 45-year-old male who had drawn up a list of negative consequences of overeating that began with a double chin and ended with a very deep concern about high blood pressure and diabetes, both of which were quite frequent on his father's side of the family. He had always had a vigorous appetite, but his weight problem had become aggravated since he had become sales manager of an insurance firm, a position that required frequent luncheon and dinner meetings with clients. He had gained 25 pounds in the past nine months, reaching his present weight of 230 pounds. There was a classical history of crash diets and rapid regaining of weight, usually to a point greater than the preceding figure. This time he had made a commitment to his family to stay with the program under the supervision of his internist and psychotherapist. His only constraint was that no appetite-suppressing medication be used.

SUGGESTIONS

Therapist: You indicated with the Chevruel pendulum that you were ready to give full emphasis to these feelings while in trance so that the inner part of your mind could get the message to use them to become a balanced eater.

Please raise your right hand in front of you with the palm facing away, and focus upon your fingers as you have done several times before. Let the feelings of heaviness come into your hand as your eyes maintain their fixed focus. . . . As you feel your hand moving down, let the heaviness in your eyes increase until they want to close . . . good . . . let them close and let your arm come to rest in your

lap . . . letting go . . . your whole being relaxed . . . drifting . . . drifting . . . drifting to an eating situation where you have an inexhaustible supply of food in front of you. . . . Signal with your right index finger when that image or that idea is clear to you. . . .

Okay . . . [Dissociation is suggested:] I'm going to ask you to describe the scene, and as you talk you become more and more involved in the scene until part of you feels like it is right there in the scene and the main part remains right here with me watching what is happening. . . .

Client: I see myself in the restaurant. . . . There is a huge smorgasbord table spread out in front of me piled high with wonderful food. . . . It all looks and smells so appetizing. . . .

T: Imagine yourself with an unlimited appetite . . . begin feeding yourself from the heaping plates . . . and imagine that it is like time-lapse photography. . . . As the food goes into you . . . it is processed almost immediately . . . and you can see the effects of the food . . . as if weeks and weeks of eating were being condensed into minutes. . . .

C: I can taste the food on the back of my tongue and just feel the swallowing. . . . The skin under my chin is filling out. . . . It seems to be getting larger and fuller until my chin seems to blend into this under-skin. . . . I can hardly see the neck line. . . . It looks almost like a frog's neck, and my head is forced upward a way, by the mass under my chin . . . that's really weird-looking. . . .

T: Keep on with your eating. . . . See where your image leads you as you continue eating. . . .

C: Now I see myself beginning to get larger around my chest and middle. . . . A funny thing is happening . . . now I can see myself only from the back, and I am no longer sitting on a chair but on a bench, and my back end is beginning to drape over it. . . . I see the midseam in the back of my jacket pulling apart . . . as though it might give way any moment. . . . Now it shifts again and I am looking at the front of me . . . I can hardly recognize myself. . . . My eyes are deep in my head with big rolls of cheek. . . .

T: How are you feeling?

C: Terrible . . . yet I still see myself eating . . . and getting more and more bloated . . . hardly a large enough opening in my face for the food to be put in. . . . I don't know if I could stand up on my legs if I tried. . . .

T: Intensify the image . . . [Client comanagement is suggested:] Bring it to the point where it will be most helpful to you in managing your daily eating program. . . .

C: I'm beginning to get a sickish feeling inside. . . . That's hardly human. . . . I can't seem to recognize myself. . . . It stopped feeding itself. . . .

T: Good . . . make use of this image when your inner mind needs it to help you become a balanced eater. . . . Now condense future time. . . . See that image begin to restore itself as the eating becomes a balanced eating. . . . When the figure of yourself is back to where it pleases you . . . signal with your right index finger . . . Count yourself back to the here and now . . .

Aversive Metaphor for Chocolate Eaters

Marvin Stock, M.D.
Toronto, Ontario, Canada

When you mentioned your *problem* with chocolate, I told you how I understand that, and that I will tell you of my personal experience. Years ago, when I was a young adult in medical school, I suffered from acne. The dermatologist repeatedly informed me that my adolescent acne was maintained, actually *made worse*, by *the chocolate* I regularly consumed. Despite the *disfiguring* acne, I found it impossible to stop. The years went by. At last I was at the stage where I could work with actual patients in the outpatient department. I found the O.P.D. filled with fascinating and *challenging*

problems, each one the equivalent of a detective story.

One day my teacher and I were presented with an unusual problem. He was a young man in white coveralls and a chef's hat. Now one of the first things that was required of us medical students, as part of our learning, was to guess the patient's age and occupation, the problem, and then the solution. Looking at the young patient, the most obvious things about him were the numerous *green and yellow stains* on his coverall. Naturally I first considered which occupations would produce stains of that sort. However, it turned out that he worked at Laura Secord, with chocolate, and none of the fillings used were that color. As is the custom, we asked him why he had presented himself at the O.P. department, and he said, "Look." He removed his chef's hat and the coveralls and stood there in his underwear. He was *covered* with large *boils*, each *boil* like a *volcano erupting*, *pus*, *yellow* in some areas, *green* in other areas. It had *seeped through* the material of the uniform and produced the green and yellow stains. By the time we had established the connection between the pus stains on his garment and the *erupting boils*, the aroma of *putrefaction* had reached us, the typical *revolting smell of pus* from BACILLUS PYOCYANEUS.

My teacher explained this was quite common among chocolate workers. A light *dusting* of sugar provides just the right *condition* for *bacteria* and *mold to grow*. With my *vivid imagination* I could see hordes of chocolate *workers covered* with all kinds of *vile skin lesions*. My *stomach heaved* the *premonitory acid* to the *back* of the *mouth that precedes vomiting*. I quickly made up my mind to *renounce chocolate* and *felt better*. Needless to say, my acne cleared rapidly after that. That was a *worthwhile* experience.

Later in medical school, in the course on nutrition, we were given the most advanced and detailed analysis of foods, and in the breakdown of chocolate, it turns out there is always *5%-10% of unrecognizable organic material*. Now what could that mean?

Our professor informed us that this represents *the remains of insects*, and *rodent droppings* that could not be washed off the cocoa bean during manufacturing. Furthermore, during the manufacturing process, similar *unwanted animal life falls into the vats* all the time. I was so glad that I had rejected chocolate before.

Now I suggest when *you look at chocolate*, you do what I have done, you *imagine* for a moment that you have *microscopic vision* and see those bits and *pieces, up to 10%, dispersed through the chocolate*. When you *do* so effectively, just be prepared for a *pleasant surprise*.

Symbolic Imagery: The Dial Box Shrinking Technique

Mark S. Carich, Ph.D.
Collinsville, Illinois

INTRODUCTION AND INDICATIONS

This technique has the hypnotized client imagine a dial with different degrees or levels that indicate reduction of the specified behavior. For example, the client may imagine a dial ranging in intensity from 0 to 10. This method may be beneficial in "shrinking" a symptom, whether it is a "need" or desire, pain, a cognitive belief or perception, or a behavior. [Another illustration of this type of method is Hammond's master control room technique in Chapter 11.]

THE TECHNIQUE

The client is instructed to imagine or visualize a dial that controls the intensity of the symptom. It is important to tailor the metaphor to the sensory modalities that the client uses. For example, if the client is capable of imagining sounds, it is important to emphasize the clicks when turning down the dial. The actual details of the dial or control box may be left to the client's imagination and liking.

SUGGESTIVE WORDING.   And now visualize a box with a dial on it. Do you see the dial box? [Obtain verbal or nonverbal confirmation.] That's it, and now visualize the dial, and notice the different degrees of intensity, perhaps ranging from 1 to 10. [Obtain verbal or nonverbal confirmation.] Become aware of the level of *[e.g., pain, desire, problematic behavior]*. What level do you feel it on a scale of 1 to 10? [Alternatively: "What level is this currently on the dial box?"] Now allow yourself to turn it down. [Pause] That's it, visualize yourself turning the sensation down to a comfortable level. [Obtain input about the process.] What are you feeling? Is it comfortable? [If a "no" answer is obtained, have the client explore the symptom and decide its various attributes, characteristics, sensation, etc.] And notice how easy it is to turn the dial. Notice how easy it is to control *things*. [Have the client practice modifying the intensity of the symptom. This procedure may also be tape recorded for use in self-hypnosis. With each practice session the client may be able to decrease the intensity toward a manageable level or reinforce symptomatic control.]

The Attic of the Past

Eleanor S. Field, Ph.D.
Tarzana, California

INDICATIONS

This technique may be used with habit disorders such as obesity or smoking. Instead of "trading down" to another kind of oral habit or addiction, the patient is encouraged to "trade up" instead by ascending the stairs to the attic of the past.

SUGGESTIONS

And with each step you climb toward the attic, at the same time you go deeper and deeper relaxed. One, going up toward the attic of the past. Two. [Etc.]. At five you reach the landing and turn as the stairs take you in another direction. Six, smelling the pleasant, familiar smell of the cedar. Seven, experiencing the warmth of the air. Eight. Nine. Ten. As you open the doors to the attic, the rafters appear to reach in every direction, and the rickety old floor cracks beneath your feet.

Before your eyes are several large old chests and several large cartons. You might wonder what they contain. You might like to take a moment now and rummage through one of the old chests and come upon a past experience of your life that was particularly pleasant, and joyful, perhaps even a peak experience for you. When you come upon that experience, lift a finger on either hand that indicates "yes" for you. Now, really reexperience that situation in every way, see it in every detail, what you look like, the colors you are wearing, the surrounding environment. Feel the joyous and pleasant feelings associated with that experience, and any other feelings that are a part of that time of your life. Hear the sounds involved with that episode. Smell the smells associated with that time. Take a few moments and do just that. [Pause]

Would it be all right to share that experience with me? [If "yes," allow the patient to do so. If "no," or following the patient's sharing, continue as follows.] Before we move on, please title your experience, like the name of a book or movie. Now move forward or backward over the river of time and come upon another such experience, perhaps an anniversary, wedding, graduation, or the birth of a child. [Repeat the process, accessing three or four positive episodes, going backward or forward over the river of time or the highway of life.]

Now I'd like you to descend the stairs from the attic of the past, and as you do so, it might be especially nice if you could bring those experiences back with you. Perhaps you could put them in that big knapsack that lies near the door of the attic. Perhaps you might like to put them in a jar, the one over there with the pretty lid. Perhaps you might just like to keep them within your psyche or your innermost mind.

Close the doors to the attic and descend the stairs. Ten, coming down. Nine, beginning to leave the smell of the cedar behind you. Eight, carrying those valuable experiences back with you. Seven, almost to the landing now. Six. [Pause] Five, turning again toward your initial direction. Four. Three. Two. One, leaving the attic of the past, knowing you can return there on your own, whenever you please, and having with you those valuable experiences from out of your past.

And I now make the suggestion to you that each and every time you have the desire to eat at a time you know is not in your best interest, or eat something which is not in the realm of becoming the "slim, trim, thin you" [or whatever you have the desire to reach for a cigarette, etc.], instead, I suggest that you think of the title of one of your past peak experiences, and allow yourself to take a few moments to relax and reexperience it again in every detail, with all the sounds, smells, colors, and especially the good feelings, the feelings of accomplishment, of attainment of goals, and whatever sensations are related to that experience.

And won't it be exciting for you to realize that you can do just that, and you don't even need to sit or lie down to do it. You can be anywhere you happen to be at that time. And won't it be especially exciting when five weeks or five months from now, I really don't know when, you look back at today here in this office, and you have achieved this present goal of becoming the "slim, trim, thin you" [or the person who no longer desires a cigarette, etc.]. And you'll realize that you were able to become the person you wanted to be, entirely on your own, utilizing all of your courage, your own control, and especially your very own life experiences to make the present and future happen for you, as you wanted it to happen, having achieved your goal and knowing you can maintain it for the rest of your life.

TREATMENT OF EATING DISORDERS

Suggestions to Modify Body Attitude

Eric J. Van Denburg and Richard M. Kurtz, Ph.D.
Chicago, Illinois, and St. Louis, Missouri

INTRODUCTION AND INDICATIONS

The authors documented that these suggestions may produce attitudinal and phenomenological changes in hypnotically responsive subjects. In support of traditional clinical wisdom, they also found that the suggestions were primarily effective when the subject was amnestic for the suggestions. Thus their amnesia suggestions have also been included with their other suggestions. (*Ed.*)

SUGGESTIONS

Now listen very carefully. I want you to concentrate on your bodily appearance, form a picture of how you look in your mind and listen to what I say. During the next two weeks you are going to think over and over again—"How attractive I am, how good looking I am, how beautiful I am." These ideas will spring into your mind over and over again. You will think about your bodily appearance and you will be very satisfied with how you look. When you see yourself in a mirror, you will be very pleased with all aspects of your body. You will like everything about your body. Everything you do—putting on a coat, adjusting your clothes, combing your hair—will remind you of your body, and you will think how good-looking you really are. You will think over and over—"How attractive I am, how good looking I am." These ideas will come to you naturally, over and over again. You will find yourself thinking this over and over—it will seem very natural—it will not seem silly and you will not feel the least bit embarrassed by the idea that your body is very attractive. These thoughts will simply spring into your mind over and over again. [Repeat suggestions again.]

SUGGESTION FOR AMNESIA

. . . I want you to forget that I gave you this suggestion—you will carry out the suggestion—but you will not remember that I gave it to you. No matter how hard you try you will not be able to remember that I gave you this suggestion. The harder you try to remember the more difficult it will become. You'll completely forget about my suggestion about your body as if it never happened. This is the one thing that you cannot remember. You are going to wake up in a few minutes. You will feel refreshed, wide awake, and in a good mood. I will count from 1 to 5 and with each count you will be more fully awake.

Altering Body Image

Hans A. Abraham, M.D.
Palm Beach, Florida

You are comfortably seated by the side of a beautiful mountain lake, the blue of the sky reflected in the mirror-like surface of the lake. There are sailboats with billowing white sails sailing into the distance, the ripples in their wake representing the past, as they spread further and further until they disappear in the surface of the water. There is a small island not far from the shore with beautiful trees, dark green oaks, reddish brown beech trees, yellow-green birches and the lacy branches of the weeping willows reaching to the surface of the water. There's a rustic bridge, slightly curved upward with a wooden rail leading to this island. *You can see yourself standing on that bridge at 125 pounds* [give the weight that the patient desires to achieve], *beautiful, strong, happy.* Under the bridge, reflected in the water — we know this is a distorted image — is your likeness at 180 pounds.

Pick up a pebble, right there, and toss it into the lake. [Have the patient indicate with an ideomotor signal when he/she observes the splash of the stone in the water.] Circular waves quickly spread from that splash obliterating the obese image. These ripples are the past, just like the wake of the sailboats. You know that sailboats go forward only, no matter which way the wind blows. Sailboats go forward only, just as you go forward only toward the newfound image. This image will be in your subconscious mind wherever, whatever, whenever you eat. This image will guide your eating habits from now on, and you are looking forward to the time when you will reach the beautiful image on that bridge.

Suggestions for Increasing Food Intake

Harold B. Crasilneck, Ph.D., and
James A. Hall, M.D.
Dallas, Texas

INTRODUCTION

The authors (Crasilneck & Hall, 1985) emphasize that increased food intake in medical patients may result in complications, such as "food shock" if there is acute overfeeding or the possibility of irritating eroded esophageal mucosa in severely burned patients. Thus hypnotherapy should proceed under close supervision from the primary care physician. Eleven of twelve patients were reported to have responded positively to these suggestions. (*Ed.*)

SUGGESTIONS

Because of the power of the unconscious mind, you can and will accomplish any goal necessary. . . . I give you the strongest of strong suggestions that you will be hungry . . . you will be hungry for meals and if, on the advice of your doctor, supplementary feedings are necessary for your health and recovery. . . . you will also tolerate these well. . . . You will be hungry, you will ingest and digest your food easily . . . food will taste good . . . you will enjoy eating, for you will do all in your power to sustain life . . . you will feel hungry and you will eat to satisfy your hunger. . . . You will be able to tolerate more and more food as prescribed by your physicians . . . food will be a source of comfort in the fact that in eating the food you are getting well . . . you will tolerate the increase in food easily, consistently, until you have reached the desired goal advised by your physicians.

Suggestions for Presenting Symptoms in Anorexia Nervosa

Meir Gross, M.D.
Cleveland, Ohio

INTRODUCTION

Gross (1984) identified target symptoms for hypnotic intervention with anorexia patients. The modeled suggestions were from a case study included with his original report. (*Ed.*)

SUGGESTIONS FOR RELAXATION

One of the earliest beneficial effects of hypnotherapy on the anorexic is relaxation, which reduces the level of hyperactivity. Whether through self-hypnosis or regular sessions with a hypnotherapist, the patient is able to calm her overactive neuromuscular system.

SUGGESTIONS FOR CORRECTING BODY IMAGE

The anorexic patient has a notoriously distorted body image. To help her realize this, the hypnotized patient is shown photographs of her emaciated body, and a healthier body image is then suggested. Asking the patient to draw pictures of herself is also instructive. Often, she will draw a normal torso but attach it to hugely distorted hips. Once the therapist realizes that only part of the body image is distorted, he can concentrate primarily on this portion. During trance, the patient is asked to touch each part of her body, including the stomach and heart, and especially the parts of most distorted image. After a time, the patient comes to understand that her conception of that part of her anatomy is not real.

SUGGESTIONS.   Touch your body and concentrate on the feelings you get. Feel the softness of your skin, the warmth of your body and the size of any part, especially your limbs. Touch your thighs and calves and feel their real size, how round and nice they are shaped. Does it make you think about the wonders of creation, of man's creation, of your own creation, of the wonder and beauty of it? That's right. These wonders are yours to enjoy and admire.

DEFECTS IN INTEROCEPTIVE AWARENESS

The anorexic has no perception of sensations from her own internal organs, especially hunger. Because of this, she cannot even perceive the sensation of satiety, and, when hunger can no longer be blocked, she will eat huge amounts of food without being able to stop. Vomiting becomes an artificial means of control, and the use of laxatives an everyday measure of reducing. Hypnosis can help unblock these sensations.

SUGGESTIONS.   Concentrate on your stomach and the sensation you feel coming from it. You can recognize the feeling of hunger and respond to them by eating small amounts. At the same time you can tune yourself to the feeling of satiety, being able to respond by stopping eating at that point. Being able to be perceptive to hunger and satiety will give the security of eating according to the needs of your body, letting your body regulate it like a clock. You can trust your body and its sensation, letting it

be controlled automatically with much confidence on your part.

SENSE OF EFFECTIVENESS AND NEED FOR CONTROL

Most anorexics lack self-esteem. Perfectionistic to extremes, anything they do seems unsuccessful and not good enough, which may be the main reason most of them also suffer depression.

SUGGESTIONS.   See yourself as you would like to be five or ten years from now. Realize how independent and self-sufficient you can be with complete control over your life.

HYPNOSIS AS A TOOL FOR THERAPEUTIC ABREACTION

Sometimes a traumatic event is the source of anorexia. Early trauma, not discussed during regular sessions, might be revealed during hypnotic age regression. Recognition of this childhood event and working through the abreacted feelings can lead to successful resolution of anorexia.

SUGGESTIONS.   Now you are watching the movie of your life going backwards from the present time to your childhood. If you see anything upsetting, raise your right finger. I will stop the movie, and you can tell me about it. [If the event is too traumatic, the therapist can remind the patient that it is only a "movie."]

HYPNOSIS TO OVERCOME RESISTANCE

As already mentioned, one of the major difficulties in psychotherapy of anorexic patients is overt or covert resistance. At the very beginning of therapy, the patient will object to any pressure to increase food intake and direct suggestions may actually antagonize her. When hypnotherapy is present as a tool for weight control, it is often accepted. Properly presented, self-hypnosis will pose no threat to the patient's personal sovereignty, since it becomes a means of gaining further control over herself.

A therapist can seize on something important to the patient to introduce self-hypnosis, and, at the same time, indirectly suggest better eating habits in order to improve her performance, e.g., in tennis, etc. The therapist can emphasize that in self-hypnosis, the patient will gain complete control and that even in heterohypnosis the operator does not control the subject.

Metaphors for Bulimia and Anorexia

Michael D. Yapko, Ph.D.
San Diego, California

INTRODUCTION AND CONTRAINDICATIONS

Yapko (1986) has stressed the potential importance of addressing family enmeshment, perfectionism, poor self-esteem, and distorted body image, and of using behavioral prescriptions as well as hypnosis in treating anorexia. He emphasizes the importance of individualizing treatment to unique dynamics and personality. Metaphors are one important component of his treatment. He stresses, however, that such techniques may be contraindicated in cases when the physical condition of the patient is too poor for meaningful engagement, when the patient is too fragile, unmotivated, or suicidally depressed, or when the patient does not have rapport with the clinician. (*Ed.*)

IDEAS FOR METAPHORS

Erickson (Rosen, 1982) described the habits of a particular species of woodpecker which lives in the Black Forest in Germany. This particular species of bird feeds her offspring a predigested meal by catching beetles, swallowing them, digesting them, and then regurgitating them into the mouths of the baby birds. While this interesting story about a natural phenomenon engages the conscious mind, for the individual with an eating disorder who engages in the bulimic behavior of bingeing and purging, a pattern not at all unrelated to the eating disorder of anorexia (in fact, some refer to these patterns that frequently occur in tandem as "bulimorexia"), the unconscious mind can begin to work on developing the recognition of seemingly strange behavior as purposeful, a strategy of reframing. In the author's own clinical practice, this same metaphor has been used successfully on numerous occasions, with the following additions to the metaphor:

. . . and in the world of nature, things are so finely balanced . . . and each stage of the life cycle leads to the next . . . and when the baby birds are old enough to obtain food for themselves in order to live their lives naturally . . . and constructively . . . the mother bird no longer needs to self-induce vomiting . . . and that pattern stops naturally one day . . . simply because it is no longer necessary . . . and there are no recorded instances of deviant woodpeckers who keep up a pattern that has outlived its usefulness. . . .

Metaphors may also be utilized to facilitate a recognition of differences between "thin, attractive" exteriors and the overall quality of the individual. Metaphors about glamorous individuals who were dishonest or otherwise flawed may serve this purpose, shifting the personal worth from an emphasis on appearance to an emphasis on personal integrity.

Hypnosis may also be used to facilitate greater awareness of and responsiveness to internal cues about one's physical needs. Metaphors about the various signal systems of the body such as pain, thirst, fatigue, and illness are framed as keys to survival while fostering the recognition that not all signals are easily detected and that many can easily be overlooked if one is motivated to do so. Regression to the initial learning experiences of body signals indicating the need to go to the bathroom, eat and drink may be a useful hypnotic pattern as well. Metaphors, such as the temperature drops that signal winter's arrival to seasonal plants and migratory birds, the signals of sexual attraction that stimulate reproduction, and the signals through which animals mark their individual territory, may enhance awareness for the vital role natural signals play when properly noticed and responded to. Building a strong awareness for and responsiveness to internal cues as a goal of treatment of the anorectic is necessary not only to successfully treat the anorexia, but also to reduce the chance of an overcompensatory weight gain from occurring once the client begins to eat more normally again.

SMOKING, ADDICTIONS, AND HABIT DISORDERS

INTRODUCTION

S MOKING AND OTHER addictions are some of the most difficult problems that health and mental health professionals treat. A review of the smoking cessation literature reveals an average success rate of about 25% on six- to twelve-month follow-ups with smokers. Clearly there is still much to be learned about curing addictive behavior of all kinds, whether smoking, alcohol and drug abuse, obesity, or sexual addiction.

Although far too many of the published papers on hypnosis for smoking cessation are anecdotal, there is enough research available to at least begin evaluating the helpfulness of hypnosis with smoking. We find that a single session approach with hypnosis (e.g., like the Spiegels') results in about 17%–25% success in most studies (Berkowitz, Ross-Townsend, & Kohberger, 1979; Shewchuk, Dubren, Burton, Forman, Clark, & Jaffin, 1977; Spiegel, 1970), although Stanton (1978) had a 45% success rate and Grosz (1978a) reported 31% abstinence at six months. It is my suspicion that hypnosis fares no better than other approaches when it is used for a single session.

However, when we examine hypnotic treatment programs with a four or five session format, success rates are found to dramatically increase (Holroyd, 1980; Orr, 1970). Crasilneck and Hall (1985) report a 64% success rate on over one-year follow-ups (11% who could not be located on follow-up are included in the failure rate). Using a five session approach, Watkins (1976) successfully treated 67% at six-month follow-up. Comparable abstinence rates of 60% were found by Nuland and Field (1970) after four weekly sessions. In planning a multi-session treatment program, it is recommended that one of the hypnosis sessions be conducted approximately two to three weeks following the first appointment. This counsel is offered because the average number of days between initial abstinence and relapse for smokers has been found to be 17 days (Marlatt, 1985).

Group hypnosis has also been utilized with quite positive effects in most (Kline, 1970; Sanders, 1977), but not all, cases (Pederson, Scrimgeour, & Lefcoe, 1975). When compared with individual hypnotherapy, group hypnosis seems to be somewhat less effective (Barkley, Hastings, & Jackson, 1977; Grosz, 1978a,b; MacHovec & Man, 1978; Watkins, 1976). But effectiveness may be enhanced in group hypnosis by using individualized suggestions and extending the length of group sessions (Holroyd, 1980).

Individualizing hypnotic suggestions to the unique motivations and concerns of patients also appears prominently related to more effective outcome (Nuland & Field, 1970; Sanders, 1977; Watkins, 1976). In fact, a review of hypnosis and smoking literature (Holroyd, 1980) found that four of the five most successful studies emphasized the use of individualized suggestions, while all ten of the reports that achieved less than 40% success utilized the same standardized suggestions with everyone. Consequently, I want to reemphasize the importance of tailoring hypnotic work to the motivations and needs of the patient. The value in providing you with the multitude of suggestions in this chapter (and, indeed, in this book) is in presenting you with many different alternatives for intervening with the unique patients who will seek your services.

It is particularly recommended that you query patients concerning the benefits and payoffs derived from smoking (e.g., to cope with nervousness or anxiety, as a social facilitator, for rebellion and to establish independence, to give oneself an excuse to take a break). Most especially, determine if smoking has been used to cope with feelings of frustration and anger. This has been found to be the most common single relapse event among smokers, alcoholics, and drug abusers (Marlatt, 1985). Addictive patients need help in expressing anger constructively and in engaging in appropriate assertive behavior, rather than creating an altered state of consciousness or distracting themselves with a chemical.

Feelings of low self-efficacy and powerlessness, which may be treated with suggestions for ego-strengthening, also seem to be vitally important in relapse prevention efforts with smoking and other addictions (Candiotte & Lichtenstein, 1981; DiClemente, 1981; McIntyre, Lichtenstein, & Mermelstein, 1983; Rist & Watzl, 1983). Some ego-strengthening suggestions specific to smoking and addictions may be found in the work of several of the contributors to this chapter.

Hypnosis with Habit Disorders

Hypnosis has been successfully used with a variety of habit disorders including thumbsucking, nailbiting, trichotillomania, skin (and acne) picking, tongue thrusting, and bruxism. Suggestions for several of these conditions are contained in sections of the book pertaining to children, dentistry and dermatology. At the conclusion of this chapter, however, you will find suggestions that may be used with nailbiting and trichotillomania (hair pulling).

HYPNOSIS WITH SMOKING AND ADDICTIONS

Smoking Suggestions

Joseph Barber, Ph.D.
Los Angeles, California

And as you continue, I want to talk to you, in a way that feels most receptive, for you. And I want to talk to that aspect of your mind, that is most interested in hearing, what I have to say; that is most interested in helping you to get, what you want. And you know what you want.

EXPLORATION OF RESISTANCE

And I would like you to let yourself become aware, even as you continue attending to your breathing, I would like you to let yourself become aware, of *any possibility*, for ambivalence, that you may feel. For instance, if you have any ambivalence now, with respect to stopping smoking, let yourself become aware, of that, ambivalence. A particular idea, or word that you may become aware of, may seem silly to you, or it may seem unreasonable, or it may seem perfectly reasonable. It doesn't really matter. If you have *any* ambivalence at all, you can just allow yourself, to describe that now, without disturbing the rest of your experience at all. If you have any ambivalence at all, if you have any good reason at all, or any silly reason at all, why you shouldn't stop smoking, just talk with me about that now, without disturbing the rest of your experience at all. Can you think of any possible objections at all? [Listen to response. Use ambivalence to assess and deal with potential obstacles to stopping smoking. Don't accept "no ambivalence."] That's fine.

YOU USED TO SMOKE

Just let yourself know, almost as if you are sending a kind of signal throughout your mind, a signal of clarity, in which you acknowledge that you are, clear about the fact, that you now have no ambivalence. That you really are *thor-* *oughly* interested, and willing, with full intention, to carry out this plan, to stop smoking—because you are a man/woman who used to smoke. You no longer smoke. And, as you have indicated, there is *no* reason on earth, that is sufficient, to justify your *ever*, picking up a cigarette again. You are a man/woman who used to smoke. And you no longer smoke. You no longer need to do that.

And it may feel almost as if you can, hear in your mind, the echoing words, "I am a man/woman who used to smoke." And those words can serve as a kind of, comfort, a kind of, acknowledgment to you, of the power, behind what you have done, of the efficacy, of your own ability, to do what you have chosen to do.

UNDERMINING RATIONALIZATIONS

And yet, sometimes, we can confuse ourselves, with rationalizations, no matter how good our intentions, no matter how clear our plan. And that's all right too. Because, if you have a child, or if someone else you love, say, had for some reason, a really strong craving, to eat poison, you wouldn't let them eat that poison, would you? Not even if it tasted very good. No, of course not. Not even if that person gave you excellent reasons why it would be okay for them to eat that poison. No, of course not. You might be amused, or even surprised, by the inventiveness of the reasons they might give you. *But you would never take the reasons seriously*, would you? No, of course not. You can be delighted, by the creativity *you* might show, in developing really interesting, really inventive, rationalizations. But you won't take them seriously, will you? No, of course not.

FREE FROM THE PRISON

And as you continue resting deeper and deeper, and allowing yourself to hear the things I'm saying to you, effortlessly, I want you to know that, you may occasionally have, very brief, very interesting, but possibly very peculiar, experiences over the next several hours or days, or even weeks, possibly even months. Every now and then, you might have a sense, of a kind of image perhaps, or a feeling, possibly just the vaguest feeling, of looking, back over your shoulder. Every now and then, you might just have a sudden sense of, looking back over your shoulder at the high, white, walls, of a kind of prison. A prison which, you know, held you for some reason, perhaps long forgotten. But now, you know, you have liberated yourself. You are no longer a prisoner there.

Every now and then, you may have a sudden, odd, fleeting sensation of looking back over your shoulder at the high, white walls of a prison. A prison, that once held you, for some reason. But *now*, you have liberated yourself from that prison. You are no longer a prisoner there. And you can just feel, the delight, of that recognition! You may be able to hear, or even somehow feel the, discomfort, of the prisoners who are still there. And you may probably feel compassion for them. But you can also, *fully enjoy*, the clear air, of your freedom.

ENHANCING SELF-ESTEEM

And you can feel really proud, of your decision to become free, and to remain free. In fact, you may be surprised over the next while, at sudden, fleeting feelings—perhaps familiar, perhaps now—feelings of real pride, and well-being. Pride, that you have chosen, to take care of yourself. Pride that you have chosen, to free yourself. Pride that you have chosen to stand by, what *you* know to be right. And you can even feel pride that you have chosen to let this experience be one, that is calmer, more comfortable, easier, than you may once have expected. You are free now.

You can enjoy the process now, of learning to *live* freely, and of continuing to enjoy the unencumbered experience, of living the way *you* choose; of making even small, freely chosen movements, with your hands, simply because you choose to. You no longer have to

do something because, someone else once convinced you that you must. You are now free to choose to care for yourself, and to do so, freely.

FLUIDS AND EXERCISE

And you know that it's very important, beginning now and over the next several days, to care for yourself in other ways, as well. To become more clearly aware of your needs, and to let yourself begin to discover how to satisfy those needs. It's important that you begin to drink more water. It's important that you begin to be more physically active. And you can really *enjoy*, feeling good about your body. As you become more physically active, it can *really feel*, pleasurable, to notice, how well your body works. To notice how freely your limbs can move, to notice how, well your lungs can *begin* to work. To notice how good it feels to be *more* physically active, and to somehow enjoy the, kind of special tiredness you get, from becoming physically active.

SELF-HYPNOSIS TRAINING

I also want to remind you, that *this* experience, right now, of comfort and well-being, this is your experience, not mine. And the ability, to create, this experience, is your ability, not mine. And you can really enjoy discovering how to use, your ability to create this experience whenever you need to. Anytime that you would like to feel, more comfortable than you do, anytime that you would like to feel relief from a sense of stress or tension or discomfort, all you have to do is sit back, in a chair, or a sofa, or a bed—just to rest back, and to take a *very* deep, *very satisfying* breath, and hold it, hold it, for just a moment. And [exhaling] then as you let it *all* the way out, these feelings of comfort, and well-being, just automatically wash over you, like water in a hot tub.

Any time that you feel anxious, or feel a craving, or feel tense, all you have to do is take a *very* deep, *very* satisfying breath, and hold it, hold it for a moment. And then [exhaling] as you let it *all the way out*, these feelings, of comfort and well-being, just come washing over you, like water in a hot tub.

And you can take comfort in knowing, that if *any* feelings *were* bothering you, they no longer need to. You can take a special kind of pleasure, in knowing, that *you* were able to relieve yourself of that discomfort, very quickly, very easily, and in a way that, can simply make you feel *more* confident, and *more* proud of yourself. You don't have to depend upon anything else, for this kind of comfort.

FAIT ACCOMPLI

You are beginning a process, that will take several days, and some of that time will be *much* more comfortable than others. And I don't know when it will be — perhaps in a week, maybe in a month, maybe even in six months — I don't know exactly when it will be, when you'll just kind of automatically one day look back at this time, and be *so* pleased, at what you have done. To feel so pleased with yourself, for what you did, back then.

And now, I'd like you to let yourself rest *even* a little more deeply. And take this experience of comfort, deeply inside you, and *really* appreciate, for the moment, how well you're feeling. Be aware of the excitement that you probably feel, and the anticipation. And when I see you again, I'm going to be very interested, in hearing you tell me, how much more easily the days have gone, than you thought they would.

Hypnotic Suggestions for Smoking Cessation

T. X. Barber, Ph.D.
Ashland, Massachusetts

[Following an initial induction focused on relaxation, calmness of body and mind, and drowsiness, with a sense of so much time:]

Calmness is spreading throughout your mind and body. So calm. Ready to feel and experience new things in a new way, with a calm open mind. Getting the feeling of how good it is to be alive with a calm, peaceful mind. At peace with yourself, at peace with everything around you, feeling so good to be alive.

FEELING ALIVE AND STARTING A NEW LIFE

Beginning to get a feeling of how good it is to be alive, to be conscious, to be able to think and feel and know and understand. To have a mind, to be able to remember and dream and sense and taste and smell and hear and see. To be able to feel, to be fully alive, to have feelings and strength and consciousness. It's so good to be alive, so good to be aware. Starting now, you begin more and more to get a feeling as if you're starting a new life. Starting now, you are going to determine to make your life as good as you possibly can, every day. To utilize all that wonderful energy and health and strength and being that's been given to you. To utilize the consciousness and the intelligence and the awareness and the love and the ability to think and to feel. And to see with your eyes and hear with your ears, and to be fully alive starting now, every day.

Every day determined to live in a new way. The old life will change as you determine that starting now you can live fully, completely, every day. To be more and more determined to live with full enjoyment, with full health, to the utmost of your ability, every day. Every precious day in your life as you determine that you will no longer wish to chance illness or an early death. That was part of our old life where things didn't matter very much. We weren't aware of how good it is to be conscious and aware and fully alive, and to have health and strength and energy, and to live every day fully and completely, and to enjoy everything around us.

Starting today, you begin to get more and more the feeling that you have just come to earth. You're starting to live in a new way. Starting a new life. You begin to see everything again as if it's fresh and new. You begin to see your body and mind again in a new way, as if you've forgotten how wonderful it can be to be alive, and to feel good and strong and healthy, and to know that you are doing your utmost everyday to live fully. You begin to enjoy every day, the stars, and the sun, and the sky, and the birds, and the trees. And every person you meet, you see them in a new way. You begin to feel so good to be alive.

SUGGESTIONS FOR SELF-HYPNOSIS AND RELIEF OF TENSION

Whenever you feel any signs of tension, you'll be able to relax by taking a deep breath, and breathing out slowly as you hear these words deep in your mind: "I can be calm. I can be relaxed. I can feel so good to be alive." Whenever you have any thoughts that bother you, or any tensions or any feelings of tension that lead to smoking, you'll be able to overcome them by taking a deep breath, breathing out slowly, and feeling yourself relaxing. As you hear these words and say them to yourself: "I can be calm. I can be relaxed. I can feel so good to be alive."

INCREASING MOTIVATION

Starting now and every day, you'll feel so good, as your determination increases that you're going to live in a new way with full health, with full capacity, with full enjoyment, knowing that every day you're doing your best to live fully, to fulfill whatever reasons you were placed on this earth, to fulfill them for yourself and everybody you love. Starting now, you will no longer wish to chance illness or an early death. In fact, as time goes on, you'll begin to enjoy living more and more each day. And smoking will become less and less important, very quickly. Smoking will seem more and more silly, more and more something you learned to do many, many years ago when you were young. You learned to smoke to feel big and part of a group, to be like others. But you don't need that anymore. You are now mature. You are now free. You don't need that any-

more. In fact, as time goes on, smoking will seem so trite. It will seem kind of silly. You will feel so sorry for people who smoke as time goes on. You will begin to become as aware that people who are smoking are chancing illness and early death, that in a way they are almost willing to commit slow suicide. That they don't really care about themselves and about life and about being fully alive, and really living. And they just don't know.

SUGGESTIONS FOR SELF-TALK AND INTERNAL DIALOGUE

You'll hear yourself saying things like: "I'm so glad I don't smoke. I'm so glad that I've stopped smoking. It's so good to feel strong and healthy, and to know that I've had the strength to conquer this miserable habit." When you see other people smoking, you'll feel very sorry for them. You'll feel so sad that they are willing to chance an early death or sickness because of such a habit. You'll feel so sad when you see people who smoke.

Starting now, your determination rises to live fully every day, to enjoy every day as much as possible, to live your life as fully every day as you possibly can. Smoking will become less and less important, and whenever you think of a cigarette or anybody offers you a cigarette or you smell cigarette smoke or have any associations to cigarettes, you'll hear in the back of your mind: "STOP!" And you'll hear it very, very strong. It may be my voice, but it will combine with your own background voice, the voice in your own mind saying, "STOP, I don't need it anymore. I'm no longer a puppet, I don't need to smoke the way I learned to. I had to learn to smoke years ago, but I've outgrown that now. I'm no longer a child. I'm no longer a puppet. I now control my life. I start living today fully, completely, enjoyably, with all my powers, knowing that every day I will do my best to live as fully as I possibly can for myself, for everyone I love, and for the meaning and preciousness of life."

So whenever any thought of smoking comes to your mind, you'll hear these words in the back of your mind: "STOP! I don't need it anymore. I am free." These words will become stronger. This STOP will become stronger and stronger as time goes on. And you'll hear it and you'll take a deep breath. And as you breathe out slowly, you'll relax and you'll feel calm and relaxed, and good to be alive.

Starting now, more and more every day, to become more and more aware. You have decided and determined to make your life, that one precious life that you have, complete and full, and to fulfill all the potentials, all the beauty, and strength, and health, and love that you have. As this determination gets very, very strong, you will think of smoking as more and more trite, and more and more silly. And you'll feel more and more sorry for people who smoke. And a strong thought will be in the back of your mind: "I don't smoke. I'm not a smoker anymore. I've stopped. I shall live all my life with full health and enjoyment." As time goes on, you'll be able to utilize this as you hear the word "STOP." You'll hear it strong in the back of your mind. You'll take a deep breath and breathe out slowly and feel yourself relaxing as you hear these words: "I can be calm. I can be relaxed. I don't wish to smoke anymore." As life goes on you will find it can be so good as you feel the strength, and health, and full vitality of your being coming to the fore more and more every day.

Let these thoughts now go deep into your mind as you become more and more alert. Quite alert now, you are becoming very alert as you open your eyes.

Hypnosis and Smoking: A Five Session Approach

Helen H. Watkins, M.A.

Missoula, Montana

INTRODUCTION

This an individualized method of treatment aimed at the reduction of smoking which is based on the motivations of each client. Specialized suggestions and specifically tailored fantasies are then initiated to undermine rationalizations and to reinforce the person's commitment to stop smoking. Six-month follow-up rates with this approach are 67% still not smoking. (*Ed.*)

SESSION I.   A smoking history is obtained to determine the client's reasons for smoking, why he wants to stop, under what circumstances he smokes, how much, what feelings he derives from smoking, how long he has been smoking, and what happened when he tried to stop previously. In addition, information is obtained about any pertinent medical history, any emotional disturbances of significance, and relevant medication.

Between the first and second appointment, the history is studied and about three suggestions and two visual images are chosen and typed on cards. These are read to the client in the subsequent sessions. The cards feed back to the client his own reasons for quitting, attack rationalizations for smoking, provide substitutions and undermine his motivations for continuing the habit. Examples of suggestions that were designed for one particular client will be presented below.

SESSION II.   Self-hypnosis is taught with his hand stretched out above eye level, focusing on the finger of choice. It is suggested that the more he concentrates on his finger, the heavier the hand becomes, and as the hand becomes heavier it will move down to a state of relaxation, but he will not enter a deep state of relaxation until the hand is all the way down. When the hand is down, he is relaxed more through the suggestion of muscle relaxation, abdominal breathing and imagery. In this relaxed state, the cards are read to him. After that he is given about one minute to meditate about all the ways he can fight the smoking habit. Then self-arousal is suggested by silently counting up to five.

At the end of the second session, the client is asked to phone in each day to report his progress. These daily phone calls are important to allay fears of failure, give support, and provide suggestions to root out trouble spots. It is also important for the therapist to make a commitment: "If you don't phone me by 10:00 p.m., I will call you." Such commitment provides an alliance against the enemy—the smoking habit.

SESSION III.   This session involves repetition of the previous session, exploration of any smoking behavior, along with support, plus the use of appropriate therapeutic measures to correct problem areas that continue the habit. For example, if dealing with anger is a problem area, then the client is helped to release anger in a constructive way.

SESSION IV.   Self-induction is done by the client along with learning the suggestions and visualizations on the cards. Between the fourth and fifth session, the client is asked to practice the self-induction daily.

SESSION V.   The client is asked to repeat the self-induction technique, rephrase the suggestions in his own words, picture the imageries, meditate, and arouse himself to complete alertness. This technique is now a tool the client can use in the future should he have the desire to return to smoking. At the end of this session, the client is told that the therapist will send him a questionnaire periodically for one year to determine his smoking status.

RELAXATION SUGGESTIONS

You tell me that smoking calms your nerves, that (1) it is relaxing and settles you down, but what's so good about a cigarette that (2) shortens your breath, and gives you a dry, cotton feeling in your mouth? A cigarette may seem relaxing because you pause to reach for a cigarette, remove it from the pack, light it, and take a deep inhalation. It gives you a tension-free relaxing moment. But there are other ways to get the same effect, the same relaxing moment. I'm going to teach you a substitute way to

get the same effect, by taking a deep breath in, letting it out slowly and telling yourself to relax. Do that now. Take a deep breath in, let it out slowly and tell yourself to relax. [The numbered inserts apply only to this client.]

VICTORY SUGGESTIONS

You tell me you want to feel a sense of victory over your smoking habit—a sense of willpower and self-control—a feeling of winning over this vice. You can have this feeling by doing the following: Every time you pick up a pack of cigarettes and then put that pack down again, this feeling of victory will come over you. You will feel good and strong. It's like winning one battle after the other. Each time you repeat this behavior of saying no to a cigarette, either in fantasy or reality, you will be winning one battle after the other until the final victory—the victory over your smoking habit. [I have the client experience this scene in fantasy. The good feeling he derives from putting down the pack is the immediate reinforcement which tends to increase future probabilities of his actually putting down the pack without smoking. This is in line with current behavior modification theory.]

ANGER SUGGESTIONS

You tell me that you smoke to put a damper on your anger and frustrated feelings. You can see that smoking is one way you handle anger, but you and I both know that smoking is no solution to this problem. Smoking ends up hurting you physically and it cannot discharge or control your feelings. If you are angry at someone, express those feelings in a constructive way. If this is not appropriate, then release your anger via exercise, or beating a pillow, or imagine you have a small rubber ball in your hand and knead it as you would dough. Try that now. Just imagine there is a soft rubber ball in your hand and squeeze it. Keep working the ball until your hand is tired.

COST IMAGERY

Cigarettes cost $ ____ a pack. You tell me that you smoke up to two packs a day. That means you pay at least $ ____ a day for cigarettes. Multiply $ ____ by 7 and the result is $ ____ a week. If you multiply $ ____ by the number of days in a year, then the total amount you are paying for cigarettes in a year is $, and for what? For a habit that makes you miserable. Wouldn't you like to use that money for something else—for something that would make you happy instead of miserable? If you stop smoking you deserve to spend the money you save by buying something that won't go up in smoke. Think now what you would like to buy with the $ ____ you would save in a year's time, something perhaps that you have always wanted but felt it was too much of a luxury. In your imagination right now buy this item, and experience using it. Feel the pleasure you derive from it. Experience this pleasure while I am silent for a minute. [In this imagery, I motivate the client by picturing a desirable long-term goal to which he can commit himself. If so inclined, I suggest to him after arousal from the relaxation that he save the money he doesn't spend for cigarettes in a glass jar and watch the money accumulate daily.]

DAY-OF-NOT SMOKING IMAGERY

Imagine that the day has come that you no longer smoke. You are walking across campus to this building. The air is fresh; the sun is shining; and it's a beautiful day. You woke up this morning feeling good about yourself and your world. You like the way you're handling your life. For one thing, the feeling of being a slave to a cigarette no longer haunts you. *You are in control*, not the cigarette. You have more energy; your throat is clear; and you know your lungs are clearing. You feel great, and the more you think about how good you feel, the more energetic your step becomes. Continue walking across campus now while I am silent for a minute.

EXCUSE FOR A BREAK

Suggestions may be given justifying a break without smoking.

SOCIALIZATION

Suggestions may be offered showing that a cigarette interferes with socialization in that it separates the smoker from the other person, making listening and sharing more difficult. Client fantasizes intently listening to someone without a cigarette.

PACIFIER

Clients who use cigarettes as a pacifier may have suggestions customized to them denying emotional control and safety via cigarettes.

KEEPING HANDS AND MOUTH BUSY

For clients who use cigarettes to occupy their hands, substitute activities may be suggested.

IMAGES

The following images may be used with one minute of concentration at the end of the description.

1. *Hospital scene*. Describing hospital setting sometime in the future with patient lying in bed listening to the doctor saying, "I'm sorry , but I can't do much for you now. I told you years ago you should stop smoking. Too bad you didn't. All I can do now is give you medication for temporary relief."
2. *Exercise*. Aversive experience of hiking, becoming short of breath, sitting down, panting, and putting out a pack of cigarettes, then making the connection between the panting and the cigarettes.
3. *Tobacco smell*. Aversive experience of tobacco smell on clothes, furniture and dirty ashtrays.

Smoking Control

David Spiegel, M.D., and
Herbert Spiegel, M.D.
Stanford, California; New York, New York

The essence of our hypnotic instruction for smoking control is the following: (1) For my body, smoking is a poison; (2) I need my body to live; (3) I owe my body respect and protection.

This dialectical restructuring strategy is expanded upon during the hypnosis:

1. For my body smoking is a poison. This point is especially important because it emphasizes that fact that smoking is not so much a poison for you as it is quite specifically a poison for your body. Your body is like a trusting, innocent child that has to take into it anything that you put into it even if it is damaged by it. Like an infant, your body cannot tell you in words that it is being poisoned. It tells you through the symptoms you experience, the cough, the shortness of breath, the chest pain. These are your body's ways of telling you it is being poisoned by cigarette smoke, so "For my body, smoking is a poison."

2. I need my body to live. Your body is the precious physical plant through which you experience life. You are not the same as your body but you cannot live without it, so "I need my body to live."

3. I own my body respect and protection. This point emphasizes the fact that for you to do what you wish to do with your life, you need to treat your body in such a way that it can enable you to do it. You cannot put sugar in the gas tank of your car and expect it to drive you into the mountains. Likewise, putting poison in your body hampers its ability to enable you to do what you wish to do, so "I owe my body respect and protection."

Subjects are instructed to practice this exercise every one or two hours at any time they have an urge to take a cigarette. In this way they are instructed to restructure their approach to the smoking problem by concentrating on an affirmation experience, i.e., protecting their body from poison, rather than fighting smoking.

Suggestions for Smoking Cessation

Harold B. Crasilneck, Ph.D., and
James A. Hall, M.D.
Dallas, Texas

You will not crave excessively for a habit negatively affecting your health. . . . Your mind can block the perception of discomfort, as when your finger felt insensitive to the pressure of the sharp nail file. . . . Your mind will function in such a manner that you will no longer crave for a habit that has negatively affected your life with every drag of cigarette smoke you have taken into your lungs. . . . You will block the craving for tobacco . . . a habit that is causing your heart and your lungs to work much harder than necessary, forcing your lungs to labor beyond all necessity, stressing and straining these vital organs . . . like a car constantly driven in low gear . . . constantly laboring uphill . . . stressing and straining the motor. . . . But because of the great control of your unconscious mind, the craving for this vicious and lethal habit will grow steadily and markedly less until it rapidly reaches a permanent zero level. . . . You simply will not crave for cigarettes again. . . . You will be relaxed and at ease, pleased that you are giving up a habit which has such a negative effect upon your life and well-being. . . . You are improving your life by giving up cigarettes and you will continue to do so. . . . You will not smoke cigarettes again. . . . You will not be hungry or eat excessively . . . your craving will reach a permanent zero level . . . through the virtually omnipotent and godlike power of your unconscious mind, you can and you will be able to resist a craving that is harmful to your body . . . you will treat your body with kindness and consideration . . . your body that serves you so unselfishly . . . you will no longer consciously or unconsciously choose to impose this undeserved burden of smoking on your heart, your lungs, your circulation, and the vital organs of your body . . . you will treat your body with kindness, as if it were your closest friend . . . you will find that through the immense power of your unconscious mind you will be able to overcome this old, outgrown, outworn addiction, which we now know, statistically, robs you of four minutes of life with every cigarette you smoke. . . . You will be able to give up this dirty and unhealthy habit. . . . As you permit your body to rid itself of this undeserved burden of smoking, your lungs will again become efficient, your red blood cells will carry more oxygen to all your vital organs, you will feel more alert and alive . . . and you will have a justifiable sense of pride for having worked toward and accomplished this important, healthy, worthwhile goal. . . . You are no longer a smoker, you are using your own free will, you are treating yourself in a healthy, proper manner. . . . You will not be excessively nervous or tense . . . you will not gain excessive weight . . . you will exercise, you will walk a mile a day, if your physician approves . . . you will sleep well . . . your craving for tobacco will be minimal and will rapidly decline to a zero level at a rapid pace.

Smoking Cessation

Richard B. Garver, Ed.D.
San Antonio, Texas

RESPONDING TO CONDITIONED ENVIRONMENTAL CUES

We structure hypnosis for smoking in three sessions. The first two sessions occur on consecutive days, the third session is held two weeks later. In the first session, a history is taken, followed by determining how much the patient has smoked, how long, and how many packs/day. Then it is determined when the patient smokes (for instance, when first awakening in the morning, with a cup of coffee, while driving to work, arriving at work, on the phone, during stressful times, after meals, etc.). These times and situations in which the patient smokes are explained to the patient as environmental cues which trigger the smoking response. Then, during the hypnosis session of the first day, it is suggested to the patient: "When these environmental cues occur, there will be another unconscious program that will respond, instead of the smoking program. An unconscious non-smoking program will respond, to be relaxed, calm and comfortable, without a cigarette." In each of these situations, this new response ("relaxed, calm and comfortable, without a cigarette") is paired with each one of these environmental cues. The patient is also told that, "There will be no other unconscious substitute, other than the one that we have agreed upon. No other substitutes, such as increased eating, or drinking, or nailbiting, or any other unproductive behavior. You may have no urge whatsoever to smoke when this new program of being 'relaxed, calm and comfortable without a cigarette' works perfectly. However, there may be times that the old smoking program will respond as well and you may have an urge to smoke. If you do, you are to say, 'No,' and if necessary, take a few deep breaths which will reduce the urge noticeably, if not eliminating it, but certainly reducing it to a tolerable level."

When the patient returns on the second day, all of these situations are again discussed. Usually, in over half of the response situations, the patient has been relaxed, calm, and comfortable without any urge to smoke. At the times when there is an urge to smoke, usually it is tolerable, and when met with the decision, "No," and with a few deep breaths, the urge disappears. Any urges that persist are identified as difficult times, and during the second hypnosis session, these times which were teased out as being the more difficult ones are now given special attention and the unconscious mind is asked to give the patient additional help and reinforcement at these times. It is suggested to the patient: "Day by day this new program gets stronger as it's being used, and the old smoking program gets weaker since it is not being used. The new one is stronger, the old one weaker, until the new one replaces the old." This sometimes is completed within a few days, and other times it may take two or three weeks.

SELF-HYPNOSIS TRAINING

At the end of two weeks, the patient returns for a session in which he/she is taught self-hypnosis, which should help him/her during any specific times that have remained difficult. It is explained that he will be able to use the self-hypnosis technique in many other situations. Reference is made here to the article that I published (Garver, 1984). The eight steps proposed there have been modified to six simple steps that I go over with each patient. The steps are designed for the patient to do the self-hypnosis exercise in one minute or less, and to limit the conscious screening that often occurs (e.g., thinking too much about the suggestion before it is given and critically thinking about it after it is given).

The six steps are as follows: The first step is to plan the suggestion before going into hypnosis. This reduces the tendency, once in hypnosis, to do too much thinking. It is also suggested that patients plan the suggestion, thinking about the event or time that they are planning, which should ideally be within the next hour or two. They are instructed to think of themselves in the situation, responding to the situation exactly as they would like to respond. For instance, suppose they are concerned about an important meeting and being too anxious or nervous. Instead of saying that they will not be anxious or nervous, they will picture how they would like to respond, and the positive suggestion may be given: "I will go to that meeting and I will feel comfortable. I'll feel relaxed, calm, and in control, and will remember everything that I have planned for."

After the planning of the positive suggestion, the second step is the entry cue. This is a cue

that they learned for entering hypnosis (for instance, to focus on a spot, take a deep breath and hold it, release the breath, and let their eyes close). Once in hypnosis, the third step is to count slowly backwards from 100 to 95. When they are counting, they cannot be thinking or worrying about the suggestion. As soon as the number 95 is reached, the suggestion is given (Step 4) as it was planned, in a positive and simple statement. As soon as the suggestion has been given, the fifth step is to count 95, 94, 93, 92 91, 90. When they are counting, they cannot think about or criticize the suggestion. As soon as the counting reaches 90, the exit cue is given. This may be any exit (awakening) cue that the patient has learned to come out of a hypnotic state.

These six steps are explained intellectually to the patient, and then modeled while the patient observes. Next, the patient is taken step by step through these self-hypnotic procedures before he leaves the office.

Suggestions Regarding Smoking

Steven Gurgevich, Ph.D.
Tucson, Arizona

GENERAL INSTRUCTIONS

A patient's program for smoking cessation begins in the waiting room, where there is a conspicuous sign that says, "If you still enjoy smoking, ashtrays are located in the patio." The smoking cessation program involves seeing the patient on three consecutive days with a follow-up in one week. He or she is also asked to make telephone calls to the office/answering service on a daily basis upon arising each morning to announce, "This is , I am not smoking today."

SUGGESTIONS

After the patient is able to demonstrate trance phenomenon (e.g., arm levitation, hypnoanesthesia), the following suggestion is offered:

Today, I don't know how long you will wait to discover the pleasure of non-smoking. Today, I wonder how long you will wait to discover the pleasure in non-smoking.

When you began smoking, you taught your body to suppress its natural reaction to burnt tobacco particles. Now you may begin to forget those unconscious instructions and allow your body to remember what it does best. I don't know if your body will go back to coughing out uninvited guests. . . . I don't know how badly burnt tobacco will smell within your nose. . . . I don't even know what your unconscious mind will begin associating to tobacco particles as you begin enjoying fresh, clean air.

These suggestions oftentimes are embellished with visualizations of linings of the lungs, bronchial tubes, etc., and with greater detail of the suppression process that was achieved in order for the patient to become a successful smoker. This allows for associating achievement and success to non-smoking with greater ease, as it can now be viewed as a natural state that preceded his conditioning as a smoker.

Suggestions to Modify Smoking Behavior

Harry E. Stanton, Ph.D.
Hobart, Tasmania, Australia

INTRODUCTION

Stanton (1978) outlined his one-session approach to smoking cessation. He begins with ego-enhancing suggestions "that the patient will feel physically healthier, more relaxed, more calm and unworried, more self-confident, self-reliant, independent, and be able to think more optimistically and positively." He then feeds back to the patient his own reasons for wanting to stop smoking. More direct suggestions concerning smoking are then given. (*Ed.*)

SUGGESTIONS

You are confident, completely confident, that you are going to overcome the cigarette smoking habit. . . . You will be able to let go of the habit so easily. . . . You will wonder why you ever bothered to smoke. . . . You won't miss smoking at all. . . . From this moment on, whenever you think of having a cigarette, if you automatically reach for one, if someone offers you one, you will say "No" . . . a voice will echo through your mind, "No! No! No! . . . Smoking is a foolish, stupid habit . . . it hurts me physically. . . . it damages my health. . . . I am not going to smoke again." You will completely overcome the cigarette smoking habit. . . . You will find you are able to do this. . . . Know in your mind, now, that you will be able to do this. . . . It is easy and you can do it. . . . Your mind can and should control your body. . . . When you stop smoking, and you can do so from this moment, you will feel physically better, healthier, your breathing easier, your senses sharper . . . and you will also feel mentally better, pleased that you have been able to control your body . . . happy that you are in control . . . happy that you are strong enough to stop smoking so easily. . . . You do it, not me. . . . It is your triumph . . . your victory. When you see others smoking around you, you will feel delighted that you don't smoke. . . . You'll say to yourself, "I'll never smoke again . . . the sight and smell of cigarettes is unpleasant . . . I haven't any desire to smoke at all. . . . I have no need to smoke . . . it doesn't help me in any way and I feel so much better when I don't smoke."

Make your decision now. . . . You will completely overcome the cigarette smoking habit and stop smoking now . . . and you will never smoke again. . . . It is easy and you can do it. . . . You will feel no sense of loss or unhappiness . . . instead you'll feel good, happy, proud of yourself. . . . Once you make this decision to stop smoking, no force will be able to change this decision. . . . You will be completely confident that you will stop and stop permanently.

You don't need to smoke cigarettes. . . . From now on, if you think about smoking, and this will happen very infrequently, you will immediately take a deep breath, let go and relax, and you will realize in your mind that you don't need to smoke. . . . You are in complete control and your decision to stop smoking cannot be reversed.

FURTHER TECHNIQUES

[Stanton's (1978) approach next utilizes Walch's (1976) red balloon technique, imagining throwing cigarettes one at a time into the basket of a hot air balloon, symbolizing throwing away all needs, desires and wishes to smoke. The balloon then floats away, carrying away desires to smoke. Finally, Stanton had patients imagine coping imagery in situations where they used to smoke. (Ed.)]

Another visualization is to have the patient imagine himself in a room, writing on a blackboard. The blackboard is divided into two halves and on the lefthand side he writes a reason for smoking. Once he has done so, he imagines himself erasing what he has written. On the righthand side of the board he then writes, much larger, a reason why he should stop smoking, and this he leaves intact. He then goes back to the lefthand side of the board and writes up another reason for smoking and again wipes this out immediately after he is finished putting it up. This process is repeated, and the end result is a blackboard with a blank lefthand side and a righthand side containing a number of reasons written largely why the patient should cease smoking.

Suggestions Applicable for Smoking, Obesity, and Other Addictive Behaviors

Doris Gruenewald, Ph.D.
Laguna Hills, California

INTRODUCTION

It is to be understood that all suitable preliminaries (e.g., pertinent history, reason for refer

ral, motivation, discussion of hypnosis, questions pertaining to it, etc.) have been observed. Suggestions are given following the induction of hypnosis. [Appropriate pauses should, naturally, be included to allow imagery and perceptions to develop. Head nods or ideomotor finger signals may also be used to alert the therapist to the pace of the patient's progress. (Ed.)]

CHECKING MOTIVATION AND OBTAINING COMMITMENT

Imagine a cigarette on the desk (or table) in front of you . . . one single cigarette. And as you look at it more and more intently, you notice a curious thing happening. The cigarette seems to be moving, ever so slightly, in the direction away from you. It's moving just a little, but noticeably. You become more and more fascinated as you relax even more deeply, watching the cigarette moving away from you, as if pulled by an invisible force. It's moving, moving. [Keep repeating these suggestions as indicated.]

You begin to realize that soon it is going to reach the edge of that desk (table). You have the thought that only you can allow it to fall off, or to stop it from falling off. The thought keeps occurring to you that only if you are really and genuinely ready to quit smoking can this cigarette fall off the desk (table). You know, without any great surprise, that once it has fallen, that's the end of your smoking. This cigarette stands for all the cigarettes in the world that could be yours to smoke. But when you let it fall off, you know that cigarettes will no longer exist for you.

SPECIAL ROOM WHERE SMOKING DOES NOT EXIST

[After using a stairway or escalator technique for deepening, the patient enters a special room.] Make yourself comfortable in this very special, beautifully furnished and appointed room. As you do, you notice that there are no ashtrays, and it dawns on you that you have entered a place where smoking does not exist. Not just that you have to refrain from smoking while in this room. On the contrary, this room is a space where smoking just does not exist. That thought gives you a great feeling of peace and serenity. You realize, dimly at first, and then more and more distinctly, that you have acquired (created) a space inside you that will be forever yours . . . and into which you can go (retreat, withdraw) any time you need to do so . . . whether it is to turn away from the . . . inevitable temptation to smoke . . . or for some other reason, like unwinding, becoming relaxed and at peace with yourself, or whatever.

The idea of this room, and you know and accept that it is an idea, will remain with you from now on, for you to make use of at your own choosing. You will not have to go into hypnosis to do it. All you need is to let yourself think, "my room," and all that you are now experiencing will arise, like an echo of this situation: the ambience, the relaxed feeling, the realization of an environment where smoking does not exist to you . . . even if you are in a room or other place with people who smoke . . . that need not concern you at all. [Expand on these suggestions, if appropriate.]

STOP SIGN IMAGERY

[The two modules of suggestions above may be used singly or in combination. In either case, preface these suggestions, or add to them the image of a stop sign which arises as soon as an urge to smoke is experienced. That would include reaching for a pack, going out to buy some, getting ready to light up, etc. (Of course, cigars and/or pipe smoking are included.) The stop sign is intended to introduce a delay factor.]

As you heed that stop sign, you have a little time to think whether you really want that cigarette . . . and mostly your answer will be "no" . . . and the urge passes . . . until the next time . . . when you will repeat the "stop sign" procedure.

[This technique is in the interest of reinforcing the patient's sense of control. In suitable cases, I may add provision for less than complete success — "if occasionally your answer is 'yes,' it does not mean that you failed — it just means that this one time it didn't work, and you started over again."]

APPLYING THESE SUGGESTIONS TO OVEREATING

The suggestions above lend themselves to adaptation for control of overeating. However, during treatment it must be brought out that food is necessary for life (in contrast to smoking, etc.) and should be enjoyed. The focus should be on control of what is eaten and when, with emphasis on dietary knowledge, thorough chewing, a more leisurely pace, etc.

EGO-SUGGESTIONS FOR FEELINGS OF ACHIEVEMENT

[In the case of other addictions, the complete absence of the substance in question must be reinforced. The pleasure issue is addressed as follows (or with some variant thereof).]

You can take great pleasure in your growing ability to do what you have decided to do. There will be a sense of real achievement, so much greater than any feeling of deprivation that you are very likely to experience at times. Your joy in gradually or even suddenly achieving your goal outweighs everything else, even in the face of an occasional setback which is almost inevitable. If that happens, it is, and can be experienced as, an isolated incident. It does not spell the collapse of what you are building up, only a small interruption.

[Conclude with repeating the main points, placing emphasis on what appears prominent in the individual patient. Where indicated, be sure to instruct the patient to continue or seek out medical consultation.]

Suggestions for Rational Self-Talk for Smoking and Other Addictions

D. Corydon Hammond, Ph.D.
Salt Lake City, Utah

INDICATIONS

A prominent cognitive therapy method for facilitating impulse control is "self-talk." Rational-emotive therapy and other cognitive approaches stress the importance of undermining irrational self-talk by patients and replacing it with positive internal dialogue. Any of the kinds of suggestions given at a conscious level in these therapeutic approaches may also be given or reinforced in hypnosis. The following suggestions, modeled after concepts of Albert Ellis, seem particularly indicated with patients who engage in negative, self-defeating internal dialogue. Furthermore, some patients are more intellectualizing and seem to prefer approaches that emphasize rationales rather than the stirring of emotions. These kind of suggestions may be particularly helpful with such patients. The reader should also refer to "Hypnotic Strategies for Managing Cravings," found in Chapter 12.

SUGGESTIONS

It's interesting to realize, how we sometimes deceive ourselves. Some people tell themselves, "This is *too* hard," when they feel the urge to smoke. Occasionally, briefly, momentarily, it can be hard, but what makes it *too* hard? Naturally it can sometimes be difficult to learn new habits, but you've done many difficult things before. [Pause] The only thing that makes not smoking "*too* hard," is our irrationally telling ourselves that it is. So remember, there may be a few times when it is briefly hard to remain a non-smoker, but it's not *too* hard. In fact, I wonder if you'll be surprised to notice, how much easier it is to stop smoking, than you'd imagined it would be.

Occasionally when something is difficult, some people say to themselves, "I can't stand it," and then give in to a tempting urge. They are deceiving themselves. Of course they can "stand it." When we choose not to smoke a cigarette, we're not going to explode. We won't evaporate. For the first few hours, choosing to respect our bodies, may not be entirely pleasant or *completely*, easy, but we *can* stand it. There is no logical reason why life *should always*, be perfectly comfortable, and completely pleasant. But when we choose to do things that are not entirely easy, we grow as people, and you feel good about yourself. Remember, you don't *have to* have a cigarette when you feel a momentary urge to smoke. You don't *need* it. You briefly *want* it for a moment, *but* you also *want* to respect and protect your body, and [cite patient motivations]. So you can admit an occasional, brief urge to smoke, but then choose to ignore it and respect yourself.

Suggestions for Smoking Cessation

William C. Wester, II, Ed.D.
Cincinnati, Ohio

INTRODUCTION

Wester advocates an approach that is individualized to the patient. Suggestions illustrative of his method are reprinted below. A very positive aspect of his approach is that he has patients send progress postcards for 10 days, and six-month and one-year follow-up cards. Examples of postcards that have been received from patients who had positive responses are reviewed at the end of the session. (*Ed.*)

INCREASING MOTIVATION AND DECREASING WITHDRAWAL

As you are enjoying that experience with your conscious mind, your subconscious is now very aware. You are going to experience some interesting things in the next few days and for weeks to come. You don't have to try to figure out why—just enjoy what your subconscious mind is doing for you. Your motivation to quit smoking is going to be higher than it has ever been. Each day you will find yourself feeling more relaxed, comfortable, confident and very much in control. There will be less tension, less anxiety, less tightness and little or no withdrawal. As a result of being more relaxed, confident, comfortable and in control, there will be no need for a cigarette.

RESPECT YOUR BODY

Your subconscious is also going to remember something very important. Your body is very important to you and you need your body to live. You want to respect and care for your body. Smoking is a poison to your body. Since you do not want to poison yourself in any way you will stop smoking immediately and continue to be an ex-smoker. Remember, your body is important to you and you need your body to live.

AVERSIVE SUGGESTION

[This suggestion is not necessary in all cases. Use it when the patient tells you that something strong is needed to get him/her to quit.] We know that if you took a regular drinking glass (8–10 oz.), filled it completely with tar and nicotine from cigarettes, and drank it, you could be dead before 12 minutes. You do not want to poison yourself—even slowly—and therefore will stop smoking immediately and remain a non-smoker. [Positive motivations elicited from the patient may be introduced at this point.]

In addition to respecting your body, you can feel so proud that you are now in control and no longer subject to this bad and dirty habit. Everywhere you go people will appreciate the fact that you are not smoking—no longer making people feel uncomfortable.

TIPS FOR NEW EX-SMOKERS

Over the years, I have found that a personal approach enhances the hypnotic procedures. At the end of the hypnosis session, I give all of my patients the following "Tips for New Ex-Smokers." I go over the list step by step making special suggestions based on the history.

1. Clean and store away all ashtrays.
2. Exercise if there is any withdrawal tension. Check with your physician regarding proper exercise if you have any health problems.
3. If there is an urge to smoke—sit down and relax, take a deep breath, hold it for 5–10 seconds and release it slowly.
4. Increase fluid intake—juice, water, diet drinks, etc. (no caffeine).
5. Decrease caffeinated coffee and alcohol.
6. If needed, get a supply of sugarless gum or use carrot/celery sticks if you feel you need something in your mouth. 7. Talk with another non-smoker or someone who has recently quit for any positive strokes.
7. Send your daily postcards for 7–10 days.
8. Keep thinking—"I am now an ex-smoker."
9. Call if you have any problem. Do not smoke that first cigarette and you will be fine.

Aversive Metaphor for Smoking

Marvin Stock, M.D.
Toronto, Ontario, Canada

INDICATIONS

There is an emphasis in modern hypnosis on using positively focused suggestions. Nonetheless, particularly when more positive methods are not entirely successful, and when the patient has high hypnotic talent and is capable of experiencing ideosensory phenomena, aversive suggestions may potentially contribute to favorable outcomes. Aversive methods also seem indicated when they are congruent with the patient's expectations for therapy. Dr. Stock has offered us an indirect, subtle option for conveying aversive suggestions. Note the interspersed suggestions that appear in italic. They may be set off by a very slight emphasis, different tonal quality or pause. (*Ed.*)

METAPHOR

Years ago, while I was a medical student at the *U* of Toronto, after being virtually *locked in* . . . by a *dark* and *dirty* winter . . . I was determined to get away . . . to make a complete *change* . . . from all that *dirt* and slush.

By March, I had assessed the options . . . and I chose the outdoor *freedom* of farm life. I arranged a contract from May 15 to August 15 . . . on a mixed farm . . . which happened to be in the middle of tobacco growing country. After being *stuck* . . . in the *dirt* and dark . . . *what a welcome relief it was* . . . *the broad expanse of sky* . . . *wide open spaces* . . . *fresh air*.

There was so much I enjoyed about the life. The arrangement between the farmer and the land . . . he *cared* for the fields . . . and they grew crops for him . . . the arrangement with the barnyard animals . . . in return for feeding . . . *looking after* their stalls . . . they would provide all kinds of *amusement* . . . and *work hard if called on. The beauty and strength of those work horses* . . . *and how well they responded to control* . . . such a contrast to the noisy and *smelly* tractor.

And I still think about the evenings; the work of the day completed. And you know what it is like at 8:00–8:30 p.m. in June or July. The light is golden . . . it slants across the fields casting long shadows. The birds are quieting down. I'd usually take a walk . . . from the house . . . down the lane to the road . . . five or six dogs as companions . . . it was all so peaceful and quiet. On my right there was a ten acre field of wheat . . . made more golden by the light. I

could follow the course of the breeze across the field . . . a constantly changing wave pattern tilting the wheat before it . . . and as it did so, carrying the sound of gently rustling heads of wheat . . . carrying the sweet scent of the hay. Whether it was the beauty of the time . . . or the peace and quiet . . . it was a golden *opportunity* to *think* . . . about the *day* . . . the *future*. When the lane reached the road . . . I would usually turn right . . . prolonging the walk beside the bright gold wheat.

The character of the countryside abruptly turned *somber* when I reached the first of the many tobacco farms in the area. Now if one of the dogs would dash after a ground hog into the tobacco field and not return . . . I would have to *crawl* through the fence to fetch it. Walking the furrows between the tobacco plants . . . I observed many *unexpected* things. For example, the *grayish stain on the leaves* . . . the residue of the chemical *sprayed to* kill *fungus*. There were regular spraying days. When we were downwind, the spray made us gag . . . *and five-year-old Henrietta would always* vomit. *Now the tobacco leaf is broad* . . . *so birds flying over the field* inevitably spatter the leaves *with the pale green of their droppings. In the slanting evening light, there were* long shadows *cast by the* half-eaten bodies *of grasshoppers* . . . *bees* . . . *flies* . . . caught *and* lying suspended *in the cobwebs* fastened to the leaves. I made certain they wouldn't stick to my pants by walking around them.

And you know those little drying houses called kilns [pronounce "killins"]? Sometimes the door was left ajar and if the dog chase ended there . . . I found it unpleasant to enter because the frightening bats were flying wildly about . . . I thought they might stick in my hair. Now the tobacco leaves hang to dry from the lines . . . as they age, they *wrinkle* and turn *yellowish-brown. You can see where those bats had been sleeping* . . . *for the leaves below are streaked yellow by their feces.*

No matter how much I enjoyed farm life . . . *time passes* . . . the day arrives *where no matter how* reluctant . . . *how* difficult . . .

you do have to say goodbye *and* get on with life.

In September, I returned to medical school . . . *strengthened* by the experience. On the first courses that semester was public hygiene. We were divided into groups of ten and required to visit manufacturing facilities to check their hygienic procedures. By good luck our group was assigned to a cigarette manufacturing *factory* for rating. We learned that by law, one out of every 200 cigarettes was removed from the line . . . and placed under a 30-power microscope. On first looking through the eyepiece . . . everything is *murky brown*. Then if you *focus* . . . you see the cut tobacco leaf, and suddenly with more *precise focusing* . . . *you see other things* . . . quite unexpected. Tiny *bits* . . . pale *green* . . . pale *yellow*. I recognized these from my experience in the summer . . . the tobacco *leaves spattered by birds* . . . and the *bat droppings on the drying tobacco leaves* . . . *and* other fragments . . . cross-sections of insects . . . torsos, limbs . . . the insects that had been lying half eaten in the cobwebs . . . we became quite expert at determining which was the *eye of* the grasshopper . . . or fly . . . or bee. And then the reason for the law . . . other pieces . . . dark grayish brown . . . these turned out to be *rat droppings. We were informed the law permitted* up to six pieces *per cigarette . . . more than six, and the batch was destroyed. Now we were curious as to how this could be. It turned out the leaf was transported from the kilns* [*"killins"] straight to the cutting room of the factory . . . no washing process . . . the cut leaf is then placed in bins to await wrapping in paper . . . and the bins are a favorite* nesting place for rodents . . . *who leave their* urine *and* feces *willy-nilly.*

Now I ask you . . . to wonder . . . just how long it takes that group of medical students to refuse to put cigarette to lips . . . *let alone* light up . . . *and permit* penetration *of that smoke* . . . and all it contains. To this very day . . . I find it *uncomfortable* to even touch a cigarette . . . for I know what is inside.

General Strategies for Overcoming Pleasure-Producing Habits

M. Erik Wright, M.D., Ph.D.

INTRODUCTION

Erik Wright (1987), a former President of the American Society of Clinical Hypnosis, outlined six major approaches for use with habit or addictive disorders.

1. STRATEGY OF POSITIVE FUTURE CONSEQUENCES.
This strategy concentrates on highlighting the long-term rewards from overcoming the habit, while simultaneously stressing the decrease in the negative side effects. Wright emphasized such long-term benefits as health, self-esteem, appearance, and financial reward. Either age regression or age progression might be utilized by Wright in emphasizing such positive consequences.

2. STRATEGY OF NEGATIVE ACCENTUATION. Wright believed there were times to confront patients with the long-term negative consequences from a destructive habit, while at the same time devaluing the short-term pleasure.

3. STRATEGY OF SUBSTITUTING ALTERNATIVE MEANS OF GRATIFICATION. Other methods may be found for reducing tension that are less destructive.

4. STRATEGY OF CONSCIOUS DECISION-MAKING. Instead of responding in a habitual, automatic fashion, patients are required to take responsibility for making a conscious choice if they indulge a destructive habit.

5. STRATEGY OF ENVIRONMENTAL CHANGE. Another of Wright's strategies was to change the social and environmental context in which a habit could occur.

6. STRATEGY OF SELF-REWARD. The last tactic was to encourage self-reinforcement for changes and successes.

NEGATIVE ACCENTUATION: CONFRONTATION WITH FUTURE CONSEQUENCES

The following illustrative suggestions and interaction with a patient demonstrate Wright's technique of negative accentuation. His style of using this technique is different from many who use aversive imagery in that he personalizes the process, concentrating on *natural* consequences that are specific to the patient.

Although this method is less popular in hypnotherapy today than it was in the past, with certain difficult patients it may prove beneficial to have the patient to imagine highly specific negative consequences—for instance, hacking coughs, choking on the thick phlegm in the morning, burning holes in clothes, the smell, and health consequences. It is important, in my opinion, that this technique not be relied upon as a central strategy, but rather be used in combination with other techniques and suggestions. However, when patients have difficulty completely stopping smoking in response to other suggestions, and have during assessment identified many negative consequences, this technique may be considered along with exploration of the underlying functions of continuing the addictive disorder. In such cases, however, it seems very wise to follow Wright's model of checking the acceptability of this approach with the patient through ideomotor signals before proceeding to actually offer suggestions. Note, in the modeling provided below, how respectful Dr. Wright is in his use of aversive methods. (*Ed.*)

ILLUSTRATIVE SUGGESTIONS.   T: You listed two distressing experiences that were important to you in making your decision to become a nonsmoker: first, the heavy yellow crud that you have so much trouble with in bringing up from your lungs in the morning; second, the 10 to 15 minutes of deep coughing and wheezing each night when you first hit the sack.

C: Right, both of them really worry me. They were part of the reason I saw my doctor.

T: There is no question about your getting pleasure out of smoking in the past and in the present. These two bad reactions can help you reach your goal of becoming a nonsmoker instead of just being things that have frightened you as threats to your health. I would like to ask the inner part of your mind if it would be okay for you to intensify the frightening feelings that each of these experiences arouses in you, so that these feelings are not just pushed out of mind as soon as the event is over, but that they remain up front in your memory. If you should reach for a cigarette, not only will you have a vivid recall of how you felt when these events happen, but you might even have the events begin right there and then.

C: I don't see how that would be any worse than what actually happens. I have had some terrible feelings about both of these experiences. [The client closes his eyes and relaxes and the right index finger, the "yes" finger, rises up.]

T: Good. Your inner mind seems strongly committed to nonsmoking. . . . Give yourself the signal to go into trance . . . and drift ahead in time to tomorrow morning. . . . You are in the bathroom, and you are ready to try raising the heavy phlegm from your throat. . . . Signal with your right index finger when you are ready for this. . . . [The client's finger rises.]

T: Fill your thoughts with wondering how hard it will be to bring it up this time . . . Will it be slimy yellow or green? . . . Will there be some flecks of blood in it? . . . Feel yourself gagging as you struggle to bring it up. . . . When you finally manage to bring it up . . . look at it . . . feel disgust and anger at the cigarettes that have done this to you . . . at yourself for letting it happen. . . . It will disappear when you are a nonsmoker. . . . More smoking will make it heavier, slimier, harder to bring up. . . . Tomorrow morning . . . when you clear your throat . . . flood your mind with these thoughts. . . . More smoking . . . worse crud . . . No smoking . . . clear throat. . . . Let the inner part of your mind consider this. . . . Does it want to use these suggestions each morning for as long as you need support to become a nonsmoker? . . . [The client's right index finger indicates "yes."]

Now move yourself ahead in time until night. . . . You are just stretching out on the bed when the first coughing attack starts. . . . Feel how deeply the cough reaches down into your lungs. . . . Feel the bed shake with each coughing spasm. . . . It feels as if your belly button wants to pop out with all the straining to get the smoke poison out of your lungs. . . . Feel yourself beginning to wonder how much more the lungs can take before the smoke poison is cleared out. . . . No smoking . . . no poison. . . . Tonight . . . if the coughing begins . . . focus on the coughing . . . how it feels . . . how hard your lungs are working to clear out the past residue of smoke poisoning. . . .

Each time you make a move for a cigarette . . . let each of these images flood into your mind . . . feel the strain in your lungs . . . then decide whether you want to smoke the cigarette. . . . It remains your decision. . . . The more unpleasant and vivid these images are . . . the easier it will be to become a nonsmoker. . . . It is worth the effort. . . . After you have signaled yourself to return to the here and now . . . the inner part of your mind will continue to rehearse these images and make them available to you immediately whenever you need them to sustain your decision to be a nonsmoker. . . .

COMMENT

Some hypnotherapeutic procedures involving negative accentuation do not limit themselves to actual life experiences of the client. The client may be encouraged to create highly aversive fantasies about cigarettes and smoking during the trance state, and then, with strong posthypnotic suggestions, to evoke these aversive fantasies and their concomitant psychosomatic stresses whenever there is a temptation to smoke.

RELAPSE PREVENTION SUGGESTIONS TO SUBSTITUTE AN ACTIVITY FOR SMOKING

[The suggestions that follow illustrate part of Wright's (1987) technique of substituting a nonintrusive activity to relieve a smoker's social strain:]

[After recalling a memory associated with these feelings:] Let this sense of comfort, of well-being, of confidence flow through your body like a pleasurable force . . . so real that you can feel it in your body. . . . Some people feel it like a color . . . or a muscle sense . . . or an inner glow. . . . Each person knows what it is, even though different words are used. . . . It is more than an absence of strain or tension. . . . It is a positive strength that is your own . . . that can grow as you learn to recognize it . . . that can help you to reduce big problems to manageable size. . . . Signal with your right index finger as you feel that special strength in you. . . . [The client signals.] Very good. . . .

[The therapist suggests the substitute activity:] As you enjoy that feeling of strength moving in you . . . gently let your thumb and index finger begin to turn the ring on your fourth finger. . . . [The therapist identifies the substitute activity with wellness:] As you move it around, it seems to bind that feeling of well-being ever more strongly into your consciousness as well as into your subconscious self . . . making it a part of you . . . belonging to you . . . yours to call on when you need it. . . .

[The therapist offers a posthypnotic suggestion concerning autohypnosis:] Should you feel stress building up . . . that thumb and index finger can begin to move the ring . . . and you will be able to put yourself in trance to draw on this sense of well-being, of confidence in yourself. . . . Whatever is confronting you can be brought back into manageable size . . . to be dealt with . . . sometimes in part, if you are not ready to deal with all of it. . . . And then you can either continue the trance or terminate it as you deal with the situation. . . .

[The therapist reassures and protects the client:] As you practice with this feeling . . . you will become increasingly secure in your capacity to cope realistically. . . . You will be able to talk and act while in the trance situation. . . . Even if you do not give yourself the signal to terminate your own trance . . . it will terminate when the need is fulfilled. . . .

[Confirmation is sought from the client:] Tell me how you will use this new skill. . . . [The client presents some situation, step by step.] Very good . . . now let yourself go very relaxed . . . and give yourself the signal to be in the here and now. . . .

Illustrative Suggestions with Smokers

Paul Sacerdote, M.D., Ph.D.
Riverdale, New York

[After obtaining sufficient depth through fractionation I verbalized as follows:]

Through the experience of having learned during the last 10 minutes to produce a state of hypnosis, you have established in your brain new circuits, new pathways, and new patterns of activity through which your brain learns to assume better and fuller control of your body. Your brain is the communications center; every second it receives millions of bits of information from every part of your body and from the outside; it coordinates this information, reaches decisions, and sends out orders and instructions. . . . Therefore, your brain is in full control and will continue to control your hands and will keep your hands from picking up cigarettes, from holding cigarettes, from lifting cigarettes, from lighting cigarettes. . . . Your brain also controls your lips and your entire mouth and will keep them from holding any cigarette, from puffing on any cigarette. . . . Your brain controls the muscles of your chest, of your shoulders, and of your diaphragm and will keep them from pumping any more tobacco smoke into your lungs. . . .

New patterns and new circuits have already become activated in your brain; among other changes, you will experience prolongation and continuity in your periods of enjoyment and satisfaction, while episodes of irritation and frustration will seem to be quite short. . . . During the next few days additional patterns become established in your brain and you begin to experience calmness and comfort instead of the usual rushed feeling. Therefore, you begin to discover that you can accomplish many things well and efficiently with much less effort than before while your brain is completely eliminating any wish or need to smoke.

[I then added specific posthypnotic suggestions that upon reopening his eyes he would find himself in "a pleasant and interesting posthypnotic state"; that during this state his right hand would take a pencil and begin to write on a sheet of paper the word "sleep" several times until his eyes became heavy and closed; that when the pencil would become too heavy and fall out of his hands he would find himself in a deep and relaxed sleep. His need to be in control permitted him to write the word "sleep" 10 times before any response to the posthypnotic suggestion of falling asleep became evident.

While the patient was "asleep," I repeated to him all the previous suggestions and added that, if he needed to, he could dream, using the dreams for his own needs and pleasure, but feeling free to forget or recall them without having to tell me about them. Noticing the rather prompt development of REM's (rapid eye movement), I assumed that he was indeed responding to the suggestion, congratulated him for his understanding response to my suggestions, and then added the following verbalizations:]

Every hour and every day that you go without smoking permits your body to eliminate the nicotine and the carbon monoxide that are now in your system, while tar and other impurities will gradually be removed from your lungs until they may become again as healthy as the lungs of a person who had never smoked. . . . Gradually you are beginning to develop a dislike for cigarettes, and it will be enough for you to see cigarettes, to see or hear advertisements about cigarettes, or to smell cigarettes or cigarette smoke for you to immediately think of a cigarette that has just been stubbed out, to see it, and to smell it as it is smoldering and gradually releasing that stale disgusting smell. . . . You will always be aware of and avoid traps that anybody, even you, may set for you by tempting you with a cigarette puff "just to see how well hypnosis works."

A Posthypnotic Suggestion and Cue with Smokers

Brian M. Alman, Ph.D.
San Diego, California

Occasionally, when I'm having a social cocktail, I know it is an enjoyable and relaxing diversion. This is a time when I may also take better care of myself. A very healthy thought to remember at these times is that I can avoid smoking. I may smell that many people are smoking around me. I may hear other people coughing and see their eyes watering. But as I sip my drink and hear the ice clinking against the clear glass, I may be reminded that my lungs can be clearer than theirs. The clarity and freshness in my lungs can be maintained by avoiding cigarettes.

HYPNOSIS WITH HABIT DISORDERS

Hypnosis with Nailbiting

Harold B. Crasilneck, Ph.D., and James A. Hall, M.D.
Dallas, Texas

INTRODUCTION

Crasilneck and Hall (1985) typically explore the possible psychodynamic meaning of nailbiting and assess family interaction to determine if there is a functional purpose to the symptom. The following types of hypnotic suggestions are then given. Afterwards, if the patient is a child, he or she is asked to learn appropriate methods for caring for his/her fingernails. (*Ed.*)

SUGGESTIONS

When you begin to put your hands toward your mouth, there will simply be an automatic and opposite withdrawal movement. You will no longer wish, nor desire, to continue this outgrown, unwanted habit that injures your hands and embarrasses you before your family and friends. . . . As you begin to discontinue the habit of biting your nails, you will feel a sense of well-being and self-approval. You will begin to respect your fingernails and hands and be proud of them. Each time that you successfully avoid nailbiting, you will feel proud of yourself for accomplishing a worthwhile and desirable goal.

Erickson's Suggestions for Nailbiting

Milton H. Erickson, M.D.

. . .I don't think you really like those stubby fingernails of your either. And you have been biting them since you were four years old . . . and I feel rather sorry for you, because for _____ years you have been biting your fingernails and you have never gotten anything more out of it than a teensy, teensy little piece of fingernail; and you have never had a decent-sized piece of fingernail to chomp on. _____ years of frustration! Now what I am going to suggest to you is this: You have ten fingers. Certainly you can spare one on which to grow a decent-sized fingernail, and after you have grown a decent-sized fingernail on it, bite it off, and have something worth chewing on.

Suggestions for Nailbiting

David Waxman, L.R.C.P., M.R.C.S.
London, England

One of the most important factors in successful treatment is to be found in strengthening the patient's desire and motivation to stop the habit. This is equally necessary in child, adolescent or adult, first in the waking state, and subsequently repeated during hypnosis. Once again, the deeper the trance, the more rapid and effective treatment is likely to be. The procedure seems to be particularly successful when the patient is female:

As you grow up . . . you will become more and more attractive. You will not want your appearance to be spoilt by ugly hands. Nice hands and shapely nails will make you even more attractive . . . and you will want to make every effort to stop biting your nails, and spoiling them. With my help . . . you will be able to stop biting them altogether . . . and then they will soon begin to grow.

Commence treatment with the routine ego-strengthening and then proceed in the following manner:

As your nerves become stronger and steadier . . . as you become calmer and more relaxed, each day . . . so, there will be no reason for you to go on biting your nails.

You will no longer *want* to bite them . . . you will *stop* biting them. If at any time you do start to bite them, without realizing what you are doing . . . *the moment your fingers touch your mouth . . . you will know immediately what you are doing . . . and you will be able to stop yourself right away . . . before you have done any damage at all.*

From now on . . . you will stop biting your nails . . . they will begin to grow . . . and you will feel proud of your hands.

Strong, authoritative, direct suggestions under hypnosis will often succeed in stopping the habit altogether. Where a very deep trance or somnambulism can be obtained, the prohibition may be rendered much more effective by telling the patient that he will experience a strong feeling of distaste whenever he puts his fingers in his mouth:

Whenever you start biting your nails . . . the moment you put your fingers in your mouth . . . you will get a horrible bitter, nasty taste in your mouth.

This will become stronger and nastier . . . and will make you feel sick.

Conditioning a feeling of nausea to the habit in this way may help greatly in establishing control. When this particular method is used, however, fairly frequent sessions will be necessary, and even when the nails begin to grow the suggestions may need to be reinforced about once a fortnight, for a time. Increasing motivation is a much superior method and the results are likely to be more effective.

An alternative method is to *permit the biting of one or two nails, whilst allowing the others to grow.* Once this succeeds, it is surprising how often and rapidly the habit is abandoned altogether.

Whilst the patient has actually stopped biting her nails after one or two sessions, she may substitute a habit of picking them instead. This occurs more in adults and adolescents than in the case of children. It is not difficult to deal with, since the inclusion of specific suggestions prohibiting this as well will usually cause it to stop.

Suggestions for Nailbiting

Don E. Gibbons, Ph.D.

Every time you bit your nails from now on, you will have to bite them with your hand turned *completely upside down* from the way you usually hold it. You are going to be absolutely unable to bite your nails in the way you have been doing it, because every time you start to bite your nails in the usual way, you are going to *have to turn your hand completely over* before you do.

Every time you feel like biting your nails, your desire to *stop* biting them is going to be felt too. And this is what is going to make you do it in such an awkward and uncomfortable way. You won't be able to express one desire without expressing the other one at the same time, so if you do let yourself bite your nails, you won't let yourself enjoy it.

And when you do turn your hand upside down to bite your nails, you will soon find that this position is *so* uncomfortable, that your desire to bite your nails is going to get weaker and weaker, until your desire to bite your nails is *so* weak, and it is just *so* much trouble, that you will just give it up completely.

Suggestions with Trichotillomania

Marianne Barabasz, Ph.D.
Pullman, Washington

INTRODUCTION

Trichotillomania, compulsive hair pulling, is estimated to be a chronic habit disorder of 8 million people (Azrin & Nunn, 1978). There are many case reports in the behavior modification literature, with varying success rates, using methods like aversive self-stimulation (e.g., snapping a rubber band on the wrist), covert sensitization, self-monitoring and stimulus control procedures (Bornstein & Rychtarik, 1978; Levine, 1976; Mastellone, 1974; Saper, 1971). There are also case reports of the successful use of hypnosis with this condition (Galski, 1981; Rowen, 1981; Spiegel & Spiegel, 1978). Barabasz (1987) successfully used the following permissive suggestions to treat trichotillomania in three of four cases. She used the restricted environmental stimulation technique that she and her husband developed to enhance hypnotic responsiveness.

SUGGESTIONS

You will be acutely aware whenever you put your hand to your head, then it is entirely up to you, you have the power, the control, no one else, no habit controls you. You can pull your hair if you want to or you can choose to control the habit.

Suggestions for Scalp Sensitivity with Trichotillomania

T. J. Galski

INCREASING AWARENESS OF BEHAVIORS PRECEDING HAIR PULLING

Become immediately aware of reaching up to pull your hair. Feel your fingers wrap around a lock of hair . . . feel the texture, the softness and silkiness of the hair wrapped around your fingers. . . . When you become aware of your arm reaching up and your hair wrapped around your fingers, another interesting feeling can occur—just touching your hair in these circumstances can serve as an emotional trigger for your scalp to become very sensitive, sensitive as when you get a bad sunburn and touching the sunburned area can make you cringe! . . . [Patients may only be minimally aware of the discomfort.] The awareness of hair-pulling behaviors will immediately be followed by letting go of your hair, relaxing, . . . inhaling . . . letting all normal sensations be restored. There'll be no need to soon reach up again with any urge to pull out your hair.

CONCENTRATION, ACADEMIC PERFORMANCE, AND ATHLETIC PERFORMANCE

INTRODUCTION

T HE FIRST SECTION OF this chapter will present suggestions that have commonly been used to enhance motivation for learning, concentration, study skills, reading ability and to overcome text anxiety. The next section of the chapter will contain several suggestions that have been gleaned from the literature for enhancing creativity. The final section of this chapter will provide a brief overview of the applications of hypnosis to athletic performance along with suggestions for sports hypnosis.

Research

Through the years hypnosis has been used in a number of ways in academic performance. In particular, it has been used to reduce generalized anxiety and test anxiety. Excessive anxiety lowers intellectual efficiency and may impair performance, but hypnosis, especially learning self-hypnosis skills, gives the student a self-management tool. Although one study did not find hypnosis helpful (Egan & Egan, 1968), Eisle and Higgins (1962) and Mellenbruch (1964) reported positive results, as did Lodato (1969) in a single case report. With 130 undergraduate students, Goldburgh (1968) documented that hypnosis was more effective than a tranquilizer or "expressive-directive" treatment.

Attempts to enhance learning and recall through hypnosis have been another focus of research. Haggendorn (1970) gave graduate students hypnotic suggestions to stimulate interest in and retention for lecture material, and found improved recall. But a variety of other studies have found hypnosis to be ineffective for this purpose (Fowler, 1961; St. Jean,

1980; White, Fox, & Harris, 1940) and found that it does not increase recognition for previously learned material (Council on Scientific Affairs, American Medical Association, 1985).

There have also been many studies concerning the ability of hypnotic suggestion to enhance reading ability and concentration. Knudson (1968) documented increased reading speed and comprehension with four sessions (24 subjects) at 11-week follow-up. Compared to a control group, subjects in a study by Mutke (1967) similarly showed improved reading speed and comprehension with hypnosis. Holcomb (1970), experimenting with seventh grade students, found significant increases in speed of reading, but only slight increases in comprehension. Improved reading and spelling skills were also obtained by Krippner (1963, 1966), and Wagenfeld and Carlson (1979) reported a successful adult case utilizing ego-strengthening to alter a negative self-concept. Koe and Oldridge (1988) additionally reported mildly positive effects on reading from hypnotic suggestions. Finally, alert trance (Banyai & Hilgard, 1976), rather than relaxation or drowsiness suggestions, has also been used with reading and study skills. In a tangentially related study, Liebert, Rubin, and Hilgard (1965) found fewer learning errors (in learning word-number pairs) in a group given suggestions in alert trance versus a traditional hypnotic procedure. Oetting (1964), whose suggestions are included in this chapter, described his alert trance approach but without any outcome data. But Donk, Vingoe, Hall, and Doty (1970) documented that alert trance increased reading speed more than traditional hypnotic induction or conversation. Recently, Wark (1989), using his alert trance procedure that is included in this chapter, documented positive increases in reading comprehension in nine university students. No control group was used.

There are negative results as well, however, concerning the effects of hypnosis on reading. Swiercinsky and Coe (1971) used Oetting's alert trance approach with 58 university undergraduates with no effects. Using alert trance, Willis (1972) also failed to find an increase in reading speed between a waking suggestion and hypnosis group, but only one session was used. Cole (1977, 1979) similarly failed to find improvements in reading and test-taking skills with either traditional hypnosis or waking suggestions *over what a class for improving study skills produced* (which presented similar information).

Thus we cannot be sure at this time how much the use of hypnosis is truly capable of enhancing reading speed, comprehension, or concentration during studying. Hypnosis has been successful in some studies, and unsuccessful in others. Further research is needed.

It should also be noted that there has been some experimental work done on hypnosis and creativity. Raikov (1976) had subjects in deep hypnosis roleplay someone famous and talented in art, music, etc., and reported positive results, as did Dave and Reyher (1978) with real life problems. Bowers and Bowers (1979) also documented a relationship between level of hypnotic capacity and creativity, leading them to conclude: "The personality characteristics that allow one person to be more susceptible to hypnosis than another coincide to some extent with those characteristics that make him more creative. Perhaps the ease with which one can deconventionalize experience and accept the unrealistic and fantastic contributes both to susceptibility and creativity" (p. 378). But, on the other hand, results are inconclusive since some experimental work has failed to find hypnosis capable to enhancing creativity (K. Bowers, 1968; K. Bowers & van der Meulen, 1970). Gibbon's suggestions in this chapter model Raikov's approach to enhancing creativity.

Hypnotic Enhancement of Athletic Performance

References to the use of hypnosis to enhance sports performance have been made in the literature for a long time (e.g., Lindemann, 1958; Mitchell, 1972; Narcuse, 1964a, 1964b; Schultz, 1932). In 1964, Narcuse found that of 125 Japanese Olympic athletes, only 20% had invested time in developing a means of coping with performance anxiety, and few of them had done this systematically or reliably. In contrast, today cognitive training and hypnosis training are widely utilized with Olympic athletes and a wide variety of professional athletes.

It is my recommendation that you individually design hypnotic training for athletes based on their particular needs. A training plan may be formulated by determining which of ten overall strategies are needed with the individual athlete:

1. Enhance sensory awareness and muscle control.
2. Increase concentration, control internal dialogue, and decrease awareness of unimportant external stimuli.
3. Control anxiety, anger and emotionality.
4. Enhance motivation and enthusiasm.
5. Increase energy, feelings of invigoration, and endurance.
6. Enhance performance skill.
7. Increase self-esteem, confidence, and self-efficacy.
8. Control perception of time and focus on the present experience (time contraction or expansion).
9. Resolution of unconscious blocks or conflicts.
10. Management of discomfort.

Under these ten strategies we may identify the specific hypnotic *techniques* that will allow us to accomplish the goals, such as age regression (e.g., to outstanding performances), imagining an ideal model, mental rehearsal, use of end-result imagery, age progression, direct suggestions, progressive relaxation, symbolic imagery techniques, ideomotor signaling for unconscious exploration, amnesia (e.g., for past defeats), ego-strengthening methods, positive internal dialogue, alert trance, suggestions for time distortion or (temporary) time reorientation, the protective shield technique, analgesia and so forth.

In the last section of this chapter you will have an opportunity to study a sampling of suggestions that are used in sports hypnosis. You will also find it beneficial to consult Jencks' suggestions for increasing energy and for invigoration found in Chapter 8.

ENHANCING ACADEMIC PERFORMANCE

Suggestions for Enhancing Academic Performance

Don E. Gibbons, Ph.D.

IMPROVING STUDY SKILLS

As a result of what I am about to tell you now, you will find many helpful improvements taking place in your study habits, and in the effectiveness with which you utilize your abilities in studying. Whenever you have any studying to do, you will find that you will be in just the right mood for it. You will *really feel like studying,* and as a result, you will be able to dig into the material with a lot more energy and a lot more enthusiasm than you usually have. You will be able to use your study time much more effectively; for you will be able to concentrate much more easily and to remember with much less effort what you have learned.

Each time you complete a period of study, you will find that you experience very strong feelings of pride, achievement, and accomplishment because you have been able to perform so effectively and so well. These feelings will reward you for the time you have spent in study, and you will come to look forward to your study periods in the same way that a trained athlete looks forward to a good workout. It will be a source of deep personal satisfaction to you that you are able to use your abilities so fully and so well, and you are going to be thrilled and delighted at the results.

TAKING EXAMINATIONS

From now on, you will be able to approach your examinations calmly and to feel calm and relaxed as you take them. When you enter the room in which the test is being given, the act of walking through the doorway will serve as a stimulus that will release within you a great wave of additional peace and tranquility, confidence and calm. And it will drive out completely any tension which might be reawakened by your starting to take the test, so that by the time the test begins, you will be in just the proper mood to function most effectively.

You will be able to recall a great deal of information which might otherwise be blocked because of tension. Your mental processes will be much more flexible, and you will be able to draw on vast reserves of potential which will enable you to concentrate much more easily on the questions asked and your answers to them.

You will be able to remain perfectly relaxed and calm throughout the entire test as the ideas, facts, and concepts continue to flow smoothly into your awareness and to organize themselves naturally and almost spontaneously, as if they were flowing onto the paper by themselves. You are going to be thrilled and delighted at how much easier the entire process of taking examinations is going to be, and at how much better you will be able to perform.

FACILITATING CLASS PARTICIPATION

From now on, you will find that the subject matter of all your classes has taken on a great deal more meaning. You will want to ask many more questions in class, and you will be very interested in the answers which are provided, both to your own questions and to the questions of others.

As you continue to participate more and more in the give-and-take of class discussion, you will become ever more interested in everything that is being presented. You will become more and more absorbed in the content of what is being taught, as each new fact and concept to emerge becomes more vivid and more interesting than those which have gone before.

As time continues to pass, your personal involvement will continue to grow, for you will constantly be discovering new ways to relate the material to your own life and experiences. And these applications will give rise to still more questions, resulting in an even greater desire to know.

As these new questions are satisfied in turn, the process will continue at an ever-increasing rate, for the more your aroused curiosity is fed, the stronger it is certain to become.

ACHIEVEMENT MOTIVATION

Please extend both arms straight out in front of you, palms facing inward, about four inches apart. Now I would like you to imagine that there is a large rubber band stretched around your wrists holding them close together, as they are now. This rubber band represents all the negative thoughts and feelings which have been holding you back and preventing you from attaining your true potential; and as I continue speaking, you will begin to notice a force pulling your hands apart, until the rubber band will suddenly snap and you will be free of all these negative thoughts and feelings once and for all. Feel the force beginning to pull at your outstretched hands now—tugging and tugging as it slowly draws your hands apart. Feel your wrists drawing farther and farther apart, and feel the rubber band stretching tighter and tighter between them. Soon the band will snap, and you will finally be free of these negative influences. It's ready to break; ready to break. *Now!* You are *free!*

Now you can rest your hands comfortably in your lap, as you continue listening to my voice. Let yourself relax completely now and think back to a time in the past when you were in a totally positive frame of mind, looking forward to a complete and certain success. This need not be a great success in the usual sense of the term—it's the positive feeling that counts. Everyone has experienced this type of feeling at one time or another, even if only in childhood. So take your time, and when you have thought of the kind of situation I am describing, let your imagination focus on it clearly and capture the mood once more. And when you have caught this mood once again, you can signal me by raising the index finger of your right [or left] hand.

[After the subject has responded:] All right. Now just hold this mood for a moment, and feel it growing even stronger.

Now, as the mood continues to grow ever clearer and stronger by the second, you are going to be able to carry it back with you and to call it up again whenever you wish. The mood will persist for a while after the trance is terminated, and whenever you need to, you are going to be able to act and feel in just this manner once again. You are going to be able to act and feel as if you were going toward a predetermined and certain success. You are going to be able to *act as if it were impossible to fail.* For this is the key which will enable you to continue to tap into your true potential and to employ your abilities to the fullest in pursuit of the goal you have chosen.

The Memory Bank

Douglas M. Gregg, M.D.

INDICATIONS

These are suggestions for enhancing memory. The metaphors concerning checking and banking will be most appropriate with older adolescents or adults. (*Ed.*)

SUGGESTIONS

As you drift along deeper and deeper relaxed, concentrating your mind more and more, you are receptive to and you accept suggestions about memory and recall. The art of memory is the art of attention and retention. You must pay attention to anything in order to remember it. People who do not pay attention, do not remember. To remember something you must pay attention. For instance, you think of the name, you look at the man, you associate them. You *want* to know the man's name. You *really want* to remember. This is the process that you use to remember anything: you concentrate your mind, you think, you look, listen, associate, and remember.

In being able to recall something you have to have stored the information properly; you have to put the facts in your memory bank before you can recall them. You have an excellent memory; you are going to use it; you are going to pay attention. You must very literally pay attention, close attention. That way you store the facts properly in your memory bank and they are ready for you when you want or need them.

From this moment on, every day, you utilize your good memory, you use your good memory every day. You always pay attention. You pay attention to exactly what is going on around you, to exactly what is being said, to exactly what you hear, and exactly what you see, so that when you need to go into your memory bank to make a withdrawal, you have already deposited something to withdraw. The facts are properly stored and they are ready for you. They are ready for you whenever you want or need them.

Your memory bank is just like any other bank. When you go into a bank to withdraw some of your money, you do not hold them up with a pistol. You fill out a withdrawal slip or write a check and have it cashed. You do the same thing with your memory bank. It is not necessary to force your memory bank to give you the information. You simply concentrate your mind, request the information, relax, and let it drift up to your conscious awareness.

You have a good memory, you have an excellent memory. This is true for every single living human being. It is part of the way we are made. You need only to use your memory properly. Force only leads to frustration. In order to recall anything, you simply let your subconscious mind know what you want. Anything you want to know then comes into your conscious awareness naturally and easily. If it does not come immediately, forget about it, forget about it, forget about the *process* of remembering it. Do not try to force it. The information that you want washes up on the sands of your conscious awareness in a few moments . . . sometimes when you least expect it. Any information that you want comes into your conscious awareness . . . naturally and easily.

One way to promote recall is to go down the alphabet. What is the name of that hotel? A, B, C, or D? Oh, D, that is it! It is the Delaware Hotel. You use a hook, a hook which you stretch down into your memory, into your subconscious mind, and you use it to withdraw your answer.

Another technique: If you want to remember where you left something, go through the motions of what you were going through or what you were doing at the time you left it. You retrace your steps mentally.

By retracing the steps, you write a check, and it is cashed in the memory bank. To write a mental check, do something that is associated with the information you want. You want something from your memory bank. You do not know what it is. However, you do know some other bit of information that is associated with what you want or that is related to it. You use that bit of information as the check you write in order to get a withdrawal from the memory bank of your subconscious mind. Knowing and practicing this technique tremendously increases your ability to recall. You are surprised and amazed at how precisely accurate and effective your memory is. Your memory has always been good. By properly training and utilizing the memory system that you have in your subconscious mind, you are able to obtain maximum recall. You provide yourself with maximum deposits. You develop maximum recall. You have an excellent memory . . . always alert and active.

Now, all of these suggestions are very important, for they represent the proper way to utilize your good memory, the excellent memory that you have. First, you make the proper deposit in the memory bank by paying attention; you concentrate your mind, you think, look, listen, associate, and remember. Second, when you want to make a withdrawal from the memory bank, your memory, your recall is always successful because you make the withdrawal in the proper manner. You do not force it; you utilize some natural association that you already know in order to bring out the information that you want. All of these suggestions improve your memory, your recall; they take complete and thorough effect upon your mind, emotions, body and spirit as they seat themselves in the deepest parts of your subconscious mind, reinforcing themselves over and over again as you drift down deeper now . . . way down . . .

As you drift down deeper now . . . way down . . . so calm, so comfortable . . . relaxed, you realize that all of these suggestions are completely and totally effective and available to you throughout your life whenever you need them. Growing more and more comfortable . . . more and more confident . . . feeling calm and serene and secure in the knowledge that these suggestions which are now seated permanently in your subconscious mind are available for your use whenever you need them. As you sink down deeper relaxed, all of these suggestions are implanted firmly and permanently in the deepest parts of your subconscious mind; completely and thoroughly effective . . . always automatically available as you drift down deeper and deeper relaxed, deeper relaxed.

Academic Study Suggestions

Stanley Krippner, Ph.D.

ELEMENTARY SCHOOL

Every time you read a word or a sentence correctly, you will feel very good inside. You will feel proud of yourself because you read so well. You will enjoy the feeling that reading well gives you. You will want to read some more words and sentences. You will become interested in reading books and magazines and newspapers. Every time that you read something correctly, and understand what you read, your interest will increase. You will want to read another book, or another magazine, or another newspaper. Sometimes you will make mistakes while reading. These mistakes will not bother you because we all make mistakes. None of us is perfect. However, when you read a

word or a sentence very well, you will be pleased and happy. You will want to read more and more.

As you relax, you begin to stop worrying. You stop worrying about reading. You begin to think how much you would like to read better. You begin to think how much you would like to improve your reading ability. You know that you can read better if all the muscles of your body are relaxed. If all of your muscles are relaxed, you will be able to pay closer attention to what you read. You want very much to relax your muscles while you read and to be completely at ease. You want very much to relax all the little muscles in your eyes while you read. This will help you to read with your eyes wide open so that you will not miss any of the letters. If your eyes are wide open, you will not miss any of the words. If your eyes are wide open you will read much better.

HIGH SCHOOL

Before you start to study this evening, form an outline of the work you wish to accomplish so that you, by following your outline, study very efficiently. You will accomplish a great deal as you follow this outline.

When you are studying this evening, you will find that your concentration is so intense that you will be interested in nothing but your [e.g., mathematics] assignment.

COLLEGE

As you begin to study [e.g., chemistry], your mind will quickly grasp the information at hand. Each important fact will make a profound impression upon you. You will be able to recall the information easily when future events demand it.

At (e.g., 8:00 p.m.) you will be absorbed in completing your history term paper. For the following three hours, you will want to do nothing else. Barring emergencies, nothing will interrupt you. If your friends enter the room you will, with as much tact as necessary, send them away.

When you start working on your paper, you will organize your references and other material according to an outline of the general formation of your paper. As you plan your paper, you will become very eager to make your plan a reality and put the ideas into writing.

Concentration Suggestions

William T. Reardon, M.D.
Wilmington, Delaware

If you would like to improve your power of comprehension, concentration, memory, and recall, practice your relaxation [self-hypnosis] for one-and-one-half to two minutes just before you start to study, take an examination, have an interview, or do anything that is usually disconcerting to you.

When you open your eyes, you will be able to concentrate on the work that is to be done. Concentrate to such a degree that you will absorb the material like a sponge taking up water, making an indelible mark in your mind so you will be able to recall it any time in the future. You will get twice as much work done in half the period of time.

The things that used to be distractions will no longer bother you, whether they were persons, places, or things. You will be able to take your examinations with a relaxed body, a clear sharp mind, with no butterflies in your stomach. You won't be able to explain how and why things come so easily to you. Don't try to analyze it; no one knows how it works. Just let it happen and it will happen.

Suggestion for Concentration

Brian M. Alman, Ph.D.
San Diego, California

[This suggestion is phrased as a patient may deliver it to herself in self-hypnosis.] While I sit reading, my mind will be focused on the words and thoughts in this book. Just as a funnel can direct and concentrate water flowing into it— my eyes can channel and focus my concentration onto the words and concepts in this book.

Suggestions and Success Imagery for Study Problems

Jeannie Porter, Ph.D.
Murray Bridge, South Australia

INTRODUCTION

Within a broad clinical context embracing the varying aspects of the learning process, this paper presents a set of specific suggestions in conjunction with use of *success imagery*. Guidelines are given for posthypnotic suggestion and contingency management. Success imagery adopts the approach of idealized-self-imagery (ISI) proposed by Susskind (1970) as a confidence training technique. Principles of self-fulfilling prophecy and operant reinforcement shape change in self-perception towards successful outcome responses. While relaxed under hypnosis, the patient is taught to imagine his "ideal self"—the person he knows he is capable of being—if present inhibiting influences were to be removed. The technique is directly comparable to Maltz's (1973) use of "target imagery" in programming the subconscious to realize self-fulfillment, as goals are successively set on a conscious level and achieved through the ongoing activity of the subconscious working to bring about the "desired end."

Since most study problems are seen to intimately involve the self-concept (Porter, 1975), however, it would seem essential to convince the student seeking help that he can change (Gindes, 1951, p. 84) before he can set his targets and formulate what "success" means to him within his own unique perception of the world (Combs, Avila, & Purkey, 1971). Only then will a change in self-concept, from labeling himself a "doomed failure" to a "potentially successful and aspiring person," enable him to begin to expect success and break out of the "failure syndrome" (Porter, 1975). The role of the therapist is to feed this expectancy with his own belief in the person's potential (Porter, 1974). With the first taste of success, confidence begins to grow and social reinforcement from others strengthens the possibility of future success where once failure had been expected. Success begins to bring success as a self-fulfilling prophecy (Rosenthal & Jacobson, 1968).

This paper ascribes to the concept of mastery as emphasized by Gardner (1976). Mastery becomes an active therapy goal aided in achievement by use of self-hypnosis and self-management exercises. One would hope to engender an "attitude of activity" (Raikov, 1976), while maintaining belief in the self and inducing self-programming. It is pointed out that in creating this image for himself, the student already knows within himself what he is truly capable of doing. Given the removal of present barriers, limitations, and inhibiting influences, this success image will become more and more a reality until soon it is no longer an image but the student's actual self that has been allowed free and full expression. The therapist conveys his belief that this will be the case very soon, thus adding his own belief to the student's to increase the expectancy of change and to catalyze (Bednar, 1970) the change process.

INSTRUCTIONS FOR DAILY USE

Further instructions are given to the student for daily use, first under hypnosis and then reinforced in the discussion on awakening. It is explained that each time he flashes this success image as a total percept into his mind, the student will speed the realization of his goal through known principles of learning and receptivity of mind at stages of "natural trance." He is asked to bring the success image to mind, just long enough for it to seem real, without any particular effort, giving full reliance to belief and imagination to effect the change (Gindes, 1951). The times specified for daily use are:

1. First thing in the *morning* on wakening, before stirring, as the student eases from natural sleep into wakefulness—the hypnagogic state of "natural trance."

2. Last thing at *night* as the student drifts comfortably into natural sleep from normal wakefulness—the hypnopompic state of "natural trance."

3. *Before each meal*—pausing before taking the first mouthful to "flash" the success image into his mind for a few seconds. This invokes the added operation of the Premack (1959) principle, whereby the strong positive primary reinforcer of food follows the conscious evocation of the "success image" at the mental level. By association, food being linked since birth with positive consequences, this strengthens the adoption of the positive image of the self into the person's cognitive structure and allows it to become a determinant of the individual's inner and outer life (Combs et al., 1971).

4. As *many times as possible* during the day—especially in moments of boredom, inactivity, or negative feeling states, to switch the mood to a positive, self-enhancing one and away from a negative, self-defeating one.

5. Whenever *self-hypnosis* is used, as discussed later. Students who find it difficult to "imagine themselves" are given alternative methods. A student can "let his mind go blank" as though it becomes a blank television or movie screen and then imagine the film rolling and the screen showing a film of himself acting out the "success image." With poor visualizers, a change of wording to *"feeling as if"* rather than "imagine" or "think" seems sufficient.

SPECIFIC STUDY SUGGESTIONS

The following suggestions present content rather than exact wording. Actual paraphrasing should be uniquely adapted to the patient's level of understanding and emotional state at the time. It also seems more natural and acceptable to repeat the same types of suggestions on different occasions with slightly altered wording rather than to use direct repetition. Ordering of suggestions can be made flexible, with deletions made of more threatening ones on earlier inductions and of irrelevant ones for the particular individual. Format is best discussed prior to the actual induction, thus establishing agreement as to what to expect in the therapeutic segment of the trance and enhancing acceptance (Porter, 1974). The suggestions include:

Work efficiently without being fatigued by the sheer effort of study, it will come naturally and easily. . . .

- Enjoy the learning process, find it easy and natural to study and to learn. . . .
- Ability to learn and recall information, to integrate new information with what you already know, and answer appropriately any oral or written questions. . . .
- Spend adequate time to ensure success. Take sufficient rest pauses to remain alert and efficient. . . .
- Have increasing belief in your own abilities and certainty that you will succeed.
- Gain ability to switch on the internal success mechanism within the mind, instead of the failure mechanism . . .until very soon you forget even how to switch on the failure mechanism.
- Treat failures as merely pointers to a new path to success.
- Have general confidence in your ability to do not only what you have to do but also what you want to do.
- Maintain a pleasant balance between work and pleasure while remaining always on an overall path to success. . . .
- As belief in your own abilities increases, you will see potential as unlimited. . . .
- Given the opportunity to learn and the ability, you can do anything if you have the desire.
- Do the necessary practice and have the determination to bring success, but you will be able to do this without having to strive unduly. . . . The entire process will be enjoyable and pleasant and you will have the overall conviction that you can be a success. . . .
- Have an increasing sense of achievement and accomplishment.

USE OF POSTHYPNOTIC SUGGESTION

Since study problems are usually associated with high tension and anxiety levels, a simple technique for self-management of anxiety is introduced under hypnosis and further elaborated on awakening. A handout sheet gives a basic rationale as to why it should work. This is given at the session's close.

RELAX/LET GO FIVE BREATHS.   Initially, the student is asked to take five slow, deep breaths, thinking at the same time to *relax* as he breathes in and to *let go* as he breathes out. This encourages awareness of the natural body response of relaxation that comes with exhalation and its use in control of inner emotional states. Under hypnosis, the student is then told that during the day he can evoke this *same* control with ever increasing facility — merely by pausing whenever he experiences some inner disturbing negative thought or feeling state, or feels under pressure from external influences, and repeating the process as just experienced under hypnosis. By taking the five deep breaths, he calls on the body's natural resources to relax and, with the conscious mental commands of "relax" and "let go," chooses to exert control in the situation and acquires inner strength and calmness to deal with present demands.

Thus the student has been given a posthypnotic suggestion. When he actually uses the suggested self-management exercise, he further strengthens it by invoking a self-induced posthypnotic suggestion. With repetition, the control becomes more immediate, and the student's confidence in his own ability to cope generally increases. The student knows a technique that he can use without others becoming aware. At any time during the day, in any situation, he can attain inner control without the necessity of even relaxing first.

RELAXATION, ENERGY, AND CONFIDENCE VERSUS TENSION, TIREDNESS, AND FEAR (REC/TTF). Following the same principles as the above self-management technique, the student is told that he can pair his breathing rhythm with further mental conditioning. Most students wish to feel they can dispel debilitating tension interfering with concentration, tiredness impeding progress, and fear producing confused thinking. Ridding the mind of negatives is not sufficient, however, as other debilitating emotions or thoughts will quickly fill their place. In this instance, the three positive opposites of the negative states "tension, tiredness, and fear" are deliberately internalized by thought concentration, viz. "relaxation, energy, and confidence."

Again the exercise is initially carried out under hypnosis. With attention directed to relaxing with breathing, active concentration is then given to *breathing IN*: relaxation, energy, and confidence; and *breathing OUT*: tension, tiredness, and fear. With each subsequent inhalation/exhalation, it becomes easier for the person to feel he really is drawing in with the pure life-giving air these qualities he wishes to absorb and become permanent within him, while letting go with the stale, impure air the distressing inner states he wishes to reject as no longer affecting him.

Use of the exercise during the day again employs a "self-induced posthypnotic suggestion," which gains in strength on repetition. Anything from five to ten breaths are taken as concentration is given to the mental taking in/letting go, the number of breaths depending on what seems natural and sufficient at the time.

CONCENTRATE AND RECALL. The command to "concentrate and recall" is given as a direct posthypnotic suggestion under a deeper stage of hypnosis toward the end of the session. The student is instructed when he enters the study situation and prepares to commence the task at hand, to briefly pause and say three times firmly and slowly to himself, "concentrate and recall." This command is presented as directing the subconscious to release to him the necessary energy to continue working, to remove all barriers or limiting influences whether past or present, and to allow him to think clearly and work efficiently without strain.

CONTINGENCY MANAGEMENT

In order to reinforce the person's increasing control over when and where he studies (Thoresen & Mahoney, 1974) for his time to be spent more effectively, the student is asked to decide on specific places where he will study. Within the home environment, it may be at a desk in a particular room. At the learning institution, it could be in the library. Once decided, he goes to the specific place to study. The chosen localities become the places of work. Other places are free space where he has no obligation to himself to even think of work. This discrimination makes it much easier to work. If the student is jaded, he leaves his place of work. Away from his place of work he is free to let go and relax, with no associated guilt. In giving himself permission to take times to relax and recuperate, he returns to the selected study environment with a readiness and ability to concentrate and work effectively.

DISCUSSION OF PROCEDURE

In the author's experience, the following general format has proven useful in progressing through therapy sessions. Usually, three sessions seem sufficient for most student needs, with the first two one week apart and the third session two weeks later. With some students, a fourth "booster session" after another four weeks removes any lingering blocks or resistances. The student then continues with the use of self-hypnosis and the self-management exercises to fully master his problem (Lazarus, 1971). An outline of the complete procedure by session follows.

I. Session 1
  A. Contingency management is introduced and explained.

B. With the initial induction, the student is introduced to the experience of hypnosis and conditioned to a "cue signal" to allow quick induction on subsequent occasions. This cue signal is later used for self-hypnosis induction.

C. Hypnosis is reinduced using the "cue signal," then deepening follows.

1. Suggestions. A paraphrased version of Stanton's (1977) form of rational-emotive therapy suggestions [see Chapter 5 on ego-strengthening] is used. These suggestions seem more directly relevant to this specific type of problem as general strengthening suggestions than the more commonly used ego-strengthening suggestions of Hartland (1971).

2. Specific study suggestions are used. (See detailed explanation above.)

3. Relax/let go with five breaths is used as the posthypnotic suggestion to induce self-management. (See detailed explanation above.)

II. Session 2

A. Contingency management is discussed and reinforced.

B. Hypnosis is induced using the cue signal.

1. Wolberg's (1965) suggestions are paraphrased as noted below (designed here to remove any blocks or resistances without having to bring them to the conscious level).

a. You will have a desire to yield, give up, relinquish the symptom, difficulty, problem.

b. The desire will grow so strong that it will make you want to do whatever is necessary to relinquish, give up, the problem.

c. As this happens, you will enjoy the experience of becoming increasingly free of the past problem, difficulty, symptom.

d. You will be so much more relaxed, feel so much better in yourself and at ease, that it will no longer be necessary to have that particular problem,

it will lose its hold over you as it loses its meaning for you.

e. You will be able to go through the day without even thinking about the former problem, symptom, difficulty.

f. You will find that you feel good as you realize the problem (is leaving) has left you, it no longer needs to be there, and has lost its power and influence over you. You are free of its former effects, and no longer need to consider it as belonging to you or as being part of you or your personality.

g. When you indeed get to the point when you want to give up the symptom, problem, difficulty, and are ready and willing to give it up completely, it will simply vanish and no longer be there. It will no longer be necessary to you, and with its disappearance it will no longer be part of you or your personality.

h. With this change, you will grow in strength day by day, becoming happier and more content within yourself, stronger and healthier in every respect, as you become free to be yourself.

2. The relax/let go exercise is reinforced.

3. REC/TTF with breathing is introduced as another posthypnotic suggestion inducing self-management. (See detailed explanation above.)

C. Hypnosis is reinduced.

1. Rational-emotive therapy suggestions are used.

2. Specific study suggestions are used.

3. Self-hypnosis is taught to the cue signal.

III. Session 3

A. The use of contingency management and self-hypnosis is reviewed.

B. Hypnosis is induced.

1. Wolberg's (1965) suggestions are used.

2. The relax/let go exercise is reinforced.

3. REC/TTF is reinforced.

C. Hypnosis is reinduced.

1. Rational-emotive therapy suggestions are used.

2. Specific study suggestions are used.
3. "Concentrate and recall" is given as a direct posthypnotic suggestion.
4. Self-hypnosis is reinforced.

It should be appreciated that the procedures outlined are intended only as guidelines. Each individual case presents unique difficulties that may require modification in procedure. Clinical experience, however, has shown four sessions to be generally sufficient to establish a carry-over to self-management.

This method has been shown to be clinically useful for patients with problems of attention span, concentration, recall, creative thought and problem-solving, phobic withdrawal, recurrent failure, lack of direction and motivation for achievement, test anxiety, and performance fear. Although these behavioral aspects are inherent to the study problem, they are also common to other confidence and relationship difficulties. With ingenuity, this general procedure can become applicable to more extensive behavioral management.

Caution should be exercised in application of this general procedure to depressive cases. Concurrent psychotherapeutic management is mandatory to prevent lack of control precipitated by fantasy escape into self-hypnosis. The same applies to cases of social withdrawal. Self-hypnosis is introduced only when its possible adoption as an alternative escape mechanism is outweighed by the benefits already realized by growing self-management as a general coping skill to allay anxiety states.

Personal clinical experience supports particular application of the procedure to adults returning to study or seeking academic advancement outside of study hours. This is especially true of housewives returning to the school situation or work force out of interest or financial necessity and of business executives trying to keep abreast of the rapidly expanding advances in technology. In such cases, performance pressure often exacerbates anxiety and feeds uncertainty and confusional thought. Adolescents also become prime candidates when faced with society's demands for self-identity

and goal-setting. As for young children, the procedure should be tailored to current needs, with modification to age comprehension level and minimization of complexities. Selective choice of pertinent steps are matched to the child's needs and implemented through clear presentation, feedback understanding, and the gain of acceptance without arousing the typical resistance areas met with adults. However, for children under 10 years of age, the guided fantasy technique (Porter, 1976) is probably more amenable, since it has a wider applicability to childhood complaints and capitalizes on the child's inherent delight in fantasy. Originally proposed for the treatment of childhood insomnia, this method is also a nonthreatening procedure for study phobia, tension cramps in the writing arm and hand, disruptive acting-out behavior, and fear reactions.

Suggestions for Studying, Concentration, and Test Anxiety

Richard B. Garver, Ed.D.
San Antonio, Texas

SUGGESTIONS

As you study this material, whether it is reading it or listening to a lecture, your unconscious mind will help you concentrate. You will have very selective attention. It is as though a light that is focused everywhere begins to constrict, and the peripheral areas grow dim as the center of that light increases in intensity. And you can see and hear very clearly what it is within that narrow band of concentration. And since you are perceiving this information with great intensity, your unconscious mind will be able to store and keep it until you need it. It is important that your unconscious mind knows where to store it, not just anywhere, but to put it in a convenient place, so that you will have access to it by (*a date or an approximate time may be specified*). And so that you know right where it is, you know how to retrieve it when you need to, for whatever purpose there is, whether it is oral recitation or written examination.

METAPHOR

Imagine a board, perhaps two feet wide, that stretches across the floor in my office from one end to the other. You have plenty of room. Do you think you could walk across that board to the other side? [If a positive response is given:] Would you be willing to bet me five or ten dollars that you could? [Typically the answer is yes, they know that they can do it.] Then, I want you to imagine that I am pushing a button on my desk, and now the board stays there, but the floor parts, and what you see is a pit 20 feet below filled with rattlesnakes. Do you think this will affect your performance? [Most will say, yes, absolutely.] So you can see that it is important to make an intelligent decision about the risk versus the outcome. If the outcome is important, then you will feel strong enough to take the risk, and you will then focus on the board rather than on the snakes, and on the outcome on the other side. But, in order to get there, the focus must be on the board, rather than on the snakes.

Erickson's Suggestions for Facilitating Speed of Learning

Milton H. Erickson, M.D.

I don't know how quickly you can learn, but then we all have different learning speeds. . . . Some of us learn to type rapidly but to take shorthand very slowly; to drive a car very quickly but to play golf very slowly. We all have different learning speeds, and we differ in our learning speeds for different kinds of learnings. [What are you doing with these statements? You are raising the question of a rate of learning, but you used the word *speed*. You haven't said we have different degrees of *slowness* in learning; you've said we have different degrees of *speed* in learning, and so you have suggested a rapidity.]

Alert Trance Suggestions for Concentration and Reading

E. R. Oetting, Ph.D.

INTRODUCTION

Basically, the approach consists of training the student in the autohypnotic induction of an "alert trance." The process differs sufficiently from the usual trance induction so that it is not identified as hypnosis. In fact, it is important that the student does not visualize the training as related to hypnosis or he will bring into the situation his previous conceptions of what hypnosis involves, thus creating many of the problems that we are trying to avoid.

As usual, the preliminary orientation plays an important part in trance induction. In this situation, any reference to hypnosis is avoided, but a considerable amount of discussion of approaches to study and general principles of learning is used to establish a set so that subsequent development of an "alert trance" and training in the technique seems reasonable and appropriate to the subject. The first interview includes a discussion of the problems that the individual student has in studying. The technique is then presented as a solution to some aspect of the individual's problem, not as a general solution to all study problems. Most frequently the application is centered around a discussion of concentration. Suggestion in this preliminary stage is used to communicate the following points: (1) that the problem is a common one and that these techniques, if learned successfully, can solve it; (2) that the solution is simply a matter of learning some new techniques; (3) that these techniques can be learned easily but will require time and effort on the part of the patient; (4) that the process of learning involves presenting a set of specific cues; and (5) that learning anything is a function of the number of trials and, to be established firmly, the trials must be presented over a period of time.

It is important that the subject should be dealing with real materials right from the beginning. In our case we use standardized reading materials, but the student's ordinary study materials could be used effectively. A typical trance induction, after rapport has been established and the subject's attention has already been narrowed to the person of the hypnotist and to the topics, would occur as follows.

SUGGESTIONS

I am going to teach you how to concentrate. Really concentrating is quite easy once you learn the knack. You have not been able to concentrate because nobody has ever shown you exactly how to do it. I am going to show you how to do this, and, then we will practice the technique several times until you can do it by yourself. Here, this is going to be your desk. You will notice that the desk is entirely clear of everything but the one piece of material that you are going to work on. Now stand quietly in front of the desk by the chair. Look at the desk and at the material on the desk. You are already beginning to pay attention to the material that you want to study and learn. When you reach this point, you have decided to really get down to work. Keep your eyes right on the material. Now keep looking at it while you reach down, pull the chair out, and seat yourself comfortably. That is good. We are going very slowly now so that you can see all of the steps. Later you can go through these steps very rapidly. Now we are concentrating on them very carefully, one at a time, so that you can see how they feel, and concentrate on each one. Fine! Keep your eyes on the desk and the material in front of you while I show you something about concentration.

At any time your body is sending a lot of signals to your brain that you have learned to ignore. I want to show you some of these. Just for a moment pay attention to your legs and your feet and how they feel. All you have to do is pay attention to them and you can feel your

shoes on your feet. Keep your eyes on the book and nod when you can feel your shoes pressing against your feet. . . . You can feel the chair pressing against you and the weight of your body on the chair . . .and then against the back of the chair. . . . If you simply pay attention to it, you can feel the weight of your shirt on your shoulders . . . and on your neck . . . and you can feel your collar touching your neck. . . . All you have to do is concentrate on these feelings and you can sense them anytime that you want to. That is right, keep looking at the book in front of you. Now if you know how these muscles feel, and where they are, you can sit comfortably, smoothly, and easily. Just let your weight down on the chair and let your body and muscles take care of themselves comfortably and easily. . . . Very good! Your feet are firm and comfortable on the floor, you are balanced and comfortable in your chair. Let me show you. Here. See how your arm is free to move. Now it will reach forward. [The arm is moved by a light, firm touch.] Pull your book towards you a little bit and the rest of your body stays comfortable and easy and well balanced in the chair. Your other arm is free to pull a piece of paper toward you. [The other arm is moved, gently but firmly.] Place it in position to write. You head is free to turn from the book to the paper and you are still comfortable, balanced firmly in the chair, and at ease. That's very good.

[By this time the trance induction is already well under way. The subject has been following repeated suggestions to focus his attention on the materials in front of him. The concentration has been intensified by the gentle, but firm, movement of his arms and hands, and by strong suggestions of ease and well-being, as well as the implied suggestion of immobility of the rest of his body. The next step involves holding a pencil or finger on the same level as the subject's head but to the side so that he can just see it out of the corner of his eye.]

Now, keep your eyes fixed on the book. I am going to show you something about concentration. Can you see the pencil that I am holding up out of the corner of your eye? That's right.

Keep looking at the book. Now, look at my finger on the book. Watch the fingernail carefully. I am going to press my finger against the book. I will press harder and harder until finally my fingernail changes color. Watch carefully, and when it changes color, nod your head. Watch it very carefully so you can see the first slight change in color. Good. Now notice when you are concentrating intently on the tip of my finger, you can no longer see the pencil out of the corner of your eye, and yet now when I have called your attention back to it, you can see the pencil clearly even though your eyes are still focused right on the tip of my finger. Now look again at my finger on the book in front of you and concentrate intently just like you did before. Notice that as you concentrate . . . as you really concentrate . . . you do not notice the things around you. All you see is my finger, and the book, and the paper next to it. It is almost as though there were a spotlight shining on the book and the paper on which you will take notes. As you really concentrate you will only see the materials right in front of you that you are going to work on. Nothing else is important, and you simply don't pay any attention to anything else, you simply concentrate right here in front of you on the work you are going to do. That is very good! Now lean back and relax.

[The repetition is for adding and deepening suggestions eliminating distracting noises and peripheral vision. The field of awareness is narrowed to relevant ideas and materials, but is not restricted to a single point.]

Now I have shown you how to concentrate. You can do this at any time but to make it really work for you will require practice, repeating it over and over again. Now we also need some kind of cue or signal so that you can turn on the concentration yourself, and another signal when you stop. Then you can turn yourself on, using the signal, concentrate intently and accurately on the material, and turn yourself off afterward. Repeating this again and again when you study will make you better and better at it. The signal we will use is

a normal one of sliding forward in your chair into the exact position that you were in before, picking up your pencil, and concentrating. Now, open the book to where I have it marked. Hold it open with your left hand like this. There is a very short paragraph on this page. Read the title of the paragraph. All right, get ready . . . slide forward . . . reach over and pick the pencil up. . . . Get ready to make notes if you want to. Now, read the paragraph, find out what it says about the subject. When you finish, put the pencil down and slide back.

COMMENTARY

The student repeats this process several times in the office. We then discuss how to break down the material that he is ordinarily studying into short segments so that he can repeat the process on his own. Generally two or three sessions repeating, reinforcing, and deepening are sufficient for a student to learn a technique that he can use on himself in almost any situation, regardless of outside distractions.

The technique of developing an "alert trance state" has distinct advantages over the classical techniques for trance induction. Since it is "concentration training," the fear and criticism that would be associated with the use of "hypnosis" with students is avoided. More importantly, the student himself does not bring his preconceived ideas about hypnosis to the situation. Most students who want to be hypnotized to help with study also want to avoid the responsibility for motivating themselves and training themselves in study techniques. They tend to lean on the trance state as though it were a crutch, waiting for it to solve their problems. With this technique they are required to train themselves and to practice active studying and concentrating. From the beginning the student has the feeling of doing everything himself.

Alert Self-Hypnosis Technique to Improve Reading Comprehension

David M. Wark, Ph.D.
Minneapolis, Minnesota

THE LEVER INDUCTION

PURPOSE AND INDICATIONS.   This is a practical technique to quickly bring your mind to a state of focused tension and your body to a state of efficient relaxed calmness. Since studying is an alert activity, the typical deep induction involving drowsiness is inappropriate. The technique is called the LEVER because you lift your mind to a state of sharp focus and relax your body while holding your mind's tension. Then you lever up your mental focus a bit higher, and again relax your body. And then, a third time, you raise your mental focus and relax your body.

I have found it useful to use two levels of suggestion. The first is a basic suggestion, which focuses on the perceptible qualities of the text (color, shape, texture, etc.) and then suggests some cognitive changes (ideas will flow up from the page, attention will be focused, study will be enjoyable). When students have learned to use those suggestions, I have them move on to the advanced suggestions, designed to increase comfort, meaning, or various types of imagery.

PHYSICAL PRACTICE

Sit comfortably in your chair. Pick a spot to focus on, and attend to it alertly. Take in a deep breath, sit straight up in your chair and extend your spine right up to the sky. Keep your eyes on the target, and begin to exhale. As you do, keep your spine straight, but allow your shoulders to relax, like a cape falling over your back.

Take another deep breath while focusing on your target. Tense all the muscles below your waist — your hips and thighs, and calves and feet. Keep your eyes on the target, and slowly relax your whole body. Take a third deep breath. Tense your whole body, and observe your target while your body relaxes. Now, give yourself your suggestion.

BASIC SELF-HYPNOSIS SUGGESTIONS IN AN ALERT TRANCE

Enter an alert trance state by using the LEVER or some other exercise. Then give yourself the basic suggestions. After the suggestion, begin to study in an alert trance state.

1. Notice the paper. What color is it? Notice how clean and crisp it seems. Fingers slide over the surface, and feel how smooth. Eyes can flow across the page, going easily from side to side, seeing everything.
2. Notice the letters on the page. They seem dark and distinct. The round parts of the O's and C's are very smooth; the up and down parts of the T's and L's are tall and strong. The printing is especially vivid. The words seem to stand out very clearly.
3. And it seems that every sentence suggests images and ideas, that flow up from page to mind, directly and easily, recalling what has already been learned. The new ideas from the page and old ideas from the past seem to fit together now. New ideas come forward, and the meaning gets clearer and clearer.
4. After the reading, the learning will continue, and the meaning will get ever more clear.
5. Attention will become completely focused on the page. The only sound will come from the reading and study. The reading and study will become more and more enjoyable, more and more involving.
6. At the end of the lesson, close the book and review the learning. When the trance ends, attention will return to other things, but the learning will continue. It will become easier and easier to enter an alert trance and enjoy studying.

Advanced Comprehension Suggestions for an Alert Trance

David M. Wark, Ph.D.
Minneapolis, Minnesota

AUTHOR

[This suggestion increases comfort and motivation.]

Behind the book is an author who wrote the book. When I sit alertly focused on my page, it may sound as if the author is talking directly to me. The author is another teacher, one who really wants to get a message to me. I remember another important person, who helped me so much. I may get an image of us together, and feel how I am enjoying the learning. I may feel a real closeness to the author, and the author back to me. As I read alertly, the ideas from the author will seem to flow easily into my mind. It will seem that I can make a connection with the mind of the author.

PUZZLE

[The Puzzle suggestion is useful in increasing meaning and comprehension.]

Reading can be like putting together a jigsaw puzzle. I remember a time when I really enjoyed doing a puzzle. I saw the parts all spread out in front of me on the table. Some looked familiar, like things that I had seen before. Some had no pattern, just out-parts and in-parts, but they looked like they might fit together. I looked again and saw two bits with the same shade, and when I tried them together they fit with a click. What pleasure! More and more I pushed and fit and clicked. Soon the whole puzzle seemed to make sense. I can do that with my books.

FLOWERS

[This metaphor increases the use of visual imagery.]

A small seed lives nested in the warm, dark earth of a garden. It is just the time, just the beginning, just the very start of something to be. Slowly the warm light of the sun reaches down through the dark soil and warms the shell of the seed. The shell expands and slowly water and nutrients seep inside, around the old, hard, protective shell and into the rich inner core. A small sprout starts to push out and up, slowly at first, and then more and more confidently, up through the layers of dark soil. The sprout grows, gets stronger. It grows tall and strong in the sunlight, buds and flowers, adding color and fragrance to the garden. Then, one by one other seeds repeat, until the pattern of the planting is obvious for all to see. I can do that with my reading.

ANTS

[The metaphor of ants can be used to facilitate kinesthetic imagery.]

Some people devour and digest what they read. The soldier ants march across the field in lines and lines. They are organized and orderly. No one lags, no one gets ahead. They present a pleasing pattern to the eye. They are moving directly forward. Then an obstacle appears in the path. Somehow the ants know just what to do. Some move off to one side or the other, looking for a toe hold, a crevice, the smallest little chink to use as a foot hold. Others move directly up and over, covering the obstacle. If it is nourishing, the ants chew and digest. I can do that as I read and study.

Improving Reading Speed by Hypnosis

Raymond W. Klauber, Ph.D.
Edwardsville, Illinois

[If, upon examination, it is found that the slow reader is moving his throat, lips, or tongue, he should be told that the fastest readers move only their eyes. With proper rapport and diagnosis of the reading difficulty, the therapist could move into hypnotic techniques. After a relaxing hypnotic induction, slowly say:]

Your mind reads by ideas—in an instant, your mind grasps complete ideas through your eyes, faster than anyone could say each word. Your eyes are faster than your throat, lips, or tongue. Saying each word prevents a slow reader from achieving a pace quicker than he can speak. Without moving your throat, lips, or tongue, the meaning of the words quickly leaps through your eyes into your mind. If you like, I will teach you a way you can prevent these movements while reading. Would you like to learn such a method? If your answer is yes, raise this finger [after you touch his right index finger, wait for him to raise it]. . . . Good!

Now slowly raise the fingers of your left hand to your throat, that is, place your finger lightly about your Adam's apple [guide hands and fingers if necessary].

Now imagine that there is no movement; try to further imagine that not only does the area you are touching not move but that you no longer feel it . . . it disappears. Signal me with your right finger when you have imagined away your throat [wait for the signal and give further suggestions if necessary]. . . . Good!

The same forgetting of your throat will take place when you read. Your throat will be relaxed and comfortable. It will be still, rather than making the words you read. Lower your hand to your lap when you have imagined this in order to receive the next suggestions. . . . Good!

Now slowly raise the fingers of your left hand to your lips, that is, place your fingers lightly on your lips [guide hand and fingers if necessary].

Now imagine there is no movement, try to further imagine that not only does the area you are touching not move but that you no longer feel it . . . it disappears. . . . Signal me with your finger when you have imagined away your lips [wait for the signal and give further suggestions if necessary]. . . . Good!

The same forgetting of your lips will take place when you read. Your lips will be relaxed and comfortable. They will be still rather than making the words you read.

Without moving your throat or lips as you read, the printed words group together into ideas that quickly leap through your eyes into your mind.

Lower your hand to your lap when you have imagined this in order to receive the next suggestion. . . . Good!

Now slowly raise your left hand to your mouth and place one finger lightly on your tongue. Now imagine there is no movement, try to further imagine that not only does the area you are touching not move but that you no longer feel it . . . it disappears.

Signal me with your right-hand finger when you have imagined away your tongue [wait for the signal and give further suggestions if necessary]. . . . Good!

The same forgetting of your tongue will take place as you read. Your tongue will be relaxed and comfortable. It will be still rather than making the words as you read.

Without moving your throat, lips, or tongue as you read, the printed words group together into ideas that quickly leap through your eyes into your mind.

Lower your hand to your lap when you have imagined this in order to receive the next suggestion. . . . Good!

You have now learned to read without using your throat, lips, or tongue. However, as you read you will lightly touch your throat. lips, and tongue so that you know they don't move. You will be further assured that they aren't moving as you touch them.

You will make these movements from time to time until you are sure that you never move your throat, lips, or tongue while reading. You will make these movements without thinking about them so that you will continue to concentrate upon your reading.

Think about everything I told you. . . . When you believe that you can read as you learned today, open your eyes and be fully awake.

Gorman's Ego-Strengthening Technique Adapted for Reading

G. Gerald Koe, Ed.D.
Mission, British Columbia, Canada

INTRODUCTION AND INDICATIONS

The suggestions contributed by Koe, previously unpublished, were used in an experiment (Koe & Oldridge, 1987) with university students. They found that, with four sessions utilizing these suggestions, self-concept improved, particularly with regard to self-satisfaction and personal self-concept. Of the three sets of suggestions used in the study, the suggestions printed here were the most effective. These suggestions are recommended for use with university or high school students who need to improve reading, academic performance and self-esteem. (*Ed.*)

SESSION I SUGGESTIONS

You are now so deeply relaxed that your mind has become very receptive. In this state of deep relaxation the critical part of your conscious mind is also very deeply relaxed so that you can accept any idea you wish to accept for your own good.

Because I wish you to remain in this uncritical state, I am not going to give you any direct suggestions with regard to any of your particular problems. I am only going to ask you to think about certain words and their meanings and associations for others. I want you to think lazily of these words, to turn them over in your mind, to examine them, to let them sink deeply into your subconscious mind.

The first word I want you to think about is the word "health," and I want you now and always to couple it with the word "good." What can the words good health mean? They can mean a sense of superb physical well-being, with strong heart and lungs; perfect functioning of all the organs, nerves, glands and systems of the entire body;

firm, strong muscles, bones and joints; smooth, healthy, elastic skin and the absence of any excess fat or flesh; greater, increased resistance to all forms of infection or disease and an increasingly great measure of control of both the autonomic nervous system and the hormone glands which, between them, control all the functions and conditions of the body.

Good health means not only physical health but also a healthy attitude of mind in which the nerves are stronger and steadier, the mind calm and clear, more composed, more tranquil, more relaxed, more confident.

It can mean a greater feeling of esteem in the eyes of others, a greater feeling of personal well-being, safety, security and happiness than has ever been felt before.

It can mean others will perceive you as having complete control of your thoughts and emotions, with the ability to concentrate better and utilize all the vast resources of the memory and the full intellectual powers of the subconscious mind.

It can mean that others will perceive you as having the ability to sleep deeply and refreshingly at night and to awake in the morning feeling calm, relaxed, confident and cheerful— ready to meet all the challenges of the new day with boundless energy and enthusiasm. The words good health can mean to others any or all of these things and more. These words have tremendous power. I want you to let them sink deeply into your subconscious mind, which always can reproduce in you your dominant thoughts.

The next word I would like you to think about is success. It may mean a sense of recognition, a fulfillment of your desires.

It may mean the ability to set and achieve goals in life which people who are important to you consider to be realistic, worthwhile and progressive, and the motivation and determination to achieve those goals. It may mean the confidence to recognize that friends perceive you as being able to throw off your inhibitions, being spontaneous, expressing your feelings without fear or hesitation.

Success may mean wealth in terms of money and the things that money can buy, or security for yourself and your family. It can also show itself in the attitude of mind which gives inner happiness regardless of material possessions or circumstances. It could mean the ability to overcome some particular problem—perhaps even some problem about which you do not know. Whatever the word success means to others, I want you to use this word as an emotional stimulus to produce in you all the feelings which go with success.

Finally, I want you to think of the word motivation. What can it mean to others? It can mean a gradual but progressive strengthening of one's desire to be in charge of one's life; to destroy the old recordings of habit patterns; to play new music instead of old; to cease being a puppet to one's early conditioning and to become a creator of a new, healthy, happy, successful script in the play of life.

It can mean the gradual but progressive building of a stronger and stronger feeling of how positively others perceive you until your self-confidence is much stronger than your fear of failure and achieving high grades at university [in high school] presents no difficulty, hardship or discomfort for you.

We have all been conditioned since birth to associate words with feelings. Words are, therefore, the tools which we are going to use to produce the feelings and results which we want. And these words are health, success, and motivation.

In a few seconds, I will slowly count to three. When I do, you will come out of the hypnotic trance you are in now. You will remember the suggestions given you regarding health, success, and motivation while you were hypnotized. You will incorporate these suggestions into your self-image.

When you wake you will feel deeply relaxed. You will remember being hypnotized as an enjoyable and pleasant experience. Ready now. I am going to count to three. One—you are starting to wake up. Two—your eyes are starting to open. Three—your eyes are open

now and you are completely out of the hypnotic trance.

SESSION II SUGGESTIONS

You are now so deeply relaxed that your mind has become very receptive. In this state of deep relaxation, the critical part of your conscious mind is also very deeply relaxed so that you can accept any idea you wish to accept for your own good.

Because I wish you to remain in this uncritical state, I am not going to give you any direct suggestions with regard to any of your particular problems. I am only going to ask you to think about certain words and their meanings for others. I want you to think lazily of these words, to turn them over in your mind, to examine them, to let them sink deeply into your subconscious mind, until they become woven into the very fabric of your beliefs as to how others perceive you.

The first word I want you to think about is the word health, and I want you now and always to couple it with the word good. What can the words good health mean to others? They mean a sense of superb physical well-being, with a well conditioned, well functioning body. They can mean that the body feels full of power and strength, with greater balance and stamina, increased resistance to fatigue and disease, more slender with firm muscle tone and vibrant complexion. Good health can result in greater awareness of the body, greater control of all parts of the body, and a sense of harmony in the functioning of the body.

Good health means not only physical health but also a healthy attitude of mind, in which others see you as feeling calmer, safer, more secure; more confident and sure of yourself, happier and more self-satisfied than you ever felt before at university.

It can mean that others perceive you as being able to control your thoughts and emotions. It can mean that others perceive you as being better able to concentrate on your studies at university [in school]. It can mean that others perceive you as being able to sleep better at night. It can mean that others will perceive you as feeling calm, confident, and cheerful in the morning when you rise, ready to meet the challenges of a new day.

The words good health can mean any or all of these things and more. These words have tremendous power. I want you to let them sink deeply into your subconscious mind, which always can reproduce in you your dominant thoughts.

The next word I would like you to think about is success. It may mean that others see you as feeling a sense of worthiness or fulfillment, the attainment of your desires in terms of your achievement at university [in school]. It may mean that others see you as having the ability to set and achieve goals at university [school] which are realistic, worthwhile, and progressive, and the motivation and determination to achieve these goals. It may mean that friends see you as having the confidence to ask questions in class, to enable you to be spontaneous, to express feelings without fear or hesitation.

Success can mean higher marks at university [in school], which may mean security for you and your family. It can also manifest itself in the inner happiness that comes when you know that you have done the best you can.

It could mean the ability to overcome some particular problem that is interfering with your university achievement.

Whatever the word success means to others, I want you to use this word as an emotional stimulus to produce in you all the feelings that go with success.

Finally, I want you to think of the word motivation. What can it mean? It can mean the desire, determination, and driving force to achieve at university [school]. It can mean a gradual but progressive strengthening of one's desire to be in charge of one's life, to change habit patterns so that they facilitate the goal of high achievement at university.

It can mean the gradual but progressive building of a stronger and stronger feeling of how positively others perceive you until your self-confidence is much stronger than your fear of failure, and achieving high grades at university [in school] presents no difficulty, hardship, or discomfort for you.

We have all been conditioned since birth to associate words with feelings. Words are, therefore, the tools which we are going to use to produce the feelings and results which we want. And these words are health, success, and motivation.

In a few seconds, I will slowly count to three. When I do, you will come out of the hypnotic trance you are in now. You will remember the suggestions given you regarding health, success, and motivation while you were hypnotized. You will incorporate these suggestions into your self-image.

When you wake up you will feel deeply relaxed. You will remember being hypnotized as an enjoyable and pleasant experience. Ready now. I am going to count to three. One—you are starting to wake up. Two—your eyes are starting to open. Three—your eyes are open now and you are completely out of the hypnotic trance.

SESSION III SUGGESTIONS

You are now so deeply relaxed that your mind has become very receptive. In this state of deep relaxation the critical part of your conscious mind is also very deeply relaxed so that you can accept any idea you wish to accept for your own good.

Because I wish you to remain in this uncritical state, I am not going to give you any direct suggestions with regard to any of your particular problems. I am only going to ask you to think of your particular problems. I am only going to ask you to think about certain words and their meanings and associations for others. I want you to think lazily of these words, to turn them over in your subconscious mind, until they become woven into the very fabric of your substance and of your self-image and into the very fabric of your beliefs as to how others perceive you.

The first word I want you to think about is health, and I want you now and always to couple it with the word good. What can the words good health mean? They can mean that people will perceive you as feeling good physically; alert when studying; strong and healthy; and happy with how your body looks and responds. Good health may mean less fatigue and illness, better body weight, less muscle strain and other irritations which keep you from performing to your fullest capacity in your studies and work. It may mean friends perceive you as looking good as well as feeling good.

Good health means not only physical health, but also a healthy attitude of mind in which your friends perceive you as feeling better about yourself than ever before; more confident in and sure of your ability to analyze the material you read; calmer and more relaxed when expressing yourself; happier and more satisfied in your classes this year than ever before.

It can mean that others will feel that you are better able to control your thoughts and attention, better able to concentrate and remember information in the material you read. It can seem that friends will feel that you are able to use your subconscious mind to the full extent of your ability, allowing your subconscious mind to focus on pertinent data when needed.

It can mean that others will feel that you are able to sleep better at night; free from anxiety and self-doubt; awaking calm and confident in the morning. It can mean that friends will perceive you as feeling wide awake in the morning, eager and ready to absorb all you can from the coming day.

The words good health can mean any and all of these things and more. These words have tremendous power. I want you to let them sink deeply into your subconscious mind, which always can reproduce in you your dominant thoughts.

The next word I would like you to think about is success. It may mean that friends see you as feeling a sense of accomplishment as you improve in your reading speed and comprehen-

sion; a sense of satisfaction with this accomplishment.

It may mean that others feel you have the ability to set realistic goals in study habits. It may mean others see you as having the motivation and determination to achieve these goals. It may mean that others feel you are confident when reading or studying, easily making connections between material read and information stored in memory. It may mean that others think you easily remember important facts and information and are able to easily identify crucial issues, lead discussions, and in general be a superior student.

Success may mean wealth in terms of money and the things that money can buy, or security for yourself and your family. It can also show itself in the attitude of mind which gives inner happiness regardless of material possessions or circumstances. It could mean the ability to overcome some particular problem — perhaps even some problem about which you do not know. Whatever the word success means to others, I want you to use this word as an emotional stimulus to produce in you all the feelings that go with success.

Finally, I want you to think of the word motivation. What can it mean to others? It can mean that friends perceive you as having the desire to improve your reading. It can mean they feel you have the drive and determination to improve your achievement. It can mean they feel you have the progressive desire to change habits, to take control of your life rather than to passively respond to old feelings.

It can mean the gradual but progressive building of a stronger and stronger feeling of how positively others perceive you until your self-confidence is much stronger than your fear of failure and achieving high grades at university [in school] presents no difficulty, hardship, or discomfort for you.

We have all been conditioned since birth to associate words with feelings. Words are therefore the tools which we are going to use to produce the feelings and results which we want. And these words are health, success, and motivation.

In a few seconds, I will slowly count to three. When I do, you will come out of the hypnotic trance you are in now. You will remember the suggestions given you regarding health, success, and motivation while you were hypnotized. You will incorporate these suggestions into your self-concept.

When you wake up you will feel deeply relaxed. You will remember being hypnotized as an enjoyable and pleasant experience. Ready now. I am going to count to three. One—you are starting to wake up. Two—your eyes are starting to open. Three—your eyes are open now and you are completely out of the hypnotic trance.

SESSION IV SUGGESTIONS

You are now so deeply relaxed that your mind has become very receptive. In this state of deep relaxation the critical part of your conscious mind is also very deeply relaxed so that you can accept any idea you wish to accept for your own good.

Because I wish you to remain in this uncritical state, I am not going to give you any direct suggestions with regard to any of your particular problems. I am only going to ask you to think about certain words and their meanings and associations for others. I want you to think lazily of these words, to turn them over in your mind, to examine them, to let them sink deeply into your subconscious mind until they become woven into the very fabric of your beliefs as to how others perceive you.

The first word I want you to think about is the word health, and I want you now and always to couple it with the word good. What can the words good health mean to others? They can mean that others perceive your body is in top physical shape. It feels good to exercise and exert your body. It feels good to strive and achieve physical limits. You find exercise exhilarating rather than fatiguing. By keeping physically fit, studying comes easily because the mind feels alert in a healthy body. This feeling may reflect in your work because you spend less

time away from work as a result of fatigue or tiredness.

Good health means not only physical health but also a healthy attitude of mind. Because you know and accept your body limits you feel calm and confident in your ability to succeed in your endeavors. Knowing you approach your limits gives you a feeling of pride and confidence in a job well done.

It can mean appearing to others to be in charge of your thought processes, thinking calmly, logically, and making good decisions on the information available. Others feel you weigh and use all the information before drawing conclusions or making inferences. They feel you are able to concentrate better, remember more, and progressively gain more information each day.

It can mean friends feel you sleep more deeply at night and awake more alert in the morning ready to assimilate new material. Because you are rested, yesterday's problems are seen with a new perspective and you are able to make decisions which enhance success.

The words good health can mean to you any or all of these things and more. These words have tremendous power. I want you to let them sink deeply into your subconscious mind, which always can reproduce in you your dominant thoughts.

The next word I would like you to think about is success. It can mean high achievement in class, outstanding performance on exams; recognition and rewards. It may mean you appear calm and confident during exams, easily recalling pertinent facts and knowing that you will be successful despite transitory difficulties. You will appear to be motivated to re-read questions on exams to be sure you fully understand their implications so that you can answer completely and in a logical manner. Others will perceive you as feeling motivated to re-check answers on examinations to ensure success. If you don't know an answer, you will appear confident to allow yourself to make spontaneous guesses, knowing that your subconscious mind will help recall the correct answer.

Success may mean higher marks at university [in school] because of improved examination performance. It may also mean more security for you and your family. It can mean friends will perceive you as feeling the happiness and self-worth that comes from making the best effort you can, not only in study habits, but in exam performance. It could mean the ability to overcome some particular problem that is interfering with your exam performance. Whatever the word success means to others, I want you to use this word as an emotional stimulus to produce in you all the feelings that go with success.

Finally, I want you to think of the word motivation. What can it mean? It can mean the willingness to apply yourself for gradually increasing periods of time while studying. It can mean the determination to use the full allotment of time on exams. It can mean the willingness to ask the instructor to clarify obscure or ambiguous questions. It can mean the desire to take responsibility for your own performance onto yourself, to take charge of your life and your successes rather than letting life's forces mold and shape your performance. You appear this way to others and seem to have the perseverance and ability to achieve the goals you desire.

We have all been conditioned since birth to associate words with feelings. Words are therefore the tools which we are going to use to produce the feelings and results which we want. And these words are health, success, and motivation.

In a few seconds, I will slowly count to three. When I do, you will come out of the hypnotic trance you are in now. You will remember the suggestions given you regarding health, success, and motivation while you were hypnotized. You will incorporate these suggestions into your self-concept.

When you wake up you will feel deeply relaxed. You will remember being hypnotized as an enjoyable and pleasant experience. Ready now. I am going to count to three. One—you are starting to wake up. Two—your eyes are starting to open. Three—your eyes are open

now and you are completely out of the hypnotic trance.

Suggestions for Foreign Language Study

Don E. Gibbons, Ph.D.

Now I would like you to think of a particular nursery rhyme, bedtime story, or fairy tale which was your favorite when you were a child; or if you prefer, you can think of a motion picture or a television program which you particularly enjoyed when you were very young. I would like you to picture yourself as a young child again, listening to the story, or watching the program or the movie, and feeling completely enthralled by the performance, just as you did then. Just let your imagination go, and soon you will be able to recapture the mood completely, feeling now just as you felt then. And when you have fully caught the mood, you can signal me by raising the index finger of your right [or left] hand.

[After the subject has raised his hand:] That's fine. Now just hold the mood for a moment and continue to listen to my voice, and as you do, you will notice the feeling growing even stronger. Notice how enthralled you feel, and how easy it is to concentrate and to absorb new information, almost without any deliberate effort.

From now on, whenever you wish, you will be able to call up this mood yourself, just by thinking of a situation like the one you have chosen and letting your imagination drift backward in time until you have recaptured the feeling completely. And the more often you practice doing this, the easier it will become, and the more strongly you will be able to feel such a mood once you have captured it again.

Now the mood is completely gone, but as a result of this experience, you are going to be able to transfer to your present language study more and more of the wonder and excitement which learning and using your language used to hold for you as a child. When you are ready to begin your language homework, you will be able to call forth this same mood once again, just as I have shown you; and if the mood should start to "wear off" before you finish studying, you can take a break for a few moments and call it back again. For the more often you practice recalling and reexperiencing these feelings, the stronger your ability to reexperience them will become, and the more easily you will be able to do so.

And as a result of this change in mood and in attitude, you will find a great improvement taking place in your ability to acquire and to use foreign words and phrases; for they will not seem "foreign" to you at all, but rather, a continuation of the language learning you have always enjoyed. These new words and phrases will come to possess the same interest, the same fascination and appeal, and the same power to arouse your curiosity and to capture and hold your attention as did you own native language when you were first acquiring it. You will spend a great deal of time turning the new information over in your mind and making up games with it in order to amuse yourself, just as children often do. And consequently, you will be able to learn, to retain, and to use the new language with the same ease, the same naturalness of expression, and the same inherent grammatical sense which characterized the learning of your mother tongue as a child.

The entire process of language learning will become a natural, an enjoyable, and a spontaneous process once again, and you are going to be absolutely delighted at your progress.

Suggestions for Mathematics or Statistics Performance

Robert M. Anderson, Ph.D.
Takoma Park, Maryland

INTRODUCTION AND INDICATIONS

Some people who have facility in language studies do not have similar talents in mathe-matics or related fields such as statistics. The following suggestions have been utilized to create an analogous condition between language talent and the ability to understand and use mathematics and statistics. To personalize the suggestions, use the name and words of a specific language or languages. If the subject does not know a foreign language, the suggestions may be modified so that English (or any native language) can be used for the analogy.

SUGGESTIONS

Think for a moment how easily language(s) comes to you. Your talents, your abilities, allow you to learn vocabulary, grammar and syntax almost without effort. Consider how easily the words [*predetermined words the subject knows*] come to you, how easily you use them. The ease with which you learned and use these words is indicative of how easily you learn languages.

There are many languages in the world. Your ability would allow you to learn any one easily that you would want to learn, almost without effort, effortlessly. You would have to study some, but you would learn. And you would be pleased at your ability, just as you have been pleased and proud of yourself as you have learned [*specify the language*].

One language you have learned and mastered is English, another is . Another language that you can learn and master is the language of mathematics [or statistics, etc.]. In fact, mathematics is one of the easiest languages to learn. It is logical, with no surprises like irregular verbs or strange spellings. In mathematics, everything means what it says. Letters and numbers are the words, equations are sentences, problem solutions are paragraphs. The beauty of language is present in the beauty of mathematics, and you will see this beauty more and more as you learn mathematics.

You will see that sentences like, "Michael is a good boy," or "My car is a compact car," are merely verbal equations, showing that one side (Michael) equals the other side (good boy). "Marty and Bob are a couple," is the same as 1

+ 1 = 2 or a + b = 2 or x + y = z. And with your facility for language guiding you, you will see more and more clearly the language of mathematics. The language of mathematics will become more and more friendly to you. As you understand it as a language, its beauty, symmetry and meaning will become clearer and clearer to you. As you study mathematics, it will become like English or _____ , easy, understandable. And you'll find that you may even be surprised at first at how easily, effortlessly, you learn and recall the language of mathematics.

[To reinforce the suggestions, at the end of the session, go through a few simple problems that the patient already understands, allowing the patient to look for the analogies between language and mathematics in them.]

Examination Panic

Milton H. Erickson, M.D.

INDICATIONS

The late Dr. Erickson formulated the following suggestions that he tended to give to highly motivated subjects who had test anxiety and who were going to take an essay exam. These patients included physicians, lawyers, Ph.D. candidates, college and high school students. The central theme of the suggestions is the avoidance of perfectionism and motivating the student for "the comfortable achievement of lesser goals" (1965, p. 358). Erickson, despite myths to the contrary, did not individualize all of his suggestions. He specifically indicated that "the procedure employed with these various applicants for help was essentially constant in character" (p. 356). He reported "uniformly good" results. The essence of Erickson's overall approach was tremendous flexibility and he was willing to be both highly direct and highly indirect, depending on the patient. You will note that the suggestions he typically used with this problem are sometimes so highly directive and authoritarian that therapists who are not

exceptionally confident will probably feel uncomfortable using some of them. Erickson reported only a few failures with the technique. "All of these first-time failures occurred with subjects who developed only light trances and who could not seem to learn deep trances. The deeper the trance, the better pleased was the examinee with the examination results" (p. 358). It is, therefore, recommended that the patient be placed in the deepest trance possible prior to offering these suggestions. (*Ed.*)

SUGGESTIONS

You wish to have help in passing your examination. You have sought hypnosis and you have developed the trance state that I know to be sufficient to meet your needs. You will continue in that trance state until I tell you otherwise.

Now, here is the help you wish. Listen carefully and understandingly. You may not want to agree with me but you must remember that your own ideas have led only to failures. Hence, though what I say may not seem exactly right, abide by it fully. In so doing, you will achieve your goal of passing the examination. That is your goal and you are to achieve it and I shall give you the instructions by which to do it. I cannot give you the information that you have acquired in past study and I want you to have it available for the examination in the way I specify.

First of all you are to pass this examination, not trying in the unsuccessful ways you have in the past but in the way I shall now define. You want to pass this examination. I want you to pass it. But listen closely: *You are to pass it with the lowest passing grade—not an A or a B. I know you would like a high grade but you need a passing grade, that's all and that is what you are to get. To this you must agree absolutely, and you do, do you not*? [An affirmation was always given.]

Next, after leaving this office I want you to feel carefree, at ease, even forgetful of the fact that you are to write an examination. But no matter how forgetful of that fact you become, you will remember to appear on time at the place of the examination. At first you may not even remember why you are there but it will dawn on your mind in time, and comfortably so.

Upon taking your place, you are to read through all the questions. Not one of them will make sense, but read them all. [The purpose of this was to give the subject an unwitting appraisal of the number of questions and the amount of time each would require.]

Then get ready to write and read the first question again. It will seem to make a little sense and a little information will trickle into your conscious mind. By the time you have written it down, there will be another trickle keeping you writing until suddenly the trickle dries up. Then you move on to the next question and the same thing will happen. When the time is up, you will have answered all of the questions comfortably, easily, just recording the trickle of information that develops for each question.

When finished, turn in your examination paper and leave feeling comfortable, at ease, at peace with yourself.

Suggestions for Concentration, Studying, and Overcoming Test Anxiety

Alcid M. Pelletier, Ed.D.
Grand Rapids, Michigan

Your brain is like a computer. It is superior to a computer. As a matter of fact, your brain is the prototype for all computers. All of them have been fashioned after some of the processes of your mind.

During the first five years of your life, you learned more than you did in any other five-year period since. You learned a language, how to walk and run; you learned how to distinguish one person from another and one object from another with all their proper names. You learned your colors, how to draw between lines, perhaps a few of your ABC's, to count at least to ten. You learned how to get up and down stairs, how to get around your yard and immediate neighborhood. You learned how to write a few characters, how to draw, how to bathe, how to brush your teeth, comb your hair, and dress. One of the big achievements in learning was how to distinguish your right from your left when you put on your shoes, how to lace them, and especially how to tie a bow. To accomplish all this learning and memory, you had to study, to concentrate. You did not allow yourself to be distracted; you kept on trying until you were successful.

All of the learning, concentration, studying, and memory I have just mentioned was data which you programmed into your computer brain. Now that you are older, you daily perform these tasks, but they were not so simple when you were learning them. The same principle applies in learning, concentration, studying and memory at any age. Now you are not studying how to tie your shoelaces, you are studying math [or chemistry, anatomy, design, architecture, music, adeptness at sports, etc.]. But the same principle applies in learning your [*e.g., math*]. You learned by concentration and thinking logically even before you knew the meaning of the word "logical." Now that you know the meaning of the word and you have the interest and the need to learn, it ought to be easier for you if you have the attitude to broaden your learning.

Try an experiment in concentration. Take a ballpoint pen, discover its parts and functions, and fully describe it, its color, size, circumference, length, spring mechanisms, slip, bands, ink, etc. You can spend five or more minutes describing that ballpoint pen if you really concentrate. Then that pen will be different from other pens. Think of the possibilities of your social and personal life if you become aware of people like that. Think of how you can excel in math when you concentrate on its logistics, theorems, calculations, and accurate conclusions, make your studying exciting and you will become excited in learning.

Since your brain is like a computer, you are storing data into it every time you study and concentrate. Whatever you feed into a computer can, in turn, be retrieved from it. Now you are about to take a test, an examination—written, oral, true-false, essay, multiple choice—it really doesn't matter. What matters is that it is a test to test what you have stored in your computer brain and how effective is your trained retrievable system. Since you have placed the data in your computer, you *can* retrieve it.

Suggestions for Examination Phobia

David Waxman, L.R.C.P., M.R.C.S.
London, England

The moment you enter the examination room and pick up your paper to read the questions . . . you will become completely calm and relaxed . . . and all your nervousness and apprehension will disappear completely.

No matter how difficult the questions may seem at first sight . . . or how little you seem to know . . . you will not panic . . . because you will find that things are not as bad as they seem.

You will read *all the questions carefully and deliberately . . . you will decide upon the one that you can tackle best . . . and answer that one as fully as you can . . . without worrying about the others until you have completed it.*

As you do this . . . *you will find that you will actually remember far more than you originally thought you would.*

When you have put down all you know about this first question . . . *choose the next easiest to answer . . . and tackle that in exactly the same way.*

Continue in this way with the rest of the questions until you have written all that you can remember . . . or until the time is up.

When you have finished . . . you will find that you have remembered far more that you thought possible when you first read the questions.

[The combination of the two techniques of desensitization and ego-strengthening will usually be found to be successful. However, in all cases one must be certain that there is no other underlying neurosis or personality problem.]

SUGGESTIONS FOR AESTHETIC REFINEMENT

Suggestions for Artistic Expression

Don E. Gibbons, Ph.D.

INDICATIONS

These suggestions are designed for somnambulistic, deep trance subjects who wish to enhance their creativity as artists. Gibbons suggests that the subject be seated ready to paint when the hypnosis takes place. (*Ed.*)

SUGGESTIONS

I'm going to count backward from five to one, and by the time I get to one you will no

longer be here in the present setting; but instead, you will be seated in the middle of a lovely forest glade with your easel, paint, and brushes still before you. By the time I get to the count of one, you will be able to open your eyes and look around, and you will be able to paint what you see in rapid, steady strokes.

You will always be able to hear and to respond to my voice, and I will return you to the present setting in a while; but until I do so, every aspect of the situation to which I guide you will be completely real, and you will experience it all just as if you were actually there. And even though the experience may actually last for only a few moments, it will seem to be going on for a much longer time, so that your ability to respond to it artistically will be correspondingly enhanced. Just continue to listen to my voice now, as I begin to count backward from five to one.

Five. Your awareness of the present scene is beginning to grow dim, as you feel yourself and your equipment being transported to that lovely forest glade. Four. Your awareness of the present is dimming more and more, and you can begin to be aware of yourself seated in that lovely forest glade, with your easel and brushes before you, ready to commence painting in a few moments. And as soon as I get to the count of one, you will be able to open your eyes and look around, catching the mood perfectly as you do, and you will be able to paint as you have never painted before. Three. You can feel yourself becoming more and more aware of the forest glade around you, but keep you eyes closed until I get to the count of one and the transition has been completed. Two. Your anticipation and excitement are increasing with each passing second; for soon you will be able to open your eyes and gaze upon one of the most beautiful landscapes you have ever seen. One. Now you can open your eyes and take in all the breathtaking beauty before you, and in just a few seconds you will have caught the mood and you can begin to paint.

[After a few moments have elapsed, it may be suggested to the subject that he will be able to retain the same mood, and the same ability to express what he has seen, after the trance is terminated. He may then be requested to close his eyes once more while the suggestor counts forward from one to five:]

One. Your awareness of the forest glade is beginning to grow dim, as I return you to the scene from which you left. Two. Coming back more and more now, as your awareness of the forest glade begins to leave completely and you start to become aware of yourself back in the original setting. Three. Almost back now. And by the time I get to the count of five, the transition to the original setting will be complete. Four. Almost back. But you will remain in trance for a while, until I bring you out. Five.

Now you are back in the original setting, still very much in trance, but feeling thrilled and delighted at all that you have seen and done and retaining the mood and the memory perfectly. And when the trance is over, you will be able to paint from memory just as clearly and just as well as if you were still there in the forest.

Suggestions for Aesthetic Appreciation and Enjoyment

Don E. Gibbons, Ph.D.

The next time you read a good novel, or see a quality motion picture, stage play, or television performance, what I am about to tell you will set in motion a number of changes in your artistic sensitivity and responsiveness; and these changes will greatly enhance your appreciation and understanding of what you experience, multiplying your enjoyment many times over.

You will find that all your senses will suddenly begin to feel much keener as the event begins, and that your emotional responsiveness is also considerably enhanced. These changes will enable you to become more and more deeply involved in the experience as it unfolds; for you will be able to follow it not merely with your senses alone, but with your entire being.

As time continues, the degree of your involvement in such cultural experiences will continue to increase, as this process repeats itself. And this enhancement of your artistic responsiveness will help you to discover new depths of appreciation in life itself, as you come to possess an ever-increasing ability to experience life in a richer and more rewarding manner.

Suggestions to Enhance Musical Performance

Don E. Gibbons, Ph.D.

AINTRODUCTION

The following post-induction suggestions are intended to facilitate musical performance by encouraging a close identification with musicians whose performance the student has previously come to admire. A similar approach has been reported by Raikov (1976).

SUGGESTIONS

Now I would like you to think of some musician who plays the same instrument you do, whose playing you are especially fond of — or, if you wish, you can think of one of the great virtuosos on this instrument from the past. I'm going to count backwards from five to one; and by the time I get to one, you will be able to feel just as if you were this person, feeling as he [she] feels and playing as he [she] plays.

You will always be able to hear and to respond to my voice, and I will return you to your own identity in a while; but until I do so, every aspect of the situation to which I guide you will seem completely real, and you will be able to experience it all just as if you were really there. So just continue listening to my voice now, as I begin to count backward from five to one.

Five. Your awareness of the present is beginning to grow dim as you feel yourself being mentally transported into a new situation and into a new identity. And by the time I get to the count of one, the transition will be complete. Four. You are beginning to lose awareness of the present completely now, as my words transport you on to the identity of the person you have chosen. Three. You are becoming aware of yourself as this other person now, as the musician you have selected. Feel yourself entering this other body, and feel your identities beginning to merge. Two. You can feel great wellsprings of talent and ability flowing through every muscle and every fiber and every nerve of this new body as your identities merge completely now; and you can see yourself playing as you have never played before. One. Your identities have merged completely now, and you can see and feel yourself playing as you have never played before. Live the experience,

and enjoy it fully for a moment, and then it will be time to return.

[After a moment's pause:] Now I am going to return you to your original identity. But you will be able to carry back with you the feelings which you have experienced, and your own playing and your own confidence will be greatly enhanced as a result. By the time I get to the count of five, you will be back to your normal identity; but you will remain in trance for a while, until I bring you out.

One. Beginning to lose your awareness of yourself as the other person, and beginning to become aware of your original identity once more, here in trance, with me once again. Two. Coming back now, coming all the way back, but remaining in trance for just a while longer. Three. Beginning to be fully aware of your true identity now. Four. Almost back. Five. Now you have fully resumed your own identity, but you will still remain in trance for a while, until I bring you out.

As a result of the experience you have just undergone, you will notice a great many improvements taking place in your own musical performance. Whenever you begin to play for others, you will become completely absorbed in the music with the very first note. You will become so absorbed in the piece you are playing that all sense of self is lost, and all traces of fear and doubt are lost as well. Your timing and your concentration will be perfect, and as you and the music merge together, you will be able to tap into the feelings you have experienced just now and feel the same wonderful sense of power and ability flowing out from the innermost depths of your being and flowing on to touch the hearts of everyone who hears you play.

When the performance is ended, you will realize just how deeply you have been able to tap into the boundless wellsprings of talent and ability which lie within you, and you will experience a great surge of exaltation and a deep sense of personal fulfillment and satisfaction at the realization that you have been able to perform so well. It will always be a source of deep personal satisfaction to you that you are able to use your own vast talents so fully and so well, and you will come to look forward to each performance supremely confident that you are honing your talent to its finest possible edge, looking forward to the inevitable moment of triumph which this awareness will bring to you when the performance is completed.

[A specific situation may also be suggested which represents a special moment of triumph in the career of the artist chosen, or in the future career of the artist himself. Moreover, if the subject is able to open his eyes without disturbing his ongoing experience of trance, he may actually perform for a few moments while imagining himself in the identity of another. With the subject seated before his instrument and ready to play, an induction may be administered in the usual manner and the preceding suggestions may be administered as far as the count of two, at which time the following verbalizations may be substituted:]

You can feel great wellsprings of power and ability flowing through every muscle and every fiber and every nerve of your body as your identities begin to merge completely. One. Your identities have completely merged together now, and you can open your eyes and begin to play. Live the experience fully and play as you have never played before.

[After a moment or two has elapsed, the subject may be requested to close his eyes and the suggestions for canceling the identification may be administered as previously indicated.]

Suggestions to Enhance Writing Ability

Don E. Gibbons, Ph.D.

INTRODUCTION

The following suggestions for the enhancement of writing ability may also be presented, in conjunction with suggestions for ego-

strengthening and for achievement motivation, to assist the subject to replace recurring fantasies of failure with positive expectations of success.

SUGGESTIONS

Whenever you are engaged in creative writing, you will find that during your spare moments your thoughts will tend to turn to whatever you are writing about. These frequent moments of extra attention will keep new ideas constantly forming in your mind, even when you are consciously preoccupied with other matters.

Because of this extra attention, new ideas and associations will frequently emerge into your awareness as though unbidden; and when you begin to write, these new ideas and associations will flow even more freely, providing you with a steady stream of inspiration.

As you write, you will be able to maintain continuous contact with these vast resources of creativity which lie within you. You will be able to carry out any revisions which may be necessary as the work progresses, without any undue reluctance on your part to change what you have already written, and without striving for perfection for its own sake in those instances wherein it is more important to finish what you have begun.

You will be able to break your writing down into small segments which can be comfortably fitted into the time you have at your disposal, enabling you to maintain a pace which is both productive and enjoyable, without feeling unduly rushed or under pressure. And when each writing period is over, or each segment of the work is completed, you will experience strong feelings of pride, achievement, and accomplishment, which stem from an ever-growing realization that you are employing your abilities fully and well. Writing will thus be experienced as a spontaneous, natural, and joyful process, which will enable you to make the fullest use of your creative potential.

ENHANCING SPORTS AND ATHLETIC PERFORMANCE

Suggestions Used to Enhance Sport Performance

Keith P. Henschen, Ph.D.
Salt Lake City, Utah

The value of hypnosis in enhancing sport performance has been the subject of considerable debate over the years. Athletes, or performers of any type for that matter, are constantly seeking techniques that will help their performances. It is now understood that hypnosis can be of great value if it is correctly utilized in sports; but it can also be a disaster if it is incorrectly applied to the performance realm (Unesthal, 1983). Hypnosis is recognized as one possible tool for aiding the athlete to achieve his/her full potential.

INDICATIONS

Currently, hypnosis in sports is mainly used to control the athlete's emotional experience, that is, to control anxiety levels, to regulate concentrational demands, to stimulate aggressive behavior when appropriate, to enhance motivation, to instill self-confidence and pride, and to inhibit any psychological factors that often serve to limit physical performances. Most sport psychologists are very cautious in their use of hypnosis and agree that: (1) hypnosis is not a performance panacea, but a very useful tool; (2) hypnosis is only as good as the skill of the person using it; and (3) the athlete using hypnosis must be thoroughly trained (Ziegenfuss, 1962).

A few specific examples of how hypnosis is currently being used in athletic settings follow:

A. A performance team (volleyball, basketball, etc.) is hypnotized in a group setting and then asked to mentally visualize themselves executing precise motor skills. They are then presented a posthypnotic suggestion that

they will be able to translate these visualizations into action during a game or practice at the same level of expertise that they had visualized. Most crucial here is that, during the visualization sessions, the athletes are instructed that, while visualizing the various motor skills, there will be a concomitant physical experience in their bodies. This leads to strengthening of neural patterns through hypnotic mental imagery, which reinforces neuromuscular coordination.

B. When competing against one particular opponent, a young golfer feels stressful and consequently performs poorly. This happens over and over again against the same person, but not against other opponents. His belief of not being able to perform is reinforced every time this particular opponent is present. This is obviously an emotional problem and not a matter of poor technique. In this situation hypnosis is used to influence the emotions and attitudes of the golfer and to focus attention on particular relevant cues to improve his golf game. A suggestion such as "block out the entire environment on each shot and concentrate on the rhythm of your swing" is very constructive in this situation.

C. Many athletes have great difficulty getting to sleep, especially the night before an important contest. Suggestions such as "relaxed and calm" or "deeply relaxed and comfortable" are frequently used to facilitate relaxation and/or sleep.

D. A gymnast is experiencing fear when attempting a particularly difficult routine. She is told to visualize a "happiness room" in her mind. This is to be a completely pleasant room, decorated to her taste, with money being no handicap. Anything that makes her happy is to be placed in the room. She is told to have a television in the room and to watch herself perform the difficult routine to perfection on the TV. Then she is given a posthypnotic suggestion "relaxed and easy" as she initiates the difficult routine. In practice and meet situations, she is to visit her happiness room just prior to performing this routine.

As was mentioned previously, it is in the area of mental attitude for athletics where hypnosis is most effective. It can be applied to specific situations in sports to reduce the feelings of pressure, tension, stress and anxiety. Suggestions which have been most useful for athletes include the following:

1. Muscles are strong, relaxed and non-tight.
2. You are in complete control of your environment.
3. You are like a coiled spring—powerful and strong.
4. Feel the sensations within your muscles.
5. Focus on this skill and block out all other distractions.
6. Gain complete control of yourself.

CONTRAINDICATIONS

At present, the most difficult problems in using hypnosis in the sports setting can be categorized into two general areas: (1) opposition to its use by the uneducated and ill-informed, and (2) the lack of competent therapists who are trained to use hypnosis appropriately in athletic situations. Most of the dangers to using hypnosis in sports are identical to the dangers of using it in any situation. Many of these dangers are intrinsic to the close interpersonal relationship that develops in any form of counseling and/or psychotherapy. Hypnosis should not be used by coaches because of their vested interest in the outcome of competitions.

SUMMARY

Hypnosis is used in sports to supply motivating instructions, to boost confidence, to remove fears, to influence arousal levels, to control anxiety or pain, and to increase self-concept. Most sport psychologists advocate various techniques of self-hypnosis in sports

over other hypnotic methods. Hypnotic procedures commonly used in sports include: yoga breathing, age regression, autogenic training, progressive relaxation, awareness through movement, mental practice with imagery, and posthypnotic suggestions.

It is thought that by eliminating the psychological factors which inhibit an athlete, physical performance will be improved. Hypnosis is a technique that allows the athlete to gain control of him/herself and mitigate the effects of distracting psychological factors.

Sports Performance Enhancement

Richard B. Garver, Ed.D.
San Antonio, Texas

Essentially there are two areas that are very important and helpful: (1) control of arousal level and (2) neuromotor facilitation. Arousal level, no matter what the motivations are behind it, affects performance. It is not always necessary to psychotherapeutically work through all of the many complex issues that produce these arousal levels; they may not even be important any longer. But it is important to begin to control the arousal level even if you are working through the reasons behind it. You may still bargain with the unconscious mind to begin to help controlling the arousal level. [See Garver's method for working with study, concentration, and test anxiety problems (p. 000) for an example of his method for controlling arousal level.] The control of arousal level is important because, no matter how skillful you are or how well you use any technique, it can all be lost if the arousal level is too low or too high.

Secondly, the facilitation of neuromotor pathways is very important. Physical educators call it mental practice; psychologists call it covert rehearsal; imagers call it using visual imagery. Whatever the process, it is a mental review that the performer goes through, previewing his actual performance. This is an image of an ideal performance of a role model (like a videotape presentation of a sports performance), which is then applied in some way or adopted to the athlete's own technique and physical capacities. It is, however, very important to make sure that the image that performers have is the correct one, whether it's one developed by their coaches or one they have conceived from a book, videotape or other credible source. It is important to be able to see yourself from without (dissociated), as though looking at yourself on a videotape replay, and it is important to look out *from yourself* as you would when actually performing this particular motor skill. It is also extremely helpful to have a kinesthetic sense of what you are doing, to feel every move as well as see it. You should sense in any way (including hearing) what you are doing, and then memorize the way that you do it best. Then you need to continue reinforcing what you do right versus what you do wrong. This is essential because it does not matter how often you practice if you are practicing wrong patterns. Your unconscious mind memorizes behavioral performance both good and bad, without making a judgment about it. Thus, it is very important to memorize what is good.

The following is a technique that I have found very effective in reinforcing correct behavior patterns and releasing or ignoring incorrect or bad performance. I use the sequence of having subjects visualize what it is, how it is, how it feels, how they want to do this, and then to simply focus on doing it. I tell them, "It is important to be in the left brain when planning, but you had better be in the right brain when you are performing or you will be consciously interfering and get what I call paralysis by analysis. Thus it is important to trust whatever program is in the unconscious mind, even if it is not the best program, because it is the best that you currently have, and it will be ineffective if you try to consciously change it in some way when you are actually performing."

The cue to be used while the subject is performing and/or practicing for a performance is the following: "When you do it right, when you feel that the program has run exactly

as you want it to and the outcome is right, reach with your left hand and touch your right shoulder. That is a cue to your unconscious mind that has been established to program in that behavior. If the performance is not good, then touch your left shoulder with your right hand." Any cue may be used. What is important is that this process reinforces everything that is right and does not reinforce what has been practiced wrong. This maximizes optimal reinforcement of positive performance and minimizes any reinforcement of negative behavior.

When we recognize what we did right and what we did wrong, it can also be used in rehearsing a specific skill. For instance, after a golfer has made two or three perfect practice swings or mental images, the right shoulder may be touched to program it in, and then he can go ahead and hit the shot. The principle is to program very specifically how the person wants to perform, to be very specific about the arousal level, and to use posthypnotic cues while both practicing and performing. "Trust the unconscious program; trust the cue that will trigger the right program, the specific program that you know is there and that you are reinforcing. This is much better than trying to get rid of or not do negative behavior. If you are hitting from the top in a golf swing, the worst thing you can do is to try *not* to hit from the top. Instead, concentrate on doing something else that will prevent you from hitting from the top [the principle of using positive rather than negative suggestions]. For example, think of shifting your weight or moving your lower body through, rather than not hitting from the top. Always focus on how you want to perform."

Metaphor for Athletics/Sports Competition

Richard R. Wooton, Ph.D.
Provo, Utah

INDICATIONS

The following metaphor was used with a nationally ranked university volleyball team. It was designed for use with a team who had a tendency to lose because its members were "slow starters." The last paragraph was also designed for one of the players who had a problem with anger and when he made an error was practically of no use for a period of time until he could pull himself together. It may be used with a group induction of the entire team and tape recorded for use in self-hypnosis. (*Ed.*)

METAPHOR

I'd like to tell you about a friend of mine who used to be an outstanding runner. He was a sprinter who could run the 100 meters faster than any junior high or high school kid in his city or for several surrounding cities. He was so much faster than anyone his age that he consistently ran away from his competition. The interesting thing about him is that he seemed to run faster and faster as he approached the tape and coaches often were heard to comment on how strong and fast he was at the end of the race. He dominated all of the junior high school track meets in which he was a participant and was almost as strong throughout his high school years. He did notice while in high school that, while he consistently won, the competition seemed to be getting better. He knew that he was running as well—if not better—than he had ever run in his life, but, for some reason unknown to him, others seemed to also be getting faster. He began to realize that he often just barely beat his competitors as they got to the finish line.

This young man was such a fine competitor that he was offered an athletic scholarship at a university known for its strong track teams. He continued to compete well, but for the first time in his life he began to be aware that there were others who not only were very fast, but probably had a good chance of beating him. As hard as he would run, the competition seemed to edge ever closer, making each race one that he would barely win. The time came when, in one important event, he lost a close race and then—

little by little—even though he continued to win most of his races, he would occasionally lose. Since he knew that he was running faster and harder than he had ever run before, the whole reason for losing was a mystery to him.

He was fortunate to have a coach who cared a great deal about him personally and about his performances. The coach had a keen eye and a particularly good ability to analyze running styles. After watching the sprinter in several races, the coach came to him and said, "I think I've discovered your problem. You have always been a very strong and a very fast runner, but you have never learned to use the starting blocks and, in fact, you really do not know how to start very fast at all. The result is that you are always running faster and faster in an attempt to catch up with the competition, rather than leading from the beginning. This has resulted in your sometimes winning but sometimes losing to those who know how to come out of the starting blocks faster."

In the end, because of effective coaching and a willingness of this athlete to listen, he learned to charge out of the blocks quickly, and, while it was still possible for him to lose on occasions, he rarely lost once he had learned to put the whole race together—beginning with a fast start and ending with a strong and quick finish.

[Continuing after about a 10-second pause:] Many of you have heard of a rather famous artist who lived some years ago by the name of Vincent Van Gogh. His paintings now command a very high price even though he was not as well-known in his own lifetime—perhaps because he acted in some very peculiar ways and had such a violent temper that he would get totally out of control for periods of time. In fact, in one such period of rage he became so angry at a situation that he could not control that he cut off his own ear. The really sad thing about what he did, besides losing his ear, was that most other people simply thought that he was acting like a crazy man and they really didn't have a lot of sympathy for him. I suppose that they would have respected and befriended him more if he had acted in a more appropriate manner rather than simply looking stupid by allowing his anger to go so uncontrolled. His effort to gain attention and to show others how bad he felt, only resulted in others' not wanting to have as much to do with him and, in the final analysis, he only ended up looking kind of silly walking around with one ear!

Metaphor for Facilitating Cooperation and Teamwork in Athletics

Richard R. Wooton, Ph.D.
Provo, Utah

INDICATIONS

This metaphor was used successfully with a nationally ranked male volleyball team. It may be used to facilitate working cooperatively together as a team, rather than playing as a "group of individuals." This metaphor may be given following a group hypnotic induction, and may be tape recorded for use in self-hypnosis. (*Ed.*)

METAPHOR

Six friends of mine love to sky dive. One of their biggest thrills is getting together whenever they can so that they can fly together in a plane up into the skies, where they can prepare to make their jumps. Without question, their biggest thrill is when they jump from the plane and make a six-sided star in the sky. Now to make a star takes a lot of talent along with some courage to jump as well as a good deal of trust in your fellow jumpers. You see, not all six of the skydivers can leave the place at the same time. One must leave first, and then delay pulling the rip cord of the parachute until all of the five others have jumped one at a time. It takes great discipline and cooperation for each diver to pull his own rip cord at a different time, and yet at precisely the right time so that they can line up in a way that will give them the

proper height and configuration in order to make the star. Each has an individual job to do, but without each participant doing his or her job in exactly the right in relationship to the other jumpers, then the star cannot be made.

The star is by far the skydivers' favorite design to make because of its difficulty and also because of its beauty.— so much so that if any one of the jumpers does not make the needed response in relationship to all of the other jumpers, then the star cannot be made at all and each of the skydivers must float to the ground individually. But, again, because they enjoy making the star so much and because it is such a beautiful thing to see from the ground as well as to experience as a jumper, they immediately go back into the airplane, return to the skies, and jump again so that they can continue trying to "connect up" as well as they can with each other, and until the star turns out to be as satisfying in its structure and beauty as they would like. The dependency that the jumpers feel for one another in their group and the precision with which they contribute to the star is, indeed, one of the most satisfying experiences that they can share together.

Suggestions for Concentration

Brian M. Alman, Ph.D.
San Diego, California

SELF-SUGGESTIONS FOR CONCENTRATION BEFORE A GAME

[These suggestions may be given by the subject in self-hypnosis, and reinforced in heterohypnosis.] Whenever I lace up my shoes before a game or workout, I may notice that my mind cinches up in its focus, also. As I tighten the laces on my shoes, perhaps I am also tightening my concentration on my game to come.

SELF-SUGGESTIONS FOR CONCENTRATION IN TENNIS

As I walk onto the court I will see the net dividing the area. The net can prevent the ball from passing from one side to the other. I will find that the concentration of my attention is able to screen out distractions just as the net stops poorly hit balls.

When I first step out on the court, I can notice that there are lines marked off for the boundaries. I may be able to form boundaries in my concentration that mark those actions and events that are *in* bounds, and pay attention only to them.

I can also ignore those actions, sounds and events that are *out* of my mental bounds for this game. I can allow them to pass through me without interrupting my concentration. If I am distracted, I'll be able to see the distraction as momentary. As if I'm on automatic pilot, I can return to my game and focus.

I will grasp my racket firmly and confidently. The racket is designed for a specific purpose—to play the game most effectively. As I grip the racket, I may bring that same kind of concentration and purpose to my game.

I will associate the feeling of concentration and readiness with stepping onto the court. My stretching exercises before a match can be a complete stretch. My physical flexibility and my mental readiness can begin with those exercises.

A Cognitive-Hypnotic Approach to Athletic Performance with Weight Lifters

W. Lee Howard, Ph.D., and
James P. Reardon, Ph.D.
Columbus, Ohio

INTRODUCTION

This hypnotic training approach, adapted from the authors' original article (1986), was found to produce successful results in a controlled experimental study. The authors used hypnotic relaxation and imagery techniques to facilitate and reinforce cognitive restructuring

skills, to facilitate control of physiologic processes and to enhance athletic performance.

The Self-Directed Behavior Change Instrument (Tosi, 1973) was used with the athletes "as an exercise to facilitate high cognitive control over other processes and as an initial means of modifying self-concept. Subjects used this instrument to identify negative self-referring statements. The subjects were then directed to provide themselves with more 'rational' alternatives" (p. 252). It was emphasized that the individual, not the environment, was responsible for his thoughts and emotions (Ellis, 1962). Specific efforts were also made to identify negative ideation associated with subjects' athletic performance (e.g., concentrating on the amount of weight to be lifted, rather than the process of lifting; worrying about what others would think if they "failed"). A variety of negative cognitive sequences were presented to the athletes as a stimulus in helping them to pinpoint their own self-defeating ideations. The athletes were also encouraged to employ cognitive strategies in real life settings in their everyday lives. (*Ed.*)

COGNITIVE-HYPNOTIC TRAINING

After a general discussion of hypnosis, the subjects were hypnotized . . . and directed to experience the negative emotional states associated with the above identified situations as well as identifying the negative irrational cognitions. The therapist negatively reinforced this entire self-defeating sequence. The therapist next directed the subject to refocus on relaxing thoughts and then visualize the same sequence, visualizing himself engaging in more rational self-talk and experiencing more positive affective, physiological and behavioral responses. This self-enhancing sequence was positively reinforced by the therapist.

The above process was designed to facilitate the restructuring of negative cognitive-emotional responses to specific internally/externally disturbing situations. This process was also designed to restructure the self-concept (negative self-referring statements). The hypnotic state was next utilized to enhance physiological processes associated with increased performance via rich hypnotic imagery.

More specifically, the subjects were directed to visualize themselves performing the behavioral criterion measure (supine barbell press) while hypnotized. They were directed to practice several dimensions via hypnotic imagery: (1) psychological—elimination of negative ideation, increased focusing, elimination of distractions, (2) physiological—attaining proper levels of arousal, (3) behavioral—successful performance of the supine barbell press (facilitation of correct neural pathways).

The behavioral dimension and neural pattern facilitation were accomplished by a detailed description of the behavioral task, encouraging only positive visualization and performance. The psychological dimension was practiced via the standard cognitive restructuring process. The physiological variable (appropriate arousal level) was developed through the use of an arousal scale in which specific events and physiological variables (heart beat, perspiration, etc.) were associated with numbers on the scale. That is, on a scale of one to five (with one being the lowest arousal level and five being the highest), the subjects first associated sleep with one, walking with two . . . their best performance with five, etc., until they were able to monitor and control their arousal level. They were given instructions to perform the monitoring of arousal during their real life performances, as well as in controlling of the other dimensions mentioned.

Subjects were encouraged via hypnotic imagery to experience sensory hallucinations to facilitate physiological control associated with muscular growth. They were asked to visualize themselves in a comfortable location in which "hot, moist towels" were placed on their chest and arms. They were directed to "feel a warm, swelling, pulsating sensation" in these areas. They were also asked to visualize their body as a "giant transport system in which all available blood is being sent to the chest and arms." Next, the subjects were told to see themselves

sometime in the future with increases in muscular size in the chest and arms. The subjects were directed to visualize themselves proud and happy about the increases they had achieved, and to see others recognizing their muscular gains. All subjects were encouraged to practice the imagery techniques described above (without hypnosis) during the week.

Suggestions for Sports Performance

Don E. Gibbons, Ph.D.

INTRODUCTION AND INDICATIONS

Since even the best players can occasionally encounter a losing streak, care should be taken to avoid suggesting specific targets which might lead to a loss of faith in the efficacy of the procedure if specific levels of athletic performance are not attained. By the same token, athletes should not be encouraged by means of suggestion to train or to compete so strenuously that they run the risk of possible injury or of diminishing their resources instead of continuing to improve. However, suggestion may be employed to maximize the enjoyment of playing well, while simultaneously decreasing the fear of possible failure, thus providing the subject with positive attitudes which are highly conducive to continued growth. The following suggestions may be administered at the conclusion of an appropriate induction.

SUGGESTIONS

As a result of what I am about to tell you now, you will find that any negative aspects of sports performance which might have troubled you in the past will have greatly diminished in importance, and as times goes on, their importance will continue to decrease. With each passing day, you will find yourself adopting a much brighter outlook, in which the positive aspects of playing and the lure of success have taken on a great deal more appeal. And in this more positive frame of mind, you will come to experience wonderful new feelings of strength and energy as you find yourself looking forward eagerly to each new challenge, wanting more than ever to play and to win.

Any psychological barriers or obstacles which might have been keeping you from performing well are being eliminated. You are able to look forward to each new game, secure in the knowledge of your own abilities and of the vast potential within you for further growth. Nothing is holding you back any longer. Every barrier, every obstacle, has been removed. You are completely free to develop all the vast potential within you to its fullest extent.

And as you proceed, the success of winning will be experienced as infinitely richer and more rewarding than it has ever been before; whereas the sting of any occasional setback you may still encounter will be so considerably diminished that you will scarcely notice it. You will be able to accept any occasional reversal calmly and philosophically, as the small price which must be paid to experience the rich joys of playing and of winning. And even an occasional losing streak will no longer be of any undue concern to you. Since playing itself has become so enjoyable, you will be able to derive satisfaction from any game, regardless of the outcome.

All these changes will naturally result in marked improvements in your training, your preparation, and in everything which contributes to your actual performance. You will make sure that you get all the rest that you require, and you will be able to sleep soundly and well. You will be able to do whatever else is necessary as part of your training and preparation.

You will not waste time and energy worrying about your past or future performance; for each time you play, you will feel yourself improving. Each time you play, regardless of whether you win or lose, you will take continuing pride in your strategy and skill, and in your timing and coordination. And each time you play, you will find that you are advancing closer and closer to the goal of becoming the player that you want to be.

Endurance Suggestions with Distance Runners

J. Arthur Jackson, Gregory C. Gass, and E. M. Camp

You are now so deeply relaxed that all the suggestions that I am going to give you will be firmly fixed in the unconscious part of your mind; so firmly fixed, so deeply embedded, that nothing will remove them. Everything that I tell you that is going to happen to you, will happen exactly as I tell you. Every feeling and sensation that I tell you that you are going to experience, you will experience just as I tell you and these things will happen particularly when you run. This entire project is really an experiment on human potentialities. Exercise experts have discovered that most people tend to underestimate their own capacities and abilities. . . .

There are really two major factors that allow you to do your very best when running. The first, of course, is really wanting to do well with the exercise tasks which you are to perform. This is something with which you are already familiar. But the second one, which is even more important, is something which you may not know about. This is the fact, that if you realize in advance what things ordinarily make you think you have reached your limit, you will be able to keep on going beyond the point where you are beginning to experience them. Most people use discomfort and fatigue as signs that they should stop what they are doing. They fail to realize that discomfort and fatigue are the first signs that they are approaching their maximum performance and that they can, in fact, keep on going far beyond that point. Most people generally assume that when they start feeling uncomfortable, this feeling will get worse but, as a matter of fact, if you allow yourself to keep on going after you start to feel that discomfort, that feeling will actually diminish. I am taking it for granted that you are here because you really want to be and that you are really eager to explore your potentiality and to do your utmost on these tasks. In that case, the thing that you really must keep in mind is the importance of noticing each sign of discomfort or fatigue and using it as a stimulus to keep on going. Then put it aside in your mind and concentrate on the running itself. It is terribly important to us in this experiment, to find out exactly how much you can do with these tasks. The outcome of this experiment cannot be successful unless you cooperate by giving us your absolute maximum performance. This is not going to be easy for it is going to take every ounce of concentration, effort and willpower that you can muster. I want you to give it everything that you have got; to feel the strain all through your body and to use that strain and effort to good advantage using every resource within you. Make this a total effort.

As you run for a longer and longer period of time, you may experience certain symptoms. You may experience a feeling of heaviness in the arms; you may experience breathlessness, a feeling of tightness in your legs, or a sensation of discomfort in the chest, throat, or mouth. You will probably develop a sense of fatigue after you have been running for some time. As you start to experience any of these sensations, this will be a stimulus for you to run even harder. As a result of this, you will find that you are able to go on and actually run through this experience so that you become less aware of whatever discomfort you were experiencing. You will feel as though you could go on running for a longer and longer period of time. You will feel a greater desire to give a total effort; to use every bit of willpower that is within you. You will actually run through your most difficult period and, no matter how tired you start to become, this will act as a stimulus so that you can continue running without becoming unduly distressed. As you concentrate on my voice, so all these things that I am telling you will act on you when the time comes for you to perform the exercise task.

HYPNOTIC SUGGESTIONS
WITH CHILDREN

INTRODUCTION

Hypnotic Responsivity in Children

THE RESEARCH AND clinical literature on hypnosis with children suggests that they are usually good hypnotic subjects and typically more easily hypnotizable than adult subjects (London & Cooper, 1969). Children generally have very active fantasy lives, a characteristic of more hypnotically talented adults (Hilgard, 1979), and seem to be entranced in a world of their own much of the time. Most research suggests that as children reach adolescence, perhaps in response to socialization demands to become more rational and realistic, their hypnotic capacities tend to decline (Morgan & E. Hilgard, 1973; Morgan & J. Hilgard, 1979). Although much research has suggested that hypnotic talent reaches a peak of responsiveness between the ages of eight and twelve, there is controversy concerning the methodology of these studies (Olness & Gardner, 1988), and hypnosis has also been found to be quite valuable with preschool children (Gardner, 1977). Thus, hypnotic techniques may be of particular benefit in the practice of enlightened pediatricians, emergency room personnel, dentists, child psychiatrists, psychologists, and social workers.

Tailoring Hypnosis to Children

As you will see in the presentation in this chapter by Kohen, success in working with children requires that you adapt induction procedures and suggestions to the age of the child. Significant research has documented, for instance, that children have difficulty closing their eyes in hypnosis and will often respond better when this is not demanded (London & Cooper, 1969;

Moore & Cooper, 1966; Moore & Lauer, 1963). Developmental issues with children should be taken into account (e.g., adapting language to the age of the child and considering cognitive and perceptual skills at various ages).

Taking developmental issues into account, Olness and Gardner (1988) recommend induction techniques with children ages two to four that include blowing bubbles, pop-up books, storytelling, using a stereoscopic viewer, imagining a favorite activity, speaking to the child through a stuffed animal or doll, use of a Raggedy Ann or Andy doll, and watching an induction on videotape.

Between the ages of four and six, useful inductions may include imagining a favorite place, imagining interactions with favorite animals, imagining being in a flower garden, storytelling, imagining a chalkboard with letters of the alphabet appearing on it, imagining a television program, use of a stereoscopic viewer, pretending to be bouncing a ball, and imagining activities on a playground (Olness & Gardner, 1988).

In middle childhood (ages seven to eleven), meaningful inductions often include imagining a favorite place, activity, or music, imagining riding a bike or being carried on a magic flying blanket, imagining watching clouds change shapes and colors, or eye fixation on a point on their hand. Adolescents frequently enjoy induction procedures such as arm catalepsy, imagining driving a car, being in a favorite place or engaged in a sports activity, imagining playing or hearing music, arm levitation, absorption in breathing, and adult methods of induction (Olness & Gardner, 1988).

Sometimes parents will be resistant to the idea of using hypnosis with their children because of widespread misconceptions about hypnosis (Gardner, 1974b). Educating parents concerning myths and the nature of hypnosis, as well as the specific advantages of using hypnosis with their child, will be invaluable. You may also allay parental fears by allowing them to observe hypnotherapy with their children, although it has been suggested that this be postponed until after the initial induction (Gardner, 1974b). Some parents may additionally wish to experience hypnosis themselves to set their minds at ease. Gardner's contribution at the beginning of this chapter provides other ideas for helping parents see the advantages of child hypnotherapy.

Indications and Contraindications

Olness and Gardner (1988) suggest the following broad indications for child hypnotherapy: (1) when a child shows responsiveness to hypnotic inductions; (2) when a problem has been shown to be treatable through hypnosis; (3) when there is a positive relationship between the therapist and child; (4) when the child possesses at least some motivation to remedy the complaint; (5) when parents or guardians approve the treatment plan; and (6) when the use of hypnosis is not anticipated to cause iatrogenic harm.

In contrast, we must be cautious about acceding to parental demands to use hypnotic magic to bludgeon their children into submission. The child must possess at least some motivation for change. We should point out, once again, that mere knowledge of hypnosis does not qualify one as a child therapist. This is a subspecialty area requiring training in more than hypnosis alone. If you are not trained to treat a pediatric problem with techniques other than hypnosis, you should not be treating the patient with hypnosis. There are certainly times (e.g., enuresis) when thorough medical evaluation is indicated prior to using hypnosis. Other absolute contraindications (Olness & Gardner, 1988) for child hypnotherapy include: (1) when it would lead to physical endangerment of the patient (e.g., in athletics); (2) when the use of hypnosis might aggravate existing psychological problems or create additional ones (e.g., creating amnesia for a girlfriend who has rejected an adolescent.); (3) when it is "for fun" (stage or entertainment hypnosis); (4) when a problem may be more effectively treated by a nonhypnotic method (e.g., family therapy); and (5) when a referral source or parent asks for hypnosis based on a misdiagnosis, and the actual problem should be treated in some other way.

Areas of Application

Hypnosis has been used with a tremendous diversity of childhood problems: text anxiety, problems with studying and concentration, reading difficulties [suggestions on these topics may be found in Chapter 14], phobias (e.g., of school, animals), sleep disorders, social skill training and anxiety, conversion reactions, psychogenic amnesia, seizures, pain, bulimia and anorexia, enuresis (bedwetting), encopresis (soiling), stuttering, trichotillomania (hair pulling), nailbiting, thumbsucking, obesity, sleepwalking, tics, learning disabilities, chronic and acute pain, preparation for surgery, burns, gastrointestinal complaints, asthma, hives, allergies, warts, hyperhidrosis (excessive sweating), to increase compliance in diabetics, hemophilia, juvenile rheumatoid arthritis, dentistry, headaches, urinary retention, cerebral palsy, Tourette syndrome, cancer and terminal illness, and sports. You will find suggestions concerning some of these areas of application in the pages to follow.

Those who wish to consult excellent texts concentrated on hypnosis with children are encouraged to study Olness and Gardner (1988), Wester and O'Grady (in press) and Ambrose (1961).

Helping Parents See Specific Advantages in Child Hypnotherapy

G. Gail Gardner, Ph.D.

Parents can be of the greatest help in child hypnotherapy if, beyond alleviating their fears and misunderstandings, we show them that there are specific reasons for selecting hypnosis as the treatment of choice at a particular time. That is, parental enthusiasm and cooperation will be maximal if hypnosis is perceived not as "just another treatment" but as having its own special advantages. Of course, some of these benefits will be more relevant for one child than for another, and the hypnotherapist should vary the emphasis accordingly.

LIKELIHOOD OF SUCCESS

The parents can be told that most children are quite easily hypnotized because of several reasons, including their interest in the technique and the absence of pain or unpleasantness in hypnotic induction. Of course, the parents are cautioned that hypnosis is not effective in every case and, even for a particular child, may be helpful for some problems but not others. It may help to discuss the literature on the use of hypnosis for the problem at hand. This might alleviate parental fear that the child is being experimented upon, especially in the unfortunate but all-too-frequent event that hypnosis is being tried as a last resort.

LACK OF SIDE EFFECTS

For many medical and emotional problems, previous treatment has included drugs which produce drowsiness, nausea, or other unpleasant side effects. Parents are relieved to realize that this is not the case with hypnotherapy. Occasionally, they ask if a child can become "addicted" to hypnosis, wanting to be in hypnosis all the time, but they are reassured, especially when reminded that the purpose of posthypnotic suggestions is to carry the benefits of the hypnotic state over into the waking state.

ACHIEVING AND MAINTAINING THE CHILD'S MOTIVATION

Both parents and children often become enthusiastic when hypnotherapy is suggested, especially if other treatment techniques have failed. It relieves growing despair by offering a new approach. Increased hope then increases cooperation. If the hypnotherapy is successful, the results are usually obvious and appear quickly, thus allowing even young children to see its value.

PARENTAL PARTICIPATION

Many parents, especially those whose children have serious medical or emotional problems, experience marked feelings of helplessness. They feel that they must stand by—at best useless and more often in the way—while the "experts" work to relieve the child's distress. This is not just true of parents who feel guilty or in some way responsible for their child's problem; most parents derive a special sense of pleasure and fulfillment from helping their children and feel frustrated when this is not possible. Parents who are encouraged to assist in hypnotherapeutic sessions, or at least to encourage the child between sessions, enjoy participating with the "experts" in the helping process.

In fact, it is usually not long before a parent notes that the simple, repetitive, soothing features of hypnotic inductions are similar to the normal behavior of parents toward children in distress. Thus, participation in hypnotherapy can be seen by them as an extension of natural parenting behavior and not as part of the vast array of exotic and unpronounceable drugs, machines, paraphernalia, and concepts which comprise most treatment procedures. Parents come to regard hypnosis with an attitude of casual confidence, knowing that neither they nor we fully understand how it works, but still not looking on it as magic.

When hypnosis is presented as a state which can be used for many purposes, parents often find themselves being quite creative in using hypnotherapy for purposes other than those originally intended. Of course this assumes that the parent has had sufficient training to know when hypnosis might not be appropriate and can maintain contact with the hypnotherapist for consultation as needed. Thus, for example, one parent, whose terminally ill child had successfully used hypnosis for relief of pain and nausea, thought of trying it to help curb the child's excessive appetite when he was put on large doses of steroids; the boy cooperated well and the result was a return to normal appetite level after one hypnotic session. The same parent, however, raised thoughtful questions with the hypnotherapist and agreed to abandon her idea of possibly using hypnosis to gain more understanding of the child's concept of death when it became clear that the outcome might produce unnecessary distress for the child.

FLEXIBILITY

In addition to the kinds of creativity already described, parents are comforted and relieved to learn of other dimensions of flexibility in hypnotherapy, and this, too, maximizes hope and participation. For example, they like the idea that flexibility of wording or induction technique can bring them closer to a desired goal. Parents report successfully varying original wording in an unexpected situation. Likewise they find appealing the idea that hypnotherapy can be done with children by telephone or with the aid of a tape recorder.

Once parents are comfortable with the idea that their child can master self hypnosis, they gain a special feeling of security in knowing that this treatment modality is available to the child at any time or place. One parent of a leukemic child remarked on how nice it is that hypnosis is "so portable" and reported that this had allowed the family to feel more comfortable visiting relatives during the later stages of the child's illness. This writer deliberately avoids using any sort of "gadgetry" such as egg-timers or locking in the induction to any particular set of circumstances or environment, since these may not be always available when needed.

HOPE AND MASTERY

It is commonly known that, when a child is in distress, the parents' anxiety and despair can get communicated to the child, thus aggravating the child's distress and setting up a vicious cycle. Likewise, when parents see their children experience feelings of hope and mastery after successful use of hypnosis, the parents, too, report feeling more hopeful and peaceful about the situation. Such a positive parental attitude also gets communicated to the child, who can use it constructively to help develop still stronger feelings of hope and mastery. Thus a growth cycle of positive feeling results between parent and child.

One mother listened to her sick child's hypnotic dreams of being an eagle who could fly easily from one safe and happy place to another, and she reported her own feelings of relief and tenderness, as she heard him express previously untapped faith in his potential for self-protection and recovery. Another mother, whose family lived at a great distance from the medical center where the child was being treated, reported instances when both she and her daughter had encouraged each other by discussing the value of hypnosis for easing pain and inducing sleep. . . .

Although these kinds of successful experiences are not possible for the parents of all children, it certainly seems worth the effort of trying to educate them concerning the value of hypnosis. Though parents' initial attitudes may indeed be obstacles to progress, a positive and low-keyed approach from the hypnotherapist can usually result in the parent's becoming an ally and an asset in the effort to help the child. Unfortunately, some professionals focus only on the obstacle phenomenon and never work toward a better goal with the parents. They feel that the solution is either to abandon the idea of hypnosis altogether or to use it surreptitiously, calling it by some other name. While the latter approach may bring some success, the potential results might be far greater with the parents' active support.

Finally, a word about the ethics of using hypnosis with a child without the knowledge of the parents. As indicated in a previous paper (Gardner, 1974a), this writer is willing to call hypnosis by some other name (suggestive therapy, relaxation therapy) if it is clear that the parents are too uncomfortable with their concept of "hypnosis" and cannot benefit from professional explanation. The point here is that the parents agree with the essentials of the technique (e.g., using relaxation to reduce fear) and that the name given to it is really not that important. However, if after discussion with the hypnotherapist, the parents expressly state they do not want hypnosis to be used, then this writer would not do so. This experience, however, is quite rare, unless one or more professionals have already discussed hypnotherapy with the patients in very negative terms, usually saying either that it is dangerous or that it is ineffective for this problem.

Hypnosis with Children

Daniel P. Kohen, M.D.
Minneapolis, Minnesota

In working with hypnotherapeutic techniques with children it is fundamentally important to remember that hypnosis with children is easy but not simple, it is fun but requires concentration, and it should be conducted with respect for the child and his/her intrinsic abilities. Children learn hypnosis even more easily than adults because they are, as part of their normal growth and development, spontaneously in and out of alternative states of awareness (imagination) all day long. They are also usually highly motivated to make a change (in the problem for which they have come). A key to teaching children how to build these self-regulatory skills is trust and rapport with the clinician. The clinician's approach to and language with the child are also more important than the precise "hypnosis" induction or technique utilized.

INTRODUCING HYPNOSIS TO CHILDREN

Children *understand* hypnosis as the same as or analogous to pretending, daydreaming or imagining. Accordingly, it can and should be presented to them as "something you already know how to do but maybe didn't know you knew, or maybe didn't know you could use to help yourself with [*whatever problem they are having*]." Believing in children's ability, in their

awareness, and in their ability and desire to learn something new, I appeal in a matter-of-fact, expectant fashion to those experiences I know they must have had with daydreaming or imagination. I then build on these in order to introduce, explain, and demystify the forthcoming hypnotherapeutic experience. Thus, I may say, "You know how when you daydream you can pretend to be wherever you are daydreaming and still be where you are?" And they understand. And I might add, "And you can notice everything about whatever you are daydreaming about—what you see and hear there. Isn't that pretty neat?" And then I might matter-of-factly present a "quick opportunity" for a safe, brief hypnotic experience, designed purposely to facilitate comfort, trust, and enhance a sense of personal control:

"Well, *before* we do anything on purpose to work on the [*problem*], let's just practice some daydreaming and imagining and relaxing *together* [reassurance to the child that he/she is not alone] to remember how easy it is; . . . and then *later* [creating expectations] I'll show you how you can use the *same thing* [anchor] to *help yourself* [ego-strengthening]. So . . . just get comfortable and close your eyes and start daydreaming or pretending about something." [Note: Children under six or seven may not want to close their eyes. Clinicians must be aware of, prepared for, and comfortable with this. One might say instead, "And you can close your eyes or keep them open until they close or just look at something carefully to help you concentrate the way you want to on your daydream."]

As is critical with most if not all hypnotherapeutic suggestions for children, these statements are framed with certain principles in mind: i.e., choices that imply directly both that change will take place and that the child has options within that choice; that you believe what you are saying and that the child is competent to make a change occur; that the child is in control and you are the coach or teacher; and that you respect and believe in the child.

As the child closes eyes and/or develops fixed gaze to indicate trance has begun, simple suggestions to build the imagery are all that are required to enhance the belief in (and "depth"of) the hypnotic experience. These should be multisensory, permissive, open-ended, and general: "While you are daydreaming or pretending or imagining — I don't know which you like the best — make sure it is really fun *because* [children, like adults, need a *reason* to carry out the suggestion] you are the *boss of your imagination* [ego-strengthening]. *Notice* [an invitation to concentrate, pay attention] what you *see* there in your imagining, who is with you or maybe you're alone or with friends or family or new friends. Notice where you are, whether you're inside or outside, whether the weather is hot or cold or in between, or rainy or snowy . . . and *hear* the sounds there in your *favorite place* . . . maybe you'll hear voices of people talking, or sounds of music, or machines, or of the weather . . . or maybe it's quiet and you'll listen to the quiet . . . and *notice* the *smells* where you are imagining, and the *tastes* there. . . ."

Often I will point out to the child the importance of understanding the "natural way that the body relaxes when you focus your imagination this way." This, like other suggestions, is offered in order to demystify the experience, to enhance a sense of personal control, as well as to create awareness of physical changes that occur in relation to changes in the mind. Thus, in expectant fashion, while the child is in a hypnotic state, I will say, "You probably already noticed [and if she didn't, she will now!] that your face muscles are relaxed" [or "your neck muscles" or . . .] and that your breathing is slower than it was before, and that's because you are doing this exactly the right way . . ." [to reinforce personal control, acceptance, and take the whole thing out of the realm of "spooky or scary"]. I then build on this by adding, "And since you and your brain are the boss of your body, you can even make your relaxation even more than it already is . . . because our bodies already know how to relax . . . and we even relax a little bit each time we breathe out . . . just notice how your shoulders go down every time you breathe out . . . [pause, add "that's right" on next exhalation] so, to help relax even more, just take a slow . . . deep . . . breath . . . in . . . and . . . out . . . and when you breathe out   say 'relax' to yourself in your inside thinking . . . and just notice what happens as your shoulders go down and relax."

HYPNOSIS WITH PAIN

Hypnotic Procedure for Pain Relief

Valerie J. Wall, Ph.D.
Seattle, Washington

INDICATIONS

This hypnotic method is designed for treating pain problems in children who are between six and ten years of age. The induction and deepening verbalizations are included along with the therapeutic strategy because of the comparatively limited amount of modeling that is available concerning hypnotic work with children. All pain should not be removed hypnotically except under very selective conditions (e.g., in dental or surgical procedures) or a patient may be at risk for injury. The management of this matter is discussed by Dr. Wall in the latter part of this procedure. (*Ed.*)

PRE-INDUCTION

Today we are going to talk about ways to teach you and your body to be comfortable during what might normally be a painful procedure or injury. We know that your mind can help you be more comfortable, even when we wouldn't normally expect that to be true. Your mind is able to make its own sort of numbing medicine which it can send out through your body to help you be comfortable whenever you need to be. There are many ways in which your body is able to make numbing for you and today we need to find the way that is just right for you.

THE CLOUD CAR INDUCTION

To begin with, I'm going to ask you to use your imagination to think about something that you like to do very much. You may want to think about doing this with your eyes open or you may want to think about doing it with your eyes closed. Whichever one works best for you is the one that you need to do. I want you to start by imagining that your body is becoming very, very relaxed and very comfortable, and that your mind is busy thinking about the things I am saying to you.

Let your body feel relaxed and comfortable and let the chair you are sitting in begin to feel soft and fluffy. You can notice that this soft and fluffy feeling happens somewhat gradually, but that it is beginning to be there by now. And as you're thinking about this feeling, you can also notice that it's possible to turn that soft and fluffy feeling into a very special car just for you. We'll call this your cloud car, and it is your own cloud way toward fun and imagination, and more control of your mind and body. You may picture your cloud car in your mind's eye any way that you would like to. Get a good look at the controls, look at the size and shape. Is it fast, does it maneuver well, can it go high in the sky? All of these things can be true and what's most exciting of all is knowing that this car is completely under your control, and that you're able to drive it in a way that is fun and exciting, and relaxing and beneficial to you.

DEEPENING

I'd like you to begin to fly your cloud car now. Get very comfortable and used to the controls. You will notice that if you lean forward your car goes down, if you tip back it goes up, if you tip to the right it goes to the right, and if you tip to the left it goes to the left. These are just a few of the ways in which you can control the flight of your car. Perhaps you

would like to experiment with your car. You can begin by flying it low along the ground, or perhaps you would like to soar high into the sky and take a look at the view from up there. Whatever you do, have a good time doing it. Make your experience as real as you can, enjoy yourself, see yourself laughing and feeling the comfort of being in your own special car. [Pause]

And now that you've had a chance to fly your car a bit, I'd like you to begin to head toward that special place that you and I have already talked about. You may want to take a scenic route there, looking at the mountains or the ocean. Perhaps you'd like to fly over and check out the Pyramids or Big Ben in London, or a castle or two. Wherever you go, remember that you have a bird's eye view and that the air you are flying in is fresh and clean and relaxing, and that it feels very, very soft against your skin. After you've toured some and are ready to head toward your special place, you can let me know by moving your finger [head nodding or verbal communication are also used, depending on the youngster.]

That's fine. And now I'd like you to move toward your special place and very gradually begin to lower your cloud car to the ground. You may land very, very slowly. As you do so, look around and enjoy the sights and the sounds and the smells of your special place. And once you have landed your car, coming down slowly, drifting, gradually landing, softly on the ground, you can park your car and get ready to play in your special place.

ENHANCEMENT

And now you can enjoy the feeling of being in your special place. Perhaps as you walk you can feel the ground beneath your feet. The warmth and the comfort of walking across such a familiar and happy place, the soft freshness of the air against your skin and body, and the pleasantness of the warmth from the sun on your skin.

You can also see your surroundings. You can see the animals and the planets, the sky above and all the things that you love to have there with you. And you can make the pictures more vivid in your mind and make your experience more real by seeing and feeling being there.

Use your sense of smell. Find out what you can smell. Can you smell the freshness of the air, the fragrance of being out in nature, the freshness? Use your sense of smell to enhance your experience.

You can also use your sense of taste. Can you taste the smells? Can you taste the air? All of your senses help to make your imagination experience very, very real and vivid for you. They help to make your experience more comfortable and more fun for you. Use your imagination and your mind's eye to make your experience become very, very real.

THERAPEUTIC STRATEGY

And now I'd like you to begin to see, at a short distance away, a small area in which there is an amount of mist or fog. The interesting thing about this mist is that it's very inviting, very welcoming, and very safe for you. It's quite a special place in that you can walk over to the mist and it will assist you in making your body more comfortable. Go ahead, walk toward the mist, taking all the time you need to become familiar with how it looks. [Pause] When you get closer, perhaps you'd like to reach out and touch it with your finger. You will find that it has a pleasant feeling, that it makes your skin feel good. It may even make you tingle just a little in your fingertip as you touch it, just as if there were just a little numbing medicine there. Go ahead, have fun with the mist. You can play in it and you can enjoy it. [Pause] And as you play in it, your body is more and more able to produce its own numbing medicine inside, and send that medicine wherever you would like it to be. You can feel a sensation of happiness when you are in the mist. Your body is pleasantly warm and comfortable while you are there and you are relaxed and happy in the mist, and see yourself laughing and enjoy knowing that, that is what you're doing.

And you can know that whenever you come to the mist, you will develop greater control of mind and body together. You can bring a friend with you if you'd like, or perhaps your pet or your favorite toy. And you can enjoy playing in the mist and feeling good about yourself. If you want to, use the mist to help you with numbing your body. You can do this simply by touching the place where you need numbing medicine while you are in the mist. When you do this, your body will know that it is time for it to put numbing medicine there. And you will experience a small amount of tingling or a funny feeling in that one spot. And it's a good feeling, a feeling of confidence and well-being.

[After the youngster has been given adequate time to play in the mist, I generally encourage him/her to talk with me about his/her body sensations and other experiences while there. This is all done during trance, in order to facilitate feelings of control regarding physical symptomatology and to improve general self-confidence. Once these objectives have been obtained, the youngster is brought back out of the mist and the induction, deepening and enhancement phases are worked through in reverse order to the conclusion of trance.]

Now that you have had an opportunity to play in the mist, you can get ready to leave and gradually return to your cloud car. It is important for you to remember that the mist is always available to you and that you can return to it at anytime you so choose. The mist is always available and able to help you whenever you need it. The mist will help you to gain greater control over mind and body. The more you practice, the easier this will become, and the easier it becomes for you, the greater control and confidence you will experience over mind and body. As you return to your cloud vehicle, you can enjoy the sense of confidence and well-being which you have in knowing that you can return, and in knowing that you have gained new skills that you can use to help yourself. And as you return to your vehicle, you can step in and take charge of the controls and gradually fly your vehicle into the air and begin your journey back, flying back toward the office and back toward the chair, knowing that at any time you choose in the future you can turn your chair into a cloud vehicle and into an imagination experience which will lead you to the mist and to the comfort and confidence of being there. You can do this at any time that you need to.

And now you can gradually begin to land your vehicle in the chair and let the chair begin to feel once again more like a chair, more like the chair in the office, and more like the room in which we are sitting. And now I am going to wait here for you, and you can enjoy your journey, coming back to the chair and back to the room in which we are sitting whenever you are ready. And I'll wait for you and I'll know that you're ready to talk to me about your experience once again, when you open your eyes and are comfortable, and relaxed, and alert and refreshed.

[In the debriefing period following induction, I generally discuss the children's experiences with them, adding or guiding any therapeutic corrections that might be necessary. I also suggest to children that they have learned a skill which they can use in order to reduce or eliminate pain when necessary. However, I emphasize that pain is a necessary body signal which warns us that we are in some danger. Therefore, I ask that all children agree to report the presence of pain to a responsible adult and to make sure that they are being cared for by someone else before "shutting off" the feelings of pain. This insures that they will receive either the necessary parental or medical attention before diminishing their distress. Children are generally very responsible about this condition, as they recognize the need for adult assistance when physical injury or insult is present.]

Techniques of Hypnoanalgesia

Karen Olness, M.D.
Cleveland, Ohio,
and

G. Gail Gardner, Ph.D.

The following techniques represent methods we have used with our patients. We often use several in combination. Every technique involves suggested dissociation, either directly or indirectly. For instance, notice how the phrase "that arm" rather than "your arm" facilitates dissociation. Our list is by no means complete. Other hypnotherapists will prefer variations of our methods or will develop other methods.

DIRECT SUGGESTIONS FOR HYPNOANESTHESIA

REQUEST FOR NUMBNESS. "You know what a numb feeling is. How does numbness feel to you? [Child responds.] Good, just let that part of your body get numb now. Numb like a block of ice [or whatever image the child has used]."

TOPICAL ANESTHESIA. "Just imagine painting numbing medicine onto that part of your body. Tell me when you're finished doing that."

LOCAL ANESTHESIA. "Imagine injecting an anesthetic into that part of your body. Feel it flow into your body and notice the change in feeling as the area becomes numb."

GLOVE ANESTHESIA. "First, pay attention to your hand. Notice how you can feel tingling feelings in that hand. Then let it become numb. When it is very numb, touch that hand to your jaw [or other body part] and let the numb feeling transfer from the hand to the jaw."

SWITCHBOX. The therapist explains the idea that pain is transmitted by nerves from various parts of the body to the brain, which then sends a "pain message" back to the body. The therapist can describe nerves and their pathways or can ask the child to provide a color for nerves. The importance of accuracy varies with the age and needs of the child. Then the child is asked to choose some sort of switch that can turn off incoming nerve signals. The therapist can describe various kinds of switches, such as flip, dimmer, pull, or even a television computer push-button panel or control panel of lights. Having chosen a switch, the child is asked to begin practicing turning off the switches or the lights that connect the brain and certain areas of the body. It is useful to ask the child to turn off the incoming nerve signals for defined periods of time (e.g., 10 minutes, 15 minutes, or 90 minutes). The success of the exercise is judged by touching the child with a small gauge needle or some other sharp object and asking for a comparison with feelings on the other side where the nerve signals are unchanged.

DISTANCING SUGGESTIONS

MOVING PAIN AWAY FROM THE SELF. "Imagine for a while that that arm [or other body part] doesn't belong to you, isn't part of you. Think of it as part of a sculpture or a toy, or picture it just floating out there by itself." Some patients comfortably imagine having only one arm; others imagine three arms, one of which is dissociated.

TRANSFERRING PAIN TO ANOTHER BODY PART. "Imagine putting all the discomfort of the spinal tap into the little finger of your right hand. Tell me how much discomfort is in that little finger. Give it a numerical rating and let me know if it changes. Good. Now let it float away."

MOVING SELF AWAY FROM THE PAIN. "You said you like to go to the mountains. Imagine yourself there now. Let yourself really be there. Just leave all the discomfort and be in the mountains. See the trees and flowers. Watch the chipmunks playing. You can give them some of your food if you like. Smell the fresh air and the pine trees. Listen to the gentle wind. Listen to the running stream." In one study of adults (Greene & Reyher, 1972), it was suggested that body-oriented imagery (e.g., feeling the warmth of the sun) was less effective for hypnotic pain control than imagery that was not body oriented (e.g., looking at scenery or skiing). We do not know if these same results are applicable to children.

SUGGESTIONS FOR FEELINGS ANTITHETICAL TO PAIN

COMFORT. "Recall a time when you felt very comfortable, very good. Then bring those good comfortable feelings into the present. Let your body feel comfortable here and now. You can let comfortable feelings fill your whole body and mind completely, until there is just no room for discomfort. You can be completely comfortable, and you can keep these good feelings for as long as you like."

LAUGHTER. "Laughing helps pain go away. Think of the funniest movie you ever saw or the funniest thing you ever did or your friend did. Each time you imagine laughing, your pain becomes less and less. You may find yourself really laughing and feeling very good."

RELAXATION. "Concentrate on breathing out, for that is a relaxing motion. If you relax completely when you breathe out, you can reduce the pain. Follow your breathing rhythm. Relax more each time you breathe out. You may find that you can cut the pain in half. And then in half again. Use your energy where it will help you feel better and get better."

DISTRACTION TECHNIQUES

FOCUS ON UNRELATED MATERIAL. Young children often obtain some pain relief if the therapist tells a story, either in its original form or with ridiculous variations such as changing the characters ("Once upon a time there were three little wolves and a big bad pig") or their roles ("Once there was a wolf who cried 'Boy, boy'"). Older children may be distracted by discussion of areas of interest such as sports or music.

FOCUS ON PROCEDURE OR INJURY. This method is especially useful for children for whom cognitive mastery is a major coping mechanism. The therapist asks the child to describe the injury in detail, how it occurred, how others reacted, and so on. In the case of a painful procedure, the therapist describes various instruments and asks the child to assist by holding instruments or bandages, counting sutures, or checking the time at various points.

FOCUS ON LESSER OF TWO EVILS.   If a child feels both pain and cold, the therapist can focus on the cold. If a child is having a spinal tap and also has an IV running, the therapist can focus on the IV.

DIRECTING ATTENTION TO PAIN ITSELF

For various reasons, some children refuse or are unable to focus attention on anything but the experience of pain. The therapist can utilize this behavior to the child's own advantage. By joining with the child and asking for a detailed description of the pain, the therapist can offer subtle suggestions for change and relief. Confusion techniques also help.

LIGHTED GLOBE.   "Imagine you are inside a lighted globe and you can see yourself walking around on the inside of a map of your discomfort. Notice that discomfort very carefully. See it right now in a color you don't like. I'll ask you to check it again later. Notice what size it is. It might be the size of a grapefruit or a grape or a lemon. Even a pinhead has a size. We'll check the size again later. And notice the shape. What shape is it right now? And what is it saying to you now? How loud is it right now? Later we'll see if you can still hear it. Look again. What color is it now? That's interesting. It seems to be changing. I wonder how you did that. How small is it now? Can you change the size too? Yes. You are really in charge there in that lighted globe. You are a good map maker. You can go wherever you want. Feel whatever you want. What shape is the discomfort now? Can you still hear it?"

Older children can benefit from a technique of focusing on breathing, then shifting focus to the area of discomfort, with emphasis on the fact that it is changing. Subsequently, the therapist can ask the child to focus on a piece of music, or a smell (e.g., by bringing an open bottle of perfume near the child's nose), and on the discomfort at the same time. The child will gradually learn that the perception of two stimuli fades as the attention is shifted to one.

REINFORCEMENT

We encourage—but do not demand—that our patients practice their skills in hypnotic pain control, using variations or new methods as they see fit. The more confident children are of their ability to use these skills, the more likely it is that they will use them whenever it is appropriate to do so. Other methods of reinforcement include selected use of audiotapes, videotapes, parents acting as therapeutic allies, group meetings, and communication with other patients who have successfully used hypnotherapy for pain control.

After several practice sessions, the therapist can ask the child which type of relaxation or imagery exercise is most helpful. This can be taped and placed over the child's favorite music, if he or she wishes, and made available on a Walkman-type recorder during procedures. The child can also be encouraged to tape himself guiding himself through a relaxation exercise; this can also be placed over favorite music. Therapists should also encourage children who are skilled in pain control to help the therapist coach other children. This gives confidence to the child who is teaching, and the learner will trust that other child.

Pediatric Wound Injection— Using a Visual Distraction Technique

Steven F. Bierman, M.D.
Encinitas, California

INTRODUCTION

It is a sad paradox that the injection of local anesthesia into a wound—in order to render debridement and wound closure painless—is itself painful. In pediatrics, especially, such an unpleasant prelude often aggravates the situation for both patient and physician.

The following technique serves to eliminate the pain of wound injection. It makes simple use of the fundamental fact that consciousness (i.e., present awareness) is limited. Thus, when consciousness is preempted by pain, other stimuli are disregarded. Distraction, then, is merely the redirection of consciousness from painful to nonpainful stimuli. Of course, when distraction redirects consciousness from kinesthetic (i.e., feeling) to visual perceptions, the likelihood of anesthesia is enhanced.

PRINCIPLES

The success of this technique hinges on the following basic principles.

1. All children like to think of themselves as bigger, older, more capable.
2. Confusion is an element of all hypnotic inductions.
3. The degree of absorption of the subject is proportional to the degree of absorption and sincerity of the operator.

PREPARATION

In most cases, the presenting configuration is one of (a) consciousness, fixed and fully absorbed in (b) a stimuli-generating wound. Both members (a and b) of the system warrant preparatory attention. Accordingly, consciousness is unlimbered/unstuck by attending to the wound last while devoting serious, brow-furrowing attention to other parts. The wound is prepared by applying proparacaine 5% ophthalmic drops, after first placing a drop on the subject's hand or forearm: "Now, that may feel just cold, or nothing at all." Then, moving to the wound, "And I wonder how you will even know when it is all the way asleep?"

TECHNIQUE

What follows is a transcript of the technique, from the first moment of the encounter to the conclusion of the injection. Often, the author proceeds from this technique to trance induction and maintenance, thereby offering suggestions for wound healing, continuing comfort, etc., as circumstances require.

[Doctor enters the room, looks directly and inquiringly at the patient, momentarily disregarding parents.]

"And where is [JOHNNY]?" [The child is helpless and unimportant. With this question, he/she immediately becomes the central figure. Moreover, the child now knows something the doctor does not know, and so, is no longer quite so helpless.]

[Child indicates himself as Johnny] "Hi Johnny." Doctor extends his hand [something the child *can* refuse], "I'm Dr. Steve. You really *were* scared, weren't you?" [By affirming the fact that the child *was* scared, the physician is both "pacing" the child's internal experience and consigning that experience to the past.]

[Doctor touches or points to some unaffected part.] "Hmmmm, how is *this* part?" [Unlimbering attention.]

Child: "Okay."

Doctor: "Okay . . . [moving elsewhere], "and *this* part here?"

Child: "Okay."

Doctor: "Okay . . ." [moving again], "and *this* part here?"

Child: "Okay." [giggles, curiously]

Doctor: "So, there really is quite a lot that's okay, isn't there?" [Not waiting for an answer—building response potential. Doctor now points to blood near the wound.]

Doctor: "And I see you had some good *red* blood, didn't you?"

Child: [bewildered nod]

Doctor: "Good. Because if there is one thing I don't like it's blue blood, or that crummy old pink blood. . . . Good red blood."

Thus, the experience of bleeding is "reframed" into an opportunity for the child to witness one of his superior qualities. The doctor now introduces himself to the parent and repeats the importance of noting whether it is, in fact, good red blood.

[Doctor now turns to the wound.]

"And now I can look." [Doctor regards wound.] "Hmmm, and did you want just three stitches, or four really good ones?" [That the child wants stitches is presupposed.]

Child: "Umm, . . . just three."

Doctor: "Okay, just three stitches."

[The doctor now prepares to suture, placing sterile drapes, etc., and applies proparacaine to the wound.]

Doctor: [continues] "And you're five years old, aren't you?" [Guessing the age at one year *more* than the child's actual age.]

Child: "No. Four." [Again, the child knows something the doctor doesn't know, but the mistake is in the child's favor.]

Doctor: "Oh, I see, but smart enough to be a five-year-old . . . and do you know how to mix colors?"

[Child grimaces ambiguously.]

Doctor: "Well, do you know what happens when you mix red paint and white paint?"

Child: "Mmm. . . ." [Many children will supply the answer correctly.]

Doctor: "It's pink, isn't it?

Child: "Yeah."

Doctor: "And when you mix blue paint and yellow paint?"

Child: "Green."

Doctor: "That's right! So you *can* mix colors. And do you know how to do algebra, too . . .?" [Parents usually discharge some nervous laughter here.] "Okay, so I'm going to *show* you how to do algebra, just like a five-year-old, and mix colors. And this is just for you, Johnny; so your parents can just listen and wonder."

[Doctor now delivers a set of instructions, watching carefully for signs of maximal absorption: eyes roll upward, distracted gaze, altered facial tonus, etc. It is during this period of maximal absorption that injection proceeds. Occasionally, if the child perceives the injection, the operator desists momentarily and reemphasizes the visual/intellectual task at hand.]

Doctor: [continues] "Ready? Okay. There are

two dogs, a mother dog and a father dog. And one is blue and the other is yellow. Okay? And the two dogs have four puppies. . . . Half of the puppies are the mixed color; and the other half are the color of the mother. What are the colors of the puppies? . . . And really *think*."

The question creates a focused state of internal absorption, requiring:

1. A mathematical operation (halving four);
2. A visual operation (determining the outcome of mixing colors); and,
3. The resolution of the confusion resulting from the deletion of necessary information (the color of the mother). Similar questions — using other animals, numbers, and colors — can also be posed. It does not matter that some of the operations may be beyond the child's range of competence, so long as they capture his/her attention. However, it is best to allow for some measure of success. Two or three such questions are often used during a single procedure. Of course, the operator must always be seriously attentive and willing to repeat the question or to go on to another.

CONCLUSION

A method for painless pediatric wound injection is presented. Almost daily use of this method has proved gratifying to the author and delightfully surprising to both patient and parent.

Examples of Suggestions for Use in Pediatric Emergencies

Daniel P. Kohen, M.D.
Minneapolis, Minnesota

"As I wash it, all of the hurt can be washed away; as I wash and you breathe out, your muscles can get loose, soft, and comfortable."

A pediatric patient with abdominal discomfort, nausea and vomiting enjoyed dancing, so she was told she would be "pleased to find out how little things have to bother you, and you can be happy to see how relaxed you can become even as you breathe slowly."

"During trance several other suggestions were given. These included the 'ease of learning how to help yourself feel good'; the 'ease of pain control'; and finally 'now that you know you are safe, and going to be okay, you can allow yourself to become more and more comfortable, knowing you don't have to vomit anymore, and that you don't even have to let the hurt bother you.' After pelvic examination, and before termination of relaxation/mental imagery, the posthypnotic suggestion was given that, 'In a moment or two you can stay relaxed, even when you slowly reorient to this room . . . and then you may use this place in your mind and these good feelings to feel comfortable during further examinations, during surgery, and after surgery.' "

The following interaction took place in an emergency room setting with a boy, almost 13 years old with first-time upper gastrointestinal bleeding. He was uncooperative and staff had been previously unsuccessful in inserting the nasogastric tube. "It was apparent that T.S. was in a spontaneous, albeit unhappy trance. He was staring quietly at the blood dripping into the tubing in his arm. His gaze was fixed, He was staring quietly at the blood dripping into the tubing in his arm. His gaze was fixed, his breathing very slow, and his attention obviously focused. I then suggested to him, 'It is nice to know that the blood running is to replace what you threw up.' In a similar, direct, and matter-of-fact way, I also whispered that he was 'smart to come to the hospital when you

are sick.' Without altering his gaze or his breathing, he nodded, apparently in response to my comments. The following exchange then occurred:

Doctor: Isn't it good to know that you're going to be okay?

T.S.: [He nodded and turned his head toward me.]

Doctor: I guess it was hard when they put that tube in your nose before?

T.S.: [Shakes head no.]

Doctor: It's to clear all the blood out of your stomach so you won't have to throw up any more blood . . . and then you can begin to get better . . . so it's real important that the tube goes into the stomach. . . . Isn't it good to know that?

T.S.: Yes. [Nod.]

Doctor: Now that you know that, I know that you want to find out how to do that really easily. . . . You know those switches in your brain that turn off hurts? [This metaphoric suggestion for control was offered directly and matter-of-factly—as a foregone conclusion.]

T.S.: [A knowing nod.]

Doctor: Find the one for your nose and mouth . . . and when it's *off*, you know that will make it very easy to swallow the tube down into your stomach. The helping tube will go down easy when the switch is off . . . and, of course, your breathing tube will be very comfortable an won't be bothered . . . this goes only in the food tube . . . I'll help you. Did you notice how when you breathe in you breathe in good feelings . . . and that you breathe out bad feelings?

T.S.: Yes."

HYPNOSIS WITH ENURESIS

A Hypnotherapeutic Approach to Enuresis

Daniel P. Kohen, M.D.
Minneapolis, Minnesota

As with any clinical problem in children, the success of a hypnotic approach to enuresis is

predicated at least in part upon those things that occur "before" any "official" hypnotherapy occurs. Initially there must be the development of a sensitive and positive rapport with the child, the establishment in the mind of the parents that the clinician is both competent and confident, and the appropriate and thorough clinical assessment of the problem itself.

It is critical that a careful and comprehensive history be obtained so that the clinician can be assured that appropriate medical assessment of enuresis has taken place prior to proceeding to do hypnotherapy and teaching self-hypnosis.

The history should assure that (1) the child is over six years of age (at under age six, enuresis should be considered a normal developmental variant unless the child has been completely dry and suddenly started to wet again); (2) the absence of associated daytime wetting (which most often indicates either an important physical cause or a more profound psychological problem), (3) the absence of known physical causes of enuresis such as urinary tract infections, chronic constipation with or without soiling, urinary tract malformations, juvenile onset diabetes mellitus, diabetes insipidus, hyperthyroidism, or spinal dysraphism. Such histories can be obtained with questionnaires as well as being corroborated during an initial visit.

In the context of history taking and rapport development in the first visit, it is mandatory that the child learn that the clinician (1) believes s/he can help the child help him/herself, (2) knows that the child feels bad about this problem, (3) knows that often many things have been "tried" before that "didn't work," and (4) believes that the child's ideas, thoughts, beliefs and worries are important to the clinician. These can only be accomplished in the context of taking the history from the child, "joining" with the child, and teaching about the body without trying to go "too fast."

I often learn the details of the problem by focusing on *dryness*. Thus when a child comes in, I often ask directly, "What are you doing here?" Some are shy, embarrassed, and/or sad and prefer not to acknowledge the problem right away in this fashion. In turn, I ask instead if they would prefer to "talk about some other stuff for a few minutes before we talk about why you're here or what problems you have?" This provides respect, comfort, and relief, while also creating a positive expectation for what will follow. Ultimately I ask something like, "Lots of kids come here for different kinds of problems, some big ones, some little ones. . . . I wonder what your problem is? "I

wet the bed" is usually the answer. My response is usually to *begin the reframing by talking instead about dryness*. I might say, therefore: "I'm sorry to know that. Well, how many times a week do you wake up in the morning in a *DRY* bed? In addition to reframing the focus on dry not wet, this represents the introduction of language that will be used later in hypnosis, and thus is the "planting of seeds" for later use in the cultivation of imagination. The history is then obtained (with the parent present, but usually directed largely to the child) of the frequency of dry beds. We also learn what happens, for instance, whether the child awakens during the night or learns in the morning that the bed is wet, who changes the sheets, whether or not there is or has been punishment and the child's feelings about that, and *what the child perceives will be different when he wakes up in a dry bed every day*. This positive suggestion is offered as an expectation but also as an assessment to identify both the degree of motivation of the child for change, as well as his awareness of how the problem is affecting his life. (Often this results in a response that being dry will enable him to go on more sleepovers or to camp, which previously had been discouraged or disallowed.)

It is important briefly to ascertain the thinking of both the child and the parents about the reason for the accidents. While the response may often take the form of "he sleeps too soundly," or "it's inherited, her uncle wet until age 14," the identification and discussion of their beliefs are nonetheless important. I follow this with a brief explanation that the specific cause is not easily discovered, but that the method that I am about to teach the child can be helpful as long as the child won't mind having dry beds. Another indirect assessment of motivation, this usually results in the child's agreement that he would indeed like to be dry every day.

EXPLAINING HOW THE BODY WORKS

A simple explanation of how the body works, an important part of the approach, is another medium through which expectations and phrases that will be used during hypnosis may be easily and comfortably introduced. A drawing of the heart, kidneys, bladder, a "gate" or "door" on the bladder, a urethra, a brain, and a toilet are made while teaching about the function of each. The heart is described as a pump muscle that sends blood all over the body. The kidneys are described as a filter, strainer, or "one kid told me once that the kidney was the washing machine for the blood and he was right." The bladder is described as the place where the urine ("pee" or whatever words the family uses) is stored up.

I then stop and ask the child, if he had to pee right then, how would he know. Children often say they feel it, and some say they know they feel it because of their brain. At this point the concept of the *brain as the master computer of the body* is introduced. Using the picture that was drawn and arrows going back and forth between the brain and bladder, a story is told about the brain and the bladder communicating with one another. I present something like this:

Let's just pretend that we could listen in on the communication between your brain and your bladder even though they don't talk loud. So your bladder fills up and it sends a message to the brain like, "Hello, brain, this is the bladder speaking. I'm full." And the brain sends a message back, something like, "Well, we're busy talking now, or we're busy in class now, or we're outside playing now, so keep the gate closed and keep the pee inside because it wouldn't be very nice to pee on Dr. 's chair!" And the bladder sends a message back to the brain like, "Well, that's fine for you to say, but I really have to go; I'm really full." Then the brain says, "Well, okay, so keep the gate closed and I'll send a message to the mouth and tongue to ask where the bathroom is and if I can be excused, and then I'll send a message to the ears to hear the answer and then to the legs to stand up and walk to the bathroom, and to the hands to close the door. *Then* I'll send a message to you to open the gate, bladder, and *let the pee out in the toilet where it belongs*, and then close the gate again." And that's the way it really happens, isn't it? Even though they don't talk out loud, and they have known how to do that for a long time in the daytime, haven't they? Since you were about [*age, parent fills in the age of daytime learning*] . . . *So they already*

know how to talk to each other just fine all day long [positive suggestions, ego-strengthening about competence]. [If the child is also having some dry beds each week, I add something like:] *And even two or three nights each week they talk to each other fine.*

I then ask the child and parent what they think the brain is *doing* at night. Often the response is that the brain is asleep. Irrespective of the response, however, I continue the notion that:

The *brain is the boss of the body. The brain takes care of us*, and even when we are asleep it may be resting, but it is paying attention, taking care of us, dreaming, keeping our heart beating, our lungs breathing, telling us how to kick the covers off if we're too hot, to turn the pillow over, etc. Sometimes the brain and bladder get in the bad habit of not talking to each other at night, and they need some reminders and some training, just like you trained yourself when you were even younger. And now that bladder and that brain [dissociative suggestions] know what to do without thinking about it out loud. So, when you learn this relaxing and imagining in a few moments [or, at the next visit], *you'll learn* how to give them instructions to talk to each other just fine during the night so you can wake up in the morning in a nice, warm, comfortable, dry bed.

I often offer the suggestion, then, that they keep track of dry beds during the next two weeks, and that before going to sleep at night, they look at the drawing of the body and "just think about what we talked about. I don't know what instructions you will give your brain and bladder about how to talk to each other. Maybe you will tell them to talk to each other during the night and either have the brain wake you up so you can walk to the bathroom, open the gate pee in the toilet and walk back to your nice, warm, comfortable dry bed, *OR* maybe you'll have the brain simply tell the bladder to keep the gate closed through the night. I don't know which" [This so-called double bind suggestion is a no-lose suggestion that offers choice within the context of the desired outcome of dryness.]

Whether the "official" hypnosis session is conducted that day or at the next visit, it is done in the context of a carefully developed positive relationship of trust, of a positive expectation for success, and of a mutual understanding of how the body works.

RELAXATION AND IMAGERY
FOR ENURESIS

INTRODUCTION.   Now that you know about how the body works and have been thinking about it, I'm happy to show you how to use your inside thinking and daydreaming [or pretending or imagining] to help teach your brain and bladder how to talk to each other even better than they already are doing.

IMAGERY (INDUCTION).   Just go ahead and close your eyes and pretend or daydream something fun. Notice everything about whatever you are daydreaming about—what you see and hear there, who's there with you. Notice the smells, tastes. [Enhance the imagery with emphasis on enjoyment, on "*because* you're the boss of your imagination like you're the boss of your body."] While you are daydreaming or pretending or imagining—I don't know which you like the best—make sure it is really fun *because* [children, like adults, need a *reason* to carry out the suggestion] you are the *boss of your imagination* [ego-strengthening]. *Notice* [an invitation to concentrate, pay attention] what you *see* there in your imagining, who is with you or maybe you're alone or with friends or family or new friends, where you are, whether you're inside or outside, whether the weather is hot or cold or in between, or rainy or snowy, and *hear* the sounds there in your *favorite place*. Maybe you'll hear voices of people talking, or sounds of music, or machines, or of the weather, or maybe it's quiet and you'll listen to the quiet, and *notice* the *smells* where you are imagining, and the *tastes* there.

RELAXATION (DEEPENING).   To enhance the imagery and ego-strengthening and to deepen the experience, suggestions about relaxation are often added. For example: "You probably already noticed that your face muscles are relaxed and that your breathing is slower than it was before. That's *because* you are doing this exactly the right way, and since you and your brain are the boss of your body, you can even make your

relaxation even more than it already is, because our bodies already know how to relax, and we even relax a little bit each time we breathe out. Just notice how your shoulders go down every time you breathe out [pause, and add "that's right" on the next exhalation]. So, to help relax even more, just take a slow, deep, breath, in, and, out, and when you breathe out, say relax to yourself in your inside thinking, and just notice what happens as your shoulders go down and relax" [e.g., "just like Raggedy Ann"]. Pacing and leading according to cues from the child, proceed with progressive relaxation down the body, utilizing language comfortable for the child ("letting your muscles get loose and floppy, maybe like jello or spaghetti!").

UTILIZATION – THERAPEUTIC SUGGESTIONS.   Now that you have given your body good relaxation, keep enjoying your imagination, or maybe you're having a new daydream, I don't know. But, in another corner of your mind, just imagine that you are in your bedroom getting ready to go to bed. Let me know when you notice that in one corner of your thinking. [Head nod, finger signal, etc.] While you are noticing that, just watch yourself getting ready for bed, and notice how before you go to bed you walk to the bathroom, send a message from your brain to your bladder to open the gate, let the pee out in the toilet where it belongs, close the gate, and then walk back to your bedroom and get ready to get into your nice, warm, dry, comfortable bed.

While you do this special inside thinking practice, it's best to do it sitting up before you fall asleep. Then *remind* [they already *know*, they just need reminders] your brain and bladder that tonight while you're asleep you will have a good night's sleep, and a great dream, and during the night while you sleep if your bladder fills up with pee it will *of course* send a message to your wide awake brain to let it know. And then your brain will have *two choices*: either wake you up, wide awake, get out of bed, walk to the bathroom, send a message from your brain to your bladder to open the gate, let the pee out in the toilet where it belongs, close the gate, and then walk back to your bedroom and get ready to get into your nice, warm, dry, comfortable bed, *OR* send a message back to the bladder to keep the gate closed until you wake up in the morning *proud and happy* in your nice, warm, dry, comfortable bed.

I don't know which one your brain and bladder will choose . . . maybe sometimes one and sometimes the other, or maybe one and not the other. But before you go to sleep you can remind them to be sure and talk to each other tonight, *just the same way they talk to each other so well all day long, because your brain is the boss of your body and the main computer.* And *when* you *practice* this way, the way you are doing so well, you are really programming the computer, just the same way you teach your brain to teach you to do so many of those other things you do so well. [Include here other things that the history indicates that the patient does well without thinking about them, such as playing soccer, singing, musical instrument, grades, video games, etc.] So, the more you practice, the better you get.

Now, before you finish, take a few moments of inside thinking time to repeat those messages to yourself . . . and to let me know when you have completed that [signal]. Great! Now, keep enjoying your daydreaming for these last few moments. I don't know who will be most proud of you when you have given yourself a dry bed every morning . . . but probably you will be most proud and the . . . I don't know . . . Mom or Dad or me or who . . . but *when* you practice each day for 10 or 15 minutes, two or three or maybe only one time, be sure and do it just as easily and well as you learned today. So, start your self-relaxing by closing your eyes and thinking of something fun like you're doing now . . . it might be the same thing as now or something different but you'll find out because you're the boss of your imagining . . . and then when you're ready, you can relax your body, either from head to toe or toes upward. One kid I know starts at his belly button and goes both ways! And then when you're ready, be sure to give instructions to your bladder and brain

about how you want them to talk to each other during the night. And when you're finished, then you'll be done. When you're practicing at night you can then just fall asleep, and if you're practicing in the day, then you can just gradually come back to where you were at the start, but be sure to bring your proud and relaxed feelings with you!

[At the end of the session, I tell the patient I thought he did a wonderful job. I also ask, "What did you notice that you liked the most?" as a reinforcement, and ask him for a time commitment as to when he will practice the self-hypnosis at home. Following reinforcement about keeping track of dry beds, we then agree on a time for a return visit.]

Imagery with Bedwetting

H. E. Stanton, Ph.D.
Hobart, Tasmania, Australia

INDICATIONS AND CONTRAINDICATIONS

Enuresis is an extremely common pediatric problem, but one that requires careful evaluation, as just indicated by Kohen. Before the age of five, the majority of bedwetting does not seem linked to organic or underlying psychological or family system causes (Olness & Gardner, 1988). Situational enuresis and secondary enuresis (where there previously was good control) are somewhat more suggestive of the absence of an organic problem. However, it is recommended that a careful medical evaluation always be conducted in children over the age of five. A pediatrician needs to rule out such potential organic causes as diabetes, urinary tract infections, congenital anomalies, seizures, occult spinal dysraphism, neurological etiologies, hyperthyroidism, and potential contributors such as diuretic medications and caffeine drinks (Olness & Gardner, 1988). Functions of the symptom within the family system and historic, unconscious factors may be explored through interview assessment and ideomotor signaling. When hypnosis is used, cassette tapes may assist in reinforcing suggestions. An addition to the suggestions provided by Stanton is to suggest repetitively that the control panel "will send a message to wake you up when the dam is full and you need to pee. Then you can get up, walk to the bathroom, urinate in the toilet, and enjoy going back to sleep in your dry bed." (*Ed.*)

SUGGESTIONS

Imagine a dam equipped with gates to hold back the flow of water. When they are open, water flows through the dam; when they are closed, no water is able to pass. Their operation is controlled by a computer-controlled instrument panel. As soon as you get into bed, set the controls in such a way that the gates are closed. They are to remain that way until you awaken in the morning. At that time, change the controls on the instrument panel so that the gates will open.

Induction and Ocean Metaphor for Bedwetting

Valerie J. Wall, Ph.D.
Seattle, Washington

INDICATIONS AND CONTRAINDICATIONS

This procedure is designed for working with children between seven and twelve years of age who enjoy and have been to the beach. As cited at the beginning of Stanton's paper, it is vitally important to obtain careful pediatric evaluation for bedwetting problems prior to pursuing psychologically oriented therapy. (*Ed.*)

PRE-INDUCTION

Today I want to talk with you about learning to keep your bed dry at night and feeling a greater sense of self-confidence and control when you're sleeping at home or at a friend's house. We know that learning to have dry beds is something that people do as they grow older and develop more regular patterns of sleeping during the night. Some people do this when they are very young, perhaps two or three years of age, and other people do this when they are somewhat older. Still other people develop more adult sleeping patterns and dry beds at night when they are in middle school. I'm not exactly sure at what age you will develop these patterns; however, I am sure that you can teach your mind to have greater control over urinating so that when your body is ready, you will be able to be confident and comfortable every night.

In order to assist you in feeling dry and more confident, I am going to talk to you about a walk which you and I can take in our mind's eye, and I'm also going to talk to you about the things we can observe on this walk. We will be taking a walk, in our mind, to the beach, where there are many interesting things to see. While I'm talking with you, you can simply relax and picture the things that I am talking about. As you picture them in your mind, they may look just the way I've described them to be, or they may look somewhat different to you. Either way is fine, for you will be able to understand and remember the most important parts. You may choose to close your eyes while I'm talking to you, or you may choose to keep your eyes open. Either way is fine with me. I'd like you to choose the way which allows you to concentrate most successfully on what I'm saying and which allows you to create a very real imagination experience in your mind.

INDUCTION

To begin, I'd like you to sit comfortably in the chair, allowing all the muscles in your body to relax, and enjoy the feeling of being fully supported and at ease. Remember, that if you choose to close your eyes, this may be helpful to you in making your imagination experience more real. . . . [At this point, with the older child, I encourage children to close their eyes by suggestions for eyelid heaviness or seeing the pictures better when their eyes are closed. I do not suggest drowsiness or sleepiness, as this is somewhat disconcerting to many children.]

DEEPENING, ENHANCEMENT, AND BEGINNING OF THERAPEUTIC STRATEGY

As you and I prepare to go on our walk, you may notice that we are in a very pleasant surrounding in which there are numerous plants, and some small and rather friendly animals. You may also see larger animals which are friendly and curious about our presence here. One other thing to notice is that we are on a definite path, and that pathway seems to be leading gradually toward a small hill, which slopes down in the direction of the ocean. While we are still quite a ways from the ocean, you can notice that it is some ways off in the background. As we walk along this path, you can watch the animals playing, the birds flying, and notice the peacefulness and yet the amount of busy-ness occurring around you in the lives of the small animals.

It is a very pleasant time of day, perhaps the late afternoon, with the sun about halfway down to the horizon. As we walk along this pathway it becomes more tranquil and peaceful, with many interesting events going on around us. However, you can feel calm and at ease. We are gradually approaching a small slope which leads down to another flat area between the ocean and us. As we go down this slope, we can travel at an even and smooth pace without unnecessary hesitation or unnecessary hurrying. As we reach the next level, the sunlight is somewhat less bright. However, there is still ample light and it is not yet dusk. This level of the pathway is even calmer, and we can feel the tranquility, peacefulness and comfort of this area of the path, as we walk along through the grasses and brush, through the little bushes

and flowers. There continue to be animals of interest to us along this part of the path. However, the animals are somewhat less active than before; they seem more drowsy, as if they know that evening will be coming in a while. And now, perhaps, you can see ahead of you another slight slope downward, and this slope leads to the beach.

Once again, as we approach this slope, you know that it is possible to walk down it at an even pace, a pace which demonstrates to you your control of your muscles. You are able to walk down the slope without having to run or to go very slowly, and as you go down the slope you can see in front of you the wide sands of the beach. It's a beautiful beach with waves coming up on the shore. The sunlight here is very tranquil and the ocean is very beautiful. As you walk along the beach, you will notice the shells, and the seaweed, and the seashore animals that live here.

Of particular interest is an area of rocks where there are some tide pools that have formed. The water inside these tide pools is contained perfectly within them by the rocks, and it provides the perfect home for the seashore plants and animals. We know that the tide of the ocean, which rises and falls, and the waves, which move rhythmically, are controlled by the force of gravity which comes from the moon. The moon acts sort of like a master control above the ocean and the tide pools. It contains them well within the ocean beaches, and allows the tide pools to stay in their basins. The moon maintains control over the tides and the tide pools, and provides a comfortable home for the animals of the beach. The moon does this for the oceans and the beaches and the beach animals in the same way that your mind can do this for you.

In the same way that the moon controls an even and steady rhythm for the ocean, so your mind can maintain an even and steady rhythm for you while you sleep. This rhythm will allow you to sleep comfortably and allow you to maintain control over your bladder. By doing this, you will be able to experience the comfort and confidence of dry beds. As you prepare to come back from your walk along the beach, you can enjoy knowing that this is a place to which you can return at any time, a place where you can learn greater control of mind and body together. Greater control of mind and body allows you to feel more confidence in yourself and in your physical growth. The more often you return and the more often you practice, the easier it will become for you to have control of mind and body together. The easier it becomes, the easier it will be for you to practice and the more confidence you will experience. You will find that this is very pleasant and easy for you to do, and that your learning and development will improve on a regular basis as you come back to the ocean in your mind's eye and practice what you have learned.

And now I would like you to begin walking back across the ocean sand toward the path that brought you here. And as you walk back across the beach, you will come to the gentle slope that leads you down to the beach. You will find that it is very easy to walk back up this slope, and that you can do so at a regular and controlled pace, which is just the same as the walking rate you maintained on the beach. And you can walk back across the second flat area where the animals were a little more sleepy, and notice how comfortable and contented they are. These animals live up from the beach in a dry area and enjoy the warmth and comfort of the dry sand and grasses around them. And you can continue across this area up towards the next slope. Once again, you can walk up this hill at a comfortable and even pace, on to the first flat area where our path began. Here the animals are more active and playful, just as they were before. And they, too, are comfortable and happy in the warm, dry grasses and sand of their homes.

RE-ALERTING

And when you have walked across the path and up the slopes and across the flat areas, you can begin to sense that you are returning closer to being in the chair in this room. And you can

return from your imagination experience whenever you are ready, knowing that you can revisit the pathway, the slopes, the flat areas, the sand, the ocean, and the tide pools at any time. You will know the sun and the moon will always be above to guide your progress. And whenever you are ready, you can open your eyes and return to this room alert, relaxed, and refreshed, feeling an increased sense of confidence and well-being. And I'm going to be quiet now, and you can open your eyes whenever you feel that you are ready.

[After the induction and therapy phase, I discuss with children their responses to the therapeutic metaphor. I have included the concept of a walkway which either changes directions or moves into different areas across slopes in order to assist youngsters with maintaining an even pace across phases of sleep. This is incorporated along with the metaphor of the moon's control over the tide pools, as there was some research done in the Stanford Sleep Research Lab in the late 1970s which suggested that bed wetting might be tied to inappropriate neurological triggering when moving from one phase of sleep to another.]

Suggestions with Enuresis

Franz Baumann, M.D.
San Francisco, California

You can wake up all the way when you need to empty your bladder. You can learn how good it feels to empty your bladder completely. You can learn to control the flow of urine from your bladder through your penis. You can learn to enjoy fully the feeling of urine coming from your penis. Because this enjoyment is such a good feeling, you will want to be fully awake for it at all times. You can practice stopping and going every single time you urinate. Every time you do this you can learn that *you are the boss* of your bladder and urine. You can have a wonderful feeling of pride every time you put your urine where you really want it, namely, into the toilet. You can do all these things because they make you happy. [They are taught to repeat these suggestions in self-hypnosis before going to sleep.]

Erickson's Suggestions with Enuresis

Milton H. Erickson, M.D.

This is the second day of January . . . and you have wet the bed, your parents say, every night for twelve years. You know that and I know that, so now let us forget about it. Let us talk about something that is really important. Now, this is the second of January, and I don't think it would be reasonable, not the least bit reasonable in any way, for me to expect you to have a permanently dry bed two weeks from now. And you know, by that time January will be practically over, and then February is a short month. Does anybody want to dispute that? It is a short month, and I certainly don't think you ought to start a permanently dry bed before March. It doesn't seem reasonable that you do it before then, but I will tell you what you might be interested in doing. In a couple of weeks from now [I point to the calendar on the wall], I would like to have you puzzle mentally over this question: *In two weeks from today, will it be on Wednesday, or will it be on Thursday, that I will have a dry bed for the first time?* Two weeks from now, *will it be on Wednesday, or will it be on Thursday, that I will have my first dry bed*? And you will have to wait until Friday morning to know for certain, and so that Friday you will come in to tell me whether it was Wednesday or whether it was Thursday. . . .

[Later, after some progress the suggestions were given:] February is such a short month . . . that you really ought not to have a dry bed, reasonably speaking, more than three times in any one of those four weeks of February—three times in succession in any one of those weeks. Now that doesn't mean you can't have one dry

bed or two dry beds, but I don't think it would be reasonable to expect more than three dry beds in any one of those four weeks. . . .

[After still more progress it was suggested:] Now, I still don't know when your permanently dry bed will come about, but you are Irish and St. Patrick's Day is a very nice day; but when I think about how your father and mother have treated you, I think April Fools' also would be a very nice day. There is one thing I would like you to get straight, Joe, and that is that when you have your dry bed, whether it is on St. Patrick's Day or April Fools' Day or any day in between, *that day is your business*. It is none of my business. It is nobody else's business either.

Enchanted Cottage Suggestions for Enuresis

Don E. Gibbons, Ph.D.

As you look around the room we have entered, here in the enchanted cottage, you see a fireplace at the far end of the room, with a warm log fire burning brightly, and beside the fireplace is an easy chair, which looks so comfortable that you decide to go over and curl up in it for a while.

Our journey here has made you sleepy, and as soon as your curl up in the chair and begin to watch the fire, you find yourself starting to drift off to sleep, soundly and comfortably, there in that soft easy chair.

Now you are sleeping very soundly. But in just a minute or two, you are going to have to go to the bathroom. And as soon as you begin to feel that you have to go to the bathroom, you are going to start to move around, and you will open your eyes and wake up before you have wet. Your eyes will open, and you will be completely awake before you actually start to do anything. And when you do open your eyes, you will be back here with me, and not in the cottage anymore. We can go back to the cottage after you have gone to the bathroom. But first, you will open your eyes and wake up, ready to go to the bathroom before you have wet. And from now on, whenever you are asleep at night, you will wake up before you have wet, just as you are going to do now.

Any time now, you are going to feel that you have to go to the bathroom, and you will begin to move around, and your eyes will open before you have wet.

SUGGESTIONS FOR THUMBSUCKING

Erickson's Suggestions for Thumbsucking

Milton H. Erickson, M.D.

Your father and mother want you to stop sucking your thumb, and they told you that they were going to bring you to me and make you stop. I'd like you to understand one thing: your thumb is your thumb; your mouth is your mouth. If you want to suck your thumb, you go right ahead. Your Daddy can't boss me; your Mommy can't boss me; and I'm not going to boss you. *But if you want to, you can boss your thumb, and you can boss your mouth, and you can go ahead and suck your thumb as much as you like.*

[. . . I pointed out to him that I thought it awfully unfair that he sucked only his left thumb; that his right thumb was just as nice a thumb and it was entitled to just as much sucking, and that I was astonished (that he wasn't sucking his right thumb as well). Little Jimmy thought that he was at fault. Being a nice, bright boy, Jimmy should be willing to suck *both* thumbs. But, you see, what happens is that as surely as Jimmy sucks *both* thumbs he has cut down sucking his left thumb by about fifty per cent. He has reduced his habit. And what about that forefinger, and the other three fingers? *When you start dividing, you start conquering.*]

Now, let us get one thing straight. That left thumb of yours is your thumb; that mouth of yours is your mouth; those front teeth of yours are your front teeth. I think you are entitled to do anything you want to with your thumb, with

your mouth, and with your teeth. They are yours, and let us get that straight. I want you to do anything you want to do. . . . One of the first things you have learned when you went to nursery school was to take turns. You took turns with this little girl and with that little boy in doing things in nursery school. You learned to take turns in the first grade. In fact, you learned to take turns at home. When Mother serves the food she serves it first to one brother, and then it may be your turn, then it may be sister's turn, then it is Mother's turn. We always do things by turns. But I don't think you are being right or fair or good in always sucking your left thumb and never giving your right thumb a turn. . . . Your left thumb has received all of the sucking. . . . The right thumb hasn't had a turn; the first finger hasn't had a turn; not a single other finger has had a turn. Now I think you are a good little boy, and I don't think you are doing this on purpose. I think you really would like to give each of your fingers a proper turn. [Can you imagine giving a turn to ten separate digits? Can you imagine a more laborious task in the world? And Jimmy strove manfully to give his fingers an equal turn at sucking. Next I pointed out:] You know, Jimmy, you are over six years old now, and soon [in two months] you will be a big boy of seven; and you know I have never seen a big boy or a big man that ever sucked his thumb, so you had better do all of your sucking before you are a big boy of seven. [No longer a mere six. He would be joining the big kids when he turned seven years old.] And you know, Jimmy, I don't know a single big kid that sucks his thumb, so you'd better do plenty of thumb sucking before you join the big kids. You'd really better get plenty of it.

Suggestions with a Four-Year-Old Thumbsucker

Lawrence M. Staples, D.M.D.

INTRODUCTION

Gretchen was four years old and sucked her thumb "continuously," in spite of anything that her parents could do to stop her. The young lady happened to come to my office with her mother and an older sister. Out of curiosity she came into the operatory while her older sister was having dental service rendered, and she saw her older sister calmly reposing in a deep state of hypnosis. After older sister's dental period was over, Gretchen came running into my operatory and said she wanted to "hippatized . . . hippatized like big sister." My first thought was to merely give Gretchen a ride in the dental chair, but she insisted that she be "hippatized."

INDUCTION AND SUGGESTIONS

[Following an induction utilizing her teddy bear:] You are now doing just what big sister was doing a few moments ago, which means that you are being big, and some day you will be big like big sister, for you really are getting bigger and bigger and smarter and smarter every day. And pretty soon you will be big like big sister and will go to school just like big sister, for you really are getting bigger and bigger, and smarter and smarter every day. And pretty soon you will be big like big sister and will go to school just like big sister, because you are getting bigger and bigger every day . . . and pretty soon you will be so very big that you will not suck your thumb anymore. Of course lots of little girls and boys suck their thumbs, perhaps I sucked my thumb when I was a very little boy, but if I did, as I grew bigger and bigger, like lots of little boys and girls, I stopped sucking my thumb because I had grown big, and I'll bet pretty soon you are going to get so very big that you will not suck your thumb anymore. Perhaps it will be next month, perhaps you will be so big by tomorrow, or perhaps it will be by the next day, and when that thumb goes up to your mouth you will say, "Naughty thumb, I am not going to suck you anymore, because I am a big girl now. You just stay out of my mouth. Big girls don't suck thumbs. That's just what little people do. I am getting to be a big girl. You, Mr. Thumb, stay out of my mouth." Yes, Gretchen, you are getting to be a big, big girl, you have been hippatized just like big sister, and you will pretty soon be big and you will not suck your thumb anymore, not any, anymore.

MISCELLANEOUS PEDIATRIC PROBLEMS

Metaphor for a Boy with Behavioral Problems

Norma P. Barretta, Ph.D., and
Philip F. Barretta, M.A.
San Pedro, California

INDICATIONS

This is a metaphor that was designed for use with the family of a boy with severe behavioral problems. The father was busy, the mother handicapped, and there was an irresponsible older brother and an older sister who wished to leave home. Parts of the metaphor that were designed for each family member are specified in brackets.

METAPHOR

Once upon a time, there was a herd of wild horses roaming the hills of southern California, eating the scrub grass, and running through the valleys. [Boy] This herd of horses had many beautiful, wild horses in it. None of these horses had ever been around human beings, and none had ever been broken to do work. None of the horses in the herd could be controlled by human beings. All of their lives they had roamed free.

In the valley below the mountains where the horses ran, there was a town where many farmers lived and worked. As you know, farmers often have horses on their farms to help with the work and to give rides to the farmers and their families. When any of these farmers needed a good horse to help them with the farm work, they went to the Bee Haven [behaving] Ranch.

The Bee Haven Ranch was a famous ranch in that part of southern California, for the rancher who owned the land was an excellent trainer of horses. In addition to training horses, the ranch raised bees and made an excellent honey which was sold in the town.

At the Bee Haven Ranch there were all kinds of horses and they all had jobs for which they were trained. There was a strong and dependable work horse. This work horse [Father] was smart and knew just how to best help the rancher with the duties and responsibilities at the ranch. Sometimes the strong work horse worked longer hours than even the rancher, making sure all the jobs on the ranch got finished. This horse was a steady worker. The rancher knew he could depend on this well trained work horse.

There was also a group of well trained show horses at the Bee Haven Ranch. These were being trained for the circus. [Sister] This team of show horses consisted of four snow white horses who knew exactly what the world would expect of show horses. They had been trained for this job, and they were ready to join the circus. They were in the final stages of training, and the rancher was just about ready to send the snow white show horses to the circus. As they waited for the final days of their training, the show horses worked together and worked with other, not-so-well-trained horses to help

the rancher in the horse training activities at the ranch.

[Mother] The ranch also had a lovely horse named Lady who was the rancher's wife's horse. Lady had recently fallen and had hurt her knee. Lady was being treated by the vet. Lady could not help the rancher with the training of other horses while she was sick, but she was still strong and would soon be able to help the rancher again. Lady would never be able to carry heavy loads again, the vet told the rancher, but she could help with some of the easier training jobs.

[Brother] A team of brown horses that were supposed to go to the Budweiser stables was also at the ranch. These horses had been well trained, at least as well as the snow white show horses, but did not like to remember their training. The brown horses did not like to work together and did not like to remember all the things they had been taught by the rancher and the steady work horse. These brown horses knew what to do, but they didn't like to do what was good, so they just played around all day and didn't learn their lessons and didn't help the rancher.

As you can see, the brown horses would not make good work horses and would not make good show horses. It is very difficult to know what to do with such horses. The rancher at the Bee Haven Ranch is getting ready to catch the wild horses in the hills and train them to be good work horses.

When the rancher catches the wild horses, he saves them from starvation (from overpopulation) and provides warm, safe homes for them. Wild horses, when there are too many of them, can get into trouble. So, the rancher will catch some and make them into good, dependable work horses. It is important, too, that when the rancher starts to train the wild horses only the best horses on the ranch share in the training duties. It would not be a good idea for the wild horses to learn the brown show horses' bad habits. The training of the wild horses must follow the examples of the steady, dependable work horse, the snow white show horses, the lovely horse Lady, and the rancher himself.

Hypnosis in the Treatment of Tourette Syndrome

David N. Zahm, Ph.D.
Lawrenceburg, Indiana

INTRODUCTION

Gilles de la Tourette syndrome is typically diagnosed in childhood, and boys display this problem three times more frequently than girls. Zahm (1987) has stressed that the clinician must have a good understanding of pediatric hypnosis (Olness & Gardner, 1988) in order to be effective. He finds that parents have often been frustrated with previous failures in controlling the tics and will usually be rather skeptical of hypnosis. Parents may be willing to experiment with hypnosis, however, after medication has failed or produced negative side effects.

Zahm explains the organic etiology of TS, but stresses the mediating effect of anxiety and stressful life circumstances. Thus, it is explained, the relaxation and focused concentration of hypnosis may serve to reduce tic frequency. Parental myths and misconceptions about hypnosis must be dispelled, since the parents' involvement is crucial. The author further recommends that parents be invited to observe at least one hypnotic session. Children are encouraged to practice self-hypnosis but the responsibility for practice is left with the child, thus avoiding power struggles. Zahm obtains a baseline measure of the frequency of the tics and then sees the patient twice a week for outpatient hypnotherapy. Frequent sessions facilitate rapid mastery of skills, greater encouragement to practice self-hypnosis, additional reinforcement of suggestions, and increased awareness of treatment gains. A self-hypnosis practice record may facilitate compliance. He finds that children often respond well with a directive approach that might be offensive to adults. (*Ed.*)

SUGGESTIONS

[These suggestions are given following hypnotic induction and deepening.]

On each word that I say, you may let all other thoughts—all other feelings—all other sounds fade, fade away into the distance so that everything that I tell you you may take to help you with your tics. As I talk to you, you may let yourself relax more and more completely, and without even thinking about it, your mind automatically makes each suggestion a part of your everyday life, helping to solve your problems. As you drift along, you feel yourself relax, deeper and deeper relaxed—way down—so that more and more you know that you are the boss of your body. You can control your tics—all your tics [list specific tics]. Now, right now, you can begin to control your body and relax and be rid of your tics. You have control, you have the say. You are relaxed and very, very comfortable now and are able to control your tics. Now, very good, you can and will be able to control your tics and relax other times, whenever you wish. You are the boss, you can make your body do what you want it to. You can relax your muscles and make your body stop your tics—stop [list specific tics].

Now, as you drift along deeper, deeper relaxed, deeper, deeper relaxed—way down, you feel very, very sure that you are able to relax and control your own muscles. These suggestions may sink down, down into your memory and you will be able to completely remember. You know that you are the boss of your own body, and that you can relax and stop your tics—all your tics [list specific tics].

You can use this very nice, calm, relaxed feeling to help you throughout the week. Whenever you are tense or uptight, you can relax, just like now, and feel the tension leave your body. Each time you practice at home, you will be better able, better and better all the time, to relax and control your tics. You are getting better and better—relaxing and able to control your tics. You know what to do whenever you are upset or tense, just relax and calm yourself—you're the boss of your own body, you have the ability to control your muscles and stop your tics. Each time you practice, you get better and better, more and more relaxed and able to control your body.

Now that you fully understand and are able to enjoy and use this pleasant relaxation, I want you to begin to become more alert, beginning to wake up, feeling very, very good—refreshed and very comfortable. You remember that each time you practice, either at home or here, you will be able to better relax and enjoy this calm sense of relaxation. Soon it will be time to be fully alert, fully awake. Feeling fresh, feeling fine. And as you awake, now awake, you remember and feel fine, feel very good.

A New Hypnobehavioral Method for the Treatment of Children with Tourette's Disorder

Martin H. Young, Ph.D.
Worcester, Massachusetts
and

Robert J. Montano

INTRODUCTION AND INDICATIONS

The authors describe an innovative treatment method for children with Tourette's Disorder that utilizes self-hypnosis with habit reversal and response prevention techniques. They documented its effectiveness in three case studies and made suggestions for further controlled research in their original publication, from which the description of their technique is adapted (Young & Montano, 1988). The original article may be consulted for further details, literature review and references.

Their method offers an encouraging treatment option since psychotherapy has proven of limited effectiveness for patients with tics. The authors recommended that the clinician should limit the children's target choices (for change) to tic behaviors that are the most easily managed and the most distressing, so that too many tic behaviors are not targeted. They also suggested that this technique may have the poten-

tial to embarrass the child when he or she becomes increasingly aware of the tic behaviors. (*Ed.*)

PROCEDURE

At the time of the initial interview a detailed description of each tic behavior was obtained. The salient characteristics of each tic behavior included: when it occurs, which muscle groups are involved, and its frequency, intensity, and duration. This was requested independently from both the parents and the child. Baseline data were collected by parents, at home, after the initial visit.

The treatment design has three major phases: (1) discrimination training and skill acquisition; (2) skill application and problem resolution; and (3) generalization, symptom mastery, and maintenance.

DISCRIMINATION TRAINING AND SKILL ACQUISITION.   A commonly described characteristic of individuals who have tics is that they tend to be unaware of the type, frequency, and intensity of their tic behaviors. The first step in phase one is to increase the patients' awareness of tics and to help them to discriminate the tic from other motor behaviors. This was accomplished in the following manner.

Two methods were used to enhance awareness of tic behaviors. The first method consisted of asking the children to identify the tic behaviors they would like to decrease first, and then, both parents and children were asked to separately record the frequency of this tic. This was performed at a time when the tic behaviors were known to occur and could be conveniently recorded for one hour. The second method was designed to help the children discriminate the tic behavior from other motor behaviors by directly observing themselves alone in a mirror or face-to-face with a parent for 15 minutes a day.

Simultaneously, self-hypnosis training was initiated. A naturalistic approach (Gardner & Olness, 1981) utilizing a muscle relaxation induction technique with visual imagery for deepening of the trance state was used. Children were interviewed for activities they found enjoyable and relaxing. These were incorporated into the suggestions for deepening of the trance by visual imagery. Instructions for progressive muscle relaxation training (Jacobson, 1973) included suggestions for the children to let their arms "go floppy like a rag doll." Instructions to deepen the trance state were facilitated by using imagery and asking the children to think of activities they have found enjoyable (i.c., fun, pleasant), different sensations associated with these activities, and suggestions of being in control of themselves.

For example, "Now that your arms feel floppy, think about something that you've done or would like to do that you really liked and found fun. Imagine yourself being there again . . . the feelings you had . . . the smells, sounds, and the things you saw. Notice how good you feel right now . . . how in control you are of your body, feelings, and thoughts." Children were initially given an audiotape of their first training session with the therapist and were instructed to listen to the tape for approximately 15 minutes twice a day.

SKILL APPLICATION AND PROBLEM RESOLUTION.   The children were requested to identify the subjective urge that precedes their tic behaviors in imagination, as part of the instructions in the use of the symptom-prevention technique. Self-hypnosis aided the children by increasing their ability to concentrate and focus on this urge. The therapist determined the muscle response that competed with the tic behavior as part of the instructions in the use of the habit-reversal technique. During self-hypnosis, the children were asked to imagine their tic behavior occurring. They were asked to select and apply which of the above two procedures would be most successful in decreasing their tics.

GENERALIZATION, SYMPTOM MASTERY, AND MAINTENANCE.   The children were instructed to continue self-hypnosis practice in imagination, while applying their chosen technique for approximately 15 minutes a day. During the treatment session, the children were instructed to practice self-hypnosis with their chosen technique to decrease their tiquing behavior. Generalization, outside the treatment session, occurred by instructing the children to use their chosen technique during periods of high-frequency tics. Recording of tic behaviors by the children and their parents continued. Symptom mastery was defined as the time when the tic behavior was no longer occurring or when the children reported that they felt adequate self-control. Parents continued to monitor their children's progress and were instructed to utilize verbal praise and special privileges and/or activities to positively reward their children for achieving symptom mastery.

Recurrence of tics is common among children with TD following initial treatment. Therefore, a relapse-prevention technique (Marlatt & Gordon, 1980, 1985) was employed as a precautionary measure to insure treatment gains. Relapse prevention consisted of discussions with both children and their parents about the probability of tic behaviors recurring. The children were asked to think about how they would respond if relapse occurred and then to imagine during self-hypnosis how to respond successfully. They were then instructed to utilize this approach if and when relapse occurred. Parents were instructed to expect relapse to occur and to support their children's efforts at self-management.

SUMMARY

This hypnobehavioral method appears to be an extremely effective psychotherapeutic procedure for the treatment of TD. It utilizes self-hypnosis to allow the child to self-select one of two promising treatment techniques: habit reversal and response prevention. Furthermore, the present method represents a brief treatment model which can be easily applied by the clinician and learned by the child.

Self-hypnosis plays multiple roles in this approach and can be incorporated into a cognitive interpersonal model that is multi-interactional. First, self-hypnosis provides the means by which the child can successfully achieve greater self-awareness, motivation, and concentration. This helps the child maintain focused interest in treatment. Second, self-hypnosis permits children to self-select habit-reversal or response-prevention techniques to control their tic behaviors in imagination. Third, self-hypnosis facilitates reduction of symptoms in imagination. Fourth, self-hypnosis helps children to modify cognitions and perceptions. This allows children to conceptualize their tic behaviors as being within their control and, therefore, subject to change. Fifth, self-hypnosis facilitates the child's sense of self-efficacy. Sixth, self-hypnosis permits the child to reduce symptoms and develop mastery in real life. Therefore, self-hypnosis is felt to decrease both overall feelings of stress as well as the targeted tic behaviors.

Technique with Asthmatic Children

Harold B. Crasilneck, Ph.D., and
James A. Hall, M.D.
Dallas, Texas

Look at a spot on the ceiling. As you continue looking at this spot, you will begin to relax as much as possible. You will notice that your eyelids begin to feel heavy . . . yes . . . starting to flutter . . . and so just let them close and relax just as much as you can. Let your arms and hands hang limp at your side . . . your body is so relaxed . . . your legs and feet at ease.

[If the patient is younger than 13 years of age, we usually hold the child's hand to establish the best rapport and sense of security possible. Children are then told the following:]

How cooperative you can be indicates that you are in a state of hypnosis. If you can cooperate with your mind, you can also relax every muscle in your body, but especially the muscles that control the breathing in your chest . . . and you can become much more

relaxed and as you feel yourself relaxing still more, squeeze my hand, yes. . . . Good . . . just relax as much as you can. Now I want you to imagine that you are looking at your television set at home . . . can you see it? Good, now you are going to see the set come on and a movie of cowboys riding on horses. As you see this, nod your head. . . . Good. . . . You will notice that the horses are running very fast and they are breathing hard and fast . . . like your breathing . . . can you see this? Can you feel this? . . . Good . . . but now the horses are beginning to run more slowly. . . . Breathing is becoming slower and easier and your breathing is slowing down. [The therapist should talk in tempo to the patient's breathing rhythm.] . . . That's it. . . . The horses are slowing down . . . slower now . . . walking . . . breathing almost normal. . . . The wheezing is much less . . . so relaxed. . . . The television scenes fade out. . . . Just let yourself be as comfortable as possible . . . all over . . . secure, relaxed and at ease. I take your hand again. Now I give you the suggestion that you will smell a nice odor. . . . You can smell this nice odor. . . . You can smell this nice odor and when you do . . . squeeze my hand. . . . Good. . . . Now a very deep and sound state of relaxation . . . and breathe deeply and slowly, deeply and slowly . . . enjoying the nice odor and you see that your rapid and hard breathing is slowing down . . . your wheezing is less . . . relaxed, so relaxed and at ease . . . free from tension. . . . Your lungs and chest muscles are so relaxed. Smelling the nice odor and now you see your breathing is deep and relaxed, taking deep relaxed breaths . . . so relaxed and at ease. Now the odor is gone. I release your hand. Anytime you need to relax yourself you can do so . . . by closing your eyes and giving yourself these same suggestions just as I have or anytime you are ready to work with me. . . . If I take out my fountain pen and tap it on my desk five times, you can enter this same depth of trance. Do you understand? . . . Good. . . . Remember that you can enter this deep state and your asthma will become controlled. As I slowly count from ten to one, backward, you will be fully awake and your breathing will be normal and the asthma will be gone.

Suggestions with Dyslexia

Harold B. Crasilneck, Ph.D., and
James A. Hall, M.D.
Dallas, Texas

INTRODUCTION

Although there has been relatively little use of hypnosis in treating dyslexia, Crasilneck and Hall (1985) anecdotally report that three-fourths of the dyslexic children treated through hypnosis demonstrated moderate to marked improvement. (*Ed.*)

SUGGESTIONS

Your vision is simply going to improve. . . . You can recognize words with much more ease. . . . Once you have learned the word, it will make an impression upon your unconscious brain and mind, and recall of this word in the future will be much easier. . . . Your memory for words that you learn will become implanted in your mental processes and will be recalled in a smooth, coordinated fashion. There will be an excellent coordination between your eyes, your brain, and your memory . . . and your reading capabilities will continuously improve until they return to normal. . . . You will be much less anxious and much less afraid in your reading and learning habits. . . . Your reading is going to improve consistently.

Hypnotic Suggestions with Stuttering

Harold B. Crasilneck, Ph.D., and
James A. Hall, M.D.
Dallas, Texas

[After hypnotizing the patient to the deepest level, the following suggestions are given:]

Your speech will be very soft-spoken, relaxed and at ease. . . . Your previous fears and tensions and staccato and jerking type of talking will be replaced by a smooth and flowing manner of speaking. . . . Your fears of talking to strangers, to groups of people, on the telephone, reciting in class will be greatly reduced because of the great power of your unconscious mind. . . . Your speech will be soft, secure, and you will be much more relaxed and at ease, pleased that you can speak without stammering or stuttering. . . . Now speak in a whisper without stammering or stuttering and hear how your voice sounds.

Personalized Fairy Tales for Treating Childhood Insomnia

Elaine S. Levine, Ph.D.

INTRODUCTION

Levine (1980) used indirect hypnotic suggestions presented through the medium of audiotaped childhood fairy tales tailored to each child. In two cases, after the audiotape was played at bedtime for six consecutive nights, the maladaptive behaviors were successfully eliminated. The outline of her procedure is presented here. Excerpts from the fairy tales used in two case examples may be seen in her original article. (*Ed.*)

PROCEDURES FOR THE TREATMENT

The procedures for creating the indirect hypnotic tape can be summarized into five steps:

1. Hypotheses about the child's primary stresses and conflicts are drawn from discussions with the parents and, if the child is old enough, with the child himself/herself.
2. A list of the child's likes and dislikes are generated from a discussion with the child. The list should include the child's favorite

fantasy figures, colors, foods, and animals, as well as preferred activities.

3. A fairy tale is created in which:
   - The child's favored objects and activities are woven into the plot (use of the child's preferences and avoidance of the child's dislikes assures a positive cathexis to the fairy tale).
   - The fantasy figures interact with the child in the story.
   - The fantasy figures demonstrate appropriate ways of dealing with the stresses that were targeted as central concerns of the child.
   - It is suggested at the ending of the fairy tale that a fantasy figure falls asleep in the child's lap, and the child also sleeps in order not to disturb the new fantasy friend.

1. An audio recording of the fairy tale is made. Suggestions of relaxation, comfort, happiness and self-confidence are included.
2. The child is informed, "This recording will make going to sleep much easier and much nicer. Simply play this tape each night before you get into bed, and it will help you feel more and more relaxed each night."

Suggestions with School Phobia

David Waxman, L.R.C.P., M.R.C.S.
London, England

INDICATIONS AND CONTRAINDICATIONS

Waxman (1989) appropriately recommends that parents must always be involved in therapy for school phobia. Parents may be an important part of the problem, for example, through pushing the child too hard for achievement or being overly critical. School phobia may likewise be symptomatic of family problems requiring a broader focus than simply hypnosis with the child. Where individual hypnosis is deemed appropriate, ego-strengthening suggestions like the following may be a useful part of the hypnotherapy. (*Ed.*)

SUGGESTIONS

Every day . . . (at such and such a time) . . . you will get into the habit of working for at least two hours or so . . . without fail.

You will be able to *think more clearly* . . . you will be able to *concentrate much more easily.*

You will become . . . *so deeply interested and absorbed in what you are studying* that you will be able to *give your whole attention to what you are doing* . . . to the complete exclusion of everything else.

Because of this . . . you will be able to *grasp things and understand them more quickly . . . more easily . . . and they will impress themselves so deeply upon your memory that you will not forget them.*

With every treatment that you have . . . *your memory will improve enormously . . . and your work will become easier and easier.*

You will not only be able to remember what you have learned . . . but you will be able to recall it without difficulty . . . whenever you need to do so.

A Science Fiction-Based Imagery Technique

Gary R. Elkins, Ph.D.
Temple, Texas
and
Bryan D. Carter, Ph.D.

INTRODUCTION AND INDICATIONS

The authors recommend that this technique should be used flexibly and indicates that it has been found to be useful with children between six and thirteen. It has proven effective in trance induction and in the treatment of a variety of problems including school phobia, adverse chemotherapy reactions, fear of swallowing and choking, secondary enuresis, and as an adjunct in treating hyperactivity syndrome. (*Ed.*)

THE TECHNIQUE

In the initial session, rapport is built and pre-induction talk centers around a discussion of science fiction, space travel and movies with which the child is familiar. We have found it useful at this stage to have short movie strips, audio or videotapes, or books available for viewing.

The child is then invited to go on a science fiction adventure and take a ride in a space ship "in his imagination." The child is then asked to relax and the following approach is used:

I want you to relax and get ready to go on an adventure in a space ship. Just sit back in the "cockpit" of your space ship. Now put on your "space helmet" and your "oxygen mask." Now take a deep breath of oxygen through your mask. With each breath you take you can relax even more and get ready to "take off" into space on an adventure. When you are ready to begin your adventure you can close your eyes. Very good. Now you can see the instrument panel in front of you and hear the roar of the engines. When you are ready you can reach out and "fire the rockets" and climb into space. Feel the pressure of the seat as you lift off. Very good. You can look out the window of the space ship and see the stars as they go by. See all the pretty stars and the beautiful and interesting planets.

Now, in space there is no gravity and you can have a lot of fun with this. Your body is becoming very light and your hands and arms can begin to drift upward because they feel weightless. Very good. Now you can land on a friendly planet to have a good adventure and "learn something new." You can relax even more as you land your spaceship on the planet and your arms return to the sides of the chair. Good. Now you can step out the door of the space ship to look at the planet.

Here the therapist may call forth any number of imaginary characters, devices, and scenes as helpful therapeutic approaches to coping and problem resolution. In the treatment of children with pain the following has been utilized:

Now, look around at the trees and buildings on this planet. I want you to meet someone you have wanted to meet. You can see "Dr. Zargon" coming toward you. He is a very famous space traveler and the doctor for this galaxy. As he shakes your hand you can see him smile and you feel good. That's right. Now, Dr. Zargon knows that you have a problem with pain and you know he can help you. Dr. Zargon has a "super ray machine" that he can focus on the pain and cause it to go away. And as it goes away you may feel a tingling feeling or a warm sensation where the pain was. Now as Dr. Zargon focuses this machine on the pain, the tingling feeling or warmth begins. Very good. As the different feeling begins, you can let Dr. Zargon know by raising your right hand. That's right.

Similar suggestions are given until the goal for that session has been reached. In terminating the session the child is told: "Now you feel very good and relaxed and it is time to return to your space ship and to return to Earth."

The child is encouraged to return to conscious alertness whenever he is ready. Afterwards it is useful to have the child discuss the experience and any objects or characters he perceived which were or were not specifically suggested. This reinforces prior suggestions and provides valuable information which can be used in future sessions.

If possible the child's parents may be involved in the hypnotherapy sessions and/or audiotape recordings of the session may be made and given to the child for use at home. The parents may be helpful in encouraging and leading the child through specific images and suggestions at home during practice sessions.

TIME REORIENTATION: AGE REGRESSION, AGE PROGRESSION, AND TIME DISTORTION

INTRODUCTION

Age Regression

Age regression as a therapeutic technique has been described since at least the late 1800s. Although Erickson's (Erickson & Rossi, 1979, 1989) "February Man" technique of inserting new memories or creating new endings for historical events appears innovative, as early as 1889 Janet described the use of very similar techniques in his work with Marie (Ellenberger, 1970; Janet, 1889). The technique of hypnotic age regression and particularly particularly became more popular among those working with victims of trauma ("shell shock" and "war neurosis") following World War I (Wingfield, 1920) and World War II (Watkins, 1949).

Age regression is commonly described as being either a partial or a complete regression. Partial regression refers to a state wherein the patient has a divided sense of consciousness: part of her feels the regressed age, and part of her is aware of her adult perspective. In a complete regression or revivification, the patient may seem to lose such dual awareness; for example, he feels four years old, seemingly without a knowledge of future events that transpired. A great deal of research through the years has focused on the nature of revivification and age regression.

SCIENTIFIC RESEARCH ON AGE REGRESSION

There is a very small amount of evidence suggesting that there may be some quite limited physiological or neurophysiological regression in revivification. For example, it has been possible to regress excellent subjects to infancy and elicit a Babinski reflex and similar phenomena that simulating subjects (actors) could not produce (Gidro-Frank & Bowersbuch, 1948; Raikov, 1980, 1982; True & Stephenson, 1951). It has been pointed out, however, that this may be the result of depressed muscle tone which allows this response to be elicited in adults (Barber, 1962), a challenge that should be examined in controlled research. Further supporting the evidence for a lack of a genuine physiological regression during age regressions, Aravindakshan, Jenner, and Souster (1988) failed to find a change in auditory evoked response morphology in the direction of those seen in children. On the other hand, Kupper (1945) provided evidence of changes in EEG patterns when a subject was regressed to various ages prior to age 18, the age at which a seizure disorder developed. Clearly, further well-controlled research would still be beneficial on the extent of physiological regression that may take place.

In contrast, there is a tremendous amount of evidence concerning the degree of genuine regression that occurs in cognitive and perceptual processes during revivification experiences (Asher, Barber, & Spanos, 1972; Barber, 1962; Bynum, 1977; Crasilneck & Michael, 1957; Fellows & Creamer, 1978; Gard & Kurtz, 1979; Gordon & Freston, 1964; Hoskovec & Horvai, 1963; Leibowitz, Graham, & Parrish, 1972; Nash, Johnson, & Tipton, 1979; O'Brien, Kramer, Chiglinsky, Stevens, Nunan, & Fritzo, 1977; O'Connell, Shor, & Orne, 1970; Orne, 1951; Perry & Chisholm, 1973; Porter, Woodward, Bisbee, & Fenker, 1972; Reiff & Scheerer, 1959; Roberts, 1984; Sarbin, 1950; Sarbin & Farberow, 1952; Schofield & Reyher, 1974; Silverman & Retzlaff, 1986; Spiegel, Shor, & Fishman, 1945; Staples & Wilensky, 1968; Taylor, 1950; True, 1949; Young, 1940). Such research has examined tests of memory, cognitive and intelligence tests, projective test performance, Bender-Gestalt test performance, Piagetian-based tests of cognitive developmental level and illusion tests to which children respond in predictable ways. Although Reiff and Scheerer (1959), Erickson and Kubie (1941) and others suggested that there is a reinstatement of childhood cognitive patterns with an ablation of adult memories, most of the research demonstrates that this is not truly the case. For instance, subjects who are regressed to a certain age are found to have higher IQ scores than when they were that age (Sarbin, 1950). The cognitive performance of age-regressed subjects is generally found to exceed norms for the regressed age and thus is not a reinstitution of childhood mental processes.

Thus, overall there is an overwhelming body of evidence suggesting that age regression is not truly a return to the childhood experience any more than hypnotically suggested amnesia, blindness or deafness is the functional equivalent of its physiological counterpart (Nash, 1988). Age regression does not allow subjects to return to previous modes of mental functioning.

Truly, however, age-regressed subjects may in some cases retrieve memories and information that was not originally available to them consciously, perhaps especially under circumstances where emotional trauma has created a block to memory (Nash, Johnson & Tipton, 1979; Sheehan & McConkey, 1982; Smith, 1983). On the other hand, subjects have been shown to be clearly capable of filling in gaps of memory with confabulated information, of distorting information, and of being influenced in what is "remembered" by leading questions or suggestions (Council on Scientific Affairs, American Medical Association, 1985; Pettinati, 1988). Nevertheless, despite the fact that hypnotized subjects may distort or produce false information, there is abundant evidence of startling and accurate information that may also be retrieved through the use of hypnosis. A particularly dramatic case (Fromm, 1970) demonstrated how a Japanese-American man, unable to speak or understand Japanese, was able to speak Japanese fluently, accurately and in a age-appropriate manner when regressed to early childhood (when he had lived in a relocation center during World War II).

The fact that hypnosis may at times impressively facilitate the recall of information and yet also produce recall of inaccurate information presents a forensic dilemma that is beyond the scope of this clinically oriented volume. Nonetheless, it is incumbent upon clinicians to be aware of these facts and issues and to realize that careful forensic hypnosis guidelines must be followed when litigation or court testimony is involved. For this reason I have included Garver's summary overview of such guidelines at the end of this chapter. Forensic hypnosis may be of clear value in providing investigating leads, but these leads must always be corroborated through independent sources because of the possibility of inaccuracy. Those interested in forensic work should thoroughly study Pettinati (1988), Laurence and Perry (1988), Scheflin and Shapiro (1989), and Sies and Wester (1987).

Although research has severely questioned the degree to which regression reinstitutes cognitive, perceptual, or physiological states from the past, clinicians may find it interesting that experimental evidence thus far suggests that during an age-regression experience there may be a reinstitution of the affective aspects of the regressive situation (Nash et al., 1979). And, in fact, the most effective age regressions in experimental work appear to be those associated with affect-laden events (Nash et al., 1979; Sheehan & McConkey, 1982). This research suggests that under conditions of emotional arousal, such as those encountered in our clinical work, memory may be more effectively revived.

PAST AND FUTURE LIVES

When the technique of age regression is discussed, questions about the possibility of regression to past life experiences are often raised. This controversy stemmed in large part from the famous Bridey Murphy case (Bernstein, 1956), in which a lay hypnotist hypnotized a woman who subsequently imagined herself to be the reincarnation of an Irish woman. Credible hypnosis experts immediately debunked this idea (Kline, 1956), and in fact investigative reporters discovered background experiences of the woman that accounted for her seemingly inexplicable knowledge about Ireland (Gardner, 1957).

The phenomenon of source amnesia (Evans & Thorn, 1966) thus seems adequate to account for this and the many similar cases (Barker, 1979; Edwards, 1987a, 1987b; Harris, 1986; Hilgard, 1986; Wilson, 1982), where investigations have both revealed flaws in the accounts of the subjects and have also identified that they had been exposed to historical information in the past that was related to their presumed past lives. In cases that have been investigated where the regressed subject supposedly spoke in another language, a linguist found the claims to be patently false (Thomason, 1984, 1986-87). Carefully controlled research (Baker, 1982) has also confirmed that having the experience of regressing to a "past life" is based on a combination of the expectations of the subject and of suggestions and the demand characteristics from the hypnotherapist. But, despite scientific evidence to the contrary, there has never been a dearth of gullible individuals willing to believe in anything from abductions by UFOs to people living inside the earth under the north pole (Hines, 1988). Thus, there continue to be individuals who will promulgate a belief in regression to previous lives, most of them lay hypnotists.

However, there are also skilled and respected professionals like Barnett (1981) and Cheek (Rossi & Cheek, 1988) who believe that it is possible to regress patients to birth experiences and even prebirth uterine experiences. Despite fascinating recent evidence about the ability of the fetus to hear, which may give one pause to wonder, regressions to uterine or birth experiences seem to me more likely to consist of projective processes. However, if a patient should spontaneously "regress" to such an experience, it may still be useful in promoting therapeutic change. From my point of view, such "believed-in imagining" may, because it is believed by such a patient, be a catalyst for altering perceptions and at the same time provide a face-saving excuse that some patients need.

CAUTIONS AND GUIDELINES IN USING AGE REGRESSION

In introducing the topic of age regression, we should begin with some cautions. Many years ago, Wolberg (1964) warned us that, "We may conjure up a situation permitting us to track down the origin of each of the patient's symptoms. Having done this, we should probably find, in most cases, that the symptoms themselves would not vanish. The expectation that recovery of traumatic experiences will invariably produce an amelioration or cure of the patient's neurosis is founded on a faulty theoretic premise" (p. 321). Although I have found age regression to be a powerful and highly effective technique, bear in mind that not all patients need or benefit from age regression. Nor is insight always a necessary precondition for change. Motivated patients will often benefit from suggestive hypnosis. Furthermore, adaptive functions that are being served in the present may be ignored if one looks almost exclusively to the past.

It is strongly recommended that you do not age regress a patient without first obtaining permission from their unconscious through an ideomotor signal. When a "no" signal is given, one should respect and work through the patient's defenses (Hammond, 1988f; Hammond & Miller, in press).

Another helpful guideline is: the less experience you have in using hypnotherapy, the more structure you should maintain (reducing ambiguity rather than being vague or permissive) in doing a regression. You will find it helpful to pinpoint an incident with ideomotor exploration (Hammond & Cheek, 1988; Rossi & Cheek, 1988) and then do the regression to that specific incident. Regressing patients to specific, identified events seems to improve the quality of age regressions. The ego strength and capacity of the patient to uncover trauma and to handle the intensity of the abreaction should also be taken into account. When treating borderline and psychotic patients, for example, the emphasis should be on ego-strengthening and using self-hypnosis for self-control. Age regression and abreactive work can be done, but must be approached more cautiously and preferably in controlled, inpatient settings. Alternatively, in working with fragile or severely disturbed patients, one may use dissociative age regression techniques and methods like Kluft's fractionated abreaction and slow leak techniques, which may be found later in this chapter.

A final consideration in conducting age regression and abreactive work is your own capacity to handle the expression of intense affect without panicking and prematurely terminating the experience. If patients sense that even their therapist cannot handle the emotions and intensity within, it becomes truly frightening for them. Not all therapists feel comfortable facilitating such intense experiences; some may choose instead to refer patients to another therapist for this portion of their therapy.

METHODS OF FACILITATING AGE REGRESSION

Less experienced therapists often try to facilitate age regressions in relatively light hypnotic states. Some degree of hypermnesia or improved memory may be obtained, but unless the patient is very hypnotically talented the results will often be limited and disappointing. Erickson (1952) often worked at deep levels of trance when doing age regression, using extended length interviews. He reported that he commonly only gave important suggestions after patients had been in trance for over 20 minutes. Wolberg (1964) also reserved extended time interviews for age regression work. I likewise prefer to have the patient in deeper levels of trance and I usually do a *minimum* of 15–20 minutes of induction and deepening work prior to beginning an age regression.

There are a variety of methods for facilitating an age regression. In the first part of this chapter you will find several modeled examples of verbalizations illustrating various methods. Stanton's contribution demonstrates imagery techniques for producing regression. My own contribution illustrates a straightforward method for producing regression after identifying a specific event through ideomotor signaling. Brown and Fromm's contribution will provide you with tips for enhancing the quality of the regressions.

INDIRECT AGE REGRESSION.   It should also be noted that when age regression is being used for metaphoric work, it may often be facilitated informally through simply using phrases like, "Remember when . . .," "A long time ago, when you were very, very young . . .," or "As children . . ." For example: "You can probably remember as a little boy how painful it was when your best friend moved away" [assuming you know this event occurred]. A metaphor about loses and getting over losses may then be used. This type of informal regression often does not produce the high quality regression experience that is desired in working with trauma, but is usually sufficient for metaphoric work involving earlier life experiences. Examples of this type of informal (metaphoric) regression may be seen in my two metaphors later in the chapter.

REVIVIFICATION.   If you are interested in the type of wording that is used in facilitating a full age regression (revivification), you will find this modeled in the sections by Brown and Fromm and by Greenleaf. One of Erickson's contributions also illustrates one of his methods for facilitating a full regression. His technique of age regression by disorientation is one wherein a state of confusion is induced in the patient. The patient is disoriented as to what day of the week it is, and then the week and date, and finally concerning what month and year it is. After completely disorienting the patient for time and place, the patient is reoriented to the earlier age. We should mention, however, that a partial age regression is generally sufficient for therapeutic work and is much easier to obtain than a full revivification. The advantage of a partial regression is that the patient will feel emotionally involved in the experience, and yet will have the advantage of an adult perspective that can be applied in reframing and working through negative past events.

ABREACTION AND REFRAMING

Skills in conducting hypnotic induction, deepening and age regression to a past event are relatively easy to teach. It is, however, much more difficult to readily impart skills for how to facilitate intense abreactions and to then cognitively reframe and work through trauma in such a manner that it provides a corrective emotional experience. It is beyond the scope of this book to systematically describe all the steps and details in this process. You should consult hypnotherapy textbooks (e.g., Hammond & Miller, in press; Watkins, in press) for more detailed information concerning abreaction, working-through, strategies in age-regression work, and working with resistance to age regression. Some limited information and modeling concerning abreactive technique will be found, however, in Kluft's contributions to this chapter. Erickson's suggestions for dissociating affect and content and his screen technique illustrate dissociative regression techniques for reducing the intensity of an experience. Kluft's fractionated abreaction and slow leak techniques demonstrate other ways of doing gradual abreactive work. Some models of working-through techniques are also provided in the contributions by Wright and Barnett. Please bear in mind that the working-through of intense material from the past is an advanced hypnotherapy skill deserving of your thorough and careful study, as well as supervision.

Age Progression

"Age progression," "time projection," "pseudo-orientation in time into the future," "mental rehearsal," "process imagery," "goal imagery," "success imagery," "end-result imagery" are all terms that have often been used in a rather fuzzy and sometimes interchangeable manner in hypnosis. All of these terms refer to future-oriented therapeutic work, but they are not all synonyms for the same thing.

I conceptualize mental rehearsal in hypnosis as essentially being the parallel to this technique as it is discussed by cognitive behavior therapists; that is, the patient is asked to mentally, covertly roleplay an anticipated future situation. In an elaboration on this method, the patient may be asked to imagine an ideal role model handling a situation effectively, and then to imagine himself reacting similarly. Mental rehearsal has also been called process imagery (Zilbergeld & Lazarus, 1987) — imagining the process or means by which you will eventually accomplish the end result.

End-result, goal, or success imagery are terms, as I conceptualize them, that refer to imagining oneself in the future, after changes have already taken place, experiencing what life and oneself are now like as a result of the changes. However, we do not need to be in a trance state to do this. Each of us, right now, can close our eyes and construct such an image. One step beyond this is what Erickson referred to as time projection or pseudo-orientation in time, and what is often called age progression. This consists of having patients in deep trance imagine themselves in the future, but because of the depth of trance and degree of hypnotic talent, the experience has an intensity and quality of reality to it that a more consciously willed experience does not possess.

The difference between end-result imagery and age progression is like the difference between consciously remembering an event from your childhood versus undergoing a complete age regression and having a revivification of a childhood experience while in a deep trance. Erickson likened this to the difference between conscious fantasies (mental rehearsal, success imagery) and "unconscious fantasies" (age progression). The deeper trance experience is truly "believed-in imagining" wherein the experience is very intense and seems quite real to the subject. When we consider the research that documents how utterly real and convincing a confabulated (or therapist-suggested but inaccurate) age regression may feel to a subject, why shouldn't age progressions have the potential to feel just as actual and real?

I refer to this group of methods as goal-directed hypnotherapy techniques, and each one of them may be helpful and beneficial. They all seem compatible with Alfred Adler's teleological or future-oriented approach to treatment, wherein people are perceived as being basically goal-oriented. From this perspective, we may see ourselves as moving forward toward goals in the future at least as much as we are impelled from behind by causes in the past. The problem is that many of our patients are moving toward irrational goals and/or using their imaginations in self-defeating rather than constructive ways. Erickson certainly appreciated the value of such an orientation when he said that we should have an "appreciation that practice leads to perfection, that action once initiated tends to continue, and that deeds are the offspring of hope and expectancy" (1980, Vol. 4, p. 397).

Because of limitations in the hypnotic talent level of patients and in the confidence and experience level of therapists, mental rehearsal (process imagery) and end-result imagery are the future-oriented hypnotic techniques used most commonly in everyday clinical work. However, age progression should also be appreciated as a powerful method. In considering this technique, Erickson (1980, Vol. 4) realized that "the patient could respond effectively psychologically to desired therapeutic goals as actualities already achieved" (p. 397).

This section begins with an outline and illustration of Erickson's technique of time projection. Afterwards, you will have an opportunity to study verbalizations of several other clinicians as they illustrate their use of process and goal imagery techniques. Finally, Erickson's future-oriented self-suggestion technique concludes this section.

Time Distortion

The hypnotic phenomenon of time distortion may consist of a subjective sense of either time contraction or of time expansion. How does one go about producing time distortion? Sometimes this phenomenon occurs spontaneously, simply by hypnotizing someone. It may also be suggested to patients.

AREAS OF APPLICATION.   Time distortion may be of particular value in working with acute and intractable pain, in childbirth training, in helping patients endure unavoidable but miserable experiences or suffering (e.g., hospitalization, cancer), in athletics, in treating obesity (making the time between meals seem to go by very rapidly), in treating cravings and withdrawal symptoms, with hypnoanesthesia, and in treating anorgasmia and retarded ejaculation. It may also be of value in conducting a time distorted review of experiences from the past. Time distortion may even be used to have patients conduct internal reviews of learnings in therapy and to review potentially disturbing dreams (Rossi & Cheek, 1988). In working with severe trauma, time distortion may be suggested (in an age regression) so that the traumatic event will be subjectively experienced in a much shorter period of time.

RESEARCH IN TIME DISTORTION.   Although time distortion is frequently mentioned, modern texts on hypnosis are amazing barren of information about this phenomenon. There is an extensive literature on this topic, however. Cooper (1948, 1952) began initial research in this country on time distortion, and later allied himself with Milton Erickson to investigate this topic (Cooper & Erickson, 1954). Through the years there have been a variety of other investigations (Cooper & Rodgin, 1952; Erickson & Erickson, 1958; Graef, 1969; Loomis, 1951).

Barber (Barber & Calverly, 1964) challenged time distortion as a hypnotic phenomenon in much the same way that he has challenged almost everything else in hypnosis. Orme (1962, 1964, 1969) demonstrated that, as with other hypnotic phenomena, there are individual differences in the hypnotic capacity to experience this phenomenon. And Weitzenhoffer (1964) directly challenged Barber's (Barber & Calverly, 1964) claims and documented that deeply hypnotized subjects experienced time distortion significantly more than waking control subjects.

Unique pioneering research with what we may conceptualize as major time reorientation was pioneered by Fogel and Hoffer (1962), and extended by Aaronson (1968a, 1968b), Zimbardo, Marshall, and Maslach (1971), and Sacerdote (1977). This research examined the implications of altering perceptions of past, present and future time—for example, contracting a sense of past time while expanding a sense of present and future time. If you are interested in examining suggestions for time reorientation, you may refer to Sacerdote's contributions on eliciting mystical states in Chapter 3 and refer to my textbook (Hammond & Miller, in press).

TIME DISTORTION THROUGH SUGGESTIONS.   When you want time distortion, you may simply give suggestions for the patient to experience it. In most clinical contexts and with most problems, this is the most practical approach and patients often respond positively to these suggestions. For example, one may simply suggest, "A lot of time will pass. But pass very rapidly" (Erickson & Rossi, 1979, p. 374). Or, as I have heard a couple of different colleagues suggest: "You will have all the time you need, in the time you have."

Thus, Erickson (Rossi & Ryan, 1985, p. 194) explained:

You do not have to use an awfully extensive verbalization for time distortion. Yesterday I gave just this amount of verbalization to subjects who had never before demonstrated time distortion: "You are waiting for a bus on a cold, wet, rainy day. You're in an awfully hurry to get downtown, and that bus is two minutes late. Your appointment downtown is important, and you've just got to be there on time. And waiting those two extra minutes for that bus seems like waiting all day. Then once it arrives, the bus seems to poke along all the way to town. Now it's a nice sunny day, and you're going downtown, and you're not in a hurry. A friend comes along and talks to you, and the bus is two minutes late the way it was the other time. But this time you're ready to swear that the bus is ten minutes ahead of schedule!"

Kroger and Fezler (1976) emphasized the use of imagery conditioning and of standardized, multisensory images to produce hypnotic phenomena. The interested reader may consult their book for two examples of structured images designed to produce and train subjects in experiencing time contraction and time expansion.

TIME DISTORTION TRAINING.   There are situations, however, when therapists or physicians desire to make extensive use of time distortion and to have a patient reliably experience it in self-hypnosis. These situations may include working with severe chronic pain, in psychotherapy where extensive exploration of past events is anticipated, in therapy with multiple personality disorder or other patients with a background of extensive trauma, and when anticipating using hypnosis as the sole anesthetic for surgery. Experimentalists who want to use time distortion may likewise desire an added confidence that their subjects have been carefully prepared to experience this phenomenon.

In situations such as these and where you have the luxury of preparation time, it may be desirable to specifically train the patient to more fully experience this hypnotic phenomenon. The last section on time distortion by Cooper and Erickson (1959) has, therefore, been reprinted. It is filled with beneficial clinical nuances and provides modeling in phrasing suggestions that will be beneficial in brief interventions aimed at producing time alteration, in more thorough time distortion training, and in experimental work. Specific time distortion training may enhance the patient's ability to experience time contraction or expansion.

It is well-known that Erickson often preferred to conduct four to eight hours of "trance training" with patients, both to augment their hypnotic performance and to become thoroughly familiar with their capacities to experience the various phenomena. You are encouraged to consult Cooper and Erickson (1959) for further details concerning training, and particularly for a review of some of Erickson's fascinating cases in which time distortion was used. For the benefit of clinicians, suggestions that may have particular value have been printed in italics so that they may pick them out more easily.

AGE REGRESSION AND ABREACTION

Ideomotor Identification Followed by Partial Regression

D. Corydon Hammond, Ph.D.
Salt Lake City, Utah

INTRODUCTION

Through ideomotor signaling you may ask patients, "Is there some past event or experience responsible for the beginning of this problem?" When an affirmative response is given, the next step is to obtain the patient's permission to explore this event: "Then would it be all right with your unconscious mind for us to go back and explore, and understand, and resolve whatever it was that happened when you were X years old?" If a signal of "no" is given, we must work through the resistance before proceeding. When a signal of "yes," is given, I then use the following suggestions to facilitate a regression to the specific event identified as relevant to the problem.

SUGGESTIONS

Then allow your unconscious mind to begin reorienting you back in time, orienting you back to that event at the age of _____ . Drifting back through time, perhaps as if you're drifting back through a long tunnel, drifting back through time, to that event at the age of _____ . And it will feel almost as if you're reliving that experience again, thinking and feeling as you thought and felt then. Allow you unconscious mind to take you back to that event, and when you're there, your "yes" finger will float up to signal me. [Pause. Allow time for the reorientation; however, if a signal has not been given after about 30 seconds, repeat the suggestions. After receiving a "yes" signal:] Tell me where you are and what's happening. [Note the use of the present tense.]

Imagery Methods of Facilitating Age Regression

H. E. Stanton, Ph.D.
Hobart, Tasmania, Australia

INDICATIONS AND CONTRAINDICATIONS

Dr. Stanton models two methods for facilitating age regression through the use of imagery. Naturally, use of such methods presupposes that the patient is talented at visualizing. These methods may be used for promoting a dissociated regression in which the patient feels one step distanced from intense material. Alternatively, the patient may be asked to enter the scene pictured and experience it firsthand. Dr. Stanton's methods are permissive and allow the patient considerable latitude in determining what time or event to select for regression. This may be desirable with seasoned clinicians and relatively stable, psychologically-minded patients. But for the less experienced hypnotherapist and with less stable patients, this lack of structure introduces an extra element of unpredictability. There is less certainty concerning what event will be selected from the past. Less experienced therapists may want to impose more structure in conducting a regression. (*Ed.*)

THE BOOK OF TIME

Imagine that you have before you the book of time, in the pages of which you will find photographs spanning your entire life. As you open the book, it reveals a picture of yourself at your current age. Turn back the pages one year, and see the photograph of yourself as you then were, and you can be there again, feeling the things you felt then, having the knowledge you then had. Continue turning the pages if you wish, going back further and further into your past, knowing you are able to stop at any point in order to explore more fully the experiences

you had at that time. Whenever you so desire, you can return to your present age by going forward through the pages of the book of time.

BOOKSHELVES

Visualize yourself going into a pleasant room, its walls lined with bookcases. Filling these bookcases are diaries, one for every year of your life. Should there be some problem worrying you at the present moment, you may wish to use these diaries to find relevant information from your past. Or you may simply wish to find out more about your past life. To help you do this, stored in drawers beneath the bookshelves are old photographs, report cards, letters, and other memorabilia.

Improving the Quality of the Age Regression

Daniel P. Brown, Ph.D., and Erika Fromm, Ph.D.
Cambridge, Massachusetts, and Chicago, Illinois

Suggestions can be designed in various ways to improve the quality of the regression and to achieve genuine age regression. . . . To increase the likelihood of reinstating previous modes of functioning over current adult functioning, the therapist can directly suggest:

You will find yourself thinking, acting, feeling, and behaving like a child of [specify suggested age]. No matter what you find yourself doing, you will experience yourself exactly as you did when you were [x] years old. You will temporarily forget your current ways of thinking, acting, feeling, and behaving until the next time you hear me say these words, "Soon you will find yourself growing up again."

He may also suggest a change in the body image, especially for regression to childhood:

You are younger and younger, and your body is getting smaller and smaller . . . your arms and legs seem smaller and smaller . . . your whole body seems smaller and smaller . . . the room which you are in seems so large as you look around . . .

The reinstatement of previous modes of functioning is for the most part quite unstable. The regressive experience characteristically fluctuates between revivification and . . . age regression. In order to bias the fluctuation in favor genuine age regression, the therapist must help the regressed patient temporarily suspend his orientation to the therapeutic context and adopt the context of the regressed situation. The hypnotist does this in a number of ways. Once the therapist has suggested the regression, he should give the patient enough time to orient himself to the new level of functioning. The hypnotist should pause before giving any further suggestion. A graded suggestion is also useful: ". . . and the longer you find yourself to be [x] years old, the more you will actually experience yourself once again as an [x]-year-old." A finger signal may be added: ". . . and whenever you feel exactly the way you did when you were [x] years old, the index finger will lift up." As most patients did not know the hypnotist when they were children, he must explicitly suggest an alteration in the way he is perceived. An open-ended suggestion will allow the patient the freedom to imagine the hypnotist in a way that best fits the internal experience of the age regression: "I will be a person you know and like. Who am I?" The age-regressed patient may say that the hypnotist is a teacher, a relative, a sibling, a parent, a friend. The hypnotist then uses the information from the patient's history to play the part chosen for him as well as possible.

Thus, the hypnotist structures the situation to favor a context congruent with the regressed situation, giving task-appropriate suggestions that will elicit childlike responses. Giving suggestions that demand adult-appropriate response will interfere with genuine age regression. For instance, if the patient is regressed to the age of five years, the therapist must relate and talk to the patient as if he were talking to a five-year-old. And he must word the inquiry with the regressed patient in the present, not in the past tense—not "What happen*ed*?" but

"What *is* happening?" Talking to the patient in the present tense, as if the childhood experience were happening right now, favors the occurrence of a genuine age regression. . . . The therapist must also treat the patient as if the patient were a child. To develop a context appropriate for the age regression, the therapist may need to engage the "child" in fantasy, sit down on the floor and play at mental age of the regressed patient.

Some highly hypnotizable patients with a talent for age regression may manifest two additional features of age regression. If they are capable of an open-eyed trance, they may open their eyes and hallucinate a childhood setting to which they are regressed. That is, they perceive the office in which they currently are as if it were, say, their school room. Yet, they also see the therapist's office when they open their eyes. Because of trance logic (Orne, 1959), perceiving two realities with open eyes simultaneously is not necessarily a problem for the age-regressed patient (Sheehan & McConkey, 1982). Other patients are capable of experiencing themselves simultaneously as the regressed child and the observing adult (Fromm, 1965a; Laurence & Perry, 1981). Still others, by dividing the ego into an experiencing part and an observing part (Fromm, 1965b), alternate between the experience of the regressed child . . .and the observing adult. . . . Such patients can be given "hidden observer" (Hilgard, 1977) suggestions to help then achieve a fuller age regression:

Now, often it is possible for people who are hypnotized to comment in some way on their experiences, what they are feeling at the time, the various sensations and experiences they feel while they are hypnotized. You're back in the classroom and five now, and you are deeply hypnotized. In a little while I am going to tap you on the shoulder, when I do that, I want that other part of you that can comment on these experiences to tell me what you are feeling at the time, just simply tell me what's happening. When I tap you on the shoulder again, the other part of you will go, and you will be right back to where you are now, five years of age. So when I tap you the first time, the other part of you can tell me what you are feeling and thinking and when I tap you again you will be back, to five years of age. I'll tap you the first time now. Describe to me the feelings and thoughts you have at this moment. (Sheehan & McConkey, 1982, p. 126)

When regressing a patient to a very young age, it is a good idea to have the patient imagine being in a warm and safe setting, perhaps being surrounded by warm blankets or feeling the comforting presence of the mother or teddy bear. Because a very young child does not understand language, the hypnotherapist must also prearrange a nonverbal signal to bring the patient back to the verbal level, where he understands language: "The next time you feel the touch on your arm like this [therapist touches patient], you will no longer be six months old but will be [therapist names an older age]."

Suggestions to Facilitate Revivification

Eric Greenleaf, Ph.D.

INDICATIONS

Greenleaf's (1969) suggestions were prepared to facilitate full age regression. As a regression approaches full revivification, the patient loses adult perspectives and increasingly has the *perception* of more fully being the regressed age. Although full revivification is not usually necessary in clinical practice and often requires much more deepening to obtain, the following verbalizations serve as a useful model for facilitating more complete regressions. (*Ed.*)

INTRODUCTION

The regression suggestions were devised to include both standardized and individuated methods. A number of possible "ways" into the experience of regression are introduced to the subject, who may then resist one or the other while still complying with the general directive to "regress."

SUGGESTIONS

[Following induction and deepening:] Now that things are becoming deeper and easier with every minute, I'm going to tell you about the pleasant, interesting experience you're about to have. You may wish to listen very carefully to the interesting things I'm about to tell you, but they'll register in your unconscious mind whether you pay close attention, or just sit back and watch the hands of the clock going round and round in reverse. You've probably begun to feel that pleasant, quiet air of expectation, something like kids feel when they know they're about to get a present with no strings attached; before they know it, the birthday is there, even if it seems far in the future or long ago.

BEGIN DISSOCIATION INDUCTION

Now I'd like you to imagine that you're watching a small child who looks very much like you. He's wearing handsome party clothes, and he looks very, very pleased and happy because he's about to play with the presents at his fourth birthday party. Can you see him clearly? What is he wearing? Do his shoes buckle or lace? Can he tie his own shoes? Very good. [Subject is encouraged to develop and respond to the image of himself as a child.]

While you watch him, and see all the nice things he does, I'm going to continue to talk to your unconscious mind. So, while your conscious mind watches, and feels pleased at watching this four-year-old child who looks so much like you and who is so pleased with things, your unconscious mind will register *everything* that I say, without any effort on your part, as you sit, pleased and expectant, and watch this little child who looks so much like you.

[These suggestions encourage expectation of and participation in the child experience, yet they allow the subject distance and time to adjust to the new experience. There are also a number of disguised binds which allow for resistance to suggestion or individual accommodation to suggestion without retarding the direction of the regression.]

[Following this introduction, the subject is confronted with Erickson's (1964e) confusion induction. This is designed to disorient the subject as to time and place, and to prepare him for amnesia during regression. At the same time, such a technique should make the subject more amenable to the direct instructions to follow.]

REGRESSION BY CONFUSION (ERICKSON)

Everyone knows how easy it is sometimes to become confused as to the day of the week, to misremember an appointment as of tomorrow instead of yesterday, and to give the date as the old year instead of the new. Although today is Tuesday, one might think of it as Thursday, but since today is Wednesday and since it isn't important for the present situation whether it is Wednesday or Monday, one can call to mind vividly an experience of one week ago Monday, that constituted a repetition of an experience of the previous Wednesday. This, in turn, may remind you of an event which occurred on your birthday in 1958. At this time you could only speculate upon but not know about what would happen on the 1959 birthday, and, even less so about the events of the 1960 birthday, since they had not yet occurred. Further, since they had not yet occurred, there could be no memory of them in your thinking in 1958.

Now people may remember some things and forget others; often one forgets things he is certain he will remember but which he does not. In fact, certain childhood memories stand out more vividly than memories of 1960, 1959, 1958. Actually, every day you are forgetting something of this year as well as last year or of 1958 or 1957, and even more so of 1956, '55 and '54. As for 1950, only certain things are remembered identifiably as of that year and yet, as time goes on, still more will be forgotten.

Forget many things, as naturally as one does, many things, events of the past, speculations about the future; but, of course, forgotten

things are of no importance — only those things belonging to the present — thoughts, feelings, events, *spontaneous present* — only these are vivid and meaningful.

Things at age four will be remembered so vividly that you will find yourself in the middle of a pleasant life experience, not yet completed.

REGRESSION: "THE BIOLOGICAL CLOCK"

Everybody knows that clocks can go forward, to register the passing of time, or backward, to indicate time going into the past. Sometimes, in the movies, pages are taken from a calendar, or clocks run backwards, to indicate the passing of time into the past. That's how it is with "outside" time — time you can see. Many people don't know that there's also a kind of "inside" time — time you can't see. Everyone has a kind of biological clock that can *really* go forward or backward, that can really take you into the past. You can feel that inside clock, even without being quite aware of it, and we can turn it backwards just by counting; later, we can turn it back to the present, just as easily.

REIFF AND SCHEERER INDUCTION (MODIFIED)

In a little while I am going to start counting from [subject's age] back to *four*. As I count, the biological clock will start to run backwards and you'll become smaller and smaller and younger and younger, so when I reach four you'll be four years old. With each count you'll lose all memory of that year-number, so when we reach four you'll have forgotten everything that happened to you after four. That's the way the biological clock works. When we reach four you'll *really* be four, celebrating your fourth birthday. You'll move and talk and act and *think* four years old; it will be easy because you'll *really* be four and won't be able to *think* of being anything else: being four will be very happy, and being anything else will seem silly until we count again on the biological clock. So, you'll be four years old. When we reach four, you'll slowly open your eyes and look around the cozy room. I will be somebody you know and like and like to talk to.

Erickson's Confusional Method for Revivification

Milton H. Erickson, M.D.

INTRODUCTION AND INDICATIONS

One of Erickson's techniques for facilitating a revivification was to begin by producing a disorientation of the patient. This may be done in several ways. For instance, the patient may be disoriented spatially by having him or her tumble over and around in a cloud. Erickson seems to have particularly tended to use the following method of disorienting the patient temporally. (*Ed.*)

ILLUSTRATIVE VERBALIZATIONS

"You all, I believe, had breakfast this morning; or at least it is customary for you to have breakfast in the morning. You had breakfast yesterday morning, and you expect to have breakfast tomorrow morning. In fact, you expect to have breakfast next week. But last week you had breakfast in the morning, and before you had breakfast last week in the morning you had dinner on the evening before that, but before that dinner you had a lunch, and, let us see — last week . . . let us see, last week was May 6th . . . but before May 6th came May 5th, and of course, May 1st always precedes May 5th, but, of course April comes before May and you know that April also follows March just as March follows February, and February comes after January, and New Year's Day was such a delightful day, but of course it was only seven days after Christmas. And you are following along, and this happens to be May and we are back to Christmas of 1964 already, but then, you know, Labor Day preceded Christmas, and before that was July 4th,

and we are way back again." In this manner you keep going backward in your suggestions, shifting this direction and that direction a little bit at a time until your patients . . .get awfully confused. They do wait for you to make a sensible, intelligent remark to which they can attach a meaningful significance. And so you say, "You know, this is really a nice day in June, 1940, and it really is."

Watkins' Affect or Somatic Bridge

John G. Watkins, Ph.D.
Missoula, Montana

INDICATION AND CONTRAINDICATIONS

This method, summarized by the editor from Watkins (1971), should be considered for use when a patient is experiencing an emotion (e.g., depression, anxiety), compulsion, or physical sensation (e.g., pain) of unknown origin. It is vitally important, however, that the patient be considered sufficiently stable and the therapist sufficiently experienced to constructively handle an age regression where intense emotion and perhaps a revivification may be experienced. The technique is Dr. Watkins, but the summary steps and verbalizations below are mine, adapted from his important article. (*Ed.*)

THE TECHNIQUE

STEP ONE. *Obtain permission* with an ideomotor signal for "us to explore and understand what originally happened to cause this feeling."

STEP TWO. *Age regress to a recent experience* where the feeling, compulsion or sensation was felt. The therapist then facilitates the experiencing of this state again, having the patient signal when he/she is feeling it.

STEP THREE. *Intensify the feeling.* "The feeling is becoming more and more intense. It is becoming so strong that it seems as if you can think of nothing else."

STEP FOUR. *Disorient the patient and further intensify the feeling.* "You are beginning to feel confused. The room is beginning to fade away and everything is becoming very, very blurry. [Use fog if the patient likes it.] The only thing that you can experience is the feeling of _____ . The whole world is just filled with _____ ."

STEP FIVE. *Age regress the patient to the origin of symptom.* "And now this feeling is a bridge that we'll use to travel back into your past, like a railroad track consisting of _____ . And you are becoming younger, going back further and further in time, into the past, traveling back on this bridge of _____ . Everything is changing except _____ . The is the same. And you are becoming younger and younger, traveling back through time over the bridge of this feeling, back to the very first time you ever experienced this feeling, going back in your life to when you first felt this." The patient may be instructed to give an ideomotor signal when there. If necessary, verbalization can continue: "As I count from one to ten, you can finish traveling backward to an earlier time, to another place. You can experience yourself getting smaller and younger, and younger and smaller, until, by the count of ten, you'll be reexperiencing the situation that first produced this feeling. Don't try to consciously remember. Simply allow it to happen and let yourself experience it, as your unconscious mind takes you back. 1 . . . 2 . . . 3 . . . 4 . . . 5 . . . 6 . . . 7 . . . 8 . . . 9 . . . 10. Where are you? What is happening? How old are you?"

If another feeling is encountered that appears fundamental, another affect bridge may be used from this regressed age back to an even younger age. A reverse affect bridge may also follow a feeling forward from the original experience to later ones involving the same feeling.

Facilitating a Full Abreaction

D. Corydon Hammond, Ph.D.
Salt Lake City, Utah

INDICATIONS AND CONTRAINDICATIONS

It is my belief that most patients who do not display serious psychopathology and for whom the trauma is not unusually severe (e.g., brutal rape or gang rape, torture, or cult abuse) are capable of experiencing an age regression back to a negative event or traumatic episode, and enduring a full abreaction of feelings about the event. When this is possible, therapy progresses more rapidly. However, facilitating a complete abreaction also requires that the therapist is someone who is experienced and skilled in this type of work.

As indicated earlier, I always ask the patient's unconscious mind if "it would be all right for us to go back and explore, and understand, and *resolve*" whatever happened at a specified age that has already been identified as relevant to the patient's problem. Given the contraindications already stated above, it is my experience that if a patient has inner apprehensions or serious reservations about reexperiencing a traumatic event, he or she will not give permission for the regression. This is an indication for consideration of other less intense abreactive alternatives and methods of dissociative regression which require more time but are gentler.

It is generally believed that feelings associated with more specific events will probably respond more favorably to abreaction than generalized feelings toward someone that have evolved through the process of many unpleasant (but not particularly traumatic) events, although this is not always the case. It is also commonly believed in the field that the more intense a traumatic episode, the more extreme the abreaction that will eventually be required to work through the incident. In cases of particularly severe trauma, an abreaction may have to be repeated two or three times, until almost no emotion is evoked by the regression. This may be done in one of two ways: (a) In an extended time interview where the patient is given five- or even ten-minute "sleep" periods between abreactions. At the beginning of the "sleep" period the patient may be given suggestions for having "peaceful" dreams and for time distortion so that "in a few minutes of this special trance time, it can seem as if hours of peaceful, restful, refreshing sleep have occurred." (b) Abreactions may also be repeated in sessions one day, several days, or a week apart.

ILLUSTRATIVE VERBALIZATIONS

After the patient has been regressed back to the beginning of an incident, instruct him/her to, "Tell me where you are, and what's happening." Further detail may be obtained through giving the following suggestion: "You will find yourself thinking and feeling as you did then, and everything you're thinking and feeling, just say out loud." The latter suggestion may be repeated from time to time. This suggestion not only assists in identifying the emotions involved, but also frequently allows you to identify the internal dialogue—what is going on in the patient's mind and how he was interpreting what is occurring. Both as the patient reports what is happening and after the details of the incident have been reported, you should seek to intensify the expression of emotion.

As the patient reexperiences the past trauma, you may facilitate the release of the emotions associated with it through some of the following types of suggestions: "That's right. Just let all the feelings out. Just like a dam breaking, all those feelings can come out now." "Let all those feelings out. You don't have to keep them inside anymore." "And as you let those feelings out, it's as though they evaporate. As you let those feelings out, they'll no longer influence how you think, or feel, or see things. Let go of all those feelings, so that this incident will no longer influence your thoughts, or your feelings, or your actions."

After the patient has narrated the entire event, I will often have her confront the perpetrator of abuse in imagination. For instance, if a woman was incestuously molested by her father, I may ask her to imagine that he is in front of her, in the same room with us, but now unable to harm or do anything to her. She is then asked to speak directly to her father. This procedure generally facilitates much more intense expression of affect, and a great deal of reframing and working-through is accomplished simultaneously with the expression of feelings.

The suggestions below are frequently used in this process. Typically one such comment will be made, and then, after the patient has vented feelings and begins to "run out of steam," another comment will facilitate continued and more thorough expression of emotion. In this process I focus on encouraging the patient's expression of the four primary feelings of anger, hurt, fear, and guilt. "And tell *[e.g., your father, mother]* now all the things you couldn't tell him then." "Speak directly to *[e.g., your grandpa]*, as if he's here right now, and tell him about all the anger and hatred inside." "Say that to him again, even louder." "That's right. Just let all the fear out. Tell him how scared it made you." "Tell him what it was like." "And tell him how bad that hurt. Tell him what that did to you inside." "Tell him the words that go with the tears." "Tell him what your tears are saying." "That's right, just let out all that pain." "Tell him what you'd like to do to him." In some cases the patient may even be allowed to imagine acting out against the perpetrator of the trauma.

Following a certain amount of abreaction, it is sometimes useful to use ideomotor signals to determine which primary emotions are unresolved: "Now I'd like to ask that little four-year-old girl down inside, and you can communicate with me through the fingers. Are you feeling frightened? Are you feeling hurt and a lot of pain inside? Are you feeling angry? Are you feeling guilty?" Later, following reframing and interpretive work, a check can be conducted to determine that each of these feelings has been resolved and that they do not require further abreaction or interpretive work.

CONCLUSION

Depending upon the individual patient, you may select one of the many methods that follow to reduce the intensity of the cathartic experience during age regression. However, most patients who have been through a significant trauma, will sooner or later need to experience a full confrontation with and abreaction of the material. I have treated many patients who talked extensively about traumatic events with previous therapists, but on a more intellectual level, with limited release of emotion. Many of these patients consciously believed that the past experience was resolved and that the root of their continuing problems was elsewhere. Through ideomotor exploration, however, we have commonly discovered that the events were still unresolved emotionally, at a deeper level. Following age regression and more adequate abreaction, these patients became asymptomatic. Incomplete abreaction of underlying feelings has also been cited by many others as a cause of therapeutic failure (Kline, 1976; Kluft, 1982; Maoz & Pincus, 1979; Putnam, 1989; Rosen & Myers, 1947; Shorvon & Sargant, 1947; Watkins, 1949).

An Abreactive Technique

Richard P. Kluft, M.D., Ph.D.
Philadelphia, Pennsylvania

INTRODUCTION

The following technique is often used as a first step toward a complete abreaction. It encourages a distanced abreaction that diminishes the emotional charge of the event somewhat; if the patient is ready, it is followed in subsequent sessions by procedures in which there is no effort to blunt the impact of the reliving of the traumatic event.

Trance is induced by whatever method is mutually agreeable to by both therapist and patient. Clinical circumstances dictate whether the patient will envision doing this technique or experience it. For the more timorous patient, a double-distancing technique may be used in which the patient may see himself on a screen or television as he or someone just like him goes through this technique.

VERBALIZATIONS

And now it's time to learn a little more, to move closer to the health and well-being you deserve. Let's walk together through a pleasant garden, into a beautiful and stately building that feels safe and secure. Its furnishings are very luxurious, but rich, tasteful, and understated. We pass through an impressive living room and turn down an impressive hall, lined with oil paintings and sculptures on pedestals. Midway down the hall there is an especially ornate door, wooden, heavy, and intricately carved. Looking through a small window, we can see that it is a door to a library. We enter, the door opening easily. Wherever the eye may look, there are impressive volumes, each with its own story to tell. We walk along the shelves, and leaf through a number of the books. Their illustrations are so vivid that what they depict, we can see, hear, feel, taste, and smell. It is engrossing, compelling, to be drawn so completely into the worlds of these absorbing books.

Now we stop at a shelf that seems to draw us to it. There, like the volumes of an encyclopedia from another century, or the leather-bound first editions of the works of a great author from another time and place, is an impressive set of [the patient's age in years] books, numbered from one through [current age], entitled, "The Complete Life and Thoughts of *[patient's name]*." We open the volume [current age], and can see ourselves right here as we read the very book that shows us as we are. We can smile at that, and close the volume, putting it back on the shelf. And now we begin to look down the row of volumes [count down from the current age to the age you hope to explore] . . . and now we are standing right in front of volume [age that one wishes to explore]. We open the volume, and leaf through it slowly [here insert suggestions that are specifically keyed to the material that is to be retrieved or more precisely suggest what is to be explored]. And now we find what we are looking for, a series of pictures that takes us rapidly and surely into the flow of how things were, of how things felt. With each picture, we become more absorbed, more completely involved. And now, as you become more in touch with how things were, as you see yourself as you were, you will find yourself reading more rapidly than I, and involved completely. Therefore, you begin to tell me what you see, what you feel, how things were.

COMMENTARY

Again, this allows for several measures of remove, distancing, and security. For patients with multiple personality disorder, this can be modified so that the volumes bear the names of the alters, and this procedure can be used to induce co-consciousness and to facilitate fusion.

A Vigorous Abreaction Technique

Richard P. Kluft, M.D., Ph.D.
Philadelphia, Pennsylvania

INTRODUCTION

This technique is used when an effort is being made to exhaust the remaining dysphoria, recover the remainder of a trauma, and to enhance mastery. It is designed for use with extremely cooperative patients who have good ego strength, with whom the therapist has developed a good therapeutic alliance, and who have given informed consent to what is to be done. It should not be used with a patient whose equilibrium is precarious, unless the patient is in a structured setting or one can be provided if necessary. Its use with such a patient is only for the experienced and expert, and SHOULD NOT BE ATTEMPTED BY A NOVICE OR SOMEONE WITHOUT GREAT FAMILIARITY WITH ABREACTIVE TECHNIQUES.

VERBALIZATIONS

[After trance is induced and deepened (if necessary or desirable), the patient is instructed as follows:]

And now, let's go back over time, back over space, directly to [the incident]. Let the pain of [the incident] come back, and make it more and more intense, just to the point that it feels like it is happening again. Deeper and deeper into the pain. And now, let the pain stay with you. Let all the pain and all the memory return, and put into words whatever may occur. Allow all the pain to come through, at full force as I count from 1 to 10. [Count] For the next X minutes [sometimes time distortion is a desirable adjunct], allow everything to come through, full force. [Offer encouragement throughout.] And now, allow all the pain that needs to come out to do so within the next X minutes. [Count it down and reassure the patient that time is passing.] And now everything is coming out by the count of ten. [Count]

The positive aspects of this technique are the sense of mastery and closure that the patient gains. In the course of the abreaction, the patient learns to both induce and ablate the pain that is most feared.

The Fractionated Abreaction Technique

Richard P. Kluft, M.D., Ph.D.
Philadelphia, Pennsylvania

INDICATIONS AND CONTRAINDICATIONS

An abreaction can be an emotionally wrenching and physically demanding experience. Many patients whose current problems are rooted in unsettling past traumas need to confront and process these traumas in the course of their treatments; however, for a variety of reasons these patients may not be suitable candidates for traditional abreactive approaches. Some patients' anxiety tolerance is inadequate to the task. For them a full-fledged abreaction may become a retraumatization rather than a healing process; in extreme instances a decompensation or major regression may occur. Still other patients suffer physical conditions that render an exposure to prolonged and intense affect undesirable or dangerous.

Although it might seem that the obvious solution would be to avoid abreactive work with such patients altogether, often this proves to be impractical and/or impossible. Sometimes such patients stumble into traumatic material and the spontaneous breakthrough of the material begins and cannot be completely curtailed. In others, the patient's difficulties do not become appreciated until the work with painful material has begun.

For such individuals the fractionated abreaction technique was developed. It allows for the recovery of experiences in discrete bits with a minimal experience of the associated affect, which is allowed to emerge later on, in small amounts, after the patient has placed him/herself in a state of autohypnotic relaxation. In addition, subjective time distortion is used so that each encounter with the affect, however brief, is experienced as having been quite extensive in duration. The overall goal is to bring unsettling material into awareness in manageable bits and process them in a very attenuated fashion. It is first used with minimally upsetting material to assess the patient's response to it. It is not designed to be used for the first time with highly charged material.

SUGGESTED VERBALIZATION

[The patient is placed in trance in whatever manner is mutually congenial, and deepening is used.] And now let us return to where we have been before, back to that book in the library of the mind [or any other congenial metaphor] in which we found *[the incident that we have been discussing]*. We can open the book once again, at the place where we left a bookmark. As we read, the pages come alive to us with sights and sounds and feelings. Let us read together for a paragraph or so, and put into words what we see. [Note: Verbalization is essential in this technique, lest the patient abruptly encounter material that is too much to handle all at once while the therapist is unaware.]

All right. Now at the count of three, your body and mind will enter a state of profound relaxation; you may, however, want to open your eyes, and we can begin to discuss what you have learned. *The emotions can be left aside for now.* Some will enter our discussion in a mild and gentle manner. The remainder will gradually percolate to the surface of the mind in the course of the week, *only* when your body and mind are profoundly relaxed in a state of self-hypnosis, when you are ready to allow them to be processed. One, two, three.

[The materials are discussed in great detail, over and over. Before terminating the trance, one says:] And as you study and work over what you have found, always in a state of profound relaxation and peace, you will find that small bits of feeling can rise to the surface of the mind, always in amounts that you can handle with no difficulty. *Although they will actually only be with you for a few moments, these moments will feel very impressive and complete; in fact, by the time we next meet, those feelings will have been completely metabolized, completely processed, and trouble you no longer.* If at any time in your autohypnotic work you do begin to feel some distress that is more than we have agreed is useful, you will immediately allow that feeling to slide away, and remain away, and you will call me so that we can consult together on its management.

The Slow Leak Technique

Richard P. Kluft, M.D., Ph.D.
Philadelphia, Pennsylvania

INTRODUCTION AND INDICATIONS

The slow leak technique was developed for work with patients who had some or all of the following features: they were anxiety phobic, had poor anxiety tolerance, and/or were physically compromised. Such patients are not optimal candidates for the more strenuous experience of a traditional abreaction, which makes considerable demands upon both their physical and emotional resources. At first glance it might seem that all abreactive work should be avoided with such individuals. However, often a clinician will find himself confronted with a patient who, despite his or her limitations, has begun to abreact a traumatic experience spontaneously or has unexpectedly begun to do so in the course of psychotherapy. On occasion, unique circumstances may make it necessary to initiate an abreactive process with such a patient.

An effort was made to devise an approach that would allow the transformation of the abreactive process in such patients from an overwhelming experience that had the potential to become an additional (and potentially dangerous) traumatization to a situation involving elements of control and mastery.

The slow leak technique is used only after the patient has been introduced to hypnosis in a positive and nonthreatening manner. It was named for the verbalizations that were utilized on the first occasion of its employment (and spoke directly of a slow leak). It is a wordy technique that relies upon the development of a metaphorical story that constitutes a constructive alternative to the dire outcome the patient anticipates will follow in the aftermath of facing painful material. In essence, it creates an expectancy that the material can and will be managed without untoward disruption. It employs an implicit pseudo-orientation in time that reassures the subject that whatever was thought to be so difficult or impossible has, in fact, already been mastered successfully.

ILLUSTRATIVE VERBALIZATIONS

BACKGROUND.   [This is a highly abbreviated version of a story that helped an elderly and timorous woman who lived near the scene of a nuclear reactor mishap. Prior to the induction of hypnosis, we had spoken at length about the proper way to dispose of toxic wastes. Hypnosis had been induced with a version of the eye-roll technique. Deepening was achieved by the use of a peaceful bucolic image in which she imagined herself walking through a lovely meadow on the edge of the woods, and then entering deeper and deeper into the forest.]

And now you have reached a beautiful place in the woods, where there is a clean flat rock, a rock where it is easy to find a comfortable place to sit. As you enjoy the unspoiled beauty of the scene, you find your thoughts going back to a time when it seemed to be in terrible danger, and you wondered whether all of this beauty and all of this serene loveliness could be preserved. Now that these woods are no longer threatened, it is possible to heave a sigh of relief and reflect back upon how this all came to pass. There was a time when you and your community did not know that you lived among dangerous and threatening toxic wastes, dreadful things left over from what had been done in the past and been long forgotten. Then, suddenly, you became aware of them, and it seemed that your way of life might be changed for the worse, that it might be destroyed or, at the least, changed forever.

That's how it seemed. The toxic wastes were beginning to escape containment. But you recall how some of the older and wiser members of the community realized that since the toxic wastes could not be contained forever, they needed to find a way to both deal with them and preserve everything they valued and they loved. Finally, after they thought and thought, and got plenty of consultation and advice, they decided to release them very, very slowly by creating a deliberate slow leak that would provide no risk at all for anyone in the environment.

It might be good to remember something that you probably have forgotten—about the time that you visited the place where the slow leak had been arranged, about how scared you were to make that visit, and about how, when you finally arrived at the scene that you had been afraid to behold, you discovered that the leak that had been arranged was so very small and the drops that came out were so minuscule and infrequent, so far apart, that you left wondering why you had allowed yourself to become so concerned and apprehensive. It's amazing at times how our apprehensions can be so much more terrible than what we really have to face. So let's spend a while longer in this beautiful place. You know, its survival is a tribute to the capacity of human beings like yourself to find, within their conscious and their unconscious ingenuity, a way to heal and to become well and whole.

Watkins' Silent Abreaction Technique

Helen H. Watkins, M.A.
Missoula, Montana

INDICATIONS

This is a symbolic imagery type of abreactive technique. It was designed for patients with strong feelings of resentment and anger. It is ideally suited for the office setting because the venting of the feelings is internal, and thus a loud catharsis in a less than soundproof environment is avoided. It has proven valuable in dealing with anger toward parents, spouses, ex-spouses, employers, and perpetrators of abuse, and in self-hypnosis tapes with women with premenstrual syndrome. In the later case, it can provide the patient with a means of

self-control and a way of draining off intense feelings during the luteal phase of the menstrual cycle. It should be noted, however, that in some cases (especially with severe abuse and multiple personality disorder) a more overt, intense abreaction is generally required. The following description and verbalizations are mine, modeled after Watkins' description of the technique, but this contribution has been credited to her because it is her technique. (*Ed.*)

THE TECHNIQUE

Have the hypnotized patient imagine walking along a path in the woods with the therapist, deepening the trance as you enjoy details of the scenery. As you walk, you approach a waist-high boulder, covered with moss and dirt. Nearby is a large hammer with an axe-like handle that is lying on the ground. Have the patient nod when he/she can see the hammer and then have him/her pick it up. Suggest that the boulder represents feelings toward a specific person, a traumatic event, etc., and symbolizes all the frustration and resentments he/she has, encompassed in this mass of stone. Some patients may wish to visualize the boulder resembling a sculpture of a person.

ILLUSTRATIVE VERBALIZATIONS.   "In a moment I want you to start beating on that boulder, hitting it harder and harder, until you're completely exhausted. And when you're worn out and too tired to go on, signal me by lifting your "yes" finger. Even though you won't be heard here in this office, you can yell and scream, and do or say whatever you wish in this place of ours beside the boulder. I'll make sure that no one will intrude on our scene in the woods. So you can feel free to hit that boulder, and yell or scream, or say whatever you want, here in the mountains, and no one will hear you. You can yell or scream the things you've only said inside before, or that you've always wished you could say, while you hit that boulder. And each time you hit it, pieces of it will break off or crumble."

Urge the patient to "keep hitting that boulder until it's completely demolished. And by that time you'll be worn out and exhausted, and you'll have gotten all those feelings out." You may typically urge the patient to continue for four, five, or more minutes.

Periodically encourage the patient with verbalizations such as, "Come on, hit it again, harder!" "Keep on going. Get it all out. You don't have to keep it inside anymore." "More, and more, and more. Keep going. Don't give up. Just keep hitting that boulder, and yelling or saying whatever you want, until you're just too worn out to continue! And then that "yes" finger can lift. But don't stop until you get it all out and are really exhausted." It is important to convey some of the anger and intensity in your voice during these verbalizations.

Occasionally, an especially inhibited patient or someone fearing loss of control may balk at hitting the rock. Explore his/her hesitancy. In some cases, you may have the patient imagine laboriously pushing the rock over the edge of the deep ravine, just behind the boulder. Another option is to dissociate the patient, having him view someone who looks like him, yelling and screaming and hitting the boulder.

POST-ABREACTION EGO-STRENGTHENING.   Next, suggest that the patient can now drop the large hammer. And together, walk up a small rise to a beautiful meadow with wild flowers, where the sun is shining and there is a gentle breeze. Describe a lovely group of trees nearby, with soft green grass underneath. Suggest that the patient can lie down on the grass and watch the clouds peacefully drifting in the sky, while you sit nearby.

The patient may now be told: "Before we go on today, I need to hear something positive that you're willing to share with me about yourself." [This requires patients to shift frames and perceive some positive things about themselves]. If there is some hesitancy, persist. Next, particularly when the patient is responsive to kinesthetic, ideosensory imagery, the patient may be told: "I want you to pay very close attention to your toes. Something interesting is going to happen. In a moment you'll become aware of a warm, glowy, tingly sensation in your toes. When you notice that feeling, signal

me with your "yes" finger [or, alternatively, "Nod your head"]. [After the signal:] Good. And notice, with a sense of curiosity, how that sensation begins to spread throughout your foot, and when it has flowed all the way up to your ankle, signal me again." Proceed in this manner up to the knees, the top of the thighs, through the trunk, to the shoulders, then down the arms, and throughout the head.

After the pleasant, warm, tingly sensation has spread through the entire body, following Watkins' model, the therapist may state: "These pleasant sensations come from your own positive feelings about yourself, from your inner resources and faith that you can resolve your problems." [Be careful to say only what you know is true about the patient.]

"And now this warm, glowing, tingly feeling can become even stronger, and when you feel it getting stronger, you can signal me again. [Pause] That's right. And this added sensation symbolizes another resource that you have. It represents energy coming from me and my belief in you, my faith that you have the strengths and resources you need to grow and solve your problems. [Be sure at this point to say what you honestly feel.] And this added energy represents my part in our relationship, as a partner in working with you to get to where you want to be. It symbolizes my caring, and respect, and belief in you and the inner resources of your unconscious mind. And you can allow yourself to feel it as a positive, strong energy, circulating all through your body."

In awakening the patient, suggest that the tingly feeling will probably be gone, but that the glow can remain.

Erickson's Age Regression Techniques

Milton H. Erickson, M.D.

INTRODUCTION

The following verbalizations illustrate several of Erickson's procedures for working through trauma or negative life experiences. They are typically dissociative regression experiences that allow the patient to begin by more gently experiencing an event and the feelings about it in a gradual, piecemeal fashion. (*Ed.*)

SUGGESTIONS FOR A DEPERSONALIZED REGRESSION

And now you can look back on last night as if it were last week or even last month—who really cares now? Just feel comfortable and just as if you were another person. Tell me what happened to that young woman [the patient] in her kitchen that scared her."

REGRESSION WITH THE VISUAL HALLUCINATION SCREEN TECHNIQUE

INTRODUCTION.   One method for reducing affective intensity is to physically dissociate the patient from the experience. Thus the patient may view the traumatic event on a visualized or hallucinated movie or television screen. During an interview, the patient may even be asked to view the event several times, from different camera angles and gradually with a zoom lens to bring the patient closer to the experience. (*Ed.*)

I later discovered that it is much easier to elicit regression with the following technique: You have the person hallucinate a movie screen, and on that movie screen is a living, moving picture. . . . My behavior suggests that I am actually looking at a movie screen. It is a nonverbal communication, a nonverbal suggestion; but my behavior—my eye behavior, my head behavior, the position of my upper torso—suggests that I am really looking right at that movie screen and that I am indeed viewing something on it. "And now a little girl appears from that direction over there, and she is walking happily along. Now she is standing still, but what is she going to do next?" And my subject is aware of my behavior; the subject looks in the direction I am looking and also

begins to see the little girl. Of course, my subject is a woman, and who is the little girl she is likely to see? It is the little girl that is herself. Once in a while a subject (or patient) will see another little girl, so then I ask: "Tell me about that little girl. What is she doing now? I don't see her clearly. I couldn't see that movement she just made. . . . What was it? . . . What is she picking up now?" And my subject tells me. Next I want to know: "You know, I think the little girl is talking to somebody, but I can't hear. Will you listen carefully and tell me what she is saying? Now tell me, what is she saying?" So my subject tells me. I may then add: "No! She said that! And now she is going to do some thinking, and will you tell me what she is thinking?" And so my subject begins to tell me what that little girl is thinking. Now I ask: "And how do you suppose she feels? Can you notice how she is feeling? Does she feel the way her feet are placed on the ground? Does she feel the swing moving?" . . . Next I say: "You know, as you swing up there a voice here beside me can talk to me. And a voice beside me can talk to me." And so she keeps on swinging, and playing with the doll, and making mud pies, and what not; and a voice down here talks to me and tells me what the little girl up there is thinking and doing, because I really can't know those particulars.

SYSTEMATIC SURVEY OF EARLY CHILDHOOD MEMORIES

INTRODUCTION.   It seems that sometimes Erickson had a patient systematically survey the learnings and memories throughout early childhood. We only have the following brief glimpse of some of his verbalizations available in his writings. (*Ed.*)

This was governed and directed by the therapist by intruding such statements as: "And in that first year what a wealth of fundamental learning, from diapers to pretty things and sounds and colors and noises;" or, "And then you come to the second year, creeping and walking and falling and using the toilet like a

good little baby and saying little sentences";
and, "Of course, there comes the third year and
language is growing, words, so many, the parts
of the body, the little hole in your tummy, and
you even know the color of your hair."

DISSOCIATING AFFECT AND CONTENT

INTRODUCTION.   Erickson believed that we try
too often to recover entire experiences all at
once. As an alternative in working with a
subject capable of amnesia, Erickson would
have the patient reexperience the emotions associated with the event, but without knowledge
of what caused the emotions. He would then
uncover the content (or sometimes just a part of
the content), and then create an amnesia for it.
Finally, the patient would retrieve and integrate
the complete memory, including affect and
content. This method is most successful with
highly talented hypnotic subjects who are capable of experiencing amnesia. (*Ed.*)

ILLUSTRATIVE VERBALIZATIONS

Erickson provided us with detail on how he
initially introduced this technique to the hypnotized patient so as to minimize resistance: "You
point out to a patient that there are various
ways of remembering things. Undoubtedly,
when we cover up a memory, we usually cover
up a lot more than the memory itself" [e.g., an
address, a place, other things that happened
that year]. . . . Does the year need to be covered up? All the other things that happened that
year? You thus emphasize that the patient
undoubtedly covered up many things that
didn't need to be covered up. So why not
uncover every one of those things that are safe
to uncover and be sure to keep covered up the
things that are not safe to uncover? You then
define the situation as one from which the
patient can withdraw at any time. You point
out, 'Suppose you did accidentally uncover
something you didn't want uncovered. How

long do you think it would take you to cover it
up again?'"

The patient in trance may be told that it is
perfectly possible to remember the intellectual
facts of something, but not to remember the
emotions associated with it, and vice versa. You
may then give a truism and metaphoric illustration: "Every once in a while, almost everyone
has the experience of feeling discouraged and
down, and yet we don't really know why. We
sense that there must be some reason, but we
just can't put our finger on why we feel that
way."

"You can *experience* all your feelings about
something that occurred at age X without being
able to *remember* just what caused those feelings. When you next open your eyes you will
have an unusually clear *memory* of all that, but
without the *feelings* you had then." Apparently,
Erickson sometimes gave posthypnotic suggestions to awaken and recall an aspect of the
trauma, rather than restricting all the work to a
formal hypnotic state. This technique is further
illustrated in Erickson's dialogue from a spe
cific case:

"Now after you awaken I will ask you casually, 'Are you awake?' In a moment you will say
'yes,' and as you say 'yes,' there will come over
you all the horrible feeling that you experienced
sometime before the age of ten . . . , but you'll
have just the feelings. You won't know what the
thing is that caused those feelings. You will just
feel feelings, and you won't know what is
making you feel so miserable. And you will tell
us how miserable you feel. [Pause] Get a firm
grip on those horrible feelings. You won't know
about them until after I ask if you are awake
and you say, 'yes,' and at that moment those
feelings will hit you hard. Do you understand
now?"

After therapeutic work: "Now the next time I
awaken you, I have a different kind of task for
you. When next I ask you casually if you are
awake, you will say 'yes,' and then there will
come to your mind something that could have
scared you years ago. But you won't feel any
emotions at all, is that all right? It won't scare
you, is that all right? . . . You'll just remember,

'Yes, when I was a little kid I was scared.' That's the way you'll remember it. You will be able to laugh about it and take an adult person's view." Erickson would emphasize, "It will be just a memory, as if it happened to somebody else."

"But then there were other pictures, some of them taken when we were *very* young, that we couldn't remember at all. They were interesting, but we had no memory of them, no feelings associated with them. The picture showed us the details, or if it was an old home movie, we would have seen all the facts of what occurred, but we didn't have any feelings associated with it. And in a similar way, you'll find that you can remember details, facts that happened, but it will be as if they happened to somebody else. Your unconscious mind will bring up some facts and information about what happened, but none of the feelings, just the content and details, but without any feelings about it. Do you understand?"

After working singly with affect and content, Erickson then facilitated a full recall of the experience: "And when I ask you if you are awake and you will say 'yes,' then immediately this entire episode will flash into your mind very vividly. Is that all right? . . . Completely, intellectually and emotionally complete. So that you will know what your feelings *were then* and everything about how you felt *then*, even knowing yourself then." Another of Erickson's suggestions to facilitate the final integration of the repression was to tell the patient, "As you review that, you can now experience an appropriate balance of *thinking* and *feeling* about the whole thing."

Since this is a unique method, you may appreciate the opportunity to review still other suggestions that Erickson used with a different patient: "All right, you are in a deep trance. I would like to explain a few things to you. You know what a jigsaw puzzle is? You can put a jigsaw puzzle together in two ways: You put it together right side up, and then you will know what the picture is; you can put it together reverse side up, and there you have just the back of the jigsaw puzzle. No picture on it—just blankness and no meaning, but the puzzle

would be together. The picture of the jigsaw puzzle is the intellectual content. . . . The back of it is the emotional foundation, and that will be without any picture. It is going to be just the foundation. Now you can put that jigsaw puzzle together by putting two pieces on one corner together, two pieces in the middle together, two pieces in another corner together, two pieces in a third corner, two pieces in a fourth corner, and then, here and there, you can put two or three pieces together. You can put some of the pieces together face up, some pieces together face down. You can put them all together face down, put them all together face up, but you do what you want to do . . . Suppose you haul out from your unconscious just a few little pieces of that unpleasant memory." After processing the feelings he got back, Erickson had him experience an amnesia for what he recalled. "Suppose you reach down into your repressions and bring up a few pieces of the picture." After talking about the content that he remembered, Erickson said: "That is fine, now you shove that down. Now bring up some more pieces of emotion." Afterwards Erickson had the patient re-repress the material and bring up more content. As already stated, this process may continue back and forth, creating an amnesia for each aspect after it's experienced, and providing rest periods as needed after intense abreaction and before the final recall of the complete memory.

Gradual Dissociated Release of Affect Technique

D. Corydon Hammond, Ph.D.
Salt Lake City, Utah

I have often used another variant of Erickson's technique of dissociating affect and content in successfully working with severe trauma in cases of multiple personality. A personality who holds both the content and feelings of a memory is asked by the therapist to give back feelings only to the appropriate personality (most commonly the host). The therapist then negotiates with the host personality to establish a willingness to receive these feelings back for a limited period of time (e.g., 30 seconds). When agreement has been reached, the personality holding the feelings is told that when a cue word ("NOW") is given, he/she should give back only feelings (no content) for the prescribed period of time, which the therapist will monitor. This personality is then instructed that in a moment he will see the number 100 as he looks up and to the right. This number, he is told, signifies the amount (percentage) of feeling that he currently has inside about the traumatic incident. After the carefully timed abreaction is concluded, the host personality is given soothing, calming suggestions and allowed to rest or sleep while imagining being in a peaceful, secure setting. The other personality is then asked to look up and to the right and to verbalize the number he sees. This number has often been reduced to one in the range of 60-85. Later in the hypnotic session, or in another session, this process may be repeated until the number is sufficiently reduced that the patient is willing to recall the content of the memory along with the remainder of the feelings.

Sickness and Immunity Metaphors

D. Corydon Hammond, Ph.D.
Salt Lake City, Utah

INDICATIONS

There are many methods of interpreting and helping the patient to reframe negative life events. Metaphors are one of those methods. This is an example of what I refer to as trauma metaphors. This type of metaphor may be useful with victims of incest, grief, divorce, and other types of past trauma. This particular metaphor is even more useful with a patient who is also kinesthetic.

THE METAPHORS

Remember a time when you got the flu, and how completely *miserable* you can feel. Remember how your *stomach* feels, when you're sick like that, and how your *head* feels. [Pause] And there's the *nausea*, and sometimes the congestion. And when you're *so sick* like that, it *drags on*, seeming *endless. And you wonder if it will ever be over*. [Pause]

And you feel so *exhausted*, worn out, and *depressed*. And you may recall how miserable the *high fever* is, how hot you feel. And with high fevers, sometimes our *perceptions become so altered, distorted*. You lay around, and don't do much, and time passes so slowly. And sometimes our sleep is so fitful, and we have nightmares, or *confused, mixed-up dreams*. And we can't seem to think very clearly.

And sometimes you get the cold sweats, perhaps in part because it gets *frightening*. You start having *vague fears, that you won't get over it*, or that maybe it's more serious than you imagined. And at these times, *you feel so alone*, so *cut off* from the world. Although sometimes *we cut ourselves off* when we're sick, because we feel so rotten, and because we're afraid we'll make others sick or miserable. We can't imagine anyone wanting to be with us. And so *the world can seem uncaring*, and not understand how really sick you feel. And yet this is the time when you really want and *need attention*, and tender loving care.

But as really miserable and bad as that was, *you got over it. It ended*. And it really wasn't very long before, *you began forgetting* how bad it was. You were so completely miserable. It *seemed* endless, and like torture, but *you lived through it*, and before long, *forget how bad it was*. And later, you just vaguely remember that it happened, a long time ago. *But it doesn't continue to influence you*. And after a while, you can hardly even remember it at all, and *rarely ever think about it*. There's no need. It was just something *long ago*, and so many happy and wonderful things happened later, that they can just sort of obscure, and outweigh that brief period, long ago. And with *this* pain, that you've been through, even though it was much worse than the misery of the flu, it also, will seem this way. And later, it will be hard to remember, how bad it was.

ADDITIONAL OPTION.   And as I think about this, I wonder if you ever had chicken pox? I did. And the misery that *you've* been through, is maybe kind of like that experience, of having chicken pox. I found that it can leave some marks on you. It usually leaves a scar or two behind. But they're usually in places where other people can't see them, and where they won't show, or interfere. And it just becomes a part of you, that you seldom even think about.

IMMUNITY METAPHOR FOR REFRAMING

And when we're miserable and hurting, we usually don't realize a hidden benefit, in the suffering. Through the process of suffering, without any conscious awareness, we *inwardly change*. After something has happened, like the chicken pox or the measles, we develop some immunity. We've been influenced in such a way, that in a sense, *we've grown stronger, much stronger*, internally. It's as though, because of the adversity and suffering — even though we seldom recall the experience later — we've been made *stronger*, more immune to some things, for having lived through it. And we also change, in that we also have a greater sense of compassion and empathy for others, who suffer. And we can appreciate, that without unpleasant experiences in life, you wouldn't be able to so fully enjoy and appreciate how wonderful the beautiful, happy times are.

And as you reflect for a moment about the suffering *you've* been through, you can feel a sense of *inward strength*, realizing that *you* survived this. [If the suffering is current: "As you reflect on the suffering you're going through, you can know that as miserable as it is, it will end, and you will be stronger for it."] As they say, a smooth sea, never made a skillful sailor. And this pain and struggle *have made you stronger*, like a tree strengthened by the winds. Those painful experiences have formed [will form] a foundation of strength. And therefore, deep inside, you can have an inner sense, that having survived the pain of *this*, you have the strength to cope with *anything*, that comes along.

Metaphor of an Injury, Scab, and Healing

D. Corydon Hammond, Ph.D.
Salt Lake City, Utah

INDICATIONS

This is a trauma metaphor that is valuable in working with incest, rape or trauma victims, as well as with patients struggling to work through divorce. It consists of truisms about a virtually universal experience, tending to facilitate acceptance by the patient. It is my belief, however, that metaphors are primarily part of the reframing and working-through process and, as such, are best reserved until after an abreaction has been facilitated. The abreaction will release outdated emotions, lower patient defenses, and create an openness to accepting subsequent therapeutic suggestions. Stated another way, experiencing precedes conceptualization.

THE METAPHOR

We've all had the experience of scraping a knee, or an arm, or an elbow. And after we're injured like that, *when it's first beginning to scab over*, it's still soft, and kind of bloody, and many people don't like to look at it, and kind of wince when they see it. And that may even make us feel self-conscious. *And when it's still raw and painful*, we don't want people to touch it, because the wound is still too painful and fresh. But it can be nice when there are people who show care, and who are nurturing and show us the tender loving care we need, without touching the hurt directly.

But then, after a little while, as a natural part of the healing process, it scabs over to protect us, and that part of us can get very hard, as a defense to protect us for a while, while processes within ourselves, natural healing processes are gradually taking place. And that healing takes a little time.

And because of that scab, we're very aware of that hurt for quite some time. But inside, healing is taking place. After most of the healing process has already been automatically occurring inside, the outer protective hardness and scab begin to disappear, breaking off from the outer edges toward the middle, so that the less sensitive parts, that weren't as seriously wounded, are able to disappear first. And often the very core of it takes a little longer to recover and regenerate.

Sometimes, when we're young and don't know better, we're tempted to keep picking at it and bothering it, which only reopens and exposes the wound too soon, so that it takes even longer to mend, and leaves a scar. So you don't want to take off that protective scab *right away*. You want to allow a certain amount of time that's necessary, for natural healing to occur. And if someone is wise and caring enough to help us, and gently lubricate the scab and keep it oiled to soften it up, then it may heal without even leaving a scar.

But *most of us* in the process of growing up got some scars, that later, may be little reminders that something happened a long time ago, but which doesn't have to mean much later on. And after a while, we hardly even have to notice it. In fact, I have several scars that remind me that I was hurt once, a long time ago, but I really can't even remember just what that was. And later, in the couple of cases when we can remember what caused a scar, we don't feel anything any longer. We just remember that something happened a long time ago, but it doesn't hurt anymore, in remembering.

And with this pain that *you've* been through, I think you'll find that your healing process is really very similar to what happens with your body. [This is the bridging association; suggestions very specific to the patient's needs may now be made.]

THE COLLAGEN METAPHOR

And sometimes when there has been a particularly deep scar, with modern techniques and advancements, our healers of today have learned how to overcome that. For instance, we can take some collagen, and inject it, which is, of course, a little painful. But that little pain that is caused by the doctor is well worth it, because we have discovered now how to inject new things into that space, so that new tissue grows to replace the old, gaping hole. And it fills in with new life, so that the scar no longer remains, and something new and wonderful has replaced it.

And in a similar way, with the spaces where there has been pain, and suffering, and anger, new things can fill those spaces. You'll find that you can let go of those old, outdated, painful feelings, that belong to the past. And there are new feelings, and new meanings that you can allow to fill those spaces, where the old feelings were stored. And when your unconscious mind can sense you letting go of old, outdated feelings, your "yes" finger can float up. [Following an affirmative reply:] Good. And when your unconscious mind feels the empty spaces that are left, being filled in with positive, new, good feelings, your "yes" finger can float up again.

[After an affirmative reply, suggestions may be reinforced. For obvious reasons, it is infinitely easier for patients to let go of old feelings after they have already, earlier in the interview, reexperienced the past events and had a cathartic release and working-through of the experience.]

Example of an Analytical Procedure for Reframing

E. A. Barnett, M.D.
Kingston, Ontario, Canada

INDICATIONS AND INTRODUCTION

The following excerpts illustrate a method referred to as ego-state reframing (Hammond, 1988f; Hammond & Miller, in press) for the working-through and reframing of feelings. This method may be used following the identification of a problematic past experience. It is recommended that an abreaction be facilitated prior to using this reframing technique. When abreaction is done without cognitive restructuring the therapist runs the risk of simply creating a transitory emotional release. On the other hand, when emotional experiencing of the event does not precede the conceptualization process, the experience becomes overintellectualized and may well be ineffective.

Barnett's method illustrates the manner in which a therapist may use the metaphor of an adult ego state helping a child ego state to work through negative emotions. It is essentially a method, following catharsis, for facilitating self-healing. It will be apparent that Barnett uses a transactional analysis model for conceptualizing this process. For further details about the rationale of this method and additional examples, consult Barnett (1981).

Note in the case example how Barnett initially determines the primary emotions involved in the incident. He subsequently encounters initial resistance and, therefore, begins by facilitating a more dissociative regression and gently moves the patient into a partial regression. There is then greater affective involvement on the part of the patient. After obtaining the details of the experience and at least some emotional release, the reframing process is illustrated. (*Ed.*)

UNDERSTANDING THE REPRESSED EMOTION(S) AND THE ASSOCIATED FEELINGS OF GUILT

"I would like you to give all of your 40 (present age) years of wisdom and understanding to four-year-old John, and when this has been done, the yes finger will lift. . . ." "Is there more information that needs to be divulged before full understanding can be attained?" If so, this information should be imparted to the 40 year old John (Adult) by the four-year-old John (Child/Parent) ego com-

plex, and this can be done at an entirely unconscious level with the ideomotor signals as the only evidence that this has been accomplished.

RECOGNITION OF THE CURRENT IRRELEVANCE OF THE PREVIOUSLY REPRESSED EMOTION

"Four-year-old John, with the wisdom and understanding that you now have, do you still need to keep those old tensions?" At this point the specific emotions identified as being repressed can be enumerated individually. . . .

"Are you keeping those old out-of-date uncomfortable feelings for protection?" A yes answer to this question means that the therapist must renew his efforts to persuade the Adult of 40-year-old John to convince four-year-old John that he (40-year-old John) is now able to protect himself and he needs no further protection from four-year-old John's outdated feelings. Four-year-old John needs to be reassured that 40-year-old John has ready access to his own protective emotions should the need arise. If necessary, four-year-old John can be asked to hand over all his outdated, uncomfortable feelings and responsibilities to 40-year-old John, who is now quite capable of protecting every part of the personality complex. If 40-year-old John has been sufficiently convincing, the question as to whether these old tensions are necessary should now receive a no response. This procedure may have to be repeated before this reply is attained. Sometimes four-year-old John remains convinced that he must retain his old protective emotions for one reason or another. He should then be asked, "Do you need to keep these uncomfortable feelings *all* of the time?" A no to this question should be followed by a direction to four-year-old John to be certain of the kind of circumstances when he feels that he needs all of his uncomfortable tensions and confirm this fact with ideomotor signals. He is then asked to be equally certain of those circumstances where the uncomfortable feelings are not necessary and be persuaded to discover means of relinquishing these feelings at such times. This maneuver does not abolish symptoms but it does establish considerable control over them.

"Are you keeping these tensions to punish yourself with?" A more difficult situation arises when old tensions are deemed to be necessary not for protective reasons but for self-punitive reasons. When the Parent remains convinced that it is still its duty to punish the Child (in spite of the intervention of the Adult), a renewal of this intervention is called for. The objective is to convince the Parent that the Child did not do anything that could be regarded as bad, even though it may have originally merited parental disapproval, and the punishment so far meted out by the Parent should now be regarded as having been more than adequate. To aid the Parent, the therapist can make such statements as the following: "I know that you have done a great job in disciplining four-year-old John and have done so to the best of your ability, but the time has come for you to forgive him. I believe that you can do this if 40-year-old John will make sure that all will go well and if four-year-old John can assure you that he really did not mean to create so much distress by his behavior." In this way the Parent is given a means of relinquishing the arduous responsibility of maintaining a punitive stance toward the Child and can then be encouraged to take care of four-year-old John in other, more appropriate, protective, nurturing and loving, parental ways.

RELINQUISHING THE REPRESSED AND REPRESSING EMOTIONS

While the Parent ego state has agreed to stop punishing the Child (and the Child has recognized that the old outdated feelings need no longer be retained), it must nevertheless be empowered to discover means of relinquishing its repressing activity. It may need to obtain permission from other parts of the personality to accomplish this; it also needs to find improved ways of relating internally with the Child. All of these new behaviors must be discovered if the Child/Parent conflict is to come to an end. The Adult ego state is that part of the individual's personality with the resources and the communications within the personality to accomplish this task. With ideomotor questioning, it is easy to switch from addressing the unconscious Adult to communicating with the Child/Parent ego state complex simply by labeling states by their respective ages.

"Four-year-old John has agreed that these old tensions are no longer necessary. Forty-year-old John, using all of your wisdom and understanding, I would like you to find a way for four-year-old John to let go of all of these unnecessary, outdated, useless old tensions. When this has been accomplished, the yes finger can lift to let me know." Fortunately, this state is usually accomplished readily, even though it may take some time for the unconscious mind to find an appropriate solution. It is wise to assure the patient that the solution need not be known at a conscious level. In some cases, no solution is found. Invariably this is because a strong Parent has decided to retain a punitive position.

RECOGNITION OF THE RESOLUTION OF THE CHILD/PARENT CONFLICT

At this stage, a solution of the conflict between the Child and the Parent has been found but not yet applied. It is now necessary to apply this solution to see if it is acceptable to all parts of the personality.

"Four-year-old John, 40-year-old John has now found a means by which you can let go of all of the old, out-of-date, unnecessary tensions that you have been keeping. Please use that way right now and let go of all of those tensions. When you have done so, let me know by raising the yes finger." In most cases the yes finger is promptly raised and the therapist knows that the conflict is probably at an end. Nevertheless, he should then confirm that the tensions have been relinquished by saying, "If you have really let go of all of the old tensions, John, you should now be feeling very comfortable inside, more comfortable than you have felt for 36 years. If you are really very comfortable, the yes finger will lift again."

An even better confirmation of this relief from tension comes if there is a spontaneous smile. A simple confirmation of this inner comfort is the *smile test*, in which the previously distressed ego state complex is asked to indicate its relief by smiling, as follows: "Four-year-old John, if you are really feeling comfortable, you can give me a nice smile to let me know." The presence of a really happy smile is excellent proof of total relief from the original tension. Conversely, any difficulty in giving that smile will alert the therapist to the probability that some old tension remains.

CASE EXAMPLE

[This dialogue follows suggestions for age regression to "the first experience that has anything whatever to do with" a problem of anxiety attacks.]

Dr.: When you are at that very first experience that has anything whatever to do with it — you do not need to become consciously aware of it — but when your deep inner mind is there, your head will nod for yes. [Head nods.] Now I want you to go through that experience just in your deep inner mind — your conscious mind doesn't need to know about this — and when you have done that, again your head will nod for yes. [Head nods.] That experience you have just gone through . . . is it a scary experience? [Head nods.] Makes you feel sad? [Nods.] Makes you feel angry? [Nods.] Guilty? [Nods.] Is it sexual? [Head shakes.] Are you five years of age or younger?

Pt.: About five.

Dr.: You're five years of age. Okay. Five-year-old Vera, what's happening? What's happening at five years of age? [The patient is beginning to look extremely sad and is obviously on the verge of tears.] You're feeling very sad, scared and angry. What's happening there? Five-year-old Vera, if it is okay to talk to me about it, just nod your head. If it is not, shake your head. [Head shakes.] Okay, you needn't talk about it. Does 28-year-old Vera know all

about it now? [Shakes.] Can you tell her all about it? [Nods.] Will you tell her? [Nods.] Okay. [Pause] Does she know all about it now? [Nods.] Can she now feel all of that scared feeling and all of that sad feeling and all of that angry feeling? [Nods.] She can? Oh, good. Do you think that you are going to be able to tell me anything about it at all? [Nods.] Okay, five-year-old Vera. It is really scary, is it? [Nods.] And sad? [Nods.] Okay, bring it all forward. What's happening now? Where are you?

Pt.: I'm waiting at home. [Tearfully.]

Dr.: You are? What for?

Pt.: For my Mum.

Dr.: Oh?

Pt.: She's late.

Dr.: Oh, dear.

Pt.: I'm afraid of being left alone.

Dr.: I see. What are you afraid of?

Pt.: I don't know where to go if she doesn't come home.

Dr.: Yes . . . what happens?

Pt.: Well, I cry.

Dr.: Is there anyone about?

Pt.: No.

Dr.: Are you in the house?

Pt.: Yes. [Looking frightened.]

Dr.: Very scared? Do you cry for a long time before she comes?

Pt.: No.

Dr.: Does she come soon?

Pt.: About five or ten minutes.

Dr.: And how do you feel when she comes?

Pt.: Relieved. [With a sigh.]

Dr.: Did she say anything that bothers you?

Pt.: No.

Dr.: Does she ask you how you are? [Nods.] Does she give you a cuddle? [Nods.] Do you feel safe? [Nods.] Okay, 28-year-old Vera, did you hear all of that?

Pt.: Yes.

Dr.: There is five-year-old Vera still feeling scared and still feeling hurt. Would you please give her all of your comforting, your wisdom and your understanding? When you have done that, nod your head for yes. [Nods.] Five-year-old Vera, now you've heard that, do you still need to keep that scared feeling, that hurt feeling, that angry feeling any longer? If you do, nod your head for yes, but if you don't, then shake your head for no. [Shakes head for no.] Okay, 28-year-old Vera, five-year-old Vera has told me that she doesn't need to keep that old scared feeling any longer. Would you please find a way for her to let go of it? When you have found a way, nod your head for yes.

Pt.: [Nodding.] I've found a way.

Dr.: Five-year-old Vera, there is a way now. There's a way you can let go of that scared feeling right now. You can feel safe to change that sad feeling into a happy one. Let that old angry feeling go and be loving. When you have done that, let me know by nodding your head. [Pause.] Five-year-old Vera, can you do it? [Shakes head slowly.] Okay. [Pause.] Now, 28-year-old Vera, five-year-old Vera can't do it yet. She is still keeping some uncomfortable feelings. I want you to really understand what it is she is keeping. Maybe, five-year-old Vera, you can tell me what it is that is making you feel so bad. [Pause.] You haven't told me about something that is bothering you. What is it? [Pause.] Are you still angry with her — with Mum for not coming? [Pause.] Do you feel guilty about being angry with her?

Pt.: [Sighs.]

Dr.: Do you feel guilty about being angry with her? [Nods.] Is there anything else that you want to tell us, five-year-old Vera? If there is, nod your head for yes; if there isn't, shake your head for no. [Pause.] [Shakes.] Okay, 28-year-old Vera, talk to five-year-old Vera again and see if you can get her really to feel good. When you have done that, nod your head for yes. [Pause.] [Nods.] Five-year-old Vera, now you've heard that, do you still need to keep those old, out-of-date, uncomfortable feelings any longer? [Pause.] [Head shakes.] Good. Twenty-eight-year-old Vera, five-year-old Vera now says she doesn't have to keep those uncomfortable feelings anymore. They're out of date, they're finished with. It's all past. It's over, and I am going to ask you to please find a way for

her to let go of those uncomfortable feelings for good. When you have found a way, nod your head for yes. [Pause.] [Nods.] Five-year-old Vera, you can now let go of those uncomfortable feelings. Let go of those uncomfortable feelings right now, and when you have done that, just nod your head to let me know that you have done it. [Pause.] [Nods.] Now if you really have let them all go, five-year-old Vera, you should be feeling very good inside. Good, comfortable feelings, so good to let go of all that pain and unnecessary uncomfortable feeling. When you are feeling really good inside, perhaps you can give me a smile which says, yes, I am feeling good.

Desensitization: An Example of Rapid and Repetitive Memory Evocation

M. Erik Wright, M.D., Ph.D.

INTRODUCTION

Distressing memories, whether stirred by one of the projective techniques or by some other precipitating event, may lose their emotional intensity and impact through a process of desensitization. Desensitization can be achieved by having the client repeatedly relive the painful memory while the therapist offers suggestions to dissipate the emotional hurt, as in the following example.

FACILITATIVE SUGGESTIONS

Therapist: This time you will go through this entire stressful experience again, but it will occur at a much more rapid pace. You will experience every detail of the situation again as I count from TWENTY to ZERO. . . . [The therapist suggests reduction of hurt:] But as I reach the ZERO count you will also note a significant discharge of some of the emotional intensity tied up with the remembrance of this episode in your life. . . . Let yourself begin the experience . . . TWENTY . . . NINETEEN . . . etc. . . . ELEVEN. . . . You are well into the experience and it is beginning to come to an end. . . . NINE, etc. . . . TWO. . . . The episode is ending . . . ONE . . . ZERO. . . . The episode is over. . . . Take a deep breath. . . . [The therapist suggests emotional calmness to dissipate hurt:] Go more deeply into trance and have a quiet calmness flow through you as the pain, hurt, and stress of this episode dissipate and decrease. . . . [The process is repeated:] Let us ask the inner part of your mind if it would be helpful to once more go through this experience at an even more rapid pace, with an even greater decrease in the stored tensions that remain in some form right up to the present. . . . The "yes" finger signaled that it was okay. . . . So, once more . . . etc.

COMMENTARY

Desensitization, abreaction, or whatever one chooses to call the release process is beneficial for many clients in the assimilation and detoxification of past painful experiences that, in terms of the current status of the individual, no longer need to arouse undue distress. With repetition and reliving under hypnotic trance, the "alien" quality dissipates, the episode begins to assume manageable proportions, and a better psychological perspective about the memory evolves.

Forensic Hypnosis Guidelines: The "Federal Model"

Richard B. Garver, Ed.D.
San Antonio, Texas

1. The investigative hypnotic examination should be the responsibility of a psychologist or psychiatrist with specific training in its use.

2. The interrogative part of the conference should be accomplished by a law enforcement officer with special training in conducting interviews in the hypnotic environment.

3. The mental health professional and the law enforcement investigator should work as a team. It is wise and discretionary that they not be informed about the facts of the case in any detail, lest the inquiry become biased and contaminate the information desired. The law enforcement interviewer should not be involved in the investigation of the case, and the mental health professional should be independent of responsibility to the prosecution or investigating agency.

4. All conferences of the interview team with the individual to be hypnotized should be videotaped. Before the hypnotic interview, a brief mental evaluation of the interviewee should be conducted by the mental health professional.

5. Before the hypnotic interview, the person to be questioned should be given an opportunity to provide a conscious, detailed recital of the experience. It is important to have a record of what the witness describes in conscious recall before the hypnotic interview.

6. While conducting the interview, the consultation team should be careful not to prompt the witness with any new components to the description of his/her experience and should be especially careful not to alter the perceptual reality of the incident in any way.

7. The number of people present in the room during the interview should be kept to a minimum, but may include the prosecuting and/or defense attorneys, the case agent, a chaperone when appropriate, or a close friend or family member at the request of the interviewee.

8. Finally, all information gleaned from the hypnotic interview must be independently corroborated by other evidence before it is used as an investigative lead or is presented in court.

AGE PROGRESSION

Erickson's Time ProjectionTechnique

D. Corydon Hammond, Ph.D.
Salt Lake City, Utah

INDICATIONS AND CONTRAINDICATIONS

Erika Fromm has expressed her belief that age progression procedures are contraindicated with seriously depressed and suicidal patients. Erickson still used this method, however, with quite depressed patients. Nonetheless, I urge great caution in utilizing it with seriously depressed patients who may project themselves negatively into the future, stimulating further feelings of hopelessness. This technique may be used with couples as well as individual patients, but it is not recommended for use it with couples who are highly discouraged or teetering on the brink of divorce.

STEPS IN THE TECHNIQUE

STEP 1: TRANCE TRAINING. All of Erickson's subjects were described as somnambulistic and he specifically indicated that this technique was generally used with a deep trance (Rossi & Ryan, 1985, p. 196). Subjects should also, ideally, be capable of experiencing amnesia.

STEP 2: IDENTIFY HOPES AND WISHES FOR THE FUTURE. After deeply hypnotizing the patient, while in the trance, have him meditate about and identify his hopes and wishes for the future.

STEP 3: (OPTIONAL) REVIEW PAST HISTORY AND PATTERNS. Have the patient visualize or hallucinate a series of TV sets (Erickson had the patient hallucinate "crystal balls"), like in an appliance store with a whole wall of TV sets. Instruct the patient that he will be able to see himself in a variety of situations (in moving pictures) and at different times in his life. He will be able, therefore, to observe his behavior, reactions and patterns at different times, to compare, to contrast, and to discern the threads of continuity between different ages. This review may also include reviewing achievements and learnings that have occurred in therapy.

STEP 4: DISORIENTATION AND CONFUSION REGARDING TIME. "The deeply hypnotized subject is reminded of the current date; told that the seconds, minutes, and hours are passing; that tomorrow is approaching, is here, and now is yesterday; and that as the days pass, this week will soon be over and then all too soon next month will be this month . . . and do it easily and gradually without rushing the subject." (Erickson, 1980, Vol. 4, p. 400). In this manner the patient is disoriented first for the day, then the week, then the month, "culminating in an amnesia for time, place, and situation, but with an awareness of the general identity of the self" (p. 425). Erickson recommended that we not be too specific in defining the future period of time, allowing the future dates to be selected by the patient.

The following confusional suggestions, transcribed verbatim from one of Erickson's (Erickson & Rossi, 1989) cases in 1945, further illustrate his method of reorienting the patient in time. In this particular case age regression was employed, but the direction of movement in time is simply reversed in age projection:

Time can change, can it not? And I want you to forget something. I'm not going to tell you just what it is. But you are going to forget something gradually, slowly, easily, and comfortably. It almost seems as if it might be Monday [the day is Sunday], or perhaps it might be Saturday, or as if it might even be Friday. [Going backwards because this is to be a regression.] And I want it to seem that way, and I would like to have you feel a bit amused as you begin to get confused about the date, and enjoy it . . . And since you don't know what day it is, it will be hard to tell what week it is. It has to be this week, but what week is this week? Is it the last week in May or the first week in June? [It was actually June.] Or maybe it isn't either one. I want you to enjoy that. June, May, May, June, and the first thing you know the thought of April will come into your mind [because this is an age regression]; and it can't be June, it can't be May, it can't be April. And now as you experience that feeling, I want you to realize you have forgotten something else. You forget it is May, and if you think it is April or March, or even if you think it is February—March, April, May, and June are forgotten, and now I want you to discover you are not certain whether it is 1944 or 1945 [actually it's 1945].

[At another time the following suggestions were used:] Now listen carefully to me. It's 1942, is it not? And time is changing, changing, and soon it won't be 1942. Soon it won't be 1941. Many things are slipping from your mind, and you are forgetting and forgetting and forgetting and forgetting, and you are just a little girl—just a little girl and feeling happy. Now you can talk to me.

What day of the week is it? You really don't know, do you? You have more important things to think about.

After the patient had received further trance training, the following suggestions for time projection into the future were then used (Erickson & Rossi, 1989):

And now I want you to understand, listen carefully and understand, that time is going to change again. And it is now June, 1945. And I'm going to change time again. I want you to forget June, 1945. Forget, June, 1945, *and yet be able to listen to me and understand me. And time is going to change and you won't know what day it is, or what month it is, and you won't even care.* You will be comfortable, sleeping deeply and soundly. *You won't even care what day it is.* All you want is to sleep. And now time is changing, and I want you to realize that time has changed very quickly. Still you don't know the day and you don't care. Soon it is going to be August, 1945. August, 1945. And it is really going to be August, 1945; *and before it will be August, 1945, many things must happen to you.* Many different things. And slowly I want those things to happen to you. I want them to go through your mind [or the patient could see them on TV sets or crystal balls]— every day in July and every day in the first week of August. I want these days to be clear in your mind until slowly you begin to recall even the last week in June, 1945. *And now sleep and let time go by until it*

is August, 1945. Just keep sleeping as time goes by, as things happen to you—many things happen. And in August, 1945, you are going to come to see me. You are, are you not? *When it is August, 1945, I want you to sleep with your eyes open, and talk to me, and tell me those things that happened the last week in June, and in the weeks of July and the first week of August* [an implied directive type of suggestion, allowing the patient to take whatever internal time was necessary, and then providing a behavioral response when it was completed]. And you've got to tell me about . . . , what you did, and how you did it.

STEP 5: PSEUDO-ORIENTATION IN TIME INTO THE FUTURE.

The patient is now projected into the future. After being oriented in time, interact with the subject as if both patient and therapist are now in the future. This step is illustrated in the following suggestions that were used by Erickson (1980, Vol. 4, pp. 401-402):

"As I remember, I saw you last about two months ago. You came in to report your progress. I put you in a trance and had you visualize yourself in crystal balls so that you could give me full accounts. Now, suppose you remember tonight all the things you said and saw that night about two months ago. Never mind anything I saw or did; remember only the things you said and saw and did while you were giving me the report. [This was to prevent him from recalling anything about preliminary or subsequent hypnotic inductions, particularly in relation to time projection.] Now review all those things, some of them go way back to our first meeting and even way back to the beginning of the problem you brought to me. Think them over carefully, clearly, extensively, and then discuss things for me."

You now have the patient evolve "fantasies in keeping with their understandings of actually attainable goals" (1980, Vol. 4, p. 422). Erickson found "there was no running away of the imagination, but a serious appraisal in fantasy form of reality possibilities in keeping with their understandings of themselves" (p. 422).

Erickson indicated that he would provide "elaborate instruction" to the patient "to ensure a calm, comfortable feeling and to induce an overwhelming interest in whatever the writer might have to say" (Vol. 4, p. 405). He further explained: "Then I ask the patient who has altered his time orientation to think comprehensively about stressful matters—about those things that worry him and make him fearful in his current life situation. And since he can look upon those things from his reoriented vantage point as having occurred in the past, he now can employ hindsight in their resolution!" (Rossi & Ryan, 1985, p. 196). In facilitating the patient's analysis, you may ask questions like, "How was it that you finally . . ." and "What was it that happened?"

Prior to suggestions for amnesia, you may present confident suggestions concerning what the patient has accomplished in the future. For instance, "You now know that you can, you are confident. In fact, you have succeeded, and there is nothing that you can do to keep from succeeding again and again" (Erickson, 1980, Vol. 1, p. 172).

STEP 6: EXTENSIVE SUGGESTIONS FOR AMNESIA. Erickson (1980) indicated that "every effort was made to keep them unconscious by prohibitive and inhibitive suggestions. By so doing, each patient's unconscious was provided with a wealth of formulated ideas unknown to the conscious mind. Then, in response to the innate needs and desires of the total personality, the unconscious could utilize those ideas by translating them into realities of daily life as spontaneous responsive behavior in opportune situations" (Vol. 4, p. 421). If at all possible, he did not want this process to be one wherein the patient simply consciously imagined the future and remembered it following hypnosis. "For the patients, special understandings for the future were developed in their unconscious minds, and their actual life situations presented the reality opportunities to utilize those ideas in responsive behavior in accord with their inner needs and desires" (p. 422). "Furthermore, [because of the amnesia] their behavior was experienced by them as arising within them and in relation to their needs in their immediate life situation" (p. 422).

The following suggestions from one of Erickson's (Erickson & Rossi, 1989) cases illustrate this step:

I want you to keep that knowledge in your unconscious. Do you understand? I want you to keep this knowledge in your unconscious and not to discover it until later this summer. Do you understand? Just as you repressed and forgot painful things in the past, I want you to repress this knowledge until the right time comes for it to burst out into your understanding, so that you can actually have the experience of finding yourself. . . . Do you understand? *And I want it to be a tremendously pleasing surprise to you* (p. 225).

STEP 7: (OPTIONAL) REPETITION OF THE ENTIRE PROCEDURE IN THE NEXT INTERVIEW. It appears that on occasion Erickson had the patient repeat the entire age progression experience in the following session. It may have been that he felt this would further formulate the goals and images at an unconscious level in the patient's mind and provide further repetition of suggestion.

STEP 8: POSTHYPNOTIC SUGGESTION. After the completion of the age projection experience, you may once again give positive, confident suggestions to the patient: "You now know, deep inside, that this is how it will be. You have actually experienced it." "You now know that you can, you are confident. In fact, you have succeeded, and there is nothing that you can do to keep from succeeding again and again" (Erickson, 1980, Vol. 1, p. 172).

Age Progression to Work Through Resistance

Richard B. Garver, Ed.D.
San Antonio, Texas

[After the induction, the following suggestions are given:] "It's now (*e.g., 1995, or some year in the future*) and you can see yourself in a situation that is safe and as comfortable as it can be. And I would like for you to tell me when you are there, and how you feel, and how you look."

[If responses are very negative or depressed, then appropriate supportive psychotherapy is helpful, but if they tend, as they often do, to be positive, then it is important to say:] "Well, I'm glad things are going better for you. I wonder if you could tell me, because frankly I just forget, what it was that helped you the most when you and I were working on this in therapy five years ago? I remember we worked on a lot of things, but what was it that seemed to really make a difference that helped you change your behavior?"

Often the patient will say, "Oh, it was dealing with that issue about my father, or it was helping control my emotions differently from the way I did when I was a teenager," etc. Thus, when we come back to the present, we can often use that insight from age progression which the patient was unable to see prior to projecting himself into the future. Perhaps this technique provides patients with enough distance to look more objectively at their problems and to provide their own answers.

Suggestions Following Age Progression with Public Speaking

Don E. Gibbons, Ph.D.

As a result of your experience, you *know* that without anxiety you can perform efficiently and well before a group. And as you think back upon your experience now, you are feeling a great deal of pride, achievement, and accomplishment in the knowledge of how well you performed.

Imagery of the End Result

Errol R. Korn, M.D., and
George J. Pratt, Ph.D.
LaJolla, California

INTRODUCTION AND INDICATIONS

As we have already indicated, age progression may be used with subjects capable of deep trances. However, when time does not permit sufficient trance deepening, with less talented subjects, and in self-hypnosis, end-result imagery may also produce very beneficial results. The following two contributions by Korn and Pratt (1988) model such interventions. Such goal imagery may be beneficial whenever you are working with individuals who have specific goals toward which they are working. These techniques present a very positive approach to promoting behavior change, recognizing that people are motivated from in front, toward goals, as well as being pushed from behind by the influences of the past. These techniques have applicability with business success, sales, athletic performance, and such problems as obesity, smoking, academic achievement, parenting, low self-esteem, and relationship or interpersonal problems. These types of suggestions may also be recorded on tape, along with induction and deepening, for subjects to use for reinforcement at home. (*Ed.*)

SUGGESTIONS

[Following induction.] Imagine now that you are in a very large room. A private, very comfortable room. It may be a room in your own house. It is a room of safety and of comfort. You feel good when you are in this place.

Now imagine yourself seated in a large, comfortable chair. Feel your body sink into the chair. In front of you is a television set with a very large screen. On your chair are buttons and dials that will allow you to control every aspect of this television set.

Now in your mind, formulate a goal that you would like to work on. It can be any goal—short-term or long-term. It can be a goal related to your personal life, or to your job. Now turn the television set on and allow a picture to appear. You see yourself. You are experiencing the goal, already achieved. You have done it. Imagine a scene that could only take place if you had accomplished your goal. [Pause]

Experience the scene fully. Use the fine controls of the television set to slow the scene down, to study the details. Make it move more quickly. Add people, or change the set or the music. It's your program, it's your goal.

Now feel yourself being drawn into the picture, so that you become the person on the screen. Instead of looking into the television set, you are merging with the person who accomplished the goal. Again, this could only take place if your goal was achieved. Spend the next few moments completely experiencing the imagery of your fully realized goal. [Awaken the subject upon completion.]

Mental Rehearsal: The Protective Shield

Errol R. Korn, M.D., and George J. Pratt, Ph.D.
LaJolla, California

[Following induction:] To experience your personal power, you must be certain that you are a special person, a person who truly contributes to the community. You can be that person. You are already becoming that person. Now, you need to find the safety and protection that you need. And then, you can begin to step forward, to take the risks that will allow you to make the changes that you need to make in the world and in your life.

Imagine, all around you, a protective shield, or a bubble. The shield, or the bubble, is completely transparent. It can be as far away from you as you please, or as close to you as your second skin. You are in control—you choose the size and shape of your protection. The bubble is visible only to you. Nobody else can see it. It is like a one-way mirror; you move outward, but only the things that you allow in, will get in. You can choose who, or what you want inside the bubble—people, ideas, incidents, physical surroundings. You can keep your fears outside the bubble.

Spend the next few moments experimenting with the bubble. Experience it. Make it larger. Make it smaller. Feel its texture, or consider its absence of texture. Move around within it. Feel it move around you. [Pause] Practice using the bubble, not only while you're listening . . ., but at anytime when you are relaxed and safe. The bubble is your own place, a place where you are completely safe and in control.

As you begin to feel your own breathing, and the energy that it brings back to your body, focus on this idea: This protective shield will help you to become more powerful. You will be able to express your personal power, more and more, with every day that passes. Your strength will come from inside of you. Virtually anything will be possible. And your power can affect others. Not only will you believe in yourself; others will believe in you as well. You will be able to feel this energy come up from within you, whenever you wish.

Now, as you have done before, breathe the energy back into your body. Feel the energy move to all parts of your body. When you are completely back in the present time, simply open your eyes, feeling alert and awake.

Mental Rehearsal of Presentation and Sales Skills

Errol R. Korn, M.D., and George J. Pratt, Ph.D.
LaJolla, California

Bring to mind a presentation that you have to make in the near future. It may be a sales presentation to a client, it may be a speech to a gathering of your peers or your superiors, it may be a simple meeting. Imagine yourself getting a good night's sleep—focus on feeling as though you're falling asleep . . . and that you're waking refreshed. Imagine dressing as you would dress on the day of the presentation, feeling very good about yourself. You are smiling.

At the place where the presentation is to take place, imagine yourself walking into the room. Your audience, or your client, is eagerly awaiting your arrival. You are several minutes early, comfortably early. There is little pressure. The people are interested in what you have to say.

Before giving your presentation, take a deep breath. Use your physical cue, touching your thumb and your finger together on your nondominant hand. For a brief moment, visit your place of safety. Imagine your protective shield around you. And now, return to the meeting.

Imagine the faces and the potential questions. The real questions. Imagine the points that you will cover. Understand each question beyond just the words; you understand WHY each question is asked, what the underlying emotional concerns would be. You are intuitive, you are sensitive to their thoughts and ideas.

Now imagine the result. A positive result. A handshake, a job well done, the sale closed, the promise of a contract. The nods of approval, the smiles, the anticipation of working together again. A standing ovation from your public speaking audience.

Next, picture yourself under the worst possible conditions. The room is noisy, the people are not at all cooperative. They're rude. They're interrupting you. You're forgetting your key points. You're losing your cool. After imagining the worst possible conditions, you feel better. You know that the presentation will seldom become as rough or as difficult.

You are back in control. You are again in the positive environment. People want to buy what you have to sell. They are very pleased to see you. You rehearse the presentation once again. Take your time; think through every point. . . .

Now, as you have done before, breathe the energy back into your body and feel the energy move to all parts of your body. When you are completely back in the present time, simply open your eyes, feeling alert and awake.

Suggestions for Goal-Imagery

Alcid M. Pelletier, Ed.D.
Grand Rapids, Michigan

You remember that we use hypnosis in age regression, to help you go back to deal with an issue or event you did not understand, to settle some unfinished business. We all live in the present, which tomorrow will be the past, and the future becomes the present. Time is always moving. You can see the future in fantasy to make the present move progressively happy and successful.

Fantasies are good to have. Unrealistic fantasies can be fun and entertaining, then discarded as one would shut off a TV set. Realistically achievable fantasies can provide the material for you to establish and work at accomplishing your goals. Then, when the tomorrows become the present, fantasies will become realities.

Just as you went *down* the road, or a corridor, or stairs to go back into the past, you can go *up* that same road, corridor, or stairs to envision your future. You can see the pleasant future happening to you, or, if you prefer and it is more helpful, you can be an observer watching it happen to someone else. And then afterwards, you can imitate the model. You may select either method; simply select the method which will give you the greatest revelation and that will be the most beneficial to you.

By looking into the future, you are establishing goals—let's say five-year goals. For the present, you will need to determine how to really make it happen so it won't always remain a fantasy. To do so, you will break that five-year goal into five shorter one-year goals. Each of these years will be broken down into 12 months. Each of those months will be broken down into weeks. Thus, each week you are achieving some of your goals, until you realize that the future is now. You can write all those goals down after you come out of hypnosis, and then, on a weekly basis, review your pleasurable and successful progress. Looking into the future, you are concerned about relationships. See them as you desire them to transpire. [Pause] You are concerned about a career, work, an occupation. See that self efficiently functioning in the choice of work. [Pause] You are concerned about health possibly. You are concerned about finances. See the process unfold without careless debt. [Pause] You can also see interest in hobbies, recreation, travel, personality improvement or whatever you realistically desire, and see the process you must go through to realize these achievements. [Pause] You are making things happen, even some things that you haven't done before, but that you can realistically accomplish.

Now you won't be saying, "When I get around to it . . .," "One of these days, I'll . . .," "When I get the chance, I will . . .," or "Soon, I'll. . . ." Instead, you will make things happen. You are making some things happen now. There is power in this, and you can come to realize that the future is now.

End-Result Goal Imagery for Sales Productivity

Don E. Gibbons, Ph.D.

Now I would like you to think of some major incentive which you are working toward, and which you would like to achieve in the future. It might be taking an ocean cruise, or seeing a child graduate from college, or building your dream house—in fact, it could be almost anything. But whatever it is, this goal should be an important one, and one which is within your power to achieve as a result of your own efforts.

And when you have the goal firmly in mind, I would like you to picture yourself transported into the future, savoring the fruits of your achievement and enjoying the knowledge that the goal for which you have worked so long and so hard is finally yours. Continue to hold the image in your mind, and to focus on it, and soon it will be just as if you were really there.

Let yourself begin to live the experience now. You have achieved what you have set out to attain, and the fruits of your efforts are yours to enjoy. Live the fulfillment of your goal and allow yourself to experience all the joy and the satisfaction which come from knowing that your ambitions have at last been realized. Let yourself savor the thrill of achievement and

bask in the warm rewarding glow of a job well done.

And as you allow yourself to let go completely and experience this event fully, savoring your triumph and all its fruits, the feelings of satisfaction and achievement are becoming clearer and sharper and more intense with every passing moment.

In a little while, I'm going to return you to the present time. But until I do, let yourself continue to enjoy the fulfillment of the goal which you have worked so hard to attain, as the feelings of achievement and satisfaction continue to grow, and each passing second finds them stronger than they were before.

[After a two-minute interval of free fantasy:] It's time to return to the present now, to the time from which you left. You are beginning to return to the present time, and the scene you have been experiencing in your mind is beginning to fade, but you will still remain in trance for a while, until I bring you out. You will feel renewed and recharged as a result of your experience, and you will possess a heightened resolve to succeed in the attainment of your goal.

And now the scene is fading more and more, almost gone. Now the scene is completely gone, and you are back with me in the present. You are feeling renewed and recharged, and more determined than ever to succeed in the attainment of the goal you have envisioned, for its benefits and attractions are now so much more clearly apparent than they were before.

Erickson's Self-Suggestion Technique

D. Corydon Hammond, Ph.D.
Salt Lake City, Utah

INDICATIONS

This technique is included in this section on goal-directed hypnotherapy techniques because it is a procedure that assists the patient in focusing on the future and on establishing highly specific goals. This is also a technique with particular value for "resistant" patients who will not accept direction from authority, and with "scalp collectors" who have been to many therapists without success. Such patients often come to hypnotherapy seeking a "hypnotic miracle" after everything else has failed. This procedure places the burden of responsibility for results on the patient himself, rather than on the therapist trying to promote change. It will probably be most effective with intelligent patients who basically already possess insight concerning what they need to do, but who are not translating insight into action.

After this method has been used successfully and a patient has found it effective, it may also be recorded on tape for use in self-hypnosis, having the patient speak inwardly to him or herself. Erickson originally used the procedure itself as a hypnotic induction, having patients speak with their eyes closed. However, when there is no resistance to induction itself, I prefer to induce trance before using the procedure.

THE TECHNIQUE

[Induce a trance and then suggest:] You can speak in a hypnotic state, without awakening, just as you can talk in the dreams of the night. And in a moment, still remaining in a hypnotic state, I want you to begin to review your problem and your goals. I want you to review your problem and goals slowly, thoughtfully, and carefully. And as you do so, simply the sound of your voice, will take you deeper and deeper into a hypnotic state, in which you can continue talking to me, without any interruption of your story and review. So, in a moment, as I tell you to begin, you can slowly, thoughtfully describe your problem from beginning to end. Describe your problem in detail, and the very specific goals you have for yourself, going deeper and deeper into trance as you speak. Now, begin to slowly describe your problem." [Pause for the patient's description.]

Good. Now in a moment I want you to speak again. I want you to slowly, carefully, and thoughtfully indicate what you need, and what you want. And as you *slowly* speak, with each word, your unconscious mind can take you deeper and deeper into trance. The mere sound of your voice, will take you into a deeper and deeper state, in which you can continue to talk to me, listen to me, answer questions, and do anything asked of you. And you will find yourself in such a deep state, that you will be under a most powerful compulsion, to do precisely what is indicated. Now, meditatively, thoughtfully, slowly, review precisely what you need and what you want. [Pause. If necessary, occasionally help the patient to be more specific, for example, by asking, "When?" "How often?"]

All right. Now continue to drift into a deeper, and sounder trance, deeper with every breath you take. And as you continue to go deeper, in a moment I'm going to have you outline the therapy, and the actions that will be necessary, to accomplish what *you* want. Once again, as you speak, you will continue to go into a deeper, and more profound trance, with every sound of your voice, and with every word you speak. Simply the sound of your voice, will take you into such a deep hypnotic state, that you will find yourself compelled and constrained, to do exactly that which is indicated. So, in a moment, when I stop speaking, I want you to slowly, thoughtfully, meditatively, describe specifically what you will need to do. Now, slowly, thoughtfully, describe exactly what you need to do. [Pause. As necessary, very briefly question the patient for greater specificity and detail.]

Very good. And continue drifting deeper, and deeper into comfort. In a moment, I'm going to ask you to speak again. And I want you to specify in great detail, precisely what's necessary, and exactly what *you will do*, so that you'll reach your goals. As you speak, you can do so with an increasing effortlessness, allowing your unconscious mind to take over, and take you into a deeper, and more profound trance, with each sound of your voice. And you find yourself in such a deep trance, that the things you indicate are necessary, the suggestions you give to yourself, will profoundly influence your thoughts, and feelings, and actions. You are in such a deep trance, that you will feel impelled from deep within you, to do precisely what is indicated. Now, thoughtfully, slowly, and in detail, indicate exactly what *you will do*, so that you'll have what you want. [Pause]

Very good. Now just rest, into an even deeper, and sounder state, as each breath takes you into a deeper hypnotic sleep. [Pause] Now in a moment, I want you to speak again. And once again, as you speak, each sound of your voice will take you deeper; so deep, that you'll find yourself under a most powerful compulsion, to do exactly what is indicated. Now I want you to slowly, emphatically, and in full and comprehensive detail, to affirm again, precisely what *you will do*. [Pause]

[Repeat this last step once or twice more to provide repetition of suggestion.]

Now before awakening you, I want to point out, that I have offered you no advice or suggestions. Every suggestion has come from you, yourself. And these suggestions will sink deep into your unconscious mind, and profoundly influence your thoughts, and feelings, and your behaviors. And you will find yourself under a powerful compulsion, arising from deep inside you, to do everything that you have indicated. You will feel unconsciously impelled, deeply compelled, to do the things that you yourself have indicated. [Awaken the patient.]

Time Distortion Training

Training Patients to Experience Time Distortion

Linn F. Cooper, M.D., and
Milton H. Erickson, M.D.

In this section, those techniques will be considered whereby a subject, already trained in the production of the more common phenomena characteristic of the trance state, is taught to experience time distortion and to perform the various sorts of tasks discussed in this treatise.

Although a small percentage of "good" subjects will produce many of the phenomena under discussion on the first attempt to elicit them, it is most important for investigators to realize that the training of subjects for time distortion in hypnosis usually requires considerable time, effort, and skill. Methods that succeed with one subject may fail with another, and a keen appreciation of, and sensitivity to, the delicate interpersonal relationship involved in hypnosis is of paramount importance, along with resourcefulness, and the willingness to try original and varying approaches. By and large,

training in time distortion requires from three to 20 hours (best spent in daily sessions), not including the time required for the training in hypnosis per se. Furthermore, once learned, the ability decreases with lack of use and retraining may then be necessary to restore the former level of proficiency. With sufficient effort, and the proper technique, the phenomenon can probably be produced, to varying degrees, in the majority of subjects. A casual approach to the work is almost certain to lead to disappointment.

In general, it may be said that time distortion, and related phenomena, depends upon a high degree of withdrawal, by the subject, into his hallucinated world, with an accompanying lack of awareness of his surroundings as such. This state of detachment, in which the subject becomes completely engrossed in his hallucinatory experience, constitutes the first goal in training. When achieved, subjects will report that, during their task performance, they were quite unaware of their surroundings. Indeed, some subjects have reported that, at the termination signal, they experienced a slight "jolt" or "shock." One subject gave evidence of her engrossment in a different world by referring to the termination of the task by saying, "When you *called me out*, I was combing my hair." When she said this, she was still in the trance state, reporting on the performance of a just-completed task. Sudden noises likewise will "jolt" a subject who is hallucinating during time distortion, and sometimes they will destroy the production.

A most helpful suggestion to encourage withdrawal from the physical world is, *"During these experiences you will be completely unaware of your surroundings in the waking world."*

Prior to the starting signal, while the experimenter is assigning the task, subjects generally think about what they will do. Then, with the starting signal, well-trained subjects find themselves in the hallucinated world, living the assigned experience. This may or may not proceed along the lines they had planned, but it generally satisfies the conditions stipulated in the instructions, and is subject to volitional direction by the subject. Thus, not only does he do what was suggested to him but, within this limitation, he will carry out decisions as he is faced with them, just as he does when awake. One subject, for instance, whose wrist became uncomfortable while hallucinating the writing of a large amount of material, interrupted the writing long enough to go into the bathroom and put some alcohol on the lame wrist (this was, of course, hallucinatory activity only, and involved no actual movement).

The well trained subject does not consciously construct the details of his hallucinated world, but rather finds himself among them. In other words, whatever be the mechanism of fantasy production, it is spontaneous and effortless. This is in sharp contrast to the case of the waking subject who is asked, say, to imagine that he is looking at his house. Here he is likely deliberately to construct the image from his knowledge of it, and this is accompanied by more or less effort, depending upon how good a visualizer he is. And even then his productions generally lack what Dunne refers to as "reality tone," which is so characteristic of

hallucinatory experience. One of our subjects exemplified this in describing how he went about putting himself into a self-induced trance state. He said, "I first imagine myself in a certain situation as, for instance, lying on a rubber raft off a beach. I look about me and visualize the raft, the water, and so forth, and imagine that I feel the warm sun on my back and hear the waves. After a while, *everything comes into focus*, and I'm 'actually there.'"

We have always used the word "Now" as a starting and termination signal, and have avoided concurrent reporting almost entirely. Concurrent reporting is the reporting on an experience, by the subject, as he is actually living it, and is, of course, common practice in experimental hypnosis. We avoid it because we believe that it tends to prevent the subject from becoming detached from his surroundings in the physical world, and hence from learning time distortion. Obviously, experience proceeding in distorted time cannot be reported concurrently, for it proceeds too rapidly relative to world time.

It would seem that reality tone is in some way dependent upon a free flow of material from the unconscious. Since most persons dream, it may be well to cite dreams, pointing out to the subject that they are a form of hallucinatory experience, that they show reality tone and time distortion, and that the dreamer is quite unaware of his surroundings. This will give him an idea of the sort of thing that we are after. And in order to encourage a free and spontaneous flow of material from the unconscious, it is probably advisable to instruct the subject to permit free association to guide his imagery during his early training. Some such suggestions as the following may be used:

"When I give you the starting signal by saying, 'Now,' you will let some sort of visual image, or scene, come to you. It makes no difference what it is. As you watch, other images will come, of their own accord, one after another. These images will become more and more clear and more and more real, so that eventually you will find yourself 'actually there' in another world. You will be a part of that

world, which will be just as real as the waking world, and you will truly live such experiences as you have there. After a while I shall say to you, 'Now, make your mind a blank,' whereupon a hallucinatory activity will cease. I shall then ask you to tell me what you saw or did, but you need tell me only what you wish of your experience."

The subject is thus introduced to the use of a starting signal and a termination signal.

The subject should be allowed several minutes (allotted time) for such an exercise.

The next step is to assign definite tasks. These tasks should be familiar ones, and the instructions should be as general as possible. This permits the subject a wide range of action, with a minimum of limitations. We may simply instruct him to do anything he wishes. At first we may tell him that he is to *imagine* himself in such a place, or doing such and such a thing. Soon we discontinue the use of the phrase "to imagine" and tell him that he *will be* in such a place, or *will do* so and so, adding that *"it will be very real, so that you will actually live the experience."*

As training progresses, a series of tasks is run with completed activities. In these, it is important to assure the subject, after the activity suggestion, that he will "have plenty of time between signals to complete the task." In order to be certain that the allotted time is long enough for him to complete the task, it may be assigned first with no allotted time, allowing the subject to signal when he has finished. Having noted the world time, the task is then repeated, using the world time as the allotted time. By employing this technique with a number of tasks, the subject is introduced to the use of completed activities that he can finish within an allotted time.

Examples of such tasks follow:

"When I give you the starting signal by saying 'Now,' you will . . .

". . .take a walk."

". . .buy a pair of shoes."

". . .watch a movie 'short'."

". . .order a meal in a restaurant."

". . .draw a picture."

". . .polish your shoes."

". . .change a tire on a car."

". . .hear a record."

Here again, a report of each task, with its seeming duration, should be obtained.

Early in training, the seeming duration may be way out of proportion to the amount of activity reported. As the work progresses, this disproportion tends to disappear, and the amount of activity becomes more appropriate to the experiential time.

Next, continuous activities with a suggested personal time and an allotted time are introduced. The "finishing" of such activities consists, of course, in the activity having continued for the suggested personal time. Here again, it may be well to run the activity first as a task without an allotted time, allowing the subject to signal when he has finished. It can then be repeated, using the world time interval as the allotted time. With this, the subject should be assured that "when the time (suggested personal time) is up, the termination signal will be given." These activities are introduced by telling the subject that he will be at a certain place, or doing a certain thing. *The reliving of pleasant past experiences is a type of task that is useful at this stage of training.* However, any familiar type of activity is quite satisfactory, such as the following:

"When I give you the starting signal by saying 'Now,' you will . . .

". . .be at a beach."

". . .be in the country."

". . .be in school."

". . .be at work."

". . .be on a vacation."

". . .be taking a walk."

". . .be at a movie."

". . .be taking a drive in a car."

etc.

The subject should be asked for a report after each task, and the seeming duration of the experience should be asked for. Time distortion will soon become evident to the experimenter and, at some point in the training, it is advisable to point out to the subject the difference between the seeming duration and the clock reading during his experiences. This will help him to realize that time distortion is a fact, and that he himself can experience it quite naturally. In this way, the subject will become accustomed to finishing "completed" activities and "continuous" ones (with a suggested personal time) within an allotted time.

The next step is to run a series of tasks, either completed or continuous (with suggested personal time), using at first an allotted time long enough to permit the subject to finish the task and then, in repeating it, gradually to decrease the allotted time in steps of from 10 seconds to 30 seconds. The subject, "caught short" at first, will soon learn to adjust to the shorter allotted time, and will fit his hallucinatory experience into the interval allowed him, without hurrying or compromising in any way. Thus he learns to work with short allotted times. How far the process can be carried is not known at present.

A few words are in order concerning *suggested personal time*. This is used, as a rule, only with continuous activities, and may be introduced by such an expression as, "*You will spend 10 minutes (of your special time) doing so and so.*" Or, the experimenter may say, after the activity instructions, "*You will do this for 10 minutes.*"

Some subjects readily accept this early in their training; others have difficulty doing so. The difficulty seems to arise from at least two factors—a residual awareness of surroundings and consequently of world time, and a deep conviction that it "just is impossible." Practice, and use of a deeper trance, will help overcome the first difficulty. With the second, it may help to point out to the subject that he has on many occasions during his training himself experienced the variability of subjective time in relation to world time. The results of some of his earlier tests will convince him of this when shown to him.

Repeated assurance, to the subject, that he will have plenty of time for his task is of great importance during training, and should be used frequently. Such suggestions should be given with conviction, and it is often wise to repeat them many times. Examples are:

"You will have plenty of time."
"You will not have to hurry."
"You will have all the time you need."
"Relax and take your time."
"You can loiter over it if you wish."
"Remember, you have an unlimited supply of special trance time at your disposal, so take as much of it as you need."
"You are to do this slowly, without hurrying."

We have found the following technique useful, at times, in teaching the subject to work with short allotted times. It consists merely in suggesting a series of 10 tasks, each with an allotted time of 10 seconds, with reporting deferred until the series has been completed.

0 sec.: "When I give you the starting signal by saying 'Now,' you will get a haircut . . .

10 sec.: "Now."

20 sec.: "Now, blank. At the next signal you will wash your car . . ."

30 sec.: "Now."

40 sec.: "Now, blank. At the next signal you will buy a pair of shoes . . ."

50 sec.: "Now."

etc.

Another helpful technique is to repeat a given task over and over, keeping the allotted time constant. Although the subject may not be able to finish it at first, he often will learn to do so, without hurrying in the slightest, after repeated attempts. This will facilitate high degrees of time distortion in subsequent tasks.

To encourage progress, the activity instruction should be followed by such suggestions as the following, given repeatedly, and with conviction:

"You will finish this, without hurrying."
"Remember, you're going to finish this task, and you won't hurry."
"You will take as much time as you need to finish the task without hurrying."
"You will finish the task."

A most interesting technique, learned from Erickson and applicable to a very wide range of suggestions is, after an affirmatory suggestion, to ask the subject the question, "*Won't you?*" thus:

"You will finish, won't you?"

The subject, in answering "Yes," increases the likelihood of his carrying out the suggestion.

This technique may be used with commands in the following way: "Take as much time as you need in order to finish the task. You'll do this, won't you?"

Even further affirmatory reinforcement may be obtained by adding, "Are you sure?" after the subject has answered "Yes" to the above question.

As is pointed out elsewhere, the hallucinatory productions with which we deal in these experiments are, in certain important respects, different from most dreams. On the other hand, the nocturnal dream is the commonest form of experience that resembles them, and in which time distortion is present. Therefore, *in some subjects, production of a few hypnotically-induced dreams may serve as a useful introduction to hallucinatory experience of the sort we seek to develop.* If the dreams are produced, we explain to the subject that we shall ask for no more of them, but shall strive for productions that are identical with waking experience, that are continuous, "real" experiences, which he will actually *live.* Thus they will "make sense," and will be rich in detail, and will contain no omissions or gaps. We must frequently suggest that *the experiences will be "very, very real, so that you will actually live them."* This is extremely important.

At some point during training, it is desirable to discuss time with the subject. How this is done will vary with different experimenters. We generally employ some such approach as the following:

"There are two kinds of time: one, the time the clock tells us, the other, our own sense of the passage of time. The first of these is known as physical, or solar, or world time. It is the time used by the physicists and the astronomers in their measurements, and by all of us in our work-a-day life. The second is called personal, or subjective time. Einstein refers to this as 'I-time.'

"It is this subjective time that we are most interested in here. One of the most important

things about it is that it is very variable. Thus, if several persons are asked to judge the length of a five minute interval as measured by a clock, they may have very different ideas as to the duration of the interval, depending upon the circumstances in which each person finds himself. To those who were enjoying themselves, or who were absorbed in some interesting activity, the interval might well seem shorter. On the other hand, to those in pain or discomfort, or anxiety, the five minutes would seem much longer. We call this time distortion, and the most familiar example of it is found in the dream. You yourself have probably often noticed that you can experience many hours of dream life in a very short time by the clock.

"Now, it has been repeatedly demonstrated that subjective time appreciation can be hallucinated just as you can hallucinate visual or auditory sensations, in response to suggestion during hypnosis. The subject thus actually experiences the amount of subjective time that is suggested to him. So, in a sense, you have a 'special time' of your own, which you can call on as you wish. Moreover, you have an unlimited supply of it. It is the time of the dream world and of the hallucinated world, and since it is readily available, you will never have to hurry in these tests. Furthermore, it bears no relation whatever to the time of any watch, which, consequently, you will ignore.

"Knowing these things, you can now relax and take your time."

Certain suggestions other than those pertaining to specific tasks have proved useful. Among these are the following:

"As we practice these tasks, they will become easier and easier for you."

"With practice, the experiences will become more and more clear, and more and more real, so that you will actually live them."

"With each experience, you will go deeper and deeper asleep."

"The experiences will come of their own accord, promptly and effortlessly, when I give you the starting signal."

"The experiences will stop immediately, as I give you the termination signal."

Throughout the training, advantage is taken of the following:

1. The inherent tendency toward spontaneous time distortion in hallucinated activities.
2. The effort and the need on the part of the hypnotized subject to carry out suggestions, especially to finish a completed activity.
3. The fact that, at the beginning at least, familiar activities are more readily hallucinated than unfamiliar ones.
4. The fact that the interest and curiosity of the subject, and his feeling of being productive, tend to improve cooperation and performance. Advantage can be taken of this by giving him sufficient understanding of what he is doing so that he accepts and does not reject it.
5. The tendency to improve with practice.

In all training, it is of utmost importance for the experimenter to give the subject his undivided attention when addressing him. Subjects are quick to detect the slightest deviation from this approach, and may resent highly any evidence that they themselves are not the sole object of the experimenter's interest and attention. Thus, they can often tell, by changes in his voice, when the experimenter is thinking of something else, or turning his face away, as in looking at his notes, etc., even though their eyes are closed.

It must be remembered that subjects vary widely in their capabilities as regards time distortion in hypnosis. After a few hours of training, the experimenter will have obtained a fair idea as to a given subject's ability to acquire this skill. For routine experimental work, it has been our policy to continue training with only those who are promising.

Summary of Suggested Steps in Time Distortion Training

D. Corydon Hammond, Ph.D.
Salt Lake City, Utah

1. *Experiencing a continuous activity without suggestions for personal time.* Example: "You are listening to a record."
2. *Experiencing a continuous activity with suggestions for personal time.* Example: "You're going to listen to a record for 15 minutes."
3. *Experiencing a completed activity without suggestions for personal time.* Example: "You're going to cook a meal."
4. *Experiencing a completed activity with suggestions for personal time.* Example: "You will spent 15 minutes cooking a meal."
5. *Experiencing a continuous activity, in an allotted period of time, without suggestions for personal time.* Example: "You're listening to a record." [Subject is allotted two minutes, without telling him or her the amount of time.]
6. *Experiencing a continuous activity, in an allotted period of time, with suggestions for personal time.* Example: "In the next two minutes you're going to listen to an entire record, and you'll find that you have all the time you need." [Subject is allotted a certain number of minutes, and on subsequent trials, the amount of time is reduced.]
7. *Experiencing a completed activity, in an allotted period of time, without suggestions for personal time.* Example: "You're going to watch a television program, without hurrying, and will have all the time you need." [Subject is allotted three minutes, without telling him or her how much time is allotted.]
8. *Experiencing a completed activity, in an allotted period of time, with suggestions for personal time.* Example: "In the next three minutes of time by the clock, you're going to watch one of your favorite TV programs, without any sense of rushing. And you'll find you have plenty of time to thoroughly enjoy it."

After each experience, patients may be questioned about their experience. For example: "Tell me what you experienced." "What was that like?" "How long did it seem to you?" "Were you able to finish?" "Was it real to you?" "Did you experience it from beginning to end?"

USE OF A METRONOME IN FACILITATING TIME DISTORTION

A metronome may be used to facilitate time distortion in an office or experimental setting. The hypnotized patient may be told: "In a moment I am going to turn on a metronome, and it will tick at one tick per second. I would like you to listen to the metronome carefully, as it makes a sound once each second. And you will continue hearing the sound of the metronome in the background of your awareness, as it continues to make one sound each second. And with each sound of the metronome, you'll go deeper and deeper into trance. And the metronome will beat once each second, and each sound will take you deeper."

The therapist subsequently has two options. First, after a period of time, the metronome may be gradually slowed down (e.g., to one beat every 2–4 seconds), or speeded up (e.g., to 2–4 beats/second). Patients will typically become lethargic, depressed and slowed in motor behavior when the metronome slows down. They will become hyperactive, happier, and finally manic as a metronome is speeded up. Second, the metronome may be left at the same speed, but it may be suggested that it is slowing down or speeding up. For example, "As you listen to the metronome, it will begin going faster and faster." This method often produces impressive demonstrations, but is more limited in clinical applications.

TIME DISTORTION IN EXPLORATORY HYPNOSIS

Psychotherapists will particularly find it instructive to review case reports in Erickson's (Cooper & Erickson, 1959) chapter on clinical and therapeutic applications of time distortion. Brief elaboration of one of these cases may prove instructive.

A dental hygienist consulted Erickson for a phobic response of anxiety, nausea and fainting at the sight of blood. She wanted hypnosis to remedy the problem, but to not let her know

until it was over. After inducing a somnambulistic trance "the suggestion was offered that, first of all, it might be well to have her experience, as a means of keeping her hypnotized [as she desired] and as a measure of giving her satisfaction, the various common phenomena of the hypnotic trance" (p. 177). Trance training in the hypnotic phenomena was conducted for another 50 minutes.

She was then told, while still in trance, that there remained a couple more phenomena which she could enjoy. One of these was related to time and would really center around a stopwatch, which was exhibited to her. With every effort to be instructive, she was reminded of the rapidity with which time passed when she was pleased, how slowly when bored, the endlessness of a few seconds' wait for an intensely regarded outcome of a matter of doubt, the rapidity with which a mere word could cause to flash through the mind the contents of a well liked book or the events of a long, happy trip and the tremendous rapidity and momentum of thought and feelings.

Against this background, a detailed elaboration was presented of the concept of distorted, personal, special or experiential time as contrasted to clock time. Extensive discussion was also offered of the "normal tempo" of distorted or experiential time.

When she seemed to understand, the explanation was offered that this hypnotic phenomenon could be initiated for her by giving simple instructions which she could easily accept fully. These instructions would be followed by the starting signal of "Now," at which time the stopwatch would be started. Then, when the phenomenon had been completed, she would be told to stop. This explanation was repeated until she understood fully.

Then with compelling, progressive, rapid, emphatic, insistent intensity, she was told, "Begin at the beginning, go all the way through in normal experiential tempo with a tremendous rush of force, skipping nothing, including everything, and reach a full complete understanding of everything about *Blood—Now*."

She reacted to the word "blood" by a violent start, trembled briefly, became physically rigid, and clenched her fists and jaw. She appeared to be in acute physical distress but too rigidly involved physically and mentally to break into disruptive actions.

Twenty seconds later, at the commend "Stop," she relaxed, slumped in the chair and breathed hard. Immediately she was told emphatically, "You now know, you understand, you no longer need to fear. You don't even need to remember when you are awake, but your unconscious now knows, and will continue to know and to understand correctly, and thus give to you that ease you want." She was asked if she wished to awaken or to think things through. (Cooper & Erickson, 1959, pp. 177-178) [This was successful in resolving her problem.]

This case illustrates how Erickson seems to have often used time distortion in the process of unconscious exploration. He would train patients to experience time distortion, sometimes taking them through the kinds of hypnotic training exercises discussed in the previous section. Then, in the guise of another training "experiment," he might give the following type of suggestion:

You have many times taken a trip in a car and enjoyed it immensely. The car was moving very rapidly. You saw this sight, you saw that scene, you said this, you said that, all in an ordinary way. The car moved fast but you were sitting quietly, just going along. You could not stop the car, nor did you want to. The telephone poles were so many feet apart and they came along one by one and you saw them pass. You saw the fields and they passed by, large fields, small fields, and you could only wait quietly to see what would be in the next field, and to see whether the next house would be brick or frame. And all the time the car went along and you sat quietly, just saw, you thought, all in your own way, at your own speed, just as it happened, and the car just kept going. You did not need to pay attention to the car, *just to what next would happen*, a field, a house, a horse or *whatever was next*.

However, this experiment will not be a car ride. I have just used it to explain more fully to you. I could have described going through the cooking of a dinner—peeling potatoes, washing carrots, putting on pork chops—*anything that you could have done*.

Now I'm going to give you much more time than you need to do this experiment. I will give you twenty seconds of world time. But in your special time, that twenty seconds will be just as long as you need to complete your work. It can be a minute, a day, a week, a month or even years. And you will take all the time you need.

I will not tell you yet what your experiment or task is. As soon as you nod your head to show that you are ready, I will start the stopwatch and give you the signal *now* and very rapidly I will name the task [as had been done in previous "experiments"] and you will start at the beginning of it, the very beginning, and go right through to the end, no matter how far away it is in time. Ready? All right, listen carefully for the click of the watch, my signal, and the name of the task. *Now—from Childhood to Now—Remember!* (The *Now* was repeated as literally a double signal.) (Cooper & Erickson, 1959, p. 171) [Twenty seconds later this patient was told to stop, asked if she was through, and asked if she would be willing to share what had been reviewed after awakening.]

In a similar case, following training to "systematically" teach the patient "a working knowledge of time distortion," Erickson gave the following suggestions:

With this stopwatch I will give you an allotted world time of twenty seconds. In your own special experiential time, those twenty seconds will cover hours, days, weeks, months, even years of your experiential life. When I say "Now," you will begin the experiment. When I say "Stop," you will be finished. During that twenty seconds of world time, you will sit quietly, neither speaking nor moving, but mentally, in your unconscious, you will do the experiment, taking all the experiential time you need. This you will do thoroughly, carefully. As soon as I give you the starting signal, I will name the experiment and you will do it completely. Are you ready?

Now—Go through all the causes of your problem. *Now.*

Stop. (Cooper & Erickson, 1959, p. 185)

It is interesting to note how Erickson talked about providing "intensive" and "systematic" training to patients who were excellent hypnotic subjects. Most of these patients could have undoubtedly responded at least to some extent to brief, straightforward suggestions for time distortion. Nonetheless, Erickson invested the time to "train" these patients to respond more fully when he anticipated using time distortion as an important aspect of his intervention.

REFERENCES

Aaronson, B. S. (1966). Behavior and the place names of time. *American Journal of Clinical Hypnosis, 9,* 1–17.

Aaronson, B. S. (1968a). Hypnotic alterations of space and time. *International Journal of Parapsychology, 10,* 5–36.

Aaronson, B. S. (1968b). Hypnosis, time rate perception, and personality. *Journal of Schizophrenia, 2,* 11–14.

Aaronson, B. S. (1971). Time, time stance, and existence. *Studium Generale* (Springer Verlag), *24,* 369–387.

Abarbanel, A. R. (1978). Diagnosis and treatment of coital discomfort. Chapter in J. LoPiccolo and L. LoPiccolo (Eds.), *Handbook of Sex Therapy.* New York: Plenum.

Abramson, M., Greenfield, I., & Heron, W. T. (1966). Response to or perception of auditory stimuli under deep surgical anesthesia. *American Journal of Obstetrics & Gynecology, 96,* 584–585.

Abramson, M., & Heron, W. T. (1950). An objective evaluation of hypnosis in obstetrics: Preliminary report. *American Journal of Obstetrics & Gynecology, 59,* 1069–1074.

Adam, L. (1976). Sleep-assisted instruction. *Psychological Bulletin, 83,* 1–40.

Ader, R. (Ed.). (1981). *Psychoneuroimmunology.* New York: Academic Press.

Aja, J. H. (1977). Brief group treatment of obesity through ancillary self-hypnosis. *American Journal of Clinical Hypnosis, 19,* 231–234.

Alexander, F. M. (1910). *The Use of the Self.* London: Re-Educational Publications.

Alexander, L. (1974). Treatment of impotency and anorgasmia by psychotherapy aided by hypnosis. *American Journal of Clinical Hypnosis, 17*(1), 31–43.

Alman, B. (1983). Bypassing hypnotic susceptibility scales. Paper presented at the Annual Scientific Meeting of the American Society of Clinical Hypnosis, Dallas, Texas.

Alman, B., & Carney, R. E. (1980). Consequences of direct and indirect suggestions on success of posthypnotic behavior. *American Journal of Clinical Hypnosis, 23,* 112–118.

Alman, B. M. (1983). *Self-Hypnosis: A Complete Manual for Health and Self-Change.* San Diego: International Health Publications.

Ambrose, G. (1961). *Hypnotherapy with Children* (Second Edition). London: Staples.

Anderson, J. A. D., Basker, M. A., & Dalton, R. (1975). Migraine and hypnotherapy. *International Journal of Clinical & Experimental Hypnosis, 23*(1), 48–58.

Antich, J. L. S. (1967). The use of hypnosis in pediatric anesthesia. *Journal of the American Society of Psychosomatic Dentistry & Medicine, 14,* 70–75.

Araoz, D. L. (1980). Clinical hypnosis in treating sexual abulia. *American Journal of Family Therapy, 8*(1), 48–57.

Araoz, D. L. (1982). *Hypnosis & Sex Therapy.* New York: Brunner/Mazel.

Aravindakshan, K. K., Jenner, F. A., & Souster, L. P. (1988). A study of the effects of hypnotic regression on the auditory evoked response. *International Journal of Clinical & Experimental Hypnosis, 36*(2), 89–95.

Asher, L. M., Barber, T. X., & Spanos, N. P. (1972). Two attempts to replicate the Parrish-Lundy-Leibowitz experiment on hypnotic age regression. *American Journal of Clinical Hypnosis, 14,* 178–185.

Auerbach, A. H., & Johnson, M. (1977). Research on the therapist's level of experience. In A. S. Gurman & A. M. Razin (Eds.), *Effective Psychotherapy: A Handbook of Research.* New York: Pergamon.

August, R. V. (1960a). Obstetrical hypnoanesthesia. *American Journal of Obstetrics & Gynecology, 79,* 1131–1138.

August, R. V. (1960b). Hypnosis: An additional tool in the study of infertility. *Fertility & Sterility, 11,* 118–123.

August, R. V. (1960c). Hallucinatory experiences utilized for obstetric hypnoanesthesia. *American Journal of Clinical Hypnosis, 3,* 90–92.

August, R. V. (1961). *Hypnosis in Obstetrics.* New York: McGraw-Hill.

Azrin, N. H., & Nunn, R. G. (1978). *Habit Control in a Day.* New York: Simon & Schuster.

Bakal, P. A. (1981). Hypnotherapy for flight phobia.

American Journal of Clinical Hypnosis, 23(4), 248–251.

Baker, E. L. (1981). An hypnotherapeutic approach to enhance object relatedness in psychotic patients. *International Journal of Clinical & Experimental Hypnosis, 29*, 136–147.

Baker, E. L. (1983a). The use of hypnotic dreaming in the treatment of the borderline patient: Some thoughts on resistance and transitional phenomena. *International Journal of Clinical & Experimental Hypnosis, 31*, 19–27.

Baker, E. L. (1983b). Resistance in hypnotherapy of primitive states: Its meaning and management. *International Journal of Clinical & Experimental Hypnosis, 31*, 82–89.

Baker, E. L. (1983c). The use of hypnotic techniques with psychotics. *American Journal of Clinical Hypnosis, 25*, 283–288.

Baker, R. A. (1982). The effect of suggestion on past-lives regression. *American Journal of Clinical Hypnosis, 25*(1), 71–76.

Bandler, R., & Grinder, J. (1975). *Patterns of the Hypnotic Techniques of Milton H. Erickson, M.D.* (Volume 1). Cupertino, CA: Meta Publications.

Bandler, R., & Grinder, J. (1978). *Frogs into Princes: NeuroLinguistic Programming.* Moab, Utah: Real People Press.

Bandura, A. (1969). *Principles of Behavior Modification.* New York: Holt, Rinehart & Winston.

Bandura, A. (1977). Self-efficacy: Toward a unifying theory of behavior change. *Psychological Review, 84*, 191–215.

Bandura, A. (1981). Self-referent thought: A developmental analysis of self-efficacy. In J. H. Flavell & L. D. Ross (Eds.), *Cognitive Social Development.* New York: Cambridge University Press.

Banyai, E., & Hilgard, E. (1976). A comparison of active-alert hypnotic induction with traditional relaxation induction. *Journal of Abnormal Psychology, 85*(2), 218–224.

Barabasz, A F., & Barabasz, M. (1989). Effects of restricted environmental stimulation: Enhancement of hypnotizability for experimental and chronic pain control. *International Journal of Clinical & Experimental Hypnosis, 37*(3), 217–231.

Barabasz, A. F., & McGeorge, C. M. (1978). Biofeedback, mediated biofeedback and hypnosis in peripheral vasodilation training. *American Journal of Clinical Hypnosis, 21*, 28–37.

Barabasz, M. (1987). Trichotillomania: A new treatment. *International Journal of Clinical & Experimental Hypnosis, 35*, 146–154.

Barber, J. (1977). Rapid induction analgesia: A clinical report. *American Journal of Clinical Hypnosis, 19*, 138–147.

Barber, J., & Adrian, C. (1982). *Psychological Approaches to the Management of Pain.* New York: Brunner/Mazel.

Barber, J., Donaldson, D., Ramras, S., & Allen, G. D. (1979). The relationship between nitrous oxide conscious sedation and the hypnotic state. *Journal of the American Dental Association, 99*, 624–626.

Barber, T. X. (1962). Hypnotic age regression: A critical review. *Psychosomatic Medicine, 24*, 286–299.

Barber, T. X., & Calverly, D. S. (1964). Toward a theory of "hypnotic" behavior. *Archives of General Psychiatry, 10*, 209.

Barber, T. X., Spanos, N. P., & Chaves, J. F. (1974). *Hypnosis, Imagination and Human Potentialities.* New York: Pergamon.

Barber, T. X. (1984). Hypnosis, deep relaxation, and active relaxation: Data, theory, and clinical applications. Chapter in R. L. Woolfolk & P. M. Lehrer, *Principles and Practice of Stress Management.* New York: Guilford Press, pp. 164–166.

Barker, D. (1979). Correspondence. *Journal of Parapsychology, 43*, 268–269.

Barker, P. (1985). *Using Metaphors in Psychotherapy.* New York: Brunner/Mazel.

Barker, W., Rodenheaver, G. T., Edgerton, M. T., et al. (1982). Damage to tissue defenses by a topical anesthetic agent. *Annals of Emergency Medicine, 11*, 307–310.

Barkley, R. A., Hastings, J. E., & Jackson, T. L. (1977). The effects of rapid smoking and hypnosis in the treatment of smoking behavior. *International Journal of Clinical & Experimental Hypnosis, 25*, 7–17.

Barlow, D. H., & Cerny, J. A. (1988). *Psychological Treatment of Panic.* New York: Guilford.

Barnett, E. A. (1981). *Analytical Hypnotherapy.* Kingston, Ontario: Junica.

Bartlett, E. E. (1966). Polypharmacy versus hypnosis in surgical patients. *Pacific Medicine & Surgery, 74*, 109–.

Baumann, F. (1981). Hypnosis in the treatment of urinary and fecal incontinence: A twenty-year experience. Chapter in H. J. Wain (Ed.), *Theoretical & Clinical Aspects of Hypnosis.* Miami: Symposia Specialists Inc.

Bednar, R. L. (1970). Persuasibility and the power of belief. *Personnel & Guidance Journal 48*, 647–652.

Bennett, H. L. (1988). Perception and memory for events during adequate general anesthesia for surgical operations. Chapter in H. M. Pettinati (Ed.), *Hypnosis & Memory.* New York: Guilford, pp. 193–231.

Bennett, H. L., Davis, H. S., & Giannini, J. A. (1984). Nonverbal response to intraoperative conversation. *Anesthesia & Analgesia, 63*, 185. (Abstract)

Bennett, H. L., Davis, H. S., & Giannini, J. A. (1985). Nonverbal response to intraoperative conversation. *British Journal of Anaesthesia, 57*, 174–179.

Bensen, V. B. (1971). One hundred cases of post-anesthetic suggestion in the recovery room. *American Journal of Clinical Hypnosis, 14*, 9–15.

Benson, H., Rosner, B. A., Marzetta, B. R., & Klemchuk, H. M. (1974). Decreased blood pressure in borderline hypertensive subjects who practice meditation. *Journal of Chronic Disease, 27,* 163–169.

Benson, H., & Wallace, P. K. (1972). Decreased blood pressure in borderline hypertensive subjects who practice meditation. *Circulation, 46,* (Supplement II), 130.

Berkowitz, B., Ross-Townsend, A., & Kohberger, R. (1979). Hypnotic treatment of smoking: The single-treatment method revisited. *American Journal of Psychiatry, 136,* 83–85.

Bernstein, M. (1956). *The Search for Bridey Murphy.* New York: Doubleday.

Best, J. A., & Hakstian, A. R. (1978). A situation-specific model for smoking behavior. *Addictive Behaviors, 3,* 79–92.

Betcher, A. M. (1960). Hypnosis as an adjunct in anesthesiology. *New York State Journal of Medicine, 60,* 816–822.

Beutler, L. E. (1983). *Eclectic Psychotherapy: A Systematic Approach.* New York: Pergamon.

Bierman, S. F. (1988). Painless wound injection through use of a two-finger confusion technique. *American Journal of Emergency Medicine, 6*(3), 266–267.

Bishay, E. G., & Lee, C. (1984). Studies of the effects of hypnoanesthesia on regional blood flow by transcutaneous oxygen monitoring. *American Journal of Clinical Hypnosis, 27*(1), 64–69.

Bishay, E. G., Stevens, G., & Lee, C. (1984). Hypnotic control of upper gastrointestinal hemorrhage: A case report. *American Journal of Clinical Hypnosis, 27*(1), 22–25.

Bliss, E. L. (1980). Multiple personalities. *Archives of General Psychiatry, 37,* 1388–1397.

Bonke, B., & Verhage, F. (1984). A clinical study of so-called unconscious perception during general anesthesia. Unpublished manuscript cited in H. L. Bennett, Perception and memory for events during adequate general anesthesia for surgical operations. Chapter in H. M. Pettinati (Ed.), *Hypnosis and Memory.* New York: Guilford.

Bonello, F. J., Doberneck, R. C., Papermaster, A. A., et al. (1960). Hypnosis in surgery. I. The postgastrectomy dumping syndrome. *American Journal of Clinical Hypnosis, 2,* 215–219.

Bonilla, K. B., Quigley, W. F., & Bowen, W. F. (1961). Experiences with hypnosis and surgical service. *Military Medicine, 126,* 364–370.

Bootkin, R. R. (1977). Effects of self-control procedures for insomnia. Chapter in R. B. Stuart (Ed.), *Behavioral Self-Management: Strategies, Techniques & Outcomes.* New York: Brunner/Mazel, pp. 176–195.

Bornstein, P. H., & Rychtarik, R. G. (1978). Multicomponent behavioral treatment of trichotillomania: A case study. *Behavioral Research & Therapy, 16,* 217–220.

Borysenko, J. (1987). *Minding the Body, Mending the Mind.* Reading, Mass.: Addison Wesley.

Bowen, D. (1973). Transurethral resection under self-hypnosis. *American Journal of Clinical Hypnosis, 16,* 132–136.

Bowers, K. S. (1968). Hypnosis and creativity: A preliminary investigation. *International Journal of Clinical & Experimental Hypnosis, 16,* 38–52.

Bowers, K. S., & van der Meulen, S. J. (1970). Effect of hypnotic susceptibility on creativity test performance. *Journal of Personality & Social Psychology, 14,* 247–256.

Bowers, P. G., & Bowers, K. S. (1979). Hypnosis and creativity: A theoretical and empirical rapprochement. Chapter in E. Fromm & R. E. Shor (Eds.), *Hypnosis: Developments in Research & New Perspectives.* New York: Aldine, pp. 351–379.

Brauer, R. O., & Spira, M. (1966). Full thickness burns as source for donor graft in the pig. *Plastic & Reconstructive Surgery, 37,* 21–30.

Braun, B. G. (1984a). Uses of hypnosis with multiple personalities. *Psychiatric Annals, 14,* 34–40.

Braun, B. G. (1984b). Hypnosis creates multiple personality: Myth or reality? *International Journal of Clinical & Experimental Hypnosis, 32,* 191–197.

Brice, D. D., Hetherington, R. R., & Utting, J. E. (1970). A simple study of awareness and dreaming during anesthesia. *British Journal of Anaesthesia, 42,* 535–542.

Brown, P. (1985). Hypnosis as an adjunct to the psychotherapy of the severely disturbed patient: An affective development approach. *International Journal of Clinical & Experimental Hypnosis, 33,* 281–301.

Brown, D. P., & Fromm, E. (1986). *Hypnotherapy & Hypnoanalysis.* Hillsdale, N.J.: Lawrence Erlbaum.

Browne, R. A., & Catton, D. V. (1973). A study of awareness during anesthesia. *Anesthesia & Analgesia, 52,* 128–152.

Brownell, K. D. (1982). Obesity: Understanding and treating a serious, prevalent, and refractory disorder. *Journal of Consulting & Clinical Psychology, 50,* 820–840.

Brunn, J. T. (1963). The capacity to hear, to understand, to remember experiences during chemoanesthesia: A personal experience. *American Journal of Clinical Hypnosis, 6,* 27–30.

Bynum, E. (1977). Hypnotic age regression: An experimental investigation. Doctoral dissertation, Pennsylvania State University. *Dissertation Abstracts International, 38*(5-B), 2394–2395.

Byrne, S. (1973). Hypnosis and the irritable bowel: Case histories, methods and speculation. *American Journal of Clinical Hypnosis, 15,* 263–265.

Callan, T. D. (1961). Can hypnosis be used routinely in obstetrics. *Rocky Mountain Medical Journal, 58,* 28–30.

Candiotte, M. M., & Lichtenstein, E. (1981). Self-efficacy and relapse in smoking cessation programs. *Journal of Consulting & Clinical Psychology, 49,* 648–658.

Caritis, S. N., Edelstone, D. I., & Mueller-Heubach, E. (1979). Pharmacologic inhibition of pre-term labor. *American Journal of Obstetrics & Gynecology, 145,* 557–578.

Carnegie, D. (1966). *How to Win Friends and Influence People.* New York: Pocket Books.

Chapman, L. F., Goodell, H., & Wolff, H. G. (1959a). Augmentation of the inflammatory reaction by activity of the central nervous system. *American Medical Association Archives of Neurology, 1,* 557–572.

Chapman, L. F., Goodell, H., & Wolff, H. G. (1959b). Changes in tissue vulnerability induced during hypnotic suggestion. *Journal of Psychosomatic Research, 4,* 99–105.

Cheek, D. B. (1959). Unconscious perception of meaningful sounds during surgical anesthesia as revealed under hypnosis. *American Journal of Clinical Hypnosis, 1,* 101–113.

Cheek, D. B. (1966). The meaning of continued hearing sense under general chemo-anesthesia: A progress report and report of a case. *American Journal of Clinical Hypnosis, 8*(4), 275–280.

Cheek, D. B. (1981). Awareness of meaningful sounds under general anesthesia: Considerations and a review of the literature 1959–1979. Chapter in H. J. Wain (Ed.), *Theoretical & Clinical Aspects of Hypnosis.* Miami: Symposia Specialists, pp. 87–106.

Cheek, D. B. (1986). Using hypnosis with habitual aborters. Chapter in B. Zilbergeld, M. G. Edelstien, and D. L. Araoz (Eds.), *Hypnosis: Questions and Answers.* New York: Norton, 1986, pp. 330–336.

Cheek, D. B., & LeCron, L. (1968). *Clinical Hypnotherapy.* New York: Grune & Stratton.

Chiasson, S. W. (1964). Hypnosis in postoperative urinary retention. *American Journal of Clinical Hypnosis, 6,* 366–368.

Cialdini, R. B. (1988). *Influence: Science & Practice* (Second Edition). Glenview, IL: Scott, Foresman & Co.

Clarke, J. C., & Jackson, J. A. (1983). *Hypnosis & Behavior Therapy: The Treatment of Anxiety & Phobias.* New York: Springer.

Clarke, J. H., & Persichetti, S. J. (1988). Hypnosis and concurrent denture construction for a patient with a hypersensitive gag reflex. *American Journal of Clinical Hypnosis, 30*(4), 285–288.

Cole, R. (1977). Increasing reading and test-taking skills with hypnosis and suggestion. Unpublished doctoral dissertation, Texas A & M University. *Dissertation Abstracts International, 37*(8-A), 4859.

Cole, R. (1979). The use of hypnosis in a course to increase academic and test-taking skills. *International Journal of Clinical & Experimental Hypnosis, 27*(1), 21–28.

Colgan, S. M., Faragher, E. B., Whorwell, P. J. (1988). Controlled trial of hypnotherapy in relapse prevention of duodenal ulceration. *Lancet, 11*(1), 1299–1300.

Combs, A. W., Avila, D. L., & Purkey, W. W. (1971). *Helping Relationships: Basic Concepts for the Helping Professions.* Boston: Allyn & Bacon, 1971.

Conn, J. H. (1972). Is hypnosis really dangerous? *International Journal of Clinical & Experimental Hypnosis, 20,* 61–70.

Coons, P. M. (1980). Multiple personality: Diagnostic considerations. *Journal of Clinical Psychiatry, 41,* 330–336.

Cooper, L. F. (1948). Time distortion in hypnosis. *The Bulletin, Georgetown University Medical Center, 1,* 214–221.

Cooper, L. F. (1952). Time distortion in hypnosis. *Journal of Psychology, 34,* 247–284.

Cooper, L. F., & Erickson, M. H. (1954). *Time Distortion in Hypnosis.* Baltimore: Williams & Wilkins.

Cooper, L. F., & Erickson, M. H. (1959). *Time Distortion in Hypnosis.* Baltimore: Williams and Wilkins.

Cooper, L. F., & Rodgin, D. W. (1952). Time distortion in hypnosis and non-motor learning. *Science, 115,* 500–502.

Cooper, L. M., & London, P. (1976). Children's hypnotic susceptibility, personality, and EEG patterns. *International Journal of Clinical & Experimental Hypnosis, 24,* 140–148.

Copeland, D. R. (1986). The application of object-relations theory to the hypnotherapy of developmental arrests: The borderline patient. *International Journal of Clinical & Experimental Hypnosis, 34,* 157–168.

Corley, J. B. (1965). Hypnosis and the anesthetist. *American Journal of Clinical Hypnosis, 8,* 34–36.

Council on Scientific Affairs, American Medical Association. (1985). Scientific Status of refreshing recollection by the use of hypnosis. *Journal of the American Medical Association, 253,* 1918–1923.

Courtois, C. A. (1988). *Healing the Incest Wound.* New York: W. W. Norton.

Crasilneck, H. B. (1979). The use of hypnosis in the treatment of psychogenic impotency. *Australian Journal of Clinical & Experimental Hypnosis, 2,* 147–153.

Crasilneck, H. B. (1980). Clinical assessment and preparation of the patient. Chapter in G. Burrows and L. Dennerstein (Eds.). *Handbook of Hypnosis & Psychosomatic Medicine.* Amsterdam: Elsevier/North Holland.

Crasilneck, H. B. (1982). A follow-up study in the use of hypnotherapy in the treatment of psychogenic impotency. *American Journal of Clinical Hypnosis, 25*(1), 52–61.

Crasilneck, H. B., & Hall, J. A. (1985). *Clinical Hypnosis: Principles & Applications.* Orlando: Grune & Stratton.

Crasilneck, H. B., McCranie, E. J., & Jenkins, M. T. (1956). Special indications for hypnosis as a method of anesthesia. *Journal of the American Medical Association, 162,* 1606–1608.

Crasilneck, H. B., & Michael, C. M. (1957). Performance on the Bender under hypnotic age regression. *Journal of Abnormal & Social Psychology, 54,* 319–322.

Crowley, R. (1980). Effect of indirect hypnosis (rapid induction analgesia) for relief of acute pain associated with minor podiatric surgery. *Dissertation Abstracts International, 40,* 4549.

Cullen, S. C. (1958). Current comment and case reports: Hypno-induction techniques in pediatric anesthesia.

Anesthesiology, 19, 279–281.

Daniels, E. (1962). The hypnotic approach in anesthesia for children. *American Journal of Clinical Hypnosis, 4,* 244–248.

Dave, R., & Reyher, J. (1978). The effects of hypnotically induced dreams on creative problem solving. *Journal of Abnormal Psychology.*

Davidson, J. A. (1962). An assessment of the value of hypnosis in pregnancy and labour. *British Medical Journal, 5310,* 951–953.

DeAmicis, L. A., Goldberg, D. C., LoPiccolo, J., Friedman, J. M., & Davies, L. (1984) Three-year follow-up of couples evaluated for sexual dysfunction. *Journal of Sex & Marital Therapy, 10*(4), 215–218.

Deabler, H. L., Fidel, E., Dillenkoffer, R. L., & Elder, S. T. (1973). The use of relaxation and hypnosis in lowering high blood pressure. *American Journal of Clinical Hypnosis, 16,* 75–83.

Deiker, T., & Counts, D. K. (1980). Hypnotic paradigm-substitution therapy in a case of hypochondriasis. *American Journal of Clinical Hypnosis, 23*(2), 122–127.

Deiker, T. E., & Pollock, D. H. (1975). Integration of hypnotic and systematic desensitization techniques as in the treatment of phobias: A case report. *American Journal of Clinical Hypnosis, 17,* 170–174.

Deyoub, P. L., & Epstein, S. (1977). Short-term hypnotherapy for the treatment of flight phobia: A case report. *American Journal of Clinical Hypnosis, 19,* 251–254.

DiClemente, C. C. (1981). Self-efficacy and smoking cessation maintenance. *Cognitive Therapy and Research, 5,* 175–187.

Doberneck, R. C., McFee, A. S., Bonello, F. J., Papermaster, A. A., & Wangensteen, O. H. (1961). The prevention of postoperative urinary retention by hypnosis. *American Journal of Clinical Hypnosis, 3,* 235–237.

Donk, L. J., Vingoe, F., Hall, R., & Doty, R. (1970). The comparison of three suggestion techniques for increasing reading efficiency utilizing a counterbalanced research paradigm. *International Journal of Clinical & Experimental Hypnosis, 27*(2), 126–133.

Golden, W. L., Dowd, E. T., & Friedberg, F. (1987). *Hypnotherapy: A Modern Approach.* New York: Pergamon Press.

Dubovsky, S. L., & Trustman, R. (1976). Absence of recall after general anesthesia: Implications for theory and practice. *Anesthesia & Analgesia, 55*(5), 696–701.

Egan, R.M., & Egan, W. P. (1968). The effect of hypnosis on academic performance. *American Journal of Clinical Hypnosis, 11,* 30–34.

Ebert, B. W. (1988). Hypnosis and rape victims. *American Journal of Clinical Hypnosis, 31*(1), 50–56.

Edelstien, M. G. (1981). *Trauma, Trance, & Transformation.* New York: Brunner/Mazel.

Edwards, P. (1987a). The case against reincarnation: Part 2. *Free Inquiry, 7*(1), 38–47.

Edwards, P. (1987b). The case against reincarnation: Part 3. *Free Inquiry, 7*(2), 38–49.

Eich, E. (1984). Memory for unattended events: Remembering with and without awareness. *Memory & Cognition, 12,* 105–111.

Eich, E., Reeves, J. L., & Katz, R. L. (1985). Anesthesia, amnesia, and the memory/awareness distinction. *Anesthesia & Analgesia, 64,* 1143–1148.

Eisle, G., & Higgins, J. (1962). Hypnosis in education and moral problems. *American Journal of Clinical Hypnosis, 4*(4), 259–261.

Eliseo, T. S. (1974). Three examples of hypnosis in the treatment of organic brain syndrome with psychosis. *International Journal of Clinical & Experimental Hypnosis, 22,* 9–19.

Elkins, G. R. (1984). Hypnosis in the treatment of myofibrositis and anxiety: A case report. *American Journal of Clinical Hypnosis, 27*(1), 26–30.

Elkins, G. R., & Carter, B. D. (1981). Use of a science fiction-based imagery technique in child hypnosis. *American Journal of Clinical Hypnosis, 23*(4), 274–276.

Ellenberger, H. F. (1970). *The Discovery of the Unconscious.* New York: Basic Books.

Elliotson, J. (1843). *Numerous Cases of Surgical Operations Without Pain in The Mesmeric State.* Philadelphia: Lea and Blanchard.

Ellis, A. (1962). *Reason and Emotion in Psychotherapy.* New York: Lyle Stuart.

Ellis, A. (1986). Anxiety about anxiety: The use of hypnosis with Rational-Emotive Therapy. Chapter in E. T. Dowd and J. M. Healy (Eds.), *Case Studies in Hypnotherapy.* New York: Guilford, pp. 3–11.

Erickson, M. H. (1952). Deep hypnosis and its induction. Chapter in L. M. LeCron (Ed.), *Experimental Hypnosis.* New York: Macmillan, pp. 70–114.

Erickson, M. H. (1959). Further clinical techniques of hypnosis: Utilization techniques. *American Journal of Clinical Hypnosis, 2,* 3–21. [Also reprinted in E. L. Rossi (Ed.), *The Collected Papers of Milton H. Erickson on Hypnosis, Volume 1,* pp. 177–205.]

Erickson, M. H. (1960). Psychogenic alteration of menstrual functioning: Three instances. *American Journal of Clinical Hypnosis, 2,* 227–331.

Erickson, M. H. (1963). Chemo-anaesthesia in relation to hearing and memory. *American Journal of Clinical Hypnosis, 6,* 31–36.

Erickson, M. H. (1964). The confusion technique in hypnosis. *American Journal of Clinical Hypnosis, 6,* 183–207.

Erickson, M. H. (1964b). The burden of responsibility in effective psychotherapy. *American Journal of Clinical Hypnosis, 6,* 269–271.

Erickson, M. H. (1965). Hypnosis and examination panics. *American Journal of Clinical Hypnosis, 7,* 356–357.

Erickson, M. H. (1966). The interspersal hypnotic technique for symptom correction and pain control. *American Journal of Clinical Hypnosis, 8,* 198–209.

Erickson, M. H. (1973). Psychotherapy achieved by a reversal of the neurotic processes in a case of ejaculation praecox. *American Journal of Clinical Hypnosis, 15*(4), 219–221.

Erickson, M. H. (1980). *The Collected Papers of Milton H. Erickson on Hypnosis, Volumes 1–4.* Edited by E. L. Rossi. New York: Irvington.

Erickson, M. H. (1983). *Healing in Hypnosis: The Seminars, Workshops & Lectures of Milton H. Erickson, Volume 1.* Edited by E. L. Rossi, M. O. Ryan, & F. A. Sharp. New York: Irvington.

Erickson, M. H. (1985). *Life Reframing in Hypnosis: The Seminars, Workshops, & Lectures of Milton H. Erickson, Volume 2.* Edited by E. L. Rossi and M. O. Ryan. New York: Irvington.

Erickson, M. H. (1986). *Mind-Body Communication in Hypnosis: The Seminars, Workshops, & Lectures of Milton H. Erickson, Volume 3.* Edited by E. L. Rossi & M. O. Ryan. New York: Irvington.

Erickson, M. H., & Erickson, E. M. (1958). Further considerations of time distortion: subjective time condensation as distinct from time expansion. *American Journal of Clinical Hypnosis, 1,* 83–88.

Erickson, M. H., & Kubie, , L. S. (1941). The successful treatment of a case of acute hysterical depression by a return under hypnosis to a critical phase of childhood. *Psychoanalytic Quarterly, 10,* 583–609.

Erickson, M. H., & Rossi, E. L. (1974/1980). Varieties of hypnotic amnesia. *American Journal of Clinical Hypnosis, 16*(4). Reprinted in E. L. Rossi (Ed.), *The Collected Papers of Milton H. Erickson on Hypnosis, Volume III.* New York: Irvington, pp. 71–90.

Erickson, M. H., & Rossi, E. L. (1975). Varieties of double bind. *American Journal of Clinical Hypnosis, 17,* 143–157.

Erickson, M. H., & Rossi, E. L. (1976). *Hypnotic Realities.* New York: Irvington.

Erickson, M. H., & Rossi, E. L. (1979). *Hypnotherapy: An Exploratory Casebook.* New York: Irvington.

Erickson, M. H., & Rossi, E. L. (1989). *The February Man: Evolving Consciousness & Identity in Hypnotherapy.* New York: Brunner/Mazel.

Esdaile, J. (1846/1976). *Mesmerism in India.* New York: Arno Press.

Evans, C., & Richardson, P. H. (1988). Improved recovery and reduced postoperative stay after therapeutic suggestions during general anesthesia. *Lancet, 2*(8609), 491–493.

Evans, F. (1979). Hypnosis and sleep: Techniques for exploring cognitive activity during sleep. Chapter in E. Fromm & R. Shor (Eds.), *Hypnosis: Developments in Research and New Perspectives.* New York: Aldine, pp. 139–183.

Evans, F., Gustafson, L. A., O'Connell, D. N., Orne, M. T., & Shor, R. E. (1966). Response during sleep with intervening waking amnesia. *Science, 152,* 666–667.

Evans, F., Gustafson, L. A., O'Connell, D. N., Orne, M. T., & Shor, R. E. (1969). Sleep-induced behavioral response: Relationship to susceptibility to hypnosis and laboratory sleep patterns. *Journal of Nervous and Mental Disease, 148,* 467–476.

Evans, F. J., & Thorn, W. A. F. (1966). Two types of post-hypnotic amnesia: Recall amnesia and source amnesia. *International Journal of Clinical & Experimental Hypnosis, 14,* 162–179.

Ewin, D. M. (1974). Condyloma acuminatum: Successful treatment of four cases by hypnosis. *American Journal of Clinical Hypnosis, 17*(2), 73–78.

Ewin, D. M. (1978). Clinical use of hypnosis for attenuation of burn depth. In F. H. Frankel & H. S. Zamansky (Eds.), *Hypnosis at its Bicentennial.* New York: Plenum.

Ewin, D. M. (1979). Hypnosis in burn therapy. In G. D. Burrows, D. R. Collison, & L. Dennerstein (Eds.), *Hypnosis, 1979.* Amsterdam-New York: Elsevier/North Holland Press.

Ewin, D. M. (1983). Emergency room hypnosis for the burned patient. *American Journal of Clinical Hypnosis, 26,* 5–8.

Fagan, J., & Shepherd, I. L. (1970). *Gestalt Therapy Now.* New York: Harper & Row.

Fava, G. A., & Pavan, L. (1976–77). Large bowel disorders. I. Illness configuration and life events. *Psychotherapy & Psychosomatics, 27,* 93–99.

Feinstein, A. D., & Morgan, R. M. (1986). Hypnosis in regulating bipolar affective disorders. *American Journal of Clinical Hypnosis, 29*(1), 29–38.

Fellows, B. J., & Creamer, M. (1978). An investigation of the role of 'hypnosis,' hypnotic susceptibility and hypnotic induction in the production of age regression. *British Journal of Social & Clinical Psychology, 17,* 165–171.

Fermouw, W. J., & Gross, R. (1983). Issues in cognitive-behavioral treatment of performance anxiety. Chapter in P. C. Kendall (Ed.), *Advances in Cognitive-Behavioral Research: Volume 2.* New York: Academic Press.

Fey, W. F. (1958). Doctrine and experience: Their influence upon the psychotherapist. *Journal of Consulting Psychology, 22,* 103–112.

Figley, C. R. (1978). *Stress Disorders Among Vietnam Veterans.* New York: Brunner/Mazel.

Finer, B. L., & Nylen, B. O. (1961). Cardiac arrest in the treatment of burns, and report on hypnosis as a substitute for anesthesia. *Plastic & Reconstructive Surgery, 27,* 49–.

Finkelstein, S. (1984). Hypnosis and dentistry. Chapter in W. C. Wester II., & A. H. Smith, Jr. (Eds.), *Clinical Hypnosis: A Multidisciplinary Approach.* Philadelphia: J. B. Lippincott, pp. 337–349.

Fischer, R. (1971). A cartography of the ecstatic and meditatives states: The experimental and experiential feature of a perception-hallucination continuum are considered. *Science, 174,* 897–904.

Fogel, B. S. (1984). The "sympathetic ear": Case reports of a self-hypnotic approach to chronic pain. *American*

Journal of Clinical Hypnosis, 27(2), 103–106.

Fogel, S., & Hoffer, A. (1962). Perceptual changes induced by hypnotic suggestion for the posthypnotic state. I. General account of the effect on personality. *Journal of Clinical & Experimental Psychopathology & Quarterly Review of Psychiatry & Neurology, 23*, 24–35.

Fowler, W. (1961). Hypnosis and learning. *Journal of Clinical & Experimental Hypnosis, 9*, 223–232.

Frank, E., Anderson, C., & Rubinstein, D. (1978) Frequency of sexual dysfunction in "normal" couples. *New England Journal of Medicine, 299*(3), 111–115.

Fredericks, L. E. (1980). The value of teaching hypnosis in the practice of anesthesiology. *International Journal of Clinical & Experimental Hypnosis, 28*, 6–12.

Freytag, F. K. (1961). *The Body Image in Gender Orientation Disturbances.* New York: Julian Press.

Fricton, J. R., & Roth, P. (1985). The effects of direct and indirect suggestion for analgesia in high and low susceptible subjects. *American Journal of Clinical Hypnosis, 27*, 226–231.

Friedman, H., & Taub, H. A. (1977). The use of hypnosis and biofeedback procedures for essential hypertension. *International Journal of Clinical & Experimental Hypnosis, 25*, 335–347.

Friedman, H., & Taub, H. A. (1978). A six-month follow-up of the use of hypnosis and biofeedback procedures in essential hypertension. *American Journal of Clinical Hypnosis, 20*, 184–188.

Fromm, E. (1965a). Hypnoanalysis: Theory and two case excerpts. *Psychotherapy: Theory, Research and Practice, 2*, 127–133.

Fromm, E. (1965b). Awareness versus consciousness. *Psychological Reports, 16*, 711–712.

Fromm, E. (1970). Age regression with unexpected reappearance of a repressed childhood language. *International Journal of Clinical & Experimental Hypnosis, 18*, 79–88.

Frumkin, L. R., Ripley, H. S., & Cox, G. B. (1978). Changes in cerebral hemispheric lateralization with hypnosis. *Biological Psychiatry, 13*, 741–750.

Fuchs, K, Brandes, J, & Peretz, A. (1967). Treatment of hyperemesis gravidarum by hypnosis. *Hanfuah, 72*, 375–378.

Fuchs, K., Marcovici, R., Peretz, B. A., & Paldi, E. (Panelists). The use of hypnosis in obstetrics. International Congress of the Israeli Society of Hypnosis in Psychotherapy & Psychosomatic Medicine. Haifa, Israel (1983). Cited in H. B. Crasilneck & J. A. Hall (1985). *Clinical Hypnosis: Principles & Applications.* Orlando: Grune & Stratton.

Fuchs, K., Paldi, E., Abramovici, H., Peretz, B. A. (1980). Treatment of hyperemesis gravidarum by hypnosis. *International Journal of Clinical & Experimental Hypnosis, 28*, 313–323.

Fuller, A. K. (1986). A method for developing suggestions from the literature. *American Journal of Clinical Hypnosis, 29*(1), 47–52.

Gaal, J. M., Goldsmith, L., & Needs, R. E. (Nov. 1980).

The use of hypnosis, as an adjunct to anesthesia, to reduce pre- and post-operative anxiety in children. Paper presented at the Annual Scientific Meeting, American Society of Clinical Hypnosis, Minneapolis.

Galski, T. J. (1981). The adjunctive use of hypnosis in the treatment of trichotillomania: A case report. *American Journal of Clinical Hypnosis, 23*(3), 198–201.

Gard, B., & Kurtz, R. M. (1979). Hypnotic age regression and cognitive perceptual tasks. *American Journal of Clinical Hypnosis, 21*, 270–277.

Gardner, G. G. (1974). Parents: Obstacles or allies in child hypnotherapy? *American Journal of Clinical Hypnosis, 17*(1), 44–49.

Gardner, G. G. (1974b). Hypnosis with children. *International Journal of Clinical & Experimental Hypnosis, 22*, 20–38.

Gardner, G. G. (1976). Hypnosis and mastery: Clinical contributions and directions for research. *International Journal of Clinical & Experimental Hypnosis, 24*, 202–214.

Gardner, G. G. (1977). Hypnosis with infants and preschool children. *American Journal of Clinical Hypnosis, 19*, 158–162.

Gardner, M. (1957). *Fads and Fallacies in the Name of Science.* New York: Dover.

Garver, R. B. (1984). Eight steps to self-hypnosis. *American Journal of Clinical Hypnosis, 26*(4), 232–235.

Garver, R. B. (1987). Investigative hypnosis. A chapter in William Wester (Ed.), *Clinical Hypnosis A Case Management Approach.* Cincinnati: Behavioral Science Center, 1987.

Gaskin, I. M. (1978). *Spiritual Midwifery.* Summertown, TN: The Book Publishing Company.

Gerbert, B. (1980). Psychological aspects of Crohn's disease. *Journal of Behavioral Medicine, 3*, 41–58.

Gibbons, D. E. (1971). Directed experience hypnosis: A one-year follow-up investigation. *American Journal of Clinical Hypnosis, 13*, 101–103.

Gibbons, D. E. (1979). *Applied Hypnosis & Hyperempiria.* New York: Plenum.

Gibbons, D., Kilbourne, L., Saunders, A., & Castles, C. (1970). The cognitive control of behavior: A comparison of systematic desensitization and hypnotically induced "directed experience" techniques. *International Journal of clinical & Experimental Hypnosis, 12*, 141–145.

Gidro-Frank, L., & Bowersbuch, M. K. (1948). A study of the plantar response in hypnotic age regression. *Journal of Nervous & Mental Disease, 107*, 443–458.

Gillett, P. L., & Coe, W. C. (1984). The effects of rapid induction analgesia (RIA), hypnotic susceptibility, and severity of discomfort on reducing dental pain. *American Journal of Clinical Hypnosis, 27*, 81–90.

Gilligan, S. G. (1987). *Therapeutic Trances.* New York: Brunner/Mazel.

Gindes, B. C. (1951). *New Concepts of Hypnosis.* New York: Julian Press.

Gindhart, L. R. (1981). The use of a metaphoric story in

therapy: A case report. *American Journal of Clinical Hypnosis, 23*(3), 202–206.

Glick, B. S. (1970). Conditioning therapy with phobic patients: Success and failure. *American Journal of Psychotherapy, 24*, 92–101.

Golan, H. P. (1975). Hypnosis: Further case reports from the Boston City Hospital. *American Journal of Clinical Hypnosis, 12*, 55–59.

Golan, H. P. (1989). Temporomandibular joint disease treated with hypnosis. *American Journal of Clinical Hypnosis, 31*(4), 269–274.

Goldburgh, S. J. (1968). Hypnotherapy, chemotherapy, and expressive-directive therapy in the treatment of examination anxiety. *American Journal of Clinical Hypnosis, 11*, 42–44.

Goldmann, L. (1986). Awareness under general anesthesia. Unpublished doctoral dissertation, Cambridge University.

Goldmann, L, Shay, M. V., & Hebden, M. W. (1987). Memory of cardiac anesthesia. Psychological sequelae in cardiac patients of intra-operative suggestion and operating room conversation. *Anaesthesia, 42*(6), 596–603.

Gordon, D. (1978). *Therapeutic Metaphors.* Cupertino, CA: Meta Publications.

Gordon, J. E., & Freston, M. (1964). Role-playing and age regression in hypnotized and nonhypnotized subjects. *Journal of Personality, 32*, 411–419.

Gorman, B. J. (1974). An abstract technique for ego-strengthening. *American Journal of Clinical Hypnosis, 16*(3), 209–212.

Graef, J. R. (1969). The influence of cognitive states on time estimation and subjective time rate. Unpublished doctoral dissertation, University of Michigan, Ann Arbor.

Greene, R. J., & Reyher, J. (1972). Pain tolerance in hypnotic analgesia and imagination states. *Journal of Abnormal Psychology, 79*, 29–38.

Greenleaf, E. (1969). Developmental-stage regression through hypnosis. *American Journal of Clinical Hypnosis, 12*(1), 20– 36.

Grinker, R. R., & Spiegel, J. P. (1945). *Men Under Stress.* Philadelphia: Blakiston.

Grinker, R. R., & Spiegel, J. P. (1943). *War Neuroses in North Africa.* New York: Josiah Macy, Jr. Foundation.

Gross, M. (1984). Hypnosis in the therapy of anorexia nervosa. *American Journal of Clinical Hypnosis, 26*(3), 175–181.

Grosz, H. J. (1978a). Nicotine addiction: Treatment with medical hypnosis, part 1. *Journal of the Indiana State Medical Association, 71*, 1074-1075.

Grosz, H. J. (1978b). Nicotine addiction: Treatment with medical hypnosis, part 2. *Journal of the Indiana State Medical Association, 71*, 1136-1137.

Gruber, L. N. (1983). Hypnotherapeutic techniques with affective instability. *American Journal of Clinical Hypnosis, 25*, 263-266.

Gurman, A., & Kniskern, D. (1978a) Deterioration in marital and family therapy: Empirical, clinical and conceptual issues. *Family Process, 17*, 3-20.

Gurman, A., & Kniskern, D. (1978b) Research on marital and family therapy: Progress, perspective and prospect. Chapter in S. Garfield & A. Bergin (Eds.), *Handbook of Psychotherapy & Behavior Change.* New York: Wiley.

Gustavson, J. L., & Weight, D. G. (1981). Hypnotherapy for a phobia of slugs: A case report. *American Journal of Clinical Hypnosis, 23*, 258-262.

Haggendorn, J. (1970). The use of posthypnotic suggestions on recall and amnesia to facilitate retention and to produce forgetting for previously learned materials in classroom situation. Unpublished doctoral dissertation, University of Tulsa. *Dissertation Abstracts International, 30*(10-A), 4275.

Haley, J. (1973). *Uncommon Therapy: The Psychiatric Techniques of Milton H. Erickson, M.D.* New York: W. W. Norton.

Halfen, D. (March 12, 1986). What do "anesthetized" patients hear? *Anesthesiology News,* p. 12.

Hall, C. W. (1980). *Psychiatric Presentations of Medical Illness: Somatopsychic Disorders.* New York: SP Medical & Scientific Books.

Hall, H. R. (1982-1983). Hypnosis and the immune system: A review with implications for cancer and the psychology of healing. *American Journal of Clinical Hypnosis, 25*(2-3), 92-103.

Hammond, D. C. (1984a). Myths about Erickson and Ericksonian hypnosis. *American Journal of Clinical Hypnosis, 26*, 236-245.

Hammond, D. C. (1984b). Hypnosis in marital and sex therapy. Chapter in R. F. Stahmann & W. J. Hiebert (Eds.), *Counseling in Marital & Sexual Problems* (Third Edition). Lexington, Mass.: Lexington Books, pp. 115-130.

Hammond, D. C. (1985b). An instrument for utilizing client interests & individualizing hypnosis. *Ericksonian Monographs, 1,* 111-126.

Hammond, D. C. (1985c). Treatment of inhibited sexual desire. Chapter in J. Zeig (Ed.), *Ericksonian Psychotherapy. Volume II: Clinical Applications.* New York: Brunner/Mazel, 415-428.

Hammond, D. C. (1988a). Utilization & individualization in hypnosis. Chapter in D. Corydon Hammond (Ed.), *Hypnotic Induction & Suggestion: An Introductory Manual.* Des Plaines, IL: American Society of Clinical Hypnosis.

Hammond, D. C. (1988b). Will the real Milton Erickson please stand up? *International Journal of Clinical & Experimental Hypnosis, 36*(3), 173-181.

Hammond, D. C. (Ed.). (1988c). *Hypnotic Induction & Suggestion.* Des Plaines, IL: American Society of Clinical Hypnosis.

Hammond, D. C. (1988d). A clinical approach of a psychologist to PMS. Chapter in W. R. Keye (Ed.), *The Premenstrual Syndrome*. New York: Saunders, pp. 189-198.

Hammond, D. C. (1988e). The psychosocial consequences of Premenstrual Syndrome. Chapter in W. R. Keye (Ed.), *The Premenstrual Syndrome*. New York: Saunders, pp. 128-141.

Hammond, D. C. (Ed.) (1988f). *Learning Clinical Hypnosis: An Educational Resources Compendium*. Des Plaines, IL: American Society of Clinical Hypnosis.

Hammond, D. C., & Cheek, D. B. (1988). Ideomotor signaling: A method for rapid unconscious exploration. In D. C. Hammond (Ed.), *Hypnotic Induction & Suggestion: An Introductory Manual*. Des Plaines, IL: American Society of Clinical Hypnosis, pp. 90-97.

Hammond, D. C., Hepworth, D., & Smith, V. G. (1977). *Improving Therapeutic Communication*. San Francisco: Jossey-Bass.

Hammond, D. C., & Miller, S. (in press). *Integrative Hypnotherapy: A Comprehensive Approach*. New York: W. W. Norton.

Hammond, D. C., & Stanfield, K. (1977). *Multidimensional Psychotherapy*. Champaign, IL: Institute for Personality & Ability Testing.

Harris, M. (1986). Are "past-life" regressions evidence of reincarnation? *Free Inquiry*, *6*(4), 18-23.

Hartland, J. (1971a). *Medical & Dental Hypnosis* (Second Edition). London: Balliere Tindall.

Hartland, J. (1971b). Further observations on the use of "ego-strengthening" techniques. *American Journal of Clinical Hypnosis*, *14*, 1-8.

Heiman, J., & LoPiccolo, J. (1983). Clinical outcome of sex therapy: Effects of daily versus weekly treatment. *Archives of General Psychiatry*, *40*, 443-449.

Henker, F. O. (1976). Psychotherapy as adjunct in treatment of vomiting during pregnancy. *Southern Medical Journal*, *69*, 1585-1587.

Hilgard, E. R. (1977/1986). *Divided Consciousness: Multiple Controls in Human Thought & Action*. New York: Wiley.

Hilgard, J. R. (1970). *Personality and Hypnosis: A Study of Imaginative Involvement*. Chicago: University of Chicago Press.

Hilgard, J. R. (1979). Imaginative and sensory-affective involvements in everyday life and hypnosis. Chapter in E. Fromm & R. E. Shor (Eds.), *Hypnosis: Developments in Research & New Perspectives*. New York: Aldine, 1979, pp. 483-517.

Hilgard, J. R., Hilgard, E. R., & Newman, D. M. (1961). Sequelae to hypnotic induction with special reference to earlier chemical anesthesia. *Journal of Nervous & Mental Disease*, *133*, 461-478.

Hilgenberg, J. C. (1981). Intraoperative awareness during high-dose fentanyl-oxygen anesthesia. *Anesthesiology*, *54*, 341-343.

Hill, N. (1963). *Think & Grow Rich*. Greenwich, Conn.: Fawcett.

Hines, T. (1988). *Pseudoscience and the Paranormal: A Critical Examination of the Evidence*. Buffalo: Prometheus Books.

Hinshaw, J. R. (1963). Progressive changes in the depth of burns. *Archives of Surgery*, *87*, 993-997.

Hodge, J. R. (1959). Management of dissociative reactions with hypnosis. *International Journal of Clinical & Experimental Hypnosis*, *7*, 217-221.

Hodge, J. R. (1972). Hypnosis as a deterrent to suicide. *American Journal of Clinical Hypnosis*, *15*(1), 20-21.

Hodge, J. R. (1976). Contractual aspects of hypnosis. *International Journal of Clinical & Experimental Hypnosis*, *14*, 391-399.

Hodge, J. R. (1980). Hypnotherapy combined with psychotherapy. In T. B. Karasu and L. Bellak (Eds.), *Specialized Techniques in Individual Psychotherapy*. New York: Brunner/Mazel, pp. 400-425.

Hodge, J. R.(1988). Can hypnosis help psychosis? *American Journal of Clinical Hypnosis*, *30*(4), 248-256.

Hodge, J. R., & Babai, M. (1982). Strategies and tactics in hypnotherapy. Presentation to the annual scientific meeting, The American Society of Clinical Hypnosis, Denver, Colorado (October).

Hodge, J. R., & Wagner, E. E. (1964). The validity of hypnotically induced emotional states. *American Journal of Clinical Hypnosis*, *7*, 37-41.

Holcomb, L. (1970). The effects of hypnosis on the reading remediation of seventh grade boys. Unpublished doctoral dissertation, University of Oregon. *Dissertation Abstracts International*, *31*(5-A).

Holroyd, J. (1980). Hypnosis treatment for smoking: An evaluative review. *International Journal of Clinical & Experimental Hypnosis*, *28*, 341-357.

Holroyd, J., & Maguen, E. (1989). And so to sleep: Hypnotherapy for Lagophthalmos. *American Journal of Clinical Hypnosis*, *31*(4), 264-266.

Horowitz, S. L. (1970). Strategies within hypnosis for reducing phobic behavior. *Journal of Abnormal Psychology*, *75*, 104- 112.

Hoskovec, J., & Horvai, J. (1963). Speech manifestations in hypnotic age regression. *Activitas Nervosa Superior*, *5*, 13-21.

Howard, W. L., & Reardon, J. P. (1986). Changes in the self concept and athletic performance of weight lifters through a cognitive-hypnotic approach: An empirical study. *American Journal of Clinical Hypnosis*, *28*(4), 248-257.

Hunter, M. E. (1988). *Daydreams for Discovery: A Manual for Hypnotherapists*. Vancouver: SeaWalk Press.

Hutchings, D. D. (1961). The value of suggestion given under anesthesia: A report and evaluation of 200 consecutive cases. *American Journal of Clinical Hypnosis*, *4*, 26-29.

Jackson, J. A., Gass, G. C., & Camp, E. M. (1979). The relationship between posthypnotic suggestion and endurance in physically trained subjects. *International Journal of Clinical & Experimental Hypnosis*, *27*(3),

278-293.

Jacobson, E. (1973). *Teaching and Learning. New Methods for Old Arts*. Chicago: National Federal for Progressive Relaxation.

Janet, P. (1889). *L'Automatisme Psychologique*. Paris: Felix Alcan.

Jencks, B. (1977). *Your Body: Biofeedback at its Best*. Chicago: Nelson-Hall.

Jencks, B. (1979). *Exercise Manual for J. H. Schultz's Standard Autogenic Training and Special Formulas (With Appendixes on Procedures with Children and Advanced Autogenic Training)*. Des Plaines, IL: American Society of Clinical Hypnosis.

Jones, C. W. (1977). Hypnosis and spinal fusion by Harrington instrumentation. *American Journal of Clinical Hypnosis*, *19*, 155-157.

Kaplan, H. S. (1983). *The Evaluation of Sexual Disorders*. New York: Brunner/Mazel.

Kaplan, H. S. (1979) *Disorders of Sexual Desire*. New York: Brunner/Mazel.

Kaplan, H. S. (1983). *Evaluation of Sexual Disorders*. New York: Brunner/Mazel.

Kardiner, A., & Spiegel, H. (1947). *War Stress & Neurotic Illness*. New York: Hoeber.

Karoly, P., & Jensen, M. P. (1987). *Multimethod Assessment of Chronic Pain*. New York: Pergamon Press.

Kelly, M. A., McKinty, H. R., & Carr, R. (1988). Utilization of hypnosis to promote compliance with routine dental flossing. *American Journal of Clinical Hypnosis*, *31*(1), 57-60.

Kelsey, D., & Barron, J. N. (1958). Maintenance of posture by hypnotic suggestion in patients undergoing plastic surgery. *British Medical Journal*, *1*, 756.

Kilmann, P. R., Boland, J. P., Norton, S. P., Davidson, E., & Caid, C. (1986). Perspectives of sex therapy outcome: A survey of AASECT providers. *Journal of Sex & Marital Therapy*, *12*(2), 116-138.

Klauber, R. W. (1984). Hypnosis in education and school psychology. Chapter in W. C. Wester & A. H. Smith (Eds.), *Clinical Hypnosis: A Multidisciplinary Approach*. Philadelphia: J. B. Lippincott.

Klein, K. B., & Spiegel, D. (1989). Modulation of gastric acid secretion by hypnosis. *Gastroenterology*, *96*(6), 1383-1387.

Kleinhauz, M. & Beran, B. (1984). Misuse of hypnosis: A factor in psychopathology. *American Journal of Clinical Hypnosis*, *26*, 283-290.

Kline, M. V. (1956). *A Scientific Report on the Search for Bridey Murphy*. New York: Julian Press.

Kline, M. V. (1970). The use of extended group hypnotherapy sessions in controlling cigarette habituation. *International Journal of Clinical & Experimental Hypnosis*, *18*, 270-282.

Kline, M. V. (1976). Emotional flooding: A technique in sensory hypnoanalysis. Chapter in P. Olsen (Ed.). *Emotional Flooding*. New York: Human Sciences Press.

Kluft, R. P. (1982). Varieties of hypnotic interventions in the treatment of multiple personality. *American Journal of Clinical Hypnosis*, *24*, 230-240.

Kluft, R. P. (1983). Hypnotherapeutic crisis intervention in multiple personality. *American Journal of Clinical Hypnosis*, *26*, 73-83.

Kluft, R. P. (1985a). Using hypnotic inquiry protocols to monitor treatment progress and stability in multiple personality disorder. *American Journal of Clinical Hypnosis*, *28*, 63-75.

Kluft, R. P. (1985b). Hypnotherapy of childhood multiple personality disorder. *American Journal of Clinical Hypnosis*, *27*, 201-210.

Kluft, R. P. (1986). Preliminary observations on age regression in multiple personality disorder patients before and after integration. *American Journal of Clinical Hypnosis*, *28*, 147-156.

Knudson, R. A. (1968). A program for improving reading efficiency through the use of suggestion. Unpublished doctoral dissertation. *Dissertation Abstracts International*, *29*(1-B), 359.

Koe, G. G., & Oldridge, O. A. (1988). The effect of hypnotically induced suggestions on reading performance. *International Journal of Clinical & Experimental Hypnosis*, *36*(4), 275-283.

Kohen, D. P. (1986). Applications of relaxation/mental imagery (self-hypnosis) in pediatric emergencies. *International Journal of Clinical & Experimental Hypnosis*, *34*, 283-294.

Kohl, R. (1962) Pathological reactions of marital partners to improvement of patients. *American Journal of Psychiatry*, *118*, 1036-1041.

Kolodny, R. C., Masters, W. H., & Johnson, V. E. (1979). *Textbook of Sexual Medicine*. Boston: Little, Brown & Company.

Kolough, F. T. (1962). Role of suggestion in surgical convalescence. *Archives of Surgery*, *85*, 304-315.

Kolough, F. T. (1964). Hypnosis and surgical convalescence: A study of subjective factors in postoperative recovery. *American Journal of Clinical Hypnosis*, *7*, 120-129.

Korn, E. R., & Pratt, G. J. (1988). *Release Your Business Potential*. (Cassette recording). New York: John Wiley & Sons.

Krane, R. J., Siroky, M. B., & Goldstein, I. (1983). *Male Sexual Dysfunction*. Boston: Little, Brown & Company.

Kratochvil, S. (1970). Prolonged hypnosis and sleep. *American Journal of Clinical Hypnosis*, *12*(4), 254-260.

Krauss, D. (1983). The physiologic basis of male sexual dysfunction. *Hospital Practice*, *2*, 193-222.

Krippner, S. (1963). Hypnosis and reading improvement among university students. *American Journal of Clinical Hypnosis*, *15*, 187-193.

Krippner, S. (1966). The use of hypnosis with elementary and secondary school children in a summer reading clinic. *American Journal of Clinical Hypnosis*, *8*(4), 261-264.

Kroger, W. S. (1970). Comprehensive management of

obesity. *American Journal of Clinical Hypnosis, 12*(3), 165-175.

Kroger, W. S. (1977). *Clinical & Experimental Hypnosis* (Second Edition). Philadelphia: J. B. Lippincott.

Kroger, W. S., & Fezler, W. D. (1976). *Hypnosis and Behavior Modification: Imagery Conditioning*. Philadelphia: J. B. Lippincott.

Kumar, S. M., Pandit, S. K., & Jackson, P. F. (1978). Recall following ketamine anesthesia for open-heart surgery: Report of a case. *Anesthesia & Analgesia, 57*(2), 267-269.

Kupper, H. I. (1945). Psychic concomitants in wartime injuries. *Psychosomatic Medicine, 7*, 15-21.

Kuriyama, K. (1968). Clinical applications of prolonged hypnosis in psychosomatic medicine. *American Journal of Clinical Hypnosis, 11*(2), 101-111.

LaBaw, W. L. (1970). Regular use of suggestibility by pediatric bleeders. *Haematologica, 4*, 419-425.

LaBaw, W. L. (1975). Autohypnosis in hemophilia. *Haematologica, 9*, 103-110.

LeBaron, S., & Zeltzer, L. (1985). Hypnosis for hemophiliacs: Methodological problems and risks. *American Journal of Pediatric Hematology & Oncology, 7*(3), 316-319.

Lait, V. S. (1961). Effect of hypnosis on edema: A case report. *American Journal of Clinical Hypnosis, 3*, 200.

Lankton, C. H. (1985). Elements in an Ericksonian approach. *Ericksonian Monographs, 1*, 61-75/

Lankton, C. H.., & Lankton, S. R. (1989). *Tales of Enchantment*. New York: Brunner/Mazel.

Lankton, S. R., & Lankton, C. H. (1983). *The Answer Within*. New York: Brunner/Mazel.

Laughlin, H. P. (1967). *The Neuroses*. Baltimore: Reese Press.

Laurence, J. R., & Perry, C. (1981). The "hidden observer" phenomenon in hypnosis: Some additional findings. *Journal of Abnormal Psychology, 90*, 334-344.

Laurence, J. R., & Perry, C. (1988). *Hypnosis, Will and Memory*. New York: Guilford.

Lazarus, A. A. (1971). *Behavior Therapy & Beyond*. New York: McGraw-Hill.

Lazarus, A. A. (1981). *The Practice of Multimodal Therapy*. New York: McGraw-Hill.

Lazarus, A. A. (1989). *The Practice of Multimodal Therapy* (Second Edition). Baltimore: John Hopkins University Press.

Leavitt, F., Garron, D. C., Whisler, W. W., & Sheinkop, M. B. (1978). Affective and sensory dimensions of back pain. *Pain, 4*, 273-281.

LeBaron, S., & Zeltzer, L. (1985). Hypnosis for hemophiliacs: Methodological problems and risks. *American Journal of Pediatric Hematology & Oncology, 7*(3), 316-319.

Leckie, F. H. (1964). Hypnotherapy in gynecological disorders. *International Journal of Clinical & Experimental Hypnosis, 13*, 11-25.

Leckie, F. H. (1965). Further gynecological conditions treated by hypnotherapy. *International Journal of*

Clinical & Experimental Hypnosis, 13*(1), 11-25.

Leiblum, S. R., & Rosen, R. C. (1988). *Sexual Desire Disorders*. New York: Guilford.

Levine, B. A. (1976). Treatment of trichotillomania by covert sensitization. *Journal of Behavior Therapy & Experimental Psychiatry, 7*, 75-76.

Levine, E. S. (1980). Indirect suggestions through personalized fairy tales for treatment of childhood insomnia. *American Journal of Clinical Hypnosis, 23*(1), 57-63.

Levinson, B. W. (1965). States of awareness during general anaesthesia. *British Journal of Anaesthesia, 37*, 544-546.

Levinson, B. W. (1969). An examination of states of awareness during general anesthesia. Unpublished doctoral dissertation, University of Witwatersrand, South Africa.

Levitan, A. A. (1985). Hypnotic death rehearsal. *American Journal of Clinical Hypnosis, 27*(4), 211-215.

Levitan, A. A. (1987). Hypnosis and oncology. Chapter in W. C. Wester, *Clinical Hypnosis: A Case Management Approach*. Cincinnati: Behavioral Science Center, pp. 332-356.

Lewenstein, L. N., Iwamoto, K., & Schwartz, H. (1981). Hypnosis in high risk surgery. *Ophthalmologic Surgery, 12*, 39-.

Lewis, S. A., Jenkinson, J., & Wilson, J. (1973). An EEG investigation of awareness during anaesthesia. *British Journal of Psychology, 64*(3), 413-415.

Lieberman, M. A., Yalom, E. D., & Miles, M. B. (1973). *Encounter Groups: First Facts*. New York: Basic Books.

Liebert, R. M., Rubin, N., & Hilgard, E. R. (1965). The effects of suggestion of alertness in hypnosis on paired-associate learning. *Journal of Personality, 33*, 605-612.

Leibowitz, H. W., Graham, C., & Parrish, M. (1972). The effect of hypnotic age regression on size constancy. *American Journal of Psychology, 85*, 271-276.

Lief, H. (1977) What's new in sex research? Inhibited Sexual Desire. *Medical Aspects of Human Sexuality, 11*(7), 94-95.

Lief, H. (1985). Evaluation of inhibited sexual desire: Relationship aspects. Chapter in H. S. Kaplan (Ed.), *Comprehensive evaluation of disorders of sexual desire*. Washington, D.C.: American Psychiatric Press.

Lindemann, H. (1958). *Alone at Sea*. New York: Random House.

Lodato, F. (1969). Hypnosis as an adjunct to test performance. *American Journal of Clinical Hypnosis, 6*, 276-279.

Loftus, E. F., Schooler, J. W., Loftus, G. R., & Glauber, D. T. (1985). Memory for events occurring under anesthesia. *Acta Psychologica, 59*, 123-128.

Logsdon, F. M. (1960). Age regression in diagnosis and treatment of acrophobia. *American Journal of Clinical Hypnosis, 3*, 108-109.

London, P., & Cooper, L. M. (1969). Norms of hypnotic susceptibility in children. *Developmental Psychology, 1*, 113-124.

Loomis, E. A. (1951). Space and time perception and distortion in hypnotic states. *Personality*, *1*, 283.

LoPiccolo, L. (1980) Low sexual desire. Chapter in S. R. Leiblum & L. A. Pervin (Eds.), *Principles & Practice of Sex Therapy*. New York: Guilford, 29-64.

Lugan, W. G. (1963). Delay of premature labor by the use of hypnosis. *American Journal of Clinical Hypnosis*, *5*, 209-211.

Lynn, S. J., Neufeld, V., & Matyi, C. L. (1987). Inductions versus suggestions: Effects of direct and indirect wording on hypnotic responding and experience. *Journal of Abnormal Psychology*, *96*, 76-79.

Lynn, S. J., Weekes, J. R., Matyi, C. L., & Neufeld, V. (1988). Direct versus indirect suggestions, archaic involvement, and hypnotic experience. *Journal of Abnormal Psychology*, *97*(3), 296-301.

MacHovec, F. J., & Man, S. C. (1978). Acupuncture and hypnosis compared: Fifty-eight cases. *American Journal of Clinical Hypnosis*, *21*, 45-47.

Mainord, W. A., Rath, B., & Barnett, F. (1983). Anesthesia and suggestion. Paper presented at the 91st Annual Convention of the American Psychological Association, Los Angeles. Cited in H. L. Bennett, Perception and memory for events during adequate general anesthesia for surgical operations. Chapter in H. M. Pettinati (Ed.), *Hypnosis and Memory*. New York: Guilford.

Maltz, M. (1960). *Psycho-Cybernetics*. New York: Prentice-Hall.

Mann, H. (1973). Suggestions based on unlimited calorie, low carbohydrate diet. *A Syllabus on Hypnosis and a Handbook of Therapeutic Suggestions*. Des Plaines, IL: American Society of Clinical Hypnosis, pp. 81-83.

Mann, H. (1981). Hypnosis in weight control. Chapter in H. J. Wain (Ed.), *Theoretical and Clinical Aspects of Hypnosis*. Miami: Symposia Specialists, Inc.

Maoz, B., & Pincus, C. (1979). The therapeutic dialogue in narco-analytic treatments. *Psychotherapy: Theory, Research & Practice*, *16*, 91-97.

Margolis, C. G., Domangue, B. B., Ehleben, C., & Shrier, L. (1983). Hypnosis in the early treatment of burns: A pilot study. *American Journal of Clinical Hypnosis*, *26*(1), 9-15.

Marks, I. M., Gelder, M. G., & Edwards, G. (1968). Hypnosis and desensitization for phobias: A controlled prospective trial. *British Journal of Psychiatry*, *114*, 1263-1274.

Marlatt, G. A. (1985). Situational determinants of relapse and skill-training interventions. Chapter in G. A. Marlatt & J. R. Gordon, *Relapse Prevention: Maintenance Strategies in the Treatment of Addictive Behaviors*. New York: Guilford, pp. 71-127.

Marlatt, G. A., & Gordon, J. R. (1980). Determinants of relapse: Implications for the maintenance of behavior change. Chapter in P. O. Davidson & S. M. Davidson (Eds.), *Behavioral Medicine: Changing Health Life Styles*. New York: Brunner/Mazel, pp. 410-452.

Marlatt, G. A., & Gordon, J. R. (Eds.). (1985). *Relapse Prevention*. New York: Guilford.

Marmer, M. J. (1959). *Hypnosis in Anesthesiology*. Springfield: Charles C. Thomas.

Maslach, C., Marshall, G., & Zimbardo, P. G. (1972). Hypnotic control of peripheral skin temperature: A case report. *Psychophysiology*, *9*, 600-605.

Mastellone, M. (1974). Aversion therapy: A new use for the old rubber band. *Journal of Behavior Therapy & Experimental Psychiatry*, *5*, 311-312.

Master, W., & Johnson, V. (1970) *Human Sexual Inadequacy*. Boston: Little Brown & Co.

Masters, W. H., Johnson, V. E., & Kolodny, R. C. (1977). *Ethical Issues in Sex Therapy & Research*. Boston: Little, Brown & Company.

Masters, W. H., Johnson, V. E., Kolodny, R. C., & Weems, S. M. (1980). *Ethical Issues in Sex Therapy & Research, Volume 2*. Boston: Little, Brown & Company.

Matthews, W. J., Bennett, H., Bean, W., & Gallagher, M. (1985). Indirect versus direct hypnotic suggestions— An initial investigation: A brief communication. *International Journal of Clinical & Experimental Hypnosis*, *33*, 219-223.

Matthews, W. J., Kirsch, I., & Mosher, D. (1985). Double hypnotic induction: An initial empirical test. *Journal of Abnormal Psychology*, *94*, 92-95.

Matthews, W. J., & Mosher, D. L. (1988). Direct and indirect hypnotic suggestion in a laboratory setting. *British Journal of Experimental & Clinical Hypnosis*, *5*(2), 63-71.

May, R. (1958). Contributions of existential psychotherapy. Chapter in R. May, E. Angel, & H. F. Ellenberger (Eds.), *Existence: A New Dimension in Psychiatry & Psychology*. New York: Simon & Schuster, 37-91.

McConkey, K. (1984). The impact of an indirect suggestion. *International Journal of Clinical & Experimental Hypnosis*, *32*, 307-314.

McIntyre, K. O., Lichtenstein, E., & Mermelstein, R. J. (1983). Self-efficacy and relapse in smoking cessation: A replication and extension. *Journal of Consulting & Clinical Psychology*, *51*, 632-633.

Meares, A. (1983). A form of intensive meditation associated with the regression of cancer. *American Journal of Clinical Hypnosis*, *25*(2-3), 114-121.

Meares, A. (1979). Regression of cancer of the rectum following intensive meditation. *Medical Journal of Australia*, 539-40.

Meichenbaum, D. (1971). Cognitive factors in behavior modification: Modifying what people say to themselves. Paper presented at the Fifth Annual Meeting of the Association for the Advancement of Behavior Therapy, Washington, D.C.

Mellegren, A. (1966). Practical experiences with a modified hypnosis-delivery. *Psychotherapy & Psychosomatics*, *14*, 425-428.

Mellenbruch, P. (1964). Hypnosis in student counseling.

American Journal of Clinical Hypnosis, 7(1), 60-63.

Melzack, R. (1975). The McGill Pain Questionnaire. In R. Melzack (Ed.), *Pain Measurement & Assessment.* New York: Raven.

Millar, K., & Watkinson, N. (1983). Recognition of words presented during general anesthesia. *Ergonomics, 26,* 585-594.

Miller, S. (1977). Dialogue with the higher self. *Synthesis 2.* San Francisco: Institute for the Study of Humanistic Medicine, 285-300.

Mills, J. C., & Crowley, R. J. (1986). *Therapeutic Metaphors for Children and the Child Within.* New York: Brunner/Mazel.

Minalyka, E. E., & Whanger, A. D. (1959). Tonsillectomies under hypnosis: Report of Cases. *American Journal of Clinical Hypnosis, 2,* 87-89.

Mitchell, W. M. (1972). *The Use of Hypnosis in Athletics.* Stockton: Mitchell.

Mody, N. V. (1960). Report on twenty cases delivered under hypnotism. *Journal of Obstetrics & Gynecology in India, 10,* 3-8.

Monteiro, A. R. de C., de Oliveira, D. A. (1958). Amigdalectomia sob hipnose [Tonsillectomy under hypnosis]. *Medicine Cirsugia Formaria, 267,* 315-320.

Moore, R. K., & Cooper, L. M. (1966). Item difficulty in childhood hypnotic susceptibility scales as a function of item wording, repetition, and age. *International Journal of Clinical & Experimental Hypnosis, 14,* 316-323.

Moore, R. K., & Lauer, L. W. (1963). Hypnotic susceptibility in middle childhood. *International Journal of Clinical & Experimental Hypnosis, 11,* 167-174.

Morgan, A. H., & Hilgard, E. R. (1973). Age differences in susceptibility to hypnosis. *International Journal of Clinical & Experimental Hypnosis, 21,* 78-85.

Morgan, A. H., & Hilgard, J. R. (1979). The Stanford Hypnotic Clinical Scale for Children. *American Journal of Clinical Hypnosis, 21,* 148-155.

Mosconi, G., & Starcich, B. (1961). Preparacion del parto con hipnosis (Preparation for childbirth with hypnosis). *Review of Latin American Hypnosis Clinics, 2,* 29-34.

Moss, C. S. (1965). *Hypnosis in Perspective.* New York: Macmillan.

Mozdzierz, G. J. (1985). The use of hypnosis and paradox in the treatment of a case of chronic urinary retention/"bashful bladder." *American Journal of Clinical Hypnosis, 28*(1), 43-47.

Muehleman, T. (1978). Age regression as a possible enhancement to conception: A case report. *American Journal of Clinical Hypnosis, 20*(4), 282-283.

Murphy, J. K., & Fuller, A. K. (1984). Hypnosis and biofeedback as adjunctive therapy in blepharospasm: A case report. *American Journal of Clinical Hypnosis, 27*(1), 31-37.

Murphy, M. B. (1988). A linguistic-structural model for the investigation of indirect suggestion. *Ericksonian*

Monographs, 4, 12-27.

Murray-Jobsis, J. (1984). Hypnosis with severely disturbed patients. Chapter in W. C. Wester II & A. H. Smith, Jr., (Eds.), *Clinical Hypnosis: A Multidisciplinary Approach.* Philadelphia: J. B. Lippincott, pp. 368-404.

Murray-Jobsis, J. (1985). Exploring the schizophrenic experience with the use of hypnosis. *American Journal of Clinical Hypnosis, 28,* 34-42.

Mutke, P. (1967). Increased reading comprehension through hypnosis. *American Journal of Clinical Hypnosis, 9*(4), 262-264.

Narcuse, G. (1964a). "Agari" no tsisaku ni tsuite (On a treatment of stage fright). *Olympia, 6,* 29-.

Narcuse, G. (1964b). Hypnotic treatment of stage fright in champion athletes. *Psychologia, 7*(324), 199-.

Narcuse, G. (1965). The hypnotic treatment of stage fright in champion athletes. *International Journal of Clinical & Experimental Hypnosis, 13,* 63-70.

Nash, M. R. (1988). Hypnosis as a window on regression. *Bulletin of the Menninger Clinic, 52*(5), 383-403.

Nash, , M. R., Johnson, L. S., & Tipton, R. D. (1979). Hypnotic age regression and the occurrence of transitional object relationships. *Journal of Abnormal Psychology, 88,* 547-555.

Nash, M. R., Lynn, S. J., & Givens, D. L. (1984). Adult hypnotic susceptibility, childhood punishment, and child abuse: A brief communication. *International Journal of Clinical & Experimental Hypnosis, 32,* 6-11.

Newton, B. W. (1982-83). The use of hypnosis in the treatment of cancer patients. *American Journal of Clinical Hypnosis, 25*(2-3), 104-113.

Norcross, J. C. (1986). *Handbook of Eclectic Psychotherapy.* New York: Brunner/Mazel.

Norcross, J. C., & Prochaska, J. O. (1982). A national survey of clinical psychologists: Affiliations and orientations. *The Clinical Psychologist, 35*(3), 1, 4-6.

Nowlis, D. P. (1969). The child-rearing antecedents of hypnotic susceptibility and of naturally occurring hypnotic-like experience. *International Journal of Clinical & Experimental Hypnosis, 17,* 109-120.

Nuland, W., & Field, P. B. (1970). Smoking and hypnosis: A systematic clinical approach. *International Journal of Clinical & Experimental Hypnosis, 18,* 290-306.

O'Brien, R. M., Kramer, C. E., Chiglinsky, M. A., Stevens, G., Nunan, L., & Fritzo, J. (1977). Moral development examined through hypnotic and task motivated age regression. *American Journal of Clinical Hypnosis, 19,* 209-213.

O'Connell, D. N., Shor, R. E., & Orne, M. T. (1970). Hypnotic age regression: An empirical and methodological analysis. *Journal of Abnormal Psychology, 76* (Monograph Issue No. 3, Pt. 2).

Oetting, E. R. (1964). Hypnosis and concentration in study. *American Journal of Clinical Hypnosis, 7*(2), 148-151.

Olness, K., & Gardner, G. G. (1988). *Hypnosis and*

Hypnotherapy with Children (Second Edition). Philadelphia: Grune & Stratton.

Omer, H. (1987). A hypnotic relaxation technique for the treatment of premature labor. *American Journal of Clinical Hypnosis, 29*(3), 206-213.

Omer, H., Darnel, A., Silberman, N., Shuval, D., & Palti, T. (1988). The use of hypnotic-relaxation cassettes in a gynecologic-obstetric ward. *Ericksonian Monographs, 4*, 28-36.

Omer, H., Friedlander, D., & Palti, Z. (1986). Hypnotic relaxation in the treatment of premature labor. *Psychosomatic Medicine, 48*, 351-361.

Orme, J. E. (1962). Time estimation and personality. *Journal of Mental Science, 108*, 213.

Orme, J. E. (1964). Personality, time estimation, and time experience. *Acta Psychologica, 22*, 430.

Orme, J. E. (1969). *Time, Experience, & Behavior*. New York: American Elsevier.

Orne, M. T. (1951). The mechanisms of hypnotic age regression: An experimental study. *Journal of Abnormal & Social Psychology, 46*, 213-225.

Orne, M. T. (1959). The nature of hypnosis: Artifact and essence. *Journal of Abnormal and Social Psychology, 58*, 277-299.

Orr, R. G. (1970). Hypnosis helps reluctant smokers. *Practitioner, 205*, 204-208.

Parloff, M. B., Washow, I. E., & Wolfe, B. E. (1978). Research on therapist variables in relation to process and outcome. In S. L. Garfield & A. E. Bergin (Eds.), *Handbook of Psychotherapy & Behavior Change* (2nd Edition). New York: Wiley.

Pearson, R. (1961). Response to suggestions given under general anesthesia. *American Journal of Clinical Hypnosis, 4*, 106-114.

Pederson, L. L., Scrimgeour, W. G., & Lefcoe, N. M. (1975). Comparison of hypnosis plus counseling, counseling alone, and hypnosis alone in a community service smoking withdrawal program. *Journal of Consulting & Clinical Psychology, 43*, 920.

Pelletier, A. M. (1979). Three uses of guided imagery in hypnosis. *American Journal of Clinical Hypnosis, 22*(1), 32-36.

Pennebaker, J. W., & Beall, S. K. (1986). Confronting a traumatic event: Toward an understanding of inhibition and disease. *Journal of Abnormal Psychology, 95*(3), 274-281.

Pennebaker, J. W., Kiecolt-Glaser, J. K., & Glaser, R. (1988). disclosure of traumas and immune function: Health implications for psychotherapy. *Journal of Consulting & Clinical Psychology, 56*(2), 239-245.

Pennebaker, J. W., & O'Heeron, R. C. (1984). Confiding in others and illness rates among spouses of suicide and accidental-death victims. *Journal of Abnormal Psychology, 93*, 473-476.

Perry, C., & Chisholm, W. (1973). Hypnotic age regression and the Ponzo and Poggendorff illusions. *International Journal of Clinical & Experimental Hypnosis, 21*, 192-204.

Perry, C. W., Evans, F., O'Connell, D. N., Orne, E. C., & Orne, M. T. (1978). Behavioral response to verbal stimuli administered and tested during REM sleep: A further investigation. *Waking & Sleeping, 2*, 35-42.

Peterson, G. F. (1981). *Birthing Normally: A Personal Growth Approach to Childbirth*. Berkeley: Mindbody Press.

Pettinati, H. M. (1982). Measuring hypnotizability in psychotic patients. *International Journal of Clinical & Experimental Hypnosis, 30*, 404-416.

Pettinati, H. M. (Ed.). (1988). *Hypnosis & Memory*. New York: Guilford.

Pettinati, H. M., Horne, R. L., & Staats, J. M. (1985). Hypnotizability in patients with anorexia nervosa and bulimia. *Archives of General Psychiatry, 42*, 1014-1016.

Poncelet, N. M. (1982). The training of a couple in hypnosis for childbirth: A clinical session [Videotape]. Western Psychiatric Institute and Clinic Library, 3811 O'Hara Street, Pittsburgh, PA 15213.

Poncelet, N. M. (1983). A family systems view of emotional disturbance during pregnancy. *Clinical Social Work Journal, 11*, 1.

Poncelet, N. M. (1985). An Ericksonian approach to childbirth. Chapter in J. K. Zeig (Ed.). *Ericksonian Psychotherapy: Volume II*. New York: Brunner/Mazel, pp. 267-285.

Porter, J. (1974). Personalistic considerations for the hypnotherapist drawing from both humanistic and learning orientations. *Australian Journal of Clinical Hypnosis, 2*, 101-105.

Porter, J. (1975). Self-hypnosis for study success. *S.A. Teachers Journal, 1*, 14.

Porter, J. (1976). Self-hypnosis as self-management for student problems involving the self-concept. Paper presented to Murray Park College of Advanced Education, Adelaide.

Porter, J. (1978). Suggestions and success imagery for study problems. *International Journal of Clinical & Experimental Hypnosis, 26*(2), 63-75.

Porter, J. W., Woodward, J. A., Bisbee, C. T., & Fenker, R. M. (1972). Effect of hypnotic age regression on the magnitude of the Ponzo illusion: A replication. *Journal of Abnormal Psychology, 79*, 189-194.

Premack, D. (1959). Toward empirical behavior laws: I. Positive reinforcement. *Psychological Review, 66*, 219-133.

Price, D. D., & Barber, J. (1987). An analysis of factors that contribute to the efficacy of hypnotic analgesia. *Journal of Abnormal Psychology, 96*(1), 46-51.

Prochaska, J. O., & DiClemente, C. C. (1984). *The Transtheoretical Approach: Crossing the Traditional Boundaries of Therapy*. Homewood, IL: Dow Jones-Irvin.

Pryor, G. J., Kilpatrick, W. R., Opp, D. R., et al. (1980). Local anesthesia in minor lacerations: Topical TAC vs lidocaine infiltration. *Annals of Emergency Medicine, 9*(November), 568-571.

Putnam, F. W. (1989). *Diagnosis & Treatment of Multiple Personality Disorder*. New York: Guilford.

Putnam, F. W., Guroff, J. J., Silberman, E. K., Barban, L., & Post, R. M. (1986). The clinical phenomenology of multiple personality disorder: A review of 100 recent cases. *Journal of Clinical Psychiatry*, 47, 285-293.

Raikov, V. L. (1976). The possibility of creativity in the active stage of hypnosis. *International Journal of Clinical & Experimental Hypnosis*, 24, 258-268.

Raikov, V. L. (1980). Age regression to infancy by adult subjects in deep hypnosis. *American Journal of Clinical Hypnosis*, 22(3), 156-163.

Raikov, V. L. (1982). Hypnotic age regression to the neonatal period: Comparisons with role playing. *International Journal of Clinical & Experimental Hypnosis*, 30, 108-116.

Rath, B. (1982). The use of suggestions during general anesthesia. Unpublished doctoral dissertation, University of Louisville.

Rausch, V. (1980). Cholecystectomy with self-hypnosis. *American Journal of Clinical Hypnosis*, 11, 124-130.

Rausch, V. (1987). Dental hypnosis. Chapter in W. C. Wester, *Clinical Hypnosis: A Case Management Approach*. Cincinnati: Behavioral Science Center Publications, pp. 85-95.

Read, A. D. (1944). *Childbirth Without Fear*. New York: Harper Brothers.

Redd, W. H., Rosenberger, P. H., & Hendler, C. S. (1983). Controlling chemotherapy side effects. *American Journal of Clinical Hypnosis*, 25, 161-172.

Reiff, R., & Scheerer, M. (1959). *Memory and Hypnotic Age Regression: Developmental Aspects of Cognitive Function Explored Through Hypnosis*. New York: International Universities Press.

Reyher, J., & Wilson, J. (1973). The induction of hypnosis: Indirect vs. direct methods and the role of anxiety. *American Journal of Clinical Hypnosis*, 15, 229-233.

Rist, F., & Watzl, H. (1983). Self-assessment of relapse risk and assertiveness in relation to treatment outcome of female alcoholics. *Addictive Behaviors*, 8, 121-127.

Roberts, D. (1984). Hypnotically induced age regression versus age regression in response to task motivation instructions on five developmental tasks. Doctoral dissertation, Hofstra University. *Dissertation Abstracts International*, 45(5), 1594B.

Rock, N. L., Shipley, T. E., & Campbell, C. (1969). Hypnosis with untrained nonvolunteer patients in labor. *International Journal of Clinical and Experimental Hypnosis*, 17(1), 25-36.

Rodger, B. P. (1982). Ericksonian approaches in anesthesiology. Chapter in J. K. Zeig (Ed.), *Ericksonian Approaches to Hypnosis & Psychotherapy*. New York: Brunner/Mazel.

Rosen, H. (1953). *Hypnotherapy in Clinical Psychiatry*. New York: Julian Press.

Rosen, H., & Myers, H. J. (1947). Abreaction in the military setting. *Archives of Neurology & Psychiatry*, 57, 161-172.

Rosen, S. (1982). *My Voice Will Go With You: The Teaching Tales of Milton H. Erickson*. New York: W. W. Norton.

Rosen, S. (1985). Hypnosis as an adjunct to chemotherapy in cancer. Chapter in J. K. Zeig (Ed.), *Ericksonian Psychotherapy: Volume II*. New York: Brunner/Mazel, pp. 387-397.

Rosenberg, S. W. (1983). Hypnosis in cancer care: Imagery to enhance the control of the physiological and psychological "side-effects" of cancer therapy. *American Journal of Clinical Hypnosis*, 25(2-3), 122-127.

Rosenthal, R., & Jacobson, L. (1968). *Pygmalion in the Classroom: Teacher Expectation and Pupils" Intellectual Development*. New York: Holt, Rinehart & Winston.

Rossi, E. L. (1986). *The Psychobiology of Mind-Body Healing: New Concepts of Therapeutic Hypnosis*. New York: W. W. Norton.

Rossi, E. L., & Cheek, D. B. (1988). *Mind-Body Therapy*. New York: W. W. Norton.

Rossi, E. L., & Ryan, M. O. (1985). *Life Reframing in Hypnosis: The Seminars, Workshops, and Lectures of Milton H. Erickson, Volume 2*. New York: Irvington.

Rossman, M. L. (1987). *Healing Yourself: A Step-by-Step Program for Better Health Through Imagery*. New York: Walker & Co.

Rowen, R. (1981). Hypnotic age regression in the treatment of trichotillomania. *American Journal of Clinical Hypnosis*, 23, 195-197.

Russell, D. E. H. (1986). *The Secret Trauma: Incest in the Lives of Girls and Women*. New York: Basic Books.

St. Jean, R. (1980). Hypnotic time distortion and learning: Another look. *Journal of Abnormal Psychology*, 89(1), 20-.

Sacerdote, P. (1970). Theory and practice of pain control in malignancy and other protracted or recurring painful illnesses. *International Journal of Clinical & Experimental Hypnosis*, 18, 160-180.

Sacerdote, P. (1974). Convergence of expectations: An essential component for successful hypnotherapy. *International Journal of Clinical & Experimental Hypnosis*, 22(2), 95-115.

Sacerdote, P. (1977). Applications of hypnotically elicited mystical states to the treatment of physical and emotional pain. *International Journal of Clinical & Experimental Hypnosis*, 25, 309-324.

Sacerdote, P. (1978). *Induced Dreams*. Brooklyn: Theo Gaus.

Samuels, M., & Bennett, H. (1973). Create your imaginary doctor. Chapter in M. Samuels & H. Bennett, *The Well Body Book*. New York: Random House.

Sanders, S. (1977). Mutual group hypnosis and smoking. *American Journal of Clinical Hypnosis*, 20, 131-135.

Saper, B. (1971). A report on behavior therapy with outpatient clinic patients. *Psychiatric Quarterly*, 45, 209-215.

Sarbin, T. R. (1950). Mental age changes in experimental

regression. *Journal of Personality*, *19*, 221-228.

Sarbin, T. R., & Farberow, N. L. (1952). Contributions to role-taking theory: A clinical study of self and role. *Journal of Abnormal Psychology*, *47*, 117-125.

Sargant, W., & Slater, E. (1941). Amnesic syndromes in war. *Proceedings of the Royal Society of Medicine*, *34*, 757-764.

Saucier, N., Walts, L. F., & Moreland, J. R. (1983). Patient awareness during nitrous oxide, oxygen, and halothane anesthesia. *Anesthesia & Analgesia*, *62*, 239-240.

Scagnelli, J. (1976). Hypnotherapy with schizophrenic and borderline patients: Summary of therapy with eight patients. *American Journal of Clinical Hypnosis*, *19*(1), 33-38.

Scagnelli-Jobsis, J. (1982). Hypnosis with psychotic patients: A review of the literature and presentation of a theoretical framework. *American Journal of Clinical Hypnosis*, *25*, 33-45.

Scheflin, A. W., & Shapiro, J. L. (1989). *Trance on Trial*. New York: Guilford.

Schmideberg, M. (1959). The borderline patient. In S. Arieti (Ed.), *American Handbook of Psychiatry, Vol. 1*. New York: Basic Books.

Schneck, J. M. (1966). Hypnoanalytic elucidation of a childhood germ phobia. *International Journal of Clinical & Experimental Hypnosis*, *14*, 305-307.

Schofield, L. J., & Reyher, J. (1974). Thematic productions under hypnotically aroused conflict in age regressed and waking states using the real-simulator design. *Journal of Abnormal Psychology*, *83*, 130-139.

Schover, L. R., & Jensen, S. B. (1988). *Sexuality & Chronic Illness*. New York: Guilford.

Schover, L., & LoPiccolo, J. (1982) Treatment effectiveness for dysfunctions of sexual desire. *Journal of Sex & Marital Therapy*, *8*(3), 179-197.

Schultz, J. H. (1932). *Das Autogene Training*. Leipzig: Verlag.

Schwartz, M. (1963). The cessation of labor using hypnotic techniques. *American Journal of Clinical Hypnosis*, *5*, 211-213.

Schwartz, M. F., & Masters, W. H. (1988). Inhibited sexual desire: The Masters & Johnson Institute model. Chapter in S. Leiblum & L. Pervin (Eds.), *Sexual Desire Disorders*. New York: Guilford, pp. 229-242.

Scott, D. L. (1969). Hypnosis as an aid to anesthesia in children. *Anesthesia*, *24*, 643-644.

Scott, M. J. (1960). *Hypnosis in Skin & Allergic Diseases*. Springfield, IL: Charles C. Thomas.

Secter, I. I. (1964). Dental surgery in a psychiatric patient. *American Journal of Clinical Hypnosis*, *6*, 363-371.

Sheehan, P. W., & McConkey, K. M. (1982). *Hypnosis & Experience: The Exploration of Phenomena & Process*. Hillsdale, N.J.: Lawrence Erlbaum.

Shewchuk, L. A., Durren, R., Burton, D., Forman, M., Clark,, R. R., & Jaffin, A. R. (1977). Preliminary observations on an intervention program for heavy smokers. *International Journal of Addictions*, *12*,

323-336.

Shorvon, H. J., & Sargant, W. (1947). Excitatory abreaction: With special reference to its mechanism and the use of ether. *Journal of Mental Science*, *43*, 709-732.

Sies, D. E., & Wester, W. C. (1987). Admissibility of hypnotically refreshed testimony. Chapter in W. C. Wester (Ed.), *Clinical Hypnosis: A Case Management Approach*. Cincinnati: Behavioral Science Center Publications, pp. 226-273.

Silverman, P. S., & Retzlaff, P. O. (1986). Cognitive stage regression through hypnosis: Are earlier cognitive states retrievable? *International Journal of Clinical & Experimental Hypnosis*, *34*, 192-204.

Simonton, D. C., Matthews-Simonton, S., & Creighton, J. L. (1978). *Getting Well Again*. Los Angeles: Tarcher-St. Martins.

Sinclair-Gieban, A. H. C., & Chalmers, D. (1959). Evaluation of treatment of warts by hypnosis. *Lancet*, *2*, 480-482.

Smith, D. S. (1982). Trends in counseling and psychotherapy. *American Psychologist*, *37*, 802-809.

Smith, M. C. (1983). Hypnotic memory enhancement of witnesses: Does it work? *Psychological Bulletin*, *94*, 387-407.

Smith, M. S., & Kamitsuka, M. (1984). Self-hypnosis misinterpreted as CNS deterioration in an adolescent with leukemia and vincristine toxicity. *American Journal of Clinical Hypnosis*, *26*, 280-282.

Snow, L. (1979). The relationship between "Rapid Induction" and placebo analgesia, hypnotic susceptibility an chronic pain intensity. *Dissertation Abstracts International*, *40*, 937.

Spark, R. F., White, R. A., & Connoly, P. B. (1980). Impotence is not always psychogenic. Newer insights into hypothalamic-pituitary-gonadal dysfunction. *Journal of the American Medical Association*, *243*, 750-755.

Spiegel, D., Detrick, D., & Frischholz, E. (1982). Hypnotizability and psychopathology. *American Journal of Psychiatry*, *139*, 431-437.

Spiegel, H. (1970). A single-treatment method to stop smoking using ancillary self-hypnosis. *International Journal of Clinical & Experimental Hypnosis*, *18*, 235-250.

Spiegel, H., Shor, J., & Fishman, S. (1945). An hypnotic ablation technique for the study of personality development. *Psychosomatic Medicine*, *7*, 273-278.

Spiegel, H., & Spiegel, D. (1978). *Trance & Treatment*. New York: Basic Books.

Spinhoven, P., Baak, D., Van Dyck, R., & Vermeulen, P. (1988). The effectiveness of an authoritative versus permissive style of hypnotic communication. *International Journal of Clinical & Experimental Hypnosis*, *36*(3), 182-191.

Stalb, A. R., & Logan, D. R. (1977). Hypnotic stimulation of breast growth. *American Journal of Clinical Hypnosis*, *19*, 201-208.

Stanton, H. (1975). Weight loss through hypnosis. *American Journal of Clinical Hypnosis, 18*, 34-38.

Stanton, H. E. (1977). The utilization of suggestions derived from rational-emotive therapy. *International Journal of Clinical & Experimental Hypnosis, 25*(1), 18-26.

Stanton, H. E. (1978). A one-session hypnotic approach to modifying smoking behavior. *International Journal of Clinical & Experimental Hypnosis, 26*, 22-29.

Stanton, H. E. (1989). Ego-enhancement: A five-step approach. *American Journal of Clinical Hypnosis, 31*(3), 192-198.

Staples, E. A., & Wilensky, H. (1968). A controlled Rorschach investigation of hypnotic age regression. *Journal of Projective Techniques, 32*, 246-252.

Stein, C. (1963). The clenched fist technique as a hypnotic procedure in clinical psychotherapy. *American Journal of Clinical Hypnosis, 6*, 113-119.

Stein, C. (1972). Hypnotic projection in brief psychotherapy. *American Journal of Clinical Hypnosis, 14*, 143-155.

Stein, V. T. (1980). Hypnotherapy of involuntary movements in an 82-year-old male. *American Journal of Clinical Hypnosis, 23*(2), 128-131.

Steinberg, S. (1965). Hypnoanesthesia — A case report in a 90 year old patient. *American Journal of Clinical Hypnosis, 7*, 355.

Sternbach, R. A. (1982). Medical evaluation of patients with chronic pain. Chapter in J. Barber & C. Adrian (Eds.), *Psychological Approaches to the Management of Pain*. New York: Brunner/Mazel, pp. 21-39.

Stolzy, S., Couture, L. J., & Edmonds, H. L. (1986). Evidence of partial recall during general anesthesia. *Anesthesia & Analgesia, 65*, S154. (Abstract)

Stone, J. A., & Lundy, R. M. (1985). Behavioral compliance with direct and indirect body movement suggestions. *Journal of Abnormal Psychology, 94*, 256-263.

Strupp, H. H. (1955). An objective comparison of Rogerian and psychoanalytic techniques. *Journal of Consulting Psychology, 19*, 1-7.

Stuart, F., & Hammond, D. C. (1980). Sex therapy. Chapter in R. B. Stuart, *Helping Couples Change*. New York: Guilford, pp. 301-366).

Stuart, F., Hammond, D. C., & Pett, M. (1986). Psychological characteristics of women with inhibited sexual desire. *Journal of Sex & Marital Therapy, 12*(2), 108-115.

Stuart, F., Hammond, D.C., & Pett, M. (1987). Inhibited sexual desire in women. *Archives of Sexual Behavior, 16*(2), 91-106.

Stunkard, A. H., & McLaren-Hume, M. (1959). The results of treatment for obesity. *Archives of Internal Medicine, 103*, 79-85.

Surman, O. S., Gottlieb, S. K., & Hackett, T. P. (1972). Hypnotic treatment of a child with warts. *American Journal of Clinical Hypnosis, 15*, 12-14.

Surman, O. S., Gottlieb, S. K., Hackett, T. P., & Silverberg, E. L. (1973). Hypnosis in the treatment of warts. *Archives of General Psychiatry, 28*, 439-441.

Susskind, D. J. (1970). The idealized self-image (ISI): A new technique in confidence training. *Behavior Therapy, 1*, 538-541.

Swiercinsky, D., & Coe, W. (1971). The effect of "alert" hypnosis and hypnotic responsiveness on reading comprehension. *International Journal of Clinical & Experimental Hypnosis, 19*(3), 146-153.

Sylvester, S. M. (1985). Fear in the management of pain: Preliminary report of a research project. Chapter in J. K. Zeig (Ed.), *Ericksonian Psychotherapy: Volume II*. New York: Brunner/Mazel, pp. 464-472.

Tasini, M. F., & Hackett, T. P. (1977). Hypnosis in the treatment of warts in immunodeficient children. *American Journal of Clinical Hypnosis, 19*, 152-154.

Taylor, A. (1950). The differentiation between simulated and true hypnotic regression by figure drawings. Unpublished masters thesis, The City University of New York.

Taylor, C. B., Farquhar, J. W., Nelson, E., & Agras, S. (1977). Relaxation therapy and high blood pressure. *Archives of General Psychiatry, 34*, 339-342.

Terman, S. A. (1980). Hypnosis in depression. Chapter in H. Wain (Ed.), *Clinical Hypnosis in Medicine*. Chicago: Symposia Specialists.

Thakur, K. (1984). Hypnotherapy for anorexia nervosa and accompanying somatic disorders. Chapter in W. C. Wester & A. H. Smith (Eds.), *Clinical Hypnosis: A Multidisciplinary Approach*. Philadelphia: J. B. Lippincott, pp. 476-493.

Thomason, S. (1984). Do you remember your previous life's language in your present incarnation? *American Speech, 59*, 340-350.

Thomason, S. (1986-87). Past tongues remembered? *Skeptical Inquirer, 11*, 367-375.

Thoresen, C. E., & Mahoney, M. J. (1974). *Behavioral Self-Control*. New York: Holt, Rinehart & Winston.

Thorne, F. C. (1967). *Integrative Psychology*. Brandon, VT.: Clinical Psychology Publishing Co.

Tinterow, M. M. (1960). The use of hypnotic anesthesia for a major surgical procedure. *American Surgery, 26*, 732-737.

Toomey, T. C., & Sanders, S. (1983). Group hypnotherapy as an active control strategy in chronic pain. *American Journal of Clinical Hypnosis, 26*(1), 20-25.

Tosi, D. J. (1973). Self directed behavior change in the cognitive, affective, and behavioral motoric domains: A rational-emotive approach. *Focus on Guidance*, December.

Truax, C. B., & Carkhuff, R. R. (1967). *Toward Effective Counseling and Psychotherapy: Training & Practice*. Chicago: Aldine-Atherton.

True, R. M. (1949). Experimental control in hypnotic age regression states. *Science, 110*, 583-584.

True, R. M., & Stephenson, C. W. (1951). Controlled experiments correlating electroencephalogram, pulse, and plantar reflexes with hypnotic age regression and induced emotional states. *Personality, 1*, 252-263.

Tucker, K. R., & Virnelli, F. R. (1985). The use of hypnosis as a tool in plastic surgery. *Plastic & Reconstructive Surgery*, 76, 140-146.

Turk, D. C. (1980). A cognitive-behavior approach to pain management. Paper presented at the American Pain Society, New York, 1980.

Unestahl, L. E. (1983). *The Mental Aspects of Gymnastics*. Orebro, Sweden: Veje Publishers.

Van Denburg, E., & Kurtz, R. (1989). Changes in body attitude as a function of posthypnotic suggestions. *International Journal of Clinical & Experimental Hypnosis*, 37, 15-30.

Van der Hart, O. (1981). Treatment of a phobia for dead birds: A case report. *American Journal of Clinical Hypnosis*, 23, 263-265.

Van der Hart, O. (1985). Metaphoric hypnotic imagery in the treatment of functional amenorrhea. *American Journal of Clinical Hypnosis*, 27(3), 159-165.

Van der Kolk, B. A. (1984). *Post-Traumatic Stress Disorder: Psychological & Biological Sequelae*. Washington, D.C.: American Psychiatric Association.

Van Dyke, P. B. (1970). Some uses of hypnosis in the management of the surgical patient. *American Journal of Clinical Hypnosis*, 12, 227-232.

Van Gorp, W. G., Meyer, R. G., & Dunbar, K. D. (1985). The efficacy of direct versus indirect hypnotic induction techniques on reduction of experimental pain. *International Journal of Clinical & Experimental Hypnosis*, 33, 319-328.

Vingoe, F. J. (1968). The development of a group alert-trance scale. *International Journal of Clinical & Experimental Hypnosis*, 16(2), 120-132.

Wadden, T. A., & Anderton, C. H. (1982). The clinical use of hypnosis. *Psychological Bulletin*, 91, 215-243.

Wadden, T. A., & Flaxman, J. (1981). Hypnosis and weight loss: A preliminary study. *International Journal of Clinical & Experimental Hypnosis*, 29, 162-173.

Wagenfeld, J., & Carlson, W. (1979). Use of hypnosis in the alleviation of reading problems. *American Journal of Clinical Hypnosis*, 22(1), 51-56.

Wagner, G., & Green, R. (1981). *Impotence: Physiological, Psychological, Surgical Diagnosis & Treatment*. New York: Plenum.

Wakeman, R. J., & Kaplan, J. Z. (1978). An experimental study of hypnosis in painful burns. *American Journal of Clinical Hypnosis*, 21(1), 3-12.

Walch, S. L. (1976). The red balloon technique of hypnotherapy: A clinical note. *International Journal of Clinical & Experimental Hypnosis*, 24(1), 10-12.

Walker, B. B. (1983). Treating stomach disorders: Can we reinstate regulatory processes? In R. Hozl & W. E. Whitehead (Eds.), *Psychophysiology of the Gastrointestinal Tract: Experimental & Clinical Applications*. New York: Plenum, pp. 209-233.

Walker, L. G., Dawson, A. A., Pollet, S. M., Ratcliffe, M. A., & Hamilton, L. (1988). Hypnotherapy for chemotherapy side effects. *British Journal of Experimental &*

Clinical Hypnosis, 5(2), 79-82.

Wark, D. M. (1989). Alert self-hypnosis techniques to improve reading comprehension. Unpublished paper.

Watkins, H. H. (1976). Hypnosis with smoking: A five-session approach. *International Journal of Clinical & Experimental Hypnosis*, 24, 381-390.

Watkins, H. H. (1980). The silent abreaction. *International Journal of Clinical & Experimental Hypnosis*, 28(2), 101-113.

Watkins, J. G. (1949). *Hypnotherapy of War Neuroses*. New York: Ronald Press.

Watkins, J. G. (1971). The affect bridge: A hypnoanalytic technique. *International Journal of Clinical & Experimental Hypnosis*, 19, 21-27.

Watkins, J. G. (1986). *Hypnotherapeutic Techniques, The Practice of Clinical Hypnosis, Volume I*. New York: Irvington.

Watkins, J. G. (in press). *Hypnotherapeutic Techniques: Volume II, Hypnoanalytic Techniques*. New York: Irvington.

Waxman, D. (1978). Misuse of hypnosis. *British Medical Journal*, 2, 571.

Waxman, D. (1989). *Hartland's Medical & Dental Hypnosis* (Third Edition). London: Bailliere Tindall.

Weitzenhoffer, A. M. (1964). Explorations in hypnotic time distortions. I. Acquisitions of temporal reference frames under conditions of time distortion. *Journal of Nervous & Mental Disease*, 138, 354.

Weitzenhoffer, A. M. (1989). *The Practice of Hypnotism, Volume 1 & 2*. New York: Wiley.

Werbel, E. W. (1960). Experiences with frequent use of hypnosis in a general surgical practice. *Western Journal of Surgical Obstetrics & Gynecology*, 68, 190-191.

Werbel, E. W. (1963). Use of posthypnotic suggestions to reduce pain following hemorrhoidectomies. *American Journal of Clinical Hypnosis*, 6(2), 132-136.

Werner, W. E. F., Schauble, P. G., & Knudson, M. S. (1982). An argument for the revival of hypnosis in obstetrics. *American Journal of Clinical Hypnosis*, 24, 149-171.

Wester, W. C. (1987). Hypnosis for smoking cessation. Chapter in W. C. Wester, *Clinical Hypnosis: A Case Management Approach*. Cincinnati: Behavioral Science Center Inc. Publications, pp. 173-182.

Wester, W. C., & O'Grady, D. O. (Eds.). (in press). *Clinical Hypnosis with Children*. New York: Brunner/Mazel.

White, R., Fox, G., & Harris, W. (1940). Hypnotic hypermnesia for recently learned material. *Journal of Abnormal & Social Psychology*, 35, 88-.

Whorwell, P. J., Prior, A., & Faragher, E. B. (1984). Controlled trial of hypnotherapy in the treatment of service refractory irritable-bowel syndrome. *Lancet*, 2, 1232-1233.

Whorwell, P. J., Prior, A., Colgan, S. M. (April 1987). Hypnotherapy in severe irritable bowel syndrome:

Further experience. *Gut, 28*(4), 423-425.

Wiggins, S. L., & Brown, C. W. (1968). Hypnosis with two pedicle graft cases. *International Journal of Clinical & Experimental Hypnosis, 16*, 215.

Willard, R. D. (1977). Breast enlargement through visual imagery and hypnosis. *American Journal of Clinical Hypnosis, 19*, 195-200.

Williams, J. E. (1973). Stimulation of breast growth by hypnosis. *Journal of Sex Research, 10*, 316-326.

Willis, D. C. (1972). The effects of self-hypnosis on reading rate and comprehension. *American Journal of Clinical Hypnosis, 14*(4), 249-255.

Wilson, I. (1982). *All in the Mind*. Garden City, N.Y.: Doubleday.

Wingfield, H. E. (1920). *An Introduction to the Study of Hypnotism*. London: Balliere Tindall.

Witztum, E., Van der Hart, O., & Friedman, B. (1988). *Journal of Contemporary Psychotherapy, 18*(4), 270-290.

Wogan, N., & Norcross, J. C. (1985). Dimensions of therapeutic skills and techniques: Empirical identification, therapist correlates, and predictive utility. *Psychotherapy, 22*, 63-64.

Wolberg, L. R. (1948). *Medical Hypnosis, Vol. 1 & 2*. New York: Grune & Stratton.

Wolberg, L. (1954, 1967, 1987). *The Technique of Psychotherapy*. Orlando: Grune & Stratton.

Wolberg, L. R. (1964). *Hypnoanalysis*. New York: Grune & Stratton.

Wolberg, L. R. (Ed.). (1965). *Short-Term Psychotherapy*. New York: Grune & Stratton.

Wolfe, L. S., & Millet, J. B. (1960). Control of postoperative pain by suggestion under general anesthesia. *American Journal of Clinical Hypnosis, 3*, 109-112.

Wollman, L. (1960). The role of hypnosis in the treatment of infertility. *British Journal of Medical Hypnotism, 2*, 3.

Wright, M. E. (1987). *Clinical Practice of Hypnotherapy*. New York: Guilford.

Yapko, M. D. (1986). Hypnotic and strategic interventions in the treatment of anorexia nervosa. *American Journal of Clinical Hypnosis, 28*(4), 224-232.

Yapko, M. D. (1988). *When Living Hurts: Directives for Treating Depression*. New York: Brunner/Mazel.

Young, M. H., & Montano, R. J. (1988). A new hypnobehavioral method for the treatment of children with Tourette's disorder. *American Journal of Clinical Hypnosis, 31*(2), 97-106.

Young, P. C. (1940). Hypnotic regression—Fact or artifact? *Journal of Abnormal & Social Psychology, 35*, 273-278.

Zahm, D. N. (1987). Hypnosis in the treatment of tourette syndrome. Chapter in W. C. Wester, *Clinical Hypnosis: A Case Management Approach*. Cincinnati: Behavioral Science Center, pp. 319-331.

Zeig, J. (1980). Erickson's use of anecdotes. Chapter in: J. Zeig (Ed.), *A Teaching Seminar with Milton H. Erickson, M.D.* New York: Brunner/Mazel, pp. 3-28.

Zelling, D. A. (1986). Snoring: A disease of the listener. *Journal of the American Academy of Medical Hypnoanalysis, 1*(2), 99-101.

Ziegenfuss, W. B. (1962). Hypnosis: A tool for education. *Education, 82*, 505-507.

Zilbergeld, B., & Ellison, C. R. (1980) Desire discrepancies and arousal problems in sex therapy. Chapter in S. R. Leiblum & L. A. Pervin (Eds.), *Principles & Practice of Sex Therapy*. New York: Guilford, 65-101.

Zilbergeld, B., & Evans, M. (1980, August). The inadequacy of Masters & Johnson. *Psychology Today, 14*(3), 28-43.

Zilbergeld, B., & Hammond, D. C. (1988). The use of hypnosis in treating desire problems. Chapter in S. R. Leiblum & R. C. Rosen (Eds.), *Sexual Desire Disorders*. New York: Guilford Press, 192-225.

Zilbergeld, B., & Lazarus, A. A. (1987). *Mind Power: Getting What you Want Through Mental Training*. Boston: Little, Brown & Co.

Zimbardo, P. G., Marshall, G., & Maslach, C. (1971). Liberating behavior from time-bound control: Expanding the present through hypnosis. *Journal of Applied Social Psychology, 1*, 305-323.

Zimmer, E. Z., Peretz, B. A., Eyal, E., & Fuchs, K. (1988). The influence of maternal hypnosis on fetal movements in anxious pregnant women. *European Journal of Obstetrics & Gynecology & Reproductive Biology, 27*(2), 133-137.

Zisook, S., & DePaul, R. A. (1977). Emotional factors in inflammatory bowel disease. *Southern Medical Journal, 70*, 716-719.

CREDITS

Chapter 3

Techniques of Hypnotic Pain Management was reprinted with permission from: Barber, J., and Adrian, C. (1982). *Psychological Approaches to the Management of Pain*. New York: Brunner/Mazel.

Altering the Quality of Discomfort: Example of Leg Pain was reprinted with permission from: Wright, M. E. (1987). *Clinical Practice of Hypnotherapy*. New York: Guilford Press.

Transformation of Pain was reprinted with permission from: Golden, W. L., Dowd, E. T., and Friedberg, F. (1987). *Hypnotherapy: A Modern Approach*. New York: Pergamon Press.

Erickson's Suggestions for Pain Control were reprinted with permission from: (a) Erickson, M. H. (1983). *Healing in Hypnosis: The Seminars, Workshops, and Lectures of Milton H. Erickson, Volume 1*. Edited by E. L. Rossi, M. O. Ryan, and F. A. Sharp. New York: Irvington. (b) Erickson, M. H. (1985). *Life Reframing in Hypnosis: The Seminars, Workshops and Lectures of Milton H. Erickson, Volume 2*. Edited by E. L. Rossi and M. O. Ryan. New York: Irvington. (c) Erickson, M. H. (1986). *Mind-Body Communication in Hypnosis: The Seminars, Workshops, and Lectures of Milton H. Erickson, Volume 3*. Edited by E. L. Rossi and M. O. Ryan. New York: Irvington.

General Principles for Alleviating Persistent Pain was reprinted with permission from: Rossi, E. L., and Cheek, D. B. (1988). *Mind-Body Therapy*. New York: W. W. Norton.

Religious Imagery of Universal Healing for Ego-Strengthening and Pain was reprinted with permission from: Wright, M. Erik. (1987). *Clinical Practice of Hypnotherapy*. New York: Guilford Press, pp. 167-168.

The "Sympathetic Ear" Technique with Chronic Pain was adapted with permission from: Fogel, B. S. (1984). The "sympathetic ear": Case reports of a self-hypnotic approach to chronic pain. *American Journal of Clinical Hypnosis, 27*(2), 103-106.

Reactivation of Pain-Free Memories: An Example of Intensifying and Relieving Pain was reprinted with permission from: Wright, M. E. (1987). *Clinical Practice of Hypnotherapy*. New York: Guilford.

Hypnotically Elicited Mystical States in Treating Physical and Emotional Pain was reprinted with permission from: Sacerdote, P. (1977). Applications of hypnotically elicited mystical states to the treatment of physical and emotional pain. *International Journal of Clinical and Experimental Hypnosis, 25*(4), 309-324.

Active Control Strategy for Group Hypnotherapy with Chronic Pain was adapted with permission of publisher from:

Toomey, T. C., and Sanders, S. (1983). Group hypnotherapy as an active control strategy in chronic pain. *American Journal of Clinical Hypnosis, 26*(1), 20-25.

Quotes in Erickson's Interspersal Technique for Pain were adapted with permission from: Erickson, M. H. (1966). The interspersal hypnotic technique for symptom correction and pain control. *American Journal of Clinical Hypnosis, 8*, 198-209.

Pain Reduction was reprinted with permission from: Jencks, B. (1977). *Your Body: Biofeedback at its Best*. Chicago: Nelson-Hall.

"Body Lights" Approach to Ameliorating Pain and Inflammation (Arthritis) was reprinted with permission from: Rossi, E. L., and Cheek, D. B. (1988). *Mind-Body Therapy*. New York: W. W. Norton.

Suggestions with Postherpetic Neuralgia ("Shingles") is copyrighted (1989) by Diane Roberts Stoler, Ed.D. and all rights are reserved. No portion of this material may be reproduced, republished or used for any commercial purpose without permission of Diane Roberts Stoler.

Suggestions to Reduce Pain Following Hemorrhoidectomies was reprinted with permission from: Werbel, E. W. (1963). Use of posthypnotic suggestions to reduce pain following hemorrhoidectomies. *American Journal of Clinical Hypnosis, 6*(2), 132-136.

Suggestions for Pain Control was reprinted with permission from: Gibbons, D. E. (1979). *Applied Hypnosis and Hyperempiria*. New York: Plenum Press.

Suggestions with Migraine was reprinted with permission from: Anderson, J. A. D., Basker, M. A., and Dalton, R. (1975). Migraine and hypnotherapy. *International Journal of Clinical and Experimental Hypnosis, 23*(1), 48-58.

Diminution Rather than Elimination of Headache was reprinted with permission from: Secter, I. I. (1964). Dental surgery in a psychiatric patient. *American Journal of Clinical Hypnosis, 6*, 363-371.

Suggestion for Symptom Substitution was reprinted with permission from: Elkins, G. R. (1984). Hypnosis in the treatment of myofibrositis and anxiety: A case report. *American Journal of Clinical Hypnosis, 27*(1), 26-30.

Chapter 4

Hypnosis and the Anesthetist was reprinted with permission from *American Journal of Clinical Hypnosis*, 1965, *8*, 34-36.

Summary Steps for Preoperative Hypnosis to Facilitate Healing was reprinted with permission from: Rossi, E. L., and Cheek, D. B. (1988). *Mind-Body Therapy*. New York: W. W. Norton.

Ericksonian Approaches in Anesthesiology was reprinted with permission from: Rodger, B. P. (1982). Ericksonian approaches in anesthesiology. Chapter in J. K. Zeig (Ed.), *Ericksonian Approaches to Hypnosis and Psychotherapy*. New York: Brunner/Mazel. (Quotes taken from pp. 317-321, 323-328.)

Examples of Preoperative Suggestions was reprinted with permission from: Barber, J., and Adrian, C. (1982). *Psychological Approaches to the Management of Pain*. New York: Brunner/Mazel.

Preparation for Surgery was reprinted with permission from: Sylvester, S. M. (1985). Fear in the management of pain: Preliminary report of a research project. Chapter in J. K. Zeig (Ed.), *Ericksonian Psychotherapy: Volume II*. New York: Brunner/Mazel, pp. 464-472.

Rapid Induction Analgesia was reprinted with permission from: Barber, J. (1977). Rapid induction analgesia: A clinical report. *American Journal of Clinical Hypnosis, 19*, 138-147.

Surgical and Obstetrical Analgesia was reprinted with permission from: Rossi, E. L., and Cheek, D. B. (1988). *Mind-Body Therapy*. New York: W. W. Norton.

Techniques for Surgery was reprinted with permission from: Kroger, W. S. (1977). *Clinical and Experimental Hypnosis* (Second Edition). Philadelphia: J. B. Lippincott.

Chapter 5

Suggestions for Raising Self-Esteem was reprinted with permission from: Barber, T. X. (1984). Hypnosis, deep relaxation, and active relaxation: Data, theory, and clinical applications. Chapter in R. L. Woolfolk and P. M. Lehrer, *Principles and Practice of Stress Management*. New York: Guilford Press, pp. 164-166.

Barnett's Yes-Set Method of Ego-Strengthening was adapted with permission from: E. A. Barnett, *Analytical Hypnotherapy*. Kingston, Ontario, Canada: Junica, 1981.

Ego-Enhancement: A Five-Step Approach was adapted with permission from: Stanton, H. E. (1989). Ego-enhancement: A five-step approach. *American Journal of Clinical Hypnosis, 31*(3), 192-198.

Suggestions Derived from Rational-Emotive Therapy was reprinted with permission from: Stanton, H. E. (1977). The utilization of suggestions derived from rational-emotive therapy. *International Journal of Clinical and Experimental Hypnosis, 25*(1), 18-26.

Suggestions to Facilitate Problem Solving was reprinted with permission from: Gibbons, D. E. (1979). *Applied Hypnosis and Hyperempiria*. New York: Plenum Press.

An Abstract Technique for Ego-Strengthening was reprinted with permission from: Gorman, B. J. (1974). An abstract technique for ego-strengthening. *American Journal of Clinical Hypnosis, 16*(3), 209-212.

The Prominent Tree Metaphor was reprinted with permission from: Pelletier, A. M. (1979). Three uses of guided imagery in hypnosis. *American Journal of Clinical Hypnosis, 22*(1), 32-36.

The Seasons of the Year: A Metaphor of Growth was reprinted with permission from: Gindhart, L. R. (1981). The use of a metaphoric story in therapy: A case report. *American Journal of Clinical Hypnosis, 23*(3), 202-206.

Suggestions for Emotional Enrichment was reprinted with permission from: Gibbons, D. E. (1979). *Applied Hypnosis and Hyperempiria*. New York: Plenum Press.

Stein's Clenched Fist Technique was adapted from: Stein, C. (1963). The clenched fist technique as a hypnotic procedure in clinical psychotherapy. *American Journal of Clinical Hypnosis, 6*, 113-119.

Suggestions for Ego-Strengthening was adapted with permission from: Hartland, John. (1971). Further observations on the use of "ego-strengthening" techniques. *American Journal of Clinical Hypnosis, 14*, 1-8.

Suggestions for Self-Reinforcement was reprinted with permission from: Gibbons, D. E. (1979). *Applied Hypnosis and Hyperempiria*. New York: Plenum Press.

Chapter 6

Methods of Relaxed Breathing was reprinted with permission from: Jencks, B. (1977). *Your Body: Biofeedback at its Best*. Chicago: Nelson-Hall, pp. 139-143.

The Autogenic Rag Doll was reprinted with permission from: Jencks, B. (1973). *Exercise Manual for J. H. Schultz's Standard Autogenic Training and Special Formulas with Appendixes on Procedures with Children and Advanced Autogenic Training*. Des Plaines, Illinois: American Society of Clinical Hypnosis, pp. 42-44.

Rational-Emotive Suggestions About Anxiety was reprinted with permission from: Ellis, A. (1986). Anxiety about anxiety: The use of hypnosis with Rational-Emotive Therapy. Chapter in E. T. Dowd and J. M. Healy (Eds.), *Case Studies in Hypnotherapy*. New York: Guilford, pp. 3-11.

The Closed Drawer Metaphor was reprinted with permission from: Alman, B. M. (1983). *Self-Hypnosis: A Complete Manual for Health and Self-Change*. San Diego: International Health Publications, pp. 118-119.

He Who Hesitates Is Lost: A Metaphor for Decision-Making was reprinted with permission from: Yapko, M. D. (1988). *When Living Hurts: Directives for Treating Depression*. New York: Brunner/Mazel.

De-Fusing Panic was reprinted with permission from: Hunter, M. E. (1988). *Daydreams for Discovery: A Manual for Hypnotherapists*. Vancouver: SeaWalk Press.

A Reframing Approach for Flight Phobia was reprinted with permission from: Bakal, P. A. (1981). Hypnotherapy for flight phobia. *American Journal of Clinical Hypnosis, 23*(4), 248-251.

Hypnosis with Phobic Reactions was reprinted with permission from: Gibbons, D. E. (1979). *Applied Hypnosis and Hyperempiria*. New York: Plenum Press.

Example of Treating Phobic Anxiety with Individually Prepared Tapes was reprinted with permission from: Wright, M. E. (1987). *Clinical Practice of Hypnotherapy*. New York: Guilford Press.

Treatment of Lack of Confidence and Stage Fright was reprinted with permission from: Waxman, D. (1989). *Hartland's Medical and Dental Hypnosis* (Third Edition). London: Bailliere Tindall, pp. 295-297.

Overcoming Anxiety over Public Speaking was reprinted with permission from: Gibbons, D. E. (1979). *Applied Hypnosis and Hyperempiria*. New York: Plenum Press.

Suggestions with TMJ and Bruxism was reprinted with permission from: Golan, H. P. (1989). Temporomandibular joint disease treated with hypnosis. *American Journal of Clinical Hypnosis, 31*(4), 269-274.

Erickson's Suggestions with Bruxism was reprinted with permission from: Erickson, M. H. (1985). *Life Reframing in Hypnosis*. Edited by E. L. Rossi and M. O. Ryan. New York: Irvington, pp. 39-40.

Suggestions to Promote Dental Flossing was reprinted with permission from: Kelly, M. A., McKinty, H. R., and Carr, R. (1988). Utilization of hypnosis to promote compliance with routine dental flossing. *American Journal of Clinical Hypnosis, 31*(1), 57-60.

Imagery with Hypersensitive Gag Reflex was reprinted with permission from: Clarke, J. H., and Persichetti, S. J. (1988). Hypnosis and concurrent denture construction for a patient with a hypersensitive gag reflex. *American Journal of Clinical Hypnosis, 30*(4), 285-288.

The copyright for Denture Problems and Gagging is reserved by the author.

Illustrative Suggestions with Tooth Extraction was reprinted with permission from: Finkelstein, S. (1984). Hypnosis and dentistry. Chapter in W. C. Wester II., and A. H. Smith, Jr. (Eds.), *Clinical Hypnosis: A Multidisciplinary Approach*. Philadelphia: J. B. Lippincott, pp. 337–349.

Dental Hypnosis was adapted and reprinted with permission from Rausch, V. (1987). Dental hypnosis. Chapter in W. C. Wester, *Clinical Hypnosis: A Case Management Approach*. Cincinnati: Behavioral Science Center Publications, pp. 85–95.

Suggestions for Operative Hypnodontics was reprinted with permission from: Kroger, W. S. (1977). *Clinical and Experimental Hypnosis* (Second Edition). Philadelphia: J. B. Lippincott.

Erickson's Approach with Bruxism in Children was reprinted with permission from: Erickson, M. H. (1983). *Healing in Hypnosis*. Edited by E. L. Rossi, M. O. Ryan, and F. A. Sharp. New York: Irvington, pp. 123–124.

Chapter 7

Clinical Issues in Controlling Chemotherapy Side Effects was adapted with permission from: Redd, W. H., Rosenberger, P. H., and Hendler, C. S. (1983). Controlling chemotherapy side effects. *American Journal of Clinical Hypnosis*, *25*, 161–172.

Suggestions for Chemotherapy Patients was reprinted with permission from: Levitan, A. A. (1987). Hypnosis and oncology. Chapter in W. C. Wester, *Clinical Hypnosis: A Case Management Approach*. Cincinnati: Behavioral Science Center, pp. 332–356.

Hypnotic Suggestions with Cancer Patients was reprinted with permission from: Crasilneck, H. B., and Hall, J. A. (1985). *Clinical Hypnosis: Principles and Applications* (Second Edition). Orlando: Grune and Stratton.

Imagery to Enhance the Control of the Physiological and Psychological "Side Effects" of Cancer Therapy was adapted with permission from: Rosenberg, S. W. (1983). Hypnosis in cancer care: Imagery to enhance the control of the physiological and psychological "side-effects" of cancer therapy. *American Journal of Clinical Hypnosis*, *25*(2–3), 122–127.

Breast Cancer: Radiation Treatment and Recovery, copyright 1989 by Diane Roberts Stoler. All rights reserved. No portion of this material may be reproduced, republished or used for any commercial purpose without permission of author.

Hypnosis as an Adjunct to Chemotherapy in Cancer was reprinted with permission from: Rosen, S. (1985). Hypnosis as an adjunct to chemotherapy in cancer. Chapter in J. K. Zeig (Ed.), *Ericksonian Psychotherapy: Volume II*. New York: Brunner/Mazel, pp. 387–397.

Hypnotic Death Rehearsal was adapted with permission from: Levitan, A. A. (1985). Hypnotic death rehearsal. *American Journal of Clinical Hypnosis*, *27*(4), 211–215.

Chapter 8

Erickson's Reframing Suggestion with Pruritus was reprinted with permission from: Erickson, M. H., and Rossi, E. L. (1979). *Hypnotherapy: An Exploratory Casebook*. New York: Irvington, p. 227.

Suggestions for Itching was reprinted with permission from: Jencks, B. (1977). *Your Body: Biofeedback at its Best*. Chicago: Nelson-Hall.

Hypnotic Technique for Treating Warts was reprinted with permission from Crasilneck, H. B., and Hall, J. A. (1985). *Clinical Hypnosis: Principles and Applications* (Second Edition). Orlando: Grune and Stratton, pp. 374–375.

Suggestions for Warts (Modeled after Hartland) was reprinted with permission from: Gibbons, D. E. (1979). *Applied Hypnosis and Hyperempiria*. New York: Plenum.

Suggestions for Vaginal Warts is copyrighted 1989, by Diane Roberts Stoler, Ed.D. All rights reserved. No portion of this material may be reproduced, republished or used for any commercial purpose without permission of Diane Roberts Stoler.

Suggestions with Condyloma Acuminatum (Genital Warts) was reprinted with permission from: Ewin, D. M. (1974). Condyloma acuminatum: Successful treatment of four cases by hypnosis. *American Journal of Clinical Hypnosis*, *17*(2), 73–78.

Suggestions for Immunodeficient Children with Warts was reprinted with permission from: Tasini, M. F., and Hackett, T. P. (1977). Hypnosis in the treatment of warts in immunodeficient children. *American Journal of Clinical Hypnosis*, *19*(3), 152–154.

Evoking Helpful Past Experiences and Medical Treatments: Example with Skin Rash was reprinted with permission from: Wright, M. E. (1987). *Clinical Practice of Hypnotherapy*. New York: Guilford Press, pp. 66–67.

Suggestions with Pruritus was reprinted with permission from: Kroger, W. S., and Fezler, W. D. (1976). *Hypnosis and Behavior Modification: Imagery Conditioning*. Philadelphia: J. B. Lippincott.

Suggestions with Burn Patients was reprinted with permission from: Crasilneck, H. B., and Hall, J. A. (1985). *Clinical Hypnosis: Principles and Applications* (Second Edition). Orlando: Grune and Stratton.

Emergency Hypnosis for the Burned Patient was reprinted with permission from: Ewin, D. M. (1983). Emergency room hypnosis for the burned patient. *American Journal of Clinical Hypnosis*, *26*, 5–8.

Hypnosis in Painful Burns was adapted with permission from: Wakeman, R. J., and Kaplan, J. Z. (1978). An experimental study of hypnosis in painful burns. *American Journal of Clinical Hypnosis*, *21*(1), 3–12.

Ideomotor Healing of Burn Injuries was reprinted with permission from: Rossi, E. L., and Cheek, D. B. (1988). *Mind-Body Therapy*. New York: W. W. Norton.

Direct Suggestions in Emergencies with the Critically Ill was reprinted with permission from: Rossi, E. L., and Cheek, D. B. (1988). *Mind-Body Therapy*. New York: W. W. Norton.

Suggestions for Use of Spontaneous Trances in Emergency Situations was reprinted with permission from: Wright, M. E. (1987). *Clinical Practice of Hypnotherapy*. New York: Guilford.

Painless Wound Injection Through Use of a Two-finger Confusion Technique was reprinted with permission from: Bierman, S. F. (1988). Painless wound injection through use of a two-finger confusion technique. *American Journal of Emergency Medicine*, *6*(3), 266–267.

Symphony Metaphor was reprinted with permission from: Hunter, M. E. (1988). *Daydreams for Discovery: A Manual for Hypnotherapists*. Vancouver: SeaWalk Press.

Healing Imagery was reprinted with permission from: Hunter, M. E. (1988). *Daydreams for Discovery: A Manual for Hypnotherapists*. Vancouver: SeaWalk Press.

Prolonged Hypnosis in Psychosomatic Medicine was reprinted with permission from: Kuriyama, K. (1968). Clinical applications of prolonged hypnosis in psychosomatic medicine. *American Journal of Clinical Hypnosis*, *11*(2), 101–111.

Further Suggestions for Facilitating Prolonged Hypnosis was reprinted with permission from: Kratochvil, S. (1970). Prolonged hypnosis and sleep. *American Journal of Clinical Hypnosis*, *12*(4), 254–260.

Vascular Control Through Hypnosis was reprinted with permission from: Bishay, E. G., and Lee, C. (1984). Studies of the effects of hypnoanesthesia on regional blood flow by transcutaneous oxygen monitoring. *American Journal of Clinical Hypnosis*, *27*(1), 64–69.

Suggestion for Control of Bleeding was reprinted with permission from: Erickson, M. H. (1985). *Life Reframing in Hypnosis*.

Edited by E. L. Rossi and M. O. Ryan. New York: Irvington, p. 121.

Suggestions for Control of Upper Gastrointestinal Hemorrhage was reprinted with permission from: Bishay, E. G., Stevens, G., and Lee, C. (1984). Hypnotic control of upper gastrointestinal hemorrhage: A case report. *American Journal of Clinical Hypnosis*, 27(1), 22–25.

Teaching the Other Side of the Brain was reprinted with permission from: Hunter, M. E. (1988). *Daydream for Discovery: A Manual for Hypnotherapists*. Vancouver: SeaWalk Press, Ltd.

Once Learned, Can Be Relearned was reprinted with permission from: Hunter, M. E. (1988). *Daydream for Discovery: A Manual for Hypnotherapists*. Vancouver: SeaWalk Press, Ltd.

Hypnosis with Blepharospasm was reprinted with permission from: Murphy, J. K., and Fuller, A. K. (1984). Hypnosis and biofeedback as adjunctive therapy in blepharospasm: A case report. *American Journal of Clinical Hypnosis*, 27(1), 31–37.

Hypnotherapy for Lagophthalmos was reprinted with permission from: Holroyd, J., and Maguen, E. (1989). And so to sleep: Hypnotherapy for Lagophthalmos. *American Journal of Clinical Hypnosis*, 31(4), 264–266.

Suggestions for Involuntary Muscle Jerking was reprinted with permission from: Stein, V. T. (1980). Hypnotherapy of involuntary movements in an 82-year-old male. *American Journal of Clinical Hypnosis*, 23(2), 128–131.

Suggestions for Insomnia was reprinted with permission from: Erickson, M. H. (1986). *Mind-Body Communication in Hypnosis*. Edited by E. L. Rossi and M. O. Ryan. New York: Irvington, pp. 145–146.

Snoring: A Disease of the Listener was reprinted with permission from: Zelling, D. A. (1986). Snoring: A disease of the listener. *Journal of the American Academy of Medical Hypnoanalysis*, 1(2), 99–101.

Hypnotic Techniques and Suggestions for Medical-Physical Complaints was reprinted with permission from: Jencks, B. (1977). *Your Body: Biofeedback at its Best*. Chicago: Nelson-Hall.

Paradoxical Self-Hypnotic Assignment for Chronic Urinary Retention or "Bashful Bladder" was reprinted with permission from: Mozdzierz, G. J. (1985). The use of hypnosis and paradox in the treatment of a case of chronic urinary retention/"bashful bladder." *American Journal of Clinical Hypnosis*, 28(1), 43–47.

Hypnosis in Postoperative Urinary Retention was adapted with permission from: Chiasson, S. W. (1964). Hypnosis in postoperative urinary retention. *American Journal of Clinical Hypnosis*, 6, 366–368.

Hypnotic Paradigm-Substitution with Hypochondriasis was reprinted with permission from: Deiker, T., and Counts, D. K. (1980). Hypnotic paradigm-substitution therapy in a case of hypochondriasis. *American Journal of Clinical Hypnosis*, 23(2), 122–127.

Suggestions with Asthma was reprinted with permission from: Gibbons, D. E. (1979). *Applied Hypnosis and Hyperempiria*. New York: Plenum.

Erickson's Metaphor with Tinnitus was reprinted with permission from: Erickson, M. H., and Rossi, E. L. (1979). *Hypnotherapy: An Exploratory Casebook*. New York: Irvington, pp. 117–118.

Chapter 9

Suggestions for a Comfortable Delivery was reprinted with permission from: Barber, J., and Adrian, C. (1982). *Psychological Approaches to the Management of Pain*. New York: Brunner/Mazel, pp. 174–176.

The Hypnoreflexogenous Technique in Obstetrics was reprinted with permission from: Fuller, A. K. (1986). A method for developing suggestions from the literature. *American Journal of Clinical Hypnosis*, 29(1), 47–52.

Management of Antenatal Hypnotic Training was reprinted with permission from: Waxman, D. (1989). *Hartland's Medical and Dental Hypnosis* (Third Edition). London: Bailliere Tindall.

Erickson's Childbirth Suggestions was reprinted with permission from: Rossi, E. L., and Ryan, M. O. (1986). *Mind-Body Communication in Hypnosis: The Seminars, Workshops, and Lectures of Milton H. Erickson, Volume III*. New York: Irvington, pp. 120–121.

An Ericksonian Approach to Childbirth was reprinted with permission from: Poncelet, N. M. (1985). An Ericksonian approach to childbirth. Chapter in J. K. Zeig (Ed.). *Ericksonian Psychotherapy: Volume II*. New York: Brunner/Mazel, pp. 267–285.

Childbirth Script, copyright 1989 by Diane Roberts Stoler. All rights reserved. No portion of this material may be reproduced, republished or used for any commercial purpose without permission of Diane Roberts Stoler.

Preparation for Obstetrical Labor was reprinted with permission from: Kroger, W. S. (1977). *Clinical and Experimental Hypnosis* (Second Edition). Philadelphia: J. B. Lippincott.

Suggestions with Untrained Patients in Labor was reprinted with permission from: Rock, N. L., Shipley, T. E., and Campbell, C. (1969). Hypnosis with untrained nonvolunteer patients in labor. *International Journal of Clinical and Experimental Hypnosis*, 17(1), 25–36.

Hypnotic Relaxation Technique for Premature Labor was reprinted with permission from: Omer, H. (1987). A hypnotic relaxation technique for the treatment of premature labor. *American Journal of Clinical Hypnosis*, 29(3), 206–213.

Use of Immediate Interventions to Uncover Emotional Factors in Pre-Abortion Conditions was reprinted with permission from: Cheek, D. B. (1986). Using hypnosis with habitual aborters. Chapter in B. Zilbergeld, M. G. Edelstien, and D. L. Araoz (Eds.), *Hypnosis: Questions and Answers*. New York: Norton, 1986, pp. 330–336.

Suggestions for Hyperemesis was reprinted with permission from: Crasilneck, H. B., and Hall, J. A. (1985). *Clinical Hypnosis: Principles and Applications* (Second Edition). Orlando: Grune and Stratton.

Suggestions for Hyperemesis Gravidarum was reprinted with permission from: Waxman, D. (1989). *Hartland's Medical and Dental Hypnosis* (Third Edition). London: Bailliere Tindall.

Suggestions with Psychogenic Amenorrhea was reprinted with permission from: Kroger, W. S. (1977). *Clinical and Experimental Hypnosis* (Second Edition). Philadelphia: J. B. Lippincott.

Suggestions with Leukorrhea was reprinted with permission from: Leckie, F. H. (1965). Further gynecological conditions treated by hypnotherapy. *International Journal of Clinical and Experimental Hypnosis*, 13(1), 11–25.

Chapter 10

Responsibility to a Fault: A Metaphor for Overresponsibility was reprinted with permission from: Yapko, M. D. (1988). *When Living Hurts: Directives for Treating Depression*. New York: Brunner/Mazel.

Different Parts: A Metaphor was reprinted with permission from: Yapko, M. D. (1988). *When Living Hurts: Directives for Treating Depression*. New York: Brunner/Mazel.

Enhancing Affective Experience and Its Expression was reprinted with permission from: Brown, D. P., and Fromm, E. (1986). *Hypnotherapy and Hypnoanalysis*. Hillsdale, NJ: Lawrence Erlbaum, pp. 172–174.

Can Hypnosis Help Psychosis was reprinted with permission from: Hodge, J. R. (1988). Can hypnosis help psychosis? *American Journal of Clinical Hypnosis*, 30(4), 248–256.

Suggestions for Creative Self-Mothering was reprinted with permission from: Murray-Jobsis, J. (1984). Hypnosis with severely disturbed patients. Chapter in W. C. Wester II and A. H.

Smith, Jr., (Eds.), *Clinical Hypnosis: A Multidisciplinary Approach.* Philadelphia: J. B. Lippincott, pp. 368–404.

Hypnotherapeutic Techniques with Affective Instability was reprinted with permission from: Gruber, L. N. (1983). Hypnotherapeutic techniques with affective instability. *American Journal of Clinical Hypnosis, 25,* 263–266.

Hypnotic Suggestions to Deter Suicide was reprinted with permission from: Hodge, J. R. (1972). Hypnosis as a deterrent to suicide. *American Journal of Clinical Hypnosis, 15*(1), 20–21.

Hypnosis with Bipolar Affective Disorders was reprinted with permission from: Feinstein, A. D., and Morgan, R. M. (1986). Hypnosis in regulating bipolar affective disorders. *American Journal of Clinical Hypnosis, 29*(1), 29–38.

Chapter 11

Hypnotherapy with Psychogenic Impotence was reprinted with permission from: Crasilneck, H. B. (1982). A follow-up study in the use of hypnotherapy in the treatment of psychogenic impotency. *American Journal of Clinical Hypnosis, 25*(1), 52–61.

Changes in Preference Metaphor was reprinted with permission from: Hammond, D. C. Treatment of inhibited sexual desire. Chapter in J. K. Zeig (Ed.), *Ericksonian Psychotherapy, Volume II,* New York: Brunner/Mazel, 1985, pp. 415–428.

Suggestions for Impotence and Anorgasmia was reprinted with permission from: Alexander, L. (1974). Treatment of impotency and anorgasmia by psychotherapy aided by hypnosis. *American Journal of Clinical Hypnosis, 17*(1), pp. 34, 37, 29, 42.

Suggestions with Sexual Dysfunctions was reprinted with permission from: Gibbons, D. E. (1979). *Applied Hypnosis and Hyperempirlu.* New Yorln Plenum Press

Suggestions for Premature Ejaculation was reprinted with permission from: Erickson, M. H. (1973). Psychotherapy achieved by a reversal of the neurotic processes in a case of ejaculation praecox. *American Journal of Clinical Hypnosis, 15*(4), 219–221.

Hypnotic Ego-Assertive Retraining was reprinted with permission from: Waxman, D. (1989). *Hartland's Medical and Dental Hypnosis* (Third Edition). London: Bailliere Tindall.

Suggestions to Increase Interpersonal Effectiveness was reprinted with permission from: Gibbons, D. E. (1979). *Applied Hypnosis and Hyperempiria.* New York: Plenum Press.

The Jazz Band Metaphor for Family Interaction was reprinted with permission from: Barker, P. (1985). *Using Metaphors in Psychotherapy.* New York: Brunner/Mazel, pp. 132–135.

Chapter 12

Weight Control was adapted by the authors from: Spiegel, H., and Spiegel, D. (1978). *Trance and Treatment: Clinical Uses of Hypnosis.* New York: Basic Books. [Reissued by American Psychiatric Press, Inc., 1987].

Suggestions for Decreasing Food Intake was reprinted with permission from: Crasilneck, H. B., and Hall, J. A. (1985). *Clinical Hypnosis: Principles and Applications* (Second Edition). Orlando: Grune and Stratton, pp. 200, 430–431.

The first group of suggestions in Hypnosis in Weight Control was reprinted with permission from Mann (1973), and the last suggestions were adapted with permission from Mann (1981).

Weight Control Suggestions was reprinted with permission from: Stanton, H. E. (1975). Weight loss through hypnosis. *American Journal of Clinical Hypnosis, 18*(2), 94–97.

Miscellaneous Suggestions for Weight Control was reprinted with permission from: Kroger, W. S., and Fezler, W. D. (1976). *Hypnosis and Behavior Modification: Imagery Conditioning.* Philadelphia: J. B. Lippincott.

Further Suggestions for Management of Obesity was adapted with permission from: Kroger, W. S. (1970). Comprehensive management of obesity. *American Journal of Clinical Hypnosis, 12*(3), 165–175.

Erickson's Suggestions with Obesity were reprinted with permission respectively from: (a) Erickson, M. H. (1983). *Healing in Hypnosis.* Edited by E. L. Rossi, M. O. Ryan, and F. A. Sharp. New York: Irvington, p. 268. (b) Erickson, M. H. (1985). *Life Reframing in Hypnosis.* Edited by E. L. Rossi and M. O. Ryan. New York: Irvington, p. 184. (c) Erickson, M. H., and Rossi, E. L. (1979). *Hypnotherapy: An Exploratory Casebook.* New York: Irvington, p. 31.

Negative Accentuation: Vivifying the Negative During Trance was reprinted with permission from: Wright, M. E. (1987). *Clinical Practice of Hypnotherapy.* New York: Guilford.

Suggestions to Modify Body Attitude was reprinted with permission from: Van Denburg, E., and Kurtz, R. (1989). Changes in body attitude as a function of posthypnotic suggestions. *International Journal of Clinical and Experimental Hypnosis, 37,* 15–30.

Suggestions for Increasing Food Intake was reprinted with permission from: Crasilneck, H. B., and Hall, J. A. (1985). *Clinical Hypnosis: Principles and Applications* (Second Edition). Orlando: Grune and Stratton.

Suggestions for Presenting Symptoms in Anorexia Nervosa was adapted with permission from: Gross, M. (1984). Hypnosis in the therapy of anorexia nervosa. *American Journal of Clinical Hypnosis, 26*(3), 175–181.

Metaphors for Bulimia and Anorexia was reprinted with permission from: Yapko, M. D. (1986). Hypnotic and strategic interventions in the treatment of anorexia nervosa. *American Journal of Clinical Hypnosis, 28*(4), 224–232.

Chapter 13

Hypnosis and Smoking: A Five-Session Approach was reprinted with permission from: Watkins, H. H. (1976). Hypnosis and smoking: A five-session approach. *International Journal of Clinical and Experimental Hypnosis, 24*(4), 381–390.

Smoking Control was adapted from: Spiegel, H., and Spiegel, D. (1978). *Trance and Treatment: Clinical Uses of Hypnosis.* New York: Basic Books. [Reissued by American Psychiatric Press, Inc., 1987].

Suggestions for Smoking Cessation was reprinted with permission from: Crasilneck, H. B., and Hall, J. A. (1985). *Clinical Hypnosis: Principles and Applications* (Second Edition). Orlando: Grune and Stratton.

Suggestions to Modify Smoking Behavior was reprinted with permission from: Stanton, H. E. (1978). A one-session hypnotic approach to modifying smoking behavior. *International Journal of Clinical and Experimental Hypnosis, 26*(1), 22–29.

Suggestions for Smoking Cessation was adapted and reprinted with permission from: Wester, W. C. (1987). Hypnosis for smoking cessation. Chapter in W. C. Wester, *Clinical Hypnosis: A Case Management Approach.* Cincinnati: Behavioral Science Center Inc. Publications, pp. 173–182.

General Strategies for Overcoming Pleasure-Producing Habits was reprinted with permission from: Wright, M. E. (1987). *Clinical Practice of Hypnotherapy.* New York: Guilford Press.

Illustrative Suggestions with Smokers was reprinted with permission from: Sacerdote, P. (1974). Convergence of expectations: An essential component for successful hypnotherapy. *International Journal of Clinical and Experimental Hypnosis, 22*(2), 95–115.

A Posthypnotic Suggestion and Cue With Smokers was reprinted with permission from: Alman, B. M. (1983). *Self-Hypnosis: A Complete Manual for Health and Self-Change.* San Diego: International Health Publications.

Hypnosis with Nailbiting was reprinted with permission from: Crasilneck, H. B., and Hall, J. A. (1985). *Clinical Hypnosis:*

Principles and Applications (Second Edition). Orlando: Grune and Stratton.

Erickson's Suggestions for Nailbiting was reprinted with permission from: Erickson, M. H. (1983). *Healing in Hypnosis*. Edited by E. L. Rossi, M. O. Ryan, and F. A. Sharp. New York: Irvington, pp. 259-260.

Suggestions for Nailbiting was reprinted with permission from: Waxman, D. (1989). *Hartland's Medical and Dental Hypnosis* (Third Edition). London: Bailliere Tindall.

Suggestions for Nailbiting was reprinted with permission from: Gibbons, D. E. (1979). *Applied Hypnosis and Hyperempiria*. New York: Plenum Press.

Suggestions with Trichotillomania was reprinted with permission from: Barabasz, M. (1987). Trichotillomania: A new treatment. *International Journal of Clinical and Experimental Hypnosis, 35*, 146- 154.

Suggestions for Scalp Sensitivity with Trichotillomania was reprinted with permission from: Galski, T. J. (1981). The adjunctive use of hypnosis in the treatment of trichotillomania: A case report. *American Journal of Clinical Hypnosis, 23*(3), 198-201.

Chapter 14

Suggestions for Enhancing Academic Performance was reprinted with permission from: Gibbons, D. E. (1979). *Applied Hypnosis and Hyperempiria*. New York: Plenum Press.

Suggestion for Concentration was reprinted with permission from: Alman, B. M. (1983). *Self-Hypnosis: A Complete Manual for Health and Self-Change*. San Diego: International Health Publications.

Suggestions and Success Imagery for Study Problems was reprinted with permission from: Porter, J. (1978). Suggestions and success imagery for study problems. *International Journal of Clinical and Experimental Hypnosis, 26*(2), 63-75.

Erickson's Suggestions for Facilitating Speed of Learning was reprinted with permission from: Erickson, M. H. (1985). *Life Reframing in Hypnosis*. Edited by E. L. Rossi and M. O. Ryan. New York: Irvington.

Alert Trance Suggestions for Concentration and Reading was reprinted with permission from: Oetting, E. R. (1964). Hypnosis and concentration in study. *American Journal of Clinical Hypnosis, 7*(2), 148-151.

Improving Reading Speed by Hypnosis was reprinted with permission from: Klauber, R. W. (1984). Hypnosis in education and school psychology. Chapter in W. C. Wester and A. H. Smith (Eds.), *Clinical Hypnosis: A Multidisciplinary Approach*. Philadelphia: J. B. Lippincott.

Suggestions for Foreign Language Study was reprinted with permission from: Gibbons, D. E. (1979). *Applied Hypnosis and Hyperempiria*. New York: Plenum Press.

Examination Panic was reprinted with permission from: Erickson, M. H. (1965). Hypnosis and examination panics. *American Journal of Clinical Hypnosis, 7*, 356-357.

Suggestions for Examination Phobia was reprinted with permission from: Waxman, D. (1989). *Hartland's Medical and Dental Hypnosis* (Third Edition). London: Bailliere Tindall.

Suggestions for Artistic Expression was reprinted with permission from: Gibbons, D. E. (1979). *Applied Hypnosis and Hyperempiria*. New York: Plenum Press.

Suggestions for Aesthetic Appreciation and Enjoyment was reprinted with permission from: Gibbons, D. E. (1979). *Applied Hypnosis and Hyperempiria*. New York: Plenum Press.

Suggestions to Enhance Musical Performance was reprinted with permission from: Gibbons, D. E. (1979). *Applied Hypnosis and Hyperempiria*. New York: Plenum Press.

Suggestions to Enhance Writing Ability was reprinted with permission from: Gibbons, D. E. (1979). *Applied Hypnosis and Hyperempiria*. New York: Plenum Press.

Suggestions for Concentration was adapted with permission from: Alman, B. M. (1983). *Self-Hypnosis: A Complete Manual*

for Health and Self-Change. San Diego: International Health Publications.

A Cognitive-Hypnotic Approach to Athletic Performance with Weight Lifters was adapted with permission from: Howard, W. L., and Reardon, J. P. (1986). Changes in the self concept and athletic performance of weight lifters through a cognitive-hypnotic approach: An empirical study. *American Journal of Clinical Hypnosis, 28*(4), 248-257.

Suggestions for Sports Performance was reprinted with permission from: Gibbons, D. E. (1979). *Applied Hypnosis and Hyperempiria*. New York: Plenum Press.

Endurance Suggestions with Distance Runners was reprinted with permission from: Jackson, J. A., Gass, G. C., and Camp, E. M. (1979). The relationship between posthypnotic suggestion and endurance in physically trained subjects. *International Journal of Clinical and Experimental Hypnosis, 27*(3), 278-293.

Chapter 15

Helping Parents See Specific Advantages in Child Hypnotherapy was adapted and reprinted with permission from: Gardner, G. G. (1974). Parents: Obstacles or allies in child hypnotherapy? *American Journal of Clinical Hypnosis, 17*(1), 44-49.

Techniques of Hypnoanalgesia was reprinted with permission from: Olness, K., and Gardner, G. G. (1988). *Hypnosis and Hypnotherapy with Children* (Second Edition). Orlando: Grune and Stratton.

Examples of Suggestions for Use in Pediatric Emergencies was reprinted with permission from: Kohen, D. P. (1986). Applications of relaxation/mental imagery (self-hypnosis) in pediatric emergencies. *International Journal of Clinical and Experimental Hypnosis, 34*, 283-294.

Suggestions with Enuresis was reprinted with permission from: Baumann, F. (1981). Hypnosis in the treatment of urinary and fecal incontinence: A twenty-year experience. Chapter in H. J. Wain (Ed.), *Theoretical and Clinical Aspects of Hypnosis*. Miami: Symposia Specialists Inc.

Erickson's Suggestions with Enuresis were reprinted with permission from: Erickson, M. H. (1983). *Healing in Hypnosis*. Edited by E. L. Rossi, M. O. Ryan, and F. A. Sharp. New York: Irvington, pp. 175-177.

Enchanted Cottage Suggestions for Enuresis was reprinted with permission from: Gibbons, D. E. (1979). *Applied Hypnosis and Hyperempiria*. New York: Plenum Press.

Erickson's Suggestions for Thumbsucking was reprinted with permission from: Erickson, M. H. (1983). *Healing in Hypnosis*. Edited by E. L. Rossi, M. O. Ryan, and F. A. Sharp. New York: Irvington, pp. 117-118, 263-264.

Hypnosis in the Treatment of Tourette Syndrome was reprinted with permission from: Zahm, D. N. (1987). Hypnosis in the treatment of tourette syndrome. Chapter in W. C. Wester, *Clinical Hypnosis: A Case Management Approach*. Cincinnati: Behavioral Science Center, pp. 319-331.

A New Hypnobehavioral Method for the Treatment of Children with Tourette's Disorder was adapted with permission of publisher from: Young, M. H., and Montano, R. J. (1988). A new hypnobehavioral method for the treatment of children with Tourette's disorder. *American Journal of Clinical Hypnosis, 31*(2), 97-106.

Technique with Asthmatic Children reprinted with permission from: Crasilneck, H. B., and Hall, J. A. (1985). *Clinical Hypnosis: Principles and Applications* (Second Edition). Orlando: Grune and Stratton.

Suggestions with Dyslexia was reprinted with permission from: Crasilneck, H. B., and Hall, J. A. (1985). *Clinical Hypnosis: Principles and Applications* (Second Edition). Orlando: Grune and Stratton.

Hypnotic Suggestions with Stuttering was reprinted with permission from: Crasilneck, H. B., and Hall, J. A. (1985). *Clinical Hypnosis: Principles and Applications* (Second Edition). Orlando: Grune and Stratton.

Personalized Fairy Tales for Treating Childhood Insomnia was reprinted with permission from: Levine, E. S. (1980). Indirect suggestions through personalized fairy tales for treatment of childhood insomnia. *American Journal of Clinical Hypnosis, 23*(1), 57–63.

Suggestions with School Phobia was reprinted with permission from: Waxman, D. (1989). *Hartland's Medical and Dental Hypnosis* (Third Edition). London: Bailliere Tindall.

A Science Fiction-Based Imagery Technique was reprinted with permission from: Elkins, G. R., and Carter, B. D. (1981). Use of a science fiction-based imagery technique in child hypnosis. *American Journal of Clinical Hypnosis, 23*(4), 274–276.

Chapter 16

Improving the Quality of the Age Regression was reprinted with permission from: Brown, D. P., and Fromm, E. (1986). *Hypnotherapy and Hypnoanalysis.* Hillsdale, N.J.: Lawrence Erlbaum.

Suggestions to Facilitate Revivification was reprinted with permission from: Greenleaf, E. (1969). Developmental-stage regression through hypnosis. *American Journal of Clinical Hypnosis, 12*(1), 20–36.

Erickson's Confusional Method for Revivification was reprinted with permission from: Rossi, E. L., Ryan, M. O., and Sharp, F. A. (Eds.). (1983). *Healing in Hypnosis: The Seminars, Workshops, and Lectures of Milton H. Erickson, Volume I.* New York: Irvington, p. 254.

Watkins' Silent Abreaction Technique was adapted from: Watkins, H. H. (1980). The silent abreaction. *International Journal of Clinical and Experimental Hypnosis, 28*, 101–113.

Erickson's Age Regression Techniques were reprinted with permission from: (a) Erickson, M. H., and Rossi, E. L. (1979). *Hypnotherapy: An Exploratory Casebook.* New York: Irvington, p. 357. (b) Rossi, E. L., Ryan, M. O., and Sharp, F. A. (Eds.). (1983). *Healing in Hypnosis: The Seminars, Workshops, and Lectures of Milton H. Erickson, Volume I.* New York: Irvington, pp. 255–256. (c) Erickson, M. H., and Rossi, E. L. (1979). *Hypnotherapy: An Exploratory Casebook.* New York: Irvington, pp. 453–454. (d) Erickson, M. H., and Rossi, E. L. (1979). *Hypnotherapy: An Explor-*

atory Casebook. New York: Irvington, pp. 34, 318–319, 321–322, 326, 348, 349, 350.

Example of an Analytical Procedure for Reframing was adapted with permission from: Barnett, E. A. (1981). *Analytical Hypnotherapy.* Kingston, Ontario, Canada: Junica. Pp. 143–148 and 151–156.

Desensitization: An Example of Rapid and Repetitive Memory Evocation was reprinted with permission from: Wright, M. E. (1987). *Clinical Practice of Hypnotherapy.* New York: Guilford Press, pp. 83–84.

Forensic Hypnosis Guidelines: The "Federal Model" was adapted from Richard B. Garver, "Investigative Hypnosis," a chapter in William Wester (Ed.), *Clinical Hypnosis: A Case Management Approach.* Cincinnati: Behavioral Science Center, 1987.

Imagery of the End Result was reprinted with permission from: Korn, E. R., and Pratt, G. J. (1988). *Release Your Business Potential.* (Cassette recording). New York: John Wilcy and Sons.

Mental Rehearsal: The Protective Shield was reprinted with permission from: Korn, E. R., and Pratt, G. J. (1988). *Release Your Business Potential.* (Cassette recording). New York: John Wiley and Sons.

Mental Rehearsal of Presentation and Sales Skills was reprinted with permission from: Korn, E. R., and Pratt, G. J. (1988). *Release Your Business Potential.* (Cassette recording). New York: John Wiley and Sons.

End-Result Goal Imagery for Sales Productivity was reprinted with permission from: Gibbons, D. E. (1979). *Applied Hypnosis and Hyperempiria.* New York: Plenum Press.

Erickson's Self-Suggestion Technique was adapted from: Erickson, M. H. (1964). The burden of responsibility in effective psychotherapy. *American Journal of Clinical Hypnosis, 6,* 269–271.

Training Patients to Experience Time Distortion was reprinted with permission from: Cooper, L. F., and Erickson, M. H. (1959). *Time Distortion in Hypnosis.* Baltimore: Williams and Wilkins.

Quotations in Summary of Suggested Steps in Time Distortion Training were reprinted with permission from: (a) Cooper, L. F., and Erickson, M. H. (1959). *Time Distortion in Hypnosis.* Baltimore: Williams and Wilkins. (b) Erickson, M. H. (1985). *Life Reframing in Hypnosis.* Edited by E. L. Rossi and M. O. Ryan. New York: Irvington. (c) Erickson, M. H., and Rossi, E. L. (1979). *Hypnotherapy: An Exploratory Casebook.* New York: Irvington. (d) Rossi, E. L., and Cheek, D. B. (1988). *Mind-Body Therapy.* New York: W. W. Norton.

NAME INDEX

SUBJECT INDEX